P9-AEV-665

THOMAS JEFFERSON
AND THE
NEW NATION

Thomas Jefferson in 1800. Portrait by Rembrandt Peale.

THOMAS JEFFERSON
AND THE
NEW NATION

A BIOGRAPHY

Merrill D. Peterson

New York · Oxford University Press · 1970

Preface

THE PRESENT WORK grows out of a line of inquiry commenced some twenty years ago. In the Preface to *The Jefferson Image in the American Mind*, in 1960, I forewarned the reader that the book dealt not with Thomas Jefferson but with his shadow, not with the "living" but with the "posthumous" figure, not with the history he made but with what history made of him. *Thomas Jefferson and the New Nation* treats the historical Jefferson, and in this sense—in the sense of shadow and substance—may be viewed as a biographical companion to the former work.

The Jefferson Image suggested that the historical Jefferson could never be truly discovered. The point strikes me even more forcibly now after more years of research and reflection. Jefferson became so much a part of the nation's ongoing search for itself, so deeply implicated in the whole epic of American democracy, that succeeding generations were unable to see him clearly and objectively in his own life and time. This is, I think, less the case today than it used to be, for in our kinetic age the epic itself has gradually receded from view and the twin hysterias of exaltation and denunciation that once surrounded the Jefferson symbol have given way to a more neutral climate in which scholars might assert their legitimate claims and seek to restore the integrity of the historical personage. Even now, however, the student of Jefferson cannot be truly detached and disinterested. I have not been, though I have sought that "disciplined subjectivity" someone has defined as the essence of the historian's craft.

In addition to the first obstacle—the obstacle presented by the Jefferson image—the biographer must also contend with the obstacle of the man himself. He was so closely identified with the first half-century of the nation's history that the human figure fades into the events massed around it. His life exhibited seemingly bewildering conflicts and contradictions, and it is not easy to resolve these elements in the flow of experience. He was a prodigy of talents. The tributaries of his mind ran in all directions. To trace their channels into the main stream is only half the problem, for the terrain itself belongs to another intellectual world, which challenges understanding on its own terms and yet must be translated into the grammar of our own time. Although he left to posterity a vast corpus of papers, private and public, his personality remains elusive. Of all his great contemporaries Jefferson is perhaps the least self-revealing and the hardest to sound to the depths of being. It is a mortifying confession but he remains for me, finally, an impenetrable man.

All this is said not by way of apology for what follows but simply to disclaim any intention of revealing that Platonic abstraction, the *real* Jefferson, or of offering a definitive life of the man. So far as such a life is attainable, it is being written by Dumas Malone in his magnificent series, *Jefferson and His Times*, of which three volumes have thus far appeared. And in a different medium, the medium of editorial scholarship, Julian P. Boyd is producing the authoritative work in his monumental edition of *The Papers of Thomas Jefferson*, still a longer way from completion. These are the greatest of all works of Jefferson scholarship. My own is a cockboat by comparison. In the course of the work I have sometimes been asked, in tones ranging from curiosity to dismay, if anything important remained to be said about Jefferson. I have usually replied that he is one of those men about whom the last word can never be said, that he demands continual re-study and re-evaluation, and quite aside from the merits or the faults of my own effort, it was one I felt bound to make as a part of my own education. I hope, of course, it may also be of use to others.

Within the limits of a single volume I have tried to write a basic narrative of Jefferson's life formed by my own understanding of its place, its problems, and its importance in the history of the United States as the first revolutionary new nation. Such an approach is necessarily selective. The emphasis throughout is on Jefferson's public career, though this cannot be isolated from his private affairs, and also on the fascinating traffic between Jefferson's mind and the surrounding environment. I have aimed at neither a "personal" nor even an "intellectual" biography but, rather, at a history of Jefferson in the making of the new nation. The conceptual scheme expresses, it seems to me, the paramount interest of Jefferson to our time. Each American generation has had its own perspective on the founding and the founders. In the case of my generation, which came of age in the Second World War and has witnessed shattering global upheaval for a quarter-century, the experience throws into sharp relief the nation's beginnings in another age of revolution, "the age of the democratic revolution," in Robert R. Palmer's conception, and its struggles to survive and prosper in the turbulent Atlantic world. The United States holds a very different position in today's world—the lamb has become the lion—yet its early history may help to recall Americans to a spirit and a purpose still valuable and, one trusts, not without relevance to old and new nations alike in our time. No other founder had a longer or larger influence on the life and the hopes of the New World prodigy than Thomas Jefferson. Rising to fame as a leader of colonies in revolt against an empire, he embodied the nation's aspirations for freedom and enlightenment, and throughout most of his life he was intellectually and politically engaged not only in American affairs but in the affairs of a world unhinged by war and revolution.

Without forcing the multitudinous events of Jefferson's life into an arbitrary pattern, I have thought they might be interpreted, on the whole, in the light of three dominant motifs: democracy, nationality, enlightenment. The terms are meant as symbols for whole clusters of principles and actions and passions, not altogether coherently arranged. By *democracy* I refer to the gradual emergence in Jefferson of a revolutionary creed of liberty, equality, and popular government. By *nationality* I mean to embrace his sense of the newness of the new nation, his *amor patriae*, all his directives toward independence, cultural or political or economic, and his efforts to define America's place in the community of nations. By *enlightenment* I wish to emphasize Jefferson's thrust beyond nationality to the cosmopolitan fraternity of science and philosophy, his commitment to the civilizing arts, to education, to progress, to rationality in all things, and his participation in the eighteenth century campaign to enlist man in the cause of nature and nature in the service of mankind.

The research for this study is grounded in Jefferson's voluminous papers. For the period to 1790, I have relied mainly on Boyd's comprehensive edition—seventeen published volumes to this point. For the rest I have made use of earlier editions but have relied principally on the microfilm reprints of various manuscript collections, especially those of the Library of Congress and the Massachusetts Historical Society, as well as on the Jefferson Papers of the University of Virginia. The reader is referred to the Select Bibliography for further information on sources. After considerable agonizing I have omitted footnotes or any other form of notation. In a work of synthesis and interpretation, addressed more to readers than to scholars, making no pretensions to definitive treatment, and on a subject so much researched and written about as Jefferson, it seemed to me that footnotes would place an unnecessary burden on the text. Complete notation would be very burdensome indeed to the general reader and partial notation merely an annoyance to the interested scholar. So I have allowed the book to stand free of the scaffolding. I have also taken the liberty of modernizing eccentric spelling, punctuation, and capitalization in nearly all quoted passages from personal letters.

I wish to acknowledge the services of three great libraries where virtually all the research was conducted: The Library of Congress, Widener Library of Harvard University, and, above all, Alderman Library of the University of Virginia. I am deeply indebted for financial support to three exemplary institutions: The Thomas Jefferson Memorial Foundation for continuing assistance over seven years, the John Simon Guggenheim Memorial Foundation for a fellowship at the inception of this work, and the Center for Advanced Study in the Behavioral Sciences for a fellowship and many auxiliary aids which enabled me to bring the work to completion. Several of my colleagues at the Center read the manuscript and offered their comments and suggestions. I have also profited from the work of my graduate students and the intellectual stimulation of my friends in the Corcoran Department of History of the University of Virginia. My thanks go finally to Hildegarde Teilhet and her crew at the Center for the proficient typing of the manuscript.

Charlottesville   M. D. P.
September 1, 1969

Contents

One · Prologue to Fame

*

Beginnings in Albemarle   3

A Williamsburg Education   10
Student of Law   16
Lawyer, Builder, Husband   20

Manner of the Man   28

*

Two · Philosopher of Revolution

*

The Burgessess, May 1769   32

Troubled Virginia   37
Enlightenment—Democracy—Nationality   45
Empire Theory and the American Cause   69
Congress and the Declaration of Independence   79

Philosophy of the Declaration   92

*

Three · Virginia Reformer

*

From Philadelphia to Williamsburg   97

The Virginia Constitution	100
In the House of Delegates	107
Lands	113
Crime and Punishment	124
Religion	133
Education	145
Other Reforms	152

At Monticello   158

*

Four · War Governor

*

State of the State   166

The Case of Governor Hamilton	174
Against the Southern Thrust	183
Invasion	203

Censure and Vindication   236

*

Five · Withdrawal and Return: Congressman

*

Agony at Monticello   241

The Notes on Virginia	247
The Vagabond Congress	265
National Cornerstones	273
A Strategy of Trade	288

Passage to Europe   293

*

Six · Minister to France

*

Seasoning in Paris   297

Commercial Diplomacy   303
Negotiating with France   314
The Vaunted Scene   330
To the Bastille   370

Hail and Farewell   385

*

Seven · Secretary of State

*

The Reluctant Nominee   390

Agenda in New York   395
Conflict in Philadelphia   419
Struggles with Hamilton   446
The Ordeal of Neutrality   479

Epilogue of Diplomacy   507

*

Eight · Withdrawal and Return: Vice President

*

Return to Felicity   518

Farming   523
Monticello Renewed   538
Adams and Jefferson   543
Science and Politics   576
The Terror of '98   590
The Election of 1800   625

Verdict in the House   642

*

CONTENTS

Nine · President: First Administration

*

Inauguration 652

Reconciliation and Reform   660
President, Congress, Court   681
Man in the White House   702
Louisiana!   745

Unquiet Empire 789

*

Ten · President: Second Administration

*

Inauguration 801

Trials of Foreign Policy   805
The Burr Conspiracy   841
The Embargo   874

Failure and Triumph

*

Eleven · Sage of Monticello

*

In Retirement 922

Kaleidoscope in Twilight   929
Founding the University   961
Unquiet Sage   988

Death in Jubilee 1005

*

Select Bibliography 1011

Index 1049

List of Illustrations

Thomas Jefferson in 1800. Portrait by Rembrandt Peale.

Monticello, the first version. Accepted elevation, 1771.
General plan of Monticello. Jefferson's drawing, 1772.
The Declaration of Independence July 4, 1776. Detail from the painting by John Trumbull.
A page from Jefferson's draft of the Bill for Proportioning Crimes and Punishments, 1778.

follow page 144

The Maison Carrée at Nîmes.
The Virginia Capitol. Plaster model.
Minister to France. Replica of the portrait by Mather Brown, 1786.
Jefferson in 1789. Marble bust by Houdon.
Secretary of State. Portrait by Charles Willson Peale, 1791.

follow page 368

Monticello renewed. Elevation, west front, and plan of first floor and dependencies. Drawn by Robert Mills, about 1803.
The President. Portrait by Gilbert Stuart, 1805.
The President. Medallion portrait by Gilbert Stuart, 1805.
The President. Portrait by Rembrandt Peale, 1805.
Sage of Monticello. Portrait by Thomas Sully, 1822.

follow page 720

Plan of the University of Virginia. Engraving by Peter Maverick from a drawing by Jefferson in 1822.
The University of Virginia. Engraving by B. Tanner, 1827.
Jefferson at eighty-two. Plaster life mask by John H. I. Browere, 1825.
Jefferson's design and inscription for his tombstone.
Monticello, west front, after Jefferson's death. Engraving after a painting by George Cooke.

follow page 912

THOMAS JEFFERSON
AND THE
NEW NATION

CHAPTER ONE

Prologue to Fame

I confess, there are some men's constitutions of body and mind so vigorous, and well framed by nature, that they need not much assistance from others; but by the strength of their natural genius, they are, from their cradles, carried towards what is excellent; and, by the privilege of their happy constitution, are able to do wonders. But examples of this kind are few; and I think I may say, that, of all men we meet with, nine parts of them are what they are, good or evil, useful or not, by their education. It is that which makes the great difference in mankind. The little, or almost insensible, impressions on our tender infancies, have very important and lasting consequences: and there it is, as in the fountains of some rivers, where a gentle application of the hand turns the flexible waters into channels, that make them take quite contrary courses; and by this little direction, given them at first, in the source, they receive different tendencies, and arrive at last at very remote and distant places.

John Locke, Some Thoughts Concerning Education. *1693.*

To BECOME my own biographer is the last thing in the world I would undertake," Thomas Jefferson remarked in his seventy-second year. "No. If there has been anything in my course worth the public attention, they are better judges of it than I can be myself, and to them it is my duty to leave it." Few men ever left a richer or more abundant record of a life well spent. From the time he became conscious of his own fame and of posterity's immense stake in the events with which he was associated, Jefferson dutifully preserved the annals of his journey. Unfortunately, the road to fame is not so well documented. He did, it is true, five years after declining to become his own biographer, write for his family an unvarnished chronicle of his life to mid-passage, but this "autobiography," as valuable as it is, sheds little light on the child who became the man.

"The tradition of my father's family," Jefferson began his account, "was that their ancestors came to this country from Wales, and from near the mountain of Snowdon, the highest in Great Britain." This ancestor could not be definitely established. There had been Jeffersons in Virginia from the earliest times, but the great descendant traced the family line no farther back than his grandfather, Thomas Jefferson, Jr., who lived in Chesterfield County (then part of Henrico) some distance below the falls of the James River. Like a number of small planters, as well as large, Thomas turned his eyes to the virgin lands west of tidewater, and in 1718 patented several hundred acres at Fine Creek in what would become Goochland County. Upon his death thirteen years later, his youngest son Peter inherited these James River lands, which he promptly settled, if indeed he had not already done so.

Peter was then twenty-three or twenty-four years of age, a strongly built man with great force of mind and considerable ambition. His education, as his son would say, "had been quite neglected," and his circumstances were modest at best; but casting his lot with the new upcountry society, he quickly rose in the social scale, becoming a large landholder, a prominent member of the county squirearchy, and as a self-taught surveyor and mapmaker carved a niche for himself in the history of the province. Contributing to this rise was his marriage into one of the princely families, the Randolphs. "They trace their pedigree far back in England and Scotland, to which let every one ascribe the merit he chooses." Thomas Jefferson, the democrat, could thus lightly dismiss the aristocratic pedigree that helped to secure position and influence for himself and his children.

Jane Randolph was nineteen, the eldest daughter of Isham Randolph, of Dungeness, some miles farther up the James, when Peter Jefferson married her in 1739. "Captain" Randolph had been a seafaring man, sojourning a good deal in England, where Jane was

4

born, before he settled down on a plantation seat in the Virginia piedmont. He thereafter played a prominent role in the military affairs of the colony. Botany was his amusement, as it was for so many planters, and he knew such eminent botanists as Peter Collinson in England and the Philadelphian John Bartram, who stopped at Dungeness on his southern excursion in 1738. Peter Jefferson's courtship there probably commenced about this time. He had become acquainted with the Dungeness branch of the family through his best friend, William Randolph, Isham's nephew, whose great estate Tuckahoe lay thirty miles or so to the east. The intimacy of these two men, William and Peter, would exert an influence on the latter's distinguished son beyond the incident of maternity.

The son, the first to Peter and Jane Jefferson, was born at Shadwell, in what soon became Albemarle County, on April 13, 1743. In this wilderness country, many miles up the Rivanna River from its confluence with the James, Peter Jefferson had patented a thousand acres in 1735, then cleared a tract for planting and built a modest frame dwelling, to which he brought his wife and two infant daughters not long before the birth of his son. The place, named for the London parish where his wife was born, lay in verdant rolling countryside between ramparts of the Southwest Mountains opening vistas of the Blue Ridge beyond the valley to the west. When the County of Albemarle was created in 1744 it embraced the entire Rivanna region. Indians called Saponi, of Sioux stock, once inhabited the region, but there were no Indians now except those who passed through, often stopping at Shadwell, on the road to the capital 120 miles or so to the east; and bear and buffalo had surrendered the forests to wolf and deer. The first settlers came in the 1730's; Jefferson thought his father the third or fourth in the region. They were nearly all, as he was, enterprising planters packing west from crowded or worn-out lands. His own landholdings, though they rapidly increased, were never as large as some of his neighbors'. As the region filled up, the gap widened between the magnates owning many thousands of acres, with the slaves to work them, and the mass of small farmers, many with fewer than a hundred acres. This was a frontier in the provincial Virginia fashion, free and open to middle-rank men of Peter Jefferson's means and enterprise but utterly recalcitrant to the leveling influence so often claimed for

5

the American frontier. If his son felt the force of the frontier, if the West constantly tugged at his mind, it was not from growing up in a democratic frontier society.

What counted in this respect was his emotional response to the natural landscape, his sense of the freedom and simplicity of up-country life, and, above all, his identification with Virginia pioneering and exploration. The last came chiefly through his father. Not only had he been in the vanguard of Virginia's westward settlement —always a source of pride to his son—but he had penetrated the Alleghenies, traversed the uncharted wilderness of southwest Virginia to extend the boundary with North Carolina begun by William Byrd many years before, and with his partner in this expedition, Joshua Fry, professor of mathematics in the College of William and Mary, drew the first correct map of the province. All of this happened when Jefferson was a child. His adventurous mind must have been touched by it. Something in Albemarle seemed to excite the westering imagination. Peter Jefferson's physician-friend and neighbor, Dr. Thomas Walker, also explored the mountain vastness, and later became the young Jefferson's preceptor on the West and the Indians. Walker was the leading spirit of the Loyal Company, a speculative enterprise in southwest Virginia in which Jefferson's father had a share. George Rogers Clark, conqueror of the Northwest during the American Revolution, and Meriwether Lewis, who later journeyed to the far Pacific, were natives of Albemarle, while William Clark, brother of the former and, in time, partner of the latter, only missed being born there. All would figure prominently in the life of Albemarle's most famous son. He was neither pioneer nor explorer, but the West was in his thoughts from an early age. The West was nature writ large, and though his own preference was for the humanized middle state between the wild and the civilized, such as he never ceased to celebrate in his native country, nature in the large had an enduring fascination for him. And his response to the softer and smaller, the tamed yet unspoiled and endlessly beautiful natural world of his childhood, enforced a sense of man's relationship to his environment that colored all his values. The openness, the freedom, the simplicity he found in this world set him on the road to the democratic ethic of his mature years.

Jefferson would never think of any place as home but the Albemarle of his birth. Actually, he spent six of the first nine years of his life at Tuckahoe. William Randolph died in 1745 leaving a will that requested his "dear and loving friend" Peter Jefferson to move down to Tuckahoe and look after his three motherless children until the son, four-year-old Thomas Mann Randolph, came of age. Peter honored the request, at least for a period of years, and packed off his entire family (there were now four children and a fifth on the way) to Tuckahoe. Thomas's earliest memories accordingly, were not of the simple farm house at Shadwell but of the airy and commodious frame and brick mansion on the James. "It is in the form of an H and has the appearance of two houses, joined by a large saloon; each wing has two stories, and four large rooms on a floor . . . the saloon that unites them is of considerable magnitude and on each side are doors. . . ." If it answered perfectly the purposes of Virginia hospitality, as the author of this description thought, Tuckahoe perfectly suited as well the needs of two families. Peter managed the large Randolph plantation, together with his own farms at Fine Creek and Shadwell, and was frequently away from home on surveying expeditions. His son's schooling commenced at the age of five. In a little one-room plantation schoolhouse Thomas and his sisters and cousins learned their reading, writing, and arithmetic from a private tutor.

About nine years old when the family returned to Shadwell, Thomas was promptly placed in a classical school conducted by the Reverend William Douglas, from Scotland, at his parsonage some distance to the east in Goochland County. In those days, of course, the classical languages were the indispensable foundations of education. His father had never acquired them, but he was sufficiently cultivated to know their value, for which his son was eternally grateful. "To read the Latin and Greek authors in their original is a sublime luxury . . . ," he said many years later. "I thank on my knees him who directed my early education for having put into my possession this rich source of delight; and I would not exchange it for anything which I could have then acquired, and have not since acquired." Perhaps he did not learn a great deal from the Reverend Mr. Douglas. Jefferson remembered him as "but a superficial Latinist, less instructed in Greek," though he got from him the rudiments of these languages as well as of French. In 1758, after several years

7

with the Reverend Mr. Douglas, he went to school with "a correct classical scholar," the Reverend James Maury. This delightful gentleman belonged to a prominent Virginia family of Huguenot descent and was among the better educated men of the province. He it was who, in 1763, brought to court the celebrated case of the Parson's Cause, which humbled the Anglican clergy and rocketed Patrick Henry to fame. Maury's Fredericksville parish, the first in the region, included part of Albemarle; in later years Jefferson, like his father before him, would serve on its vestry. The schoolhouse built of logs lay about a dozen miles from Shadwell, too far for commuting from home. For two years the young scholar soaked up Greek and Latin, got a mere smattering of English literature, perhaps a little geography and history and mathematics, and doubtless a heavy dose of the Bible. Partly because he boarded with the Maury family, riding home weekends, he was also introduced to the master's library of some four hundred volumes, by far the largest he had seen. Here at Maury's school he came to know the pleasures of study and caught his first glimpse of the world of learning.

He would remember these schooldays as among the happiest of his life. No friendships ever seemed sweeter than those he made then. Among his school chums were young James Maury, later American consul at Liverpool for many years; Dabney Carr, whom Jefferson loved as a brother and who would wed his sister Martha; John Walker, perhaps the only close friend Jefferson would ever lose; and James Madison—the *other* James Madison—afterwards president of the College of William and Mary. Their favorite pastime was hunting in mountains alive with deer, fox, turkey, partridge, and other game. Like most country boys, Thomas took to hunting at an early age, though loyalty to nature seemed to curb his ardor. It was later said that he would never shoot partridge or hare "settin" but would "scare em up" first to give them a sporting chance. He was a good horseman in the Virginia fashion, but for exercise and diversion preferred walking in the woods and fields. Nature should be observed from the ground, not from five feet up in the air. Besides, a horse gave the body "but a kind of half exercise." From the little that can be known of his schooldays, Jefferson comes through not as the "All American Boy" but as the exceptionally diligent student. Even after classes were dismissed, "he used to be seen with his

Greek Grammar in hand while his comrades were enjoying relaxation." Not averse to games and fun, he studied first and played later. If a holiday was granted, the younger Maury recalled, "he would withdraw from the noisy crowd of his school fellows, learn the next day's lesson, and then, rejoining them, begin the day's pleasure."

He was only fourteen, and had not yet entered Maury's school, when he lost his father in 1757. Peter Jefferson had established himself as a first citizen of the county—local magistrate, county surveyor, county lieutenant (the chief military officer), even member of the House of Burgesses for a time. The pathway to power had been blazed for his son. He had also become wealthy, at least in land and slaves and the accoutrement of the tobacco planter. Had he lived longer he might have built the mansion that his estate plainly authorized; but this was left to his son. The "Colonel's" landholdings, mostly in Albemarle, amounted to about 7500 acres. Two-thirds of this, including the Monticello property, would eventually go to Thomas. The will made provision for the widow and all eight children, the youngest being two-year-old Randolph, but as was customary the distribution of the patrimony favored the first son. His mother lived many years yet. By his own reckoning she was a zero quantity in his life. He was especially fond of two of his sisters, Jane, the eldest, who shared his love of music, and Martha, who married Dabney Carr. With his only brother, Randolph, so much younger, he was never close. Indeed, except for the strong example and guidance provided by his father, his life course would not have been very different had all the members of his family been erased from the picture. He owed his father a great deal, not in companionship, for they were frequently apart, perhaps not even in affection, but in the tone and direction given to his life. Habits of industry, system, and responsibility are acquired early, and in Jefferson's case they were learned first from his father. He later expressed some astonishment that, when this force was removed at a tender age and there was no one to turn to, he did not lose his bearings, fall into bad company, and become quite worthless to society. Instead, the early thrust to maturity hardened the grain of habits already acquired.

Jefferson would have nothing to do with management of his inheritance until he came of age. Meanwhile it was in the hands of executors who also acted as guardians. In January 1760, when he was going on seventeen, he wrote a letter—the first from his pen that survives—to the principal executor, John Harvie. "I was at Col. Peter Randolph's [another executor] about a Fortnight ago," the letter began, "and my Schooling falling into Discourse, he said he thought it would be to my Advantage to go to College, and was desirous I should go, as indeed I am myself for several Reasons." He went on to explain that the move would put a stop to the distraction and the expense of company at Shadwell, widen his acquaintance with the world, and of course further his education. After two years at Maury's school he was ready for a richer and more varied fare. That he should go anywhere but the College of William and Mary seems not to have occurred to him or to his guardians. The College was in ill-repute in certain quarters; and some Virginia sons of well-to-do families still went to England for education, though the College of New Jersey, in Princeton, under Scottish Presbyterian auspices, was increasingly favored as an alternative. But the young gentleman of Albemarle set his sights on the provincial college. Here a new chapter opened.

A Williamsburg Education

This youth of seventeen who came down from the hills to Williamsburg in 1760 had taken on the physical characteristics so commonly ascribed to him in later years. He was tall and lanky, with large hands and feet, and seemed to be growing right out of his clothes. As straight and strong as a gun-barrel, he had the sinewy broad-shouldered vigor of his father. His tousled hair was of a reddish color, his eyes light and hazel, his face ruddy and freckled. His head, like his body, was spare of flesh. Lips thin and compressed suggested a mind in thought, while the angular nose and projecting chin added forcefulness to a countenance otherwise mild. He gave the appearance of the fresh country lad he was, rather more awkward than graceful, and by no stretch could he be considered handsome or polished at this stage. But he was bright, amiable, eager, and full of bounce, which more than compensated for any deficiency in looks.

Williamsburg was a new scene. To begin with it was a town, that rarity in Virginia young Jefferson had not known before. It was also the provincial capital, seat of empire in the New World, about as little felt in Albemarle as His Majesty's government across the ocean, but, nevertheless, the hub of Virginia politics, society, and culture. Close to 1500 people lived in the town. During "publick times" in the spring and fall, however, when the General Court and the House of Burgesses were in session, the population doubled. Between the College at one end and the Capitol at the other stretched a mile-long thoroughfare, Duke of Gloucester Street, through which coursed a colorful parade of humanity. In the years ahead Jefferson came to know every feature of this artery and its tributaries—the Bruton Church where he sometimes worshiped, the Raleigh Tavern where he danced and flirted and on occasion minded weighty affairs of state, the shops he patronized, the houses he visited. Williamsburg was not showy; but for the porticoed Capitol and the splendid Palace of the governor it might have been mistaken for a good English town. In the surrounding country were the princely estates of tidewater aristocrats who wielded power at Williamsburg. Sons of several of these patrician families—Harrisons, Burwells, Pages, and others—were among Jefferson's classmates at college, and he easily made his way into their society, so much grander than anything he had known in the upcountry.

Jefferson lived and studied for two years in the College. Chartered by the Crown in 1693, receiving its name from the reigning sovereigns, and floated on the profits of Virginia lands and tobacco, the College had a distinctive public character. It had a religious character too, being founded in part to provide ministers for the established Church of England and being under the control of the Church; but unlike the sister colleges to the north—more emphatically ecclesiastical in character—William and Mary failed miserably in this object. Few of the planters' sons who went there chose a ministerial career, with the result that the College was constantly at war with itself, torn between the brazen secularism of the community it served and its clerical mission. The College had grown into a miscellaneous assortment of schools: a preparatory or grammar school presided over by a master; an Indian school, the Brafferton, intended to Christianize the natives, also with a single master; the philosophy school, which was the equivalent of a liberal arts college, with two professors; and the divinity school, similarly staffed. Not more than a hundred students were enrolled in all the schools. Over the whole sat a president, who also usually occupied the position of commissary, as agent of the Bishop of London in the colony, and the pulpit of the Bruton Church, and who at the time of Jefferson's entrance into the College was a notorious drunkard. Jefferson, of course, enrolled in the philosophy school where "systems of logick, physicks, ethicks and mathematicks" were dispensed by the two professors.

"It was my great good fortune, and what probably fixed the destinies of my life," Jefferson wrote in his autobiography, "that Dr. William Small of Scotland, was then Professor of Mathematics, a man profound in most of the useful branches of science, with a happy talent of communication, correct and gentlemanly manners, and an enlarged and liberal mind. He, most happily for me, became soon attached to me, and made me his daily companion when not engaged in the school; and from his conversation I got my first views of the expansion of science, and of the system of things in which we are placed." This gentleman, the single non-clergyman on the faculty, had only recently come to the College, and he remained but six years. Judging by his later friendship, after his return to England, with James Watt, Erasmus Darwin, and others of the Birmingham scientific circle, Small was a man of talents not far below the mark assigned to him by his favorite student. He had been swept up in the enlightened thought of the age. His teaching was rational and scientific rather than religious and didactic; and he gave this cast to Jefferson's mind. He was, in fact, the first truly enlightened or scientific man the young student had encountered. Because of some rowdyism that led to the dismissal of his other teacher, the professor of moral philosophy, Jefferson was fortunate in having Small not only for mathematics, natural philosophy, and natural history but also for logic, ethics, rhetoric, and belles lettres. In fact, except for a few months, Small was his only regular teacher; and Jefferson continued in his company after leaving the College and commencing the study of law.

His choice of law as a profession was influenced more by chance and circumstance than by the conscious bent of his own mind. He never professed to love the law in the way he professed, repeatedly, to love science or the arts. A dark and gloomy study, the law was out of tune with his cheerful nature. The law was not his mistress but a profession of service and, incidentally, of livelihood. Now approaching twenty years of age, without the fortune to support a splendid retirement or any desire to spend his life planting tobacco, he sought a vocation that would challenge his mind, supplement his income, and render him useful to society. In Virginia the options were very few. The ministry held no charms for him, nor did any branch of the military service; like most Virginians he knew nothing of trade, which was a British monopoly; and there was no art or science or literature in which the colonial could make a career. Had he lived nearer the center of empire he might have found a calling that answered to his strongest impulses. And in retrospect it seems clear he might have excelled in almost any field of learning. (If the estimates of "historiometry," the technique of measuring the intelligence of historical figures, are to be credited, his IQ was about 150, in the same rank as Galileo, Handel, Michelangelo, and some other geniuses.) But in Virginia, on the fringes of empire, only law, and possibly medicine, though Jefferson always held a low opinion of the art, offered a calling at once learned and useful, if not especially profitable, and one which a gentleman could pursue while attending to his country estate. At Williamsburg the youth discovered models for emulation: Peyton Randolph, the king's attorney, who had been educated at the Inner Temple in London; Edmund Pendleton, the very popular home-grown product; and above all George Wythe, also native-born, bred, and educated, who became Jefferson's mentor. The magnates who sat on the Governor's Council and exercised great influence were, for the most part, planters, not lawyers; but as the contest with the mother country came on, and Virginians thought seriously about rights and government, a new generation of professional lawyers, their roots in the native land, rose to prominence. Themselves a part of the ruling class, they did not dethrone it but infused it with their own learning and ambitions. Jefferson and Patrick Henry were among the first of this Revolutionary generation of lawyers. Henry, who preceded him, came to the bar after six weeks of desultory reading while Jefferson spent five years in exhaustive preparation.

The presence of George Wythe in Williamsburg fixed Jefferson's determination and squelched any fugitive thoughts of going abroad for study. It was Small who brought master and pupil together. A man of the most exalted character and learning, entirely without the benefit of formal schooling, Wythe had become, as was said, "a scholar by the indispensable progress of his own industry in his closet." About thirty-five years of age when Jefferson came under his wing, he was already an ornament of the bar and on the point of learning the most eminent in the profession. To his knowledge of English and Roman law he brought a command of the whole field of humanistic learning and an irrepressible enthusiasm for classical languages and literature. "Mr. Wythe" it was said, "not only labored through an apprenticeship, but almost through life in the dead languages." Jefferson himself had spent several years in the same apprenticeship, and he did not in any formal sense continue it in Williamsburg. The burden of his education under Small was rational and scientific; but this new direction did not exclude the older one. His Attic and Roman tastes were further cultivated by Wythe, who pursued law and politics under the spell of the ancients. In a course of reading over five years, Jefferson learned law as a branch of the history of mankind. The relationship of master and pupil ripened into affectionate friendship through life. Wythe went on to become a signer of the Declaration of Independence, first professor of law at William and Mary, and finally chancellor of Virginia. Jefferson never tired of singing his virtues—integrity, generosity, patriotism, love of liberty—and thought he might be best remembered as "the Cato of his country without the avarice of the Roman."

The Williamsburg chain of influence from Small to Wythe terminated in the Royal Governor, Francis Fauquier, remembered by Jefferson as the ablest man ever to fill that chair. "They were"—Small, Wythe, and Fauquier—"inseparable friends, and at their frequent dinners with the governor (after his family had returned to England) he admitted me always to make it a *partie quarée*. At these dinners I . . . heard more good sense, more rational and philosophical conversations than in all my life besides. They were truly Attic societies." Coming to Virginia in 1758, the Governor had made himself popular with the leading gentry by exhibiting in his own character the fashionable culture to which they aspired. Elegant, urbane, learned, and witty, a man of almost Chesterfieldian manners, he brought the tastes and amusements of the metropolis to the province. He dabbled in science, patronized art and music, and introduced the taste for French literature and philosophy so much the vogue in England. The Governor, who was himself musical, recruited his young friend for the amateur ensemble that performed weekly at the Palace. Having taken up the fiddle on his own while still in school Jefferson found the first opportunity for instruction in Williamsburg. He must have attained at least a modest proficiency to play in Fauquier's concerts. The Governor's example of "taste, refinement and erudition," which he is said to have impressed on the colony, was not lost on Jefferson. However, he rejected the elegant vices that accompanied the Governor's virtues. Although he occasionally played at cards or backgammon or laid a bet on a horse race, he escaped the extravagant fashion of gambling, "the rage for playing deep, reckless of time, health, or money," that Fauquier was charged, not quite fairly, with spreading like wildfire among the great families.

Small, Wythe, and Fauquier: this Williamsburg circle was Jefferson's university. Small, the Scotsman, was his preceptor in mathematics, natural science, and modern philosophy; from him came the impulse toward scientific rationalism. Wythe extended his lines to the ancient world while at the same time opening before him a generous and humane path to the law. Fauquier, the man of the world, introduced him to the life of cultivated manners, taste, and sensibility, showing its pitfalls as well as its charms. All were, in their fashion, men of the Enlightenment. All were, if not heretics, suspiciously unorthodox in their religious opinions. All were models of conduct. Jefferson afterwards called Williamsburg "the finest school of manners and morals that ever existed in America." And the peak of felicity for him was undoubtedly the *partie quarée* around the Governor's table. Looking back on his youth for the instruction of his grandson, Jefferson said that when under temptations and difficulties he would ask himself, "What would Dr. Small, Mr. Wythe, Peyton Randolph, do in this situation? What course in it will insure me their approbation?" He never doubted that this way of deciding his conduct led him more truly than any mere process of reasoning through the "jaundiced eye of youth."

Student of Law

Once launched on his legal studies, Jefferson was more often at Shadwell than in Williamsburg. As he came of age his responsibilities to his family, his farms, and his country increased, but he was a "hard student" at all times, and in this period drove himself relentlessly. To get a good legal education in Virginia, or anywhere in North America, was more difficult, in some respects, than obtaining a good scientific education in the Congo today. There were no schools, no texts, no American law reports, and few books of any kind. The completion in 1769 of William Blackstone's grand outline, *Commentaries on the Laws of England,* marked a tremendous advance. Within a few years Blackstone was as popular in America as in England. But the work came too late for Jefferson, and in retrospect he was grateful for having missed the "honeyed" smoothness and treacherous systematizing of Blackstone's packaged course in four volumes at the commencement of his studies.

Jefferson started with Sir Edward Coke, that dreary and crabbed seventeenth-century legalist whose *Institutes of the Laws of England*—a "painful" work as he warned the reader in the preface—was unquestionably the fundamental treatise. Had he gone to the Inns of Court he would probably have started at the same place, but in England he would have found a highly organized legal profession that not only controlled entrance into this estate but sharply distinguished its various jurisdictions—common law, civil law, admiralty law, law of nations, and so on—and parceled out the business among tribes of specialists—barristers, solicitors, scriveners, and the like. In the simpler American world all of this was thrown together in disordered profusion. The practice was neither specialized nor even professionalized in the sense of conforming to rigid standards of its own. It developed helter-skelter in response to the needs and pressures of the community. Indeed, before it could develop very far at all, the law became so mixed up with the rising nation's political life that two generations passed before it began to acquire a life of its own. The process of training and admission to the bar was similarly free and loose. There were no patterned roads, as exemplified in the contrasting cases of Henry and Jefferson. The usual practice, however, was for the aspirant to read and work as an apprentice in a lawyer's office. Wythe started Jefferson along this route, but after a few months, whether because of the student's responsibilities in Albemarle or because of his manifest capacities of self-discipline, he turned him loose on an ambitious program of reading. Thereafter, only at brief intervals was Jefferson an apprentice. He disapproved of the system anyway, thinking it "rather a prejudice than a help" because it diverted the aspirant from books to business. "The only help a youth wants is to be directed what books to read, and in what order to read them," he said.

"Well, Page," Jefferson wrote from Shadwell to his college chum John Page, "I do wish the Devil had old Cooke [Coke], for I am sure I never was so tired of an old dull scoundrel in my life." It was enough to make one wonder if the quest for happiness through knowledge was not all humbug and delusion! But Jefferson struggled through the first part of the *Institutes, Coke upon Littleton,* an extended commentary on the classic treatise on tenures written in Law French during Edward III's time, then went on to other parts of the *Institutes,* treating statutory law since Magna Charta, criminal law, and jurisdiction; and he finally came to admire the "uncouth but cunning" legalist. Coke, of course, was best known to history as the common-law champion of English rights and liberties against the Stuarts, which was bound to ensure his reputation with the Americans as they took up what many believed to be the same cause nearly a century and a half later. In the aftermath of that struggle Jefferson would say of him, "a sounder Whig never wrote, nor of profounder learning in the orthodox doctrines of the British constitution, or in what were called British liberties." Blackstone, the champion of parliamentary supremacy become tyrannical, was a Tory by comparison, and in his later years Jefferson attributed the decline of Whig principles in the legal fraternity to the displacement of Coke's "black-letter text" by Blackstone. But in the 1760's, though his reading of Coke obviously faded into his developing political opinions, he was more immediately influenced by the jurist's precise ways of deciphering the mysteries of the common law, by his historical method, and his conception of legal science. Once alerted by Coke, Jefferson dug back to the roots of things before Magna Charta, before the Norman Conquest; unlike Coke, he came

17

to believe that these ancient Saxon foundations of English liberty had been corrupted in the succeeding centuries. His principal guides here were the work of Henry Bracton and the digest of Alfred's laws. Bracton, not Coke, he discovered, was the true foundation. Written a few years after Magna Charta, in technical Latin "abounding in terms antiquated, obsolete, and unintelligible but to the most learned," he later said, it gave the common law its ultimate form at exactly the point of division of the unwritten from the written, or statutory, law. Jefferson moved forward from Coke too, using Matthew Bacon's digest, various reports of cases, and treatises by Lord Kames and others.

But law was not to be studied in an intellectual vacuum. It was kindred of all the sciences and ought to be part of a large and varied diet of reading. Not long after Jefferson finished his own studies and began to practice, a young aspirant looked to him, as he had looked to Wythe, for direction. Although declining this responsibility, he supplied a complete course of reading all carefully scheduled for daily exercise. It was enough to rattle the brain of any man, so formidable a regimen, in fact, that Jefferson himself probably never followed it strictly; yet it conveys his own ardor for learning and the athletic rigor of the pursuit as well as the copious outlines, beyond mere technical competence, of his mentor's instruction. It was first necessary, Jefferson informed the aspirant, that a solid groundwork be laid: Latin and French, mathematics, natural philosophy, natural history—this was the minimum. Then the regular study of law might commence, mixed, however, with "its kindred sciences." From dawn until eight a.m. should be employed in the physical sciences, sparing some time for ethics and religion. Jefferson named the specific texts to be read under each of eight headings. From eight to noon, the best hours of the day, should be devoted to the black-letter of the law. From noon to one p.m., politics, beginning with Locke and Sidney. In the lazy hours in the afternoon, history, proceeding from ancient through modern to English and American. (At least the last appears in the 1814 revision of the letter, the only available text.) The evening hours until bedtime, usually about ten o'clock for Jefferson, should be given over to imaginative literature of all genres ("Shakespeare must be singled out by one who wishes to learn the full powers of the English language"), criticism, rhetoric, and oratory, on which Jefferson was very explicit. He also recommended the habit he had formed after getting through Coke of "commonplacing" pertinent cases and striking things encountered in his reading, sometimes adding his own reflections. These "commonplace books" reveal his careful way of working and provide a partial index to his reading from student days until the Revolution.

He was no recluse in these years. He could not escape company or the round of plantation visiting even had he wanted to—it was the custom of the country. If he was somewhat shy and reserved and inclined, as Page said, "to tear himself away from his dearest friends, and fly to his studies," he also had the normal youthful craving for companionship, male and female, and good times. Trudging the same round day after day at Shadwell he sometimes yearned for the gayer social life of Williamsburg.

This was especially true at the beginning of his legal study when he was caught up in a youthful romance. The lady, actually only sixteen years of age, was Rebecca Burwell, to whom he had been introduced by a college classmate, her brother, at the Burwell family seat, Fairfield, in York County. Back at Shadwell he was desperately afraid that this ripe young virgin would be plucked from the vine while he carried on his affair with old Coke. He did not wish to lose her, still less was he ready to take her. Not only was there Coke to think about, with all that involved, but he had vague ideas of a journey to England and other faraway places, perhaps Italy, where he could pick up a good violin. These ideas never matured. The farthest he traveled from home during the next twenty years was New York, which he visited on a northerly journey in 1766. At any rate, returning to Williamsburg in the fall of 1763, Jefferson saw Rebecca again. They danced at a ball in the Apollo Room of the Raleigh Tavern. Mustering all his courage, carefully rehearsing everything in advance, he determined to declare his affections. "But, good God!" the poor wretch wrote to Page the next morning, "When I had an opportunity of venting them, a few broken sentences, uttered in great disorder, and interrupted with pauses of uncommon length, were the too visible marks of my strange confusion!" Some days or weeks later he managed to make his little speech. It was not a proposal but the promise of a proposal to come, after he had arranged his own future. The damsel listened, returned no answer, and parted from this beau who could so coolly put romance on the shelf. Not long afterwards Jefferson learned of her engagement to Jacquelin Ambler. "Well the Lord bless her, I say! . . . Many and great are the comforts of a single state. . . ." He seems to have been none the worse for this amorous adventure. During the next several years, reconciled to the single state and the male companionship he usually preferred anyway, Jefferson took a harsh view of woman-kind in general. They would not cheat him of his freedom! "Marry!" he quoted a poet, "When I am old and weary of the world. . . ." He would rather be prudent than sorry; and it was not the last time he set duty, reason, and his emerging sense of destiny above the promptings of the heart. "Bold in the pursuit of knowl-edge," as he remembered himself in these young years, he would let nothing come in his way.

Lawyer, Builder, Husband

In 1767, three years after he came of age, Jefferson was admitted to the bar of the General Court. The highest court in the colony, it consisted of the Governor and Council and had appellate and origi-nal jurisdiction in both criminal and civil cases. Members of the Council, being appointed for life by royal grace and favor from among the leading families, having legislative and executive responsi-bilities as well, were not generally known for their legal or judicial attainments. It was a highly respectable court nonetheless, in part because of the advocates who appeared before it. Wythe and Pen-dleton were especially eminent at this time. Both men had risen from modest beginnings. One, Pendleton, was a striking figure, with a nimble mind and much popularity; the other, his rival, without surface brilliance of any kind, distinguished himself by plodding erudition. One was more learned, the other more successful in court. To an extent the contrast between them would be repeated in the two rising co-adjutors, Jefferson and Henry, though they seldom confronted each other at the bar. As Edmund Randolph observed, "Mr. Jefferson drew copiously from the depths of the law, Mr. Henry from the recesses of the human heart." Whatever advantage Jefferson derived from superiority of learning was canceled by

Henry's golden throat and folksy ways, which built for him a following Jefferson could never match. His deficiencies as a speaker were often noted in later years. As a lawyer, however, he seems to have acquitted himself respectably. Randolph, who knew him at the bar, said he was an impressive speaker who easily fixed the attention of his audience without the artifices of oratory.

At least half of the young lawyer's practice was in the county courts. These ruling bodies were even less judicial than the high court in Williamsburg; the litigation tended to be petty, the fees smaller; and the practice necessitated riding the circuit of the county seats. By law the two practices were to be kept separate, but the attorneys paid no attention to the law and pleaded indiscriminately in both jurisdictions. Like a plague of locusts, the pettifoggers of the counties descended on the General Court and, as Jefferson complained, "consumed the harvest." During the Revolution he tried to correct the evil by enforcing the separation of the two practices. Then men of legal science would not have to go marauding in the counties to make a living and the bar of the General Court would become the nursery of future judges. But the growing herd of lawyers had no interest in this system. Jefferson submitted to the drudgery of county practice and made the best of it. Mounted on horseback, his servant Jupiter in tow, he attended the courts of most of the counties of Virginia during seven years of practice. The circuit had its small rewards. It gave him firsthand knowledge of the society and politics of his native country and it established connections that would be useful to him later on. There was an *esprit*, an air of good humor and good fellowship, on the circuit that he enjoyed. And the court days were not without amusement. His account books, which he started with his law practice and in which he recorded every trifling expenditure to the end of his days, show that he attended the races, gambled occasionally at dice or cards, saw puppet shows, a "legerdemain man," an elk, a tiger, "a great hog," heard musical glasses, a woman sing, an organ grinder, and so on. Williamsburg offered plays and concerts and dances. Everywhere he searched out books for his growing library; once he bought a violin.

The account books with other records prove that he was a busy lawyer and, in the circumstances, a successful one. In Virginia, of course, litigation revolved around land and estate—there was little else. Not surprisingly, most of Jefferson's cases concerned tenures in one form or another, a subject grounded in *Coke upon Littleton*. His load of cases steadily increased, peaking in 1773, when he had more than 500 divided more or less evenly between the two jurisdictions, and dwindling the following year when the onrush of revolution closed the courts. Partly because the fees were fixed by law—a lingering trace of the old prejudice against lawyers—the financial return was rather paltry. The annual income on the average of seven years did not exceed $2000, and he was lucky if he collected three-quarters of this. Adding the tobacco income from his farms, he grossed in the neighborhood of $4000 a year, which was a substantial but far from princely income in pre-revolutionary Virginia. For him, as for Henry, as for John Adams in Massachusetts and so many others, the law laid the groundwork for a political career. His future was in the forum not at the bar. None of his cases produced public repercussions or became celebrated in the way the Parson's Cause brought instant fame to Henry. But his practice led to a widening circle of acquaintances and influence; even more important, it cultivated habits of mind that proved to be remarkably creative in the work of state-making. When he abandoned the practice in 1774 he did not abandon the law; rather he turned his legal skills to the greater cause of the Revolution.

The turn from law to politics had commenced five years earlier. In 1769 he took his seat in the House of Burgesses as a representative of Albemarle. This was almost sure to come in time: the service went with his position in the county. Still it was unusual for the freeholders to elect a young man of twenty-six who had not yet learned the ropes in the county magistracy. In the normal course one rose to the Burgesses on the ladder of local offices. Such had been his father's case. Jefferson reversed the procedure, starting at the top and taking in the local offices from that point. At least it does not appear that he was a justice of peace before he was a burgess; and he succeeded to the posts of county lieutenant and county surveyor, both formerly held by his father, in 1770 and 1773 respectively. Clearly the Albemarle gentry had taken the measure of young Jefferson and decided to promote him at once to the head of the class. Perhaps they were impressed by his legal attainments or his business-like approach to farming or, most of all, his enterprise in opening the Rivanna River to navigation. This was his first important public service and one that in later years he would count among the most useful. Until he came of age scarely a canoe navigated the Rivanna. Tobacco was transported overland to the stream's juncture with the James. Jefferson took a canoe, explored the river, and located the obstructions to navigation. He then started a subscription among his neighbors. Finally, with legislative authorization, the river was cleared as far as the falls at Milton just below Shadwell. Henceforth, the Rivanna floated most of the county's tobacco and produce to market.

As he was entering the public stage, Jefferson was also beginning to build at Monticello. The "little mountain" to which he gave the Italianate name was part of his father's original grant and had been a favorite haunt since he was a boy. It was now the chosen spot for his country seat. He began sawing lumber and planting fruit trees there in 1767; the next year he let a contract to level the summit; and in 1769 the foundations were dug, the brick kilns fired, and hardware ordered from England. He tried to get his English agent to send over an architect as well, but without success. He became his own architect. The versatility he demonstrated in this endeavor marked a permanent trait, exploding in all directions. The offspring of the meagerness of his cultural environment, it also expressed a powerful creative impulse in the man himself. Others might be content with what was; he could think only in terms of what should be. And he would not allow trifling obstacles, like those in the bed of the Rivanna, to bar his way.

To build a house with any pretensions to elegance in his remote country was difficult. But to rear it on a densely wooded summit seemed an act of folly. There was no precedent for it in America or in England; and though his reading of the Romans might have suggested the idea, it appears to have been entirely original with him. The simplest explanation is that he liked the view. From this eminence he surveyed a splendid panorama of nature, waves of forest, rolling hills and deep valleys, sharply etched, to the west, against the noble background of the Blue Ridge. The place appealed to his commingled sense of the beautiful and the sublime. He had probably read Edmund Burke's *Philosophical Inquiry into the Origin of*

Our Ideas of the Sublime and the Beautiful and noted his distinction between beauty in the classical sense of harmonious form and the sublime with its evocations of the boundless, the incomprehensible, the awesome in nature which, in Burke's view, communicated feelings of exaltation and power to the beholder. Whether or not he intended it, Jefferson achieved the latter in the setting and the former in his house. On the mountain nature was softened, proportioned, and improved by man; but all around wild nature inspired admiration and awe. The grandeur of the spectacle uplifted him. He felt bigger and nobler for having it at his command. "Where has nature spread so rich a mantle under the eye?" he exulted. "Mountains, forests, rocks, rivers. With what majesty do we ride above the storms! How sublime to look down into the workhouse of nature, to see her clouds, hail, snow, thunder, all fabricated at our feet! And the glorious sun when rising as if out of distant water, just gilding the tops of the mountains and giving life to all nature."

Learning to be his own architect, Jefferson first looked around his native country for models. The great plantation houses in the lowlands, Rosewell, Brandon, Westover, and others, some of which he knew well, were too elaborate, and the rough plans he obtained of newer and more modest dwellings did not suit him. So he turned to books. Later, when he felt he had earned the right, he was a harsh critic of Virginia building generally. Except for the Capitol in Williamsburg, no public building merited respect; and he cursed the prejudice against brick and stone and the sway of Georgian style in domestic architecture. "The genius of architecture seems to have shed its maledictions over this land." Searching for the first principles of the art, he acquainted himself with the books of certain English architects, Robert Morris and James Gibbs in particular, and they in turn led him to the master, the sixteenth-century Italian Andrea Palladio, whose *Four Books of Architecture*, virtually unknown in America, was the fountainhead of the art in Europe. Palladio had returned to Roman antiquity for his models—to surviving monuments where they existed, as in the case of theaters, temples, basilicas, and so on, and to the descriptions left by Vitruvius, Pliny, and others of Roman country villas. It was the last, of course, that now interested Jefferson. These villas, like his own, usually commanded an extensive landscape—Palladio recommended building on an eminence—and as they were planned for productive estates employing slave labor, Jefferson discovered that their requirements, as in the relationship of the master's house to the service quarters, were remarkably similar to his own. But the greater and more enduring appeal of the Renaissance Italian to the Revolutionary Virginian lay in an aesthetic that not only confirmed but gave visible statement to his Newtonian faith in a rational and harmonious universe. In architecture the scientific modernist went back to the ancients because there, rather than in the vernacular of his own time and place, he found a definition of beauty that was as universal, chaste, and orderly as the laws of nature. The lesson of Palladio was that there were laws of architecture, equivalent to mathematical and physical laws, and that they were articulated in the buildings of ancient Rome. Escaping from mindless provincialism along this route, Jefferson ran the risk of falling into academic dogmatism. But he realized that in matters of taste, no less than in morals and politics, nature had constituted utility as the standard, thus the mind was free to adapt and transform the purest models in the light of environment and use. For himself, of course, and for the culture of his own country, he believed the classical ideal best expressed the dignity of free men in a free environment.

Palladio's influence made itself felt gradually, and never completely, in the design of Monticello. The early sketches show a one-story central block with pediment and flanking wings. Its principal source seems to have been a plate in Morris's *Select Architecture*. Later, after assimilating Palladio, he added a classical portico and other touches. The final plan combined features of both its predecessors. The elevation he drew exhibits a two-story central portico, Doric capitals below, Ionic above, with wings supporting a low attic story. Inside, a large entrance hall with staircase, a parlor or saloon, and a library on the second floor filled the central mass, while the wings housed the master's suite and the dining room and smaller bedrooms above. A Palladian villa in outline, the building was not a literal copy of anything. Many detail drawings, of orders, pediment, entablature, interior ornament, and so on, carefully calculated and scaled to correct classical proportions, show that Jefferson, who probably learned drafting skills from his father, had become a good craftsman. By 1772, when the house plan was settled, he had also worked out its relationship to the service buildings. Abandoning the first idea of a great terraced rectangle adjoining the house at one end, he decided instead on two L-shaped wings running out from the house. While this conformed to the idea of the Palladian court-yard, Jefferson imaginatively adapted it to his own taste and situation by sinking these service wings into the slopes of the hillside at basement level, facing them outward rather than inward, and roofing them as terraces that flowed from the house to the lawns and gardens.

In planning his gardens Jefferson followed the new landscape style in vogue in England. He encountered it in the books of William Shenstone and Thomas Whately and in the aesthetic theory of William Hogarth. The object of landscape, as distinguished from gardens in the formal French mode, was to reproduce artfully the beauties of nature in country estates. And since these beauties were irregular, waving, and rustic in outline—romantic rather than classical—Jefferson's style in gardening contrasted sharply with his style in architecture. This was not a contradiction, since one complemented the other; the mingling revealed a man whose tastes, far from being narrow, were generous and eclectic. He made elaborate plans, including a park stocked with wild animals and embellished with cascading falls, temples (Chinese, Grecian, Gothic), and so on. But many years passed before these plans came to fruition, on a scale well below what he had envisioned.

The house itself was completed in about a dozen years, but the upper portico seems to have been omitted, and the service wings, or dependencies, existed only on paper until Jefferson rebuilt Monticello along its present lines in the 1790's. In a sense, he was always building Monticello. It was a lifelong passion, not simply as an object of taste and beauty but as an object of workmanship. He enjoyed building. A reflective or contemplative interest in the art did not satisfy him. He was excited more by the process itself than by the ultimate product. This went, too, for the other fine arts, such as music, that caught his fancy.

Jefferson took up residence on the mountain in November 1770. At the time only the little pavilion that in time would fix the terminus of the south service wing had been completed. "I have here but one room," he wrote, "which, like the cobbler's, serves me for parlor, for kitchen and hall . . . for bed chamber and study too." A devastating fire at Shadwell caused him to make the move somewhat earlier than he had anticipated. The fire consumed most of his papers together with a library estimated in monetary terms at £200 sterling, though it was the books, not the money, that he treasured. He set out at once to repair the loss, and within a few years boasted a library second to none in Virginia. His ambitions in this direction are suggested by the spacious quarters set aside in his house for the library. By the fall of 1770, too, Jefferson had commenced a courtship which, while its outcome remained uncertain, provided further incentive for him to hurry with the building of Monticello.

The lady was Martha Wayles Skelton, an attractive widow of twenty-three who resided at her father's place, The Forest, near Williamsburg. Jefferson had known Bathurst Skelton, the deceased husband, at college, and John Wayles, Martha's father, at the bar. By his own industry and cunning, both as a lawyer and trafficker in lands and slaves, Wayles had accumulated a large fortune. Martha, his eldest daughter, was the principal heir. Precious little is known of her. The fleeting glimpses that survive portray her as petite, pretty, vivacious, and unusually accomplished in the pleasing arts cultivated by Virginia belles. Indeed it is said that she favored Jefferson over several other suitors in part because he shared her love of music. He, at any rate, gave his sentineled heart to Martha and took her as his bride. They were married at The Forest on New Year's Day, 1772. After a round of festivities and a leisurely journey from the lowlands, they began housekeeping in Jefferson's bachelor quarters, transformed into "Honeymoon Lodge," at Monticello. The first child, Martha, was born in September. Of the six children born over ten years, only two survived infancy. The pain and the sorrow killed Martha. Jefferson, who regarded conjugal love, like religion, as an exclusively private matter, hid the emotional traces of his marriage from the world. Yet it was clearly a happy marriage even with its sorrows. He came to prize domestic felicity above any other. In his view the burden of attaining it rested mainly on the wife, whose whole life ought to revolve around husband, hearth, and children. Martha evidently measured up to the standard—and died under it.

John Wayles's death in 1773 led to a doubling of Jefferson's estate. He would never be so rich again. He came into possession, on behalf of Martha, of some 11,000 acres of land and 135 slaves. However, he promptly sold over half the land to cover his share, about £4300, of Wayles's debts to English creditors. Unfortunately, the bonds given him by purchasers of the lands, which were the security of his own bonds to the creditors, were finally paid off in depreciated Revolutionary currency as worthless as "oak leaves," as Jefferson said, and unacceptable in England. So he had to liquidate the debt all over again. In fact, it dogged him the rest of his life. The two valuable estates retained from the legacy, Elk Hill at the confluence of the Rivanna and the James, and Poplar Forest, to the west in Bedford County, were at first managed from Monticello, and there was a good deal of going and coming between these places. The management of so large an agricultural estate—over 10,000 acres with about 180 slaves, divided among three extensive plantations and several smaller ones—was not unlike the government of a miniature state. As the Revolution approached, Jefferson found less and less time for the affairs of this private domain, and two decades would pass before he could give it his earnest attention.

What manner of man was this thirty-year-old Virginian about to step to the center of the Revolutionary stage? Certain dominant traits of mind and character had formed a personal style destined to have profound public effects. While no complete accounting is possible at this point, before he was really known to history, some of the controlling features of his personality might be discerned.

One is struck, first of all, by the young Jefferson's intellectuality. He was pre-eminently a student, strenuous in the pursuit of knowledge. His mental discipline, his appetite for books, his omniverous curiosity, all marked the trait. He approached the world through his understanding rather than his feelings. It would be misleading to call him bookish, especially if that adjective is meant to suggest the pedant or the closeted philosopher, for he was neither of these; yet, far more than most men, he was dependent on books and inclined to take his knowledge from them rather than from direct acquaintance. As a result, his understanding spanned an immense field but spanned much of it at second- or third-hand, which gave a certain airiness to his traffic with reality. He gained a vantage point above or outside of things-as-they-are—the hard crust of history—from which to perceive, as through the eye of reason, things-as-they-might-be. The Baconian axiom, "knowledge is power," became the core of his faith; and he was never more typically a man of the Enlightenment than in his conviction that reason and inquiry would lead men away from whatever was false or capricious or twisted in human affairs toward the truth inherent in the natural order of things. With this went a tendency, already evident in law and architecture, to run everything back to its source, whence its inner nature could be defined, and to proceed from that point. A radical tendency, it would usually have radical effects. Because the quality of intellectuality was so marked in Jefferson, the principal wellsprings of his thought should be plainly defined. First in the course of education, though not in ultimate influence, was classical philosophy and literature. Second, modern scientific rationalism and natural religion, to which he was introduced by Dr. Small and the trio of tutors in Williamsburg. And third, English law and history, which became for him the main road to revolution.

A close companion of Jefferson's intellectuality was a characteristic forbearance and reserve in his intercourse with his fellow men. In part, this simply expressed his deference to the forms and proprieties of civilized society; but there was an added quality of austerity in Jefferson that, by Virginia standards, seemed more in keeping with the Puritan type. He was by all appearances an amiable and sociable person, never harsh or disagreeable, and he had a remarkable talent, seemingly effortless in its motions, for drawing men to him. But appearances could be deceiving. Most men caught him at the easy glasslike surface he exposed to the world. As Albert J. Nock has observed, "He was the most approachable and the most impenetrable of men, easy and delightful of acquaintance, impossible of knowledge." He kept a tight rein on his emotions. Only once in his youth, when he made "improper advances" to the wife of a friend, did the control slacken, and the narrowness of the escape may have caused him to strengthen his hold. He did not lack a sense of humor, yet it could not be considered a strong point of his personality. He was too fussy. What was ludicrous in life was more likely to be cause for regret than for amusement. Expecting so much of men, and of nations too, he could not laugh at their follies, least of all at his own. He discovered early, as early as his admission into the circle of mature scholars at Williamsburg, that high seriousness was the condition of any worthy endeavor, and he turned from this purchase of his youth, in the words of a favorite poet, "big with holy hope of nobler time to come." It remains to be seen what effects these traits would have in his public career. But one thing seems clear: he was not, in his nature, born for the public. The Pendletons and the Henrys and the Adamses—men who opened themselves freely to the currents of life and politics—were, but not Jefferson. None of the heroes of his early life was associated with political power. Intellectual and moral power yes, power of state no. Like Seneca he would "rather be quiet than in arms." And when arms swept him up, he could never resign himself to his fate. He held back, begrudging commitment to the public role, yet unable to make it in any other; and this pattern of forbearance, with its cycles of withdrawal and return, ran through his life.

No less characteristic was Jefferson's penchant for methodical industry, order, and system. In this he proved to be a rigorous man of business, like his father. He hated idleness. He was fond of detail. His personal records—Account Book, Garden Book, Farm Book, and so on—exhibit a profusion of minutiae. He recorded from year to year, for instance, the exact time and place of planting a given vegetable, when it sprouted, when it ripened and came to the table. His meteorological observations, regularly three times a day, extended over several decades. All was neatly ordered and arranged. He enjoyed poetry when young and heartstrong, even wrote a verse or two; but he was not a poet by nature and, as he matured, had little call for this muse. In nothing he ever undertook did he lack facts; and he felt more at home in the realm of empirical data than in the realm of abstractions. The logic of facts took nothing for granted. It dissolved phenomena into component elements, analyzed them, defined their natural relationship, then reconstructed the parts to express the newly discovered truth. Such at least was the intent. Clarity, precision, proportion—these qualities of his architecture expressed an essentially mathematical spirit—a Newtonian as well as a classical aesthetic—in the service of utilitarian objectives. Jefferson could not surrender gracefully to life. His whole tendency was to combat the chaos of experience and submit it to the dictates of reason which, of course, he identified with the laws of nature.

Related to this, though seemingly at odds with the traits of intellectuality and reserve, was the fundamentally activist temper of Jefferson's mind. With him, as with enlightened thinkers generally, ideas were meant to act on the world, not simply to reflect it. This functional interest in ideas exalted useful knowledge, practical workmanship, and mastery of nature. Even in the arts he was not primarily a passive observer or auditor; his greatest enjoyment came from participation. His temperament rejected the conventional dualism of mind and body, thought and work, theory and practice. He espoused bodily health and activity as the necessary condition of mental vigor; and partly for the same reason, he distrusted overly civilized environments cut off from physical nature. He loved to tinker, to work with his hands, as Monticello would demonstrate. The versatility that would become one of his claims to fame, the result of the workman-like temperament nurtured by his own environment, was already evident in the young Jefferson who, in James Parton's memorable description, "could calculate an eclipse, survey an estate, tie an artery, plan an edifice, try a cause, break a horse, dance a minuet, and play a violin."

An activist must, of necessity, be an optimist as well. The world of experience was malleable to the hammers of the mind. Only gloomy and hypochondriac souls thought differently. "My temperament is sanguine," Jefferson told John Adams in his seventy-third year, and he might have said the same in the thirtieth. "I steer my bark with Hope in the head, leaving Fear astern."

CHAPTER TWO

Philosopher
of Revolution

Charles Townshend: *Will these Americans, children planted by our care, nourished up by our indulgence until they are grown to a degree of strength and opulence, and protected by our arms, will they grudge to contribute their mite to relieve us from the heavy weight of that burden which we live under?*

Colonel Isaac Barré: *They planted by your care? No! Your oppressions planted 'em in America. They fled your tyranny to a then uncultivated and inhospitable country where they exposed themselves to almost all the hardships to which human nature is liable, and among others to the cruelties of a savage foe. . . .*

They nourished by your indulgence? They grew by your neglect of 'em. As soon as you began to care about 'em, that care was exercised in sending persons to rule over 'em. . . .

They protected by your arms? They have nobly taken up arms in your defence, have exerted a valour amidst their constant and laborious industry for the defence of a country, whose frontier while drenched in blood, its interior parts have yielded all its little savings to your emolument. And believe me, remember I this day told you so, that same spirit of freedom which activated that people at first, will accompany them still.

From the debate in the House of Commons on the Stamp Act, 1765.

THOMAS JEFFERSON entered the councils of the American Revolution in May 1769. Taking his seat in the House of Burgesses, he ceased to be an onlooker and became a mover and shaper of events. Pomp and circumstance befitting His Majesty's government in the Dominion of Virginia accompanied the initiation of the delegate from Albemarle. On the morning of May 8, standing with other newly elected burgesses in the Council chamber of the Capitol, he took the oath of office and, before returning to the House, watched the fanfare for the governor as he arrived in an elegantly liveried carriage drawn by six white horses. The Governor, Norborne Berkeley, Baron de Botetourt, had come to Virginia the previous year in succession to Francis Fauquier, dead and buried beneath the stone slab of the Bruton Church. He was a nobleman, of course, but significantly, unlike Fauquier and indeed all the royal governors since 1705, who had been lieutenants of titular heads in England, Lord Botetourt bore the commission of a full-masted viceroy, which the Virginians interpreted as a mark of respect from George III in troubled times. They looked upon this courtly but amiable man as a harbinger of peace and friendship.

Ceremony was the life of royalty. The burgesses—Jefferson one of the troop of perhaps 90 or 100 actually present—answer His Excellency's summons to attend him in the Council chamber. Gentlemen, he commands, return to the House and choose a speaker. They obey, and unanimously re-elect Peyton Randolph to that honorable post. The Governor, duly informed, again summons them and the burgesses again evacuate their benches and march to the other chamber, crowding around the room where the Council is seated at the great table. The Speaker is presented; the Governor reads his speech from the throne; the House retires. These formalities completed, it is now ready for business; not quite, however, for "a most humble and dutiful address" thanking His Excellency for his "very affectionate speech" must be drafted. The new member from Albemarle was given this task, and though his draft was virtually rewritten in committee, the address may be reckoned the first, and certainly the most innocuous, of Jefferson's state papers.

33

After all this parade, the assembly session lasted only ten days. The Speaker at once laid before the House an explosive piece of unfinished business from the previous meeting. In February 1768 the Massachusetts House of Representatives had adopted a vigorous protest against Parliament's Townshend Acts, and by a circular letter to the other colonial legislatures had appealed for united action. The Virginia House had answered with a circular letter of its own urging support of Massachusetts. It was the correspondence evoked by this action that was now laid before the house.

The several acts passed by Parliament in June and July 1767, and known collectively by the name of their principal sponsor, Charles Townshend, Chancellor of the Exchequer, revived the great controversy ignited by the Stamp Act of 1765. The repeal of that measure in the face of massive colonial resistance had given grounds for hope that the imperial government, though it persisted in claiming the right, would not again assert the power of taxing the colonists or otherwise interfere in their internal affairs. But Townshend shattered this illusion. Seizing on the distinction the Americans had supposedly made between *internal* taxes, which were prohibited, and *external* taxes, which were conceded, at least in so far as levied for the regulation of trade, Townshend proposed to collect £40,000 a year by duties in American ports on paper, glass, lead, paints, and tea. The act was a brazen reassertion of Parliament's sovereignty, a clear test of the power claimed by the Declaratory Act, which had passed on the repeal of the Stamp Act, to bind the colonists "in all cases whatsoever." The duties were *external*, but revenue, not trade, was their object; and the anticipated revenue was so paltry that the colonists could not fail to see the political motive and purpose of the act. This was further disclosed by the provision to pay the revenue into a special fund to support, in part, the salaries of royal governors, judges, and other colonial officials, thereby freeing them from dependence on the provincial legislatures. A companion of the revenue measure looked to the more vigorous enforcement of all trade laws by the establishment in Boston of an American board of customs commissioners directly responsible to the British treasury. Still another measure, the most audacious of all, suspended the New York Assembly for failure to furnish quarters and supplies for His Majesty's troops as required by the Quartering Act. New York's grudging eleventh-hour compliance lifted the suspension before it could take effect; but it was this act which submitted the very existence of a colonial government to the will of Parliament that particularly agitated the Virginians in 1768. Meanwhile, as Virginia and most other colonies endorsed the Massachusetts circular letter, the imperial government reacted angrily. All the governors were ordered to treat the letter as a subversive document and to dissolve, if necessary, any assembly that united in the protest against the Townshend Acts. Lord Botetourt carried the directive to Virginia. The Burgesses were under no misapprehension on this point and they had learned of new invasions of American rights brewing in Parliament, for instance, a proposition to transport American malcontents to England for trial.

Such was the challenge to the Burgesses in May 1769. Of course, it must be met. Jefferson may have been surprised that the Governor had chosen to risk a confrontation by convening the assembly. If he expected to pacify the Virginians, he was sadly mistaken. On May 16 the House unanimously adopted four resolutions: first, that the sole right of levying taxes on the inhabitants of Virginia rests with the local government; second, that the united action of the colonies to secure redress of grievances is lawful; third, that all trials for treason or other crimes committed in Virginia must be conducted locally with a jury from the vicinage; and fourth, that the King again be petitioned to intervene on behalf of the rights and liberties of his colonial subjects. A "humble address" to the King was adopted the next day. Immediately, the Governor summoned the House to attend him in the Council chamber. "Mr. Speaker and Gentlemen of the House of Burgesses," he announced, "I have heard of your resolves and augur ill of their effect. You have made it my duty to dissolve you; and you are dissolved accordingly."

Without further ado the burgesses, or rather ex-burgesses, reassembled in the Apollo Room of the Raleigh Tavern and there adopted a non-importation agreement, known as the Association, which bound the signers not to import or to buy any goods taxed by Parliament for the purpose of raising revenue in America. A long list of contraband articles was drawn up and measures taken to circulate the agreement. The Virginians were following the example of merchants and town meetings in the Northern ports; but for the first time a colonial legislature, stripped of its official status and re-constituted under its own authority, engaged in an act of rebellion. Several assemblies similarly situated now followed the Virginia example. The principal aim of the Association was to force repeal of the Townshend duties by unprecedented economic coercion of the mother country. In Virginia, where there were few cities or native merchants, the enforcement was poor; in the major seaports it was more effective. The merchants and treasury in Britain felt the effects, and partly for this reason the new ministry under Lord Frederick North in 1770 brought about the repeal of all the duties, except the one on tea, and by other actions as well sought to conciliate the colonists. The experiment would have lasting consequences for Jefferson's career. He became a convert to the principle and the strategy of commercial coercion not only in the Revolutionary struggle against the mother country but in the larger campaign for national independence in the decades ahead.

In 1770 the American resistance promptly collapsed, despite North's vindication of the principle, in the continuing tax on tea, of the right and the power of Parliament to tax the colonists. Jefferson refused to accept the outcome. Nothing fundamental had been settled. Whatever the conciliatory gestures of the North ministry, the only security for America lay in a constitutional principle no closer to resolution than at the start of the controversy. In the spring, with some others of the same mind in Williamsburg, he signed additional articles of the Association demanding total repeal of the obnoxious duties and looking to the formation of county committees to enforce the agreement. But the movement had fallen beyond recovery at this stage. The Governor had charmed Virginians into a state of fawning admiration and treacherous insensibility to danger, Jefferson later said. Deftly playing the part of friend and reconciler, finessing every difficulty, Botetourt made himself so beloved by Virginians in the few remaining months of his life that when he died the assembly voted to erect a statue of the noble lord in Williamsburg, where it remains to this day a monument of that "colonial subservience" Jefferson deplored.

The second crisis in the contest with the mother country passed in 1770. Jefferson had witnessed the first, brought on by the Stamp Act, and played a modest role in the second, while in the third sure to come he had a still undisclosed appointment with destiny. As he went about the business of law and farming, building and marrying, politics began to have an important place in his life. Service in the assembly plunged him into the center of the colony's affairs. His reading shifted from law and literature, which had predominated, to the theory and practice of government, and with it went a change in the contours of his mind. Virginia was also changing. While it is difficult to say how conscious he was of these shifting contours of society and politics in his native country, it is equally difficult to explain his own career and convictions without taking some account of them.

Troubled Virginia

The remarkable unity of Virginia in support of the Revolution has tended to give a deceptively simple picture of the society and the impulses that moved it. In no colony was there greater solidarity in the ruling class or greater deference in the mass of people to the leadership. Nowhere did the Revolutionary movement produce so little internal discord or was the transition to independence accomplished with such ease. The smoothness of the entire operation has pointed up the importance of two causative factors. First, the structure of politics in Virginia consolidated power in a close-knit gentry class. Power was riveted solidly to wealth, breeding, and status. The House of Burgesses, which one historian has called "a tobacco planters' club" and others have seen as one huge cousinship, consisted of men who ordinarily had passed through the same experience, shared the same interests, and converged in the same outlook. Jefferson, however much he deviated from the type, was a member of the club and could always count half a dozen or more blood relations at the Capitol. Oligarchy was undergirded by democracy—the country democracy of all the landholders. But the electoral system favored the first gentlemen of the counties, and from ingrained habits of deference the freeholding yeomen looked to them for leadership.

The second factor, flowing from the first, was the extraordinary consensus among the leaders on the constitutional basis of Virginia's resistance to the mother country. Until the 1760's the colony had, in fact, enjoyed a high degree of self-government. When this period of "salutary neglect" ended after the Seven Years War, and the imperial government reasserted its claims, the Virginians described the movement as an assault on their ancient liberties and put forth their own claims, carefully buttressed with the defenses of the English constitution, to exclusive jurisdiction over the internal polity. From the Stamp Act forward, certainly, none of the leaders doubted the rightness of this position, though they might disagree on the means of holding it. The idea had been latent for some time. An astute observer in 1759 wrote of the gentry: "They are haughty and jealous of their liberties, impatient of restraints, and can scarcely bear the thought of being controlled by any superior power. Many of them consider the colonies as independent states, unconnected with Great Britain otherwise than by having the same common king." The House of Burgesses claimed for itself co-ordinate jurisdiction in Virginia with the House of Commons in England. Any interference from outside, any subordination of the representative body in Virginia, threatened gentry rule and could not be tolerated. The gentry, therefore, formed a united front against Britain. And precisely because they lacked other pressing grievances, they settled on the constitutional principle that, while it may also have been right and good in itself, secured their own power. When Jefferson finally worked the constitutional argument to a finish in 1774 he drew upon depths of thought and feeling in Virginia as well as upon his own capacious intellect.

Yet, admitting the importance of these forces of solidarity and consensus, revolutions are not made in the absence of social stress nor are the principles invoked an accurate reflection of the reality that moves them. If there were no sharp class or sectional or ideological or interest divisions in Virginia, such as could be found in other colonies, and if the gentry ruled without challenge except from abroad, it does not follow that the gentry had no serious problems of its own. It did; and the anxieties within the ruling class poisoned the imperial relationship. In their quarrel with the mother country Virginians objectified the tensions and strains of their own society. The process was largely unconscious. Jefferson himself was scarcely aware of it. But to a greater degree than anyone recognized, Virginia's antagonism to Britain arose from the ruling elite's troubles about itself.

Grave economic problems afflicted the colony in the 1760's. A debt of half a million pounds had been contracted in the imperial war against France; and lacking specie, the only way the colony would retire it was by the issuance of paper money. But the home government put a stop to this practice that threatened the sterling debts owed to British creditors. Currency remained a problem. Far more serious, however, was the sharp decline of tobacco prices. The planter's income dwindled while he continued to pay high prices to the British merchants who supplied him. The value of his lands and slaves depreciated. Some planters went under. The courts were crowded with suits for debts, and *capias* issued in great number, even against wealthy families. Several successive years of short crops added to the trouble. Planters observed a cooling trend in the climate and feared it would soon cease to support tobacco. Jefferson himself, guided by his thermometer at Monticello, came to this opinion sometime later. In the tidewater, planters worried over "our low land worn out soil." Everywhere the sordidness of slaves and the insolence of overseers stirred complaint. Worst of all, the shrinkage of income, rather than enforcing austerity, was accompanied by reckless extravagance. Chasing the fantastic image of themselves as transplanted English country gentlemen, the great planters lavishly indulged their taste for luxury, refinement, and idle pleasure. "Extravagance hath been our ruin," moaned one of the grandees in 1768. John Wayles, soon to become Jefferson's father-in-law, felt the same gloom. "In 1740," he observed, "I don't remember to have seen such a thing as a Turkey carpet in the Country except a small thing in a bedchamber. Now nothing are so common as Turkey or Wilton Carpets, the whole furniture, rooms, elegant, and every appearance of opulence." Had the Virginians risen to such heights to decline so soon? The history of some of the great families seemed to point the downward direction. William Byrd III had turned a great patrimony into a £100,000 debt. "Wild Bob" Carter, eldest son of Landon Carter of Sabine Hall, was a notorious rake. And ruin impended for the mighty Nelsons in the third generation. These squandering legatees of Virginia wealth and power, these ungrateful sons, figured in the general malaise which only a radical purgative could cure.

But if Virginians must castigate themselves for wanton extravagance, it was not as if they alone were to blame—the British merchants had lured them into the trap. On the whole, the planters were content to work within the mercantilist system, sending all their tobacco to the mother country, where 90 per cent of it was re-exported, after adding £200,000 a year to the British treasury and lining the merchants' pockets with the profits of the trade. The planters thus had no control over the market; yet such were the advantages of the system, especially the British mercantile expertise to which the Virginians laid no claim, that the trade laws were never a serious grievance against the mother country. The great irritant in this colonial subservience was credit, not trade. As Jefferson later explained it: "The advantages made by the British merchants, on the tobacco consigned to them, were so enormous, that they spared no means of increasing those consignments. A powerful engine for this purpose was the giving of good prices and credit to the planter, till they got him more immersed in debt than he could pay, without selling his lands and slaves. They then reduced the price given for the tobacco, so that let his shipments be ever so great, and his demand of necessaries ever so economical, they never permitted him to clear off his debt. These debts had become hereditary from father to son, for many generations, so that the planters were a species of property, annexed to certain mercantile houses in London." There is special pleading in this account, but what matters in the present context is the way Virginians viewed their plight; and, unquestionably, they attributed it in large part to this vassalage under British credit. Jefferson estimated the planter debts at two to three million pounds at the time of the Revolution. To unfriendly observers at the time, to historians since, the desire to throw off these debts was the hidden motive of the Virginia gentry's zeal for independence. The evidence fails to support this view, and as Jefferson's own experience would testify, the debts were not thrown off. Falling deeper and deeper into arrears, the planters directed their anger against Britain through her merchants, above all the Scottish resident factors who, coming to Virginia at mid-century, bought and sold to everyone and spread the web of debt and credit over the whole society.

Land rich, the planters too easily assumed that if forced to it they could sell parcels of their holdings to pay off their debts. But since nearly everyone was in the same boat, and specie or currency in any form exceedingly scarce, there were few buyers even at sacrifice prices. Indebtedness had become a chronic evil from which there seemed to be no escape.

The problem erupted in local politics in 1766. The death of John Robinson in May disclosed a major scandal in the ruling class. For nearly thirty years Robinson had held both the powerful offices of treasurer and speaker of the House of Burgesses. The clique that gathered around him, receiving his favors and doing his bidding in return, has been not inaccurately compared to a modern political machine. Now, after his death, it was discovered that Robinson had embezzled £100,000 from the Virginia treasury in order to help his friends in distress. (The paper money remitted during the war was to be retired when collected in the form of taxes, but instead of burning it as the law required, Robinson loaned it to hard-pressed planters, expecting that the transactions would be covered before they came to public notice.) Approximately 240 gentlemen were the beneficiaries of this largesse. They included Jefferson's father and his future father-in-law, who were indebted to the treasury for £52 and £445 respectively. The debts fell now to Robinson's estate, which in turn owed the money to the province. The administrator of the estate, Edmund Pendleton, patiently pressed the planters for payment. Many suits were instituted, and many of the debtors became bankrupts, if indeed they were not already. At the end of the Revolution the public account was finally closed in depreciated paper money, but before the Revolution the Robinson scandal shook the ruling class, wounded its morale, and damaged its prestige. Corruption and influence, it seemed, had spread from English shores and infected the virtuous heart of liberty in America. Virginians trembled for the future.

The Robinson affair did not split the ruling gentry since they had better reasons to stick together; but it joined with other influences to alter the complexion of Virginia politics. Men like Patrick Henry and Richard Henry Lee, "young hot-heads," Governor Fauquier called them, helped to expose the scandal and then used it to break the virtual monopoly of the Robinson coterie in the affairs of the assembly. Lee's ambitions were allied with the Potomac region, Henry's with the piedmont, both previously neglected in the distribution of power, and allied too, for both men, with more aggressive opposition to the mother country.

The "hot-heads" had won the first challenge a year before in the debate on the Stamp Act. In the waning hours of the assembly session, after most of the burgesses had gone home, Henry offered his resolutions against the Stamp Act and, in this connection, reputedly put down shouts of treason with the defiant line, "If this be treason, make the most of it." The resolutions, or most of them, were adopted over the strenuous opposition of Speaker Robinson, Peyton Randolph, and other members of the old guard. They did not disagree with the principle of these resolutions, which focused the constitutional claim of "no taxation without representation," one which they had, in fact, only a year before solemnly declared a "sacred birthright." But these gentlemen thought the resolutions too bold, perhaps treasonable now that the Stamp Act had become law, and quite aside from fiery implications for the contest with Britain, the resolutions and their upstart backers threatened the reign of the tidewater junto in Virginia. So the larger struggle for power enclosed a smaller one; and while the Virginia Stamp Act Resolves ignited a continent, they also shifted the balance of power in the Virginia gentry. The Robinson affair following in quick succession confirmed the change with added leverage. In general, power moved to the younger gentry, geographically to the upcountry and the Potomac; but these new forces did not so much take over as they were taken into the old leadership. It was a remarkable vindication of a law of conservative politics, phrased by a modern sociologist as "restriction by incorporation." Rather than lose the scepter altogether, the tidewater magnates consented, not without bitterness, to share it.

When Jefferson came into the House he naturally gravitated to the Lee-Henry pole, somewhat to the left of center—though it may be misleading to speak of poles when the political spectrum was so narrow. Lee and Henry remained suspect, but Jefferson was accepted by the old leaders as well as the new and thus helped to allay the little frictions between them. He had known Henry a long time, since a rollicking Christmastime in Hanover County before he entered college. As a law student he had stood in the door of the

House of Burgesses to hear Henry's great speech on the Stamp Act. "He appeared to me to speak as Homer wrote," Jefferson later recalled. From that moment, certainly, his own course in the imperial struggle was fixed. He always credited Henry, seven years his senior, with setting "the ball of revolution" in motion, and whatever he may have said about the Forest Demosthenes after their political estrangement, he insisted on the "exact conformity" of their opinions at this time. What he later said—that Henry was lazy, ignorant, coarse, ambitious, demagogic, and so on—was a fair summation of old guard opinion in the 1760's, though Jefferson had better ground for it. In the end Henry became the most conservative of provincials, while Jefferson, following the popular path he had blazed through densities of aristocratic conceit at the onset of the Revolution, became the hero of American democracy.

Certain areas of British policy in the 1760's not only aroused opposition in Virginia but slashed at the nerves of competing interests within the ruling class. This was notably the case with western lands. In the years between 1745 and 1754 the Governor and Council had granted over a million acres of Trans-Allegheny lands to several speculative companies. Different interests and coteries—a Robinson-Nelson group in the lower tidewater, a Lee-Washington-Mason group in the Potomac region, the Walker interest with which Jefferson's father was associated in Albemarle—jockeyed for favor and influence on Virginia's great frontier. So long as the French were in the Ohio Valley the home government encouraged this movement, believing that Virginia settlers would form a bulwark against the enemy. Various problems, including the war that followed, prevented the land companies from fulfilling the conditions of their grants, and the grants lapsed. After the fall of Fort Duquesne the Virginians attempted to revive the expansionist policy. The British ministry, on the other hand, more concerned now to keep peace with the Indians on the frontier, checked the Virginians at every turn. The Governor was enjoined from making grants on pain of removal from office, and the Royal Proclamation of 1763 prohibited settlement beyond the mountains. The policy broke down five years later. The companies, still without valid title to a single acre, faced a new obstacle in the form of the Grand Ohio, or Vandalia, Company, based in Philadelphia but with influential friends at court in

England, which capped four years of bargaining and intrigue by securing a huge proprietary grant lying south of the Ohio. Claiming jurisdiction in this area, Virginia revived the old grants, issued new patents, and pushed expansion westward, until new British restrictions in 1774 halted the march, so far as it could be halted by law. In this enterprise the Virginians stood together on the issue of provincial versus Crown control but, otherwise, they were not always united among themselves. There was rivalry between the companies; the favors of Governor and Council were unevenly distributed; policies or tactics that benefited one speculative interest often injured another; and the common people were left out of the reckoning altogether. Here again the smaller inner struggle generated some of the heat for the larger one. Jefferson himself, a sworn non-speculator, had only a remote personal interest—the inherited share of dubious value in Walker's Loyal Company—in this business, but western lands and expansion claimed his attention politically. And the more he studied the matter the more convinced he became that no satisfactory solution was possible within the imperial framework.

Looking back at this time in later years, Jefferson complained of "the dull monotony of colonial subservience." What he meant, apparently, as he suggested in his autobiography, was that thought and action were "circumscribed within narrow limits," not only by imperial rule but by colonial habits of mind. Insulated in his little quarter of the globe, Jefferson's mind had nevertheless opened to the enlightened spirit of his age, and he wished to give it effect in the laws of Virginia. But what could be accomplished while the provincial mind was enthralled and an imperial authority 3000 miles across the ocean fixed the country's destiny? During his first brief session in the assembly he sought with one of the senior members to secure legislation to ameliorate the condition, or possibly even permit the manumission, of slaves. The effort failed, and the senior member, Richard Bland, who had taken the lead, was "denounced as an enemy of his country." The Established Church, like slavery an essentially colonial institution in Jefferson's eyes, enforced a "bigoted intolerance" at war with human rights, the peace of society, and religion itself. Yet Virginians, who cared little for the Church, could do nothing about it, except stave off such "pernicious projects" as the establishment of an American episcopate, which would further undermine local autonomy. The obstacles to improvement, Jefferson later said, were more of habit and despair than of reflection and conviction. As he began to see government through the eye of first principles, he discovered many defects in both the Virginia and the English practice. The colonial judiciary, especially the mixing of legislative and executive powers in the General Court, assailed every sound principle. The case of John Wilkes, widely publicized in Virginia during Jefferson's first years on the political scene, vividly dramatized the corruption and deterioration of the home government. Wilkes's four successive elections to, and expulsions from, Parliament after his return from political exile seemed to prove that King and Parliament were tyrants at home as well as in America. The English constitution, although the whole world had been taught to admire it, appeared badly shattered. Jefferson increasingly despaired of its reform and feared the contagion of corrupt influence and arbitrary power in provincial affairs. Alienated from the source of authority, he in common with many other Americans set out to discover what the grounds of authority should be.

Enlightenment—Democracy—Nationality

The American Revolution was an intellectual as well as a political event. The political course to 1776 and beyond is well known in its outer manifestations. The inner movement of thought and sentiment —the history of the Revolutionary mind—remains obscure. Jefferson, who helped to make that mind and who epitomized the philosopher-statesman of the era, was remarkably inarticulate about the processes of thought that conducted him to the revolutionary event. Perhaps he did not understand them himself. Their channels were intricate, devious, and partly hidden from consciousness. Gradually, the heterogeneous elements, dissolved from their old associations, crystallized into a new body of thought. The future would disclose the full range of new associations, but the theoretical framework was set in 1776. It was articulated as a creed, notably in the Preamble of the Declaration of Independence, not as a philosophy, however. Jefferson, as has often been said, never reduced his thought to a system. He was distrustful of philosophical systems generally—

45

they were prisons of the mind. Thought with him was an instrument for reshaping life, not for reflecting it in some grand cosmic design. His philosophy was eclectic, dynamic, and pragmatic. Any attempt to give it the logical coherence of a finished system would be to rob it of the freedom and flexibility essential to its mission. So the philosophy was left in fragments, profuse but disordered, compatible but strangely dissimilar; and to reassemble them into something like the organic unity they must have had in his own mind is at once a difficult and treacherous undertaking. Even the fragments are distressingly scarce before 1776; but many things may be inferred from his reading, his writings, his education, and his experience.

Viewed as an intellectual movement, the Revolution drew on a cultural heritage as old as Western civilization itself. Picking and choosing from the vast concourse of traditions—Classical, Christian, English, Modern—the Americans, not omitting their own incipient tradition, framed a Revolutionary ideology that, while addressed to the unique task of national independence, exploited the sources and ideas and rhetoric of latent democratic revolution in the Western world. Certain dominant configurations emerged from this gathering of forces. For the purpose of analysis in Jefferson's thought, they may be broadly defined in terms of the critical spirit of the age in which he lived, the Age of Enlightenment, the central tradition of law and government on which he drew, the English, and the still shadowy but developing consciousness of the native environment. The terms are rough correlatives of the paramount themes of Jefferson's career in nation-building: Enlightenment, Democracy, Nationality.

Jefferson was the pre-eminent American exponent, along with Benjamin Franklin, of the eighteenth-century Enlightenment. Whether the Enlightenment is considered an intellectual movement, a temper of mind, or a climate of opinion, whether it is dismissed, denounced, or admired, Jefferson was one of its legitimate children, in the end one of its authentic geniuses. Its progenitors were English, Newton and Locke in particular, to whom Jefferson added Lord Bacon to form his trinity of heroes. His early exposure, beginning with the lesser trio in Williamsburg, was mainly to English and Scottish votaries of the Enlightenment. It had invaded the Continent, of course, and Jefferson was familiar with the writings of Montesquieu, Voltaire, Beccaria, Buffon, and several others before the Revolution; but it was not until he took up residence in Paris in the 1780's, then the capital of the Enlightenment, that he plugged the currents of his mind into the wider movement and became something of a *philosophe* himself.

The controlling assumptions of enlightened thought were so thoroughly assimilated in Jefferson's mind that he cannot possibly be understood apart from them. First, untrammeled free inquiry in the pursuit of knowledge. Nothing was to be taken for granted; everything was to be questioned, taken apart, traced back to its origins, and reconstructed in the light of intelligence. "Everything," Diderot enjoined in the great *Encyclopédie*, "must be examined, everything must be shaken up, without exception and without circumspection." Philosophy was a method of inquiry, not a static system of truths; and empirical science on the Newtonian model was good in all fields, the moral and social together with the physical. As Ernest Cassirer has said, the cosmos was no longer to be looked at but permeated. Second, the object of inquiry is the discovery of the natural order of things. Newton had demonstrated the order of the physical universe; Linnaeus had begun to put order into the chaos of life; and Locke, on the same empirical principles, had pointed the way to a science of mind. Were there not universal laws, roughly equivalent to the law of gravitation, in the moral and social realms? There were, the eighteenth-century philosophers insisted, but they lay buried under the rubble heaped up over the centuries by dogmatic authority and superstition. The political economists were gradually approaching the conception of an autonomous economic order governed by immutable laws of nature. The Newtonian model, which exalted a divine Creator, gave assurance that the laws of nature were universal, harmonious, and beneficent. Nothing in nature could be disharmonious, as Jefferson often said. Man, so long alienated from nature, could now begin to feel at home in it. Third, reason is the principal agent of criticism and inquiry—reason, that is, not as "eternal verities" but as a method of verification. Aggressively secular, enlightened thinkers exposed bigotry and superstition, denounced airy "metaphysical" speculation, and leveled the walls of mystery and authority separating man from nature. They did not claim omnipotence for reason, however. As the century advanced, more and more thinkers looked to the affections, or feelings, for a unifying principle in the moral world. And as Bacon taught, the mind should be freed from the burden or rationalizing grand mysteries beyond finite understanding in order to attack the concrete obstacles to human happiness in everyday life. The faith was utilitarian. "It is by witness to works rather than by logic or even observation that truth is revealed and established," said Bacon. "It follows from this that the improvement of man's lot and the improvement of man's mind are one and the same thing." Finally, the end of enlightened thought is happiness. "Man is unhappy only because he does not know nature," the *philosophe* Holbach declared. Knowing nature, man might come into harmony with the order of things and avail himself of its laws to secure happiness. Whether or not the "pursuit of happiness" was a right, as Jefferson would claim, it was certainly man's deepest desire. Individuals, like societies, differed in their definitions of happiness; hence an easy freedom, tolerance, and pluralism should reign in the determination of goals. Most, though not all, enlightened thinkers agreed that individual happiness, far from being a selfish propensity, was founded in social affections. Thus the pursuit involved an active and, on the whole, practical and humanitarian commitment to the well-being of others. Progress, one of the keynotes of the Enlightenment, was ensured by the conviction that man had all the necessary equipment to take possession of nature in the interest of the species. Illimitable progress, rather than the perfectibility of man, was the captivating vision. As Jefferson himself cautiously summed up this reasoned faith: "Although I do not, with some enthusiasts, believe that the human condition will ever advance to such a state of perfection as that there shall no longer be pain or vice in the world, yet I believe it susceptible to much improvement, and most of all, in matters of government and religion; and that the diffusion of knowledge among people is to be the instrument by which it is effected."

Jefferson's affinities to the ancient world were anchored in the world of thought of his own century. Perhaps in no way was he a more typical representative of the Enlightenment than in his deep feeling for antiquity. For the Enlightenment embraced, in Peter Gay's phrasing, both an "appeal to antiquity" and a "pursuit of modernity," the former being in the service of the latter. Hence it is quite misleading to polarize these two intellectual worlds and to say that Jefferson, for example, struck a balance between the "humanistic" interests of one and the "naturalistic" interests of the other. In fact, both were essentially humanistic by virtue of being essentially naturalistic, and one infused the other, just as Jefferson's appeal to classical forms infused a modern architecture. Men of the Enlightenment found in the pagan world of Greece and Rome a basis of perspective on their own age, one that liberated them from the claims of Christianity, and also furnished them with a whole armory of weapons for the assault on dogma, bigotry, and superstition. Except for the classical millennium, succeeded, it must be remembered, by the Christian "Dark Ages," there was scarcely an edifying page in the history of mankind. Darkness shadowed the ancient world too; nonetheless, the ancients exhibited ideals of learning, virtue, beauty, cultivation, the dignity of man, and the freedom of mind for the emulation of moderns. Their intelligence groped with fundamental problems of nature, religion, conduct, and governance. The questing mind of Socrates, the Horatian idyl to the art of living, Cicero on the duties of life, the competing moral schools of Cynics, Stoics, and Epicureans who yet united in the command "Follow Nature," Lucretius who conducted his own war of science against religion, the serenity of Seneca, the political wisdom of Tacitus, Tacitus who Jefferson thought "the first writer in the world without a single exception"—these and so many other classical authors threw shafts of light on the perplexities of modern men struggling for enlightenment.

Jefferson, like most of his contemporaries, was more attentive to Rome than to Greece. The Romans had absorbed what was best in Greek civilization and overcome its crucial weakness by the creation of a universal rule of law, the *jus gentium*, applicable to the farthest reaches of empire, to which, of course, the Western world fell heir. Politically, however, Rome too was a failure. Corruption, luxury, and ambition sank the republic in the second century of the Christian era. Not surprisingly, enlightened men, especially in America, focused their eyes on the republic and on Livy, Tacitus, and the others who sadly recorded its history and rebuked its sequel. Was the England of George III very different from Nero's Rome? The republic, indeed the entire course of ancient history, furnished a rich storehouse of analogies to eighteenth-century philosophers. The appeal to antiquity was not an antiquarian exercise; it had vitality, though with shallow men it could be a mere conceit, a badge of superficial learning. Some made a cult of antiquity and waxed nostalgic over "golden ages." Jefferson was not afflicted in this way. The darkness of the ancient world struck him fully as much as the light. He found virtually nothing to admire in ancient governments; and in time he would discover serious deficiencies in ancient morals. But none of this lessens his debt to the ancients.

In Jefferson's early thought on fundamental questions of religion and morals classical strains are subtly interwoven with the modern. In his youth, perhaps at college, perhaps soon after, he lost his inherited Anglican faith and became a convert to deistic natural religion. "I had never sense enough to comprehend the articles of faith of the Church," he later wrote in declining to be godfather to a child, "and it has always appeared to me that comprehension must precede assent." He did not sever all ties with the Church but was clearly alienated from it as early as 1770, by which time, too, the "episcopal palace" probably recognized him as an enemy, the dissenting sects as a friend, and the rising generation as a patron of the widest latitude in religious matters. He had no respect for the Established Church on any ground, and his reading of the modern rationalists, principally English and Scottish, conveyed him to that convenient via media of the Enlightenment, natural religion, between orthodoxy and atheism. The catalogue of his library in 1815 lists many of the English deistic tracts and treatises of the early eighteenth century, but with three or four exceptions one cannot be certain that Jefferson acquired and read these works when young. He probably did, for he would not have troubled himself at a later time. The works of these ponderous theologians—Matthew Tindal, Samuel Clarke, Thomas Chubb, Conyers Middleton, and others—together with those of more edifying philosophers like Lord Bolingbroke, belonged to a particular stage of religious controversy and staled rapidly. It was the stage that established two main propositions for enlightened men. First, that the Christianity of the churches was unreasonable, therefore unbelievable, but that stripped of priestly mystery, ritual, and dogma, reinterpreted in the light of historical evidence and human experience, and substituting the Newtonian cosmology for the discredited Biblical one, Christianity could be conformed to reason. Second, morality required no divine sanction or inspiration, no appeal beyond reason and nature, perhaps not even the hope of heaven or the fear of hell; and so the whole edifice of Christian revelation came tumbling to the ground.

Jefferson reached his own religious convictions along the lines of these propositions. He was a theist whose God was the Creator of the universe. Such a God exemplified workmanship and design; all the evidences of nature testified to His perfection; and man could rely on the harmony and beneficence of His work. Such a God could not be identified with the God of the Bible as commonly known. Tindal's *Christianity as Old as the Creation,* one of the classics of Deism, may have convinced Jefferson of the sufficiency of the laws of nature, the superfluousness of revelation, to explain the creation and the simple duties of man. He later attributed great influence to Middleton's writings. Middleton was both classical scholar and theologian. His *Life of Cicero* became a favorite with Jefferson. His *Letter from Rome,* a landmark in the pursuit of historical Christianity, explored its mythopeic origins in pagan idolatry and superstition, while the *Answer to Waterland* denied the literal inspiration of the Gospels and raised other doubts of Scriptural authority. From Middleton, rather than from Hume's scoffing *Essay on Miracles,* Jefferson probably learned to apply the test of historical evidence in religion and to withhold assent from the miracles and related supernatural phenomena. The same lesson was taught by Bolingbroke, that whirligig of eighteenth-century thought, whose writings Jefferson "commonplaced" at length. He copied Bolingbroke's Lockian injunction: "No hypothesis ought to be maintained if a single phenomenon stands in direct opposition to it." And also numerous passages that disparaged the Biblical God in comparison with the God of nature, rebuked Scriptural authority, and ridiculed sectarian pretensions to truth. He was inclined to agree with Bolingbroke's famous maxim on the tacit alliance between priests and atheists against true religion. In later years he traced the corruption of Christianity to the "whimsies" and "mysteries" excogitated by Plato's "foggy brain," inspiring "endless systems of mystical theology"; but at this stage, while never an admirer of Plato, he was not prepared to load the awful responsibility on him. Dismissing revelation, divine grace, and the future state of Christianity, dismissing, in short, the religion of the churches, Jefferson believed that natural reason and the evidence of the senses provided a sufficient basis of religion and ethics. Indeed, for the young Jefferson religion was absorbed in ethics; and he looked to the classical moralists, more than to the Christian, for his principles of conduct. He recognized, however, that this was only his private judgment. Others might disagree, and their truths, if reached after the same patient inquiry, were no better or no worse than his.

The conviction that religion is a private concern, that it merits honest inquiry, and that multiplicity of belief is the result, distinguishes Jefferson's thought on the subject. Unlike many Enlightenment thinkers, especially in the later and more radical stage, he did not form intellectual conceits about religion or scoff at faiths more pious than his or envision a grand unifying "religion of humanity." In a letter to a young nephew in 1787, he prescribed the method of inquiry he approved and had doubtless tried to follow himself. Fix reason firmly in her seat, he advised, shake off all bias in favor of novelty as well as all "servile prejudices" of orthodoxy, and boldly question everything, beginning with the existence of God. The religion of your own country merits respect—study it with care. "Read the Bible, then, as you would read Livy or Tacitus." Events that contradict the laws of nature must be weighed in the light of testimony, credibility, pretensions to inspiration, and so on. "The pretension is entitled to your inquiry, because millions believe it." Examine the character of Jesus. Was he the son of God? Read all the histories of Jesus, those of both the evangelists and the pseudo-evangelists. "Do not be frightened from this inquiry by any fear of its consequences," Jefferson said. "If it ends in a belief that there is no God, you will find incitements to virtue in the comfort and pleasantness you find in its exercise, and the love of others which it will procure you. If you find reason to believe there is a God, a consciousness that you are acting under his eye, and that he approves you, will be a vast additional incitement. . . . Your own reason is the only oracle given you by heaven, and you are answerable, not for the rightness, but [the] uprightness of the decision."

The uprightness of the decision: this conviction that true belief is the result of an open mind and the courage of one's own understanding was the essence of Jefferson's doctrine. It was quite the opposite of both lazy conformity to prevailing canons of piety and aggressive hostility to religion. It called for persevering search of truth, not one and absolute, since the experiences of men and the composition of their minds are much too varied to admit that, but for the truth as one sees it. The doctrine would have profound public effects, for religion conceived in this way could have no public authority. Moreover, the doctrine reveals Jefferson's concern for the place of religion in his life; and although skeptical inquiry at the threshold of maturity led him to assign it a rather small place within the bland scheme of natural religion, there is no reason to question the uprightness of his decision or his continuing responsibility to the quest for religious truth.

Religion was valuable chiefly as an adjunct of morality. Partly for this reason Jefferson never formulated a creed, and his library catalogue assigned religion to a sub-division of a sub-division under moral philosophy. Whether one acted on right principles considered as the rule of God or considered as the rule of nature made little difference. For himself, the latter was clearly indicated. In the ripeness of years he distilled a secular code from the teaching of Jesus, the purest system of morals ever taught, he then thought; but when young he could not separate the purities from the impurities of theology. He copied a passage from the contentious Bolingbroke denying that Christ revealed "an entire body of ethics." Instead of the hodgepodge of inscrutable utterance, allusion, and parable contained in the gospels, Bolingbroke recommended a code derived from the ancient moralists. "A system thus collected from the writings of ancient heathen moralists, of Tully, of Seneca, of Epictetus, and others, would be more full, more entire, more coherent, and more clearly deduced from unquestionable principles of knowledge."

Jefferson turned to these ancients less for a code than for a posture of conduct. Not committing himself to one school or another, he took what he wanted from both Stoic and Epicurean. The former, as exemplified in Epictetus, Seneca, and Marcus Aurelius, emphasized freedom from passion, aloofness from the swirling currents of life, and resignation to fate, all to be achieved by stern self-discipline. The latter, the Epicurean, allowed more latitude to human passions and pleasures and was more cheerful generally. The Stoic creed, with its ideal of brotherhood, had been absorbed into Christianity, while the Epicurean had been smothered under the odium of libertinism. A seventeenth-century philosopher, Pierre Gassendi, much admired by men of the Enlightenment, had rescued Epicurus from this fate and, at the same time, established him as a classical precursor of the physics of Galileo and Newton. Jefferson read Epicurus through the eyes of Gassendi. Pleasure, rightly understood, conduces to virtue, for one cannot live a pleasurable or happy life without honor, goodness, and peace of mind. And since pleasure and pain, unlike virtue, which is an abstraction, are immediately experienced, the basis is laid in these sensations for an empirical science of ethics.

On the whole, Jefferson's posture was Epicurean. His desire to cultivate the senses, his concern for bodily comforts, his confidence in man's power to control events, his commitment to the pursuit of happiness—these directives were Epicurean. But the stiffer, the more ascetic, Stoic strain was always present and at times, when he sickened of the world, uppermost. His early commonplace book of the poets and philosophers, *The Literary Bible*, contains generous samples of melancholia, together with many fatalistic aphorisms and ordinances of self-denial. If much of this can be dismissed as youthful posturing, the fact remains that Jefferson's emotional reticence toward the world was characteristically Stoical. Like most men he found room in his life for both attitudes and shifted the accent according to his mood. In the final analysis, as Adrienne Koch has said, he employed rigorous Stoic self-discipline to the attainment of the Epicurean good life.

But what was the foundation of morality once the props of Christianity had been removed? Taking their cue from the ancients, who had found the moral in the natural, the enlightened thinkers developed a naturalistic ethics within the framework of empirical science. Human nature was the starting point for a moral Newtonianism. Early efforts to locate the source of moral judgement in reason failed. Reason was not an exciting force; it might be the stem but could not be the root of morality. The capacity to reason, in which men differed greatly, seemed to have no direct relation to moral capacity. So the inquiry turned to the sentiments or feelings.

One school, originated by Hobbes but popularized in the eighteenth century by Bernard de Mandeville, located the source of moral action in self-love. Jefferson was familiar with these teachings—several of Mandeville's books were in his library—and was repelled by them. The idea that selfishness led to virtue, that private vices produced public benefits—Mandeville's famous axiom—seemed to him a cynical assault on morality, in the same way that Machiavelli assailed the moral foundations of politics. He found his solution in the "moral sense" school of Lord Shaftesbury, Francis Hutcheson, and others. The ubiquitous Scot Henry Home, Lord Kames, whose writings on law, theology, natural history, and moral philosophy Jefferson mined when young, was the principal conveyer of this doctrine. He may have been introduced to Kames by Dr. Small. In any event, the moral philosophy taught by that good man was surely of this school.

Formulations differed, but in general the doctrine held that man is equipped with an inner sense of right and wrong, and that it approves conduct tending to the public good or, as Hutcheson put it, "the greatest happiness of the greatest numbers." Why is it, Jefferson asked, that benevolent actions give us pleasure? "Because nature hath implanted in our breasts a love of others, a sense of duty to them, a moral instinct, in short, which prompts us irresistibly to feel and to succor their distresses. . . ." (The fact that Jefferson used *instinct* interchangeably with *sense* suggests the deeper biological basis of the doctrine in his conception than in the formulations of leading proponents.) To act viciously is to be miserable; to act virtuously is to be happy—and to increase the happiness of mankind. The individual calculus of pleasure and pain, in the sensationalist psychology derived from Locke, thus had its social counterpart in a calculus of public happiness. "The Creator would indeed have been a bungling artist, had he intended man for a social animal, without planting in him social dispositions," Jefferson observed. Such a marvelous contrivance for harmonizing pleasure and virtue, self and society, implied a divine artificer, of course. Reason came into the system as a cultivator and regulator of the moral sense: the head informed and guided the natural dispositions of the heart. The moral sense was universal, as much a part of every man as the senses of sight and hearing; its exercise was defective from the want of education or other circumstances. The fact that what was deemed virtue in one country was deemed vice in another did not disprove its existence. An internal directive toward the right and the good, it did not determine external standards. Utility, as Jefferson said, determined these. "Men living in different countries, under different circumstances, different habits and regimens, may have different utilities; the same act, therefore, may be useful, and consequently virtuous in one country which is injurious and vicious in another. . . ." He thus affirmed his belief in the fundamental uniformity and equality of mankind, while at the same time making allowance for the variations produced by history, culture, and environment. What was useful was good in Jefferson's philosophy; what was good was natural; and what was natural—an inherent human endowment—laid claim to the status of inalienable right.

The moral sense philosophy, with its facile logic and easy optimism, proved very useful to Jefferson, as to many of his contemporaries. In the breakdown of religious authority, it provided a secular analogue of Christian conscience. It helped to save him from nominalism and skepticism and, politically, from traffic with the Hobbesian Leviathan. The moral world had not been abandoned to chance. The same directing forces subsisted in the social as in the solar system. As the law of gravitation was the regulating power of one, the moral sense was the regulator of the other. Around the doctrine gathered Jefferson's faith in a divine Creator, in common humanity, and the natural sociability of mankind. It was the cohesive force in a philosophy pivoted on sense experience, wide open to the diversity of thought and the contentiousness of civil life, and running pell mell to individualism.

Jefferson's political thought, though it became the quintessence of Enlightenment liberalism, had its roots in English law and government. The American revolutionaries were fortunate in their heritage. The tradition of the English constitution gave a concreteness to their claims of personal and political liberty, even a color of legality to revolution itself, that no other modern revolutionaries possessed. Thus it has sometimes seemed that the Americans, far from finding a new political paradise, were simply regaining the one that had been lost somewhere in the tumultuous English past. The recovery strain is especially evident in the young Jefferson. He approached government from the law, and precedent was nine-tenths of the law. He approached law as a form of history. History, as the esteemed Bolingbroke had said, was philosophy teaching by example. Law was its most objective expression. Jefferson did not look to the past for political models. "History, in general, only informs us what bad government is." It was full of admonitions. More positively, however, historical investigation disclosed the sources of both truth and error in the modern constitution of society. By possessing this knowledge men might cultivate what was good, eradicate what was bad, and so, in a sense, escape altogether the tyranny of the past. Jefferson became an authentic spokesman of this hope of the Enlightenment, this vindication of human nature against the past, which seemed to be the peculiar mission of America. But he reached the position gradually. The progression of his political thought before the Revolution has been described as a movement from history to theory. It was that, and at the same time a movement from the particularism, the local patois, of English law and government to the rationalism and universalism of the natural rights philosophy. In the preliminary stage of the controversy with the mother country, he joined his fellow colonials in the appeal to the English constitution. And even after the ultimate appeal to nature in 1776, the shadow of the English heritage hovered over Jefferson's mind. His political imagination, partly clouded by old historical ideas, had not yet caught up with the principles of reason. The two main ideas that had great powers of prepossession in Jefferson's mind concerned the Saxon origins of English liberty and the "balanced" government of the English constitution.

Jefferson's study of law led him to the Anglo-Saxon conception of English liberty. The seeds were planted by the invading tribes from Germany in the fifth and sixth century, according to this theory. Tacitus, who had described these tribes in *Germania*, credited the Saxons with great virtue and political wisdom, and modern commentators embroidered his celebrated account. The Saxons, it was held, introduced into England an elective kingship, an annual assembly of tribal chiefs, the witenagemot—the true forerunner of Parliament—trial by jury, and the common law. The polity was pre-feudal. It presented an idyllic picture of simple independent farmers free of rents, entails, and other burdens. The Norman Conquest brought feudalism to England, and in the view of some commentators virtually destroyed the ancient Saxon laws. Against Norman tyranny the nation sought to reclaim the rights it had lost. The recurring struggle thenceforth characterized English history. Magna Charta opened a new epoch by restoring, substantially, the original constitution. Usurpation ever threatened, however, and under the Stuarts in the seventeenth century English liberty and self-government were again destroyed. The Long Parliament, the Commonwealth, the Restoration—these turbulent chapters were brought to a close by the Glorious Revolution of 1688. Alas, corruption and vice and new forms of oppression—standing armies, septennial parliaments, ministerial influence—soon spoiled the promising new epoch. In the eyes of belligerently libertarian Englishmen of the eighteenth century, at home and in the colonies, salvation lay in return to the track of the ancient constitution.

Such, in general, was the Saxon myth. Jefferson encountered it in whole or in part in the writings of legal commentators, historians, political theorists, and pamphleteers: in Tacitus, in "old Coke," in Lord Kames's *Historical Law Tracts*, Sir John Dalrymple's *Feudal Property*, Henry Care's *English Liberties*, Obadiah Hulme's *Historical Essay on the English Constitution*, Sir Robert Molesworth's *An Account of Denmark*, the "Cato Letters" of John Trenchard and Thomas Gordon, the martyred Algernon Sidney's *Discourse on Government*, which Jefferson thought "the best elementary textbook on the principles of government," the *History of England* by the Huguenot Paul de Rapin-Thoyras, which he always considered the most faithful ever written, and in numerous other works.

The Saxon myth in some form pervaded English historical thought. It entered into the prevailing Whig interpretation of the eighteenth century. Traces of it could be found even in David Hume's *History of England*, the great witness against the Whig theory. Hume was an ingratiating writer. Jefferson later recalled the enthusiasm with which he devoured the *History* when young—"and the length of time, the research and reflection which were necessary to eradicate the poison it had instilled into my mind." He must have eradicated the poison well before 1776, for beyond the admission of Saxon virtue there were few opinions in Hume's work he could approve, and he commenced a lifelong campaign against its insidious

58

influence. Hume was a rank Tory apologist, he repeatedly insisted, who having begun with the vindication of the Stuarts wrote backwards, perverting all prior history, praising feudalism, deriving the constitution from the Norman Conquest, so as to sustain the enormities of the Stuarts. "It is this book which had undermined the free principles of the English government," he said. The Whig theory, identified with the ascendancy of Parliament after 1688, held to the idea of an immemorial constitution from ancient Saxon times. Thus the common law existed continuously, "time out of mind," undisturbed by conquest or usurpation, and Parliament, too, rested on the ancient foundation. Coke and the lawyer combatants of the Stuarts had invented this myth. In the eighteenth century it became the historical justification of the Whig ascendancy.

Jefferson absorbed the general theory, of course, but without at first realizing the implications, subscribed to a radical version. Unlike Coke and the Whig apologists, he believed that the Conquest had broken the line of continuity by introducing feudal tyranny, corrupting the common law, and so on; and that after all the struggles to root out these evils, they persisted, like some cancerous disease, in the English polity. So Jefferson celebrated the Saxon past as a kind of golden age, still to be recovered, rather than as a baptismal confirmation of the present regime. Many of the modern writers he read on English history and government—Trenchard and Gordon, Rapin, Hulme, James Burgh—held this view as part of a reform ideology. The heirs of a radical tradition born in the tumults of the seventeenth century, these "commonwealthmen," as they have been named, rejected the complacent Whig optimism of the age, decried luxury, vice, corruption, and arbitrary power, demanded the reform of Parliament, the purification of religion, the freedom of the press, the end of standing armies and other oppressions. Their voices were scarcely heard in Hanoverian England; but they struck a responsive chord in American breasts. The principles of the "commonwealthmen" fell in with emerging native ideals. If England had strayed so far from the paths of the ancient constitution, the Americans should look to its preservation on their own distant shore. Molesworth had shown how other northern nations, Sweden and Denmark in particular, sprung from the same Saxon origins as England, had lost their liberties during the past century. Heavy taxes, armies and navies, aristocratic influence at court, despotic kingship—these were parts of the story that Jefferson found sufficiently instructive to record in his commonplace book.

Early committed to the Saxon myth, Jefferson never abandoned it. His lifelong interest in the Anglo-Saxon language expressed a linguistic passion, involved as well, however, with the roots of law and government. Saxon laws of tenure and descent served him well in the reform of Virginia institutions commencing in 1776. And before that, in 1774, he invoked the Saxon myth to justify the colonists' claims against the mother country. This revealed a characteristic habit of mind: the appeal to ancient sources in behalf, not of conservatism, but of change and revolution. A good illustration is the little essay, "Whether Christianity is a Part of the Common Law," written in his commonplace book, perhaps about 1774. Interested at this time in the legal foundations of the Established Church, he questioned the doctrine first clearly enunciated by Sir Matthew Hale at the King's Bench in 1676, and solemnly repeated by Blackstone nearly a century later, that "Christianity is parcel of the laws of England." If true, Christianity must have been taken into the common law before Magna Charta, for it was never given the protection of statutory law. But the original Saxons were pagan; two centuries passed between the invasion and their conversion to Christianity, and the common law was in existence throughout. Jefferson searched the sources of the half-millennium before Magna Charta and found no evidence of Christianity's incorporation into the common law. The silence of Bracton, himself an ecclesiastic, offered cogent evidence of a negative kind. It was true that the codification of King Alfred in the ninth century incorporated the Ten Commandments and two or three chapters of Exodus. But the adoption of a part implied rejection of the rest; even more to the point, as Jefferson discovered in a French treatise on Anglo-Norman law, the interjection of ecclesiastical law into common law was an "*hor d'œuvre* of some pious copyist," "an awkward Monkish fabrication," proven a fraud by the whole nature of Alfred's laws. The ultimate fraud, however, originated in the seventeenth-century treatise of Sir Henry Finch. Finch mistranslated a phrase from an opinion in the Yearbook of 1458. The opinion held that the common law credited those laws of the Holy Church that were in ancient writing, *en an-*

cien scripture, that is, those precedents of the canon law shown to be part of the common law. But Finch rendered the Latin phrase as "holy scripture," thus installing bigotry and superstition in English law. "In truth," Jefferson concluded, "the alliance between church and state in England has ever made their judges accomplices in the frauds of the clergy; and even bolder than they are." His methodical inquiry, whether or not it led him to the right conclusion, proved his commitment to the rational laws of "our Saxon ancestors," which, far from existing in England's "immemorial constitution," had to be rediscovered under layers of fraud and usurpation.

The theory of "balanced government" had its origin with Aristotle, its revival with the late Renaissance political craftsman Machiavelli, and its modern exemplification in the English constitution. The celebrated freedom of the English government—the freest in the world—was a product of the balanced power of King, Lords, and Commons, each representing one of the great orders of society, royalty, nobility, and populace, and embodying in principle the three classical forms of government: monarchy, aristocracy, and democracy. These pure forms left to themselves ran to corruption: despotism, oligarchy, mobocracy. But properly mixed and balanced in association with the orders of hierarchical society, each checked the vices of the other without alienating or forfeiting the benefit of any one. This tripartite balance was the widely esteemed genius of the English constitution. The Americans not only looked to it for their freedom within the empire but conceived their provincial governments on the same model, at least in the royal colonies. The Royal Governor, the Council, and the Assembly became the rough colonial equivalents of King, Lords and Commons.

The theory was in the air, so to say, and Jefferson could not escape it. Its *locus classicus* in the eighteenth century was the eleventh book of the Baron de Montesquieu's *Esprit des lois.* Jefferson read this famous work around 1770. From it he made twenty-seven entries in his commonplace book—more than from any other book or author. He did not copy from Book XI, as it happens, probably because he took the exposition for granted, although Montesquieu introduced some new wrinkles. He admired this most astute of philosophers for the relativistic theory that associated laws and government with "climate" or, more generally, the entire cultural environment of a people; for the perception that the spirit of republican government was "virtue," a civic spirit subordinating selfish interests to the general welfare; for the generous humanitarianism of the work, as shown in the discussions of slavery and crime and punishment; for the advocacy of civil liberties and religious toleration; and for penetrating observations on federative republics, especially in ancient times. All of this was grist for Jefferson's mill. Yet he probably had reservations about Montesquieu even at this early stage, and two decades later he was an avowed antagonist. The theory of the English constitution was one thing, the perfection of its working quite another. He could not join wholeheartedly in the glorification of the English system in the years before the Revolution; and it would become an impertinence after the Americans evolved a system of their own. The aura of authority, the ensnaring charms of the *Spirit of the Laws*, easily led men into political heresies, Jefferson came to believe. The worst of these was the idea that a republic could exist only in a small territory, since the welfare of the whole could not make itself felt in a large state. Another reflected Montesquieu's class bias: his adherence to a hierarchical society and to aristocratic "honor" as the impulse of liberty.

In the reign of George III the Americans concluded, with the dissident Whigs in England, that this marvelous machine of reciprocating attractions and repulsions, this political counterpart of Newtonian law, the English constitution, had broken down. King and Parliament had combined to upset the balance. The Glorious Revolution established the supremacy of Parliament, more especially of the House of Commons. Locke, whose famous *Treatise on Civil Government* rationalized the event, clearly enunciated the principle: "the legislative must need be the supreme [power], and all other powers in any members or parts of society derived from and subordinate to it." Well and good; but it was not long before King and ministry, the latter becoming with the rise of the cabinet system a new fourth wheel of government, corrupted the new balance of the constitution by wickedly employing favors, bribery, and intrigue in the debasement of Parliament. George III, whose education was Tory, as Jefferson pointedly observed, pursued the scheme to alarming lengths. An invisible government, centered in the "King's Friends," manipulated Parliament for its own interest against the public. If the King was the author of the system, Parliament had co-alesced with him until the checks and balances of the constitution were meaningless or, as Thomas Paine bluntly said, "farcical." The old party distinctions, Whig and Tory, had also become meaning-less. Politicians were locked into the system. "Influence," the favorite word to describe its operation, bought elections with honors, titles, pensions, money, and offices. The Commons was dominated by sev-eral self-perpetuating cliques who fought not over principles but spoils. The "democratic" branch had never represented more than a tiny fraction of the nation, and it was becoming steadily less repre-sentative all the time. Septennial election further weakened the spring of the popular will. "As standing water stinks . . . ," wrote James Burgh, "so a standing house of commons, will ever be a stand-ing pool of corruption." The great check on the Crown, the power of the purse, was no longer effective. According to the theory, the King, receiving his authority from the people and responsible to them for maintaining the constitution, should check any extrava-gance of Parliament, thus redressing the balance. Bolingbroke of-fered the old prescription in *The Idea of a Patriot King*. But George III, unable to return to this discredited Tory model, perfected the system of "influence," which instead of correcting the balance cor-rupted it.

The Americans observed the course of deterioration and feared for their own governments. Taxes, armies, monopolies, venal offices —all the arms of the octopus were reaching out to the colonies. The dissident "old Whigs" and radical heretics in England warned the colonials of their fate. The hope, of course, was that England would reform. Americans closely followed the career of John Wilkes, not only because the Crown's suppression of his voice and his rejection by the Commons dramatized the tyranny of the government, but also because they looked to Wilkes and his agitated following to spur reform. At the peak of the agitation, between 1768 and 1771, Wilkes was quoted in the gazettes published in Williamsburg more often than any other man. Jefferson encountered him there, and he obtained Wilkes's speeches for his library. In the end Wilkes proved a disappointment, and there was no one to take his place. The ob-stinacy of Parliament to reform left the Americans no promising av-enue of appeal except to the King, which was not very hopeful, actually, in view of his collusion with Parliament. Nevertheless, unrepresented in Parliament, increasingly scornful of its authority, the Americans were dependent on the King in theory and in fact. In 1774 Jefferson pointedly reminded His Majesty that he was "the chief officer of the people, appointed by the laws, and circumscribed with definite powers, to assist in the working the great machine of government, erected for their use, and consequently subject to their superintendence." This sounded a little like Bolingbroke: the "patriot king" as the great balance-wheel of the constitution. But Jefferson had shrugged off the Tory implications contained in the theory of balanced government. Only the awkward status of the colonies within the empire, all owing allegiance to a common sovereign, forced him to appeal to the Crown. He was a "True Whig" of 1688, a champion of legislative supremacy in the English constitution, in the American practice, and in political theory generally. It is notable that John Adams admired Bolingbroke's political theory but regretted his heretical religious opinions, while Jefferson accepted the latter but rejected the former. They were both Whigs in fact, yet their contrasting responses to Bolingbroke, the putative "father of modern toryism," would be reflected in the different emphases the two men gave to executive (monarchical) and legislative (democratic) power in the governments of the new nation. But these differences were unimportant before 1776 when American patriots agreed on the melancholy deterioration of balanced government in England and worried for the survival of this genie of freedom in America.

The ideas of Saxon origins and balanced government were so firmly implanted in Jefferson's mind that, while they could be transformed, they could never be uprooted. The Saxon myth persisted in curious ways. In the main, however, as a historical foundation of the rights of Englishmen, it was assimilated into a rational creed of liberty. Locke had pointed the way. When rights were subsumed under the law of nature, history was of no account. Rationalism conquered history. Jefferson did not go as far as Locke in this respect, for he appealed to ancient liberties to buttress the rational argument and to render concrete what otherwise was ethereal. The theory of balanced government was also historical, identified as it was with English constitutional development and premised on a historically given structure of power corresponding to the hierarchical orders of society. To erase from the political mind the vocabulary of orders, even in a society where there were none, and the forms of the classical trivium, and the categories of King, Lords, and Commons, was not easy. Jefferson encountered less difficulty than some of his notable contemporaries, John Adams for instance. Gradually, one form, one order, one category, democracy, effaced the others; and the old theory was transformed into a new theory of "separation of powers." Now the functional powers of government, legislative, executive, judicial, rather than the historically given orders, were to be checked and balanced, regarding nothing but natural rights and the sovereignty of the people. Driven by the force of the Revolution, Jefferson recast his essentially English political theory, retaining its strong constitutional and democratic elements, in the intellectual mould of the Enlightenment.

The American Revolution was a national as well as democratic movement—a colonial revolt that gave birth to a revolutionary ideology. It was accompanied by a growing consciousness of nationality, the sense of common experience and common culture, of unifying habits, beliefs, and aspirations, all parts of the process by which a people comes to identify itself as a nation. How far this had gone in the thirteen mainland British colonies by 1776 is problematical, and downright conjectural in Jefferson's case. The chicken-and-egg problem of whether revolution emerged from nationality or nationality from revolution is unsolvable. But more than most new nations the Americans achieved political independence before they had a conscious tradition and culture of their own; indeed the unique feature of the American fabric of nationality was its self-conscious creation in response to the achievement of nationhood. The frame came before the picture; in a sense, the Americans painted the picture themselves. Yet the process of transforming colonial Englishmen and assorted Europeans into Americans had been going on for a century and a half, and it was greatly accelerated by the alienation of affections after the Seven Years War. John Adams, more given to reflection on past times than his Virginia friend, observed in later years that "the Revolution was in the minds of the people, and this was effected from 1760 to 1775, in the course of fifteen years before a drop of blood was shed at Lexington." Jefferson, though he did not say, probably agreed in principle. His own emotional identifications were more Virginian than American or continental before 1775, and the transmutation of provincial loyalties into unifying national loyalties was another part of the process, as real in Massachusetts as in Virginia. But the inner revolution toward Americanism had already begun in him and would burst forth with tremendous energy once independence was declared.

Every philosophical American was aware of the debate among European savants on the prospects of the New World. The Abbé Raynal's *Histoire des deux Indes*, one of the most influential works of the age, brought the matter to a head in 1770. Whether America, North and South, should be considered a boon to civilization or a return to barbarism on a fantastic scale, whether America promised regeneration or degeneration for mankind, was the troubling question. Jefferson took it up when occasion offered in 1780, siding with the optimists against Raynal and others. To this school America, or at least the Northern British colonies, appeared as the land of Enlightenment dreams. Europeans caught between the impulses of primitivism and civilization, of retreat to nature and rush to progress, witnessed in America the emergence of civilization from nature. Here was a laboratory for the testing of eighteenth-century ideas. Beginning in the Lockian "state of nature," the Americans had an opportunity to create a new order of mankind. To many Europeans, Benjamin Franklin personified the ideal: provincial and cosmopolitan, rustic and philosopher, a man equally at home in the simple American world and the sophisticated salons of Europe. This hopeful New World image, as well as its dark opposite, crossed the Atlantic and forced its way into the consciousness of colonials. They began to think of themselves as Americans, to trace out the contours of the native environment, differentiating it from the European world they had fled, and to define its unique promise.

Montesquieu had taught that different physical and social environments give rise to different beliefs, manners, and laws. Human nature is everywhere the same but laws and government are moulded by circumstances of time and space, in a word by the culture of a people. What, then, was the American case? Or perhaps there were thirteen separate cases. Serious differences among the colonies became painfully evident in the First Continental Congress as delegates forged a common front against the mother country. Yet, sharing the same grievances, driven by the same fears, they perceived with increasing clarity that similar lines of development, under similar conditions, had produced a collective basis of national existence. "Love of freedom," in Edmund Burke's opinion the leading feature of American character, ran across the face of the country and up and down the social scale. It was not an abstract thing, as in most of Europe, but the sovereign force of law and opinion. The governments of the colonies were remarkably alike. Everywhere the public will centered in a representative assembly. Since a kind of revolutionary legitimacy was already contained in these bodies, it was unnecessary to go in search of it. English political institutions had been not merely adapted but transformed in the American environment. For example, the theory and practice of representation: as Bernard Bailyn has observed, the colonists developed the idea of "attorneyship," wherein the representative literally re-presents the will of his constituents, while in England the prevailing theory ran to unitary or collective representation, Parliament being considered the assemblage of one nation with one overriding interest. Hence the idea that the Americans were *virtually* represented in Parliament made sense in England, where in fact not nine out of ten of the subjects of the realm were *actually* represented; but it made no sense at all in the colonies. In the light of peculiar American conditions, some imported institutions, such as the establishment of religion, began to seem incongruous with the society. Multiplicity, not uniformity, characterized religious life in America—the laws should be adapted to this condition. The wide diffusion of property meant that a more democratic frame of government was practical in America without incurring the risk, so much emphasized in conventional political wisdom, of splitting power from property. Characteristics of this kind, which philosophers abroad were already conceptualizing as "the American character," became more and more obvious to the colonists in the course of controversy with the mother country; and by 1776 some of them, like Jefferson, were ready to seize upon these *differentiae* for the reconstruction of civil life.

In his great Revolutionary pamphlet *Common Sense*, Thomas Paine dwelt on the absurdity of a continent's being governed by an island. "In no instance hath nature made the satellite larger than its primary planet; and as England and America, with respect to each other, reverse the common order of nature, it is evident that they belong in different systems. England to Europe: America to itself." This idea, too, had been breaking into American consciousness for some time. A quarter-century earlier Franklin, in his *Observations Concerning the Increase of Mankind*, noted that the population of the mainland colonies had doubled in twenty-five years, while the population of England had remained virtually stable. "What an accession of power to the British Empire by sea as well as land! What increase of trade and navigation. What numbers of ships and seamen," Franklin rejoiced. Clearly, he had a maritime conception of empire, an "empire of the deep," rated largely in trade, ships, and seamen. This was the prevailing conception. Under it the colonies were outposts of British dominion on the seas. They were not *in* and *of* the empire but existed *for* the empire. It was, Adam Smith wrote bitingly in 1776, an empire of "a nation of shopkeepers" run for "the sole purpose of raising up a people of customers." But Franklin, by locating the future grandeur of the empire in America, sounded a new note with startling implications. The perimeter was to become the center!

Before 1775, few if any Americans, whatever their hidden desires, admitted the intent of raising an independent empire. They advocated an empire of equal self-governing states owing allegiance to a common King. But this did not fit the British scheme. So gradually, almost imperceptibly, the earlier vision of America as the foundation of future British glory changed into a vision of America as potentially an empire within itself. This was a continental conception, though not excluding the maritime; and it looked to an empire of free and equal states, "an empire of liberty," as Jefferson would soon call the American experiment. It embraced the great West beyond the Appalachians, perhaps beyond the Mississippi, as well as the Atlantic seaboard. American nationality, inchoate and untried, was thus invested with high promise. Fulfillment was far off, but as independence dawned the promise grew in magnificence until it seemed, with Thomas Paine, that this new nation had it in its power "to begin the world over again."

Empire Theory and the American Cause

Many forces fed into the American Revolution, but the movement fed upon one great issue, the constitutional authority of Great Britain over the colonies. A struggle involving other and diverse interests and principles was conducted largely as a contest on the nature and limits of the English constitution. Jefferson addressed himself to this great question in *A Summary View of the Rights of British America* in 1774. Written as instructions for the Virginia delegates to the First Continental Congress, the tract was published on both sides of the Atlantic without his permission or ascription of authorship, though he quickly became known as the author and on that recognition moved to the front rank of America's patriot leadership.

Following the crisis of 1769, American resistance collapsed everywhere. The Virginians, Jefferson remarked, "seemed to fall into a state of insensibility to our situation." The new ministry in London headed by Lord North, a court favorite, showed strength at home and caution abroad. For three years North gave the American radicals no new fuel to stoke the furnace of agitation. Yet the Declaratory Act was still on the books and the Townshend duty on tea remained in force. In Virginia, returning prosperity and the popularity of the new Governor, Lord Dunmore, whose ardor for granting lands and pushing Western claims endeared him to many planters, contributed to the uneasy calm. Awaiting a new signal of alarm, Jefferson found it in 1773 in the British response to the burning of a revenue cutter, the *Gaspee,* off the coast of Rhode Island. A vice-admiralty court of inquiry was empowered to send the culprits to England for trial. The culprits were never identified, but this calculated usurpation could not be ignored, Jefferson thought. At the opening of the assembly in the spring of 1773 he met with several of the "hot-heads," Henry, Richard Henry Lee, Francis L. Lee, Dabney Carr, perhaps one or two others. They agreed to a series of resolutions calling for the institution of committees of correspondence in each colony to facilitate intercommunication and union in the common cause. Local committees had already been appointed in Massachusetts towns. But Jefferson always believed that the resolutions drawn up by his little group, introduced in the House, passed and circulated throughout the country were the first looking to colony-wide committees in a system of collective action. The Governor, sensing the threat of a revolutionary underground, promptly prorogued the House. Within a few months every colony but Pennsylvania had a committee of correspondence.

Before the legislature next met, in May 1774, the Tea Act had been passed, the Boston Tea Party had occurred, and British retaliation had commenced against Massachusetts. The Tea Act, which undercut colonial merchants by the special privileges it gave to the East India Company in the American market, little concerned Virginians. But they were aroused by the first of a series of measures, the Coercive Acts, against the sister colony to the north. News of the Boston Port Act reached Williamsburg while the assembly was in session. The trade and livelihood of a great city were to be sacrificed to revenge the action of a few militants who dumped several hundred chests of tea into Boston harbor. "This is administering justice with a heavy hand indeed!" Jefferson exclaimed. The little cadre of the previous year, minus Dabney Carr, now dead, again took the lead. They met, rummaged through John Rushworth's *Historical Collections* for precedents and forms drawn from the Puritan Revolution in England, and as Jefferson recalled, "cooked up a resolution . . . for appointing the 1st day of June, on which the port bill was to commence, for a day of fasting, humiliation, and prayer, to implore Heaven to avert from us the evils of civil war, to inspire us with firmness in support of our rights, and to turn the hearts of the King and Parliament to moderation and justice." They prevailed on Robert Carter Nicholas, "whose grave and religious character was more in unison with the tone of the resolution," to sponsor it in the House. It passed without opposition. The Governor, as on the push of a button, dissolved the assembly.

The burgesses reconvened, as it were, at the Raleigh Tavern and took the longest step yet recorded toward independence. The incipient revolutionary body declared that an attack on one colony should be considered an attack on all, instructed the Virginia committee of correspondence to propose the meeting of a continental congress, recommended to the counties the election of delegates to a convention to meet in Williamsburg on August 1, and adopted an

Association, more strongly armed than its predecessors, to interdict trade with Great Britain. The fast day, soon after the burgesses returned home, was a stunning propaganda success. "The people met generally, with anxiety and alarm in their countenance," Jefferson recalled, "and the effect of the day, through the whole colony, was like a shock of electricity, arousing every man, and placing him erect and solidly on his center." The counties chose delegates to the provincial convention, which in turn concluded its work in August by electing delegates to the First Continental Congress, convened in Philadelphia in September. A little "tea party" in Boston had mushroomed into a mighty storm uniting the continent.

Jefferson, from his part in this movement, might have been elected one of the seven delegates to the Congress had he taken his seat in the convention at Williamsburg. But falling sick on the road, he never reached the capital, and had to forward copies of his proposed instructions to Peyton Randolph and Patrick Henry. The paper was read by the members, admired by many, but thought too bold. Jefferson afterwards concurred in this judgment, saying that "the leap" he proposed was "too long as yet for the mass of our citizens." The difference between his paper and the humble instructions adopted by the convention showed, he added, "the inequality of the pace with which we moved, and the prudence required to keep front and rear together." The cooler heads of men like Randolph, Wythe, Pendleton, and Washington ensured a united, if slower, march toward the goal. The Virginia instructions of 1774 still turned on the constitutional distinction, worked out by John Dickinson several years earlier, between *external* and *internal* legislation, Parliament having rightful authority in one sphere but not in the other. Jefferson's paper, on the other hand, denied Parliament's authority altogether, or any connection with the mother country except through the King, and turned on natural as well as legal rights. "The young ascended with Mr. Jefferson to the source of those rights," Edmund Randolph recalled the division, "the old required time for consideration, before they could tread the lofty ground. . . ." Published by his friends as the *Summary View* in Williamsburg, at once reprinted in Philadelphia and in England, Jefferson's hastily penned instructions opened a new chapter in the polemics of the Revolution.

Yet, if the chapter was new, it was not without antecedents in Virginia. The *Summary View* carried to logical conclusion a line of argument broached by Richard Bland a decade earlier. In *The Colonel Dismounted* (1763) and, above all, his *Inquiry into the Rights of the British Colonies* (1766), Bland held that the colonies had never been part of the realm of England, hence could not of right be subject to the laws of Parliament, where they were not represented, but being dominions of the King, the colonies and the colonists owed him the same allegiance as his subjects in England or Scotland or Ireland. Bland seemed to lack the courage of his own premises, however. Jefferson, who admired this bookish elder statesman and upon his death at the beginning of the Revolution purchased his valuable library, later characterized Bland's rambling and indecisive argument: "He would set out with a set of sound principles, pursue them logically till he found them leading to the precipice which he had to leap, start back alarmed, then resume his ground, go over it in another direction, be led by the correctness of his reasoning to the same place and again back about and try other processes to reconcile right and wrong, but finally left his reader and himself bewildered between the steady index of the compass in their hand, and the phantasm to which it seemed to point." Jefferson took the compass and threw the phantasm of Parliament overboard.

From the beginning of the contest with the mother country the colonists had searched for some halfway house between total subjection to the authority of Parliament and its total rejection. Some, like James Otis of Massachusetts, had appealed to fundamental constitutional guarantees, such as the right to consent to taxes, which Parliament, supreme but under the law, could not transgress. Dickinson and many others had drawn the line between internal and external legislation. In imperial relationships any line was difficult, however; and just as it was anachronistic, with Otis, to regard Parliament as a high court that would void its own unconstitutional acts, it was equally so, and equally futile, with Dickinson to expect a body that since 1688 had made a fetish of its own "sovereign and uncontrollable authority" to yield limitations on its powers, regardless of hoary sanction or precedent. No modern Whig, not even the few, like Lord Chatham and Edmund Burke, friendly to the colonial cause, questioned the supremacy of Parliament. Burke's approach was to reconcile parliamentary supremacy and colonial rights on the level of expediency. "The question with me is," he said, "not whether you have a right to render your people miserable, but whether it is not your interest to make them happy." The Declaratory Act, "the system of 1766," set the proper course by claiming the right to legislate for the colonies while refraining from its exercise. But the colonists after 1774 demanded a solution founded in right and principle. Burke was no true friend of this cause; indeed he condemned "the dangerous spirit of disquisition," the fondness for "metaphysical questions," the speculation on rights and liberties, a foolish ministry had let loose in America. The myopia that persisted in treating issues of principle as issues of policy was a reproach to Whig politics. The Americans, seeking but not finding a halfway house, moved toward a theoretical position wholly incompatible with the Whig conception of the English constitution. What had been deemed liberty for Englishmen in 1688 was now deemed tyranny for the Americans. Returning to the ancient distinction between the realm and the dominions, Jefferson, together with the Adamses in Massachusetts and James Wilson in Pennsylvania, set forth the new theory of the imperial connection in which the colonies were equal self-governing states owing allegiance to the King.

The *Summary View* began with the proposition that the Americans were the sons of expatriated men who "possessed a right, which nature has given to all men, of departing from the country in which chance, not choice, has placed them, of going in quest of new habitations, and of there establishing new societies, under such laws and regulations as to them shall seem most likely to promote public happiness." This alleged natural right had no standing in English law, as Jefferson knew. Blackstone stated the rule: an English subject could not by any act of his own throw off his natural born allegiance. Jefferson could find the right of expatriation in Cicero, Grotius, Locke, and other eminent authorities, though he cited none of them. Instead he appealed to the example of the Saxon ancestors who had left the wilds of northern Europe and settled in England without their mother country ever making any claim of superiority over them. "And it is thought that no circumstance has occurred to distinguish materially the British from the Saxon emigration. America was conquered, and her settlements made and firmly established, at the expense of individuals, and not of the British public. . . . For themselves they fought, for themselves alone they have a right to hold." Much the same claim, it may be noted, had been made for the Americans in Parliament years before, during the debate on the Stamp Act, by Colonel Isaac Barré, whose speech on that occasion Jefferson considered one of the most eloquent ever uttered.

Exploiting the past for political ends, Jefferson was less interested in the historical truth than in the moral truth of the proposition. But he was not ready to dismiss history altogether, for to do so would be to dismiss the English constitution and imperial connection of any sort, and he was not ready for that. Proceeding with the argument, he conceded that when Britain discovered the commercial value of the wilderness colonies she extended protection to them. Receiving these aids, the colonists did not thereby submit themselves to British sovereignty. Certain errors crept into the relationship because the early settlers, being laborers not lawyers, failed to see the implications of practices that were, in fact, usurpations. Thus they were victimized by the "ficticious principle that all lands belong originally to the king . . . and accordingly took grants of their own lands from the crown." But this was the feudal principle introduced into Saxon England by William the Norman. The Americans, like their Saxon ancestors, claimed the wilderness lands in absolute dominion, disencumbered of any superior, whether feudal lord or king, and so escaped the terrible fate that overcame England. "America was not conquered by William the Norman, nor its lands surrendered to him or any of his successors." In principle, that is; in fact, feudalism sneaked in. So long as it worked easily the error went undetected. Only in recent decades had His Majesty's exactions on lands and control of grants caused severe hardship and the usurpation become evident. Confusion arose too, Jefferson said, from the early emigrants' adoption of the common law. They brought with them the rights of expatriated men, that is, natural rights, but they voluntarily chose to govern themselves by English law. Similarly, they chose to submit themselves to a common sovereign, the British monarch, "who was thereby made the central link connecting the several parts of the empire thus newly multiplied."

Jefferson dealt at length with the encroachments of Crown and Parliament on American rights. Freedom of trade, which he called a "natural right," fell before arbitrary power in the middle of the seventeenth century. Considering itself heir to the powers of the deposed king, Charles I, Parliament took the fatal step of legislating for the dominions. The trade and navigation acts from that point forward instanced a despotism without parallel in English annals. Yet Jefferson did not propose going back to the true principle. The commercial system, rightly conducted by the Crown, was one of the benefits of the empire. "The true ground on which we declare these acts void is that the British Parliament has no right to exercise authority over us." Until the reign of George III other violations of American rights had occurred at such distant intervals as to muffle alarm; since then they had followed in swift succession. "Single acts of tyranny may be ascribed to the accidental opinion of a day; but a series of oppressions, begun at a distinguished period, and pursued unalterably thro' every change of ministers, too plainly prove a deliberate, systematical plan of reducing us to slavery." Jefferson passed in review these oppressive measures beginning with the Revenue Act of 1764 and ending with the Boston Port Act. It was the responsibility of the King to check these encroachments; but not only had he failed in this duty, he had arbitrarily used his executive powers in the colonial governments, dissolving assemblies, refusing assent to some laws for trifling reasons, delaying consideration of others, interfering with the organization of legislative bodies, granting lands and advancing the terms of sale, standing an army among the people, and subordinating the civil to the military power. These charges against the King anticipated the long indictment in the Declaration of Independence. Jefferson's stated purpose in 1774, however, was not to convict the King but to reform him. "No longer persevere in sacrificing the rights of one part of the empire to the inordinate desires of another: but deal out to all equal and impartial right," he implored. "Let no act be passed by any one legislature which may infringe on the rights and liberties of another. This is the important post in which fortune has placed you, holding the balance of a great, if a well poised empire." The advice, unrelieved by humility or praise, was scarcely calculated to arouse the sympathies of George III. Nor was Jefferson's defiant conclusion: "The God who gave us life gave us liberty at the same time: the hand of force may destroy, but cannot disjoin them."

75

What was the purpose of the *Summary View?* Not conciliation, for Jefferson's language was anything but conciliatory. Did he and the other Americans who set forth this new theory of empire actually expect it to be adopted by the authorities in England? No, they were not naïve. There was, to be sure, historical basis for it in the tradition of the English constitution. In Jefferson's opinion the relationship of the colonies to England was exactly the same as that of Scotland after the accession of James I and before the Act of Union: equal states under a common king. And he was quite familiar with the case of Anglo-Irish, who claimed with some success at law the equality of their parliament with the English; yet their case was not as good as the American, for Ireland had been conquered by English arms. The idea of dominion status, not without precedent in history, also pointed to a creative solution to the problems of a multiplying empire; and Britain, after losing the American colonies, would slowly come to the conception of a "commonwealth of nations" anticipated by Jefferson and his American compatriates. But the conception was impractical given the structure of British politics in the reign of George III. That monarch gloried in the supremacy of Parliament and was intimately involved with it. The new theory of empire demanded the King's separation from Parliament—a monarch *above* many parliaments rather than *in* one Parliament. Besides, no English Whig could accept the idea that Parliament should be deposed and the Crown exalted in imperial affairs. Yet this seemed to be what the American militants advocated. Lord North sneered, "Their language therefore was that of toryism." The aberration was more glaring in Wilson's 1774 tract, *Considerations on the Nature and Extent of the Legislative Authority of the British Parliament,* than in the *Summary View.* Wilson made explicit what Jefferson left implicit: the King should be the colonies' protector, negative unjust acts of Parliament, and exercise his "prerogative" to regulate trade. The logic of the argument led embarrassingly to the aggrandizement of royal power, unless, of course, an imperial parliament miraculously came into being; but neither Jefferson nor Wilson advocated this, and when one was proposed in the First Continental Congress it was defeated. If Jefferson was not naïve, not a Tory, not a parliamentary unionist, what then, was he driving at?

He was advancing the contest to the next stage, not knowing where, once this act was played out, he would go next. The basic premise, that the Americans were expatriated men, a distinct people, endowed with natural rights and free to shape their institutions as they pleased, pointed directly to independence. But he still shrank from this last resort. Like Bland, whom he criticized for failure to leap the precipice of parliamentary authority, Jefferson, too, had a precipice, and he drew back, retreated along devious and at times treacherous trails of history and theory, rather than follow his premises to conclusion.

Events were rapidly driving him to that conclusion. The Congress at Philadelphia adjourned on October 26. "The colonists have taken such grounds that Great Britain must relax, or inevitably involve herself in civil war," John Dickinson, one of the delegates, wrote. "The first act of violence . . . will put the whole continent in arms from Nova Scotia to Georgia." He was right, in the main. Congress endorsed the Suffolk Resolves of Massachusetts, which declared the Coercive Acts unconstitutional and void, urged the formation of an independent government in that beleaguered colony, called the people to arm, and backed strong economic sanctions against Britain. Resolutions of the Congress repudiated the authority of Parliament, without specifically endorsing the new theory of empire. The system of non-intercourse copied with little change the Virginia Association. Local committees were to be elected throughout the country to enforce the economic coercion. In Virginia they were already in operation. Jefferson was a member of the Albemarle committee. With the suppression of commerce the county courts closed, and the local committees became the effective governing bodies. The Association brought the revolutionary movement to every man's door. The agreement served as a kind of loyalty oath; one either signed or faced suppression, boycott, or disrepute. In Virginia most merchants joined the planters in signing. Independent militia companies also sprang up in the fall of 1774. Jefferson found himself a private in the ranks—even his overseeer was a sergeant—of the Albemarle company. The issue in the colonies was no longer between parties seeking different paths to conciliation, but between a radical party pushing toward independence and a moderate party holding back, still hopeful of conciliation. Jefferson kept in step with the radicals but patiently awaited the King's response to disillusion the moderates.

Nothing official had been heard from the King when the second provincial convention met at Richmond, out of the way of the Governor, in March 1775. Reports were discouraging, however. In his recent address to Parliament George III set a mad course of coercion and was applauded for it. Patrick Henry boldly announced in Richmond, "The war is actually begun," and vowed, "Give me liberty, or give me death." The old guard, still in control of the reconstituted Burgesses, wished to stand pat on the platform of Congress, pending the King's answer to the Virginia petition. But Henry moved a resolution to put the colony in a state of defense, not only at the local level, where volunteer companies were already forming, but colony-wide by raising an army. Jefferson spoke in favor of the motion. It passed, narrowly, though with little immediate effect. Jefferson also introduced a resolution denouncing the Governor for innovations in the established usage of granting lands. Poor Dunmore had just fought an Indian war, Dunmore's War, to defend the colony's claim to the Ohio Valley; but the Virginians, while grateful, would not brook royal interference with land policy. The Governor lost all standing in April, not long after the convention adjourned, when he succumbed to panic and removed the powder from the magazine at Williamsburg to a British vessel in the James, sent off his family, and barricaded himself in the Palace. Henry, in a grandstand play, put himself at the head of the Hanover militia and marched to the capital. The moderates spiked the burgeoning crisis, however. The militia turned back before reaching the capital.

The first shot had already been fired in Massachusetts. The encounter at Lexington and Concord, Jefferson wrote, "has cut off our last hopes of reconciliation, and a phrenzy of revenge seems to have seized all ranks of people." Incongruously, at this time, Dunmore called the assembly into session. The object was to deal with Lord North's "conciliatory proposition," under which Parliament would forbear to tax the colonies if they, individually, would make regular contributions to support the civil government and defense of the empire. Jefferson wrote Virginia's reply to the North proposal. In language firm but temperate he said that the plan "only changes the form of oppression, without lightening the burden." Parliament had no right to meddle in any way with the provincial government. "For us, not for them, has government been instituted here. . . ." A perpetual tax set by Parliament and subject to its disposal was totally unacceptable. "It is not merely the mode of raising but the freedom of granting our money for which we have contended." The plan made no provision for lifting other oppressions. It asked money of the colonies but continued the monopoly of their trade. And while this olive branch was held forth in one hand, the other unsheathed the sword—"a style of asking gifts not reconcilable to our freedom." Finally, now pledged to a common cause, the union of the colonies, Virginia could not accede to terms on its own authority. Jefferson praised Lord Chatham's more generous plan of reconciliation, brutally beaten down in Parliament, and invoked the God of Justice to point the way to peace.

On June 10 the House unanimously adopted Jefferson's resolutions, after passing over the moderate answer prepared by its own committee. By this time the Governor had taken refuge aboard a British man-of-war in York River, and Jefferson was on the road to Philadelphia. The convention had added him to the congressional delegation to serve in the place of Peyton Randolph, called from Philadelphia to preside over the House of Burgesses. That body would not convene again. The transition to revolutionary government was already far advanced in Virginia. Jefferson, having devoted his energies to this movement, now entered the continental theater in Philadelphia.

Congress and the Declaration of Independence

The Second Continental Congress had been in session several weeks when Jefferson took his seat in the downstairs chamber of the Pennsylvania State House (Independence Hall) on June 21, 1775. The assemblage was young, spirited, and distinguished. Benjamin Franklin, at sixty-nine, was the oldest member; Jefferson, at thirty-two, almost but not quite the youngest. Fifty to sixty members were usually in attendance. Omitting the Virginians, Jefferson recognized only one vaguely familiar face, Elbridge Gerry of Massachusetts, whom he had met in New York nine years before on his northern tour. His career in the future would cross Gerry's in unpredictable ways, as it would with many of these patriots: John Jay, an austere New Yorker, two years his junior; John Langdon, a Yankee commoner; the aristocratic Rutledge brothers, John and Edward, of South Carolina; John Dickinson, Pennsylvania's reluctant revolutionist; Charles Thomson, another Pennsylvanian and secretary of the Congress; and, of course, the leading zealots, John and Samuel Adams of Massachusetts. Next to Franklin, worshipped from the start, Jefferson was at once drawn to the bluff man from Quincy, John Adams, whose personality was of another genre but whose politics at this stage agreed with his own. The men who came to this Congress were accustomed to lead—all were generals bidding for new distinctions, commands, and followings—and while all were Americans, they were provincials still in their traits, attitudes, and interests. "Fifty gentlemen meeting together, all strangers, are not acquainted with each other's language, ideas, views, designs," Adams observed. "They are therefore jealous of each other—fearful, timid, skittish." If Jefferson found it difficult to keep front and rear ranks together in Virginia, it would be more difficult in Philadelphia, and infinitely more important because the cause of continental union depended upon it. Delicacy, tact, patience, a willingness to subordinate personal or parochial views to unity of action, were essential.

Jefferson's reputation had gone before him. As Adams recalled, he brought into Congress "a reputation for literature, science, and a happy talent of composition." His writings were known and admired for what Adams called their "peculiar felicity of expression." It was in this area, as a legislative draftsman, that he made his mark in Congress. On the floor of the House he never uttered a word, unless to untie some procedural knot. Yet his persuasive powers were not confined to a masterful pen. "Though a silent member of Congress," Adams said, "he was so prompt, frank, explicit, and decisive upon committees and in conversation, not even Samuel Adams was more so, that he soon seized upon my heart." Of course, he was an acquisition for the radicals. Lee and Henry, among the Virginia delegates, were on that side; but Henry's talents were exclusively oratorical and Lee's lay mainly in that line. The connection Lee established with the two Adamses aided the radical cause. Unfortunately, it also contributed to jealousy and division, especially in the Virginia delegation, where Lee was unpopular with moderate leaders like Harrison and Pendleton. Commanding the respect of all, Jefferson helped to hold the Virginia delegation together; and by virtue of his talents for legislative business and the drafting of papers, the radicals gained a valuable recruit from the most populous and most powerful of the thirteen colonies.

Just after he arrived in Philadelphia, news of the Battle of Bunker Hill reached the city. Amidst martial fanfare the next day, Congress sent off George Washington to take command of the Continental Army near Boston. Jefferson wrote home "that the war is now heartily entered into, without a prospect of accommodation but through the effectual interposition of arms." As civil war became the massive reality, he hesitated to embrace independence, which, as Adams said, was "a hobgoblin of . . . frightful mien." While not a "hobgoblin" for Jefferson, it clearly was for others, and he preferred to march in measured steps, in full force, to the Rubicon. Adams and several others wished to make the crossing at once, believing that only then would the country unite in the prosecution of the war. The Pennsylvania delegation under Dickinson, with strong support in the middle colonies, remained anxious for reconciliation. The prevailing sentiment seemed to be to fight and, for the present, keep the imperial quarrel open to negotiation. Jefferson could accept this, as could Adams and Dickinson, each with his own accent.

Jefferson's first important assignment came in connection with the Declaration of the Causes and Necessity for Taking Up Arms. A committee had reported, but the House, dissatisfied with the report, recommitted it and at the same time added Jefferson and Dickinson to the committee. The Virginian was asked to prepare a new draft. He did so with great care and deliberation, then presented the result. Dickinson objected to the paper as unnecessarily harsh and offensive. In this impasse the committee, as Jefferson put it, "indulged" Dickinson by asking him to try his hand. His draft, incorporating large parts of Jefferson's, was approved in committee and, subsequently, in the House. The Declaration was thus the product of collaboration at arm's length between Jefferson and Dickinson. Addressed not only to Great Britain but to the "Opinion of Mankind," the Declaration justified the appeal to arms as a cruel necessity forced by violent and tyrannical authority. "Our cause is just. Our union is perfect. Our internal Resources are great, and, if necessary, foreign Assistance is undoubtedly available." In strong but elevated language, the Declaration pledged unyielding resistance, "being with one Mind resolved to die Freemen rather than to live Slaves." With equal firmness it rejected independence, pleading instead for the restoration of union and concord. Jefferson's text had made the same appeal but less bluntly and without disclaiming independence. He had wished to express the true theory of imperial relations in the manifesto. Dickinson put a gloss on this question, alluding ambiguously to the theory without affirming it or explicitly repudiating the authority of Parliament. Dickinson's hand improved the style of the document if it somewhat weakened its theoretical basis. Yet both men aimed to produce the same effect: the justification of armed resistance not to divide but to reunite the empire on terms compatible with American liberty.

Having composed the Virginia reply to Lord North's "conciliatory proposition," Jefferson was asked to perform the same service for Congress. His argument was the same but the pitch was higher. He had not, in the Virginia answer, reflected on the motives of the British ministry in advancing this specious proposition; now he said it was "held up to the world, to deceive it into a belief that there was nothing in dispute between us but the *mode* of levying taxes" and to put the colonies in the wrong if they spurned the overture. In truth, this was far from the case, and the world when led to reflect on the bold succession of oppressions over the past eleven years would "believe with us, that nothing but our own exertions may defeat the ministerial sentence of death or abject submission." Congress adopted Jefferson's draft virtually unchanged. It also adopted a second humble petition to the King, again begging his intervention on the side of peace. Jefferson expected nothing from this appeal penned by Dickinson. Its cringing tone disgusted him and many of the delegates, yet it seemed necessary in order to mollify Pennsylvania.

Congress had other business than the drafting of manifestos, replies, and petitions. It was engaged in war. Officers had to be commissioned, a supply system organized, money raised, military regulations promulgated, strategy planned, Indian tribes won over or neutralized, new channels of trade opened, alliances broached, the union of the colonies consolidated. In the summer of 1775 the extent, the duration, and the course of the conflict were, as Jefferson said, "among the secrets of providence." Congress proceeded under a cloud of uncertainty, but it was best, he reflected, to be prepared for the worst.

When Congress adjourned briefly in August, Jefferson attended the Virginia convention at Richmond before going on to Monticello. The convention and its executive arm, the Committee of Public Safety, under Pendleton, ruled the province. Henry, panting for military glory, was put in command of Virginia's gathering forces, and operations were soon under way against Dunmore's paltry contingent of redcoats, loyalists, and blacks pillaging and plundering with the aid of several men-of-war in the vicinity of Norfolk. The convention elected a new set of delegates to Congress. Jefferson received the third highest vote, just behind Randolph and Lee, which was a fair indication of his standing in Virginia politics, though it must be remembered that several of his seniors—Henry, Pendleton, and Washington notably—were now unavailable for congressional service.

Detained at Monticello by the death of an infant daughter, Jefferson hurried back to Philadelphia early in the fall. The expedition against Quebec was in full tilt—Montreal fell to General Montgomery in November—and Jefferson confidently expected Canada's accession to the American union. He was busy with committees in the early morning hours, then in the House until late afternoon, and back to committee business late into the night. Congress set up a navy, appointed a secret committee of correspondence to arrange for foreign aid and support, and authorized several additional colonies, including Virginia, to establish their own governments, as Massachusetts was doing. The door was thus opened to internal revolution as Congress moved ever closer to independence. The radicals, generally, hailed this development, for they were eager to exploit the opportunity for democratic reform at home; the moderates, on the other hand, feared the specter of democracy that hovered ominously over the movement toward independence. In November, Congress learned of the King's refusal to receive the "Olive Branch Petition" —the second humble address—and his proclamation placing the colonies in a state of open rebellion. Congress answered by a disavowal of the authority of Parliament and a reaffirmation of allegiance to the King, though this was now a shabby fiction. Writing to a good friend, John Randolph, the attorney general, who had declared his loyalty to Britain and was about to leave Virginia, Jefferson made his last profession of affection for the empire and laid the blame for its impending dissolution squarely on the shoulders of George III. "In an earlier part of this contest out petitions told him that from our King there was but one appeal," he said. "The admonition was despised and that appeal forced on us. To undo his empire he has but one truth more to learn, that after colonies have drawn the sword there is but one step more they can take. . . . We want neither inducement nor power to declare and assert a separation. It is will alone which is wanting and that is gaining apace under the fostering hand of our King."

Near the end of the year Jefferson returned to Monticello. He was worried about his wife's health. Congress sat in continuous session, marking time on the great issue. The Virginia delegates, having only one vote together, agreed to spare him for awhile. He did not expect to be gone long, but his mother's death, followed by his own illness, kept him at home until early May. The personal malady was an "inveterate headache," which struck him periodically over the years, usually at times of emotional stress. (The first mention of the affliction is in a letter of March 1764 when he learned Rebecca Burwell would marry another.) At home he turned his thoughts to the reconstruction of Virginia's government and also, it seems, to the confederation of the colonies or states. He annotated a plan of union Franklin had prepared and extended his reading in the history of confederations both ancient and modern. But this problem, while much discussed, would not come on the carpet in Congress until after independence was declared, when Jefferson's mind reverted to Virginia. Reading in January the King's recent speech to Parliament, in which it was unctuously claimed that Britain had planted, nursed, and cared for the colonies, Jefferson indignantly rushed to his books to refute the pretension, filling in the details of the case outlined in the *Summary View*. "A King who can adopt falsehood, and solemnize it from the throne, justifies the revolution of fortunes which reduces him to a private station," he asserted after ransacking Hakluyt, Raleigh, Stith, and other authorities on the early English settlement of the New World. Presumably he intended this brief for publication, but it was technical and antiquarian, hardly calculated for the immediate crisis, so he filed it away.

A tract exactly calculated for the crisis was Thomas Paine's *Common Sense*. Published anonymously in Philadelphia in January, it spread the doctrine of independence across the land. Jefferson read the pamphlet at Monticello. Saying nothing about it at the time, he later praised its contribution, with all of Paine's services to the American cause, when most men preferred to forget him. A commoner by birth, a radical by temperament, a revolutionist by profession, Paine, though a newcomer to the American scene, perceived the absurdity of the imperial connection, the promise of continental union, and the greatness of the cause not only for Americans but for all mankind. "The sun never shone on a cause of greater worth. 'Tis not the affair of a city, a county, a province, or a kingdom; but of a continent—of at least one eighth part of the habitable globe. 'Tis not the concern of a day, a year, or an age; posterity are virtually involved in the contest, and will be more or less affected even to the end of time, by the proceedings now." Paine stripped the issues of their conventional legalistic dress and nakedly disclosed the "common sense" of independence. His political rhetoric was quite new. Earthy, naïve, direct, it addressed the people in their own language and evoked a qualitatively different response than the erudite polemics of constitutional warriors. He did not toy with error but strangled it; he did not toss truth into the philosophical air but grasped its stark simplicity. Appealing to the "simple voice of nature and reason," Paine pooh-poohed the elegant myth of balanced government, ridiculed monarchy and hereditary succession, and scoffed at the "papistical" idea of English parentage of America. Jefferson could agree with most of what Paine said, but he could not possibly have written *Common Sense*. The Virginian's language was elegant, not vulgar; his mind craved the historical and legal authority Paine contemptuously dismissed; his comparatively sedate politics reflected his membership in a governing class with which, of course, Paine had no associations and whose methods he eschewed. Yet the essentially naturalistic assumptions of Paine's pamphlet went right along with Jefferson's philosophy, and bringing these assumptions to bear on the question of national independence helped to free him from the inhibitions of law and history.

Independence had made great strides when Jefferson resumed his seat in Congress on May 14, 1776. Privateering had been authorized, American ports thrown open to all the world but Britain, and energetic steps taken toward securing foreign aid. The colonists had suffered a serious reversal in Canada, but the British had evacuated Boston. The military balance sheet, if not encouraging, was far from desperate. The middle colonies, in particular, still shied away from independence. "The novelty of the thing deters some," Franklin wrote from Congress in April, "the doubts of success, others, the vain hope of reconciliation, many." When Jefferson arrived Congress was just winding up debate on John Adams's motion calling on all the colonies to establish their own governments. The motion, "a machine to fabricate independence" in Adams's calculation, passed on May 15. On the same day the Virginia convention unanimously instructed its delegates to propose a declaration of independence, as well as to support foreign alliances and the confederation of the colonies. The convention proceeded at once to declare the independence of Virginia and to frame a government for the new state, adopted on June 28.

In Congress, meanwhile, compliant with the Virginia instructions, Lee introduced a resolution stating that the colonies "are, and of right ought to be, free and independent states." The laggards were coming up to the mark; even in the continent's mid-section, revolutionary patriot parties mobilized against the proprietary governments to force the issue of independence. "Every post and every day roles in upon us, Independence like a torrent," Adams rejoiced. The Lee resolution, incorporating as well the provisions for alliance and confederation, came up for consideration in committee of the whole on June 8. Jefferson recorded the arguments advanced pro and con in this debate. The spokesmen for the opposition—Jefferson mentioned Dickinson and Wilson, of Pennsylvania, and Robert R. Livingston and Edward Rutledge of New York and South Carolina respectively—narrowed the issue to one of timing. Congress should defer the final step until the united voice of the people drove them to it. The middle colonies, while ripening, were not yet ripe; and since their delegations were either expressly forbidden or unauthorized to vote for independence, premature forcing of the issue must produce secession from the union with all its perils. The more prudent course, the opponents said, was to await the outcome of the present summer's campaign, concentrating meanwhile on the formation of an alliance with France and consolidation of the union. To this the radicals, led by Adams and Lee, replied that a declaration of independence would simply recognize the *de facto* situation; that public opinion was ahead of Congress, even in the middle colonies, where the influence of proprietary power and immunity as yet from enemy attack, not the majority voice of the people, held them back; that the European nations would neither trade nor treat with rebel colonies until they established their independence *de jure;* that fears of secession were exaggerated, and military affairs might not for some time wear a brighter aspect than now. The debate continued on into the evening, was adjourned, and resumed the following Monday. A compromise was then adopted: the independence resolution would be postponed for three weeks, until July 1, and a committee appointed at once to prepare a declaration likely to be wanted at that time. The moderates won a brief reprieve; the radicals won the contest.

On the next day Congress appointed a committee of five, Jefferson, Adams, Franklin, Livingston, and Roger Sherman of Connecticut, to prepare the Declaration of Independence. (Two other committees were presently appointed to report a plan of treaties and a plan of confederation.) The naming of so young a man to head the committee caused some surprise. The resolution coming from Virginia, a Virginian was naturally named first; and Lee, standing as the sponsor, seemed the obvious choice. Adams later said Lee was passed over because of his unpopularity within the Virginia delegation. The probabilities are, however, that Lee did not want the job. He, too, had an ailing wife at home and wished for leave, not alone for that reason but also to share in the work of constitution-making at Williamsburg. Lee got his wish, while Jefferson remained, unhappily, in Philadelphia. The committee met, perhaps without Franklin, ridden by gout; and Jefferson agreed to prepare a draft of the Declaration. Adams remembered a conversation which began with Jefferson asking him to draw the paper:

"Oh! no.

"Why will you not? You ought to do it.

"I will not.

"Why.

"Reasons enough.

"What can be your reasons.

"Reason first—You are a Virginian, and a Virginian ought to appear at the head of this business. Reason second—I am obnoxious, suspected, and unpopular. You are very much otherwise.
Reason third—You can write ten times better than I can.

"Well, if you are decided I will do as well as I can."

The recollection, if not correct in every detail, suggests how it
happened that Jefferson became the author of the Declaration of
Independence. Fortune of circumstance played a part; but his genius
alone converted a merely political and diplomatic document into a
monument of human liberty.

In his quarters on the second floor of a brick house at Seventh
and Market Streets, during the third week of June, presumably before and after business hours in Congress, Jefferson composed the
original draft of the Declaration of Independence. Only a fragment
of the draft survives. What he called the rough draft, though it was
almost certainly the second or perhaps even the third, was submitted
to Frankin and to Adams for their corrections. "Their alterations
were two or three only, merely verbal," he recalled. He then went
through the work again, making many verbal changes and several
additions. Satisfied now, he propped up the little portable writing
table built to his own design by a previous landlord, and penned the
fair copy of the Declaration. He reported this to the committee, and
from there, unaltered, it went to Congress on June 28. This fair
copy has been lost, but it can be reconstructed from duplicates Jefferson himself made apparently when the Declaration was before
Congress.

In form the Declaration of Independence presents a syllogistic
argument in three parts: a major premise stated in the introductory
part, the Preamble; a minor premise, also stated there but demonstrated at length in what is sometimes misleadingly called the body
of the work; and a conclusion following from the premises. The
primary purpose, as stated in the opening paragraph, was to convince the world of the rightfulness of the colonies' separation from

Great Britain. Jefferson went beyond this, however, and seized the occasion to advance in axiomatic terms a political ideology for the new nation. This was compressed in the complex major premise of the second paragraph: just governments are founded on equal rights and the consent of the governed, and "whenever any form of government becomes destructive of these ends, it is the right of the people to alter or to abolish it, and to institute new government. . . ." Without attempting to define all the equal and "unalienable" rights, he epitomized them in the captivating phrase "life, liberty, and the pursuit of happiness." The strategy of the argument turned on the asserted "self-evidence" of the major premise. A moral truth beyond powers of demonstration, it carried immediate conviction to men of reason and good will. (If it did not, of course, the whole argument collapsed.) The minor premise was this: George III has repeatedly usurped the rights of the Americans with the design "to reduce them under absolute despotism." The demonstration took the form of a bill of indictment against the King—a list of eighteen incisively paragraphed charges, authenticated in historical events, and artfully exhibited as proof *prima facie* of guilt. The indictment issued against the King rather than Parliament because Congress had repudiated the latter authority, leaving allegiance to the King the only legal bond. Congress had not, it may be noted, formally adopted Jefferson's theory of empire as developed in the *Summary View*, and except for a passing allusion it refused to do so now when he attempted to smuggle it into the Declaration. The conclusion of the argument followed automatically. A corollary of the right to throw off a tyrannical government is the right to institute just government. So the Americans absolved themselves of allegiance to the British Crown and solemnly declared "that these United Colonies are and of right ought to be free and independent states."

Jefferson later said that in drafting the Declaration he turned to neither book nor pamphlet nor writing of any kind. This was not quite correct. He drew his charges against the King from the preamble of the constitution he had just drafted for Virginia and sent to Williamsburg. The Virginia Declaration of Rights, drawn by George Mason and available in Philadelphia before the middle of June, probably influenced the phrasing of the philosophical second paragraph. And Jefferson may have resorted to the *Summary View* for the passage on the imperial relationship struck by Congress. But ideas, as he once said, were of all things in nature the least capable of confinement or of exclusive appropriation. The ideas in the Declaration belonged to everyone and to no one. They were part of the climate of opinion, and they passed as coin of the realm among American patriots in 1776. Years afterwards, responding to criticism of the Declaration as a hackneyed performance, Jefferson lucidly stated his view of the task: "Not to find out new principles, or new arguments, never before thought of, not merely to say things which had never been said before; but to place before mankind the common sense of the subject, and to justify ourselves in the independent stand we are compelled to take. Neither aiming at originality of principle or sentiment, nor yet copied from any particular or previous writing, it was intended to be an expression of the American mind, and to give to that expression the proper tone and spirit called for by the occasion."

Yet the Declaration bore the unmistakable stamp of the author's genius. It possessed that "peculiar felicity of expression" for which he was already noted. It was simple, clear, and direct; crisp and angry when this was the tone required, as in the arraignment of the King; gracious and elevated in the soft passages enunciating the rights of man; solemn and stately in the concluding pledge of "our lives, our fortunes, and our sacred honor." Its rhetoric was faintly aristocratic, shrinking from the boldness, the enthusiasm, the popularity of Paine's writing, for example. But Jefferson was not penning a manifesto, and graciousness cannot be counted a fault in a production addressed to the opinion of mankind. Even so, he may have learned something from *Common Sense*, for the Declaration, far beyond any of Jefferson's earlier writings, suppressed recondite legalisms to fundamental human values and capsuled large ideas in electrifying phrases. In a document of less than 1500 words, most of it a bill of particulars against the reigning sovereign, ideas could not be developed, nor indeed even stated; they could only be conjured up by magical words and phrases in trim array. Jefferson managed to compress a cosmology, a political philosophy, a national creed in the second paragraph of the Declaration. This was a triumph. It raised the American cause above parochialism, above history, and united it with the cause of mankind. A philosophy of human rights attained timeless symbolization in words that inspired action; action became thought and thought became action. It was, as Hannah Arendt has said, "one of the rare moments in history when the power of action is great enough to erect its own monument."

Congress heard the Declaration on Friday, June 28, and promptly laid it on the table pending disposition of the Virginia resolution on independence. During the three-week interval just passed several of the delegations from the middle colonies received new instructions, representatives of the new revolutionary government in Pennsylvania came into Congress, and the Rutledge-dominated South Carolina delegation gradually gave ground. When the vote came on July 2 only New York, whose delegates approved the resolution but who were bound by previous instructions, was not recorded in favor. Congress then took up the Declaration, scrutinizing and debating it line by line for two and one-half days. The author squirmed under this ordeal. The introductory part was quickly approved, but Congress made many changes, mostly stylistic, some of substance, in the body of the work. It tempered overly vehement or extravagant expressions against the King, eliminated certain pejoratives, and here and there made a ceremonious bow to historical objectivity. For instance, "he has suffered the administration of justice totally to cease in some of these states" became "he has obstructed the administration of justice." The change was a gain for directness as well as balance. Most of the charges, it might be observed, concerned invasions of the representative assemblies, pointing up the crucial importance of this issue. Congress eliminated altogether the longest, angriest, and climactic count in Jefferson's indictment: the King's "cruel war against human nature itself" by the traffic in slaves. It was struck, Jefferson said, at the behest of South Carolina and Georgia, who wished to continue the African trade. But Congress had other reasons as well for removing this piece of bombast. True, as Jefferson knew from Virginia experience, the Crown had suppressed legislative attempts to stop the importation of slaves. But the Virginians had been motivated perhaps less by humanitarian than by selfish considerations, such as protecting the value of their property in slaves and securing their communities from the dangers of an ever-increasing slave population. It ill became the Americans, north and south, who had profited from this infernal traffic to lay the blame on George III. The charge simply did not ring true. And Jefferson's bloated rhetoric gave it away. Congress also cut deeply into the concluding portion of his composition, eliminating the capsuled restatement of the empire theory, which was water over the dam, and about two hundred additional words superfluous to the case. Jefferson seemed to feel that the Declaration, after passing through the gauntlet of Congress, emerged a weaker document. In fact, it gained in every respect. Congress corrected him precisely where he had allowed himself to go astray: in entering technical legal points, in making loose, circuitous, or wordy statements, and in using declamatory language. Cleared of these aberrations, the intrinsic merits of the work stood in bolder relief than when it passed from Jefferson's hands.

Adopted on the evening of July 4, the Declaration of Independence was promptly printed and put into circulation. Four days later, on a warm sunshiny Philadelphia morning, before a great concourse of people in the State House yard, it was publicly proclaimed for the first time. The people returned their huzzahs, then tore down the King's arms before the State House, and rang bells and lit bonfires on into the evening. It is pleasant to think that Jefferson shared in this celebration. He may not have, however. Congress worked without let-up. The Declaration of Independence, he realized, was no ordinary state paper, yet its immediate significance lay not in causing anything but in affirming an accomplished fact. It did not at once become popular. And several years passed before his authorship was generally known. It was some time, in fact, before he felt a marked pride in the authorship. In part, this was owing to the irritant of congressional tinkering; mainly, however, it was because neither he nor anyone else realized the far-reaching implications of the document. But the Declaration heralded the future, not alone in America but the world around; and in the longer run of time Jefferson's destiny rode with it.

Jefferson's progress from Virginia burgess to American revolutionist in seven years followed the main road of the patriot cause, beginning with the protective defense of traditional rights and liberties and ending with the radical ideology that became the birth-right and creed of a new nation. The line of advance intellectually ran, in general, from law to theory, from history to reason, from the prescriptive guarantees of the English constitution to the natural rights of man. In the course of asserting their claims within the empire, the colonists became increasingly disenchanted with the home government, distrustful of its designs, and anxious for the security of their own polities. They began to think for themselves and to search out their own identity; and swept along by the dialectics of the controversy, they assumed theoretical positions that placed them at odds not alone with the principles and practices of the imperial government but with the principles and practices of government everywhere. Discovering the bankruptcy of one system of politics, they invoked a new system. Viewed abstractly, it was founded on the ideas of the Enlightenment. But these ideas had a traditional base in English law and government, which facilitated the transition. Moreover, in America, the ideas were virtual mirror images of emerging social and political realities only dimly perceived before the birth of revolutionary consciousness. As liberal ideas called attention to these native realities, so did they enable Americans to release the substance of English liberty from its corrupted and constricted forms. The patriots did not invent these ideas, but they organized and condensed them into a revolutionary ideology, then proceeded to put it to work in the civil life of the new nation. Without quite realizing the implications for their own institutions, much less the world-wide import of what they had done, the patriots of 1776 had launched a radical new experiment in democracy.

In the philosophical second paragraph of the Declaration of Independence, Jefferson crystallized the ideas of that "transforming radicalism of the mind" that was, as Bernard Bailyn has said, the essence of the American Revolution.

First of all, *equality:* "all men are created equal." With Jefferson this was an article of science as well as of faith. All men were equal because all stemmed from a single divine creation. In an earlier draft he had written "that from that equal creation" they derive inalienable rights, but he dropped this infelicitous phrasing in favor of "they are endowed by their Creator." Believing in the unity of the human species—metaphorically, at least, in the Mosaic account of creation—and its indestructible place at the end of "the great chain of being,"

Jefferson considered all men equals in the order of nature, just as if the race had been carried forward by creation rather than generation. All men possessed an innate moral sense, the faculty of reason, and essentially the same biological needs. Hence the doctrine of equality was grounded in the facts of natural history.

Second, *natural rights:* "they are endowed by their Creator with certain unalienable rights; that among these are life, liberty, and the pursuit of happiness." The law of nature was furnished with the rights of man—a liberating, not a coercive law. Locke and other modern theorists had deduced the fundamental rights from an imaginary "state of nature." Jefferson neither liked nor used this fiction. The natural state of man was the social state; man realized his true nature as a civilized being. Moreover, the concept implied, as some said, that men gave up their natural rights when they entered under government. But these rights were not only antecedent to government, the whole object of government was to protect individuals in them. Even Locke, whose famous *Second Treatise* was the prototype of the theory, had been more concerned to establish the supremacy of Parliament than the supremacy of man. Jefferson's doctrine ran toward releasing the powers of free individuals. Government might help in this, especially by guarantees of liberty; but it must always be remembered that the moral right precedes the legal guarantee. The more striking departure from Locke was Jefferson's substitution of "the pursuit of happiness" for "property." In his *Essay on Human Understanding,* Locke had made the pursuit of happiness the mainspring of human action, yet he did not think it a natural right, as suggested by its omission from the *Second Treatise.* The idea of happiness, individual or social or both, as the supreme end was a commonplace of eighteenth-century thought. Jefferson declared it a right. Everyone had the right to pursue happiness in his own way, according to his own experience, his own talents, his own balance of pleasure and pain. There could be no objective definition of this good, therefore no way a government could obtain it for the multiplicity of citizens. Reason and the moral sense provided safeguards against the extravagances of individualism. Virtue being essential to happiness, and virtue consisting in the duty to others, it was negated by mere selfishness. Because the pursuit was a public activity, in part, dependent on public well-being, all men had a stake

94

in the *res publica* and should have a voice in its affairs. Property, on the other hand, Jefferson apparently considered a civil rather than a natural right. Without the protection of the property that a man derived from his own labor, there could be no life, liberty, or happiness. So Jefferson did not intend to depreciate the right of property when he omitted it from the Declaration, but considering it an instrumental value, as a means to human happiness, and recognizing its civil character, he could not elevate property to the status of inalienable right.

Third, the *sovereignty of the people:* "that to secure these rights, governments are instituted among men, deriving their just powers from the consent of the governed." Sovereignty passed in 1776 from the Crown to the people of the newly free and independent states. There was no crisis of legitimacy: the people of each state possessed the ultimate authority, and they set about, through the device of civil contract, erecting legitimate governments on the old foundations. Always before sovereignty had been attached to the law-making power; the American theory placed it in the people, thus subordinating the rulers to the ruled. Always before sovereignty had been assumed to be one and indivisible—the British had conjured up the specter of an *imperium in imperio* to frighten the colonists. The American theory united sovereignty in one authority, the people, but delegated and divided the operative powers of government. Always before governments had swallowed up the rights of the people. The American theory made government responsible to the people, limited it to securing their rights, safety, and happiness, and bound it under a fundamental written law. Taking man as the starting point, the Declaration of Independence downgraded the role of government. At best government was, as *Common Sense* said, but "a necessary evil" in the work of securing the blessings of society. "Society is produced by our wants and government by our wickedness; the former promotes our happiness *positively* by uniting our affections, the latter *negatively* by restraining our vices." Jefferson agreed entirely, though he never said it so well. The conception of popular sovereignty, barely evoked in the Declaration, possessed many as yet unexplored or even undetected convolutions. Indeed the American democratic experiment would be largely an effort to come to grips with it.

Finally, the *right of revolution:* "that whenever any form of government becomes destructive of these ends, it is the right of the people to alter or to abolish it, and to institute new government." As the people made government so could they unmake it. The principle of revolution, which brought the American polity into being, was thus built into its foundations. The principle should be held under the dictates of prudence and forbearance, of course, in the manner of the patriots of 1776; and there could be no cause to exercise the right at all so long as government was free and popular. Nevertheless, the right of revolution was an inflammatory doctrine. It ignited combustible materials in other nations and conferred political legitimacy on radical democratic forces in the new nation.

The Declaration of Independence endowed the American Revolution with high moral purpose united to a theory of free government. Without this, the independence of thirteen colonies, three million people strung along the western Atlantic seaboard, would have been a significant but scarcely an epochal event in the history of mankind. As it was, it opened an age of revolution in old and new nations that is not yet spent. "We have it in our power to begin the world over again," *Common Sense* declared. This was inspired prophecy. Jefferson did not speak in these terms, and very few of the patriots of 1776 shared Paine's earth-shaking vision. The larger vision, this sense of destiny beyond national frontiers, came later, filtered through the French Revolution. Focusing on the task at hand—a war to wage, trade to secure, governments to erect, a federal union to form—the Americans had first to comprehend and work out the creed Jefferson had given them in the building of their own nation.

CHAPTER THREE

Virginia Reformer

You and I, my dear friend, have been sent into life at a time when the greatest lawgivers of antiquity would have wished to live. How few of the human race have ever enjoyed an opportunity of making an election of government—more than of air, soil, or climate—for themselves or their children! When, before the present epoch, had three millions of people full power and a fair opportunity to form and establish the wisest and happiest government that human wisdom can contrive?

John Adams, Thoughts on Government, in a Letter from
a Gentlemen to his Friend. *Philadelphia, 1776.*

T HE REMAINDER of the story of Jefferson's service in Congress is little more than a footnote to the events that culminated in the Declaration of Independence. Throughout July and August, while his thoughts turned increasingly homeward, he worked in the day-to-day business of Congress. He took copious notes on the beginnings of the two-year-long debate on the Articles of Confederation, but made no significant contribution of his own. He served on numerous committees, among them the first of all congressional investigations, which looked into the failures of the Canadian campaign. Of the several reports he wrote, one at least had lasting importance: it first proposed the Spanish dollar as the standard money unit of the new nation. He communicated with his friends at home, exhorting them to rise above considerations of local defense and to throw the resources of the commonwealth behind the greater cause of the Union.

Virginia was secure. The pesky Dunmore, with his motley crew of Tories and blacks, dropped the royal standard and fled during the summer. The new government was in operation, lacking only the imprimatur of an official seal to dignify its acts. "We are very much at a loss here for an engraver to make our seal," John Page wrote to Jefferson. "Can you get the work done in Philadelphia?" Jefferson located an artist, but the seal was not actually cut until three years later in Paris. The United States waited even longer for its Great Seal. On July 4 Jefferson was appointed with Benjamin Franklin and John Adams to report an appropriate design. Adams proposed the figure of Hercules resting on his club, shunning sloth and pleasure, and beckoned by Virtue to ascend her rugged mountain. Franklin preferred a Biblical image: Moses in priestly robes causing the sea to overwhelm mighty Pharaoh, while a pillar of fire in the clouds evoked divine presence. Jefferson liked this, and proposed for the reverse side the figures of "Hengist and Horsa, the Saxon chiefs from whom we claim the honor of being descended, and whose political principles and form of government we have assumed." The confusing array of symbols, for all their incongruity, nevertheless fairly represented the different pasts Americans claimed heir to in 1776. Unable to agree among themselves, the distinguished committee recommended a thoroughly unhistorical plan submitted by the artist, Pierre Eugene Du Simitière. The Great Seal as finally approved by Congress in 1782 retained only its motto, *E Pluribus Unum.* A fitting emblem of the Union! But the spirit of the Revolution was better captured in the motto proposed by Franklin and Jefferson, one the Virginian later made his own: "Rebellion to Tyrants is Obedience to God."

Jefferson was more interested in revolution than in union. Without the latter the former must fail, of course, but the work of confederation was bound to lumber along for years, hobbled by the war's exigencies and the jangling interests in Congress. It was not yet a field for enduring accomplishment in the governing of men nor, as essentially the foreign department of the newly independent states, could it become the principal field until they were placed on proper foundations. The time was ripe for revolutionizing the colonial governments. It was, as Adams said, "a time when the greatest lawgivers of antiquity would have wished to live." Jefferson, with a sense of history and of his place in it no less acute than Adams's, wished to be a lawgiver to the new age. He was determined to seize the opportunity while the Revolutionary spirit flamed in every patriot breast. It would not last. "From the conclusion of the war we shall be going down hill," he later reflected. "It will not then be necessary to resort every moment to the people for support. They will be forgotten, therefore, and their rights disregarded. They will forget themselves, but in the sole faculty of making money, and will never think of uniting to effect a due respect for their rights."

So he must return to Virginia. There the work of reformation was under way, and Jefferson, three hundred miles from the scene, was deeply disturbed by the conservative course it was taking. In the opinion of many Virginians, the work was finished and done with upon the adoption of a constitution some days before Congress proclaimed independence. Such men were separationists—rebels against Britain but conservatives at home. Jefferson was a revolutionist. He had hoped that the Virginia delegates might have been recalled from Congress for a short time in order to have a voice in the making of the constitution. "In truth," he wrote to a friend in Williamsburg, "it is the whole object of the present controversy; for should a bad government be instituted for us in future it had been as well to have accepted the bad one offered to us from beyond the water without the risk and expense of contest." But in the momentous spring of 1776 Virginia could not be without a delegation in Congress. And had Jefferson got his wish he would not, in all probability, have become the author of the Declaration of Independence. He had to content himself with submitting a proposed constitution from afar, relying on his old teacher, George Wythe, to carry it to Williamsburg. It was late June when Wythe arrived at the convention. The weather was hot, the delegates were tired, and they had so far agreed on a plan of government widely at variance with this fresh proposal from Jefferson that they had not the patience to discuss it. They found it convenient, nevertheless, to tack on Jefferson's preamble, the parent of his arraignment of George III in the Declaration of Independence, and to incorporate two or three propositions of his in the finished document.

The constitution fell far below Jefferson's expectations, thus deepening his anxiety to return home. He was anxious in any event. Martha was not well; and the desire to be near his family was as strong as the spur of public responsibility. Against his declared will, the convention had re-elected him to another term in Congress. No sooner was he notified than he resigned, vaguely begging "the situation of my domestic affairs." But his correspondence with friends at home during the same months makes it abundantly clear that he was eager to take up the work of reformation where the convention had left off. He retired from Congress on September 2, and after a month at Monticello, took his seat in the House of Delegates, the old Burgesses, at Williamsburg.

The Virginia Constitution

The constitution Jefferson drafted and placed in Wythe's hands in Philadelphia was an epitome of his political science in 1776. Actually, this was the third draft. As one who believed the framing of new republican constitutions "the whole object of the present controversy," he probably gave to the task more time and thought than ever he did to the drafting of the immortal Declaration. There he boldly sketched the philosophy of the new nation; here, in planning a government for his countrymen, he endeavored to implement that philosophy and to secure the rights declared in the fundamental law of the new commonwealth. While some of his patriot friends looked upon the achievement of independence as the end toward which the Revolution aimed, it was for Jefferson only the beginning. The ultimate justification of American independence was moral: in the obligation to conform all conduct to the standard of right raised in the Declaration. Rhetoric was cheap, as Jefferson knew. Philosophers had talked of "natural rights" and "self-government" for centuries, but when had these theories been reduced to practice? Where had a government been instituted by "the consent of the governed"? Where had the rights of "life, liberty, and the pursuit of happiness" been held sacred? This was the harder part. And while it could not be finished in a day, a year, or a century, while it could never be accomplished with the nicety of abstract theory, the strongest possible beginning ought to be made lest the noble principles of 1776 be hooted down the corridors of time.

The constitution adopted at Williamsburg was undoubtedly more representative of Virginia political opinion than Jefferson's draft. Mainly the work of George Mason, a Fairfax planter close to the Lees, it steered a middle course between the conservatism of Edmund Pendleton, Carter Braxton, and the old guard generally, and the liberalism of Jefferson, Wythe, and many young Virginians. It did not in any way alter the distribution of power in Virginia society. It continued the freehold suffrage qualification under which one-third or more of the adult white males were disfranchised. It continued a system of representation in the legislature favorable to the smaller eastern counties. It actually increased the oligarchical power of the fountainheads of local justice and administration, the county courts. The most conspicuous change was in the executive office. Stripped of the vestments of monarchy, the Governor was annually elected by the General Assembly, and required to act with the consent of an eight-man Council of State, also elected by the assembly. Judges too, except for the self-perpetuating county courts, received their appointments from the assembly. All powers thus resided in the legislative body. In creating a bicameral legislature, Senate and House of Delegates, and in attacking such "monarchical" abuses as plural-officeholding, the convention went some farther way toward constituting an old and familiar Whig theory of government. The Virginia convention's originality lay not in the constitution but in Mason's Declaration of Rights appended to it. This was a magnificent achievement, even if its authority was uncertain. There were distressing disparities between the Declaration and the constitution, between the equalitarian phrases of the one and the aristocratic features of the other. The Virginia Declaration of Rights nevertheless set a model for governments of free men the world over.

Jefferson at once became the Virginia constitution's severest critic. His lifelong quarrel with it picked up more and more democratic accents in progress with his political opinions. He argued, first of all, that the constitution was illegitimate—a mere ordinance or statute with no permanent and binding power on the government. The convention that framed the constitution was, as he correctly observed, the Revolutionary successor of the House of Burgesses, its members elected in April 1776 to perform the *ordinary* business of government. "They could not, therefore, pass an act transcendent to the powers of other legislatures." The term "convention" as then employed in Virginia in no way conveyed the idea, still nebulous, of a constitutional convention: an especially elected body of delegates to draw the fundamental law of the state. This is what was necessary, Jefferson thought, for without it succeeding legislatures might freely alter the constitution to please themselves. Jefferson stated his objection through Edmund Randolph at the time of the convention's meeting. But Pendleton, Mason, and Patrick Henry, to whom Randolph talked, "saw no distinction between the conceded power to declare independence,"—a more than ordinary power the convention had exercised—"and its necessary consequence, the fencing of society by the institution of government." The fact that Jefferson went ahead and submitted his own proposal to the body whose rightful authority he denied suggested that his objection was captious and might not have occurred to him had he been in Williamsburg.

But Jefferson was not being frivolous. He was attempting to work out the practical means whereby a people, taking sovereignty to themselves, may create a government of their own choosing. There was, in his opinion, a vast difference between the revolutionary act of independence and the institution of government according to principles that alone jusified the act. "Necessities which dissolve a government, do not convey its authority to an oligarchy or to a monarchy. They throw the authority back, into the hands of the people . . . and leave them to shift for themselves." Thus figuratively thrown back into the Lockian "state of nature," how were the people to form a government over themselves? Neither Locke nor any theorist of the people's sovereignty had answered this question. It was to be answered in the actual process of state-making in the American Revolution.

As finally and fully developed, the process included three elements: a convention emanating from the people for the purpose of framing a constitution, popular ratification of the document, and provision for its periodic amendment and revision. None of the first constitutions, hastily framed in the face of the enemy, exhibited all these cardinal elements, nor did Jefferson or anyone grasp the finished theory in 1776. He had a good idea of it, however. It is interesting to notice in this connection the advanced position taken by numerous citizens of Albemarle County in the summer of 1776. In a document of unknown authorship, the citizens protested the undemocratic features of the new constitution and instructed their delegates, one of whom was Jefferson, to press for certain changes, to be followed, when made, by popular ratification of the entire plan of government. "It is our opinion," said Jefferson's constituents, "that among the rights, of which men cannot deprive, or divest their Posterity, the most important is that of approving, or disapproving, their own laws; which power ought forever to remain with the whole body of the people." The Albemarle instructions agreed on so many points with Jefferson's opinions as to warrant the inference that he had a hand in their preparation. Of the three draft constitutions he wrote, only the second demanded popular ratification. To the third, which Wythe took to Williamsburg, he appended a note proposing that the constitution, after approval by the convention, "shall be referred by them to the people to be assembled in their respective counties and that the suffrages of two thirds of the counties shall be required to establish it." But the convention, assuming the authority to establish as well as to frame the constitution, paid no attention to Jefferson's proposal; and in the long campaign he waged against the constitution of 1776, its failure to receive "the consent of the governed" was never the main ground of complaint. He made allowance for the hazard of popular ratification during the war. "True it is," he reflected, "this is no time for deliberating forms of government. While an enemy is within our bowels, the first object is to expel him." The same apology, if such it was, will not do for still another constitution he drafted, in 1783, for submission to a reform convention that never materialized. The war was over and despite the successful example of popular ratification of the Massachusetts constitution of 1780, he made no similar provision in his new proposal. In all but the very first of his draft constitutions, on the other hand, Jefferson supplied a method for regular amendment and revision by the consent of the people. He regarded this feature as indispensable if republican government was to advance "hand in hand with the progress of the human mind," and he made its omission from the Virginia constitution a leading count in his indictment.

The fact is that Jefferson, with many others, at first fumbled and groped in searching out a practical means of implementing the principles of the Revolution. "In truth," he reflected years later, "the abuses of monarchy had so much filled all the space of political contemplation, that we imagined everything republican which was not monarchy. We had not yet penetrated to the mother principle, that governments are republican only in proportion as they embody the will of the people, and execute it." If this can be said with respect to the foundations of authority, it can also be said with respect to the structure of government.

Here Jefferson was in substantial agreement with the moderate Whigs at Williamsburg. The question of the Senate was unusually perplexing. He had been disenchanted with the widely acclaimed "balance" of the English constitution, wherein the opposing forces of King, Lords, and Commons supposedly functioned with the perfection of the Newtonian laws of motion; still he was sufficiently influenced by the theory to conclude that the two houses of a consistently republican legislature ought to be bottomed on different principles and interests. How, then, should the upper house, the Senate, be differentiated from the popular branch of the legislature? In his first draft, Jefferson proposed life appointment of the senators, thus placing himself, on this issue, in the aristocratic camp of Pendleton and Braxton. He copied the same provision in the second draft, then pulled back, struck it, and called for election of senators to terms of nine years by the lower house. This was repeated in the final draft. The convention's solution was to have the Senate elected on a district basis, each district being composed of several counties, but by the same voters as elected representatives to the so-called popular branch. Jefferson disliked it. "I have ever observed that a choice by the people themselves is not generally distinguished for its wisdom," he avowed to Pendleton. The Senate should be entirely independent of the people and gifted with greater wisdom. Just how this would be achieved by making the senators elective of the lower house he did not explain. Perhaps he calculated on the maturer age, thirty-five years, he would require of senators and the combination of long terms with no re-eligibility. Confessing he would submit to almost "any thing rather than a mere creation by and dependence on the people," he nevertheless opposed return to the principle of life appointment and, as for the solution adopted in several states of basing the senate on property, he tartly remarked, "my observations do not enable me to say I think integrity the characteristic of wealth." He continued for some years to be troubled by the make-up of the Senate, perhaps less because it flouted conventional political theory than because it was, in fact, a lackey of the House of Delegates. In the final analysis he was unable to devise a basis of the Senate that satisfied both the demands of Whig political science and his republican convictions. When he again turned his hand to the reform of the Virginia constitution in 1783, he acquiesced in the system of election it provided.

Shedding aristocracy was a problem, but shedding monarchy was as easy as throwing off a badly frayed coat. The executive of Jefferson's plan was in some details even weaker than the one agreed upon at Williamsburg. His governor, whom he called Administrator, was elected annually by the House. He was ineligible for re-election until the expiration of three years after a term of service, whereas the convention allowed the Governor three consecutive annual terms. On balance, however, Jefferson's executive was definitely the stronger. He envisioned the Council as purely consultative, "to give advice to the Administrator when called on by him." Such an arrangement would have lightened Jefferson's later ordeal as Governor under the constitutional mandate to act with the "advice and consent" of the Council on all questions. Jefferson's plan also concentrated greater appointive powers in the Governor. The constitution continued the colonial practice of filling vacancies in the county courts on nomination of the respective court. Jefferson gave the appointments entirely to the executive. The provision, together with another making sheriffs and coroners elective, would have gone some way toward curbing the power of the courthouse cliques. Although Jefferson was to learn from hard experience the necessity of strengthening the executive, it would be many years before he would advocate the most obvious means of accomplishing the objective: election by the people.

Jefferson was farthest at odds with his compatriots in Virginia and elsewhere on the related issues of suffrage and representation.

His unhesitating advocacy of a broadly popular suffrage and of equal representation of the people in the legislature held the promise of making his constitution a vital instrument of democratic government. Although he did not entirely abandon the freehold suffrage qualification, he reduced it by more than one-half and, further, extended the suffrage to all taxpayers. Moreover, he ensured the enfranchisement of still other Virginians by a unique measure of both economic and political democracy: every person of full age who did not own fifty acres of land was entitled to a government appropriation of so many acres as necessary to make up that amount. Jefferson thus revived the old colonial importation or headright system, under which a fifty-acre grant was awarded to the person responsible for settling an immigrant in Virginia, and turned it toward democratic ends. But if he hoped to overcome the resistance of the planter class to universal white male suffrage by, in effect, making every man a freeholder, he was quickly disappointed. Young Randolph could not recall that any delegate in the convention uttered a word against the traditional freehold suffrage. It remained the rock of conservative influence for decades to come. Jefferson's reform would also eliminate special property qualifications for officeholders. Public office would be thrown open to a large electorate virtually identical with the community. Jefferson proposed to achieve fair and equal representation geographically by proportioning the legislature to the rule of numbers. Under the county-unit system of representation which the convention perpetuated, the tidewater counties controlled one-half the Senate and nearly one-half the House, though they possessed well under half the population and were steadily losing ground to the interior sections. The question was one of interest as well as of principle. The wealth and privilege of the state centered in the east. Jefferson identified himself with the aspirations of the west. But the point of equal representation struck him as "capital and fundamental" on whatever ground it was put, and he would not rest easy until it could be obtained.

Most of the remaining differences between Jefferson's plan and the one adopted at Williamsburg fall into the general category "rights and liberties." In view of his staunch advocacy of a federal Bill of Rights in 1788, it is surprising he did not add a similar document to the proposed Virginia constitution. He endeavored, he later said, "to reach all the great objects of public liberty" in the constitution itself. In fact, he reached only a few of them. The Virginia Declaration of Rights contained guarantees of the right against self-incrimination, the right of *habeas corpus*, and freedom from unwarranted searches and seizures, none of which were to be found in Jefferson's drafts. He upheld these rights, of course. They were in the common law. But in 1776 he evidently did not think it essential to give them constitutional protection. On the other hand, he incorporated in his constitution a number of liberal reforms—on religion, slavery, descent of lands, punishment of crimes—that were strangers to the Virginia constitution.

That frame of government proved utterly recalcitrant to change. Several times during the next fifty years Jefferson rode full tilt against it, each charge more democratic than the last, and each time he retired in defeat. But if he could not revamp the Constitution, he might, for the present, turn one of its vicious principles, the unfettered power of the assembly, to virtuous ends, and endeavor to achieve by ordinary legislation those fundamental reforms in Virginia law and institutions he had hoped to accomplish at one stroke by a liberal constitution.

In the House of Delegates

The House of Delegates Jefferson entered in October 1776 was, with the exception of several members like himself, the same body as formed the constitution. He took his seat, occupied by an alternate in his absence, by virtue of his election to the convention in April. Soon after he arrived in Williamsburg, a messenger from Congress notified him of his election as a joint commissioner, with Benjamin Franklin and Silas Deane, to negotiate a treaty of alliance at the Court of Louis XVI. Duty, the pleasures of France, the delightful company of Dr. Franklin—all inclined him to accept the charge. Although more sanguine than most men about the prospects of American arms, he knew the capital importance of the French mission, and he was honored by so distinguished an appointment. For three days he groped toward a decision; finally, on October 11, he dismissed the messenger with a letter politely declining the commission. The circumstances of his family, he explained, neither permitted him to leave them behind nor to expose them to the dangers of the crossing. "I saw, too," he later reflected, "that the laboring oar was really at home, where much was to be done, of the most permanent interest, in new modeling our governments. . . . " No task seemed more urgent to him, or more agreeable, since it permitted him to live as he was accustomed and be near his ailing wife. She joined him in Williamsburg. During Wythe's absence in Philadelphia, the Jeffersons occupied his modest house, which still stands facing the Palace green, a monument to an age of gentle simplicity.

A revolution had come, but the only noticeable change in the old capital was the new face in the Governor's Palace. Patrick Henry had been elected first Governor of the Commonwealth. The conservatives had put up an opposition in the person of Thomas Nelson, Sr., long-time secretary of the colony; but the popular orator drew support from both moderate and liberal men, and thus carried the election handily. It was a tribute owing to his unrivaled leadership in the Revolutionary movement. Despite his reputation as a "radical," Henry was satisfied with the new frame of government. The conservatives had nothing to fear from him. His powers were forensic; he was amiable and pliable; he was a Virginian to the core of his being, no less attached to the old ways than his arch-antagonist Edmund Pendleton. In 1776 Henry's great work was done; the work of his young friend and comrade Thomas Jefferson was just beginning. Henry led Virginia to the Revolution, but lacking either talent or zeal for constructive reform, he could not consolidate it. This was to be Jefferson's role. Elevated to the governorship, jealously guarded as it was, Henry lost much of the influence he formerly had. The vacuum he left in the legislative chamber, Jefferson hastened to fill. The delegate from Albemarle was one of the half-dozen most popular figures in the assembly. While this counted for much, the fact that he knew what he wanted, that he had a program for correcting abuses, righting wrongs, and expanding liberty, counted for more. Developing this line of politics, Jefferson did not displace Henry in the affections of the people—no one could do that —but made his brand of demagogical politics unnecessary to successful leadership in a republic of free men.

In the House of Delegates most of the faces were familiar. In the Speaker's chair sat Edmund Pendleton, one of Jefferson's prized friends among the elder statesmen of Virginia. The two men heartily liked and respected each other, though their political swords were usually crossed. Genial, unaffected, and judicious, Pendleton embodied the virtues of the ruling class without either its wealth or its vices. Jefferson did not feel the same esteem for other leaders on the conservative side, such as opulent Benjamin Harrison, of Berkeley, with whom he had served in Congress, and Robert Carter Nicholas, the former treasurer and guardian of the Church. He was perhaps not yet well acquainted with George Mason, who best represented the moderate element in the assembly and whose authorship of the Declaration of Rights commended him to Jefferson. The master of Potomac's Gunston Hall was a man of marvelous force and presence. A successful planter with a large family and a distinct preference for private life, he shied away from the leadership that might have been his. During the next several years, when he served in the assembly, Jefferson found him to be perhaps his "most steadfast, able and zealous" colleague. Looking back on the time from the perspective of nearly half a century, Jefferson also remembered the assistance of two other men, more eager and more advanced in their opinions than Mason but lacking his influence. One was George Wythe, who returned from Congress in 1777, the other the new delegate from Orange, James Madison. A delicate little man, reserved, always garbed in black, and without surface brilliance of any kind, Madison was wise and learned beyond his twenty-five years. He had been educated at the College of New Jersey, in Princeton, where he acquired clear ideas of civil and religious liberty from its Scottish Presbyterian president, John Witherspoon. Several months earlier, in the convention, he had posted his liberal colors by proposing a crucial amendment to the article on religion in the Declaration of Rights. But Madison was not a man to invite instant attention or friendship. Jefferson came to know and respect his abilities during the first session of the assembly. Not until three years later, however, when he was Governor and Madison a member of the Council, did they become intimate. In the years ahead Jefferson drew long and well on "the rich resources of his luminious and discriminating mind."

There were, of course, factions and followings in the government, and Henry was even accused of leading a party. Jefferson carefully skirted these political entanglements, with the personal animosities they often involved. The cordiality of his relations with men who were notorious enemies of each other—Henry and Pendleton, Lee and Harrison—bespeaks a mild temperament, a studied courtesy, and a revulsion from the dubious glories of political gladiators. This fact, combined with his forwardness in legislative business and the force of his ideas, ensured his ascendancy in the House of Delegates. Given the convenience of political labels, it is tempting to label Jefferson a "radical." A committed revolutionist, even if a gentle one, could hardly be anything else. And so he seemed to many Virginians of the old order. He was, certainly, more advanced in his thinking and objectives than the great host of his contemporaries in and out of Virginia. Yet he had none of the typical radical's rage against the past, intolerance of opposition, and perfectionist aspirations. With other philosophers of the time, he made a god of nature; yet, without idealizing the past, he embodied history in the cause of the future. He did not compromise his political convictions; but he recognized that they were *his* convictions, to be enjoyed with the same confidence he accorded to others, that perfect agreement was as unnecessary as it was unattainable, and that force could never substitute for reason and persuasion in republican government. He had no blueprint for a new society. He was, at bottom, attached to Virginia society, wishing only to reform its abuses—its feudal holdovers, unnatural privileges, its slavery, and massive ignorance. He would not go to radical lengths to achieve his objectives. And even his most progressive reforms were streaked with conservatism. If democracy was his destiny, he had yet to escape from the chrysalis of Whiggery in which he was born.

The initiative passed to Jefferson on October 12. On that day the House of Delegates gave him leave for the drafting of two bills: one for the abolition of the law of entail, the other for a general revision of the laws of the Commonwealth. He reported the former two days later. In retrospect, he bracketed it with three other measures, those calling for the abolition of primogeniture, for freedom of religion, and for general education, and viewed the whole "as forming a system by which every fiber would be eradicated of ancient or feudal aristocracy; and a foundation laid for government truly republican." Such measures were, as he said, "indicative of the strength and general pulse of reformation." But he also believed the entire code of law should be revised "with a single eye to reason, and the good of those for whose government it was framed."

The Revision of the Laws occupied Jefferson throughout his years in the assembly. The bill passed on October 26, and a few days later the two houses jointly elected a committee of five with instructions to repeal, amend, or revise the laws in force, to introduce others, and then to report the whole for the action of the legislature. Of the members nominated to undertake this work of "magnitude, labor, and difficulty," Jefferson received the most ballots, thus becoming chairman of the committee of revisers, whose other members were Pendleton, Mason, Wythe, and Thomas Ludwell Lee.

The committee met at Fredericksburg on January 3, 1777, to settle on a plan of operation. Disagreement arose on the first question: "whether we should propose to abolish the whole existing system of laws, and prepare a new and complete Institute, or preserve the general system, and only modify it to the present state of things." It was Pendleton, "contrary to his usual disposition in favor of ancient things," who advocated the former, and bolder, approach. As a philosopher of enlightenment, wishing to reform law "with a single eye to reason," Jefferson might have been expected to place himself unreservedly on the side of a new code. But law, for him, was a science of learning as well as of reason, and he shunned system-making heedless of the historic fabric of the law. He thought a completely new code or institute "would involve us in ages of litigation, and render property uncertain until, like the statutes of old, every word had been tried, and settled by numerous decisions, and by new volumes of reports and commentaries." Law should be reasonable, but stability and familiarity were essential elements of the law's reason. The question was settled in Jefferson's favor, though somewhat ambiguously, for what actually came to pass fell between two stools. For the most part the revisal simply recast the existing body of law, after discarding what was obsolete and useless; on the other hand, however, it introduced many new principles unknown to the law of Virginia in 1776. At Fredericksburg, the committee divided the work among themselves. But Lee died soon after and Mason resigned. Jefferson took over most of the portions assigned to them. The committee agreed on the style to be followed in drafting its bills. In general, it was thought better "not to vary the diction of the ancient statutes by modernizing it, nor to give rise to new questions by new expressions," but the style of the later statutes—involute, verbose, redundant—was to be reformed in favor of plain and direct diction.

The three remaining members of the committee finally submitted their report to the assembly in June 1779. "We had in this work," Jefferson wrote in his autobiography, "brought so much of the Common Law as it was thought necessary to alter, all the British statutes from *Magna Charta* to the present day, and all the laws of Virginia from the establishment of our legislature . . . which we thought should be retained, within a compass of one hundred and twenty-six bills, making a printed folio of ninety pages only." This was a triumph of brevity. Actually, though, the published *Report* omitted a good deal that was law in Virginia, and it exempted certain statutes from the final bill repealing all prior acts and ordinances. Before this time, too, a number of bills had been lifted out of the revisal, usually at Jefferson's instigation in order to quicken the pace of reform. Some of these were adopted in the ordinary course of legislation. But the major corpus was not taken up by the assembly until 1785, when to Jefferson's undying gratitude, "by the unwearied exertions of Mr. Madison, in opposition to endless quibbles, chicaneries, perversions, vexations and delays of lawyers and demi-lawyers, most of the bills were passed by the legislature, with little alteration." He was justifiably proud of the Revision of the Laws, even though the original aim of a revised code miscarried. The *Report* was never acted on as a unit; and the revisal became, to employ Madison's figure, "a mine of legislative wealth," rather than a single great monument of legislation. And a mine, it should be added, not only for Virginia but for many new American states over several decades.

The revisal, ample and compendious as it was, did not exhaust the labors of this republican Solon. In the day-to-day affairs of state Jefferson served on numberless committees and drafted reports and bills on every variety of subject. As Julian P. Boyd has observed, "He was in himself a veritable legislative drafting bureau." All this immense industry helps to reveal the mind of the Virginia revolutionist.

Lands

Jefferson's bill to abolish entail, enacted on November 1, 1776, pulled down the first of the pillars of landed aristocracy in Virginia. He subsequently proposed as part of the revisal the abolition of primogeniture, and the bill was adopted on Madison's motion in 1785. These measures, together with others abolishing quitrents and disposing of unappropriated lands, decisively settled the question of whether feudal or freehold tenure would prevail in the new state. Very likely the question would have been settled in the same way without Jefferson's assistance; in fact, social and economic forces having little to do with law had perhaps already settled it. Jefferson's bills capped the development and exalted the principle of freehold tenure.

From his earliest law reading Jefferson formed the opinion that entail and primogeniture—indeed all aspects of feudal tenure—were perversions of the common law. By the law of entail estates were perpetuated from generation to generation through a particular line of descent. By its twin, primogeniture, the lands and slaves of a person dying intestate passed exclusively to the eldest son. An estate held in fee tail might be alienated by a device known as "docking," which required a special act of the legislature. In 1774 Jefferson himself had applied to the Burgesses for permission to dock the entail on certain lands inherited by Martha. The procedure proved troublesome and doubtless contributed to his censure of it in the preamble to the abolition bill. Primogeniture could be avoided by the simple act of drawing a will. Wills were increasingly the practice among the great families. Land was plentiful in Virginia, thus the principal factor that sustained these feudal relics in England was absent. But the pride, opulence, and power of aristocratic families knew no country and continued to furnish motives for the perpetuation of great estates. The privilege of the laws had raised up a "patrician order," Jefferson said. "To annul this privilege, and instead of an aristocracy of wealth, of more harm and danger, than benefit, to society, to make an opening for the aristocracy of virtue and talent, which nature has wisely provided for the direction of the interests of society, and scattered with equal hand through all its conditions, was deemed essential to a well-ordered republic." Annulling the privilege, dissolving all property rights connected with it, the General Assembly at the same time fixed in the laws of Virginia the individualistic system of freehold tenure. Owners of land and slaves in *fee tail* were possessed of their estates in *fee simple*—that is, in absolute dominion, without limitation to a class of heirs or restriction on alienation—and intestate estates were henceforth to be divided equally among all the children. This was, in Jefferson's opinion, the system of reason and nature.

It was also "the happy system of our ancestors." In *A Summary View*, Jefferson had traced the introduction of feudal tenure in England to the alien Normans. The Saxons had held their lands in absolute dominion, but William the Conqueror granted the lands to the Norman barons in return for feudal dues and military services. There arose the fiction that all the lands originally belonged to the king, were received as gifts from him, and were forever beholden to him. This fiction founded on conquest was carried to America. But America had not been conquered by the Normans. The Saxon law of possession should have prevailed here. Instead, the Americans received their lands from the Crown, encumbered with quitrents acknowledging a superior, and were unable freely to hold or to alienate, as they did their personal property. In so far as this was so the Americans were servants of kings and lords rather than themselves free and independent lords of the soil.

Jefferson revived the argument in correspondence with Pendleton during the summer of 1776 when, as Pendleton dryly remarked, "it may be deciding by the sword in New York, whether we shall have any lands left to dispose of." The discussion in the letters centered on quitrents, only one element of the feudal tenure Jefferson wished to abolish. Pendleton favored continuing the system by transferring the right to these dues from the Crown to the Commonwealth. "To hold of the commonwealth by the payment of a certain sum, cannot interfere with the dignity of Freeman," Pendleton said. Jefferson objected, pointing to the danger of a perpetual and independent revenue, as well as to the rights of individuals. His reading of history told him that feudal tenure arose at a specific time for a specific purpose, Norman military discipline and defense, which had long since passed away. "Is it wanting with us for the purpose of military defense? . . . Are not we better off for what we have hitherto abolished of the feudal system? Has not every restitution of ancient Saxon laws had happy effects?" The conservative Pendleton could only smile at his young friend's enthusiasm to go forward by returning to the eighth century. "I highly esteem the old Saxon Laws in general," he remarked, "but cannot suppose them wholly unalterable for the better after an experience of so many centuries."

When the bill on entail came before the House in October, Pendleton opposed it and according to Jefferson offered an amendment that would merely give to the tenant in tail the discretion to convey his estate, both land and slaves, in fee simple. Jefferson dallied with the compromise, but seeing it would defeat his principle rejected it. The act as passed made mandatory the conversion to fee simple tenure, thus carrying out the proposal first advanced in his draft constitution. The Speaker continued his rear-guard action when the revisers met at Fredericksburg. The question of primogeniture was now on the carpet. He wished to preserve it, but finding no support proposed that the committee adopt the Hebrew principle of awarding the eldest son a double portion of the father's estate. "I observed," Jefferson recalled in his autobiography, "that if the eldest son could eat twice as much, or do double work, it might be a natural evidence of his right to a double portion; but being on a par in his powers and wants, with his brothers and sisters, he should be on a par also in the partition of the patrimony; and such was the decision of the members."

The committee went on to determine the precise course of descents, accounting for all possible circumstances, under the rule of co-parceny. The bill Jefferson drafted generally followed the committee's outline. The fundamental departure from the common law was, of course, in admitting all the children to the inheritance. The common law preference for "the worthiest of blood," beginning with the eldest son, had been carried all through the elaborate chain of descent, and had excluded kindred of certain degrees from representation. Thus bastards, aliens, and half-bloods could not inherit in

England. Jefferson manifested his humanity by admitting all three to representation. In the opinion of St. George Tucker, the distinguished Virginia jurist of Jefferson's time, the act of 1785 not only abolished primogeniture but introduced and established principles "in direct opposition to those of the common law, and scarcely agreeing with it in any one principle." It was "enlightened reason" replacing "feudal barbarism."

In later years it was not uncommon for the sons of the "old regime" to imagine that the overthrow of entail and primogeniture had accomplished at one stroke a virtual democratic revolution in Virginia society. Jefferson never made this mistake. He believed the laws "laid the axe to the foot of pseudo-aristocracy." But they did not destroy it. Only the "pseudo-aristocrats" themselves had a stake in that idea. The institution of fee simple tenure in the law of the commonwealth, while a radical act, was not socially revolutionary. A keen observer of the Virginia Tidewater early in the nineteenth century saw the same great inequalities of wealth and of social rank as in colonial times: "Here and there a stately aristocratic palace, with all its appurtenances, strikes the view; while all around, for many miles, no other buildings are to be seen but the little smoky huts and log cabins of poor, laborious, ignorant tenants. And, what is very ridiculous, these tenants, while they approach *the great house,* cap in hand, with all the fearful, trembling submission of the lowest feudal vassals, boast in their court-yards, with obstreperous exultation, that they live in a land of freemen, a land of equal liberty and equal rights." Jefferson had wished to change this picture, not by a leveling equalitarianism but by creating opportunities for "the aristocracy of virtue and talent" to rise. The eradication of entail and primogeniture—hopeless vestiges of feudalism—was only the first measure of his system. Unfortunately, he did not have the same success with the others.

The republican order Jefferson envisioned was bottomed on a mass of small, independent farmers. The husbandman was a poetic figure for him, associated with all the sturdy virtues a free government expected of its citizens; and agriculture was the most natural, as it was the most worthy, of all occupations. "Those who labor in the earth are the chosen people of God, if ever He had a chosen people, whose breasts He has made His peculiar deposit for substantial and genuine virtue." This was not simply an ideal, such as philosophers and poets of other times and places had conjured with. It was rooted in the American environment. It grew from Jefferson's effort to define and interpret the values and the arts of a pioneering society with an immensity of land at its disposal. In 1776 the Trans-Allegheny West was in its infancy. Most of it, the vast expanses of forest and prairie stretching westward to the Mississippi, was claimed by Virginia. But the question of what should be done with these lands, whether profiteering speculators or common farmers should become the beneficiaries, was a question as yet vaguely defined and far from settled. Jefferson first seriously turned his thoughts this way in 1774. Gradually he evolved a policy designed to turn the western lands into a resource of freedom and democracy. The West, new Virginia, became in his eyes a ready-made substitute for the revolution he was unable or unwilling to effect in the landed order of old Virginia.

Before Virginia could make policy for the lands on the western waters, she had first to re-establish her claim to them. While a colony her unappropriated lands belonged to the King to hold or to grant at his pleasure. At least, the principle was universally assumed until Jefferson denied it in the *Summary View*. "From the nature and purpose of civil institutions," Jefferson there declared, "all the lands within the limits, which any particular party has circumscribed around itself, are assumed by that society, and subject to their allotment; this may be done by themselves assembled collectively, or by their legislature, to whom they have delegated sovereign authority; and if they are allotted in neither of these ways, each individual of the society, may appropriate to himself such lands as he finds vacant, and occupancy will give him title." An amazing statement! Not only did Jefferson assert that the local government was rightfully sovereign with respect to its land and boundaries—repudiated by all colonial precedent—but also that individuals might themselves take title to land after the manner of John Locke's theory of property. Jefferson too, like Locke, was dealing in theory, not in law; but when Virginia became independent the theory could be put into practice.

His draft constitution contained several provisions on the subject of Virginia lands. One defined the boundaries of the new state in conformity with the "sea to sea" charter of 1609. This first positive assertion of Virginia's jurisdiction beyond the mountains was copied into the constitution of 1776. The unappropriated lands within these boundaries were thus vested in the commonwealth to be disposed of on its authority, subject to the extinguishment of Indian titles. During the previous quarter-century, however, huge areas of the West had fallen into the hands of profiteering adventurers and land companies, who had obtained grants from the Crown, or negotiated purchases from the Indians, or both. Were these claims to be recognized? The question was complicated in the extreme, involving the interests of many Virginians and non-Virginians, and Jefferson did not propose to settle it by an outright constitutional bar to the claims. But he made his intention abundantly clear by providing that no purchases should be made of the Indians except by the authority of the General Assembly and "on behalf of the public." With one minor change, the convention adopted Jefferson's proposal. Some days earlier, probably under the influence of Jefferson's draft, for it was the only one to go into this question, the convention also adopted a resolution which condemned all private purchases from the Indians and ensured preemption rights to squatters on unappropriated lands. Still another proposal by the absentee delegate in Philadelphia contemplated the creation of new free and independent states in the West. But where Jefferson's draft made this mandatory, the constitution as adopted left it at discretion. Mason was against it entirely, and Article XIV of his Declaration of Rights explicitly barred the creation of new states within the limits of Virginia.

In sum, Jefferson's plan of government gave shape to a new policy for the West. Virginia asserted her political jurisdiction, which carried with it the heavy responsibility of defending this great domain. The lands would be alienated, after Indian titles were extinguished, to common farmers. And if Jefferson had his way, independent, self-governing states would be erected in the West. Significantly, he included these articles in the section of the draft constitution entitled "Rights Private and Public," under the subdivision "Lands," along with the provisions on entail and primogeniture and the fifty-acre grant. These were all spokes in the wheel of a freeholders' republic. The value of the lands as a source of public wealth and power did not seem to interest him at this juncture. The lands should not be sold but given away, he told Pendleton. "I am at the same time clear," he added, "that they should be appropriated in small quantities."

Once Virginia's western claim was officially declared, the land companies that sought to turn the West into a gigantic commercial adventure had no recourse but to Congress. Here they were not disappointed. The Articles of Confederation as first recommended to Congress placed the entire backcountry under its jurisdiction. The so-called landless states—those without western claims of any sort— took up the cause under the banner of union and common benefit from the western lands. This sounded good. But the intimate association between representatives of these states in Congress and powerful speculative interests centered in Philadelphia suggested that the land companies, and not the people, would benefit from congressional jurisdiction. The issue became the stumbling-block to the completion of the Confederation. Jefferson, in 1776, was aware of the stakes in the game, though it took him a little time to comprehend the rules and the characters of the players. Unlike so many of the prominent men of his day he never himself meddled in western lands and seemed to have no connections with speculative interests, though they were avid seekers of political influence. They lobbied at Williamsburg, for the assembly had yet to settle all the outstanding claims to ownership of Virginia soil.

Jefferson openly encountered the speculators in the first session of the assembly. The occasion was a conflict in the Kentucky lands. In March 1775 the Transylvania Company, headed by Judge Richard Henderson of North Carolina, acquired from the Cherokee some 20 million acres of land between the Cumberland and Kentucky rivers. Here Henderson planned to erect a new proprietary colony, Transylvania, which he hoped would be confirmed by charter from the King. In April, Daniel Boone led the first party of settlers into the region. Boonesborough was founded, a land office opened, and rudimentary government established. The coming of independence, followed by the unqualified assertion of Virginia's charter claims, upset Henderson's plan. He sought recognition from Congress but was unsuccessful. He turned to Williamsburg, now disclaiming any thought of "such an absurdity" as the erection of an independent government, but forcefully petitioning for title to the soil on the basis of Indian deed. Meanwhile, a group of settlers at Harrodsburg, in Kentucky, declared their opposition to Transylvania, acknowledged themselves citizens of Virginia, and begged to be represented in the government at Williamsburg. On October 8 the two "delegates" elected by the Harrodsburg meeting, Gabriel Jones and George Rogers Clark, presented the settlers' petition and asked to be recognized. They could not be seated in the House since the Kentucky region was then an appendage of the huge southwestern county of Fincastle; but a committee of three was appointed to bring in a bill which would convert this appendage, including most of Transylvania, into a distinct county. Jefferson was a member of this committee together with Nicholas and Braxton, both tidewater oligarchs with land company connections. Braxton, the chairman, reported a bill calling for the simple division of Fincastle. By some fast legislative footwork Jefferson blocked the bill's passage and got it recommitted to a new committee headed by himself. At the outset, at least, he seemed to have had no definite objective other than courting western favor. But as the struggle wore on during the next six weeks, he took the position that Fincastle should be divided into three counties, and incorporated this, with other liberal features, into the bill he drafted. He then secured its passage, thereby giving to the people on the southwestern frontier a net increase of four representatives. The position of leadership he assumed among the western delegates added greatly to his political capital. Either bill, Braxton's as well as Jefferson's, struck decisively at Henderson's ambitions by the extension of Virginia government to Kentucky. The question of ownership of the soil was left in suspension.

Land titles on the frontier were in a state of chaos. The pretensions of the land companies contributed to the situation. For several years, against discouragements first from the royal government and then from the revolutionary government, pioneers had traversed the mountains and settled on lands claimed by absentee proprietors. The settlers might be forced to make payment at any time on pain of eviction. But even if they had the means it was not always clear to whom they should pay. And after Dunmore's departure in 1775 no land office was open in Virginia. The government sold no lands; no lands could be patented. Pressure mounted on the frontier, especially in Kentucky lands. In 1776 the convention assured the squatters they might purchase the lands they occupied when a land office opened; and the next year the assembly taxed these people as if they had legal title to 400 acres. These were stopgaps. The liberals, led by Jefferson and Mason, favored a two-part program: first, the settlement of the multifarious and irregular claims outstanding; second, the establishment of a permanent policy for the disposal through a land office of the remainder of Virginia's domain, so far as cleared of Indian titles. Mason drafted the bill for the first object, Jefferson for the second. Introduced in January 1778, both bills met formidable eastern opposition. The tidewater, generally, showed little enthusiasm for Virginia's thrust westward. It drained off population, depreciated land values, offered a refuge for draft-dodgers and deserters, and incited costly Indian war. Conservative leaders like Harrison and Braxton had connections with northern land companies seeking to profit from Virginia lands. The liberals and western allies, anxious to secure these lands with settlers, nevertheless made progress in 1778. The House declared new claims prior to the opening of a land office invalid, and also permitted settlers to preempt 400 acres of land at whatever price the government might finally decide. At the fall session, after repeated delays, the land companies presented their claims. Henderson settled, rather handsomely, for "compensation" in the amount of 200,000 acres on the Green River in Kentucky, subject to Virginia law. The leading claimant from the North, the Indiana Company, received nothing, and such was the verdict on all the speculative combines except the old Loyal Company of Virginia, which was subsequently confirmed in its title to 200,000 acres in southwest Virginia.

The bills drafted by Mason and Jefferson, finally enacted by the assembly in the spring of 1779, were obvious twins. Mason's Bill for Settling Titles to Unpatented Land sought to clear away the existing chaos. It confirmed valid titles, granted 400 acres at a nominal price to all settlers prior to January 1778, and set up a commission empowered to render judgment on disputed claims. The bill passed with few changes.

Jefferson's Bill for Establishing a Land Office, on the other hand, was badly treated. It set up four classes of rights to Virginia's unappropriated lands: importation rights, native rights, military rights, and treasury rights. Any person qualifying under one or more of these classes was entitled to so many acres of land. The first class revived the colonial practice of headrights. The second was unprecedented, though consistent with the 50-acre grant provision of the draft constitution: every free-born native of the commonwealth since its establishment was entitled to 75 acres of land upon his or her marriage. Military rights referred to land bounties awarded in varying amounts to officers and soldiers in the Revolutionary armies. Treasury rights would arise from purchases through the Land Office at a set price of £40 per 100 acres, the equivalent in the state's depreciated currency of the old colonial price of ten shillings the hundred. But the House massacred Jefferson's plan for spreading property among common farmers. It eliminated altogether the grants to immigrants and natives. Of the many other changes made in the bill, one was especially significant. In the case of purchases not exceeding 400 acres, the bill authorized issuance of land warrants at any county court, while the act required purchasers, the small with the large, to obtain warrants from the Register of the Land Office at the capital. Virginia was a huge state. Jefferson's proposal to decentralize this business was clearly in the interest of the small settler in the backcountry. The one crucial omission from the bill, as from the act, was a limitation on the number of acres an individual might patent—a surprising omission in view of Jefferson's declared preference for small grants and his acquaintance with the insatiable appetites of speculators. Probably its cause lay in the desire to turn the lands into a source of revenue for the state, which was strongly felt as the costs of war mounted. Whatever the cause, the omission contributed to the defeat of Jefferson's democratic aims and to monopolization of a large part of the most valuable lands in the West.

Jefferson took the lead in legislation on still another part of the land problem in Virginia, the Tory estates. Most of the Loyalists, never very numerous, had followed Dunmore's example and left the state; the few who remained were effectively suppressed, though they became a nuisance when British armies invaded Virginia. The estates of these British subjects were both real and personal, involving not only valuable lands and improvements but planter debts amounting to perhaps three million pounds. Jefferson's sensitive regard for the rights of personal liberty and property did not extend to Tories. Their only standing at law was as enemy aliens; and his policy toward them, reflecting the feelings of most patriots, was tinged with malice. But he cast his eyes on the Tory estates from cold calculations of dollars and cents. He sought to bolster the state's credit and increase its revenue. In January 1778, simultaneous with the introduction of the Land Office bill, which had the same objects partially in view, the assembly passed Jefferson's Bill for Sequestering British Property. The act did not disturb titles or confiscate property; rather, it provided for the administration of Tory estates by government appointed commissioners and payment of the income into the treasury. In addition, it authorized the discharge of private debts owed to British subjects by legal tender payments into a state fund. The provision was confiscatory, in fact, since Virginia money had already depreciated four or five times over and would become, as Jefferson said, as worthless as oak leaves. But Virginians were required to accept it in payment of their debts, so it seemed fair enough to force it on enemy creditors. Surprisingly, comparatively few debtors took advantage of the law. Jefferson was one of them, motivated more by its public than its private benefits; for he subsequently repaid his British creditors in full value, and the Treaty of Paris in 1783 exacted no less.

From a financial standpoint, sequestration was a fiasco. The following year Jefferson drafted, and the assembly passed, a bill for the confiscation of Tory estates. The apologetical preamble suggests that he had little taste for this harsh measure. It marked, as he conceded, "a departure from that generosity which so honorably distinguishes the civilized nations of the present age." He resorted to the ancient common law of escheat and forfeiture for justification. The law of escheat derived from Jefferson's hated Normans. It was feudal, being founded, according to the eminent Blackstone, "upon this single principle, that the blood of the person last seized in fee-simple, is by some means or other, utterly extinct and gone; and since none can inherit his estate but such as are of his blood and consanguinity, it follows as a regular consequence, that when such blood is extinct, the inheritance itself must fail; the land . . . must result back again to the lord of the fee, by whom . . . it was given." Jefferson took this antiquated law, blended it with the English rule barring the transmission or inheritance of real property by aliens, and made the commonwealth, rather than feudal lord or king, bene-ficiary of the corrupted titles. The procedure called for the use of inquests to determine if the holders of real estate were, in fact, British subjects; if they were the property reverted by way of escheat to the commonwealth. The legality of the system was beyond question. It belonged to common law. It was specifically recognized by a provision of the constitution lifted from Jefferson's draft. It represented, nevertheless, an astounding revival of feudal practice. All the states confiscated British property, and some of them were far less generous than Virginia; but there alone, ironically by the most enlightened statesman of his time, was confiscation carried out in the shadow of feudalism.

Jefferson's attempt to prop up the state finances by the seizure and sale of Tory estates failed dismally. The return to the treasury in depreciated currency scarcely paid the state for its trouble. These measures, unlike his endeavors on behalf of the Virginia pioneers, had no place in his reform program. He did not conceive of the break-up and sale of Tory estates—far less extensive in Virginia than in several other states—as a means of distributing property among the common people. It did not have this effect, but neither did it have the effect Jefferson intended.

Crime and Punishment

The reform of criminal codes was a favorite pastime of the Enlightenment. All over Europe projects were afoot. Philosophers competed for prizes offered for humane solutions to problems of crime and punishment. Monarchs planned new and liberalized penal codes for their countries. Reformers gave a helping hand to criminals wasting away in jails and dungeons. Some of these stirrings reached Jefferson by way of books. He read the Marquis Beccaria's seminal work, *An Essay on Crimes and Punishments*, in the original Italian, copying long passages into his commonplace book. Similarly, *The Principles of Penal Law* by William Eden, a pioneer English reformer and collaborator with the great humanitarian John Howard. Montesquieu, Helvetius, Kames, even Blackstone put ideas of penal reform in Jefferson's head.

In this sphere there was no distinctly colonial body of law. Virginians were hanged, whipped, and pilloried; they were branded, dismembered, and cropped; but rarely were the crimes or the punishments set forth in any Virginia law. The English law, common and statute, was simply taken for granted. Only where local conditions required modifications, as in the case of slavery, did the provincial government concern itself. As an attorney practicing before the General Court, Jefferson had many opportunities to observe the vagaries and the brutalities of criminal justice in Virginia. Only in the privacy of his study, however, did he seem to entertain ideas of reform.

When the committee of revisers first met, the criminal law falling to Jefferson's portion, he got agreement on certain leading principles. The most important of these was that capital punishment should be abolished for all crimes except treason and willful murder. He had incorporated this principle in his proposed constitution. Proceeding from it now, he took up the several score of crimes which, as felonies, carried the death penalty, and to each of them assigned the punishment suited to reason. The lifting of the death penalty thus called forth a total reconstruction of criminal law. If Jefferson did not quite accomplish this, he made an important contribution of his own in one of the cornerstones of the revisal: A Bill for Proportioning Crimes and Punishments in Cases Heretofore Capital.

No other mere draft of legislation reveals so much of the mind and style of its author. It was definitely humanitarian in principle and design. Had it been enacted into law, Virginia would have taken the longest stride forward of any of the states and set an example to the whole of Christendom. Yet the bill contained shocking lapses from humane and liberal standards, which can only be attributed to the force of traditionalism in Jefferson's thinking. The subject was agreeable to his scholarly impulses. He avidly researched the books in his library, reviewed the passages earlier copied into his commonplace book, and wrote long notes as he went along. He lavished meticulous care on the drafting of the bill. "In style I have aimed at accuracy, brevity and simplicity . . . ," he explained to Wythe. "Indeed I wished to exhibit a sample of reformation in the barbarous style into which modern statutes have degenerated from their ancient simplicity." In the copious margins of the text, Jefferson bared the massive erudition of the bill: extracts from ancient laws (in An-glo-Saxon, Latin, Old French, and English), citations of learned sources, references to Beccaria and other philosophers, and little notes and queries suggested by his own reflection. This was all very artfully done, with more than a trace of pedantry, but glorious withal. Here the philosopher declared his precedence to the states-man! An exquisitely penned copy of the bill for his own keeping suggests his pride in it simply as a work of legislative draftsmanship.

The bill expressed Jefferson's passion for order and system in a curiously perverse way. In the stately preamble, he said it was the duty of lawmakers "to arrange in a proper scale the crimes which it may be necessary to repress, and to adjust thereto a corresponding gradation of punishments." This was the rational approach, but Jef-ferson did not follow it. Instead, he set up three basic classes, or grades, of punishment—life, limb, and labor—and then fit the crimes into this oversimplified system. One crime was related to another not so much by its nature as by its penalty. From the standpoint of legal science, Jefferson's classification was useless, perhaps even a re-trograde step. More promising was his enunciation of three cardinal principles derived from Beccaria and other votaries of reason. First, since punishment is an evil in itself, it is justified only so far as it produces greater happiness through the reformation of the criminal and the future prevention of the crime. From this it followed, among other things, that capital punishment should be "the last mel-ancholy resource" of society. Second, punishments more severe than necessary to prevent crimes defeat their object by, in Jefferson's words, "engaging the benevolence of mankind to withhold prosecu-tions, to smother testimony, or to listen to it with bias. . . ." Third, crimes are more effectively prevented by the certainty than by the severity of punishment; therefore, certain penalties should be clearly associated with certain crimes and justice should be swift and sure, protected from judicial caprice and special dispensation of any kind. As Jefferson remarked to Pendleton, "Let mercy be the character of the law-giver, but let the judge be a mere machine." The whole tendency of the philosophy ran to the moderation of punishments. And this was the dominant tendency of Jefferson's bill. However, there were alarming chinks in its humanity.

In that category of "crimes whose punishment goes to *Limb*," Jefferson embraced rape, polygamy, sodomy, maiming, and disfiguring. All but polygamy were felonies (it was finally omitted) and there was local legislation covering two forms of mayhem endemic to Virginia: the gouging out of eyes and the biting off of ears. Travelers were shocked by these barbarous customs. "I have seen a fellow, reckoned a great adept in gouging," one outlander observed, "who constantly kept the nails of both his thumbs and second fingers very long and pointed; nay, to prevent their breaking or splitting . . . he hardened them every evening in a candle." These were hideous crimes. To them Jefferson applied the hideous punishment of the law of retaliation. No sooner had he done so than he was repelled by it. Presenting the bill for Wythe's inspection, he wrote, "The lex talionis, although a restitution of the Common law, to the simplicity of which we have generally found it so advantageous to return, will be revolting to the humanized feelings of modern times. An eye for an eye, and a hand for a hand will exhibit spectacles in execution whose moral effect would be questionable. . . . This needs reconsideration." It certainly did, and on the very principles declared in the preamble; but the *lex talionis* was allowed to stand in the bill as recommended by the revisers in 1779. Forty years later Jefferson was puzzled to account for the sanction given to this "revolting principle." The letter to Wythe indicates that he believed the principle had been adopted by the committee and that he "strictly observed" the decision "without being entirely satisfied with it." The committee did, in fact, give limited sanction to the principle, but Jefferson himself set up the category of "crimes whose punishment goes to *Limb*" and embraced mayhem, the most common of these crimes, within it. The old Saxon law, which exhibited the *lex talionis*, was a kind of political fetish with Jefferson. Always before it had been employed for liberal ends; here the effect was reactionary, as if he had been bewitched, though that was certainly not the case. He was fully convinced of the inhumanity and the inutility of maiming and stigmatizing offenders of certain crimes. Yet he proposed the very thing that revolted him and the sentiments of mankind. Other explanations failing, it seems probable that he was trapped by a misplaced desire for simplicity, such as he found in his threefold classification, and by the deceptive symmetry of "an eye for an eye and a tooth for a tooth."

Some other provisions of the bill embodied the same error. For example, "Whosoever committeth murder by poisoning shall suffer death by poison." But it was in this category of "crimes whose punishment extends to *Life*" that Jefferson made his principal contribution: the limitation of the death penalty to crimes of treason and murder. Manslaughter became a capital offense on the second conviction. Counterfeiting was punishable by labor and forfeiture of goods. But circumstances altered principles. Counterfeiting was a grave problem during the war, sapping the strength with the credit of the state, thus partaking, as it had of old, of the crime of treason; and in 1779 the assembly passed a bill drafted by Jefferson making it a capital offense. The bill on crimes and punishments lifted the penalty of forfeiture from the victims of suicide. Like Beccaria, Jefferson believed suicide not properly punishable. "As to the example, we need not fear its influence," he noted. "Men are too much attached to life to exhibit frequent instances of depriving themselves of it. At any rate, the quasi-punishment of confiscation will not prevent it." One of the fascinating curiosities of English law was the statute enacted in the reign of James I by which the mother's concealment of the death of a bastard child was made murder. In 1702 one Ann Tandy was convicted and executed in Virginia for the crime; and some years later the Burgesses took the unusual step of re-enacting the English statute, thus providing the only reference to the crime of murder in the colonial statutes. The law inferred guilt from the act of concealment, for the mother would choose to murder the child rather than to disgrace herself. Jefferson found the reasoning untenable. "If shame be a powerful affection of the mind, is not parental love also? Is it not the strongest affection known? Is it not greater than even that of self preservation?" Regardless of the moral arguments against the law, Jefferson thought there could never be justification for substituting presumption of guilt for the proof of it. In a note on breach of prison, a capital offense at common law, Jefferson gave full effect to the rule of the liberal penologists against laws at war with the sentiments of the heart. "It is not only vain, but wicked, in a legislator to frame laws in opposition to the laws of nature, and to arm men with the terrors of death. This is truly creating crimes in order to punish them," he declared. "The law of nature impels every one to escape from confinement; it should not therefore be subjected to punishment." Jefferson's bill released prison-breakers from penalty—a logical extension of the doctrine of natural rights. The bill abolished one of the least defensible features of English justice, the benefit of clergy. Under this privilege, which had originated as a protection of clerics in the civil-ecclesiastical conflicts of the Middle Ages, persons who could read Scripture were excused from punishment on first conviction of most felonies. Although criminal statutes steadily encroached on the privilege, it was recognized in Virginia until 1796.

Contracting the scope of capital punishment and such brute penalties as whipping, pillorying, and ducking, Jefferson had to devise some alternative method of punishment which, on the principles of the bill, ought to look to the reform of the criminal. Fines, forefeitures, and reparations might be relied upon to an extent, but they were insufficient. Imprisonment was not then a normal punishment for crimes. Prisons were rude jails, primarily places of custody for persons awaiting trial, execution, or discharge. The modern prison, or penitentiary, system developed logically from the philosophy of the eighteenth-century penal reformers. Already there were anticipations of the new system in Europe, but Jefferson learned nothing of these until later. He proposed instead a system of employing criminals at hard labor in the public works—mines, galleys, ship-yards, foundries, roads, and so on. Thus the third and largest of his three categories: "crimes punishable by *Labor*."

Manslaughter, arson, burglary, horse stealing, larceny, and such crimes were to be punished by hard labor. Jefferson intended to carry the system into effect by a companion bill. The malefactors would "have their heads and beards constantly shaven, and be clothed in habits of coarse materials, uniform in color and make, and distinguished from all others used by the good citizens of this commonwealth . . . so they may be marked out to public note as well while at their ordinary occupations, as when attempting to escape from the public custody." Where he found the germ of this system is uncertain. It may have stemmed from his own reflections. He suggested one possible literary source, however, in Sir Thomas

More's *Utopia*. Of the punishment of thieves in the land of nowhere, More wrote, "And they themselves be condemned to be common labourers: and, unless the theft be very henious, they be neither locked in prison, nor fettered in gyves, but be untied to go at large, labouring in the common work. . . . All and every one of them be apparelled in one colour. Their heads be not polled or shaven, but rounded a little above the ears." Closer at hand than this sixteenth-century work, the Pennsylvania constitution of 1776 authorized imprisonment at hard labor for punishment of crimes not capital; but this was not the same proposal as Jefferson's. In fact, there is more reason to believe that the direction of influence ran the other way: that his bill influenced Pennsylvania's adoption in 1786 of the system of "hard labor, publicly and disgracefully imposed." It failed after a brief trial, as Jefferson was to learn. "Exhibited as a public spectacle, with shaved heads and mean clothing, working on the high roads, produced in the criminals such a prostration of character, such an abandonment of self-respect, as, instead of reforming, plunged them into the most desperate and hardened depravity of morals and character." Regarding the experiment as conclusive, he turned, with the Pennsylvania reformers, to the penitentiary system on the principle of solitary confinement. While in Europe he learned of the success of this experiment in England and obtained from an architect in Lyons the plan of a prison adapted to solitary confinement. This plan, sent to Virginia, left its mark on the state penitentiary erected at Richmond a decade later. The peculiar horrors of the solitary system soon led to its replacement, but that is another story in no way involved in Jefferson's life.

When Madison, in 1785–86, systematically introduced each of the bills included in the *Report* of the revisers with a view to approximating the original aim of a revised code, the Bill on Crimes and Punishments proved a major stumbling-block. Twice introduced, debated at length, it was finally defeated in the House by a single vote in December 1786. Madison thought, so he reported to Jefferson, that most of the objections to the bill had been argued away. He did not explain these objections except to say, "The rage against horse stealers had a great influence on the fate of the Bill." Horse stealing had been a capital offense since the middle of the century; dozens of culprits had been hanged for it. Jefferson's bill would punish the crime with three years labor and reparations to the injured party. If a "rage against horse stealers" hurt the bill's chances, it is altogether probable that the mild punishments it proportioned to other crimes caused feelings of uneasiness among the legislators. There is no evidence that the *lex talionis* contributed to the bill's defeat. Virginians seemed to prefer "our old bloody code," as Madison put it. A decade later some of the good features of Jefferson's bill were finally enacted into law.

One provision of Jefferson's bill is significant because of its bearing on a notorious episode in the Revolutionary annals of Virginia. "No attainder shall work corruption of blood in any case," Jefferson wrote. While thus thinking to do away with one of the most revolting features of bills of attainder, Jefferson also assumed that such bills might be proper. Only a few months before, in May 1778, he had drafted the statute attainting Josiah Philips and his accomplices of high treason. Philips was a rank Tory who retired into the Dismal Swamp after Dunmore's exit and at the head of an insurgent band repeatedly sallied forth to pillage and terrorize the countryside. Captured once, he escaped and eluded all efforts of the government to take him dead or alive. The Governor, Patrick Henry, referred the problem to Jefferson. It was discussed in the House. A resolution to attaint Philips passed, and Jefferson drew the bill enacted on May 30, apparently without a whisper of dissent. The act accused Philips (and others unnamed) of levying war against the commonwealth and gave him one month to appear and submit himself to proper trial, at the expiration of which, if he remained at large, he would stand convicted of treason and become the lawful prey of any man. The attainder never actually took effect. Philips and three confederates were brought in within the month, tried on the charge of robbery, convicted, and hanged. They were quickly forgotten, but the act of attainder was not. It was later recalled to the republican mind of Virginia as a shocking example of legislative tyranny, violating the rights of individuals and usurping the powers of the judiciary. Jefferson, who felt the censure, defended the attainder of Philips. A special and limited act of attainder is always a legitimate instrument, he said in 1815, in the case of a person charged with heinous crime and who cannot by any other means be brought to justice. "No doubt that these acts of attainder have been abused in England as instruments of vengeance by a successful over a defeated party. But what institution is insusceptible to abuse in wicked hands?"

But this begged the question. His proposed revision of the Virginia constitution in 1783 prohibited bills of attainder; the United States Constitution barred them; and the execrable institution had few defenders anywhere. Did Jefferson really believe in 1815 that the question was one of its abuse? Probably not. Two considerations may help to make his role in the Philips case understandable. First, the original state constitutions, including Virginia's, imposed no bar to bills of attainder, and several of the Revolutionary governments used them. Pennsylvania attainted 490 persons of high treason in a single act; New York similarly attainted 59 persons. While such examples take none of the sting from Virginia's single act of attainder, they help to put it in perspective, and also to put Jefferson, who drew it, in the currents of passion and error with his Revolutionary comrades. Second, Jefferson always found the greatest difficulty in admitting a mistake either to himself or to others, even at the cost of deepening the guilt of the original error. After his renunciation in 1783, the defense of his actions in the Philips case offers the only evidence of continuing endorsement of the practice. Conscious of his own rectitude, he resented the imputation of trampling on the rights of liberty by the attainder of a traitorous scoundrel during the war. His pride was involved, and rather than admit the error as a Revolutionary aberration, he was led into a course of reasoning blatantly at odds with his own principles.

The Revolution was accomplished in Virginia without a single execution for treason, tending to bear out Jefferson's opinion that, despite occasional violence and unavoidable miscarriages, the record over-all was one of forbearance, moderation, and substantial justice. In the face of enemies within and without, the infant state had the problem of identifying those in allegiance. The test oath—a kind of naturalization oath—became the instrument of citizenship. Non-jurors (those who did not take the oath) were restrained, laws were enacted against Loyalists, and others to punish treason and lesser crimes stabbing at the state's existence. Jefferson subscribed to all these measures—the pains and penalties of revolution. With respect to treason, he may have influenced the statute enacted in 1776. The statute marked a great advance over the English law by narrowing the scope of the crime, defining the evidence required for conviction, and doing away with the hideous aftermath of hanging. In the Bill on Crimes and Punishments, he had only to embody the essential provisions of the treason statute of 1776.

Religion

The Church of England was established in the infancy of the Old Dominion and reigned virtually free of challenge for more than a century. Buttressed and safeguarded by many laws both local and English, aided by a long tradition, the Anglican Church functioned as an arm of the government. Its clergy, creed, and worship held a privileged status, while all others were subject to varying degrees of restraint, and it exacted support from believers and non-believers alike. The principles of the Revolution rendered this state of affairs intolerable. Jefferson at once set himself the task of tearing up the establishment by its roots. His draft constitution contained this sweeping clause: "All persons shall have full and free liberty of religious opinion, nor shall any be compelled to frequent or maintain any religious institution." This was too big a step for the Virginia convention. The constitution of 1776 pleaded mute. The Declaration of Rights, however, stated the true principle: "all men are equally entitled to the free exercise of religion according to the dictates of conscience." If the realization of this right became an object of legislation, the establishment was doomed.

The dissenting sects and others, secular liberals like Jefferson, who opposed the "spiritual tyranny" of the Anglican Church were alert to the opportunity. The first legislative assembly was crowded with petitions calling for disestablishment. "These brought on the severest contest in which I have ever been engaged," Jefferson reflected many years later. Soon after taking his seat, he was appointed to a nineteen-member committee on religion charged with the responsibility of reporting on these numerous petitions. The conflict must have been intense, resulting in stalemate, for after a month's deliberation the committee was discharged and the matter thrown into the House. On November 19 the House agreed to a set of six resolutions, all but one of which supported the liberal position as formulated in resolutions Jefferson had drafted. A new committee was now appointed, Jefferson again a member, to bring in a bill founded on the resolutions. Before this could be accomplished, the House drew back and instructed the committee to report a moderate bill. The upshot of these maneuvers was the act of December 1776 repealing oppressive acts of Parliament and exempting dissenters from taxes to support the Church. While this was an advance, it did not disestablish the Church or secure full freedom of religious conscience. Virginians might still be punished for heretical opinions, either under common law or Virginia statutes. Parish levies on members of the Church were suspended but not abolished. Finally, the act expressly reserved decision on the question, "Whether a general assessment should not be established by law, on every one, to the support of the pastor of his choice, or whether all should be left to voluntary contributions." This was a new issue going beyond the fate of the Established Church. It rapidly became the crucial issue in the long campaign for religious freedom. The climax came a decade later, when Jefferson was in France, with the enactment of his remarkable Bill for Establishing Religious Freedom.

When late in life Jefferson penned his epitaph, he named the Virginia Statute for Religious Freedom one of the three achievements for which he wished to be remembered. More than a statute, it was an eloquent manifesto of the sanctity of the human mind and spirit. It gave mature expression to convictions that, though they might have been reached wholly along the untroubled path of reason, were, in fact, tempered and formed in the crucible of religious controversy in Virginia. In denouncing the establishment and in advocating the fullest freedom in religious concerns, Jefferson drew on his experience as well as his philosophy.

Theological differences played a part in Jefferson's early alienation from the Virginia Church; but the Church was notably indifferent to theology in any case, so it could not have contributed materially to his growing disaffection. He came to oppose the union of Church and State in any form or dogma; and as the abuses of the Anglican connection more and more pressed upon him, he targeted it for dissolution in the holy cause of the Revolution. A pernicious colonial survival, the establishment in his eyes served neither religion nor liberty. The clergy, weak, indolent, and ineffectual, shared the worst vices of the community. "It is a melancholy fact," recalled a leading churchman of the next generation, "that many of them had been addicted to the race-field, the card-table, the ball room, the theatre—nay, more, to the drunken revel." The Church had failed in its moral and spiritual mission. Largely for that reason, and despite its privileged status, as Jefferson observed, a majority of Virginians were dissenters on the eve of the Revolution. The offices of some of the parishes had actually been taken over by dissenters. Such anomalies made a mockery of the establishment. Possessing little intrinsic strength, the Church depended all the more on the support of civil authority, which was extrinsic in its nature. First, on the faintly aristocratic governing bodies of the parishes, the vestries, which levied tithes, looked after church property, cared for the poor, and so on. Second, on protective statutes such as required religious services according to the articles of the Church of England, restricted marriage to its forms, and punished heresy. Finally, and ultimately, on the ecclesiastical authority of the Crown. Independence abolished the latter. Practically, it had never been important. The establishment had always been essentially colonial rather than imperial, and not even Jefferson made it one of the grounds of revolt against Britain. Yet political independence was a calamity for the Church. At least one-third of the Anglican ministers affirmed their loyalty to Britain, while still others silently opposed the patriots. In New England, on the other hand, the Congregational clergy enlisted in the cause of liberty. What subtracted from the Church's strength added to the power and prestige of the strangely allied forces marshaled under the banner of religious freedom.

The Baptists, numbering in excess of five thousand, formed the spearhead of sectarian opposition. Whether in spite of persecution or because of it, they had grown remarkably during the previous decade. Writing to a friend in Pennsylvania in 1774, the young Madison bemoaned "the state and liberty of my country," citing the imprisonment of five or six Baptist preachers in neighboring Culpeper. "That diabolical Hell conceived principle of persecution rages among some and to their eternal infamy the Clergy can furnish their quota of imps for such business." These preachers were of a particularly enthusiastic Baptist sect, the Separates. Their revivalistic style of preaching, their coarse and provocative manners, their itinerant ministry, their appeal to the poor and ignorant combined to make them obnoxious not only to easygoing Virginians of the Anglican faith but to the less zealous, better-educated Presbyterians and old-style Baptists as well. "They cannot meet a man upon the road but they must ram a text of Scripture down his throat," said a prosecutor of these evangelists. The invariable charge against them was "disturbance of the peace."' Under the English Act of Toleration, which legally extended to Virginia, dissenting Protestants were permitted to hold religious services provided their ministers and places of worship were registered. Most dissenters were content to work within the generous limits of the Act of Toleration. But the Separate Baptists, not finding them convenient, willfully violated the regulations society thought necessary for its peace and order, thereby furnishing the civil magistrates, prodded by the Anglican clergy, the handle of their persecution. In 1772 they began petitioning the House of Burgesses for religious freedom.

Jefferson became an outright champion of this cause in 1776. Prior to independence he had followed with concern the developments in the religious life of Virginia and unquestionably given a good deal of thought and study to the relationship between civil and ecclesiastical authority. His little essay on the fraudulent incorporation of Christianity into the common law has been noted. "We might as well say that the Newtonian system of philosophy is a part of the common law, as that the Christian religion is," he declared. As usual with him, history proved a convenient handmaid of his convictions. When he came to advocate the cause in the assembly he drew upon formidable legal and historical knowledge. Among his papers are several of the "scraps" he worked from: a list of the acts of Parliament and of the Virginia assembly concerning religion, a series of notes and observations on these acts, notes on episcopacy, on heresy, and so on. These notes, together with an abstract of Locke's views, formed the basis of a speech, probably delivered in November 1776, which compressed his whole philosophy of the subject.

Jefferson did not often rise to address the House, nor was he an eloquent speaker; but when the principle was as important as this one, he wished to expose it thoroughly to view, and the known strength of his ideas assured him a careful hearing. He first discussed the injuries of the establishment, with a detailed accounting of the statutory oppressions inseparable from it. Heresy might be punished by death; denial of the Trinity was punishable, on the third offense, by three years' imprisonment; Unitarians and freethinkers might be declared unfit parents and have their children taken from them; Roman Catholics were excluded from the mantle of toleration and burdened with legal disabilities; periodic church attendance was compulsory; profanity carried a fine of ten pounds for each offense; and so on. Yet, Jefferson observed, "most men imagine that persecution is unknown to our laws." He conceded that the statutes were dead letters for the most part. There were a few Virginians—Catholics, Unitarians, heretics—on whom the penalties might fall. "Happily, the spirit of the times is in favor of the rights of conscience." But when was this ever a sufficient reliance? "Everyone should know under what law he lives, and should not be obliged to recur to the spirit of the times for protection." Now, while the spirit was sound and union against the common enemy a necessity, now was the time to fix every right on firm foundations. Over one-half the inhabitants were dissenters from the Church they were nevertheless taxed to support, and despite the voluntary support many gave to the ministries of their choice. This, too, was a form of persecution. What kind of attachment might these people feel toward a government that so flagrantly, and in the face of declared principle, discriminated against them? Political realism as well as abstract right demanded that all religions be placed on a footing of freedom and equality.

Jefferson then posed this fundamental question: "Has the state a right to adopt an opinion in matters of religion?" His answer was an unequivocal no. The conclusion followed logically from the contract theory of government. Men unite in government to secure those rights they cannot secure themselves. The rights of conscience are not submitted to civil authority, first, because men are answerable for them solely to God, and second, because their exercise does no injury to others. Jefferson later gave memorable statement to the principle in the *Notes on Virginia:* "The legitimate powers of government extend to such acts only as are injurious to others. But it does me no injury for my neighbor to say there are twenty gods or no god. It neither picks my pocket, nor breaks my leg." In all this and more he simply followed Locke, particularly the first *Letter Concerning Toleration*. But as Jefferson observed in his "Notes on Locke," the great Whig failed to push his principles to conclusion, declining to extend freedom to Catholics, athiests, and some others. "It was a great thing to go so far . . . but where he stopped short, we may go on." Significantly, Jefferson, with Madison and others of the liberal persuasion, dropped the term *toleration*, which implied an official and preferred religion, in favor of the term *liberty*. The religious liberty advocated in 1776 involved both freedom *from* the privileges and oppressions of a state church and freedom *to* worship according to the dictates of conscience without legal hindrance or discrimination of any kind.

Irrespective of the question of right, as Jefferson went on to show, the intervention of government in the affairs of religion was neither necessary nor advantageous to either one. Some men feared the consequences of government showing religion to the door, turning it out like a pauper to struggle in the world of ideas, both sacred and profane, for a place in the minds of men. Such men hungered for Truth infallible and absolute. But it would forever elude them, Jefferson warned. "Millions of innocent men, women and children, since the introduction of Christianity, have been burnt, tortured, fined, and imprisoned; yet we have not advanced one inch towards uniformity. What has been the effect of coercion? To make one half the world fools, and the other half hypocrites." The history of progress in religion as in philosophy was the history of the march of free inquiry and private judgment against the coercion and error of public authority. "It is error alone which needs the support or government," Jefferson declared. "Truth can stand by itself." Religious differences were beneficial to the peace and order of society: "The several sects perform the office of a *censor morum* over each other." They were equally beneficial to religion, setting up a virtuous competition among the sects and forcing them to develop their own resources rather than to depend on external support.

As already recorded, the first contest in the assembly ended in a halfway measure. Dissenters of every description declined to stop there. During the next several years they kept the initiative and, propelled increasingly by the force of an idea, pressed the assembly to finish the work. The next victory came in 1779: repeal of the laws requiring members of the Anglican Church to contribute to its support. This pushed the establishment into irretrievable ruin, though vestiges of its exclusive status remained for a time. An act of the assembly in 1780 legalized marriages performed by non-Anglican clergy, and it was later liberalized in 1784 to overcome Baptist objections. The vestries continued for some years yet to discharge civil functions, such as the care of the poor. Not until 1802 were the parishes deprived of glebe lands for the support of the clergy.

These were details. Much more important was the new ground of contest: government support of Christianity as the established religion of the Commonwealth. Religious freedom being extended to all citizens, all sects and persuasions being put on an equal footing, churchmen and some other religionists, with strong political backing, called for a general assessment of all citizens for the support of all Christian ministers. The act of 1776 had specifically reserved this question for later decision. And in 1779, after the doom of the old establishment, its friends introduced the first general assessment bill. They sought thereby to prop up the decaying edifice of the Anglican Church, but the scheme committed them to a principle of far greater import. Historically, in America and throughout the Christian world, "the establishment of religion" meant official sanction and support of a single state church. In the course of religious controversy in Virginia, however, the concept acquired a new meaning: state encouragement and support of Christianity without preference as to sect.

The position staked out by liberals and dissenters in the early stages of the controversy was sufficient to meet the new challenge. Of course, their arguments had been directed against the existing establishment, and none of Jefferson's statements on record emphatically barred simple tax support of different faiths without discrimination. Yet this was the whole tone and tenor of his doctrine. If required to be more explicit about it, he certainly would be, and without revising anything. He believed with Locke that religion consists in "the *inward* persuasion of the mind," that a church is "a *voluntary* society of men," and that the jurisdiction of civil government cannot extend to either. He was far too sophisticated in his views of government, far too convinced of the tenderness of the private conscience, to believe that religious liberty, so conceived, could be secured under the patronage of the state. He would have been equally opposed to the introduction of government support for all religions —the Jewish, the Mohammedan, the Hindu with the Christian— though such a program would have overcome powerful objections of another kind. "Hands off" was the only acceptable policy. Thus Jefferson's doctrine necessarily involved *the separation of church and state,* even if none of the reformers had yet uttered that doctrine.

Still, men who conceded the injustice of a state church might see nothing unjust or illogical in a general establishment of religion, all supporting the minister or church of their choice. It was partly to close off this fortuitous development that Jefferson drafted his Bill for Religious Freedom. Drawn in 1777 as part of the Revision of the Laws, it was not introduced in the House until two years later. The delay was probably a question of timing. The first protests against the "general assessment" plan reached the Assembly in the spring of 1777, and it was discussed in subsequent sessions, but the time grew ripe for it only after the old establishment was disposed of. Neither Jefferson's bill nor the first version of the plan to establish the Christian religion could command a majority in 1779 or for several years to come. The issue was well understood by the people. The contending principles and measures were identified with the two giants of Virginia politics, Jefferson and Henry. Starting as a champion against the Church, the famous orator came around to the cause of churchmen and conservatives like Pendleton and Nicholas without, in his opinion, the least change of principle. In 1784 the assembly entered upon the climactic stage of the long controversy. It called up a bill, principally sponsored by Henry, to levy "a moderate tax or contribution annually for the support of the Christian religion, or for some Christian church, denomination or communion of Churches, or for some form of Christian worship." The bill, somewhat more liberal than its predecessor, justified government support of religion not on any grounds of ecclesiastical authority but on the recognized power of the state to diffuse knowledge (Christian knowledge in this case), restrain vice, and preserve the peace of society. The idea that the state might thus, in the name of peace and morals, do what it could not do in the name of religion seemed to underscore the need to raise a wall of separation between church and state. The old dissenter coalition of rationalists and sectarians—the Presbyterians alone wavering for a time—blocked passage of the bill in 1784 and, under Madison's vigorous leadership, defeated it in 1785. Seeking to cap the climax, Madison then brought forward Jefferson's Bill for Religious Freedom.

As Jefferson reflected in his autobiography, he had drawn the bill "in all the latitude of reason and right" regardless of principles that might already have been established in law. Like the Declaration of Independence, to which it was a corollary, the great statute had more importance as an eloquent manifesto than as substantive legislation. But while the Declaration might be criticized for want of passion, the Statute for Religious Freedom burned with an ardor that belied mere rationality. Jefferson poured into the preamble—four times the length of the act itself—all his rage against the cant, the falsehood, the hypocrisy, the self-righteousness, the corruption, and the tyranny associated with the history of the alliance between Church and State. He did not stop with the assertion that it is "sinful and tyrannical" to compel a man to support opinions he disbelieves, but argued, no doubt with the assessment plan in mind, "that even the forcing him to support this or that teacher of his own religious persuasion" deprives him of liberty and the ministry of "incitement to earnest and unremitting labours for the instruction of mankind." He condemned religious tests and discriminations. He roundly declared "that the opinions of men are not the object of civil government, nor under its jurisdiction." The assembly struck this clause, but the statute in its entirety made evident how far the general cause of intellectual liberty—freedom of mind—was involved in Jefferson's argument for religious liberty. Of all men's convictions those of a religious nature were the most tender, most subjective, most private, and therefore, Jefferson believed, the least subject to authority or compulsion of any degree.

After several amendments which Madison termed "frivolous," the bill passed into law on January 16, 1786. Apparently no objection was raised to the enacting clause, only to the radical preamble. The legal effect of the statute was to make positive and unambiguous what had heretofore been the result of essentially negative actions, such as repeal laws and the defeat of the general assessment scheme. Never satisfied to leave fundamental rights to the hazard of statute, Jefferson had added an unusual final clause declaring that, though the act could not bind succeeding legislatures, nevertheless "if any act shall be hereafter passed to repeal the present or to narrow its operation, such act will be an infringement of natural right." Succeeding assemblies heeded the admonition. Reporting the conclusion of the campaign in which he shared equal honors with his friend in France, Madison grandly announced that the statute "extinguished forever the ambitious hope of making laws for the human mind."

The fame of the Virginia Statute for Religious Freedom rapidly spread beyond American shores. No other act of legislation so pointedly enforced the reality of the American Revolution on the enlightened heads of Europe. On the scene in Paris, proud of the honor the statute did to his country as well as to himself, Jefferson saw to its propagation. Before the year 1786 ran out, he reported to Madison on the wide acclaim. "I do not mean by the governments, but by the individuals which compose them. It has been translated into French and Italian, has been sent to most of the courts of Europe. . . . It is inserted in the new Encyclopédie, and is appearing in most of the publications respecting America. In fact it is comfortable," Jefferson continued, "to see the standard of reason at length erected, after so many ages during which the human mind has been held in vassalage by kings, priests and nobles; and it is honorable for us to have produced the first legislature who has had the courage to declare that the reason of man may be trusted with the formation of his own opinions."

The statute was the great testimony to Jefferson's conviction that "reason is the only oracle" of man. The question naturally arises of how far Jefferson's perfervid rationalism was hostile to the religion he professed to free. The statute repudiated the assumption common to most religions that there is an absolute standard of right and truth not to be known by reason alone. It denied to any religion the aid of civil authority to extend its sway. Was this position, expressing attitudes of skepticism, rationalism, and secularism, compatible with the ends of the statute: the full measure of religious profession and the strict neutrality of the state? Was Jefferson not arraying the state on the side of a new religion of enlightenment? These are questions for the logician, and he is not apt to be satisfied with Jefferson's logic. Theological presuppositions lurk in all great measures of legislation. Yet to find fault with the statute on this ground is but a sophistical way of quarreling with its principles and purposes.

Churchmen then and for generations after openly quarreled with them, charging that Jefferson was motivated by hostility to the Episcopal Church and, indeed, to all Christian profession or religious life of any kind. Nothing could be more mistaken. As a philosopher has said, "The power and eloquence of Jefferson's writings on religious freedom is due largely to his evident religious devotion." Unlike the anti-clericalism of the Old World, his hatred of establishments and priesthoods did not involve him in hatred of religion. He wished for himself, for all his countrymen, not freedom from religion but freedom to pursue religion wherever reason and conscience led, and the more sensitive and upright the pursuit the more respect it won from him. He attempted to say as much but, of course, the onus of his public work and utterance was on the side of tearing down, so he must appear to many as a mere destroyer of religion. His own deepest convictions he kept to himself, nor did the public know of the generous support he gave to various churches throughout his life. In 1777, for example, he subscribed six pounds to the annual support of the Reverend Charles Clay, St. Anne's Parish, Charlottesville. Jefferson may have had no personal call for the Reverend Mr. Clay's services but his neighbors did. His contribution—nearly twice the amount subscribed by any other parishioner—proved Jefferson's readiness to accept the consequences of his own principle: the voluntary support of churches and ministers.

In the liberality of his mind, as in his entire personality and background, Jefferson obviously had more in common with the mild and genial Episcopalians than with the evangelical Baptists and "New Light" Presbyterians who furnished the battalions for the campaign generaled by Madison and himself. It was a strange alliance: rationalists and enthusiasts, secularists and sectarians, skeptics and believers united by their common opposition to the established order. They were able to co-operate, in part, because they were so far apart, appeals to reason giving no practical trouble to sectaries who relied on the converting presence of the Holy Spirit. Thus by the unique logic of American history the seekers after God and the seekers after enlightenment were allies in liberty. Some of Jefferson's friends, like his boyhood chum John Page, were stunned by his stubborn support of the "bigoted and illiberal" folk after they had stolen the flocks and disrobed the shepherds of the "rational sect." "Nothing but a general assessment can prevent the State from being divided between immorality and enthusiastic bigotry," Page told Jefferson. The warning carried a partial truth, as Jefferson would discover in the course of time. Whatever the long-run effect of the newer sects on Virginia piety and morality, they were to do irreparable injury to the state's reputation for liberality and enlightenment. Yet even had Jefferson calculated this loss, it could have had no weight with him. "Reason and free inquiry are the only effectual agents against error." What he shared with Baptist ranters was more fundamental than his intellectual distaste for them. He looked to schools, not to churches, to improve the mass of people. Moreover, while Page with so many others thought the old church would go steadily downhill without public support, Jefferson's belief in the salubrity of freedom promised a better future for the Episcopalians. Viewing the progress several decades later, Bishop William Meade observed that "nothing could have been more injurious to the cause of true religion in the Episcopal Church, or to its growth in any way, than the continuance of either stipend or glebes." The revival of the Church commenced, Meade thought, when she was "thrown upon her own resources."

Jefferson's motives on the side of religion were entirely creditable, yet it would be quite erroneous to imply that he was motivated primarily by concern for religion. Religious freedom absorbed him most earnestly where it intersected intellectual freedom. The martyrs of science and philosophy, rather than the martyrs of religion, won his highest admiration. Both sectarian religionists and secular liberals sought separation of church and state; but the former feared most the power of the state to corrupt and tyrannize the church, while the latter feared, above all, the inquisitorial tendencies of the church. Religion and philosophy in all their amplitude do not comprehend the earnestness of Jefferson's purpose, however. A republican statesman who had made "the pursuit of happiness" his creed, he believed that the "voluntary system" would tend to produce loyalty in the state, moderation in the government, and peace and harmony

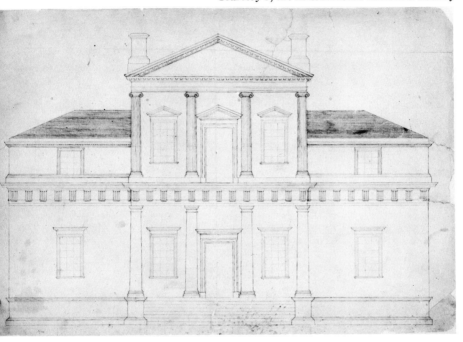

Monticello, the first version. Accepted elevation, 1771.

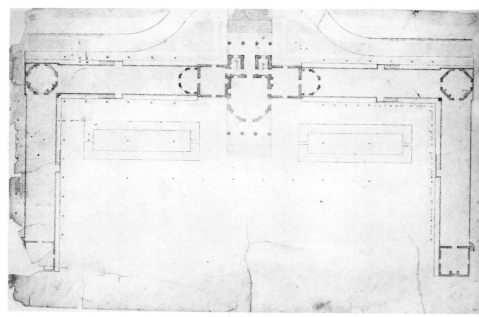

General plan of Monticello. Jefferson's drawing, 1772.

e Declaration of Independence July 4, 1776. Detail from the painting by John Trumbull.

22.23.Car.2. Whosoever on purpose and of malice fore-
c.1.
-thought shall maim another, or shall disfi-
-gure him by cutting out or disabling the tongue,
slitting or cutting off a nose, lip or ear, brand-
-ing, or otherwise, shall be maimed or disfi-
-gured in like sort: or if that cannot be for
want of the same part, then as nearly as
may be in some other part of at least equal
value and estimation in the opinion of a
jury, and moreover shall forfeit one half
of his lands and goods to the sufferer.

si soit le jugement tiel que il perde autiel membre come il avera tollet al pleintiffe. et si la pleynte
soit faite de femme que avera tollet a home ses membres, en tiel cas perdra la femme la une meyn
par jugement, come le membre dount ele avera trespasse.' Britton. c.25. Fleta. B.1.c.40 Ll.Aelfr.19.40.

* maiming was felony at the com: law. Britton. c.25
'mahemium autem dici potent, ubi aliquis in aliquâ
parte suî corporis loesionem acceperit, porquam ef-
factus sit inutilis ad pugnandam: ut si manus am-
-putetur, vel pes, oculus privetur, vel scerda de
osse capitis levetur, vel si quis dentes proecisores
amiserit, vel castratus fuerit, et talis pro maha-
-miato poterit adjudicari.' Fleta. L.1.c.40. 'et volons
que nul mahéme ne soit tenus forsque de membre
tollet dount home est plus feble à combatre, en
sicome del oyl, ou de la mayn,
ou del pée, ou de la tête debruse, ou de les dentz
devant.' Britton. c.25. for further definitions see Bracton.
L.3.c.24.§.3.4. Fonch. L.B.3.c.12. Co.L.126.a.b.288.a.
3.Bl.121.&.Bl.205. Stamf.P.C.L.1.c.41. I do not find
any of these definitions confine the offence to wilful &
malicious definitions of it. 22.23.Car.2.c.1. called the
Coventry act has the words 'on purpose and of
malice forethought'. nor does the Com: law prescribe
the same punishment for disfiguring as for maiming.
* the punishment was by retaliation. 'et come ascun
appele serra de tele felonie atteint et attende jugement.

25.E.3.st.5.c.2. Whosoever shall counterfeit any coin
current by law within this Commonwealth, or
any paper bills issued in the nature of money,
or of certificates of loan on the credit of this
Commonwealth, or of all or any of the United
States of America, or any Inspectors notes for
tobacco, or shall pass any such counterfeited
coin, paper, bills, or notes, knowing them to be
5.El.c.11. counterfeit; or, for the sake of lucre, shall diminish
18.El.c.1.
2.9.W.3.c.26 case, or wash any such coin, shall be condemned to
15.16.G.2.c.28.
7.Ann.c.25. hard labor six years in the public works, & shall forfeit
all his lands and goods to the Commonwealth.

* by the laws of Aethelstan and Canute this was punished
by cutting off the hand. ȝif ƿe mynetere ful pulpe,
rlea man þa hano of. ðe he þ ful mio pohtre. I rezz
upon ða mynez ʒmiþþan: in English characters and
words ' if the minter foul [criminal] went, slay the
hand off, that he the foul [crime] with wrought, and set
upon the mint - smithery.' Ll. Aethelst. 14.' I reðe
open ðir faire pynce. ðolize ðʒna hanoa ðe he
þ faire mio pohtre. ' et si quis praeter hanc, fal-
-sam fecerit, perdat manum quacum falsam con-
-fecit'. Ll. Cnuti. 8. it had been death by the Ll. Aethelredi
sub fine. by those of H.1. 'si quis cum falso denario inven-
-tus fuerit — fiat justitia mea, saltem de dextro pugno
et de testiculis. Anno 1108. operae pretium vero est au-
-dire quam severus rex puniit in pravos. Monetarios
enim fere omnes totius angliae fecit ementulari, et
manus dextras abscindi, quia monetam furtive cor-
-ruperant. Wilkins id. et anno 1125. when the Com: la
became settled it appears to have been punishable by
death. 'est aliud genus criminis quod sub nomine
falsi continetur, et tangit coronam domini regis, et ut
-timum inducit supplicium, sicut de illis qui falsam
fabricant monetam, et qui de re non reproba, faciunt

42055   Note 3 in

A page from Jefferson's draft of the Bill for Proportioning Crimes and Punishments, 17 in the society. The circumstances of war and revolution and nation-building gave an urgency to considerations of this kind. Writing to Jefferson in 1779 the Reverend John Todd, a leader of the famed Hanover Presbytery, stated the shared conviction "that people of different sentiments in religion will be all one in their love and fidelity to the State which secures to them everything dear and valuable: and the more catholic and friendly one to another, and free from *pride* and *envy* when the State rewards all men according to their merit." Two years later Jefferson thought the experiment had proved itself in New York and Pennsylvania, more varied religiously than Virginia. Unparalleled harmony prevailed amidst widest diversity. "They have made the happy discovery, that the way to silence religious disputes, is to take no notice of them." It would not prove quite so simple, but the history of American society justified his optimism.

Education

The backbone of Jefferson's republic was a system of public education. "If a nation expects to be ignorant and free in a state of civilization, it expects what never was and never will be," he once observed. The state of civilization being one of organization and power, of progress and improvement, it demanded commensurate means of enlightenment. Without the diffusion of knowledge through all the ranks of society, adapted to its different degrees and conditions, individuals could neither attend to their own happiness nor, as citizens, secure the freedom and the welfare of the state. It was axiomatic with Jefferson that the people were the only safe depository of their rights and liberties, always provided, however, that they were adequately informed and instructed. Education was too important a matter to be left to chance. It must be planned and carried out as a paramount responsibility of republican government.

Jefferson's "quixotism for the diffusion of knowledge," as he styled it, thus sprang from his political principles. The men of his class, favored by wealth and family, educated at private hands, had brought the country to freedom and self-government amidst colossal ignorance. There were no schools for children of the common people. Too many were raised up in the ignorance in which they were born. Much of Virginia was but a step or two removed from the reckless, brawling frontier, where education was a luxury and communal responsibility unformed, while the settled eastern portion was dominated by an haughty aristocracy notably more conscious of its rights than of its social obligations. Except for slavery, which added to the problem but raised peculiar dangers of its own, the ignorance and torpor of the people presented the main obstacle to the success of the republican experiment.

The Revision of the Laws gave Jefferson his first opportunity to attack the problem. Several acts of the old assembly relating to the College of William and Mary fell to Pendleton's portion, but the revisers agreed that a "systematical plan of general education" should be proposed and turned the entire subject over to Jefferson. He drafted three bills. The most important, A Bill for the More General Diffusion of Knowledge, in 1778, offered the blueprint of a system of education adapted to the condition and the capacity of everyone, as Jefferson thought, and reaching the objects of republican citizenship. The preamble defined two such objects. First, "to illuminate, as far as practicable, the minds of the people at large," which was called the most effectual means of preventing the degeneration of free government into tyranny. Second, to ensure "that those persons, whom nature hath endowed with genius and virtue, should be rendered by liberal education worthy to receive, and able to guard the sacred deposit of the rights and liberties of their fellow citizens, and that they should be called to that charge without regard to wealth, birth or other accidental condition or circumstance." There was nothing contradictory in these objects; but the first involved rudimentary instruction of the mass of citizens, while the second looked to the superior cultivation of the "natural aristocracy" from whom the state might draw its leaders. Citizenship and leadership: education for both ought to be supported at the public expense so far as practicable. To the question of which object was more important, Jefferson answered "that none is more important, none more legitimate, than that of rendering the people the safe, as they are the ultimate, guardians of their own liberty."

His method of reducing a problem to its components, analyzing them, then reassembling the parts into a new system was well displayed in the plan of general education. He projected three distinct grades of education—elementary, middle, and higher—the whole rising like a pyramid from the local communities. The latter, unfortunately, had almost no existence in Virginia. Jefferson proposed to create them. Counties would be laid off into *hundreds*, or *wards*, each of a size and population suitable for the maintenance of an elementary school. "At these schools all the free children, male and female, resident within the respective hundred, shall be entitled to receive tuition gratis, for a term of three years, and as much longer, at their private expense, as their parents, guardians or friends, shall think proper." Of course, the schools would teach reading, writing, and arithemtic. The aims of primary education included moral improvement, the acquisition of skills necessary for the common personal and business transactions of life, and instruction in the rights and duties of citizens. The last of these particularly absorbed his attention in 1778; and he specifically directed instruction in the history and experience of other ages and nations so that young citizens may come to recognize tyranny in embryo and exert themselves to crush it. Instead of drawing their moral lessons from the Bible, the children were to take the histories of Greece, Rome, Europe, and America as their texts. The Bible called for more mature judgment than children possessed, and was precluded in any event in a secular state. History furnished a secular guide to morality and promised to be even more useful as a monitor of the civil polity. "History, by apprizing them [the children] of the past, will enable them to judge of the future . . . it will qualify them as judges of the actions and designs of men; it will enable them to know ambition under every disguise it may assume; and knowing it, to defeat its views." This was expecting a good deal of the judgment of children! Jefferson was no Rousseau. His knowledge of the psychology and the learning processes of children was never very great. The design of an educational system deeply interested him; the theory of teaching it embodied clearly did not. He simply assumed with Locke that young minds were formed by the impressions passed before them, hence the right curriculum could make the right kind of citizens. Children were but incipient adults to him. Combined with the secularism and utilitarianism of his educational plan was a rationalism and a verbalism that were already being challenged by such European thinkers as Rousseau and Pestalozzi.

Above the hundred schools, freely educating all children, were the grammar schools, twenty in all, laid off in districts embracing several counties. These schools were also to be maintained by the state; however, most of the pupils coming from homes "in easy circumstances," they would be charged tuition and board. The exceptions were the "public foundationers," perhaps sixty or seventy of the most promising geniuses who, being also from poor families, would be annually chosen after rigorous examinations in the lower schools and awarded, in effect, state scholarships. One-third of these scholars would be eliminated after the first year's instruction, the remainder after two years, excepting the best scholar of each school, who would be at liberty to continue four more years. "By this means," Jefferson wrote of his ingenious selection system, "twenty of the best geniuses will be raked from the rubbish annually, and be instructed, at the public expense, so far as grammar schools go." And they would go to the teaching of the classical languages, English grammar, geography, and the higher branches of mathematics. At the top of the pyramid stood the College of William and Mary, which Jefferson sought by a companion bill to convert into a state university offering instruction in all the sciences. Every year ten seniors "of the best learning and most hopeful genius and disposition" would be chosen from the grammar schools of the state to be sent to the university, "there to be educated, boarded, and clothed, three years" on the public account.

William and Mary was to become not only a university but the supervisory head of the entire system of education. The College would determine the course of instruction in the lower schools, for example. Jefferson's plan for his alma mater, like the general education bill, was influenced in part by the desire to divorce education from religious guidance. Most of Virginia's private schoolmasters were Anglican clergymen. And, of course, the College was an Anglican institution. Publicly supported from its founding, the College was now of great interest to the commonwealth, for it was the only seminary "in which those who are to be the future guardians of the rights and liberties of their country may be endowed with science and virtue, to watch and preserve the sacred deposit." Jefferson proposed to amend the College's charter in three main respects. First, the self-perpetuating governing body of Anglicans would be replaced by a secular board receiving its appointment annually from the General Assembly. Second, the professorships would be raised from six to eight covering the principal fields of knowledge. Third, the public revenue of the College would be increased and placed on a secure footing.

Nothing came of this bill, but in 1779, when he became Governor, Jefferson was elected a visitor of the College, and he attempted in this capacity to make some limited progress toward his objectives. Restrained by the charter to six professorships, he succeeded in replacing three of them, in Divinity, Oriental Languages, and Greek and Latin, with professorships in Law and Government, Anatomy and Medicine, and Modern Languages. (Jefferson favored instruction in the ancient languages but felt it belonged to the academy or grammar school.) One of the professorships, called the Brafferton after the estate of its English donor, would be transformed from its stated mission, the conversion of the Indians to Christianity, into a kind of anthropological chair for the study of the American Indians. These changes struck very advanced secular and utilitarian notes in keeping with the idea of a university rather than a college. Their actual effect was small, however, and the assembly never got around to revising the charter or acting on other parts of Jefferson's bill. Nothing could erase the College's reputation as a Church institution. "The religious jealousies, therefore, of all the dissenters, took alarm lest this [the bill] might give an ascendancy to the Anglican sect . . . ," Jefferson accurately reported. "Its local eccentricity, too, and the unhealthy outward climate, lessened the general inclination toward it." Finally, the success of his own measure for removing the capital from Williamburg hurt the College by severing its connections with the seat of government. Decades later, when Jefferson revived his dream of a university, he brushed aside the claims of his alma mater and built from the ground up.

Still a third bill, for establishing a state-supported library, completed Jefferson's system. The function he had in mind for the library is obscure, but presumably it was to serve the needs of both public officials and scholars. He was zealous for the collection of historical records and artifacts, for the encouragement of learned inquiry in all areas, and, of course, he could not conceive of education without libraries. Years later, reflecting on the continuing education of adult citizens, he said "that nothing would do more extensive good at small expense than the establishment of a small circulating library in every county." But nothing ever came of this, or of the library bill proposed as part of the revisal in 1779.

The general education bill was nine-tenths of the system; the rest rose from it and could scarcely rise without it. "What a plan was here to give stability and solid glory to the republic!" The bill first went to the House in December 1778, then again a year and one-half later, and for a third time in 1785, when it passed in the House but died in the Senate. It was reconsidered and rejected for the last time the next year. "The necessity of a systematic provision on the subject was admitted on all hands," Madison informed Jefferson. The leading objections to the plan were "1. the expense, which was alleged to exceed the ability of the people. 2. the difficulty of executing it in the present sparse settlement of the Country." The objections mortgaged the future to exigencies of the present. Virginia *was* poor. But she would grow poorer still without the education of her people. The plan *was* impractical for large parts of the state. Each hundred was supposed to cover an area of five or six square miles at most—children could not be expected to traverse a greater distance daily—but many such areas had but a scattering of people. Yet the bill might have been revised to take account of this problem. There were still other objections, for the plan reached deep into the society and touched a number of sensitive interests. Religionists generally distrusted its secularism, while the Presbyterians in particular opposed the influence of William and Mary over the schools. The bill posed a threat to the county courts by the creation of potentially new units of local government, the hundreds or wards, with popularly elected officials called aldermen to administer the schools and perform other duties, such as poor relief and tax assessment, which were assigned to them by other bills of the revisal. Taxation to support the schools would fall most heavily on the propertied class, and from a purely selfish viewpoint the rich felt no interest in paying for the education of the poor. Whatever the reasons for the defeat of the plan, it was a terrible disappointment to Jefferson. "I think by far the most important bill in our whole code is that for the diffusion of knowledge among the people," he wrote to Wythe from France, which he thought the best school in the universe to cure Americans of the folly of seeking public happiness without public enlightenment. "Preach, my dear Sir, a crusade against ignorance; establish and improve the law for educating the common people," he implored. "Let our countrymen know . . . that the tax which will be paid for this purpose is not more than the thousandth part of what will be paid to kings, priests and nobles who will rise up among us if we leave the people in ignorance."

Regardless of defeat, Jefferson's Bill for the More General Diffusion of Knowledge was a landmark in the history of American education. The principle of public education was not new: common schools had existed in New England for generations. In fact, the principal difficulty of Jefferson's plan was the attempt to introduce a system borrowed from the close-knit town environment of New England into the spread-out rural environment of Virginia. But the plan broke sharply with the essentially religious ideal of New England education, substituting for it the citizen-republicanism of the new nation. Public responsibility for the enlightenment of the people was founded in the interest all men felt in freedom and self-government. Also significant was the conception of a complete and unified educational system, from the common schools at the bottom to the university at the top. There were no models for this, and whatever the possible literary sources of the idea—John Knox's sixteenth-century Scottish Presbyterian *Book of Discipline* has been suggested—it appears to have been an independent product of Jefferson's republican imagination. Three years of elementary education—all that Jefferson's plan guaranteed—seems very niggardly by modern standards, which must also condemn omission of the compulsory principle. But that principle was unheard of for many years yet, and a larger commitment to common schooling would have been hopelessly unrealistic. Jefferson perhaps would not have advocated it in any event. He did not believe the mass of citizens either required or were susceptible to education at advanced levels. But nature had sown talent and energy as liberally among the poor as the rich. As

Sir William Petty had observed a century earlier, "many are now holding the plough which might have been made fit to steer the state." The state had an obligation both to nature and to itself to prevent these abilities from running to waste. Jefferson's selection scheme aimed to scale education to merit; and he unreservedly placed the state on the side of talent by proposing to tax the entire community for the education of its most promising offspring of adversity. An audacious experiment indeed! It carried elitist overtones, though it was no part of Jefferson's purpose to establish an elite, even a natural one. Unfortunately, the current neologism of the educators, "meritocracy," did not occur to him, for that is precisely what he had in mind when he spoke of "natural aristocracy." The ideal could find no place in the democratic ideology of public education in nineteenth-century America, and only recently have educators begun to catch up with it.

Other Reforms

Next to education as a means of improving the lot of his countrymen, Jefferson set his heart on the eradication of slavery. But he never underestimated the resistance he would meet on this question, and he would let it lie rather than risk the loss of all power of accomplishment by untimely advocacy of so arduous a cause. He had warmly denounced the African slave trade in his draft of the Declaration of Independence. His proposed constitution for Virginia prohibited holding in slavery any person henceforth coming into the country. In 1778 the assembly, while not going this far, slammed the door on the foreign slave trade. Although Jefferson's authorship of the statute cannot be definitely established, he claimed responsibility for it and there is no one else to whom it can be as fairly assigned. The original bill sought to encourage the private manumission of slaves, which existing law made virtually impossible, and firmly declared an anti-slavery position. As enacted the statute simply raised a bar to foreign importation.

The greater question of emancipation came before the revisers in connection with the codification of colonial slave laws. The bill they reported, and the assembly enacted after several amendments in

1785, contained no provision for emancipation and was for the most part "a mere digest" of the old laws. The principal difference lay in the limits set to the increase of slaves by confining this status henceforth to the descendants of female slaves currently in Virginia. The provision alone, by limiting the source of replenishment, would have gone some way toward eliminating slavery. As finally enacted, the bill did not have this effect. The revisers, according to Jefferson, prepared a plan of gradual emancipation under which all the slaves born after the passage of the act would become free at the age of adulthood and be colonized outside the limits of Virginia. "It was thought better that this should be kept back," Jefferson later wrote, "and attempted only by way of amendment, whenever the bill should be brought up." But, of course, he was abroad when the bill came up, and the amendment was never offered, perhaps because, as he observed, "the public mind would not yet bear the proposition." While he continued to favor the plan of gradual emancipation, first published in the *Notes on Virginia* in 1785, neither he nor any other prominent Virginian was ever willing to risk friends, position, and influence to fight for it.

Jefferson's work on the Revision of the Laws gave him a liberal education in most of the branches of political science. One of these, citizenship, was thrown into vast confusion by the American Revolution. Jefferson drew the principal bill intended to clarify the matter; detached from the *Report* of the revisers, it was enacted in 1779. The statute took over the basic English formula of *jus soli*, founding citizenship on native birth; however, both the conditions and the principles of the Revolution caused important departures from English law. (Jefferson drafted and introduced, also in 1779, the revisers' bill prescribing the oath of fidelity as the Revolutionary test of citizenship in Virginia.) The question of United States citizenship was covered in obscurity, but by extending to the citizens of the other twelve states all the rights, privileges, and immunities of the citizens of Virginia, Jefferson's bill placed his state in the path of the Confederation. The bill also offered liberal terms of naturalization. Jefferson had indicted George III for "obstructing the laws of naturalization of foreigners, and refusing to . . . encourage their migration hither." Indeed, English law did not recognize the validity of naturalization. The encouragement of immigration was, for Jefferson, the positive counterpart of his hostility to slavery, for as the number of slaves declined and Negroes were "colonized" their places would be "filled up by free white laborers." To accomplish this he was against any religious bar, such as the exclusion of Catholics, which Pendleton had proposed; he sought, unsuccessfully, to add the inducement of modest land and monetary grants to immigrants; and he placed naturalization on the simple basis of residence and oath of fidelity.

Of greater theoretical, if not practical, interest was still another feature of the citizenship statute. It declared that every citizen has a "natural right of expatriating himself" and laid down the method of exercising the right. The right arose logically from the principles of the Declaration of Independence. Free men could not be forced to remain members of that state "in which birth, or other accident may have thrown them." The right was unknown to English law, and Blackstone denied it any standing in the law of nations. The ancients had given precedence for it, however, and Jefferson, if he did not find it in Cicero, must certainly have discovered it in Locke. The Americans themselves had exercised the right, and they invited the citizens of other nations to do the same by coming hither. It became a fixed article of Jefferson's creed, and one might say of the American creed, though not in explicit legal terms. No sister state copied Jefferson's innovation. Virginia law ceased to recognize it in 1783, when the first citizenship statute was replaced by a less liberal one. And despite Jefferson's later efforts as Secretary of State, the right of expatriation—man's natural right to live on any portion of the earth that pleases him—went unrecognized in United States law.

Among the principal tasks Jefferson undertook during the first busy session of the General Assembly—any one of them enough to give him a name in history—was the organization of the Virginia judiciary. The constitution merely named the different courts of law to be established; their actual establishment, their powers, jurisdictions, procedures, and so on, was left to legislation. As chairman of the committee appointed to this work, Jefferson drew five bills, each covering a separate court. At the time only the inferior county courts were open for business. The old courts of more extensive jurisdiction remained closed to protect planters from suits for the recovery of debts. Wishing to set the entire judicial system in operation, Jefferson tried to allay the fears of debt-ridden planters by a measure to suspend executions for debts during the wartime interruption of Virginia's trade. But this compromise was unacceptable to the House. It promptly passed Jefferson's Bill for Establishing a Court of Admiralty, with jurisdiction over prizes, and deferred action on the others. The House never acted on the measure "for better regulating the proceedings in the County Courts"—all Jefferson's efforts to reform them failed. In 1778, when the planters were authorized to liquidate their debts in paper money, the House finally approved the bills for establishing a General Court and a High Court of Chancery, both to receive appeals from the county courts and to have original jurisdiction where they were incompetent, and also a Court of Appeals with ultimate jurisdiction in civil cases.

The judicial system thus established made no important departure from English practice. Jefferson liked to point to the innovation of jury trial in the Court of Chancery; but the reform did not last, and it is more significant that the Virginians chose to continue a separate court of chancery, or equity, rather than to mix this jurisdiction with the common law jurisdiction of the General Court. The latter course was advocated in England by the celebrated jurists Blackstone and Mansfield. Jefferson and the Virginians, on the other hand, thought it a matter of fundamental importance to keep the settled common law, which reached nine-tenths of the disputes before the courts, untroubled and uncorrupted by questions of equity. "This proportion then of our rights is placed on sure ground. Relieve the judges from the rigour of text law, and permit them, with pretorian discretion, to wander into its equity, and the whole legal system becomes uncertain. This has been its fate in every country where the fixed, and the discretionary law have been committed into the same hands." He recognized the dangers of the Court of Chancery, dispensing justice where the common law gave no relief, but thought they might be guarded against, as by the introduction of jury trial, and that they were less than the dangers to be apprehended from opening the common law courts to discretionary justice. The opinion was thoroughly characteristic of him. He wished always to bind judges, legislators, and executives to the fixed letter of the constitution and the laws, and where this was impossible always to keep the exceptions from spoiling the rules. The principal defect of the judicial system set in motion in 1778 arose from the inability of the General Court rapidly to dispose of all the business that crowded upon it. Even so the course of justice was several times speedier than in lazy colonial days. The bottleneck would have been avoided had the assembly not eliminated Jefferson's provision for assize courts as accessories to the General Court. The problem was overcome a decade later by the establishment of district courts.

Jefferson's name is omnipresent in the legislative history of Virginia during these formative years of statehood. He headed the committee of the House that brought in a fresh proposal for the settlement of the long disputed western boundary with Pennsylvania. For three successive sessions he was the protagonist of the House in a quarrel with the Senate over the asserted power of the latter to alter or amend money bills. Where there were bad feelings between rival factions Jefferson was the conciliator. In 1777, for example, he was appointed a committee of one to bring in a bill settling the terms of appointment of delegates to Congress, an issue that had embittered the Lee and Harrison factions. He remained on good terms with Governor Henry, who turned to him for counsel and assistance on matters too delicate to discuss openly, such as the attainder of Philips and George Rogers Clark's first expedition above the Ohio. He drafted and reported bills on every conceivable subject: the outfitting of soldiers and sailors, prices chargeable at grist mills, regulations for smallpox inoculation. He was responsible for the plan to move the capital from Williamsburg to Richmond, thus inaugurating the westward migration of the seats of government of many states. As he failed in several of his great enterprises, so he failed in a number of small ones; but these too reveal his mind and his hopes. He proposed to establish a state postal system, supplementing the national one, with a postmaster general, postriders and postroads running east and west across the north-south line of Congress, all with the view to promoting "the more general diffusion of public intelligence among the citizens of this commonwealth." He proposed a state system of vital statistics, a matter formerly in the hands of the parish clergy. But the assembly showed little interest in either of these measures.

Perhaps he attempted too much too soon. Disappointed by mindless and selfish opposition to reform, he had need of the philosophy commended to an impatient cohort a dozen years later: "the ground of liberty is to be gained by inches . . . we must be contented to secure what we can get from time to time, and eternally press forward for what is yet to get. It takes time to persuade men to do even what is for their own good." What he sought, most of all, was to create a more favorable public climate for the freedom and happiness of his countrymen. In order to create, it was first necessary to destroy—feudal holdovers, aristocratic privileges, the religious establishment. But Jefferson was not a happy destroyer and the balance of his effort was on the constructive side. Freedom was many things —suffrage and representation, land and mobility, education and learning—all interwoven in his republican design.

His creed, of course, was the simple philosophy of human rights of the Declaration of Independence. He had no Platonic conception of the perfect society. He had no thought of overthrowing the past and legislating for man as if he were just emerging from the state of nature. The Lockian idea of government originating in contract from that primitive state, while a useful fiction in the consummation of the Revolution, was rejected as a rule of action in the work of reconstruction. "For the nation was not dissolved, was not annihilated; its will, therefore, remained in full vigor: and on the establishing of the new organs, first of a convention, and afterwards a more complicated legislature, the old acts of national will continued in force, until the nation should, by its new organs, declare its will changed." The problem, then, was to save what was good and to reform what was bad in the received institutions. Jefferson worked for realizable goals, which is not to say that practicality was his standard but rather that he kept the needs and conditions of his own country in view and adjusted his principles and objectives to what, in his opinion, the society could sustain. His confidence in the reforming power of law was great, too great, in fact, for he expected much more from laws promoting the alienability and equalization of property, to cite one example, than they could accomplish apart from fundamental social change. He was a creature both of history and of reason. Either could lead him astray, and did; but as long as these two lights of truth converged steadily in his mind, bringing fact and logic, the actual and the ideal, the past and the future, into the alliance he found particularly congenial, the results were likely to be brilliant. It may be misleading to label him liberal or conservative, democratic or aristocratic, radical or moderate, for he was all these things in degrees and in different contexts. He called himself a Whig, which is the historical term, in America, that best describes his political outlook. He was a Whig, however, in a revolutionary situation, when there was both the opportunity and the determination to embody principles in the foundations of a new experiment. Embarked in this way, exalting reason, striking at privilege, opening rights, and releasing talents, Jefferson's direction was inescapably democratic in the line of American progress.

During Jefferson's three years in the Virginia assembly, the future of American independence was being decided in the camps and on the battlefields east of the Potomac and in the regal courts of Europe. General Washington led his tattered and beaten army from the heights above New York City across New Jersey to the rolling farmlands west of Philadelphia; then, after two desperate years when the question was not one of victory but of survival, Washington pursued the enemy back to New York and again camped his army on the bluffs above the Hudson. Nothing had been lost, only time had been gained. Jefferson kept himself posted on the ravages and fortunes of the war as best he could. During the bleak winter of Valley Forge, his friend John Harvie, who was with Congress some miles further west of Philadelphia, occupied by the British, told him of "the avarice and disaffection of the people here," "the shivering limbs of our poor naked soldiers," and "an almost universal discontent in the Army." "The waste of the enemy wherever they move is a scene of cruelty and distress," Harvie gloomily reported. If Jefferson was downcast by these things, he never admitted it. He was cheered by the surrender of Burgoyne's army at Saratoga, and when it was followed five months later, in February 1778, by the consummation of the French Alliance, he put aside any doubts he may have had for the outcome of the war.

Partly because of his optimism on this point, it never occurred to him that he served his country any less than the generals, the congressmen, or the ministers abroad by choosing a modest station suited to his public talents. He enjoyed a full life during these years, never long or far from his fireside, and free to indulge his intellectual curiosity. Twice annually, in the spring and in the fall, he journeyed to Williamsburg for the meetings of the assembly, which consumed perhaps four or five months of a year. His attendance was regular except when his wife was ill or expecting. She presented him with his first and only son in May 1777. He died, unchristened and unnamed, after three weeks of life. On August 1, 1778, "at 1 o'clock and 30 minutes A.M.," as he precisely noted in his prayer book, his third daughter, Mary, was born. Called Maria, or, affectionately, Polly, she grew to maturity with her sister Patsy, six years older. Jefferson's anxiety for his wife's recovery kept him away from the House of Delegates until the end of November, when he was brought in under the custody of the sergeant-at-arms. Of course, his public business was not confined to sessions of the assembly. Most of the work on the Revision of the Laws was done in his own library and could not have been done anywhere else. As county lieutenant of Albemarle he was responsible for the militia, for the recruitment and draft of regular soldiers, and, for a time, the supervision of prisoners-of-war lodged in the county. But these were minor duties. For the most part, while not in Williamsburg, he was the dutiful husband and father, the master of Monticello, and the student of everything that rubbed the surface of his mind.

Building, landscaping, and other improvements at Monticello continued to absorb him. He could not do as much as he would have liked because of wartime scarcities of labor and material. His attempts to recruit a house joiner, stonecutter, and other workmen in Pennsylvania failed. Despite these difficulties he was laying brick at Monticello almost from the moment he returned from Philadelphia. He began stocking his park with deer and drew the finished plan of his orchard, already well advanced. One of the local casualties of the Revolution was the experiment in Mediterranean fruits and viniculture started in 1774 by the middle-aged Italian immigrant, Philip Mazzei, whom Jefferson had enticed to settle on an adjoining property. Mazzei had planted his exotic vines and trees, imported Italian laborers, and planned an agricultural company, all with Jefferson's ardent patronage. In the fall of 1778 he brought from Colle, Mazzei's place, several shoots of a dying orange tree, one of a dead olive, and nursed them with the devotion of a true horticulturist. Not much else remained of the promising experiment. Now Mazzei was departing on a mission to his native Tuscany to raise money for the American cause he had made his own. This experiment, too, was doomed to failure.

"Tho' much of my time is employed in the councils of America I have yet a little leisure to indulge my fondness for philosophical studies," Jefferson wrote to an Italian correspondent and friend of Mazzei's, Giovanni Fabbroni. He wished to exchange information that would provide "a comparative view of the two climates," suggesting his method of taking daily high and low temperatures at Monticello. Mazzei and his friends had excited Jefferson's interest in things Mediterranean. He hoped the United States might cultivate trade and friendship with these sun-drenched countries, and receive from them workmen skilled in both agriculture and the fine arts. "I believe that had our country been peopled thence we should now have been farther advanced in rearing the several things which our country is capable of producing," he wrote to Lee in Congress. Other ventures were less speculative. Thus the critical shortage of salt in the early years of the war caused Jefferson to interest himself in a project to extract salt from sea water by means of large iron pans, which he had manufactured by his friend, the ironmaster Isaac Zane, in Frederick County.

On June 24, 1778, he made observations on the eclipse of the sun, a major astronomical event. At Williamsburg, as he learned from observers there, the eclipse was total. "Lightning bugs were seen as at night." It was not so dramatic at Monticello; the day was cloudy, and besides he had no timepiece he could depend on. All of which prompted him to write to David Rittenhouse, in Philadelphia, reminding him of his promise to make for Jefferson an accurate clock, "which being intended for astronomical purposes only, I would have divested of all apparatus for striking or for any other purpose, which by increasing its complication might disturb its accuracy." The belief that there was a correlation between the simplicity of a thing's construction and the accuracy of its purpose, it might be noted, was not limited to Jefferson's opinion of clocks. Rittenhouse was an ingenious mechanic, who had constructed a mechanical model of the solar system, commonly called the Orrery, which Jefferson greatly admired. (His bill to reform William and Mary in 1779 included provision for the Board of Visitors to engage Rittenhouse in the construction of "so great an ornament of astronomical science.") He thought Rittenhouse "the greatest of astronomers" and stood in awe of him. Imploring the astronomer, who was a good Whig, to shun affairs of state, he remarked, "No body can conceive that nature ever intended to throw away a Newton upon the occupations of a crown." It was a worshipful letter, conveying the sense of a man who felt himself in touch with greatness, the greatness of scientific inquiry, which Jefferson prized above any other.

Another letter, written in May 1777 to John Adams, marked the beginning of a brilliant epistolary dialogue. Again it is significant that Jefferson took the initiative, reaching out in this instance to a statesmen he admired and a man whose republican heart beat in unison with his own. Adams was then chairman of the Board of War in Congress, and Jefferson wrote to him matter-of-factly on subjects within his purview. He spoke of the needlessness and oppressiveness of a compulsory draft of soldiers; he repeated a suggestion earlier made to Adams in Philadelphia for closing the breach between the large and the small states on the delicate point of representation in the confederate government; and he urged "speedy and frequent communication of intelligence" from Congress. The primitive state of public intelligence troubled Jefferson throughout the war, and long after the war. Delays in printing the journal of Congress caused uneasiness, he told Adams. "In our assembly even the best affected think it an indignity to freemen to be voted away life and fortune in the dark." The postal system also required attention. "Our people merely for want of intelligence which they can rely on are become lethargic and insensible to the state they are in." Adams received Jefferson's letter ten days later in Philadelphia, as if to prove the point. Replying on the same day, he dealt with each of Jefferson's complaints in his characteristically open way, concurred in them, and closed with a warm appeal to "come and help us." "We want your industry and abilities here extremely. . . . Your Country is not yet, quite secure enough, to excuse your retreat to the delights of domestic life. Yet, for the soul of me," he added poignantly, "when I attend my own feelings, I cannot blame you."

No one blamed him then, but it is significant that Adams, and probably others, viewed Jefferson's station as more a private than a public one and was vaguely disturbed about it.

Early in 1779 Jefferson was diverted from his accustomed rounds by the arrival in the neighborhood of some 4000 English and German prisoners-of-war, the remains of the army Burgoyne had surrendered at Saratoga, commonly known as the Convention Army. Quartered for a year in the environs of Boston, the troops had been a heavy drain on the food and fuel supplies of the New England metropolis and a tempting prize to the British fleet cruising off shore. Congress ordered their removal to the area of Charlottesville. In the dead of winter, marching 700 miles over "break-neck roads," experiencing hardships of every description, the troops at last reached their destination, "the climax of all bad things," in the middle of January. Charlottesville, "this famous place we had heard so much of, consisted only of a Courthouse, one tavern, and about a dozen houses." The officers scurried about the countryside to find houses to rent. The soldiers were quartered on a wooded hill overlooking the town. "When they first reached here," wrote a German officer, "they found a few buildings, barracks *in name*, but *in fact*, nothing but some logs laid one upon another, without any covering, and the snow three feet deep on the ground." The barracks were to have been ready, but the unusual snows had scattered the workmen. No stores of bread had been laid in, much of the meat refrigerated in the ground had spoiled, and for days the troops made a diet of Indian corn. The populace round about gave a stony welcome to these Royalists and "dogs of Royalists," the Hessians, and feared that the want of provisions would create a dangerous situation.

The conditions and the spirits of the troops gradually improved, however. They finished the barracks, each consisting of a single room 24′ x 14′, built without windows and with precious few nails, adding chimneys and other improvements, caking the chinks between the logs with the orange-red mud of Albemarle—336 of these cabins, twelve in a row, four rows making a square, seven squares ranged across the top of the hill. Unfortunately, the weather was more freakish than usual during the early months of the year. After the heavy January snows, the weather turned mild, even warm, in February—peach trees and cherry trees put on their blooms—reverted to freezing cold in March, turned mild again, and wound up its crazy gyrations on April 17 with a blizzard that "totally blasted the forest and caused untold loss and hardship." Undaunted, the Germans sowed seed in the spring, and soon neatly trimmed and paled gardens, said to attract visitors from sixty miles around, adorned the tree-stumped hill. It was all very delightful, Jefferson thought. "There is little doubt that their own gardens will furnish them a great abundance of vegetables through the year. Their poultry, pigeons and other preparations of that kind present to the mind an idea of a company of farmers rather than of a camp of soldiers." The English, meanwhile, built a church and makeshift theater. "Having thus found the art of rendering captivity itself comfortable," as Jefferson observed, the troops seemed quite satisfied with their situation.

The officers made themselves as comfortable as possible in the places they had rented, often from Virginians who would sooner have the hard money rents than their own roofs over their heads. One of the articles of the Saratoga Convention provided that the officers were not to be separated from their men. This proved advantageous, for the officers not only cared for the needs of the troops but gave an honorable assist to the Virginia regiment of guards in the enforcement of discipline. Major General William Phillips, the British commanding officer, lived at Blenheim, Colonel Landon Carter's estate, while Major General Friederich von Riedesel, his German counterpart, with family in tow, rented Colle from Mazzei. Baroness Riedesel was a spirited trooper, affectionately known to the Brunswickers as "Madame General." She rode a horse astride, playfully sang Italian arias in exchange for farmers' butter, and fretted endlessly about Virginia rattlesnakes, wood ticks, and thunderstorms. Finding Mazzei's modest dwelling too small for his family— there were three young daughters—the Baron had a larger one built nearby. He kept the fields in production and set out his own gardens. "Very soon we wanted nothing," the Baroness noted in her charming memoirs. Jefferson later said that Riedesel's horses destroyed in one week what was left of Mazzei's vinicultural labors, "which from every appearance, would in a year or two have established the practicability of that branch of culture in America." Actually, most of the destruction seems to have been done by the horses of several British officers who briefly tenanted the place before the Riedesels' coming; and it is doubtful that Mazzei's experiment would ever have proven itself.

The hospitality enjoyed by the English and German officers at the seats of Virginia gentlemen suggests a kind of international community among men of rank and breeding that even the hatreds of war could not abate. Jefferson despised royalty and its trappings, but he was charmed by Phillips, Riedesel, and their like. He opened his doors to them, entertained them, loaned them books, tried to make them comfortable in the strange and primitive country they inhabited. There was a studied politeness in these relationships. Public questions were never discussed. Music was the happy *divertissement* when the Europeans were guests at Monticello. "As all Virginians are fond of Music," a German officer wrote home, "he is particularly so. You will find in his house an elegant harpsicord, pianoforte, and some violins. The latter he performs well upon himself, the former his lady touches very skillfully and who," he added, "is in all respects a very agreeable, sensible and accomplished lady." An English staff officer who played violin duets with Jefferson called him "one of the best amateur violinists" he ever knew. The opportunity to play with others, to make an ensemble, was rare at Monticello, and Jefferson must have made the most of it while it lasted. In writing to Fabronni, he wondered if it would not be possible to locate skilled tradesmen in Italy, where music was cultivated by every class, who would migrate to Virginia and who, in addition to serving as cabinet makers, stonemasons, and so on "could perform on the French horn, clarinet or hautboy and bassoon, so that we might have a band . . . without enlarging . . . domestic expenses." But the closest he ever came to realizing the dream of a "domestic band of musicians" was in 1779 with the captives he treated as guests.

The guests appreciated Jefferson's kindness and did what they could to repay him. One of the German officers, on departure, left to him all his music. Of course, the general officers entertained him in their temporary homes. On April 11 the following note was addressed to him from Blenheim: "Major General Phillips sends his Compliments to Mr. and Mrs. Jefferson, requests the favour of their company at dinner on Thursday next at Two o'clock to meet General and Madame de Riedesel. Major General Phillips hopes Miss

Jefferson will be permitted to be of the party to meet the young Ladies from Colle." Sometime later, when Jefferson was Governor of the sovereign state of Virginia and Phillips was commanding His Majesty's forces there, he contemptuously addressed the Governor as "Thomas Jefferson, Esquire." Jefferson was properly offended. But nothing harsh or rude disturbed this beguiling interlude of courtesy and civility in the midst of war. "The great cause which divides our countries is not to be decided by individual animosities," Jefferson wrote to Phillips. "The harmony of private societies cannot weaken national efforts. To contribute by neighborly intercourse and attentions to make others happy is the surest way of being happy ourselves."

Jefferson was not simply voicing an ideal of personal conduct; he was also seeking to refute the proposition that between nations at war "humanity was kicked out of doors." No sooner had the prisoners arrived than many Virginians called for their removal. They were 4000 more mouths to feed out of the state's stock. They were enemies in the bowels of the country. But Jefferson, when he learned in March that the Governor was considering the removal of all or part of the troops, indignantly opposed the measure in a lengthy and carefully reasoned letter to Henry. Still another forced removal of the Conventioners would be a breach of faith, he said. He pointed to the financial rewards of the prisoners' presence in Albemarle, recommended a sensible plan of provisioning, expatiated on their health and happiness, countered fears on the point of security, and so on. Above all, he emphasized humanitarian considerations. "It is for the benefit of mankind to mitigate the horrors of war as much as possible." Applying the principle to the case at hand, his argument was unanswerable. The Convention Army was left undisturbed for the present. Over the next two years, however, he would realize what a gossamer thing were the cosmopolitan sentiments of humanity and philosophy in a country at war, and he would be forced to approve what he had so vehemently disapproved in his address to Henry.

CHAPTER FOUR

War Governor

Certainly it must be a happy Climate, since it is very near the same Latitude with the Land of Promise. Besides, as Judea was full of Rivers, and Branches of Rivers; so is Virginia: *As that was seated upon a great Bay and Sea, wherein were all the conveniences for Shipping and Trade; So is* Virginia. *Had that fertility of Soil? So has Virginia, equal to any Land in the known World. In fine, if any one impartially considers all the Advantages of this Country, as Nature made it; he must allow it to be as fine a Place, as any in the Universe; but I confess I am asham'd to say any thing of its Improvements, because I must at the same time reproach my Country-Men with a Laziness that is unpardonable. If there be any excuse for them in this Matter, 'tis the exceeding plenty of good things, with which Nature has blest them; for where God Almighty is so Merciful as to work for the People, they never work for themselves.*

    Robert Beverley, The History of the Present State of Virginia, *1705.*

T HE GENERAL ASSEMBLY elected Jefferson Governor of Virginia on June 1, 1779. John Page, then at the head of the Council of State, was his principal rival for the office, though as Jefferson hastened to assure his old friend, "it was their competition, not ours," and the margin of victory was "too insignificant to give you a pain or me a pleasure had our dispositions toward each other been such as to have admitted those sensations." Nor were Page's feelings any different. His political strength lay in the tidewater, where he was a prince among planters; while Jefferson succeeded to Patrick Henry's following in the interior; but neither man was a creature of section or of party, and Jefferson's political course brought him into ever-increasing conflict with Henry. The "Forest Demosthenes," having completed the three consecutive terms allowed by the constitution to Virginia's governors, retired for a time to the seclusion of his modest estate Leatherwood. He remained a power to be reckoned with, however, as Jefferson was to discover before his governorship ended.

Honored by the office, Jefferson had no taste for it. He knew how far the duties of the chief magistracy of Virginia must break in upon his domestic happiness; yet he knew too that the public's claim on his services could not rightly be denied. "In a virtuous government, and more especially in times like these," he wrote to a friend, "public offices are, what they should be, burthens to those appointed to them which it would be wrong to decline, though foreseen to bring with them intense labor and great private loss." His election accurately measured his prominence in the state, and in view of his accomplishments both in Congress and in the assembly, his elevation to the state's highest office was as logical as it was merited. He was in Williamsburg at the time, having taken his seat in the House of Delegates early in May. He did not seek the governorship, but neither did he attempt to dissuade the friends who were active on his behalf. When formally notified of the assembly's decision, he responded with characteristic modesty. "My great pain is, lest my poor endeavours should fall short of the kind expectations of my country. . . ." This was one of the pleasantries the occasion demanded; it was not a confession of feebleness. And yet, if Jefferson paused at the threshold of the governorship, wracked by doubt, it can easily be forgiven him. Hitherto his abilities had been exhibited in the legislative chambers of the Revolution. Only now were they brought to the test of executive leadership in a crucible of foaming discord and disaster.

The Revolutionary War had entered a new and ominous phase. The British commander in chief, Sir Henry Clinton, unable to destroy General Washington's army in the North, determined to "unravel the thread of rebellion from the southward." Savannah fell to the British in December 1778, Augusta a month later, and in May the redcoats probed the defenses of Charleston. How far Clinton meant to pursue this strategy remained to be seen, but it broke upon the Virginians with lightning swiftness on May 10. A British fleet under Admiral Sir George Collier sailed into Hampton Roads, landed 1800 troops, which seized Portsmouth, raided the surrounding country, burned several towns, captured 130 vessels, destroyed 3000 pounds of tobacco and quantities of military and naval stores, and after sixteen days of plunder and ravage, returned to their ships and sailed back to New York without the loss of a man. Collier boasted, "the whole trade of the Chesapeake is at an end, and consequently the sinews of rebellion destroyed." Not since the departure of the Royal Governor's fleet in 1776 had Virginia been set upon. Surprisingly, in view of Collier's extraordinary success, nearly eighteen months were to pass before she was invaded again. Clinton was not yet ready for Virginia. The Carolinas must first be conquered. An early, hesitant probe of the strategy that would make the Chesapeake the principal theater of the war, first by disruption of supply lines, finally by conquest, the Collier expedition was a foretaste of things to come. The commonwealth, meanwhile, sped all possible assistance southward in the hope of defeating the enemy there.

"I see no better purpose to which they can apply their army in America," Washington sadly reflected on the enemy campaign in the South. The British had centered their operations in the North for three and one-half years, yet the southern states were more vulnerable on almost every count. And Virginia, the richest and largest of all the states, was the epitome of the whole. If instruction were needed on the defenselessness of her situation, it was furnished at Portsmouth. Chesapeake Bay and the several broad rivers emptying into it invited an enemy superior at sea. By blockading the bay at its mouth, the enemy could shut up the trade in tobacco which was the lifeblood of the state's economy. The rivers were navigable far into the interior, giving easy access to the principal towns and estates. Jefferson was convinced "that our only practicable defense was naval," but so ill-conceived and wasteful was the state's work in this sphere that he concluded six weeks after taking office, "we should be gainers were we to burn our whole navy" and start over. Virginia's naval investment exceeded that of any other state. Yet her total force consisted of three ships and a brig, mounting sixty-two guns altogether, four armed galleys, and a few boats, all badly cared for and chronically undermanned. Adequate naval defense was beyond the state's means in 1779, if indeed it was ever attainable, and Jefferson could only look, somewhat wistfully, to the aid of the French fleet.

The prospect on land was not much better. From the long, exposed coastline, the low country stretched upwards to 150 miles toward the Blue Ridge, with scarcely hill or vale to break its surface. Rivers and forests provided the only natural defenses against the marchings of armies. In the mountains and on the frontiers far beyond, there was the constant menace of hostile Indians aided and abetted by the British at Detroit and Pensacola. As Jefferson summed up the situation in 1780: "While we are threatened with a formidable attack from the northward on our Ohio settlements and from the Southern Indians on our frontiers convenient to them, our eastern country is exposed to invasion from the British army in Carolina." After subtracting the Ohio country, ceded to Congress in 1781, Virginia dwarfed the United Kingdom in size, and the more exposed portion east of the Alleghenies was as large as all New England. Thinly dispersed over this vast surface was an agricultural population estimated at something in excess of one-half million inhabitants, of whom approximately four in ten were slaves. The slaves were submissive, though a zero quantity at best in the reckoning of military strength. Among the whites were still a few Tories, pocketed in the Chesapeake region and in the mountains; but far more serious than Tory disaffection was the general languor of a rural populace, accustomed to peace, jealous of authority, and unmindful of danger. Habit alone would bring them to their senses, Jefferson later reflected, "a habit which must be purchased by calamity, but cannot be purchased too dear."

The defense of the country rested on the militia. Organized by county, the militia enrolled every able-bodied freeman between the ages of sixteen and fifty, with certain exceptions. While Jefferson was Governor it numbered fifty thousand. If the whole of the militia, including several thousand in the remote Trans-Allegheny counties, were distributed across the land east of the mountains it would have furnished but one makeshift soldier to the square mile. Supposedly like so many Cincinnati, militiamen rushed from the fields at the sound of alarm, then resumed their peaceful occupations after the suppression of danger. They were required by law to furnish themselves with arms, but most of the serviceable arms had been sent out of the state and, as a rule, only the mountain men—sharp-shooting riflemen—were well armed. "It is a melancholy fact," a Virginian wrote after the invasion of Portsmouth, "that there were not arms enough to put in the hands of the few militia who were called down . . . of which those which were to be had, a great number were not fit for use." Whether armed or not, untrained, un-disciplined militia, strangers to battle, ebbing and flowing like the tides, were no match for British regulars. Excessive reliance on mili-tia was vociferously denounced in Congress and the camps of the Continental Army. Jefferson was quite aware of the militia's short-comings, but it was easier to denounce the system than to embody a sufficiency of regular troops for the state's defense. At the beginning of the contest, the state had done so. "Finding, however," as Jeffer-son explained, "that the dangers of our being invaded became less, our legislature made a tender of these battalions to the continental service." The ranks of the eleven Virginian battalions in the Conti-nental Army were but two-thirds full in June 1779, and recruits were desperately hard to find. Without a respectable force of regu-lars in the state, except for the regiment of guards at the Charlottes-ville barracks, the Governor was under constant pressure to fill up the Continental Line and succor the states to the southward. For the defense at home, there was only the shadow army of the militia.

The state's plight stemmed in part from acute financial disorders. Virginia had early embarked with Congress and the other states on the experiment of paying for the war with paper money. "I think nothing can bring the security of our continent and its cause into danger, if we can support the credit of our paper," Jefferson wrote in 1777. But depreciation had already set in, and by the time he be-came Governor the situation was desperate. The government's need for funds rose steadily. The presses printed more and more bills. As the volume swelled, their buying power diminished. The paper could not be maintained as legal tender, on a par with gold and sil-ver; so in May the assembly bowed to the inevitable and lifted all penalties for discounting the state's paper. Currency inflation under-mined the government's credit, soaked up its purchase funds, bred disaffection among soldiers and civilians alike, and let loose all the mean arts of pecuniary fraud and chicane. "The inundation of paper money appears to have overflowed virtue," one Virginian commiserated in June, "and I fear will bury the liberty of America in the same grave."

Virginia was not lacking in economic resources, but no application of them stemmed the torrent of depreciated paper. Her citizens were deeply averse to paying taxes to support a war originated in opposition to taxation. Light as the tax burden was, the habit of delinquency quickly took hold. Half the counties failed to meet their tax obligations in 1779. The amounts assessed steadily increased, but not as rapidly as the currency in which they were paid depreciated. Thus the government's revenue always lagged behind its needs. In May the legislature resorted to taxation in specifically enumerated commodities, but problems of collection and transportation were enormous. "Taxation is become of no account," Jefferson declared in June. At this time he hoped to realize substantial revenue from two statutes he had initiated in the assembly. The Land Office Act provided for the sale of western lands, partly with the aim to "increase the annual Revenue, and create a Fund for discharging the Public Debt." Five months later Congress bowed to the demand of the landless states and strongly protested this act. By holding out the prospect of "savage freedom" on the Ohio, it was wildly charged, the Virginia law "afforded both an asylum and a temptation for desertion." Some pointed to the increased burden of frontier defense exacted by the law. Untold thousands moved west and many who stayed home made fortunes in land warrants; still the finances of the state continued to deteriorate. Equally disappointing was the act of June 4 confiscating the property of British subjects. The statute remained on the books until 1784, but four months after its passage Jefferson advised the legislators to cast their eyes elsewhere for funds. The pleadings allowed by the courts were blocking the law's effects, "throwing the subject into a course of legal contestation which . . . may not be terminated in the present age."

Jefferson had once thought that public solvency could be secured by one of two steps: "Either to procure free trade by alliance with some naval power able to protect it: or, if we find there is no prospect of that, to shut our ports totally to all the world, and turn our laborers into manufacturers." Freed from British shackles, Virginia's tobacco entered the ports of France, Spain, Holland and their possessions in the West Indies. Tobacco brought hard money, and the sinews of war flowed from the trade. The French alliance of 1778 held the promise of naval protection. As already noted, however, the trade of the Chesapeake was easily bottled up by the British, and the risks of capture at sea were high. The tobacco trade was not enough. In June the new governor saw no escape from financial disaster except by "a plentiful loan of hard money." To secure loans, the government contracted with commercial agents abroad and sent special emissaries of its own, like Philip Mazzei, whose project to obtain assistance from Italian princes Jefferson had warmly supported. But nothing was accomplished. There was thus no alternative, as Jefferson saw it, even without a formal embargo, to the development of domestic manufacturers.

The weaving of cloth, the tanning of leather, the forging of iron, the making of gunpowder—simple manufactures of this kind made rapid strides in Virginia during the war. Jefferson took a keen interest in them. He embarked on a particularly ambitious enterprise at the outset of his governorship: the establishment of a large public arms factory on the James River. As he explained the plan to Benjamin Harrison, Speaker of the House of Delegates: "The depending on the transportation of arms across an element on which our enemies have reigned, for the defence of our Country, has been already found insecure and distressing. The endeavors of five years aided with some internal manufactures have not yet procured a tolerable supply of arms. To make them within ourselves, then, as well as the other implements of war, is as necessary as to make our bread within ourselves." The assembly authorized him to contract with the French firm of Penet, Windel & Company to build and operate the factory for the state and also to cut a canal around the Great Falls at Richmond in order to open navigation between the factory's site at Westham and the lower James. The project failed, mainly because the French government barred the emigration of munitions workers. The public foundry already at Westham turned out arms and munitions, though not at all on the scale envisioned by Jefferson's plan. Virginia remained dependent on outside sources of supply, not only for arms but many other articles of manufacture as well. Had transportation overland from the north been more convenient, or at sea less perilous, the situation would have been tolerable. Unfortunately, little reliance could be placed in either.

The system of government was badly designed for the exigencies of war that accompanied its revolutionary birth. Recoiling from the horrors of monarchy, the framers of the Virginia constitution had created a weak executive bridled by the legislature. Annually elected by the General Assembly, and rigidly separated from it, the chief magistrate was enjoined to "exercise the Executive powers of Government according to the laws of the Commonwealth; and . . . not, under any pretense, exercise any power or prerogative by virtue of any Law, statute, or Custom of England." The Governor could not very well rise above the level of the legislature; and nearly everyone agreed that the legislature of 1779 was not the equal of the body that brought on the Revolution and established the government. It was more democratic but less able, larger but less experienced, more complaining but less constructive. In addition, the constitution required the governor to work hand-in-glove with the Council of State. He could not make appointments, grant pardons, call out the militia except on advice of the eight-man Council. In a very real sense, the Council *was* the executive power, with the Governor merely its head. Almost invariably in executive matters, Jefferson spoke in the first person plural—the executive "we" not "I". Executive control over the cumbersome administrative apparatus was also limited. Military and commercial affairs were superintended by the Board of War and the Board of Trade respectively. Both were appointed by the assembly, an arrangement productive of confusion and delay since they must necessarily act under the executive. The Governor commanded the militia and relied on the local officers in the counties for its efficient functioning. In military as in civil administration, the government was decentralized, in conformity with the facts of geography, economics, and social organization.

Strength, energy, and dispatch, such as the times demanded, were simply not built into the Virginia government. The same could be said of the new governments in the sister states, for all were founded on Whig principles. The executive was usually the creature of popularly elected legislative bodies; and in this regard the Virginia executive was neither the weakest nor the strongest. But whether a wartime governor was weak or strong depended less on the constitutional powers of his office than on the political temperament he brought to it. George Clinton and William Livingston, governors of New York and New Jersey respectively during most of the war, gained reputations for vigor and resourcefulness. Their powers exceeded those of the Virginia governors, and allowance must be made for the greater compactness of the societies they represented, as well as for the almost constant presence of the contending armies; yet their personal inclinations toward forceful leadership probably counted for more. Jefferson's inclinations ran to the contrary. It would be exceedingly difficult for him to supply the kind of personal leadership that alone could overcome the deficiencies of executive power in the Virginia system. While no admirer of the frame of government, his objections at the time he became governor did not touch on the question of executive powers. A firm Whig, he believed in the strict separation of powers, the popular will embodied in the legislature, the supremacy of the constitution and the laws. Soon after he retired from office, he had reason to reflect on a proposition, first put forward in 1776 and later revived, to create a wartime dictator in Virginia. His impassioned denunciation of the scheme suggests his conception of the governor's office. "One who entered into this contest from a pure love of liberty, and a sense of injured rights," he wrote, "who determined to make every sacrifice, and to meet every danger, for the reestablishment of those rights on a firm basis, who did not mean to expend his blood and substance for the wretched purpose of changing this matter for that, but to place the powers of governing him in a plurality of hands of his own choice, so that the corrupt will of no one man might in future oppress him, must stand confounded and dismayed when he is told, that a considerable portion of that plurality had mediated the surrender of them into a single hand, and, in lieu of a limited monarchy, to deliver him over to a despotic one!" He thus took his bearings from the republican principles of the Revolution.

The Case of Governor Hamilton

Such was the state of affairs when Jefferson, sanguine and undismayed, took up residence in the Palace he had visited as a youth in the days of the Royal Governors. His wife and daughters stayed at The Forest until in the August doldrums they all returned to Monticello. Family housekeeping commenced at the Palace in September. It was hardly on a palatial scale, and would be even less so when the government moved to Richmond the following April.

Jefferson had sponsored this move in the second year of the Revolution, chiefly on the grounds of the greater security and centrality of Richmond. The assembly finally and reluctantly consented just after his election. As grandly conceived by Jefferson, the new capital was to occupy six large public squares, each with a handsome edifice of brick brilliantly porticoed. But none of this work had even begun in 1780. Richmond, picturesquely set upon the hills above the murmuring cascades of the James, was a sleepy village of about 1800 inhabitants. "It is indeed a lovely situation," wrote a young lady unhappily transplanted from Williamsburg, "and may at some future period be a great city, but it will at present afford scarcely one comfort of life." Wishing to be as comfortable as possible, Jefferson rented perhaps the most elegant establishment in town—a brick house and garden on Shokoe Hill. There he brought his family, servants, and household goods—forty-nine boxes containing books, furniture, chandeliers, china, pictures, etc.—on a cold day in April, and there he remained with but one brief respite at Monticello until the government was forced to abandon Richmond a year later.

The work of the Governor involved the multitudinous details of countless transactions. The promulgation and execution of the laws, relations with Congress, Indian affairs, the care and exchange of prisoners-of-war, public works such as the gun factory and the lead mines, trade, taxes, purchasing and disbursement of funds, the raising of troops and the ordering of militia, naval affairs, fortifications, logistical support of the army—all these matters and others unmentioned occupied the Governor more or less constantly. As a rule, decisions were made "in Council." Jefferson met with the Council regularly at ten o'clock in the morning, laid the day's business before it, then proceeded to carry out the Council's actions. Clerks were employed to keep records and copy official letters, but the Governor, meticulous on all points of form and system, performed a large share of the drudgeries of the office.

The arrival in Virginia of a military escort bearing Sir Henry Hamilton and other British captives of Colonel George Rogers Clark's momentous conquest of Vincennes in the Illinois country at once confronted the new governor with a delicate problem. Hamilton's reputation for infamy had gone before him. As the Lieutenant Governor of Detroit in command of British operations in the Northwest, he had made formidable alliance with the Shawnee, Miami, and other tribes, and incited savage warfare on the distant Virginia frontier. "The Famous Hair Buyer General," Clark labeled him. He was a prize captive, and Clark, a state officer under state orders, sent Hamilton with part of the captured garrison to Virginia that they might receive the justice due them. At length, after a horrendous journey of three months through 1200 miles of wilderness, most of it on foot, the prisoners reached their destination, Chesterfield Court House. There Hamilton and his principal accomplice, Captain Guillaume La Mothe, were mounted, handcuffed, and marched to Williamsburg. Arriving on the evening of the next day, Hamilton later reported, "We were conducted to the Palace where we remained about half an hour in the Street at the Governor's door, in wet cloaths, weary, hungry, and thirsty, but had not even a cup of water offered to us." A jeering mob gathered, then followed them to the jail, where a tiny cell already inhabited by five common criminals and another of Hamilton's accomplices, Phillip Dejean, awaited them. "The next day," to continue Hamilton's account, "we three were taken out about 11 oClock, and before a number of people our handcuffs taken off and fetters put on in exchange—I was honored with the largest which weighed eighteen pounds eight ounces." Thus put in irons, they were further ordered by the Governor and Council "confined in the dungeon of the publick jail, debarred the use of pen, ink, and paper, and excluded all converse except with their keeper."

This cruel and unusual punishment embroiled Jefferson in a prolonged controversy. Despite the trouble it caused him, he seems never to have regretted the executive's action and always took full responsibility for it. The vengefulness of his feelings toward Hamilton may appear strangely out of character, particularly in view of the humanitarian plea he had recently made on behalf of the Convention prisoners; but those feelings were enmeshed in Jefferson's anxiety for the West, and when viewed in this context they are not so surprising.

In Jefferson's eyes British power in the Northwest presaged a dangerous extension of the Province of Canada and, more immediately, threatened the very survival of the new Virginia counties in Kentucky. The agent of this power was the Lieutenant Governor of Detroit. No doubt he took orders from the London government, but under his agency, the Indians, often with Tory troops, terrorized the Ohio frontier. Such was the destruction wrought by "the infernal rage and fury of those execrable Hellhounds" that in the summer of 1777 the Kentuckians withdrew into two garrisoned towns, and dared not venture forth to plow their fields or cut wood or herd cattle without arms. Dreadful atrocities were reported, and the Indians took scalps by the score to Detroit. "No people could be in a more alarming position," Clark said.

A native of Albemarle, Clark had settled in Kentucky in 1775. The following year the frontiersmen chose him to represent their claim to the protection of the government at Williamsburg. He was successful in this mission: the Kentucky settlements became an organized part of Virginia. But Clark realized the hopelessness of Kentucky's situation while the British held sway above the Ohio. The capture of Detroit was the obvious solution. As a first step in this ambitious enterprise, he formed the idea of conquering the towns in the Illinois country to which British power flowed from Detroit as along the fingers of a great outstretched hand. In the fall of 1777 he again journeyed over the mountains to lay his plan before the authorities in Williamsburg. Governor Henry favored the proposed expedition, declining, however, to hazard its chances by submission to the assembly or, on the other hand, to take full responsibility for it. He therefore called a council of three "select men," of whom Jefferson was one. How well Jefferson knew Clark is uncertain, but he instantly saw in this hardy and intrepid frontiersman a born leader of men—the hoped for savior of the West—and he gave himself wholly to Clark's bold enterprise. If successful, it would secure Kentucky, strengthen Virginia's disputed claim to the Northwest, open the Ohio River to trade with the Spanish at St. Louis and New Orleans, invite settlement beyond the mountains, and prepare the way for the decisive stroke on Detroit. What a leap forward of Jefferson's westering vision of an "empire of liberty"! In January 1778, Clark received his secret instructions. Money and supplies were placed at his disposal, and he was empowered to raise a troop of volunteers, allegedly for the defense of Kentucky. Jefferson and the others privy to Clark's true objectives gave assurance that the conquerors of Illinois would be rewarded with liberal grants of land.

Proceeding to Pittsburgh to assemble boats, ammunition, and supplies, Clark then descended the Ohio to the falls (the present-day site of Louisville), established a fortified base nearby, and from there embarked on the river with 170 men. At Fort Massac the troops landed and marched eighty miles to Kaskaskia. They took the town by surprise on July 4. Cahokia and the lesser villages in the vicinity soon fell; and in August the American flag flew over Vincennes on the Wabash nearly 200 miles to the east. None of these towns was defended. They were chiefly populated by Frenchmen, who generally welcomed the Americans and far outnumbered the few British officers and soldiers. The French used their influence to wean the Indians from their new allies, the British, telling them that their old father, the King of France, had come back to life and wished the tribes to make peace with the Big Knives. By bluff and cunning diplomacy at Kaskaskia, Clark won over several of the more powerful chiefs. "The British cause lost ground daily . . . ," he wrote, "and in a short time our influence over the Indians extended to the River St. Joseph and the lower end of Lake Michigan." Gloom descended with the winter snows, however. Supplies ran low. Hamilton's agents were once again among the Indians, and in December he retook Vincennes with a mixed force of regulars, redmen, and French volunteers. Clark's situation was desperate. "We saw but one alternative," he said, "which was to attack the enemy in his stronghold." Calculating the obvious madness of an attack "through a drowned country in the middle of winter" to catch the enemy off-guard, Clark resolved to try it after learning that Hamilton had sent his Indians to the Ohio preparatory to the spring campaign. He set out with his men on February 8. The unusual warmth of the season had turned the country into a veritable marshland. Alternately wading and marching for sixteen days "through difficulties far surpassing anything we had ever experienced," Clark came in sight of Vincennes on February 23. The town welcomed the Americans and joined in besieging the fort. It surrendered after a fight of eighteen hours, giving up seventy-nine prisoners and quantities of stores. Hamilton sought generous terms of capitulation from Clark, such as had been allowed to Burgoyne's army at Saratoga, but in vain. In effect, if not in law, he was forced to "surrender at discretion." His honor wounded, suffering Clark's contempt and the taunts of the victorious militia, Hamilton had yet to taste the dregs of the cup of humiliation at Williamsburg.

The Council of State publicly condemned the prisoner-of-war as a kind of war criminal. He was placed in irons because, in words that were doubtless Jefferson's, "They find that Governour Hamilton has executed the task of inciting the Indians to perpetuate their accustomed cruelties on the citizens of these states, without distinction of age, sex, or condition, with an eagerness and activity which evince that the general nature of his charge harmonized with his particular disposition." Proclamations and other papers implicating Hamilton seemed to place this point beyond reasonable doubt. But having established Hamilton's zeal in the incitement of Indian warfare, Jefferson and his colleagues went on to conjure up the demoniacal monster, The Hairbuyer, of the frontiersman's frightful imagination. The only witness actually to appear before the Council was one John Dodge, a native of Connecticut who had become an Indian trader in Detroit before the Revolution and, at its outset, been imprisoned by Governor Hamilton for disloyalty to Great Britain. Escaping two years later, he published at Philadelphia a sensational account of his captivity, and subsequently journeyed to Williamsburg to revenge himself on Hamilton, Dejean, and La Mothe. "They will be hanged without redemption," Dodge vowed. Despite the highly questionable character of Dodge's testimony, the Council accepted it and proclaimed its truth. Indeed, the Council's indictment of Hamilton was founded on little more than frontier opinion and rumor and the treacherous testimony of John Dodge.

Jefferson did not often allow his feelings to dictate to his judgment, but the celebrated case of Governor Hamilton exhibited the fault. He always justified the Council's action on "the general principle of National Retaliation." The original order, which was published in the *Virginia Gazette* and widely circulated, contrasted the British treatment of American prisoners-of-war, "savage and unprecedented among civilized nations," with the "moderation and humanity" practiced by the Americans. Since the British had apparently learned nothing from the American example, the time had come to try another method of persuasion. The Detroit butcherers were "fit subjects to begin on with the work of retaliation." Apparently the Governor was not aware of the improvement that had recently occurred in the lot of American prisoners. In any event, conscious of his own feelings of humanity and revolted by British "enormities," whether on the frontier, in Portsmouth, or in the pestilential holds of prison ships, Jefferson seemed convinced that an example of retaliation in the case of so distinguished an officer as Governor Hamilton would produce salutary effects. This was the official justification of his conduct, and Virginians applauded the courage of the example. Undergirding it, however, were considerations that could not be stated officially. Jefferson was closely identified with Clark's Illinois campaign. Its objectives were, in his view, of first importance both militarily and politically. They were realized beyond his fondest expectations: Virginia authority extended to the Wabash and beyond, greater security on the frontier, Kentucky's bond with the mother state strengthened. And the captive of Clark's conquest was the symbol not alone of the principal object yet to be attained but of the warfare that had brought untold suffering and sacrifice on western Americans. Was it not just as well as politic to celebrate his captivity? Had not Hamilton and his confederates forfeited honorable treatment by the betrayal of civilized warfare? Was it not imperative to take every precaution against Hamilton's escape or early parole? The new nation was playing for big stakes in the West. Jefferson would go to almost any lengths to see that they were won in the ultimate treaty of peace.

Three weeks after the spectacle at Williamsburg, General William Phillips, commander of the British prisoners in Albemarle, interceded on Hamilton's behalf. From the liberality Jefferson had shown toward him, Phillips was puzzled by the treatment of Hamilton. "I am led to imagine," he wrote, "it must have been very dissonant to the feelings of your mind to have inflicted so severe a weight of misery and stigma of dishonour upon the unfortunate gentleman in question." Unless there was mitigation of Hamilton's punishment, Phillips warned, the British would retaliate on Virginia prisoners. For the British general, the issue turned on the nice distinction between prisoners at *discretion* and prisoners on *capitulation*. Assuming for the sake of argument that Hamilton was the beast depicted by Jefferson, said Phillips, Clark might assuredly "have put the Lieut. Governor and every other person to the sword." But Clark granted a capitulation, "and it matters not how barbarous the disposition of the Lieutenant Governor might have been previous to the surrender, the capitulation was assuredly sacred, and should remain so. . . ." To this Jefferson answered that although Hamilton had capitulated, he had done so without any terms respecting the manner of confinement. Supposing that Phillips had not seen the straightforward surrender Hamilton had signed, Jefferson enclosed a copy for his perusal. In the usage of nations Hamilton might be a prisoner on capitulation, but he was liable to the treatment accorded prisoners at discretion, that is, said Jefferson, "gentle and humane, unless a contrary conduct in an enemy, or individual, renders a strict treatment necessary."

Jefferson at once forwarded Phillips's letter to General Washington and submitted the case to his decision. He had at first approved the Council's action, but now, on deeper reflection, thought that Hamilton's capitulation, regardless of its terms, "placed him upon a different footing from a mere prisoner at discretion." He allowed it might be expedient to continue Hamilton's confinement "from motives of policy and to satisfy our people." If so, he recommended the publication of a full and documented report of Hamilton's cruelties. No such report was ever made. Nor did Jefferson alter his opinion of the case. Washington's letter nevertheless had its effect. Hamilton's shackles were struck at once. In October the prisoners rejected paroles they thought too confining and offered, according to Hamilton, "from no other motive than to lay us open to the malice of the first informer," John Dodge. The paroles were, in fact, much more severe than those granted the Convention troops. Dejean and La Mothe soon changed their minds and accepted the paroles. Hamilton stood his ground. Meanwhile, having been taken to Chesterfield County, his health and circumstances improved. Finally, on October 10, 1780, he accepted a parole which, while still restricting his freedom of speech, permitted him to go to New York and await exchange.

By then Virginia's obstinacy in the Hamilton case seriously embarrassed the whole delicate business of prisoner exchange. Jefferson had refused to be bullied by British irons clamped on Virginia captives; he had rebuffed captive American officers paroled to Virginia in exchange for Hamilton; and only two weeks before issuing the final parole, he had informed Washington of the Council's grim determination to retain Hamilton. "You are not unapprised of the influence of this officer with the Indians, his activity and embittered zeal against us; you also perhaps know how precarious is our tenure of the Illinois country, and how critical is the situation of the new counties on the Ohio." Washington was not unaware of these things, nor was he inclined to interfere with the state's handling of Governor Hamilton. On the other hand, he was faced with the practical problem of prisoner exchange, and Hamilton had become a sticking point with the British. It was this consideration that finally forced Jefferson to retreat from "the hard necessity" he had so long felt.

All the while Jefferson kept an eye cocked on the frontier. Clark's victory at Vincennes upset Hamilton's plan for the summer of 1779 and brought a season of comparative calm to the Ohio. But Detroit, the key to peace, stood unmolested, and the Shawnee and other tribes breathed defiance of the Big Knives. Upwards to a thousand Virginia fighting men—men who became increasingly precious as the British advanced in the Carolinas—were employed in the West. The logistical difficulties were formidable. Hard money was non-existent, and the Illinois traders refused Virginia paper. Spanish New Orleans was a potential source of supplies. It could not be too much relied upon, however, because of the risks of the traffic and the tedious roundabout process of making payment on New Orleans bills with hard earned funds accumulated in France from the sale of Virginia tobacco. These troubles, combined with pressure from Congress, caused Jefferson in January 1780 to order Clark "to withdraw to the eastern [i.e. southern] side of the Ohio all the forces not absolutely necessary to sustain the spirits of the inhabitants of the Illinois, and for their real defence." Still determined to strengthen Virginia's position, Jefferson worked out with Clark a plan of operations for the succeeding summer. First, a fort was to be built near the mouth of the Ohio. The Mississippi trade would thus be secured, the neighboring Indian tribes subdued, and government firmly planted in the Illinois. Jefferson envisioned more than a military outpost. Land was promised to settlers around the fort, civil officers were to be appointed, and "a town of importance" was expected to rise. Second, Clark was to employ a force of regulars authorized by the assembly—only half the number Jefferson had wished—either in chastising the hostile tribes or in an expedition against Detroit, as circumstances might dictate. Jefferson prayed for the latter, and harder, of these alternate courses, but the Shawnee and their like, "troublesome thorns in our sides," could not be ignored. "The same world will scarcely do for them and for us," he reflected. Clark triumphed over the Shawnee during the summer. And a post, named Fort Jefferson, was established just below the mouth of the Ohio. Unfortunately, it was poorly situated for the purposes of trade and Jefferson's cautious recommendations for dealing with the neighboring tribes who claimed the land were neglected. Falling prey to hunger and attack, the fort was abandoned in June 1781.

Ardent, clearheaded, and persevering in his policy toward the West, Jefferson saw his ambitions exceed his grasp. Congress was either cool or downright hostile to Virginia's venture above the Ohio, and Virginia at this stage looked askance on congressional intervention. Faced with more pressing demands from other quarters, the state was unable to support Clark's command with the men and resources Jefferson knew to be necessary for complete success. In 1781, when the country lay stripped and naked before British arms in the East, the Governor was to make one last effort to drive the enemy from the Northwest. It was doomed to disappointment. He had finally to be satisfied with the gains already won. They proved sufficient in the final reckoning of 1783, and the entire Union became the beneficiary of Virginia arms and pioneering. The intensity of Jefferson's devotion to this enterprise antedated his governorship and had yet to show its fairest side in works of national statesmanship during three decades.

Against the Southern Thrust

One dominant force, the British thrust from the southward, controlled Jefferson's governorship. For the present Virginia was safe;

but invasion from the sea was a constant menace, and every triumph of British arms in the Carolinas brought the war closer to Virginia soil. Jefferson gauged the situation with increasing clarity. Hopes for a speedy conclusion of the war were set aside. The tempo of the executive, slow and cautious at first, quickened to the alarm, gathering energy with the acceleration of its movements. Spun upon the axis of military necessity, Jefferson struggled to perform duties for which he professed to have neither taste nor talent and, at the same time, to maintain the civilian deportment that alone suited his character and his principles.

One of his first objectives on taking office was to fill up the Virginia regiments in the Continental Army. Early in the war he had pleaded with friends at home to reconcile the defense of the state to the greater cause of the Union. Both military and political considerations recommended this course, and despite trials and difficulties, he never wavered from it. Neither was he able, however, to complete the Virginia Line according to the quota assigned by Congress. In the spring of 1779, Virginia was reported deficient one-third of its quota. The debt to the Continent was bound to increase, if for no other reason because of the expiration of short-term enlistments. Just before he entered office the General Assembly enacted legislation, which he had drafted, to meet the problem. The Governor was empowered to appoint an officer in every county to raise recruits for the duration of the war; the officers received premiums for the men they enlisted; bounties in land and money and other inducements were offered to the volunteers; and a draft was ordered in districts that failed to furnish them. Jefferson diligently implemented this measure. Every other month an officer rode "the circuit of the country" to gather the recruits. But few came forward, and the punitive draft was so feeble, distasteful, and unproductive that, Jefferson remarked, "we have not thought them worth the expense and trouble of gathering up." Supplementary acts of the assembly in the fall failed to improve Virginia's account with the Continent. It is difficult to say where the fault lay. The legislators might have offered stronger inducements: premiums and bounties figured in paper money were not as large as they seemed. The Governor could not, in the physical circumstances of Virginia, have ridden the circuit to rouse volunteers, even assuming his character admitted such activity.

Perhaps he might have made more effective use of influential men in the counties. But more than likely the blame, if such it was, lay in that nebulous thing, the public, whose ardor had cooled remarkably after four years of war. "But tell me," Henry queried his successor, "do you remember any instance, where Tyranny was destroyed and Freedom established on its ruins among a people possessing so small a share of virtue and public spirit?" But Jefferson's faith in the people and their attachment to the Revolution would not permit him even to entertain Henry's question, much less answer it.

Neglect of the Continental Army was not peculiar to Virginia. In fact, her record bettered that of most states. So depleted were the ranks in the fall, 1779, Washington resorted to the detestable expedient of calling 12,000 militia from nearby states. By this time, too, more urgent demands upon Virginia came from the South. "We have at present very pressing calls to send additional numbers of men to the southward," Jefferson informed Washington. "No inclination is wanting in either the legislative or executive powers to aid them, or to strengthen you: but we find it very difficult to procure men." Within two weeks, on December 9, Washington ordered the 2000 troops of the Virginia Line at Morristown, under Brigadier General William Woodford, to march to the aid of beleaguered Charleston. The Governor had legislative authority to send southward 1500 militia and as many of the state troops as could be marched under the terms of their enlistments. The latter, several small cavalry troops and a depleted regiment of infantry, were reserved for the defense of the commonwealth; but when other measures failed Jefferson used the power delgated by the assembly. He did not at this juncture order any militia to South Carolina, a last recourse in any event, and with nearly all the state's regulars marching south and west (the regiment raised for Clark's campaign) it was painfully obvious that the militia was the sole reliance for the state's defense.

Jefferson seemed less alarmed by this prospect than some others in his administration. In November the Board of War advised the Governor to expect a visit from the British in the winter months and recommended a series of defense measures. Governor and Council immediately approved most of these. The executive was cool to a plan for concentrating arms and militia in the exposed eastern counties, however, and flatly rejected the Board's call for the appointment of a general officer to direct the state's defense. "Civil bodies tho [they] may dictate to, are illy calculated to direct military ones," the Board declared. "The vigor and dispatch, necessary to military movements, can only be derived from full powers concentrated in one man. . . ." While Jefferson appreciated the merit of this position, it was one his political convictions would not permit him to endorse. Irrespective of its merits, the executive had no authority to appoint a general officer until an invasion or insurrection actually occurred and forces of resistance were organized.

An invasion seemed imminent on December 22, when Jefferson received a report, transmitted by the governor of Maryland, of a British naval expedition to the Chesapeake. Confirming intelligence reached Williamsburg some days later. Writing from Morristown on December 11, Washington advised that a powerful naval force carrying 8000 troops was about to sail from New York: "Their destination *reported* to be for Chesapeake Bay, on a combined operation in the 1st. place against the French Squadron there, and afterwards to attempt the rescue of the Convention troops." On the first report, Jefferson ordered precautionary measures, unhappily aware, with the Board of War, "that no place is defensible against a considerable force of the enemy." Defensive works were thrown up at York and Portsmouth, military stores removed from this sector, the few regulars concentrated there, recruits forming for South Carolina detained, and the Conventioners readied to march over the Blue Ridge. Jefferson deferred an immediate call for militia, pending opinion of the assembly. The procedure was unusual, suggesting some indecisiveness on the Governor's part. But for him to have called the militia in force on the mere suspicion of an invasion, founded on the first fragmentary report, would also have been unusual. Moreover, he was keenly aware of the economy wave that had swept over the assembly and seriously cut back both the land and the naval forces of the state. In addition to the expense of militia service, he was mindful of "the difficulties which attend a general call of the militia in the field, the disgust it gives them more especially when they find no enemy in place, and the extreme rigor of the season." The assembly's advice, if any, is unrecorded, and it promptly adjourned on December 24. Jefferson called a few militia in the eastern counties in order, as he later said, "to convince the French of our disposition to protect their ships." For the rest, he quietly awaited the crisis. When it failed to materialize, his judgment was vindicated. Charleston, as he later learned and all along suspected, was the destination of Clinton's army. By the middle of January even "the most timid," he observed, had recovered from the panic, and the recruits marched southward.

Responsibility for the direction and disposition of Virginia's men and arms involved the Governor more or less constantly in decisions calling for the rapid assessment of numerous imponderables, for discerning judgment of military requirements and opportunities, and, above all, for an encompassing view of Virginia's commitments. These swept a wide arc from Charleston in the South, to the farthest reaches of the Ohio, and to the camps of the Continental Army in the East. Endeavoring always to employ Virginia's overtaxed resources in the best interest of the Continent, Jefferson was puzzled to determine where that interest lay from one crisis to the next. Nor could he forget his first obligation to defend the state's exposed frontiers. He had made the fateful decision, in which the legislature gave him little alternative, to risk the state's defense to the militia, whose "radical defects" he knew as well as anybody. But manpower was among the least of his problems. Men could not fight unless armed, equipped, clothed, and fed; and the pesky problems of supply were as stubborn as any he ever encountered.

The shortage of firearms caused genuine alarm in the summer of 1779. Returns from the state magazines showed at most 4000 stand of serviceable muskets. The invasion at Portsmouth had once again demonstrated that militiamen called from the field went home with their weapons. The stock was further depleted by arms furnished to the Virginia Line and to South Carolina. Rumors of invasion were afloat in the summer; and so when a vessel loaded with arms for delivery to Congress "seemed to be guided by the hand of providence into one of our harbors," the Council ordered the seizure of 5000 muskets for Virginia's use. Jefferson was absent at the time, but when Congress censured the action, he warmly defended it. Virginia could, he said, establish a right to 10,000 stand of arms freely furnished, with many other articles, to the Continent. In the distress then felt, the seizure was fully justified. "They were it's true the property of our friend, but of friends indebted to us for those very articles. They were for the common defence too, and we were a part of the body to be defended." The arrival from France of three vessels ladened with arms and military stores, the acquisitions of a resourceful commercial agent, replenished the state's stock in October. So rare was the safe conduct of any goods from Europe to the Chesapeake that Jefferson asked the assembly to award the agent, Jacques Le Maire, the brevet commission of lieutenant colonel. Meanwhile, his hopes for filling the arms gap by domestic manufacture were dashed by the failure of the contract with Penet, Windel & Company. Cannon, other ordnance, and military hardware were manufactured in modest quantities at Westham and Fredericksburg, and Jefferson gave these public works every assistance, including authorization for the purchase of Negro slaves to keep them in operation. But there were never enough arms.

Other shortages plagued the government in the autumn and winter. The late harvest was "the most unfavorable . . . ever known since the settlement of this Country," Jefferson said. The wheat crop gave little more than seed for the next planting, and Virginia went begging for flour to neighboring states she usually supplied. Maryland's executive approved the purchase of 2000 barrels of flour in that state, but before most of this could be forwarded, a new governor acting under a new statute seized the flour. Jefferson, considering the need desperate, protested the seizure. "Accustomed at all other times to furnish subsistence to others," he wrote, "it is the first instance where providence has exposed us to the necessity of asking leave to purchase it among our friends." But the seizure stood. A request to Congress for large quantities of flour to supply the Convention troops also failed. Still determined to alleviate the distressing shortage and the exorbitant prices of provisions, Jefferson proclaimed an embargo on export by land or water. He exercised judgment in its enforcement, however, approving trade in provisions that benefited the commonwealth. The British island of Bermuda, for example, depended on the United States for grain and gave precious salt in return. So precious, indeed, had salt become that it was rationed to families by county magistrates and could not be carried from one place to another except under bond. Without salt there could be no meat; and in order to obtain it Jefferson kept open the

Bermuda trade. Rum was an item almost as indispensable to armies as salt. The government endeavored to supply rum. Thinking it less than a prime necessity, Jefferson practiced restraint in this regard. The law required the Governor's approval of all purchase requisitions on the state's account; thus he was almost daily occupied in the tedious business of finding suppliers, comparing prices, estimating needs, making contracts, setting priorities, scrutinizing accounts, and —the worst of all his aggravations—paying the bills.

Financial deterioration, well under way when Jefferson became Governor, rapidly passed beyond recovery and left the state prostrate two years later. He at once saw the necessity of reducing the quantity of paper money in circulation. "Every other remedy is nonsensical quackery," he declared. He was a little inclined to look for fiscal scapegoats. "It is a cruel thought that when we feel ourselves standing on the firmest ground in every respect," he wrote to Richard Henry Lee, "the cursed arts of our secret enemies combining with other causes, should effect, by depreciating our money, what the open arms of a powerful enemy could not." No doubt there were such enemies—the avaricious and the speculators, the faint-hearted and the weak-headed—but Virginia's financial plight did not require their efforts. When the returns of the tobacco trade declined, when foreign loans failed to materialize, and revenue from the confiscation and land office acts fell so far below expectations, Jefferson was put at wits' end to devise other means of bolstering the state's finances. On no other subject did he defer so entirely to the assembly. The Revolution was partially staked on the principle of "fiscal liberty," and Jefferson had no desire to contradict it by entering the most jealously guarded of all the areas of legislative jurisdiction. Unfortunately, the assembly's only wisdom, aside from sudden bursts of frugality such as reduced the state's land and sea forces in the fall of 1779, was to increase taxes and speed up the printing presses. Fresh additions to the government's revenue were promptly wiped out by inflation. Public creditors declined to pay taxes because their bills had not been paid; the government could not pay its debts with the promptness the inflationary spiral required because citizens were delinquent in their taxes. And so the vicious circle went, gathering momentum from one session of the assembly to the next. The depleted treasury, as Jefferson observed during the December crisis, "presented an absolute obstacle to every military endeavor." It was his responsibility to enforce the revenue laws. For assistance where it counted, at the local level, he depended on the county governments, which were slow and stubborn. In this area, as in others, he governed with a gentle hand, believing that the good citizenry with burdens enough already would not endure a harsh one.

The deterioration of both state and Continental currencies led Congress to adopt drastic measures of reform early in 1780. The first of these, in February, assigned to each state a quota of supplies to be collected and delivered for the Continental Army. Thus Virginia was to supply so much corn, hay, flour, and rum. The state, in return, was forgiven two-thirds of the money she had previously been asked to raise monthly. The plan substituted supplies in kind for drafts of money to supply the army. The second resolution of March 18, projecting a "new plan of finance," was a companion of the first. The states were to retire the depreciated Continental currency by means of tax collections payable at the rate of 40 "continentals" to one dollar in coin. For each $20 of the old money thus collected the state could then issue one dollar of new, which Congress pledged to redeem in coin after five years. Meanwhile, Congress would print no money, relying on state supplies. Obviously, the plan required the full co-operation of the states. Since the two currencies circulated on an equal basis, state bills as well as Continental had to be retired. It was a hazardous experiment. James Madison, who had just taken a Virginia seat in Congress, summed up the situation: "An old system of finance discarded as incompetent to our necessities, an untried and precarious one substituted and a total stagnation in prospect between the end of the former and the operation of the latter." Madison favored the plan but was apprehensive for its success and deeply troubled by Congress' surrender of the one real power it had over its own affairs. So long as Congress exercised the power of issuing currency, the government had a margin of independence from the states. Now, as Madison explained to Jefferson, that was gone. "Since the resolution passed for shutting the press, this power has been entirely given up and they [Congress] are now as dependent on the States as the King of England is on the Parliament. They can neither enlist pay nor feed a single soldier, nor execute any other purpose but as the means are first put into their hands." Unless the states rose to the occasion, the tottering edifice of Union would fall in ruins.

Jefferson, too, was apprehensive. "The period . . . which will intervene between abolishing the old and establishing a new system of finance, will be distressing to the last degree," he observed. In the House of Delegates the plan met with strong opposition led by Patrick Henry, now back in harness. It was "repudiation," Henry charged. Under his influence the House defeated implementing legislation. But after he took leave of the assembly, the bill was revived and passed by a small margin, with the condition that its operation be suspended until a majority of the states enacted similar legislation. The condition was satisfied, as Jefferson had hoped, before the enemies of the plan could overturn it at the fall session. Unfortunately, it did not abate the twin evils of inflation and depreciation in Virginia. In order to see the government through the transition period, the assembly authorized another large issue of the old currency, thus at once cheapening the new. Balances still owed to Congress continued to drain the treasury. In May Congress urged payment in the amount of $1,900,000 so that the Army might be put on a footing to co-operate with the French forces soon to arrive. Jefferson made strenuous efforts to comply and by June 30 had scraped together nearly three-quarters of the total. As Madison had predicted, since the ability of the people to pay taxes derived from the sale of their commodities, the requisition of the latter made the former more difficult than before.

Virginia was already launched on the experiment of taxation in kind. The Provision Law enacted by the General Assembly in May 1779 assessed every white male of sixteen years of age or older and every female slave of like age the annual payment of one bushel of wheat, the equivalent in other grain, or twenty-eight pounds of tobacco. The repugnance of the tax, combined with problems of collection and storage and transfer, made the law, with its successors, an administrative nightmare. Jefferson probably did not welcome Congress' resort to the same expedient, though it sharply reduced Virginia's dollar payments. The state's compliance with the supply requisitions of Congress necessitated new executive powers. The assembly authorized the Governor to appoint commissioners in the counties to search out and purchase provisions at stipulated prices. The commissioners might break down doors, exact penalties for hoarding, and seize supplies. They were to hire, and if need be seize, wagons, boats, and men for transporting provisions. Congress left the states to struggle as best they could with the problem of moving the supplies to the armies. In Virginia it proved to be a task of Sisyphus. Jefferson assured Congress of "the strongest disposition" to contribute the quotas assigned but, though provisions were collected, he could not promise their delivery. "Transportation by land has been little practiced in this country. We have therefore few wagons, and a great part of these have been lately drawn to the southward. Transportation by water has been cut off for some time by the privateers which have been constantly cruising in our bay. . . . To them are added at present eight [enemy] frigates . . . In this situation nothing can venture out of our rivers." Some weeks later, on July 27, Jefferson was unable to say precisely what part of the quotas had been furnished, but he confessed disappointment at the state's performance.

Men, money, supplies: these were the items of account with the Continent. After summarizing the state of the account for the President of Congress in July 1780, Jefferson reflected on the circumstances that had prevented full and timely compliance. "It will doubtless occur," he wrote, "that some of these requisitions were difficult in their nature, that others were new in experiment, and all of them on as large a scale as the people think themselves equal to. In states more compact, experiments, tho' new, and difficult, are made with promptitude, their defects soon discovered and readily supplied. In those of greater extent they are carried into execution with less vigor and punctuality, and the time for complying with a requisition expires frequently before it is discovered that the means provided were defective. The time necessary for convening the legislature of such a state adds to the tardiness of the remedy, and the measure itself is so oppppressive on the members as to discourage the attempting it, but on the last emergencies." Perhaps he was too much inclined to find fault with circumstances; but he spoke from hard experience and what he said was undeniably true.

While the Governor labored at these tasks in the early months of 1780, the British to the south grew stronger and still other enemies threatened in the southwestern part of the state. Indians of the Cherokee nation lived in settlements stretching for hundreds of miles along the Virginia and Carolina backcountry. Most of the Cherokees were "friendly," as a result of treaties forced upon them in 1777. Others withdrew to the Chickamauga River where, under the haughty chief Dragging Canoe, they started new towns, and assisted from the British posts in Florida, took to the warpath. They were badly punished by a joint expedition of North Carolina and Virginia in the spring of 1779, but violence flared again a year later. Jefferson ordered an expedition under the command of William Campbell to attack the hostile towns, and at the same time asked Clark's co-operation from Kentucky. Well aware of the frontiersmen's aversion to all Indians—"the only good Indian is a dead Indian"—Jefferson was anxious to protect the friendly Cherokees from harm. The state incurred much trouble and expense to supply them with clothing, liquor, and other scarce necessities. "Their present distresses are so great," Jefferson said, "that we have bought up every thing proper for them in our own country without regard to price." By purchasing their friendship, he hoped to defeat the machinations of British agents. He urged the same policy on the governors of the Carolinas. "The attachment which each settlement will by these means acquire to the particular state under whose patronage it is, perhaps will be a bond of peace, and will lead to a separation of that powerful people." Divide and rule, aid the friendly in peace, exterminate the incorrigibles—this was Jefferson's Indian policy. And in 1780 he wanted by every means possible to minimize the costly diversion of Virginia's manpower to Indian warfare. He was but partially successful. Before the attack on the Chickamaugas could be carried out, British agents prevailed on the chiefs of the old towns to resume their war-like ways. Retaliation was swift, as Virginia and Carolina backwoodsmen destroyed the towns in December 1780. Thereafter the danger lessened, but it was not extinguished.

More dangerous was the spirit of disaffection and insurgency that erupted in the southwest at this time. "Nothing can produce so dangerous a diversion of our force, as a circumstance of that kind if not crushed in its infancy," Jefferson wrote to Clark in the spring. Trouble had flared in the area before, but it now assumed a threatening aspect from the progress of British arms in the South, which rallied the disaffected and raised the prospect of Tory uprisings along a wide front. The disturbances centered in Montgomery County, whence came the lead for the bullets of American guns. William Preston, head of the Montgomery militia, alerted Jefferson to the conspiracy. As many as fifteen of the insurgents were operating under British commission, he said. Their principal object was the lead mines. Jefferson commended Preston for the measures he had already taken to capture the ringleaders, urged him to employ only legal means, and suggested he call new recruits from the vicinity to guard the mines. By July, however, the conspiracy had spread to several neighboring counties. Jefferson now ordered Campbell to forget the Chickamauga for the present and combine his force with the militia Preston had summoned to "take in hand these parricides." The border captains sent spies among the conspirators, discovered the plot before it could be sprung, and took captive about 60 men. Jefferson advised leniency toward the small offenders, if repentant, and prosecution of the ringleaders for high treason. He had nothing further to do with the proceedings in the case, which were sufficiently notorious to enrich the language with the euphemism "lynch law," derived from Charles Lynch, manager of the lead mines, who took a leading part, and also to cause the legislature later to pass an act of immunity for Lynch, Preston, and others who had suppressed the insurrection. An open insurrection, which must have been very damaging at that place at that time, was thus averted at a heavy price. The discontents that fed insurgency increased with the war's hardships until they became a factor in all of Jefferson's calculations.

Three days after he commenced his second term in office, Jefferson learned of the fall of Charleston to Clinton's army. The disaster, which actually occurred on May 12, was not unexpected, but coming on top of a mountain of troubles, and after he had strained every resource to help the city, he found it the least welcome event of the war. Public morale fell to a new low. The people grumbled at taxes and inflation, suspected everyone of growing rich but themselves, and in the spring elections exchanged many delegates of rank and experience for new men promising better things. The government was still recovering from the upset of its removal to Richmond. The boards of war and trade, handicapped by the move, ceased functioning in April. The General Assembly at its May session formally abolished these administrative monstrosities and, "for conducting the public business with the greatest expedition," authorized the Governor to appoint a commercial agent, a commissioner of the navy, and a comissioner of the war office. By other acts as well, the legislature seemed impressed with the need to strengthen and streamline the executive. It stiffend the Governor's powers to procure and transport provisions, authorized him to restore the navy it had dismantled six months before, and gave him a number of "extraordinary powers" in case of invasion or insurrection. While encouraged by these measures, Jefferson was disappointed by the failure of the legislature to meet the full request of Congress for militia and regulars to join the Southern Army.

The surrender of Charleston swallowed up nearly the whole of the Virginia Line. "There is really nothing to oppose the progress of the enemy northward but the cautious principles of the military art," Jefferson advised the commander in chief. Before the end of May, General Cornwallis crossed the Santee River with an army of 4000 men, steadily augmented as it advanced by recruits among the native inhabitants, who were the more susceptible to British intimidation as the hopes of American arms faded. North Carolina had neither the guns to arm nor the food to subsist its militia in the field. Jefferson concentrated his efforts, first, on forwarding the Continental troops of Maryland and Delaware detained on their march to Charleston, fortunately as it turned out, for want of wagons; and second, on assembling the force of 2500 militia that the legislature had now authorized for service in the Carolinas. On June 11 Jefferson informed Washington that the total force "in and about to be in motion" to oppose Cornwallis numbered 10,000 men; but the bulk of it was raw Virginia and North Carolina militia deplorably armed and accoutered. "Your Excellency will readily conceive that after the loss of one army our eyes are turned towards the other, and that we comfort ourselves that if any aids can be furnished by you without defeating operations more beneficial to the general union, they will be furnished." But this was poor comfort indeed. Congress could send no more than token assistance southward, and Washington dared not risk the further depletion of his army in the North. Later in the month, when Clinton returned to New York, Jefferson perceived Washington's embarrassment, "being situated between two fires," unable to attend to the new one in the South lest the old and still larger one in the North escape control. It became painfully evident that Virginia must shoulder the burden of southern defense.

The fact that Charleston was in enemy hands twenty-four days before news of the event reached Richmond pointed up the seriousness of the communications gap. Jefferson had already set up a team of express riders, stationed at intervals between the Virginia capes and Richmond, to speed intelligence of the long awaited arrival of the French fleet. (As it happened, on July 11, the fleet sailed into Rhode Island rather than Virginia.) The lamentable delay and unreliability of intelligence from the southward suggested the same remedy on a larger scale. To gather and transmit proper information from the vicinity of the enemy camps, Jefferson sought a sensible and judicious person with some knowledge of military affairs. He turned to a young acquaintance, James Monroe, who had served bravely and well in the Continental Army, left it for mysterious reasons, and then, after a period of deep perplexity and despair, commenced the study of law under Jefferson's tutelage. Believe me, Monroe wrote to him some months later, "I feel that whatever I am at present in the opinion of others or whatever I may be in future has greatly arose from your friendship." Jefferson's offer of a confidential mission precisely suited to his young protégé's talents and ambitions strengthened the bond between them, and thus had a significance far outrunning the mission itself. Jefferson directed Monroe to proceed southward from Richmond, stationing riders at forty-mile intervals to the vicinity of Cornwallis's army, from thence transmitting anything of military import, and opening channels of communication to commanders in the field and heads of government. At the same time, he arranged with Congress for the northern extension of the express line to Philadelphia. Monroe's first dispatch reached Richmond within forty-eight hours, which clipped five days off the time normally required by the post. Riders were sometimes negligent to the point of treachery, and commanders in the field unco-operative, but the express line largely fulfilled Jefferson's expectations. Congress was grateful for his innovation, and at the end of June undertook to maintain the full line at the expense of the Continent.

Unfortunately, no good tidings came from the South. Congress placed General Horatio Gates, the somewhat tarnished hero of Saratoga, in command of the Southern Army. Soon after arriving at headquarters the middle of July, he reported that the condition of the army was even more distressing than Jefferson had led him to expect. Only 1500 of the promised Virginia militia were on the scene; many were without arms, tents, and other necessities; all were obliged to forage for food. Jefferson attended to Gates's needs as best he could and congratulated him for advancing on the enemy. But the advance was more daring then wise. With a ragged and untried army numbering about 3000 men, Gates encountered Cornwallis at Camden on August 16, and was utterly crushed. One-third of the Americans were killed, another third captured, and the remainder, Gates at their head, fled in wild disorder. A more complete defeat could hardly be imagined. Jefferson was particularly disheartened by the behavior of the Virginia militia, as reported in vivid detail by its commanding officer, General Edward Stevens. On first fire the enemy charged with bayonets; the militia panicked and ran like a torrent, bearing all before them. "Their cowardly behavior has indeed given a mortal wound to my feelings," Stevens said. "I expect that near one half of the Militia will never halt till they get home." Stevens's mortification deepened when the stragglers, after being rounded up and ordered forward again, deserted in great number, as if to prove "they never had any intention of rendering their Country service." Jefferson refused to lose heart. "Instead of considering what is past . . . ," he philosophized to Stevens, "we are to look forward and prepare for the future."

In this spirit he returned to the arduous task of rebuilding the Southern Army. Fully realizing the difficulty of stopping the enemy in North Carolina, he knew it would be infinitely more difficult, and painful, to wage the combat on Virginia soil. Determined to act with all the vigor the laws permitted, he ordered the impressment of provisions, wagons, and other essentials; he pleaded with county lieutenants to arrest militia deserters, try them at court-martial, and exact the legal penalty of eight months' duty as regular soldiers; and he called for 2000 militia reinforcements to march south with new levies of Continental troops at the earliest opportunity. Jefferson told Washington nearly 7000 regulars and militia had been ordered from Virginia. But this was on paper. The number who actually marched fell well below the 5500 Jefferson, with his usual optimism, had counted on. Even so, many of the Virginians went south in an atrocious condition, and logistical support was as precarious as ever despite resourceful measures to overcome the bottleneck in transportation. "Sickness, Death, and Desertion," Gates repeatedly warned, "must certainly be the dire result of sending troops into the field" so badly equipped. "I must beg Sir this may be seriously consider'd by the Executive, whom I must request, will not send any men into the field, or even to this camp, that are not sufficiently clad, well furnished with shoes, blankets, and every necessary for immediate service, as I have not a single article here to supply them with." Jefferson patiently replied that adherence to this rule "would amount to a stoppage of every man." If the General wanted soldiers he would have to take them raw and ragged. Gates did not blame Jefferson for the situation; in fact, he thanked him for the "great care and assiduity" he showed. It was difficult to know who to blame. Jefferson refrained from blaming anyone. He sent the troops on, meanwhile trusting that Congress would eventually respond to his pleas for support.

For the rest, good news mixed with bad. At the beginning of October he cheered Clark's devastating blow to the Indians on the Ohio and, a few days later, the backwoodsmen's gallant victory over a joint force of British and Loyalists at King's Mountain, which aroused the flagging patriotism of North Carolina and sent Cornwallis hustling to safe quarters. Encouraged by Clark's success, Jefferson turned his thoughts once again to the long-deferred campaign against Detroit. To the south, time, at least, had been gained. But what of the eastern frontier? In September Gates had forwarded intelligence obtained from British deserters of a plan concerted between Cornwallis and Clinton to invade Portsmouth. Jefferson thought it most unlikely Clinton would provide the men for such an expedition, especially when the French could send a superior fleet to the Chesapeake; but he at once transmitted the report to Congress, observing that should the enemy "in this, as in so many other instances, go directly contrary to the principles of reason, they would find us in a condition incapable of resistance for want of small arms." Reason being a poor reliance in warfare, he would have felt more secure had the French fleet decided to pass the winter in the Chesapeake. But Washington, to whom he made this suggestion, assured him it was impossible: the enemy had blocked up the fleet at Newport since its arrival and, contrary to the Governor's opinion, continued its superior. Meanwhile, Washington informed him of an embarkation preparing in New York and bound, it was thought, either for Virginia or the Carolinas. Jefferson felt no more alarm at this report than at Gates's earlier one. He still thought an invasion improbable; if attempted, nothing could stop it, so he took no precautionary measures, except to employ an engineer attached to the Southern Army, Colonel John Christian Senf, in the long-term project of surveying the country of the lower James with a view to improving defensive capabilities there.

Senf was well along in this work when, on October 20, an enemy fleet stood in for Cape Henry, and during the next two or three days discharged its force of infantry and horse, commanded by Major General Alexander Leslie, on either side of the James River estuary. The army was first thought to number 5000 men, about twice its actual size. Jefferson learned of the invasion from General Thomas Nelson, who commanded a tiny corps of Virginia regulars on the lower James. "I hope you will lose no time in ordering a body of men down, that we may at least attempt an opposition," he pleaded. "I shall endeavour to collect a force from these counties, but the confusion is so great that much cannot be expected . . . . I never was in so bad a part of the Country for intelligence. The enemy might have secured every pass before I had any account of their landing." On receiving this report, which accurately conveyed the defenseless and bewildered state of the invaded country, Jefferson roughed out a breathless agenda of executive action: "Call on Lawson's troop of horse. . . . Call 10,000 troops. viz. . . . . Stop troops going on to Southward . . . Call vessels and stores from Ship yard . . . Provide batteaux at Foundry . . . Order away Conventioners . . . Beeves from Warm Springs come to Barracks . . . Officers . . . . Commrs. of provision law . . . Stores etc. at Wmsburg . . . Write to General Nelson Gates Congress. . . ." Obviously, Jefferson assumed the enemy would move up the James. Great numbers of militia were called, but his main reliance was on the militia and regulars already assembled and destined for the Southern Army. They were reluctantly, and temporarily, diverted to the task of driving the invaders back to their ships. "On this contemptible naval force," Jefferson wrote, "hangs the fate of an army; and yet contemptible as it is . . . it does not appear to be in danger."

While the enemy was thus unchallenged at sea, the want of arms, also of cavalry, checked effective opposition on land. Because the Convention troops furnished "perpetual fuel to that smothered fire," disaffection, and now a tempting object to the invasion army, Jefferson sought their removal to Maryland. (Only the more dangerous British troops were actually moved at this time.) As October gave way to November, no encounter, no action of any consequence occurred. The plains of Virginia spread like a brown carpet before the redcoats, but they showed no appetite for conquest and settled instead at Portsmouth. "Their movements have been truly incomprehensible," Jefferson noted with a trace of exasperation. "I rather believe that Lord Cornwallis had expected to have been in this state at this time, that they were intended to join him here; that his precipitate flight has left them without an object, and that they wait for further orders." Events soon verified Jefferson's hunch. Clinton had sent the expedition to the Chesapeake with the intention of establishing a permanent post, creating a diversion in favor of Cornwallis, disrupting the Virginia supply lines to the Southern Army, and rallying the disaffected on the lower James. But when Leslie learned of Cornwallis's retreat after the crippling blow at King's Mountain, he sent south for further orders. When they arrived about the middle of November, he embarked his whole force for Charleston. "But this is an end of all golden dreams in Chesapeake," Clinton sighed in New York.

Leslie's abortive expedition proved either the soundness of Jefferson's military sense or the weakness of the enemy's in the fall of 1780, but he took no comfort from this. It once again exhibited the defenseless state of the tidewater country, which the British could exploit at their convenience. With Leslie's departure the Governor returned to the principal business of reinforcing the Southern Army. As he did so, he gave the General Assembly a shrewd estimate of military prospects. "This event tho' relieving us in a certain degree by opening again the door to our commerce and also by putting it in our power to avail ourselves of the whole resources of our country, seems yet to call for an increase rather than abatement of military preparation," he said. "Should those now leaving us proceed to reinforce the hostile army already in the south: should the same be the object of a new embarcation said on good authority to be preparing in New York; we shall but too probably and speedily see our retreating enemy treading back their footsteps and menacing this country with a force to which the southern states have yet seen nothing equal. South Carolina and Georgia we are to consider as weighing nothing in our scale. North Carolina has been exhausted by the ravages of two armies. On this state therefore rests the weight of the opposition; and it is infinitely important that our efforts be such as to keep the war from our own country. Nor does it seem that we have a moment to lose, should the enemy be disposed to lose no time on their part." He concluded by asking the legislature for additional powers to procure supplies and transport, the money "to set every wheel in motion," and "men to form a permanent army."

The past several months had been wearisome to the last degree, and the months ahead promised to be worse. Since the Battle of Camden, Jefferson had been riveted to his desk, immersed in a thousand details that held no real interst for him, making plans and issuing orders that all too often crumbled at the touch of immitigable circumstance. He was uncomplaining. His sense of duty and devotion to the cause ensured that. But he felt keenly the impoverishment of his private life. He last visited Monticello in August. It was probably on that summer holiday, so harshly interrupted by the news of Camden, that he planned an ingenious contrivance for his house. "In his parlour," wrote one of the German officers, "he is creating on the ceiling a compass of his own invention by which he can know the strength as well as direction of the winds." But this was a rare pleasure. During the entire length of his governorship, Jefferson wrote scarcely a letter in which he permitted himself to indulge his curiosity on literary, scientific, and artistic subjects. He was all business. Anything in the course of executive business that awakened his slumbering intellectual interests—the running of a boundary line according to celestial observation, planning the government buildings at Richmond, securing Indian artifacts and records, purchasing for the state Diderot's *Encyclopédie*—gave him special delight. These were only crumbs from the executive table. In November a Virginia delegate to Congress placed in the Governor's hands an elaborate series of questions concerning the state of Virginia which François Marbois, secretary to the French minister, desired to have answered. "I am at present busily employed for Mons. Marbois without his knowing it," he was soon writing, "and have to acknowledge to him the mysterious obligation for making me much better acquainted with my own country than I ever was before." However, neither the leisure nor the requisite books were available to him in Richmond. He set the work aside until his retirement.

By September, not long after his last holiday at Monticello, he had decided to retire from office at the earliest opportunity. Confiding this decision to Lee, he wrote, "The application requisite to the duties of the office I hold is so excessive, and the execution of them after all so imperfect, that I have determined to retire from it at the close of the present campaign. I wish a successor to be thought of in time who to sound whiggism can join perserverence in business, and an extensive knowledge of the various subjects he must superintend. Such a one may keep us above water even in our present moneyless situation." What he meant by "the close of the present campaign" remains to conjecture. He presumably did not mean the expiration of his term of office, which ran to June, and of course he was eligible for a third term. At about the same time, he informed Page of his decision and suggested that he succeed him. Page flatly rejected the idea but could not persuade Jefferson to drop his plan. Hearing reports of it again in December, Page humored his old friend and beseeched him to stay on, not just for six months but for eighteen. "I know your love of study and retirement must strongly solicit you to leave the hurry, bustle, and nonsense your station daily exposes you to," Page wrote. "I know too the many mortifications you must meet with, but 18 months will soon pass away. Deny yourself your darling pleasures for that space of time, and despise not only now, but forever, the impertinence of the silly world." No one, unless possibly Lee, who was unpopular, was as eminently qualified for the office as he, nor was this merely a personal opinion, Page assured Jefferson. Whatever his reasons may have been, Jefferson dropped any thought of retiring in midstream and grimly resolved to stay on the job until June 1781.

Invasion

The new year began ominously. The traitor Benedict Arnold invaded the state from the coast, slashed through the low country, spreading panic as he went, and put the government itself to flight. It was a crippling blow to Virginia's morale. Some glittering military exploit was needed to revive it. Jefferson sorely taxed himself and the resources of the state in an effort to capture the perfidious author of Virginia's humiliation. All to no avail. He did not lose heart, but the fates seemed to have spiked all his guns. Even his little successes wore the face of disaster. As the energy of government increased, the more ineffectual it became, until it appeared to collapse altogether. In May, Cornwallis administered the last stroke in a long train of misfortune. The British army overran Virginia, and as if to add a crowning touch chased Jefferson within an inch of his life from Monticello, whither he had gone to escape "the impertinence of the silly world."

Leslie's expedition had in no way altered Jefferson's determination to combat the enemy outside of Virginia's borders. The state should be the arsenal, not the battleground, of the Southern Army. In this view he was encouraged by Congress, by Washington, and the commanders in the South. One of Washington's most trusted officers, General Nathaniel Greene, had been appointed to relieve Gates, who left the remnants of his military reputation at Camden. On November 16, Greene arrived in Richmond accompanied by "the Baron" Frederick William von Steuben, Inspector General of the Continental Army, assigned now to Greene's staff and ordered by him to command in Virginia "to put things in the most proper train for forwarding the reinforcements of men, and supplies of every kind to the Southern Army."

Greene and Steuben were two of the ablest officers on the Continent. Their assignment to the southern theater suggested that it was at last receiving the attention Jefferson had claimed for it. He welcomed them with the utmost cordiality and good will. Greene, a Yankee humbly born, corpulent, squint-eyed, lamed in one leg, and cocksure in his thirty-eighth year, had risen to great heights since that fateful day in 1775 when he marched the Rhode Island militia to Boston. Steuben, the Prussian drillmaster, was older than his friend, stocky in build, haughty in bearing, with soft lips, piercing dark eyes, and hair dressed in a slender queue after the manner of his former master and hero Frederick the Great. He had come to America in search of military glory, and after a period of three years spent in disciplining Washington's troops found himself, to his enormous satisfaction, one of the half-dozen top generals in rank. How little Jefferson understood either of these men, or they him, as they sat at the Council table in November! Remarkably different though they were, the two generals had much in common. In their inglorious staff positions under Washington, Greene as Quartermaster General, Steuben as Inspector General, both had aspired to line command. They prided themselves on being students of the military arts. In these matters they thought alike and had unshakable confidence in each other. Neither had any acquaintance with the southern country, so little suited to conventional rules and tactics, and they were quick to find fault with the government of Virginia. It is notable that Jefferson, despite much provocation, never found fault with either of them but, on the contrary, went out of his way to praise their talents and enterprise. He saw no more of Greene after he presented his requisition for the Southern Army and rode south to assume command. Steuben remained behind, dishing up to Virginians his "plate of *sauerkraut* dressed in the Prussian style" and hoping to prove to them, as he had earlier in the North, "by the force of 'God damns' that my cookery was the best."

Jefferson turned at once to the business of filling Greene's requisition. The assembly responded well to his appeal for an acceleration of military effort. That "last of all opppressions," in Jefferson's opinion, a draft, previously a punitive measure only, was authorized. Three thousand recruits enlisted for three years would hopefully complete the state's quota, however. Additional taxes were voted to pay the bounties; also, stiffer penalties for desertion and the harboring of deserters. Clothing, provisions, and wagons were to be obtained by a combination of purchase and levies on the citizenry. And the treasurer was empowered to emit an additional six million pounds in paper money. Jefferson seemed confident the executive could now meet Greene's requests on every article but that of guns. The state had attempted to arm its militia when necessary, he explained to Steuben, but Congress was responsible for arming Continental troops. If Jefferson wanted any instruction in the horrible poverty of the Southern Army, he received it in a typically lofty letter from Greene, expressing his shock at the wretched condition of the troops he had come to command. "Your troops may literally be said to be naked, and I shall be obliged to send a considerable number of them away into some secure place and warm quarters, until they can be furnished with clothing. . . . There must be either pride or principle to make a soldier. No man will think himself bound to fight the battles of a State that leaves him to perish for want of covering; nor can you inspire a soldier with the sentiment of pride whilst his situation renders him more object of pity than envy." A year earlier the Governor might have needed this sermon, but not now.

Steuben, meanwhile, hurried up reinforcements to Greene. There was no cause, he advised the Governor at the outset, to keep corps of regulars in the state, where no enemy was to be seen, nor bodies of militia that exhausted the state's magazines. All troops not destined for the Southern Army should be discharged, Steuben said; and this was promptly done. Complaining alternately of the insufficiency of the troops authorized and the poor provision of those actually raised, the Baron had great difficulty readying even a small detachment for the march. The executive must understand, he lectured, "the inhumanity of enlisting men and letting them die by inches." Too many of the recruits sent down from the counties were totally unfit, being decrepit old men or mere striplings. The recruiting system had operated on the principle of filling quotas rather than of furnishing fit soldiers. Some men made a profession of enlisting, pocketing the bounty, deserting, then enlisting again—an evil compounded by the assembly's fondness for short enlistments. Jefferson assisted the Baron in his attack on these abuses, but rot had sunk so deep into the system that measures to eradicate it produced costly delay and downright resistance. In other branches of military activity as well, Steuben took some of the burden off Jefferson's shoulders. With the help of his experience and forthright example, the executive set about to reform the war administration, eliminating waste and inefficiency, removing official deadwood, and appointing new and able officers to key posts. Unfortunately, no sooner had this work begun than Arnold's invasion threw everything into confusion.

Jefferson was forewarned of a possible invasion. On December 9,

Washington briefly mentioned at the end of a long letter, "I am at this moment informed from New York, another embarkation is taking place . . . supposed to be destined Southward." Steuben received the same intelligence, so similar to other reports in the previous weeks. Neither he nor Jefferson paid much attention to it. Preoccupied with the effort to support Greene, they resented any diversion to local defense. Had the Governor supposed Virginia threatened on every word of an enemy embarkation conjectured for the South, he would have had the militia constantly in the field, with disastrous results for the Southern Army.

In the present instance, the next news reached the Governor on a mild Sunday morning, the last day of the year. Twenty-seven sail of ships had been sighted entering the Virginia capes. Whether friend or foe, what force the ships carried, and what their destination might be—these things were as yet unknown. Jefferson ordered General Nelson to the lower country armed with full powers to act as exigencies should require. He informed Steuben and Benjamin Harrison, Speaker of the House, and, for the rest, awaited further information. None came until the following Tuesday morning: the fleet was British and it had advanced to near Jamestown. "From a fatal inattention to the giving us due notice of the arrival of a hostile force," he later reflected, "two days were completely lost in calling together the Militia." Always placing a high value on prompt intelligence, so singularly lacking in his crisis, he rightly emphasized the costliness of the delay; yet he might have posted the enemy's movements more carefully and made more efficient use of the intelligence he did receive.

In any event, he wasted no time on the 2nd of January. The Council met. Forty-six hundred militia were called into the field. Orders issued for removing official records and military stores to Westham, a few miles above the falls. And preparations were made for marching the remainder of the Convention troops across the Blue Ridge. The second and third of these measures were precautionary. Williamsburg was then believed to be the enemy's object. Taking full advantage of wind and tide, however, Arnold swiftly sailed up the river, destroyed the battery at Hood's intended to guard the upper James, and landed a force of 1500 at Westover, on the river's north shore where it bends toward Richmond. Jefferson was stunned. Even the elements had conspired with the enemy! "Winds favoring them in a remarkable degree," he remarked, "they almost brought the first news themselves of their movements." Richmond was the enemy's object. He ordered out the militia of the adjacent counties and asked Steuben to take command of the citizen army tumbling from the countryside to repel the invaders.

But not tumbling fast enough. On the 4th of January, two days after the first orders, only scattered militia were on the road to Richmond—more scattered at the redcoats' approach—and only 200 were in the town. The place was indefensible. Jefferson sent his wife and daughters to Tuckahoe, and at seven-thirty in the evening, as cannon announced the enemy, took his own solitary leave of the capital. He rode on horseback, was constantly active, yet managed to keep a record of his movements on scraps of paper taken out of his pocket at moments of rest. He went to Westham, stopping first at the foundry a mile below, to see that the records, arms, and stores earlier directed to these places were sent across the river. Mounting again about midnight, he rode another eight miles to Tuckahoe to look after his family. Early the next moring he returned to Westham, later crossed the river to Manchester, and there had a view of the enemy on the heights of Richmond. During the preceding eighteen hours, attending chiefly to the safety of records and stores, he had never been far in advance of the enemy. From Richmond, Arnold sent a detachment to Westham in search of stores; finding none, the troop succeeded in destroying the cannon foundry nearby. Jefferson, meanwhile, set out in futile search of Steuben. Riding up and down for two days—one horse had aready collapsed under him—he finally returned to Manchester through drenching rains and over heavy roads. Steuben was attempting to marshal the militia on the south side of the James, but the utmost confusion prevailed. He knew nothing of Nelson's movements on the opposite side, had the services neither of quartermaster nor of commissary, had exhausted his supply of arms on the militia coming in, and was frantic to discover the whereabouts of arms and stores sent off in several directions.

From the occupied capital Arnold sent a deputation to Jefferson proposing a ransom for its safety. He rejected it, of course. Arnold had neither the intention nor the capability of holding the town;

and after twenty-four hours, during which some houses and stores were burned, he retraced his steps to Westover. When Arnold reached there on the 7th he had completed a circuit of sixty-six miles in little more than two days and inflicted heavy damage at no expense to himself. At Westover he was reinforced by 400 troops whose transports had been separated from the main squadron off the capes. But by this time an equal force of Virginia militia was marshaled against him, and the fateful winds still blew from the east. Steuben's vigilance prevented the enemy from crossing the river. "Should they loiter a little longer and he be able to have a sufficient force," Jefferson informed Washington on the 10th, "I shall flatter myself they will not escape with total impunity." Almost at the moment of his writing, the enemy embarked on a fresh westerly wind, beating Steuben to Hood's where he had hoped to be ready for them. Informed of Steuben's approach, Arnold landed his army in the night and sent forward a detachment of 300 men. It encountered an advance party of 240 militia commanded by Colonel Clark, who had come to Richmond several weeks earlier to plan the next summer campaign in the West. Firing from ambush, Clark's men killed or wounded perhaps as many as thirty of the redcoats before fleeing from their bayonets. The next day Arnold made good his retreat down the river, landed on the 14th, and after collecting provisions around Pagan Creek marched to Portsmouth and rapidly covered himself behind barricades on the spot Leslie had abandoned.

Little ammunition had been spent or blood spilled on either side. Arnold's mission was the same as Leslie's earlier. And so far as it aimed at destroying stores and disrupting support of the Southern Army, his raid was a *tour de force*. After his return to Richmond, Jefferson gave Washington a full account of the physical damage: 300 muskets, some artillery pieces, and several tons of powder lost; quantities of clothing, artisans' tools, quartermaster's stores, including 120 sides of leather, destroyed; the boring mill and roof of the foundry consumed, but furnaces and chimneys secure; and the greater part of the papers of the Auditor and the Council of State gone. "Within less than 48 hours from the time of their landing and 19 from our knowing their destination they had penetrated 33 miles, done the whole injury and retired," he said. That the loss of records and stores was not greater was largely owing to Jefferson's diligence. But far greater were the damages that eluded his precise methods of accounting. Arnold succeeded in creating a diversion in favor of Cornwallis. Jefferson understood this, but unless he ignored the invasion, as he told Greene, he could not defeat the object. "When they came we were getting in a fair way of providing both subsistence and men. They have amazingly interrupted both operations." The militia ravenously consumed the provisions collected for Greene, tied up the meager facilities of the quartermaster, and so long as they were in the field, stopped the execution of the law for raising regular troops. Government was discredited by the invasion. Charges of supineness and neglect fell all around the Governor. Arnold's injury to the state's morale was quite incalculable. It was not so much the damage he did that hurt as it was the state's helplessness to return the blow. This slashed the tender nerve of Virginia pride, and the wound cut all the deeper because its author was the notorious traitor and parricide. Jefferson felt the humiliation, frankly conceded it, but unlike others who in losing honor lost all he did not exaggerate its importance or become demoralized in the face of it.

Against mounting difficulties, he set about repairing the losses and reopening the southern channel of men and materials. When the enemy barricaded itself at Portsmouth, the opposing force numbered 3700 men, nearly all militia, divided into three encampments: at Fredericksburg under General George Weedon for the protection of the iron works and other facilities there; near Williamsburg under the ailing Nelson; and on the opposite side of the river under Steuben until General J. P. G. Muhlenberg returned from furlough. Steuben advised Jefferson the enemy could not be dislodged, though it could be held in place. A small force would be sufficient; accordingly, the excess militia, who could not be armed anyway, should be discharged. By thus economizing on the state's defense, more men and supplies could be sent to Greene. Most stocks were desperately low in the weeks following Arnold's devastation. Of muskets, there were 3300 in service, two-thirds as many waiting repair, and only 68 in the magazines. Of shirts, shoes, and blankets, the situation was distressing to the last degree. The militia "are lousy dirty and ragged," a commander told the Governor. Ammunition stocks were all but gone. Lead, an article Virginia had furnished in great quantities to the Continent, was running dangerously low, partly from disaffection, partly from the ravages of the enemy, and a little later from the failure of the principal vein at the mines. No battle was lost for "the want of tacks," but this annoying deficiency held up the covering of wagons in February. Even money was exhausted for a time, not from any negligence of the legislature, which continued to authorize abundant issues, but from the enemy's destruction of the state's "money press." Only a single press was now available to the government, "and that has the newspapers, the Acts of Assembly, the advice and directions of the Executive, and many other things to print, so that money hardly gets its portion of time." These perplexing problems, while hardly novel, became terribly urgent toward the middle of February when Jefferson learned that Greene was retreating in all haste to Virginia.

The invasion offered instruction on a number of points concerning the state's defense. Steuben and several of the new staff officers spotted weaknesses and proposed reforms to the Governor, who was nearly always receptive, though less often able to effect changes. Colonel William Davies, a bluff, plain-speaking, and resourceful officer, in charge of assembling and equipping the state recruits at Chesterfield Court House, proved to be particularly useful. The troubles he had encountered during the invasion led him to conclude "that the former management of the military stores of this country was never adapted to the defense of it," and he soon proposed major reforms. The management of military stores was the responsibility of the Commissioner of the War Office, Colonel George Muter, a conscientious but weak administrator. Steuben, looking for the invasion's scapegoat, formally charged the Commissioner with neglect of duty, presented his case to the legislature, and forced Muter's resignation. Jefferson at once appointed Davies to the post. Given more latitude than Muter, showing more initiative and energy, Davies was to make himself indispensable in the trying months ahead.

Steuben took particular interest in a project to erect a small fort at Hood's, on a narrow, angular channel of the James, and when the work did not proceed as rapidly as expected he vented his rage on Jefferson. For sometime Jefferson had planned fortifications on each of the four principal rivers at the first points where the passage of vessels could be prevented. Priority was assigned to the James, at

Hood's. In November he informed the legislature that cannon had been removed there from the easterly posts, where they were quite useless, construction begun, and preliminary plans of the works sketched by Colonel Senf. These were submitted to the assembly, but it took no action on the proposal. After Arnold demolished the guns at Hood's and descended the river, Steuben directed Senf to finish his plans. They called for a battery of eight heavy cannon and several field pieces, blockhouse, redoubt, and barrack for a permanent garrison of sixty men, palisades, revetment, and impediments on an extensive scale. "This I insist on in the name of the United States," the Prussian thundered. "This shall be done," Jefferson promised. He must have been startled when he received Senf's request for men and materials two weeks later—10 artisans, 40 laborers, 560,000 bricks, wagons, and so on—but if he had misgivings on the state's ability to build the fortification, he kept them to himself. Labor, hard to obtain at any price, was the biggest obstacle. Steuben went to Jefferson and told him in blundering and blustering English that he meant to call a corps of militia from the surrounding counties to erect the fort or, that failing, to commandeer slave labor. Jefferson replied, "The Executive have not by the laws of this State any power to call a freeman to labor even for the public without his consent, nor a slave without that of his master." Steuben grudgingly bowed to the law upon being assured that voluntary laborers would be engaged and, he thought, made available at Hood's with the necessary materials on a specific day, February 7. The day passed and no workmen appeared. Steuben filed an indignant protest: "If Government think the work unnecessary [or if] they have it not in their [power] I have only to beg they would for my own justification give me their opinion in writing. I must beg your Excellency to consider that the shameful opposition made to the last incursion of the Enemy falls in some measure on me as the Commanding Officer in the state and I cannot but reckon it among my misfortunes to have been here at the time." Jefferson promptly gave him the explanation he demanded. The executive had not agreed to furnish the workmen at a specific time. Steps had been taken to hire both artisans and slaves, thus far with disappointing results. "Sensible that a necessary work is not to be abandoned because their means are not so energetic as they could wish them," he said, "and on the contrary that it is their duty to take those means as they find them and to make the most of them for the public good, they propose to pursue this work, and if they cannot accomplish it in a shorter, they will in a longer time."

And "a longer time" it would be. Jefferson tried first one means and then another to procure laborers. When the responsible officers failed, he turned to influential men in each of five counties surrounding Hood's, requesting them to hire the needed slaves. When this too failed ("Those who do not spare their labourers from principle will not for hire," one of the gentlemen sadly informed Jefferson), he proposed to the freemen of these counties a two months exemption from militia duty in exchange for eight days' labor. But the bargain, and a more liberal one later extended, had little appeal. Finally, Jefferson *ordered* every man of Prince George County to furnish a workman for a brief time in return for credited militia service. By then, however, the British were on the James again, and the few artisans and laborers at Hood's scampered. The fort was never finished. It might have been had Jefferson adopted Steuben's methods or come to his own final expedient at an earlier date. In this as in other matters, Steuben's arbitrary methods exacted a price he was reluctant to pay, and proceeding on characteristically sanguine expectations of public sacrifice, he had first to exhaust all voluntary remedies before resorting to the hated expedient of forced labor.

Virginia's shameful opposition to Arnold emphatically proved the error, if proof were wanting, of risking the state's defense to militia. Perhaps even the militiamen were convinced. "They have been so much harassed lately," General Nelson reported, "that they would give nearly half they possess to raise Regulars, rather than to be subject to the distresses they feel at leaving their plantations and families." Jefferson appreciated the defects of a citizen "army on paper". The disgraceful performance of the militia at Camden had instructed him further. And after Leslie's invasion he had suggested the formation of a "permanent army" to the legislature. The theory of militia—"the natural strength of a Nation, the cheapest and surest defence, on whose protection we are ultimately to depend"—appealed to Jefferson's republican feelings. He never raised his voice in the widespread and wholesale condemnation of militia. He took pride in their valorous achievements, at Saratoga, at King's Moun-

tain and elsewhere; and where humiliation and defeat was their lot
he made allowance for all the failings of leadership and arms and
supply they were helpless to overcome. Nevertheless, the problems
and difficulties he encountered in the wartime practice of the theory
were enough to make the British yoke seem almost inviting.

Militia duty, being rather like the payment of taxes, should fall
with equality and justice, which required exact returns from the officers, regular rotation, and careful bookkeeping by the Governor.
Jefferson was scrupulously fair, though he could not overcome all
the delinquencies of county lieutenants and field commanders. In
theory, militiamen were to respond at the call of alarm and accept
the lot of soldiers until relieved or discharged. But they were, for
the most part, farmers with families dependent on their labors.
Where did the obligation to their families end and the obligation to
the state begin? Drawn into the service, they remained more citizens
than soldiers and easily found excuses for returning to their firesides,
which while desertion in the eyes of the law appeared in a different
aspect to them. Their misfortunes were often heart-rending. A
county lieutenant thus explained to the Governor why 240 of his
men left the field and came home in the spring of 1781: "As meany
of them who will Now have goe [back] has Not a Creature to act
for them but a wife and Small Children, unavoidable they will
lose their Crops and of Corse thear famaly starve." He assured the
Governor that they "always Discovered the Greatest Alacrity and
Zeal in our Cause," and observed "that if their Conduct is not altogether Defensible, it is not so bad but might be plead in their Excuse."

Jefferson was moved by such pleas in the name of humanity. He
realized, moreover, that in the face of "murmerings almost amounting to mutinies," or of widespread desertion, it was sometimes foolish
to stand on impeccable rules of military discipline. But the pitfalls of
too freely temporizing with discontented militia were equally obvious. He checked his feelings and, with few exceptions, adhered to
a stern and impartial course. "We are sensible that the circumstances
of hardship . . . are just and have to lament that the public situation should have called such hardships into existence," he wrote typically to one petitioner, "but they must perceive that it will be vain
for them to sow or plant and leave the enemy to reap." Losses of

food for the camps and the sinews of war were, nevertheless, among the hidden costs of the militia system. How its costs compared with those of a regular army could not be determined, but experience exploded the idea that it was cheap. No possible mode of carrying on the war, Jefferson told the legislature, "can be so expensive to the public and so distressing and disgusting to individuals as by militia." Militiamen served for such short terms—Jefferson attempted to standardize the term at two months—that dividends of training and experience were unappreciable. They were "here today and gone tomorrow." They had to be freshly supplied each time they came into the field. And nothing was more annoying than their habit of carrying guns from the field. Jefferson repeatedly pressed officers to recover the arms, and before his term was over actually committed the anomaly of *disarming* the militia not on active duty.

Just as the theory, and the law, of the system assumed that every man furnished his own weapon, it also assumed that men were called to service in the defense of their own homes and firesides. In fact, of course, they were called to distant parts, out of the state, where they were subjected to the rigors of the continental Articles of War. Incongruously, as James Innes, a top-flight militia commander, philosophized to Jefferson, the militia belonging to the country most in danger were the least effectual in combating the enemy. "The feelings of the man, may in a fatal moment, swallow up the sentiments of the patriot," Innes said. "During my little experience in the Northern Army, I learned by observation one truth—which I ever found invariable—which was that no militia could ever be drawn from the part of the Country immediately invaded. The strong impulses on the heart . . . forever produced inactivity, but transfer the scene of war from their own doors, and the very men who before had been so tame and inactive, flew to arms with fierceness and unanimity, and were of very important service." Governor Clinton of New York, among others, also noted this paradox, and Jefferson seems to have been convinced of its truth. Within the state, at any rate, he preferred to rely on militia called from a distance. But he placed little trust in militia called to service beyond the state's borders. So he exerted every effort to send Greene regulars. Unfortunately, no sooner was the recruiting system set in motion after one invasion than it was immobilized by the next, for it could not function in any county whose militia was in the field. His hopes for escaping this vicious circle were not very high in 1781. For all its faults the country was stuck with the system, and must either cherish the militia or give up the contest.

Dissatisfaction with the militia as the state's sole means of defense was one of the reasons Jefferson convened the assembly in special session on March 1. (The call went out on January 23.) "Whether it be practicable to raise and maintain a sufficient number of regulars to carry on the war is a question," he impassively announced to the assembly. He did not seek to answer it; that was the assembly's job, but he transmitted a plan developed by Steuben for the establishment of a regular army. The assembly demurred. The treasury was empty. Legislation authorized the issuance of £10,000,000, half again as much if exigencies required, and pledged the public faith to redeem the bills in specie at the old ratio of forty to one. The act further provided that Virginia paper should be legal tender in the discharge of all debts, thus restoring the principle abandoned nearly two years before. The principle, maintaining a parity of specie and paper on a fixed ratio, had been impracticable then; it was now hopelessly so, and a fraud on creditors besides. The paper actually had less than half the legally stipulated value and was falling rapidly. Some of the consequences were described by the officer commanding the regiment of guards for the Convention troops in Winchester: "The Regiment have just received their pay at 40 to one, but it is of little value to them. Every merchant here refused to receive it for goods, and those persons who will take it demand three hundred or more for one." The problems encountered by procurement officers—commissaries, quartermasters, purchasing agents—may well be imagined. Jefferson could only listen to their troubles, throw them more and more paper that bought less and less, expand the despised alternative of impressment, and trust their ingenuity. Finally, in March, he requested the legislature to extend the time allowed for the execution of the acts of the previous session for recruiting the quota of Continental troops and for supplying the army with provisions, clothes, and wagons. The invasion had interrupted the former and so far delayed the printing and promulgation of the latter that the time set for execution had passed before it could be received in the counties. Jefferson was criticized for these delays, which were perhaps longer than necessary. He did not scruple to enforce the stiff supply act, however, having directed the county magistrates to assess the levies of wagons, provisions, and clothing at once. "While we have so many foes in our bowels and environing us on every side, he is but a bad citizen who can entertain a doubt whether the law will justify him in saving his country, or who will scruple to risk himself in support of the spirit of a law where unavoidable accidents have prevented a literal compliance with it." The assembly approved Jefferson's extra-legal actions in this instance.

Arnold had delayed everything. In December the assembly had resolved to send a special emissary to Congress beseeching immediate assistance in the form of men, arms, ammunition, clothing, and other necessities. But it was February before Benjamin Harrison, the appointed emissary, journeyed northward. "Have you cried aloud to Congress, and to *The Commander in Chief of The Army*, for succor; have they listen'd to your cry?" Gates implored the Governor. He assured the rusticated General, "I have been knocking at the door of Congress for aids of all kinds, but especially of arms ever since the middle of summer." Repeatedly called on the carpet by Greene for failure to fill his November requisition, Jefferson politely suggested that he too should take his complaints to Congress. "Every moment . . . brings us new proofs that we must be aided by our Northern brethren," he went on. "Perhaps they are aiding us, and we may be uninformed of it. I think near half the enemy's force are now in Virginia and the states south of that. Is half the burthern of opposition to rest on Virginia and N. Carolina?" His hopes now rode on Harrison's mission, not alone for military assistance in the South but also for the settlement of other serious matters: the continuation of the illicit Bermuda trade "without umbrage to Congress or the French minister," removal from the state of the 1400 German Conventioners and release from the task of provisioning the English prisoners transferred to Maryland, assistance in the transportation of a valuable cargo belonging to the state but held in Rhode Island, and the immediate shipment of four tons of powder to Pittsburgh for Clark's campaign.

Harrison skillfully attended to all this business and reported encouraging progress to Jefferson on February 19. The next day Congress voted to add the Pennsylvania Line to the Southern Army, to furnish 10,000 suits of clothes, 400 wagons, and sufficient arms and military stores. As Harrison foresaw, Congress would discover "very great difficulty in their carrying their resolution into effect, they being extremely poor and their credit but low." The problem of moving any supplies from the North, or from Europe, was illustrated by the balky cargo at Newport. It had been dispatched from Nantes on the ship *La Comité* in May 1780. The ship was taken as a British prize, then recaptured by American privateers and brought to Rhode Island, where one-half of its cargo of arms, clothing, and other military supplies was awarded to its former owner, the Commonwealth of Virginia. Informed of this odyssey in September, Jefferson directed the Virginia delegates in Congress to arrange for the conveyance of the precious cargo to Virginia. With the assistance of the French minister, it was finally loaded on a French frigate, where it still reposed in February. Jefferson expected to receive it when several French warships came to Virginia about this time but was disappointed. On April 3 Madison informed him the cargo was in harbor at Philadelphia. Realizing its "infinite importance" to the state, the delegates decided to forward it immediately by land. There arose, however, "insurmountable difficulties." The shipment got into transit near the end of April and reached the state magazines one week before Jefferson's retirement from the governorship. Such were the exasperations of "circumstances beyond his control."

On the issues of the Bermuda trade and the Convention prisoners, Harrison had little success, though the latter was finally settled to Virginia's satisfaction; but he accomplished the remaining, and in Jefferson's eyes more important, task assigned to him: the purchase and shipment of powder to Clark at Fort Pitt. As long ago as September, after hearing of Clark's devastation of the Indian towns above the Ohio, he had begun planning the next campaign in the West, with Detroit the object. "Could that post be reduced and retained it would cover all the States to the south-east of it," he wrote to Washington. Virginia could not carry out so large an enterprise unassisted. He therefore reversed standing policy and asked that it be pursued jointly with the Continent.

Various factors entered into this decision, among them the hard realities already stated. Of fundamental importance, as he suggested to Washington, was the fact that Congress was about to resolve the divisive issue of western lands on terms acceptable to Virginia. Those lands would be ceded to Congress by Virginia and the other claimant states, then disposed of for the benefit of all the people, rather than of a few speculators, and formed into new self-governing states. The cession would remove the only obstacle to the completion of the Confederation. When finally effected, as Jefferson had every confidence it would be, Virginia's lands north of the Ohio River would become the property of the Union. And the expedition against Detroit in the coming spring, as it would be for the "general good," ought to be at the "general expense." Washington at first responded coldly to Jefferson's overture but subsequently promised to furnish Clark all possible assistance at Fort Pitt, perhaps even a detachment of Continental troops. Jefferson, meanwhile, moved ahead with his plans. Recent intelligence warned of a powerful confederacy of British and Indians forming to terrorize the frontier in the spring. "Should this take place we certainly lose in the south all aids of militia from beyond the Blue Ridge besides the inhabitants who must fall a sacrifice in the course of the savage irruptions. There seems to be but one method of preventing this," he said, "which is to give the Western enemy employment in their own country." Clark came to Richmond in December, and Jefferson spent Christmas Day 1780 penning his orders, which ran to approximately 2800 words. Everything was covered in detail: the force numbering 2000, mostly crack militia from nine western counties; arms, munitions, supplies of all kinds, their anticipated quantities and locations; the times and places of rendezvous, calculated on Clark's leaving Fort Pitt no later than March 15 so as to drop down the Ohio and move up the Wabash soon after the ice broke.

But the plans, so carefully laid, went all awry. Not long after Clark left Richmond in January with a brigadier general's commission, the militia officers of three of the counties informed the Governor their men would not march. Jefferson cast about for replacements, but Clark's anticipated force steadily dwindled. The commandant at Pittsburgh, Colonel William Brodhead, a Continental officer, was jealous of Clark and threw obstacles in his path. Aside from authorizing the powder, Congress showed little interest in Clark's project. The expedition was doomed long before the sorely frustrated General set forth on the Ohio in August. Jefferson was disappointed, of course. He was right in the importance he attached to the project, not in the short-range, but in the longer course of history. The Treaty of Peace would confirm American sovereignty in the Northwest, but British power and Indian alliances were left undisturbed. Had Clark's campaign succeeded, the United States would have been spared much trouble and grief in the years ahead. Yet in 1781 that issue had almost no bearing on the question of victory or defeat in the war against Britain.

"History," General Greene wrote to a Virginia officer, "affords no instance of a nation being so engaged in conquest abroad as Virginia is at a time when all her powers were necessary to secure herself from ruin at home." Jefferson might have answered this, and other charges of "going on some wild goose Chase," by another vindication of the military as well as political soundness of aggressive policy in the West. But the argument was circuitous, and Greene could not wait for the roundabout relief it promised to the Southern Army. He crossed the Dan River into Virginia, on February 14, with Cornwallis in hot pursuit. "Unless our Army is greatly reinforced I see nothing to prevent their future progress," he warned Jefferson. The militia rallied in the southern counties. Greene gathered new strength. While Cornwallis lingered in North Carolina, he seized the initiative, recrossing the Dan on the 21st. It was a tense moment. Jefferson felt he could have been of more service to Greene at the Dan, and also better prepared to meet the enemy in Virginia, had the General kept him posted on the movements of the two armies. Not until he was in Virginia did Greene apprise the Governor of his retreat. To improve communication Jefferson sent his own confidential representative, Major Charles Magill, to Greene's headquarters. Gates had welcomed Monroe in a similar capacity; but Greene, underscoring "the necessity for secrecy," gently rebuffed the Governor and kept Magill at arm's length. Although he bore Jefferson no personal ill-will, Greene, with typical military conceit, believed the prosecution of war to be the business of generals, and he deeply distrusted the Virginia government. "I have long endeavored to impress upon the different Legislatures the impossibility of accommodating the operations of the Army to civil convenience . . . ," he lectured Jefferson on another occasion. "Indeed civil polity must accommodate itself to the emergencies of war, or the people submit to the power of the enemy." No sensible man, certainly not Jefferson, disputed the need for such "accommodation," but he insisted on the authority of civil government to determine its conditions, bounded by what a free people could accept; and this required the confidence of military commanders, as well as ultimate superiority over them. Carefully avoiding fruitless argument on so basic a disagreement, Jefferson must, nevertheless, have been affronted by the preaching tone of Greene's letters and his use of Steuben, a man of monumental ineptitude off the drillgrounds, as the main pipe of comunication with the Virginia government.

While Greene artfully parried Cornwallis in North Carolina, Jefferson entered eagerly into a plan to capture Arnold and rout the invaders from Portsmouth. A virtual stalemate prevailed there: except to forage, the British never ventured from behind the barricades, and the Virginians lacked the strength to expel them. But the longer the enemy remained, the greater the dangers of timidity and disaffection in the surrounding counties. Jefferson frustrated this in part by a timely proclamation aimed at the British practice of taking unarmed citizens and, on the pretext they were prisoners-of-war, extorting pardons with the condition they would not in any way assist the enemies of Britain on pain of life and fortune. The practice was, as Jefferson declared, unauthorized by the law of nations, though perfectly consistent with the British view of the war as a rebellion. Regardless of the principle, the policy jeopardized the patriot cause wherever the British were in a position to exchange the safety of the citizen for his loyalty. "They have conquered South Carolina by paroles alone," Jefferson said. "They will conquer us also if we admit their validity." By his January proclamation such paroles were null and void, and citizens who did not avail themselves of release were ordered behind the enemy lines. Subsequently, when British umbrage threatened death to civilians who violated their paroles, Jefferson promised retaliation in kind on enemy prisoners-of-war.

Having brought this danger under control, he was still anxious to revive Virginia's flagging morale by some exploit at Portsmouth. A spectacular scheme to send a "fire ship" into the enemy fleet, its sole means of escape, aborted; and nothing came of a cloak and dagger plan to capture Arnold. Then a stroke of fortune put it in the power of the French fleet to answer his persistent pleas for assistance. Late in January, a fierce gale crippled the British squadron off Gardiner's Bay, Long Island, at last securing the ascendancy of the French navy. "Heavenly Storm!" A detachment under Commodore Tilly soon sailed from Newport, arriving in the Chesapeake on February 15. But unable to take his strongest ship of 64 guns into the shallow waters of Elizabeth River, where the enemy vessels lay at anchor, the Commodore returned as abruptly as he had come.

The disappointment was momentary. On February 28 Jefferson heard from Washington of a joint sea and land operation planned at the highest level against Arnold at Portsmouth. Washington had ordered a detachment of 1200 troops commanded by General Marquis de Lafayette to march from the Hudson to Head of Elk, at the upper reaches of the Chesapeake, fall down the bay on transports, and in concert with the militia around Portsmouth and the French squadron lead the expedition against Arnold's forces. (Washington was as yet uninformed of Tilly's departure from Virginia waters.) Jefferson, with Steuben and others, worked feverishly to mobilize men, provisions, ordnance, and articles of all kinds. With unabashed eagerness, dreams of glory dancing before him, young Lafayette drove his troops hard, arriving at Head of Elk on March 3, three days ahead of schedule. There he waited until boats could be gathered and a French squadron could command the bay. In a long letter to Jefferson, he sketched in bold words the preparations wanted of Virginia, emphasizing men, boats, and horses. Jefferson had already called for militia reinforcements of 1100 men, which he estimated would place a total of 4000 Virginia militia, plus another 1000 from North Carolina, at Lafayette's command.

A week passed, and Jefferson was dismayed to learn from Steuben "of the refusal of considerable numbers of militia within certain counties to come into the field, and the departure of some others in defiance with their arms." Excessive duty, desertion with impunity, and downright fear contributed to this disobedience. The fear arose, Jefferson thought, from a widespread rumor "that the militia now called on are intended to storm the enemy's works at Portsmouth." In fact Lafayette did intend to storm Arnold's fortifications, though Jefferson continued to entertain the idea of a siege. "Were it possible to block up the river," he told Washington, "a little time would suffice to reduce them by want and desertion and would be more sure in its event than an attempt by storm." At any rate, the crisis would not admit of disobedience by militia. He referred Steuben's complaint to the assembly with recommendation for amendment of the Invasion Law. Stiffening amendments were introduced and debated but finally defeated. Meanwhile, he ordered additional militia into the field to make up for deficiencies that baffled all his calculations.

Impressment offered the only means of obtaining boats and horses. The deserted and plundered Virginia navy was useless in this crisis, as in every other. Fearing inadequate naval protection at Portsmouth, Jefferson took the extraordinary measure of directing the impressment of private vessels and crews on the James and Appomattox rivers. He asked the assembly for authority but did not wait to receive it. One ship and three brigs mounting a total of 36 guns, exceeding the combined power of the state vessels in readiness, were thus drawn into service. The greater need was for small craft to carry men and cannon across the James. Jefferson had first issued orders to obtain boats of this description, under armed guard apparently, when Tilly was at the mouth of the James. The orders were renewed in March. Nevertheless, he had to report to Lafayette a shortage of boats.

The impressment of horses was an even more arduous, and indeed inflammatory, business. If Virginians were not necessarily averse to parting with their horses, they expected outlandish prices for them. "The Thirteen United States are not rich enough to remount the two regiments of this state," Steuben declared. Horses taken under impress warrants were appraised by two citizens, who knew their own property was as likely to be taken as another's and, therefore, had a personal interest in inflated prices. "To retain the horses at such enormous prices threatens ruin on one hand," Jefferson said, "on the other, to discharge them endangers an enterprise which if successful would relieve us from an enemy whose presence is attended with continued expense, fatigue and danger." He referred the problem to the assembly, which promptly authorized the executive to appoint appraisers charged with the responsibility of affixing just prices. But, once again, he had waited until the crisis was upon him. The problem was not wholly one of valuation and price. The much harassed Continental Quartermaster in Virginia, Richard

Claiborne, insisted the needed horses could be obtained only with an armed force. With Steuben's support, he repeatedly asked Jefferson's authority to employ a troop of militia in this work. The executive repeatedly denied the application. An impress force was "as unnecessary as it was new," Jefferson said. The fact was that citizens had parted with their horses "too easily by delivering them to every man who said he was riding on public business and assumed a right of impressing." The militia had troubles enough already, and while the executive could not prevent commanding officers from ordering militia to assist the Quartermaster, it could not itself countenance their employment in this capacity. "We did not think proper to resign ourselves and our Country implicitly to the demands of a Quarter-master," Jefferson indignantly wrote, "but thought we had some right of judgment left to us."

He was perhaps peculiarly sensitive to the issue because a little earlier, without a stitch of legislative authority, he had told Greene to taken horses for his cavalry, and the abuses committed by Greene's officers in this nasty business caused an uproar in the assembly at the very time hundreds of the beasts were demanded for Lafayette's expedition. It was alleged that valuable stud horses and brood mares were taken, that fine covering horses were castrated, that others unfit for service were impressed at exorbitant prices. Jefferson felt some responsibility for these abuses, which of course stung the Virginians' pride in good horseflesh and made them all the less willing to part with their mounts. He sent vigorous protests to Greene, appealing for corrective action; but he was not prepared to support the angry resolution of the assembly calling for the return of all horses valued in excess of £5000 Virginia money. Few could be had at that price, and their return would accomplish nothing. So while urging Greene to rectify abuses, Jefferson told him to ignore the resolution as "inconsistent with the public good." This bold exercise of executive discretion showed that Jefferson would not allow trifles of economy and punctilio to override military requirements. In the circumstances of Caliborne's appeal, however, when passions ran high against impresses generally and especially of horses, he did not think it either desirable or necessary to substitute force for reason and persuasion.

The pressures and frustrations became too much for Steuben. On

March 9 he exploded to the Governor: he would "not be answerable for the consequences" of a slack militia, he would give "no future orders for impressing horses or any thing else," he would, unless he received immediate satisfaction from the government, bare its failings to the Marquis and the commander of the French fleet "that they may not engage too far in an enterprise which there is no prospect of carrying through." Steuben had had mixed feelings about the Portsmouth expedition from the start. He was jealous of the dashing Marquis, many years his junior but his senior in rank, and was singularly devoted to Greene. "The Baron wishes to be with you," his aide-de-camp wrote Greene near the end of February. "He would rather Obey in an Army, than Command in Virginia." Steuben was rapidly losing what popularity he had in Virginia, partly from clumsy handling of staff and line officers, partly from constant badgering of the government. On the other hand, the Portsmouth expedition held out the prospect, however dimly, of fame and glory. This overruled contrary feelings, and the apprehension of losing that stake, or of another failure at the expense of honor, prompted Steuben's angry outburst under the strain of preparing for the expedition. Jefferson did not make light of it. He at once conveyed Steuben's letter to the House of Delegates and also to Lafayette. If the state's support of his command fell short of expectations, he assured the Marquis, the fault did not arise from any want of zeal in the executive. "Mild laws, a people not used to war and prompt obedience, a want of the provisions of war and means of procuring them render our orders ineffectual, oblige us to temporize and if we cannot accomplish an object in one way to attempt it in another." Lafayette's answer was like a cheerful breath of spring to the Governor. He thanked Jefferson for the exertions already made, confident that new ones would ensure the success of the operation, and understood that, of course, every measure must be accommodated to the temper of the people. "Long since have I been used to those inconveniences that are so far compensated by the numberless blessings of a popular government."

Lafayette wrote from Williamsburg, having arrived there with an advance party on March 14. It is not likely he journeyed to Richmond, though Jefferson assuredly met him there, for the first time, at a critical hour in April. But Jefferson was prepared to love this celebated young Frenchman whom Mazzei described to him as "sensible and clever, lively, smart and modest, and all together one of the most amiable characters I ever saw." He might have wished that other commanders showed the same plucky, uncomplaining spirit of Lafayette: "When we are not able to do what we wish, we must do what we can." Steuben, fortunately, soon recovered his composure and apologised for his conduct. He did not so much blame Jefferson for his difficulties as he did the lethargy of the people, the laxity of the laws, and the bureaucracy that botched the best efforts of the executive. Yet the responsibility, if it was to be meaningful, had to be placed somewhere in particular. The appeal to "circumstances" was self-defeating. As one whose entire training inculcated responsibility under military chain of command, Steuben could not comprehend, much less accept, the justification Jefferson offered—and underscored for effect—in his letter to him: "*We can only be answerable for the orders we give, and not for their execution.*" An executive disclaiming responsibility for the execution of its orders must have struck Steuben as strange. On the usual administrative canons it was untenable. Yet in the actual context of "obstinacy of spirit or want of coercion in the laws" Jefferson's assertion was perfectly reasonable.

In the end, the expedition against Portsmouth went astray not from any backwardness on the part of Virginia but from the tardiness of the French fleet. Its commander, the Chevalier Destouches, was under orders to sail from Newport for the Chesapeake on March 7; unaccountably, he was delayed more than twenty-four hours, long enough to permit a British squadron reinforcing Arnold to overtake him outside the Virginia capes. He fought a brief, indecisive action on March 16, laid off during the night, and discovered the next morning that the British ships had quietly sneaked into the James. Risking nothing further, he returned to Newport. Thus ended one of the intriguing "might have beens" of the war. For it is not unrealistic to suppose that the design on Portsmouth would have succeeded with the necessary naval support. "With a naval superiority our success would have been certain," Lafayette insisted. And success at Portsmouth would have altered British strategy. Had Cornwallis then rushed to Arnold's rescue, the climactic battle of the Revolution might have been fought in Virginia while Jefferson

was Governor, thus redounding to his fame, rather than at Yorktown months later, when the victory could not erase the defeats and
disappointments of his leadership.

As it was, the enemy at Portsmouth doubled its strength and now
threatened to break out at any time. Jefferson stoically turned to the
task of dismantling the project that had cost so much trouble and
expense. At the same time he made a crucial decision on the strategy
now to be be pursued. On March 27 Steuben presented his plan to a
military board convened at Williamsburg. He would draw together
the 4000 Virginia militia before Portsmouth and by forced marches
lead them to Greene's camp. The Baron, of course, discovered
sound military reasons to support the plan that agreed so precisely
with his feelings and desires. "After four weeks' suspense," he un-
burdened himself to Greene, "our hopes of doing anything are destroyed and the Marquis returns to the Northward, leaving me exposed to nothing but affront, whilst every prospect of glory was reserved for others." The military board, consisting of Lafayette,
Weedon, and a French colonel, endorsed Steuben's plan, and he set
out for Richmond at once. Two days later he met with Jefferson
and the Council. After discussing the plan at length, they rejected it
as unjustifiable in the present circumstances, the enemy having been
greatly reinforced in Virginia. Steuben was crushed. Weedon,
who owed his command to Steuben, sourly commented, "I was fearful our scheme would be rejected by the Executive who have not an
idea beyond local security." The impudence of the man challenges
belief! Greene was more restrained, though he complained of the
presumptuousness of the executive in vetoing a plan of operations
recommended by the Continental officers commanding in the state.

But events rapidly proved the folly of Steuben's strategy and the
wisdom of the executive's decision. The plan assumed, first of all,
that Arnold, or rather General William Phillips, who now commanded at Portsmouth, would not break out and overrun the state.
There was an element of sophistry in this reasoning, for Steuben admitted to Greene that the enemy troops would in all probability
advance through the country when they pleased. No reliable intelligence came from the enemy's camp, but within three weeks Phillips
started his advance. Secondly, Steuben calculated that Greene,
greatly strengthened from Virginia, would overwhelm Cornwallis

before he could repair his damaged army or receive assistance from Phillips. But both Greene and Cornwallis, to say nothing further of Phillips, upset the calculation. Greene had already elected a totally different strategy. "I think it will be our true plan of policy to move into South Carolina. . . . This will oblige the enemy to follow us or give up their posts there." Thus Greene abandoned the center in order to recover the rear. Cornwallis decided to leave Greene alone and march his army from Wilmington to Virginia, the real seat of rebellion in the South.

Jefferson did not foresee this course of events as the spring bloom returned to Virginia. He still viewed the southern theater as "the interesting scene of action to us." In its critical decision of March 29, the executive had voted to reinforce Greene with a minimum of 1500 militia; and on through April and part of May, despite Phillip's ravages along the James, the state continued to succor Greene's army. Jefferson wrote to Lafayette near the end of April: "The British force may harass and distress us greatly but the Carolinas alone can subdue us. . . . We therefore think it our first interest to keep them under in that quarter, considering the war in our own Country but as a secondary object." Knowing better than ever that Virginia could not alone withstand the enemy armies in the South, he took a bolder tone toward "our Northern Brethren." On this ticklish subject, he bared his feelings to the French minister, the Chevalier de la Luzerne. "The Northern States are safe: their independence has been established by the joint efforts of the whole," he said. "It is proved as far as testimony can prove any thing that our enemies have transferred every expectation from that quarter and mean nothing further there than a diversion in favor of their Southern arms. It would be unfortunate indeed should it be again proposed to lose a campaign in New York and to exhaust on that the efforts of the Confederacy as those of Spain on Gibraltar,* to give up Provinces in the South for towns in the North." Though he did not exactly say so, Jefferson clearly felt that Washington, fearing to lower his guard at New York, fearing his army would evaporate if divided or marched south, played into the British hands. Washington supposed that he thereby created a useful diversion in favor of southern arms

* A reference to the Spanish ally's almost exclusive interest in acquiring Gibraltar from Great Britain.

when, in fact, it was really Clinton who was diverting him. In Jefferson's opinion, as he told Luzerne, the solution lay in large part with French sea power. "Should a superiority on the Continental Seas be obtained by our fleet, it will save everything from North to South. If the detachments of the British Army can once be insulated, they will be whittled down by the militia, by famine, by sickness and desertion to nothing." He was right on both counts. Washington's army and the French navy did, in due time, come to Virginia, but too late for him to share the glory of their victory.

The problems of the Governor were essentially no different from before, but they threatened to pass out of his hands entirely. "The affliction of the people for want of arms is great," he wrote tiresomely to Congress, "that of ammunition is not yet known to them." And to the Virginia delegates: "It is impossible to give you an idea of the distress we are in for want of lead." Fortunately, he had anticipated this deficiency, rummaged the state for quantities to meet immediate needs, and pushed, successfully, to get the mines back in operation. The state's credit was all but gone. The British conquest of the Dutch free port of St. Eustatius in the Caribbean deprived Virginia of a principal outlet for tobacco. At the end of March the state's Commercial Agent, David Ross, informed Jefferson that tobacco could not be sold in Philadelphia and merchants flew from Virginia money. "Sweet Virginia goes on as usual," a fellow countryman remarked of Ross's efforts in Philadelphia. "The agent is sent up to purchase an immense quantity of articles without a farthing of cash in his pocket: As to the credit of the state, I don't believe anybody would trust her for half a crown." But Ross was not easily defeated. If tobacco would not do, he would try hemp; and he managed, with hemp, to pay for repairs of 2000 stand of arms in May. Promising reforms had been made in the quartermaster department, but it was hopelessly bogged down in the state's financial and moral troubles. More than once Claiborne told Jefferson his department must shortly collapse altogether for want of money. He depended for wagons, teams, and forage on the county commissioners of the Provision Law; if they failed him, or if the supply thus obtained was used up, he must either purchase or impress, and he might succeed in neither. When Jefferson directed him to furnish wagons for the transportation of ammunition from the northward,

Claiborne threw up his hands: "However easy it was for your Excellency to issue such an order, the business is attended with so many difficulties that I am very fearful it will not be in my power to comply with it." *He* would not be answerable for orders he had not the means to execute!

The Governor could scrape through problems such as these. How he was to cope with the breakdown of authority in the militia system and the recruiting system was more difficult to discern. The calls on the militia were exceedingly heavy in April, when upwards to one-half of the men in the camps around Portsmouth and 1500 with Greene were due for replacement. Jefferson carefully chose the counties now to be called with a view to minimizing interference with recruitment. Most recruits were, in fact, drafted. The draft was restored in counties whose militia were recalled, suspended in counties with militia in the field or freshly called. But results were poor all around. In May, Steuben had 954 men in the Virginia Line, about one-sixth of the quota. Seven of the eleven counties ordered to send militia reinforcements to Greene applied for excuse—the Council indulged only one. Specific examples illustrate the range and the seriousness of the problem: *Charlotte:* Of its rank and file numbering 565, some 142 were on duty at Portsmouth, 170 marched with Greene from the Dan, 30 volunteered on the same occasion, and 70 were with General Lawson's corps—412 in service, leaving but 153 men to answer the executive's call for 156. *King George:* The militia of this Potomac county was occupied with the protection of life and property close at hand from enemy vessels raiding and plundering along the river as far north as Alexandria; furthermore, not one-third of the militia had servicable arms, and there were no gunsmiths to repair the others. *Fayette:* This Kentucky county had furnished men to Clark and had scarcely enough bodies at home to hold its forts against the Shawnee; it therefore begged to be excused from the draft of eighteen men for the Continental Army. *Montgomery:* Disaffection had spread to half the militia, who would withdraw to the mountains or start another insurrection rather than obey the laws; many of the others were exposed to the savages and could not leave their families at this dangerous season. *Hampshire:* Open insurrection had broken out in this county at the northern tip of the state. The trouble began with defiance of a collector. "A certain John Claypole Said if all the men were of his mind they would not make up any Cloathes, Beef or men and all that would Join him Should turn out. Upon which he Got all the men present to five or Six and Got Liquor and Drank king George the thirds health, and Damnation to Congress." Claypole, thereafter, rallied a great number. Jefferson instructed the county lieutenant to mount loyal militia, sweep down in the night, "and take them out of their beds." Not for two months were the insurgents rounded up and order restored in Hampshire. As discontents deepened and multiplied, government drifted in an expanding vacuum of power. Jefferson can only be accused of understatement in what he wrote to the Virginia delegates in Congress: "Should this Army at Portsmouth come forth and become active (and as we have no reason to believe they came here to sleep) our affairs will assume a very disagreeable aspect."

Phillips came forth on April 18. At six-thirty the next morning, Jefferson received a dispatch from Colonel Innes commanding the troops at Williamsburg: fourteen sail of enemy vessels dragging numerous flat-bottomed boats at their sterns were standing up the James. Still suffering the grief of his infant daughter's death but three days earlier, the Governor called the Council into session, and within an hour issued orders to the militia of nine counties to rendezvous in all haste at Richmond, Petersburg, and Manchester. Soon, more militia and also volunteer cavalry were called. Richmond was feared to be the enemy's object; accordingly, Jefferson prepared for its abandonment. Records and stores were promptly removed. "We can never proceed with any degree of certainty in any of our public works while the enemy command the rivers," Davies observed. On his advice the government moved works and magazines to Point of Fork, far up the James at its juncture with the Rivanna. As events unfolded, Richmond did not appear to be Phillips's destination. He aimed at disruption and depredation in advance of Cornwallis. On the 20th, a sizable detachment of infantry and cavalry landed near Jamestown and marched on Williamsburg. Innes quickly withdrew his inferior force, and the enemy retraced their steps to the James. Another detachment on the Chickahominy took possession of the shipyard, burned its buildings and some vessels and stores, then chased after Innes. His alertness and agility, while it occupied his pursuers, kept them at a distance, until by a circuitous route he approached Richmond from the east. Meanwhile, the fleet carried the main body of troops farther up the James. It lay opposite Westover on the 23rd, when Phillips feinted toward Richmond. The capital was indefensible as before. Of the militia called there but 500 had reported, only 200 of them armed. Jefferson prepared to leave the city. Neither he nor Steuben, who was on the south side of the James, had yet unraveled the enemy's plan or organized an effective resistance.

The Prussian was disconsolate as ever. Militia came in slowly, arms were wanting, cavalry was wanting, the fort at Hood's was not half finished: "Every thing is in the same confusion as when Arnold came up the River." On the 24th, while reconnoitering the fleet, Steuben watched it ascend the river toward City Point on the southern side of the confluence of the Appomattox and James. There Phillips landed his force of approximately 2300 men, declaring his object to be Petersburg, a few miles to the west. At Petersburg, Steuben marshaled about 1200 militia of Muhlenberg's command, and in the heat of the following day, April 25, battled the enemy for two hours, at first disputing the ground "inch by inch," then, ammunition exhausted, making an orderly retreat across the Appomattox. Steuben congratulated the militia on its performance. After burning tobacco and warehouses in Petersburg, Phillips marched to the place called Osborne's, or Coxe's Dale, on the south bank of the James. Here Captain James Maxwell, Commissioner of the Navy, had ranged his pitiful fleet, adding several impressed vessels, for a last stand. A curious engagement between land and sea forces followed. The British set up a deadly fire of musket and cannon from shore positions. Some of the ships surrendered, others were destroyed by enemy fire, still others were burned or scuttled by their officers. None escaped. As one participant recalled, "we saved nothing but the clothes we had on." Two days later, the 29th, Phillips marched to Manchester.

If Phillips had any intention of attacking Richmond on the opposite bank, he was dissuaded by the view it suddenly presented: 900 Continental troops with Lafayette at their head. The Marquis, on hearing at Baltimore of Virginia's plight, left baggage, artillery, and stores behind, and by forced marches under the most trying conditions reached Richmond in ten days. It was a timely arrival. The British retired to their waiting fleet in the James, burning as they went. "Six or eight hundred of their picked men of light infantry with General Arnold at their head . . . ," Jefferson gloated, "fled from a patrol of 16 horse every man into his boat as he could, some pushing north and some south as their fears drove them." Before reaching the camps at Portsmouth, the fleet abruptly turned about, ascended the river, and came to anchor at Brandon, just below Hood's, where the troops landed. "We have not yet heard which way they went or whether they are gone," Jefferson informed Washington on May 10, "but having about the same time received authentic information that Lord Cornwallis had on the 1st instant advanced from Wilmington half way to Halifax we have no doubt putting all circumstances together but that these two bodies are forming a junction."

Jefferson braced himself for this gloomy event. It was essential, he told the county lieutenants, "to turn out . . . as many men as there are arms to be found in the County." One-tenth should be mounted and equipped as cavalry. Other troops of cavalry, earlier authorized by the assembly at his request, were also in formation. In a country as wide and open as Virginia, especially when the enemy commanded the rivers, a formidable cavalry was indispensable. On the surface, nothing should have been easier. But the people had been so revolted by the commandeering of horse as to put the objective out of reach. And instead of Virginia gaining the benefit of its cavalry potential, it fell to the enemy by plunder. Determined to reverse this disastrous course, Jefferson formed the policy of requiring the removal, and military impress as necessary, of all servicable horses from within twenty miles of the enemy. A first step toward the proclamation of martial law in the areas of the contending armies, Jefferson's action was subsequently sanctioned by the legislature. He kept his wits about him, however, and urged "a high tone of conduct" upon the responsible officers, lest the people take umbrage as before and defeat the measure.

Evidences of panic and collapse were all around him. Claiborne declared "all faith in the public agents is lost and the citizen will do nothing without being compelled by military force." Jefferson stayed at his post and almost alone gave some semblance of direction to the government. During Phillips's invasion, as in Arnold's before, the members of the Council scattered. The Council did not again meet, for want of a quorum, until May 7, and from May 15 through the remainder of his term in office Jefferson was without its services. The assembly was to convene on May 7, but neither house could muster a quorum. The members present issued a call to meet in Charlottesville on May 24. Jefferson now put everything in motion to transfer the seat of government to Charlottesville. Davies had already centered the operations of the War Office at Point of Fork some miles below. Steuben made this inland location his training grounds for recruits intended for the Southern Army. The dispersal of the government from Richmond added to the sum of confusion. But it was unavoidable. Richmond was surely in Cornwallis's line of March. Jefferson kept in constant touch with the different commands and departments as the government endeavored to draw its energies together again at the base of the Blue Ridge.

More support was coming from the North. By May, after agonizing delay, no one could doubt that Washington, Congress, and the nothern public were at last awake to the needs and opportunities of the southern states. The Virginia congressmen maneuvered and scraped to obtain 2000 rampart muskets which, after being sawed to proper size and repaired, were shipped to Virginia. The Board of War promised more arms. Ross's agent in Philadelphia, on the credit of private citizens, purchased and dispatched hundreds of guns and tons of powder. To these shipments was added the cargo of *La Comité*. By the end of May, for the first time in Jefferson's governorship, the state had a sufficiency of arms. Soldiers too were coming. Troops of the Pennsylvania Line under General Anthony Wayne, after weeks of exasperating delay, finally marched to join Lafayette. "No means in the power of Congress will be left unessayed to give you all necessary aids," the President assured Jefferson. What a welcome change! For months Jefferson had pleaded and plotted for this commitment. On May 16 Washington wrote that he would soon meet with General Rochambeau to plan a summer campaign looking to the relief of the southern states. When the two commanders met at Wethersfield, Connecticut, they decided to move their combined armies against New York, and thereby force Clinton either to risk its loss or recall troops from the South. The decision was disappointing. It favored Virginia only with a questionable diversion at New York. But the French fleet was as yet incapable of wresting the Chesapeake from the British, and Washington declined to risk his army in an overland march of 450 miles in the heat of the summer. The commanders agreed, however, to resort to the alternate plan, a campaign in Virginia, should circumstances dictate. They did, after Jefferson went into retirement.

Unopposed in his march, Cornwallis joined forces with the British army in Virginia, at Petersburg, on May 20. Five days later he crossed the James, and with the reinforcements he then received led an army of 7000 men. His first objective was to destroy Lafayette's army, vastly inferior, yet the principal force in the state. "The boy cannot escape me!" Cornwallis gloated. Lafayette retreated above Richmond in a northerly direction, holding to the upper part of the country and hoping to effect a juncture with Wayne. "We are in the outmost want of Cavalry," he informed Jefferson. General Banastre Tarleton's intrepid dragoons moved with lightning speed, plundering the stables of fine mounts all along the line of march, until it became impossible, Lafayette said, "either to stop or reconnoiter their movements, and much more so to send impressing parties around their camp." Despite the handicap, Lafayette made good his escape. Cornwallis gave up the chase halfway to Fredericksburg, turned about, and ravaged the defenseless country to the south. Before leaving his camp, he sent Tarleton's dragoons and Colonel Simcoe's rangers on separate missions to the west: the former to rout the government at Charlottesville and capture the Governor, the latter to destroy the arms and stores under Steuben's protection at Point of Fork.

Steuben was eagerly preparing to march southward at the head of 500 recruits equipped and outfitted at Point of Fork. Believing his usefulness to the state was at an end, he had written to Greene on May 14, "I will with pleasure fly to put myself under your orders and I beseech you . . . to call me as soon as possible, for be assured I am heartily disgusted at the conduct and proceedings in this quarter." Greene also wanted Steuben, "an officer educated in the Prussian school," and orders calling him south were already on the way. Cornwallis's presence, Lafayette's retreat—all the needs of the state that so far exceeded Greene's—did not deter Steuben. He was blocked, however, first by the pressure of events, second by a resolution of the assembly holding the recruits in the state, and finally by Lafayette's order. The responsibility of protecting the magazines at Point of Fork fell to him. As Lafayette retreated northward, the security of that place came into jeopardy. Steuben directed the removal of the stores to the south bank of the James, whence they were to be transported beyond the mountains. In the midst of this work, on June 4, he was surprised by Simcoe's rangers. By the ruse of kindling superfluous campfires over a long stretch of the river's north bank, Simcoe led Steuben to believe the entire British army lay opposite. Beating a hasty retreat in the night, he abandoned most of the stores to the enemy's torch the next morning. The loss was of minor importance. But Steuben's conduct was such that, as Lafayette reported to Washington, "every man, woman and child in Virginia is roused against him." Jefferson, certainly, never "roused against him." Despite serious differences between them, he had trusted the Baron, humored his faults, and quieted his enemies. But nothing now could prevent the legislature, enraged by Steuben's flight, from voting an inquiry into his conduct; and while he remained in Virginia he lay under its shadow.

Tarleton was foiled in his objectives by an alert militiaman, Jack Jouett, who spotted the white-coated dragoons on the main road at Louisa, mounted his steed, and sped along a back trail to Charlottesville heralding their approach. On his way, at sunrise June 4, he stopped at Monticello to warn the Governor and several members of the assembly who were his guests. They breakfasted, then descended the mountain to the town. The assembly convened hurriedly, and just as hurriedly adjourned to meet again at Staunton, across the Blue Ridge, on June 7. As Tarleton swooped down on the fleeing delegates, capturing some of them, a detachment under Captain McCleod took the road to Monticello. Jefferson, meanwhile, ordered his favorite horse freshly shod at Shadwell, looked after his papers, and sent his family to a neighboring plantation. What passed through his mind as he occupied himself in this deliberate manner for nearly two hours, it is impossible to say; but in view of the infamous reputation of Tarleton's legion, he must have contemplated Monticello with mournful affection. Alerted to McCleod's approach, he walked to the road between Monticello and adjacent

Carter's Mountain, where his horse awaited him. Riding up the mountain, he stopped and trained his telescope on Charlottesville. The scene dispelled any lingering hope that he might reverse his steps. He went on and took refuge with his family. Not for many years did anyone suggest that the "flight" to Carter's Mountain was an act of pusillanimity.

McCleod, arriving a few minutes after the prey departed, proved to be as considerate of Monticello as Jefferson could have wished. Martin, one of the house servants, met the Captain at the door and escorted him through the house. "On reaching the study, the depository of the Governor's papers," according to a family tradition, "McCleod gazed about him a few moments, and then locking the door gave Martin the key, and bade him refer any of his soldiers inquiring for it to himself." Nothing was disturbed. After eighteen hours, McCleod rejoined Tarleton. The dragoons followed the Rivanna down to the main army on the James. Here Cornwallis set up headquarters at Jefferson's Elk Hill plantation. In later years he bitterly recalled the "spirit of total extermination" the British commander loosed on this property: the barns and fences burned, the crops in the field and the quantities of corn, wheat and tobacco destroyed, the number of horses, cows, sheep, hogs eaten or carried away, and the number of slaves, 27, captured. "Had this been to give them freedom he [Cornwallis] would have done right," Jefferson reflected, "but it was to consign them to inevitable death from the small pox and putrid fever then raging in his camp." This, indeed, was the fate of most of the slaves, and Jefferson recovered only five of them.

Before these events took place, actually before his narrow escape at Carter's Mountain, the curtain fell on the agonizing drama of Jefferson's governorship. His term of office expired on June 2. This was the day fixed for his retirement, though he in effect occupied the office until Tarleton chased the government from Charlottesville. Not until June 12, after the assembly convened at Staunton, was General Nelson chosen as his successor. It was the least propitious time imaginable—at the piercing crescendo of all the havoc and defeat Virginia had endured—for Jefferson calmly to withdraw from the scene. "You will then judge the situation of this country," Richard Henry Lee solemnly wrote to the Virginia congressmen, "without either executive or legislative authority, everything in the greatest possible confusion, the enemy far superior in force to that with the Marquis, and practicing everything that force and fraud can contrive."

Infected by the panic that struck the state, Lee took a chapter from the book of the ancient republics and proposed that Congress dispatch Washington to Virginia vested with dictatorial powers. A faction of the assembly also looked for salvation from a dictator, though their candidate, so Jefferson believed, was Patrick Henry. The subject was delicate, the proceedings of the House of Delegates veiled in obscurity; but the motion to appoint a dictator was apparently introduced by George Nicholas, seconded by Henry, and after some debate defeated. Jefferson afterwards learned as much from an eyewitness. He was writing the *Notes on Virginia* at the time, and entered a passionate denunciation of the scheme in that work. The experience of the past two years, while it had lowered still further his opinion of the Virginia constitution, had in no way diminished his attachment to republican government. He did not disguise to himself or to others the perilous situation of the state. In one of his last acts as Governor, he had pleaded with Washington to return to his countrymen, assured "that your appearance among them, would restore full confidence of salvation, and would render them equal to whatever is not impossible." But he looked to Washington for generalship, not dictatorship. "The very thought alone was treason against the people . . . a people mild in their dispositions, patient under their trial, united for the public liberty, and affectionate to their leaders." Writing in retrospect, Edmund Randolph stated Jefferson's opinion more pointedly than he ever did himself: "The power which may have saved Rome, would have made Virginia revolt."

Rage succeeded to panic. On June 12 the House of Delegates resolved on an inquiry into the conduct of the executive. This motion, too, was made by young Nicholas, though Jefferson believed, as with the former one, "his natural ill-temper was the tool worked with by another hand"—the hand of Patrick Henry. By the terms of resolution, the executive, not simply the Governor, was called on the carpet. And, of course, the Council being an integral part of the executive authority, no inquiry of the sort proposed could be fairly pressed on the Governor alone. Yet this was the upshot of the resolution. Several members of the Council threatened to resign if the sword of censure hung over them. Faced with the dilemma of either depriving the state of a lawful executive or of simply by-passing the record of the Council, the assembly chose the latter. Jefferson viewed the resolution as an implied censure of him; accordingly, with his friends in the assembly, he invited the inquiry as a means of vindication.

In July he addressed Nicholas for information on the charges against him. Nicholas replied, "I shall exhibit no charges but only join in an enquiry," and then proceeded to list five, which were later revised and enlarged to the number of eleven. All referred to Arnold's invasion: Why had the executive not acted on the receipt of Washington's notice of an embarkation? Why had not lookouts been stationed at the capes? Why had there not been carriages for heavy artillery? Why had the fortifications at York and Portsmouth been abandoned? And so on. Jefferson sought affidavits where pertinent and penned his own impatient answers. In December he attended the House of Delegates as a member solely on this business. A committee was appointed to conduct the inquiry, but neither Nicholas nor anyone else offered information. There was no inquiry. The committee simply reported to the House that the original resolution had stemmed from rumors which, in its opinion, were groundless. After the delegates heard the report, Jefferson rose and read the paper he had prepared during the summer. The House then, without further ado, voted Jefferson a resolution of thanks in which, after amendment, the Senate concurred: "The Assembly wish in the strongest manner to declare the high opinion which they entertain of Mr. Jefferson's Ability, Rectitude, and Integrity as chief Magistrate of this Commonwealth, and mean by thus publicly avowing their Opinion, to obviate and to remove all unmerited Censure."

But the assembly, while it might obviate, could not prevent censure, and it pursued Jefferson through life and beyond the grave. He was stung by the original resolution, far beyond anything that had befallen him in public life. As usual, he checked his feelings and avoided personal recrimination. "If pride of character be of worth at any time," he had observed, "it is when it disarms the efforts of malice." For whatever reason, his critics were disarmed in 1781, the assembly relieved of embarrassment, and Jefferson accorded the expression of public gratitude he deserved, though not without the tormenting suggestion that some censure might be merited.

His governorship could not be reckoned brilliant or even successful. Yet if faithfulness to duty, courage in distress, calmness and forecast of mind, devotion to republican principles, flexibility in the face of danger, and an enlarged view of Virginia's place in the grand strategy of the Union—if these things were important, then Jefferson was more deserving of praise than of blame. He certainly never claimed more for himself. He knew, and frankly conceded, how far character and training unsuited him to the role of a wartime governor, and he endorsed the assembly's choice of a military commander, General Nelson, to succeed him. But he knew that some circumstances are unyielding, that some evils are mild when compared with the evils likely to result from their suppression, and, as he stated to Lafayette, "that public misfortunes may be produced as well by public poverty and private disobedience to the laws as by the misconduct of public servants."

The panic that accompanied his retirement was unjustified. The government had not collapsed. The assembly was in being, the War Office and other administrative departments continued to function, and the executive was fully restored by the middle of June. The state maintained its independence and the loyalty of its people. Its military strength constantly increased while Cornwallis exhausted himself in useless marches. "Overrunning a Country is not to conquer it," Lafayette wisely observed of the lord commander's movements, adding by way of illustration, "and if it was construed into a right of possession, the French could claim the whole German Empire." Virginia's situation would have been much worse had the executive, bowing to the wishes of Steuben and Greene, stripped the state of all defensive capabilities in the spring. The nucleus of defense remained. Lafayette's force engaged Cornwallis until fresh militia could be mobilized, until Steuben's recruits were diverted from a fruitless march southward and drawn into the field, and until Wayne's army arrived from Pennsylvania. All of this occurred at the time of Jefferson's retirement. By the middle of June, Lafayette's army, now numbering perhaps 8000 men, was superior to the enemy's. The second division of the French fleet, with 24 warships and 3000 troops, lay poised in Caribbean waters. Congress was making every endeavor to aid Virginia. And Washington closely watched the developments there. When Cornwallis, in short order, withdrew his fever-ridden army into Yorktown, the outcome was a military certainty. Going into retirement, Jefferson could not foresee in detail the culmination of this chain of events; but he had never once doubted the ultimate triumph of American arms, and he turned to the long deferred pleasures of private life confident of an early victory and an early peace.

CHAPTER FIVE

Withdrawal and Return:

Congressman

Our style and manner of thinking have undergone a revolution more extraordinary than the political revolution of the country. We see with other eyes; we hear with other ears; and think with other thoughts, than those we formerly used. We can look back on our own prejudices, as if they had been the prejudices of other people. . . .

The people of England not having experienced this change, had like-wise no ideas of it. They were hugging to their bosoms the same preju-dices we were trampling beneath our feet; and they expected to keep a hold upon America, by that narrowness of thinking which America dis-dained. What they were proud of, we despised; and this is a principal cause why all their negotiations, constructed on this ground, have failed. We are now really another people, and cannot again go back to ignorance and prejudice. The mind once enlightened cannot again become dark.

Thomas Paine, Letter to the Abbé Raynal. *Philadelphia, 1782.*

D AYS AND MONTHS of anguish, eighteen dreary months, descended on Jefferson after his retirement. The Nicholas resolution wounded him more than he was at first willing to admit. The charges themselves were a mere impertinence; but to be exposed to the public on the suspicion of delinquency, to be made a mark for the slings of malice and the sport of rumor and gossip, to be forced to defend a record that needed no defense—all this was painful and more than a little disillusioning. The adulation of the public he could do without, but he did require its respect. Duty as high-minded as he believed his to be was insupportable in the face of censure. It poisoned his affections, and he determined to quit the public stage forever. The December resolution of the assembly cleared him of ill-founded suspicion or blame, but the wound, being to the spirit, could "only be cured by the all healing grave."

Sickened to his heart's core, Jefferson nursed the injury and embraced suffering as the only solace in a cruelly misshapen world. The response, so out of proportion to the offence, revealed sensitivities of no ordinary degree. Perhaps there lurked in Jefferson's consciousness some unavowed sense of failure or inadequacy such as men accused him of. He had learned that governing was a perilous thing, perhaps unworthy of further venture in his case. Several years later he confessed to a friend how ill-suited he was to a scene of troubles. "I do not love difficulties. I am fond of quiet, willing to do my duty, but irritable by slander and apt to be forced by it to abandon my post." Writing thus, the memory of his retirement from the governorship may not have entered his head, but the words suggested that ordeal. It was followed by a succession of personal misfortunes and one final, almost mortal, blow. Worn down by the grueling pace of the last five months in office he was chased from Monticello before he could catch his breath. At Poplar Forest, where he took refuge with his family, he fell from a horse and was immobilized for several weeks. His James River plantation was ravaged, the slaves carried away and consumed by pestilence, the tobacco crop destroyed. As a result, he found it hard to pay his taxes the following year. Apprehensions for his wife's health rose steadily while she was carrying their sixth child. A daughter was born in May 1782. Martha sank beyond recovery and died in September. Jefferson seemed to pass the threshold of misery.

All through these months his friends in Congress and the General Assembly tried to soothe his feelings and draw him back to the public stage. But without success. In July 1781 he was notified of his appointment as a commissioner to negotiate peace with Great Britain. He promptly drafted his refusal, then held the letter for four weeks. Again, as five years before, he was tempted by a European mission. But he must yield the opportunity, he said, in order to confront his accusers in the fall session of the legislature. Writing from Congress, Edmund Randolph hastened to assure him that he might discharge this obligation and still reach France before the negotiations commenced. He replied that there were still other obstacles, unspecified, to his acceptance of any public post. "I have taken my final leave of everything of that nature, have retired to my farm, my family and books from which I think nothing will ever more separate me." Randolph shot back: "If you can justify this resolution to yourself, I am confident, that you cannot to the world." Madison agreed. Jefferson's conduct in the fact of adversity, while it manifested "a keen sensibility and strong consciousness of rectitude," could not be justified by philosophy or patriotism. Even before the adoption of the December resolution, the assembly showed its confidence in the former governor by electing him to Congress. He declined to serve; and after leaving Richmond the day before Christmas wrapped himself in a mantle of oblivion uninterrupted by word or letter for a period of three months. The silence was broken, though not the oblivion, by another "act of renunciation": the repudiation of his Albemarle constituents who again elected him to the House of Delegates. His protégé James Monroe, just now embarked in politics as a member of the House, took alarm at Jefferson's absence. The talk of the streets and the corridors was full if it. "It is publicly said here," Monroe reported, "that the people of your county informed you that they had frequently elected you in times of less difficulty and danger than the present to please you, but that now they called you forth into public office to serve themselves." He implored Jefferson to overcome his morbid resolution and shoulder the burden of republican service. To this appeal, the Speaker of the House, rejecting Jefferson's resignation, added the threat of arrest and attendance in custody of the sergeant of arms should he persist in his disobedience.

Jefferson deigned no reply to the Speaker, but to Monroe he wrote a long and pathetic letter which revealed the tortures of his soul and set forth, with what reason he could muster, the grounds of his defense. His beloved Martha had given birth to her last child twelve days before. She was slipping from him. He did not, however, offer her illness as his excuse. He returned instead to the feelings that had motivated his retirement: the exhaustion of political ambition, the preference for private life, the care of his disordered estate, the obligation to his family, and, above all, the distressing evidence "that by a constant sacrifice of time, labour, loss, parental and friendly duties, I had been so far from gaining the affections of my countrymen which was the only reward I ever asked or could have felt, that I had even lost the small estimation I before possessed: that however I might have comforted myself under the disapprobation of well-meaning but uninformed people yet that of their representatives was a shock on which I had not calculated. . . ." He then undertook to refute the proposition that "the state may command the political services of all its members to an indefinite extent." Reason and law were against it. "This would be slavery and not that liberty which the bill of rights has made inviolable. . . . This to men of certain ways of thinking would be to annihilate the blessings of existence; to contradict the giver of life who gave it for happiness and not for wretchedness, and certainly to such it were better that they had never been born. However with these I may think public service and private misery inseparably linked together, I have not the vanity to count myself among those whom the state would think worth oppressing with perpetual service. I have received a sufficient memento to the contrary," he bitterly concluded. More because of his wife's condition than his own apology, the House left Jefferson to his misery. At the fall session, however, after her death, he was ordered into custody, appeared in the House, and obtained release for good cause.

During the first few months of retirement, Jefferson picked up the threads of an idealized private life that, like a phantom, seemed always to escape his grasp. He took an increasing interest in the education of his eldest daughter, Patsy. His sister Martha Carr and her six children, a "sacred charge" since the death of their father, came to live at Monticello; and to Peter Carr, in particular, Jefferson was a devoted guardian and tutor. There was little he could do in the distressed situation of Virginia to improve his estate. The practice of law offered an obvious recourse, and Jefferson took it, though not very seriously. Early in 1782 he undertook at Madison's urging to prepare a defense of Virginia's title to the western territory; but it was interrupted by his wife's illness and never completed. Unquestionably the most important product of these months was the *Notes on the State of Virginia*. Whatever his countrymen might think of his withdrawal from public life, they, and indeed all Americans, had reason to be grateful to him for this work. Commenced in the fall of 1780, set aside after Arnold's invasion, Jefferson brought it near completion during the weeks of enforced idleness at Poplar Forest, leaving only a few gaps to be filled up after his return to Monticello later in the summer.

There, in the first blush of spring the following year, Jefferson received a memorable visitor, the Chevalier de Chastellux, a member of the French Academy and a major general in Rochambeau's army encamped at Williamsburg. When he returned to France, Chastellux published his *Travels in North America*, subsequently translated into English. His felicitous portrait of Monticello and its master was the first to present Jefferson to the world in philosophical colors. The amiable Frenchman at first found Jefferson "serious, nay even cold," but within two hours they were as intimate as if they had spent their lives together. They walked up and down Jefferson's little mountain, conversed on all variety of subjects—politics, natural philosophy, fine arts—and passed an entire evening around a bowl of punch, spouting the bardic verses of Ossian, in whom they discovered a mutual enthusiasm. "Let me describe to you a man, not yet forty, tall, and with a mild and pleasing countenance, but whose mind and understanding are ample substitutes for every exterior grace. An American, who without ever having quitted his own country, is at once a musician, skilled in drawing, a geometrician, an astronomer, a natural philosopher, legislator, and statesman . . . a philosopher, in voluntary retirement from the world, and public business, because he loves the world, inasmuch only as he can flatter himself with being useful to mankind. . . . A mild and amiable wife, charming children, of whose education he himself takes charge, a house to embellish, great provisions to improve, and the arts and sciences to cultivate; these are what remain to Mr. Jefferson, after having played a principal character on the theater of the new world, and which he preferred to the honorable commission of Minister Plenipotentiary in Europe." Chastellux described Monticello in some detail, for it had a charm, an elegance, a character not to be found in other Virginia mansions. "Mr. Jefferson," he observed, "is the first American who has consulted the fine arts to know how he should shelter himself from the weather." The visit of four days passed like so many minutes, Chastellux recalled, and he set out to view the spectacle of the Natural Bridge convinced that his host was a supremely enlightened man. "It seemed as if from his youth he had placed his mind, as he had done his house, on an elevated situation, from which he might contemplate the universe."

Chastellux saw little of Mrs. Jefferson, which is a pity, for it would be pleasing to know something more of her than that she was "mild and amiable." Of course, she was also charming and accomplished in the manner of Virginia ladies of that day. But what else she was, what set her apart, what she contributed to the life of her husband other than six children in ten years (three of them living) and an abiding love—on the person of Martha Jefferson history is silent. Death lingered at her bedside for four months. Jefferson was never out of calling and daily attended her as a nurse. When she died on September 6, according to his eldest daughter's recollection, he fell into a state of insensibility from which it was feared he would not revive. When he did, his torment was indescribable. "He kept [to] his room three weeks, and I was never a moment from his side. He walked almost incessantly night and day, only lying down occasionally, when nature was completely exhausted, on a pallet that had been brought in during his long fainting fits. . . . When at last he left his room, he rode out, and from that time he was incessantly on horseback, rambling about the mountain, in the least frequented roads, and just as often through the woods. In those melancholy rambles, I was his constant companion," Patsy said, "a solitary witness to many a violent burst of grief. . . ."

From this stupor Jefferson gradually emerged in October. Monticello was now full of anguished memories. He found himself "absolutely unable to attend to any thing like business," and saw in prospect "a gloom unbrightened with one cheerful expectation." Then, in November, Congress threw him a lifeline: renewal of the commission as Minister Plenipotentiary to negotiate peace. Congress acted on the well-founded assumption that the loss of his wife had caused a change in Jefferson's sentiments toward the public service. He lost no time accepting the appointment. In little more than three weeks he was on the road to Philadelphia to embark for France. Jefferson had lost a wife; the country regained a statesman.

With overtones of heroic mythos, the passing of Jefferson's beloved freed him from the prison he was making for himself and returned him to the path of destiny. "Before that event my scheme of life had been determined," he wrote to Chastellux on the very day he announced his return to duty. "I had folded myself in the arms of retirement, and rested all prospects of future happiness on domestic and literary objects. A single event wiped away all my plans and left me a blank which I had not the spirit to fill up." His withdrawal served him well. Not only did he have the *Notes on Virginia* to show for it, but it also taught him to take adversity in stride, stoically shore up his feelings, and view his favored life of retirement with more becoming modesty. These lessons did not change his character, or overcome its pivotal ambivalence, but they improved its balance and resiliency. After passing through the great private ordeal of his life, he returned to the public a stronger and wiser man.

The Notes on Virginia

"The subjects are all treated imperfectly, some scarcely touched on," Jefferson wrote of the *Notes on Virginia* in 1787. "To apologize for this by developing the circumstances of the time and place of their composition, would be to open wounds which have already bled enough." Of all Jefferson's compositions this one alone assumed the character of a book; yet it did not begin as one or with intentions of publication. It began in response to the request of the secretary of the French legation, François de Marbois, for information on the state of Virginia. The information might have been furnished in perfunctory fashion, as indeed it was, so far as furnished at all, by the secretary's informants in other states. But Jefferson converted the occasion into an opportunity for the intellectual discovery of his own country. In the philosophic view Americans were yet strangers to the land. Its rivers and mountains, its flora and fauna, its laws and institutions and productions—"What a field have we at our door to signalize ourselves in!" Jefferson exclaimed. The information sought by an enlightened foreigner for his government was information of infinitely greater value to the enlightened patriot. And thus, as Jefferson answered Marbois's queries, the manuscript became a vehicle for the interpretation of his country to himself.

While he had no desire to appear before the public as an author, and was actually averse to it, Jefferson sensed that the work so modestly begun had taken a character to interest other Americans of a philosophical turn of mind. He returned the answers to Marbois in December 1781, but this was not the end of it. His friend Charles Thomson, Secretary of Congress and a fellow counsellor of the American Philosophical Society, encouraged him to present it to that body. Jefferson held off. Some parts required more complete and reliable data. He continued his investigations, communicated with well-informed friends, and as leisure permitted, revised and enlarged the manuscript until, in 1784, it had "swelled to nearly treble bulk." By then many persons in Virginia, Philadelphia, and other places had seen or heard something of Jefferson's "Notes." They wished to possess it. Being now too much for manuscript copies, such as he had endeavored to provide, Jefferson decided "to print a dozen or 20 copies to be given to my friends, not suffering another to go out." He opposed outright publication from the fear that his severe strictures on slavery and the Virginia constitution would expose him to renewed censure in his native state and prove more a hindrance than a help to the reform of these institutions. The plan for a limited edition was deferred until Jefferson, at last, reached Paris. An edition of 200 copies was ready for private distribution in the spring of 1785.

The book was born. It contained no avowal of authorship, however, and he still hoped to confine his opinions to a small circle, whose co-operation he asked to prevent the book from falling into untrustworthy hands. But a corps of secret agents on two continents could not have prevented this. On the decease of a friend who had received a copy, the book came into the possession of a French bookseller. Jefferson had no choice but to make the best arrangement he could for French translation and publication. Even worse was the prospect of a botched English edition, retranslated from the already botched French. So in 1787 he arranged for the publication of the *Notes* in England, submitting also to the acknowledgment of authorship. Meanwhile, Madison overcame his opposition to the circulation of the book in Virginia. He sent numerous copies home, a total of thirty-seven to George Wythe alone for distribution to favored students in the College. His political feelings, still tender after six years, could not be protected in any event. The book had escaped his control. Months before the English edition crossed the Atlantic, American newspapers were publishing the work piecemeal. The first, and unauthorized, American edition appeared at Philadelphia in 1788. Four editions in four years, with many more to come: such is the record of a book Jefferson never meant to write and, having written it, seemed determined to keep from the general public.

Viewed in one aspect the *Notes on Virginia* was simply a glorified guidebook, descriptive, crammed with facts, informative on a broad range of subjects from cascades and caverns to weights and measures, all treated in clear, effortless prose touched with philosophy. Viewed in the light of eighteenth-century knowledge, it was a work of natural and civil history, uniquely interesting as a guide to Jefferson's mind as well as to his native country. Taking his cue from the Baconian faculties of the time—memory, reason, and imagination—Jefferson divided all knowledge into three great branches: history, philosophy, and fine arts. Each in turn was subdivided until every species of knowledge found its logical place. When he first made a catalogue of his library in 1783, he classified the books according to this system. History, the principal realm occupied by the *Notes on Virginia,* was divided between natural and civil. Much of Jefferson's discussion of Virginia society and government belonged to the field of civil history; other parts of it, such as the strictures on slavery and the constitution, belonged in his system to the realm of philosophy, including among its lesser branches ethics, law, and politics.

Natural history was one of the two vast fields of scientific inquiry in the eighteenth century. For Jefferson, as for most Americans, it was a more spacious, a more agreeable, and a more practical field of investigation than natural philosophy, which embraced astronomy, physics, and chemistry. Natural history comprehended the entire earth as a scene of life: land, water, and climate, the kingdoms of plants and animals, the races and the descent of man. Some of the particular sciences were peculiarly attractive to Americans. Botany, for example, was not only useful, it might be pursued as a charming pastime. "No country gentleman," Jefferson observed, "should be without what amuses every step he takes into his fields." Both botany and zoology had been reduced to orderly system by the Swedish naturalist Linnaeus. Even the untutored investigator could discover, describe, and classify according to the Linnaen system. A triumph of rationality, it appealed to Jefferson's mind; and the infinitely subtle gradations of plant and animal life confirmed his faith in the perfection of the divine Creator. The study of American nature was, moreover, a patriotic as well as a scientific obligation. Astronomy and physics—all the sciences Jefferson called "mathematical" and considered of greater import in the long run—were the same the world around. But America had its own natural history, and from this standpoint was still a *terra incognita*. The unique task of American science lay along the paths of self-discovery. This conviction animated Jefferson's scientific work, set the tone of the *Notes on Virginia*, and, with that book, secured him a reputation among the savants of two continents. It was, according to Charles Thomson, "a most excellent Natural History not merely of Virginia but of North America and possibly equal if not superior to that of any country yet published."

Marbois's twenty-two queries came to Jefferson's hand in a jumble. Questions on colonial laws and charters and the constitution preceded questions of a geographical nature, for instance, and some questions combined incongruous subjects. Jefferson sorted and arranged the whole under twenty-three heads, the order proceeding from the natural through the civil to the generally social and moral. Viewing Virginia as an environment of life, he thought it important to begin with nature, which so profoundly conditioned every human part. The greater Virginia he described, broken in the middle by the Allegheny Mountains, had no geographical unity. But the coastal and the western rivers might be joined together, or nearly so, making strong bonds between the two regions. Questions of western navigation and commerce occupied him when he revised the original manuscript. He described all the principal rivers from the James to the Missouri in remarkable detail, traced their courses, measured their length and breadth and depth, noted their rapids and other obstructions to navigation, and so on. His interest was factual and utilitarian; still he could not refrain from observing that the Ohio was "the most beautiful river in the world," and that the passage of the Potomac through the Blue Ridge, at Harper's Ferry, was "one of the most stupendous scenes of nature . . . . worth a voyage across the Atlantic." A lover's pride in the bigness and grandeur of his country shone through Jefferson's prose, without any traces of the braggadocio that was later to characterize native depictions of American nature. He was capable of wildly subjective emotion, as in his response to the Natural Bridge, which was located on his own property in Rockbridge County. "It is impossible for the emotions arising from the sublime to be felt beyond what they are here; so beautiful an arch, so elevated, so light, and springing as it were up to heaven! The rapture of the spectator is really indescribable." Even here, however, the paroxysm was momentary, the sublimity faded, as he became the geometrician again and exactly measured every element of the "semi-elliptical" arch through the mountains. The Potomac passage was similarly affecting. Regarding it as a stupendous monument of "a war between rivers and mountains, which must have shaken the earth itself to its very center," he supposed that an ocean had once filled the valley behind the Blue Ridge until the waters rose to a great height, broke over, tore the mountain down from its summit to its base, and cut the channel of the Potomac.

The notion of an inland sea suggested explanation for the phenomenon of shells discovered in Virginia, as in other countries, thousands of feet above sea level. The curiosity was of unusual interest because of its implications for the emerging science of historical geology. Two schools of thought, Neptunists and Vulcanists, were at loggerheads on the theory of the formation of the earth's crust. The Neptunists held that it emerged gradually from a universal ocean. The theory easily disposed of the mystery of shells atop mountains, and it appealed to learned and unlearned alike because of its compatibility with the Biblical deluge. The Vulcanists held that the earth's chaotic surface was formed by volcanic explosion from intense heat within its bowels. On this theory the shells were supposed to have been thrown from the earth's bed onto the mountains by a gigantic convulsion. Jefferson, neither Vulcanist nor Neptunist, rejected both explanations. Nothing in the history of nature pointed to a force sufficient to warrant the Vulcanists' conclusion. Equally "out of the laws of nature" was the hypothesis of a universal deluge —an opinion that contributed to Jefferson's reputation as an infidel. Still a third solution to the riddle of the shells had been advanced by Voltaire: they were not shells at all but calcareous earth and stone formed by some process of nature into the image of shells. Jefferson took this position in the first edition of the *Notes on Virginia*. When David Rittenhouse, among others, disagreed, he reconsidered, altered the text, and stamped Voltaire's hypothesis unproven with the others. "Ignorance is preferable to error; and he is less remote from the truth who believes nothing, than he who believes what is wrong." Yet the theory of "mineral simulacra" of shells was the only one that did not run in the face of the laws of nature. It had the singular merit, moreover, of being subject to Jefferson's personal investigation. It was founded on observation of a spot of earth near Tours, in France. In 1787 Jefferson visited Tours to satisfy his curiosity in this matter. "What are we to conclude? That we have not materials enough yet to form any conclusion." He began to think the entire question "beyond the investigation of human sagacity." And soon historical geology, as differentiated from the useful applied science of mineralogy, appeared a senseless muddle: "the dreams about the modes of creations, inquiries whether our globe has been formed by the agency of fire or water, how many millions of years it has cost Vulcan or Neptune to produce what the fiat of the Creator would effect by a single act of will, is too idle to be worth a single hour of any man's life." His own idle hours with the mystery of the shells revealed both the strength and the weakness of Jefferson's scientific attitude. A hard-headed skepticism toward all explanations not grounded in observed facts of nature and a dominant utilitarian purpose. But impatience with imaginative generalizations which, while neither verifiable nor useful, held the promise of entire new orders of truth. The early geologists were wrong, yet they were on the right track, the track of evolution, while Jefferson slumbered in the pious faith of divine creation "by a single act of will."

In treating the animals of Virginia, Jefferson entered the first important rebuttal of European theories of degeneracy in the New

World. Georges Louis Leclerc, Comte de Buffon, the greatest naturalist in the world—"the pope of eighteenth century zoologists"—had said the New World exhibited fewer species than the Old and, of the animals common to both, those of the former were smaller, meanly formed, "very few ferocious, and none formidable." The niggardliness of American nature was owing to three facts: the coldness of the climate in comparison with other lands in similar latitudes, the excessive moisture that overlaid the ground and filled the atmosphere, and the very newness of America from the standpoint both of geologic time and human habitation. Buffon was a Neptunist. The American continent had emerged more recently from the deluge; it was, accordingly, more primitive. "In these melancholy regions," Buffon wrote depressingly, "nature remains concealed under her old garments, and never exhibits herself in fresh attire; being neither cherished nor cultivated by man, she never opens her fruitful and beneficient womb. . . . In this abandoned condition, every thing languishes, corrupts, and proves abortive. The air and the earth, overloaded with humid and noxious vapours, are unable either to purify themselves, or to profit by the influence of the sun, who darts in vain his most enlivening rays upon this frigid mass, which is not in a condition to make suitable return to his ardour. Its powers are limited to the production of moist plants, reptiles and insects, and can afford nourishment only for cold men and feeble animals." The savages of America formed no exception to the rule of degeneracy, according to Buffon. But it was left to others to take the next step, condemning the transplanted European to waste and decay in the wretched New World. The Abbé Raynal, the Swedish naturalist Kalm, the Dutchman De Pauw, the Scotsman William Robertson, whose *History of America*, published in 1777, won a large audience—these freely elaborated the theory until Buffon himself was moved to refute their extravagances.

Jefferson's vindication of American nature attacked the Buffon theory in its conclusions rather than in its premises. That the natural environment basically determined institutional life was the assumption of the age. But whether America was, in fact, comparatively more humid, whether moisture was unfriendly to animal growth, whether there had been a deluge or America had emerged late from it, were questions scientists could not answer. Prompted by Franklin, Jefferson later pursued evidence to prove that Europe was actually more humid than America; but knowledge of these matters was still very primitive, as he said in the *Notes*, giving neither proof nor disproof of degeneracy theories. He proceeded instead on the assumption that America was equally adapted with Europe to animal life. "Let us then take a comparative view of the quadrupeds of Europe and America, presenting them to the eye in three different tables, in one of which shall be enumerated those found in both countries; in a second, those found in one only; in a third, those which have been domesticated in both." The truth would then emerge from comparisons of number and size. He put his friends to work weighing and measuring animals "from the mouse to the mammoth." "I Killed a bear, not fat which waighed 410 lb after he was Quartered," Archibald Cary reported, "and have seen much larger but had no oppartunaty of Trying their Weight." Weasel and woodchuck were never more meticulously gauged and scaled than by James Madison! As the data came in, Jefferson filled up his tables. They remained very imperfect, as he conceded, not only because comparable weights were unavailable for comparable animals, but also because the state of the science and the differences in nomenclature between the two continents often made it impossible to identify the comparable animals. Nevertheless, so far as the evidence went, Jefferson was justified in his conclusions: that of the quadrupeds common to both continents, those of America were generally as large; that the types peculiar to America were much more numerous than those peculiar to Europe and built on as generous a scale; that while the domestic animals were perhaps smaller in America, the cause was to be found in the miserable animal husbandry of the country rather than in its climate; and finally, taking all the tables together, that America produced more than her share of the world's quadrupeds. As great a zoologist as Buffon was, in Jefferson's opinion, he showed "more eloquence than sound reason" in support of his theory.

One animal particularly, the mammoth, fascinated Jefferson, and it furnished the *coup de grâce* in his encounter with Buffon. Tusks, grinders, and bones of this huge creature of Indian legend had been found on the Ohio. While Governor of Virginia, inspired perhaps by Marbois's queries, Jefferson had asked George Rogers Clark to procure the necessary bones to reconstruct a skeleton of this most desirable of all objects of natural history. Not for many years was the mission accomplished, by Colonel William Clark (of Lewis and Clark fame) under Jefferson's auspices; but thus began Jefferson's long interest in paleontology, his one great passion in pure science. Certain European naturalists, including Buffon, had said that the relics of the so-called mammoth belonged to the family of elephant. But the elephant, Jefferson pointed out, was a native only of the torrid zone and its skeleton was probably but one-fifth that of the mammoth. He thought the mammoth a distinct species, "the largest of all terrestial beings," and believed it still roamed the frozen northland. The Old World elephant was but a mouse to the New World mammoth! "It should have sufficed to have rescued the earth it inhabited, and the atmosphere it breathed, from the imputation of impotence in the conception and nourishment of animal life on a large scale; to have stifled, in its birth, the opinion of a writer, the most learned, too, of all others in the science of animal history . . . that nature is less active, less energetic on one side of the globe than she is on the other."

There was a touch of the fabulous in Jefferson's account of the mammoth, as if to answer European pessimism with a tale of American giants; but he checked himself and kept the discussion on a high plane. Although his comparative data supported a claim for American superiority, he asked only for equality, consistent with the enlightened principle of uniformity in the operations of nature. He had no desire, not yet anyway, to encourage a delusion the opposite of Buffon's: America the land of noble savagery or Arcadian simplicity in contrast to the civilized decadence of Europe. It was against this romantic conception, nourished by the primitivism of Jean Jacques Rousseau, that Voltaire, Buffon, and the partisans of civilization had risen in protest. Jefferson did not take sides in this contest. But in the *Notes on Virginia*, as it happened, the criticism was all on one side, and several of the book's most eloquent passages contributed mightily to the idealization of American nature. Revolutionary nationalism accented nature. Philosophical Europeans, responding to the achievement of the American Revolution, established correlations between the natural environment of the Americans and the principles of liberty. The New World image projected by Raynal, Buffon, and the other degenerationists was fading fast, at least as to the United States, when Jefferson undertook to refute it. The *Notes on Virginia* blended in with the ascendant revolutionary cult of America, though idealization was far from Jefferson's intention.

For the Abbé Raynal the great crime of the New World was the ruthless slaughter, plunder, and enslavement both of the Indian aborigines and the imported Africans. Jefferson treated at considerable length each of these races, the conquered and the enslaved, as well as his own race of conquerors.

For all his enlightenment, Jefferson suffered the color prejudice of Western man. He believed the race of "whites" of superior beauty, possibly of superior intellect, though morally no better or worse than others. Civilization in the United States was the white man's enterprise and responsibility. Any other hypothesis was inconceivable to him. But he did not idealize the prospect. From the end of the Revolution the country would probably be "going down hill." In Virginia the people had yet to secure a constitution of their own or the education of their posterity; they would, he feared, become caught up in the race for riches, forget about their rights, and lose their chance of happiness. The natural history of government, as he always said, was for liberty to lose and tyranny to gain ground. Such had been the fate of Rome, and Britain's sun had already set. What saved him from pessimism was the dominant fact of the American environment: "an immensity of land courting the industry of the husbandman." The economic values of agriculture concerned him, of course, but the moral values were of first importance. Agricultural industry put man into relationship with the natural world, and through that to the divine Creator; it nourished a virtuous way of life; it secured dignity, competency, and independence, so essential to the support of free government. "It is the manner and spirit of a people which preserve a republic in vigor," he wrote. Jefferson's hymn to the husbandman became famous:

> Those who labor in the earth are the chosen people of God, if ever He had a chosen people, whose breasts He has made His peculiar deposit for substantial and genuine virtue. It is the focus in which He keeps alive that sacred fire, which otherwise might escape from the face of the earth. Corruption of morals

in the mass of cultivators is a phenomenon of which no age nor nation has furnished an example. It is the mark set on those, who, not looking up to heaven, to their own soil and industry, as does the husbandman, for their subsistence, depend for it on casualties and caprice of customers. Dependence begets subservience and venality, suffocates the germ of virtue, and prepares fit tools for the designs of ambition. This, the natural progress and consequence of the arts, has sometimes perhaps been retarded by accidental circumstances; but, generally speaking, the proportion which the aggregate of the other classes of citizens bears in any State to that of its husbandmen, is the proportion of its unsound to its healthy parts, and is a good enough barometer whereby to measure its degree of corruption. While we have land to labor then, let us never wish to see our citizens occupied at a work-bench, or twirling a distaff.

This was an ideal, drawn from poetry more than from observation, and not meant to describe any American reality; but it was meant as a moral directive consonant with the American environment. In 1782 Hector St. Jean Crèvecœur struck the same bucolic note in his *Letters from an American Farmer*, which became the bible of a European cult of republican simplicity. It was not so much the farmer or farming that Jefferson, or Crèvecœur, idealized, but a state of life midway between the primitive and the civilized, possessing the virtues of both and the vices of neither. This dreamy state captured his feelings and his hopes for the culture of man in America.

For Jefferson, clearly, the American land was a regenerative force. Taking up the application of the degeneracy theory to "the race of whites," Jefferson focused on Raynal's statement of amazement that America had not yet produced a good poet, an able mathematician, or a man of genius in any science. In war Washington, in physics Franklin, in astronomy Rittenhouse: these names, Jefferson declared in answer, would be remembered long after the philosophy defrauding the Western day was forgotten. America, "though but a child of yesterday," with a population not one-third that of Great Britain or one-sixth that of France, had contributed her full share to the world's genius. He claimed nothing in poetry but, with ill-disguised indignation, asked for time. "When we shall have existed as a people as long as the Greeks did before they produced a Homer, the Romans a Virgil, the French a Racine and Voltaire, the English a Shakespeare and Milton, shall this reproach be still true, we will inquire from what unfriendly causes it has proceeded, that the other countries of Europe and quarters of the earth shall not have inscribed any name in the roll of poets." The European reproach to American culture rang down the years. Jefferson's response, while more realistic and restrained than many to come, unmasked the patriotic ardor that animated his entire vindication of American nature.

The Virginia philosopher keenly perceived the dilemma of the American Indian and, in a sense, entered into it himself. As children of nature, the aborigines were admirable. They recalled man to his original freedom. He sometimes wondered if their condition, without organized government, was not the best; it was certainly preferable to the government of "wolves over sheep" as in Europe. But civilization was the natural state of the white man. As he pushed back the wilderness, the Indian way of life was doomed. Fortunately, these people possessed equal powers of body and mind with the whites; hence they could be civilized, fully incorporated into the white man's society, indeed racially amalgamated as well. Ultimately, the Indians could be saved from extinction only by losing their racial identity—by becoming Americanized.

Buffon had condemned this race to stupidity and impotence. Mere automatons of nature, feeble in body and mind, without manly ardor or parental affection, their fundamental defect, according to Buffon, was one of sexual incapacity. The picture was false, Jefferson said. In a superficial view certain characteristics of the race (the beardlessness of the males, the fewer childbirths of the females) supported the theory; but these were cultural rather than physical characteristics. "With them it is disgraceful to be hairy on the body," for example. "They say it likens them to hogs. They therefore pluck the hair as fast as it appears." Making allowance for the "circumstances of their situation which call for a display of particular talents only"—talents of war and chase—"we shall probably find that they are formed in mind as well as in body on the same module with the *Homo sapiens Europaeus*." Even in their savage state the Indians showed the germ of higher talents. "They astonish you with strokes of the most sublime oratory; such as to prove their reason and sentiment strong, their imagination glowing and elevated." Jefferson introduced into the *Notes* the affecting speech of the Mingo Chief Logan, related to him at Williamsburg in 1774. The speech had been published before, in the United States, England, and France, but the *Notes* gave it immortality. Schoolboys across the land later declaimed this grave lament on the white man's murderous destruction of the chief's family and his proud revenge, closing with the familiar line, "Who is there to mourn for Logan? Not one."

Jefferson's interest in the redmen was essentially anthropological. The *Notes* provided an informed summary of the numbers and locations of the tribes of North America. He described his own careful excavation of a large barrow in Albemarle and speculated on the origin of the aborigines. Whether they were the product of a "special creation," as Buffon and Lord Kames thought, or descended from an ancient people—Hebrew, Tartar, Carthaginian—was a much debated question. In Jefferson's opinion they were of the same race as the people of Northern Asia, Tartar, having probably crossed from one continent to the other by way of the Bering Strait. The conjecture was not original; but he went on to argue against the principal authorities that the migration had been from North America to Asia rather than the other way around. He inferred the greater antiquity of the Americans from the greater profusion of tongues and dialects among them. At any rate, the comparative study of languages held the key to the puzzle of origins. He lamented that many tribes had passed away without leaving any record of the languages they spoke. At the time of writing the *Notes*, he commenced a remarkable collection of Indian vocabularies, eventually numbering some forty tribes. He thus employed the tools of ethnology, archaeology, and linguistics in his study of the Indians.

Jefferson's vindication of the American Indian was at the same time a vindication of the American environment; the children of Africa, on the other hand, had no natural place in that environment, and his solution for them was not amalgamation but expulsion. The double standard toward Indians and Africans was at least two centuries old. The great Hispanic priest Las Casas, while he had envisioned a Christianized utopia for the Indians of the New World, had condemned the Negroes of the dark continent of the Old World to perpetual slavery. The Indians of the Northern latitudes had not, with few exceptions, been enslaved, which seemed to Jefferson all the more reason to bring them under a different rule than the unfortunate blacks, redeemed by neither nature nor civilization. But this rule did not justify their enslavement.

Jefferson's impassioned denunciation of slavery occurred in answer to the query on "the particular customs and manners" of Virginians. Basically, his position was a moral one, founded in the immutable principles of human liberty. No abolitionist of later time ever cried out more prophetically against slavery. "And can the liberties of a nation be thought secure when we have removed their only firm basis, a conviction in the minds of the people that these liberties are the gift of God?" he demanded. "That they are not to be violated but with his wrath? Indeed I tremble for my country when I reflect that God is just. . . ." He even threatened "supernatural interference"—an event unheard of in his philosophy—should civil emancipation fail to take place. But Jefferson was moved as much by the debasement of the master as by the misery and oppression of the slave. Like Montesquieu, he believed that slavery created an evil social environment, retarded public improvement, and corrupted the master class. "The whole commerce between master and slave is a perpetual exercise of the most boisterous passions, the most unremitting despotism on the one part, and degrading submission on the other. . . . The man must be a prodigy who can retain his manners and morals undepraved by such circumstances." And he added, "With the morals of the people, their industry also is destroyed." Jefferson sketched the plan of gradual emancipation earlier withheld by the revisers, and looked hopefully to young men growing up, who had "sucked in the principles of liberty as it were with their mothers' milk," to turn the fate of this question. Young men still in college: this was the audience Jefferson wished to reach. Outside a small circle of friends, they were the first Americans to receive his book.

The colonization feature of the plan of emancipation led Jefferson into a discussion of the racial attributes of the Negro; and here he broached opinions that seriously embarrassed his philosophy. It was unthinkable, he said, to incorporate the mass of freed blacks into the commonwealth. "Deep-rooted prejudices entertained by the whites; ten thousand recollections, by the blacks, of the injuries they have sustained; new provocations; the real distinctions which nature has made; and many other circumstances, will divide us into parties, and produce convulsions, which will probably never end but in the extermination of one or the other race. To these objections, which are political," Jefferson continued, "may be added others, which are physical and moral." The color of the Negroes, "that immovable veil of black," which in its "eternal monotony" was aesthetically inferior to "the fine mixtures of red and white" of the Caucasians, posed a powerful objection to the racial blending that must ensue from a simple act of emancipation. There were differences of figure, of hair, of glandular function, all unfavorable to the Negroes. "Many of their advocates," among whom Jefferson counted himself, "while they wish to vindicate the liberty of human nature, are anxious also to preserve its dignity and beauty." In a moral view the Negroes had several engaging, if somewhat child-like qualities. But they had little capacity for reflection or forethought; in reason they were much inferior to the whites, in imagination "dull, tasteless, and anomalous"; and, while sexually ardent, their affections were neither tender nor lasting. Many Negroes, unlike the Indians, had associated with the whites, some were liberally educated; yet never had Jefferson known a black to utter an eloquent thought, compose a piece of music, paint a simple picture, discover a single truth. The criticism came with ill grace from the man who demolished Raynal for employing the same line of argument against the American whites!

Great allowance ought to be made for "the difference of condition," Jefferson conceded, but too many proofs offered that the inferiority of the Negroes was not the effect merely of their servile status. The slavery of ancient Rome was infinitely more wretched than the American; nevertheless, the Roman slaves excelled in the arts and sciences. "But they were of the race of white," Jefferson reasoned from the analogy. "It is not their condition then, but nature, which has produced this distinction." The very thought was treason to his heart and head. Still he advanced the opinion, though "a suspicion only" and "hazarded with great diffidence," "that the blacks, whether originally a distinct race, or made distinct by time and circumstances, are inferior to the whites in the endowments both of body and mind."

Honest, disinterested, and no doubt true to his personal observation and knowledge, Jefferson's opinion was also a product of frivolous and tortuous reasoning, of preconception, prejudice, ignorance, contradiction, and bewildering confusion of principles. Was he not simply voicing the master's conceit in observing that, while the Negroes "seem to require less sleep," they are disposed to sleep more than the whites? Their disposition to theft he readily ascribed to condition, but the transiency of their griefs he supposed a defect of nature, never stopping to consider the slaves' inordinate need for a psychological mechansim to check grief. The analogy to Roman slavery was badly misplaced. The discussion of the comparative beauty of the two races betrayed an insensibility to standards other than his own. Many of his observations, paraded as scientific, were but thinly disguised statements of folk belief about Negroes. This was blatantly true of his causual reference to the uniform preference shown by the orangutan for the black woman over the female of his own species. Yet even Buffon, "the greatest scientist in the world," had credited this notion. Deplorably, Jefferson was not out of tune with the scientific teaching of his day. Edward Tyson's monumental treatise on the orangutan, with which Jefferson was probably familiar, had established the close proximity of ape to man, and from this some scientific and pseudo-scientific observers—it is not always easy to distinguish them—went on to infer the Negro's intermediate place in the chain of being. Whether the Negro was equal or inferior to European man, if the latter whether his inferiority stemmed from genetic or environmental causes, and whether he was to be considered a different species or an inferior variety of the same species, the offspring of a unitary or a separate creation of God—these questions scratched the minds of the Enlightenment. The tendency was toward a humane, generous, and hopeful view of the Negro, as in *Esprit des lois* or, even better, the later work of Jefferson's philosophical friend in Paris, the Marquis de Condorcet, which he began to translate into English and never finished. But there were heretics, like the great Hume, who argued the natural inferiority of the Negro.

Jefferson's basic assumptions touching race were liberal and enlightened, but they were upset by his observation from the post of a Virginia planter. He could account for the observed inferiority of the Negro in one of two ways: either the Negro was a distinct species with an ancestry other than the white man's or an environmentally produced variety of the same species. But neither explanation was satisfactory. The first degraded a whole race of men in the order of Creation, exploding the equality doctrine founded in the unity of the species. The second was inconsistent with the conception of a fixed chain of being wrought by the Creator in the beginning. If the Negro was created equal, he could not lapse in the scale of being; if created unequal, time and improvement could not raise him on the scale. Jefferson evaded the problem, declining to accept either the explanation that assailed his faith in human equality or the explanation that played havoc with the system of nature. Nevertheless, overwhelmed by the physical distinctions between the races and the limited testimony of his senses, he raised the awful doubt of Negro inferiority.

Why? A quarter-century later, still not allowed to forget what he had written, Jefferson said, "It is impossible for doubt to have been more tenderly and hesitatingly expressed than it was in the *Notes on Virginia*, and nothing was farther from my intention than to enlist myself as the champion of a fixed opinion, where I have only expressed a doubt." Fair enough, in view of the abuse he had taken. Yet his "doubt" had been the conclusion of a long argument that carried the tone of conviction, and the opinion he chose to "hazard" was inferiority rather than equality. He might have been expected to place the emphasis on the inhibiting effects of slavery. In defense of the noble redmen he repeatedly appealed to "the circumstances of their situation." He argued that the conquest of the wilderness would ameliorate the American climate. Even the size of the asses of America was the effect of circumstances, not of nature. Yet he was unable to see the Negro in the same light. He reproached his countrymen for their failure to view either of the minority peoples living among them as subjects of natural history, which was to say, in effect, that these races were still unknown to scientific intelligence. Perhaps he wished, by broaching the subject, to open the way to investigation. But he broached it, it will be recalled, in order to demonstrate the practical impossibility of incorporating the emancipated blacks into the free American society. The twin imperatives were emancipation and colonization. To support, in his own mind to justify, the latter, he offered his damning appraisal of Negro capacities. Perhaps in this way he hoped to hasten a solution—the only workable one in his opinion—to the most menacing problem of the new nation.

Still, in the final analysis, what is astounding is that he chose to advance any conclusion at all, albeit a guarded one. He always commended the skeptical attitude: believe nothing rather than what is unproven. "To justify a general conclusion, requires many observations, even where the subject may be submitted to the anatomical knife, to optical glasses, to analysis by fire or by solvents. How much more then where it is a faculty, not a substance, we are examining; where it eludes the research of all the senses . . . ," as in the case of a race of men little known to natural history. Instead of adhering to this rule, he reached a tentative conclusion on the Negro that he knew to be indefensible morally and unproven scientifically. He soon retreated under fire from assorted Christians, speculators, abolitionists, and political enemies, though the latter usually seized upon his condemnation of slavery. Unable to affirm the natural equality of the Negro, unwilling to deny it, he suspended judgment and closed his mouth, meanwhile keeping his mind open and, as a practical matter, adhering to the liberal principle. "Whatever be their degree of talent," he declared, "it is no measure of their rights."

The *Notes on Virginia* ensured Jefferson a scientific and literary reputation to accompany his reputation as a political philosopher and statesman. Its information on all sorts of phenomena natural and civil, its sometimes dazzling erudition, its flights of speculation— these made it a book fit for the appetites of learned men. The circle of its readers steadily increased as the restraints on its circulation were lifted and as its author became better known to the American people. While never a popular book, it was constantly involved in public discussion. In Virginia, particularly, its politcal parts became virtually a handbook of liberal opinion. The *Notes on Virginia* acted as a catalyst in several fields of intellectual activity. It set an enviable standard for the writing of state histories and, of course, spurred this enterprise. It stimulated the investigation and inventory of the natural resources of the new nation. When Jedediah Morse, "the father of American geography," published his pioneer work in

1785, all he had to do with respect to Virginia and the vast western domain was to reprint the account from the *Notes on Virginia*. (Some travelers offered Jefferson's depiction as their own!) It set the stage for the literary battles of the next half-century between the Old World and the New. Much of the book, having served its purpose, soon became outmoded, and Jefferson never found the leisure to revise it as he wished to do. It would be longest and best remembered for the triumphant vindication of American nature. "Mr. Jefferson," an American scientist later declared, "in stepping forward as he did in favour of American power, may be almost said to have proclaimed emancipation a second time."

The Vagabond Congress

Jefferson was at Ampthill, Archibald Cary's place down the James, having his children inoculated against smallpox, when he was notified of his reappointment as Minister Plenipotentiary to negotiate peace. There was no time for delay. He placed little Polly and the infant Lucy in the care of their Aunt Eppes, arranged the management of his affairs, and left Monticello accompanied by ten-year-old Patsy, whom he was determined to keep at his side, on December 19. They were in Philadelphia a week later. Jefferson armed himself for the negotiations, poring over papers in the office of the Secretary of Foreign Affairs, and wondering if he would have anything to do upon his arrival in Paris but to toast the victory. Dispatches from the commissioners on the scene had already announced a preliminary accord. Then the brief stopover he had planned lengthened to a month, as the French warship in which he was to sail lay locked in ice below Baltimore.

The month passed pleasantly enough. Jefferson attended the meetings of the American Philosophical Society, then struggling to recover from the war's paralysis. He dipped into his pocketbook to help the cause of "useful knowledge," and at one of the meetings proposed that the Society present the King of France with an orrery to be made by the great Rittenhouse. (The Society agreed to the resolution, but the orrery was never completed.) He drew up at this time the first "catalogue" of his library, listing as well the books he wished to procure in France. From it Madison compiled a desideratum of some 300 titles to be embodied in a report to Congress recommending, unsuccessfully, the establishment of a congressional library. With Madison he concerted the first of many ciphers to be employed in political correspondence in order to evade snoopers and tattlers on both sides of the Atlantic.

The resumption of his friendship with Madison proved of lasting consequence. They lived under the same roof in Philadelphia, ate at the same table, and spent long hours in conversation. After the passage of a month, the friendship became something more, a partnership of two philosophic statesmen, enduring with scarcely a ripple between them as long as they lived. They had unlimited confidence in each other. Each in his own station was the eyes and the ears and the helping hand of the other. Madison, younger by several years, readily acted the part of the faithful lieutenant, undertaking assignments from Jefferson such as he would never ask him to perform. Yet Madison was a general in his own right, "the greatest man in the world," Jefferson called him in 1790; and in the constant exchange of ideas and services between them the account balanced. Men who were enough alike to work together, yet sufficiently different to complement each other, their alliance was remarkably beneficial. Madison had the more penetrating mind, sharp, probing, and persistent. Jefferson was the bolder thinker, more inventive, more talented in generalization and synthesis, and easily caught up in any idea that promised improvement to mankind. Madison had the keener sense of realities: he helped to keep Jefferson's political feet on the ground. In the new nation's search for an equilibrium between liberty and power, Jefferson's stress typically fell on the first term of the equation, Madison's on the second. Jefferson possessed the gift of brilliant rhetoric, Madison of skillful analysis. Jefferson had political magnetism, Madison none. About Jefferson there was an aura of greatness from the moment he stepped into fame: he stood, like his house, on a mountain, and celebrated himself in splendid achievements. Madison radiated neither mastery nor charm, but he had infinitely more patience with the drudgeries of politics and shone in caucuses and committees. Men respected Madison, even in opposition. They worshiped, or hated, Jefferson.

Toward the end of January 1783, Jefferson and his daughter

rode to Baltimore to board the French frigate *Romulus* for passage to France. Again he was delayed, by winter ice and a British fleet blocking Chesapeake Bay. No flag of safe conduct having been asked or received for Jefferson's passage, his capture was a calculable certainty were he to venture forth. "I am exceedingly fatigued with this place," he wrote to Madison after a fortnight, "as indeed I should be with any other when I had neither occupation nor amusement." He was soon rescued. Reports that a provisional treaty had been signed reached Congress the middle of February, and Jefferson's orders were suspended. Returning to Philadelphia, he waited another month to learn what final disposition would be made of him. When the earlier reports were verified, Congress gave him his discharge. The disappointment he felt at the defeat of his plans was submerged in the glad tidings of peace. On April 11 he sent a letter of congratulations to the commission in Paris, and the next day departed for Virginia.

He did not intend to fall back into the retirement he had so recently left. Stopping at Richmond, he discussed public affairs with members of the assembly. Under Madison's prodding at Philadelphia, he had enlisted in the campaign to strengthen the Confederacy. The first point to be gained from the states was the power of Congress to raise its own revenue by means of an impost. No doubt Jefferson lobbied for this measure at Richmond. With the end of the war, the question of a convention to "new model" the Virginia constitution was seriously agitated. Nothing was closer to Jefferson's heart. The chances of a convention seemed to him good. When he collected his family and returned to Monticello in May, he prepared a new draft constitution which, as noted earlier, made some advances over his previous thinking. He sent it to Madison and later incorporated it in the *Notes on Virginia*. But the convention never materialized. In June the assembly placed Jefferson at the head of the newly elected delegation to Congress. The news probably came as no surprise. He had discussed congressional duty with Madison in Philadelphia, and he could not have avoided the subject in Richmond. If he would accept employment in Congress, the assembly was eager to put him there. And so, after a lazy summer at Monticello, Jefferson again parted with his two younger daughters, arranged his affairs, and set out for Philadelphia, Patsy in tow, the middle of October. He traveled a westerly route, through the Shenandoah Valley bedecked in fall colors, leisurely viewing caves and caverns and the spectacle at Harper's Ferry—scenes new to his eye and depicted in the *Notes on Virginia*—thence to Philadelphia.

Unfortunately, a soldiers' mutiny had driven Congress from Philadelphia. It was temporarily quartered in the insignificant village of Princeton, New Jersey, "utterly undecided," as Madison informed his friend, "both as to their ultimate seat and their intermediate residence." Jefferson hurried off to Princeton, and took his seat on November 4, the same day Congress adjourned to reconvene at Annapolis, Maryland, three weeks later. Wherever Congress might set, he meant to settle Patsy in Philadelphia, the metropolis of America, for her education. He now arranged for her to live with the widowed mother of his friend, the genial poetaster, composer, and gadgeteer Francis Hopkinson, and canvassed the city for the best tutors in French, music, dancing, and drawing.

His familiar letters to Patsy, which commenced on his arrival at Annapolis, portray a keenly solicitous and demanding father. His wife gone, he clutched his daughters to his heart, the eldest especially, and transferred to them his hopes of personal happiness. "I have placed my happiness on seeing you good and accomplished," he told Patsy, "and no distress which this world can now bring on me could equal that of your disappointing my hopes." It was a dreadful onus to place on a child. Patsy carried it better than her younger sister. The daily regimen Jefferson prescribed was rather forbidding: "From 8 to 10 o'clock practice music. From 10 to 1 dance one day and draw another. From 1 to 2 draw on the day you dance, and write a letter the next day. From 3 to 4 read French. From 4 to 5 exercise yourself in music. From 5 till bedtime read English, write etc." Patsy was to write by every post. "Inform me what books you read, what tunes you learn, and inclose me your best copy of every lesson in drawing." Father was crushed when weekly epistles, and the drawings, failed to arrive. Mixing endearments with admonitions, his letters usually taught some little lesson in deportment. "Take care that you never spell a word wrong. . . . It produces great praise in a lady to spell well." "I do not wish you to be gayly clothed at this time of life, but that what you wear should be fine of its kind; but above all things, and at all times let your clothes be clean, whole, and properly put on. . . . Nothing is so disgusting to our sex as a want of cleanliness and delicacy in yours." "Determine never to be idle. No person will have occasion to complain of the want of time who never loses any." The man who found himself equal to whatever he undertook expected the same ability and application in his children. Deeply devoted to her father, Patsy did her best, which was really very good, and continually promised to do better; but sometimes she was at her wits' end to please him.

After the peregrinations of the past year, Jefferson was glad to come to rest at last in Annapolis. James Monroe, newly elected to Congress, had arranged temporary quarters for them in the home of a widow lady. Then in February the two men rented a house, hired a French major-domo, and lived quietly as two bachelors until Jefferson's departure in May. Annapolis was a charming, pleasure-loving town. It boasted a theater but no church, and "plays, balls, concerts, routs, hops, fandangoes and fox hunting." Jefferson did not partake of these amusements. He hated the cold, and the winter in Annapolis was "severe beyond all memory." Through most of it he was ill: a prolonged infection, with intermittent high fever, later complicated by his old headache affliction. Not until spring was he on the mend. The public business was demanding; but since Congress was slow to organize, and then frequently stalled for want of a quorum, he read a good deal and worked sporadically on the *Notes on Virginia*.

A young Dutch nobleman, Gijsbert Karel van Hogendorp, whom Jefferson befriended at Annapolis, portrayed him in words that have the ring of authenticity. "Retired from fashionable society," Hogendorp said, "he concerned himself only with affairs of public interest, his sole diversion being that offered by belles lettres. The poor state of his health, he told me occasionally, was the cause of this retirement; but it seemed rather that his mind, accustomed to the unalloyed pleasure of the society of a lovable wife, was impervious since her loss to the feeble attractions of common society, and that his soul, fed on noble thoughts, was revolted by idle chatter. . . . He has the shyness that accompanies true worth, which is at first disturbing and which puts off those who seek to know him. Those who persist in knowing him soon discern the man of letters, the lover of natural history, Law, Statecraft, Philosophy, and the friend of mankind." Hogendorp persisted. Jefferson liked him, thought him brilliant, took him into his household, fed his curiosity about things American, and seemed to open his heart to this presumptuous young man.

Congress was in deep trouble as the nation emerged from the war. The Confederation had slowly gathered strength in the presence of the common enemy; now, the enemy gone, the incentive to tighten the continental belt seemed gone too. When Congress failed to obtain additional powers from the states, the promising nationalist movement of the later war years subsided, and several of its young leaders, like Madison and Alexander Hamilton, of New York, retired in disgust. New faces predominated in the Congress Jefferson entered at Annapolis, itself a symbol of congressional impotency. The problem began with obtaining a quorum. The presence of a majority of the states was required to transact any business at all. Seven states must concur in the adoption of ordinary legislation, nine in decisions of greater import. These numbers proved formidable in themselves; but when it is considered that most of the states in attendance were represented by only two delegates, who must therefore concur if the vote of that state was to affect the decision on any question, the predicament of Congress becomes truly staggering. "There are 8 states in town, 6 of which are represented by two members only," Jefferson wrote to Madison in February. "Of these two members of different states are confined by the gout so that we cannot make a house. We have not sit above 3 days I believe in as many weeks. Admonition after admonition has been sent to the states, to no effect." The numbers changed from time to time, but the problem was constant. What could it signify but indifference to the government of the Union or inability of the states to support it? Jefferson preferred the latter, the more charitable, explanation. While he advocated the accession of new powers and the more vigorous employment of existing ones, he made every allowance for the havoc wreaked by the war in most of the states. "The greatest difficulty we find is to get money from them. The reason is not found in their unwillingness, but in their real inability." The Confederacy had labored under this difficulty for years; now, however, it reflected itself in the niggardly policy of the states toward their delegations, if any, in that "vagabond, strolling, contemptible crew," the Congress of the United States. Jefferson felt it in his own purse. He was on public duty for four months before he received one cent of pay. Other congressmen were in tighter straits. "There is really no standing this." And, of course, good men would not stand it for long. Everyone's energies were quickly exhausted in vain efforts to do business, and the interminable sessions, which necessarily followed from the lack of an executive head, were beyond endurance. After all was said of the feebleness of Congress on the point of constitutional powers, the fact remained, in Jefferson's opinion, that it lacked the political backing of the states, the internal organization, the caliber of leadership required for the effective exercise of the powers it had.

Jefferson at once encountered the problem in the ratification of the treaty of peace. When Congress finally reconvened on December 13, he was appointed to a committee to report on the definitive treaty. The report recommending its approval was submitted in his hand three days later. Seven states only being present, when the Articles of Confederation required the assent of nine to a treaty, the question of how Congress should proceed caused heated debate. Nor was it merely an abstract question. The treaty, having been signed on September 3, allowed six months, until March 3, 1784, for the exchange of ratifications to take place in Paris. Congress was reaching the ultimate point of time for ratification, after which the British government could regard the treaty as void. A number of congressmen ingeniously argued that seven states were competent to sanction the treaty. Jefferson called this course "a dishonorable prostitution of our seal," and led the opposition, less on grounds of law than of policy. The treaty was a solemn engagement. In the nature of the Confederation, its enforcement would rest with the states. Although nine states had approved the treaty in its provisional form, several of its articles—on the return of Tories and the restitution of confiscated estates, for instance—were already resisted. What excuses and evasions might not be found if the treaty was riveted on the states by a body representing less than one-third of the whole citizenry! The only statesman-like course was to remove every possible source of cavil. If this was true with regard to the United States, it was equally true with regard to Britain. Jefferson did not minimize the risks of delay. War was kindling in Europe, and if France were to be involved Britain might jump at the opportunity to scrap or amend the treaty. But the risks of fraud and deception were far greater, he thought. It would be easy enough to explain a delay; it would be impossible to explain or to justify an improper ratification, should Whitehall choose to make a point of it. Jefferson had the votes to defeat the move for immediate ratification. Having done so, he yielded to the opposition, "very restless on the loss of their motion," and proposed to meet them on "middle ground." He prepared a resolution declaring ratification by seven states so far as they were competent and requesting the commissioners in Paris to obtain an extension of three months for the exchange of the treaty. In this way the integrity both of the Confederation and of the treaty would be protected. The resolution appeased the opposition. Fortunately, events made it unnecessary. On January 13 the delegations from Connecticut and New Jersey took their seats. Nine states formally endorsed the treaty on the next day. The instrument of ratification was Jefferson's report of December 16. He also wrote the public proclamation. So the author of the document declaring American independence became, seven and one-half years later, the author of the state papers announcing its consummation.

The celebration of the peace was anti-climactic in Annapolis. Just before Christmas, Congress witnessed the imposing spectacle of George Washington's resignation as Commander in Chief. Since taking leave of his officers in New York on December 4, the General had been on a homeward journey that was one long triumphal procession. He arrived in Annapolis on December 19, and only on the next day announced his intention of surrendering his sword to Congress. Jefferson was named chairman of a committee hurriedly appointed to make the arrangements for Washington's "public audience," set for the noon hour, December 23. People crowded the Maryland State House, the meeting place of Congress, to witness the ceremony. "The spectators all wept, and there was hardly a member of Congress who did not drop tears." The General's hand shook, his voice faltered, it was said, as he read his solemn address. "Having now finished the work assigned to me," he concluded, "I retire from the great theatre of Action; and bidding an Affectionate farewell to this August body under whose orders I have so long acted, I here offer my Commission, and take my leave of all the employments of public life." So saying, he drew his commission from his chest and presented it to the President of Congress, who replied in an address that showed "the shining traces of Jefferson's pen." The ceremony concluded, Washington "bid every member farewell and rode off from the door, intent upon eating his Christmas dinner at home." Jefferson had little liking for ceremony of any kind, but the voluntary retirement of the victorious general who might have become a Caesar was an event so honorable to the young republic that it left an indelible impression on his mind.

National Cornerstones

Jefferson must have wished that Congress had the "august" character Washington generously attributed to it. "Our body was little numerous, but very contentious," he recalled in his autobiography. "Day after day was wasted on the most unimportant questions." On one occasion of "trifling but wordy debate," a member asked him how he could sit impassively while men spouted nonsense. "I observed to him, that to refute indeed was easy, but to silence was impossible; that in measures brought forward by myself, I took the laboring oar, as was incumbent on me; but that in general, I was willing to listen; that if every sound argument or objection was used by some one or other of the numerous debaters, it was enough; if not, I thought it sufficient to suggest the omission, without going into a repetition of what had been already said by others: that this was a watse and abuse of the time and patience of the House, which could not be justified." He observed that Washington and Franklin, with whom he had served in the old Burgesses and in Congress respectively, had never spoken more than ten minutes on any question. "They laid their shoulders to the great points, knowing that the little ones would follow of themselves." It was a good example, and he followed it. In Congress he showed the same talent for legislative business, for modest leadership, and for bold political design he had earlier demonstrated in Virginia affairs. Immediately, without a trace of effort, he became the dominant figure. Indeed, whatever merit Congress had during his five months of service was mainly owing to his presence.

When the treaty of peace was out of the way and Congress had the majority, at least for a time, to tackle its new problems, Jefferson reported the formidable agenda to the Governor of Virginia: "1. Authorizing our foreign ministers to enter into treaties of alliance and commerce with the several nations who have desired it. 2. Arranging the domestic administration. 3. Establishing arsenals within the states, and posts on our frontiers. 4. Disposing of the Western territory. 5. Treaties of peace and purchase with the Indians. 6. Money." His hand was present in all but the third item of the agenda. He chaired the principal committees and wrote the principal reports. In connection with the fourth and sixth items, his contributions were of the highest importance. But the list does not begin to encompass Jefferson's work in Congress. As the head of the Virginia delegation, no doubt remembering his own experience as governor, he inaugurated a regular system of communication with the state government. Only in this way could the Confederation gain the support it required. Questions stemming from the treaty, questions of commerce and navigation, questions of congressional power— none could be settled satisfactorily, even with the best will in the world, unless there was co-operation between the governments. "We seem to blunder here more for want of information than design," Benjamin Harrison, the Governor, told Jefferson. Harrison was grateful for the new plan of correspondence. Each member reserved the right to dissent from the reported views of the delegation as a whole, a right often exercised by two of the five Virginians in particular. With Monroe and young Samuel Hardy, whose one foible was excessive good humor, Jefferson was on the best of terms. With Arthur Lee and John F. Mercer, men of distinguished northern Virginia families, his relations were less fortunate. Both were vain and quarrelsome, both fed on faction and intrigue, both lusted for the same office, the Secretary of Foreign Affairs, which Robert R. Livingston had vacated and because Jefferson stood in the way of their ambitions, they often opposed him.

Judged by the space he gave to the subject in his autobiography, Jefferson thought his attempt to establish "a visible head of the government," though unsuccessful, worthy of historical notice. In 1776 he had advanced the idea of a "committee of the states" to exercise executive powers during the recess of Congress. The Articles of Confederation made provision for this incipient executive, but Congress had never put it to work. Jefferson hoped to remedy the deficiency. The idea that the business of the Confederation must grind to a halt in the recess of Congress was, of course, preposterous. In the eyes of foreign nations, the adjournment of Congress virtually effaced the government of the United States. Keeping Congress in more or less permanent session was equally preposterous, and Jefferson associated this idea with the notorious ills of that body. Three months a year ought to be a sufficient term, he thought. "Then," as he explained to Hogendorp, "intelligent men from each state will be pleased to enter Congress for a short period, whereas now it is a sacrifice. . . . We will never again have in such a Congress obscure men who do its business badly." In January he moved the appointment of a committee of the states, to consist of a member from each state, empowered during the recess of Congress to exercise executive responsibilities. The resolution was sent to a committee he headed. The report as finally submitted, then amended, did not go the lengths Jefferson wished. He conceived of the interim executive as a device to strengthen the Confederation; Congress agreed only to a committee of caretakers. Such a committee was appointed prior to adjournment in June. Soon after it went into operation, as Jefferson recalled, the members quarreled, "split into two parties, abandoned their post, and left the government without any visible head, until the next meeting in Congress." The plan was not revived. In addition to all the congressional bickerings and fears of executive authority, the Articles of Confederation offered a very poor framework in which to rig an independent executive. The lesson was not lost on Jefferson, nor on the framers of the Constitution three years hence.

Money was the ubiquitous problem of Congress. Jefferson, first as a member, then as chairman of the Grand Committee, struggled to make economies in the domestic administration, procure funds from the states, and meet pressing obligations at home and abroad. In these difficult matters he often found himself at odds with the Philadelphia banker Robert Morris, the former Superintendent of

Finance, whose wizardry, practiced with so much success at the close of the war, no longer cast a spell over Congress. But this was all patchwork. Jefferson's plan for a national system of coinage, on the other hand, was a landmark in monetary history. Here, too, he clashed with the financier.

Jefferson's connection with the subject went back to 1776 when he first recommended the dollar as the standard money unit of the new nation. Nothing was done until Morris revived the subject six years later. Coinage and monetary reckoning were in a state of chaos. Congress minted no money, and while the states were free to do so, the supply of domestic coins fell far short of the demand. As a result, English and French guineas, Spanish pistoles, Portuguese "joes," and many other coins circulated side by side, their values varying from one part of the Union to another. As Morris observed, "The ideas annexed to a pound, a shilling, and a penny are almost as various as the States themselves. . . . A farmer in New Hampshire for instance can readily form an idea of a bushel of wheat in South Carolina weighing sixty pounds and placed at one hundred miles from Charleston, but if he were told that in such situation it is worth twenty-one shillings and eight pence, he would be obliged to make enquiries and form some calculations before he could know that this sum meant in general what he would call four shillings." The situation was productive of fraud and, of course, it obstructed trade among the states. Morris asked for a standard money unit based on silver. By intricate calculations he fixed the unit at the 1440th part of a dollar, this being the one by which the currencies of all the states save one were divisible without a fraction. The new money would thus be intelligible in terms of the old. The mint, which he also urged Congress to establish, would turn out coins in several denominations: two copper coins of five and eight units, and silver coins rising in decimal proportions of 100, 500, and 1000 units. While his report languished in Congress, he proceeded independently with his plan for a mint and actually had specimen coins struck before Congress killed the project in 1783. By then Morris had resigned.

Jefferson revived the subject. He avoided the controversial, and subsidiary, question of a mint and returned the discussion to the primary point of the money unit. The paper he then prepared, Notes on Coinage, while not actually a legislative report, assumed that character in history. A remarkably lucid analysis of a complex problem, it was intended to overcome congressional reluctance to tackle an issue covered with confusion and difficulty. It also set forth a clear alternative to the financier's system of coinage. Jefferson adopted the dollar as the unit of coinage, and attached it to gold as well as silver; but what distinguished his plan was the use of the decimal ratio to proportion the values among the different coins. "Every one knows the facility of decimal arithmetic. . . . The bulk of mankind are school boys thro' life. . . . Certainly in all cases where we are free to choose between easy and difficult modes of operation, it is most rational to choose the easy." And what could be easier than a system of coins in multiples and divisions of ten: the dollar, ten dollars, one-tenth and one-hundredth of a dollar. Morris's unit, on the other hand, preserved the monstrous strength of calculation required of monetary systems the world around. A loaf of bread, one-twentieth of a dollar, or five cents, would be 72 units; a pound of butter, 20 cents, 288 units; a horse, perhaps $80, 115,200 units; and so on. Morris conceded the desirability of the decimal ratio, but he thought it necessary to devise a unit consonant with the existing currencies. His merchant's head told him that no merchant kept his books in dollars, and that however convenient a scheme such as Jefferson's might appear in the abstract, it was not in keeping with the life of trade. To this objection Jefferson replied: "The conversion of the merchant's accounts is but a single operation. Once done it is done forever. He is skillful and equal to the task. Tho' the adoption of the Financier's Unit may relieve this one operation of the merchant yet it would throw the difficulty on the farmer who knows what a dollar is but not what the Financier's Unit is. The farmer is ignorant." The planning of a system of coinage was "a work proper . . . to mathematicians as well as merchants," Jefferson said. Seldom would he have the opportunity to demonstrate so pointedly and so conclusively the superiority of a statesmanship founded on rational principles to one founded on narrowly practical considerations.

The theory, in this instance, would prove sound in practice. Jefferson left Congress before he could offer his plan in the form of a resolution. He had communicated it to several of his colleagues, however, among them David Howell, of Rhode Island. Howell had an odious reputation as an obstructionist and a demagogue, in keeping with the reputation of his state; but Jefferson was friendly with this professor turned politician and found him a staunch ally in several contests. Pleased with the Notes on Coinage, Howell sent a copy to the Governor of Rhode Island, who saw to its publication in *The Providence Gazette*. When the subject was again brought forward in 1785, mainly on Howell's initiative, Congress reprinted the newspaper version of Jefferson's plan and proceeded to adopt its basic principles. In Paris, meanwhile, Jefferson was preparing the Notes on Coinage for what he supposed to be its first publication. The dollar thus became the money unit of the United States, and history was made by the adoption of the decimal system in the coinage of a nation. Several years passed before the system was implemented by the first secretary of the treasury, Alexander Hamilton.

The fortuities that guided Jefferson's plan of coinage to a happy conclusion were somewhat less evident in the case of his plans for the West. Two ordinances, one a plan of government for the western territory, the other a system of land survey and sale, were cornerstones of national policy, meriting rank with Jefferson's most important legislative accomplishments. The first, however, while enacted into law in 1784, remained a dead letter and was practically erased from the page of history by the famous Northwest Ordinance of 1787; the second ordinance was not enacted, though major parts of it survived in the first federal land law of 1785. The way was prepared for these plans by Congress's acceptance, after prolonged and angry controversy, of Virginia's cession of lands northwest of the Ohio. From the time Jefferson transmitted Virginia's original act of cession in January 1781, the creation of a national domain scarcely admitted of doubt; but whether it would be premised on Virginia's declared title to these lands, and therefore formed on the conditions she laid down, was a question to exhaust the talents of legal casuists and land speculators. Virginia stood firm, reserving tracts of land to satisfy bounty claims on the state, combating the pretensions of land companies, and calling for the formation of new republican states to be admitted to the Union on an equal footing with the original thirteen. Congress received Virginia's final act of cession in February 1784. A committee recommended its acceptance in the form of a deed executed by the Virginia delegation. At first only five states approved. New Jersey, the main opponent, offered an amendment declaring that acceptance should not amount to an acknowledgment of Virginia's title. "We told them we were not authorized to admit any conditions or provisoes," Jefferson reported the debate, "that this acceptance must be simple, absolute and unqualified or we could not execute." The amendment was lost, the subject dropped. Then the dissenting member of the Pennsylvania pair asked leave to change his vote, and this, with the vote of the New Hampshire delegation just arrived, furnished the majority. Never did a state have so much difficulty disposing of an empire! Jefferson, with Madison, Joseph Jones, and several others, had played a leading part in the entire transaction, as honorable to Virginia as it was beneficial to the nation.

Jefferson's thoughts were never far from the West, and now, in 1784, he sought to fix its future. Time was running out. The debt-ridden and land-hungry poured across the mountains, pushed down the Ohio, the Kanawha, the Kentucky, and the Cumberland. Treaties must be made with the Indians. An orderly system of land survey and sale must be instituted. Provision must be made for the temporary government of these lands, extending westward to the French towns of the Illinois and southward, pending cessions from North Carolina and Georgia, to the Spanish border. The British in their posts on the Great Lakes, the Spanish in command of the great river that drained the entire country, had it in their power to do untold mischief. The Kentuckians, looking down the Mississippi, grew restive under Virginia's sovereignty. There was no holding them, Jefferson thought, and he advocated their independence from the mother state and admission to the Union.

As Jefferson studied these problems, he realized that political ties alone would not secure the West. Economic ties were also necessary. The waters flowing to the Mississippi furnished the natural arteries of western commerce; but the hazards of this traffic, the difficulty of upstream navigation, along with Spanish control at New Orleans, seemed likely to check the Mississippi trade for some time to come. The bulk of western commerce might, therefore, be drawn to the Atlantic, helping to bind the Union together even as it expanded. Navigation being essential to an extensive inland commerce,

Jefferson believed the principal competition would be between the Hudson River and the Potomac. Geography had declared in favor of the Potomac, provided its upper waters, with those of the Ohio, were joined and cleared for navigation. Virginia ought to undertake this great work, Jefferson argued. "This is the moment in which the trade of the West will begin to get into motion and to take its direction. It behooves us then to open our doors to it." And not only through the Potomac system. The James and its headwaters reached toward the Kanawha, thence to the Ohio. The development of both the James and the Potomac systems would complete a vast network of navigation such as promised "to pour into our lap the whole commerce of the Western world." In March Jefferson outlined his plan in a long letter to Washington and begged him to put himself at the head of the Potomac project. "What a monument of your retirement would it be!" Washington was no stranger to the subject, having dreamed of a Potomac route to the West before the Revolution. In the summer he toured some of the western country, where he had speculative holdings, and on his return persuaded the legislature to adopt elaborate plans to extend the navigation of the Potomac and the James. Hopes rode high for a few years. But the design of a Virginia commercial empire in the West was doomed to failure. Jefferson followed its course, meanwhile offering his solution to the manifold problems of allocating and governing this new and unpredictable domain.

He reported his plan of government when Congress accepted the Virginia cession on March 1, 1784. The national domain was a reality. Whether the title deed to the land itself, as distinguished from the right of political jurisdiction, still belonged to the Indian tribes or had fallen to the Americans by right of conquest was another issue awaiting settlement. Jefferson worked at this problem too; and it would finally be resolved, technically in favor of the Indians, practically of the Americans. Whatever the solution, he simply assumed the advance of civilization over the whole domain. Obviously, a plan of government was needed. The fact that Congress had no delegated authority to govern territory was irrelevant, for the constitutional limits were breached, irrevocably, when Congress acquired the lands it had no authority to acquire. "The public interest, the necessity of the case," as Madison later said, "imposed upon them the task of overleaping their constitutional limits." But how should the country be laid off into political jurisdictions? Should Congress deal with the problem piecemeal, making political arrangements as exigencies of settlement beyond the mountains required, or should it draw a blueprint of government for the entire West? And what should be the character of this government? A centralized colonial administration like the old imperial government, with Congress taking the place of King and Parliament? Or a government consonant with the principles of the Revolution? Far-reaching questions of this kind had been bandied about Congress for months. Nothing had been decided when Jefferson was appointed chairman of a committee to "prepare a plan for temporary government of western territory." He interpreted this vague commission in all possible latitude. The committee deliberated several weeks, then reported the plan of Jefferson's authorship. Congress adopted it, after amendment, as the Ordinance of 1784.

The first feature of Jefferson's plan was its application to all the territory ceded *or to be ceded* to the United States. It thus encompassed the entire western country between the Mississippi and the British and Spanish borders, though approximately one-half of this area was not yet under congressional jurisdiction. Jefferson divided the whole into fourteen states, arranging them longitudinally in two tiers, one bounded by the Mississippi on the west and the meridianal line drawn from the falls of the Ohio to the tip of Lake Michigan on the east, the other from this line to the meridian of the mouth of the Kanawha, with one state to be formed between this line and the Pennsylvania border. These lines were crossed by parallels allowing each state two degrees of latitude. The approach was severely geometrical, taking almost no account of physiographical features. At an early stage of his plan Jefferson had attempted to do so, but cartographical knowledge of the West, which he possessed thoroughly, was as yet too imperfect. Moreover, he was working under a mandate contained in the Virginia cession to organize states not less than 100 nor more than 150 miles square. If the political geography was arbitrary, it was not entirely through fault of his own. It was abritrary, too, where it touched the old states. The Kanawha meridian fixed the western boundary of several states some degress east of existing claims, cutting off a large chunk of Virginia, for example.

Congress approved Jefferson's geographical divisions with but one or two modifications. But it eliminated the names he had thought to give ten of the proposed states. These curious polysyllables—Cherronesus, Assenenisipia, Metropotamia, Polypotamia, Pelisipia, and so on —provoked an unending stream of hilarity and ridicule. Congress mercifully dropped them, less because it objected to the names themselves than because the subject was premature. The names, most of them Indian derivatives with classical endings, were not as eccentric in Jefferson's generation as they would seem later, and they testified to his mingling of Roman civility with American wildness.

The great idea of the Ordinance of 1784 was the creation out of the wilderness of new republican states eventually to be taken into the Union on perfect equality with the original states. Many had advocated the basic principle, Jefferson for the first time in 1776 in connection with the Virginia Constitution. While generally accepted in 1784, the opposition was sufficient three years later to prevent a guarantee of the equality of new states from being written into the federal Constitution. The progression to statehood, on Jefferson's plan, would be in three easy stages. In the earliest stage all the free adult males would meet together to form a temporary government modeled on the constitution and the laws of one of the states. When the free inhabitants numbered 20,000 they would be authorized to call a constitutional convention for the purpose of establishing permanent self-government. The final stage, statehood, would be attained when the population of a territory equaled the population of the least numerous state, approximately 160,000 in 1784. The plan allowed wide freedom to the territories and their inhabitants. Manhood suffrage was guaranteed at the outset. Not a single state had as yet taken this step toward democracy! Control by the central government was severely limited, thereby encouraging the freedom and initiative of a pioneering people. They were to elect their rulers, make their own laws, lay off counties and townships to suit themselves. Congressmen who imagined a frontier populated by marauding banditti incapable of self-government—and many respectable men held this opinion—sought to increase the measure of congressional control. An amendment to this end failed, though at the last minute Jefferson acquiesced in an amendment empowering Congress to take measures necessary for the preservation of peace and order in any of the new lands prior to the organization of temporary self-government.

In so far as Jefferson's plan placed restrictions on the territories, they were in the form of five so-called "compact" articles. The new governments must be republican in form, subject to the jurisdiction of Congress, liable for the payment of the federal debt, and forever remain a part of the United States: thus far the "charter of compact" merely embodied conditions implicit or explicit in Virginia's deed of cession. The fifth and final article was totally unprecedented: "That after the year 1800 of the Christian era, there shall be neither slavery nor involuntary servitude. . . ." Jefferson thus proposed that Congress, without a shadow of authority, pre-empt the decision on the question of slavery in the territories. He had deep convictions on many important questions of public policy, such as religious freedom and common schools. He did not attempt to decide these questions for the westerners. Slavery had become in his mind a matter of fundamental national importance overriding considerations of local autonomy. The majority of congressmen agreed with him, yet the anti-slavery clause was lost. Jefferson's own delegation abandoned him. Of the southern delegates only his good friend Hugh Williamson, of North Carolina, voted with him. But for the absence of a New Jersey delegate, ill in his lodging, the clause would have been retained. "Thus we see the fate of millions unborn hanging on the tongue of one man," Jefferson later reflected, "and heaven was silent in that awful moment."

Factors intrinsic and extrinsic rendered the Ordinance of 1784 ineffectual. Delays in the extinguishment of Indian titles and the failure of Congress to enact Jefferson's land law presented the first obstacles, for these were prerequisites of any political organization in the West. Then it was discovered that the plan's political divisions were impractical. Many congressmen came to this conclusion, among them James Monroe, who traveled in the West after leaving Annapolis in 1784 and again the following summer. "A great part of the territory is miserably poor," he reported to Jefferson, "especially that near Lakes Michigan and Erie, and that upon the Mississippi and the Illinois consists of extensive plains which have not had from appearances and will not have a single bush on them, for ages."

So, Monroe said, with reasoning history would make laughable, the territories as bounded by Jefferson "will perhaps never contain sufficient numbers of inhabitants to entitle them to membership in the confederacy." He and other critics were right, however, in seeing that the low ratio of land to people in Jefferson's plan would delay the progress to statehood; indeed confusion and delay might occur at the start from the provision making the settlers rather than Congress responsible for organization of the territories. The defects of Jefferson's rigid grid also became evident: some of the proposed states were inconveniently divided by mountains and rivers or deprived of effective navigation.

In 1786 Monroe was named chairman of a committee to devise a modified plan of government, and this became the entering wedge to upset Jefferson's plan entirely. Fear that the virgin lands would drain off the population of the East to its economic harm, distrust of the frontier as a scene of lawlessness, apprehension of western power in the Union—these sentiments were not new, but now they produced a reaction led by Rufus King and Nathan Dane, of Massachusetts, against Jefferson's plan of government. The result was the Northwest Ordinance of 1787. As the title indicates, it was framed solely for the area above the Ohio River, from which three to five states were to be carved. Like Jefferson's plan, the new one provided for territorial government through stages culminating in statehood. It also restored Jefferson's anti-slavery clause in a modified form. But it tore from his plan the provisions for democratic self-government. The Ordinance of 1787 legislated a freehold suffrage, combined with residence qualifications, and high property qualifications for officeholders. It imposed a centralized colonial government, "similar to that which prevailed in these States previous to the Revolution," in Monroe's opinion, with Congress-appointed governor, secretary, and judges. Its "compact" articles, so very different from Jefferson's, also breathed hostility to the West, for they purported to fix the fundamental laws and institutions of the new lands forever, even after statehood was attained. Still, with all its defects, the Northwest Ordinance was a more workable offspring of his original conception of an expanding continental empire of free and independent states. Monroe's fears were not unjustified, but the American "empire of liberty" followed a different course from European colonial empires.

Jefferson's land ordinance of 1784 projected the rectilinear land survey system of the American West. Anyone who has flown across the prairies of the Old Northwest or the Great Plains beyond, and viewed the seemingly endless rectangular patchwork of the fields below, is familiar with the effects of the system. It is not quite the one Jefferson planned with Hugh Williamson and the other members of his committee, however. That plan called for dividing the land into "hundreds"—Jefferson's favorite Anglo-Saxon unit—of ten miles square, lines running due north and south at right angles, which would then be subdivided into lots one-mile square. This was a unique conception: the use of parallels and meridians to bound lands uniformly over a vast area regardless of topography. It could only have originated in a country planning to take possession of an immense unexplored terrain, and at a time when rational philosophers were at the helm of state. Addicted to decimal measurement, Jefferson proposed to use the geographical (or nautical) mile surveyed by a chain of 100 links, 100 chains to the mile, 10 square chains to the acre, 1000 acres to the square mile, 100,000 acres to the hundred. The large lots of this grid were on a scale more suggestive of southern than of northern practice. The plan also incorporated the southern system of indiscriminate settlement, even prior to survey, provided, however, that the final grants conform to the grid. Jefferson reported the plan just before he left Congress in May. When finally brought to a vote, it was defeated, only twenty-three delegates being present. Revived and revised at the next session, it eventuated in the Land Ordinance of 1785. This plan, the basis of the federal survey system, retained the rectilinear grid on the smaller scale of six-mile square townships, rather than hundreds. It abandoned altogether decimal measurement and indiscriminate settlement, substituting for the latter the New England practice of discriminate settlement after survey.

One of the innocent restrictions Jefferson had thought to place on the republican governments of the territories was that they "shall admit no person to be a citizen who holds any hereditary title." Congress kept the requirement of republican government but dropped this clause, no doubt because it would be interpreted as a direct slap at the controversial Society of the Cincinnati. The Society had been organized the previous year by a group of army officers, General Steuben at their head. The elitist character of a society of military officers was objectionable; and the provision for hereditary membership through the eldest son sent shivers through the country. A fiery pamphlet accused the Society of aiming at hereditary aristocracy. Several state legislatures passed resolutions against it. As the alarm spread, Washington, who had been named temporary president of the Society, was puzzled what stand he should take and asked Jefferson's opinion. "The subject has been at the point of my pen in every letter I have written to you," Jefferson replied in the middle of April. While acquitting the Society of devious intent, military or monarchical, he nevertheless felt that it ran contrary to the spirit of American institutions, that the dangers men feared from it were, even if remote, founded in all human experience, and that Washington's association with the Cincinnati sullied his character and renown. Passing through Annapolis a week or so later on his way to the first national meeting of the order in Philadelphia, the General stopped at Jefferson's house, dined in style, and talked of the Cincinnati. "It was a little after candlelight, and he sat with me till after midnight, conversing almost exclusively on that subject." He left, Jefferson later recalled, "with a determination to use all his influence for its entire suppression." In this he was not successful, though his impassioned appeal to the officers resulted in the elimination of the hereditary principle. The victory belonged in some part to Jefferson.

When spring came to the village at the mouth of the Severn, and Congress seemed, week after week, on the point of winding up its affairs, Jefferson pondered a summer trip across the mountains as a commissioner of his state in fixing the ultimate boundary with Pennsylvania. Congress had other plans for him. On May 7 he was appointed Minister Plenipotentiary to join Benjamin Franklin and John Adams in the negotiation of treaties of amity and commerce with European nations. The American ministers abroad had for some time been engaged in commercial negotiations of the highest interest. Jefferson had been one of a committee charged with the reformulation of policy on this subject. The committee's report lay untouched for several months. Then, on May 7, being officially informed that John Jay, one of the ministers, was sailing for home, Congress appointed him to the vacant post of Secretary of Foreign Affairs, named Jefferson as his replacement in Europe, and adopted the new instructions he had helped draft and would now receive.

His career as a legislator thus came to an abrupt and final close. Now the long-deferred career in diplomacy on the European stage opened before him. While he professed to be indifferent to the appointment, the haste with which he penned "valedictory" letters to friends and loved ones in Virginia, settled his affairs, and abandoned Annapolis suggests feelings of another kind. He had come out of retirement with the expectation of going to Europe. Instead, he had landed in Congress, and his experience with the "justlings of states" in that vagabond and lackluster body, while remarkably creative on his part, had not been pleasant. So with no apparent regrets he set out for Philadelphia four days after his appointment.

He lingered there two weeks, packing Patsy's trunk as well as his own, fetching a favorite servant, Jame, from Monticello, and awaiting the papers he was to take to Paris. His plans for a prolonged absence had been laid eighteen months before; he had only to reactivate them. To his entourage he added a secretary, William Short, a young friend and protégé unhappy with his prospects as a member of the Governor's Council and anxious to serve Jefferson in Europe. Balloon ascensions were all the rage in Philadelphia. Jefferson witnessed three of them. (He had read one of the first books devoted to the wonderful discovery of the French Montgolfier brothers a year before.) A serious breach in the Franco-American alliance also drew his attention. A disgruntled Frenchman named Longchamps brutally attacked the secretary of the French legation, Marbois, in the streets of Philadelphia. The affair dragged on. Jefferson, meanwhile, co-operated with Marbois in taking the exact measurements of a four-year-old bull: more ammunition against Buffon. Discovering that the cost of printing his manuscript in Philadelphia was prohibitive, he packed it up, and all in readiness near the end of May, departed for Boston to catch a ship bound for France.

A Strategy of Trade

"I mean to go thro' the Eastern states in hopes of deriving some knowledge of them from actual inspection and enquiry which may enable me to discharge my duty to them somewhat the better," Jefferson explained his overland journey to Edmund Pendleton. Much of the United States he had not seen—most of it he would never see. Only twice had he crossed the Delaware. Now duty happily comported with desire, and he sought first-hand knowledge of the country to the east. With the commerce of the Chesapeake he was familiar, of course, and all the staple producing states had much in common. He had been an easy choice to replace Jay, a New Yorker, on the European commission, for in addition to his other merits he was a Virginian. The interests of the South deserved an advocate in a body whose other members were Franklin and Adams. But Jefferson did not regard himself as the representative of a section. In foreign commerce the United States was "one nation," he insisted. The diversified productions and extensive carrying trade of the eastern states thus claimed his attention. With his usual penchant for order and system, he devised a questionnaire covering all aspects of trade for the purpose of eliciting information from merchants and officials as he passed through the principal cities.

The future of American commerce, perforce of American wealth and power, was very uncertain in 1784. The return of peace had brought prosperity more delusive than real. Americans found ready markets and good prices for their productions, but they let their starved appetites for European finery run away with them, buying far more than they could afford, depleting the country's money stock, and saddling it with a huge debt. The signs of economic depression—money scarcity, falling prices, stagnation of trade—had begun to appear when Jefferson traveled to Boston. In Connecticut, he learned, European imports exceeded exports in more than a tenfold proportion. The carrying trade of the eastern ports languished. Key industries, like shipbuilding and whaling, failed to revive after the war. With respect to the mainstay of Virginia's economy, tobacco, production was well below prewar levels, and the planters were still in the grip of the Scottish merchants. These were some of the alarming weaknesses. While their causes were various, Jefferson agreed with most Americans in tracing the manifold problem to a common root: Great Britain.

From the first, the economic hopes of the new nation had been tied to the kite of commercial freedom. The United States stood ready to trade freely with all comers who would recognize its independence and enter into liberal commercial arrangements. "Our plan is commerce," *Common Sense* had declared, "and that, well attended to, will secure us the peace and friendship of all Europe; because it is the interest of all Europe to have America as a free port. Her trade will always be a protection. . . ." Acting on this calculation, Congress, in 1776, adopted the "plan of treaties." It failed of conspicuous success except in the case of France, where, however, the treaty of commerce was coupled with a treaty of alliance involving political commitments inconsistent with the "commerce only" principle of the original plan. That plan, for all the troubles it encountered, was the natural offspring of the union between revolutionary necessity and revolutionary aspiration. Seen in the light of the policies of nations, rather than of their forms of government, the American Revolution looked to the dissolution of mercantilism and the liberation of trade, together with a new openness, trust, and pacific temper in the international community. It was this emphasis on commercial freedom that made the Revolutionary event and the simultaneous publication of Adam Smith's *The Wealth of Nations* something more than a coincidence; that gave substance to the Earl of Shelburne's abortive project for a commercial union between Britain and the United States at the conclusion of the war; and that conveyed the message of the American Revolution to many enlightened Europeans who, while they exalted commercial freedom, either feared or had little hope for republican government.

Jefferson had no direct responsibility for the "plan of treaties" and probably had not thought much on commercial questions before he returned to Congress. But he was in complete accord with the spirit of the standing policy. "Our interest," he wrote in the *Notes on Virginia*, "will be to throw open the doors of commerce, and to knock off all its shackles, giving perfect freedom to all persons for the vent of whatever they may chuse to bring into our ports, and asking the same in theirs." With the conclusion of the war, it was thought that nations reluctant to treat with a rebel government would be eager to treat with a legitimate one whose only interest was mutual trade and profit. To take advantage of these friendly dispositions, Congress had appointed the three-man European commission. The undertaking had assumed a new importance. Lacking the old privileges of trade within the empire, the Americans had secured few privileges of trade outside of it, and so they suffered the same colonial dependence as before the Revolution. It became increasingly evident that Britain, though she had lost the thirteen colonies, was determined to hold the Americans in commercial vassalage. The Earl of Sheffield, in his influential *Observations on the Commerce of the United States*, in 1783, had demonstrated how easily it could be done. Exploit the feebleness of the Confederacy. Exploit the British merchants' mastery of the American market. Above all, destroy the American carrying trade by imposing the navigation law that had secured its growth within the imperial system. A new ministry, with other dispositions than the discredited Shelburne ministry had shown toward the United States, adopted this line of policy. The crippling blow fell in July 1783. An order in council excluded American ships from the British West Indies; and this, together with the restoration of old restrictions in the French and Spanish colonies, closed off the most profitable branch of American trade.

There were several possible lines of attack on the problem, and in different contexts Jefferson advocated all of them. When moral and political considerations were uppermost, he held up the ideal of a hermit nation. "Were I to indulge my own theory," he wrote characteristically, "I should wish them [the Americans] to practice neither commerce nor navigation, but to stand with respect to Europe precisely on the footing of China. We should thus avoid wars, and all our citizens would be husbandmen." He thus expressed his sense of the unique opportunities of American society, which modified the orthodox canons of European political economy. "But this is theory only," he hastened to add, "and a theory which the servants of America are not at liberty to follow." The people were accustomed to foreign commerce; great interests depended upon it; it was essential for the disposal of agricultural surpluses. Jefferson never let the dreamy ideal control his search for a viable system of political economy. A variation of the insular approach looked to the development of internal commerce. The Americans are peculiarly blessed and have no need of foreign trade, no cause to incur its vices, enmities, and debaucheries, Richard Price counseled in 1784. "They are spread over a great continent, and they make a world within themselves." The English radical was gifted with prophesy. In time the Americans would realize his conception of a great home market—"a world within itself"—but few had as much as a glimpse of it in 1784. Even with regard to western navigation, Jefferson, and nearly everyone else, viewed inland commerce as an accessory to foreign commerce. Still another strategy called for the creation of a countervailing system of mercantilist restrictions by the United States. Jefferson was not averse to retaliatory measures of this kind. In the condition of American affairs he did not believe trade should be left to regulate itself, though that was his theoretical preference, of course. He helped to draft the congressional address of April 30, 1784, recommending that the states "vest Congress with so much power over their commerce as will enable them to retaliate on any nation who may wish to grasp it on unequal terms; and to enable them . . . to pass something like the British navigation act." The Confederacy must be strengthened primarily, in his opinion, for the purpose of regulating foreign trade. But the states held back, defeating a truly national system, and regulation by the states severally raised more problems than it solved. Madison and some other nationalists inclined to believe that so long as the vacuum of commercial power existed in the Confederacy there was really nothing to do but to fill it. Jefferson, always sanguine, did not take this desperate view. The front door to commercial regulation was closed but the back door was already open. In its power to make treaties the United States could act as "one nation," and so acting not only develop its commercial system but strengthen the bonds of Union as well.

The new instructions Jefferson helped to draft for the European commission carried forward the liberal policy with some practical modifications. Each party to a commercial treaty should be free to carry exports and imports to or from the other in its own bottoms. Duties should be based on the principle of the "most favored nation," which simply offered a guarantee against treatment less favorable than accorded another nation. The principle was European, far short of the American objective of free trade. Although the commission was authorized to go as far toward the ultimate goal as conditions might permit, it was recognized that the "most favored nation" formula offered the only realistic starting point. Mercantilist prejudice and practice, deeply embedded in the European states, had to be reckoned with. Jefferson willingly accepted this concession to expediency, yet was steady in his pursuit of the goal. With respect to the American colonies of European powers, trade was to be put on a reciprocal footing if at all possible; at the very least, United States ships and productions must be admitted into direct trade with these possessions. This was asking a good deal when scarcely a foreign port in the Western Hemisphere was open to American vessels. Other provisions covered the rights of enemy aliens and neutral carriers in time of war—matters of pacific and humanitarian import under the law of nations, in which Jefferson built on the work already begun by Franklin.

Congress authorized commercial treaties with sixteen European states, as well as the Barbary powers. The decision to pursue this general European plan was of considerable importance. Freedom from British domination was to be found in the widening of markets. A strong minority in Congress, primarily New England men, advocated a different approach, one which would give precedence to a commercial treaty with Britain. The restoration of the British trade to something like its old footing was so vital, in their opinion, that it should not be complicated by trifles; and no doubt some objected to the European plan because it would tend to pivot on France, thereby increasing that nation's influence in American affairs. Jefferson opposed the re-establishment of a partial connection with Britain. And he envisioned the French treaty not as a new axis of American commerce replacing the discredited British one, but rather as the point of departure for the creation of a far-flung system.

It was an incredibly ambitious undertaking: nothing less than a diplomatic mission to convert all Europe to the commercial principles of the American Revolution. The end in view was a system of purely commercial relations with foreign states, which, being based on the exchange of mutual surpluses for mutual wants, need not plunge the new nation into the blood-drenched rivalries of the Old

World or, alternately, force the country into isolation and penury. Clearly, however, the end could not be reached along purely commercial lines. In order to overcome mercantilism it was first necessary to play the mercantilist game and exploit trade as a political weapon. Although no threats were issued, it was well understood— Congress had so declared—that nations declining to enter into treaty relations with the United States would be liable to discriminatory regulations in the American market and would, of course, be denied other valuable privileges in peace and in war. How much these considerations could be made to count in the European balance of power depended on the progress of reform at home. But in the end every nation, on a rational view of its own interest, must see the advantages of entering the American consortium.

Instructions in hand, gathering what information he could as he traveled northward, Jefferson first stopped in New York. He lodged on Maiden Lane, next door to Crèvecœur, the French consul, known to Jefferson not only as the author of the *Letters of an American Farmer* but also as an ardent horticulturist who had earlier written to him about the reported talent of Virginians in distilling potatoes. From Virginia, Jefferson had sent him seeds of cypress, cedar, magnolia, and myrtle, a bushel or two of each. In his letters at this time, Crèvecœur was despondent over the prospects of French commercial success in the United States. The French merchants in New York were a bad lot, and the goods shipped not much better. Perhaps he did not speak so candidly to Jefferson, but he would soon hear a good deal of this problem. In New Haven, Jefferson took a holiday, touring Yale College in the congenial company of Ezra Stiles, the president. The Puritan educator thought the Virginian "a most ingenious naturalist and philosopher, a truly scientific and learned man, and every way excellent." They exchanged information on their respective colleges, talked of electrical apparatus, and speculated on the bones of the mammoth. As Jefferson passed through New England he made mental notes on the character of the people, checking these impressions with his knowledge of the Virginians. Writing to Chastellux months later, he thought the different characters, North and South, might be depicted schematically:

In the North they are	In the South they are
cool	fiery
sober	voluptuary
laborious	indolent
persevering	unsteady
independent	independent
jealous of their own liberties, and just to those of others	zealous for their own liberties, but trampling on those of others
interested	generous
chicaning	candid
superstitious and hypocritical in their religion	without attachment to pretentions to any religion but that of the heart

"These characteristics," Jefferson said, "grow weaker and weaker by gradation from North to South and South to North, insomuch that an observing traveller, without the aid of the quadrant may always know his latitude by the character of the people among whom he finds himself." Cued by Montesquieu, he ascribed these differences to a cause, the comparative warmth or coldness of the climate; and, of course, in Pennsylvania, with its moderate climate, the two characters blended "to form a people free from the extremes both of vice and virtue."

Jefferson had hoped to reach Boston in time to accompany John Adams's wife and daughter across the Atlantic, but he was too late, and while still uncertain of his passage, journeyed into New Hampshire as far as Portsmouth. When he returned to Boston, the General Court appointed a committee to confer with him on the commerce of the state. "No small part of my time too," he wrote Elbridge Gerry, his Massachusetts ally in Congress, "has been occupied by the hospitality and civilities of this place which I have experienced in the highest degree." Jefferson's reputation had preceded him. A Boston newspaper thus announced his presence: "Governor Jefferson, who has so eminently distinguished himself in the late glorious revolution is a gentleman of a very amiable character, to which he has joined the most extensive knowledge. He is mathematician and philosopher, as well as a civilian and politician, and the memorable declaration of American independence is said to have been penned by him." The tribute suggests Jefferson's rising fame as the author of the Declaration of Independence as well as his reputation, even before the publication of the *Notes on Virginia,* for philosophy.

He finally booked passage on the *Ceres,* a merchant ship owned by Nathaniel Tracy, of Newburyport, himself one of the passengers. The ship weighed anchor for England on the morning of July 5, 1784. "We had a lovely passage in a beautiful new ship that had made one voyage before," Patsy later reported. "There were only six passengers, all of whom papa knew, and a fine sun shine all the way, the sea as calm as a river." Jefferson amused himself learning Spanish with the aid of *Don Quixote* and a dictionary he had purchased in New York. Tracy was an amiable companion, possessing a great fund of commercial knowledge, and Jefferson recorded his answers to the questionnaire prepared in New York. After a fast crossing of twenty days, father, daughter and servant landed at Cowes. Detained for a time by Patsy's illness, they embarked for Le Havre on June 30, suffered the agonies of the Channel crossing, and, arriving on French soil, encountered the everlasting hardships of the foreign traveler. The nuisances of baggage and customs! Jefferson read French like a native but could speak the language scarcely at all. "It is annoying to see how they cheat strangers," Patsy noted. Journeying overland along the Seine to Paris, she thought it "the most beautiful country" she had ever seen, though the siege of beggars at every stop was disagreeable. "One day I counted no less than nine while we stopped to change horses." Thus the Virginians had their first encounter with the paradox of the beauty and the misery of France.

They first lived as transients in Paris, then in the middle of October settled in a handsome house, the hôtel Landron, as it was called, in a fashionable quarter of the city. With the aid of Chastellux, Patsy was entered in the stylish convent-school, the Abbaye Royale de Pentemont. "It is a house of education altogether the best in France, and at which the best masters attend," Jefferson wrote. "There are as many Protestants as Catholics, and not a word is ever spoken to them on the subject of religion." (He later had occasion to question this assurance.) Short, who soon arrived from Virginia, and David Humphreys, secretary of the commission, joined Jefferson's household. Humphreys had been one of Washington's trusted aides during the war. Jefferson was charmed by this elegant gentleman who, with Joel Barlow, John Trumbull and several other Yale men, belonged to a patriotic literary circle known to history as the Hartford Wits. The mission on which they were engaged was limited to two years. But it would be half-a-decade and another revolution later before Jefferson returned to his native land.

CHAPTER SIX

Minister to France

North America is become a new primary planet in the system of the world, which while it takes its own course, in its own orbit, must have effect on the orbit of every other planet, and shift the common center of gravity of the whole system of the European world. . . . It is earth-born, and like a giant ready to run its course."

Thomas Pownall, A Memorial . . . to the Sovereigns of Europe.
London, 1780.

It is not enough that the rights of man be written in the books of philosophers and inscribed in the habits of virtuous men; the weak and ignorant must be able to read them in the example of a great nation. America has given us this example.

Condorcet, The Influence of the American Revolution on Europe.
Paris, 1786.

IN THE VILLAGE of Passy outside Paris the venerable Dr. Franklin still presided, as he had for eight years, over the fortunes of the American Revolution in Europe. The friends of liberty and enlightenment had beaten a path to his door, and Jefferson made haste to follow it in August. Franklin, seventy-eight years old now, surfeited with honors, worn down by the cares of his office, punished by gout and a bladder stone so painful he could not bear the joltings of a carriage or even write without discomfort, was impatient to return home, and he could muster little enthusiasm for the ambitious project his young friend brought from Congress. Later in the month John Adams, with his wife and two children, came on from his post at The Hague and rented an elegant mansion in Anteuil, just beyond Passy. Adams doubted the success of the commission, but he took heart from Jefferson's appointment. "He is an old friend with whom I have often had occasion to labor on many a knotty problem, and in whose abilities and steadiness I always found great cause to confide."

These three giants of the Revolution, who had last labored together on the "knotty problem" of the Declaration of Independence, met officially at Passy on August 30 and more or less daily thereafter until their commissions to the various countries were put in a train of execution. "We proceed with wonderful harmony, good humor, and unanimity," Adams reported after six weeks. Even Franklin, with whom he had quarreled and whose popularity he resented, seemed amicable. With Franklin, Jefferson had anticipated no difficulty. Their tempers were as congenial as their politics, and Jefferson rejoiced in the old man's fame. With the astringent New Englander, he had been put on guard by Madison and Randolph, who had observed Adams critically from their former posts in Congress. Since he had gone abroad, they warned, Adams had become vain, cantankerous, morbidly suspicious of Congress, of the French, and of course of Franklin. Only after many months of scrutiny did Jefferson lower, though not by much, his high opinion of Adams. "He is vain, irritable and a bad calculator of the force and probable effect of the motives which govern men," he wrote to Madison. "This is all the ill which can possibly be said of him." He was honest, utterly disinterested, and often wise. Both Adams and Franklin were happy with Jefferson. Through him the official circle, not forgetting Humphreys, became agreeable all around.

Jefferson's relationship with Franklin, now almost a recluse at Passy, was for the most part confined to official business; but his relationship with Adams, the captivating Abigail, and their children, quickly ripened into a family friendship that brightened Jefferson's dreary initiation into Paris and glowed for many years. He dined often at Anteuil, which was a domestic idyll straight from America. He enjoyed the company of John Quincy, 17, and his older sister "Nabby." The whole family was charmed by the Virginian's sparkling conversation and gracious manners. Adams had earlier made some choice friends in the French capital, to whom he introduced the newcomer from Virginia. Americans kept turning up. The phenomenon of "the American in Paris" was born about 1784: merchants, adventurers, artists, scientists, fashionable sycophants—strangers all, as Abigail said—visited the American ministers and usually expected invitations to dinner. In January the Marquis de Lafayette returned from a triumphant tour of the United States. Jefferson had already been introduced to Lafayette's family. Their magnificent new home on the rue de Bourbon became the center of the American colony. No mere native of the land could equal the gallant Frenchman's enthusiasm for the United States. Lafayette's desire to serve, combined with his fame and position, smoothed many a path for Jefferson both in official and social circles.

If the universe were a gaily colored ball surrounded by a gaseous intellectual nebula, then Paris was the center of the universe. The city was not easily discovered, however. Jefferson lived on its lonely fringes for several months. Sights, diversions, people: he seldom babbled about these commonplace things in his letters, and those he wrote home during the first season offer surprisingly few glimpses of the kaleidoscopic scene. Man's conquest of the air was still the craze of Paris. Each flight of the gaudy silk bubbles was more daring than the last, until one exploded at a height of 1600 feet, making martyrs of its pilots, in an attempt at aerial navigation of the English Channel. The craze, too, burst. Jefferson regretted it, for he envisioned great things from "the aeronautical art." It was only a temporary setback. "As the birds and fish prove that the means exist, we may count on human ingenuity for its discovery." He looked askance upon another pioneering venture, Friedrich Anton Mesmer's fantastic probings across the boundaries of the conscious mind. Mesmerism was the sensation of Paris. The doctor's flamboyant style, the mumbo-jumbo of "animal magnetism," and the bewitching sorcery of the séance won a fashionable following for this alleged new science of healing. The Queen was a patron. Lafayette was an ardent disciple and actually lectured on Mesmerism before the American Philosophical Society in 1784. Jefferson, with most learned men, regarded Mesmerism as quackery. This was the verdict, in essence, of a royal commission on which Franklin served in 1785. Another bubble burst; and if the discovery of hypnosis dangled from the occult trappings, Jefferson and his peers can scarcely be blamed for failing to recognize it.

He kept his American friends informed of these rages and of all useful discoveries. Phosphorous matches: "They are a beautiful discovery. . . . The convenience of lighting a candle without getting out of bed, of sealing letters without calling a servant, of kindling a fire without flint, steel, punk etc. are of value." The Argand cylinder lamp: "It gives a light equal as is thought to six or eight candles." The screw propeller: "It is in fact a screw which takes hold of the air and draws itself along by it: losing indeed much of its effort by the yielding nature of the body it lays hold of to pull itself on by." Jefferson thought the invention could be applied to water with much greater effect.

The newcomer was alarmed by the low opinion of the United States prevalent in Europe, at court, in public print, among merchants, everywhere outside the small circles of ardent admirers of the American Revolution. Opinion and fact were wide apart. He blamed the disparity on English newspapers which blanketed Europe with lying stories of riot and anarchy in the United States. While with one hand he combated these false reports, with the other he urged the invigoration of the American government, citing the reports as evidence of the need. "All respect for our government is annihilated on this side of the water, from an idea of its want of tone and energy," he wrote Elbridge Gerry. "It is a dangerous opinion to us, and possibly will bring on insults which will force us into war." For months after his arrival he expected war between Austria and Holland and their respective allies over the navigation of the Scheldt. It would not likely involve the United States, but Britain, he warned, would surely exploit the opportunity to embarrass American peace and trade. Jealousy of the new nation's commercial rivalry, even more fear of its doctrine, Jefferson thought, was largely responsible for the British propaganda barrage.

His European initiation was edged with sadness, loneliness, and miseries of the body as well as of spirit. No sooner had he got settled than the illness that had plagued him in Annapolis returned. He continued his work and correspondence, but kept to his house most of the winter, during one stretch for six weeks without stirring. "A seasoning as they call it is the lot of most strangers: and none I believe have experienced a more severe one than myself," he wrote in March. By then the sun, "my almighty physician," had returned; he was walking four or five miles a day, and hoping to complete his recovery in the south of France. During this dreary siege Lafayette returned from America with a letter telling him of the death of little Lucy, "a Martyr to the Complicated evils of teething, Worms and Hooping Cough," the physician reported. Nothing could return this sun of his happiness.

Long accustomed to drawing information of home and friends from a thousand channels, Jefferson felt isolated and forgotten at so great a distance, dependent on the dreadfully slow transatlantic pipeline. Some letters, he remarked, "like the histories of ancient times . . . detail to us events after their influence is spent." And the letters seldom told him what he wanted to hear. "Political events are scarcely interesting to a man who looks on them from high ground. There is always war in one place, revolution in another, pestilence in a third interspersed with spots of quiet. These chequers shift places, but they do not vanish; so that to an eye which extends itself over the whole earth there is always a uniformity of prospect." Of political correspondents he could find enough, Jefferson wrote an old friend in Richmond, and there were always the newspapers forwarded from the United States. "But I can persuade nobody to believe that the small facts which they see daily passing under their eyes are precious to me at this distance: much more interesting to the heart than events of higher rank." Home was much in his thoughts. He had not been in Paris four months before he revived a favorite plan to seat his most congenial friends, Madison, Monroe, and Short—one or two others were sometimes mentioned—in the neighborhood of Monticello. "Looking back with fondness to the moment when I am again to be fixed in my own country, I view the prospect of this society as inestimable."

There were also distresses of an official nature. The question of salaries and allowances of the ministers abroad had for years been a bone of contention with Congress. At home accused of living like kings, the ministers, comparing their establishments with those of other nations, claimed they could not even keep up appearances. When Jefferson was appointed, Congress struck $2000 from the ministers' salaries and discontinued the allowance of an outfit—furniture, clothing, carriage, and so on. Congress seemed determined the ministers should not "eat the bread of idleness" and, Franklin added dryly, "that we may not eat too much, our masters have diminished our allowances." Jefferson immediately went into debt $4000, and though he lived modestly, about as they had in Annapolis, he told Monroe, he could not possibly repay it out of his annual salary. There was no end of expenses—of court, of fashion, of household— to be avoided only at the sacrifice of national dignity. The Americans were, unquestionably, "the lowest and most obscure of the whole diplomatic tribe," and Jefferson, of course, was the most obscure of the Americans. As yet he was virtually unknown in Europe, in diplomacy untried, and his position, while of ministerial rank, hung on a two-year commercial project most of the embassies little understood or cared about.

Life assumed a sunnier aspect in the spring. Not only was his health restored, but he was appointed to succeed Franklin as Minister to France. Franklin was returning home at last, and Congress had decided to keep but two ministers abroad, one in England, where Adams was appointed, and one at Versailles. Jefferson celebrated with a festive dinner. The Adamses were there, also the Lafayettes, Luzerne (the former Minister to the United States), John Paul Jones, and several others, American and French. On May 17 he presented his credentials to Louis XVI and went through the usual ceremonies. What they were, he did not care to remember and could not be troubled to describe. He was utterly indifferent to the pomp and pageantry of the Court. His curt dismissal of the subject contrasted with the lofty and effusive account Adams gave of his reception at the Court of St. James's. It had not been pleasant for the Adamses, against the soft spring beauty of Anteuil, to contemplate London. Most of all they regretted the loss of Jefferson's companionship. "He is one of the choice ones of the earth," Abigail said. Jefferson presented them with a copy of the *Notes on Virginia*, just off the press, and bade them adieu. "The departure of your family has left me in the dumps," he wrote Adams several days later. The afternoons, when he had often been at Anteuil, now hung heavily and he imagined himself a fit candidate for "the dark and narrow house of Ossian." He and Adams still had business to transact—the unfinished work of the commission—so they would not be out of touch. Franklin retired with his laurels in July. Jefferson afterwards said it was "an excellent school of humility" to step into the position of so great a man. When being presented to strangers in Paris as Minister of the United States, they were apt to say, "So you are Dr. Franklin's replacement?" And Jefferson would answer, "No one can replace him, sir; I am only his successor."

The succession raised Jefferson's diplomatic stature, put him more at ease with Europe, clarified his objectives, and enhanced the prospects of accomplishment. Although his responsibilities touched other countries, they centered increasingly on France, the surest friend of the United States in an alien world. He succeeded to Franklin's policy as well as his office, for Jefferson was equally convinced with him that France alone gave the infant nation weight in Europe and that rupture of the alliance would lead the country back into colonial subserviency. Requiring more becoming quarters now, he at length rented the elegant Paris hôtel of the Comte de Langeac, located at the end of the Champs Elysées near the city wall passed on going to Versailles. "It suits me in every circumstance but the price—being dearer than the one I am now in—it has a clever garden to it." His desire for gracious living, which Paris might gratify above any other place in the world, upset all resolutions of mean economy. He added a *maître d'hôtel* to his staff of servants, acquired a carriage, powdered his hair in concession to fashion, frequented splendid salons, and by all the outer insignia of life appeared perfectly at home in Paris. The one thing still necessary was the presence of his younger daughter. "I must have Polly," he wrote to her uncle Eppes on learning he would be away from America for at least three more years. Although this emptiness remained for some time, the cup of his happiness gradually filled, not with work only, but with the infinitely varied pleasures of mind and spirit.

Commercial Diplomacy

Considered from the standpoint of political economy, the American Revolution aimed to emancipate commerce from the myriad restrictions with which the jealous nations of Europe beggared their neighbors and exalted themselves in the benighted age of mercantil-ism. How far Jefferson had absorbed the new doctrine of "perfect liberty" of trade may be gleaned from one of many summary state-ments: "Instead of embarrassing commerce under piles of regulating laws, duties and prohibitions, could it be relieved from all its shack-les in all parts of the world, could every country be employed in producing that which nature had best fitted it to produce, and each be free to exchange with others mutual surpluses for mutual wants, the greatest mass possible would then be produced of those things which contribute to human life and human happiness; the numbers of mankind would be increased, and their conditions bettered." With this idea Jefferson went to Europe and, despite frustrations and disappointments, with it he would return to America. The aspi-ration was not unrealistic. It had a dynamism of its own, but more substantial was the inducement of American trade: necessities of life and materials for manufacture which the United States stood ready to exchange with any nation on a footing of freedom and equality. Of course, mercantilist prejudice and practice had to be reckoned with. Jefferson willingly adapted principles to specific situations without yielding the one or suffering total defeat from the other. America's trade, he believed, was a potent political weapon. By granting or withholding commercial favors, the United States might weigh in the European balance of power to the advantage of its own strength and well-being. No trading nation could be indifferent to America's effort to achieve economic independence by opening new channels to the commerce that had built Britain's supremacy. Ameri-can idealism, as embodied in Jefferson, thus plucked the strings of Old World diplomacy.

Political calculations of another kind influenced Jefferson's com-mercial diplomacy. The escape from British bondage was, as pre-viously noted, the main objective; but Jefferson also said, repeatedly, "that my primary object in the formation of treaties is to take the commerce of the states out of the hands of the states, and to place it under the superintendence of Congress, so far as the imperfect pro-visions of our constitution will admit, and until the states shall by new compact make them more perfect." The treaty-making in Eu-rope was an elaborate shadow-play, Jefferson seemed to say, for se-curing the consolidation of the American Union. "The moment these treaties are concluded the jurisdiction of Congress over the commerce of the states springs into existence." The argument that Congress might do by treaty what it could not do by legislation had dangerous implications; and, indeed, when fears of congressional usurpation in this way had been voiced in the Virginia assembly on the question of approving the Articles of Confederation in 1777, Jefferson emphatically declared that Article IX, the treaty clause, "no more gave such power over our commerce than over every thing else." By 1784, however, he was beginning to construe every power to the advantage of the Union. He had written into the commission's instructions the article declaring the United States to be "one nation" toward others: an implicit denial of state authority so far as commerce was covered by treaties. It was a very delicate point, he later informed the ministers, and swallowed with difficulty by Congress. "The majority however is for strengthening the bond of Union," he added, "they are the growing party, and if we can do any thing to help them, it will be well."

Such were the general considerations in Jefferson's mind when the commissioners went to work at Passy near the end of August. While they awaited replies to letters addressed to the envoys of the different governments at the French court, informing them of their power to treat, Jefferson drafted a model treaty. With his invariable bent toward "style and structure," he reduced the jumbled articles of existing treaties to orderly system and introduced clear and simple grammatical usage. As long as the commissioners were reforming the principles of treaties, he observed, they ought to reform their manner as well. Jefferson's model treaty expressed the "New Diplomacy" of the Age of Enlightenment. For example, Article XXIII exempted peaceful shipping from capture in time of war and gave protection to the civilians of either party then residing in the other. Franklin had unsuccessfully proposed this piece of "platonic philosophy," as Adams dubbed it, to the British commissioners during the peace negotiations. Jefferson introduced an article of his own devising for the abolition of contraband of war. This, along with the principle of "free ships make free goods," was intended to protect America's neutral commerce in case of war involving the European party to the treaty.

A treaty was concluded with Prussia on the model in 1785. Prussian commerce was of small account, but prestige attached to anything old Frederick the Great did. "Of all the powers not holding American territory, a connection with him will give us the most credit," Jefferson said. Some difficulties arose over Article IV's granting to each party the right to carry for the other and freely to buy and sell on the terms accorded the most favored nation. The commissioners showed their accommodating spirit by admitting one specific exception to these principles and further reserving the right to prohibit trade "when reasons of state require it." The benevolent Article XXIII was at once agreed to, though the recognition lost some of its force from the remote chance of belligerency between Prussia and the United States. Much more valuable to the United States, if not to the hopes of mankind, was a provision opening Prussia's neutral ports to the vessels and prizes of the United States during war with another European power. The privilege would prove of great consequence, Jefferson thought, in the event of war with Britain. Given access to Prussian ports, American vessels, both public and private, might prey on British shipping in the Baltic and cut off the supply of naval stores from Russia.

Negotiations went on with several other nations, Denmark, Portugal, and Tuscany chiefly, but no treaties were concluded. There were particular obstacles in every case. Larger difficulties of an intangible nature proved harder to overcome, however. The commissioners had counted on a growing European interest in the United States. Instead, most of the powers met their overtures with colossal indifference. "They seemed, in fact, to know little about us," Jefferson later recalled, "but as rebels, who had been successful in throwing off the yoke of the mother country. They were ignorant of our commerce, which had always been monopolized by England, and of the exchange of articles it might offer advantageously to both parties." Not understanding this, the rulers felt no disposition to offer the transatlantic stripling privileges no European country had ever before granted. The good will that had existed toward the United States in the triumph of the peace had been suffocated by the English newspapers, Jefferson added. Believing the country was falling apart, nations were wary of treaty-making. Perhaps the ministers erred in confining their negotiations to Paris, asking other countries to come to them, as it were, yet, given the magnitude of the task, the immovability of one of the commissioners and the periodic illness of the other, the alternative seemed out of the question. Had the commissioners been warmly supported at home, they might have fared better. Little more than a year after the adoption of the instructions of May 1784, John Jay, the new Secretary of Foreign Affairs, reported to Congress that, in his opinion, a purely national system for the regulation of trade should be established before more encumbering treaties were negotiated. This was certainly putting the horse before the cart, whereas the treaty policy, as Jefferson conceived it, was intended to back into a national system of political economy. Jay expressed a common nationalist view. Simultaneously, another party attacked the plan of treaties on constitutional grounds, recommending, in effect, that the entire operation be scrapped. Hearing of this from Monroe, one of the leaders of the party, Jefferson defended the right and the wisdom of the treaty policy.

By this time, however, July 1785, even Jefferson felt discouraged. From the outset he had considered the negotiation of treaties with nations holding possessions in the West Indies "the important part of our business." Trade with other European countries, such as it was, would go on covered by treaty or not. But Britain, France, Spain, Portugal, the Netherlands: not only was their commerce with the United States substantial, but entrance into their dominions took priority over everything else. In order to gain it the United States must have something to give in return. The privilege of free trade in American ports would be attractive, Jefferson thought, but it would be no privilege at all, he came to realize, if every piddling kingdom of Europe could claim it on the ordinary ground of the "most favored nation." Therefore, wishing not to embarrass negotiations with the colonial powers, the ministers "protracted designedly" with all others and anxiously awaited the expiration of their commissions.

But the new tactics met with no better success. Britain stalled, pointedly questioned the commission's authority to make a treaty binding on the states, then pretended the Americans were averse to negotiating, though Adams didn't see what more they could have done "unless we had all three flown over in an air balloon." When Adams became Minister to Britain, the task of negotiation with that court fell to him. Since the restoration of the Navigation Act in

June 1783, Britain's policy of monopolizing the trade of her American colonies had been placed upon virtually impregnable foundations by the exhaustive report of a special investigating committee appointed by William Pitt, the Prime Minister. The committee had enthusiastically endorsed the restrictive system, and government was stuck with it. The sugar islands and the Canadian maritimes could be subsisted and supplied without the commerce of the United States, it was optimistically argued. British naval supremacy rested on the monopoly of the colonial carrying trade, that "nursery for seamen," as the shipbuilders and shipowners trumpeted. "The words 'ship and sailor' still turn the head of this people," Adams remarked. "They grudge to every other people, a single ship and a single seaman." And what cause had Britain to make concessions to the United States when she already possessed 75 per cent of the Anglo-American trade? Retaliatory legislation by the state legislatures, which Jefferson applauded when it appeared in 1785, held no fears for the British, who believed their command of the American market was unbreakable. "The infatuation of that nation seems really preternatural," Jefferson remarked with more than a trace of bitterness. "Nothing will bring them to reason but physical obstruction, applied to their bodily senses. We must show that we are capable of forgoing commerce with them, before they will be capable of consenting to an equal commerce." An interdict of all commerce with Britain, he wrote to Madison, would bring that nation to its senses and purge the United States of debilitating luxuries at the same time. This was idle speculation, of course. Retaliation in the hands of miscellaneous state governments was useless, in fact positively harmful to the conception of "one nation," and the country could not do without British commerce until there was something to replace it.

The negotiations at St. James's hinged on the negotiations at Versailles and vice versa. Success at either court would provide diplomatic leverage in the other. The French government was not indifferent to the opportunity of diverting American trade from the British. Indeed, this had been the anticipated gain from French support for American independence. But circumstances demanded caution. The French economy was depressed. Merchants raised a furor when, in August 1784, American vessels were given limited entrance to the colonial ports. "As yet nothing has been opened here," Jefferson wrote soon after he became Minister, "the times did not admit it." In the regular course of diplomacy over the next four years, he would achieve modest success. But that is another story. With Spain and the Netherlands, very protective of their colonies, the commission accomplished nothing. With Portugal, a treaty was negotiated at the eleventh hour of the commission's life, only to be rejected by the government in Lisbon.

Months before their commissions expired, Adams and Jefferson were trying hard not to negotiate. Repelling Austria's advances, earlier invited, Jefferson expressed his dilemma to Jay. "Our instructions are clearly to treat. But these made part of a system, wise and advantageous if executed in all its parts, but which has hitherto failed in its most material branch, that of connection with the powers having American territory." Under the circumstances it might become necessary for Congress to adopt a defensive commercial policy, which would be hampered by commitments of small value to the United States. Earlier he had seen the plan of treaties as a means, however imperfect, of arming the Union. Now he stressed the limitations of this plan and wondered if it should not be abandoned for the frontal attack of nationalists like Madison and Jay. "My letters from members of Congress render it doubtful," he wrote Adams in September, "whether they would not rather that full time should be given for the present disposition of America to mature itself and to produce a permanent improvement in the federal constitution, rather than, by removing the incentive, to prevent that improvement." Jefferson was soon advocating coercion of the states, if need be, to strengthen the Confederacy. He continued to support the movement to vest Congress with power over commerce, the movement that eventuated in the Constitutional Convention in 1787. "*Nil desperandum*" was truly the motto of Americans: if Europe repelled their pacific overtures, they would arm "the hand of the Union" to achieve security and well-being.

This realistic awareness in no way dimmed Jefferson's vision of friendly intercourse among nations. That vision actually grew in boldness. In July 1785 he communicated to Adams a proposition to place the rights of citizenship between contracting nations on a thoroughly reciprocal basis. A citizen of the United States in England, for example, would thus have all the rights, privileges, and immunities of Englishmen. As the circle of friendship widened, men would truly become citizens of the world. The proposal is as revolutionary today as when Jefferson made it, specifically, for inclusion in the project Adams would submit to the British government. It was beyond the commissioners' authority, as Jefferson conceded, and wildly impractical. Adams shelved it. Jefferson, after mentioning it at Versailles, did the same. But the ideal of a family of mankind tugged at his mind, even as he struggled for practical solutions within the limits of circumstance.

American amity and commerce with the piratical Barbary states was a case by itself. The commission was authorized to conclude treaties with Morocco, Algiers, Tunis, and Tripoli. For two centuries the Muslim states of North Africa had preyed on the commerce of the Mediterranean, the more daring sending their fleet corsairs past Gibraltar and into the Atlantic every spring, plundering ships and cargoes, enslaving their captives in hideous workhouses, where torture, pestilence, and starvation were the lot of untold numbers. Exemption from this fate was given in exchange for lavish tribute, and the major European powers, with a heavy stake in the commerce of the Mediterranean, paid it year after year. It was an important stake for the Americans too. Jefferson estimated that before the war the countries washed by the Mediterranean annually took about one-sixth of the wheat and flour exported by the thirteen colonies, one-fourth of their dried and pickled fish, along with rice and other articles, and gave employment to 80 or 100 ships and 1200 seamen. The trade was then under the protection of the British flag. When the flag came down, the trade fell, the spoil of marauders. Moroccan capture of the American brig *Betsy* in October 1784 pointed up the urgency of the problem.

Uncertain how to proceed with the Barbary states, the commissioners sent to Congress for further instructions. Meanwhile, they sought to enlist assistance at Versailles and to obtain reliable information on the price of peace with the pirates. The King had earlier pledged to intercede for the United States in the Mediterranean, but now his ministers begged off. Diplomacy with the Barbary powers was unusually delicate and secretive. The French treaty of a century's standing with Algiers, the mightiest of these states, was about to expire; and it was not in France's interest, nor indeed in the interest of any European nation at peace in the Mediterranean, to remove obstacles to American trade east of Gibraltar. Were it not for little fish like the United States the marauders would prey on the big ones. Above all, the British, whose trade easily supported tributes, fattened themselves on Algerine piracies at the Americans' expense, Jefferson thought. Lloyds was charging 25 per cent for insurance on American vessels bound for Cadiz or Lisbon, whereas the usual rate for English vessels to these Atlantic ports was 1.5 per cent. Britain might thus virtually eliminate American freights to Spain and Portugal. Sometime later, in April 1785, Jefferson learned from the American chargé d'affaires in Madrid, William Carmichael, that the British agent in Algiers was probably exciting piratical warfare on American traders. Spain was then at war with Algiers, and Carmichael was able to throw some light on the costs of peace. Lafayette, utilizing his connections, furnished detailed accounts of the presents given by different governments on various occasions: gold, cloth, jewelry, carriages, food, and the arms, lumber, and naval stores with which Christian slaves built and outfitted the pirate vessels. From this information it appeared that the commissioners' original estimate of $300,000 as the cost of peace with the Barbary chiefs would have to be multiplied many times.

Acting without this knowledge, Congress authorized $80,000 and pressed the ministers to negotiate peace "immediately, earnestly, and vigorously," sending whatever agents they pleased to the Moorish courts. "The interests of humanity as well as commerce," Jay wrote, "urge Congress and the public to provide and to desire that no time or pains may be spared to bring this matter to an advantageous and happy conclusion." While doubting the wisdom and the policy, and smiling at the paltry means, Jefferson accepted it and awaited the arrival of the confidential agent Jay had dispatched with the official papers. The agent, John Lamb of Connecticut, required six months to reach Paris. Impatient at the delay, anxious to take advantage of the friendly disposition of the Emperor of Morocco, who had released the captives of the *Betsy* on the intercession of the Spanish minister, Jefferson arranged to send Thomas Barclay, the Consul General, to purchase peace with Morocco. (His bag of "trinkets" included a pair of gold inlaid pistols, a blue enameled gold snuff box, a crimson silk umbrella, perfume, a sword, phosphorous matches, and "a clock in the bottom of a cage, with an artificial bird, that sings every hour or when the string is pulled, and sings six times.") When Lamb finally arrived in September, he was sent to Algiers. Perhaps Jefferson and Adams together would have made no impression on the imperious Dey; but Lamb, so warmly recommended by Jay, lacked even a trace of diplomatic skill. The Algerines had recently captured two American ships off the coast of Portugal, their captive crews totaling twenty-one men. The mission to Algiers became, therefore, one of ransom and redemption as well as peace. Neither was accomplished. The price on the head of each captive was $1200; as for peace, Lamb said, "it will cost a Tower of Constantinople." At Morocco, on the other hand, Barclay negotiated in 1786 the most advanced treaty of any Christian nation with a Barbary power. No annual tribute was required, and American ships and citizens received the protection accorded the most favored nation. The treaty cost only $30,000.

From the beginning, Jefferson considered the path of diplomacy with the Barbary states not only futile and humiliating but in the long run disastrous for the United States; and despite the Moroccan peace, experience served to strengthen this conviction. No peace founded on ransom and tribute could endure. A naval war would be less expensive, more effective, and highly honorable in the United States. "Nor does it respect us as to these pirates only, but as to the nations of Europe," he told Monroe. "If we wish our commerce to be free and uninsulted, we must let these nations see that we have the energy which at present they disbelieve." He conceded that the question of war or tribute was no longer debatable; Congress had made the decision and he must obey. All the while, however, he adroitly planned for war. From information supplied by Carmichael, by the American emissaries, and friends and ministers in Paris, he formed an opinion of the contemptible weakness of the Barbary powers, of the jealousies among them, and of the interest of the Italian states, in particular, in coercive measures. No lightning blow from a great armada was contemplated; rather, a small naval force of perhaps half a dozen frigates and as many tenders to blockade the Barbary ports into submission. He learned from Lafayette that such an operation had once been employed successfully by France against

Algiers. As the scheme matured in Jefferson's mind it took the form of a confederacy among the nations at war with the pirate states to force a perpetual peace without price. In the spring of 1786, wholly without the knowledge of Congress, he communicated the proposed articles of this confederacy to the ministers of several European governments at the French court.

John Adams was acquainted with his colleague's thinking. For several years they kept up an epistolary dialogue on the question of war or tribute. The crusty New Englander, strangely enough, took the part of the dove to the gentle Virginian's hawk. Adams thought peace ought to be purchased as rapidly as possible. "At present we are sacrificing a million annually to save one gift [to the Algerines] of two hundred thousand pounds. This is not good economy. We might at this hour have two hundred ships in the Mediterranean, whose freights alone would be worth two hundred thousand pounds, besides the influence upon the price of our produce." And where, Adams asked, would the United States find a navy to pursue an offensive war? "The same facts impress us differently," Jefferson replied. Justice, honor, economy, and enduring peace called for war. Naples and Portugal would join the United States, he confidently predicted. "And many, if not most of the powers of Europe (except France, England, Holland, and Spain . . .) would sooner or later enter into the confederacy, for the sake of having their peace with the piratical states guaranteed by the whole." The anti-piratical confederacy would produce indirect benefits of the highest import. It would win European respect for the Americans, and respect, he added, is the safeguard of national interest. While Adams underscored the feebleness of the United States as an argument for peace, Jefferson thought that very feebleness one of the best arguments for war. What better occasion could the nation have for beginning a navy? "It will arm the federal head with the safest of all instruments of coercion over their delinquent members." Here, as elsewhere, he calculated the effect of diplomatic projects on the power of the American Union. He expressed his opinion even more forcefully in a letter to Monroe at this time: "Were the honor and advantage of establishing such a confederacy out of the question, yet the necessity that the United States should have some marine force, and the happiness of this as the ostensible cause for beginning it, would decide on its propriety. It will be said there is no money in the treasury. There never will be money in the treasury till the confederacy shows its teeth. The states must see the rod; perhaps it must be felt by some of them. . . . Every national citizen must wish to see an effective instrument of coercion, and should fear to see it on any other element but the water. A naval force can never endanger our liberties, nor occasion bloodshed; a land force would do both." Europe, it is sometimes said, made Jefferson a democrat; far more it made him a nationalist.

The last word, after all, belonged to Adams, the pessimist. "I perceive that neither force nor money will be applied. . . . Your plan of fighting will be no more adopted than mine of negotiating." Jefferson never sent his plan to Congress, though Congress got wind of it, no doubt as he intended, through Lafayette. In 1787 Congress resolved that the United States should enter an anti-piratical confederacy such as Lafayette had outlined, and it asked Jay to submit a report on the motion. The report was negative, essentially on the ground of Congress's inability to support the proposed confederacy. Neither was there the ability to buy peace. Not until Jefferson succeeded Adams as President would the problem be solved—by war, as Jefferson had advocated from the start.

Negotiating with France

While bringing the Prussian treaty to conclusion, preparing the Barbary negotiations, and accustoming himself to the varied rounds, official and unofficial, of the American Minister in Paris, Jefferson gradually took up the principal work of the embassy, the promotion of commercial intercourse between France and the United States. With the failure of the general European plan, he became convinced that France held the key to America's commercial problem. The British monopoly could be broken, the main avenues of American trade shifted to France and her colonies, if Versailles would abolish antiquated restrictions, open the ports to American productions, and pay for them in manufactures, oils, wines, tropical produce, and other articles. France had everything to gain. Her hopes of permanently displacing Britain in the American market as a result of the war had been cruelly disappointed; but the commercial war was still on, in Jefferson's opinion, and France might yet succeed. He did not have to look far in the French capital—to Americanists like Lafayette, to physiocrats like Dupont de Nemours, to philosophes like Morellet and Condorcet, even to the Comte de Vergennes himself—for men of influence who sympathized with the commercial goals of the American Revolution. As for the United States, the infant prodigy needed France's friendship. Britain was hostile. War was an ever-present danger. Aside from the economic benefits of a strong commercial union, it would undergird the treaty of alliance. All considered, the course of prudence for the United States, Jefferson reasoned, was to develop a Franco-American commercial axis as the first step in a free-trading system.

The ministry at Versailles seemed cordially disposed. Vergennes, Louis XVI's foreign minister, architect of the war alliance, had already initiated a plan of trade concessions calculated to maintain French ascendancy in American affairs after the war's inducements to co-operation were withdrawn. Vergennes was the acknowledged master of European diplomacy, with a sly and crafty reputation. But Jefferson, shunning diplomatic subtlety and deceit, found Vergennes, in turn, frank, honorable, reasonable, altogether an agreeable person in business, and inclined toward economic, if not political, liberalism. "His devotion to the principles of pure despotism render him unaffectionate to our governments but his fear of England makes him value us as a make weight," Jefferson thought. Fear and hatred of Britain were Vergennes's ruling passions. The United States was only a pawn on his European chessboard, yet an exceedingly useful one, and Jefferson hoped to duplicate Franklin's feat of winning for it the favors usually accorded a queen.

The first cautious ministerial attack on the old restrictive system produced the August 1784 *arrêt* opening the West Indies to trade in certain articles. Lafayette had played a leading role in this development. Popular, zealous for the American cause, craving the spotlight, the youthful Marquis was a perfect front for Vergennes's scheme, and he used him to ward off official and mercantile opposition. Unlike Vergennes, Lafayette was an ardent devotee of the United States, eager to promote its interests in any way compatible with his French nationality. Visitors to his Paris home experienced the strange sensation of being suddenly transplanted to America. One was sure to meet Americans there and to converse on things American. The Marquis spoke English as readily as French; his children, Virginia and George Washington Lafayette, spoke English and sang American songs; two American Indian boys were part of his household; an engraved copy of the Declaration of Independence hung on the wall of his study in one side of a double frame, the other side empty, "waiting for the declaration of the rights of France." Washington was his god, the Declaration of Independence his Bible. It was a sacrilege, he said, "to mention any day as the beginning of the year but the blessed 4th of July." Lafayette began his year 1785, the tenth of American independence, magnetized at Jefferson's table. Franklin's departure threw them closer together for business reasons. But their relationship was more than a business one. An intimacy sprang up between the two families; and the headstrong aristocrat, whose education was exclusively military, found in Jefferson a friendly counselor and political mentor to lead him, and France, into the promised land of republican liberty. Words could scarcely express Lafayette's admiration for Jefferson. "No better minister could be sent to France," he wrote to a friend in America. "He is everything that is good, upright, enlightened and clever, and is respected and beloved by every one that knows him." Lafayette was pleased to serve as the American Minister's aide-de-camp. He was Jefferson's liaison in nearly all matters touching the relations between the two countries. "In truth," as Jefferson years later recalled their campaign for Franco-American commerce, "I only held the nail, he drove it."

The first attack had failed, and Jefferson reviewed the entire subject in a series of conversations with Vergennes from August to December 1785. He wisely refrained from asking further concessions in the West Indies, since the government was hard pressed to hold the position taken the year before and, in fact, commenced a tactical retreat in September. He centered his efforts on opening direct trade between the two countries in the productions each could furnish the other. But here, too, he met the spirit of monopoly and a vertiable wilderness of fees, duties, and commercial regulations whose roots ran deep into the economic and political order. Especially formidable was the Farmers-General. To this company of wealthy and influential men the government "farmed out" the collection of several indirect taxes and customs' duties, including the tobacco duty. The latter filled the coffers of the King and proved very lucrative to the farmers, who were granted a monopoly in the importation of tobacco. Tobacco was America's leading export. Any attempt to free the French market for American commerce must begin with an attack on the tobacco monopoly. Yet the Farmers-General was so interwoven with the French system of finance, there seemed little chance of success. In 1783 Vergennes had collaborated with the Comptroller, Ormesson, in a move to abolish the Farmers-General. The result was Ormesson's dismissal and his replacement by Charles-Alexandre de Calonne under conditions that made him a captive of the system.

The French, of course, were still strangers to the American market. English merchants had generations of experience in managing the trade, catering to American tastes, finding vent for American productions. So it was, with the peace, that the trade flowed back into the old channels. Angry and resentful at this commercial bondage, the Americans nevertheless indulged their prejudices in favor of English wares and, falling into debt, found no way to escape the liberal credits allowed by English merchants on consignment. These credits, Jefferson said, "are the actual links which hold us whether we will or no to Great Britain." The French merchants, on the other hand, were not accustomed to advancing credit and trading on consignment; they had no established commercial connections in American ports. Their first big venture in the market, in 1783–84, had been a disaster on both sides. The French felt cheated, many abandoned the field in disgust, while the Americans looked upon their agents as "a set of needy adventurers, without fortune or character, who by importing the refuse of the French manufactures, have effectually strengthened our prejudices in favor of the British." When several of the American states embarked on commercial retaliation, they made no exception in favor of French imports. Vergennes lodged a strong protest with Jefferson. He defended the laws at court, though he privately believed they should be repealed except against Britain and other countries not in treaty relation with the United States. "The selfishness of England alone will not justify our hazarding a contest of this kind against all Europe," he told

Adams. In every conversation with Vergennes, Jefferson combated ideas of the Americans' irrevocable attachment to English manufactures, of infidelity in their commercial engagements, and so on. "Were national prejudice alone listened to," he said, "our trade would quit England and come to France." The real obstacle was the Americans' inability to make exchanges in the French market. American commerce might be coaxed from Britain if France would abolish antiquated regulations and enter into a free exchange of productions. "It will be a strong link of connection," Jefferson said, "the more with the only nation on earth on whom we can solidly rely for assistance till we stand on our own legs."

Tobacco was substance and essence of the entire proceeding. "The monopoly of the purchase of tobacco in France discourages both the French and the American merchant from bringing it here, and from taking in exchange the manufactures and productions of France." The Americans, Jefferson continued, are reluctant to enter a market where there is but one buyer, who sets the price, and that buyer one that does not engage in mercantile exchange but pays in coin. As a result, France purchased large quantities of tobacco from Britain, and of that purchased directly from Americans the coin was remitted to Britain, thus supporting the industry of the common enemy. No one in the United States or in France, except the monopolists, benefited from the enormous trade in tobacco. Jefferson proposed the abolition of the monopoly, leaving the trade freely to French and American merchants. The latter would, by their competition, ensure France's receiving the best tobaccos at the lowest prices, take their returns on the spot in merchandise, not money, and accustom the American consumer to French wares. The trade in tobacco would pave the way for other articles. To Vergennes's objection that such a change of system would imperil the King's revenue, Jefferson replied that a modest customs duty, like Britain's, would actually bring more money into the treasury. "Ma foi," said the old Count, "c'est une bonne idée." Encouraged, Jefferson pressed the matter. The time was propitious, for the Farmers-General five-year contract was up for renewal. Vergennes wished to withdraw tobacco from the contract and so advised Calonne, in whose department the business belonged. Calonne objected on fiscal grounds, adding that the negotiation of a new contract was so far advanced it was impossible to suppress the tobacco monopoly without "unravelling the whole transaction." But the true obstacle had gradually penetrated the covering veil, Jefferson observed. Calonne dared not buck the Farmers-General without risking loss of office. Jefferson kept the issue alive but no longer hoped for an early abolition of the monopoly. "I have struck at its roots here, and spared no pains to have the farm itself demolished," he wrote Patrick Henry, again Governor of Virginia, in January. "But it has been in vain. The persons interested in it are too powerful to be opposed, even by the interest of the whole country."

Two developments, meanwhile, altered the complexion of affairs. Jefferson learned near the end of the year that the monster he was combating had not one but two heads. The Farmers-General had awarded Robert Morris, of Philadelphia, an exclusive three-year contract for the supply of American tobacco. To the long-established monopoly in the purchase of tobacco was added a new monopoly in its sale. It seemed sure to depress prices in the Chesapeake, working solely to Morris's benefit, since the farm's price to him was fixed. He had struggled to slay monopoly in Europe only to find that the monster had straddled the Atlantic! At this point Lafayette, just returned from Prussia, came to Jefferson's aid. The Marquis and several men engaged with him urged Jefferson to press Vergennes for the appointment of a special committee to study means of promoting Franco-American commerce. Jefferson demurred, thinking it an improper proposal from a foreign envoy, but agreed to back it if it came from the Marquis. The proposal was made, Vergennes adopted it, Calonne acquiesced, and the so-called American Committee was appointed in January. Lafayette was a member, leading the assault on the double monopoly, ably assisted by the physiocrat Dupont de Nemours and Simon Bérard, a prominent L'Orient merchant enlisted on the side of free trade. Calonne and representatives of other government departments and the Farmers-General completed the committee of twelve. Jefferson and Vergennes remained very much in the picture as the protracted negotiations between them were replaced by the deliberations of the American Committee.

Soon after the committee commenced its work, Jefferson was called to London to join Adams in commercial negotiations with the envoys of Portugal and Tripoli. During his absence the farm's contract was renewed with provision for alteration or discontinuance at the King's pleasure. Accepting this as a foregone conclusion in any event, Jefferson pinned his hopes on a strong report from the committee, which would strengthen the King's hand, perhaps break the Morris contract, and smooth the way to freer commerce in the future. On his return at the end of April, he conferred with Lafayette and his allies, also with Vergennes. As before, the Count agreed with Jefferson's principles and objectives, but he felt the delicate financial condition of the country barred tampering with the annual revenue of 29 million livres from the tobacco monopoly. The American Committee had studied six different memoirs on the tobacco trade and considered at least as many propositions. The showdown meeting, Vergennes attending, was held at Calonne's estate in Berni on May 24. While acquiescing to the domestic monopoly, the committee resolved to break Morris's by obliging the farm to purchase annually 12,000 to 15,000 hogsheads of American tobacco over and above the 20,000 Morris had contracted to supply. The tobacco was to be carried in French and American vessels only, and purchased at prices consistent with the Morris contract. When that contract expired, no similar one was to be made.

Whether considered as a partial victory or a partial defeat, Jefferson thought the committee's decision, which the King endorsed, "the least bad of all the palliatives." He foresaw, accurately, that the farm would make all kinds of difficulty with the Berni agreement. He questioned its value, even as an expedient to keep the American trade open until the monopoly could be demolished. Nothing less would satisfy him. The committee was forced to be practical. Jefferson could afford the luxury of radicalism. "The committee's views have been somewhat different from mine," he wrote to Monroe, his confidential correspondent in Congress. "They despair of a suppression of the farm, and therefore wish to obtain palliatives which would coincide with the particular good of this country. I think that so long as the monopoly in the sale is kept up, it is of no consequence to us how they modify the pill for their own internal relief; but on the contrary the worse it remains, the more necessary it will render a reformation. Any palliative would take from us all those arguments and friends who would be satisfied with accommo-dation." He demanded the whole loaf on the familiar principle that half-a-loaf merely dulls the appetite for real reform.

The committee now turned its attention to other aspects of American commerce. Jefferson's views reached the group through Lafayette's unfailing agency. The final report took the form of a letter that Calonne addressed to Jefferson on October 22, 1786. It confirmed the concessions previously granted American trade, as in the instance of tobacco and free ports. It announced the suppression of duties on a large number of American imports from furs to ships, the reduction of export duties on French wines, and promised con-cessions on still other items. Jefferson was delighted. Viewing Cal-onne's letter as "an ultimate settlement of the conditions of our commerce with this country," he hastened its dispatch to Congress and the seaport towns.

But, alas, when shipmasters arrived claiming the benefit of these regulations for their cargoes, they found nothing changed. Calonne, whether because of real hostility to the concessions or because of the mounting fiscal crisis that would tumble him from office the succeeding April, could never bring himself to register the letter in the King's council; and thus it remained, literally, a dead letter. Not until December 1787 did it obtain the force of law. At that time Jef-ferson received assurances from Lambert, the third Comptroller General since Calonne's downfall, on the strict enforcement of the agreement of Berni. The chicaneries, vexations, and evasions prac-ticed by the Farmers-General had substantially annulled even the modest gains expected for American tobacco. Jefferson scrambled for these gains while continuing to advocate his more radical solu-tion. "By prohibiting all his Majesty's subjects from dealing in to-bacco except with a single company, one-third of the exports of the United States are rendered uncommerciable here . . . ," he preached to Vergennes's successor. "A relief from these shackles will form a memorable epoch in the commerce of the two nations. It will establish at once a great basis of exchange, serving like a point of union to draw to it other members of our commerce. . . . Each nation has exactly to spare the articles which the other wants. . . . The governments have nothing to do but *not to hinder* their merchants from making the exchange." But the power of the Farmers-General defied government itself. A mighty revolution would be needed to destroy it.

In reporting the December *arrêt* to Jay, Jefferson said the principal difficulty arose on the article of whale oil, for which he had demanded free entry but finally acquiesced in the continuance of a modest duty in order to keep the sympathetic Lambert in office. "It hung on this article alone for two months, during which we risked the total loss of the *arrêt* on the stability of M. Lambert." Next to tobacco, the precious oils of the mammoth of the deep enlisted Jefferson's diplomacy from beginning to end. He had learned of the desperate plight of the Yankee whalemen during his journey through New England. The whale fishery had flourished before the war. From barren Nantucket Island and several mainland ports, 300 ships employing 5000 hardy seamen had sailed the distant seas in search of whales, returning with cargoes that lighted millions of lamps and furnished an important item in the colonies' balance of payments with the mother country. After the Revolution, Britain levied prohibitive duties on American whale oil and rapidly built up her own fishery. The American industry was badly crippled. Nantucket whalemen, for whom the trade was a way of life, were encouraged to abandon their island and migrate to Nova Scotia or across the Atlantic, thus throwing both industry and seamen into the scale of British power. The migration began in 1784. It was checked briefly by a Massachusetts law laying a bounty on whale oil and by timely French maneuvers to defeat the British plan. Setting out to revive the French fishery, Calonne competed with the British for the Nantucketers; and a number of the clan, after striking the best bargain between the rivals, settled at Dunkirk in 1786. But Calonne's scheme was doomed to failure. Taking a different tack, Lafayette sought to open the French market to American whale oil, thereby permitting the Nantucketers to remain on their island, depriving Britain of an enormous asset, and furthering Franco-American trade. Just at the time Jefferson became Minister, a contract for the supply of American oil, free of duties, to a company franchised to light the streets of Paris and several other cities was completed under Lafayette's auspices. It helped to check the flight of the Nantucketers, who showed their gratitude by presenting the Marquis with a 500-pound cheese.

Jefferson, of course, endorsed Lafayette's objectives, though he disapproved of the exclusive privilege in the contract with the French company. Some months later a prominent Massachusetts merchant arrived in Paris asking privileges of the same kind. Jefferson took him to the Marquis's house, and the question of a contract was discussed. "I proposed, however, to the Marquis, when we were alone," as Jefferson reported the meeting to Adams, "that instead of wasting our efforts on individual applications, we had better take it up on general ground, and, whatever could be obtained, let it be common to all." When the right political path was pointed out, Lafayette took it. He pressed the matter on Calonne, with the result that the American oil was put on an equal footing with the Hanseatic towns, the most favored European nation in this article, which amounted to about a two-thirds reduction of duties. The oil must be brought in American or French ships, and the indulgence was limited to one year. Jefferson was not at all satisfied with this arrangement. By right, it represented no concession whatever, since the United States was entitled by treaty to the privileges accorded the most favored nation. Moreover, in his opinion, the duties on whale oil ought to be suppressed entirely. The indulgence, so-called, proved even less beneficial than Jefferson had expected. After a trial of two years, whale oil remained an insignificant article of commerce between the two countries, the American fishery continued to languish, while the French drained the royal treasury without supplying the nation's needs. Britain alone profited from this disastrous policy. Yet it was continued by the regulations of December 1787 for the encouragement of American commerce.

Pursuing the whale through treacherous political waters required, as Jefferson discovered, all the cunning and tenacity of the mariners' hunt. The December *arrêt* provoked "violent opposition." With an eye to appeasement, the ministry seized on the modest privileges granted the American fisheries. The first to go, in February, was the provision for an entrepôt, whereby the produce of the fisheries, including whale oil, might be re-exported from French ports without payment of duties. (Merchant ships often went from port to port in search of the best market.) Jefferson was fully informed of this change, actually participated in ministerial conferences where it was agreed upon; yet he afterwards said that the withdrawal of the privilege was meant to apply only to codfish, a minor article cheerfully sacrificed, and that its extension to whale oil arose from bureaucratic error or fraud. In truth, this was an excuse to cover his embarrassment. He had been taken off guard, and he did not realize it until he returned to Paris from a tour of the Rhineland near the end of April. Another month passed before he could bring himself to communicate the new *arrêt* to Congress. Coming so closely on the heels of a much acclaimed diplomatic victory, it was bound to be interpreted as a setback. Rather than risk a blow to American confidence in French commercial regulations, Jefferson emphasized the ministry's stubborn adherence, in the face of opposition, to other more valuable concessions it had granted. With respect to revocation of the entrepôt for whale oil, he continued to employ the fiction of trickery or error, which left him an opening to get it restored, as he promised to do at the first opportunity.

But the pressures that produced the February directive were even more formidable when Jefferson tried to overcome them in May. These pressures came from both inside and outside the government. The objective of a great national fishery, in which the ministry of marine was particularly interested, ran counter to the foreign ministry's policy of fostering American commerce. The Nantucketers at Dunkirk, to whom the success of the whale fishery was confided, artfully kept the government's hopes alive and used their influence to check American competition. The British, however, offered the more serious threat. Aided by elaborate subsidies and the Anglo-French commercial treaty of 1786, the British fishery glutted the market, underselling all rivals, and caused the Nantucketers to press for higher premiums and protection just as Jefferson again took up the American case. Britain's success was truly astounding, he said. "Before the war she had not 100 vessels in the whale trade, while America employed 309. In . . . 1788, 314, nearly the ancient American number; while the latter is fallen to about 80. They have just changed places then, England having gained exactly what America has lost. France by her ports and markets holds the balance between the two contending parties, and gives the victory, by opening and shutting them, to which she pleases." Not for many years, and after heavy financial sacrifice, could France harpoon her own needs. "Is it not better then, by keeping her ports open to the U.S. to enable them to aid in maintaining the field against the common adversary . . . ? Otherwise her supplies must aliment that very force which is keeping her under." Whether the whale fishery was viewed as a political or a commercial institution, the logic of Jefferson's position was unassailable. It concluded, of course, in the proposal to exclude European oil from France. This would not conflict with the new Anglo-French treaty, that ambiguous triumph of French physiocracy, since it granted Britain only the privileges accorded the most favored European nation. Jefferson was dumbfounded in September when an *arrêt* prohibited the importation of all foreign whale oils.

For the next two months, while also bringing to conclusion the long-delayed consular convention between the two countries, Jefferson labored to repel this new blow to Franco-American commerce. Again, in representing the matter to the Comte de Montmorin, successor to Vergennes in the foreign ministry on the latter's death the previous year, he took the tack that it was all a mistake, that the *arrêt*, despite its wording, was not meant to reverse the "uniform disposition . . . which his Majesty and his ministers have shown to promote the commerce between France and the United States," and that the exclusion really had in contemplation the nations of Europe only. He asked the issuance of an explanatory *arrêt*, lest more Nantucket whalemen flee to Britain and American merchants recoil from the uncertainties of French commerce.

Finding in his conferences with Montmorin and other ministers considerable ignorance of the whaling industry, Jefferson took the data he had studiously gathered over the years and wrote a small treatise, *Observations on the Whale-Fishery*. It exhibited his mastery of this intricate subject: the properties of different illuminating oils; the fisheries of Britain, France, and the United States; whaling as a source of naval power; whaling in all its commercial and political aspects. No more interesting or authoritative guide had been written. But its historical importance lay with a specific purpose: the reopening of French ports to American whale oil. Jefferson had a number of copies printed and sent the pamphlet to the ministers concerned. Some days later he and Lafayette conferred with Montmorin, who now agreed to exempt the United States from the prohibition. The *arrêt* was finally issued on December 7, 1788. Thus, as Jefferson wrote triumphantly to Jay, "this branch of commerce, after so threatening an appearance, will be on a better footing than ever, as enjoying jointly with the French oil, a monopoly of their markets." It was the paramount concession France made to American commerce. The government threw itself into the scale of American power, and against strong political and mercantile opposition left its own industry to the hazard of American competition.

Jefferson saw still another raw product, the rice of the steamy Carolina tidelands, as a promising article of exchange with France. Rice was the second major export of the southern states, as important to South Carolina and Georgia as tobacco was to the Chesapeake country; and, like tobacco, it suffered severely from the war. Rice exports were less than one-half of pre-war averages. Britain continued to dominate the trade—a highly profitable re-export trade on her part—through the controls of debt and credit and the excellent facilities of the entrepôt at Cowes. Of the next most important pre-war markets, the British West Indies were closed, unless carried in British bottoms, and Portugal, now supplied by Brazil, excluded American rice. The economy of South Carolina was further depressed by the need to replace 20,000 slaves lost to the ravages of war and by the virtual disappearance of the foreign market for indigo, the state's second major staple.

Taking up this problem, Jefferson endeavored to channel part of the rice trade directly to France. French consumption of rice, already large, increased yearly; yet very little was bought from the Americans. Monopoly and restriction, such as burdened the tobacco trade, had no bearing on the problem. Rice entered virtually free of duties. Versailles could do nothing. Where, then, did the trouble lie, and what could the American Minister do about it? On the basis of preliminary inquiries, he informed the Carolinians that their rice, either because of the seed or the preparation, was not adapted to the French taste, thus explaining the ascendancy of Piedmont and Levantine rice in the market. To David Ramsay, the South Carolina legislator and historian, whose *History of the American Revolution*

Jefferson was trying to peddle in France, he sent samples of the Mediterranean rice sold in Paris. "Our house of assembly was then sitting," Ramsay replied. "I produced the samples of rice on the table of the house for the inspection of the members who were planters." Ramsay also published Jefferson's letter, which made a hit with the planters. Jefferson continued in every way possible to educate the Carolinians in the culture and preparation of Mediterranean rice. When he toured the south of France in the spring of 1787, he extended his itinerary to the fields of Piedmont and Lombardy in hopes of discovering the clue to the supposed superiority of their rice. Perhaps a different machine was used to clean it, thereby lessening the number of broken grains—a culinary complaint he had often heard against the American grain. But no, the machine was the same as the one Edward Rutledge had described to him when they sat together in Congress in 1775. (As a precaution against faulty memory, however, he sent an iron tooth from a Piedmont machine to Charleston.) "It is a difference in the species of grain," he concluded, "of which the government of Turin is so sensible, that . . . they prohibit the exportation of rough rice on pain of death." Undaunted, Jefferson filled his pockets with enough grain to put the Carolinians in seed, and with greedy determination, hired a muleteer to smuggle a couple of sacks across the Appenines. What fate may have overtaken the poor muleteer, Jefferson never learned; and the Carolinians, though they dutifully planted the Piedmont seed, thought it inferior to their own and soon gave it up. Nor did they share Jefferson's enthusiasm for the upland, or dry, rice he procured from China and Africa. Some of this seed spread wild in the Georgia uplands, he afterwards learned, and the people relished it.

Despite the exacting requirements of the French cuisine, American rice found increasing favor. Jefferson came to believe it might capture the market if it could be brought directly to France. "But it is first carried and deposited in England, and it is the merchant of that country who sends it here, [drawing] a great profit himself, while the commodity is moreover subjected to the expenses of a double voyage." No respectable French mercantile house had ventured in this business, and the debtor position of the planters, combined with the liberal advances on consignment given by the merchants and the facilities at Cowes, ensured British control of the trade. Moving against these difficulties, Jefferson tried to induce solid French houses to offer attractive terms to the Carolinians. In the summer of 1787, after returning from his southern tour, Jefferson approached Simon Bérard, one of the liberals on the American Committee, and the Bérard Company of L'Orient made proposals that Jefferson sent to Charleston. They were warmly received. Jefferson had "opened the door" to release from British bondage! Several large shipments were made. Unfortunately, though they gave umbrage to the British, they lost money for the planters, who persevered nonetheless. In 1789 more shipments cleared the Charleston customs house for France than ever before. Jefferson was honored by the South Carolina Agriculture Society and lavishly praised for his efforts on the state's behalf.

On the whole, Jefferson's labors to build a Franco-American commercial system were out of proportion to the results obtained. After five years the French Revolution intervened, disrupting further progress along the lines he had laid out. Britain maintained her commercial supremacy, yet American ships and cargoes moved into new avenues of trade, above all French, partly because of his efforts. The available statistics on the trade of the two nations during this period point to several conclusions. First, the total volume, though there were ups and downs in key articles, fluctuated very little and was not significantly greater at the end of the period than it was at the beginning. Second, the trade with the French colonies far exceeded the direct trade with the mother country. And third, in both branches, the Americans had much the better of it. The balance of trade in the island commerce favored the United States on a ratio of nearly two to one, the direct trade on a ratio of perhaps five or six to one. A bonanza for the Americans, the trade was a small disaster for the French.

What, then, becomes of Jefferson's constant plea for markets? Obviously, it did not go the heart of the problem. He naturally fixed his attention on obstacles to American imports (and navigation) to the neglect of France's difficulties in making exchanges for them. He knew very well that an enduring commerce between the two countries must be more or less equal in its benefits; and near the end of his ministry especially, he was urging the French to look beyond the luxury trade in wines, oils, dyes, silks, and linens, and to adapt their industry more deliberately to the American market. But French manufacturing industry was sluggish and inefficient; the Anglo-French commercial accord of 1786 flooded the market with English goods, in the process drowning many merchants and manufacturers; and in the deepening depression of the following years capital was simply not available for the improvements Jefferson had in mind. At any rate, though he did not fully appreciate it, the difficulty of his system was less one of French markets than of French supplies. By 1789 the markets were open to an astonishing degree, largely due to his efforts and the influence of liberal commercial ideology at Versailles. The Americans exploited these markets, then transferred most of the money balance in their favor to the support of British industry. This was the very problem that Jefferson and his French allies had endeavored to overcome. As liberal commercial policy gained in official favor, the country's merchants, manufacturers, *fabricants*, and shopkeepers, who were losing by it, drifted toward revolution. The American Minister had little contact with this bourgeoisie. He moved in a narrow circle, the enlightened nobility for the most part—friends of agriculture and free trade, of America and republicanism—and so it is not surprising that some of the most disturbing realities of the French economy eluded him. Some years later, when these realities were painfully obvious, Gouverneur Morris, who succeeded him at Versailles, fastened the skeptic's slur, *visionary*, on the Jeffersonian plan of direct commerce between France and the United States.

The plan was an important phase of Jefferson's, and America's, search for a viable commercial system. It was oriented to France primarily by virtue of its being against Britain. Britain was still the enemy in his eyes, and so long as she dominated the American economy, national dignity and independence were more illusory than real. The advantages of direct trade with France were self-evident from an economic standpoint. On moral and political grounds they appeared to be overwhelming, as a means of curbing British power and of multiplying ties of interest and affection with the only nation that had earned American friendship. The true policy toward foreign nations was one of perfect freedom and equality in trade and of strict political neutrality. Unfortunately, the world was not yet ready for this policy. Denied the "natural right" of free trade, requiring foreign outlets for growing agricultural surpluses, dependent on their exchange for necessary manufactures, encircled by the colonial outposts of European powers—the United States could not escape foreign involvements or withhold itself from the balance of power in the Atlantic world or ignore the ever present danger of war, particularly with Britain. The young republic must make the best commercial arrangements it could, and everything pointed to France as the surest partner. Jefferson was thoroughly cognizant of the political risk this policy entailed—the danger that in throwing off British chains the country would put on French ones. But this risk was manageable; the risk on the other side, with the former mother country jealous of her supremacy, was not. For the new nation, France offered imposing political support in Europe and an opportunity, an entering wedge, for the free commercial system on which American wealth and welfare depended.

The Vaunted Scene

"Behold me at length on the vaunted scene of Europe!" Thus saluting a friend at home, Jefferson went on to express the ambivalent feelings—attraction and repulsion—that generations of Americans after him would experience in their encounters with the Old World. "But you are perhaps curious to know how this new scene has struck a savage from the mountains of America" he wrote with self-conscious parody. "Not advantageously I assure you. I find the general fate of humanity here most deplorable. The truth of Voltaire's observation offers itself perpetually, that every man here must be either the hammer or the anvil." And he went on to compare the misery of the European masses crushed under the weight of panoplied kings, priests and nobles with the uniform happiness of the American people. Government was a tyrant; society was a whore. "Conjugal love having no existence among them, domestic happiness, of which that is the basis, is utterly unknown." The Americans could congratulate themselves on the easy domestic felicity that kept the wine of passion unclouded and sweet. "In science, the mass of people is two centuries behind ours, their literati half a dozen years before us." On the other hand, in polite manners and breeding the Europeans were far ahead of the still unpolished Americans. "Here it seems that a man might pass a life without encountering a single rudeness." And for the lover of the fine arts Europe was a glittering paradise. "Were I to proceed to tell you how much I enjoy their architecture, sculpture, painting, music, I should want words." Yet their splendor only magnified the awful shadow cast by the hosts of the damned. "My God!" Jefferson exclaimed to another friend. "How little do my countrymen know what precious blessings they are in possession of, and which no other people on earth enjoy. I confess I had no idea of it myself. . . ."

I had no idea of it myself. In the act of discovering Europe, Jefferson discovered America as well. Not the land or people or institutions, for he came into intellectual possession of these things before he set foot in Europe; but America as a spiritual ideal, harbinger of a new era, vision of an earthly paradise, bearer of the hopes of mankind—the American dream—this seized Jefferson's heart and mind only after he was enabled to view his native land from the perspective of Europe. The Americans, having the reality, had no need to invent the dream. The Europeans, above all the French, required the dream to sustain their hopes. It was the French philosophes who made of Franklin a living exemplification of their Heavenly City. It was Lafayette, at the head of the returning soldiers, who planted the tree of liberty at Versailles. It was the Americanized Crèvecœur who conducted earthbound Europeans on a spiritual pilgrimage to the land where homely virtue and enlightenment, liberty and prosperity, dwelled together. It was the Marquis de Condorcet, philosopher of human progress, who saw in the United States a model for revolution and living proof of progress in affairs of state. This idealized image rapidly eclipsed the older theory of New World degeneracy. Jefferson reflected it back to his homeland. The more he saw of Europe, the dearer his own country became, taking a luster to all its parts that no one bound to the farther shore could know it merited.

In his growing awareness of the peculiar blessings of the United States, Jefferson was uncertain whether "Americanism" ought to be a bridge to Europe, as its devotees intended, or a protective wall against European vices. If these blessings were, in fact, peculiar, his reform-minded friends in France, Holland, England, and elsewhere were chasing after false dawns. And the blessings Europe could not attain were America's to cherish in a world happily set apart. Jefferson seemed often to hold this opinion. An almost puritanical feeling about American manners and morals led him to preach hellfire sermons against the corruptions of European education. "Of all the errors which can possibly be committed in the education of youth, that of sending them to Europe is the most fatal." Young Americans, some of whom he observed in Paris, were likely to acquire a "fondness for European luxury and dissipation . . . a partiality for aristocracy or monarchy . . . a spirit of female intrigue," all certain to make them miserable aliens to their own country. Yet, in day-to-day diplomacy, Jefferson worked to strengthen the bonds between the United States and France and to free that most efficient of all contagions, commerce. His numerous unofficial labors facilitated intercourse in the arts and sciences. He was of too liberal a mind to entertain parochial views, too admiring of Europe's civilizing arts to renounce them for America, too cosmopolitan in his principles to suppose his people held a perpetual monopoly of them. With the rumblings of the French Revolution, he seemed convinced that the European lump could be broken and he entered wholeheartedly into the movement impelled by the American example. Jefferson's stance toward Europe was, therefore, shifting and complex. He shared Franklin's catholicity of outlook, though not his easy acceptance of French society. He shared Adams's puritanical indignation toward European vice and luxury, though none of his stony austerity. Because Europe stirred very contrary feelings in Jefferson's heart it was impossible for him to formulate a simple and unambiguous conception of America's role in the Atlantic world.

Jefferson denounced Europe, yet under the cover of his rhetoric made a marriage of convenience with the wicked temptress. Except for occasional "squalls of work," the duties of the embassy left him ample time for his own pursuits. Always an early riser, he generally worked at his desk until noon. Several hours, more or less daily, were given over to correspondence, both official and unofficial. No American minister reported with such regularity to the government at home or with a keener eye to European affairs. There was always some "tedious business" to deal with: the settlement of Commodore Jones's prize account with the French government, the recovery of arms intended for the United States but seized by French creditors

during the war, the release of an American crew imprisoned for
smuggling tobacco, and so on. In the absence of a consular convention governing the rights of American citizens, they often sought
Jefferson's intervention with French authorities. The greatest discretion was necessary to keep these claims within proper bounds lest
by constantly troubling the ministry for small favors he wear out
his welcome for large ones. "Worn down every morning with writing on business, I sally at 12 o'clock into the bois de Boulogne, and
unbend my labours. . . ." Sometimes the sallies were on horseback,
more often on foot, for walking was the "sovereign invigorator" of
the body. For a summer or two he devoted every free afternoon to
the bookstores, "turning over every book with my own hands, and
putting by everything which related to America, and indeed whatever was rare and valuable in every science." He would return home
with books to occupy 250 feet of shelves. Dinner was at the peak of a
leisurely afternoon, and whether host or guest Jefferson savored the
pleasures—the wines, the cuisine, the conversation—of the French
table. Perhaps the theater, the opera, or a concert, capped by the entertainment of some glittering salon, climaxed the day. Paris shone
in all the arts. Jefferson fixed upon music in particular. "I am almost
ready to say it is the only thing which from my heart I envy them,
and which in spite of all the authority of the decalogue I do covet."

He went often to Versailles to transact business, attend the
court, or take a pleasurable excursion through the spacious avenues,
bright gardens, and classic glories of Louis XIV's monument to his
grandeur. Versailles was amusing but scarcely deserving of superla-
tives, and he wasted none on it. Nor was he enamored of the court.
A young American, Thomas Lee Shippen, whom Jefferson presented at Versailles, described the "obsequious adulation," "empty
ornament," and "unmeaning grandeur" of these regal ceremonies,
adding "that although Mr. Jefferson was the plainest man in the
room, and the most destitute of ribbands, crosses and other insignia
of rank . . . he was most courted and most attended to (even
by the Courtiers themselves) of the whole Diplomatic corps." The
corps was the most distinguished in Europe. Jefferson took a dim
view of these titled ambassadors and ministers, however. They were
not worth knowing, he said, and, in fact, he had only a trifling acquaintance with any of them. The Baron de Grimm, man of letters

and critic of the arts, struck Jefferson as the best of the tribe: "No heart, not much of any science, yet enough of every one to speak its language." The entire court followed the King to the pleasure grounds of Fontainbleau in the fall of each year. Jefferson went along, though only for several days, in October 1785. Neither his finances nor his dispositions would support an annual residence there. A more satisfying retreat was afforded by the hermits of Mont Calvaire, beyond the bois de Boulogne. He sometimes occupied an apartment there, where he could work in perfect silence and stroll in the brothers' gardens.

The American Minister moved quietly in a select social circle. He was not seeking amorous adventure. The incessant whirl from one drawing room or boudoir to another held no charms for him. He was not a celebrity, as his predecessor had been, shunned popularity, and remained as inconspicuous as his office permitted. The reading public seldom came upon his name. Chastellux, of course, portrayed him in flattering colors in his *Travels;* but this was an exception, and it embarrassed the self-effacing American. Neither through the anonymously published *Notes on Virginia*, nor through American state papers circulated in France, like the Virginia Statute for Religious Freedom, nor in other productions of his pen did he show the slightest desire to attract notice to himself.

He was known best to the initiated of the American sect. Franklin had introduced him to the Comtesse de Houdetot, a woman reputedly ugly but radiating charm, wit, and goodness, the beloved of the poet-philosopher St. Lambert, and at the time Jefferson met her the priestess of the Crèvecœur cult of Arcadian America. Jefferson was often at her salon, where the literati congregated, and they shared a mutual interest in the education of Crèvecœur's sons. When Phillip Mazzei turned up in the summer of 1785, he at once took Jefferson on an afternoon round of his friends, starting with the poet-dramatist Marmontel, Secretary of the Académie Française, then to the great chemist Lavoisier, then to Condorcet, finally to the Duc de La Rochefoucauld, an aristocrat renowned for his liberalism. With Condorcet and La Rochefoucauld, Jefferson was probably already acquainted, as he certainly was with the Abbé Morellet, translator of the *Notes on Virginia*, who belonged to the same liberal circle. Perhaps he did not yet know the two men he later described as the most powerful in France at the approach of the Revolution, Jacques Necker and the Comte de Mirabeau. The latter, "this glittering monster," he thought an unscrupulous adventurer, while Necker, the Genevese banker, showed a limited capacity for statesmanship in his desperate efforts to save the *ancien régime* from itself. Jefferson sometimes attended the fashionable salon of Madame Necker, a woman who suffered from what Virginians called "the Budge," that is, she bounced and fidgeted; and he admired the brilliant daughter and young priestess of the salon, Madame de Staël. The salons of Madame Helvetius, Franklin's great friend, and of Madame d'Holbach, whose Encyclopédist husband had written the *Système de la nature*, which Jefferson had read years before— each presented a distinctive segment of the enlightened society of Paris.

But no salon appealed to him more than that of Comtesse de Tessé, at her country place Chaville, near Paris. An abiding affection grew up between the Virginian and this captivating little lady of the *ancien régime*, Lafayette's aunt and confidante, partroness of the arts and letters, friend of liberty and humanity. The Comtesse was an enthusiastic horticulturist, Chaville a botanical paradise. Jefferson went to great pains to obtain for her whole catalogues of seeds and plants from America. At the conclusion of his ministry, she presented him a marble pedestal inscribed, in Latin, "To the Supreme Ruler of the Universe, under whose watchful care the liberties of North America were finally achieved, and under whose tutelage the name of Thomas Jefferson will descend forever blessed to posterity." The American long remembered the Comtesse as his "particular botanical friend."

The botanical exchanges Jefferson conducted between the two worlds, exchanges that found him planting Indian corn in his garden at the Grille de Chaillot, for instance, while American collaborators experimented with European varieties of grass, rice, melons, and so on, were part of a larger enterprise in the transmission of useful knowledge. "Science is more important in a republican than in any other government," he wrote many years later. "And in an infant country like ours, we must depend for improvement on the science of other countries, longer established, possessing better means, and more advanced than we are." The *Encyclopédie méthodique*, successor to Diderot's work, was in preparation when he arrived in Paris. He patronized, and silently contributed to, this project, purchased it for the College of William and Mary, and entered subscriptions for his American friends. He sent trunks full of books to Madison, who balanced the account by payments made for the education of Jefferson's nephews, the Carrs. To the Reverend James Madison, of the College, among others, he periodically passed on "the crumbs of science" from the European table. A single letter reported Jan Ingenhousz's experiments on the effects of electricity on vegetation, an impressive new theory, upsetting Newton, on the phenomenon of the rainbow, LaPlace's latest astronomical work, the alleged discovery of the lost books of Livy which, as suspected, turned out to be a hoax, and encouraging developments in the as yet infant science of chemistry, "among the most useful of sciences," he remarked, "and big with future discoveries for the utility and safety of the human race."

This Virginia Yankee's curiosity about gadgets and machines of all kinds was insatiable. From England he imported a copying press —a simple instrument for making a duplicate of a letter. He was much taken with it, got French workmen to make presses on the same principle, presented them to a number of friends, and carried a portable version on his travels. He said he would gladly have given ten times the cost of his copying press to have had it from the date of the Stamp Act. He was similarly fascinated with a new process, called polytype, for the multiplication of facsimiles of original documents, drawings, or other images. Witnessing the process at the Paris shop of the inventor, he had 100 copies of a handwritten dinner invitation struck off in 45 minutes. Remarkable! He was never content to hear or read about a new invention: he must see it. Learning of an improvement in the production of muskets by standardized interchangeable parts, he went to the inventor and with his own hand put together several musket locks, "taking pieces at hazard as they came to hand, and they fitted in the most perfect manner." The significance of this technical advance did not escape Jefferson. He reported it to Congress. Sixteen years later Eli Whitney would perform an almost identical demonstration before astonished eyes in Washington. A Swiss established in Paris, Jean Pierre Droz, had made virtually "a new art" of coinage by the invention of a machine for stamping the two faces and the edge of a coin at one stroke. Jefferson investigated and informed Congress that Droz's services could be obtained for the United States. "It would be very desirable that in the institution of a new coinage, we could set out on so perfect a plan as this, and the more so, while the work is so exquisitely done, it is done cheaper." But Congress was still far from the establishment of a mint. No new contrivance was too trifling for Jefferson's attention. For instance, the pedometer: an ingenious device strapped between waist and knee to calculate strides in walking. He conducted a little experiment, ticking off his steps from place to place in winter and summer, proving that he did indeed go at a brisker pace and with longer strides in winter—a difference of exactly 331 steps to the mile. Jefferson saw that Madison got a pedometer.

The commerce in ideas and inventions, like the commerce in goods, ought to be reciprocal, so Jefferson worked hard to overcome the debit side of the account. Fortunately, two of his countrymen, Thomas Paine, of *Common Sense* fame, and James Rumsey, "the greatest mechanical genius" he knew, came to Europe to promote two very promising inventions. Paine brought the model of his revolutionary iron bridge to Paris in 1787. Jefferson's efforts to win French acceptance of the bridge led to a lasting friendship, though, ironically, Paine got the patents and support necessary for his work in England rather than in France. Rumsey sought exclusive patents and rights for steam navigation in France. The American Minister did everything possible to help him, seeking the patronage of nobility, the imprimatur of the French Academy, and approval of Rumsey's application at Versailles. "I have been frequently at Mr. Jefferson's . . . ," Rumsey wrote admiringly. "He has got all that ease, affability, and goodness about him, that distinguishes him as a good as well as a great man." But the time was not propitious. The efforts of "the most popular ambassador at the French Court" were in vain, and Rumsey died before his dreams could be realized.

Jefferson's patience in these matters was not easily exhausted. The trials of the long ocean voyage set back his plans to introduce American plants to Europe; yet he kept defying the odds so that the Old World might enjoy the superior productions of the New. "They have no apple here to compare with our Newtown pippin. They have nothing which deserves the name of a peach. . . . Their

337

cherries and strawberries are fair, but I think less flavored." Worst of all was the corn which, he said, "cannot be eaten, either in the form of corn or of bread, by any person who has eaten that of America." A patriot's pride shown in this work. It was a task of first importance "to do justice to our country, its productions, and its genius," he declared in a letter acknowledging an honorary doctor of law degree from Harvard University, the third institution so to honor him. "It is the work to which the young men, whom you are forming, should lay their hands. We have spent the prime of our lives in procuring them the precious blessings of liberty. Let them spend theirs in showing that it is the great parent of science and virtue; and that a nation will be great in both always in proportion as it is free."

In this same letter, Jefferson noted that the natural history of America was "totally mistaken and mis-represented" in Europe. He had been in Paris little over a year when Chastellux took him to the country residence of the great Buffon. "I was introduced to him as Mr. Jefferson, who, in some notes on Virginia, had combated some of his opinions. Instead of entering into an argument," so Jefferson recalled the meeting, "he took down his last work, presented it to me, and said, 'When Mr. Jefferson shall have read this, he will be perfectly satisfied that I am right.' " Undaunted by this grand gesture, Jefferson said Buffon had confounded the American deer, or elk, with the red deer of Europe and the moose with the reindeer. "I told him that our deer had horns two feet long; he replied with warmth, that if I could produce a single specimen, with horns one foot long, he would give up the question. . . . I told him also that the reindeer could walk under the belly of our moose; but he entirely scouted the idea." Whereupon Jefferson sent to America for the specimens. John Sullivan, of New Hampshire, to whom he had applied earlier, was pressed for the horns, skin, and skeleton of a moose. The former Revolutionary general, as Jefferson subsequently learned to his dismay, conducted a regular campaign. "The troops he employed sallied forth . . . in the month of March—much snow—a herd attacked—one killed—in the wilderness—a road cut 20 miles—to be drawn by hands from the frontier to his house—bones to be cleaned etc, etc, etc. . . ." Jefferson's tilt with Buffon cost him dearly. Sullivan submitted a bill for 45 pounds! By the time it arrived, before the consignment, Jefferson had forgotten about his request. He paid, of course, and thought the moose a valuable acquisition, despite the disappointing smallness of its horns, for which he apologized to Buffon. He hoped it might be reconstructed and mounted in the King's Cabinet of Natural History under Buffon's supervision. But the great scientist was soon dead. Jefferson never learned if he had repented the error of his ways.

Science and diplomacy combined to interest the Minister in geographical explorations, for knowledge and power were uncomfortably blended in these quests of discovery. One particularly engaged Jefferson. It revolved around an eccentric Connecticut genius, John Ledyard. This self-styled "slave of accident and son of care" had sailed with Captain Cook on his third Pacific voyage. He had come to Paris with the plan of a company to trade in furs between the northwest coast of America and China. The plan had not prospered when Jefferson met Ledyard early in 1786. He urged upon him the exploration of the American Northwest by journey eastward, through Siberia to Kamchatka, thence to the North American continent, and on to the Atlantic coast. The wild scheme excited Ledyard. He became obsessed with the idea of becoming "the first circumambulator of the globe." Through Baron de Grimm, the Empress Catherine's correspondent at Versailles, Jefferson and Lafayette undertook to obtain Ledyard's freedom of passage across Russia. She refused, thinking the enterprise chimerical. Ledyard would not relinquish it, however, and after the abortion of an alternate plan to sail from England to the Pacific, he returned to the original scheme, confident Catherine would acquiesce or even approve. He actually got within several hundred miles of Kamchatka before Catherine's couriers caught up with him and turned him back. Ledyard thought he had at least solved the ethnological riddle, the relationship between the Tartars and the American Indians, that had chiefly interested Jefferson in the venture. "They are the same people—" Ledyard wrote from Siberia, "the most ancient, the most numerous of any other, and had not a small sea divided them, they would all have still been known by the same name." Jefferson saw Ledyard again a year later, in 1788, when he passed through Paris on an expedition to Africa. He promised on his return to go to America and make the continental crossing westward from Kentucky. But Ledyard never

339

returned from Africa. The path of destiny he had charted would be traveled by Lewis and Clark years later, under Jefferson's auspices of course.

In the fine arts Jefferson believed the Old World should furnish models for the New. The subject engaged him seriously chiefly in its public, or monumental, aspect. None of the commissions he performed in Paris gave him greater pleasure than two of this kind on behalf of his native state. No sooner had he arrived than he received the resolution of the Virginia assembly authorizing a statue of George Washington, with instructions to him and Franklin to select the artist and otherwise look after the execution of the work. The responsibility fell largely to Jefferson. After satisfying himself that the greatest living sculptor was the Parisian Houdon, he sent for him. Houdon leaped at the opportunity. He would gladly "leave the statues of kings unfinished," even go to America, which had not been contemplated, in order to copy Washington's features. Jefferson fell in with Houdon's thinking. Nothing should be spared in so noble a work; the statue should be life-size, and the bust, at least, taken from life. Houdon voyaged to America, "panting after glory," in company with Franklin. He returned six months later with plaster bust and measurements. The inscription for the statue provoked fanciful suggestions in Paris, including one from Jefferson, though the straightforward inscription earlier written by Madison was finally adhered to. Equally interesting was the question of dress. Benjamin West, in England, had successfully introduced modern garb into heroic portraiture. Despite his taste, and the taste of Paris, for things Roman, Jefferson thought "a modern in an antique dress as just an object of ridicule as a Hercules or Marius with a periwig and chapeaux bras." He was relieved when Washington himself deferred to the judgment in favor of modern dress. While the work went forward, Jefferson occasionally visited Houdon's studio, a cluttered museum of sculptured monuments of the great. The artist executed busts of several Revolutionary heroes—Franklin, Jones, Lafayette, Jefferson himself—and the American Minister would return home with plasters of these and others. The great noble pedestrian statue of Washington, "une Epoque dans les Arts," as Crèvecœur called it, was still unfinished when Jefferson left Paris in 1789.

Not long after, however, it would adorn the Virginia Capitol, at

Richmond, which Jefferson designed. His original plan for the new government buildings proved too ambitious for the state's resources. Rather than the complex of structures Jefferson had envisioned, the Directors of the Public Buildings decided to consolidate the whole under one roof. This single building, the Capitol, must have appropriate magnificence. The directors entreated Jefferson to consult on a plan in Paris, adding a request for drawings of a prison as well. He entered upon the assignment with the utmost deliberation. First the style was decided: Roman classical, as befitted the aspirations of the new republic. Then the model: one Palladio had made familiar to him, the Maison Carrée at Nîmes, thought by Jefferson "the best morsel of ancient architecture now remaining." Then the consulting architect: Jefferson finally chose Charles Clérisseau, who had published drawings of the antiquities of Nîmes. Finally, the adaptation of the model, a Roman temple, to the purpose at hand. Changes were made in the dimensions, the ordonance, and many details; windows were substituted for the pilasters of the outer walls; one of the three rows of columns was dropped from the portico. This last was at Clérisseau's suggestion in order to admit more light. Jefferson consented reluctantly, for he was anxious to preserve the purity of the ancient form. "What is good is often spoiled by trying to make it better," he observed. He sketched plans for the interior rooms and chambers, while Clérisseau drew the elevation and prepared a plaster model to guide workmen inexperienced in the fine art of building.

With what mortification did he then learn, in September 1785, that work was proceeding at Richmond on another, a less elegant and less costly, plan! He wrote the directors, Madison, and others imploring delay. "But how is a taste in this beautiful art to be formed in our countrymen," he demanded, "unless we avail ourselves of every occasion when public buildings are to be erected, of presenting to them models for their study and imitation?" No miserable expediency ought to decide the question between the copy of a sublime structure approved by the centuries and "the brat of a whimsical conception never before brought to light." "You see I am an enthusiast on the subject of the arts," he told Madison. "But it is an enthusiasm of which I am not ashamed, as its object is to improve the taste of my countrymen, to increase their reputation, and to reconcile to them the respect of the world and procure them its praise." His pleas were heeded. Foundations and bricks were already laid when Jefferson's plan reached Richmond many months later, but the directors endeavored to conform everything to his model. When finally completed a decade later, the Capitol gave visible form, if imperfectly, to Jefferson's grand conception. A touring Frenchman, La Rochefoucauld-Liancourt, then pronounced this building "beyond compare, the finest, the most noble, and the greatest in America." As the first monument of the classic revival, the Virginia Capitol exerted enormous influence on the public architecture of the United States.

Life for Jefferson was a perpetual study, and while on "the vaunted scene" he naturally sought to further his education by travel. Except for the brief sojourn at Fontainbleau, he had scarcely set foot outside Paris since his arrival when, in March 1786, Adams called him to London on the business of commercial treaties. Jefferson was prepared to dislike England. In friendly banter with Abigail Adams he had declared he would not give "the polite, self-denying, feeling, hospitable, goodhumored people of this country [France] and their amiability in every point of view . . . for ten such races of rich, proud, hectoring, swearing, squibbing, carnivorous animals as those among whom you are." The prejudice behind the banter was political—the freed colonial's prejudice against the mother country—and the visit to England only deepened it. Adams proudly carried his Virginia friend to court for presentation to the King. George III, who had been civil to Adams, pointedly snubbed the author of the Declaration of Independence. The Americans' overtures to the Foreign Secretary on the subject of a commercial treaty fell flat. The United States had friends in England—Richard Price, Thomas Brand-Hollis, Benjamin Vaughan, the Marquis of Lansdowne (Shelburne)—and Jefferson enjoyed their company; but they were few and without influence. Even the studied politeness of the dinner table offered no bar to English rudeness and insolence. "That nation hates us," Jefferson concluded after his visit, "their ministers hate us, and their king more than all other men."

The Adamses welcomed Jefferson as one of their own to the house on Grosvenor Square. They showed him London, from Drury Lane to the British Museum. He conceded the city was handsomer, cleaner, and roomier than Paris, though its architecture was the most wretched imaginable. In the mechanical arts, London stood at the head of the world. "I could write volumes on the improvements which I find made and making here in the arts," he wrote Charles Thomson. With the Adamses he saw the great steam mill at Blackfriars Bridge on the Thames. Powered by huge Boulton and Watt engines, it was one of the wonders of the industrial revolution. Unfortunately, he could not inspect the machinery itself. The English took extraordinary precautions against foreign larceny of industrial secrets. But not all useful inventions came from England or all thievery from foreigners. While in London he visited a shop where patented wagon wheels were made from a single piece of wood. The New Jersey farmers first perfected the process, Jefferson insisted, and Franklin had carried it to London, where it was patented, wheels produced in quantity, and exported around the world, which thought it an English discovery. Jefferson's patriotic ardor would not permit him to claim the discovery exclusively for the Americans, however. The idea was in the *Iliad*, whence the Jersey farmers, "the only farmers who can read Homer," got it! Visiting the shop of London's leading maker of harpsichords, he attempted, unsuccessfully, to promote a technical improvement introduced by his Philadelphia friend Francis Hopkinson. Patsy continued to study the harpsichord, and her father wanted her to have a fine instrument made to order in London. It was to be one of the bulkier items later carried home from Paris.

During a lull in negotiations with the Portuguese ambassador, and after talks with the Tripolitan ambassador reached an impasse, the two Americans made a leisurely tour of celebrated English country estates and gardens. Armed with Thomas Whately's *Observations on Modern Gardening*, an infallible guide as he discovered, Jefferson viewed every park, walk, riding, hedge, garden, and ornament of the spring infested English verdure with the practiced eye of a landscapist. He jotted down useful observations, supplementing Whately, on the slope of a lawn, the cost of a grotto, size of a lake or pond, style of an arch, effect of a temple or other ornament, number of deer inhabiting a park, and so on. While his taste in architecture ran to classicism, his taste in landscape ran to the baroque. Here, at least, he agreed with William Hogarth, whose provocative essay on beauty he knew, in preferring the curved and waving lines of nature to the precise formality and regularity of the classical. And because the style of English pleasure-gardening, unlike the French, generally imitated nature in rococo profusion, Jefferson was charmed by it. He liked surprises to the eye, varying levels, asymmetrical balances. "Art appears too much," he wrote of Blenheim; and he repeatedly noted disapproval of straight lines, while particularly praising a "most lovely mixture of concave and convex" in one of the gardens he toured. For him, as for Hogarth, the serpentine was the line of nature.

The New Englander did not share his companion's enthusiasm. The gardens were lovely, of course, but scarcely deserving of a chaste republican's study. "It will be long, I hope, before ridings, parks, pleasure grounds, gardens, and ornamental farms grow so much in fashion in America," Adams jotted in his diary. The historic sites they visited aroused Adams's pride in his English heritage. On the battlefield at Worcester, where Cromwell defeated Charles II, Adams was amazed to discover the farmers at the local tavern ignorant of the encounter, and he gave them a little lecture. "Tell your neighbors and your children that this is holy ground; much holier than that on which your churches stand." Jefferson undoubtedly agreed, but, except for his infernal accounting of shillings and pence, he was as silent as the grave about this and every other historic scene. At Stratford-upon-Avon they followed the tourists' custom and cut a chip from the chair in the chimney corner where Shakespeare supposedly sat. Adams entered a tribute to the poet's genius in his diary. Jefferson's dry record of the excursion runs as follows: "paid postillion 3s; for seeing house where Shakespeare was born, 1s; seeing his tomb-stone, 1s; entertainment, 4s.2d; servants, 2s; horses to Hockley, 12s." It would be wrong to conclude that because he did not record his feelings he therefore had none; but his mind was on the future, on useful knowledge rather than historical sentiments.

The Portuguese treaty continued to drag after Jefferson returned to London the middle of April. While awaiting its completion, the two ministers endeavored to reach an agreement with the chairman of a committee of British merchants on the settlement of American debts. The treaty of peace provided for the recovery of these debts, and Jefferson never questioned the justice of the measure. But the violations of the treaty on the British side, as in the refusal to withdraw from the Northwest posts and to make restitution for captured slaves, furnished the excuse to demagogues, like Patrick Henry, to keep up the spirit of opposition at home. The stalemate might be broken, Jefferson thought, if reasonable terms of repayment could be agreed upon. He recommended a term of five years, which was acceptable, but his demand for the renunciation of interest during the war was too bitter a pill for the merchants to swallow. The negotiations broke down. Jefferson, meanwhile, tried to make private arrangements with his own creditors. Spurning the protection of Virginia laws, he put a heavy burden on his estate—selling land and slaves, renting out plantations—in order to pay his just debts. "I am miserable till I shall owe not a shilling," he later wrote; "the moment that shall be the case I shall feel at liberty to do something for the comfort of my slaves." Unfortunately, that moment would never come. At length, near the end of April, the ill-fated Portuguese treaty was signed, and Jefferson hurried back to Paris.

On leaving London he paid a young American artist, Mather Brown, ten pounds for an oil portrait, so far as is known the first ever made of him. The portrait was Abigail's idea. She wished it for John and herself; and Jefferson agreed to sit for Brown if Adams would reciprocate. The Adamses actually got the replica, which they hung in their residence on Grosvenor Square, while the original went to Jefferson two years later with Brown's portrait of Adams. Brown painted a dandified Jefferson: hair powdered and rolled and tied in a queue, fancy lace, soft face, exquisitely feminine hands. It was not thought a good likeness. "It has no feature like him," Short said, adding that everyone in Paris considered it an *étude*. The opinion was shared by John Trumbull, another young American artist Jefferson met in London. He was at once taken with Trumbull. His was one of several new friendships Jefferson took back to Paris. Another was with William S. Smith, secretary of the legation and the betrothed of young Abigail Adams. Smith, Trumbull, and the Adams family were always performing little commissions for him in London, while he and Short did the same for them in Paris. He preferred to dress in English cloth, for which he apologized to the French ministry. Abigail looked after his orders for shirts, and he supplied her with silk stockings woven by the hermits of Mont Calvaire. Nothing abashed in these matters, the new Mrs. Smith asked the American Minister to obtain two corsets for her from a Parisian mademoiselle she had patronized three years before. Forwarding the corsets, Jefferson noted her failure to provide current measurements. "Should they be too small however," he added with an amusement Mrs. Smith seemed not to appreciate, "she will be so good as to lay them by a while. There are ebbs as well as flows in this world. When the mountain refused to come to Mahomet, he went up to the mountain."

The tobacco trade was on the carpet when Jefferson returned to Paris, and he was much occupied with the affairs of the American Committee, as well as the Barbary negotiations, for the next several months. Eager for every opporunity to create a favorable image of the United States in Europe, he had, in January, entered into a silent collaboration with Jean Nicholas Démeunier, who was responsible for the article on the United States in the authoritative *Encyclopédie méthodique*. Rochefoucauld had brought the two men together. Before going to London Jefferson had written out detailed answers to two sets of queries presented by Dameunier. The manuscript article of nearly 300 pages was then given to Jefferson for his observations, which he finished and returned in June. Aside from correcting Démeunier's mistakes, most of them derived, Jefferson thought, from the Abbé Raynal's *Histoire,* he supplied information on current American affairs interpreted in the most advantageous light. His true opinion of the Cincinnati, for example, left no ground for apology or equivocation; yet he urged upon Démeunier a face-saving explanation of that institution, not only in charity to the United States but to the numerous French officers who proudly wore the badge. Démeunier's article, first published in book form, disappointed him. "He has still left in a great deal of the Abbé Raynal, that is to say a great deal of falsehood, and he has stated other things on bad information." Nevertheless, it was a useful work, clearly the better for Jefferson's trouble, which Démeunier paid for "in the true coin of his country, most unmerciful compliment."

The charms of winsome romance touched the 43-year-old widower's heartstrings in August. The lady was Maria Cosway. An artist in her own right, she had come to Paris with her husband Richard Cosway, a fashionable London painter and renowned miniaturist. There Trumbull met them. He had accepted Jefferson's invitation to see and study the art treasures of Paris while making the hôtel de Langeac his home. Trumbull had brought along for engraving the first fruits of his epic enterprise in patriotic portraiture, *The Death of Montgomery* and *The Battle of Bunker's Hill;* and with Jefferson's assistance he began the composition of the still more famous painting, *The Declaration of Independence*. On an August afternoon Trumbull introduced Jefferson to the English couple at the Halle aux Bleds, the great domed grain market of Paris. A market was to be built in Richmond: how wonderful if it could be as beautiful and commodious as the Halle aux Bleds! But this utilitarian object was quickly forgotten as Jefferson fell under Maria's charms. A camaraderie seized the company, everyone of whom had dinner engagements. "Lying messengers were . . . dispatched into every quarter of the city with apologies for . . . breach of engagement." The American Minister sent his excuses to the Duchesse d'Anville; and they all drove off to St. Cloud, four miles distant, dined and toured the gallery there, returned to Paris under a glow of fireworks to match their spirits, and before separating made a late evening call on a celebrated harpist Maria admired.

Until October 5, when the Cosways returned to London, Jefferson and Maria were almost constant companions, usually with Trumbull and the Comte d'Angeville, director of the King's gallery. (Cosway was occupied with painting the portraits of the Duchesse d'Orléans and her children.) They toured the galleries, attended concerts at the Tuileries, sported at the Palais Royal, walked in the bois de Boulogne, and journeyed into the countryside. When the interlude passed, Jefferson let his memory wonder over these ecstatic days. St. Germain! "How beautiful was every object! The Port de Neuilly, the hills along the Seine, the rainbows of the machine of Marly, the terras of St. Germain, the chateaux, the gardens, the statues of Marly, the pavilion of Lucienne. . . . The wheels of time moved on with a rapidity of which those of our carriage gave but a faint idea, and yet in the evening, when one took a retrospect of the day, what a mass of happiness had we travelled over!"

The enchantress was Maria, not St. Germain. A little wisp of a woman, soft and delicate, deep blue eyes set in an oval face, with a head of frothy golden curls, she seemed to step out of one of her husband's cameos. But she possessed other charms as well. Although English, she had grown up in Florence, and the lightness of the Italian air was in her disposition, the music of the Italian tongue in her voice, the artistry of Florence in her fingertips. Introduced into London art circles when she was but twenty years of age, she soon married Richard Cosway, like Jefferson many years her senior. The marriage was not a happy one. Cosway was a vain and pompous dandy, caricatured by his enemies as "the macaroni miniature painter," jealous, or at least unappreciative, of Maria's talents, and holding her like a bird in his slightly tarnished cage of gilt. London was oppressive, but she turned their home on Stratford Place into a brilliant salon. Her musical evenings—"great concerts" they were called—became the height of fashion. It was a highly sophisticated world. Gossip connected Cosway with other women, and men buzzed around Maria like bees around a flower. "You make every body love you," Jefferson once said to her. "You are sought and surrounded therefore by all."

Jefferson's feelings toward Maria, while no doubt sexual in origin, had an airy quality that leaves no suggestion of ardent desire. They were gay and lighthearted with each other, affectionate in a pleasant way, flirting at love with neither choosing to embrace it. It was as if they were playing a game, delightfully free and even reckless, but which he at least knew all along would end in a perfectly conventional fashion. He was never happier in Paris than during this late summer of 1786, when the days, were they as long as Lapland's, would have been filled to overflowing. An evening or so after Maria's departure, Jefferson sat at his fireside, "solitary and sad," and composed a long letter to her in the form of a dialogue between his head and heart. The head upbraids the heart for its follies; the heart, unable to deny them but unrepentant, claims its rights from the prudent tyrant. "Let the gloomy Monk, sequestered from the world, seek unsocial pleasures in the bottom of his cell! Let the sublimated philosopher grasp visionary happiness while pursuing phantoms dressed in the garb of truth! Their supreme wisdom is supreme folly. . . . Had they ever felt the solid pleasure of one generous spasm of the heart, they would exchange for it all the frigid speculations of their lives, which you [the head] have been vaunting in such elevated terms. . . . Fill paper as you please with triangles and squares: try how many ways you can hang and combine them together. I shall never envy nor control your supreme delights. But leave me to decide when and where friendships are to be contracted." It wasn't that simple, however; in the end, the head (Jefferson) coolly put the heart (Maria) in its place. Reason and sentiment might divide life between them, yet, for him, one was the master, the other the servant. With the seraphic Maria he slackened the reins on his emotions but did not drop them. The following summer she was again in Paris, this time without her husband, but Jefferson saw less of her than before. "Your mere domestic cortege was so numerous, *et si imposante*, that one could not approach you quite at their ease," he apologized afterwards. Their affection endured for many years, long after he became President of the United States and she, widowed and returned to Italy, the beloved Baroness of Lodi.

During one of his perambulations with Maria, feeling friskier than usual, Jefferson attempted to jump a fence, fell hard, and dislocated his wrist. This was one of those follies the head upbraided him for. He suffered pain and sleepless nights for several days. For much longer he was unable to write except with his left hand, which required the superhuman effort reserved for such letters as the *adieu* to Maria. Short, meanwhile, was his amanuensis. The best surgeon in Paris had been called in to set the wrist, but obviously he bungled it. "The fingers remain swelled and crooked, the hand withered, and the joint having a very confined motion," Jefferson wrote nearly a year later. He had to lay aside his violin and never recovered full use of his right hand. The injury caused him to postpone a journey he had planned to the south of France in the fall of 1786. But as the months passed and the wrist failed to mend, his doctors prescribed the mineral waters of Aix-en-Provence. Government was at a standstill in February. Financial crisis had led to the extraordinary measure of convening an Assembly of Notables. This passage of affairs was likely to prove interesting—but not interesting enough to hold the American Minister in Paris. He attended the opening session of the Assembly, mapped out the tour, and took to the road the last day of February.

349

He traveled incognito with only a trunk and a servant. To complete his circuit would require more than ten weeks, but he was in no hurry. "I am constantly roving about, to see what I have never seen before and shall never see again," he wrote to Lafayette. "In the great cities, I go to see what travellers think alone worthy of being seen; but I make a job of it, and generally gulp it down in a day. On the other hand, I am never satiated with rambling through the fields and farms, examining the culture of the cultivators, with a degree of curiosity which makes them take me to be a fool, and others to be much wiser than I am." In place of ministers, dukes, and duchesses, he courted the society of gardeners, vignerons, coopers, and farmers, and at night took refuge in some simple *auberge* where, "unknown to all, unheeded, undisturbed," he dined, read, reflected, recorded the day's observations, and slept. He encountered difficulties, of course, and saw many things disagreeable to him; but, as he philosophized to a Parisian friend, "The plan of my journey, as well as of my life, being to take things by the smooth handle, few occur which have not something tolerable to offer me." His tour was a continuous inquiry, and as his notes make clear, mainly an agricultural inquiry. He traveled "to see the country and not its towns." Agriculture was the most useful field for the studious American with an eye cocked to his own country; and the mass of Frenchmen being farmers of one description or another, the countryside furnished the clues to the comparative misery or felicity of the nation. Jefferson commended his procedure to Lafayette: "You must ferret the people out of their hovels . . . look into their kettles, eat their bread, loll on their beds under the pretense of resting yourself, but in fact to find if they are soft. You will feel a sublime pleasure in the course of this investigation, and a sublimer one hereafter when you shall be able to apply your knowledge to the softening of their beds, or the throwing a morsel of meat into the kettle of vegetables." The peripatetic inquirer might thus become the wiser statesman.

Striking out through the Champagne—corn country which reminded him of the neighborhood of Elk Hill—he thought the cultivation and the cultivators poor. There were no farm houses, the people being gathered in villages, as around feudal manors, where he was sure they were "less happy and less virtuous . . . than they would be insulated with their families on the grounds they cultivate." The women too worked in the fields, "an unequivocal indication of extreme poverty," for the position of women in any society was an infallible index to its well-being. The conditions of French agriculture varied enormously from one region to another. As he moved through Burgundy and into the Beaujolais, Jefferson thought the country the richest he had ever seen. The people lived on their farms, but unfortunately, because of the system of tenancy on short leases, the husbandry was not equal to the land. He agreed with Arthur Young, the English agriculturist who toured France at about the same time: "Give a man the secure possession of a bleak rock, and he will turn it into a garden; give him a nine year lease of a garden, and he will convert it into a desert." Of French agriculture generally, Jefferson had a higher opinion than Young. The latter, of course, wrote as a professional observer and for an English audience just after the French Revolution, while Jefferson's observations on the wing were intended for no one but himself and his friends. In any event, taking things by "the smooth handle," he expressed none of the Englishman's outrage at the sight of bad husbandry and a miserable peasantry.

He came upon vineyards in Burgundy. "I mounted a *bidet*, put a peasant on another and rambled thro' their most celebrated vineyards," he reported to Short. Throughout the tour he paid the closest attention to viniculture, wines, and vintages, not with a view to American agriculture, for he discovered that the vine was "the parent of misery," but rather as a connoisseur for whom good wines had become a necessary part of the art of living. Before reaching Lyons, after two weeks of travel pelted with rain, hail, and snow, he briefly departed from his usual plan of avoiding "good dinners and good company" and stopped at a great chateau whose seigneur was known to his friends the Abbés Arnoux and Chalut. There he fell in love with a sculptured Diana, the most precious work of the chisel he had ever seen.

Bent as he was on utilitarian objects, Jefferson did not entirely ignore the fine arts in his travels. In painting and sculpture his taste was quite uncultivated. Yet he could be transfixed by a statue or a painting. He seemed indifferent to the canvases of the great masters, "the old faded red things of Rubens," for example, and saved his praise for contemporary works portraying Biblical or classical scenes in a baroque manner: Marius pleading with his assassin, by Drouais; Van der Werf's picture of Sarah delivering Agar up to Abraham; and "republican" paintings in the same vein by Jacques Louis David, leader of the neo-classical school in Paris. "I am but a son of nature," he once said to Maria Cosway, "loving what I see and feel, without being able to give a reason, nor caring much whether there be one." When his ramblings were over, in 1788, he set down some observations for the guidance of two young Americans in their European travels. Here he listed the "objects of attention for an American." Agriculture came first, then mechanical arts (forges, quarries, boats, canals, bridges), then manufactures, though it would be a waste of time to examine them minutely, since the United States would not soon become a manufacturing country. Gardens ought to be studied, for the Americans might make the noblest gardens with the least expense. "Architecture worth great attention. As we double our numbers every 20 years we must double our houses . . . and it is desirable to introduce taste into an art which shows so much." As for painting and sculpture: "Too expensive for the state of wealth among us. It would be useless therefore and preposterous for us to endeavor to make ourselves connoisseurs in those arts. They are worth seeing, but not studying." Politics were worth while so far as they influenced the happiness of a people, but one might as well see the menagerie at Versailles, with its lions, tigers and other beasts of prey, as to seek out the courts of nobility. The advice was all very American—damning in the eyes of cultivated Europeans. Utility was Jefferson's standard; but if he thereby downgraded aesthetic enjoyments, it was because he knew the American tourist would find them easily enough, whereas the discovery of the more prosaic and practical arts with which to build a civilization called for disciplined effort.

Proceeding down the Rhone Valley, Jefferson's eyes feasted on "the remains of Roman grandeur"—palaces, arches, aqueducts, amphitheaters. Nîmes abounded in antiquities, and Jefferson loved it. "Here I am, Madame," he addressed Mme de Tessé in Paris, "gazing whole hours at the Maison Quarrée like a lover at his mistress." The chaste beauty of the building riveted his attention, fully justifying his expectations for the temple chosen as the model of the Virginia

Capitol. Arriving at Aix near the end of March, he spent several days bathing his wrist, without any sensible benefit, and soaking up the sun. "I am now in the land of corn, wine, oil, and sunshine. What more can man ask of heaven? If I should happen to die in Paris," he instructed Short, "I will beg you to send me here, and have me exposed to the sun. I am sure it will bring me to life again." In the country around Aix, he studied the culture of the olive and the making of oil. Of the several useful plants of the Mediterranean —fig, caper, mulberry, apricot, and others—the olive was the least known and the most worthy of being known in the United States. The plant lived forever and grew in any soil. It might be cultivated by slaves in South Carolina and Georgia. "Having been myself an eyewitness to the blessings which this tree sheds on the poor," he wrote to one of his Charleston correspondents, "I never had my wishes so kindled for the introduction of any article of new culture into our own country." At Aix he was amused to discover that he understood the Provençal dialect more because of his command of Italian than of French. Speculating on the reason for this in a letter to Short, he also expressed his disappointment that Provençal, a language next to Italian and Spanish in point of beauty, had lost out to the French and seemed certain to disappear.

From Aix, Jefferson went to Marseilles, chiefly to gather information on the port. There he decided to venture across the Alps in order to unravel the mystery of Piedmont rice. Leaving his carriage at Nice, he mounted a mule that faithfully brought him through the mountains to Turin in four days. The road he traveled struck him as one of the greatest works of man. "It did not cost as much as one year's war." He carried with him some writings purporting to explain Hannibal's passage across the Alps, and concluded they were all guesswork. Passing through the rice country, Jefferson also saw how Parmesan cheese was made, discovered a new method of storing rice, and acquired a taste for macaroni. (Later, when Short toured Italy, he obtained for Jefferson a machine to make macaroni, seldom if ever put to use.) He went as far as Milan. The famous cathedral was "a worthy object of philosophical speculation" because of its gaudy extravagance. "On viewing the churches of Italy it is evident without calculation that the same expense would have sufficed to throw the Apennines into the Adriatic and thereby render it terra firma from Leghorn to Constantinople." And he did not believe the soul of man would be any the worse for it.

Jefferson would always regret that he did not go to Rome. "I calculated the hours . . . . . But they were exactly more than I had to spare. Was not this provoking?" he asked Maria. Nor did he see Palladio's country, which lay too far to the east. Instead, he returned to Nice by way of Genoa—a sickening sea voyage followed by a fatiguing climb on muleback. Resting briefly, he then proceeded on the westward leg of his journey. At Avignon he admired the tomb of Laura, the lovely lady of Petrarch's passion, and made an excursion to the celebrated fountain of Vaucluse. "It gushes, of the size of a river, from a secluded valley of the mountain, the ruin of Petrarch's chateau being perched on a rock 200 feet perpendicular above. To add to the enchantment of the scene, every tree and bush was filled with nightingales in full song." The nightingales along the Seine had not been the same; he had judged them inferior to the Virginia mockingbirds. The warblers of the Mediterranean had a more varied song and a fuller tone. "It explains to me . . . ," he wrote in a typical flight of fancy, "why there never was a poet north of the Alps, and why there never will be one. A poet is as much the creature of climate as an orange or palm tree. What a bird the nightingale would be in the climates of America! We must colonize him thither."

The Mediterranean spring in all its glory found the questing American on the Canal of Languedoc, "cloudless skies above, limpid waters below, and on each hand a row of nightingales in full chorus." His carriage, *sans* wheels, was mounted on a light bark and towed on the canal. "I walk the greater part of the way along the banks of the canal, level, and lined with a double row of trees which furnish shade. When fatigued I take seat in my carriage where, as much at ease as if in my study, I read, write, or observe." All in all, it was the pleasantest mode of travel he had ever come upon. The waterway linking the Mediterranean with Bordeaux via the Garonne River was a grand work of engineering, deeply interesting to the Virginian who had ideas of connecting the James and the Potomac with the waters of the Ohio. He measured its every dimension and distance, studied its locks, and investigated its sources of water.

After nine lyrical days and 200 miles on the canal, he mounted the wheels to his carriage and drove to Bordeaux. This gleaming white city, hailed by Young as the most beautiful in France, made no particular impression on Jefferson, though the celebrated vineyards of the surrounding countryside claimed his ardent attention. Six dozen bottles of "the very best Bordeaux wine" were packed up and sent to Francis Eppes in Virginia. A few months later he ordered 250 bottles of vintage sauterne for his table in Paris. With the knowledge of the vineyards gleaned on his tour, Jefferson stocked his celler in handsome style for years to come.

From Bordeaux to Nantes and by way of Tours and Orleans to Paris, Jefferson returned to his starting point on June 10. "I . . . never passed three months and a half more delightfully," he said. He might have tarried longer, perhaps taken Rome or Palladio's Vicenza into his tour, but for the anxiously expected arrival of nine-year-old Polly. Jefferson had asked the Eppeses to send her to him the previous spring. His letter arrived too late, much to the relief of the Eppeses, for the little girl put her foot down. "I am very sorry you have sent for me. I don't want to go to France, I had rather stay with Aunt Eppes." The succeeding spring found her more stubborn than ever, but she was inveigled aboard ship, attended by a servant, Sally Hemings, less than twice her age. The voyage was uneventful; the captain doted on the child, and after landing in England carried her to Abigail Adams. Polly was wretched to leave him. "I tell her that I did not see her sister cry once," Abigail reported to Jefferson. "She replies that her sister was older and ought to do better, besides she had Pappa with her. I show her your picture. She says she cannot know it, how should she when she should not know you." Abigail promised to take her to Sadlers Wells. "I had rather . . . see Captain Ramsey [sic] one moment, than all the fun in the world," Polly sulked. But soon she became as attached to Abigail as she had been to the Captain. Abigail, and John too, fell in love with her. They were dismayed when Jefferson, offering the excuse of a backlog of work, sent a servant, the faithful Petit, to fetch her. Polly refused to see him, burst into tears, and clung to Abigail as her only refuge in a deceiving world. After several days she went with Petit, arriving in Paris the middle of July.

Reunited at last with a father and sister she scarcely knew, Polly soon became everyone's favorite. Jefferson was delighted with her. "Her reading, her writing, her manner in general show what everlasting obligation we are all under to you," he wrote to Mrs. Eppes. Polly was placed in the convent school, which Abigail Adams heartily disapproved of, and under Patsy's charge rapidly adjusted. The sisters were strikingly different: Patsy, like her father, tall and angular, reddish hair, and "the sunshine of heaven" in her temperament; Polly slight-of-build, high-strung, the prettier and more bewitching of the two, and the less studious. The crimson-frocked girls visited their father weekly, often with Kitty Church, whose mother Angelica Schuyler Church, American-born but married into fashionable London society, Jefferson admired. For him no pleasures equaled those of the family circle, whether passing a leisurely hour at tea, coaxing Polly to write letters, helping with a cursed Latin text, or seated at the fire and listening to Patsy play the harpsichord.

History had marched with quickening strides during Jefferson's absence, and he hastened to catch up. The Assembly of Notables had met, listened incredulously to Calonne's report, and rather than endorse his bold program of reform had driven him from office. Even so, there was room for encouragement in the Assembly's work, and Jefferson, with Lafayette and most liberal men, was disposed to find it. He praised, for instance, the provision for provincial assemblies as an important first step toward bringing the people into the affairs of government. Calonne's retirement offered the opportunity, at last, to get the government to honor the Berni agreement. Jefferson pressed the matter as much as he dared in view of the troubles besetting the ministry. As already noted, the decree—"the sheet-anchor of our connection with France"—finally issued in December. Meanwhile, the nation's disorders mounted. Mobs raged in Paris; every scribbler denounced the government, which seemed helpless to arrest this "revolution of public opinion." "The king, long in the habit of drowning his cares in wine, plunges deeper and deeper; the queen cries but sins on," Jefferson reported. He believed reform would work its way to a peaceful conclusion, but the high confidence he felt in June subsided by September.

At the same time, affairs in Holland threatened to erupt in a European war. Foreign powers had become entangled in the long and bitter contest between the Patriot, or democratic, party, which dominated the States General of the United Netherlands, and the mingled array of royalists, aristocrats, and local burghers who supported the Stadtholder, the Prince of Orange. France was pledged to the former, Britain and Prussia to the latter. When the civil conflict produced an insult to the Princess of Orange, her brother, the King of Prussia, sent 20,000 troops into the Netherlands, and Britain prepared to enter the fray if France intervened. Jefferson pondered the effect of such a war on his own country. It promised great commercial benefits, of course, since the United States would become the neutral carrier for the belligerents. "But," he wrote to Washington, "in the first place no war can be safe for us which threatens France with an unfavourable issue. And in the next, it will probably embark us again into the ocean of speculation, engage us to overtrade ourselves, convert us into sea-ravens under French and Dutch colors, divert us from agriculture which is our wisest pursuit, because it will in the end contribute most to real wealth, good morals and happiness." The British ambassador at Versailles asked Jefferson what the policy of the United States might be in the event of war. He replied without hesitation that the country would be neutral, unless Britain should be so foolish as to attack French possessions in the West Indies, which the United States was bound by treaty to defend. "Then it will be war," the ambassador said. War was averted, and the Dutch Patriots were crushed, principally because Louis XVI, his treasury empty, his hands full at home, dishonored his commitments. The United States could take no satisfaction from France's perfidy. Britain, seeing with what ease France abandoned her friends, might think the moment propitious for regaining the lost colonies. "It conveys to us the important lesson," Jefferson wrote to Jay, "that no circumstances of morality, honor, interest or engagement are sufficient to authorize a secure reliance on any nation, at all times, and in all positions." He hoped Congress would fill the magazines and prepare for any eventuality.

Europe was turbulent from the Black Sea to the English Channel in the summer and fall of 1787. In the United States, meanwhile, a new federal constitution was framed by an assembly of notables at Philadelphia. Jefferson had applauded every effort to strengthen the bonds of union. A year before he was disturbed by alarming reports of dissension between the eastern and southern states on the question of the navigation of the Mississippi River. Congress had instructed Jay, in his negotiations with the Spanish Minister Diego de Gardoqui, to insist on the American right to navigate the river; but Gardoqui's instructions were just as emphatic on the opposite side, and after a year of fruitless talk Jay got authority from Congress, on a sharply sectional vote, to suspend the Mississippi claim for a period of twenty-five years in return for a treaty of commerce with Spain. Jefferson's Virginia friends accused Jay of selling out the West for eastern gain. In the face of angry opposition, Jay dropped the plan; but it produced a revulsion against federal measures in Virginia, west of the Alleghenies, and, indeed, in all the non-carrying states. Madison feared dire consequences. Jefferson shared his fears, and fully realized now, what he had only half believed before, that western commerce must flow to the Mississippi. "And I venture to say," he wrote Madison, "that the act which abandons the Mississippi is an act of separation between the Eastern and Western country." He did not expect Spain to relinquish the river, but he did expect it to be opened, either by the westerners themselves, perhaps in alliance with another nation, or by the agency of the United States, which was the only course consistent with the interests of the Union. The time would be ripe to pursue it when European nations jealous of American power were at war with each other.

While disturbed by the Jay-Gardoqui affair, Jefferson received the news of Shays' Rebellion with amazing aplomb. The uprising of Massachusetts' debt-ridden farmers was a frightening spectacle to Americans, but viewed from Jefferson's European perch it offered a not unpleasing picture of republican liberty flexing its muscles. The first report, from Jay, bristled with repressive outrage against the insurgents. Liberty was losing its charms, the Foreign Secretary suggested. But could it be that this immoderate reaction, rather than the insurgency, posed the real danger? Republican governors must not lose faith in the people in moments of waywardness, Jefferson lectured. "They may be led astray for a moment, but will soon correct themselves. The people are the only censors of their governors: and even their errors will tend to keep them to the true principles of their institution." Jefferson did not condone the insurgency, nor did he doubt the grievances of the insurgents, who were, in fact, very unjustly taxed; but he asked that it be weighed in the scale of European tyranny. Then a little insurgency would be found but a small price for the blessings of liberty. Abigail Adams, to whom Jefferson avowed this opinion, was indignant. "Instead of the laudable spirit which you approve, which makes a people watchful over their liberties and alert in the defense of them, the mobish insurgents are sapping the foundation, and destroying the whole fabric at once." Jefferson stood his ground. The spirit of resistance to government was so valuable on some occasions, it ought to be tolerated even when wrong. "I like a little rebellion now and then. It is like a storm in the atmosphere." He changed the metaphor, but nothing else, when he learned that Shays' Rebellion had taken a toll in lives. "The tree of liberty must be refreshed from time to time with the blood of patriots and tyrants," Jefferson flourished his pen. "It is its natural manure." The simple arithmetic of the matter was that the thirteen states had had but one rebellion in eleven years, which figured out to one rebellion per state in approximately 150 years. "What country before ever existed a century and half without a rebellion?. . . What signify a few lives lost in a century or two?" Better this insurgency and tumult, better this blood, than a European government of wolves over sheep.

This attitude conditioned Jefferson's first reaction to the Constitution framed in the shadow of Shays' Rebellion. In Philadelphia, men feared the breakdown of republican government from rampant democracy in the states; in Paris, Jefferson feared overzealous reaction to this democracy. "How do you like our new constitution?" he addressed Adams as soon as he saw it. "I confess there are things in it which stagger all my dispositions. . . ." The good it contained, he thought, "might have been couched in three or four new articles to be added to the good, old, and venerable fabric," the Articles of Confederation. He would have been satisfied with the addition of a federal commerce power, probably the tax power as well, and a separate executive and judiciary. But the convention at Philadelphia created a radically new frame of government. While the existing government was too weak, the new one promised to be too strong. "Our Convention has been too much impressed by the insurrection of Massachusetts: and in the spur of the moment they are setting up a kite to keep the hen yard in order." Unlike the adversaries of the Constitution at home, Anti-Federalists, as they were called, Jefferson was not apprehensive for the survival of the states in the invigorated system. As he assured Madison, he liked whatever strengthened the Union.

His first and principal objection was founded on European rather than American fears. The perpetual re-eligibility of the President raised dreaded monarchical alarms in Jefferson's mind. There was scarcely an evil in European countries not traceable to their kings, he said, and an American President re-eligible every fourth year would soon become a king, albeit an elective one, like the king of Poland, and like him too in that he would become the focus of foreign bribery, force, and intrigue. The recent chapter in the history of Holland also colored Jefferson's thinking on this subject. His second major objection to the Constitution, its omission of a bill of rights, seems not to have occurred to him at first. But the point was much agitated by the Anti-Federalists in the controversy over ratification, and when these reports came to hand Jefferson urged on Madison and others the addition of articles securing fundamental personal liberties. The friends of the Constitution, the Federalists, denied the need for a bill of rights, since the new government was granted no power in the sphere of personal liberties. But these rights were too important to be left to inference, Jefferson replied; and whatever the inconvenience or inefficacy of a parchment guarantee, it was far better than no guarantee at all.

As the weeks and months passed, and one state after another ratified the Constitution, Jefferson became more and more friendly toward it. "At first," he said, "though I saw that the great mass and groundwork was good, I disliked many appendages. Reflection and discussion have cleared up most of these." Some of the discussion was carried on with Lafayette and Paine. According to the Marquis, the three men debated the Constitution in a convention of their own as earnestly as if they were to decide its fate. Jefferson continued to protest the re-eligibility of the President; but finding that it excited no fears in America, chiefly because of the universal confidence in General Washington, whose election to the office was a foregone conclusion, he gave up the hope of correcting the provision. Increasingly, he concentrated on the attainable object, a bill of rights. But how could this demand be met without endangering the ratification of the Constitution? The document had been sent to the states for simple acceptance or rejection, without complicating reservations or amendments. Thus, in the mouths of Anti-Federalists like Henry in Virginia, the clamor for a bill of rights was a stratagem to defeat the Constitution. Jefferson unwittingly played into their hands. Writing to a friend in Virginia, he suggested the last four states should refuse to come under the new roof until a bill of rights was laid over it. Henry learned of the letter and used it with telling effect in the Virginia ratifying convention. "This illustrious citizen advises you to reject this government till it be amended," he declared. Henry barely failed to block ratification in Virginia, and Jefferson's letter, introduced in the North Carolina convention, contributed to the initial defeat in that state. Actually, Jefferson's plan called for the adoption, not the defeat, of the Constitution by nine states, which would put it into operation, trusting that the demand of the last four would produce the concession of a bill of rights. Virginia appeared to be the ninth state (in fact, New Hampshire ratified four days earlier) and so ought not to be a hold-out under the 9–4 plan. Moreover, unknown to Jefferson's friends at this time, June 1788, he had given up this idea in favor of the Massachusetts plan of unconditional ratification by all with recommended amendments. "It appears to me . . . from all information that its [the Constitution's] rejection would drive the states to despair, and bring an event which cannot be foreseen: and that its adoption is become absolutely necessary," he said. "It will be easier to get the assent of 9 states to correct what is wrong in the way pointed out by the Constitution itself, than to get 13 to concur in a new convention and another plan of confederation." A sense of despair over anything that would upset or impede the course of ratification had been communicated to him by Madison. In this crisis, as in others, the two Virginians compensated for each other's deficiencies. While Madison, with keen political realism, overcame Jefferson's hesitancy toward unconditional ratification, Jefferson, with superb political vision, overcame Madison's aversion to a federal bill of rights. The two men corresponded at length on this subject. Later Madison, almost singlehandedly, carried through the First Congress the first ten amendments—the Bill of Rights—to the Constitution.

While the new Constitution was winning a sure place in his political affections, Jefferson faced a crisis in the European finances of the United States. No sooner had he returned to Paris in June than he was informed by Ferdinand Grand, the Paris banker of the United States, that American funds were exhausted with no early prospect of replenishment. "We are thus left to shift for ourselves . . . ," Jefferson told poor Carmichael in Madrid. The poverty of the Confederacy was an old story, which it was hoped the Constitution would end. For years the United States had lived on borrowed money. Dutch banking houses, in particular, had raised the funds to make American remittances in Europe and to succor the credit of the infant republic. Florins borrowed in Holland kept American dollars at home where, however, there were never enough to meet domestic needs. New loans were floated in Holland in order to pay principal and interest on old loans, as well as to maintain the embassies and pay the other costs of European diplomacy. Jefferson had hoped that western land sales would replenish the Treasury and permit the government to extinguish its foreign debts. But this was a delusion. He was especially anxious to get rid of the French debt, both the part owed to the Crown and the part owed to French officers. On the former, not a franc's interest had been paid or demanded. Still it was a potential source of friction with France, and in view of the government's fiscal distress, payment of the debt amounting to 24 million livres was bound to produce a capital effect in favor of the United States. The debt to the Revolutionary officers for salaries and arrears of interest since 1785, though a trifling sum, sapped the good will of this very influential group at the French court. In 1786, and repeatedly, Jefferson pressed the home government to pay the debt with additional money borrowed from Dutch bankers, in effect transferring the French debt to private hands in Holland. The plan was politically astute, yet it risked American credit in Holland on the chance of cementing American friendship with France. Congress, thinking the risk too great, rejected the plan.

The risk was not wholly imaginary, as Jefferson learned near the end of 1787. No money came, or was in prospect, from Congress; and the Amsterdam bankers serving the United States, the brothers Willink and the brothers Van Staphorst, informed Jefferson that the loan floated a year before was but one-third filled. It would be impossible, therefore, to make remittances in Europe the ensuing year, or discharge the principal due on a small loan, or perhaps to pay the June interest amounting to 270,000 florins on outstanding loans. American credit faced collapse just when the new Constitution promised to secure it. Jefferson was at a loss what to do. Adams, who had conducted affairs with the Dutch bankers, was about to take leave of his post in London. There was no time to await instructions from Congress, more helpless than usual because of the interregnum. The bankers, meanwhile, pressed upon Jefferson their solution to the problem: the payment of a year's interest, amounting to 180,000 florins, on certain certificates of the American *domestic* debt held by Dutch speculators, as the pre-condition for filling up the current loan. It was wholly outside his or Adams's province to decide anything touching the domestic debt. Congress had made no arrangements for it. Jefferson abhorred speculation in general, scrupulously avoided it; and this particular piece of jobbery by the Amsterdam bankers struck him as a brazen attempt to exploit the foreign debt in order to reap handsome profits on the domestic. Squeezed between the jaws of an impossible proposition, on the one hand, and American default on its European obligations, on the other, Jefferson begged Adams for his advice. Adams returned a fiery blast against "the immeasurable avarice of Amsterdam." Willink and Van Staphorst were themselves speculators in American domestic securities, and by their plan would force payment at full value in Europe. Yet they were too deeply involved in American finance to do it injury. "Depend upon it," Adams wrote reassuringly, "the Amsterdamers love money too well to execute their threats." Lacking his experience in these matters, Jefferson still felt anxious. "Our affairs at Amsterdam press on my mind like a mountain." When he learned in March that Adams was going to The Hague to take formal leave as the American Commissioner there, Jefferson hurried to meet him.

Holland presented a melancholy scene. The Patriots—those who had not fled to France—were cruelly suppressed. The Orange cockade was everywhere. Jefferson passed through Rotterdam on the evening of the Prince's birthday. "The illuminations were the most splendid I had ever seen and the roar of joy the most universal I had ever heard." Catching Adams at The Hague in the nick of time, the two men went to Amsterdam, the banking capital of the world.

Their first object was to get the bankers to abandon the plan involving the domestic debt. This was accomplished, though with difficulty, Jefferson reported. The bankers agreed to push the loan on other grounds. But the million florins from this loan, if successful, would meet the country's European demands only during the current year. It would be at least another year, probably two, before the new government could make remittances to Europe. So Jefferson and Adams arranged, provisionally, for another loan of a million florins "to place the government at its ease and our credit in security during the trying interval." The estimated European account, balancing receipts and expenditures, was then drawn up for a period of three years.

Adams returned to London and soon sailed for home. Jefferson stayed on in Amsterdam for two weeks, familiarizing himself with unpleasant "money business" and anxiously watching the progress of the current loan. The condition of American credit was less desperate than he had dared hope in Paris. The Amsterdamers considered the United States "the surest nation on earth for the repayment of capital," he told Washington; the difficulty arose on the punctual payment of interest. American credit in Europe was a matter of first importance for the new government under the Constitution, which already brightened the dour countenances of bankers and brokers. A nation without foreign credit was handicapped in waging war and easily made the prey of great powers. "My wish would be to possess it in the highest degree, but to use it little," he said. In the present circumstances the principal danger lay in European speculation in the fallen domestic debt, potentially so much more profitable than the foreign. Before leaving Amsterdam, Jefferson implored the authorities at home to throw every obstacle in the way of the transfer of the domestic debt to Europe.

Jefferson saw much of interest in Amsterdam—elegant homes, wind-driven sawmills, canals and bridges, porcelain and ironwear, which he purchased—and he decided to seize the opportunity for a tour through Holland and the valley of the Rhine. He set forth at the end of March, traveling alternately by canal and road, to the Rhine at Nijmegen. "The transition from ease and opulence to extreme poverty is remarkable on crossing the line between Dutch and Prussian territory," he noted. "The soil and climate are the same.

The governments alone differ." (Six months before he had condemned misery and misrule in Holland.) Skirting the plains along treacherous roads over barren, broom-covered hills, observing the haggard populace and the run-down lands, Jefferson felt he had come face to face with unmitigated European despotism for the first time. "There are no chateaux, nor houses that bespeak the existence even of a middle class. Universal and equal poverty overspread the whole." He viewed a "sublime" gallery of paintings in Dusseldorf, observed the hog of Westphalia whence came the celebrated ham, at Cologne made inquiries about the city's world-famed millstones and commenced notes on the Rhine wines. Only when he entered Frankfort, a bustling commercial town and a republic, did he note the reappearance of wealth. Here on the fringes of the Palatinate, whence swarms of Germans had immigrated to America, he felt he was in "a second mother country." "I have been continually amused by seeing here the origin of whatever is not English among us," he wrote to Short. "I fancied myself often in the upper parts of Maryland and Pennsylvania." In Frankfort he enjoyed a reunion with a friend of Revolutionary days, the Baron de Geismar. At his garrison in nearby Hanau were several of the officers who had lived in captivity in Albemarle.

Jefferson traveled southward through Hesse and Baden as far as Strasbourg. Spring came on, the wines improved, and so, gradually, did the country. He visited the famous *Schloss* at Heidelberg, thinking it the noblest ruin he had ever seen and even more romantically situated than Petrarch's chateau at Vaucluse. He toured the great estate of the Margrave of Baden in Karlsruhe. In Strasbourg he browsed and made purchases in "the best shop of classical books" he had ever encountered, and climbed to the top of the steeple of the magnificent cathedral. Hurrying through the Marne toward Paris, he stopped briefly only in the neighborhood of Epernay to study the making of champagne.

While on the road Jefferson's observing eye fell on men and oxen straining at plows in freshly turned fields. Noting the awkward figure of the plows' moldboard, he was led to consider what its form should be. From the function of the moldboard, "to receive the sod after the share has cut under it, to raise it gradually and reverse it," he deduced that it ought to be so constructed as to oppose the least resistance to the sod. He then made rough mathematical calculations, sketched the principle of the thing, and determined exactly how it should be built. Years later, in America, Jefferson returned to the idea and perfected "the moldboard of least resistance," acclaimed on two continents as an important technological improvement. That is another story; but Jefferson's encounter with the plow on the road to Nancy in April 1788 epitomizes the *modus operandi* of this attentive traveler: eyes turned to the land and the way men live on it; the mind excited by things seen and felt in the flow of experience, reducing them to mathematical form; the man endeavoring always to add to his store of useful knowledge for the good of humanity.

Back in Paris near the end of April, Jefferson was up to his ears in whale oil for the next several months, tracking that slippery subject through another round of diplomacy. Nor had he finished with the Dutch bankers, speculators in American funds, and the vexing problem of the national credit. Encouraging reports came from Amsterdam in the spring. The current loan filled up, Congress soon approved the new loan he and Adams had negotiated. But Versailles now called for the payment of interest, and he was troubled, too, by the renewed activity of a group of speculators in American securities. They sought, among other things, to purchase the debt to the French government at a substantial discount. Spurred by the prospects of the reformed government in the United States, Dutch bankers, French intellectuals, and American adventurers, some in high places at home, others operating in Europe, speculated extensively in the foreign and domestic debt. Their profiteering schemes were obscure. Jefferson did not comprehend them in detail but perceived their injurious tendency. He again appealed to the authorities at home to stop the speculative transfer of American debt to Europe. "This is a momentous object," he told Jay, "and in my opinion should receive instantaneous attention." The rise of speculation made him more eager to shift the French debt to Holland. He proposed the consolidation of the entire foreign debt in Holland, and worked out a careful plan for funding and extinguishing it over a dozen years. Nothing came of this proposal channeled through Madison, probably because William Duer, secretary of the Treasury Board in Philadelphia, was himself at the head of a ring of Americans promoting the European speculations. Afterwards, when Alexander Hamilton put the national credit on its feet, no one remembered Jefferson's earlier efforts to prop up this prodigy. Instead, Hamilton himself, doubtless prompted by Duer, accused his cabinet colleague of culpable irresponsibility in proposing to transfer the French debt to Holland.

The ensuing winter Jefferson had an unpleasant quarrel with the Dutch bankers. Several important diplomatic objects had been postponed pending the success of the loans in Holland. One involved the payment of interest to the French officers, now threatening open agitation of their cause. Before going to Holland he had prevailed on their spokesmen to wait until July; July passed and he begged their patience until February. Even more distressing was the deferment of plans Jefferson had made to redeem Amercian captives in Algiers. In January 1787 he had enlisted the aid of an order of priests, the Mathurins, whose mission of mercy embraced the victims of Barbary piracy. Procedures and modest ransom money were agreed upon for fifteen American survivors. The plan required the greatest secrecy, indeed a feigned indifference in official quarters to the fate of the captives, lest Algiers persist in demanding a princely sum. This humane endeavor, like the obligation to the French officers, hung fire because the bankers refused to advance the money. An amount had been allocated for the secret project when Jefferson was in Amsterdam, but the bankers now contended they had been instructed by Congress to place the payment of interest ahead of any other claims whatsoever on American funds. Under this mandate, they argued in February 1789, current income from the sale of bonds must be held against the June interest. While not denying the instructions, Jefferson sharply disputed the inference that income could not be applied to other objects until the next installment of semi-annual interest was provided for. Congress must have intended that salaries and other commitments were to be paid as they arose and interest paid as it arose. Otherwise, American diplomacy in Europe was at an end, except as the bankers chose to permit it. "I have observed," Jefferson wrote to Jay, "that as soon as a sum of interest is becoming due they are able to borrow just that, and no more or at least only so much more as may pay our salaries and keep us quiet . . . . I think it possible they may choose to support our credit to a certain point and let it go no further but at their will; to keep it so poised as that it may be at their mercy. By this they will be sure to keep us in their own hands." The stalemate continued for several months. Finally, in July, after the new loan was completed and the interest paid, Jefferson received funds to discharge the arrears due foreign officers and for his "particular purpose" in Algiers. He thought Willink and Van Staphorst had exerted themselves to fill the loan because of the threat of competition from another banking house and the prompt passage of a revenue bill by the First Congress. Before leaving for home he had the satisfaction of honoring the debt to the officers, but the devious plan to redeem the captives came to nothing, as the Mathurins, like so many orders ecclesiastical as well as civil, were caught up in the whirlwind of the French Revolution.

Just before the Revolution unhinged diplomacy at Versailles, the American Minister concluded the negotiation of the consular convention that had been promised by the treaty of 1778. Congress had refused to ratify the convention signed by Franklin in 1784. Contradictory attitudes toward the consular institution, inflammatory incidents touching the consuls or envoys of both countries, obstructionism growing out of American fears of French influence—these factors contributed to the delicacy of the task that fell to Jefferson on new instructions from Congress in 1786. The business was quite deliberately pigeonholed for two years while he worked to improve Franco-American commerce and to create a conciliatory atmosphere for the settlement of the consular question. He brought it forward on his return from the Rhine, pursuing it to conclusion in November. His opinion of consular establishments in general did not differ materially from Jay's, the man chiefly responsible for defeating Franklin's project. The institution was a relic of barbarism, neither necessary nor desirable to nations that had emerged into the light of peace, liberty, and justice. Unlike Jay, however, whose aggressive feelings toward France had been a persistent obstacle to his diplomacy, Jefferson thought amicable relations between the two countries more important than theoretical and technical differences on the issue of consuls. "That this government thinks them useful," he told Montmorin, "is sufficient reason for us to give them all the functions and facilities which our circumstances will admit." Negotiating in this spirit, Jefferson achieved an accord satisfactory to

The Maison Carrée at Nîmes.

The Virginia Capitol. Plaster model.

Minister to France. Replica of the portrait by Mather Brown, 1786.

Jefferson in 1789. Marble bust by Houdon.

Secretary of State. Portrait by Charles Willson Peale, 1791.

both nations. Even Jay commended him. It was promptly ratified by the United States, the last act of the old Congress, the first of the new.

The pleasure which the Versailles court took in the American Minister was generally reciprocated at home, as earlier shown by his appointment to a second three-year term, not unanimously, but without a negative vote in Congress. Unfortunately, his French counterpart in the United States, the Comte de Moustier, was unpopular from the moment he stepped off the boat in December 1787. "He is unsocial, proud and niggardly and betrays a sort of fastidiousness toward this country," Madison summarized the general opinion of Moustier after a year's trial. Jefferson was surprised. He had warmly recommended Moustier as a generous and amiable person who would easily adapt to the American scene. Usually a good judge of character, he erred badly in this instance. Moustier suffered too, Madison said, "from his illicit connection with Madame de Brehan which is universally known and offensive to American manners." The Marquise de Brehan, the Minister's sister-in-law, had accompanied him supposedly for her health, her son's education, and love of America, or rather, Crèvecœur's image of it. Reality failed to answer her expectations, of course, and when this bucolic cultist "appeared, in a considerable company, with a three-cornered muslin handkerchief tied round her head . . . in the fashion of the Negro women in the West Indies," the native ladies thought they were being snubbed. Her disenchantment with America soured Moustier's feelings as well. A subtle treachery lurked in the Arcadian dream of America, so fashionable in French republican circles. Jefferson did not wish to kill the dream—it had become too much a part of himself—but he sought to contain it. (He reprinted Franklin's down-to-earth pamphlet, *Information to Those Who Would Remove to America*, both as a time-saver in answering inquiries and as a cheerful but honest view of the United States.) Moustier, at any rate, rapidly lost his usefulness in the United States. Jefferson presented the problem to Montmorin, who at once arranged for the Comte's return and the appointment of a successor chosen with Jefferson's blessing in 1789.

To the Bastille

The times were grave and eventful, Jefferson reported after his return to the capital in the spring of 1788. "The gay and thoughtless Paris is now become a furnace of politics. All the world is run politically mad. Men, women, children talk nothing else. . . . Society is spoilt by it, at least for those who, like myself, are but lookers on." The insouciance of Parisian society was one of its charms, and for all the gravity of his political convictions Jefferson could not suppress a sigh over the loss. He pictured himself as a mere spectator of the events propelling France toward a revolution that would make the American seem innocuous by comparison. Yet he could not entirely escape the role of a participant in the drama unfolding before him. In his circle of friends and admirers he stood as the oracle of the revolutionary nation that inspired France. Naturally, they sought his advice. How could he be indifferent? Sincerely attached to the French people, he wished they might throw off the mass of misrule and oppression. His devotion to the cause of human rights transcended narrow calculations of national interest. But cause and interest united in making him a partisan to the reformation of the Bourbon monarchy. Whatever the outcome might be, it seemed certain to introduce potent elements of republicanism into the French constitution, break the shackles on trade and industry, push back the boundaries of freedom on every side, and in this way create a stronger basis of Franco-American friendship. As France went, so would go Europe, Jefferson thought, and the destiny of the United States must be linked for a future too long to measure with the destiny of freedom in Europe.

From the convening of the Notables a reformation was assured, though no one could predict its course or extent. By the time Jefferson left Paris in September 1789, it would have gone much farther than he had any idea of in the preliminary stages. For two and a half years he had repeatedly to adjust his thinking to a course of events always leaping ahead of him. He kept expecting the movement to come to rest, the revolution to stabilize itself, at some reasonable point along the line of advance. When it did not, but rolled dizzily onward with a logic all its own, Jefferson hurried to catch

up and offer counsels of conciliation at the next favorable turn. Like
his liberal friends, Lafayette chief among them, with whom he was
in communication at all times and whose opinions usually swayed
his own, Jefferson hoped for a final settlement more on the terms of
the English constitution than the American. A nation could not go
from absolutism to democracy all at once. France had not yet had
her revolution of 1688. And Jefferson doubted she was ready for
more. Since this is what he looked for, he did not really see the revolution of 1789 until it was fast upon him. Even so his perception of
the movement was better than most men's, and he realigned his
thinking at each critical juncture with a swiftness that would put a
closet philosopher to shame. Because he responded to the French
Revolution in this *ad hoc* fashion, he thought differently about it at
different times. But the Revolution grew more and more radical, and
so did Jefferson.

In the first preliminary stage, opened by the Assembly of Notables, Jefferson supported the aristocratic resurgence against royal
absolutism in the belief it would produce a constitutional monarchy
with guarantees of individual liberty, fiscal reform, and the beginnings of popular representation, all together "a vast mass of improvement in the condition of the nation." Lafayette and most of
Jefferson's friends shared this belief. As the *noblesse*, the *parlements*,
the provincial estates, and other aristocratic bodies combated the
King, they appeared as the champions of liberty, and virtually the
entire nation cheered them on. They wrung important concessions
from the King, agreed to bear a fairer share of taxes, and gradually
evolved a program of moderate reform. Yet the nobility had no intention of surrendering its privileged status. It aimed to rule the nation, not to be absorbed into it. In any aristocratic reformation,
ancient orders and distinctions would remain, and the mass of the nation, the Third Estate, counting 96 of every 100 Frenchmen, would
be subordinate to the privileged orders of Nobles and Clergy. The
fate of the experiment with provincial assemblies in 1787 offered
useful instruction in the motives and aims of the aristocratic revolt.
As proposed by Calonne the assemblies were to be popularly elected
without distinction of rank. Jefferson thought the innovation the
most fundamental of all promised reforms. The provincial assemblies
would be perfect representatives of the people, counteracting the

evils of centralized monarchical power, and slowly setting the populace in the ways of self-government. But the nobles brought about Calonne's downfall, and the new ministry headed by the Comte de Brienne, yielding to aristocratic pressures, made the assemblies appointive bodies (one-half the members named by Brienne, the other half by co-optation), had them meet in three separate orders, and gave the presidency of each to the privileged ranks. The experiment thus lost its democratic character. The facts were clear; yet Jefferson seemed unable to recognize them, and continued for at least a year to view the provincial assemblies as incipient republican legislatures according to the mental image he had first formed of them. In this, as in the general support he gave to the aristocratic revolt of 1787–88, he allowed his fears of royal absolutism and his hopes of constitutional liberty to obscure the conservative animus and direction of the entire movement.

His perception improved markedly at the peak of the aristocratic resurgence in the spring and summer of 1788. He became as apprehensive of the nobility as he had previously been of the court, and gave up any idea that either, or both, could achieve a reformation for the good of the people. The struggle was between the centuries' old contenders, king and nobles, for "a monopoly of despotism over the people." "The nation is no otherwise concerned but as both parties may be induced to let go some of its abuses to court the public favor." A reformed constitution which curtailed the monarchy but excluded the people must still be a despotism. The question naturally arose, Jefferson reflected in a letter to Madison, "whether a pure despotism, in a single head or one which is divided among a king, nobles, priesthood, and numerous magistracy is the least bad. I should be puzzled to decide: but I hope they [the French] will have neither, and that they are advancing to a limited, moderate government, in which the people will have a good share."

But here, too, was a rub. Unfortunately, the people were not yet ready for the blessings of liberty and self-government. Jefferson doubted they would accept even a habeas corpus law if one were given to them. "The danger is that the people," he observed, "deceived by a false cry of liberty may be led to take side with one party, and thus give the other a pretext for crushing them still more." Something like this had happened in Holland, and the fiasco of the democratic revolution there colored Jefferson's counsels of moderation to the French. He was convinced the Dutch Patriots had aimed at too much democracy, thus frightening the moderate aristocrats into the arms of the Stadtholder. Events in France should take a happier turn, he thought. The "real patriots," as he called them, were united with the liberal nobility; the King, though weak and incompetent, was well-disposed toward the people; all parties showed commendable restraint; neither violence nor popular commotion threatened the advance toward a balanced constitution on the English model.

Such was Jefferson's appraisal of the situation in the fall of 1788. The King and the *parlement* of Paris had composed their differences. The momentous call had gone forth convening the Estates General in May. The popular financier Jacques Necker had been named to head the ministry. It was the quiet before the storm. In retrospect, Jefferson could be accused of bland insensitivity to the psychology of revolutionary movements. Had his temperament been different, his mind less rational, his knowledge of France better, he might have sensed, with Alexis de Tocqueville several decades later, that "the most perilous moment for a bad government is when it seeks to mend its ways."

The calling of the Estates General was an appeal to the nation, the first since 1614. The Third Estate was invited into the revolution, but whether it would have a major or a minor role depended on the forms and procedures to be followed in the convocation of the Estates General. The Patriot party, including many of Jefferson's friends—Rochefoucauld, Dupont, Condorcet, and, of course, Lafayette—demanded that the bourgeoisie have as many deputies as the nobility and clergy combined, and then pushed for constituting the assembly without distinction or vote by order, thus absorbing the old elements of estate and privilege into a single uniform nation. The first demand prevailed over angry aristocratic opposition that cost the *parlement* of Paris the popularity it had enjoyed while fencing the King. Whether voting would be by head or by order, the next crucial question, was left to the decision of the Estates General itself. But the Third Estate, being assured of a majority with the addition of liberal nobles and clerics, claimed a signal victory. The King was now virtually out of the dispute. Influenced by ministers sympathetic to the revolution, feeling the pressure of the court for money, which could be squeezed from an obstinate aristocracy by the only agency powerful enough, the people, Louis XVI must make valuable concessions. So, Jefferson said, "the dispute is between the privileged and unprivileged orders [over] how they shall divide these concessions between them." The outcome was sure, provided the Patriots did not seek too much at the threshold of power. On the whole, Jefferson thought they should ask no more than the King showed a readiness to grant and the aristocracy to tolerate, "lest they should shock the dispositions of the court, and even alarm the public mind, which must be left to open itself to successive improvements." The right of the Estates General to convene periodically, their exclusive right to raise and appropriate money, their participation in legislation, and, in time, the right to originate laws, probably a declaration of rights, possibly a habeas corpus law —this was the conciliatory agenda Jefferson set forth in January 1789.

It would soon seem hopelessly inadequate. The rise of public expectations and the surprising intransigence of the aristocracy, according to his calculations, caused Jefferson to grow bolder without, however, shifting his position as a prudent counselor of moderation. In the engine of revolution he acted as a balance wheel against dangers of extremism. He feared that in attempting too much the Patriots, like their Dutch friends, would lose everything. He feared an appeal to arms at court. He feared aristocratic reaction. He feared social chaos. He feared foreign intervention—at a time when France had lost most of her European friends. The course of the Revolution justified his fears. In this sense, then, his judgment was realistic. It was the judgment not of a radical or a visionary but of a practical statesman who refused to mix the American case with the French, who was more impressed by political than by social injustice, who wished to preserve the bonds of continuity and consensus in the society and to maintain the stability of government even in the throes of revolution. In a deeper sense, however, he was neither right nor realistic. For the Revolution proved to be a good deal more than Jefferson's idea of it. Not merely a constitutional reformation but a vast social upheaval, it could not be accomplished in the amiable spirit Jefferson advocated.

The winter of 1788–89 was the worst in memory. The Virginian had never been so cold. The mercury plummeted to 20 degrees below zero in Paris. (He had to order a new thermometer from London to take the temperatures.) Loaded carriages passed on the Seine, and thousands skated from morning to night. The laboring poor were without work. Crowds of people huddled around great fires built in the streets. To the pangs of cold were added the pangs of hunger. The summer's wheat harvest had been disastrous. At every baker's shop, long queues waited scanty allowances of bread. Soup kitchens, furnished by the well-to-do, Jefferson among them, fed the hungry; and dinner invitations to the richest houses notified the guests to bring their own bread. At Necker's request near the end of November, Jefferson sent word to America of the bread shortage and the bounty offered for cargoes of grain and flour. American shipments helped to relieve the distress, which continued for many months, though neither Jefferson nor Necker deserved the credit. Both men acted more slowly than the crisis demanded—mercantile intelligence preceded Jefferson's by several weeks. Subsequently, in July, the stormy petrel of the National Assembly, Mirabeau, recklessly accused Necker of declining an *offer* from the American Minister of great quantities of flour. Being caught in a political quarrel between Necker and Mirabeau on this seething issue was scarcely a laughing matter. With Lafayette's aid, Jefferson managed to extricate himself, and Necker, without offense.

Sensible as he was to the hardships of the prolonged freeze and the bread shortage, Jefferson seems not to have connected them with the rise of revolutionary violence in the cities and the countryside. A riot among Paris workmen in April 1789, taking a hundred lives, struck him as the "unprovoked" mischief of "abandoned banditti," therefore justly "unpitied." He did not see that the distresses of workers and peasants incited smoldering hatred of aristocratic privilege and injustice, or that mobs and riots were more than coincidental to the mounting crisis, because he viewed the Revolution as an almost self-contained political affair to be negotiated by responsible persons from above. A social revolution from below was no part of his experience or his theoretical equipment. The main effect of the bread shortage on the political rejuvenation, he thought, was the additional burden its relief placed on a treasury already drained to the bottom.

Jefferson weathered the season as best he could. One, or both, of the girls was sometimes ill, Polly seriously for a period of two or three months; and there were weeks when he seldom stirred out-of-doors. In February a distinguished compatriot, Gouverneur Morris, arrived in Paris bearing letters of introduction from Washington and others. The Pennsylvanian with a wooden leg, who had won laurels as the stylist of the Constitution, came to unravel the tangled financial affairs of Robert Morris. While attending to this business, he found time for new speculations (one of them in the French debt), for becoming a Parisian *bon vivant*, and falling in love with the enchanting Madame de Flahut. Jefferson enjoyed this amiable, if somewhat garrulous, American. He was often at the hôtel de Langeac, warming himself at Jefferson's fire, taking "a dish of tea," dining *en famille*, talking of his own affairs and of the busy scene, of which he left fascinating glimpses in his diary. The two men did not agree in their politics. Morris felt that Jefferson was too advanced, too American, too democratic, in his ideas. They were not suited to the circumstances or the dispositions of the French people. Jefferson, he said, "with all the leaders of liberty here, are desirous of annihilating distinctions of order. How far such views may be right respecting mankind in general is I think extremely problematical, but with respect to this nation I am sure it is wrong and cannot eventuate well." Morris was impressed with royalty. The sight of Louis XVI brought tears to his eyes. Mobs and murders reinforced his skepticism of the populace. By comparison with Condorcet or Mirabeau or the Abbé Sièyes, Jefferson's views were moderate; by comparison with the Pennsylvania Federalist, the only other American on the scene who recorded his opinions, they were liberal and, indeed, becoming radical.

The Estates General convened at Versailles on May 5. "Viewing it as an opera it was imposing," Jefferson remarked. The King mounted on the throne, Queen two steps down, panoplied Princes of the Blood seated below, courtly retinue, officers of the household, and guards in ancient costume all ranged about; in front of the stage, ministers of state; on the benches to one side, marshals and other great officers, on the opposite side 300 clergy in robes of all colors and the same number of nobility garbed in black and gold; finally, the bourgeoisie in somber black. It was a striking tableau of the Old Regime. The King spoke, impressively, Jefferson thought.

The Keeper of the Seals, inaudible to the crowded spectators, was followed by Necker, whose long address disappointed nearly everyone. Louis XVI left the hall to the shouts of *vive le Roi* and his imperious queen heard the sweet music of *vive la Reine* for the first time in months. The next day the three orders commenced their meetings in separate chambers of the "hall of states." For several weeks Jefferson was a daily observer, most often of the debates of the Third, which he remembered as temperate and rational despite the size of the body—600 Frenchmen "among whom there are always more speakers than listeners"—and the crowds that hissed, clapped, shouted, flowed onto the floor, and mixed with the delegates.

"It is now for the first time," he reported to Jay, "that their revolution is likely to receive a serious check, and begins to wear a fearful appearance." The Third refused to organize itself as a separate order but invited the others to join in a single national assembly. The clergy, to Jefferson's surprise, showed a willingness to coalesce. The nobles, whom he had expected to divide, stood virtually united in defense of the ancient principle of representation and vote by order. Jefferson supposed the King would end the stalemate happily for the nation by intervening on the side of the Third. But the King was mute. As the crisis entered the fifth week, Jefferson suggested a decisive course of action to the Patriots. During an evening's conversation with Short, Lafayette, and Rabaut de St. Etienne, the Protestant leader, he threw out the idea of the King coming forward in a *séance royale* with a "charter of rights" signed by himself and every member of the three orders. The dramatic idea, with its appeal to an illusory unity, caught Lafayette's fancy. Though the shining symbol of republicanism, he was still something of a courtier, still a hapless prisoner of his aristocratic heritage, and had declined to act on Jefferson's advice to burn his instructions as a noble and declare for the Third Estate. Encouraged to develop his suggestion, Jefferson sketched a proposed charter, which he sent to Lafayette and St. Etienne the next day. It embraced, with liberal amplifications, the propositions he had advanced in January. Habeas corpus and free press laws were now definitely included; the Estates General was accorded exclusive power to legislate, with the King's consent; and fiscal privileges and inequities were abolished. The nobles had consented to the last in principle; the King had vaguely promised the rest. If all parties would endorse a reasonable compromise on this plan, then disband for a time, Jefferson said, they would accomplish "more good than was ever effected before without violence, and . . . stop exactly at the point where violence would otherwise begin. Time will be gained, the public mind will continue to ripen and to be informed, a basis of support may be prepared with the people themselves." And he assured his friends that this proposal stemmed from "an unmeasurable devotion for your nation and a painful anxiety lest despotism, after an unaccepted offer to bind its hands, should seize you again with tenfold fury."

Jefferson's "charter of rights" has little importance in the history of the French Revolution, but it has considerable interest for the history of Jefferson's opinions. It marked another advance in his conception of the revolution, an advance still grounded, however, on an accommodation of king, nobles, and commoners. The Bourbon monarch was to come forth at Versailles, like William of Orange in England a century before, with a charter of compromise between tradition and progress, feudal privilege and equal rights, absolutism and republicanism. Jefferson detested monarchy in theory, yet he seemed to think the French people should enter into a contract with the King in return for certain liberties. He was no longer fond of the English "balanced constitution," at least in American affairs, yet this was his model for France. Thirty years later, when he wrote his personal account of the coming of the French Revolution, he felt that events had vindicated his judgment, and proved the "lamentable error" of those, whoever they were, responsible for the rejection of this compromise. "For after thirty years of war, foreign and domestic, the loss of millions of lives, the prostration of private happiness, and the foreign subjugation of their own country for a time, they have obtained no more, nor even that securely." He was right only if one granted that compromise such as he had advocated was politically feasible in June 1789.

The King rallied to the noblesse. "The King is honest and wishes the good of his people, but the expedience of an hereditary aristocarcy is too difficult a question for him." Had Louis been master of his own house, the issue might have been different, Jefferson thought; unfortunately, the Queen and the court held absolute sway over him. "I have ever believed," he wrote in retrospect, again disclosing his blind spot, "that had there been no Queen, there would have been no revolution." When the Third Estate constituted itself as the National Assembly and proceeded to transact the public business, the King declared its actions null and void, and, at last, in a *séance royale,* offered a program intended to unite all parties. While in line with the reforms he and the nobles had pledged—reforms such as Jefferson had advocated—the program ranged the Crown on the side of the noblesse. The King would become a constitutional monarch, but traditional orders and many privileges would be preserved. "The Nobility were in triumph, the people in consternation," Jefferson observed. A solution the Third Estate might have regarded as a victory several months, or even weeks, earlier was now completely unacceptable. "Instead of being dismayed with what has passed they seem to rise in their demands, and some of them to consider the erasing every vestige of a difference of order as indispensable to the establishment and preservation of a good constitution." Jefferson remained apprehensive as the Third Estate stood its ground against the alliance of King and nobles. Suddenly, on June 27, only four days after the *séance royale,* the clergy and nobility took seats with the Third, thus completing the union of the three orders in a single assembly. Only now did Jefferson fully embrace the radical goals of the French Revolution.

He hoped these goals might be realized peacefully through the establishment of a stable constitutional government, relying on the moderate elements in the National Assembly, backed by the King. The opportunity was real. But at the moment of their prostration at the feet of the National Assembly, the King and the "Turkish despots" around him resorted to force, provoked the violence of the populace, and dug their graves in the ruins of the Old Regime. Troops, many of them foreign, were concentrated around Paris and Versailles. Necker's abrupt dismissal on July 11 set off the explosion in Paris. Jefferson was a close observer of the events of the ensuing five days—the encounter between unarmed populace and German cavalry at the Place Louis XV, the possession of arms at the hôtel des Invalides, the storming of the Bastille—ending with the recall of Necker and the King's apparent capitulation. On the 17th the King went in a procession to Paris. "About 60,000 citizens of all forms and colors, armed with the muskets of the Bastille and Invalides as far as they would go, the rest with pistols, swords, pikes, pruning hooks, scythes, etc., lined all the streets thro' which the procession passed, and, with the crowds of people in the streets, doors and windows, saluted them everywhere with the cries of 'vive la nation.' " The King stuck the national cockade in his hat at the hôtel de Ville, "such an *amende honorable* as no sovereign ever made, and no people ever received," and he returned to Versailles amidst the joyous acclaim of "vive le roi et la nation."

Once again, and for the last time, the precious occasion was lost. The King's weakness and duplicity, the flight of refugees, reports of aristocratic conspiracy and foreign intervention—the "Great Fear" raised the vengeful fury of the populace and it spread without check. "The cutting off heads is become so much à la mode," Jefferson wrote with grim humor to Maria Cosway, "that one is apt to feel of a morning whether their own is on their shoulders." The savage murders of particularly obnoxious aristocrats and the parading of heads stirred no counter-revolutionary feelings in him, as they did in Morris. The tumult would subside once the populace had tasted blood. "I have been through it daily, have observed the mobs with my own eyes in order to be satisfied of their objects, and declare . . . that I saw so plainly the legitimacy of them, that I have slept in my house as quietly thro' the whole as I ever did in the most peaceable moments." Considering the provocation, he thought the populace behaved well, and sought to correct exaggerated reports of violence in the English press.

The aristocracy had conspired in its own destruction, Jefferson wrote at the beginning of August, "and the nation has made a total resumption of rights, which they had certainly never before ventured even to think of. The National Assembly have now as clean a canvas to work on here as we had in America." So he saw now the *democratic* revolution and also compared it with the American case. The Assembly, acting in effect as a constitutional convention, first wiped the canvas clean by abolishing feudal rank, order, and privilege. It then emblazoned the new standard of freedom and equality in the Declaration of the Rights of Man and Citizen. Jefferson had collaborated with Lafayette in drafting a declaration of rights which the Marquis introduced in the Assembly early in July; and the mon-

umental document finally enacted bears traces of the American's influence. The formation of a constitution gave much more difficulty.
All parties agreed, even the most fervent republicans, that France
should retain its monarch. But how far should his executive powers
extend? Should he have an absolute or merely a suspensive veto of
legislation? And should the legislature be constituted in one or two
houses? If the latter, should the upper house be formed as a kind of
aristocratic check on the people? These questions divided the Patriots, whose unity Jefferson considered essential to the Revolution.
When Lafayette proposed a dinner meeting of the principal leaders
at Jefferson's house, he consented at once. "The discussions began at
the hour of four," he recalled, "and were continued till ten o'clock
in the evening; during which time, I was a silent witness to a coolness and candor of argument, unusual in the conflicts of political
opinion . . . . The result was, that the King should have a suspensive veto on the laws, that the legislature should be composed of a
single body only, and that to be chosen by the people. This Concor-
date decided the fate of the constitution. The Patriots all rallied to
the principles thus settled, carried every question agreeably to them,
and reduced the Aristocracy to insignificance and impotence."

Jefferson's account, while not inaccurate, slides too easily over
one of the most significant issues in the comparative history of the
American and the French Revolutions. Turgot, a chief mentor of
the Patriots, had sharply criticized the revolutionary constitutions
of the American states for dividing the legislative power and creating an independent executive. This imitation of the English constitution, as he saw it, made no sense in a country where the people *en
masse*, undifferentiated by rank or order, were sovereign, and it
could only weaken the authority of the nation. John Adams undertook his three-volume *Defence of the American Constitutions* to refute Turgot. Adams presented his friend across the Channel with
the first volume of this cumbersome work when it appeared in 1787.
Jefferson's own *Notes on Virginia*, published in London at the same
time, incorporated his 1783 draft constitution for Virginia which
provided for a strong governor and an upper house of more distinguished character than the lower house. (The draft constitution did
not appear in Morellet's translation of the *Notes*, perhaps because he
agreed with Turgot, but Jefferson saw to its French publication in

the *Encyclopédie*.) In short, Jefferson's opinion at this time was not far from Adams's. He at once arranged for French translation and publication of Adams's volume. None appeared, however, until 1792, and that abridged. Very likely Jefferson lost interest, and may, in fact, have read the *Defence* attentively for the first time when several of his liberal friends in Paris—Mazzei, Dupont, Condorcet, and others—attacked Adams for Anglicanism, aristocratic prejudice, and distrust of the people. In 1789 Condorcet and Dupont brought out a French translation of the American John Stevens's pamphlet, *Observations on Government*, which blasted the "heterogeneous jumble" of monarchy, aristocracy, and democracy in Adams's system. The French editors supplied notes and commentary that expanded the ephemeral pamphlet into a substantial book. The work was often cited in the constitutional debates of the National Assembly to support a unicameral legislature and a weak executive against English ideas. The Patriots prevailed, as Jefferson said; but did he agree with them? A month or two earlier he would surely have sided with the minority on this issue. But the Revolution had leaped forward since then, and Jefferson, unlike Adams, went with it. The defense of "aristocracy" in America, where there was none, was quite a different matter from the perpetuation of aristocracy in France, where it was the great obstacle to reform. The establishment of an elitist upper house, even if not committed to the nobility, would provide a fortress for conservative groups against the democratic revolution. Jefferson had come to see this by August. He also believed that the French people, once they had won the stake in democracy, would come to see the wisdom of a divided legislature on the American, not the English, model.

Soon after the Patriot conference at the hôtel de Langeac—a diplomatic indiscretion for which the Minister made apology the next morning to Montmorin who, as it turned out, entirely approved of his good offices—Jefferson suffered a siege of illness. From September 1 to 9 he wrote but two letters, one of them addressed to Madison, though not sent to him for several months. This was an epistolary disquisition on the principle "that the earth belongs in usufruct to the living." It had been suggested to his mind, he said, in the course of reflection on the principles of a just society in the preceding months. The idea that one generation of men in civil society cannot bind another had extensive applications and consequences, especially in France. It was a favorite idea of Jefferson's physician, Dr. Richard Gem, an elderly Englishman, friend of the philosophes, ardent champion of the Revolution, and in the patient's recollection thirty years later, the best physician he ever met. He may have prompted Jefferson, during his illness, to consult the mortality tables, calculate the life of a generation (19 years), and develop the practical application of the idea. But it had been germinating in his mind for some time. Perhaps it began with the "little attendrissement" of a poor woman encountered on a walk near Fontainbleau in 1785. Her melancholy tale, and her tears of gratitude for the sous Jefferson gave her, first brought home to him the wretchedness produced by the unequal division of property in Europe. Returning to his fireside, he shared his reflections with a friend at home. "Whenever there is in any country, uncultivated lands and unemployed poor, it is clear that the laws of property have been so far extended as to violate natural right. The earth is given as a common stock for man to labor and live on," he wrote. It was too soon to say that American laws of property, omitting slavery, trespassed on human rights; but legislatures could not invent too many devices for dividing property from generation to generation. This was simply a more radical statement of Jefferson's well-developed principles of land tenure, which, to go farther back, stemmed from the Lockian theory of the natural right to land. The general notion was not original with him. Adam Smith, for instance, arguing from the same premises, had asserted the principle "that every successive generation of men have . . . an equal right to the earth, and to all that it possesses."

But the formulation of the principle that generations, as well as individuals, have natural rights, the application of it to the fundamental conditions of civil society, and the effort to reduce it to mathematical precision: this was at once the most original and most radical idea in the Jeffersonian catalogue. It could not have matured in America. It grew out of the European situation, specifically the situation of France in 1789. It expressed the speculative fervor of the French Revolution, the rage against the past, the assault on inequalities that amounted to a tyranny of the dead over the living; and in this light, the theory helped Jefferson justify the Revolution to his own reason. "It enters into the resolution of the questions, whether the nation may change the descent of lands holden in tail? Whether they may change the appropriation of lands given anciently to the church, to hospitals, colleges, orders of chivalry, and otherwise in perpetuity? Whether they may abolish the charges and privileges attached on lands, including the whole catalogue ecclesaistical and feudal? It goes to hereditary offices, authorities and jurisdictions; to hereditary orders, distinctions and appellations; to perpetual monopolies in commerce, the arts and sciences; with a long train of et ceteras." One generation may not form a constitution for another, or contract debts to be paid by another, or bind its successors by commitments of any kind.

The pertinence of the doctrine to France is self-evident. The issue between prescriptive rights—all the sanctions of tradition—and the "sovereignty of the living generation" would be pointedly drawn in the controversy of 1790-91 between Edmund Burke and Thomas Paine on the French Revolution. At the end of his letter—more essay than letter—Jefferson suggested that the principle would "furnish matter for a fine preamble to our [i.e. the United States] first law for appropriating the public revenue; and it will exclude at the threshold of our government the contagious and ruinous errors of this quarter of the globe, which have despots with means, not sanctioned by nature, for binding in chains their fellow men." So the doctrine gave a bearing to the United States as well, immediately with regard to the public debt, which should not be allowed to descend to the next generation. Yet this American reference had the appearance of an afterthought. In time, Madison wrote a long and cogent refutation of Jefferson's generational theory, proving its impracticability (generations are flowing waves, not fixed mathematical points) and even its elements of injustice. But, of course, the essay addressed the European more than the American condition; and Jefferson never intended rigorous application of the doctrine in public law, meaning it rather as a moral directive to society. In this sense he adhered to the doctrine throughout his life, and it entered into the spirit, if not the law, of American institutions.

The French Revolution had a long way to go when Jefferson left Paris near the end of September. The Assembly groped toward a constitution, disorders continued, bread was still scarce, civil war and foreign war threatened to upset the Revolution. Disquieting though these signs were, Jefferson radiated optimism. The juridical revolution was complete; the mass of the nation was united, with force at its disposal; public enlightenment and republicanism marched hand in hand. He felt he had witnessed, as twenty years before in America, the commencement of a new era in Europe. "I have so much confidence in the good sense of man, and his qualifications for self-government," he declared, "that I am never afraid of the issue where reason is left free to exert her force; and I will agree to be stoned as a false prophet if all does not end well in this country. Nor will it end with this country. Here is but the first chapter in the history of European liberty."

Jefferson's appointment as Minister to France still had two years to run in 1789. He returned to the United States on a six-month leave of absence, fully expecting to resume his duties in Paris after that time. He had gone to Europe on a commission of two years; events had prolonged his absence to five. Personal affairs required his attention in Virginia, and he was anxious to restore his daughters to their home and friends. Patsy was just turning seventeen, educated in the best Continental manner, but deserving now the opportunity for domestic happiness only to be found in her native country. Jefferson felt genuine affection for many French women, but the comparison of Woman in the two worlds was "a comparison of Amazons and Angels." Ironically, in Patsy's case the European temptress was Angel rather than Amazon. According to the family tradition, she had, while under the influence of the Abbaye de Pentemont, written her father for permission to become a nun, a request he had answered by abruptly withdrawing her and Polly from the school and burying the subject in awful silence.

Jefferson left everything in Paris on the assumption of an early return to his post. The business of the legation was put in the capable hands of William Short, though Congress had not seen fit to give him an official title. The lease on the hôtel was renewed; and, of course, Jefferson's books, furniture and household effects were left there. Even so, his baggage totaled 38 boxes, several trunks, and objects too bulky to pack. There were many hampers of wine, a box of food (macaroni, Parmesan cheese, raisins, almonds, dates), plants of every description, boxes of books (for Madison and Franklin and others), copies of Houdon busts, guitar, harpsichord, portraits of American discoverers (copied in the Uffizi Gallery) and of the noble trinity, Bacon, Newton, and Locke (obtained from Trumbull in London), phaeton, saddle and livery, and the handsome "crane neck" carriage made in London. There was no need for ceremonial leave from the court or sad farewells to European friends. Some of them had joined with American residents in Paris to pay tribute to the Minister on the Fourth of July. The complimentary address, after thanks for many kindnesses, lauded him as "the proper minister of that enlightened people whose cause is the cause of humanity."

In carriage and phaeton, Minister, daughters, and servants rode to Le Havre, where they were to catch a boat to Cowes, thence aboard the *Clermont* to Norfolk. At the French port the equinoctical gales descended with a fury that delayed their crossing ten days. Jefferson made his family as comfortable as possible at the British Hotel, where Nathaniel Cutting, an American merchant, offered friendly assistance. At the port Jefferson made inquiries touching the last concession he had gained for American commerce, one that permitted American ships to load salt at Honfleur, opposite Le Havre, at mercantile rates. He roamed the city, continued his correspondence, and amused himself with his children. A shepherd dog "big with pup" was added to the party; bitch, and litter, accompanied the Jeffersons to America. They crossed the Channel on October 7: "26 hours of boisterous navigation and mortal sickness." Another delay, of two weeks, at Cowes: more walks and excursions, more letters, more chats with Cutting, soon to leave "this worthy family" with regret. Jefferson penned an affectionate adieu to Maria Cosway, hoping they might enjoy a reunion in Paris with the first swallow of the spring. Trumbull, in London, had looked after Jefferson's accommodations aboard the *Clermont*, including arrangements for clearing his baggage and the convenience of boarding at Cowes. "There are two large staterooms . . . . There are *quarter galleries*, and a very good quarter deck for walking: she is new and a good sailor." In this fine vessel Jefferson sailed for home on October 23.

In the course of reassuring an American father about his touring son in Europe, Jefferson said, "He is likely to return home charged, like a bee with the honey gathered on it." Jefferson, certainly, returned home "charged"—with ideas, experiences, plans, pleasures, friendships. After five years Paris had become a second home to him. The artistic splendor of Paris, the society of his friends, their cultivated tastes and sensibilities, their speculative and humanitarian concerns, had become, not a substitute for the simpler society he had known but, like the delicacies of the French table, such an addition to his happiness that henceforth he would never feel quite complete without them. Yet, in a deeper sense, Europe had made him more profoundly American. For all the amenities of European civilization, it presented to him "no other picture than that of God almightly and his angels trampling under foot the hosts of the damned." The more he saw of it the more lustrous his image of America became.

His frame of reference was America, not Europe. This was truer in an elementary sense when he went to Europe than when he left it. Despite the sweeping clauses of the creed set forth in the Declaration of Independence, despite the rationalism and cosmopolitanism that informed his work, he had no thought, in 1776 or even in 1784, of his young country becoming the torchbearer of liberty to the world. Europe's enlightened philosophers were kindred spirits, of course, but on the entire continent, tyrannized by kings, priests, and noblemen, there was little leverage for change. As the French Revolution came on, he saw that change was possible after all, that France, if unprepared for liberty on the American plan, was nevertheless marching under the colors of 1776, and that his own country had an important stake in this political reformation of Europe. The frame was still America, but by 1789 Europe, above all France, was part of the picture. And so it remained during the next decade until finally, the hope blasted, Europe was erased and he formed a new image of American destiny in a world apart.

His business in Europe was diplomacy, not philosophy or revolution. France was an ally; she had helped the United States win its independence, which merited American gratitude whatever her motives may have been. And since the peace and independence of the new nation was still at hazard, the friendship, the power, and the prestige of France were vital to the United States. Without France the country was a cipher in the scales of European politics, with her a power of considerable weight. So Jefferson approached all questions in France, including those of reform and revolution, not as a republican dogmatist, not as a visionary theorist, not as a missionary diplomatist, but, fundamentally, as the representative of an American national interest that, in his view, was involved with the interest of France. Trade offered the most promising avenue of Franco-American co-operation. As a nation just emerging from colonial status, rich in agricultural surpluses but little else, unless possibly the carrying trade, the United States had a large stake in the liberalization of commerce, together with the whole enlightened movement for humane and pacific intercourse among nations. France sought entrance into the American market; the United States sought markets outside the old imperial system. Jefferson's commercial diplomacy found favor at Versailles. While he scored no spectacular successes, he helped to open new routes of trade and riches for his country. Easily assuming that monopolies and restrictions would fall with the progress of liberty and self-government, Jefferson believed the French Revolution would clear the way to the promised new epoch of commercial freedom. In this, too, he was destined to be disappointed.

Jefferson had impressive talents for diplomacy. He was cool, adroit, supple, resourceful, and patient. He approved Franklin's rule, "never contradict anybody." A disputant, he said, never wins an argument but only widens the gap of disagreement. So it is much better to tolerate differences, insinuate doubts, ask questions, and in this good-humored fashion discover workable grounds of co-operation. He was a very different man from his predecessor, yet he had Franklin's easy confidence and ability to relate gracefully to any situation, above all the wit to slide around rough corners without losing sight of his object. His self-possession was remarkable. William Smith, Adams's secretary, said he knew no man better qualified to pass over difficulties because "he makes his calculations for a certain quantity of imposition, which must be admitted in his intercourse with the world. When it shows itself in high colors, he has only to count ten and he is prepared for the subject. Happy state of mind—." "The quantity of imposition" at Versailles was tolerable. Jefferson genuinely liked his position, preferring it to a domestic one more exposed to the buffetings of politics. "The attaching circumstance of my present office," he remarked, "is that I can do its duties unseen by those for whom they are done." He returned home a thoroughly accomplished diplomatist, trained in Europe's leading school, yet not hardened or narrowed by the constraints of this old profession, and still faithful to the larger "cause of humanity."

He returned home persuaded that neutrality and non-entanglement in Old World politics was the true policy for the United States, yet with such strong attachments to France and Revolution that they gave a turn to his political posture. While France had nurtured his Americanism, it had also extended his vision of America's responsibility to the hopes of mankind. His attachments were founded in commercial policy; in feelings of gratitude, feelings that, in the diplomatic code of Europe, supposedly had no place in the determination of national conduct but that the young republic, acting on the principle of "but one code or morality for man whether acting singly or collectively," should not proscribe; in the reality of Revolutionary France, where he had seen American authority "treated like that of the Bible"; and finally, in the personal delights of his sojourn there, the benevolence of the people, the warmth of their friendships, the vivacity of their minds, the charm of their society. These things hung in his memory thirty years later, long after the other attachments had passed. "So, ask the travelled inhabitant of any nation, in what country on earth would you rather live? Certainly," Jefferson answered, "in my own, where are all my friends, my relations, and the earliest and sweetest recollections of my life. Which would be your second choice? France."

CHAPTER SEVEN

Secretary of State

Amidst the contentions of party, the interests of the public, even the maxims of justice and candour, are sometimes forgotten; and yet those fatal consequences which such a measure of corruption seems to portend, do not unavoidably follow. The public interest is often secure, not because individuals are disposed to regard it as the end of their conduct, but because each, in his place, is determined to preserve his own. Liberty is maintained by the continued differences and oppositions of numbers, not by their concurring zeal in behalf of equitable government. In free states, therefore, the wisest laws are never, perhaps, dictated by the interest and spirit of any order of men: they are moved, they are opposed, or amended, by different hands; and come at last to express that medium and composition which contending parties have forced one another to adopt.

Adam Ferguson, An Essay on the History of Civil Society, *1767.*

W HEN JEFFERSON disembarked at Norfolk on November 23, 1789, the newspapers at once informed him of his nomination by President Washington to the high post of Secretary of State in the new government. The honor, unexpected and unwanted, placed Jefferson in a delicate position. Several months before, when Madison sounded him out, he had declared his aversion to any post in the domestic administration, and his determination soon to retire altogether from that "mere mouser of time," public service. He soon realized that in the eyes of his Virginia countrymen, if not of his own, the President's call admitted but one answer. Official welcomes tendered the returning envoy, first in Norfolk, then by the General Assembly in Richmond, pointedly congratulated him on "the important station you are now called to by a grateful country." Jefferson responded politely but ignored the calculated persuasions of these addresses. As he journeyed westward, canvassing six years of change in a familiar society, taking stock of his friends' hopes and fears for the new government, the burden of decision weighed heavily on his mind.

The President's letter and commission reached him at Eppington on December 11. His acceptance would be very gratifying, Washington said, though he respected Jefferson's wishes in the matter. For four days he pondered his reply. He could not flatly refuse the appointment; neither was he prepared to accept it. So far as the question depended on himself, Jefferson wrote, he much preferred his post in Paris. It was familiar, its lines well charted. The new office of Secretary of State, on the other hand, embracing a mass of domestic administration together with the foreign, presented a boundless sea of troubles, which he would enter with "gloomy forebodings from the criticisms and censures of a public" easily misinformed and misled, and from which he would wish to withdraw the moment the torrent rose. "But it is not for an individual to choose his post. You are to marshal us as may best be for the public good." Jefferson thus threw the decision back to Washington, uncertain of what the outcome would be, but inasmuch as Washington had consulted his wishes, expecting he would be allowed to remain as he was.

Visiting all the way home, Jefferson and the girls reached Monticello two days before Christmas. What a tumult greeted the returned master! "The Negroes discovered the approach of the carriage as soon as it reached Shadwell . . . ," Martha recalled. "They collected in crowds around it and almost drew it up the mountain by hand. . . . When the door of the carriage was opened, they received him in their arms and bore him to the house, crowding round and kissing his hands and feet—some blubbering and crying—others laughing. It seemed impossible to satisfy their anxiety to touch and kiss the very earth which bore him." Household fires again burned at Monticello. Friends and relations—Carrs, Eppeses, Skipwiths, Jeffersons—came from all around, and in the midst of this happy reunion Jefferson labored to straighten out his private affairs. Martha, meanwhile, lost no time acquiring a suitor for her hand. She gave it to young Thomas Mann Randolph, a second cousin she had romped with as a child, the son of Jefferson's boyhood friend Colonel Randolph of Tuckahoe. Jefferson was delighted with the match. A perfectly polished Virginian, tall, handsome, studious, amply endowed with fortune and family, recently returned from Edinburgh where he had opened a correspondence with Jefferson in regard to his studies at the University, Randolph qualified as the ideal son-in-law. Marriage settlement and wedding were quickly arranged. Within little more than a month Jefferson managed to put his own affairs in order and attend to his daughter's happiness, the two main concerns of his leave.

How the leave was to be concluded, whether in New York or in Paris, remained a dilemma. One of the first callers at Monticello was James Madison, who came not only as a friend and neighbor but as the President's emissary. Anxious for the success of the bantling Constitution, disturbed by the Anti-Federalist complexion of Virginia politics, and encouraged by the public response to Jefferson's nomination, Madison regarded his friend's association with the Washington administration as a matter of "infinite importance" to the country. He was distressed by Jefferson's coolness to the office and supposed it arose mainly from a mistaken view of the quantity of domestic business annexed to the foreign department. He returned to Orange, thence to New York to report to the President, uncertain of the success of his mission. Washington soon wrote to the reluctant nominee. He had been irritated by Jefferson's gloomily compliant response to the letter bearing the commission, and now told him plainly that the decision was his alone. At the same time, cued by Madison, he endeavored to overcome Jefferson's aversion to the new office. Its duties would be less arduous than Jefferson imagined. While it was true that Congress had combined home and foreign affairs in one department, the latter, for which Jefferson was preeminently suited, was more important by far, and a division might be made should experience suggest the need. Jefferson could not mistake Washington's desire, nor be indifferent to it; yet his repugnance to the office increased "so as to oppress me extremely." No matter in what light it was viewed, the domestic post had no charms for him.

Jefferson was also feeling the force of pressures nearer home. A committee of the local citizenry, no doubt with Madison's connivance, prepared a ceremonial address to welcome the return of Albemarle's distinguished son. He received the text in the middle of January. Extolling his long career in the public councils, the citizens sympathized with his desire to remain among them and then pointedly alluded to the present crisis: "But America has still occasion for your services, and we are too warmly attached to the common interest of our Country, and entertain too high a respect for your merit, not to unite with the general voice that you continue in her councils." Jefferson pondered the appeal for three weeks before offering his response in ceremonies at Monticello on February 12.

He seized the occasion, with its complicated political overtones, for an elevated summation of his philosophy. "We have been fellow labourers and fellow sufferers, and heaven has rewarded us with a happy issue from our struggles. It rests now with ourselves alone to enjoy in peace and concord the blessings of self-government, so long denied to mankind: to shew by example the sufficiency of human reason for the care of human affairs and that the will of the majority, the natural law of every society, is the only sure guardian of the rights of man. Perhaps even this may sometimes err. But its errors are honest, solitary and short-lived.—Let us then, my dear friends, for ever bow down to the general reason of society . . . ." In this lofty response Jefferson associated the sentiments of a public he was bound to respect with the new venture in government to which their cause and his—"the holy cause of freedom"—was now committed. As all must lay aside their objections and "bow down to the general reason of the society," so he too must bow down to "the will of my country."

The die was cast. Two days later Jefferson wrote a cheerless letter of acceptance to the President. A swirl of pressures had sucked him into a position of national leadership against his will. He tried to be philosophical about it. In farewell letters to friends abroad, he stated repeatedly that the desires of others had obliged him to go into an office he neither liked nor wanted. "But these things not being created for our convenience," he grandly explained, "we have no right to decline the post in which the public authority marshals us for public service." At another time, after the agonies of the Virginia governorship, he had labeled such a proposition ridiculous. Nor was he fully reconciled to it now. The conviction that he had suffered himself to be "overpowered" accompanied him into the office of secretary of state, and he was determined to leave it as soon as decency and circumstances would permit.

He set out for New York with as little delay as possible. Martha's wedding was advanced several days. Polly was hustled off to motherly Aunt Eppes with instructions to mind her Spanish. Once again Nicholas Lewis was put in charge of affairs at home. Jefferson took to the road on March 1, accompanied by the newlyweds, who planned to settle on one of the Randolph properties, Varina, fronting the James below Richmond. At Richmond, Jefferson executed bonds for the discharge of his debts, both his own and his share of the Wayles's debt, which totaled approximately £6000, and from which, if all went well, he would be free at last in the year 1797. After bumping his way to Alexandria by stage, he laid over a day to attend a testimonial dinner in his honor. The merchants of the Potomac port lauded him for his labors at Versailles: "You have freed commerce from its shackles, and destroyed the first essay made in this country towards establishing a monopoly." Phaeton and horses, brought from Monticello, awaited him in Alexandria; and while there he purchased the noble steed Tarquin, "got by Eclipse out of Peyton Randolph's roan mare who was of the blood of Monkey, Othello and Dabster." But a heavy snow had fallen, causing Jefferson to change his mode of travel. He left the phaeton to be sent by water, and continued his passage by stage, horses following behind. Occasionally he would mount Tarquin to relieve the monotony of the coach. Thus he went, buffeted along at a pace of five or six miles an hour, stopping briefly at Baltimore, then Philadelphia, where he had a last memorable visit at Franklin's bedside, and to his journey's end at New York on March 21.

It was a Sunday. The tired traveler waited on the President after his return from church. The reunion of the two Virginians must have been a happy one. Only the President's esteem for Jefferson can explain his extraordinary patience to obtain him as secretary of state; only Jefferson's loyalty to Washington can finally explain his submission to the halter. He had brought with him two sets of medals struck in France to honor victorious commanders in the Revolutionary War; and he now presented Washington with his gold medal, authorized by Congress in 1776, together with those intended for the other officers. It was a piece of unfinished business from the Revolution, like the new government Jefferson had come to serve. After an hour's conversation, he retired to the City Tavern. Here he lodged until he could find a house. Congress was in session—few houses were to be had. He rented an "indifferent" one in Maiden Lane, going to live there on the first of June. And so, "harnessed in new gear," Jefferson set forth on still another career.

Agenda in New York

The new Secretary at once plunged into the work of his department. John Jay, newly appointed Chief Justice of the United States, had stayed on for several months as caretaker of the foreign department, but much business had been put aside for Jefferson's arrival. His staff was already complete: two chief clerks, two assistants, and a part-time translator—the entire personnel of the Department of State, which had an annual budget of about $7,000, one half of it representing the salary of the Secretary. The mission of the department in foreign affairs was reasonably clear; most of its other duties, as an unglorified "home office," had yet to be disclosed by Congress. Just before Jefferson came, it was charged with taking the census, a little later with the granting of patents and copyrights, still later with the supervision of the mint. These, together with the keeping of the seal, publication of the laws, law enforcement through district attorneys, pardons, federal relations with state and territorial governments, made a strange medley of responsibilities no minister could comprehend or, with a staff numbered on one hand, adequately attend to. The trifling ones took care of themselves, the others suffered from neglect, as the Secretary necessarily devoted nine-tenths of his time to foreign affairs.

There was as yet no "cabinet." The head of each department, State, Treasury, and War, along with the part-time Attorney General, transacted his business independently with the President. The

Constitution vested all executive powers in him. He relied heavily on the initiative and advice of his subordinates, of course, but nothing of consequence was done without his approval. The preparation of papers for the President, consultation with him (often over the breakfast table), followed by the implementation of decisions, formed the basis of Jefferson's daily routine. The President's responsibility was particularly evident in foreign affairs, not only because of their paramount importance but because he alone could speak for the entire nation. Jefferson was more of a stickler on this point than the President himself. It offered no difficulties. The relationship among the departments, on the other hand, was fraught with difficulties from the start. The shadowy lines between them, their overlapping jurisdictions, the inevitable intersections of public business occasioned administrative conflict, which then became enmeshed in personal and political differences. Washington took pains to secure a harmonious administration. The mere fact of his presence at the helm was perhaps the surest guarantee of harmony, for he commanded the loyalty of the whole nation when other forces and symbols of loyalty were still inchoate. Issues of moment touching more than one department called for concerted advice and, if possible, concerted action. As the need increased, a formal consultative body, the cabinet, was evolved. But the more the department heads were thrown together, the more vexatious their differences became; and Washington's scheme for harmonious and, as he believed, non-partisan administration collapsed.

Cordiality was the keynote in the spring of 1790. Alexander Hamilton, Secretary of the Treasury, was already the young lion of the administration. He had nailed his flag to the mast the preceding January in his Report on Public Credit, and Congress, though hesitant and divided, prepared to steer by it. Jefferson knew Hamilton principally as Madison's collaborator in *The Federalist*, the celebrated defense and exposition of the Constitution. The partnership had not withstood the shock of the minister's report, and no doubt Madison had put his friend on guard against Hamilton's aggressive leadership. The military dash and bravado of the little New Yorker, who played at the games of a Caesar, made a startling contrast to the tall, easy-gaited Virginian. There was an air of insouciance about the Secretary of State, as if he were tired or half-hearted, while Hamilton still burned with the relentless ambition that had taken him, a mere lad, from the West Indies to New York in 1773, then into the Continental Army, where his services as Washington's secretary and aide-de-camp opened up a remarkable career that had yet to satisfy his dream of grandeur for his adopted country. Jefferson had traveled the road to fame; it still lay ahead of Hamilton. Jefferson was secure in his Americanism; Hamilton flaunted his, like the nouveau he was. Jefferson's political instincts were to conciliate; Hamilton's were to command. Although Treasury was the giant among the departments, with by far the largest staff and the most influential constituency, it could not contain his energies. Treasury, too, had an access to Congress and a degree of executive independence not possessed by State, set up wholly as an arm of the President. But Jefferson did not see Hamilton as a threat in 1790. Still less did he anticipate troubles from his other colleagues. Henry Knox, the portly and amiable Secretary of War, knew guns and soldiering but little else. Like Washington and Hamilton, a veteran of the Continental Army, Knox could be counted on to take high Federalist ground on every question. He was offset by Edmund Randolph, the gifted Attorney General, who was an old Virginia friend and, in some sense, a protégé.

For several weeks Jefferson spent long hours poring over files of correspondence and bulky documents, and conferred almost daily with the President to set the course of a reinvigorated foreign policy. There was little room for complacency. Seven years after the treaty of peace, the new nation was still besieged by European empires, the Spanish to the southwest, the British to the northwest, who together occupied or controlled one-half the land area of the United States. Except for the Kentucky spearhead, the United States had still to make good its claim to the western country from the Floridas to the Great Lakes. Indian resistance, aided and abetted, as the Americans believed, by the colonial powers, checked the advance of settlement and took a frightful toll of lives. The economic loss to the nation was incalculable. Indian hostilities, together with British occupation of the posts below the Lakes, cut American profits from the fur trade, while Spain's blockage of the Mississippi navigation turned every westerner into a potential conspirator in the separatist schemes of frontier adventurers and Spanish agents. The redemption and pacification of the West constituted the paramount problem of American foreign relations. Scarcely less important in Jefferson's eyes was the release of American commerce from European thralldom, British in particular. There was no immediate prospect for the settlement of these problems. Relations with Britain remained in limbo; since Adams's departure from London two years before, formal contact between the two countries had disappeared. Similarly with Spain—nothing had occurred since the collapse of the Jay-Gardoqui negotiations, and Carmichael, in Madrid, had not even been heard from for a year. Viewing the situation broadly, the Secretary of State sometimes felt like praying for a European war, which, with all its risks, would strengthen America's bargaining power in foreign courts and enable the New World to "fatten on the follies of the Old."

The one bright spot in the picture was revolutionary France. Of the major powers only France had made important concessions to American commerce, and Jefferson expected further gains from the progress of liberal principles in Paris. In order to deal with Britain and Spain, the United States needed a place to stand in European politics. The French Alliance, while not an unmixed blessing, provided it. With France there were no critical problems; on the contrary, every step brought the two countries closer together. The Revolution had suffered some setbacks since Jefferson's departure, but as he philosophized to Lafayette, "we are not . . . to be translated from despotism to liberty, in a featherbed." He did not doubt the ultimate result. In letters of adieux to friends in Paris, written after his arrival in New York, Jefferson declared his love for France, his faith in the Revolution, his assurances of American good will, and explained that although he had reluctantly assumed a domestic station, he was reconciled to it by "the most powerful . . . opportunities it will give me of cementing the friendship between our two nations." He was far too experienced in the uncertain reckonings of the national interest to tie his foreign policy to the French kite; yet it glittered in his eyes and he hoped his country might soar with it. The political imperative of the national interest happily conspired with the obligation of fidelity and principle to France.

The first item on the Secretary's agenda was the diplomatic establishment of the United States. It was discussed in the early conversations with the President. Jefferson saw no need for representatives of a higher grade than chargé d'affaires at any court except Versailles, where only a minister carried dignity. It was agreed, however, that Britain too should receive a minister whenever the prospects for negotiation improved. Gouverneur Morris was then in London, under instructions from the President to sound out the British ministry. Although Jefferson advocated a small and unpretentious diplomatic establishment, confined to four or five countries (the others being Spain, Portugal, and, possibly, Holland) he wanted it to be respectable. The salaries of American envoys should be raised; they should be allowed outfits and private secretaries. Washington agreed. But it would not be easy to reverse the niggardly course set by the old Congress. The President worried about the scope of his authority with respect to diplomatic appointments. Could the Senate, under its power to approve persons nominated for diplomatic posts, reject the destination and the grade of the appointment as well as the person? Jefferson gave his written opinion that the Senate could not. "The transaction of business with foreign nations is Executive altogether." His strong line on this question overcame the President's caution. The Intercourse bill finally passed by Congress adhered generally to Jefferson's recommendations.

On behalf of this bill, the Secretary made his first, and last, appearance before a Senate committee. Senator William Maclay of Pennsylvania, a churlish soul who disapproved foreign embassies altogether and labeled any salary above a pittance "princely," undoubtedly voiced his opposition to Jefferson's opinions in committee; but the encounter was memorable because of the description this austere republican recorded of the Secretary of State. "Jefferson is a slender Man," Maclay wrote. "Has rather the Air of Stiffness in his Manner. His cloaths seem too small for him. He sits in a lounging Manner on one hip, commonly, and with one of his shoulders elevated much above the other. His face had a crany Aspect. His whole figure has a loose shackling Air. He had a rambling Vacant look and nothing of that firm collected deportment which I expected would dignify the presence of a Secretary or Minister. I looked for Gravity, but a laxity of Manner, seemed shed about him. He spoke almost without ceasing. But even his discourse partook of his personal demeanor. It was loose and rambling and yet he scattered information wherever he went, and some even brilliant Sentiments sparkled from him. The information which he gave us respecting foreign Ministers &ca. was all high Spiced. He has been long enough abroad to catch the tone of European folly . . . . He took his leave," Maclay concluded, "and the Committee agreed to strike out the specific sum to be given to any foreign appointment, leaving it to the President to account, and appropriated 30,000 doll. generally for the purpose." The amount was later raised to $40,000.

The appointments would be made in due course. Carmichael remained in Madrid, in baffling silence that tried Jefferson's patience; and, in the interim, William Short was commissioned chargé d'affaires at Versailles. Short was "cruelly disappointed." He had counted on Jefferson's influence to secure him the permanent post at Versailles, as minister he had hoped. To leave Paris now, he said, "would be to me like quitting the most interesting spectacle at the end of the third act." And besides, though there was no need to explain it to Jefferson, he had fallen hopelessly in love with the young wife of the venerable Duc de la Rochefoucauld. Jefferson did not in the least doubt Short's abilities, and he did his best to make them known to the President. Unfortunately, Short had no political qualifications. Jefferson could only repeat the friendly advice he had given him many times before. If he wished any public career at all, he must make a name for himself in his own country. Short was an astute observer, well regarded in French ruling circles; but his woeful refrain grew tedious, and he never fulfilled the high expectations Jefferson had for him.

With Short's help Jefferson wound up his affairs at the French capital. His lease must be terminated, his servants discharged, all except the invaluable Petit who should be prevailed upon to come to the United States as Jefferson's housekeeper. Furniture and other items, some yet to be acquired—an elegant mantle clock set between marble obelisks, an oval looking-glass, dozens of rolls of wallpaper (sky blue, pea green, crimson, brick) "eight best and thickest hair mattresses," many foods, wines, books, plants, a new copying press, pairs of Angora cats, Angora goats, bantam fowl, and as many sky larks and red-legged partridges as Petit could manage—all this, and much more, must be sent. In addition to this private business, Short was instructed to present Jefferson's letter of recall at Versailles. There was a delicacy in this, for the Comte de Montmorin and the principal officers of the *corps diplomatique* must be told, in such a way as to avoid offence, that Jefferson could not receive the customary present of the King to a retiring minister. He detested this diplomatic convention, together with the reciprocal gratuities expected of him. While in residence he had paid the usual "court fees," of course; and he now asked Short to bow to the etiquette of the court by presenting gold snuff boxes to the Secrétaire and the Introductteur des Ambassadeurs. As to the royal gift, however, which Franklin and American ministers at other courts had received before him, Jefferson thought it mercifully prohibited by the new Constitution.

But the problem was soon complicated by the discreet suggestion of the French chargé that the American government should, after many years' neglect, present some mark of its esteem to the first minister, Luzerne, and presumably to Moustier, who had recently gone home. Although deeply averse to introducing the Old World diplomatic custom into the United States, Jefferson was more anxious to avoid embarrassment with France. So he promptly worked out a policy compatible with European practice. The American present to foreign diplomats would consist of a gold medal, which Jefferson designed for execution in France, and a chain of 365 links, its gold value proportioned to the length of a minister's service in this country. Having thus committed the United States to the policy of presents, Jefferson could hardly refuse a gift from Louis XVI. For, in truth, the constitutional bar was not absolute. He might accept the gift as something demanded by custom, and following the example of Arthur Lee, deposit it in the public funds. Or he might accept it after obtaining the consent of Congress; but he had no thought of being "laid on the gridiron of debate in Congress for any such paltry purpose." The dilemma pressed upon him. What he finally did was devious, stealthy, and perhaps irresponsible. He accepted the present under the fiction it was a private matter, then turned it into cash to cover the costs of his own gifts to the King's servants. The business was confided to Short. The present, a diamond studded portrait of Louis XVI, was secretly stripped of its value, the diamonds sold, the unadorned picture sent to Jefferson.

When he balanced the account he discovered that he had, quite unintentionally, realized a neat profit. The transaction was never disclosed. It set no precedent. Neither did the policy of gifts to foreign diplomats retiring from this country. Fittingly, the fourth French Minister, Edmond Charles Genêt, who shattered so many precedents in the diplomatic line, occasioned the demise of this one.

While engaged with these endings and beginnings of diplomacy, Jefferson also gave his attention to several items of domestic policy and administration. All the reports and opinions he wrote during these early weeks in office fell on the side of a strong national government and a strong executive. His first official report dealt with the old problem of coinage. Congress had received proposals from an enterprising American connected with Matthew Boulton, in England, for supplying the American government with copper coins manufactured with Boulton's steam on the plan of Jean Pierre Droz, the inventor Jefferson had met in Paris and hoped to send to the United States, only then to watch the English snatch him from under his nose. Congress referred the proposals to Jefferson. He opposed the project. "Coinage is peculiarly an attribute of sovereignty. To transfer its exercise into another country, is to submit it to another Sovereign." The government ought to mint its own coins, he said, which was all that was wanting "to banish the discordant pounds, shillings, pence and farthings of the different states, and to establish in their stead the new denominations" on the approved decimal ratio. A year later Congress authorized the mint; and Jefferson, meanwhile, made a second unsuccessful attempt to entice Droz to America. The chaos in the nation's coinage continued for many years.

The uniform chain of connection between coins and weights and measures, all reduced to the decimal rule, had long appealed to Jefferson's reason. He was pleased to discover in the pile of papers that awaited him in New York a two-month-old resolution of Congress requesting the Secretary of State to draw up a comprehensive plan of weights, measures, and currency. The idea of deriving a universal standard from nature, the same the world around and forever, and arranged on the simplest arithmetic, was a commonplace of the Enlightenment. Entertaining this idea, with the rational hope it embodied, Jefferson was not original; but in the precision and the scope he

402

gave to it, he was unexcelled among the philosophical statesmen of his age. "I believe you are the first nation that ever produced statesmen who were natural philosophers," wrote an English savant after reading Jefferson's Report on Weights and Measures. It was this conjunction of philosophy and statesmanship that made the Report an expression of both the national spirit and its promise of universality. Actually, of all the Western nations the United States had the least need to legislate uniform standards. A gallon in the Carolinas was the same measure as a gallon in New England. But this happy uniformity, so far as it extended, ought not be left to accident. Besides the convenience that would attend the introduction of the decimal ratio, a comprehensive system of weights, measures, and money, tied to an unchangeable standard fixed in the order of nature, "accessible to all persons, in all times and places," might become the model for the entire world.

In preparing the Report, Jefferson brought himself abreast of the latest literature, profited from Madison's guidance, and checked his calculations with David Rittenhouse and other "mathematical friends." The first and most difficult problem was to determine the natural standard of measure that would "give law through the whole system." The common idea was to derive this standard from the motion of the earth on its axis. Sir Isaac Newton had determined the precise length of a pendulum in the latitude of London which would make its vibrations in one second of mean time. Finding some imperfections in this second's pendulum as a standard, Jefferson adopted the suggestion of a Philadelphia watchmaker, Robert Leslie, whose manuscript Madison showed to him, to substitute a cylindrical rod of iron, of such a length as would oscillate in a second's time. He originally proposed the 38th degree of latitude—the latitude of Monticello—but at once saw the error of this when he received from Short the plan presented by Talleyrand, the Bishop of Autun, to the National Assembly. It proposed to base the standard on the latitude of $45°$, equidistant between the equator and the poles, thus equally acceptable to all nations. Jefferson revised his plan and his calculations accordingly. Once the standard was settled, the rest was arithmetic. "Let the Second rod then . . . be the Standard of measure; and let it be divided into five equal parts, each of which shall be called a *Foot*." Such a foot would be one-quarter of an inch shorter than the current measure; it would be divided into ten inches, each inch into ten lines, each line into ten points; ten feet would make a decad, ten decads a rood, ten roods a furlong, ten furlongs a mile. The unit of capacity would be one cubic foot, to be called a bushel, though less than the common bushel. The standard of weight would be fixed by the weight of a cubic inch of rain water, the ounce, with greater and lesser weights going by the rule of tens. In order to embrace the money unit, or dollar, within the system, Jefferson proposed a slight increase in the silver content to give it a weight of one ounce exactly.

Jefferson wanted Congress to adopt a complete and integrated plan of this character, and in the original draft of his Report it was the only plan presented. But thinking that Congress would balk at "changing the established habits of a whole nation," he included a modest alternative in the final Report. The alternate plan, for which he showed no enthusiasm, would achieve invariable and uniform standards at the cost of perpetuating the bewildering arithmetic of vulgar weights and measures. Thus the gallon would be 270 cubic inches, eight gallons to a bushel or firkin, of which two would make a strike or kilderkin, of which two equaled a croom or barrel, of which two equaled a quarter or hogshead, one and one-third hogsheads a tierce, and so on. How much more difficult this system than the temporary inconveniences that would accompany the system of reason! Congress adopted neither plan. Only once, in 1792, after repeated promptings by the President, was Jefferson's Report seriously considered. It was printed, of course, and the savants of two continents joined in praise. To the end of his days Jefferson championed the cause of uniformity of weights and measures; but the moments for great innovations in society are few and far between, as he appreciated, and in the case of this one the moment quickly passed after 1790. More urgent business claimed the attention of Congress; commercial intercourse settled habits of reckoning; the spirit of national reformation gave way to intense partisanship; and the dream of universality founded on the plain dictates of reason and nature faded from councils of state. Only revolutionary France registered progress in this area by the adoption of what became the metric system. Jefferson, interestingly enough, viewed the French system as a setback. Its unit of measure was based on a quarter of a meridian of the earth as determined within the limits of France, which, aside from other difficulties, made it unacceptable internationally.

The Report on Weights and Measures was prepared, Jefferson later said, "under a severe attack of periodical headache which came on every day at sunrise, and never left me till sunset. What had been ruminated in the day under a paroxysm of the most excruciating pain was committed to paper by candlelight, and then the calculations were made." The attack came on early in May, resisted the usual dosings of "the bark" (quinine), and though it let up from time to time, kept the Secretary from his desk for most of a month's time. He was not alone in his misery. The spring was "uncommonly wet and cold," Mrs. Adams reported. Influenza swept through the city; the Adams's house on Richmond Hill became a mere hospital. The President was stricken with pneumonia. "Yesterday (which was the 5th day) he was thought by the physicians to be dying," Jefferson wrote to Monticello on May 16. But Washington sweated out the crisis, and the nation breathed easier. Both men, President and Secretary of State, were well on the road to recovery three weeks later when they joined Hamilton and several others in a fishing expedition off the coast of Long Island.

Jefferson's illness furnished the occasion, though not the cause, for his retreat from the polite society of the upstart capital. Many years later he could scarcely find words to express the shock his initiation had given him. He had left France but six months before, the watchwords of revolution fresh on his lips. Cordially received in New York, wined and dined in the best circles, he was at once placed in the city's society. "But I cannot describe the wonder and mortification with which the table conversation filled me," he recalled. "Politics were the chief topic, and a preference of kingly over republican government was evidently the favorite sentiment. An apostate I could not be, nor yet a hypocrite; and I found myself, for the most part, the only advocate of the republican side of the question." New York had been a haven of Loyalists during the war, of course, and continued to show Tory proclivities beyond most cities. Jefferson escaped his embarrassment by losing himself in the work of his department.

Government was inevitably imbued with the tone of society. Jefferson's friend the Vice President, John Adams, had started a rage for honorific titles. While still in Paris he had learned from Madison—"the most superlatively ridiculous thing I ever heard of" —the title the Senate proposed, on Adams's prompting, to give the President: "His Highness, the President of the United States of America, and Protector of their Liberties." (The House, mercifully, held out for the simple title "The President of the United States.") Adams, with many others, thought that some of the pomp and majesty of Old World courts was needed to impress the people with the dignity and authority of the new government. The flavor of a court, albeit a republican one, was everywhere. In the pompous formality and sycophancy of the "court" newspaper, the *Gazette of the United States*, for example. John Fenno, its editor, gushed flattery on the President, extolled every ceremony, chronicled the doings of every "His Excellency" and "Most Honorable" and their "Ladyships." Plain and unassuming Mrs. Washington was "the amiable consort of THE PRESIDENT." (Returning to New York in May, she was "conducted over the bay in the President's barge, rowed by thirteen eminent pilots, in a handsome white dress; on passing the Battery a salute was fired.") It was all very silly, this emulation of royalty in the American republic. The spectacle revolted Jefferson, who prayed for the disappearance of all titles but "Mister."

The President, Jefferson thought, was more the victim than the agent of these follies. Washington was used to adulation, of course, expected it, and naturally took an interest in the forms and ceremonies befitting his high office. He had himself become a ceremony— and perhaps the presidency was little more. The honor he felt in his own person reinforced his sense of the respectability owing to the chief of state. It scarcely occurred to him that an elegant state carriage, drawn by six white horses, smartly attended by liveried servants and outriders, ruffled republican sensibilities. In his character, pride and diffidence, gravity and dignity, combined to smother familiarities. Senator Maclay, after sweating out one of the President's weekly dinner parties, put him down as "a cold, formal man." "No cheering ray of convivial sunshine broke through the cloudy gloom of his settled seriousness." Jefferson revered Washington: "never did nature and fortune combine more perfectly to make a man great." Such was his considered judgment. He knew the President out of harness, shared his enthusiasms as a Virginia planter, glimpsed his convivial side, and sensed the basic simplicity of his character; yet the dominant impression for Jefferson, as for others, was one of high-toned austerity. It made the President an easy mark, Jefferson thought, for the sycophants who would surround him with the tinsel splendors of royalty.

Washington's icy Tuesday afternoon levees drew the most complaint. The three o'clock visitor to the house on Broadway was conducted past liveried servants at the entrance to the formal dining room, and there presented to the President. He stood "clad in black velvet; his hair in full dress, powdered and gathered behind in a large silk bag; yellow gloves on his hands; holding a cocked hat . . . . He wore knee and shoe buckles; and a long sword, with a finely wrought and polished hilt, which appeared at the left hip; the coat worn over the sword . . . . The scabbard was of white polished leather." The President received the visitor with a dignified bow; as others came they formed a circle around the room; at a quarter past three the door was closed and the President toured the circle, exchanging a few words with each caller. "When he had completed his circuit, he resumed his first position, and the visitors approached him in succession, bowed and retired. By four o'clock this ceremony was over." It suited Washington's personality, his convenience, and his conception of the presidential office. But it did not suit plain republicans. They supposed Washington had been duped by the high-flying Federalists of New York. Sometime later, in the fires of partisan controversy, Jefferson expressed similar sentiments; still later, he thought that the pomp and ceremony had a deeper basis in Washington's doubts for the strength and durability of republican government. "He was naturally distrustful of men, and inclined to gloomy apprehensions; and I was ever persuaded that a belief that we must at length end in something like a British constitution, had some weight in his adoption of the ceremonies of levees, birth-days, pompous meetings with Congress, and other forms of the same character, calculated to prepare us gradually for a change which he believed possible, and let it come on with as little shock as might be to the public mind." But in 1790, with a surer faith in Washington's republican character, Jefferson clung to him as the rock of national salvation.

Jefferson was more troubled by opinions than by forms. Part of the difficulty was simply one of reliable political intelligence. In Paris he had discovered that the news of the United States came filtered through the English press; now, at the other end, he found the same "lying" distortion of European events, especially of the French Revolution, and he again applied a corrective. The most authentic channel of European intelligence was the famous *Gazette de Leide*, to which he and Mazzei, in Paris, had sent communications on American affairs. The translation and publication in New York of extracts from its pages would counteract the tyranny of English opinion. For this purpose Jefferson entered into an arrangement with John Fenno, whose *Gazette of the United States*, while distasteful to him, already had the reputation of an administration organ. Toward the end of April, Fenno began to publish translations from the *Gazette de Leide*, along with other items of European news, furnished by the Department of State. The strange alliance lasted only three months. By the time newspapers and letters arrived from the Continent, the events they analyzed were ancient history; and before Jefferson could arrange for their transmission by speedy English packet, Fenno's paper had become unreceptive to the views he espoused. When the seat of government moved to Philadelphia, Jefferson found another vent for European intelligence sympathetic to the republican cause.

The dissolution of the tenuous connection with Fenno points to the beginnings of political discord in Washington's administration. When Jefferson arrived on the scene, the prospects of unity were bright, and further enhanced by his presence. The wrangling in Congress was ominous, however. In the House of Representatives a long and angry debate on the abolition of the slave trade—inferentially of slavery—was just drawing to a close. It raised a fever in the South and recalled to some minds the Cassandra warnings of Patrick Henry and others against overreaching power in the new government. "A spirit of jealousy which may prove dangerous to the Union, towards the Eastern states, seems to be growing fast among us," a Virginian warned the President in March. The "Northern phalanx" seemed to bear down all opposition. Northern congressmen, on the other hand, viewed their colleagues south of the Potomac as willful obstructionists, panderers of popular vices, "violent republicans," which, according to Fisher Ames of Massachusetts, was but another name for "the republicanism of the aristocracy of southern nabobs." The slavery debate was no more than an interlude in the controversy of far greater import on the plan submitted by the Secretary of Treasury in January for the funding of the public debt.

The belief that the new government would pay the debts of the United States was unquestionably one of the foundations of its support. Hamilton divided the whole debt, principal and accumulated interest, into three parts. First, the foreign debt amounting to approximately $11,700,000; second, the domestic debt of the Union amounting to $40,400,000; third, the debts of the several states, estimated at $25,000,000. He proposed that the federal government assume the state debts, and by a system of funding secure the whole at face value in specie. Under the funding system, public creditors would exchange their old securities for new federal "stock" bearing annual interest of something over 4 per cent on the average. Only a small portion of the stock would be eligible for redemption annually. Even under the best of circumstances, it would be many years before the debt was retired; its support, meanwhile, would represent roughly three-fourths of the entire cost of the federal establishment. Beginning in this way, "the way other nations have ended," the French chargé predicted, the Americans "will be decrepit before arriving at manhood." But the burden of so large a debt, for so long a time, held no terrors for Hamilton. Quite aside from the overwhelming importance of national credit to the power and respect commanded by a government—a point on which most statesmen were agreed—Hamilton believed this public bane, the debt, could be turned into a public blessing of incalculable magnitude. By the magic of funding—so the theory went—the debt acquires stable value, augments the productive capital of the country, and answers all the purposes of money. The Midas touch thus given to the enterprise of the moneyed class secures, in return, the consolidation of its interests with the interest of a strong national government. Servicing of the debt necessitates taxes, fiscal administration requires a national bank—the powers of the Constitution are called forth in amplitude. Viewed as a political engine, the funding system combats the centrifugal tendencies of the federal polity by creating a "union and concert of views among the creditors," which acts in some measure as a republican substitute for the Old World establishments of clergy, nobility, royalty, army and navy, and so on. These considerations of national power were of such importance in Hamilton's statecraft that, had the public debt not existed, he would have had to invent an "engine of government" equally efficacious.

The Report on the Public Credit laid the foundation of what history remembers as "the Hamiltonian system." The plan was a bold one, and Congress, anxious for direction, hastened to implement it. No difficulty arose on the provision for the foreign debt, nor indeed on the principle of funding the domestic debt of the Union. But justice was revolted by the proposal to put the original and present holders of this debt on the same footing. In the course of depreciation over the years the debt had become an article of speculation. The needs of the original creditors—soldiers, farmers, traders—for ready cash had gratified the avarice of moneyed men; the securities had been bought and sold at a fraction of nominal value. Speculation rose high after the adoption of the Constitution until, in 1790, the entire $40 million was concentrated in perhaps 15 to 20,0000 holders, of whom probably no more than one-fifth were original creditors of the Union. Hamilton's plan appeared to sacrifice the substance of justice to its shadow. Why should speculative greed be rewarded by the government? Why should the poor and the ignorant be taxed to support the nominal value of securities "filched" from them at several shillings in the pound? Their case was "a hard one," Hamilton conceded, but he flatly rejected "as equally unjust and impolitic . . . as ruinous to the public credit" the idea bruited about of a discrimination between the two classes of creditors. Madison, who had earlier rejected the idea, now took it up in Congress. Original holders should be paid in full, holders by transfer at the market value, with the difference made good to the primitive creditors. The proposal furnished a standard of justice around which opponents of Hamilton's plan rallied. They were few, however, and discrimination met defeat in February by a vote of three to one.

"This game was over, and another was on the carpet at the moment of my arrival," Jefferson recalled years later. The new game was assumption of the state debts. Had he been earlier on the scene, he would probably have concurred with Madison on the question of discrimination, though, as with him, this would have required a change of front, justified on the ground that speculation and fraud, both inside the government and in every state and town country-wide, had accompanied the introduction of Hamilton's program, thus turning the scales of justice all around. At a later day he insisted that Hamilton's debt was "artificially created" and saddled on the country by a "corrupt squadron" in Congress, many of whose members were personally interested in the public funds. In any event, it was assumption, a far more explosive question than discrimination, that agitated the Congress on Jefferson's arrival in New York. Since the Revolutionary debts of the states had been incurred in the common cause, justice and policy, said the advocates of assumption, recommended equality of treatment of state with national creditors. The measure had the further merit of doing away with the dangers of competition between two sets of creditors, one looking to the states, the other to the federal government, for command of the public revenues. But eager national creditors worried lest the addition of the mass of state debts put so great a burden on the infant government as to injure their claims. Some states, moreover, Virginia among them, had made substantial progress toward liquidating their debts, while others, Massachusetts and South Carolina in particular, still groaned under enormous debts and threatened to break the Union unless they were promptly taken up as a common charge. The problem of inequities among the states gave the most trouble. But trouble came too in other forms: jealousy of the central government, suspicion of Hamilton's purpose, fear of moneyed influence. "The Secretary's people scarce disguise their design," Maclay crankily noted in his journal, "which is to create a mass of debts which will justify them in seizing all the sources of government, thus annihilating the state legislatures and creating an empire on the basis of consolidation." The question came to a vote in the House on April 12. Assumption was narrowly defeated.

Several more weeks passed before Jefferson took any part in this "most bitter and angry contest." "I arrived in the midst of it," he wrote a quarter-century later. "But a stranger to the ground, a stranger to the actors on it, so long absent as to have lost all familiarity with the subject, and as yet unsure of its object, I took no concern in it." There is no reason to doubt his statement. He was ill much of the time; for the rest, as he told friends in Virginia, he was too much occupied with the affairs of his department to meddle in questions outside his competence. The political scene *was* strange to him; its games did not amuse him, and it was several months before he could follow them. He had come to New York "neither federalist nor antifederalist," yet persuaded by his observations in Virginia that the principal danger to the Constitution, "the wisest ever yet presented to men," proceeded from demagogic Anti-Federalism. This was the enemy, not Hamilton, whose tangled skein of credit and power he had yet to unravel.

The storm over assumption raged for more than two months, reducing Congress to a shambles, before Jefferson was drawn into it. "No assumption, no funding," its advocates cried. If they could not "milk the cow their own way, they would not suffer her to be milked at all." But the majority held firm, vote after vote, until it prevailed finally the middle of June, and sent the funding bill, *sans* assumption, to the Senate. Deadlock now settled on the upper house. As it happened, however, the Senate was already deadlocked on the residence bill—the old labyrinth of the seat of government—and this would make all the difference. Hamilton saw the opportunity to strike a bargain: the national capital in exchange for funding with assumption. But who could preside over a transaction of this magnitude? Perhaps the Secretary of State: a Unionist, a Virginian deeply interested in the location of the capital on the Potomac, an innocent bystander in the funding controversy.

As Jefferson recalled the momentous encounter, he was going to the President's one day when he was waylaid by Hamilton, "somber, haggard and dejected beyond description," who took him by the arm and walked him backwards and forwards before the President's door for half an hour. They made an odd pair: the lanky Virginian, cool and imperturbable, the brisk little New Yorker, more agitated than Jefferson had ever seen him. "He painted pathetically the temper into which the legislature had been wrought; the disgust of those who were called the creditor states; the danger of the secession of their members and the separation of the states." Nothing was said of the capital, but Hamilton begged for help to avert calamity and suggested that some of Jefferson's friends in Congress might be induced to change their votes so as to permit assumption, with the funding system, to become law. "I told him that I was really a stranger to the subject . . . but that undoubtedly, if its rejection endangered a dissolution of the Union at this incipient stage, I should deem that the most unfortunate of all consequences, to avert which all partial and temporary evils should be yielded." He asked Hamilton to dine with him the next day in the company of a friend or two. It was impossible that "reasonable men, consulting together coolly, could fail, by some mutual sacrifices of opinion to form a compromise which would save the Union." The discussion took place, Hamilton and Madison the principals, Jefferson the mediator. The Union was more important than assumption; some members must change their votes to carry the measure. "But it was observed that this pill would be peculiarly bitter to the Southern states, and that some concomitant measure should be adopted to sweeten it a little to them." The sweetener was the capital. It would go to the Potomac after a temporary residence of ten years in Philadelphia, which should appease the Pennsylvanians. The principals now undertook to obtain the votes to close the deal. Two Marylanders and two Virginians, one "with a revulsion of stomach almost convulsive," swallowed the pill; and both bills, residence and funding with assumption, became law in July.

Jefferson soon came to regret his part in this sectional bargain as the worst error of his political life. He had been "duped" by the Secretary of Treasury and "ignorantly and innocently made to hold the candle" for his fraudulent scheme to throw $20,000,000 or more of state debts to "the stock-jobbing herd." His national feelings had been enlisted to forward a system far more injurious to the Union, he came to believe, than the selfishness of congressmen and speculators whose threats Hamilton had so cleverly used to fan his fears in 1790. Perhaps Jefferson was right in this assessment; but he was neither as ignorant nor as innocent as he portrayed himself. A bystander he was, but he had eyes and ears. Speculation in the state debts was a public scandal. The full import of assumption escaped him; yet he had opinions, and while they were not favorable to the measure standing by itself, they presented no bar to compromise. "I have been and still am of the opinion," he wrote to Monroe at the time of the backstairs maneuvering, "that Congress should always prefer letting the states raise money in their own way where it can be done. But in the present instance I see the necessity of yielding . . . to the cries of creditors in certain parts of the Union, for the sake of union, and to save us from the greatest of all calamities, the total extinction of our credit in Europe." In short, he preferred to leave the debts with the states, who were perfectly capable of discharging them, but not at the price of funding, of credit, of government. The circumstances called for "mutual sacrifice and accommodation." The Potomac site, while perhaps dispensable, was a useful consideration; for aside from the political advantages of a more southerly and westerly location of the national capital, Jefferson estimated it would circulate half a million dollars annually in Virginia. Moreover, the assumption as finally passed fell several million dollars below the figure Hamilton had proposed, and the fund was scrupulously allotted among the states so as to prevent injustice to any one. Virginia, Madison assured his constituents, "will consequently pay no more to the general treasure than she now pays to the state treasury." It was only a question of who was the paymaster. But, of course, that is always the critical question in politics. Assumption opened Pandora's box, rather Hamilton's box; and whatever justifications Jefferson and Madison found for their actions in the summer of 1790, they appeared meager a year or so later.

Jefferson had actually received his first lesson in the evils of the Treasury system before he submitted to its establishment. The occasion was a minor issue, involving the paltry sum of $40,000 voted in the previous session to pay arrearages due veterans of the Virginia and North Carolina lines. Eight months passed and the money still lay in the Treasury. Theodorick Bland, of Virginia, declared on the floor of the House that a list of the soldiers to whom payments were authorized had been improperly obtained from a public office and that a parcel of knowing scoundrels was cheating the soldiers, ignorant of their claims, by purchasing assignments of pay at a fraction of value. The speculative odor was stifling in this instance. A committee reported, and Congress adopted, a series of resolutions directing the Secretary of Treasury to get on with this business, and in every case to make payment to the original claimant, unless an assignee could produce power of attorney duly attested by two justices of the peace. The resolutions were more than critical of the

Secretary: they suggested fraud, and in the context of the debate that produced them, collusion of the Treasury in the fraud. Stung to the quick, Hamilton dashed off a report to Washington. If fraud had been committed on individual claimants, Hamilton said, their redress was to the courts. To annul all contracts, the good assignments with the allegedly bad, would be to usurp the authority of the judiciary and strike at the foundation of private property. The question was a difficult one for the President. Hamilton was persuasive, as always; but, unsure of the ground, Washington turned to Jefferson for his opinion. The resolutions were passed, Jefferson said, to defeat an alleged fraud which arose, in the first instance, from improper access to Treasury information. He did not doubt that such a fraud had occurred, but neither did he furnish proof of it. He confined his argument to Hamilton's objection: that the resolutions would annul valid contracts. Under the common law, at least in Virginia, he said, the conveyance of a debt not actually in possession is void. So, contrary to Hamilton, the legislation was not retrospective. It merely directed the Treasury to refuse disbursements on invalid assignments. Law and justice commended the resolutions, and Jefferson pointedly concluded that their defeat was "solicited only to support a fraud." Washington signed the resolutions. His two secretaries had crossed swords, and the opening encounter was, as Julian P. Boyd has said, "symbolic of all that was to follow." As yet, however, neither man had taken measure of the other, and their relations remained cordial and co-operative for many months.

Further premonitions of difficulty came in Jefferson's own province of foreign affairs. All summer long Britain and Spain rocked on the verge of war. The affair took its name from Nootka Sound on the far Pacific coast, where the Spanish struck at British intruders. The United States could not be indifferent to any conflict between the great empires ringing its borders. Should the incident erupt in war, as Jefferson expected, France would be involved under the terms of the Bourbon family compact. Belligerency might be forced on the United States either from its commitments to France or in defense of its own territory. War between the European powers held both dangers and opportunities for the infant republic. On balance, Jefferson thought the opportunities outweighed the risks. A paramount object of the new government, in his view, was to enable the nation to avail itself "of the wars of others to open the other ports of America to our commerce, as the price of our neutrality." As a neutral trader the New World might indeed "fatten on the follies of the old." "Our object is to feed and theirs to fight. If we are not forced by England, we shall have a gainful time of it." This was a dangerous "if," turning on the chance of British conquest of the Floridas and Louisiana. "What a tremendous position would [British] success in these objects place us in! Embraced from the St. Croix to the St. Marys on one side by their possessions, on the other by their fleet, we need not hesitate to say that they would soon find means to unite to them all the territory covered by the ramifications of the Mississippi." On the other hand, Britain might be induced to forego conquests in the Spanish colonies, yield American claims under the treaty, and possibly offer commercial concessions in exchange for neutrality. But if the awful prospect of encirclement materialized, the United States must join in the war on Albion. This, too, might be turned to America's advantage. If he played his cards right, Jefferson thought he could win high stakes from Spain, perhaps the Floridas, perhaps the Mississippi trade. Surveying all the possibilities, the Secretary of State, like a canny broker of the national interest, prepared to negotiate with both sides and, if the developments dictated, sell to the highest bidder.

Such was the advice he embodied in a memorandum to the President on July 12. It was prompted by indirect British overtures in the person of Major George Beckwith, who had been sent to New York by Lord Dorcester, Governor of Canada. While on a similar side-wind of diplomacy a year before, Beckwith had established close connections with Hamilton. He talked to Hamilton now, holding out the bait of a treaty of commerce in exchange for American support against Spain. Hamilton reported to Washington and Jefferson. An essentially non-committal response, conforming to Jefferson's opinion, was agreed upon. Hamilton wished, with Jefferson, to exploit the crisis for America's advantage, but he was far more convinced than his colleague that the advantage lay on the side of connection with Britain. His system was bottomed on peace and commerce with that power; and the Mississippi was a subordinate object. In reporting the government's answer to Beckwith, Hamilton was reassuring on the point of negotiations, and he stepped over official bounds to warn the British agent of the obstacle Jefferson was likely to present. Should the hoped for negotiations occur, Hamilton wished to be informed of any difficulties so that they might be explained away. This was only the first instance of Hamilton's maneuvering behind the back of the Secretary of State. Not only did he disclose to British diplomacy a division of opinion within the administration, but he also offered himself as the channel for thwarting the Secretary's policy toward Britain.

Jefferson moved quickly to implement the policy of inducing Britain and Spain to bid for American guarantees. In the event of war, Gouverneur Morris was directed to assure the British of American neutrality, "*if they will execute the treaty fairly and attempt no conquests adjoining us.*" Jefferson made no mention of an alliance, though Hamilton had improperly hinted that to Beckwith. Nevertheless, Jefferson threatened Spain with an Anglo-American alliance if she failed to heed American demands. David Humphreys was sent to Madrid with instructions for Carmichael. Spain must immediately recognize the American right to navigate the Mississippi. From this point negotiation should proceed to the question of an entrepôt at the mouth of the river, and finally to the cession of the Floridas. Spanish obstinacy would be met by American force, either alone or in concert with Britain; compliance, on the other hand, would secure American friendship and protection of Spanish sovereignty in Louisiana. "In fine," Jefferson said, "for a narrow slip of barren, detached and expensive country [the Floridas] Spain secures the rest of her territory, and makes an ally where she might have a dangerous enemy." To make himself heard in Madrid, Jefferson counted on the friendly persuasions of the French foreign ministry. Short was told to press the Mississippi question at Versailles when, and if, war broke out.

Soon after the dispatch of these instructions to the three foreign capitals, Washington learned that Lord Dorcester contemplated, at the opening of hostilities, a request to the United States for the unmolested passage of British troops through American territory to the Mississippi. What should he say to such a request? Washington put the query to his advisers, in this instance Hamilton, Jefferson, Knox, Adams, and Jay. Hamilton's opinion was hopelessly snarled in narrow points of international law, but it finally came down to acquiescence in the anticipated request. The country could not risk war, least of all against Britain, with whom its interests were closely identified and whose naval power ought to be a protection. Jay's opinion was similar; Adams took a somewhat stronger line; only Knox advised peremptory refusal of the application, though he would not resist if the British marched. Jefferson advised the President to return no answer at all. He was stalling for time to give the mills of diplomacy a chance to grind. Outright rejection of the application would commit the United States prematurely. If time ran out, neutrality could be protected by granting the same privilege of passage to both belligerents. If the troops in Canada marched without our leave, the United States might keep up an altercation with Britain until events should decide whether war or peace was the more advantageous. Fortunately, Washington was not compelled to choose from these divided counsels. The application never came, and the Nootka Sound affair, after a most threatening appearance, was amicably settled in the fall. Thus American foreign policy was pivoted on the chance of an event that failed to happen. Jefferson reconciled himself to the loss of initiative but stuck to the policy.

After the dispatch of diplomatic instructions the second week of August, he accompanied the President on a tour of Rhode Island. The laggard state had rejoined the Union in the spring, and the President wished to welcome it, as he had the other New England states on an extensive tour the previous year. Crowds and ceremonies, dinners and speeches—the tour held little interest for Jefferson. A week passed and he was back in New York, drafting more papers on the foreign crisis and preparing to move his department, with the rest of the government, to Philadelphia. At the end of August he climbed into his phaeton and, with Madison's company, commenced the long journey homeward. They stopped in Philadelphia several days, then proceeded to Georgetown to reconnoiter the site of the future capital. The grandeur of the task, uniting conceptions of architecture and nationality, had an irresistible appeal to Jefferson. He turned his mind to it, and the planning of the capital occupied many of his hours as Secretary of State. From Georgetown to Mt. Vernon, via Fredericksburg to Orange and Albemarle: Jefferson was home on September 19. It was a brief visit, not much longer than the time spent on the road coming and going. Before the oaks curled their leaves in November, he and Madison returned to Philadelphia.

Conflict in Philadelphia

If he must be a prisoner of office, Jefferson was glad he could serve his time in Philadelphia. It was familiar ground. It was civilized beyond any other American city. Where else could he find so many kindred spirits, men who united wit and learning and republican principles? The beloved Franklin was dead now, Hopkinson lingered at the door, but old friends like Rush, Rittenhouse, and Thomson welcomed him into a widening intellectual circle. Philadelphia was a city of doctors—a veritable Edinburgh. William Shippen, whose son Jefferson had shepherded in Europe, taught and maintained an elegant practice; portly James Hutchinson mixed in the rough-and-tumble of politics; Rush and Caspar Wistar were scientists of note; and George Logan, abandoning the profession, had become a pioneer agriculturist on his ancestral estate, Stenton, several miles north of the city, where Jefferson spent many diverting hours. The American Philosophical Society, newly installed in a fine brick building on Independence Square, continued to be the center of many-sided scientific activity. Jefferson was at once reunited in the Society's endeavors, becoming one of its three vice presidents. (In a paper read to the Society in May 1792, Benjamin Smith Barton named the species of a new plant family, *Jeffersonia binata,* now *Jeffersonia diphylla,* not because of his political eminence, Barton said, but because of his pre-eminence in natural history.) Jefferson had complained in New York of the lack of books and libraries. It was much less of a problem in Philadelphia. In the Natural History Museum, the personal creation of the painter Charles Willson Peale, the city boasted a new marvel of science. Here could be seen, and studied, "a vast variety of monsters of the earth and main, and fowls of the air . . . in perfect preservation and in their natural shape and order," "a great collection of bones, jaws, and grinders of the incognitum," ferocious snakes, baboons, and monkeys, Indian scalps, wampum and tomahawks, a six-footed cow and other natural curiosities, together with the portraits of eminent American and French patriots. Peale idolized Jefferson, and added his portrait to the gallery in 1792. The College (soon to become the University of Pennsylvania), William Bartram's botanical garden on the Schuylkill, the Library Company, a wax works, an equestrian circus, even a theater (over Quaker objections) which some thought the equal of Paris houses—Philadelphia was not Paris, but it offered an environment in many ways congenial to Jefferson.

The city had a Quakerish reputation for coldness and reserve, but with the coming of the national government society frolicked in fashion and splendor. Philadelphia, Mrs. Adams said, was "one continued scene of parties upon parties." A young Frenchman who had yet to make his name in the world of letters, François René de Chateaubriand, arrived in 1791 in quest of the Northwest Passage. "A man landing, as I did . . . full of enthusiasm for the ancients, a Cato, who sought everywhere the rigidness of early Roman manners, must have been greatly scandalized on meeting everywhere the elegance of dress, the luxury of equipages, the frivolousness of conversation, the inequality of fortunes, the immorality of banking and gaming-houses, the noise of ball-rooms and theatres. In Philadelphia I might have believed myself in an English town. There was nothing to announce that I had passed from a monarchy to a republic." The President and his lady set the official tone, as high and formal and, in the opinion of some, as regal as before. The Philadelphia Assembly, to which Jefferson subscribed, sponsored a ball every fortnight. More elegant, however, were the soirées of the first ladies of society, Mrs. Morris, wife of the financier, and the beautiful Mrs. Bingham, whose infatuation with French fashion had made Jefferson wince even as he had admired her in Paris. Morrises and Binghams and others of their class were high-toned Federalists, of course, but politics had not yet split society in two. There was still a pleasing levity about it, reminiscent of Parisian drawing rooms before the Revolution. Jefferson might be seen at these splendid gatherings, hair powdered and scented, attired in the finest silks, blue coat, black breeches, ruffled shirt—all in the Paris mode—scattering information, amusing the company with anecdote, and charming the ladies with courtly flatteries.

He had rented a fine, large brick house on Market (High) Street, one of the city's broad thoroughfares soldiered with poplars.

The building occupied by the State Department was only three doors down and across the street; the President's establishment and the Hall of Congress were nearby. Jefferson lived on the third floor of the house for months while it was remodeled to suit his taste and convenience: a stable for five or six horses and adjoining room for three carriages, a long gallery for books, an enlarged dining room and antechamber, a veranda and garden house, and so on. The house was furnished, the gallery filled up, with the things he had acquired in Paris. They arrived, 86 packing cases, in November. Six gold leaf sofas, 44 gold leaf chairs with damask coverings, elegantly decorated tables, mirrors and commodes, blue and crimson draperies, wallpaper, statuary, and other items too numerous to mention, but all suggesting that Jefferson's house exhibited a French style beyond any other in Philadelphia. The cuisine was also French, or as nearly so as he could make it. Good French cooks were scarce, and some of the gourmet tastes he had grown accustomed to were simply unachievable. When Petit finally arrived in July, he searched the city for vanilla without success; Jefferson had to order his stock from abroad. Macaroni, too, came in this way. Guests at Jefferson's table were introduced to favorite French recipes he had copied in his own hand. His tastes were expensive. Wine was always a major item in his budget; similarly, the hired servants, who numbered four or five, and the expenses of the stable. The house rent was £100 a quarter— more than he had paid in New York. His salary never covered his expenses. The books were balanced quarterly by other income, chiefly from the sale of tobacco.

When the Secretary returned to his desk, he realized that he could not, for the present, pitch his hopes in foreign affairs on the doubtful blessings of a European war. The revised calculus of foreign policy which he made in the winter months was especially notable for the reliance placed on American commerce as a weapon of diplomacy. Jefferson had long been impressed with the potential of this weapon, whether directed to a state of war or of peace in Europe. But only with the coming of the national government could its potential be exploited. Jefferson proposed to use it, extending or withholding commercial favors as circumstances offered, with a view to advancing both the wealth and the security of the United States.

The course was set in several reports prepared between the opening of Congress in December and the following February. One of these, the Report on the Mediterranean Trade, had only an indirect bearing on Jefferson's European diplomacy. The Algerine problem remained as Jefferson had left it in Paris. All he could do was to lay before Congress the options available: war, tribute, and ransom. He continued to advocate the first, which, if successful, would permanently open the Mediterranean to American trade and command respect for the new nation in Europe. A year and a half later Congress chose the other course, voting funds to ransom the captives and to secure peace by a modest—an unrealistically modest—tribute. The riches of the Mediterranean trade continued to elude the Americans.

More central was Jefferson's Report on the Tonnage Law, prepared for the President, who later submitted it to Senate. The Tonnage Act of 1789 levied a per ton duty on foreign ships entering the ports of the United States. Although it discriminated in favor of American ships, it placed the vessels of all foreign nations on the same footing. Madison had attempted to introduce a discrimination between the vessels of nations in and out of treaty with the United States. This conformed to the abortive commercial policy of the Confederation, and Madison could rightly argue that the new government was committed to its realization. His object, of course, was to combat British restrictions while at the same time encouraging American shipbuilding and navigation. Failing in 1789, Madison resumed the fight, not once but twice, in the next session. Jefferson followed the debate in Congress with deep interest. American independence from British commercial bondage had been the goal of his strivings in France, and he hoped now to reach it through the power of the national government to legislate a system that had heretofore floundered on the contingencies of foreign treaties. From behind the scenes in the State Department, he worked to promote commercial discrimination. He and Madison defended the policy as, in fact, one of reciprocity, since it only aimed to counter British discriminations, particularly in the West Indies, and would be modified as these discriminations were removed. But to Georgia and South Carolina planters dependent on British ships and credit, to importing merchants and shippers tied into the old channels of trade, to warm friends of Britain, above all to treasury men eying the revenue collected on British tonnage and imports—to these assorted interests, Madison's project of a navigation act looked like a declaration of commercial war on Britain, and it was conveniently sidetracked during the political maneuvers over residence and funding.

Britain's gain was France's loss. The French chargé d'affaires, Louis Guillaume Otto, watched the proceedings in Congress with mounting concern. He shared with Jefferson the expectation that the revolution in American affairs, together with the Revolution in France, would bring to fruition the commercial alliance between the two countries. But the Tonnage Act, renewed in 1790 after patient deliberation, struck at the hopes of liberalization by placing the friendly commerce of France on the same basis as a commerce loaded with pains and penalties, hence, in effect, discriminating against France. In December, Otto lodged a protest with the Secretary of State. The Act, his government charged, violated the treaty of commerce of 1778, specifically by its failure to reciprocate the tonnage exemption allowed to American vessels in French ports. The protest was made under the threat of retaliation.

Jefferson reacted quickly, finishing his report within five days after he received Otto's letter. He disagreed with the Versailles construction of the treaty. The exemption from alien tonnage duties was not a special favor to the Americans but merely an application of the "most favored nation" principle, and no equivalent had been asked of the United States because it levied no such duties when the treaty was made. But diplomacy could not be threaded through the needle's eye of legal technicality. Jefferson faced a dilemma. If in the spirit of the treaty the point was conceded to France, the United States would be compelled to grant the same tonnage exemption to other countries with whom it had "most favored nation" treaties. Yet the consequences of refusal, jeopardizing the favorable standing of American commerce in France, were equally bad. Jefferson sought escape through an act of Congress that would place French vessels on the footing of natives in consideration of favors granted by the decrees of 1787 and 1788. No other nation could claim the same privilege without equal concessions. Once again he was backing into a navigation act.

Hamilton opposed the recommendation. The concession was too

high a price for the favors France had granted, and since it appeared gratuitous and voluntary, it would excite unfriendly feelings in Britain. Moreover, as he reminded Jefferson, the fund from the tonnage duty was mortaged to the payment of the public debt. "I feel a particular reluctance to hazard anything in the present state of our affairs which may lead to commercial warfare with any power . . . ." Hamilton's policy was locked in the vise of the funding system. The revenue of British trade filled the Treasury. Until the United States could manufacture for itself, Britain was its surest supplier, almost its only creditor, and its best market; and for the sake of American peace and commerce and credit, Hamilton was reconciled to the subordination entailed by the British connection. In his advocacy of the Constitution three years before, he had hailed the prospect of vigorous commercial retaliation to force the opening of British ports to American trade. Now he sang a different tune, one not unfamiliar to Jefferson but one he had not expected to hear in the highest quarters of the new government. For the first time, in the winter of 1790–91, Jefferson and Hamilton confronted each other on a major issue. For Jefferson it involved the question whether the United States would persevere in the liberal commercial policy of the American Revolution or, trapped in the web of fiscalism, acquiesce in British maritime dominion. The President approved the Secretary's report and sent it to the Senate. There Treasury influence defeated his recommendations. Jefferson thus had to scramble with the French as best he could. With Otto he took a hard line, justifying the tonnage law under the terms of the treaty, but softened the blow by holding out the prospect of a navigation act. Otto understood Jefferson's predicament. The estimable minister, he had earlier reported to Montmorin, "ought to be particularly dear to us by the affection he never ceases to show for France and by a sort of enthusiasm he communicates to persons in office for everything which concerns us."

All the while Jefferson remained hopeful for the emancipation of the French commercial system. The breakdown of French authority in the West Indies and the real distresses of the planters there gave new grounds, as he instructed Short, to press the American claim to freedom of trade with the islands. The ultimate object was a new treaty that would create a virtual commercial union between the two countries. In March 1791, when Franco-American amity was embarrassed by the tonnage question, Jefferson achieved a diplomatic *tour de force* by his official response to the homage the National Assembly of France had rendered to Benjamin Franklin. Perhaps never before in history had the death of a private citizen of one country been so solemnly mourned in another. It was a dramatic testimony of the bonds between the two nations, Jefferson said, and ought to become the occasion for cementing their friendship. Joining in these sentiments, the National Assembly called for the negotiation of a new treaty of commerce. Moustier's long-awaited successor, Jean Baptiste Ternant, departed for the United States three weeks later. Unfortunately, as Jefferson soon learned, he was not instructed to negotiate the promised treaty. And even before he arrived in the summer, it became apparent that Franco-American commerce, far from approaching a new epoch, was sliding back into an old one. It was more than Short could do to maintain previous concessions, let alone obtain new ones. The French merchants had never accepted the liberal commercial policies of ministers like Vergennes and Montmorin, philosophers like Condorcet, physiocrats like Dupont, and Americanists like Lafayette. They reaped few rewards from the American trade. Indeed, Short wrote Jefferson, they regarded it as a losing proposition, only made worse by the tonnage law, and they pointed to the evidence of seven years to show that every sacrifice made by France had done nothing to shake British supremacy in the American market. The Revolution brought these merchants of the commercial cities to power in the National Assembly. Jefferson had not understood this bourgeois animus of the Revolution. Freedom at home, protection abroad, was the merchants' cry. The evidence first came on the crucial article of tobacco. The Farmers-General was abolished, but the Assembly imposed a discriminatory duty, nearly prohibitive, on tobacco carried in American ships. Jefferson was outraged: Britain had not ventured so far! French nationalism seriously embarrassed his commercial diplomacy. He did not abandon it, but he would never find the opportunity to bring it to fruition.

Of course, Britain was incorrigible. Another key report, in December 1790, dealt with the failure of Gouverneur Morris's informal mission in London. With the passing of the Nootka crisis, this diplomatic kite fell to the ground. It had been useful nevertheless, removing all doubts as to the disposition of the British ministry. Jefferson concluded that the United States should not again renew propositions for a treaty of commerce or an exchange of ministers or for the delivery of the Northwest posts. The President concurred in this analysis, which he transmitted in a special message to the Senate in February.

At about the same time, Jefferson sent Congress his Report on the Cod and Whale Fisheries. Couched in strong language, it appeared to the British consul in Philadelphia, reporting to Whitehall, "to have been designed as the introduction or a series of proceedings calculated to promote measures very hostile to the commercial interests of Great Britain." The plight of the New England fisheries was a familiar subject to Jefferson. British bounties and trade restrictions caused much of the difficulty. "The *ex parte* regulations which they have begun for mounting their navigation on the ruins of ours, can only be opposed by counter regulations on our part." Jefferson viewed the French, on the other hand, as "co-operators against a common rival." "Nor is it in the interest of the fishermen alone, which calls for the cultivation of friendly arrangements with that nation; besides five-eights of our whale oil, and two-thirds of our salted fish, they take from us one-fourth of our tobacco, three-fourths of our live stock . . . a considerable and growing portion of our rice, great supplies, occasionally, of other grain . . . ." The fisheries had an added importance from their connection with sea power and the carrying trade. Jefferson suggested various remedies; in the main, he called for a system of counter regulations, prohibition opposed to prohibition. The British consul was not wrong in his estimate of Jefferson's report: it was part of a concerted campaign against the British commercial system.

The first gun had been sounded in Washington's annual message to Congress. One paragraph, drafted by Jefferson, recommended measures to foster the independence of American commerce and navigation. The reports on the Morris mission, the tonnage act, and the fisheries followed in rapid succession. Their cumulative effect, together with pressures exerted by interested groups in foreign trade, led a committee of the House to report a bill barring the importation of non-British goods in British vessels. Like previous attempts at a navigation act, the bill was sidetracked, principally on the Federalist plea for negotiation; and on February 23 the whole subject of commercial policy was referred to the Secretary of State for study and report. The threat of retaliatory legislation prompted the British government, at long last, to commence normal diplomatic relations with the United States; and that in turn (the news reached Philadelphia when the navigation bill was in second reading) took all the steam from retaliation. The new minister, George Hammond, arrived in August. The leading objects of his mission were, first, to obtain satisfaction of British demands under the treaty of 1783 as the *sine qua non* of withdrawal from the Northwest posts; and second, to combat the movement against British commerce. Hammond was apprised of the "extremely discordant" rift in the administration and he would seek to exploit it.

Jefferson held no illusions of British readiness to enter into reciprocal commercial arrangements with the United States. Before Hammond arrived he came into possession of a highly secret report on London's policy. This report, which was submitted in January 1791 by the Committee of the Privy Council for Trade and Foreign Plantations, gave a flattering picture of the American trade since the Revolution. Britain's share of the shipping had increased; the tonnage and tariff duties of the United States were actually less by about one-half than those levied by the states individually in 1787; British exports to the former colonies had fallen off about one-sixth, but the loss was more than offset by expanded markets in other North American colonies; and since imports from the United States had declined drastically, the balance of trade was even more favorable than before the war. The report might have been titled, "How To Grow Rich by Losing an Empire." It was a thorough vindication of the architects of British policy in 1783–84. "Government has indeed not been altogether deceived—the new system [of the Constitution] is certainly more favorable to British navigation. And there can be no doubt from the proceedings of Congress, and from all that passed in their debate during the last two sessions, particularly in the American Senate, that a party is already formed in favor of a connection with Great Britain, which by moderation on her part, may perhaps be strengthened, as to bring about in a friendly way, the object in view." The object: to detach the United States from France and to strengthen the connection with Britain. Negotiation was advised chiefly as a check on retaliatory measures, for nothing was to be conceded; as for the West Indian trade, it was not even open for discussion. Such were Hammond's instructions, as Jefferson surmised, with respect to commerce.

The Privy Council report confirmed with facts and figures Jefferson's opinion of British obduracy. He had recently learned that the Commissioners of the Treasury refused to admit as American vessels naturalized in the United States though built elsewhere. Of small moment in time of peace, the regulation would injure American neutral trade in time of war. Earlier, during the Nootka crisis, he had had a nasty taste of British impressment of American seamen. What perhaps disturbed him most in this show of British power, however, was the confession in a state paper of the highest importance of collusion with a party in the government of the United States. Many things in the early months of 1791 persuaded him that such a party existed and that Hamilton was its leader—the secret British intelligence added a crowning touch. Without knowing of Hamilton's machinations with Beckwith, Jefferson soon suspected his liaison with Hammond, and became convinced of Hamilton's unlimited hostility to his commercial diplomacy. The financial system was probably at the bottom of it. Indeed, for the first time, Hamilton's measures began to assume the character of a system in Jefferson's mind, a system permeated with fiscalism, and from what he had seen of France and learned of Britain, fiscalism was the parent of monopoly and oppression. The funding of the national debt was a necessary measure, but government should not be lashed to the predatory wheels of credit. The system was very partial in its distribution of benefits, enriching a few eastern merchants and speculators, holding nothing material for southern planters dependent on foreign markets, and, in general, checking the nation's agricultural expansion. In foreign affairs it tied the government into British politics. Despite new British encroachments on American commerce, Jefferson wrote to Monroe in April, Treasury takes the line of "passive obedience and non-resistance, lest any misunderstanding with them [the British] should *affect our credit, or the prices of our public paper.*" He was nevertheless sanguine about the prospects of commercial legislation, and he began to gather data for the report

Congress had charged him to prepare. Surprisingly enough, his principal aide in this enterprise was a Treasury officer, the Pennsylvanian Tench Coxe, an ardent economic nationalist who worked both sides of the street, Jefferson's and Hamilton's, not only because he had an eye for the main chance politically, but also because there were two distinct sides of economic nationalism, one basically fiscal, the other basically commercial, one oriented to credit, the other to markets, one British-centered, the other non-British and mainly French.

Commerce was a subordinate issue in Jefferson's Spanish diplomacy. The danger from Spain came not from strength but from weakness, which had led the colonial governors into alliances with desperate Indians and frontier adventurers and had made Louisiana and the Floridas convenient pawns on the chessboard of European politics. Yet the illusion of North American empire persisted in Madrid. A new policy came to the rescue of the old. By land grants, commercial privileges, and promises of freedom, Spain now sought to attract colonists from the borderlands. The policy struck Jefferson as rather like "settling the Goths at the gates of Rome." He wished a hundred thousand Americans would accept the invitation: "It will be the means of delivering us peaceably, which may otherwise cost a war. In the meantime we may complain of this seduction of our inhabitants just enough to make them believe we think it very wise policy for them, and confirm them in it." While still dangling the prospect of a commercial treaty before the Americans, the Spanish court declined to discuss the southern boundary or the Mississippi question. Jefferson's position was just the reverse. He was willing to discuss trade provided it in no way prejudiced the principal point to be gained, the navigation of the Mississippi. In March he boldly sketched the plan of a four-power commercial entente against Britain. To Short, Carmichael, and Humphreys, in Paris, Madrid, and Lisbon respectively, he proposed a concert along the lines of the navigation act lately debated in Congress. Could the three European countries be induced to adopt similar measures, Jefferson said, "it will form an epoch in the history and freedom of the ocean." "We would not wish to be declared the excitors of such a concert of measures," he continued, but by appealing to motives of self-interest the American ministers should "insinuate it with all the discretion and effect" they could muster. It was a long shot. Nothing came of it. In the succeeding months Jefferson's perturbations of the Mississippi question got through to the Spanish court. Two commissioners were sent to Philadelphia, and at the end of the year Jefferson learned of the court's desire to negotiate all differences in Madrid. He leaped at the opportunity, instructing Short to join Carmichael in a special mission to Spain.

Thus, over a period of twelve months, the renewed initiative in diplomacy opened promising lines of negotiation with the major powers. Whether they would reach their objects remained to be seen. Jefferson was most eager with respect to Spain. Success there would be a boon to his country commensurate with the pain and trouble of serving it. He was less hopeful of overcoming British recalcitrance; but in sending a minister His Majesty's government took the first forward step in Anglo-American relations since 1783. Continued firmness on the American side, backed by a navigation act, would surely bring results. Jefferson was little alarmed by the frictions and frustrations of the French alliance. The decree of the National Assembly calling for a new treaty of commerce, Ternant's arrival, the final establishment of a constitutional government in September—these were good omens. He was, however, disturbed by Washington's peremptory choice of Gouverneur Morris, "a high-flying monarchy man," as United States Minister to France. The Senate reluctantly consented, and Versailles hid its fears. Poor Short, awarded the consolation prize of The Hague, just as he was ordered to Madrid, vented his rage in a stream of letters to Jefferson. Thomas Pinckney, of South Carolina, soon undertook the ministerial duties at the Court of St. James's. The diplomatic establishment was at length completed.

All these developments occurred against a background of mounting tension abroad and chronic disturbance on America's frontiers. The French Revolution convulsed Europe and plunged Santo Domingo, the queen of the Indies, into a devastating slave insurrection against the French masters. If in the shifting sands of international politics the monarchs of Spain and Britain united against France, or if France, with her hands full at home, invoked the American pledge to defend her West Indies possessions, the peace and security of the United States would be jeopardized. Early in December, just as Jefferson was beginning talks with Hammond and preparing for the Spanish negotiations, reports reached Philadelphia of General St. Clair's shattering defeat by the Ohio Indians. The same fate, though less disastrous, had befallen General Harmer the year before. St. Clair's orders were to push the Indian boundary further west, which was sufficiently provocative in itself. But every American, beginning with the President and Secretary of State, believed the British incited this cruel warfare; and as they grew bolder with each success, so too did the Spanish in the Southwest. While still in New York, the government had neogtiated a new boundary with the troublesome Creeks in Georgia. But land speculators and adventurers encroached on the receding lands of the Indians. Jefferson consistently advocated a strong national line, including the use of force against intruders on the Indian lands, even if it collided with state authorities. More was involved than the rights of the Indians and the paramount authority of the national government with respect to them, for Spain exploited every disturbance on the brawling southern frontier. Indeed, no sooner had the news of St. Clair's defeat reached these quarters than the newly appointed Spanish governor, the Baron de Carondelet, dropped the pacific immigration policy of his predecessor and returned to the older policy of Indian alliance to check the Americans. The result proved embarrassing to Jefferson's Spanish negotiations, just as the Indian warfare in the Northwest spread a pall over his discussions with Hammond. Peace on the American frontiers was thus involved in peace with Britain and Spain.

The conduct of foreign affairs was inevitably enmeshed in domestic politics. The question of commerical discrimination, for example, could not be considered apart from its bearing on competing interests at home. Nor were Jefferson and Madison oblivious to these considerations. The policy was calculated to win friends in every section—from shippers chafing under the restraints of British navigation acts, from struggling manufacturers, from planters seeking wider markets—and it appeared to offer an alternative to the narrowly based fiscal program around which Hamilton's political strength was organized. It was too early to speak of parties and party conflict in 1791, but the administrative rivalry between Jefferson and Hamilton grew in intensity. The interconnections of issues of commerce and diplomacy and finance, the lack of firm policy direction from the President, the confused division of authority between the principal departments created a fluid situation which drew men who were temperamentally and politically averse into one collision after another as they competed for initiative and influence in vital areas of national policy.

The course was probably irreversible after the conflict in February 1791 on the question of the United States Bank. In the second of his great reports to Congress, Hamilton had recommended the creation of a national bank modeled on the Bank of England and combining, like that century-old institution, public convenience with private advantage. As the financial arm of the government the bank would assist in the collection of taxes and the management of the public debt. It would serve as a ready lender to the treasury. It would also constitute a fund for mounting a large paper circulation in the form of bank notes, thereby multiplying the active capital of the country and stimulating its trade and industry. This was particularly necessary in the United States, Hamilton argued, because of the deficiency of coin and credit, the retarded state of manufactures, and the settlement of the West, which soaked up capital without producing any early returns. One great bank, incorporated and fortified by the government but propelled by private enterprise and the desire for profit, would lift the economy over its difficulties. The bank was a logical corollary of the funding system, and that system alone made it possible. The government would furnish but one-fifth of the total capital of $10,000,000, the rest being subscribed by private investors, three-quarters of it in the form of public securities. The convertibility of the funded debt into bank stock would both enhance its value and augment "the *active* wealth of the country." In effect, the tiny knot of public creditors would be privileged to incorporate as a bank, empowered to engage in commercial business, and blessed with the largest account in the economy, that of the federal government. Congress enacted the Bank bill virtually as Hamilton had drafted it. Although it was strongly contested in the House of Representatives, where Madison led the fight, only twenty votes could be mustered in opposition, and fifteen of these came from the southern states.

Jefferson watched the progress of the bill with deep concern. Its

432

introduction coincided with the remonstrance of the Virginia assembly against the assumption of state debts. That measure was designed to "perpetuate a large monied interest," the memorialists charged, and it must eventually produce one of two evils, "the prostitution of agriculture at the feet of commerce, or a change in the present form of federal government, fatal to the existence of American liberty." Hamilton greeted these resolutions with gestures of defiance: "This is the first symptom of a spirit which must either be killed or will kill the constitution of the United States." Jefferson, on the other hand, after making allowance for their origin in Henry's "implacable" hostility to the new government, viewed the resolutions as a manifestation of widespread fears aroused by Hamilton's measures. He did not doubt the constitutionality of assumption; but it was precisely on this ground, where Virginia drew the line, that Madison fought the Bank bill in Congress and that Jefferson, upon its passage, sought its defeat at the hands of the President.

The constitutional question being brought to the fore for the first time, Washington was uncertain whether to sign or to veto the bank charter. While it was true that even the old Congress, under the Articles of Confederation, had chartered a bank, it was also true that the convention of 1787 had pointedly declined to include the power of incorporation among those enumerated in the Constitution. The question, therefore, became one of construction. The Attorney General's opinion, the first sought, was adverse. Jefferson's was then requested. With the crisp and categorical logic of one who had entered the realm of constitutional certitude, Jefferson presented a *prima facie* case against the bill. The Constitution was laid in the principle of the Tenth Amendment, then in the course of ratification: "all powers not delegated to the United States by the Constitution, nor prohibited by it to the States, are reserved to the States respectively, or to the people." No power to incorporate a bank was delegated. It could not be found in any of the enumerated powers, as Jefferson proceeded to show, nor could it be legitimately inferred from either of the general clauses appealed to by the bank's advocates. The power of Congress to provide for the "general welfare" was only a power to lay taxes for that purpose; the power to enact laws "necessary and proper" for carrying the enumerated powers into execution must be construed strictly or it would "swallow up all the delegated powers, and reduce the whole to one power." Jefferson acknowledged the *convenience* of a national bank but not its *necessity* for effecting the clearly defined objects of the Constitution. "To take a single step beyond the boundaries thus specially drawn around the powers of Congress," he warned, "is to take possession of a boundless field of power, no longer susceptible to definition." Not only would the creation of a bank breach the limits of the Constitution; it would also, "for a shade or two of *convenience*, more or less . . . break down the most ancient and fundamental laws of the several states," such as those against monopoly, fraud, mortmain, and alienage. No shadow of doubt crossed Jefferson's mind; yet, in conclusion, he counseled the President to bow to the will of Congress unless in his judgment the bill was clearly unconstitutional.

Washington turned finally to Hamilton, presenting him with Jefferson's and Randolph's objections for rebuttal, and meanwhile asked Madison to draft a veto message should his decision go against the bill. In a long and discursive opinion, which lost none of its force from its endless windings, Hamilton refuted every constitutional objection. Through it all ran one fundamental idea: "That every power vested in a government is in its nature *sovereign*, and includes, by *force* of the *term*, a right to employ all the *means* requisite and fairly applicable to the attainment of the *ends* of such power, and which are not precluded by restrictions and exceptions specificied in the Constitution, or not immoral, or not contrary to the *essential ends* of political society." This doctrine of *implied powers* blurred the sharp line Jefferson had drawn between the ends and means of government; every power he had strictly defined opened itself to almost limitless development. The utility of a national bank in the execution of the powers of Congress to tax, to borrow money, regulate commerce, and so on was easily shown. And it was decisive in Hamilton's judgment. Washington concurred. On February 25, within two days of receiving the opinion, he signed the bill chartering the Bank of the United States.

The issue expressed the fundamental conflict between Jefferson and Hamilton on the Constitution. Both wished a strong Union, but one sought its strength in the trust of the states and the people, the other in the amplitude of the general government's powers. Hamilton thought the Constitution "a shilly shally thing," too frail to survive. It needed every possible reinforcement. Jefferson feared an overreaching centralism. He believed in federalism as the only secure foundation of the Union; his antagonist, though he took the name Federalist, had little faith in the principle and worked incessantly to shrink the powers of the states. One viewed the Constitution as a superintending rule of political action; the other viewed it as a point of departure for vigorous statemanship. One believed that private interest corrupted public good; the other—the ghost of Mandeville looking over his shoulder—exploited selfish interests for national purposes. Jefferson, with a profound conviction in the powers of free men, was radical in the ends he pursued but generally conservative in his choice of means. Hamilton was the reverse. Untouched by Jefferson's vision, the means he employed—of organization and innovation, energy and command—disclosed a radical tendency which in time must produce radical effects.

The debate inevitably took shape on the constitutional question, but it involved much more, of course. Jefferson would almost certainly not have enunciated such a niggardly view of federal powers had he approved of the Bank as a financial institution. Tied into the funding system, the Bank would give permanence to the reign of debt and speculation and fraud. "We are ruined, Sir," he wrote to Monroe, "if we do not overrule the principles that 'the more we owe, the more prosperous we shall be,' 'that a public debt furnishes the means of enterprise,' 'that if ours should be once paid off, we should incur another by any means however extravagant' etc. etc." He took the commonsense view. A public debt was no more of a blessing than a private one, except to creditors and stockholders whose profits were wrung from the people in taxes. The Bank of the United States was only an abomination of the evils Jefferson ascribed to all banks of note issue. He loosely equated bank notes payable on demand with paper money, like the bills of credit of Revolutionary times. Either one drove out gold and silver and introduced fluctuating values into the life of trade. Commerce and industry were insecure when suspended, in Adam Smith's phrase, "upon the Daedalian wings of paper money." Bankers and public creditors had no stake in the prosperity of agriculture, commerce, and manufactures, except as they produced taxes and interest to enrich themselves. Banks ran people into debt, supported luxury and extravagance, created delusory values and delusory expectations. They did not create capital, as Hamilton implied, but diverted it from useful economic pursuits into gambling ventures in paper and stock. Jefferson recoiled from "the spirit of gaming," "the rage of getting rich in a day," which he observed in the speculative scramble for the stock of the Bank of the United States in the summer months. His friend Benjamin Rush described Philadelphia as "a great gaming house." Some men lost their reason, others their appetites, the good doctor noted with clinical interest. "The great speculators become talkative and communicative or dull, sullen, silent, and peevish." The depravity of the scene bore no resemblance to Jefferson's vision of a virtuous republican society.

He was probably most alarmed, however, by the political effects of the Bank charter. Piled on top of funding and assumption, it increased the sectional imbalance. The southern states, whether wisely or foolishly, felt little interest in a national bank. Few southerners acquired stock in it. It was designed for the convenience of merchants, not planters and farmers. The excise tax on whiskey, passed at about the same time in order to service the assumed debt, also spread resentment in southern and western quarters. The Anti-Federalist spirit still hovered over Virginia politics. Jefferson decided a week or so before he advised rejection of the Bank bill that the government should not risk further alienation of southern opinion. "There is a vast mass of discontent gathered in the South," he confided to one correspondent, "and how and when it will break God knows. I look forward to it with some anxiety." And to others he did not disguise his basically political approach to the issue. "Whether these measures be right or wrong abstractedly [sic]," he said of Hamilton's program, "more attention ought to be paid to the general opinion." "Government being founded on opinion, the opinion of the public even when it is wrong, ought to be respected to a certain degree." Treasury was "driving too fast." The precipitancy of the bank measure, when other means of financial management were available, proved it. Jefferson could not approve of the measure in the abstract or in the face of the Constitution; even more, he was convinced it was politically unsound, and he would not, in the interest of administrative harmony, take any responsibility for it.

Nor would he place himself at the head of the growing opposition to Hamilton's system. Madison was the recognized leader of this opposition; and in the reciprocity of influence between the two Virginians, it was Madison who held the edge at this time. Jefferson's position in the administration, his undiminished confidence in the President, and his aversion to political combat acted as powerful restraints. He made no effort to dramatize or publicize his quarrel with Hamilton. He was apprehensive, nevertheless, and began in February quietly to insinuate his concern to prominent men in different parts of the Union. To Robert R. Livingston in New York: "Are the people in your quarter as well contented with the proceedings of our government, as their representatives say they are?" To George Mason in Virginia: "What is said in our country of the fiscal arrangements now going on?" And after Congress adjourned early in March, to Harry Innes of Kentucky: "What is said with you of the most prominent proceedings of the last Congress?" Such inquiries were usually followed by appeals to his friends to exert their influence to change the complexion of Congress. Probing opinion, Jefferson also sought to shape it.

In the spring he was unwillingly thrust on the stage as a political gladiator against his old friend John Adams. The controversy between Edmund Burke and Thomas Paine on the French Revolution supplied the background. American opinion of the Revolution, favorable at the outset, had already begun to divide when the English polemics reverberated across the Altantic in the early months of 1791. Burke's *Reflections on the Revolution in France* captured conservative feelings for the cause of order, tradition, church, privilege, and royalty in France. No sooner was Paine's vigorous democratic reply, the first part of the *Rights of Man*, received on this side of the water than arrangements were made to publish it. John Beckley, Clerk of the House of Representatives and political accomplice of his fellow Virginians, had this purpose in hand, but before sending the pamphlet to the printer, he lent it to Madison, who then passed it on to Jefferson with instructions to return it to Beckley. But that gentleman called before Jefferson had finished. He promised to hurry Burke to his grave and then send the murderous tract to Jonathan B. Smith, whose brother was to print it. Smith was a stranger to Jefferson; so, as he later explained, "to take off a little of the dryness of the note" transmitting the pamphlet, he expressed his pleasure "that something was at length to be publicly said against the political heresies which had of late sprung up among us, not doubting but that our citizens would rally again round the standard of Common Sense." It was a casual piece of courtesy. He was dumbfounded the next week when, "without the least information or suspicion it would be published, out it comes . . . at the head of the pamphlet." Jefferson thus appeared before the public as the unqualified champion of the French Revolution. He could not disavow the endorsement, for he had indeed written it, and he rejoiced in Paine's triumph. He decided to remain silent, except as private explanations might ease his embarrassment.

The embarrassment came less from the association with Paine and his radical opinions than from the veiled reference to the "political heresies" of the Vice President. Though the gentleman was unnamed, no one mistook Jefferson's object. He candidly acknowledged it to Washington and Madison. "I tell the writer [Adams] freely that he is a heretic, but certainly never meant to step into a public newspaper with that in my mouth." The alleged heresies had filled the columns of Fenno's *Gazette* for months. The *Discourses on Davila*, as Adams called these rambling reflections on government, attacked democratic ideas of equality, progress, and popular rule. Political man was a creature of passions, Adams said, above all "the passion for distinction." To channel this selfish passion into works for the public good was the principal problem of government. A system of checks and balances founded on the different orders of society was necessary. Because of inequality of birth, of wealth, and talent in every society, a division between the few and the many was inescapable. Liberty could be had only by erecting a political balance between the two orders of *aristocracy* and *democracy*, then adding, as a presiding genius and symbol of eminence, the third order of *monarchy*. Adams's casual use of these galvanizing abstractions made him an easy target. While he did not mean, as some inferred, that nobility and kingship should be instituted in the United States—a majestic president and a high-toned senate satisfied him—his image of American government was plainly derived from the English model that Paine satirized as "this, that, and t'other." The theory had been stated earlier in the ponderous *Defence of the Ameri-*

can Constitutions, excoriated by Jefferson's friends in Paris. Now Adams was riding his hobby horse again, this time with priestly admonishment against the overbearing influence of democracy drawn from the "levelling" and "fanaticism" of the French Revolution.

Adams was hurt by Jefferson's thrust. Major Beckwith expressed astonishment that the American Secretary of State could recommend a political tract branded as seditious in England. Hamilton was "open-mouthed" against his colleague, viewing the prefatory note as an attack on both the British and American governments. As everywhere men declared themselves partisans of Burke or Paine, it became apparent that the ideological division existed in the government of the United States.

While the controversy simmered in the press, Jefferson went off on a month-long "botanizing excursion" he had earlier arranged with Madison. Their itinerary took them from New York up the valley of the Hudson to Lake George and Lake Champlain, across to Vermont and down the Connecticut River Valley, returning by way of Long Island. This was fresh country to the Virginians. The *flora* and *fauna* of the region, its scenic beauty, historic sites of Revolutionary fame—Saratoga, Ticonderoga, Crown Point, Bennington —all this was interesting to Jefferson and Madison. As they bounced along in leisurely fashion, their conversation must have turned occasionally to politics, and they probably did not overlook the opportunity to make political inquiries in the towns where they stopped. In the view of some New York Federalists the secret purpose of the Virginians' tour was to cement an alliance between the Madisonians of the South and the Clintonians of the North. The collapse of the powerful family alliance of the Schuylers and the Livingstons in January had weakened the Federalists. Robert R. Livingston, the Chancellor, seeing that the landed aristocracy he represented was becoming but a poor relation of the moneyed aristocracy headed by Hamilton's father-in-law, Philip Schuyler, joined forces with the popular Clintonians and helped elect the venturesome upstart Araon Burr over Schuyler to the United States Senate. Hamilton was troubled by this development; and the information he received from a friend in New York "that there was every appearance of a passionate courtship between the Chancellor, Burr, Jefferson and Madison, when the two latter were in town," did nothing to ease his anxiety.

Hamilton and friends imagined political intrigue where there was none. Governor Clinton, still the leader of the state despite his Anti-Federalist past, seems not to have noticed the touring Virginians, nor did they call on him. If any alliances or bargains were struck, with Livingston, Burr, Clinton, or anyone, they were very secret indeed, for they left no trace. The excursion bore fruit not in deep-laid schemes but in the innocent delights of science and agriculture, as in a grove of sugar maples Jefferson planted at Monticello.

When he returned to Philadelphia in the middle of June, the political pot had come to a boil. Caught in the polemical battle between "Burkites" and "Paineites," Jefferson found himself shamed on one side, applauded on the other. "Some persons here are insinuating that I am Brutus, that I am Agricola, that I am Philademus, etc., etc. I am none of them . . . ." The letters of "Publicola," emanating from Boston, caused the most interest. They defended the alleged "political heresies" of the Vice President, defended the English constitution from Paine's sarcasm, and lashed out at his extreme views of popular sovereignty and democratic revolution in which the Secretary of State was implicated. By his endorsement of the *Rights of Man,* Jefferson seemed, said Publicola, "like the Arabian prophet, to call upon all true believers in the Islam of democracy to draw their swords, and, in the fervor of their devotion, to compel all their countrymen to cry out, 'There is but one Goddess of Liberty, and Common Sense is her prophet.' " Publicola added to Jefferson's chagrin, for this latest gladiator was thought to be John Adams.

After Adams went home to Braintree in July, Jefferson addressed him a long letter. "I have a dozen times taken up my pen to write you," he began, "and as often laid it down again, suspended between opposing considerations." He then gave his account of the painful episode. Although they differed on the best form of government, he hoped they might differ as friends in the privacy of their own conversation. Nothing had been further from his intention than public controversy, and lest Adams suspect him of masquerading in the press under a Roman name, Jefferson declared he never had and never would. Adams's reply was friendly. He was grateful for Jefferson's letter and gave entire credit to his motives. "It was high time that you and I should come to an explanation with each other," he wrote. "The friendship that has subsisted for fifteen years between us without the smallest interruption, and until this occasion without the slightest suspicion, ever has been and still is very dear to my heart." With respect to political ideas, Adams was not aware that he and Jefferson had quarreled or, for all that, ever had a serious conversation on the subject. If Jefferson assumed that he, John Adams, wished to introduce aristocracy and monarchy into the United States, he was entirely mistaken. Adams denied authorship of *Publicola*, omitting to disclose its true author, his son John Quincy, with whom Jefferson had perambulated in Paris a few years before, now a promising young attorney in Boston. The New Englander wrote as always with an open heart; yet he could not suppress a reproach to Jefferson for giving circulation to a false or misleading interpretation of his writings. Jefferson might better have left the matter there; but, believing he was "as innocent *in effect* as . . . in intention," he sought to absolve himself entirely. Had it not been for *Publicola*, he said, his opinion of Paine's book would have gone unnoticed; furthermore, in alluding to "political heresies," he had not had Adams's writings in view. This little piece of mendacity aimed at closing the wound had the opposite effect. Jefferson protested too much, as Adams suspected. He made no answer, nor did the old friends correspond again for several years.

As the fog of political rhetoric thickened, neither man could see the other except as an enemy of the American republic. Jefferson, for his part, became a victim of volatile abstractions like "aristocracy" and "monarchy." He was correct in perceiving that a change had come over John Adams. If his system was basically unchanged, he had grown distrustful of the people, shifted the accent from democracy to the privileged orders, and, indeed, by his obsession with these European categories disclosed a treacherous intellectual flaw. It was impossible to separate the Adams of *Davila* from the reactionary tendency of Burke's *Reflections*. Yet Adams was not, even now, an uncritical advocate of the old order against the new, however frightening its appearance. His polititical vocabulary blurred the difference for Jefferson and many others. Adams, for his part, grew more distrustful still of the fickle populace and felt that Jefferson,

441

from his delusions about the French Revolution, had become a tool of democratic malcontents and Francophiles bent on running him down as an Anglican, aristocrat, and monarchist.

Jefferson placed Adams's heresies, bad as they were, on a different plane from Hamilton's. Many years later he recalled a dinner-table conversation with these men in the spring of 1792. Of the English constitution, Adams observed, "Purge that constitution of its corruption, and give to its popular branch equality of representation, and it would be the most perfect ever devised by the wit of man." Hamilton interjected, "Purge it of its corruption, and give to its popular branch equality of representation, and it would become an *impracticable* government: as it stands at present, with all its supposed defects, it is the most perfect government which ever existed." The exchange stated their differences exactly, Jefferson thought. "The one was for two hereditary branches and an honest elective one: the other, for an hereditary King, with a House of Lords and Commons corrupted to his will, and standing between him and the people." Believing in the power of ideas, Jefferson believed these theoretical preferences had a profound bearing on the future of republican government in the United States. And beginning to discover, with Madison, "a sympathy between the speeches and the pockets" of congressmen, he formed the conviction that the sophisticated "corruption" of the funding system looked to the subversion of American liberty. Hamilton denied this, of course. But he made no secret of his political convictions. In August he talked freely to Jefferson about the Vice President. He disapproved of *Davila* not because the opinions were wrong but because their publication was imprudent, tending to weaken confidence in the administration. "I own it is my own opinion," he declared to Jefferson "though I do not publish it from Dan to Beersheba, that the present government is not that which will answer the ends of society . . . and that it will probably be found expedient to go into the British form." In testimony concerning his arch rival, Jefferson scarcely qualifies as a disinterested witness; but in this instance, as in others, his own report of Hamilton's views tallies with friendly witness. The enduring effects of the Hamiltonian system lay in the directions of nationalism and capitalism. On this long view the idea of its "monarchical tendency" has often seemed the work of a demented imagination or an unprincipled demagogue. But effects and intentions, retrospective judgments and judgments in historical context, are entirely different things; and Jefferson, acting in the circumstances of his time, making the linkages authorized by the works, utterances, and sympathies of his political foes, fairly detected an animus in the proceedings carrying the government beyond the republican limits of the Constitution.

The Jefferson-Adams *contretemps* injected the ideological issues of the French Revolution into American politics. Henceforth, though the problems of the government were as mundane as before, they were increasingly colored by the hopes and the fears, the twin hysterias of enthusiasm and denunciation, sent up in the progress of an event far from American shores. Jefferson, though he regretted the personal embarrassment, thought the public controversy surrounding Paine's book was salutary. It helped "to separate the wheat from the chaff," he wrote to Paine. It dramatized the connection between the American experiment and the French Revolution. "I consider," he had earlier said, "the establishment and success of their government as necessary to stay up our own, and to prevent it from falling back to that kind of half-way house, the English constitution." He hoped "so beautiful a revolution" would "spread through the whole world." And despite revolutionary excesses that soon repelled other partisans of the cause, despite the career of exile and death that opened before many of his friends in Paris, despite evidences of official distemper toward the United States, Jefferson remained a champion of the French Revolution. The commitment was justified, but the interpolation of Revolutionary ideas and passions into American politics did as much to obscure issues as to clarify them. "The characteristic difference between your revolution and ours," the Comtesse de Houdetot suggested in a melancholy letter, "is that having nothing to destroy, you have nothing to injure, and labouring for a people, few in number, uncorrupted, and extended over a large tract of country, you have avoided all the inconveniences of a situation, contrary in every respect." Jefferson knew this truth, but the winds of European doctrine often clouded his view of it.

While thus thrust into public prominence as the champion of revolutionary democracy, Jefferson continued his intramural quarrel

443

with Hamilton. The New Yorker took the opinion against the national bank as a personal affront. The ambitions of Jefferson and his friends were first disclosed, he thought, on a bill placing the Secretary of State next in line to the Vice President in succession to the presidency. The bill failed in January 1791; revived a year later, Hamilton spurred the Federalists to defeat it as "a measure of self-defence." (Succession was fixed upon the president pro tempore of the Senate.) In his Report on the Establishment of a Mint, Hamilton opposed Jefferson's plan to conform the unit of coin to the unit of weight. Here, too, he was successful, though in other respects his ideas on mint and coinage agreed with Jefferson's, whose influence he acknowledged. He believed Jefferson's personal animosity was aroused by disagreements such as these, the small with the large; and perhaps it was, for Jefferson proceeded in the following months to snipe at Hamilton's department. When the Treasury's second officer, the Comptroller, died in April, Jefferson at once urged Washington to appoint Tench Coxe to the place. Hamilton suspected Coxe's loyalty, the more so from Jefferson's pushing his candidacy. Washington followed Hamilton's advice and nominated the Auditor, Oliver Wolcott, a stern Connecticut Federalist. Several months later the Postmaster General resigned. Jefferson espoused Paine's appointment to this office within Hamilton's department. "It seemed to be a fair opportunity for a declaration of certain sentiments," Randolph observed to Madison. In Jefferson's eyes the Post Office had great importance as the only means of circulating political intelligence. The snail-like movement of the mails retarded public discussion and posed a serious challenge to popular government. Believing he could speed up the mails, anxious, too, to lessen the influence of the Treasury, Jefferson coveted the Post Office for his own department. He was not so naïve as to expect the President to nominate Paine, or Paine, happily tooting his horn in Paris, to accept. The Massachusetts Federalist Timothy Pickering got the job. But Jefferson kept his sights on the Post Office.

It was in connection with his effort to improve the circulation of news that he helped Madison and Henry Lee in 1791 to establish a national newspaper at Philadelphia under the editorship of Philip Freneau. The uncrowned poet laureate of the American Revolution lived on the edge of poverty in New York by writing for the *Daily*

Advertiser. Madison and Lee, former classmates of Freneau at Princeton, interested Jefferson in finding an office for him. The part-time position of translator clerk became vacant when the government moved to Philadelphia. In March Jefferson offered the post to Freneau. The annual salary was only $250, but the duties of the clerkship were so inconsiderable, he said, "as not to interfere with any other calling the person may choose." It was understood that Freneau wished to establish his own newspaper, and had already made tentative arrangements to do so in Monmouth, New Jersey. Retirement to the Jersey moor appealed to him—the din of war and politics and cities had never suited the poet's true nature. He declined Jefferson's offer. But Madison refused to accept this decision as final. He was impressed by Freneau's combination of literary and polemical talents, and to enlist these in the republican cause, rather than simply to help an old friend and deserving poet, now became a major object. Preceding Jefferson to New York in the spring, he talked with Freneau there. "The more I learn of his character, talents and principles," he reported, "the more I regret his burying himself in the obscurity . . . chosen for himself in New Jersey." Madison persisted, and Freneau finally agreed to go to Philadelphia to talk with Jefferson. But stopping in New Jersey along the way, he never reached the capital city. Jefferson got his first glimpse of him, a smallish man of forty years with a touch of sadness in his deep dark eyes, from across a boarding house breakfast table in New York in May. Nothing developed then; but Madison, with Lee's assistance, resumed the negotiations in July. Jefferson added his persuasions. And Freneau, hesitant and torn between competing desires, finally agreed to trade the quiet seat in Monmouth for the prospect of fame and fortune in Philadelphia. In August, Jefferson appointed him to the clerkship, and the *National Gazette* commenced publication on the last day of October.

Because of the political storm that some months later raged around the *National Gazette*, Jefferson's motives in attending its birth assumed unexpected importance. He recognized that the republican cause, as he defined it, was making no headway in Congress and not much in the administration. Hamilton and his followers were in command and, though the President was a steadying influence, there was no limit to which they might go. Jefferson thought it necessary, therefore, to go outside the government, broadcast the issues, and form a responsive public opinion. What was needed, he told his son-in-law in May, was a national journal that "might go through the states, and furnish a Whig vehicle of intelligence." Fenno's obsequious gazette was, in Jefferson's opinion, "a paper of pure Toryism." Benjamin F. Bache's *General Advertiser* provided a mild republican antidote in Philadelphia, but, a daily, it was not suited to national circulation, and Bache declined Jefferson's overture to make it "a purely republican vehicle" for general distribution. He wished by a *national* gazette to penetrate the public mind, articulate the issues of the government in Philadelphia, and interpret European events. The plan of publishing extracts from the *Gazette de Leide*, briefly tried with Fenno, had not been forgotten. Jefferson offered Freneau access to the foreign newspapers of the State Department. But the establishment of such a newspaper was only half the battle. To get it into the hands of the people throughout the Union was the more difficult part; and so Jefferson was attentive to seemingly small matters of post offices, post roads, and postal rates, as well as a willing solicitor of subscriptions to the new *National Gazette*.

The newspaper was not begun as a party organ, for no *party* centered on the "republican interest" had as yet been organized; nor was it begun with Jefferson's auspices, for he had no editorial supervision of the newspaper and the money came from Freneau's former employer in New York. Of course, knowing Freneau's reputation as a "good whig" and a plain-speaking and hard-hitting journalist, Jefferson could rely on the *National Gazette* to combat the "political heresies" afloat in the government. Only in this sense can his intervention be described as partisan. But as the conflict within the government deepened, as the press dramatized it in bolder and bolder terms, the *National Gazette* contributed immensely to the rise of the Republican party and to the public recognition of Jefferson as its leader.

Struggles with Hamilton

It had been a torrid summer in Philadelphia. On September 2, 1791, Jefferson paid ten dollars for an odometer, fixed it to the phaeton, and journeyed home with Madison, making precise notations of the mileage from place to place along the route. He was a grandfather now. Martha and her husband and seven-month-old baby Anne were living at Monticello. The arrangement was temporary, but Jefferson would see to it that they never strayed far from his fireside. While in Philadelphia he usually wrote home every Wednesday, alternately to Randolph, Martha, and Polly; and from them he exacted the same punctuality, so that the post could complete the circuit every three weeks. But neither post nor loved ones lived up to his expectations. His letters dwelt on many things: housekeeping, the nursing of infants, news of friends abroad (to Martha especially), politics, farming, tobacco markets (for Randolph's benefit), the weather and seasonal events of frogs and bluebirds and strawberries (especially for Polly, his "botanical and zoological correspondent"). "Tell me when you shall have peas, etc., up," he had written Polly at the first hint of spring, "when every thing comes to table; when you shall have the first chickens hatched; when every kind of tree blossoms, or puts forth leaves; when each kind of flower blossoms." Not a breeze blew, not a flower bloomed, at Monticello uninteresting to him. He was there only a month and took Polly away with him. Now a lovely girl of thirteen, Polly was ready, like her sister before her, to receive the polished graces and literary refinements of Philadelphia.

The route traveled by the Virginians passed through Georgetown, close by the site of "the Grand Columbian Federal City." As became his habit, Jefferson stopped to witness its progress. This was not a casual interest. From the first Jefferson acted as the President's chief assistant in the planning and supervision of the capital city. Details relating to the purchase and sale of property, the procurement of laborers, machinery for cutting and polishing stone, even the determination of place names, received Jefferson's attention in the close liaison he maintained with the three-man federal commission on the site. Of course, the design of the city and its buildings stirred his imagination. His first suggestions were included in a comprehensive series of notes prepared for the President in August 1790, after the passage of the Residence Act. Construing the statute in all possible latitude, he proposed that sufficient land be acquired for a capital city, not simply a seat of government. The nation that had declared its own principles, formed its own government, cast its own future, ought to erect its own capital—on a scale and in a style consonant with its civic ideals. Many thought the idea ludicrous, especially in a situation as remote and unpromising as the falls of the Potomac. Jefferson helped the President to determine the exact location of the city within the constitutional "ten mile square"—several thousand acres between Rock Creek and the eastern branch of the Potomac—and to enlist the interest of the landowners in its development. The city envisioned in his early notes would be generously laid out in streets at right angles, in a checkerboard pattern, as in Philadelphia. A restriction he thought, should be placed on the height of houses, as in Paris: "it keeps the houses low and convenient, and the streets light and airy, fires are much more manageable . . . ." And he objected to the "disgusting monotony" and inconvenience produced by a uniform setback of houses and buildings. A rough sketch, made in March, was the germinal conception of the mall, the location of the capitol and executive mansion, with surrounding walks and gardens.

Major Pierre Charles L'Enfant, the French engineer who had served under Washington in the war, arrived on the Potomac about this time to lay off the city under the commission's direction. At L'Enfant's request Jefferson forwarded such plans of cities as he possessed—cities he had visited in France. But none was comparable, in his opinion, to "the old Babylon" Penn had re-created in Philadelphia. The Frenchman did not agree. The rectangular plan lacked, he said, "a sense of the real grand and truly beautiful." In June, L'Enfant unveiled his splendid scheme of radiating axes and cardinal points, together with lavish gardens, monuments, fountains, and a cascading waterfall forty feet high under the base of the Capitol. L'Enfant incorporated Jefferson's idea of a central mall, but as with everything else raised it to the nth dimension. Jefferson would have preferred more of the simplicity of Philadelphia and less of the grandiosity of Versailles. But he put aside his reservations and joined with the President in approving the L'Enfant plan. It was incredibly ambitious, indeed quite impossible of execution in the manner the egocentric Frenchman demanded. Not a lot should be sold, he argued, until the public buildings, parks, and avenues were provided; yet without the income from real estate very little could be built, and in the meantime last-ditch opponents of the Potomac capital might prevail. Thus began the conflict between L'Enfant and the commissioners, the dreamer and the realists, which rapidly threw the whole enterprise into confusion and uncertainty.

The first lots were sold at auction when Jefferson stopped at Georgetown in October. A month later the commissioners reported that L'Enfant, without a stitch of authority, had demolished a bothersome house belonging to a prominent citizen. It was apparent, Jefferson advised the President, that L'Enfant must either co-operate with the commission or be dismissed. But the temperamental engineer regarded the commissioners as a set of unprincipled politicians and speculators. Jefferson valued L'Enfant's services, and he was as interested as any man in the creation of a national capital attuned to national ideals; but law and politics, finance and administration, set limits to conceptions of grandeur. The conflict mounted to a climax in February 1792. L'Enfant's arrogance became intolerable, and Jefferson had the painful task of informing him, on the President's orders, his services were at an end. A rocky road still lay ahead.

The next step, the design of the Capitol and the President's House, also absorbed Jefferson. He wished the former to be built on one of the ancient models, like the Virginia Capitol. Architect prizes were offered for both buildings. For the President's House, he submitted, anonymously, his own porticoed and domed design based on the Villa Rotunda of Palladio, but the prize went to the professional architect James Hoban. James Thornton, an amateur like himself but less imitative of classical models, won the competition on the Capitol. Jefferson was captivated by Thornton's plan: "It is simple, noble, beautiful, excellently distributed, and moderate in size." Many thought it immoderate, however. Jefferson called in a group of architects for advice. One of them, Stephen Hallet, made the necessary alterations in scale. This was in July 1793. Jefferson's contribution to the shaping national capital, though but an episode of his tenure as Secretary of State, was perhaps more gratifying than any of his major undertakings.

Traveling from Georgetown though "five days of northeast storm," Jefferson arrived in Philadelphia on October 22, just two days before Congress convened. Polly was soon settled with a housekeeper and tutors. "She has made young friends enough to keep herself in a bustle," Jefferson informed her sister. Among several items of unfinished business claiming the Secretary's attention was a report to Congress arising from the patent application of one Jacob Isaacks for a method of distilling fresh water from the sea. The first superintendent of patents did not fully subscribe to the principle of the system. He questioned that ingenuity is "spurred on by the hope of monopoly," and thought "the benefit even of limited monopolies . . . too doubtful to be opposed to that of their general suppression." Few patents were applied for, fewer still granted—only thirty-seven during Jefferson's tenure—partly because he scrupulously guarded the privilege and investigated every claim to satisfy the statutory test of originality. In the case of Isaacks, Jefferson called in Rittenhouse and the Doctors Hutchinson and Wistar to observe demonstrations of the elaborate apparatus (a still and furnace fed with hickory logs) that had been set up in his office. This galaxy of philosophers concluded after five separate tests that Isaack's discovery marked no advance over methods already known for rendering sea water potable. The patent was denied. Jefferson's lengthy report reviewed the history of this subject, of so much interest to a seafaring nation, and proposed that the approved method of distillation be described and illustrated on the back of clearance papers given to shipmasters, with the request that all trials be reported to the Secretary of State. Although his interest in new inventions was insatiable, the care he bestowed on this and other patent claims was demanded by a jealous statute. Partly through his efforts Congress simplified the system in 1793 so as to permit the issuance of patents without the test of originality or usefulness and on the sole responsibility of the Secretary of State. Registration replaced investigaton, which overcame an intolerable burden at the price, to Jefferson's chagrin, of widening the opportunity for limited monopolies.

The year 1791 closed in a perfect siege of business. Jefferson was readying his report on commerce. There were renewed negotiatons with each of the powers. L'Enfant, public lands, Indian affairs—the latter, especially involved much time and trouble. Jefferson supported the campaign afoot against the Ohio Indians, but after giving them a good drubbing, the government should adopt, he thought, the more humane and economical policy of bribes. The cost of St.

Clair's expedition "would have served for presents on the most liberal scale for one hundred years; nor shall we otherwise ever get rid of an army, or of our debt." St. Clair's terrible defeat in November, necessitating still another expedition, buttressed his opinion on this point, as well as on the superiority of militia to regulars in frontier warfare, an opinion involved in his fears of standing army and debt. Indian affairs, primarily, caused the President to consult collectively with department heads toward the end of the year. The cabinet as a convening body was born. Increasingly thrown together with Hamilton in these meetings, "like two cocks in a pit," as Jefferson later said, the result was to intensify the rivalry between the secretaries.

Among the early subjects discussed in the cabinet none was more important than the line to be pursued in the negotiations with the British minister. George Hammond was a cocksure young man who had served his diplomatic apprenticeship at several of the European courts including Versailles, where Jefferson had had a casual acquaintance with him. He presented his credentials in November. Informal talks began. Hammond would have liked to continue these exchanges across the table; but Jefferson, averse to mixing the politeness of conversation into hard-headed diplomatic maneuver in this instance, quickly switched the negotiations into the more formal medium of written communication. He made short work of wringing from Hammond the admission that his instructions gave him no leeway with respect to commerce. What remained—it was enough —was the settlement of the issues left over from the treaty of peace. Hammond's instructions were clear: he was to obtain the execution of those articles of the treaty dealing with unpaid debts and Loyalist property as the *sine qua non* for the abandonment of the Northwest posts. On December 15 Jefferson handed Hammond the American "assignment of breaches." They were basically two: not only the posts but also the slaves carried off by the British after the cessation of hostilities. Much was made of this second grievance in the South (Jefferson had lately received a resolution of the Virginia assembly on the subject) partly because it took off some of the odium attached to the southerners on the point of the debts. Hammond agreed to furnish a counterstatement of the British position. With the cards on the table, negotiation might proceed.

Weeks, then months, passed, and nothing came from Hammond.

Jefferson suspected Hamilton's interference. At a cabinet meeting near the end of December, Jefferson had stated his intentions of recommending commercial retaliation against Britain in the report slated to go to Congress. "Hamilton opposed it violently," he subsequently wrote, "and among other arguments, observed that it was of more importance to us to have the posts than to commence a commercial war." Struck by the force of this reasoning, not wishing by commercial threats to wreck the negotiations if they held hope for the surrender of the posts, Jefferson agreed to defer the report he had promised, at least until Hammond filed his answer. From the moment this was decided in Hamilton's presence, the British minister studiously put off the counterstatement. If Hamilton had actually tipped the government's hand, it was probably not the first time, Jefferson noted. "It was observable, that whenever, at any of our consultations, anything was proposed as to Great Britain, Hamilton had constantly ready something which Mr. Hammond had communicated to him, which suited the subject and proved the intimacy of their communication; insomuch, that I believe he communicated to Hammond all our views, and knew from him, in return, the views of the British court." Jefferson felt he had again been taken in by Hamilton, whose connivance with the British minister seriously embarrassed American diplomacy. At length the President lost patience with Hammond and told Jefferson to jog him. He did so at the assembly honoring the President's birthday. Hammond delivered the statement on March 5.

The bulky memoir charged that the United States had wantonly violated the treaty from the first with grave injuries to British subjects, which were detailed in five appendices. Ninety-four charges were cited, none of them documented. "I flatter myself, my Lord," Hammond boasted to Grenville, the Foreign Minister, "that this Statement will be found . . . to contain a body of proof so complete and substantial as to preclude the probability of cavil and contradiction on the part of this government." How wrong he was! Jefferson worked nearly eight weeks on his rebuttal of Hammond, amassing quantities of data from public records and public officials, reducing them to order, and finally writing a diplomatic note of 17,000 words, plus elaborate appendices, the whole running to 250 manuscript pages, six times the length of the British memoir. It was a masterful performance, conceded even by his enemies when it was later made public.

Jefferson wrote as the American Secretary of State, not as a disinterested analyst. The memoir, while exceedingly vauable as history, ought to be read, above all, as a brilliant piece of advocacy. He did not scruple to shade the evidence within the perimeters of truth and honor. He did not refrain from fruitless recriminations. An acrimonious tone pervaded the whole. Such had been the style of Anglo-American relations, and Jefferson's production did nothing to change it. But it answered, with document and testimony, nearly all of Hammond's charges, beyond "cavil and contradiction," then went on aggressively to put the British government in the wrong. Jefferson denied the accusation of perfidy against the United States for failure to execute the article of the treaty which pledged Congress to *recommend* to the states the restitution of Loyalist property. Careful examination of the documents showed that both parties understood the nature of this article, as a sop to English opinion, with no expectation Congress would or could enforce obedience on the states. Congress made the recommendation and, as Jefferson noted in detail, the states complied in surprising degree. The provision against future confiscations of British property had not, contrary to Hammond, been violated in a single instance. It was true that several of the states had violated the fourth article by impeding the collection of British debts. However, there were mitigating circumstances. The debts could not have been paid at once; and certain questions, such as the allowance or disallowance of interest during the war, belonged to the discretion of the courts. Moreover, it could no longer be claimed that legal impediments existed. Jefferson quoted state laws, court decisions, and authoritative testimony to refute Hammond's evidence to the contrary. He was right in the main, though the persistent opposition to British creditors, especially in Virginia, received scant notice in his account. He justified any waywardness on the American side by British infractions of the treaty. Not only had the British government refused to abandon the Northwest posts, as it was obliged to do "with all convenient speed," but in violation of the same article British commanders had deliberately carried off 3000 Negro slaves during the eight months following notification of the treaty. Jefferson's conclusive proof of the latter charge fixed the onus of first breaking the treaty on the British. "It may safely be said then that the treaty was violated *in England* before it was known in America; and, *in America*, as soon as it was known." Yet Whitehall appealed to the retaliatory acts of the states as an excuse for further obstinacy, "and inverting the natural order of cause and effect, alleged that these proceedings of ours were the cause of the infractions which they had committed months and years before."

Hammond was stunned by the memoir. Having gained the upper hand, the Secretary invited the Minister to dinner, and after the cloth was removed they discussed their differences in a familiar way. Hammond said his government had heretofore heard only one side of the dispute; Jefferson's statement placed it on new ground, requiring new instructions from London before he could proceed. Jefferson surmised from the conversation "that it had not at all entered into the expectations of his court that they were to deliver up the posts." The point was pivotal for American policy, of course. Although he did not appreciate the extent to which British occupation of the Northwest was dictated by obligations to the Indians, Jefferson was justified in his suspicion of Whitehall's intentions. In March, not long after delivering his note, Hammond received from London the project for the creation of an Indian reserve and neutral barrier state in the lands above the Ohio. This was the ministry's response to St. Clair's disaster. It was hoped that Hammond's diplomacy would back up the force of Indian arms, and thus bring the Americans around to the British plan for settling the problem. But the plan was wholly unacceptable, as Hammond realized. Nothing could be done with it in the face of Jefferson's memoir. The plan never came to the attention of the American government.

Unfortunately, the force of Jefferson's *coup* was subverted by Hamilton. Several days after the "solo dinner" at Jefferson's house, when he had seemed visibly shaken by the Secretary's thrust, Hammond sent a reassuring report to his government. From Hamilton he had learned that Jefferson's paper did not represent the views of the administration, that its "intemperate violence" was regretted, that the President had not read it, nor had the cabinet agreed to it. This was misleading, in part downright false. Randolph and Hamilton read Jefferson's paper in draft. The latter suggested only one significant change, on the subject of state impediments to British creditors. Randolph, too, criticized his friend's complacent view of this subject and detected "a peculiar asperity" in the note generally. Jefferson sent his colleagues' views, together with his own, to the President, who approved the document as it was written and then submitted to Hammond. Although Jefferson's suspicions were aroused, Hamilton's underhanded conduct on this occasion never came to official notice. Had Washington learned of it, the consequences may well be imagined. Month after month passed, and Hammond made no reply to the American note. "He says, he waits for instructions," Jefferson wrote wearily in 1793, after one of his periodic needlings of the Minister, "which he pretends to expect from packet to packet. But sometimes the ministers are all in the country, sometimes they are absorbed in negotiations nearer home, sometimes it is the hurry of impending war, or attention to other objects, the stock of which is inexhaustible, and can therefore never fail those who desire but that things shall rest as they are." The British ministry buried Jefferson's memoir for a number of reasons, some of them extraneous. But the decision was a tribute to his performance as well as to Hamilton's treacherous interference; for if the former was unanswerable, the latter ensured that no answer was necessary. Nor was one ever given. Jefferson would leave office without resolving a single issue in Anglo-American relations.

He encountered inertia of different kinds in his dealings with France and Spain. Between him and the French minister Ternant, a veteran officer of the American Revolution, roughly of Jefferson's age, communication proved difficult. Both were reserved and circumspect men, to which the Frenchman added unreasoned fears of Jefferson's negotiations with Hammond. The principal object on the American side was a new commercial treaty; but, as already noted, Ternant lacked positive instructions. Under the circumstances Jefferson could do little more than lodge protests against new French restrictions, meanwhile awaiting more favorable developments. But Hamilton saw in the business of a French treaty the opportunity for forcing Jefferson into commercial negotiatons with Hammond. Let Jefferson and Ternant agree on the terms of a treaty, he said, then send it to Paris for approval or disapproval. Ternant was willing. So was the President. "I disapproved of it," Jefferson stated, "observing, that such a volunteer project would be binding on us, and not on them; that it would enable them to find out how far we would go, and avail themselves of it. However, the President thought it worth trying, and I acquiesced." He prepared the plan of a treaty exchanging the privileges of natives and fixing maximum duties on principal articles of commerce. Now it was Hamilton's turn to object. He disliked Jefferson's liberal plan and proposed instead a tariff of duties ranging upwards to 50 per cent on French goods. A treaty on this basis was impossible, as Hamilton well knew. He disclosed his little game at a subsequent cabinet meeting. Since the business of a treaty had been taken up with Ternant, he argued, it ought also to be taken up with Hammond, who was similarly uninstructed. "His scheme evidently was," Jefferson noted, "to get us engaged first with Ternant, merely that he might have a pretext to engage us on the same ground with Hammond, taking care at the same time, by an extravagant tariff, to render it impossible we should come to a conclusion with Ternant: probably meaning at the same time, to propose terms so favorable to Great Britain, as would attach us to that country by treaty." Jefferson promptly dropped the matter, though a commercial treaty with France remained a leading object. Morris was urged to press it in Paris. Jefferson later revived it with Ternant. Pending the submission of his report calling for commercial retaliation against Britain, it was highly desirable to place Franco-American trade on a more liberal footing. Otherwise, either Britain would not be singled out for discrimination or France would fail to reap the rewards. All his efforts were unavailing until war forced revolutionary France to recognize the vital importance of American trade.

Jefferson's heaviest stake was in Spanish diplomacy. A settlement with Spain opening up the Southwest would alone make his tenure in office memorable. On the American side the chance rested with the joint commissioners, Short and Carmichael, in Madrid. In March, Jefferson detailed their instructions. The paper showed more ingenuity than force of argument. Legal, historical, and moral reasons were offered in support of the American boundary claim to the 31st parallel, as provided in the treaty of 1783 with Britain; but Spain was a bystander to this treaty, while under her own accord with Britain she recovered West Florida to the 32nd parallel. Equally specious was Jefferson's plea for the American right to navigate the Mississippi. Here, too, the claim rested on a treaty engagement empty without Spanish recognition, and the dons were neither obliged nor inclined to give it. From this impasse Jefferson flew to the elevated heights of "the law of nature and nations." "If we appeal to this" he asked rhetorically, "as we feel it written on the heart of men, what sentiment is written in deeper characters than that the ocean is free to all men, and their rivers to all their inhabitants?" The right of the upper inhabitants of a river to navigate its whole length to the sea was founded in nature and reason. Indeed, said Jefferson, the segment of the Mississippi occupied by Spain ought to be considered not as part of the river but as "a streight of the sea." He went on to argue that the right to ply the river necessarily gave the right to use its shores—for mooring vessels, depositing goods, and so on. Thus was the venerable doctrine of natural rights mustered into the service of American expansion, making manifest the territorial destiny of the nation as it had earlier made manifest its freedom.

There was justice in Jefferson's position, and he buttressed it with citations to the authoritative texts in international law and to the Roman law of riparian rights; but that the "heart of men" should overrule treaty claims, that a river should suddenly become an ocean strait, that Spanish sovereignty in Louisiana should be washed away in the waters of the Mississippi—all of this only evoked smiles and sneers in Madrid. As feeble as she was in North America, Spain still gloried in empire and still weighed in the scales of European power. It was all the dons could do to suffer the upstart Americans. Yet time was on their side. If reason and justice failed to impress the Spanish court, Jefferson told the commissioners, other means of doing so would not be wanting. "The present turbid situation of Europe cannot leave us long without a safe occasion of resuming our territory and navigation, and of carving for ourselves those conveniences on the shore which may facilitate and protect the latter effectively and permanently." Unfortunately, the vessel carrying his instructions sank beneath the Atlantic, and though the diplomatic pouch was saved, it was many months in reaching its destination. Then, no sooner did the commission begin its work early in 1793 than the balance of power shifted ominously.

Spain was thrown into the scale with Britain, upsetting all of Jefferson's calculations. The Spanish negotiations, so boldly conceived, spun out in tedious charges and counter-charges on the conduct of the two governments toward the Indians. The Spanish governors in the Southwest linked the four major tribes in a defensive confederacy against the American intruders. Carondelet, in West Florida, actively incited the Indians to border hostilities which, in addition to angering Philadelphia, cost Spain the sympathies of many westerners disgruntled with the American government for its failure to secure the navigation of the Mississippi. In time, talk and protest must give way to war; by the middle of 1793, certainly, Jefferson lost hope of averting it. Not even war came to his rescue, however. In nothing he undertook did he meet with greater frustration and disappointment than in his Spanish diplomacy.

Domestic politics grew warm in 1792, lines of division hardened, and the quarrel between Jefferson and Hamilton broke into public controversy. Differences within the administration on foreign policy hastened the development, but it occurred mainly on the issues of fiscal and economic policy. The Report on Manufactures, submitted to Congress in December 1791, furnished the capstone of Hamilton's system. In this brilliant state paper, the manifesto of American industralism, Hamilton showed the advantages to the nation of industrial employments and technology, of a balanced economy embracing manufactures with agriculture and commerce, and of a home market for the varied productions of American enterprise. The principal objections to manufactures were answered in convincing fashion. If a regime of "perfect liberty of trade" prevailed among nations, the Americans might pursue agriculture to the virtual exclusion of manufactures. But, as Jefferson too had said, national policy must deal with an imperfect economic world. Viewed realistically, the goals of national wealth and power can only be attained through industrial manufactures on a large scale. And since this development works against natural currents which, together with fallacious ideas, give an unfortunate predominance to landed enterprise in the United States, the aid and patronage of the national government is required on a comprehensive plan. Banks and funded debt already made provision for investment capital; further inducements should be given to the investment of foreign capital. Labor shortage should be overcome by immigration, by the employment of women and children in factories, and by the liberal encouragement of labor-saving inventions. Roads and canals should be built to facilitate the exchange of products. Nothing would prove more efficacious, Hamilton thought, than a system of bounties: the modest protective duties collected on given foreign imports should be defrayed as subsidies to their domestic competitors. For the authority of the government to engage in these and other activities—export prohibition, drawbacks, inspection of manufactured goods, and so on—Hamilton appealed to the "general welfare" clause of the Constitution.

Jefferson disapproved of Hamilton's Report on Manufactures less as a political economist than as a republican constitutionalist. It never became a clear-cut issue between them. Hamilton's design of an industrial society was much too radical for Congress. It was, in fact, hopelessly unrealistic in 1792 in both its political and economic aspects; and the course of events in Europe soon opened unprecedented opportunities to the nation's foreign commerce, checking the incipient growth of American manufactures for nearly twenty years. So Jefferson was not required to come to grips with Hamilton's Report, and he did not. Its tendency was nevertheless disturbing. He could not help but see it as a challenge to his own system of political economy based primarily on agricultural expansion and the enforced liberalization of foreign commerce. He was not at all averse to simple manufactures of a private, or household, variety, only to large-scale enterprises publicly encouraged against the natural order of things and necessarily partial in the distribution of benefits. His interest in transportation improvements and in mechanical invention, his concern to check the adverse balance-of-payments resulting from overindulgence in imported manufactures, his passionate commitment to economic independence from Britain—in certain respects, at least, Jefferson had better credentials than his rival to espouse the cause of domestic industry and the home market. In theory, of course, he continued to favor an agricultural economy, which was especially conducive to republican virtue and to the diffusion of power among the people. But in another policy context than Hamilton's, modest proposals for the encouragement of manufactures would probably have won his support. As it was, the proposals, far from modest, had to be seen in their relations to other parts of Hamilton's design. Bounties and other aids to manufactures would perpetuate the debt. Reliance on funded debt and bank stock for the provision of capital would further enrich the privileged financial class at the expense of the mass of people. The attraction of foreign capital, from Britain undoubtedly, would add new links to the chain of bondage. For better or worse, the southern states felt little interest in manufacturing enterprise and would, presumably, reap few of the rewards. These would go to the section of the country already favored by the national government with a lavish hand; and the growth of cities and factories in the Northeast would divert the energies of the country from its westward course of empire. Hamilton planned for America as if it were England. Jefferson had a different vision of American society, more austere, more democratic, more spontaneous, more attuned to the unique task of mastering the continent. It was also more realistic in 1792 and for several decades to come; only in the longer run of history would it seem archaic.

Considerations such as these formed the shadowy background of Jefferson's thinking; the foreground was monopolized by the constitutional question which, as in the case of the Bank, was conclusive in itself. Nothing in the Constitution authorized the government to encourage manufactures except indirectly by the levy of duties on imports. Jefferson thought additional duties should be laid equal to the bounties paid by the exporting country. But the government was not free to adopt the Old World mercantilist practices championed by Hamilton. The decision on the extraordinary proposition to aid manufactures under color of the "general welfare" clause would "let us know," he said, "whether we live under a limited or unlimited government." The Bank question, touching an incident to a delegated power, was small by comparison. For Hamilton now meant to establish the doctrine, Jefferson told the President, "that the power given by the constitution to collect taxes to provide for the *general welfare* . . . permitted Congress to take everything under their management which *they* should deem for the *public welfare,* and which is susceptible to the application of money; consequently, that the subsequent enumeration of their powers was not the description to which resort must be had, and did not at all constitute the limits of their authority." The inference was warranted from Hamilton's proposition, and that had no warrant at all in the intentions of the Constitution's framers. What confidence could be placed in a government that transformed a jealously guarded constitution into a boundless charter to legislate for the "general welfare"? Leading Federalists in Congress complained that the southern contingent had conjured up the bugbear "consolidation" to paralyze the government. "The practice of crying out 'this is unconstitutional,' is a vice that has grown inveterate by indulgence." It was selfish, parochial, against the national interest, said Fisher Ames, whose own politics smelled of fish and dripped molasses. The opposite cry, "this is constitutional," also had its dangers. To force a centralizing administered system of economic development on the young country would greatly impair the national consensus. Madison once remarked that the Constitution had two enemies, "one that would stretch it to death, and one that would squeeze it to death." For him, as for Jefferson, death by stretching was the danger in 1792.

On the very day Hamilton presented his Report to the House of Representatives, the *National Gazette* printed one of Madison's occasional articles, entitled "Consolidation." Here was a more penetrating statement of Republican nationalism than any Jefferson himself wrote at this time. Earlier, before the Constitution, the danger had come from the dissolution of the central government; now, Madison warned, it came from the consolidation of the states into one big government. Congress could not regulate the infinitely varied objects of state and local concern in all the latitudes of the American Union. If it made the attempt government must become "self-directed," for the sense of so many millions of people spread over a vast surface could never be collected apart from the provincial organs of government; and, in addition, such an accumulation of powers must be vested in the executive head as to make him a virtual monarch. Governmental consolidation multiplied the causes of dissension among the people, defeating the very object most wanted: "that a consolidation should prevail in their interests and affections." In this view, strict construction and state rights served the cause of one nation. Thus, Madison concluded, "let it be the patriotic study of all, to maintain the various authorities established by our complicated system, each in its respective sphere; and to erect over the whole, one paramount empire of reason, benevolence, and brotherly affection." The alternatives were to consolidate power and divide the people or to consolidate the people and divide power. The latter offered the only sure foundation of national union.

March brought startling confirmation of still other fears—fears evoked by the mania of speculation and monopoly. A financial panic rocked New York and reverberated through the eastern cities. Its principal author was William A. Duer, a former Assistant Secretary of Treasury, a princely speculator in land and stock, Hamilton's bosom friend and his associate in a mammoth manufacturing enterprise. Playing a bullish game with public and bank stocks—by "cornering" them to create a phenomenal rise in prices—Duer borrowed money and contracted purchases on a lavish scale. When he failed to meet his obligations, the stocks collapsed, breaking Duer, sending him to prison, and ruining his numerous creditors. Losses were estimated at three million dollars. "Men are often seen to weep in the streets. Fighting and boxing are common in the Coffee house." Money was scarce. Trade sickened. Public securities slipped to dangerous lows and were, with difficulty, propped up by Hamilton. Nothing like it had been known before in the United States. Jefferson compared the panic to the South Sea Bubble of English fame and, with Republicans generally, blamed it on the Treasury system, which had given ample field to the tribe of speculators. "This nefarious business is becoming more and more the public detestation," he wrote, "and cannot fail, when the knowledge of it shall be sufficiently extended, to tumble its authors headlong from their heights." Once in an age at least, he philosophized, the people seemed "doomed by nature" to receive such painful lessons from "cunning and unprincipled men," and they would, he trusted, "now come about and get back into the tract of plain, unsophisticated common sense which they ought never to have been decoyed from."

The panic aggravated Jefferson's opposition to the Secretary of Treasury. He objected to the measures taken by the Secretary to cushion the shock. Dipping into the government's sinking fund, Hamilton threw $100,000 into the securities market to purchase federal stock at par in order to uphold the government's credit and ease the panic. Jefferson, who sat as a commissioner of the sinking fund, felt the unprecedented action looked primarily to the relief of the speculators. The stocks, he thought, should have been purchased at the depreciated market price so as to expedite the sinking of the debt. He was aware of Duer's Treasury connections but did not directly implicate Hamilton in the speculator's schemes. He accused Hamilton of wrong policy, not of wrong-doing. Yet the Secretary had contributed more than Jefferson realized to Duer's outrageous adventures. The would-be titan's downfall was precipitated by a suit brought in federal court for recovery of a debt in excess of $200,-000, the amount still outstanding in his account with the government as Secretary of the Treasury Board of the old Congress. Oliver Wolcott, the Controller, took this face-saving action when he learned of Duer's precarious situation. Hamilton did not intercede in Duer's behalf; however, for three years he had freely permitted Duer to speculate with money owed to the United States government.

Jefferson could not trace all the ramifications of the panic, but it provided him with as convincing proof as he ever wanted of the nefarious effects of Treasury's alliance with stockjobbers and adventurers. It drew out all his deep-seated fears of a society floated on the treacherous seas of money and privilege. His censure extended to manufacturing enterprise, for it was part of the same movement and must show the same effects. Hamilton and Duer were, in fact, associated with their friends in a great moneyed corporation, the Society for the Encouragement of Useful Manufactures, which was intended to exemplify the wisdom of the Report on Manufactures and attract federal largesse on top of the privileges of its New Jersey charter. SUM and the Report, the Duer panic, the whiskey excise— all brought Hamilton and his policies under mounting criticism in 1792. Despite his financial wizardy, said a New York newspaper, Hamilton had failed to reach "the heads and the hearts of the people." He had inscribed "the hieroglyphs of money" on the escutcheon of liberty and enticed men to abandon "the ordinary walks of life . . . for the golden dreams of speculation." Ironically, the nation was "on the verge . . . of ruin, by reason of prosperity"!

Political alignments in Congress began to assume a definite form in 1792. In March, for the first time, Jefferson spoke of "the heats and tumults of conflicting parties" and introduced the pronouns "we" and "they" into his political correspondence. Madison was still the leader of the "republican interest," but Hamilton and company spread suspicions of the Secretary of State. "Mr. Jefferson," Wolcott reported, "appears to have shown rather too much of a disposition to cultivate vulgar prejudices; accordingly he will become popular in ale houses, and will do much mischief to his country by exciting apprehensions that the government will operate unfavorably." A pamphlet appeared, the first in a long line of diatribes, assailing Jefferson's character and politics. (He consoled himself that he had been spared obloquy for so long, and said that its author did not half so much wish for his retirement as he did.) The press beat the drums of partisanship. The *National Gazette*, after a mild beginning, showed its true colors early in March with a violent attack on the funding system. The rival *Gazette of the United States* screamed "mad dogs," "audacious scribblers," "propagators of calumny," exhausting the vocabulary of political invective.

After Congress adjourned in May, Hamilton unbosomed himself to a friendly Virginian, Edward Carrington. His long letter on the state of the parties, afterwards reiterated in Fenno's *Gazette*, voiced opinions of Jefferson and Madison that would soon become stereotyped in Federalist discourse. As the *locus classicus* of the Federalist image of Jefferson, the epistle to Carrington has immense importance. Hamilton regarded Jefferson as the evil genius of the Virginians' partnership—a partnership in faction "subversive of the principles of government and dangerous to the Union, peace, and happiness of the country." About Madison he was frankly puzzled. Whether his apostasy was the result of Jefferson's influence or the seductions of Virginia politics, Hamilton did not know; but he was sure the older man exerted a strange hypnotic power over the younger, showed a deeper hostility to sound government, and was the more dangerous foe. Jefferson was "an avowed enemy of the funded debt," anxious for any crisis (the recent panic, for instance) that might embarrass the national credit and overturn Hamilton and funding together. Jefferson, with his friend, constantly worked for commercial warfare against Britain; if left to themselves the Virginians would embroil the United States in open war within six months. "They have a womanish attachment to France and a womanish resentment against Great Britain." Indeed, France was at the root of Jefferson's opposition. "In France, he saw government only on the side of its abuses. He drank freely of the French philosophy in religion, in science, in politics. He came from France in the moment of a fermentation, which he had a share in exciting, and in the passions and feelings of which he shared both from temperament and situation." In this intoxicated state, he could not understand the "imbecilities" of government that had occasioned the Constitution, and toward it he entertained "many doubts and reserves." The controversy on the succession bill proved, said the New Yorker, "that Mr. Jefferson aims with ardent desire at the Presidential chair." To realize this ambition the government must be rendered odious, to which nothing could prove more effectual than the subversion of its main source of energy, the Treasury. As yet the enemies of government had enjoyed no success, but failure after failure made them desperate and willing to hazard everything for power. The danger to republican government, Hamilton asserted, came not from men who, like himself, gave it order and dignity, but from political adventurers who thrived on popular fears and faction and anarchy. Jefferson was at the head of the tribe. "I read him upon the whole thus: 'A man of profound ambition and violent passions.' "

The truth or falsity of Hamilton's opinion is of less importance than the fact that he and a growing number of his followers seemed to believe it. Hamilton's doctrine on the Secretary of State not only expressed the basic assumptions of a party but set up an anti-hero for Federalist vilification. William L. Smith, a leading Treasury spokesman in the House of Representatives, provided the first outright example in *The Politicks and Views of a Certain Party Displayed*. The whole complexion of American affairs changed, Smith argued in this anonymous pamphlet, when Jefferson returned from France. Then a system was formed "as wicked, profligate and malevolent as ever disgraced the most corrupt and abandoned government." Its object: to make Thomas Jefferson President of the United States. Adams was easily cornered and demolished as a serious rival, but against Hamilton's splendid qualifications, Smith asked, what had Jefferson to offer? Charm of conversation, military exploits at Monticello, the discovery that the blacks secrete less from the kidneys, the invention of the wirligig chair—these satirical touches left indelible marks on the public image of Jefferson. Lacking legitimate claims on the public, Jefferson resorted to trickery and deception. He raised a "pretended outcry against Monarchy and Aristocracy," took on a "ridiculous affectation of simplicity," and built up a "monstrous system of detraction" in order to persuade the people they were oppressed by the Secretary of Treasury, from whom he would rescue them. As pamphlet and newspaper warfare raged in 1792, Jefferson found himself brought forward—less by his friends than by his enemies—as the "generalissimo" of a political party on which he meant to mount his own ambitions at the hazard of government itself. His fate was sealed in July when Hamilton, alarmed by the whirlwind of criticism, threw himself headfirst into the public prints against his arch rival. Thereafter, willing or no, Jefferson could not escape the leadership role thrust upon him.

It was not a role he coveted in 1792. From the first of the year his thoughts were on retirement, and the heats of politics only increased his longing for the tranquil shades of Monticello. Broaching the subject to Washington at the end of February, he said he was "heartily tired" of the office he had entered reluctantly and with a resolution to quit at the earliest opportunity. When the President, some months before, dropped the hint of his intention to retire at the end of his term, Jefferson decided "to make that the epoch of my own retirement." Washington was distressed to hear this. While reasons obliged him to retire, his example, if followed by the department heads, would send a shock through the public. He alluded painfully to "symptoms of dissatisfaction" that had lately shown themselves. Jefferson seized the opening to press his political views on the President. Treasury was the cause of these discontents, he said. A system had been contrived "for withdrawing our citizens from the pursuits of commerce, manufactures, buildings, and other branches of useful industry, to occupy themselves and their capital in a species of gambling, destructive of morality, and which had introduced its poison into the government itself." It was a fact, he continued, that congressmen "had feathered their nests with papers, had then voted for the laws, and constantly since lent all the energy of their talents, and instrumentality of their offices, to the establishment and enlargement of this system; that they had chained it about our necks for a great length of time, and in order to keep the game in their hands had, from time to time, aided in making such legislative contructions of the constitution, as made it a very different thing from what the people thought they had submitted to . . . ." Washington listened but held his political reserve. He shrank from recognizing the rift between the two secretaries. They were equally necessary to his conception of a government without parties. The resignaton of either one would tend to force a partisan character on the administration and unleash the opposition. With his Olympian conception of leadership, founded in loyalty to himself as the point of harmony and union, Washington seemed not to understand that the differences between the two secretaries went to the root of principle and, accordingly, were irreconcilable.

As the rift deepened, and without relenting in his decision to retire, Jefferson appealed to the President to stand for re-election. The public mind, comparatively calm in February, could not now, in May, endure the shock of Washington's withdrawal. Confidence in the government had slipped dangerously. Jefferson hastily summarized the causes of discontent—debt, excise, banks, panic, corruption of the legislature—hackneyed in the press. It was the belief of the "republican party," he wrote, that Hamilton's measures aimed at "a change from the present republican form of government to that of a monarchy, of which the English constitution is to be the model." The calamitous course might be reversed in the Third Congress, soon to be elected on a more numerous basis of representation by a people at least partially alerted to the issues. Nothing ensured this happy outcome, however; and since the political division in the country tended to run along geographical lines, disunion was a real danger. When we consider, Jefferson said, that most of the original opposition to the Constitution lay in the southern states; that the leading measures have favored northern interests; that the "monarchical federalists" have adopted the very constructions of the Constitution they had renounced in championing it against violent Anti-Federalists; "that the republican federalists who espoused the same government for its intrinsic merits, are disarmed of their weapons; that which they denied as prophesy, having now become true history, who can be sure that these things may not proselyte the small number which was wanting to place the number on the other side?" And this, Jefferson declared to his chief, "is the event at which I tremble, and to prevent which I consider your continuing at the head of affairs as of the last importance." In the final analysis, then, he feared the "monarchical federalists" would produce a reaction to Anti-Federalism, driving the country backwards into anarchy, violence, and disunion. It could not occur so long as Washington was at the helm. "North and South will hang together if they have you to hang on," Jefferson concluded his impassioned appeal.

The question of retirement or re-election, bristling with political thorns, was almost more than Washington could endure. On July 10, just a day before his summer's retreat to Mount Vernon, he took up the subject where Jefferson's letter had left it. After recurring to the reasons he had offered for retirement—ardent desire, physical disability, professions honorably made to his countrymen—he said Jefferson's political fears were greatly exaggerated. He did not believe there were monarchical designs on the government. He was disturbed, on the other hand, by the efforts of opposition newspapers, particularly Freneau's, to stir up discontent. If monarchy came to the United States it would come as a sequel to anarchy and discord, which the newspaper agitation tended to produce. The attacks on his administration were attacks on him, and he resented them. But he doubted that the discontents reached much beyond Philadelphia; so far as he had been able to observe, as on his travels to and from the Potomac, the people were calm and happy. In reply Jefferson went over the ground he had covered before. It was well known, he said, that the funding measures had been carried by representatives and senators personally interested in their passage. With the assistance of Madison and Beckley, perhaps others, he had been compiling the names of this "corrupt squadron," but presumably he did not show the list to Washington, who kept a stony silence on the point. The President defended assumption, however. Jefferson, with most Republicans, argued that the state debts would have been more fairly, cheaply, and easily discharged by the state governments themselves, while the Treasury plan so far inflated the national debt as to make it virtually permanent and to call forth the odious excise. A few stockjobbers grew rich on the taxes extracted from the people. He had prepared a table showing the ratio of public debt to annual revenue for several European countries in given years, from which he concluded, with a good deal of guesswork, "that tho' the youngest nation in the world we are the most indebted nation also." If he showed these figures to the President they made no impression. Finding him decided on the fiscal system, Jefferson refrained from useless argument. Three days later, on July 13, he purchased fiddle strings and muslin, paid his servants, received 1500 half-dimes of the new coinage, and, Maria in tow, followed the President's tracks for Virginia, this time for two leisurely months at Monticello.

But there was no vacation from politics in the summer of 1792. Charge and countercharge, each more reckless than the last, issued from the Philadelphia gazettes, which usually arrived at Jefferson's door in eight days, thanks to the cross-post from Richmond recently opened though his efforts. By dramatizing the divisions within the government, newspapers the country over helped to give partisan tone and character to the electoral campaigns then going on. Jefferson took no part in them. Asked to endorse his old friend Charles Clay, a candidate for Congress, he politely but firmly declined on the personal rule "never to intermeddle with elections of the people." He kept a tight rein on his partisan feelings. Some weeks before he left Philadelphia the heated New York gubernatorial contest between Governor Clinton and John Jay ended in a disputed election. Although "Clintonians" and "Jayites" were practically synonymous with "Republicans" and "Federalists" in New York, Jefferson thought, on the merits of the case, Clinton should decline an ignoble victory. The Governor's reputation as an Anti-Federalist and political manipulator troubled Jefferson. "I really apprehend," he told Madison, "that the cause of republicanism will suffer and its votaries be thrown into schism by embarking it in support of this man, and for what? To draw over the antifederalists who are not numerous enough to be worth drawing over." Though he remained on the sidelines, leaving the leadership to Madison, Jefferson was constantly solicitous for the "cause of republicanism."

Early in August the post brought news of a turn in the political warfare at Philadelphia. Fenno's *Gazette* had taken the offensive and trained its big guns on the Secretary of State. After two opening salvoes announcing that Freneau, the vilifier of the government, was also its hireling, the *Gazette* blasted Jefferson as the author of this wicked experiment, the head of a party, and the secret disturber of the public peace. "Can he reconcile it to his own personal dignity and the principles of probity to hold an office under [the government] and employ the means of official influence in opposition?" The assailant signed himself "An American." Jefferson and his friends

surmised from "the style, matter . . . [and] venom of the pieces"
he was Hamilton. Searching for a means to strike back at his
critics, Hamilton had learned of Jefferson's association with Freneau in the founding of the *National Gazette*. It suited his purpose
exactly. With his rare polemical gifts, Hamilton exploited its hints
of venality, subversion, and abuse of trust, in the process crediting
Jefferson with a larger part in the newspaper's establishment than
was his due, with an editorial influence he never had, and a party
leadership he neither coveted nor possessed. Freneau was crippled
but far from beaten. If government patronage was the issue, he
threw back at his accusers, the pittance he received as translator
clerk was not to be compared with Fenno's income as printer for
the Treasury and the Senate. Before the mayor of Philadelphia, Freneau signed an affidavit swearing that Jefferson had "at no time
urged, advised, or influenced" his establishment of the newspaper or
"ever, directly or indirectly, written, dictated or composed for it."
Hamilton, still under cover of "An American," denounced the statement as equivocal and surreptitiously sent to New York for count-
er-affidavits.

Meanwhile, at Monticello, Jefferson held council with his Virginia confederates, Madison, Monroe, and Randolph, on this startling
turn of affairs. The boldness of Hamilton's attack amazed them. The
National Gazette was fair game, of course, and Freneau's onslaught
had angered Hamilton. But it was another thing for a minister to vent
cabinet dissensions out-of-doors and make a public target of the Secretary of State. Hamilton scored heavily under a crowd of disguises.
Jefferson kept a dignified silence, while his friends put their pens to
work, not only in Philadelphia but in New York, Boston, and other
places. Hamilton soon had his hands full, trading blows with more
scribbling foes than he could count, yet never meeting the one foe
who really mattered. Jefferson's refusal to enter the field of combat
infuriated Hamilton. Seated on his lofty perch, wrapped in the mantle of philosophy, primping himself on his official dignity—how
could Jefferson be revealed for what he was, "the heart and soul of
faction," "the intriguing incendiary," "involved in all the obscurity
of political mystery and deception"! Jefferson was sly, devious, inscrutable—a Machiavellian democrat. Hamilton could neither draw
him out nor trace his tracks. Conclusive evidence incriminating Jef-

ferson in the affair of the *National Gazette* eluded him; and as he busily passed from one journalistic mask to another (Catullus, Scourge, Caesar) Hamilton brandished new accusations. Jefferson had opposed the adoption of the Constitution—a charge Madison quickly refuted by the publication of edited extracts from the accused's letters to him from Paris. Hamilton, alias "Catullus," stamped "treachery" on Jefferson's proposal of 1786 to transfer the French debt to Holland, labeling it a scheme to swindle Dutch creditors for the enrichment of the French treasury. Since the charge was supported by a passage quoted from Jefferson's letter to the Board of Treasury, it could not be treated as windy invective. But Jefferson at once produced his copy of the letter in question (he suspected Duer, secretary of the old board, of putting Hamilton on to the original) which showed that the accuser had doctored the extract passed off as genuine and cleverly twisted the meaning of Jefferson's proposal. If it was treacherous to seek the removal of a source of friction with France, while at the same time pledging to preserve inviolate the faith of the United States to all creditors, then John Adams, who endorsed Jefferson's plan, shared the infamy.

While the battle of the gazettes raged, Washington fussed at Mount Vernon to bring his quarreling secretaries to heel. Like an overindulgent parent, he found it difficult, indeed impossible, to tighten reins of authority so long slackened. His last standoffish interview with Jefferson suggested the problem was graver than he had imagined. No doubt he reflected about it, and pondered, too, Jefferson's letter of May 23; for at the end of July Washington sent to Hamilton a list of twenty-one charges made against him by "sensible and moderate men," charges, in fact, drawn almost verbatim from Jefferson's letter. Hamilton replied at length on August 18. His answers repeated for the most part what he had previously written in public defense of the funding system. On some particulars, for instance the refutation of the naïve idea that bank bills banished specie, Hamilton was clearly right. But since most of the charges turned on questions of opinion and judgment, it was not a case in which one side could be proven right and the other wrong. Hamilton denied that the debt had been "artificially" created, that the country was over-taxed, the excise odious, the Constitution violated —none of these answers touched the real grounds of Jefferson's complaint. In the New Yorker's opinion, speculation in federal securities was beneficial to the mass of citizens since the stock, operating as capital, "promotes among them industry, by furnishing a larger field of employment." The corruption charge was "malignant and false": Hamilton knew of no stockjobbers and paper-dealers in Congress, though many members owned securities. Clearly the question of what constituted improper influence on legislators, or what today would be called "conflict of interest," took a different shape in Hamilton's mind than in Jefferson's; and while the former counted the selfish interests of men a legitimate, indeed an essential instrument of legislation, his rival squeamishly recoiled from this vicious principle. Panderers to the vices of the people were "the true artificers of monarchy," said Hamilton, reiterating the time-worn conservative opinion of democracy. He flatly denied the holding of "monarchical opinions" or their advocacy in the Constitutional Convention. If the institution of hereditary kingship and nobility was the issue, the denial carried conviction; but, of course, the nub of the charge so roundly stated for political convenience lay against the tendency of Hamilton's system to transform the "pure" republican government of the Constitution into something approaching the cherished English model. And on this ground Jefferson and his friends found Hamilton's opinions, measures, and administrative conduct more English than American. The Secretary concluded his long essay with several observations on the alleged inequities of funding in the sectional balance. Even if the benefits lay predominantly in the northern scale, which he doubted, it was no argument against the policy. National credit had to be established regardless of other considerations; the government could not be blamed if forces of a political and economic character caused the benefits to flow more to one section than to another. The entire defense was calculated to appeal to the President. He shared Hamilton's national outlook and, from long acquaintance, could not doubt his loyalty to the Constitution. Moreover, the administration and the country were too far committed to Hamilton's measures for the President seriously to question their merits.

Washington had probably just received Hamilton's letter when, on August 23, he wrote to Jefferson. After alluding to fresh reports of Spanish and British intrigues on the frontiers, he again appealed for moderation and conciliation in his official family. "How unfortunate, and how much is it to be regretted then, that whilst we are encompassed on all sides with avowed enemies and insidious friends, that internal dissensions should be harrowing and tearing our vitals." Without more charity and forbearance, especially on measures fairly decided, he did not see how the government could go on. "And . . . the fairest prospect of happiness and prosperity that was ever presented to man, will be lost, perhaps forever!" Washington addressed a similar plea to Hamilton. Neither of the wayward ministers, despite nods of assent to the patriarch's wisdom, showed a disposition to reform.

Again, but with the added vexation of the journalistic outrage in Philadelphia, Jefferson went over the now familiar ground with the President. Hamilton's system, he repeated, "flowed from principles adverse to liberty, and was calculated to undermine and demolish the republic, by creating an influence of his department over the members of the legislature." Although the danger justified vigorous opposition from him, he had limited himself to private expressions of dissent, neither meddling in legislation (except when "duped" by Hamilton in 1790) nor intriguing to defeat measures he disapproved. He invited the President to compare this example of forbearance with the aggressions against him—in Congress, in the press, in the affairs of his own department. The last of these, touching the administrative rivalry between the two men, was obscured by the pyrotechnics of the gazettes. The public knew little of the intramural issue, and Washington seemed insensitive to it. But it rankled Jefferson, not because his standard of official propriety was higher than Hamilton's, though it was, not primarily because he resented the greater power and influence of the Treasury Department, though he did, but because Hamilton subverted his policy in foreign affairs, "my system," which was founded on the differential treatment of Britain and France. Supposing the President had always concurred in this system, Jefferson thought he ought to know that Hamilton's cabalistic influence forced the country into one exactly the reverse, resulting in the French stab at our navigation and continued British intransigence. On whichever ground Hamilton was judged, his own policies or his opposition to Jefferson's, he was the aggressor. The *National Gazette* episode offered further proof, Jefferson said. He explained his relations with the newspaper, hiding nothing material, praised Freneau as a "man of genius" who merited the modest patronage he had received, acclaimed the freedom of the press, and said the virtues or the faults of Freneau's gazette did not concern him. "He and Fenno are rivals for the public favor. The one courts them by flattery, the other by censure . . . . But is not the dignity, and even the decency of government committed," he asked, "when one of its principal ministers enlists himself as an anonymous writer or paragraphist for either of them?" As to the future, he again stated his determination to retire in March of the next year. "I look to that period with the longing of a wave worn mariner, who has at length the land in view, and shall count the days and hours which still lies between me and it." Meanwhile, he would mind his business, only reserving the right to appeal to his countrymen when he dropped anchor. "I will not suffer my retirement to be clouded by the slanders of a man whose history, from the moment history can stoop to notice him, is a tissue of machinations against the liberty of the country which has not only received and given him bread, but heaped honors on his head." There spoke the conceit of the Virginia aristocrat against the arrogant upstart!

Jefferson lingered at Monticello through most of September. There were the usual cares of family and estate. With habitual optimism he had overestimated the ability of his plantations to meet the scheduled installments on his debt. He sold lands occasionally, and was finally pushed to the awful extremity of selling several families of slaves. (Not wishing to have his name linked publicly with a transaction of this kind, he arranged to have the slaves sold at some distance from their Bedford plantation.) At the same time, looking forward to his retirement, he inaugurated elaborate improvements at Monticello. He had an infant grandson now, Thomas Jefferson Randolph; and little Anne, "with whom even Socrates might ride on a stick without being ridiculous," was the joy of his heart. Her illness, and the new arrival, detained him at Monticello longer than he had expected. On the road at last with Polly, he stopped at Gunston Hall to talk with George Mason, who told him anecdotes of the Constitutional Convention well suited to Jefferson's politics. Hamilton, declared Mason, had "done us more injury than Great Britain and all her fleets and armies." The old Roman died not long after—

Jefferson would miss him. Mount Vernon was virtually next door. Before breakfast the next morning, scarcely time to readjust his political senses, Jefferson sat down with Washington for a long talk.

The two Virginians were more deeply divided than they realized, but neither had difficulty appreciating the yearning of the other for retirement. Washington nevertheless confessed his willingness to make a further sacrifice to the public if necessary. Jefferson assured him "there was but one voice" on this point. As for himself, he would not recede from the decision he had made. After expressing surprise at the extent of the division within the administration, Washington said he wished to put an end to it. As Jefferson reported the conversation, "he thought it important to preserve the check of my opinions . . . in order to keep things in their proper channel, and to prevent them from going too far." Clearly, he did not think things had already gone too far. Clearly, his faith in Hamilton had not been shaken. Jefferson again tried to open his eyes to ministerial domination, corruption of the legislature, and the pantings after monarchy. All to no avail. "He finished by another exhortion to me not to decide too positively on retirement, and here we were called to breakfast."

The discussion was never resumed. The problems it addressed were abandoned to the winds of politics. Back in Philadelphia, Jefferson found the political scene more oppressive than ever. "Party animosities have raised a wall of separation between those who differ in political sentiments," he noted. Old friends, finding themselves partisan foes, crossed the street to avoid unpleasant encounters. Congress reconvened early in November. The less done in this "lame-duck" session the better in Jefferson's opinion, for the Republicans had scored impressively in the recent elections. "I think we may consider the tide of this government as now at the fullest," he wrote to Pinckney in London, "and that it will, from the commencement of the next session of Congress, retire and subside into the true principles of the Constitution." Jefferson saw encouraging signs in, among other things, the House defeat of a Federalist motion to admit department heads into its proceedings, thus crippling Hamilton's ambition to become a kind of prime minister. But the Virginia Republicans spurned Fabian tactics looking to reinforcements in the Third Congress, and impatiently launched a campaign to drive

Hamilton from the government. "Virginia moves in a solid column, and the discipline of the party is as severe as the Prussian," Ames remarked. Doubting the time was right, Jefferson nevertheless cheered the campaign from the rear. He scribbled the objectives on a scrap of paper: divide Treasury (between customs and internal revenue), abolish the Bank, repeal the excise, lower the impost, repeal the irredeemable clause in government securities, place government transactions on a hard cash basis, exclude paper-holders from Congress, and condemn a recent Treasury report. As the campaign went shakily forward in Congress, Jefferson resumed his fencing with Hamilton in the cabinet, and also in the commission on the sinking fund, which he wished to convert from a fund employed to keep securities aloft to one that actually sank the debt.

All the while he was preparing to leave office in March. He gave up the lease on his house and began to pack his furniture. Then, near the end of January, he decided to stay on. "It happened unfortunately," he explained to his son-in-law, "that the attack made on me in the newspapers came out soon after I began to speak freely and publicly of my purpose to retire this spring, and from the modes of publication, the public were possessed of the former sooner than of the latter: and I find that as well those who are my friends, as those who are not, putting the two things together as cause and effect, conceived I was driven from my office either from want of firmness or perhaps fear of investigation." How long he would continue he did not know; it would depend on those who had troubled the political waters. "When they suffer them to get calm, I will go into port." In short, wishing to avoid any repetition of the mistake he had made in 1781, he would not retire under circumstances likely to injure his reputation or the Republican cause. But why at the eleventh hour did this cloud suddenly appear so much larger than before? In fact, it was not. Hamilton, far more than Jefferson, was under attack in January. He faced investigation by Congress; Republican leaders had uncovered (and suppressed for the present) a juicy scandal in his private life; and on the very day Jefferson wrote to Randolph of the change of plans, the Senate, with an assist from the President, gave Hamilton a stinging defeat on the bill to extend funding to the small unassumed portion of the state debts. Could it be that Jefferson was moved by these brightening prospects? Or by the flattering appeals of Republican scribes, who called him "the colossus of liberty"? Philadelphia had become a ghastly inferno, he insisted; yet he found it much too interesting to leave. The demon of politics possessed him even as he yearned for retirement.

That demon drove him hard in the waning days of the Second Congress. Ignoring his earlier counsels of caution and delay, as well as his boasted standards of official propriety, Jefferson secretly joined the Virginia column in its final maneuver to discredit Hamilton. The move took the form of a series of resolutions introduced in the House by William B. Giles, a truculent young Virginian, whose "frothy manners," fondness for drink, and tendency to discourse on "canvas-back ducks, ham and chickens, old Madeira, and the glories of the Ancient Dominion" seemed not to inhibit his talents as a legislative pugilist, which had caused Madison to bring him forward as the Republican champion in the assault on the Secretary of Treasury. Giles's motives were partisan, of course, but they were not unworthy. Hamilton managed the Treasury as a private domain. A million dollars was shuffled between two continents; funds were manipulated at convenience; accounts with the Bank were veiled in obscurity. The President did not pretend to understand these intricate operations; but congressmen opposed to Hamilton's fiscal system, suspicious of his motives, baffled by his methods, demanded a close accounting from the high-handed minister. In a feat of labor his friends described as herculean, Hamilton filed a series of reports vindicating his fiscal management. The Virginians were still not satisfied. Many questions remained unanswered, and besides it would not do to leave Hamilton in command of the field.

Entering the Virginia councils at this point, Jefferson drafted a set of resolutions that indicted Hamilton's conduct and declared him unworthy of his office. It was this indictment that formed the basis of Giles's resolutions—the second set—of February 27. Even Giles could not go all the way with Jefferson. Stripped of the latter's accusations of speculative malice and fraud, the final resolutions arraigned Hamilton for technical violations of the appropriation laws, unwarranted assumption of power in fiscal management, and contempt of Congress. There were grounds for these charges, but the Republicans were drubbed on every count. Jefferson attributed the defeat to the Hamiltonian phalanx of stockjobbers, Bank directors, and devoted partisans, aided and abetted by faint-hearted Republicans. Since the result was predictable on his own reckoning, he had, in fact, committed a grave political blunder. He never acknowledged any connection with the ill-fated resolutions. The Federalists were sure he was the culprit, of course, and from the basest motives. To himself and his political intimates he justified the resolutions, not because he expected them to succeed, but because their rejection would educate the public in "the desperate and abandoned dispositions with which their affairs were conducted." If this was political wisdom, it was a curiously perverse kind. Vindicated at the hands of Congress, Hamilton appeared to occupy an impregnable position at the end of Washington's first term.

The quarrel between Jefferson and Hamilton, after threatening to wreck the administration, ended in perpetuating it for an uncertain term. Washington never offered himself for re-election, but in view of partisan dissensions his withdrawal was unthinkable, and he silently bowed to the inevitable. Jefferson and Hamilton stayed in uneasy harness. The President was much relieved and spoke optimistically of the "coalition" between the two ministers. Jefferson sought to disabuse him of this notion. Neither he nor Hamilton would yield his system and principles to the other. Pulling in different directions, each assured of the other's enmity, each accusing the other of designs to subvert the government—Jefferson to anarchy, Hamilton to monarchy—it was little short of miraculous they were kept in harness at all.

The controversy between them had yet to run its course. Beginning as an internal administrative conflict, associated with competing congressional interests and national ideologies, it assumed a much larger importance when it penetrated the public mind and became the catalyst of party conflict. Where the advantage lay in 1793, it was not easy to say. Hamilton had given direction to the government, aligned it with powerful interests, and the President, as much as he respected the Secretary of State, was committed to Treasury policies. Jefferson began to wonder if perhaps he, the President, had not become Hamilton's captive. On the other hand, for all his influence in Congress and with the executive, Hamilton had revealed himself to be a bungling political artist. The laurels of journalistic combat were frail indeed; they did not win elections, and far from making Jefferson an enemy in the eyes of the American public, Hamilton, like a wayward press agent, built up his rival as the friend and champion of the people. Against the tide of democratic opinion, rising like a force fated in nature, Hamilton was helpless. Power was in the people, in the wholesome energies of free individuals, not in the machinery of government. Forty years later Alexis de Tocqueville wrote of the American democracy: "the grandeur is not in what the public administration does, but in what is done outside it or without it." Jefferson understood this genius of democracy, Hamilton never.

The Ordeal of Neutrality

The year 1793 made its entrance to roars of acclaim for the victorious armies of revolutionary France. After a most disturbing appearance, the "conspiracy of kings" marshaled in the invading forces of the Duke of Brunswick had been turned back, and the newly proclaimed republic took the offensive, vowing never to rest until the fires of "liberty, equality and fraternity" set the whole of Europe ablaze. Jubilation swept the country. John Adams counted twenty-two "grand civic festivals," fifty-one of a lesser order, and 193 public dinners, all in celebration of the French victories. "I believe from my soul there have been more cannon fired here . . . than the French fired in achieving them." Men cropped their hair, stuck the tricolor cockade in their hats, and in deference to all that was French, made their bows to "Citizen" and "Citess." *Yankee Doodle* and the *Ça Ira* blended in song. As if to exemplify the sublimity of republican brotherhood spanning the Atlantic, the celebrated French astronaut Jean Pierre Blanchard ascended to the heavens, gallantly waving the Tricolor and the Stars and Stripes, while thousands cheered in Philadelphia.

Jefferson invested five dollars in Blanchard's feat. No doubt he witnessed it with the rest of the populace, and shared too in the rejoicing for the happy turn of affairs in Europe. The turn in his own affairs—the decision to continue in office—may have been influenced by European events. Persuaded that the republican cause in America was bound up with the fortunes of the French Revolution, that success or failure abroad would tip the political scales at home, Jefferson could not view those events with cool detachment. Reports came to him in the winter months of Gouverneur Morris's open hostility to the new republican government, whose ministers he cursed as "a set of damned rascals," and, more surprising, of Short's rancor against the extremists in France. Detecting the same sentiments in Short's letters, Jefferson pointedly censured his friend and defended the course of radicalism on what amounted to a plea of revolutionary necessity. The crimes against implacable royalty, while deplorable, were as nothing compared with the preservation of the Revolution. "The liberty of the whole earth was depending on the issue of the contest, and was ever such a prize won with so little innocent blood? My own affections have been deeply wounded by some of the martyrs to this cause," Jefferson said, alluding to the many friends he and Short numbered among its victims, "but rather than it should have failed, I would have seen half the earth desolated. Were there but an Adam and an Eve left in every country, and left free, it would be better than as it now is." Such were the sentiments, Jefferson informed the envoy, of 99 of every 100 Americans. This was hyperbole, of course, and Jefferson's brutally frank declaration conveys the misleading image of an *enragé;* but republican fevers soared in 1793, and so did Jefferson's.

February brought news of the King's execution. "Louis Capet has lost his caput" was the hardy jest of the Republican press. Jefferson shed no tears for Louis. Many Americans did, however. The ladies of Philadelphia—the ladies especially—"are open-mouthed against the murderers of a sovereign," Jefferson reported. Leading Federalists no longer concealed their enmity to the French Revolution. Despite polemical skirmishes, like the one between Jefferson and Adams two years before, the Revolution had not been a leading issue in American politics. Public opinion generally supported it, while opponents generally kept their opinions to themselves. With the execution of the King, reaction set in, and it rapidly acquired political character when France declared war on Great Britain. Contrary dispositions toward these powers were woven into the texture of American politics. Latent hostility to revolutionary democracy burst forth in the Federalist ranks as ties of affection and interest with the old country were threatened. But the mass of Americans hated and feared Britain, remembered France as a gallant ally, applauded her revolution as an extension of their own, and coupled every patriotic feeling to her beleagured cause. Jefferson recognized the political implications of this fact. It was a godsend to the Republicans. He was soon writing to Monroe: "The war has kindled and brought forward the two parties with an ardour which our own interests merely, could never excite." War and revolutionary frenzy gave the Republicans the popular initiative they had failed to gain in their opposition to Hamiltonian measures. The cause of France became "the touchstone," Republicans said, for trying the principles of men. But it was a risky game, playing politics with these combustible materials. Jefferson, as Secretary of State, endeavored to curb his partisan feelings and to meet his responsibility to the national interest. Between his roles as revolutionary ideologue and minister of state, he was caught in a cruel dilemma. While he could not resolve the dilemma, he managed it magnificently, and in the face of formidable trials emerged from the ordeal in statesman-like triumph.

Near the end of March a vessel from Lisbon brought first reports of the Anglo-French war. War had been freely predicted for two months past, even before Louis's death on the guillotine, as the certain outcome of Britain's blockade of the French coast. Jefferson kept the President informed at Mount Vernon, and when the reports were later confirmed, urged "that we take every justifiable measure for preserving our neutrality, and at the same time to provide [to the belligerents] those necessaries for war which must be brought across the Atlantic." The desire for peace and profit was as universal as it was ardent; but to realize it, to turn the European crisis to American account in all possible ways, was a task beset with difficulties. If neutrality was the policy, the French alliance might prove embarrassing. France had appointed a new minister to the United States, a young Girondin zealot, Edmond Charles Genêt, whose arrival was expected momentarily. "He has . . . more of genius than of ability," Morris had written of Genêt, "and you will see in him at first blush the manner and look of an upstart." Upstart indeed! But Jefferson cheered Genêt's coming. Diplomatic contact with France had virtually ceased. Ternant, on hearing of the King's death, had gone into "deep mourning" and discontinued his visits to the Secretary of State. Morris was, unofficially, *persona non grata* to the French republic. Washington felt enough concern for this situation to ask Jefferson to go to Paris. He would not hear of it and pointed out to the President that Genêt's coming would shift the scene of diplomacy to Philadelphia. By this time, in February, he had learned that Genêt's instructions were very cordial to the United States.

Washington hurried back to the capital. On April 19 the cabinet met at his house. Two basic questions were before the executive. In what manner, if at all, should Genêt be received? And how should the President act to maintain American neutrality? Always the aggressor, Hamilton had prepared the agenda, though it was copied in Washington's hand. Jefferson surmised the fact and called the paper merely a skeleton on which to hang the argument "that our treaty with France is void." Hamilton revived the issue of the legitimacy of the French government and, inferentially, of American commitments under the alliance of 1778, an issue Jefferson had supposed settled and laid to rest several months earlier. When the National Convention assembled after the fall of the monarchy, Jefferson took the position that this body expressed the will of the nation, and therefore ought to be recognized as the legitimate government of France. "We certainly cannot deny to other nations that principle whereon our government is founded," asserted the author of the Declaration of Independence, "that every nation has a right to change these forms of its own will; and externally to transact business with other nations through whatever organ it chooses, whether that be a King, Convention, Assembly, Committee, President, or whatever it be. The only thing essential is the will of the nation." The principle was novel, like the republic from which it sprang. Hamilton opposed it but Washington assented. Appropriate instructions went out to American embassies; payments on the French debt (briefly suspended) were resumed; and Morris was ordered to present his credentials to the French republic. In sum, this *recognition* principle, "the will of the nation substantially declared"—an enduring legacy to American government—was already operative when Hamilton used the impending arrival of the French minister as the excuse for reviving the question.

Hamilton saw a dangerous chain of troubles in the simple act of receiving Genêt. Unless pointedly qualified, the act was tantamount to recognition of the French republic; recognition admitted the continuing force of the treaties of 1778; these treaties contained articles incompatible with American neutrality, thus courting British displeasure. Under the Treaty of Alliance the United States was pledged to defend the French West Indies, while under the companion Treaty of Commerce French armed vessels were permitted to come and go freely in American ports—privileges denied to France's enemies. Anxious to avoid war with Britain at all costs, doubting the legitimacy or the virtue or the permanence of the French republic, regarding the treaties as contracts with a deposed sovereign, Hamilton thought they should be declared void, though he was willing to settle for their suspension.

Jefferson stood by the treaties, of course, including the unfettered recognition of Genêt and his government. Opinion was divided in the cabinet; the question was adjourned, and the officers, excepting Knox, turned in written opinions. Jefferson's closely reasoned argument displayed his mastery of the law of nations, his keen sense of the demands and the limits of responsibility in foreign relations, and his deep conviction that American conduct toward other nations should be founded on its own first principles. A treaty is made between nations, not between their governments, which nations may change as they please without impairment of obligations. The duties between nations are the same as between individuals. They may be excused from solemn compacts only when their performance becomes impossible or self-destructive, Jefferson said. Thus far the dangers from the alliance were imaginary. *If* affairs in France issued in "rawhead and bloody bones," *if* the West Indies guarantee threatened to engage us in war, then the United States might place its own survival above treaty obligations. Britain could not fairly complain of Article XVII's granting privileges to the belligerent vessels of France; for under the terms of the Anglo-French commercial accord of 1786 Britain granted the same privileges to the French in the case of war with the United States. Under Article XXII of the Franco-American treaty, the enemies of the former could not fit out privateers or sell prizes in the ports of the latter; but no danger was apprehended from this provision, since it did not prevent the United States from making a similar denial to France, as ought to be done. Jefferson then appealed to the leading authorities on international law (Grotius, Puffendorf, Wolf, and Vattel), ranging the pertinent passages from their works in four parallel columns. At least three of these authorities agreed on the sanctity of treaties regardless of changes in the form of government; Vattel allowed for renunciation when such a change rendered an alliance "useless, dangerous, or disagreeable," supposing, however, that the change in question was to a form of government which the other party disapproved, a supposition Hamilton had conveniently overlooked in citing this "ill understood scrap" of Vattel. It could hardly be argued, Jefferson thought, that an alliance contracted with a despotic France became "useless, dangerous, or disagreeable" when France passed into a republic. In the circumstances American neutrality would be breached, not by adherence to the treaty, but by renunciation or suspension. "An injured friend is the bitterest of foes," Jefferson warned. It was the height of folly to give France cause for war upon the American republic. Let the alliance stand, he pleaded. Washington's vote gave Jefferson the majority. Genêt would be received, the alliance maintained, trusting to events to keep them compatible with American neutrality.

But what should be done to secure that neutrality? Hamilton called for an immediate proclamation by the President. Jefferson objected so far as it would involve executive determination of a question belonging to the legislature. Viewing a declaration of neutrality as the negative side of a declaration of war, he thought the decision belonged to Congress. He had earlier supposed Congress should be summoned into special session, but on April 19, and for some time to come, he agreed with his colleagues in opposing this measure. He yielded on the question of an executive proclamation, with the understanding, however, that it simply declared the President's intention to keep the United States at peace pending action by Congress. The constitutional basis of Jefferson's position was clear. Yet he was not usually so scrupulous in his view of presidential powers. The real basis of his opposition to Hamilton's proposal lay elsewhere. He wished to keep the options open, the belligerents in suspense, and thereby force them, especially Britain, to "bid for our neutrality." Jefferson thought Britain would pay a price for neutrality both because of the contingencies of the French alliance and because of

484

her wartime dependence on American commerce to supply her colonies, feed her soldiers, and carry her goods. France was similarly dependent, though to a lesser degree, being more of a land animal. So Jefferson favored a waiting game, withholding American neutrality as a weapon of bargain. He had a particular end in view: British recognition of "the broadest neutral privileges," such as those embodied in American treaties of commerce. Some of them—"free ships make free goods," for example—had found their way into the Anglo-French accord. The fact that these *modern* principles had not gone unrecognized even by Britain, historically their major opponent, together with the pressing exigencies of war, buoyed Jefferson's hopes of a diplomatic *coup* from American neutrality.

History remembers the presidential proclamation of April 22 as the Proclamation of Neutrality. It was at once so regarded. Yet in deference to Jefferson's wishes, the word "neutrality" did not appear in the text, and he afterwards denied that it was meant to commit the government to neutrality in the strict sense. The proclamation pledged "a conduct friendly and impartial" toward the belligerents, warned citizens against hostile acts, and denied the protection of the United States for offences against "the *modern* usage of nations." The adjective was Jefferson's. He at once advised Pinckney to inform the authorities in London of the American desire for neutrality "on condition that the rights of neutral nations are respected in us, as they have been settled in *modern* times." Jefferson meant to practice this idea. By *modern* he meant—what everyone meant—a narrow definition of contraband, the security of non-contraband cargo on neutral vessels, and a realistic rule of blockade. As the leading naval power, Britain had generally refused to recognize these principles. If Britain persisted, adhering to the older rules of the *consolato del mare*, Jefferson did not mean to go to war but rather, as he explained to Madison, to adopt stiff economic sanctions against the aggressor and thereby "introduce between nations another umpire than arms."

At the same time he voiced his approval of the proclamation in letters to Virginia. "I fear that a fair neutrality will prove a disagreeable pill to our friends," he wrote soothingly to Madison, "tho' necessary to keep out of the calamities of a war." And to Monroe: "I wish we may be able to repress the spirit of the people within the limits of a fair neutrality." A "fair neutrality" was one compatible with the French alliance, on the one hand, and with the neutral rights claimed by the Americans on the other. To Hamilton, of course, Jefferson's "fair" or "manly neutrality" squinted toward France. As it worked out, however, Jefferson felt that Britain got most of the benefits while yielding nothing in return. He bitterly resented this "sneaking" Anglophile neutrality managed by his rival. And so, finally surrendering to his friends' violent opinions against the proclamation, Jefferson also called it dishonorable, unconstitutional, and impolitic, and deplored its shameful appeasement of Britain. He was embarrassed to explain his part in the birth of this prodigy. To Madison he said its intent was good, aiming only at the preservation of peace with the belligerents; unfortunately, it had been badly drawn by the Attorney General. When shown the draft, Jefferson said, he had hastily run his eye over it to see that it omitted "neutrality," not stopping to realize that even without that fateful word it might be construed as a definitive proclamation of neutrality. And so it was. Again he had been outmaneuvered by Hamilton. He was saddled with the administration of a policy he could not wholly approve and a policy condemned by the Republican friends of France.

Anxieties about the proclamation were offset in the spring by the booming public reception of Citizen Genêt, the glittering symbol of republican France, as he passed from ovation to ovation on his leisurely journey northward to Philadelphia. Landing in Charleston the second week of April, Genêt lost no time implementing his instructions to commission privateers against British commerce and to foment hostilities against the Spanish colonies. At Richmond he learned of the proclamation. It daunted him not at all in the heady acclaim he was enjoying. Reports of his precipitate actions, the popular demonstrations, the rousing appeals to French sympathies, reached Philadelphia ahead of Genêt. Already, protests from the British minister against unneutral acts of the French flag piled up on Jefferson's desk. He was mildly concerned. A good cause could be injured by too much zeal. But he was happy in Genêt's triumph. "All the old spirit of 1776 is rekindling," he exulted. Though it must be kept within the limits of neutrality, he was glad for this testimony of the people against "the cold caution of their government." In the rage for Genêt the people found their voice. "For our constituents seeing that the government does not express their mind, perhaps rather leans the other way, are coming forward to express it themselves." Not only France but the Republican party had an interest in this development.

Philadelphia gave Genêt a delirious welcome on May 16. Cannon boomed. Bells clanged. From Gray's Ferry to the City Tavern, he rode through a cheering throng. The next evening several hundred citizens met in the State House yard, acclaimed an address, then paraded noisily through the streets, swelling their ranks as they went, to make the presentation at Genêt's lodgings. "You ask who were its promoters," Hamilton wrote testily to a friend. "I answer that with very few exceptions they were the same men who have been uniformly the enemies and the disturbers of the government of the United States." The reception continued for days. "I live in the midst of perpetual festivals," Genêt remarked. The lavish banquet at Oeller's Hotel was unsurpassed in the memory of Philadelphians. A battery of artillery saluted each spirited toast; the diners, numbering perhaps 200, donned red liberty caps, hymned the *Marseillaise,* and roared approval when Genêt himself burst into patriotic song:

> Liberty! Liberty! be thy name adored forever
> Tyrants, beware, your tottering thrones must fall;
> One interest links the free forever,
> And Freedom's sons are Frenchmen all.

From other quarters, all the old Tories, as Jefferson described them —fashionable aristocrats, paper-men, merchants trading on British capital—came pledges of support for the President and neutrality. Jefferson remained aloof from the spectacle, but he was far from being a disinterested spectator.

In the midst of the furor, the youthful minister presented his credentials to the Secretary of State. For all the Girondin dash and bravado of the little Frenchman, there was about him, as Jefferson must have seen at once, the delicate aura of one who had grown up in the courtly world of Versailles. Jefferson, after a cordial exchange of greetings, took him to the President's house. The scene changed dramatically. Portraits of his late sovereign and queen hung on the wall. The President showed a cold and haughty manner. The contrast between the huzzas of the masses and Washington's chilly reception spoke volumes to Genêt. Fortunately, the Secretary of State understood him, loved France, loved the Revolution, and would espouse his cause in the government. In Charleston, Ralph Izard, an old friend of his father, had sought to disabuse Genêt of this preconceived idea of Jefferson. Izard, a leading Federalist, described the Secretary as "an ambitious and intriguing demagogue" who, together with Madison, would use Genêt so long as he was serviceable to their crooked schemes, and then drop him. "Place no confidence in them," Izard warned. Genêt would later feel Izard had prophesied his destiny, but the warning made no impression in the spring of 1793. "Tomorrow," he wrote just after his official reception, "I will have my first conference with . . . Mr. Jefferson . . . . His principles, his experience, his talents, his devotion to the cause which we defend, inspire in me the greatest confidence, and make me hope that we will reach the glorious goal which the cause of humanity in general must make us desirous of achieving."

Minister and Secretary met on a friendly footing, as men engaged in a common cause. Genêt was conciliatory in regard to his hasty actions at Charleston before the proclamation of neutrality. He was instructed, of course, to obtain every possible favor for French shipping and commerce, but he promised to respect American neutrality. Indeed, France preferred her ally as a neutral rather than as a belligerent. She had no intention of invoking the guarantee clause of the Treaty of Alliance. The West Indies ports, he announced, were thrown open to American trade. His assurances respecting the treaty vindicated Jefferson's judgment in the cabinet, while the liberation of the island commerce fulfilled a decade-long objective of American diplomacy. Genêt was also instructed to negotiate a new treaty of commerce on Jefferson's favorite plan of mutual naturalization. Alas, such a treaty would now be incompatible with American neutrality. Jefferson quietly tabled the proposition. Yet, at this juncture, Genêt appeared to embody the old dream of Franco-American commercial empire. It was the Girondin dream too, but crazily mixed up with frenzies of war and conquest troubling American peace. The danger from the French side was apparent. Could neutrality co-exist with the French alliance? Jefferson felt reassured after his first talk with Genêt. "It is impossible for anything to be more affectionate, more magnanimous than the purport of his mission," he wrote to Madison. "In short he offers everything and asks nothing." But would his colleagues in the cabinet meet Genêt fairly? He feared not. "Under pretense of avoiding war on the one side [they] have no great antipathy to run foul of it on the other, and to make a part in the confederacy of princes against human liberty."

The cabinet was becoming an established institution. "This sets almost every day on questions of neutrality," Jefferson said in May. These questions were vexing to the last degree. The statute book offered no help, though some might be found in the customary law of nations. Every question as it arose became the subject of discussion in executive conclave, testing the wits, tiring the patience, gnawing the feelings of its members. Agreement on the applicable principle —and this was often the case—was frequently accompanied by an exasperating inability to agree on details of implementation. It was unanimously agreed, for instance, that France should not be permitted to fit out privateers or sell prizes in American ports. (Article XXII of the treaty of commerce decided the question as to France's enemies.) But should the ruling be retrospective, forcing the suppression of privateers Genêt had commissioned at Charleston and the surrender of their prizes? Did the prohibition extend to the mounting of arms furnished by the belligerent as well as those acquired in the United States? Must belligerent vessels abstain from recruiting their own nationals in American ports? Were citizens of the United States barred from selling vessels armed for war to the belligerents? The negative vote Jefferson gave on each of these questions leaned to the French side. He was not for that reason any less neutral than the two, sometimes three, officers who voted affirmative. True neutrality was unattainable. Every decision, however fair its grounds, had an unequal effect on the belligerents. Jefferson bent American policy one way, Hamilton the other; and in this they represented the clash of opinion in the country at large. As the dominant naval power, without the benefit of treaty, Britain favored strict and cautious American neutrality, while France pressed the advantages not only of the Treaty of Alliance but of national sympathy for the republican cause. Neutrality was a fiction, exploited by both sides, but more effectively by the British and their friends, primarily Federalists, as the means of negating the French alliance. This was the real issue, as Jefferson had insisted from the start, though it was rapidly obscured by the unreal issue of neutrality.

Nothing so well demonstrated Jefferson's inability to direct foreign affairs the way Hamilton personally directed fiscal affairs than the fact that, largely because the maintenance of peace transcended administrative jurisdictions, the rules and regulations governing neutrality were hammered out in executive council by majority vote. The cabinet met, either at the President's house or one of the executive offices, Hamilton, lean and quick, Knox, fat and slow, on one side, Jefferson on the other, and poor Randolph more often than not in between. This is to speak figuratively. When not at Mount Vernon Washington usually attended, listened to the different opinions, and invariably bowed to the majority or cast his own vote to make a majority. Until the frenzy whipped up around Genêt, Jefferson believed the President's "penchant" was toward a "fair neutrality," and he relied on him to check the Anglicism of the Federalists. Washington tried to strike a just balance. He never seriously entertained Hamilton's project to scrap the French alliance. Although Hamilton had set his foot in Jefferson's domain, he had not supplanted the Virginian's authority in the President's eyes. But what Hamilton had failed to accomplish would be at least partially accomplished by Genêt's audacity and the invective of the Republican press. Several days after the ministerial reception, Washington called Jefferson to task for using the term "republic" to describe the governments of both France and the United States in an official letter acknowledging Ternant's recall. The irritant was the *National Gazette*, which flaunted that otherwise innocent word in attacks on the administration now aimed directly at the President's person. Freneau was a Francophile, bitterly opposed to the neutrality proclamation, and linked politically with the Secretary of State. Jefferson took the President's outburst as a hint to curb the Republican editor. "But I will not do it," he scrawled in his private record. "His paper has saved our Constitution . . . ." The President's *sang froid* was shaken. The more he was attacked from Republican quarters, and the more insolent Genêt became, the more closely he drew to his Federalist advisers.

Not the President but the Attorney General was Jefferson's

chief affliction. Edmund Randolph belonged to the inner circle of Virginia Republicanism. Jefferson had contributed to his success at the bar and in politics, and Randolph, like a grateful friend and protégé, had enrolled himself in Jefferson's cause. But he seemed less than ardent in the neutrality councils in 1793. Jefferson could endure the obstinacy of Hamilton and Knox—it was known and expected. Randolph quibbled and vacillated. Jefferson described the alignment in the cabinet as two and one-half to one and one-half, the split vote being Randolph's, which, making the majority, carried the day. "Everything . . . now hangs on the opinion of a single person," he confided to Madison in May, "and that the most indecisive one I ever had to do business with. He always contrives to agree in principle with one [Jefferson] but in conclusion with the other [Hamilton]." The affront which brought on Jefferson's disgust occurred on the question of the enforcement of neutrality. He objected to Hamilton's plan to use his customs' officers, as it would convert that service into "an established corps of spies or informers against their fellow citizens" and also add "a new and large field to a department already amply provided with business, patronage, and influence." The responsibility properly belonged in his own department, Jefferson said, utilizing the regular machinery of district attornies, grand juries, and federal judges. On this issue Randolph conceded Jefferson's point, yet sided with Hamilton. "E.R. found out a hair to split, which, as always happens, became the decision." His old friend now appeared as a political chameleon. He was angered in July when Randolph, returning from a mission to sound out Virginia opinion of administration policy, gave the President a favorable report. Outwardly, Jefferson kept up friendly relations with the Attorney General; but within the close knit Virginia circle, he threaded his distrust, causing Randolph to lose political caste there two years before the Federalists completed the wreckage of his career. Randolph was some of the things Jefferson said he was. He shilly-shallied, he split hairs, he trimmed. His irresolution favored Hamilton's ascendancy in the cabinet. Yet his offences were not of the proportion Jefferson imagined, and they arose from a conscientious effort to follow Washington's lead in striking a just balance of American neutrality. Jefferson expected dutiful obedience from his junior friend and colleague. When he did not give it and acted with seeming indifference to political considerations, Jefferson felt betrayed and responded in sullen anger.

While the administration gradually hammered out a system of neutrality, the public debate raged on, drawing fresh fuel from Genêt's antics, from the assaults of both belligerents on American commerce, from street brawls between French and English sailors, the violence of the press, and the determined effort of political foes, Federalist and Republican, to transmute all this emotion into party capital. When summer came Pennsylvania's Republican chieftains organized a Democratic Society modeled loosely on the political clubs of Paris. Soon these clubs, which championed the French Revolution, agitated public issues, and served as a kind of auxiliary of the Republican party, appeared in every part of the country. Jefferson kept to his official station, but encouraged anything tending to advance the Republican and the French cause. Society in Philadelphia was spoiled by the heats and tumults of politics. The amusement he had found in the homes of fortune and fashion turned to ashes. Old friendships were strained or broken. He had often seen John Trumbull, his artist-friend and companion in Europe, since he returned to the United States, still "collecting heads" for his historical canvases. Sometime in the early months of 1793 Jefferson invited Trumbull to dinner. Giles was in the company, and he at once, according to Trumbull, "began to rally me upon the puritanical ancestry and character of New England." At Jefferson's table the voluble Virginian launched into a tirade against Christianity and other miserable delusions in the broadest French style, "Jefferson in the meantime, smiling and nodding approbation on Mr. Giles." Trumbull roundly declared Giles a scoundrel, rose and left the house, and thereafter had only a "cold and distant" acquaintance with Jefferson. Political passions in 1793 bared all the edges of mental discord.

After giving up his house on Market Street, Jefferson found a quiet country refuge on the banks of the Schuylkill. Most of his books, furniture, and other household possessions—a total of fifty crates—were packed and shipped to the James in April, when he moved to the country. He had fewer visitors and never entertained in style. The silks and ruffles were put away in favor of more republican garb—Jefferson began to appear the Jacobin his enemies imagined him to be. Polly came to his retreat on weekends. "She passes two or three days . . . with me, under the trees," he wrote to Martha, "for I never go into the house but at the hour of bed. I never before knew the full value of trees, good grass below, and under them I breakfast, dine, write, read, and receive my company. What would I not give that the trees planted nearest round the house at Monticello were full grown." Official duties drove him hard, "like a horse under whip and spur from the start to the poll," but his thoughts turned more and more to Monticello. He needed a farm manager, tenants, workmen in different lines, and he gave what time he could to the search for them. Intending to become a plain, practical farmer at last, he talked over his plans with Dr. Logan, "the best farmer in Pennsylvania," and in correspondence with his son-in-law. Styling himself "but a tyro in agriculture," he was eager to experiment with new methods and new machinery, such as a model threshing machine he had ordered from Scotland.

Madison contemplated Jefferson's retirement with dismay. It surely ought to be deferred, he advised, until it could be "marked with justifying circumstances which all good citizens will respect, and to which your friends can appeal." Jefferson brushed aside this political appeal, retorting in language of unprecedented severity in his correspondence with Madison. "What must be the principle of that calculation which should balance against these [pleasures of private and domestic life] the circumstances of my present existence! Worn down with labors from morning to night, and day to day; knowing them as fruitless to others as they are vexatious to myself, committed singly and in desperate and eternal contest against a host who are systematically undermining the public liberty and prosperity, even the rare hours of relaxation sacrificed to the society of persons in the same intentions, of whose hatred I am conscious even in those moments of conviviality when the heart wishes most to open itself to the effusions of friendship and confidence, cut off from my family and friends, my affairs abandoned to chaos and derangement, in short giving everything I love, in exchange for everything I hate, and all this without a single gratification in possession or in prospect, in present enjoyment or future wish.—Indeed my dear friend," he closed, "duty being out of the question, inclination cuts off all argument, and so never let there be more between you and me, on this subject." At the end of July he notified Washington he would retire on September 30.

Meanwhile there was no escape. In June, Hamilton, as "Pacificus," commenced a series of articles in the *Gazette of the United States* in defense of the proclamation of neutrality. He upheld its constitutionality, declared the Treaty of Alliance in abeyance, pooh-poohed sentiments of gratitude for France, and denounced her revolution. Jefferson was shocked by the gloss Hamilton put on the proclamation. "For God's sake, my dear sir," he implored Madison, "take up your pen, select the most striking heresies and cut him to pieces in the face of the public. There is nobody else who can and will enter the lists with him." Madison had not needed Pacificus to show him the terrible mischief of the proclamation. "It wounds the national honor, by seeming to disregard the stipulated duties to France. It wounds the popular feelings by a seeming indifference to the cause of liberty. And it seems to violate the form and spirit of the Constitution . . . ," he had written to Jefferson. But simmering under the July sun of the Virginia piedmont, Madison took up the task of reply with faint heart. "I can truly say I find it the most grating one I ever experienced." In five articles over the signature "Helvidius," he never got beyond the constitutional issue. Jefferson saw to their publication in Philadelphia. The argument of Helvidius was a detailed elaboration of Jefferson's original position: that because the power to decide between war and peace belongs to Congress, the President cannot initiate a policy which, in effect, confronts Congress with a *fait accompli*. As against Hamilton's sweeping claim of executive prerogative in foreign affairs, no other position could stand the scrutiny of the Constitution; but the Constitution did not cover all exigencies, as even the Virginia Republicans were to discover in time.

The achievement of what Jefferson styled a "fair neutrality" demanded the prudent co-operation of the French minister. In this regard, first impressions had been deceiving. Within a week of his reception Genêt boldy challenged administration rulings. When Jefferson informed him that American ports could not be used for the arming of French vessels, Genêt affirmed the right from its negative as to the enemies of France in Article XXII of the treaty, an infer-

494

ence Jefferson had earlier rejected in his defense of the alliance. On June 5, Jefferson presented Genêt with a careful restatement of the government's position. The United States must prohibit acts within its borders injurious to Britain, a nation with which it was at peace. The privateers commissioned at Charleston would have to depart (a ruling Jefferson had not approved), and the granting of military commissions to American citizens would have to stop (a ruling he had emphatically approved). A week later the cabinet met to consider the cases of the brigs *Polly* and *Catherine*, the former a French privateer seized by Governor Clinton for arming in New York, the latter a French prize taken in American waters. Both, it was decided, would be held by the United States and committed to the federal district attorney for settlement at law. Genêt protested. Again Jefferson patiently stated the American position, showing it to be in accord with treaty obligations and the law of nations. The Frenchman met Jefferson's reasoning with defiance and contempt. What had he to do with "diplomatic subtleties" and "aphorisms of Vattel"! The American people would not tolerate this treatment of the French nation. "Our treaties have been unfavorably interpreted. Arbitrary orders have directed against us the action of the tribunals; indeed, my diplomatic reception excepted, I have met with nothing but disgust and obstacles in the negotiations I have been charged with."

Questions of consular jurisdiction and the French debt also gave difficulty. The consuls presumed to hold courts of admiralty on prizes. When Jefferson, in May, pointed out that the consular convention of 1788 gave no such jurisdiction, Genêt acknowledged the error and promised to correct it. Instead, he again embarked on it. After repeated warnings, the administration was finally obliged to order the withdrawal of privileges from refractory consuls. For some time before Genêt's arrival the government had been advancing payments of its debt to France in order to furnish relief for the slave-ravaged island of Santo Domingo. Genêt was instructed to improve this friendly gesture by obtaining payment of the entire balance, about $2,500,000, to be laid out in provisions. Jefferson would have liked to comply with this request, but finally agreed with Hamilton that the financial risk was too high. The decision helped to cripple the French Minister. He protested it without avail. Although the Treasury continued to make advances on annual installments, he never received sufficient funds for his larger undertakings. Moreover, hard pressed as he was, he broke faith with American creditors who had furnished supplies to Santo Domingo by diverting funds set aside on their account to new purchases for France. For this he drew another reprimand from the Secretary of State.

By the end of June, Jefferson was agonizing over Genêt's performance and wondering what to do with him. Dazzled by the brilliance of his public triumph, the little hot-head presumed to set the government itself at defiance. "I am doing everything in my power to moderate the impetuosity of his movements," Jefferson wrote to Monroe, "and to destroy the dangerous opinion which has been excited in him, that the people of the U.S. will disown the acts of their government, and that he has an appeal from the Executive to Congress, and from both to the people." Wishing at all costs to avoid a break, he gently reasoned with Genêt, coaxed and placated him, in an endeavor to set him on the right path. The envoy took Jefferson's confidence and manifest good will at face value and continued to view him as a friendy coadjutor, differentiating him in this role from his official role as Secretary of State in which he must be the agent of the President. The quaint courtesies and supple manners of the Virginian, who expressed pleasure or displeasure only in varying degrees of assent, confused the Frenchman. Yet in his most ambitious scheme Genêt might rightly claim to have had the compliance, if not the encouragement, of the Secretary of State.

As early as February Jefferson had learned vaguely of the ruling Gironde's clandestine support of Francisco de Miranda, the Venezuelan adventurer, in his efforts to foment revolution in Spanish America, as well as of Genêt's secret instructions to enlist the Kentuckians in a combined land and sea expedition against Louisiana; but nothing directly touching these matters reached the Secretary. Genêt then, late in June, asked him to furnish André Michaux, the French botanist, with a letter of introduction to the governor of Kentucky. Jefferson happily complied. He knew and admired Michaux, who had been in the United States for several years collecting botanical specimens for introduction into France—a scientific enterprise dear to Jefferson's heart—and he had only recently penned Michaux's instructions for a Trans-Mississippi expedition under the auspices of the American Philosophical Society. Unknown to Jefferson, however, the enterprise had taken on a political character since Genêt's arrival in Philadelphia. Grasses, mammoth, and the Missouri route to the Pacific were still the stated objects of Michaux's expedition, but as Genêt's appointed agent he would also go in quest of support for the western venture against the Spanish colonies. For this reason Genêt was dissatisfied with Jefferson's first letter, which simply introduced Michaux as a botanist. Jefferson obligingly tore it up and wrote another recommending the botanist as a man in the confidence of the French Minister. About a week later Genêt called on Jefferson. Making a show of speaking to him "not as Secretary of State, but as Mr. Jefferson," he read the instructions prepared for Michaux, as well as an address to the inhabitants of Louisiana, another to those of Canada, and disclosed the plans afoot to free the Mississippi, take Louisiana, and establish it as an independent state "connected in commerce with France and the United States." Jefferson responded coldly: "I told him that his enticing officers and soldiers from Kentucky to go against Spain, was really putting a halter about their necks; for that they would assuredly be hung if they commenced hostilities against a nation at peace with the United States. That leaving out that article I did not care what insurrections should be excited in Louisiana."

Perhaps Jefferson would not have made this last disclaimer, which Genêt took as a backhanded endorsement of the western project, had he known of the alliance formed between Britain and Spain several weeks earlier. Even so, the sharp distinction he made between French machinations in Kentucky and insurrections in Spanish Louisiana, while perfectly valid in law, had little support in western realities, for the Mississippi linked Kentuckians in treachery and conspiracy through all its muddy waters to New Orleans. As interested as he was in commercial union with France, he had no desire to see that ambitious nation seated at the mouth of the Mississippi. He hoped to secure the Floridas and New Orleans for the United States, on his own terms, with as little risk to peace and honor as circumstances would admit. The matter was still in the course of negotiation with Spain in the summer of 1793. But the prospect of success dimmed with each dispatch from Madrid, and the twin marplots in Philadelphia, the Spanish commissioners Viar and

Jaudenes, made such a trumpery of the United States' incitement of the Indians that a rupture seemed imminent. Already, perhaps on the possiblity of Girondin revolution in the Spanish provinces, Jefferson had told the ministers at Madrid to withhold the defensive guarantee of Louisiana earlier tendered in exchange for the navigation of the Mississippi and the Floridas. In this situation, his patience worn thin after several years of negotiation with Spain, Jefferson was little inclined to suppress French irritants. He did not lay Genêt's scheme before the President, nor did he ever make his knowledge of it a part of the official record. Near the end of August, however, the Spanish commissioners, having learned of the enterprise and the involvement of prominent Americans, such as Jefferson's old friend George Rogers Clark, brought it to official notice. Speaking for the President, Jefferson at once assured the commissioners that the United States would act to prevent American aggressions. On the same day he directed the governor of Kentucky to take appropriate measures, and when this met with an indifferent response, he wrote again in stronger terms. By then the Girondins had fallen in France and Genêt in America, and the once-postponed expedition against the Spanish colonies could not be revived. Toward it Jefferson had taken an ambivalent, perhaps even ambiguous line, which would enable him to maneuver as changing circumstances might require. It was all inconsequential, so it is difficult to say whether or not his line was the right one.

Jefferson's trust in the French Minister, ebbing fast for several weeks, finally ran out in the case of the *Little Sarah*. At a meeting of the department heads on July 5, several hours before Genêt made his startling disclosures of New World liberation in Jefferson's office, it was agreed to ask the governor of Pennsylvania, Thomas Mifflin, to determine whether or not this French prize lying in the Delaware between the city and Mud Island was arming as a privateer. Mifflin reported the next day that the merchant brig had been brought in with four guns and now mounted 14, with several swivels, and a crew of 120, some of them American. Alexander J. Dallas, secretary of the commonwealth and a leader of the Democratic Society, understood that the brig, rechristened *La Petite Démocrate*, was about to put to sea. Later that night he called on Genêt to persuade him to detain the vessel. He angrily refused, complained of ill-treatment, promised to meet force with force if it came to that, and, according to later reports of the conversation, threatened to appeal over the President's head directly to the people. The alarm reached Jefferson at his country place the next morning, which was Sunday. He hurried to the city, conferred first with Dallas and Mifflin, then went to see Genêt. He renewed Dallas's appeal: detain the vessel until the President, then at Mount Vernon but expected in the capital on Wednesday, could decide the case. Genêt flew into a rage, traversing an "immense field" of complaint, the sum of which was that the treaties had been violated, the administration had acted unconstitutionally, and he had been checked in every endeavor. The turbulence smothered Jefferson's efforts to reason with the Minister. He refused to give any assurances but said the vessel would not be ready to sail before Wednesday anyway. Taking this as a face-saving declaration, Jefferson went away confident the matter would await the President's decision.

The case of the *Petite Démocrate* was already becoming celebrated. On Monday morning the public woke to the possibility of a serious breach of neutrality. Merchants of the city held a meeting at the coffeehouse and urged strong measures. The spotlight of publicity, the scene of the challenge under the very noses of the government, made the case peculiarly delicate. Mifflin, who was charged like all governors to use force if necessary to prevent the arming of privateers, wished to know what steps he should take at this juncture. The three secretaries (Randolph was also in Virginia) met in Mifflin's office at the State House. In the opinion of Hamilton and Knox, a battery should be set up at Mud Island under a party of militia with orders to fire on the privateer if she spread sail before the President's pleasure could be known.

Jefferson dissented. Summarizing his argument in a memorandum written for the President the next day, he began with the more specific reasons and proceeded, with rising eloquence, to the more general. He felt confident the brig would not sail. The erection of a battery might "produce the fact it is meant to prevent"; if so, and if the guns fired, he warned, "it is morally certain that bloody consequences would follow," slamming the door on peace. This was too great a responsibility to be assumed by subordinate officers when the chief magistrate, to whom the people had committed their safety, was within forty-eight hours of the opportunity of judging the question for himself. Hamilton had emphasized the consequences of adverse British reaction to a breach of neutrality so flagrant as to make a mockery of the government. To this Jefferson said that Britain would have no right to complain. If the breach occurred it would be contrary to the assurances of the French Minister, and the United States would then demand satisfaction from France. In view of the evidences of good faith already given to the British, in view of American sufferance of their damnable practice of impressing our seamen to bear arms against our friends, Whitehall was not likely to make a capital case of the *Petite Démocrate*. Having borne for ten years "the grossest insults and injuries" from their late enemy, the American people ought not "to rise at a feather against their friends and benefactors," Jefferson continued with mounting indignation. "I would not gratify the combination of kings with the spectacle of the only two republics on earth destroying each other for two cannon; nor would I, for infinitely greater cause, add this country to that combination, turn the scale of contest, and let it be from our hands that the hopes of men received their last stab." In his judgment, clearly, the explosive potential of the case placed it on an altogether different footing from the generality of cases, thus making the arbitrary application of the general rule unwarranted and unwise. Hamilton also realized the stubborness of this particular transaction; indeed, for that reason, Jefferson suspected, he had seized upon it to provoke an incident fatal to the French alliance. At bottom, Jefferson's position, no less than Hamilton's on the opposite side, was dictated by commitments outside the straight-and-narrow path of neutrality. In the present instance, peace and neutrality were better served by the course Jefferson advocated.

By the time Washington returned to the capital the succeeding Thursday, the *Petite Démocrate* had hoisted anchor and fallen down the river several miles to Chester. She had not departed, but the maneuver pretty well eliminated the possibility of coercive action. The President found the relevant papers on his desk. Rage was an emotion he reserved for extraordinary provocations. He felt it now. "What is to be done in the case of the *Little Sarah*, now at Chester," he demanded of the Secretary of State, who had taken to the country with a fever. "Is the Minister of the French Republic to set the acts of this Government at defiance *with impunity?* And then threaten the Executive with an appeal to the People? What must the world think of such conduct, and of the Government of the United States in submitting to it?" He summoned the cabinet to meet the next day. Jefferson found him considerably calmed, though apparently sorry the brig had not been fired on—an action Jefferson doubted he would have ordered had he been on the spot. The President and his officers decided to refer the difficult legal questions of American neutrality to the justices of the Supreme Court, expecting in the meantime that the *Petite Démocrate* and a half-dozen vessels in indeterminate status would remain in port. But the Court declined to intervene. Left to work out its problems alone, the executive promulgated nine rules governing belligerents early in August. Long before then the *Petite Démocrate* had gone to sea. Hammond offered no protest. Jefferson might console himself in this, and in the thought that the defeat was insignificant when compared with the risks of a confrontation in arms. But he could no longer take any consolation whatsoever in the French Minister.

"Never in my opinion, was so calamitous an appointment made, as that of the present Minister of France here," Jefferson confided to Madison on July 7, the day of his disheartening interview with Genêt. "Hot headed, all imagination, no judgment, passionate, disrespectful and even indecent towards the President . . . urging the most unreasonable and groundless propositions, and in the most dictatorial style etc. etc. etc." Toward him personally Genêt was respectful and willing to listen to advice; but then at the first opportunity he would rear and buck like a wild colt. "He renders my position immensely difficult." In discrediting himself, Genêt discredited Jefferson's foreign policy pegged to friendship with France and struck at the hopes of Republicans to bury the Federalists under an avalanche of popular enthusiasm for the French Revolution. By mid-July Hamilton was moving for Genêt's recall. It was the Federalists' turn now to appeal to the people, unaccustomed though they were to that tribunal. "They know too well that the whole game is played into their hands . . . ," Jefferson remarked. Finding Genêt "absolutely incorrigible," as he reported to Madison, he saw "the necessity of quitting a wreck which could not but sink all who should cling to it." Genêt must be abandoned. The Secretary's job was to salvage what he could of the cargo.

On August 1 the four gentlemen of the cabinet took "family dinner" with the President, then got down to the business of what should be done with the Frenchman. A full and documented statement of his conduct to be prepared in the form of a letter to the American Minister in Paris for communication to the Executive Council of the French republic: agreed to unanimously. An immediate recall to be required: agreed to unanimously, Jefferson for tactful, the others for peremptory, expression. A letter to Genêt informing him of the recall action and the grounds: Jefferson against, as further incitement of the envoy, but overruled by the others. A publication of the whole record "by way of appeal to the people": Hamilton passionately advocating it, Randolph opposed, and the question adjourned to the next day. Hamilton again took up the subject, answered now by his inveterate rival. The appeal was a brazen party maneuver. Its real object was to rally the populace against France, throw the country into the arms of Britain, and destroy the incipient democratic societies. Jefferson was unusually outspoken. The measure, he asserted, "was calculated to make the President assume the station of the head of a party, instead of the head of the nation." Washington, nevertheless, favored the appeal. Knox barged in, exhibiting a pasquinade lately printed which jested with Washington's death on the guillotine. "The President was much inflamed; got into one of those passions when he cannot command himself; ran on much on the personal abuse which had been bestowed on him . . . [declared] that *by God* he had rather be in his grave than in his present situation . . . [condemned] that *rascal* Freneau," and so on. When he finished there was some difficulty resuming the question. After awhile the President said it could be deferred, and the stormy meeting ended.

Several days later Washington called at Jefferson's place in the country. The Secretary's pending resignation stared him in the face. Once again they went over the familiar ground. Washington was full of apprehension. The retirement of the minister who had become the national symbol of Republicanism would open the government to unmitigated partisanship. Jefferson alluded to the uneasiness of his situation, obliged by the laws of society "to move exactly in the circle which I know to bear me peculiar hatred." He sought to overcome the President's fears. The Republican party was sound, aiming to save, not to destroy, the Constitution; the new Congress would attempt nothing material but to establish its independence of Treasury influence; as for Genêt, though the affair caused some embarrassment, "he would be abandoned by the Republicans the moment they knew the nature of his conduct." Washington conceded the purity of the mass of Republicans, but spoke uneasily of their obsessive fears of monarchy, and he wondered if they could stop the political machine they had put in motion. He then went into the question of Jefferson's successor. Several possibilities were discussed but none suited. Like a man going to the gallows, as Washington described his predicament, he wanted to put it off as long as possible. He implored Jefferson to stay on until the end of the year. By then affairs might show a brighter prospect. Could not Jefferson readjust his own plans by a flying trip to Monticello in the fall? The Secretary demurred but agreed to think about it. Between the President's convenience and his own there was perhaps not much to choose. He consented; and without further ado proceeded to dismantle his modest household as a precaution against yielding another time.

His desk piled high with letters, newspapers, and other damning evidence bearing on Genêt's recall, Jefferson sweated over the exacting letter to Morris through torrid August days. The rough draft was taken to the cabinet on the 15th, the finished draft on the 20th. After a thorough analysis of the issues that had led to the diplomatic impasse, Jefferson indicted the French envoy for his presumption "to put himself within the country on a line with its government, to act as co-sovereign of the territory." Genêt was granted the dubious privilege of convicting himself out of his own mouth. The cabinet officers could find no fault with this masterly statement of the case. But the studied propriety of Jefferson's language, the exclusion of Genêt's provocative words and actions outside the diplomatic line, the pointed distinction between the Minister and his government—in this character the letter rankled Hamilton. Writing as "No Jacobin," he had recently presented the public his own account of Genêt's activities, premised on the assumption that the envoy was the loyal servant of his Jacobin masters in Paris whose secret purpose was to drag the United States into the war. Hamilton wished to take the same high ground toward the government as toward the minister. The issue in the cabinet discussion finally came down to a single electric phrase from Jefferson's pen. Genêt's conduct threatened to embroil the two republics and draw upon them the terrible reproach of history, Jefferson wrote, "that of liberty warring on herself." The phrase was meant, in a letter otherwise cold and forbidding, he said, "to satisfy France not only of our friendship for her, but our attachment to the general cause of liberty, and to hers in particular." But was the cause of France the cause of liberty? Hamilton denied it; even if the proposition were true, there was no need to offend France's enemies, or gratify her American friends, by asserting it. Knox agreed. So did Randolph. The President, surprisingly, favored the expression, declaring his attachment to France above any other nation and his confidence in the ultimate triumph of liberty there; then adding, as Jefferson himself would have added at this juncture, that that embattled nation sometimes failed to understand the best means of reaching the end of its strivings. Yielding to the majority, Jefferson struck the expression. For the rest, the letter was dispatched as Jefferson had written it, together with 35 documents and 32 copies of newspapers.

None of this was communicated to Genêt for several weeks. The Republican sun still shone for him as he waited impatiently for the assemblage of Congress. "We will soon be avenged," he assured the Foreign Ministry in Paris. The little firebrand had gone to New York where the French fleet, driven from Santo Domingo, mutinous, embroiled in factional quarrels among refugees, lay at anchor. While harassed with these problems, which were more than sufficient to defeat his plans for using the fleet in New World ventures, Genêt suddenly found himself arraigned in the press for threatening to appeal from the President to the people. That he had made the rumored threat was certified by Chief Justice Jay and Rufus King, the New York senator, who had got the story from Hamilton, who had got it from Mifflin and Jefferson, who had got it from Dallas, the witness to Genêt's midnight harangue on July 6. Genêt at once wrote to the President, asking that august personage to repudiate the charge. The letter was routed to Jefferson's desk. With cold formality he told the Minister he was to address his communications to the

Secretary of State; as for the present case, it was beneath the dignity of the President to interfere. Nothing abashed, Genêt promptly gave the correspondence to the newspapers. He has "thrown down the gauntlet," Jefferson told Madison, "thus forcing that appeal to the public, and risking that disgust" he had hoped to avoid.

Some weeks earlier Jefferson would have deplored the political artifice used by the Federalist chieftains to expose Genêt. Now, near the end of August, he had abandoned the wreck and wished the mass of Republicans to do likewise. So he viewed the partisan attack on Genêt with a measure of equanimity. Public addresses in support of the President against the envoy poured into Philadelphia from all parts of the country, even from Richmond, where Jefferson's sturdy republican mentor George Wythe had chaired the meeting. In the Secretary's calculation Genêt was a necessary sacrifice to preserve American neutrality, the French connection, and the Republican interest; on the other hand, the systematic campaign launched by Hamilton and his friends threatened to sink the Republicans under the weight of popular opprobrium directed against Genêt. If unopposed they might carry everything before them. Jefferson's anxieties still focused on the first danger, Genêt, when Madison, hundreds of miles from the scene and baffled by the hero's fall from grace, called the Virginia cadre into action. "The Anglican party is busy . . . in making the worst of everything, and in turning the public feelings against France, and thence in favor of England." Madison hoped through Republican assemblages in several counties to call out the true feelings of the people. This was fine, but Madison and Republicans generally did not seem to realize the necessity of abandoning Genêt. Jefferson finally got the message across and Madison toned down his resolutions. Several meetings were held and resolutions adopted, all enforcing a line of separation between the French nation and the tarnished envoy. But it was a disappointing rearguard action. The Federalists had scored heavily.

A disease more mortal than politics, the yellow fever, struck Philadelphia, mercilessly infesting the city near the end of the torrid summer until all life seemed about to stop. No movement at the wharves, streets deserted, the theater darkened, newspapers suspended, and the burial ground beginning to look like a freshly plowed field. "The fever spreads faster," Jefferson wrote on September 12. "Deaths are now about 30 a day. It is in every square of the city. All flying who can. Most of the offices are shut or shutting. The banks shut up this day. All my clerks have left me but one: so that I cannot go on with business." Washington went home on the 10th. Knox was going away, and Hamilton lay ill with the fever. Jefferson accomplished nothing by staying in the plague-ridden city. He withdrew with Polly to his house on the Schuylkill, attended to several items of business, and left for Monticello on the 17th, two weeks ahead of schedule.

Just before leaving he notified the French Minister of the request for his recall and enclosed copies of the papers sent to Morris. Genêt, stunned, replied at once with a long, ranting letter that furnished further evidence, if further evidence was needed, of his utter recalcitrance. He had only done his duty. Every obstacle had been thrown in his way. The treaties had been falsely construed. The President could not demand his recall against the will of the people. The idea of Jefferson's perfidy now entered his tortured mind. His letter suggested at least the suspicion of betrayal by the official who had pretended to be his friend. With furious energy, Genêt composed another vindication of his conduct for home consumption and sent it by special courier to Paris. (Anticipating this move Jefferson had purposely delayed notification of the Minister, thus ensuring priority for the government's case in Paris.) But the envoy was already out of favor at home. The Jacobins had come to power. Robespierre's foreign minister had already dispatched a sharp reprimand to Genêt for permitting "the brilliance of a false popularity" to place him at odds with the American government. The Jacobins wished for quiet in America; they disowned the dazzling ocean-girdling ambitions of the Girondins, sent to the guillotine in October, and pressed all-out war—at home and abroad, commercial and military—against Great Albion. The Jacobins would be happy to recall Genêt. No argument from Morris was needed. They would like the envoy's head too. Morris did not object, but this would be denied. Thanks to the generosity of the government he had abused, Citizen Genêt would be permitted to live out the remainder of a long life in the United States, a respected New York farmer and son-in-law of Governor George Clinton.

In the months and years ahead, as he reflected on his fate and learned the extent of Jefferson's complicity in his downfall, Genêt became convinced that this Janus in the cabinet had sacrificed him on the altar of political ambition. Such was the judgment he made in a vindictive autobiographical letter addressed to Jefferson in 1797, and such was his plea at the bar of history. It could not be denied that Jefferson had confided in Genêt, sympathized with his cause, egged him on, then tried to restrain him, and finally collaborated in his destruction. But neither could the over-all consistency of Jefferson's conduct be denied. He sought always to balance American peace and neutrality with the French alliance and republican ascendancy. Genêt could not be expected to appreciate the artful management this twofold commitment required of the Secretary of State. Nor could he, a man without subtlety or modulation in his own person and incapable of perceiving it in others, be expected to understand Jefferson. About America the Frenchman was incredibly obtuse, making everything of popular effusions, next to nothing of constituted authority, and supposing that true republicans, like Jefferson, were revolutionary ideologues first and patriotic Americans second. The wisdom of a later French minister was never vouchsafed to Genêt. "Jefferson, I say," wrote Pierre Adet in 1796, "is an American and, by that title cannot be sincerely our friend. An American is the born enemy of all European peoples."

Jefferson's last two months in office was like an epilogue to a turbulent drama, adding little but giving finality to the whole. The government took up temporary quarters in Germantown, out of the way of the fever. President and Secretary of State, who had met on the road, arrived there on November 1, just as rain and cold struck down the epidemic. Refugees from the city crowded Germantown. "As a great favor," Jefferson said, "I have got a bed in the corner of the public room of a tavern." Where congressmen, soon to arrive, would lay their heads he could not imagine. The cabinet met regularly. Questions of neutrality that could not be resolved under the standing rules occupied the executive officers. The question of Genêt's discharge or suspension, pending his recall, caused further discord along the usual lines, as did the discussion of the President's message to Congress. Jefferson was back in Philadelphia by the first of December. The fugitives returned. Government and life in the city resumed their accustomed rounds. But the fever had taken a huge toll. Among the victims was Jefferson's good friend and leader of the Philadelphia Republicans, Dr. James Hutchinson. He wondered "whether the Republican interest has suffered more by his death or Genêt's extravagance." Another casualty was the *National Gazette*. The paper had never paid for itself, and Freneau, who stood by Genêt to the bitter end, now gave it up, resigned his clerkship, and withdrew to rural quietude in New Jersey at last. Actually, despite casualties of this kind, the epidemic helped the beleagured Republicans. The public outrage over Genêt sickened and died, like nearly everything else in the capital, and the general disruption upset Federalist plans to exploit the affair nation-wide.

In these final months the Secretary of State endeavored to bring the British problem back into the foreground of public attention. The subordination of that problem was part of the catastrophe wrought by Genêt. Since few British privateers frequented American waters, since Hammond was on his best behavior, British infractions of American neutrality were neither dramatic nor pressing. Against all of Jefferson's calculations, the natural balance of American diplomacy was reversed in 1793. He had expected neutrality would be delicate and difficult, not with respect to France, "temperate, forbearing, and without designs on us," but with respect to the old enemy, whose "extraordinary pride, constant course of injustice and propensity to eternal war" promised trouble. "No moderation, no justice, on our part can secure us against the violence of her character, and that we love liberty is enough for her to hate us. . . ." The course of events ran to the contrary while Genêt was on the scene.

Yet the differences between Britain and the United States on neutral rights were more basic, more threatening to peace, than the issues posed by the wayward French envoy. Determined to starve the enemy into submission by blockade, the government of William Pitt formed a convention with the governments of Russia, Prussia, and Spain to cut off the supply of provisions to France, and on June 8 issued an order in council for the seizure of neutral vessels ladened with grain and flour for France and the indemnification of their cargoes in British ports. News of this "provision order" reached the

United States before the government dispersed in September. The cabinet unanimously favored protest by the Secretary of State. He wrote to Pinckney and took up the matter with Hammond. The order forced the United States into an unneutral position toward France. Britain justified it on the ground provisions were contraband and the withholding of these supplies was one of the means employed to defeat the enemy. But this was an absurd pretension, Jefferson said. "She may, indeed, feel the desire of starving an enemy nation; but she can have no right of doing it at our loss, nor of making us the instrument of it."

Before the imposing reality of the Royal Navy, Jefferson had placed in suspension the historic American principle of "free ships make free goods." He had done so reluctantly, not only because he cherished the principle together with the profits it brought to the American carrying trade, but also because this tactical retreat implicated the United States in British seizures of French goods on American vessels, with most lamentable results in the case of the Santo Domingo refugees. Genêt had wrangled at length on this point. If the United States did not take steps to protect French persons and property in American bottoms, by arms if necessary, he would advise his government to repudiate the principle written into the treaty of 1778. (In the sequel France did, in fact, revoke the principle.) Jefferson informed Genêt of his efforts to force British concurrence in the *modern* rule. He hoped the minister would desist, for as long as Britain adhered to the ancient rule, *consolato del mare*, making enemy goods liable to seizure regardless of flag, the United States was helpless to oppose her at sea. But Genêt was adamant. The British seizures assailed American neutrality—let the government bring Albion to justice on the seas. It became necessary to oppose Genêt rather than Britain. "He thus obliged us," Jefferson sadly observed, "to abandon in the first moment the ground we were endeavoring to gain, that is to say, his ground against England and Spain, and to take the very ground of England and Spain against him." The British seizure of American grain as contraband was another matter, however. Even Hamilton, who had advocated American abandonment of "ill-founded" pretensions of neutral rights, opposed this arbitrary extension of British policy.

Jefferson scarcely expected the Pitt ministry to revoke the provision order on American demand. It did not; instead, in November, it adopted a stiffer order against neutral carriers, which was applied with devastating effect in the West Indies just after Jefferson left office. Even so, diplomatically, the demand helped to balance accounts with France. Politically, it deflected some of the rising acrimony from France to Britain. Jefferson thought the matter ought to be laid before Congress, as it would be in the legislators' power to soothe France by adopting some form of commercial retaliation against Britain.

Early in December, when he was retouching the long deferred report to Congress on commercial policy, Jefferson received from the Mediterranean new evidence of British perfidy. Death had taken successive envoys, John Paul Jones and Thomas Barclay, sent to ransom the prisoners and purchase peace with Algiers. The mission, with its niggardly purse, might have failed in any event; yet while Portugal policed the Gibraltar gate the Barbary nation was perhaps sufficiently desperate to listen to American overtures. Humphreys was ordered to take up the ill-starred mission. Before he could reach Algiers, he learned of the treaty that nation had signed with Portugal. He hired a Swedish vessel to speed the alarming news to New York. The treaty was credited to British intervention. Jefferson believed that Britain aimed in this way to cripple American trade. Once again the corsairs sailed through the Strait of Gibraltar to prey on American vessels, and only the American, as other nations navigating the Atlantic were at peace with Algiers. Jefferson reported on this state of affairs to the President, who laid it before the House in a confidential message. By voting money for a naval force, Congress at last moved toward the implementation of a policy Jefferson had advocated for nearly a decade.

The retiring Secretary was largely successful, over Hamilton's opposition, in determining the substance and tone of the President's communications to Congress on the country's relations with the major powers. The unpromising state of the negotiations with Spain gave no room for disagreement. The special mission to Madrid had become a casualty of the shifting balance of European politics, and the Spanish officials' incitements of Indian aggression under a covering barrage of accusations against the government in Philadelphia had caused Jefferson to send a sharp note to the Spanish court, from which he hoped to force clarification of the issue for the decision of Congress. Waiting almost to the last day for the courier to return from Spain, Jefferson had finally to leave the matter in the same ambiguous state he had found it. With respect to France, he was reconciled to the submission and the publication of his correspondence with Genêt. To counter the partiality of this measure, however, he insisted that his correspondence with Hammond, together with the papers on the provision order, also be made public. The negotiation with Hammond was clearly at an end. The people had a right to be informed and Congress to act. Hamilton objected strenuously. It was Jefferson's last desperate effort to embroil the United States with Britain, Hamilton felt. He viewed the disputed points—the treaty, commerce, and neutral rights—as still pending, and implied that they might be amicably settled once Jefferson's influence was removed. But Washington unreservedly sided with the Secretary of State. On the question of airing the provision order, Randolph joined Hamilton and Knox in opposition only to be overruled by the President. This was the first instance Jefferson recalled of Washington's deciding on the opinion of one against three.

The publication of these documents added luster to Jefferson's name and enabled him to retire with wide acclaim. At a later day even his enemies paid him a backhanded compliment in saying he was only fit to be Secretary of State. Against Genêt he appeared as the staunch defender of American peace and neutrality, the more remarkable because of his known sympathies for France. Against Hammond he appeared as the champion of all Americans—frontiersmen, planters, merchants, shippers, and manufacturers—still under the British yoke. Documents relating to the Spanish negotiations were confided to Congress; they too offered proof of Jefferson's quickness to defend American honor and his untiring pursuit of national objectives.

Yet, while an impressive record, it included no diplomatic triumph or break-through. After the labors of nearly four years, the advance in foreign relations could be measured in inches. The movement might be considered preliminary to great strides in the future, but it did not mark the kind of achievement Jefferson had set for himself. With Spain nothing had been settled, though the mere process of inertia—the flow of rivers and people and grain—overcame the failings of diplomacy in the moribund remnant of the Spanish empire. The same process could not be relied upon with respect to Britain. Jefferson had badgered and bargained, threatened and blackmailed, but Britain was unmoved. He expected no favors from Britain and gave none. With France he had hoped to build an alliance into a transatlantic fortress of freedom. When he retired the alliance was in a shambles and only the insolence of Britain could restore it. The deterioration in Franco-American relations was an unmitigated disaster from Jefferson's standpoint. He was not responsible for it and, indeed, managed to prevent it from becoming total; but the effects on his political system were irreparable.

He was not prepared to accept this conclusion. In his last major act as Secretary of State, he placed the capstone on that system seemingly outmoded by events and shaken to its foundations. His Report on Commerce culminated a decade's work to develop a national system independent of Britain, allied with France, and directed ultimately to a reign of free exchange and pacific intercourse among nations. The Report had a curious history. It was made in compliance with a resolution passed by the House of Representatives after setting aside a navigation act in February 1791. Jefferson worked up the Report in the ensuing recess of Congress and planned to present it in the fall session; but, "taken in" by Hamilton, he deferred the recommendation of measures unfriendly to Britain until Hammond could return an answer to the demand for evacuation of the Northwest. The Report lapsed into the catalepsy of the British negotiations. Jefferson was again prepared to submit it, newly revised, expanded, and updated, at the close of the Second Congress in February 1793. But the timing troubled him. His recommendations would almost certainly get a better hearing from the Third Congress, and in the interim Genêt would have the opportunity to present the liberal propositions he was thought to be bringing from Paris, thus strengthening the case for differential treatment of the commerce of Britain and France. Cued by Jefferson, the Republican leadership in the House decided not to call for the Report. Genêt did, of course, propose a new and liberal treaty, but the circumstances of war and his own monumental ineptitude blocked the way. Urgent problems of neutrality usurped the place previously occupied by the long-range problems of peacetime commerce. A discriminatory commercial policy was one thing in 1792, when the leading maritime powers were at peace; it was another thing altogether in 1793, when they were at war. For it must then, whether founded in treaty or in statute, have the color of an unneutral act. Moreover, the injuries to the United States as a neutral were different from the injuries suffered by American trade in peacetime. In the waning hours of his ministry, Jefferson must have pondered what to do with his twice-deferred Report. He finally decided to submit it without further revision, based on the conditions of American commerce in 1792. It was a gesture of summation. But for renewed British violence on the seas, it might have passed unnoticed—a faded piece of unfinished business. Not only was the Report saved from this fate, but falling in with the turn of events, it gave form and direction to the amorphous Republican party by setting forth a counter-system to Hamilton's, "my system," as Jefferson said, which justified in hard fact and high principle aggressive opposition to the reign of Treasury policy.

"The report," it has been well said, "is an extraordinary example of the reduction to simplicity of a complicated subject." The subject is the relationship of the American economy to Europe. As an agricultural-commercial nation, its internal trade undeveloped, its industrial base exceedingly narrow, the United States must cherish its navigation, penetrate foreign markets, and seek its economic well-being in the transatlantic trading orbit. Economic policy is inseparable from foreign policy. Trade is a weapon of diplomacy—the only potent weapon in the American armory—to be employed in pursuit of the national interest, including in that term not only the security and independence of the United States but also the widening acceptance of liberal commercial principles in the international community. "Instead of embarrassing commerce under piles of regulating laws, duties, and prohibitions," Jefferson wrote in paraphrase of Adam Smith, "could it be relieved from all its shackles in all parts of the world, could every country be employed in producing that which nature has best fitted it to produce, and each be free to exchange with others mutual surpluses for mutual wants, the greatest mass possible would then be produced of those things which contribute to human life and human happiness; the numbers of mankind would be increased, and their condition bettered." Ideally, trade should be free; in fact, it is burdened with restrictions harmful to the United States and to mankind. Jefferson described these burdens, nation by nation, and drew up the balance sheet of American commerce.

The account was fairly drawn, partial to no nation other than his own; yet it required no clairvoyance to see that, in Jefferson's judgment, the principal culprit was Britain. On liberal principles it was simply absurd that an island should rule the commerce of the world. Three-quarters of American imports came from Britain; she took one-half our exports, re-exported the greater part, prohibited what she pleased, practically monopolized the navigation, and left everything at the hazard of executive decree. France too was restrictive, embarrassingly so for Jefferson's purpose; yet France neither profited from American trade nor held the nation on its tether. "But if particular nations," Jefferson wrote, "grasp at undue shares, and, more especially, if they seize on the means of the United States, to convert them into aliment for their own strength, and withdraw them entirely from the support of those to whom they belong, defensive and protective measures become necessary on the part of the nation whose marine resources are thus invaded; or it will be disarmed of its defence; its productions will lie at the mercy of the nation which has possessed itself exclusively of the means of carrying them, and its politics may be influenced by those who command its commerce." To correct this unnatural condition Jefferson proposed counter-prohibitions, regulations, and duties, working reciprocally on all nations, but in the necessity of the case working hardest on Britain. She refused to accept vessels not built in the United States as American: we should do the same as to vessels naturalized in Britain. She refused to permit American merchants to reside in her colonies: we should refuse residence to English merchants. She admitted nothing but the domestic productions of the United States in our carriers: we should admit only British productions in theirs. She excluded, with some exceptions, both the productions and the vessels of the United States from her colonies: we should prohibit American exports in British vessels. She imposed high duties on American products: we should do the same on British manufactures. And here Jefferson, although making no concession to Hamilton in principle, gave his blessing to the encouragement of manufactures in consequence of a national strategy aimed at commercial freedom and independence. "The oppressions on our agriculture, in foreign ports, would thus be made the occasion of relieving it from a dependence on the councils and conduct of others, and of promoting arts, manufactures and population at home." Ironically, the factories and workshops he had preferred to keep in Europe would the more likely result from his commercial system than from Hamilton's fiscal system. The latter reinforced Anglican connections and its political thrust was counter-revolutionary in the great conflict raging in the Western world.

No nation could object to his system, Jefferson thought, since it was founded on perfect reciprocity. Its inconveniences were nothing when compared with the loss of wealth and of power attending the current indiscriminate policy. "Free commerce and navigation are not to be given in exchange for restrictions and vexations; nor are they likely to produce a relaxation of them." But by granting favors where favors were due, by meeting prohibitions with prohibitions, the United States might, in the course of serving its own interest, bring other nations to the liberal standard.

The Report on Commerce was read in the House on December 19 and ordered to the committee of the whole. Jefferson, said the Secretary of Treasury, "threw this FIREBRAND of discord into the midst of the representatives . . . and instantly decamped to Monticello." Early in January, Madison introduced a series of resolutions based on the Report. France was stamped on its face, the Federalists charged. The movement for discrimination stemmed from the old unreasoning hostility to Britain, revived now solely for political effect. Whatever the disadvantages of the British trade, Federalists said, they were more than offset by the rewards in capital and credit, federal revenue, and dependable markets and supplies. Representatives of the eastern carrying states opposed discrimination, though they presumably had most to gain from the policy, while southerners, who had trembled at the grant of congressional power to legislate in this sphere, furnished the main support. As the anger against Britain mounted, so too did the prospect for the resolutions. But it mounted too far, bringing the two countries to the verge of war, causing the resolutions to be sidetracked in favor of a temporary embargo, and leading finally to the mission of John Jay, whose famous treaty consummated the British-centered policy of the Federalists—an astounding defeat for the Jeffersonian system.

Jefferson would observe these developments from his summit at Monticello. His retirement ended Washington's plan of a "coalition" government. For all its difficulties it had served the new nation well, checking extremism, balancing interests, commanding that element of unity so necessary if the government was to survive. But with the rise of political parties, the plan outlived its usefulness. Washington was reluctant to abandon it, and he knew this must be the consequence of Jefferson's withdrawal. One last appeal failed. He accepted Jefferson's resignation with assurances "that the opinion which I had formed of your integrity and talents, and which dictated your original nomination has been confirmed by the fullest experience, and that both have been eminently displayed in the discharge of your duty." In the critical year just passed the President had grown in Jefferson's estimation. He had failed to shake Washington's confidence in Hamilton and Treasury policy, a defeat so shattering that it robbed his partial victories in foreign affairs of character; but only later, from his Olympian perch, did he yield to his fears and view the President as a helpless captive of party. It never seemed to trouble him that he had helped to make this development inevitable.

Jefferson insisted his withdrawal from the public stage was final. He had been in the spotlight long enough, and as he wrote to an old friend, in the course of eighteen years he had had but two years at home. "It will be the second time my bark will have put into port with a design not to venture out again; and I trust it will be the last. My farm, my family and my books call me to them irresistibly." To these resolutions his Republican friends politely demurred, while the Federalists simply refused to believe them. The vauntings of pastoral quietude covered a poisonous ambition Jefferson dared not acknowledge even to himself. The retirement was only an interlude, John Adams mused. "Jefferson thinks by this step to get a reputation as an humble, modest, meek man, wholly without ambition or vanity. He may even have deceived himself into this belief. But if the prospect opens, the world will see and he will feel that he is as ambitious as Oliver Cromwell." If vanity is a qualification for seeing it in others, then Adams was a good judge. History would bear him out. While there is not the slightest reason to doubt the sincerity of Jef-

ferson's motives in seeking retirement, had he planned it as an elaborate political stratagem he could not have planned more wisely.

Jefferson lingered over goodbyes in Philadelphia, discharged his
servants, gathered the few things he had not sent by boat, took in
the Friday meeting of the American Philosophical Society, and on
the following Sunday, January 5, set forth, bumping his way by
stage, private conveyance, and on horseback to his journey's end at
Monticello on the 16th. He had, he thought, closed the last political
chapter of his life.

CHAPTER EIGHT

Withdrawal and Return:

Vice President

But there have been many and still are many who, while pursuing the calm of soul of which I speak, have withdrawn from civic duty and taken refuge in retirement. Among such have been the most famous and by far the foremost philosophers and certain other earnest, thoughtful men who could not endure the conduct of either the people or their leaders; some of them, too, lived in the country and found their pleasure in the management of their private estates. Such men have had the same aim as kings—to suffer no want, to be subject to no authority, to enjoy their liberty, that is, in its essence, to live just as they pleased.

Cicero, De Officiis.

IN HIS MIND'S EYE Monticello had long been the scene of a pastoral idyl that only now, in the ripeness of his years, took full possession of Thomas Jefferson. Successive calls of public duty had carried him far from his element and robbed him of selfhood. Too long had he lived in what he hated; too long had he neglected the things he loved—his farm and family and books. Return to the orange-red highlands of his native Albemarle—"the Eden of the United States"—was a return to the paradise of his soul.

In letters to his friends he depicted himself as a plain farmer, an "antediluvian patriarch" among his children, and a political innocent who, with Montaigne, had found "ignorance the softest pillow on which a man can rest his head." He was still capable of outraged ejaculations on the conspiracy of kings, nobles, and priests against European liberty. "I am still warm whenever I think of these scoundrels," he said, "though I do it as seldom as I can, preferring infinitely to contemplate the tranquil growth of my lucerne and potatoes. I have so completely withdrawn myself from these spectacles of usurpation and misrule, that I do not take a single newspaper, nor read one a month; and I feel infinitely the happier for it." For years he had been accustomed to writing a dozen letters a day; now weeks passed without setting pen to paper as, farmer-like, he put off letters 'til a rainy day. "My next reformation," he said, "will be to allow neither pen, ink, nor paper to be kept on the farm. When I have accomplished this I shall be in a fair way to indemnifying myself for the drudgery in which I have passed my life."

Jefferson was now fifty years of age. His hair was turning gray, but his body was as strong and trim, his countenance as mild, his mind as nimble as in his youth. After a bout with rheumatism in the fall of 1794, he imagined for a time that age had caught up with him. But the torment passed. His habits bordered on the ascetic. He rose early: the sun never caught him in bed was his boast. He neither smoked nor drank, except light wines at dinner and a single glass of water a day. He ate moderately, giving vegetables the first place in his diet. Always busy, "a miser of his time," he expected the same diligence of others, and partly for this reason would not permit games of cards under his roof. He took his own amusement on horseback, riding solitary an hour or two every day regardless of the weather. "He was an uncommonly fine rider—sat easily upon his horse, and always had him in the most perfect control." From the first breath of spring to the last gasp of autumn he spent most of his waking hours in the open air, inspecting his grounds and shops and riding over his farms. "I live on my horse from an early breakfast to a late dinner, and very often after that till dark," he said. His ruddy skin flaked and freckled under the Virginia sun. He dressed plainly, put on no airs, and in every outer aspect was the image of the Virginia farmer he professed to be.

An eminent Frenchman came to visit this American Cato in June

1796. "I found him in the midst of the harvest," the Duc de La Ro-
chefoucald-Liancourt wrote, "from which the scorching heat of the
sun does not prevent his attendance." The Duke was one of those
enlightened noblemen who in the declining years of the Old Regime
had woven fact and fancy into the gossamer dream of America. In
1789 the dream seemed about to materialize in France. Liancourt
was a leader of the Revolution. He it was who upon informing the
King of the true state of affairs just before the fall of the Bastille
heard the amazed cry, "But it is a revolt!" and retorted, "No, Sire, it
is a revolution!" When Jefferson last saw the Duke he was president
of the National Assembly and the principal author of the so-called
abolition of the feudal system. Three years later the dream turned
to ashes; he lost his estate, the head of the family, La Rochefoucald,
was murdered; and Liancourt went into exile, first in England and
then, in 1794, in the United States. From his base at Philadelphia he
made five "voyages" which took him to Canada and to Georgia and
most parts in between, studying the land and the people not as in a
dream but as they appeared to a keen and friendly sojourner. He included Monticello in his itinerary as a matter of course. The house
on the mountain's summit gradually acquired the fame of its master.
Already travelers in number beat a track to Jefferson's door. A
hard-headed Irishman, Isaac Weld, had stopped in March, and the
Comte de Volney, perhaps the most celebrated traveler of the time,
had just ended a leisurely visit when his compatriot in exile came
upon Jefferson in the harvest field.

Although there was a political bond between the Frenchman and
the American, they were men disenchanted with politics who at
once found more interesting things to talk about. "In private life,"
Liancourt recorded, "Mr. Jefferson displays a mild, easy and obliging temper, though he is somewhat cold and reserved. His conversation is of the most agreeable kind, and he possesses a stock of information not inferior to that of any other man. In Europe he would
hold a distinguished rank among men of letters, and as such he has
already appeared there; at present he is employed with activity and
perseverance in the management of his farms and buildings; and he
orders, directs and pursues in the minutest detail every branch of
business relative to them." These employments were dear to Liancourt's heart. An agricultural reformer before he was a revolutionist,

an innovator of crops and tillage and stock on his own estate, a
founder of the French Royal Agricultural Society, he at once recognized in Jefferson the republican counterpart of Europe's "improving landlord." Compared with his guest, the Virginian was a
poor amateur. Eight bushels of wheat to the acre was hardly impressive; the ancient Romans had done better. Nevertheless, in his farming as in his politics, Jefferson had escaped from the tyranny of
habit into the freedom of knowledge, and this was impressive in a
country where bad practice had hardened into a system. "Above
all," Liancourt wrote, "much good may be expected, if a contemplative mind like that of Mr. Jefferson, which takes the theory for
its guide, watches its application with discernment, and rectifies it
according to the peculiar circumstances and nature of the country,
climate, and soil, and conformably to the experience which he daily
acquires."

Jefferson's zeal for innovation and improvement extended to his
house as well as to his fields. Monticello was in noble disarray. Jefferson was tearing down his house in order to make a better one,
and the visitor had to keep a lookout for flying bricks. "Monticello,
according to its first plan, was infinitely superior to all other houses
in America, in point of taste and convenience; but at that time Mr.
Jefferson had studied taste and the fine arts only in books," Liancourt observed. "His travels in Europe have supplied him with models; he has appropriated them to his design; and his new plan
. . . will be accomplished before the end of the next year, and
then his house will certainly deserve to be ranked with the most pleasant mansions of France and England." In fact, whatever its merits,
the work of "re-edification" upset Jefferson and his family for quite
a number of years.

The patriarch directed his domestic establishment with the same
exactness and system he had shown in public affairs. "As he cannot
expect any assistance from the two small neighboring towns, every
article is made on his farm; his Negroes are cabinet-makers, carpen-
ters, masons, bricklayers, smiths, etc." In the cares of the household
he was assisted by two amiable daughters. The Frenchman thought
the younger, Miss Maria, now seventeen, "remarkably handsome"—
something of an understatement if the testimonies to her exquisite
beauty are to be credited—and he hoped that Jefferson might find

the philosophy to accept her loss in marriage and the good fortune to add a second worthy son-in-law to his family circle. Martha and her husband—more son than son-in-law, Liancourt thought—were at Monticello with their children every summer and much of the time in between. Never reconciled to their living at Varina, the distant James River plantation, Jefferson had induced Randolph *père* to part with Edgehill, a 1500-acre seat near Monticello; and despite a bitter feud between father and son the deed was done in 1792. Young Randolph soon began farming at Edgehill, though it was several years before the family actually settled there. Jefferson remained an over-anxious third party to this marriage. Martha had grown into a copy of her father, tall, bright-featured, gentle, and, from all accounts, the soul of matronly virtue. She still adored her father, once in a letter to him scolding "those who dare to think that any *new* ties can weaken the first and best of nature." On most points the new tie, Randolph, was her exact opposite. A restless, impulsive, and tormented man, whose unpredictable flights of temper were to make him a legend among his neighbors, Randolph sometimes felt like a "silly bird" among the swans at Monticello. Perhaps the "silly bird" should have taken his little swan and flown away, but his own affections were too deep to permit that, and it would have killed Jefferson. For Randolph, at least, the triangle was unhealthy. It shattered his self-esteem and threw him into fits of depression. In the summer of 1796, during Liancourt's visit, he was still suffering from a strange undiagnosed malady of body and mind that descended not long after Jefferson's retirement. The heart of the patriarch overflowed with love, but it was not selfless; and his need to remain the center of all domestic affection and management introduced a hidden flaw into the seemingly idyllic family circle at Monticello.

Jefferson's summit afforded no certain refuge from the political commotions of the world. He said his scheme was to pay no attention to them, but the world would not leave him alone and he had been too long in it to resign himself to the stoical politics he liked to imagine were his. He had been in retirement only eight months when President Washington asked him to go as a special envoy to Spain. He responded, from his bed of rheumatism, in terms that could not be misunderstood. There were earlier reports that he had actually arrived in Europe to negotiate with one or another of the great powers. The critical state of American foreign relations, together with the Whiskey Rebellion and other signposts of discontent on the home front, proved a severe test of Jefferson's political abnegation. The strife of nations and parties broke over the walls he had raised, and before a year passed he was making an experiment to determine the fastest postal route between Philadelphia and Albemarle.

Yet it was a retirement. His principal business of life now was not politics but the management of his estate. "The land left to the care of stewards has suffered as well as the buildings from the long absence of the master," Liancourt observed; "according to the custom of the country, it has been exhausted by successive culture." Jefferson hoped under his own management to make his lands bounteous again; and the outcome of this trial, so long deferred, must decide whether he and his children were to trudge through life mortgaged to British merchants or to enjoy the freedom of a great estate. His debts in 1794 were in excess of £7500, and another £1000 would be added the following year by a new judgment against the Wayles' heirs. (Randolph inherited a similar debt from his father.) The goal of debt freedom by the end of 1796 was apparently out of reach. He did not give up on it but was still struggling to reach it years later when he entered the presidency. Under so crushing a burden a man might lose the courage to pursue his vision. Jefferson, however, went ahead with his elaborate plans for Monticello at the same time that he labored to exact a profit from his lands. "I expected when I came home to be quite at my leisure," he wrote in 1796. "On the contrary, I never was so hard run with business." For all the rewards of retirement, it had its disappointments too; and he never found at Monticello the tranquility he sought.

Farming

Jefferson's land roll of 1794 shows that he was the lord of 10,647 acres. The property was divided more or less equally between Albemarle and the counties of Bedford and Campbell eighty or ninety miles to the southwest. The latter plantations, which he called collectively Poplar Forest, were under the supervision of a trusted manager, and Jefferson seldom went there. About 800 acres were under cultivation, chiefly in the prime money crop, tobacco. The lands in Albemarle were divided into several plantations, lying on either side of the Rivanna River, nearly all contiguous, and all directed from Monticello. Jefferson wanted to place Shadwell and the adjoining farms across the river under tenants, leasing his laborers with the land; but he could not perfect this system. He tilled more than 1200 acres in Albemarle. His total force of slaves numbered 152 on the roll he took in November, a decrease of about one-quarter from the roll of eleven years before. He held on to his land more tenaciously than to his slaves. In 1793 he sold Elk Hill, the James River plantation, as a contribution to his debts, though neither deed nor money passed hands for four years. After this he made only minor adjustments in his landholdings, except for handsome conveyances to his children.

Viewing his native country as a virtual Eden, Jefferson had an exalted opinion of its capabilities for agriculture. No landscape was lovelier than that upon which he gazed from Monticello—an endless panorama of fields and forests and hills—no climate was as mild and healthful, nor had nature been niggardly in her supreme gift of the soil. Perhaps he communicated his enthusiasm to his visitors; at any rate, they too formed a good opinion of the land. William Strickland, an English agriculturist who called in 1795, later wrote, "a richer district by nature there cannot be, than all those counties which lie at the eastern front of the Blue Ridge." In truth, the natural assets were matched by appalling liabilities. The surface soil, while fertile, was shallow and underlaid with hard clay almost impenetrable by the plows of that day, thus hindering the replenishment of plant food and constantly exposing the loose upper layer to leaching and erosion. The hilliness of the terrain accentuated the latter evil. The normal rainfall was quite sufficient for piedmont crops, but too often it came in huge downpours that drowned the fields and washed the precious topsoil into muddy streams and rivers. Jefferson spoke of "such rains as never came since Noah's flood," and moderately estimated the loss of soil during one summer at a year's rent. At other times the earth was so hard and dry it could not be plowed; and his well atop Monticello failed with distressing frequency. The winters, mild as a rule, sometimes froze his wheat in the ground. The land and the climate, for all their charms, were less suited to cultivation than Jefferson supposed.

He was right, nevertheless, in seeing the problem as one of art rather than of nature. Certainly he was under no illusion about the condition of Virginia agriculture, nor indeed of American husbandry generally. It was a scandal to enlightened farmers everywhere. The Virginia lands had been worked for quick profits, exhausted, then abandoned or left to beggar the wretched men who persisted in cultivating them. Bad as the situation was in New York or Pennsylvania, where the older lands yielded little more than those in Virginia, it was there at its worst, "the lowest state of degradation," in Strickland's opinion. The degradation had spread from the tidewater westward to Jefferson's Eden. A new settler described Albemarle in the 1790's, barely half a century after it had been redeemed from the wilderness, as "a scene of desolation that baffles description— farm after farm worn out, washed and gullied, so that scarcely an acre could be found in a place fit for cultivation." The causes of this rapid deterioration naturally invited speculation. Slavery was prominently mentioned. Jefferson's opposition to the institution had not abated, and he sometimes wondered if he was master enough to succeed at farming with slave labor; yet, recognizing the futility of making slavery the scapegoat, he wasted little time on the subject. Besides, he had demonstrated to his own satisfaction (though to no one else's) that Virginia slave labor was considerably less costly than English (and surely American) free labor, so the real cause of the agricultural malady lay elsewhere. The management of large estates required the employment of overseers, a class of men all too conveniently blamed by Virginia planters for the ravaging of their lands. Jefferson had the usual trouble with overseers. Seven had come and gone at Monticello during the decade of his absence. In 1793 he took pains to recruit one in Maryland, supposedly uncorrupted by the habits of the Virginia class, only to have to discharge him after a year's sorry experience; and he went through four more before 1801. But he drew up no indictment of overseers. Virginia estates lacked sufficient capital for large-scale improvements. This was part of the explanation. Another part was political: laws and policies which enriched merchants, stock-jobbers, bankers, and speculators at the expense of the landholding class. But Jefferson the farmer never gave as much weight to these political evils as some of his friends; nor did he, with some others, trace the degeneration of Virginia agriculture to democratizing laws, such as those for the divisibility of estates, which he had inspired.

Jefferson ascribed the malady primarily to a system of culture that could not fail to desolate any country where it was pursued, as in his own, over two or three generations. "The highlands where I live," he explained, "have been cultivated about sixty years. The culture was tobacco and Indian corn, as long as they would pay the labor; then they were turned out. After four or five year's rest, they would bring good corn again, and in double that time, perhaps, good tobacco. Then they would be exhausted by a second series of tobacco and corn." This remorseless "cropping" impoverished the earth. Tobacco was the first evil, "a culture productive of infinite wretchedness," but corn, especially under shallow plowing straight up and down the hillsides, was a close second. The former, it was said, enriched the planter and ruined the soil, the latter ruined both. Tobacco had been abandoned for wheat in Jefferson's part of the country. He had shifted to wheat in Albemarle in 1790 on the expectation of the rising market in Europe. He was not disappointed; but he could never get away from tobacco in Bedford, and corn was such a staple of the plantation economy he had to conquer his aversion to it. The common rotation began with wheat, followed by corn, then a year's fallow, the cycle repeated until the fields died. While exhaustion might be slower under this "three shift system," it was no less certain than under the barbarous system it replaced.

The restoration of the soil was the starting point of all improvement. Jefferson believed with the scientific agriculturists of the time that the soil held a given quantity of plant food, that it was gradually depleted under cultivation—more rapidly by some growths than by others—but that it could be constantly replenished by restorative crops in proper rotation. He had not himself been a scientific student of agriculture. He was, of course, acquainted with the agricultural revolution inaugurated in England sixty years before by Jethro Tull's famous work, *Horse-Hoeing Husbandry*. He knew some of the prolific writings of Arthur Young and opened correspondence with this great reformer's associates on the government chartered Board of Agriculture, one of whom, William Strickland, stopped at Monticello in 1795. "Should you pass by," Jefferson wrote to a neighboring farmer soon after his retirement, "you will find me more eager to talk of Home [Lord Kames] and Young than Grotius and Vattel." Like the gentlemen farmers in England, he was enchanted by the Romans, whose theory and practice had yet to be surpassed. Adam Dickson's *Husbandry of the Ancients*, a two-volume compilation of the Latin writers, was a favorite among his many books on agricultural subjects.

But he was a practical farmer, not a bookish one, and he probably learned more from George Washington and George Logan, progressive farmers like himself, than from all his books. For several years they had been applying the "English system" to their own lands. Jefferson had observed the results. Dr. Logan's careful experiments at Stenton had proven the superiority, at least in that locality, of a system that employed red clover as the principal soil improver in a nine-year rotation. Listening to the good doctor, seeing the richness of his place, Jefferson became an enthusiast for cover crops, especially red clover. The substitution of clover for unproductive fallow protected the tired lands from the baking sun and drenching rains; it enriched the soil; it furnished fodder to support livestock which, in turn, supplied the farmer with manure for his fields. Since the progressive husbandry did away with pasturage altogether, working the fields more or less continuously, the production of manure was an essential element in the plan of rotation. It also went to the principles of deep plowing first championed by Tull, for the application of manure dissolved the soil particles, thus permitting the pulverization believed necessary to good husbandry. In his own practice Jefferson was attentive to these matters of plowing and manuring, but his experimentation centered on the determination of the right crops in the right rotation. This, he thought, "the most important of all questions a farmer has to decide."

Before he left Philadelphia he had decided with Logan's advice on an eight-cycle rotation, the last three in clover. On second thought he dropped one year of clover, made other adjustments, and ended with a seven-year rotation. The plan called for the division of his farms into seven fields all equal. "In all successions of crops," he instructed Madison, "the fields must be supposed equal, each field to go through the same succession, and each year's crop to be the same. On these data the laws of combination pronounce that the number of fields and number of years constituting a complete rotation, must always be equal." Since he had 280 acres in tillage at Monticello, each field would be 40 acres; each would have its own granary, and be allotted four men and four women laborers, four horses and four oxen, a complement of plows, other implements, and so on. Such a farm on his crop rotation would support about 90 head of cattle; they, in turn, would make manure enough for spreading every field once in seven years. By commencing the rotation in each field at successive points in the seven-year cycle, the aggregate produce would be the same from year to year. The rotation ensured a balance between exhausting grain crops (wheat, rye, corn) and soil ameliorates (peas, clover, succory, vetch). It would also provide an annual crop of turnips and potatoes, primarily as animal food, though Jefferson promoted the latter, a genuine American article, as a substitute for corn in the human diet.

Such was the general system of farming Liancourt observed in Albemarle in 1796. Of course, Jefferson's plans were never fully realized. Nor is it easy to imagine under what circumstances they might have been. They expressed a rage for order and system sure to be embarrassed in the untidy and unpredictable business of farming. If agriculture were a species of architecture—if the structuring of fields and rotations were more important than the day-to-day cultivation of crops—then Jefferson would have been a superior farmer. A farmer who thinks like a mathematician is an easy object of ridicule—too easy, for ridicule diverts understanding. In farming, as in politics, Jefferson made allowance for the gap between theory and practice and seldom found it necessary to betray his responsibility to either one. The plans, the diagrams, the mathematical calculations he made for his farms served him as blueprints, rather like the architect's; and in the execution he simply did the best he could, relying on experience to correct his errors. This was the way of the thinking reformer. And in a science so little known as agriculture, reform, though it must proceed on a constructive plan, must also give a large berth to laborious methods of trial and error. Jefferson did. Still he was disappointed that his plans fell so far short of execution. His fields, sloping and irregular, were "too rough even to please the eye," he complained in 1796, "and as yet unreclaimed from the barbarous state in which the slovenly business of tobacco making left them." He never had enough cattle, usually let them forage for themselves, but not on tilled ground, thus losing the dung altogether. This was a common defect of American husbandry and certainly of Jefferson's. The slackness of slave labor, the caprices of the weather, the fluctuations of the market—all helped to upset his well-laid plans. Hopes continued to run high, but the profit account was discouraging. Two years after his return to public office he resumed the detestable culture of tobacco in Albemarle: a poignant confession of failure.

"His system is entirely confined to himself," the Duc de Liancourt noted; "it is censured by some of his neighbors, who are also employed in improving their culture with ability and skill, but he adheres to it, and thinks it is founded on just observations." Plainly, the Frenchman was not sure that it was. He admired Jefferson's "science" but thought less of his "skill." It was scarcely creditable that a man of Jefferson's knowledge should decline to enclose his fields, preferring instead to divide them by rows of peach trees—an aesthetic extravagance he could ill afford—or should allow his cattle to graze in the woods, or make no effort to control the drainage on his hillsides.

One prominent Virginian who dissented from leading points of Jefferson's system was John Taylor of Caroline. Searching for a good drilling machine in 1794, Jefferson opened an agricultural correspondence with this former political cohort. "There is a spice of fanaticism in my nature upon two subjects—," Taylor confessed, "agriculture and republicanism, which all who set in motion are sure to suffer by." Taylor did run on, dropping useful hints on many things, and Jefferson, lacking that "spice of fanaticism," had difficulty upholding his end of the account. At Hazelwood, on the Rappahannock River, Taylor had been working for years to restore his worn-out lands. His experiments led him to reject the "English system" of cover crops and manure and long rotation. He did not doubt the importance of manure; on the contrary, the best system of agriculture was that which produced the most manure. But English ideas on this subject were inapplicable to America, where it was cheaper to buy an acre of new land than to manure an old one.

Taylor had no confidence in green crops, held a high opinion of corn, and practiced a simple four-shift rotation, half in wheat and corn, half in fallow. Unmoved by these strictures, avoiding argument, Jefferson viewed his differences with the Caroline planter as more verbal than substantial. "You keep half your lands in culture, the other half in nurse; so I propose to do. . . . My years of rest, however, are employed, two of them in producing clover, yours in volunteer herbage. . . . I think that the important improvement for which the world is indebted to Young is the substitution of clover crops for unproductive fallow." In the passage of time the two Virginians, Taylor the hard-headed practitioner and Jefferson the constructive theorist, approached a middle ground.

Jefferson exchanged ideas with many persons, American and European, and not only ideas but plants, seeds, devices, and implements of husbandry. This continued an old enterprise, more directly related now to his own immediate purposes. Whenever he learned of a promising innovation in farming, he was eager to try it at Monticello and, if the experiment succeeded, to share the benefits with his fellow cultivators. He got from Washington in 1794 the seed of the succory, a "green dressing" which flourished at Mount Vernon. Planted in Albemarle it was an indifferent grower the first year but luxuriated the second. Jefferson become an ardent champion of this humble plant and awarded it a place in his rotation. On the other hand, he was disappointed in lucerne (alfalfa), giving it up after a brief trial. He never knew—no one knew—why one plant flourished and another failed; the best the agriculturist could do at this stage of the science was to follow the tedious methods of trial and error experimentation. His greatest success was with Logan's clover, but almost any ameliorative aroused his interest. For example, the "true winter vetch," a European plant he had observed in his travels abroad and wished to try at Monticello. Unable to obtain it from Philadelphia, where it was unknown, he asked Thomas Pinckney to send the seed from London. Nothing came of this, but Strickland, on his return to England sent him the vetch. Apparently, after these efforts, the plant failed, for it never entered into his rotation. During his visit the English agriculturist had given him the seed of the Swedish rutabaga, earlier imported into England, and now through Jefferson disseminated in the United States. Sheep turned turnips into manure and supplied the plantation with mutton and wool. So it went—each innovation was a link in the chain of improved husbandry. Taking a hint from Arthur Young, Jefferson began raising sheep at Monticello in 1794; but some years passed before he, with a few other Americans, turned his attention to improving the breed.

If he could be accused of negligence toward animal husbandry, the same could not be said with respect to farm machinery. Here, too, progress was painfully slow and the rewards were poor compensation for the time and money spent in securing them. He was alert to any improvement in the plow and perfected his own moldboard of least resistance; he kept a lookout for better seed drills (Young said there wasn't a good one in England); and he put the Scotch threshing machine to work in Virginia. A scale model of this horse-powered machine, sneaked out of England under Pinckney's auspices, finally arrived at Norfolk near the end of 1793. Jefferson could hardly wait to see it in action. But to construct the machine with his own labor was a much bigger job than he had counted on. It took three years. The clumsy contraption of gears and revolving beaters was mounted on a wagon and carried from one field and farm to another. While its performance was below expectations, and Jefferson hoped to find a better one, it was still a great advance over the almost universal practice of "treading" the grain from the chaff. His wheat was cleaner than his neighbors'. On the basis of his own time studies, the machine doubled his output. Earlier and speedier threshing eliminated infestation of the grain by the weevil; it also released one-half his laborers, previously employed on the treading floors, to begin the season's plowing. Jefferson never really understood machinery, only what it could do, but he liked to tinker. One of the products of his tinkering was a seed-box for sowing clover, constructed on the basis of a hint in an agricultural journal. The seed-box, he informed Taylor, "reduces the expense of seeding from six shilling to two shilling and three pence the acre, and does the business better than is possible to be done by the human hand."

Jefferson was a meticulous observer of farm operations. As Albert Jay Nock has said, his mind had something of the quality of the modern efficiency engineer.

Julius Shard fills the two-wheeled barrow in 3 minutes, and carried it 30 yards in 1½ minutes more. Now this is four loads of the common barrow with one wheel. So that suppose the 4 loads put in at the same time viz. 3 minutes, 4 trips will take $4 \times 1\frac{1}{2}$ minutes $= 6$, which added to 3 minutes filling $= 9$ minutes to fill and carry the same earth which was filled and carried in the two-wheeled barrow in $4\frac{1}{2}$ minutes. From a trial I made with the same two-wheeled barrow, I found that a man could dig and carry to a distance of 50 yds, 5 cubical yds of earth in a day of 12 hours length. Ford's Phil did it; not overlooked and having to mount his loaded barrow up a bank 2 f. high and tolerably steep.

This little study reflects Jefferson's approach to plantation management. He recorded his observations in his Farm Book, a volume of blank pages with chapter headings on every phase of farming. Here, too, was the calendar of his works and days: the fall's plowing and sowing and gathering of potatoes, corn, fodder; in the winter, clearing land, cutting firewood, repairing fences and roads, hauling wheat and floating it to market; in the spring, oxen and men set to plowing as soon as the sun warmed the earth, then planting corn, clover, peas, and so on; summer, harvest. Practically the whole force of slaves was employed in the harvest. In 1795, 17 were cradlers, 5 reapers, 7 stackers, 36 gatherers, plus cooks and loaders and carters. Working from dawn to dusk through 320 acres of wheat and rye, on both sides of the river, the harvest was finished in 10 to 11 days. The performance did not measure up to Jefferson's standards. There had been waste motion, idle time, and bottlenecks. On the basis of his inspection he drew up a new plan under which "the whole machine would move in exact equilibrio" so that the same acreage would be harvested with fewer hands in six days. But, alas, men were not machines and harvests could not be reduced to mathematical rule. The harvest the next year, though better, took the same muscle and the same time as before.

Despite the irrelevance of some of Jefferson's plans and calculations, the disjointed empiricism of others, all were informed by a unifying purpose: the improvement of agriculture for human welfare. Agriculture was his livelihood, but his zeal for improvement was actuated by interests larger than his own. By taking upon himself "the risk of a first experiment," he hoped to be more useful to his neighbors, who could not afford the risks but whose lands also cried for reform. His correspondence reached far beyond the neighborhood, of course, and so, too, might the ambit of his usefulness. The progress of agriculture and the increase of human happiness were all one. "Science never appears so beautiful," he wrote to an English coadjutor, "as when applied to the uses of human life, nor any use of it so engaging as those of agriculture and domestic economy." His idealized husbandman held the sum of human happiness. He sought it for himself, but not, after all, in the antique guise of a pastoral poem. He sought it in the modern guise of agricultural science. He really believed with Jonathan Swift "that whoever could make two ears of corn or two blades of grass to grow upon a spot of ground where only one grew before, would deserve better of mankind and do more essential service to his country than the whole race of politicians put together."

Whatever the public benefit of Jefferson's services, they probably made little if any difference in his account of profit and loss. He kept a day-to-day record of his financial transactions down to the last penny. He was forever calculating costs. (The habit stayed with him to the very end: on his deathbed he noted, "a gallon of lamp oil, costing $1.25 has lighted my chamber highly 25 nights, for 6 hours a night which is 5 cents a night & 150 hours.") Still he was not a good accountant—and anything but frugal. Prudent in small expenditures, he was lavish in large ones. His concern with costs, as with efficiency generally, seldom rose above the level of petty detail. The practice of plantation accounting, later developed to a fine point, was still in a primitive state. Jefferson itemized everything but seemed to know nothing of debit and credit accounting; hidden costs, such as depreciation, rarely entered into his reckoning; and he never actually balanced, or closed, his books. Annual income from wheat and tobacco fluctuated wildly. For the seven years 1794–1800, it probably averaged between $4000 and $5000. Since most of the Bedford tobacco was mortgaged, he looked to the produce of his Albemarle lands, to wheat primarily, for personal income. Prices were high. The crop improved in 1795, and the bumper harvest of 1796 helped to indemnify earlier losses. Then the elements turned against him. A severe winter succeeded a dry fall. (On December 24 the thermometer plunged to five degrees below zero at Monticello, breaking the low point he had stated in the *Notes on Virginia*.) In desperation he planted tobacco again, at first on a small scale but in 1798 almost exclusively. In that year the price at Richmond soared to $13 a hundred pounds. Jefferson paid $2000 on his old debts with comparative ease. The temptation to go entirely into tobacco was irresistible. But the market was a fickle temptress. The price collapsed the following year, and Jefferson, after withholding his tobacco for several months in anticipation of a rising market that never came, finally had to sell for seven dollars. He got only six dollars in 1800. If his total crop approximated 50,-000 pounds, as seems likely, the gross was only $3000. His annual account with Richmond merchants for supplies and services exceeded that amount. Clearly, after making allowance for other income, he was hard-pressed. On the whole, any net profits realized in these years took the form of capital improvements at Monticello.

His plantations were a good deal less self-sufficient in these years than later. Only the most basic supplies could be obtained locally, in Charlottesville or in Milton, the latter a now forgotten village located on the Rivanna at the head of navigation; other things came from Richmond and Philadelphia. Cash was a rarity in this rural community, and Jefferson, like other farmers, necessarily engaged in barter. He traded the work of his blacksmith for beef and butter, some of his wheat for store supplies, and a few bushels annually for whiskey. He seems never to have had a sufficiency even of corn. Clothing was a major item, for his spinners and weavers met only a fraction of the annual requisitions. Nor was he self-sufficient in labor. His records list eleven hired slaves in 1795, which represented a cost in excess of $400 a year. Many of his own slaves were mortgaged to his creditors, and, as before, he occasionally sold slaves in the effort to meet his debts. Such were his financial straits in 1796, when the new judgment on the Wayles estate went against him, that he had to mortgage away what little equity he had accumulated in his slaves in order to protect his creditors. As the old slave Isaac said of his former master, "he want rich himself—only his larnin."

In the management of his slaves Jefferson encouraged diligence but was instinctively too lenient to demand it. By all accounts he was a kind and generous master. His conviction of the injustice of the institution strengthened his sense of obligation toward its victims. It was chiefly with a view to placing his slaves "on the comfortable footing of the laborers of other countries" that he had gone outside Virginia for an overseer in 1793. It was a costly experiment, apparently without mitigating effect. There were limits to his own superintendence, but within them he would not allow his slaves to be over-driven, or whipped unless at the last resort, preferring rather to penalize the lazy and reward the industrious. He kept detailed records on his slaves, not only because it was part of good management, but because he cared about their health and welfare. The practice was to put the children to work at ten years of age, the boys at the nail forge, the girls at the spinning wheel. When they turned sixteen—and about one-half of his slaves were under sixteen—they went into the fields or learned a trade. The field hands lived in log huts clustered at convenient places over his farms, while the artisan families were similarly housed on the slopes of the mountain near their work. The house servants were privileged, of course. A number of them belonged to the Hemings family, part of the Wayles legacy, for whom Jefferson showed particular affection. He let Bob Hemings buy his freedom in 1794, the employer to whom he had been hired for a number of years having advanced the purchase price of £60. And James Hemings, who had been with him in Paris and Philadelphia and learned to cook in the French manner, won his freedom upon fulfilling the pledge to teach his art to a worthy successor. In 1796 Jefferson gave him his freedom papers and $30 to get to Philadelphia. He might have done the same for others as faithful, skilled, and enterprising as James, but the state of his affairs would not permit this indulgence, and to turn loose the mass of slaves would have been, in his eyes, an act of heartless cruelty. Until the institution itself could be extinguished, slavery was an evil he had to live with, and he managed it with what little dosings of humanity a diabolical system permitted. His anxiety for a solution to this problem increased after the horrendous slave revolts in Santo Domingo. The storm there was a portent of things to come in the southern states, he thought. He was pleased that younger Virginians, like St. George Tucker, whose *Dissertation on Slavery* he read in 1797, were reviving the plan of gradual emancipation long associated with his name. "But if something is not done, and soon done," he warned, "we shall be the murderers of our own children."

Jefferson called himself a nail-maker as well as a farmer. Realizing it would be some time before his farms were restored to profitable operation, he had, while still in Philadelphia, cast about for a modest business to help him through this trying period. He at first thought of manufacturing potash at Monticello, but finally decided in favor of nails. The manufacture was simple and required little capital; Negro boys, otherwise a nuisance, might be employed in it; and it would be useful to his neighbors. "My new trade of nail-making," he remarked, "is to me in this country what an additional title of nobility or the ensigns of a new order are in Europe." The naillery, together with the blacksmith's shop, formerly at Shadwell, was established on Mulberry Row, which ran along the southerly slope of the mountain below the mansion. Here was no pastoral Eden but belching smoke and clanging hammers. He began with one fire, turning out nails by hand. With the acquisition of a cutting machine in 1796, he added two more fires and raised the output to 10,000 nails a day. Usually a dozen boys were employed, "overlooked" by the smith, Great George, though the master himself supervised the entire operation and was frequently at the forge. According to Isaac, a blacksmith, Jefferson enjoyed making things—keys, locks, chains, and so on—in iron and brass.

The naillery was a modestly successful business, at least in the early years. It kept his family supplied with "groceries," that is store-bought goods—coffee, tea, sugar, rice, brandy—some obtained locally, some from Philadelphia, amounting altogether to $400 or $500 a year. He sold or bartered his nails at Richmond wholesale prices, counting the saving of the freight to give his product a preference with the retailers in the upper country. The system worked for a time, but then, just as he expanded his output, the merchants who dealt in English hardware caught on to his scheme and persuaded the local retailers to refuse the Monticello nails. "The two importing houses at Milton have . . . brought a deluge of British nails with a view, as is said, of putting down my work." To defeat this typically British artifice, Jefferson devised a new system. His nails were sold on consignment to single dealers in Charlottesville, Milton, and Staunton, across the mountains in the Shenandoah Valley. The dealers, each with a monopoly in his town, retailed the nails at the Richmond wholesale price plus a 5 per cent commission. The plan was not the unqualified success he had hoped for. He continued to be plagued by British competition; the consignees took the nails on credit and were slow to pay, while he had his own bills for nail rod to meet in Philadelphia; the price of the rod went up and he had trouble keeping it in stock. When the nail money stopped he was "painfully embarrassed" to pay his grocery bills. But he survived these hardships, and the nail factory operated for many years.

Jefferson had plans upon his retirement of undertaking improvements in local navigation and commerce. "I wish to heaven the spirit of mill-building and manufacturing . . . could spread itself to Albemarle," he wrote to a fellow Virginian in 1793. "We are miserably circumstanced . . . as to the disposal of our wheat. We can neither manufacture nor sell it there, and tho' we have five mill seats at the head of the navigation of the Rivanna, we cannot get mills built." The grain of the country would be worth a good deal more if it could be carried to Richmond in the form of flour; thus the importance of mills. But capital was scarce, enterprise sluggish, and engineering skills non-existent. Years before Jefferson had embarked on a project to restore the gristmill at Shadwell destroyed in the flood of 1771. This involved construction of a canal three-quarters of a mile long and eventually, as it turned out, a new dam as well. Costly and difficult, the work was repeatedly suspended. He was determined to resume it in 1793, having in the meantime incorporated a manufacturing mill in his plan. Three years passed before the work actually resumed. The first stage, the canal, was finally completed in 1803 at the astronomical cost of $20,000.

"I have sometimes asked myself," Jefferson wrote in a memorandum to himself, probably about 1800, "whether my country is the better for my having lived at all?" And he answered, "I do not know that it is," but then went on to list a number of services. The Declaration of Independence, the Statute for Religious Freedom and other acts of the Virginia Assembly—these were mentioned, of course. First in time, however, and therefore at the head of the list, was his work in opening the Rivanna to navigation. The amazing fortitude he showed in this enterprise over the years, and the manufacturing connected with it, stemmed from the conviction that it was useful to his country. He also named the introduction of olive plants from France and of upland rice from Africa. "The greatest service which can be rendered any country is, to add a useful plant to its culture; especially, a bread grain; next in value to bread is oil." Jefferson made no great discoveries in agricultural science, and indeed on his record as a practical farmer "science" established no certain superiority to common sense; yet time would vindicate the faith he exemplified in the improving sciences' works for human welfare.

Monticello Renewed

Monticello was the name of a mountain, the name of a farm, above all the name of a house. The house was an ideal: the congealed expression in brick and mortar and wood of a man's capacity to humanize his environment. As an ideal it would never be finished. Jefferson had worked a dozen years to create his first conception of Monticello—the "elegant" house described by the Marquis de Chastellux, the house where his wife died, and which he left in 1783. It no longer pleased him when he prepared to return to the mountain a decade later. He was born with an irrepressible urge to build, felt it in every house he lived in, and indulged it on every possible occasion, public or private. His passion for architecture was exuberant. Monticello did not contain it, though there it flowed long and lavishly. "They was forty years at work upon that house before Mr. Jefferson stopped building," old Isaac recalled. Monticello was the work of a lifetime, not simply a building but a continuing act of creation and recreation; "and so I hope it will remain during my life," Jefferson himself said, "as architecture is my delight, and putting up, and pulling down, one of my favorite amusements."

Perhaps there is no need to probe further into Jefferson's reasons for remodeling in the 1790's. "Architecture is my delight." Added to this personal pleasure was the satisfaction found in the instruction of his countrymen. To produce a reformation in this most useful of the fine arts, to elevate the public taste, to raise on the American landscape a shining model of republican dignity was a work of "permanent improvement" scarcely less important than improvements in agriculture. His example, to some extent his teachings, inspired the first generation of professional architects in the new nation. Men like Benjamin Latrobe and Robert Mills were his disciples even if he was not, in any formal sense, their teacher. He had learned the art almost exclusively from books, above all from the great folio volumes of Palladio, whose influence fixed Jefferson's style before he set foot outside his own country. In Europe the noble designs he had admired from afar came alive. He never saw an authentic Palladian villa—the master's creations lay beyond Jefferson's hurried steps in Italy—but Roman classicism was the fashion in Paris and several of the elegant new town houses incorporated Palladian features. He was "violently smitten" with one of these, the hôtel de Salm, which he visited almost daily, perching himself on a parapet of the Tuileries nearby and twisting his neck around to view the object of his delight. When he drew his plan for the President's House in Washington, he at first thought to take this pavilion splendidly columned in front and rear for his model, then laid it aside in favor of the purest Palladio, the Villa Rotunda near Vicenza, which he had never seen and which had, in fact, more than a decade before been his model for the Governor's House in Richmond. The neo-classical buildings he saw in Paris, in Amsterdam, and in London too, though he thought English architecture "wretched," offered a profusion of suggestion without in any way unsettling the style he had derived from books. If anything, he turned more unreservedly than before to the chaste forms of Palladio and, as in his adaptation of the Maison Carrée, beyond them to the ancient fountainhead itself. At any rate, it was while in Europe that he began to revise his conception of Monticello. Planning commenced in 1792, and all was in readiness months before he retired from office.

The house as it stood was a two-story center block with shallow wings terminating in octagonal bays. Porticoes adorned both fronts. The entrance hall, stairs on either side, led into a grand salon, or parlor, as Jefferson called it, which projected half its length toward the western portico in the form of an octagon. The dining room was in the wing to the right, the drawing room and master's quarters in the wing to the left. His library was nicely accommodated in the spacious quarters above the parlor. The "attic" space under the low horizontal roof line and above the wings on either side of the central mass contained several small bedrooms. According to the master plan of 1772, the basement was to connect at either end with long L-shaped wings sunk into the northern and southern slopes and covered with terraces on a level with the main floor of the house.

But these "dependencies" had not yet been built. Nor had the second of the two small "outchambers." "Honeymoon Lodge" stood alone at the southwest corner of the garden front.

Handsome as it was, this house no longer met Jefferson's needs on the points of size, convenience, and taste. He wanted more room to acommodate Martha and her family, Maria's when she married, at such times as they could be at Monticello; also his sisters, who often visited the highlands in the summer, and the many friends and strangers to whom he extended his hospitality. Personal convenience was probably a consideration in the expansion of his quarters on the first floor. Other considerations were aesthetic, even at the expense of convenience. In Paris he had admired the low, unpretentious elegance of houses that seemed to have but one story. He had seen second floors constructed as mezzanines with great advantage to the first. He had fallen under the spell of domes and seen how they could be managed with becoming modesty in a private residence. None of these features was novel; they were Palladian, but he had not fully understood them before. His upright center block lost its appeal, and he determined to incorporate the features he now admired in an enlarged Monticello. There was some awkwardness in this, for although these features were Palladian, like the original, he could not start over from the ground up. He had to build on to what he had.

The new design did away with the second story of the original and doubled the width of the house. This meant tearing down and rebuilding the entire east front, remounting its portico, and erecting a mezzanine floor across the length of the new portion. The one-story effect was achieved by ingeniously blending the windows of the main floor with those of the mezzanine floor. Octagonal bays at both ends of the new front duplicated an existing feature, though Jefferson sacrificed the effect of the octagons by uniting the pair at either end with arcaded loggias. The doors from the east portico led into a spacious and lofty hall. Corridors to the right and left gave access to the new rooms—three bedrooms and a library. In the former Jefferson provided for alcove beds, another Parisian touch. The space between the alcoves was barely enough to accommodate two narrow stairways to the mezzanine. Jefferson did not care for elegant staircases. By eliminating this feature he saved space and money

—one of his few gestures toward economy—and also ensured the privacy of the bedrooms above. There were five of these, accessible from corridors that joined in the open gallery above the entrance hall. There were still other bedrooms on a skylighted upper floor well obscured from outside by an ornamental balustrade that encircled the roof of the house. Only one change was proposed in the west front, the addition of a dome, but it was the crowning touch. The dome rose upon the walls that had been Jefferson's library in the old house. He apparently intended to put the dome, or "sky room," to some use, but what it was, or what use it ever actually had, is still a matter of conjecture.

Such was the new Monticello. The plan was not matured all at once, but it was fully embodied in a drawing Jefferson made in 1796. As the work progressed he figured the specifications down to the last detail. In a notebook kept for this purpose are sketches, computations, and builder's directions for cornices, columns, dome, friezes, dados, fireplaces, mantles, chimneys, windows, curtains, and so on. The house would thus become an unrivaled, and quite inexhaustible, statement of his own personality. It had no prototype. Combining elements derived from ancient models, from the Palladian revival, and French neo-classicism, all beautifully articulated with the natural setting and practical requirements of the master, it had an architectural integrity wholly its own, and so can only be described as Jeffersonian.

The new façade was an extraordinary achievement. The house clung graciously to the mountain eminence in self-assured serenity; white columns, dome, and woodwork brilliantly accented the quiet charm of native red brick; and, though the dimunitive appearance was deceptive, the treatment of the windows and the perfect symmetry of line and proportion throughout achieved coherent form scaled to the human life contained within. By the same token, however, the interior arrangements were not altogether satisfactory. Here, too, especially in the public rooms, the taste was classical. Jefferson gave the same attention to the order of his columns on the inside as on the outside; and it might be noticed that they progressed from the sturdy Doric of the portico, through the more graceful Ionic of the hall, terminating in the elegant profusion of the Corinthian in the parlor. In the disposition of his rooms he was remarkedly free from Palladian rigidities and sought, rather, his own convenience. Part of the problem was that he was remodeling, which set limitations to his freedom; besides, as a working architect Jefferson tended, even in Monticello, to sacrifice livability within to stylistic effect out of doors. The dome cost him the spacious room that had been his library, for which the elongated octagonal quarters on the first floor was a poor exchange. Being adjacent to his bedroom, the new library was a gain in convenience, of course, as were all the added rooms downstairs. But those upstairs, reached by cramped lateral stairs, poorly ventilated, and lighted from windows near the floor or from skylights, had less to recommend them.

It was many years before the house took something like a finished form. As in most of his undertakings, public and private, Jefferson refused to be intimidated by temporary obstacles and inconveniences, and he expected greater efficiency in the execution than circumstances would permit. The demolition of the east front, first scheduled for the spring of 1793, did not actually occur until three years later. Meanwhile, thousands of bricks were baked on the premises, stone and lumber brought up the mountain, and orders placed in Philadelphia and London for window frames, glass, and other articles. The old walls had been built solid; pulling them down was as big a job as putting up new ones. Jefferson had counted on completing both jobs before the return of winter, but the house was only partially covered-in when the first blast came in November and suspended building for the season. The roof was still on, so the place was habitable, if anything but comfortable. Rains poured in, brickbats flew, and once Maria tumbled through the floor into the cellar, "miraculously" without injury. When Martha came in August she took up quarters in the "outchamber" and soon gave birth to another daughter, Ellen Wayles. The walls were in place the next summer. Now the old roof had to come off and the new one laid before another winter. Jefferson's duties as Vice President interrupted his personal supervision, however, and things lagged more than usual at Monticello. Whether or not Maria was wed to John Wayles Eppes in October 1797 under her father's roof or under the blue sky above Monticello can only be guessed; but the house was both roofless and tenantless the ensuing winter and the next. There were recurrent problems of workmen and materials. "Scarcely a stroke has been done towards covering the house since I went away . . . ," he wrote to Maria on his return in March 1799. "It seems as if I should never get it inhabitable." The roof was soon finished, new floors began to be laid, and the entire family was together again at Monticello that summer. Still the house was far from finished, interior and exterior, when Jefferson became President. And although he had made several improvements in the grounds, planting trees and encircling the hilltop with several roundabouts, work had not yet begun on the gardens or on the winged dependencies of the house.

It never occurred to Jefferson to include Monticello in his record of services to his countrymen. Home, like religion, was a personal matter. Yet it had public significance of the highest import. It made certain innovations in American domestic architecture, of course, and contributed to a style still recognizable today in country mansions, especially in Virginia. More important was Jefferson's vision of human habitation formed to the life of free men. The architectural style was in itself of small consequence, though it was probably the only form the ideal could have taken at that time. Nothing luxurious, sensual, or ostentatious would do. Simplicity of line, reasoned order and proportion, a chaste dignity, at once ancient and new, beautiful and virtuous, served the civic culture of the young republic. Jefferson's classic columns rising before the wilderness framed an ideal of workmanship, beauty, and civility in the rough and tumble American world. Whether or not the Americans could appropriate it was another question. The conquest of the continent gave but narrow scope to the humanizing arts. The distance between Jefferson's cultural ideal, as stated at Monticello, and the insistent realities of American life increased with the passage of years. The Americans mastered their environment but little heeded Jefferson's example of raising it high on the scale of human values.

Adams and Jefferson

Jefferson became a candidate for the presidency in 1796 in spite of himself. He did not seek the office but the office sought him. He did not consent to run or, if elected, to serve; and lest he refuse, he was not even asked. His situation seemed to call for explanation. Having renounced public service, having repeatedly declared that nothing could drag him from the oblivion of Monticello, he found himself back on the field of combat in a contest for the nation's highest office. It had all been against his will, he protested, without concert or expectation or the lift of a finger on his part: "on my salvation I declare it." His friends would believe him; it was too much to expect of his enemies. Wasn't it marvelous, John Adams snorted, how political plants grew in the shade!

If Jefferson made no move in his own behalf, neither did he spurn the candidacy thrust upon him. He might have declared his unavailability in terms not to be misunderstood; but his candidacy was a *fait accompli* before he had knowledge of it, and he could not, consistent with his own character, set the public will at defiance. There was no escape. Nor is it at all certain that Jefferson wanted one. His attitude toward political life was always governed by some balance between reciprocal forces of attraction and repulsion, and their alternation set up the cyclical rhythm of withdrawal and return which, beyond the limits of consciousness, expressed the deep ambivalence of his nature. The cycle was again completing itself in 1796. The pastoral idyl he had imagined for himself three years earlier had not materialized. Retirement showed its darker side in crop failures, frustrations of building, dreary winters in isolation at Monticello, and cares of estate as unrelenting as his creditors. He had set out to recoup the fortune he believed he had lost by prolonged absence from home and inattention to private affairs, but after an experiment of several years devoted to these interests he could take little satisfaction in the results. "The unprofitable condition of Virginia estates in general," he said, "leaves it next to impossible for the holder of one to avoid ruin." Worst of all he began to detect feelings of self-pity and misanthropy in himself. Several years later, observing these symptoms in his younger daughter, he cited his own experience. "I remained closely at home," he recalled, "saw none but those who came there, and at length became very sensible to the ill effect it had upon my own mind . . . I felt enough of the effect of withdrawal from the world then, to see that it led to an anti-social and misanthropic state of mind which severely punishes him who gives in to it: and it will be a lesson I shall never forget as to myself." He was ready for "return to the world," though he could never actually consent to it or, once embarked, resign himself to the "splendid torments" of public life.

While thus disenchanted with his retreat to felicity, he also found that the nation's affairs still made an irresistible claim upon him. The tendency of the Federalist administration appeared even more disturbing from his private seat in Virginia than it had from his official one in Philadelphia. President Washington's retirement would create a vacuum in the national leadership. However it was filled, extreme partisanship, which the veneration for his name had checked, was sure to assert itself. The transition might well prove critical. The Republicans looked to Jefferson to convert crisis to opportunity. He gradually accustomed himself to the idea. But he neither expected nor wished to be elected President in 1796. Federalist power so impressively organized under Washington's aegis had not been spent, and Jefferson found compelling reasons both personal and political for preferring John Adams as Washington's successor. The vice presidency, on the other hand, would be tolerable. "The second office . . . is honorable and easy," he later said, "the first is but splendid misery." It carried no weighty responsibilities, yet would place him in an enviable position to steer his course as events might dictate. The calculation helped to reconcile him to return to the political arena.

Since his retirement, in Jefferson's opinion, the octopus of British policy had taken a stranglehold on the Washington administration. When British attacks on American neutral shipping brought the two countries to the verge of war in 1794, the administration, instead of adopting an experiment in commercial warfare such as he and Madison had long advocated, sent Chief Justice John Jay to London in a suit for peace. The mission was humiliating in itself, Jefferson thought, but the treaty Jay negotiated sounded the depths of national degradation. Britain was in no position to be stubborn with the United States when Jay and Lord Grenville sat down at the bargaining table in the later months of 1794. France was everywhere on the offensive: the armies of the republic had crossed the Pyrenees, invaded Italy, overrun the German Rhineland and Belgium, and all but conquered the Netherlands. An "armed neutrality" was shaping up among the Northern powers with France's blessing and the chance of American support. The monarchical coalition put together in 1793 was breaking up. Soon Britain, wracked within by sedition, grain shortages, rising unemployment, and fiscal crisis, would stand alone against France. Peace and commmerce with the United States had become vital to British survival. Yet the American envoy played his cards as if he held the losing hand.

The result was a treaty as disgusting to the Americans as it was pleasing to the British. Some satisfaction could be found in the British pledge to evacuate the Northwest posts, though this obligation descended from the Treaty of 1783. The Americans were admitted to direct trade with the British East Indies, but the far more important trade with the West Indies remained closed, except on terms too limiting and vexatious for the United States to accept. The treaty made special provision for settling the claims of British creditors on American citizens, most of them southern planters, but made no provision to indemnify the planters for slaves carried off by the enemy army. Nothing was said on the subject of impressment, nor of those principles of neutral commerce—free ships make free goods, the narrow definition of contraband, of blockade, and so on—the United States had championed from 1776 forward. The treaty assumed American acquiescence in British maritime rule and practice that had produced the crisis in the first place. No more drastic change in American foreign policy had occurred since the Revolution. Indeed for the first time since 1780 anywhere, an international treaty sacrificed the right of neutral flags to the barbarous rule of the medieval code, *consolato del mare*. France, bound by treaty to respect American commerce under liberal arrangements, could not be indifferent to this development. Article XV placed Anglo-American trade on the most favored nation basis and prohibited any new or higher tonnage duties on British vessels, yet reserved to Britain the right to impose countervailing duties on the American. So the United States not only extended valuable guarantees to a rival commercial power but ensured that favors henceforth granted to friendly nations should also go to Britain. As Madison observed, "It was hardly imagined that we were soon to grant everything to Great Britain for nothing in return; and to make it a part of this bad bargain with her, that we should not be able to make a good one with other nations." The commercial clauses of the treaty would draw the teeth of Republican doctrine and prevent legislation aimed at curbing British power. All considered, Jefferson said of Jay's work, it was "nothing more than a treaty of alliance between England and the Anglomen of this country against . . . the people of the United States."

The terms of the treaty became public only after it was ratified by the Senate in June 1795. A whirlwind of indignation rolled across the land. The treaty dismayed the Federalists, and men might read the Republican scribes' denunciations by the light of Jay's burning effigies. "So general a burst of dissatisfaction never before appeared against any transaction," Jefferson reported to Monroe, now the American Minister to France. The treaty would demolish the Federalists, he casually predicted. However, increasingly drawn into this political vortex, he grew alarmed at the resurgence of the Federalists under Hamilton's leadership. They had got themselves into "a defile, where they might be finished," he observed, but the Republicans, misled by a false security, failed to press the attack and were once again outmaneuvered by Hamilton. "Hamilton is really a colossus to the anti-Republican party. Without numbers, he is a host within himself." Only Madison could furnish an antidote strong enough for his poison. "For God's sake take up your pen," Jefferson begged his friend. The poison had infected the mass of merchants, at first open-mouthed against the treaty but now fearful of the political consequences of its defeat. "They have feared the shock would be too great, and have chosen to tack about and support both treaty and government, rather than risk the government. Thus it is," Jefferson said, "that Hamilton, Jay, etc., in the boldest act they ever ventured on to undermine the government, have the address to screen themselves, and direct the hue and cry against those who wish to drag them into light. A bolder party stroke was never struck." That the treaty was a blatant party measure Jefferson had not the slightest doubt. And, like Madison, he emphasized its commercial character: "an attempt of a party, which finds they have lost their majority in one branch [the House of Representatives] of the Legislature, to make a law by the aid of the other branch [the Senate] and of the executive, under color of a treaty, which shall bind up the hands of the adverse branch from ever restraining the commerce of their patron-nation."

The treaty was the capstone of the Hamiltonian system. How

547

else could its terms, so favorable to Britain, so insulting to France, be explained? Jefferson pondered the treaty at the same time he received the news of continuing French triumph in Europe. The latter conditioned his view of the former. With the establishment of the Executive Directory in France, the Revolution had been stabilized at last; and as liberation spread over Europe, Britain became isolated and vulnerable. It had really been in America's power, Monroe wrote from Paris, to dictate terms to Britain, provided she had been made to believe in our opposition. "Accomplishing this point, everything would have been accomplished; for of all possible calamities with which they are threatened now, a war with us is that which they most dread: not so much indeed from the fear of our maritime force, as the effect it would produce upon their commerce, by which they alone are enabled to support a war." Placing the Jay Treaty in this context, reading it after indulging lighthearted fancies of leaving his peas and clover for awhile, going to England in the fall, dining with General Pichegru in London, to "hail the dawn of liberty and republicanism in that island," Jefferson judged it to be a willful abdication of American interests.

For a time he held to the slender hope that Washington would refuse to sign the treaty. His faith in the President had been badly shaken several months earlier by the public denunciation of the democratic societies. No event prior to the Jay Treaty produced a stronger reaction at Monticello. These popular societies, thirty-five of them scattered from Maine to Georgia, championed the French Revolution and Republican men and measures. The Hamiltonians artfully accused them of fomenting the Whiskey Rebellion of 1794. A massive force of 15,000 militia, accompanied by Hamilton, overwhelmed a handful of fleeing insurgents against the whiskey excise in western Pennsylvania. Washington journeyed to the site, and after his return to the capital lashed out at the societies in language that betrayed intolerance of political opposition from outside the official channels of government. The denunciation was a bold act of repression, Jefferson said. "It is wonderful indeed, that the President should have permitted himself to be the organ of such an attack on the freedom of discussion, the freedom of writing, printing and publishing." He found it increasingly difficult to escape the conclusion that Washington had become the captive of the Anglican and "monocratic" party.

For Jefferson and for Republicans generally, Washington's decision to sign or not to sign the treaty became a final test of his politics. He withheld his signature in July on Secretary of State Randolph's plea to demand prior British repeal of a new order in council damaging to American trade. The next month Randolph was the victim of a bizarre plot fashioned by the British Minister Hammond, and Oliver Wolcott and Timothy Pickering, the successors to Hamilton and Knox in the cabinet. A British man-of-war had intercepted a dispatch from the French Minister in which Randolph appeared as the petitioner of a bribe. After tailoring the dispatch to their purposes, the Federalist marplots called the President to Philadelphia. Pickering pointed the accusing finger to Randolph: "That man is a traitor!" The plot worked. Believing that Randolph schemed to defeat the treaty as a favor to France, Washington signed it without further ado. The next day, in the presence of the accusers, he confronted the hapless Secretary, his friend and confidant of many years, with the incriminating document. Angered and humiliated, Randolph resigned at once, accused Washington of "treachery unexampled since Tiberius," and wrote a long public vindication in which he portrayed himself as the "meditated victim of party spirit" —a "not guilty" plea history is now inclined to accept. Jefferson read Randolph's *Vindication* with interest. It continued for him the secret cabinet history he had once known intimately, and it confirmed his judgment of the Jay Treaty. As for Washington, he erred with integrity, though the cost of his integrity was becoming unbearable. "I wish," Jefferson said, "that his honesty and his political errors may not furnish a second occasion to exclaim 'curse his virtues, they've undone his country.'" As for Randolph, he stood acquitted of charges of bribery and treason, but Jefferson shed no tears over this man's misfortunes. Had Randolph been firm in 1793, had he succeeded to Jefferson's policy as well as to his office, the President would have been kept from habitual concert with the Hamiltonians. The Republicans owed nothing to Randolph; to sustain him in a personal vendetta against the President was unthinkable. It was, in fact, the principal problem of the Republican leadership in the later months of 1795 to work out a strategy of opposition to the treaty free of the odium and disgrace of attacking the President, whose halo, while dimmed for many, still awed the mass of Americans.

Jefferson was a sometimes impatient bystander to the final Republican assault on the treaty. Though signed and ratified, its future waited on appropriations by the House of Representatives; and there the Republican majority tried to stifle the embryo monster. The strategy took form in the Virginia House of Delegates in November. Resolutions voted at Richmond asserted the right of the lower house of Congress to share in the making of treaties, to withhold appropriations, and to approve or disapprove stipulations on subjects, such as foreign commerce, within its legislative jurisdiction. Especially pleasing was the concession wrung from the ablest of the Virginia Federalists, John Marshall, that the treaty in all its commercial parts still fell under the power of the House of Representatives. At the opening of Congress in December, Washington confounded his foes by deferring communication of the treaty. "The situation is truly perplexing," Madison informed his friend. "It is clear that a majority, if brought to the merits of the Treaty are against it. But as the Treaty is not regularly before the House, and an application to the President brings him personally into the question . . . there is great danger that enough [congressmen] will fly off to leave the opponents of the Treaty in a minority."

Republican tempers simmered for three months. At Monticello, Jefferson commenced an inquiry into the powers of the House with respect to treaties. Finally, on March 1, after the exchange of ratifications in London, Washington sent the treaty to the House. The next day Edward Livingston, the young lion of the New York clan, seized the initiative with a resolution calling upon the President to lay before the House the instructions given to Jay in 1794 together with other pertinent papers. Such papers could be considered pertinent to the business of the House only on the assumption it possessed certain powers of decision as to treaties. Madison was dismayed by this turn of events. Apparently still uncertain of the correct constitutional ground, he worried too lest Livingston's motion force a showdown with the President. Untroubled by these doubts at Monticello, Jefferson applauded the radical move. Unfortunately, he did not complete the inquiry Madison had forced upon him. Defeated by his own party on an amendment softening the Livingston resolution, Madison had no choice but to fall in with it. The resolution passed by a decisive majority. The President, just as decisively, refused the call for papers. "The absolute refusal was as unexpected as the tone and temper of the message are improper and indelicate," Madison wrote. Jefferson searched his files for evidence that Washington had earlier taken a different view of the powers of the House. Had he searched a little farther he would have discovered that he too, in the case of the Creek Treaty of 1790, had earlier taken a different view, one in accord with the position he now combated. In response to the President, the Republican majority reaffirmed its rights in the matter. But this riposte did not decide the abstract question of constitutional law, nor was it ever finally decided. As the House proceeded to the substantive question, the majority "daily melted down" until at the end, April 30, it had become a minority by two votes.

The defeat deeply embarrassed the Republicans. Surveying the entire proceeding, Madison thought it "the most worrying and vexatious business" he had ever experienced, "and the more so," he told Jefferson, "as the causes lay in the unsteadiness, the follies, the perverseness, and the defections among our friends, more than in the strength, or dexterity, or malice of our opponents." The Republicans had yet to learn the discipline of party leadership. The effectiveness of the Federalists could not be discounted, however. They had frightened men with the danger of war. They had rallied merchants, bankers, and plain citizens in public meetings and deluged Congress with petitions. They had, at the last moment, pulled a rabbit out of the hat: a treaty negotiated by Thomas Pinckney with Spain, providing for the settlement of the southern boundary and the opening of the Mississippi to navigation. Fearing the effect of an Anglo-American rapprochement on her North American colonies, Spain chose a rapprochement of her own. The Pinckney Treaty fulfilled an old objective of Jefferson's diplomacy, ironically under Federalist auspices. It appealed strongly to western Americans, and to Republicans generally; but it stood little chance of ratification if the mainly Federalist and eastern interests associated with the Jay Treaty were sacrificed. Satisfying both interests, sacrificing none, was the simple solution.

Far from the scene, Jefferson wrote no postmortem analysis of the Republican debacle in Congress. He was disappointed but, sanguine as ever, lifted his gaze to the farther horizon. The treaty had been a "dear bought victory" for the Anglomen, he assured Monroe. "It has given the most radical shock to their party which it has ever received: and there is no doubt they would be glad to be replaced on the ground they possessed the instant before Jay's nomination extraordinary. They see that nothing can support them but the colossus of the President's merits with the people, and the moment he retires, that his successor, if a Monocrat, will be overbourne by the republican sense of his constituents, if a Republican he will of course give fair play to that sense, and lead them into channels of harmony between the governors and the governed. In the meantime, patience." Jefferson thus acknowledged what everyone tacitly assumed: the contest on the Jay Treaty was the opening gun in the presidential campaign.

The campaign was well advanced months before Washington issued his Farewell Address in September 1796. As early as January, John Adams was primping himself as "heir apparent." And Madison wrote to Monroe in February: "The Republicans, knowing that Jefferson alone can be started with hope of success, mean to push him." With friends and collaborators as close as Jefferson and Madison it is difficult to believe one would push the other into anything without his consent, yet this seems to have been the case. The subject of the presidency had entered into their correspondence more than a year before. Jefferson hoped that Madison would succeed to the highest office. Under no other helmsman would the nation's "political bark" be so safe, he wrote. As for himself, the insinuations of his enemies that he coveted the office had forced him to face the question in the privacy of his own heart and mind. And he did, finding them as quiet as the grave. To the old reasons—"reputation, tranquillity, labor"—were added others since his retirement—age and health and family—which still more insuperably barred the door. "The little spice of ambition which I had in my younger days has long since evaporated, and I set still less store by a posthumous than present name." The subject was closed. But Madison persisted. He would not for a moment entertain the idea of his own candidacy. "You ought to be preparing yourself, however," he warned, "to hear truths which no inflexibility will be able to withstand." These truths he reserved for "the latitude of a free conversation." Presumably the conversation occurred in the spring of 1795 when Madison and his bride of a few months, Dolley Payne Todd, visited Monticello. Presumably, too, Madison ran through the reasons why Jefferson should lead the Republicans. He possessed a national reputation; he had served with distinction in France and as Secretary of State; his name was identified with the Republican cause at home and abroad; and his retirement set an example of political abnegation meriting the esteem of his countrymen. Madison, on the other hand, was eight years Jefferson's junior; his career had been exclusively congressional; for years he had been in the thick of partisan controversy; and he lacked the arts of popularity. Besides, he intended soon to retire himself, overcome his bachelor ways, and devote his attentions for a time to a charming wife and fine estate. It was unthinkable that both Virginians could withdraw from the national scene. If Madison surrendered the reins of Republican leadership it had better be to Jefferson.

What part of this ground the two men traversed in "free conversation" at Monticello cannot be known. One thing seems certain: Jefferson did not consent to his name being brought forward in the forthcoming presidential contest. Doubtless other Republican leaders, like William B. Giles and the New Yorker Aaron Burr, who stopped at Monticello, tried their persuasions with no better results. Although events connected with the Jay Treaty revived Jefferson's interest in national affairs, he avoided any discussion of the presidency during this period, indeed until the election was over; nor did the political associates who placed his name at the head of the ticket discuss the subject with him. It was only half a day's ride from Montpelier to Monticello, but Madison did not make the trip in 1796. "I have not seen Jefferson," he explained to Monroe early in the fall, "and have thought it wise to present him no opportunity of protesting to his friends against being embarked in the contest." Silence was the only form of consent he could expect from Monticello.

Jefferson did not lead the Republicans in 1796—the role still belonged to Madison if to anyone—but he was the virtuous symbol around whom Republicans nation-wide could rally and unite. In newspapers, broadsides, and pamphlets, Jefferson was presented as the "steadfast friend to the rights of the people," while his opponent was portrayed as the "champion of rank, titles and hereditary distinctions." In Pennsylvania, where Jefferson's old friend John Beckley, Clerk of the House of Representatives, conducted a popular campaign without parallel, a Republican handbill invited the voters to compare the political views of the two candidates: "*Thomas Jefferson* first drew the declaration of American independence—he first framed the sacred political sentence that all men are *born* equal. *John Adams* says this is all a farce and a falsehood; that some men should be born kings, and some should be born nobles. Which of these, freemen of Pennsylvania, will you have for your President?" Republicans extolled Jefferson's character, his services, his philosophy. He was enlightened, dignified, modest, a man of unsullied integrity, without artifice, passion, rancor, or any ambition other than the freedom and well-being of his countrymen. "Of no party but the great party of human benefactions, he will allay the heats of our country, heal its divisions, and calm the boisterous elements of political controversy—Under the administration of a man, untinctured by party spirit, citizens may smoke the calumet of peace . . . , and every citizen sit down in quiet under his own vine and fig-tree." His retirement offered the surest proof of republican character. Like the renowned Cincinnatus, it was said, "he knows how to support the burden of high office with dignity, or to resign it without a sigh." Federalists heaped upon Jefferson fully as much abuse as their own candidate received. Under the pen name *Phocion*, South Carolina Congressman William L. Smith, probably assisted by Hamilton as usual, elaborated the partisan image he had drawn four years before. His stinging pamphlet, *The Pretensions of Thomas Jefferson the Presidency Examined*, denounced the candidate as an enemy of religion, of national credit, of Union, and of President Washington. Worst of all, Jefferson was a philosopher, and though not a very good one, his talents would be better employed as president of a university than as president of a great nation. The satire was heavy-handed, but the Federalists seemed determined to fashion a ludicrous, as well as a frightful, image of the Virginian.

Jefferson observed the campaign from his serene heights with mixed emotions. "In truth," he wrote when it was all over, "I did not know myself under the pens either of my friends or foes. It is unfortunate for our peace, that unmerited abuse wounds, while unmerited praise has not the power to heal." The wounds inflicted in Virginia probably hurt him most. It was said that he had been sued in federal court by British creditors for an amount exceeding the value of his entire estate—a story denied by John Marshall, with whom it allegedly began. Another libel charged a secret political alliance with Aaron Burr, his running-mate, entered into when the New Yorker visited Monticello in the fall of 1795—an allegation of bargain and corruption denied in a sworn deposition by two of Jefferson's neighbors present at Monticello when Burr called. His Virginia enemies raked up the old accusations of official negligence, personal cowardice, and resignation under fire when he was governor of Virginia. This was the kind of political ammunition the Federalists had been looking for, and they spent it freely in the propaganda barrage. It struck a sensitive nerve in Jefferson. His friends, old Dr. Currie in Richmond, John Taylor, John Beckley, and others, rushed to his defense. The charges probably had no bearing on the outcome of the election, but neither Jefferson nor his friends could ever put them to rest.

Of more direct consequence was the suspicion that Jefferson and his party were the puppets of France. Cultivating this idea, the Federalists received unexpected assistance from the alleged puppeteers on the eve of the election. Angered and dismayed by the Jay Treaty, the Directory resolved to treat American neutral shipping in the same manner as was permitted to Britain, to suspend normal diplomatic relations, and give the go-ahead to the plan of its minister in Philadelphia, Pierre Adet, to "revolutionize" the American government by securing the ascendancy of a man and a party known to be friendly to the French nation. French influence in American affairs was an old story, much exaggerated by men under British influence; but in this instance it was open and blatant. Timing his action with a view to maximum impact in the Pennsylvania election, Adet published four diplomatic notes between November 2 and 21. These notes, which had the color of campaign documents, announced the new policy of the Directory and appealed to the American people for a change in their government. The Republicans won a narrow victory in Pennsylvania in spite of Adet; and in the country generally his "diplomatic blunderbuss," like Genêt's in 1793, injured the friends rather than the enemies of France. Coming on the heels of Washington's Farewell Address, with its stern warning against "the insidious wiles of foreign influence," Adet's maneuver enabled the Federalists to point an accusing finger at their political foes. Nor were they wholly without blame. Republican leaders deplored Adet's intervention and bore no direct responsibility for it. Yet they had contributed to the impression in French governing circles that the American electorate was divided between a British party and a French party, and that once the latter attained power everything would be arranged to the satisfaction of France. Monroe had suggested as much in Paris. Incurable Francophiles, like Benjamin F. Bache, editor of the foremost Republican newspaper, the *Aurora,* which published Adet's pronouncements, daily nurtured the idea. In the political heats generated by the Jay Treaty, the opposition could not avoid impaling itself on the horn of French policy.

While all this was true, Adet acted on a calculation as fallacious as Genêt's before him. What it left out, as a former French official in the United States informed his government the next year, was the large "middle party" submissive to no foreign power and composed of the country's best men regardless of party affiliation. "This party, whose existence we have not even suspected, is the American party which loves its country above all and for whom preferences either for France or England are only accessory and often passing affections." And Adet too, after the tumult of the election, recognized this truth. Jefferson himself, so far as is known, never commented one way or another on Adet's misguided intervention in his behalf. Federalist zealots saw in the episode certain proof of Jefferson's subservience to France. Adet knew better. "Mr. Jefferson likes us because he detests Britain . . . ," the Minister reported to his government, "but tomorrow he might change his opinion of us if tomorrow Britain should cease to inspire his fears. Jefferson, though a friend of liberty and enlightenment, an admirer of the efforts we have made to break the bonds and dispel the ignorance which burden the human race, Jefferson, I say, is an American and, as such, he cannot be sincerely our friend. An American is the born enemy of all the peoples of Europe."

When the electoral vote was tallied, Adams emerged the victor 71 to 68. Jefferson had carried Pennsylvania, the southern states, except South Carolina, evenly divided, and a portion of the Maryland vote. As the recipient of the second highest vote he was elected Vice President, though of the opposite party from the President. The candidates entered by both parties for the second office were victims of political stratagems inseparable from the electoral system. Thomas Pinckney, the Federalist candidate, if supported fairly by all the electors of his party would have ended in a tie with Adams; but to avert this result, which would drop the contest into the House of Representatives, it was only necessary for some of the Federalist electors to deny their votes to one of the candidates. Hamilton preferred Pinckney to Adams, no warm admirer of the Treasury system, stubbornly independent, and, in Hamilton's opinion, a poor bet to defeat Jefferson. So he plotted to bring Pinckney in ahead of Adams by splitting the South Carolina vote between the native son and the Virginian. Suspecting this treachery, Adams's friends in New England threw more than enough votes away from Pinckney to offset the defection in South Carolina. The bitter seeds Hamilton sowed in the Federalist ranks would sprout dragons in the course of time. In the case of Aaron Burr, the other half of the Republican ticket, the Virginians had defected. Burr felt betrayed. Yet it does not appear that the Republicans nationally or in several of the states ever endorsed the New Yorker. The Virginia electors were pledged to Jefferson but not to Burr, and he received only one of the state's 21 electoral votes. Burr's reputation was already tainted. The Virginians distrusted him; and he now distrusted them. Jefferson would soon get to know Burr better. Whatever opinion he may have formed of him before or during his flying visit in 1795, he had no part in Burr's candidacy or in the slap administered by the Virginia Republicans.

Jefferson descended from his lofty perch in December when it appeared the electoral vote would be uncomfortably close. He wrote to Madison on the 17th that should he and Adams end in a tie, he wished the choice to go to the New Englander. He had always been his junior in office; he could accept second place a good deal more gracefully than Adams. And if this was not reason enough, he would consider himself fortunate to trade the presidency for a post safe from political buffettings and requiring his presence in Philadelphia only one-third of every year. A rumor was abroad that he would accept the first office but not the second. In fact, he said repeatedly, the reverse was true. "If I am to act . . . a more tranquil and unoffending station could not have been found for me, nor one so analogous to the dispositions of my own mind. It will give me philosophical evenings in the winter, and rural days in the summer." Political wisdom and personal preference were in perfect accord. Now was not the time to take the helm. Let Adams ride out the storm that had been brewing for four years and was about to burst.

Madison, in Philadelphia, could more readily assess the advantages of Jefferson's position. He urged acceptance of the vice presidency—a plea quite unnecessary—and drew Jefferson's attention to the prospects of political conciliation under Adams. "You know that his feelings will not enslave him to the example of his predecessor. It is certain that his censures of our paper system and the intrigues at New York for setting Pinckney above him have fixed an enmity with the British faction. Nor should it pass for nothing, that the true interest of New England particularly requires reconciliation with France as the road to her commerce, add to the whole that he is said to speak of you now in friendly terms and will no doubt be soothed by your acceptance of a place subordinate to him." Adams and moderate Federalists were, in fact, soothed by Jefferson's expressions in his letter of the 17th, which Madison quietly circulated in Philadelphia. The Hamiltonians were alarmed. This shameful piece of "hypocrisy" and "Jacobinical intrigue," they warned, masked "a deep design to cajole and deceive the public." Hamilton himself was soon writing, "Our Jacobins say they are well pleased, and that the *Lion* and the *Lamb* are to lie down together. Mr. Adams' *personal* friends talk a little in the same way. . . . If Mr. Adams has *Vanity*, 'tis plain a plot has been laid to take hold of." Republicans who but the other day were denouncing Adams as an apostate from the principles of American liberty now lavished him with compliment. The *Aurora* lauded his "republican character," such a welcome change from the ostentatious Washington; and even the Virginia firebrand, William B. Giles, was heard to say, "The old man will make a good President too." As the election year came to a close, men who had been bitter foes rubbed their tired eyes in amazement at the prospect of political concord founded in the renewal of the Revolutionary alliance of Adams and Jefferson, Massachusetts and Virginia.

Word of these developments had not reached Monticello when Jefferson took up his pen to write a warm, congratulatory letter to his old friend. No one could congratulate him with more disinterestedness, Jefferson said. "I have no ambition to govern men. It is a painful and thankless task. Since the day too on which you signed the treaty of Paris our horizon was never so overcast." Condolences, not congratulations, seemed to be in order; but Jefferson prayed that Adams might preserve the peace, warned him against the schemes and tricks of his "arch-friend" in New York, and pledged his loyal support. Having written the letter Jefferson laid it aside, discouraged by the difficulty of making himself believed, and worried, perhaps, lest his expressions of magnanimity and cordiality convey more than he intended. Only after reading Madison's heartening report from Philadelphia did he mail the letter. Still hesitant, he took the precaution of enclosing it under cover of his answer to Madison, who should intercept or forward the epistle as he thought best. "If Mr. Adams can be induced to administer the government on its true principles, and to relinquish his bias to an English constitution," Jefferson stated, "it is to be considered whether it would not be on the whole for the public good to come to a good understanding with him as to his future elections. He is perhaps the only sure barrier against Hamilton's getting in."

Madison was startled by the suggestion of an understanding, perhaps a coalition, between Adams Federalists and Republicans. If this was the kind of overture that lurked in the honeyed phrases of his friend's letter to Adams, it should go no farther. Seeing that it did not, Madison offered Jefferson half a dozen reasons for his action. Adams's conciliatory feelings toward Jefferson were already advertised, likewise Jefferson's toward him. Any forwardness on the Virginian's part might prove offensive to a man of Adams's prickly temperament. Moreover, overt expressions of friendship would cause embarrassment should subsequent events call for vigorous opposition to the administration. Nor could the interests of the Republican party, only now feeling its strength and demanding opposition as its life's blood, be neglected. Already, Madison noted, Republican zealots groaned at the idea of a rapprochement. Adams had everything to gain by it, the Republicans everything to lose. True policy lay in cultivating the New Englander's better nature, separating him from the High Federalists, and giving a fair start to his executive career without, however, compromising the freedom and independence of the Republican organization. Jefferson thanked his friend for suppressing the overture. While his feelings were as he stated them, there was a delicacy and probably too much mischief in the attempt to convey them. On this cautious note, January 30, the dialogue on conciliation closed, to be resumed when Jefferson arrived at the seat of government.

He had wanted to avoid the official ceremony of inauguration in Philadelphia, but out of respect for the public suffered himself to go through with it with as little formality as possible. On February 20 he was back on the road he had traveled so many times in the past. Exchanging his phaeton and pair for the anonymity of the stage at Alexandria, and announcing a later arrival than he planned, Jefferson meant to sneak into the capital unnoticed. In this he was unsuccessful. A troop of artillery met him at the gates of the city, signaled his approach, and marched before him bearing aloft a banner inscribed "Jefferson, The Friend of the People." He at once called on Adams. Cordiality was the keynote. For several weeks the friends of both men had laid the ground for reconciliation. Adams, though for some time troubled by Jefferson's traffic with Paine, Freneau, Bache, and other "pernicious" characters, never doubted his talents and love of country. Jefferson, though disappointed by Adams's retreat from the principles of 1776, "never felt a diminution of confidence in his integrity, and retained a solid affection for him." The friendliness of these professions easily survived the test of the first meeting.

The ice broken, Adams called on Jefferson the next morning, March 3, at Madison's lodgings, and broached the problem of France. The success or failure of the new administration hung on the resolution of this crisis. France marauded American commerce, and diplomatic relations between the two countries had collapsed.

Several months previous Washington had recalled Monroe, alleging failure to cushion the shock of the Jay Treaty in Paris and subservience of his embassy to partisan designs in the United States. In response to this "unpardonable" affront, the Directory snubbed Monroe's replacement, Charles Cotesworth Pinckney, leaving no avenue to negotiation. Jefferson believed that Hamilton and his lieutenants in Washington's cabinet, which Adams was about to inherit, aimed at war in alliance with Britain. The calamity might be averted if Adams assumed a posture perfectly neutral and independent at the outset. "I do not believe Mr. Adams wishes war with France; nor do I believe he will truckle to England as servilely as has been done," he wrote hopefully to Madison. The Virginian and the New Englander had different opinions of the French Revolution, but neither supposed the differences touched vital national interests. Adams, for his part, wished the benefit of Jefferson's experience and prestige in the present crisis. This was the object of his visit on March 3.

His first wish was to send Jefferson to Paris. The idea was a natural one—several of Adams's friends advocated it. "Indeed," he later wrote to one of them, "I made a great stretch in proposing it, to accommodate to the feelings, views and prejudices of the parties." Unfortunately, the dispatch abroad of the "crown prince" posed serious difficulties. Jefferson concurred, adding his personal repugnance to a European mission. So Adams unfolded the plan of a bipartisan commission. Pinckney, still cooling his heels in Paris, was mentioned, also Elbridge Gerry, Adams's close friend in Massachusetts, a moderate Federalist, who would be acceptable to the Republicans, and finally, Madison. Madison was the key to the plan. Would he go? Jefferson did not know but agreed to ask him. As expected, Madison declined. What passed between the two Virginians on this occasion is unknown. Madison had turned down foreign posts before and was about to take a well-earned rest from active service; but, more than likely, political considerations, such as those he had earlier stated to Jefferson, controlled the decision. On March 6 Jefferson and Adams dined at Washington's table. After leaving, as they walked down the street to their lodgings, Jefferson explained the result of his inquiry. Adams, somewhat embarrassed, said that objections had been raised to Madison's appointment and he had already dropped the idea. Jefferson suspected the reason. Years later Adams recalled that he had mentioned to Wolcott the plan of joining Madison in a French mission. Wolcott at once fell into "a profound gloom," then pouted, "Mr. President, we are willing to resign." Amazed, Adams discovered on further inquiry that Federalists in the cabinet and in the Senate would not tolerate the conciliatory gesture he had planned. As Jefferson remembered that evening stroll with his old friend, they came to Fifth Street "where our road separated, his being down Market Street, mine off along Fifth, and we took leave; and he never after that said one word to me on the subject or ever consulted me as to any measure of the government."

The spirit of an *entente cordiale* set the tone of the inauguration on March 4 and lingered wistfully for several weeks. Jefferson took the oath of office in the Senate chamber. Concluding his little address with an encomium on the "eminent character" who had preceded him in the office, Jefferson prayed he might be "long preserved for the Government, the happiness, and prosperity of our common country." The ceremony completed, the Vice President led the Senate to the lower chamber for the inauguration of the President. A brilliant assemblage filled the hall. Washington entered to shouts of applause, repeated when Adams, followed by his secretaries, marched down the aisle and mounted to the Speaker's chair. Attired in drab gray, a sword dangling at his side, Adams looked to Washington and Jefferson on his right, the former in black, the latter in a long blue frockcoat. Adams, Washington, and Jefferson: these three giants of the American republic had so much in common and felt so much confidence in each other that they could never quite acknowledge, much less understand, the forces that drove them apart. They sat together on the same platform for the last time, and for a fleeting moment the twenty-one-year-old nation seemed united with its history. When the hubub subsided, Adams rose to deliver his inaugural address. It was elegantly done, on his own view "the sublimest thing ever delivered in America." With an eye to the "heresies" that had been alleged against him, Adams spiritedly declared his loyalty to the Constitution and to republican government. "What other form of government, indeed, can so well deserve our esteem and love?" It had secured for America "immortal glory with posterity." Pledging to administer the government without favor to party or section, Adams extended the hand of friendship to all who would unite with him for the good of the nation. As to foreign nations, he expressed "an inflexible determination" to maintain peace, faith, and honor within the system of neutrality so long sanctioned by the American people. Concluding with a solemn invocation of divine providence, Adams then took the oath of office. Resuming his seat briefly, he rose, bowed all around, and left the hall, followed by Jefferson and Washington, after an amusing byplay on the matter of precedence. Most of huzzas were for the retiring President, who in a few days was on the road to Mount Vernon and peace at last.

Republicans were delighted with Adams's address. He had, said the *Aurora*, "declared himself the friend of France and of peace, the admirer of republicanism, the enemy of party." Some Federalists objected to his "temporizing." But the euphoria of harmony lingered. "God grant it may continue," a Federalist judge wrote, "and serve to allay that vile party spirit which does so much injury to our country." It was not destined to last, however. Cast as Washington's successor, Adams dared not hazard an abrupt change of administration or abdication of responsibility to the Federalist party. It was a pretty thought that parties might vanish, or even become friends, but a President who acted on this expectation in 1797 would soon find himself alone and helpless. With a more than average capacity for self-delusion, Adams bowed to the party yoke without knowing he was putting it on. He sealed his fate by the decision to retain Washington's cabinet: Pickering, Wolcott, and James McHenry, all High Federalists and Francophobes, who took their orders from Alexander Hamilton. The implications of this decision were at once apparent to Jefferson on March 6. Every effort would be made to keep foreign policy on a collision course with France, and nothing would be left untried to alienate Adams from him. So he went his own way, hoping for the best but fearing the worst.

Jefferson tarried in Philadelphia several days after the inauguration. Caught up in the city's society once again, he seemed to enjoy it. He attended a great farewell banquet in Washington's honor. (The Vice President's toast: "Eternal union of sentiments between the commerce and agriculture of our country.") He attended a meeting of the American Philosophical Society. He replenished his wardrobe, buying boots, coat, and waistcoat. He renewed his acquaintance with elk (75 cents) and elephant (50 cents). On the 13th, after settling his bill for ten days board, wood, and wine at Francis' Hotel, he returned to Virginia. It was "a delicious spring." Cherry and peach trees popped into bloom as he neared home. Monticello was empty. He expected to accomplish miracles of building before going to Philadelphia in the fall. But Adams disappointed him by calling Congress into special session to deal with the French crisis. Jefferson was back in Philadelphia on May 11.

Adams's "war message," as the Republicans dubbed it, dispelled the illusion of harmony. Recent dispatches from France showed the determination of the Directory to force its will upon the United States by a combination of insult, plunder, and blackmail, the President declared. He called upon Congress to strengthen the country's defenses on land and sea, not with an immediate view to war but with a view to commanding respect for the mission he intended to send to France in a last desperate effort to preserve the peace. The executive secretaries had withdrawn their opposition to the special mission though not to a bipartisan one. Adams did not know it but he had Hamilton to thank for that. The New Yorker, with sharper political calculation than he usually showed, made his underlings see that the mission was necessary to disarm the Republicans. If it failed, as he expected, high policy at home and abroad would be without effective opposition.

While the cabinet labored to put together an acceptable three-man commission, Congress fell into bitter wrangling over the President's preparedness program. In the Senate, where Jefferson presided, the Federalists had a clear majority. In the House the opposition blocked most of the "warlike" measures. Republicans turned on Adams in a rage: the hand held out to them two months before concealed a dagger! The stream of invective again poured from the *Aurora*. The response strengthened the Federalists' conviction that "the infernal French disease" was an incurable, and increasingly dangerous, affliction of Republicanism. In Geneva, Holland, and Spain "republicanization" by way of collaboration between native revolutionaries and the French armies had ended in conquest and subjection. Was this not the fate France decreed for the United States? French hostility, Adams declared in his message, showed "a disposition to separate the people from the government." Extreme Federalists might find fault with the mildness of this expression; to the Republicans it meant that their motives and aims had no title of patriotism.

Once again, as in 1793, Jefferson found himself at the center of a political inferno. The passions of debate extended to the streets and into the parlors; the pleasures of society, so refreshing in March, turned to ashes in May, and as the dreary session dragged on into June and then July, Jefferson saw few but political friends and talked little but politics. Political opinions, he reminded himself, ought to be as inoffensive in social intercourse as opinions in philosophy or mechanics. Unfortunately, his countrymen were a long way from that elysium. Recurring to an old thought, he wondered if the high style of partisanship in the United States was not "inseparable from the different constitutions of the human mind, and that degree of freedom which permits unrestrained expression." "Foreign influence" was the hue and cry. It was just, but, Jefferson observed, those most guilty of the evil were loudest in the cry. Whatever the President's intentions, the "British faction" in control of the administration aimed at war. The plan, supposedly, was to negotiate peace while preparing for war, but this was a transparent fraud, which could not succeed with Congress or the Directory. "The struggle to keep us [in session], while pretending to negotiate for peace, from provoking war by putting ourselves into all its attitudes, will be arduous and doubtful," Jefferson observed. In truth, Congress had nothing to do. The panic induced by Adams's address quickly subsided under the sobering news of events in Europe. Napoleon Bonaparte's victories over the Austrians, the failure of the Bank of England, mutiny in the British fleet, revolutionary agitation in Ireland, Lord Malmsbury's negotiations with the French—these events cooled the "war party," Jefferson said, and revived the spirit of peace in Congress. The next act would be played in Paris. The three envoys named to the special commission, C. C. Pinckney, John Marshall, and Elbridge Gerry, were moderate Federalists of varying hues. The commission, while partisan, was better than Jefferson had expected it to be.

The letters the Vice President wrote during the meeting of Congress suggest at least the outlines of the policy he would have pursued had he been President. Peace was the great object. "Interest and honor are also national considerations," he conceded. "But inter-

est, duly weighed is in favor of peace even at the expense of spoliations past and future; and honor cannot now be an object"—it had
been insulted by Britain for years. Exhortations of national honor
and dignity left him cold, not because he was any less patriotic than
the exhorters but because he suspected they were war-mongering.
He dreaded war: "I anticipate the burning of our seaports, havoc of
our frontiers, household insurgency, with a long train of et ceteras."
In war Louisiana and the Floridas might become French colonies,
for Spain could not hold them. War would multiply the debt with
all its evils. War conducted on the side of Britain would give a head
to foreign influence fatal to the republic. War would not unite but
divide the nation. "Our countrymen have divided themselves by
such strong affections, to the French and the English, that nothing
will secure us internally but a divorce from both nations; and this
must be the object of every real American, and its attainment is
practicable without much self-denial." Here he echoed the sentiments of "non-entanglement" expressed in Washington's Farewell
Address. Older commitments to the French republic seemed to have
no place in this new calculus of the national interest.

War being the great behemoth of danger, Jefferson would have
avoided bluster and recrimination, put off provocative military measures, and assumed a posture of friendship toward France. The European conflict moved rapidly to a climax. The present campaign
was probably the last, so it seemed better for the United States to
"rub through this fragment of a year" as it had four preceding ones.
He would have admitted the justice of the Directory's complaint
against the Jay Treaty, for, in fact, that abomination threw American "neutrality" into the scales of British power and provoked the
decrees of the Directory that led to the present crisis. His enemies
charged he would abrogate the treaty. While he never suggested
that, it was not at all clear how he proposed to maintain the treaty
and at the same time pacify the French in 1797. He certainly would
have seized every opportunity to force the British into a straight-
and-narrow respect for American neutrality. Failing in this, he
might have been expected to experiment with commercial coercion,
perhaps an embargo of American trade, such as he would adopt a
decade later. "War is not the best engine for us to resort to," he
wrote in a memorable restatement of an old position, "nature has

given us one *in our commerce*, which, if properly managed, will be a better instrument for obliging the interested nations of Europe to treat us with justice." Indeed, he declared, had his commercial policy been adopted at an earlier time, "we should at this moment have been standing on such an eminence of safety and respect as ages can never recover."

Clearly, Jefferson continued to believe that Britain held the nation in bondage, hence any policy risking war with France fastened the chains of oppression. The danger was greater now than before. The oppression was greater; moreover, Britain was going down in Europe and would sink the United States too if it did not get clear of the wreck. In a remarkable flourish, written for Gerry's benefit in May, Jefferson summed up the ledger of British monopoly and influence:

> When we take notice that theirs is the workshop to which we go for all we want; that with them center either immediately or ultimately all the labors of our hands and lands; that to them belongs either openly or secretly the great mass of our navigation; that even the factorage of their affairs here, is kept to themselves by factitious citizenships; that these foreign and false citizens now constitute the great body of what are called our merchants, fill our seaports, are planted in every little town and district to the interior country, sway everything in the former places by their own votes and those of their dependents, in the latter, by their insinuations and the influence of their ledgers; that they are advancing fast to a monopoly of our banks and public funds, and thereby placing our public finances under their control; that they have in their alliance the most influential characters in and out of office; when they have shown that by all these bearings on the different branches of the government, they can force it to proceed in whatever direction they dictate, and bend the interests of this country entirely to the will of another; when all this, I say, is attended to, it is impossible for us to say we stand on independent ground, impossible for a free mind not to see and to groan under the bondage in which it is bound.

The only surprise, he concluded, was that the British party had "been able so far to throw dust in the eyes of our citizens, as to fix on those who wish merely to recover self-government the charge of subserving one foreign influence, because they resist submission to another."

In this same letter Jefferson recurred to the unpleasant subject of his relationship with the President. Gerry had Adams's ear and offered himself as a friendly intermediary. Jefferson confessed that the maneuvers of the British faction to alienate the President from him made him uneasy on the point of Adams's trust. "It cannot but damp the pleasure of cordiality, when we suspect that it is suspected. I cannot help fearing, that it is impossible for Mr. Adams to believe that the state of my mind is what it really is; that he may think I view him as an obstacle in my way." He had no desire to influence the executive councils and from the nature of his office could not. If only Adams would understand . . . . But as the party warfare thickened in the spring, so did the President's suspicions of Jefferson. Assuming a posture of opposition to France Adams inevitably drew closer to the High Federalists for whom Jefferson was the enemy. In letters to Gerry, Adams repelled warnings of British influence and Hamiltonian intrigue, arguing rather that the danger came from a French party subversive of American independence since 1778. When Jefferson supplied fresh proofs of his association with this party, Adams reluctantly concluded the Vice President was his enemy too.

The *coup de grâce* was a letter addressed to Adams from Georgetown in June. The author, Uriah Forrest, an old personal friend and Federalist zealot, had been privy to certain "disgraceful insinuations" and "barefaced assertions" made by the Vice President in a confidential letter to Peregrine Fitzhugh, a Maryland Republican with whom Jefferson corresponded on agricultural and political topics. Covering a number of the latter, Jefferson pointedly criticized Adams for endangering the peace of the country. Although Fitzhugh was enjoined to hold these sentiments in confidence, he showed the letter to his friends, among them his kinsman Forrest. Struck by the discrepancy between the public reports of cordiality and the censorious tone of the letter, Forrest committed the major part to memory, then wrote it down and sent it to Adams. The revelation was "a serious thing," Adams replied; he was grateful to Forrest for putting him on guard against Jefferson's cunning. "You can witness for me how loath I have been to give him up," he said in reporting the affair to his son John Quincy. "It is with much reluctance that I am obliged to look upon him as a man whose mind is warped by prejudice and so blinded by ignorance as to be unfit for the office he holds. However wise and scientific as a philosopher, as a politician he is a child and a dupe of party!" Adams thus subscribed, grudgingly, to the canonized Federalist opinion of Jefferson. The Virginian, at the same time, though he knew nothing of the Forrest letter, believed Adams had become a "dupe of party." The breach between them was complete.

The estrangement was part of a crowded political canvas. Jefferson entered his new office in the expectation it would be "honorable and easy." He was rapidly disappointed. He became, as he complained, "the property of the newspapers, a fair target for every man's dirt." And powerless as his office was, he discovered that he had been thrust into another and unofficial role, that of party leader, in which he was the second most powerful figure in the country. The two roles, official and unofficial, were quite compatible. Had the *entente* materialized he would have felt a measure of responsibility to the administration; as it was, he could oppose and criticize without any of the disquieting ambiguity of his position in 1792–93. He could no longer escape the leadership of the Republican party. Madison had withdrawn to Montpelier. The only first-rate man the Republicans could boast in Congress, Geneva-born Albert Gallatin, who had already caught Jefferson's eye, lacked the credentials for national leadership. As Vice President, Jefferson was nothing. As party leader, he was everything. Upon him Federalists and Republicans alike, one in fear, the other in hope, fixed their gaze.

The alacrity with which he stepped into this new role has never ceased to amaze students of his character. The change from the retired master of Monticello to the downright politician, all in a few months' time, was a remarkable instance of Jefferson's adaptability to the political environment. He urged greater discipline on the Republicans in the House. He took an active part in building up the Republican press, assisting new party organs and political pamphleteers like James T. Callender. This most scurrilous of Republican scribes had fled Edinburgh in 1793 under indictment for sedition founded on his tract, *The Political Progress of Britain*, which Jefferson admired. If the author's "advertisement" of the American edition may be credited, it was reprinted in Philadelphia on Jefferson's recommendation. In June 1797 Jefferson befriended this poor, woebegone refugee, and under the mask of charity opened his purse to support his writings. Jefferson penned many ingratiating letters to political leaders in key states, to dissident Federalists like Edward Rutledge in South Carolina, to moderates like Gerry, and to valued allies like Aaron Burr. These letters were all studiously calculated for political effect. With Burr, in particular, Jefferson's connections were entirely political; and his elaborate overture to the New York chieftain in June was prompted by the desire to work out a strategy for "the penetration of truth into the Eastern States." Later in the month, obviously gratified by this mark of confidence, Burr traveled to Philadelphia to map plans with Jefferson. At Francis' Hotel, where Jefferson lodged, surrounded by congressmen, in quarters that had neither the elegance nor the privacy he had craved as Secretary of State, he found many opportunities for conversation easily blending philosophy with the politics of the day. His enemies wondered what treasonable schemes were hatching in this nest.

The vice presidency, Federalists came to believe, was an imposing front behind which the incumbent deviously, secretly, conducted a campaign against the government. Sly old Fisher Ames, fearing something of this kind in December, had warned that Jefferson's election to the second office would be disastrous. "In the Senate that will bring him into no scrapes . . . , responsible for no measures, acting in none that are public, he may go on affecting zeal for the people; combining the *antis*, and standing at the head, he will balance the power of the chief magistrate by his own. Two Presidents, like two suns in the meridian, could meet and jostle for four years, and the Vice would be first." To combat the danger Federalist politicoes spared no effort to expose the Vice President, to flush him out of his privileged sanctuary, and arraign him before the public in all the colors of political depravity. Nothing would do so well as Jefferson's own hidden words and deeds. Fortune smiled on the Federalists at the opening of Congress, and it was many years before Jefferson could trust his pen again.

The damaging document was a letter Jefferson had written to Philip Mazzei on April 19, 1796. Most of it concerned the Florentine's private affairs in Virginia, but Jefferson digressed to give his old friend a quick view of the changed political scene in the United States. He said that "an Anglican monarchical, and aristocratical party has sprung up, whose avowed object is to draw over us the substance, as they have already done the forms, of the British government." The mass of citizens remained republican, but against them were the executive, the judiciary, the Senate, traders on British capitals, speculators, stockjobbers, and so on. "It would give you a fever were I to name to you the apostates who have gone over to these heresies, men who were Samsons in the field and Solomons in the council, but who have had their heads shorn by the harlot England." Mazzei should not be alarmed, however. The Americans would "awake and snap the Lilliputian cords," and so preserve their hard-won liberty. Written in the angry aftermath of the Jay Treaty, the letter was an accurate summation of Jefferson's political views, though especially combustible because the rhetoric was highly compressed. Mazzei, quite combustible himself, turned the political portion of the letter into Italian and saw to its publication in a Florentine newspaper. The Paris *Moniteur* picked it up and lectured the "ungrateful children" of France, "their true mother country," for submitting to the harlot; and this French version, turned back into English, appeared in the American press in May 1797.

Jefferson met with the published letter while en route to Philadelphia. He at first thought he must buckle on his armor and take to the newspapers. Yet this posed difficulties. He could not disavow what he had in substance written. Nor could he altogether avow it, since in completing the circuit of three languages his own words had been altered in one or two particulars. For example, where he had referred to the *forms* of the British government, meaning "birth-days, levees, processions to parliament, inauguration pomposities, etc.," the letter as published referred to the *form*, meaning monarchy. Furthermore, since to avow was to defend, he would be compelled to go into proofs, explanations, and secret transactions which must, as he said, "embroil me personally with every member of the Executive, with the Judiciary, and others still," indeed with the nine-tenths of the people of the United States who worshipped Washington's character. So he decided to remain silent. Federalist pundits took his silence as admission of guilt: the treasonous guilt of maligning the government of the United States, of emboldening

French insult and aggression, above all of libeling General Washington. Who but Washington and his colleagues were the "Samsons in the field and Solomons in the council" of the infamous letter? Years later, not long before he died, Jefferson said his allusion had been to the Society of the Cincinnati; but the explanation seems not to have occurred to him in 1797, and had he made it few, least of all the Federalists, would have believed him.

With the publication of the Mazzei letter Jefferson stood accused of defaming Washington, and not only Washington but the American character of which he was the hero. The political value of this exposé was beyond calculation. It tumbled the lofty philosopher from his pedestal into the ranks of slanderers like Bache, Paine, and Beckley. Disclosing his deceit toward the first President, it showed, some said, the fundamental duplicity of Jefferson's character. The Federalists had labored to bathe their party in the radiance of Washington's fame. The Farewell Address, so largely Hamilton's work, was a testament to their success. Federalist policy was identified with the national interest, with patriotism, with Washington's name; and partisan opposition was denied any title of legitimacy. Hamilton spoke for himself when he later acknowledged that Washington had been "an *Aegis very essential to me,*" yet it might have been said of the party generally. In Jefferson's opinion the personification of the Federalist party was the paramount fact of American political life until March 4, 1797, and he was not a little distressed that the candor of his own pen should now help to perpetuate this idolotrous influence.

His tone toward Washington was normally respectful. The Mazzei letter was, in this regard, an aberration. He thought Washington a great and good man who had been misled, gulled by flattery, and captured by the gang around him. Whether this view was any less flattering than the one which saw him as the conscious agent of Federalist power is an interesting question; for Jefferson, at any rate, it enabled him to reconcile his exalted idea of Washington's character with his profound distrust of Washington's administration. While Washington was President, Jefferson observed, the Republicans were virtually paralyzed by the spell he cast over the American public. For the people would always support him "without appealing to their own reason or to anything but their feelings toward him"; and his mind was "so long used to unlimited applause that it could not brook contradictions, or even advice offered unasked." Once Washington withdrew into retirement, Jefferson expected the magic of his name to fade too, ushering in the epoch of political self-possession. He was disappointed for a number of reasons, of which the Mazzei letter was more symptom than cause. Yet that letter, by serving to portray him as the assassin of Washington, helped the Federalists to bring back the charisma and to vilify him for wishing to obliterate it.

What Washington himself thought of the epistle can only be surmised. After his retirement to Mount Vernon, he did not see Jefferson again, nor did any letters pass between them—negative evidence in itself of their alienation. Seeds of suspicion and distrust had been planted in Washington's mind for years. Jefferson's anxiety to remove them had, in fact, occasioned the last of his letters to Washington, in the summer of 1796. He had learned that "a miserable tergiversator," Henry Lee, had been "dirtily employed in sifting the conversations of my table" and carrying the crumbs to Washington in order "to sow tares between you and me." To Jefferson's assurances of unfailing friendship, Washington responded with assurances of his own, saying he discredited all reports of Jefferson's enmity. Presumably the seeds sprouted with the disclosure of the Mazzei letter, and they came to harvest in Washington's mind four or five months later. Peter Carr, Jefferson's favorite nephew, who should have known better, wrote to Washington over the fictitious signature of John Langhorne, apparently with a view to eliciting political sentiments useful to the Republican cause in Virginia. Washington replied in a non-committal fashion. There the matter might have ended but for a Federalist snooper in the Charlottesville post office, "Clerk John" Nicholas, who informed the old hero that the Langhorne letter emanated from "the very headquarters of Jacobinism" and gave further proof of the "vile hypocrisy" of the author of the Mazzei letter. This time Washington was not incredulous. "Nothing short of the evidence you have adduced," he wrote Nicholas, "corroborative of intimations which I had received long before, through another channel, would have shaken my belief in the sincerity of a friendship, which I had conceived was possessed by me . . . ." In retirement, observing the conceit of France and the refractoriness of

the Republicans, Washington grew more and more fearful of subversion of the government. He could no longer separate this fear
from Jefferson—was he not chief of the subverters? So political
enmity slid into personal enmity, and Washington credited the testimony of a village gossip for the proof of suspicions he had earlier
repressed. Of course, Jefferson had no responsibility whatever for
the Langhorne letter. Any enmity he felt toward Washington was
political, not personal, and he was quite incapable of the silly little
scheme concocted by his nephew. Not for some time, in fact, did he
learn of this episode which closed the book, rather sadly, on a long
friendship.

The controversy over the Mazzei letter coincided with Jefferson's assumption of the Republican leadership. The former was not
necessary to the latter, but by raising Federalist censure to new
heights, by publicly exhibiting the Vice President in partisan garb,
by stinging his pride, it enabled him to accept his new role with
something like cheerfulness. Such an experience at an earlier time
would have excited all his old loathing for politics and sent him
scurrying back to Monticello. But not now. If he became more
guarded with his pen, he neither disguised his opposition to the
Adams administration nor evaded the responsibilities of leadership.
There were grave political risks in the advocacy of pacific policy
toward France in 1797, yet Jefferson ran the risk and severed the
lines of retreat to domestic conciliation and compromise. On July 1,
a few days before Congress adjourned, he attended a festive dinner
at Oeller's to welcome James Monroe, the recalled envoy from
France and defender of the old alliance. The party was a Republican
affair. Jefferson was toasted "The man of the people." Not only to
Federalists but to some Republican moderates as well, it was a celebration of Jacobinism. One of the latter, John Rutledge, Jr., the
young South Carolinian he had befriended in Paris years before, was
shocked by Jefferson's presence in such company. "It was a complete medley . . . . Here you saw an American disorganizer and
there a blundering Irishman—in another corner a banished Genevan
and in another a French Spy—on one side a greasy Butcher and on
the other a dirty Cobbler . . . ." Young Rutledge had recently
written his uncle that Jefferson was "a wonderfully great and good
man but I really believe that the severe persecution he has lately un-

574

dergone (and which continues) has occasioned a little fresh bias."
Now, after the Monroe fete, Rutledge was the more convinced, and
soon he would be counted among the most violent of the Federalists.

Several days later Jefferson exchanged "the roar and tumult of
bulls and bears" for the prattle of his grandchildren at Monticello.
He had left home in May as the Vice President; he returned in July
as the leader of the Republican party. There was no suspension of
politics when he entered his sanctuary. Madison, Monroe, and the
Albemarle friend and congressman Wilson Cary Nicholas, a comparative newcomer to the inner circle, came to the mountain to confer on political tactics. They reviewed Jefferson's silent treatment of
the Mazzei letter. Only Monroe thought he should take to print.
Monroe himself was preparing to do so in defense of his conduct as
minister to France. Jefferson, while rather cool to the project, lent
Monroe a helping hand. The notorious Reynolds affair, for five
years a well-kept secret among half-a-dozen Republicans including
Jefferson, blew up in the summer months. Beckley fed the scandal
to Callender, and he published it in a tract Jefferson neither approved nor disapproved. Although his scrupulous respect for privacy in affairs of personal honor would never permit him to indulge
his own pen on this tawdry episode in Hamilton's career, he could
not forbid it to hacks like Callender.* The political implications of
the publication must have been discussed at Monticello, especially as
it seemed likely for a time to produce a duel between Hamilton and
Monroe, whom the New Yorker held responsible. And there were
other political questions, such as the encroachment of the federal judiciary on freedom of speech, which began to agitate Jefferson. He
wrote few political letters during this season. The risk was too high
—he had learned his lesson. The affairs of state, while discouraging,
were not at the point of crisis, nor would they be as long as Americans and Frenchmen talked in Paris. So Jefferson found time and repose for children and grandchildren, building and farming, and
for intellectual activities that even in critical hours held high claim
on his mind.

* The affair had its beginnings in the controversy of 1790 over the ar-
rearages of soldiers' pay. (See pp. 414-15.) James Reynolds was one of a group
of speculators engaged in buying up the soldiers' certificates. The next year,

575

Science and Politics

When Jefferson journeyed to Philadelphia for the inauguration he carried with him a box of fossilized bones, the remains of some great unknown creature lately uncovered in Virginia. He had written a paper to announce this discovery to the scientific world from the rostrum of the American Philosophical Society. On the recent death of its second president, David Rittenhouse, the Society had elected Jefferson to the chair; and so he came to Philadelphia to be installed not only in the second office of the government of the United States but also in the first office of American science. He took the chair at the Society's evening meeting on March 10. On his left sat Joseph Priestley, the distinguished chemist, philosopher, revolutionary, and dissenting theologian, who had fled persecution in England, and on his right the peripatetic French rationalist Volney, also a refugee in the land of freedom. Jefferson, Priestly, Volney: a philosophical triumvirate of the Enlightenment. There was the usual business of the Society, and papers on "The Big Naked Bear" of the Delawares and

---

with blackmail his object, Reynolds employed the charms of his wife Maria to seduce Hamilton. Hamilton fell into the trap, and into the lady's boudoir, and was soon paying handsomely. When the amour ceased, and when fortune turned against Reynolds, this rake exposed Hamilton to three Republican congressmen, one of them Monroe, not only as an adulterer but as a speculator in the public funds as well. The Republicans, who were then, in 1792, looking into the Treasury, were especially interested in the charge of public misconduct. When they confronted Hamilton he confessed the adultery in order to save his public reputation. The three Republicans, apparently satisfied on the latter point, had no wish to make a scandal of Hamilton's private life. Nor did Jefferson, who knew of the affair. But in 1797 John Beckley, who also knew of it, and who had recently been dismissed by the Federalists from his position as Clerk of the House of Representatives, gave the entire story to Callender, without consulting Jefferson, Monroe, or others in the Republican leadership. As the affair was told by Callender in his *History of the United States for the Year 1796*, Hamilton was both an adulterer and a partner with Reynolds in corrupt financial transactions. Hamilton now defended his public morality by confessing his private vices in his *Observations* on Callender's tract. Jefferson, although not entirely satisfied that Hamilton had, in fact, cleared himself of public misconduct, showed no interest in pursuing the matter after Hamilton himself blasted his political future.

on the properties of land and sea air; but the feature of the meeting was Jefferson's "Memoir on the Discovery of Certain Bones of a Quadruped of the Clawed Kind in the Western Parts of Virginia."

These bones had been discovered by diggers of saltpeter in a limestone cave in Greenbrier County, beyond the Blue Ridge, in 1796. A local resident, John Stuart, had sent them to Monticello. For years, since his famous encounter with Buffon, Jefferson had been collecting the relics of mysterious vertebrate giants; no objects of natural history were more interesting to him, and the bigger they came the better he liked them. He was especially excited by this new discovery, for the bones belonged to an animal apparently unknown to science. Judging from the huge claws eight inches long, he thought it probably of "the family of lion, tiger, panther, etc., but as preeminent over the lion in size as the mammoth is over the elephant." Communicating this information to Rittenhouse, he named the animal the great-claw, or megalonyx. Although eager to write an account of the discovery for inclusion in the fourth volume of the Society's *Transactions*, soon to be published, Jefferson put it off in the hope that important missing parts of the skeleton would be found in the diggings. And more bones were found, but not the thigh bone necessary to fix the animal's stature, nor any teeth. He finally ventured to write the memoir anyway, and in February packed up the bones he had for presentation to the Society.

Arriving in Philadelphia he came upon an article recently published in London which shook his classification of the animal. The article described the skeleton of a huge creature unearthed in Paraguay, brought to Madrid, and mounted in the Royal Cabinet of Natural History. (Jefferson had actually received a sketch and description of the skeleton in 1789, but, unhappily, had forgotten all about it eight years later.) The animal had great claws and measured 12 feet long and 6 feet high; however, it was classed not with the lion but with the non-carnivorous sloth, hence named great-sloth, or megatherium. Jefferson at once recognized the similarities between this specimen and the one he was about to describe in Philadelphia, yet shunned the conclusion that they were, in fact, the same. The London article was "only an abstract" of a paper written by the French naturalist Cuvier; the engraving of the skeleton, reproduced in the magazine, struck him as unreliable; and so many bones were missing, particularly in his own specimen, there was no sure basis of analogy. Jefferson mentioned the abstract in a postscript to his paper; in fact, he went further, cautiously toning down his classification of the animal. Yet he stuck to the name, megalonyx, and compared it to the lion. With the largest of the bones on the table before him, he told the Society that the animal was at least three times the size of the lion and undoubtedly as worthy an antagonist of the mammoth as the lion was of the elephant. Buffon was long dead, but Jefferson was still combating his theories of New World pygmyism.

Having described the animal as best he could, Jefferson went on to argue that it continued to exist, like the mammoth, somewhere in the dark forest beyond the American frontier. He cited accounts of early adventurers in Virginia who mentioned lion-like creatures, of images carved on rock above the Ohio River, and tales of Indians and pioneers of "terrible roarings" and "eyes like two balls of fire" aglow in the forest. Of course, it was part of the economy of nature to check the rapid multiplication of so powerful a destroyer, and so megalonyx was probably the rarest of living creatures. "In fine," he concluded, "the bones exist: therefore the animal has existed. The movements of nature are in a never ending circle. The animal species which has once been put into a train of motion, is still probably moving in that train. For if one link in nature's chain might be lost, another and another might be lost, till this whole system of things would evanish by piece-meal." At bottom, Jefferson's faith in a divinely ordered universe made it impossible for him, as indeed for Buffon and most of the naturalists of his generation, to credit the extinction of species; and thus despite his enormous contribution to paleontology as a collector and a spokesman, he denied the proposition essential to the establishment of this young science.

In this particular instance, science would have been better served had Jefferson been able to overcome the prepossessions that caused him to link the mysterious creature to the leonine species. The excitement of the discovery conquered his usual skepticism of airy hypothesis. When he returned to Philadelphia for the meeting of Congress in May, he met with an impressive folio volume on the Paraguayan animal, which had been published in Madrid the preceding year. Here were the original descriptions and drawings of the skeleton mounted in Madrid—the authentic basis of Cuvier's paper and the London abstract. Very likely the Virginia megalonyx was the same animal. Yet Jefferson was not entirely convinced. "Since this discovery [of megalonyx] had led to questioning the Indians as to this animal," he informed Stuart, "we have received some of their traditions which confirm his classification with the lion." The nature of this questioning he did not explain, but he and his colleagues in the American Philosphical Society had not been inactive. At the May meeting they discussed a plan to amass information on the antiquities of North America, including the skeletons of giant creatures. Not for several years would Jefferson concede the identity of megalonyx and megatherium. Scientific judgment was still uncertain, so he had no cause for embarrassment; and in the end Cuvier himself, the first true scientist of fossil quadrupeds, paid high tribute to Jefferson for his work in paleontology as in the other sciences.

The episode is a notable instance of Jefferson's diligence in matters of scientific investigation and, at the same time, of the national pride that infused the enterprise. All his attachments, he once said, were to "science, and freedom, the first born daughter of science." Freedom was the first principle of inquiry, inquiry the beginning of freedom. The despots of the world, supported by slavish ignorance, feared science because they feared freedom. Priestley's riotous enemies in England, Jefferson told an admirer from that country, "think they have quenched his opinions by sending him to America, just as the pope imagined when he shut up Galileo in prison that he had compelled the world to stand still." Truth had no country. Men of science the world around spoke the same language and engaged in the same search even as their countries warred upon each other; and it always seemed to Jefferson that the relations among nations ought to be copied from the fraternal community of science. In republican America, certainly, there was no cause for political dissensions to impair the quest for knowledge. Science was apolitical. What did it matter whether a man called himself a Republican or a Federalist if his work contributed to the upbuilding of civilization in America and the improvement of mankind? When Jefferson accepted the presidency of the Philosophical Society he confessed to have one clear qualification for the post: "an ardent desire to see knowledge so disseminated through the mass of mankind that it may at last reach the extremes of society, beggars and kings." He held this post through all the years of his presidency and on into 1814. In the dual role of public leadership, in science and in government, he saw nothing incompatible; indeed he believed they were mutually supporting.

Unfortunately, his political foes did not agree. They ridiculed his scientific attainments, called him philosopher, visionary, speculator—opprobrious terms the rough coefficients of which were revolutionary, infidel, and incompetent—and set down science as a positive liability to statesmanship. Years later Jefferson reflected, "Of all the charges brought against me by my political adversaries, that of possessing some science has probably done them the least credit." And the least good, for, he added, "Our countrymen are too enlightened themselves, to believe that ignorance is the best qualification for service." The attack began in 1792, subsided, revived in 1796, and exploded from the moment of his election to the vice presidency.

His appearance on the platform of the American Philosophical Society offered a fitting picture for Federalist diatribe. William Cobbett, the English bookseller who had just commenced publication of *Porcupine's Gazette* in Philadelphia, was amused by the solemn discourse on an old bone and, taking note of Volney and Priestley, wondered what fate awaited the nation from this "triumvirate of *atheism, deism,* and *nothingism.*" Among the Federalist scribes Peter Porcupine was the master of invective. The Vice President was a regular recipient. Mocking his own would-be assassins sometime later, Peter printed his last will and testament. "To Thomas Jefferson, philosopher," one clause began, "I leave a curious Norway spider, with a hundred legs and nine pair of eyes; likewise the first black cutthroat general he can catch hold of, to be flayed alive, in order to determine with more certainty the real cause of the dark colour of his skin . . . ." As a philosopher Jefferson was a straw man, but had he believed him to possess solid merits, Cobbett would have thought no better of him in affairs of state. According to Cobbett, "if one characteristic more than another could disqualify Mr. Jefferson for the Presidency, it would be the charge of being a philosopher." Robert Goodloe Harper, the South Carolina Federalist, while more respectful, concurred in this opinion. "He possesses much knowledge, chiefly however of the scientific kind, the least useful for a statesman, whose business it is to judge and act, not to write books." A man who is "always pursuing certain visionary theories of the closet, which experience constantly contradicts . . . cannot be relied on for the performance of any duty, which might require . . . a manly decisive conduct in difficult situations." And so, Harper concluded in a public letter, "With this opinion of Mr. Jefferson, I might think him fit to be a professor of a college, President of a Philosophical Society, or even Secretary of State; but certainly not the first magistrate of a great nation." The republic of Jefferson's vision was one in which freedom and science advanced hand in hand—a republic of science. In the Federalist mind, Jeffersonian science—air balloons, philosphical plows, mammoth bones, salt mountains, the Negro's kidneys, vibrating pendulums, wirligig chairs—was absurd, and Heaven preserve the nation from the whimsies of its projector. "Science and government are two different paths," a Federalist tract summed up the argument in 1800. "He that walks in one, becomes, at every step, less qualified to walk with steadfastness or vigour in the other."

A direct challenge to Jefferson's reputation as a scientific man occurred within a month of his return to office. In the pages of *Porcupine's Gazette*, Luther Martin, Attorney General of Maryland, vehemently objected to the inclusion of "The Story of Logan, the Mingo Chief" in the program of readings and recitations of a Philadelphia actor. The story, of course, had been popularized by Jefferson's account in the *Notes on Virginia*. Already an American legend in 1797, it was the theme of drama and verse and Logan's tragic plaint the *ne plus ultra* of savage eloquence. In this impassioned utterance at the conclusion of Lord Dunmore's War in 1774, Logan blamed Michael Cresap for the murder of his family. From this circumstance the ensuing blood bath on the upper waters of the Ohio was sometimes called Cresap's War. Jefferson, who introduced the speech in the *Notes* to refute Buffon's aspersions on the Indians, went along with Logan and described Cresap as "a man infamous for many murders" on the frontier. In all the years since 1775, when the story was first published, no one had challenged its truth. Now Martin declared that the speech was a fraud and that Jefferson, by broadcasting it, had libeled an innocent man, the late Captain Cresap. Like the philosopher he was, said Martin, Jefferson had a ridiculous hypothesis to establish, the equality of the American savage with the civilized European, and he picked up Logan's story without stopping to verify it or to consider its injury to the good name of Cresap. The vindication of that name was a point of honor with Martin, for Cresap's daughter, now dead, was the mother of his children.

This profession of motive was transparently false. The more Jefferson pondered the matter the more convinced he became that Martin acted as "the cat's paw" of party. "After letting this matter remain uncontradicted for upwards of twenty years it has now been raked up from party hatred, as furnishing some with the design of writing me down." The timing of the letter, the place of its initial publication, its barbs and innuendo, the entire absence of evidence against the traditional account—Martin obviously had more interest in smearing the Vice President than in clearing the name of his father-in-law. Yet his motives are not easily assessed. A Marylander to whom Jefferson made inquiry supposed that Martin must have acted in "a state of drunkenness from which he is scarcely ever free." He was a sick man, often depressed, a Federalist but forever scarred by his Anti-Federal past, as well as by fondness for drink and an unruly temperament. In short, the Federalist leaders would not have trusted Luther Martin, for all his talents at the bar, as a "cat's paw" to tickle the Vice President. The attack was political because Martin made it so, and because in the climate then existing any blemish on Jefferson's character was bound to have political repercussions.

Had it been only for these repercussions, had it been merely an attack on Jefferson as a political man, he would have adhered to his rule of silence in such matters; but Martin struck at his reputation for science and truth, and this was a different matter. Intellectually, he was committed to the principles Logan's speech had been evinced to prove; moreover its truth or falsity, unlike political opinions, was open to investigation. So Jefferson quietly commenced an inquiry, pursued for nearly three years, to establish the authenticity of the story of Logan and Cresap. Witnesses to these events of a quarter-century past still lived. Jefferson knew some of them; as the investigation proceeded he learned of others who volunteered their testimony. In effect, he made himself the annalist and the historian of this small but illuminating episode in the American past. The methods he employed were in striking constrast to the invective and bombast of his enemies.

While Jefferson prepared to overwhelm his assassin with facts, that intemperate gentleman wrote more public letters. Furious that Jefferson would not enter into the contest at his own level, or even acknowledge his letters, Martin said that he condemned himself by his "obstinate, stubborn silence." In Maryland the Attorney General's accusations were having the desired political effect. The Governor, John Henry, tried to cool the controversy but was nearly consumed by it. Before his election to this post in November 1797, Henry had been in the United States Senate where, despite his party affiliation, he had formed a high opinion of the Vice President. He expressed this opinion at Annapolis, Martin's letters being the subject of conversation, and pointedly declared "that men of sense and moderation ought not to suffer their minds to be led awry by the wicked, malicious reports unprincipled men were daily circulating." He was astonished at the result. "Innocent and natural as this conversation appears, it nevertheless instantly kindled a flame which flew through all the boarding houses and so violently agitated the minds of the majority of the legislature, that I verily believe if they . . . had the power they would have displaced the man whom a few days before they had elected to the chief office in the state without a dissenting voice." Instead they elected to the Senate seat vacated by Henry a Federalist of the same violent stripe as Luther Martin. Compared with the animosities released by the Mazzei letter or the furies that raged around Jefferson in 1798, Luther Martin's vendetta was an annoying side-show. Still it was singularly instructive to Jefferson and his friends. The Federalist press participated in Martin's malice and misrepresentation, and in at least one instance that came to Jefferson's attention closed its columns to authentic testimony on Logan's speech. Truth, justice, probity—the rules of scientific inquiry itself—seemed to be at stake in the party struggle.

All the while Jefferson was quietly amassing documentary evidence, letters, depositions, versions of Logan's speech—two dozen separate items—some solicited, some unsolicited, some obtained by old friends like Mann Page, Harry Innes, and James Brown, some obtained from total strangers like the Reverend John Heckwelder, a

Moravian missionary to the Delawares who had known Logan, John Sappington, the killer of Logan's brother, and General John Gibson, the recipient of the famous address. By 1800 Jefferson was ready to publish these "fragments of evidence, the small remain of a mighty mass which time has consumed," and he did so in the form of an appendix to the *Notes on Virginia*.

The story as reconstructed from this evidence was more complex than he had imagined, yet in its essentials consistent with what he had believed since first hearing Logan's speech repeated by Dunmore's officers in Williamsburg. It was necessary to distinguish four separate massacres on the Ohio below Fort Pitt in the bloody spring of 1774. Frontiersmen, mostly Virginians, were occupying this land claimed by the Shawnee. Logan, a Cayuga sachem, whose Indian name was Tah-gah-jute, had married a Shawnee and established a settlement at the mouth of Yellow Creek on the north bank of the Ohio. As a boy he had frequented the Moravian mission and been baptized in the name of the Secretary of the Province of Pennsylvania. Among whites and Shawnee alike he was known as a friend of the Long Knives. Fears of Indian attack spread up and down the river in April. The frontiersmen looked to Cresap, later commissioned a captain by Dunmore, for leadership. At the head of a party on the south shore near Wheeling, he laid ambush and killed two Indians, then quickly moved down the river to Grove Creek and killed several more, including some of Logan's family settled there. The next day Cresap's party went up the river to Yellow Creek. However, Cresap dropped out, leaving Daniel Greathouse in charge. The party stopped at a place called Baker's Bottom, opposite Yellow Creek, where there was a tavern. When six or seven Indians from Logan's settlement came to the tavern the next morning, Greathouse and his men got them drunk and massacred everyone. Logan's brother and sister "big with child" were among the victims. Other Indians, on hearing the shots, paddled across the river to investigate. Some fled, some were killed. At this point Logan went on the warpath.

So the famous speech had erred in blaming Cresap for all the murders that extinguished Logan's blood from every living creature. Jefferson acknowledged the error but did not think it mitigated Cresap's crime. For in the massacre at Yellow Creek, Greathouse was only pursuing the example set by Cresap. Further evidence brought to light at a later time suggested that Cresap was more directly implicated in the final murders than Jefferson claimed; even so, at the end of his researches the guilt remained where Logan had placed it. "Logan imputed the whole to Cresap . . . : the Indians generally imputed it to Cresap: Lord Dunmore and his officers imputed it to Cresap: the country, with one accord, imputed it to him: and whether he was innocent, let the universal verdict now declare." The documents spoke for themselves. As to the authenticity of the Indian's utterance, which Martin had denied, the evidence was equally convincing. Many of Jefferson's informants reported hearing the speech at the time, some at Dunmore's headquarters when peace was made—the same speech they had later seen in the newspapers or in the *Notes on Virginia*. Men who knew Logan, like the Moravians, believed him fully capable of such eloquence. In the final analysis, the point rested on the testimony of one man, General Gibson, who had been sent by Dunmore to obtain Logan's consent to the treaty. The Mingo spoke in his native tongue. Gibson, a man of some learning and also the father of a child by Logan's murdered sister, translated and took the words down in English. In his deposition Gibson gave an exact account of the incident and vouched for the accuracy of his translation. Another deponent testified that Gibson, on showing the speech in Pittsburgh, had said it was but "a poor picture of the original."

Jefferson's manner of treating the subject in his pamphlet-appendix, ignoring Martin altogether and relying, as he said, on "exact information of the historical past," caused rejoicing among his friends and proved definitive during his lifetime. When the controversy was revived after his death, the new accusers found one gaping hole in his scholar's armor. Regrettably, he had suppressed the one piece of testimony most damaging to his case. His old friend George Rogers Clark, the once idolized hero of the West, professed a "perfect recollection" of the entire transaction, which he related in a detailed narrative. Clark had known Cresap and been a member of his party in April 1774. The Marylander deserved a medal for good conduct, in Clark's opinion, and should not be blamed for any of the murders Logan charged to him. The speech was unquestionably Logan's, but he had been misinformed, Clark stated. On hearing it, Cresap had smiled and said he had a mind to tomahawk Greathouse. Why did Jefferson suppress Clark's letter? Not simply because it was favorable to Cresap, for he published other testimony of this character. And not simply because Clark alone of all the witnesses boasted a venerable name. Jefferson plainly did not think the Kentuckian's narrative trustworthy, and rather than expose it for what it was, "an attempt to rub out blood with whitewash," as Irving Brant has said, Jefferson mercifully buried it in his private papers. While his action may be regarded as a mark of charity for an old warrior who had lost all character for judgment, the indulgence was quite mistaken. Jefferson assumed the stance of a historian: let the documents speak, he said, and the testimony of all witnesses declare. But he withheld a singularly important document of a singularly important witness. The verdict would probably not have been different had he published Clark's narrative; and had he done so he would have removed the only basis for cavil with what was, in truth, a remarkable vindication of sober intelligence against vicious partisanship. Under Jefferson's barrage of facts Luther Martin was as silent as the grave. It would have been pleasant to dismiss him altogether, but in the passage of time Jefferson would have to fight off this "impudent Federal bull-dog" again and again, and with a good deal less success.

If Jefferson felt a somewhat romantic attraction for the American Indian, the methods and aims of his study were in the best tradition of science in his time. He had suggested the broad field open to investigation in the *Notes on Virginia*. Now as president of the American Philosophical Society he made a special point of advancing knowledge of the aborigines. Evidence of an archaeological nature tending to prove the red man capable of the civilizing arts was especially welcome. Languages remained Jefferson's principal interest. For years he had been placing his "blank vocabularies" into the hands of friends able to fill them up with the corresponding words of the different tribes. By comparing these languages with one another and also with Asiatic tongues, Jefferson hoped to construct the anthropology of the redmen. Supposing that the large number of radically different languages among the Indians could only have developed over an immense time, he had ventured the opinion in the *Notes* that these people were of greater antiquity than those of Asia, possibly as old as mankind itself. The opinion was a minority one. The Indians were generally traced to Asia, and thence back to the common cradle of the human race.

A prominent New York minister, the Reverend William Linn, challenged Jefferson's opinion in 1798. He replied that it had been "hazarded" on the state of knowledge a decade and a half ago; much had been learned since then, and there was still much more to learn. "My object being the true facts, I do not permit myself to form as yet a decisive opinion, and therefore leave the slight one I had hazarded to the result of further enquiry." When all the vocabularies were collected and then laid beside the Empress Catherine's great compendium of the Asiatic languages, perhaps men would be able to draw conclusions. Linn participated in Jefferson's enterprise but refused to credit his scientific purpose. In the presidential campaign two years later he blasted Jefferson as an infidel, including in his array of evidence the "profane" opinion advanced in the *Notes* that the Indians were indigenous to America. Politics and science did not mix, nor did religion and science. Benjamin Smith Barton, a colleague in the Philosophical Society, though he too disagreed with Jefferson on important points of Indian ethnology and linguistics, was considerably more generous than Linn. Recognizing Jefferson's leadership in this area of scientific investigation, Barton dedicated his book, *New Views of the Origin of the Tribes of Natives of America,* to him.

Describing his collection of vocabularies to Benjamin Hawkins, federal agent to the Creeks, Jefferson said he was "afraid to risk it any longer, lest by some accident it might be lost." So he was about to publish it. Unfortunately, he did not act on this premonition, which materialized in 1809, the whole collection being lost in the course of moving his household from Washington to Monticello. He wanted his collection to be as complete as possible before sending it forth. In 1800, when he wrote to Hawkins, he still did not have the languages of the great nations south of the Ohio. Hawkins would get for him the Choctaw, another the Chickasaw, and so on. But then entirely new tribes came into the white man's ken, even an entirely new kind of communication. From William Dunbar, in Natchez, Jefferson received the first information of "the language by signs" among the Plains Indians and hardly knew what to make of it.

The opening of the Mississippi Territory in the last years of the century commenced a new chapter in the natural history of America. Jefferson was exhilarated by every scrap of scientific intelligence from the unknown land. Andrew Ellicott, L'Enfant's successor in laying out the national capital, went down to run the boundary along the 31st parallel, as provided under the Pinckney Treaty, and he sent Jefferson his astronomical observations. In Dunbar, with whom he opened correspondence in 1799, Jefferson found a man whose learning and passion for inquiry equaled his own. "Sir William," the youngest son of a Scottish lord, who had lived near Natchez under the Spanish and only now became an American citizen, was unquestionably "the first character" for science and philosophy in that part of the world. He made the first meteorological observations in the Mississippi Valley. These records, together with the harvest of his curiosity on many subjects—Indians, astronomy, geography, agriculture—he sent to Jefferson, who referred most of it to the Philosophical Society.

Jefferson was captivated by the stories of wild horses of beautiful mien and strange colors roaming the lands west of the Mississippi. He wrote to Philip Nolan, the young man he had been told knew more about these mustangs than anyone else. Nothing was known in the Old World, Jefferson explained, of the horse in a state of nature, and with the rapid advance of civilization in America it would soon be too late to obtain this knowledge in the New. "The present then is probably the only moment in the age of the world, and the herds . . . mentioned the only subjects of which we can avail ourselves to obtain what has never yet been recorded, and never can be again in all probability." Nolan was a remarkable man, as Jefferson soon learned. For several years he had ranged far and wide in Texas rounding up wild horses, then breaking them, for the supply of the Spanish regiment in Louisiana. In Texas when Jefferson's letter reached New Orleans in 1799, he was expected at any time at the head of a cavalcade of a thousand mustangs. The next year, after the Spanish government became suspicious of Nolan's activities and revoked his license to trade in Texas, he planned to journey east with a string of horses, stopping at Monticello along the way to talk with Jefferson and present him with one of the beasts. Nolan was more than a horse-trader. He had mapped the north Texas country and explored all the way to the Rio Grande. Obviously he had more in mind than horses, as his association with the intriguing border commander, Brigadier General James Wilkinson, also suggests. From no American of that day could Jefferson have learned as much not only about wild horses but about the lands of the great Southwest. Instead of going east in 1800, however, Nolan set out on his fourth expedition to Texas, this time in defiance of the Louisiana government, and he met violent death near the Brazos River early in 1801. Decades later Edward Everett Hale used his name for *The Man Without a Country*, a character and a story with no resemblance to the historical Philip Nolan.

There was always a touch of the fabulous in Jefferson's intercourse with the West. Another, and more prosaic, side of his scientific personality expressed itself in agriculture. Nothing could be more prosaic than the plow, yet it was "the most useful of the instruments known to man," in Jefferson's opinion. While he was Vice President he presented his moldboard of least resistance to the agriculturists of two continents. He had worked out the mathematical principles of this improvement while in France. From New York, in 1790, he had sent the first model, cut in a block of wood, to his son-in-law. In retirement he had joined the mathematically perfect moldboard to the common bar share plow and tested it in his own fields. The results were amazing: the plow of his invention cut a furrow two inches deeper than the one it replaced, owing solely to the difference of resistance. Strickland saw the plow at Monticello and returned to England with a small model. In recognition of this and other contributions to the cultivator's science, Jefferson was elected an honorary member of the English Board of Agriculture in 1797. The Board mailed him books and reports and expressed further interest in the moldboard. In the early months of the next year he had a finished model executed in Philadelphia and wrote a detailed account of his invention in both its theoretical and practical aspects. After rigorous scrutiny by his mathematical friend Robert Patterson, model and paper were sent to London. The same paper was read before the Philosophical Society and printed in its *Transactions*, while another model went on exhibit in the Society's hall. Jefferson's moldboard was widely copied. He never thought of patenting it, for he opposed, in principle, the monopoly of any useful idea. How useful the invention actually proved to be is a matter of conjecture. But Benjamin Latrobe, the young architect and engineer, expressed wonderment at the performance of Jefferson's plow, and so did many others. In 1806 the Agricultural Society of Paris thought the invention worthy of a gold medal. Jefferson had made further improvements by then; still later he had the moldboard cast in iron. In time, of course, it was superseded, not by better moldboards, but by new and better plows.

Even an invention as practical as this one did not escape the jests of his political enemies. Jefferson paid no attention. By sharing his discovery with all nations, including "harlot" Britain, he testified to the cosmopolitanism of science. The societies of scientists, he once observed, "are always at peace, however their nations may be at war . . . they form a great fraternity spreading over the whole earth." What dreams might nations not realize if they would arrange their relations on the fraternal model of science! In the letter transmitting his account of the moldboard to Sir John Sinclair, Jefferson reflected sadly on the enormous gap between the two worlds of science and politics. "I am fixed in awe at the mighty conflict to which two great nations [Britain and France] are advancing and recoil with horror at the ferociousness of man. Will nations never devise a more rational umpire of differences than force? . . . Wonderful has been the progress of human improvement in other lines. Let us hope . . . that nations will at length be sensible that war is an instrument entirely inefficient toward redressing wrong; that it multiplies instead of indemnifying losses." His enlightened views addressed the future. Even as he wrote the drums of war were beating in his own country, and before long Jefferson, with many of his friends, witnessed the fanaticism of political man in America as in Europe.

The Terror of '98

In the annals of Jeffersonian Republicanism 1798 was the year of terror. It was, or rather seemed, an American Thermidor, a revolution of the right, a "reign of terror" not by the Jacobins but against them. It created a politics of hysteria, made opposition a crime, audacity a virtue, and turned breasting fears into insane political cults. The Jeffersonian Republicans survived this ordeal but were maimed by it. Some of them, assisted by Jefferson himself, raised their own cult around the "terror of '98."

Congress was in doldrums when the year began, waiting for the breeze from France that would propel the nation toward peace or war. Rumors filled the air, Jefferson reported, alternately favorable and unfavorable. "I begin to fear, not war from them [the French] but that they will refuse to have any settlement with us, only perhaps confining their depredations to provision vessels going to their enemies, and to enemy's goods in our ships, according to the English example: and that this may excite a war cry with us." Then he added, "The best anchor of our hope is an invasion of England." He was only half in earnest. Had he been primarily concerned with the balance of power in Europe, he could not have entertained this hope in any aspect; but, of course, he was primarily concerned with checking British maritime dominion, so much more pressing on the United States than French armies whether viewed as liberators or conquerors. Still, in a longer view of American interests, he could not embrace the hope, as he was careful to emphasize in other letters. "The subjugation of England would indeed be a general calamity," he said in sober truth. Jefferson continued to trace the American predicament to false commercial policy. Had the country earlier employed its commerce to force justice from Britain, instead of permitting its incorporation into Pitt's war machine, France could have been held at bay. When peace returned the error ought to be corrected. At present, while France belligerently contested British spoliation of the American trade, the nation had no weapon to command respect from either one. So the Federalists attempted to substitute a military engine for the discarded commercial one. The final provocation was all that was wanting to start a war.

The calm was unnerving. It was almost impossible to do business in the stormy political atmosphere at Philadelphia. From the moment of his arrival, Jefferson said, he had determined for the first time in his life to stand on the ceremony of the first visit, even with his friends, so as to sift out those who chose a separation. Pending the news from France, Congress had nothing to do, so it occupied its time with partisan brawls and recriminations. Day after day Jefferson walked to the historic hall on Chestnut Street to preside over the Senate. The chamber on the upper floor struck an English observer as both elegant and convenient, "just fitted in point of size for the accommodation of the Senators 26 [actually 32] in number, each of them having a large red morocco chair appropriated to him with a desk before it . . . , the whole furniture and arrangements being much superior to our House of Lords." The Vice President sat in a large, red, high-backed chair, slightly elevated, behind a mahogany table festooned with silk. His situation in this high-toned body was anything but pleasant. Being small, informal, and virtually leaderless, the Senate could not function without personal good humor, a commodity in dwindling supply even as to the Vice President himself. "More than once he has heard, in debates, and in terms which could not be mistaken, philippics pronounced against the author of the letter to Mazzei." The debates of the Senate were not reported, but such was the testimony of a Federalist member. The House of Representatives never had elegance and was fast losing all reputation for decorum. When the Connecticut Federalist Roger Griswold accused the Vermont Republican Matthew Lyon of wearing a wooden sword during the Revolution, the Vermonter spat in his face and narrowly escaped expulsion for the insult, which Griswold avenged personally on the floor by beating Lyon with his cane. Jefferson commented on the three-week-long imbroglio: "These proceedings must degrade the General Government, and lead the people to lean more on their state governments, which have been sunk under the early popularity of the former."

One of the vehicles of party rancor in the House was the Foreign Intercourse bill. Economy-minded Republicans sought to eliminate appropriations for the embassies in Prussia and Holland. Joshua Coit, of Connecticut, thought the move exhibited the abominable "political enthusiasm" of the Mazzei letter, which he read to the assembly. The Federalists seemed determined to make that letter a taboo against every expression of opposition, Albert Gallatin replied. "If we complain of the prodigality of . . . the Administration or wish to control it by refusing to appropriate all the money which is asked, we are stigmatized as disorganizers; if we oppose the growth of systems of treaties, we are charged with a design of subverting the Constitution and of making a revolution; if we attempt to check the extension of our political connections with European nations, we are branded with the epithet of Jacobins." The Federalists had turned everything around, the shrewd Genevan declared. The doctrine of the Mazzei letter was the doctrine of liberty. "Revolutions and Jacobinism do not flow from that line of policy we wish to see adopted. They belong, they exclusively belong to the system we resist; they are the last stage, the last page in the book of the history of government under its influence." Answering Gallatin, the ultraist Harper condemned the Mazzei letter, charged Jefferson with manipulating the "venal press," and ascribed to him the "war system"—war against Britain—that had guided the Republicans since 1793.

Little that passed in the political greenhouse at Philadelphia escaped Jefferson's senses. Monarchical fears, long present in his mind, now became a virtual obsession. It was the doctrine of the Mazzei letter, as Gallatin put it, "that a monarcho-aristocratic faction . . . wish to impose upon us the substance of the British government." Federalists insisted its author imputed this design to Washington; actually, Washington's presence at the helm had acted as a check on these fears. Adams was another matter. His prepossessions about government, his vanity, his political vulnerability made him highly susceptible to influence from the "monarcho-aristocratic faction." The evidence for this belief was inconclusive, but its political persuasiveness overcame all obstacles. From the standpoint of creating a popular ideology, it was in the Republican interest to portray Adams in monarchical colors, whereas the attempt would have been folly in the case of Washington.

In response to these fears and desires, Jefferson revised his conception of the party conflict in the early months of 1798. Earlier he had emphasized the economic basis of the division between the parties, accentuated by differences on the federal system and on foreign policy. Now he dusted off the old terms "Whig" and "Tory," reminiscent of the American Revolution, and fixed their meaning in the ideology of his party. "It is well understood that two political sects have arisen within the U. S.; the one believing the executive is the branch of our government which most needs support; the other that like the analogous branch in the English government, it is already too strong for the republican parts of the Constitution, and therefore in equivocal cases, they incline to the legislative powers; the former of these are called Federalist, sometimes aristocrats or mono-crats and sometimes Tories, after the corresponding sect in the Eng-lish government of exactly the same definition: the latter are still re-publicans, whigs, Jacobins, anarchists, disorganizers, etc." The names Federalist and Republican would not do, he said, because the mass on both sides were federalist *and* republican. All other terms were slanders, except Whig and Tory, which exactly described the issue between the parties. Toryism was associated with monarchy and ar-istocracy, of course—with opposition to the principles of the Ameri-can Revolution. Jefferson kept his antennae extended for reports, anecdotes, and rumors of this heresy. The "anas" he recorded dur-ing these several months were mostly of this sort, for example:

> On his second election as vice president, when there were several votes cast for George Clinton, Adams said in the Senate chamber, gritting his teeth, "damn 'em, damn 'em, damn 'em, you see that an elective government will not do."
>
> On going out of office in 1794, Hamilton alluded to party dif-ferences and said, "I avow myself a monarchist; I have no objec-tion to a trial being made of this thing of a republic, but . . . ."
>
> In an after-dinner conversation with Jefferson, the President expatiated on the vital importance of a strong senate, thinking ours not durable enough. As to trusting a popular assembly for the preservation of our liberties, Adams said it was the merest chimera imaginable.

These scraps of gossip and conversation from the President's table, from the congressional mess at Francis' Hotel, from the streets and the Senate corridors, Jefferson deemed worthy of record. The Con-stitution was threatened, he had no doubt, more mortally under Adams than under Washington; and monarcho-aristocratic Toryism described the threat in the political vocabulary of the time.

The suspense ended, the storm broke, in March. On the 5th, Adams prepared Congress for the failure of the mission to France; two weeks later he announced the end of negotiation and called for the prompt enactment of defense measures. This "insane message," Jefferson wrote to his Virginia friends, produced great effects: "Exultation on the one side, and a certainty of victory; while the other is petrified with astonishment." The President did not ask a declaration of war, but war was his aim in the guise of defense, Jefferson believed. (Unknown to him, Adams had, in fact, drafted a war message but discarded it in favor of the defense message of March 19.) However deplorable the Directory's rejection of American overtures, it offered no motive for war "plausible enough to impose even on the weakest mind." What, then, could account for the extraordinary impetuosity of the Federalists? War was a cover, he speculated, either for the monarcho-aristocratic conspiracy so long contemplated or for a disunionist scheme lately broached in the eastern states. However this might be, a war system would terrorize the opposition. Already the war fever was taking its toll among the Whigs in the House. The party would try its strength on three countermeasures, Jefferson said. First, a call for the executive papers bearing on the negotiation. "For if Congress are to act on the question of war, they have a right to information." Thus far Adams had withheld the envoys' dispatches. Second, a legislative countermand of Adams's order lifting the ban on the arming of merchantmen. This order, announced in the message, opened the way to armed conflict at sea. It was not overturned. Third, the adjournment of Congress at the earliest opportunity, permitting the legislators to return to their constituents. Jefferson was especially keen on the last point. In his conception it amounted to a popular referendum on the question of war. He had no doubt of the result: "it will be a means of exciting the whole body of the people from the state of inattention . . . , it will require every member to call for the sense of his district by petition or instruction; it will show the people with which side of the House their safety as well as their rights rest, by showing them which is for war and which for peace; and their representatives will return here invigorated by the avowed support of the people." The idea was impractical of course, treacherous from the Federalist standpoint, too exotic for the Republicans; yet in the light of subsequent events it had genuine merit.

Near the end of March, Jefferson felt "the most gloomy apprehensions." A treaty of alliance with Britain was rumored. The Senate was passing bills to purchase and arm vessels for convoy duty, to buy foundries, and to fortify the coast, this last measure the only one Jefferson could approve. How long could one-half the lower house stand up against the rest of the government? "In fact, the question of war and peace depends now on a toss of cross and pile. If we could but gain this season," he reiterated to Madison, "we should be saved." For the present, the first item on the agenda was the call for papers. Charges that Adams had misrepresented the negotiation in Paris and withheld the dispatches in order to incite a war were embarrassing the administration. "The Jacobins want them. And in the name of God let them be gratified . . . ," one Federalist pleaded, confident the dispatches would sink the Jacobins. On April 2 the High Federalists, by supporting the demand, invited the Republicans into the trap of their own making, and on the next day Adams, with a sigh of relief, forwarded the dispatches. Now the bizarre tale unfolded: how Talleyrand, the Minister of Foreign Relations, kept the envoys dangling for three months in Paris; how his agents, mysteriously named X, Y, and Z in the dispatches, demanded a large loan and a *douceur* as the price of treating; and how the Americans defended their nation's honor against swindle and intrigue. "The Jacobins in the Senate and House were struck dumb," Mrs. Adams gloated.

The Federalists saw to publication of the dispatches. Jefferson said it "produced such a shock on the republican mind, as has never been seen since our independence," and carried over to the war party many "wavering characters" anxious to wipe off the imputation of Jacobinism. The stupidity of Talleyrand's conduct, more than its depravity, which was not unexampled, astonished Jefferson. He did not attempt to defend it, yet the consequences of accepting the administration's version of the XYZ Affair were too frightful to contemplate. So he offered excuses and mitigations for France. The swindle, if actually attempted, was Talleyrand's private venture, unknown to the Directory, Jefferson said. On coming into office, in his May address, Adams had insulted France, and this on top of the outrage of the Jay Treaty had created the vindictive obstacle to negotiation. Despite these asperities, which led Talleyrand and his huckstering crew to toy with the commissioners, the French government wanted no war with the United States. Indeed, except in the mind of the war party, the negotiation was not at an end, for it was learned that Gerry, differing with his colleagues, remained in Paris to prevent a rupture. Jefferson's extenuations and half-truths had the useful function of enabling him to keep his eye on the domestic political enemy against the temptation offered by an illusory foreign one. He was right in his twin convictions that France desired peace and that the Federalist leadership wished to push matters to extremities. But by glossing over the XYZ Affair he put himself and his party in an exceedingly vulnerable position. Thrown on the defensive by the publication of the dispatches, which spoke for themselves, the Republicans had somehow to adhere to peace without risking the odium of cowardice and treason. In practical terms this meant consent to reasonable measures of defense but opposition to measures calculated on war. It was a narrow line. Jefferson was unsure the Republicans could walk it.

"Whatever chance was left us of escaping war after the publication of the dispatches," he wrote home in May, "the President's answers to the addresses pouring in on him from the great towns . . . are pushing the irritation to a point to which nobody can expect it will be borne." John Adams gloried in his new-found popularity. "We are wonderfully popular," Mrs. Adams remarked, "except with Bache & Co. who in his paper calls the President old querilous [sic], Bald, blind, cripled [sic], Toothless Adams." The President's bombastic speeches and answers to the numerous addresses of loyalty inflamed the war spirit. Even Hamilton, who was playing a more cautious game, thought them "intemperate and revolutionary." "Nor is it France alone," Jefferson observed, "but his own fellow citizens, against whom his threats are uttered." For Adams assailed "the delusions and misrepresentations" of party, "the calumnies and contempt against Constituted Authorities," and "the profligate spirit of falsehood and malignity" against the government. To the stout-hearted "soldier-citizens" of New Jersey, he declared that "the degraded and deluded characters may tremble, lest they should be condemned to the severest punishment an American suffers—that of being conveyed in safety within the lines of an invading enemy." No one could doubt for whom these grotesqueries were intended. Jefferson thought they must lead to a sedition bill silencing the Republican press.

The anti-Jacobin hysteria first settled on Philadelphia and then like a giant octopus lashed its arms to the farther reaches of the Union. The Federalist press screamed invasion, subversion, and revolution. "Our time, though delayed by the great projects of France in

Europe . . . will certainly come, when we are to be invaded by a body of their troops, who are expected to be joined by their friends among us, our Jacobins." *Ça Ira*, the *Marseillaise*, and the other French tunes, earlier so popular in Philadelphia, were hissed off the stage, and the spirited national hymn *Hail Columbia!* made its debut. In defiance of the tricolored French cockade, Federalists mounted the black cockade, said to have been the badge of the Continental Army, but jeered by Republicans for its resemblance to the British emblem. The President entered heart and soul into this spring madness. On May 7 nearly 1200 young men, suitably cockaded, paraded to martial music through Market Street to a swelling throng before the President's house. The young men came to offer their services in war against France. Adams, in full military regalia, received their delegation, heard their address, and answered with a rousing lecture on the ancestral piety that, he said, had inspired the American Revolution. The young men withdrew and proceeded to the State House yard. Adams's address was read to the cheers of the multitude and the ceremonies closed with *Hail Columbia!* The President had proclaimed May 9 "a day of solemn humiliation, fasting and prayer" throughout the United States. The churches and meetinghouses in Philadelphia were filled. There had been rumors of a Jacobin plot to terrorize the city on this sacred day. A few scuffles occurred—a sham battle of the cockades—and the lighthorse patroled the streets that night—but nothing disturbed the public peace. Years later, when old men traded clouded memories, Adams freely recalled the spectacle for Jefferson: "When even Governor Mifflin himself thought it his duty to order a patrol of horse and foot . . . ; when Market Street was as full as men could stand by one another, and even before my door; when some of my domestics, in frenzy, determined to sacrifice their lives in my defence; when all were ready to make a desperate sally among the multitude . . . ; when I myself judged it prudent and necessary to order chests of arms from the war office, to be brought through by lanes and back doors; determined to defend my house at the expense of my life . . . . What think you of terrorism, Mr. Jefferson?" The Sage of Monticello paid no attention to the parting jibe. He believed then, as in 1798, that the terror and the frenzy were whipped up by Federalist madmen, of whom Adams was indubitably one, and apparently, fifteen years later, the ancient delusion hung in his memory.

The old man at Quincy playfully supposed Jefferson was "fast asleep in philosophical tranquility" when these events took place. He was not so fortunate. "Party passions are indeed high," he wrote on May 9. "Nobody has more reason to know it than myself. I receive daily bitter proofs of it from people who never saw me, nor know anything of me but through Porcupine and Fenno. At this moment all the passions are boiling over, and one who keeps himself cool and clear of the contagion is so far below the point of ordinary conversation, that he finds himself insulated in every society." Once again the torment of politics settled over him. "Politics and party hatreds destroy the happiness of every being here. They seem, like salamanders, to consider fire as their element." Far pleasanter to contemplate the "Game of Goose" he had purchased for his grandchildren! Or to lose himself in intellectual diversions. According to tradition he found escape from the political tumult in Philosophical Hall. "I have changed my circle here according to my wish," he told Martha, "abandoning the rich, and declining all their dinners and parties, and associating entirely with the class of science." He later recalled "delightful conversations" with Benjamin Rush, which "served as an anodyne to the afflictions of the crisis through which our country was then laboring."

The war party overrode the thinning ranks of the opposition in Congress. Acts to renounce the French treaties, to suspend trade, to establish a navy department and build frigates, to authorize the capture of French ships, to raise new regiments of infantry and establish a large provisional army, to expel aliens and stamp out sedition, to borrow money and lay direct taxes—such legislation took the country to the Rubicon and the Federalists apparently had every intention of crossing it. Yet they held back, counting on France to force the decision. Some High Federalists criticized these Fabian tactics. "If we hesitate or pause now," one said, "the Jacobin faction will revive, and all the avenues for French poison and intrigue be again opened . . . . Nothing but an open war can save us and the more inveterate and deadly it shall be, the better will be our chance for security in the future." Open war would place the Republicans in an intolerable position. The longer it was averted, the more impatient the people must become with the evils of taxes, standing army, and oppressive laws. Such measures were sold to the public under the pretense of a threatening French invasion. What was to be done with this war machine when the invasion failed to materialize?

The inner circle of High Federalists around Hamilton had two grand objects in view. First, war against France, openly declared in due time, perhaps in outright alliance with Britain, for the joint conquest of the Spanish dominions from Louisiana to the Antilles and on down to South America. Under cover of the French war, the American army and the British fleet would descend on the tottering Spanish empire. The plot took form before the XYZ crisis broke. The chief plotters on the American side were Hamilton, who expected to command the army, Secretary of State Pickering, and Rufus King, the American Minister in London. King was in touch with the British foreign office, of course, and also with the first engineer of the enterprise, Franciso de Miranda, the aging Venezuelan adventurer and revolutionary. Britain was ready to commence the "revolution of South America," King wrote to Pickering in April, as soon as Spain fell under French arms. In the same month Miranda sent a personal emissary to Philadelphia to lay the plan before Adams. The President had known nothing of it. When it was broached, he would have nothing to do with it. The country was at peace with Spain, and Adams hoped, through the quasi-war with France, to create an American naval power independent of Britain. Hamilton and his allies, backed by the British Minister, Robert Liston, aimed at an alliance associated with the Miranda project. They were constrained but not squelched by the President's opposition. Conquest, both at home and abroad, was their mission. As King advised Hamilton in July, the enthusiasm and union excited in the United States could not last without "some sufficient object that will interest and employ the passions of the Nation. The mere defensive system of the [European] enemies of France," he went on, "has been a principal cause of her success, and if we adopt the error we shall be exposed to greater risks than by a bold and active system, which, exclusive of being the most certain means of safety, would promise the acquisition of great and lasting advantages."

Jefferson had no knowledge of this fantastic secret project. Of course, the war strategy was likely to encompass designs on Spain, since she offered tempting prizes of conquest, while France herself could be profitably attacked only in her commerce; and the Directory's known interest in the re-establishment of French empire in North America furnished an additional motive to the war party. This much Jefferson probably took for granted. But the audacity of the Hamiltonians exceeded even his imagination. In regard to the second object, domestic use of the war machine, Jefferson lacked neither information nor imagination. It was intended to terrorize the opposition and bring about a monolithic government on the English model. Exploitative taxes, standing army, British alliance, and so on were elements of this grand design, but it was best revealed by the Alien and Sedition Laws of 1798.

The laws were enacted during the second gyration of the war boom in mid-June. It began with the unauthorized publication in the *Aurora* of Talleyrand's long letter of March 18 to the envoys, in which he reviewed the French grievances and again spurned the commission, yet offered to negotiate with Gerry, who was believed friendly. Publication of the still secret document handed the Federalists a wonderul opportunity to denounce Republican subservience to France. Two days later, June 18, John Marshall returned to a hero's welcome in Philadelphia. Weary of the seemingly interminable session of Congress, Jefferson had planned to go home, but he decided to stay in the city to see what turn Marshall's reception gave to affairs. On the whole, Jefferson thought his Virginia kinsman a very able man whose huge land speculations and legal practice, unfortunately, had bound him hand and foot to Federalist moneyed interests. While this doubtless laid the foundation of political distrust, it had not yet placed Jefferson at swords' points with Marshall. The envoy was not at his lodgings when Jefferson called, so he left a note regretting—telling slip of the pen!—he had been "so lucky as to find that he was out." Whether Marshall warmed or cooled the war party, Jefferson could not be sure at the time, but before long he was writing scathingly of "the XYZ dish cooked up by Marshall." Rarely again would he speak a kind word for the Richmond Federalist. Apparently he held Marshall responsible for the escalation of the crisis in June mainly because upon his return Congress ordered the printing of 10,000 copies of the entire XYZ corpus for public distribution. This unprecedented act raised popular feeling to a still higher pitch.

Meanwhile, indeed on the very day Marshall returned, Jefferson found himself on the griddle of Congress and the press for aiding and abetting Dr. George Logan's personal mission to Paris. This newest "Jacobin plot" was uncovered several days after the self-appointed envoy's departure. Logan was one of Jefferson's dearest friends, a fellow agriculturist, a Republican, a Quaker, and an enthusiast for the French Revolution. Something of an eccentric too, he had the wild idea he could throw himself into the breach between France and the United States. Although Jefferson had some inkling of his plan, since he had furnished Logan a routine certification of citizenship and good character—the nearest equivalent of a passport—he later said with complete truth that the Doctor's venture was "dictated by his own enthusiasm, without consultation or communication with any one." The suddenness of his departure, added to his prominence and party connections, produced "a real panic" in the city. He was "Jefferson's envoy extraordinary"! He was the secret agent of the American Jacobins to concert invasion plans with the armies of France! *Porcupine's Gazette* screamed, "Watch, Philadelphians, or the fire is in your houses and the *couteau at your throats* . . . . Take care: when your blood runs down the gutters, don't say you weren't forewarned of the danger." In Congress, Harper gravely accused leading American Jacobins, presumably Bache, Logan, and Jefferson, of a "traitorous conspiracy" with their French masters. Treasury Secretary Wolcott rushed to New York to meet a returning traveler said to be bearing letters from France. He found and intercepted a packet addressed to Bache, which proved to be harmless, and a private letter to Jefferson from his friend Fulwar Skipwith, the Consul General in Paris, which he commandeered but left to his biographer to publish two generations later. Jefferson worried about Mrs. Logan. He rode out to Stenton, taking a circuitous route in order to elude snoopers, and begged this gentle lady to defy the accusers by making her rounds in the city as before. "He spoke of the temper of the time and the late acts of the legislature with a sort of despair," Deborah Logan remembered their conversation, "but said he thought even the shadow of our liberties must be gone if they attempted anything that would injure me." She acted on Jefferson's advice—it was a painful experience. Cobbett at once informed the public of Jefferson's trip to Stenton: "Quere: What did he do there? Was it to arrange the Doctor's *valuable manuscripts?*" Evidence of the "traitorous correspondence," no doubt. "Porcupine gave me a principal share in it, as I am told," Jefferson reported the affair to Madison, "for I never read his papers."

It was a maxim with Jefferson that "Falsehood will travel a thousand miles while truth is putting on her boots." Falsehood ran under whip and spur in June. Federalist versifiers hailed the "warlike spirit," derided the slinking Jacobins, and added new touches to their parody of Jefferson, half devil, half buffoon.

> Now each Jacobinic face
> Redden'd with guilt, with fear, disgrace,
> While thro' the land, with keenest ire,
> Kindles the patriotic fire!
> See Jefferson with deep dismay,
> Shrink from the piercing eye of day,
> Lest from the tottering chair of state,
> The storm should hurl him to his fate!
> Great Sire of stories past belief!
> Historian of the Mingo Chief!
> Philosopher of Indian's hair!
> Inventor of a rocking chair!
> The Correspondent of Mazze'!
> And Banneker less black than he!
> With joy we find these rise from coguing
> With Judge M'Kean, and "foolish Logan,"
> And reeling down the factious dance,
> Send Deborah's husband off to France,
> To tell the Frenchmen, to their cost,
> They reckon'd here without their host;
> Whilst thou, to smooth the ills of life,
> Held sweet communion with the wife.

Out of the sea of political violence emerged the Alien and Sedition Laws. The former was acutally but one of three laws enacted against aliens. The Naturalization Act raised from five to fourteen years the period required for citizenship; the Alien Enemies Act empowered the President to confine or banish aliens of an enemy coun-

try during a state of war; the Alien (or Alien Friends) Act authorized the President summarily to deport aliens deemed dangerous to
the peace and safety of the United States. The sponsors of this legislation held that two large foreign-born groups, the French and the
Irish, constituted a subversive fifth column. Political refugees of the
Irish rebellion had fled to the United States, where, as Rufus King
protested in London, they at once "arrayed themselves on the side
of the malcontents." A lodge of the Society of United Irishmen was
discovered in Philadelphia in the spring of 1798. Cobbett published
an inflammatory pamphlet: *Detection of a Conspiracy Formed by
the United Irishmen, with the Evident Intention of Aiding the Tyrants of France in Subverting the Government of the United States
of America.* The Polish patriot and veteran of the American Revolution, General Thaddeus Kosciusko, with whom Jefferson had become friendly on his return visit to America, was prominently
linked to the alien conspiracy against American liberty. Among the
numerous French refugees were several "philosophers," always the
indispensable "pioneers of revolution," according to Harper. Jefferson thought these philosophers, like his friend Volney, whose slashing attack on priestly religion, *The Ruins*, he had begun to translate,
were the main targets of the Alien bill. He had learned at first-hand
the risks of that vocation. "It suffices for a man to be a philosopher,
and to believe that human affairs are susceptible to improvement, to
look forward, rather than back to the Gothic age, for perfection, to
mark him as an anarchist, disorganizer, atheist and enemy of the
government."

As passed by the Senate, the Alien bill was "worthy of the
eighth or ninth century" in Jefferson's opinion. One of its provisions
would have required him, for example, to send a messenger 70 miles
for the written permission of a federal judge before sitting down to
dinner with a foreign guest at Monticello! Although this objectionable provision and some others were eliminated in the House, Jefferson did not think much better of the finished bill. The Republicans
had opposed it. "The people will oppose, the States will not submit
to its operation . . . ," Livingston had declared. "Thus, sir, one of
the first effects . . . will be disaffection among the States; and opposition among the people to your Government; tumults, violations,
and a recurrence to first revolutionary principles." To these senti-

ments Jefferson would only add the bill was "in the teeth of the Constitution." No authority could be found for it, and the Federalists had appealed to the dangerous concept of inherent national sovereignty to sanction it. Adams signed the bill into law on July 6. By then most of the Frenchmen, including Volney, and other "dangerous aliens" like Kosciusko, had left American soil. Despite the administration's zeal, no alien was actually deported under the arbitrary provisions of this law.

The Sedition Act, on the other hand, was generously enforced. Twenty-five persons were arrested, fourteen indicted, and ten tried and convicted, all Republican printers and publicists. Jefferson had predicted the passage of a sedition bill as early as April 26, several weeks before one was introduced in Congress. "The object . . . is the suppression of the Whig presses," he said. For years, at least as early as Washington's denunciation of the Democratic Societies, he had observed Federalist intolerance of opposition. Only a crisis was wanting to arm it. An incident in Virginia a year before had alerted him to the danger. The grand jury of the federal Circuit Court at Richmond made a presentment against Samuel J. Cabell, the representative of Jefferson's own congressional district, upbraiding him for the dissemination of "unfounded calumnies against the happy government of the United States . . . [in order] to separate the people therefrom, and to increase or produce a foreign influence ruinous to the peace, happiness, and independence of the United States." Jefferson at once fastened on this perversion of the grand jury "from a legal to a political engine." The federal judiciary was implicated, specifically in the person of Judge James Iredell, whose high-handed charge to the jury invited the presentment. After his return to Virginia in July 1797, Jefferson drafted a petition to the General Assembly in which he pleaded not only the natural right of correspondence between a representative and his constituents but also the state's right to interpose its authority as necessary to safeguard freedom of opinion. He went on to request legislative action against the Richmond grand jurors, either by impeachment or by law of *premunire*, an old English proceeding invented to punish the introduction of papal authority against the authority of the crown. He wrote to Monroe in defense of the petition: "It is of immense consequence that the States retain as complete authority as

possible over their own citizens. The withdrawing themselves under
the shelter of a foreign jurisdiction, is so subversive of order and so
pregnant of abuse, that it may not be amiss to consider how far a
law of *premunire* should not be revived and modified, against all citizens who attempt to carry their causes before any other than State
courts, in cases where those other courts have no right to their cog-
nizance." In thus rushing to the defense of civil and political liberty
Jefferson ran headlong into state rights remedies likely to prove as
mortal as the disease. The petition, without any ascription of authorship, came before the House of Delegates in December. A resolution of that body denounced the Cabell presentment as a violation
of "the fundamental principles of representation" and "the natural
right of speaking and writing freely," but omitted any mode of redress at law. So the assembly stopped short of Jefferson's objective.
The radical principles and tactics he pursued in this matter foreshadowed the course he would take in opposition to the Sedition Act.

The Sedition Act made it a federal crime, punishable by fine and
imprisonment, for anyone to enter into conspiracy impeding the
operations of the federal government or to publish "any false, scandalous and malicious writing" against the government, Congress, or
the President. Aimed at "domestic traitors," it was conceived as a
companion to the Alien Act. As first proposed in the Senate it was
also a treason bill, vaulting constitutional safeguards by the prescription of death for adherence to France and lesser penalties for failure
to divulge knowledge of treason. But these sections were omitted
from the bill passed by the Senate on July 4. Federalists noted nothing ironic in the date. A Fourth of July rally toasted Adams:
"May he like *Samson*, slay thousands of Frenchmen with the
jawbone of Jefferson." Whether or not Jefferson was a direct target
of the Sedition Act—some of his friends feared he was—he could not
fail to notice the omission of the Vice President from the officers of
the government placed under the mantle of protection.

In the House the bill came under heavy fire from the dwindling,
yet stubborn, Republican ranks. It was unconstitutional, they said,
since Congress had no delegated power in this sphere, and indeed
the First Amendment guarantee of freedom of speech and press
withdrew the entire subject from the national authority. The Federalists denied that the amendment gave immunity to libelous assaults

on the government; they appealed to the sovereign authority of any government to protect itself, and said that, even without the benefit of statute, the federal courts could punish sedition under common law. The claim of federal jurisdiction over common law crimes was a bold one. Gallatin and his little band rejected it and wondered why, if the courts already had the authority to punish sedition, any statute was necessary. The answer was that it was desirable to introduce certain ameliorations in the common law of seditious libel. First, the jury should be authorized to return a general verdict, that is, guilty or not guilty, rather than simply a verdict on the fact of the publication of the alleged libel by the defendant. In this, as in their entire campaign of repression, the Federalists followed the British example, specifically Fox's Libel Act of 1792. But they went a step further by admitting truth as a defense of the libel. By thus relaxing the common law the Federalists prided themselves on their liberality. The Repubicans were unimpressed. The statute was retrograde since it assumed an authority where none existed and where none was wanted. The real purpose of the measure was political: to cripple and destroy the Republican opposition under the pretense of saving the country from anarchists, demagogues, and incendiaries. This was the cant employed against the patriots of every nation where rulers exalted their own despotic power. And in the climate of fear and suspicion the Federalists had created, what would be the benefit of the boasted safeguards? As it turned out they were of no use whatever to the defendants tried under the Sedition Act.

Jefferson was hard at work at Monticello when the act was finally signed into law on July 14. He had earlier planned to leave by June 1, then on the 18th, the day of Marshall's return, but he did not get away until the 27th. On the day before he had heard the first reading of the bill in the Senate and learned that Bache had been hauled into federal court for common law libels of the President and the government—evidence that the Federalists would not be bound by statutory authority. Staying at his post for seven cruel months, Jefferson had helped to stave off still more violent measures and to keep up the flagging hopes of Republicans throughout the Union. To the end of his days he believed this was one of his best services. While he now despaired of stemming the Federalist tide in Congress, he still expected it to recede as rapidly as it rose. The people were Republican. War scare, land tax, standing army, and Alien and Sedition Laws were sure to produce a reaction. Had the Federalists declared war, the prospects would have been dim. Jefferson had expected it, so had Adams, and almost every leading Federalist favored war outright to the ambiguous quasi-war—a war of frigates and privateers—that existed. Just why it was not declared is a difficult question. In July the congressional strategists watched helplessly as the opportunity slipped from their grasp. "Half measures are seldom generally intelligible, and almost never safe, in the crisis of great affairs . . . ," Fisher Ames wrote to Pickering with Machiavellian cunning. "Internal foes can do twice as much harm as they could do in an open war. The hope of peace is yet strong enough to furnish the means of popular influence and delusion; at any rate, it chills the spirit of the citizens, and distracts them in the exercise of duty." Jefferson, on the other hand, took comfort in the continuing "hope of peace." Of course, if France warred on the United States every American must rally to the defense of his country. But he had never thought this likely, unless from unsufferable provocation. France had too many reasons for wishing peace with the United States. Moreover, the prospects for peace in Europe were good. If the country could scrape through the ensuing winter without being overborne by the war party, everything should turn to rights. Finally, in his last message to Congress, Adams had declared he would not send another minister to France *unless* on assurances he would be properly received. For all his thunder he had not slammed and bolted the door to peace.

Jefferson reached Monticello on July 3. (Along the way he accepted the honor of a public reception on Sunday, a fact "trumpeted from one end of the continent to the other, as irrefutable proof of his contempt for the Christian religion, and his devotion to the new religion of France.") He had much to think about, more of it political than suited his taste, yet he found time and wit in this season of madness to write an essay on Anglo-Saxon grammar. He wrote few letters, not a single one for seven weeks after his return, and when he commenced again usually relied on messengers rather than trust the post. To a Maryland Republican who sent a press report alleging subversive activities against him, he replied that his principles were those of the people and well known, whereas "the delusion of the people is necessary to the dominant party." It was pointless to answer calumnies, he said, for while putting down one, twenty new ones would spring up. To an Irish refugee bewildered by the stumbling of the American republic, he sketched a long view of the phenomenon. "The system of alarm and jealousy which has been so powerfully played off in England, has been mimicked here, not entirely without success. The most long-sighted politician could not, seven years ago, have imagined that the people of this wide extended country could have been enveloped in such delusion, and made so much afraid of themselves and of their own powers, as to surrender it spontaneously to those who are maneuvering them into a form of government, the principal branches of which may be beyond their control. The commerce of England, however, has spread its roots over the whole face of our country. This," he said, "is a real source of all the obliquities of the public mind . . . ." Virginia was safe, however—an asylum for all the persecuted.

Although Jefferson repeatedly stated that the disease would produce its own remedy, he decided in the summer months to administer a shock treatment to aid the recovery. The political therapy took the form of the Virginia and Kentucky Resolutions. These famous resolutions had a double character. Called forth by oppressive legislation of the national government, notably the Alien and Sedition Laws, they represented a vigorous defense of the principles of freedom and self-government under the United States Constitution. But since the defense involved an appeal to principles of state rights, the resolutions struck a line of argument potentially as dangerous to the Union as were the odious laws to the freedom with which it was identified. One hysteria tended to produce another. A crisis of freedom threatened to become a crisis of Union. The latter was deferred in 1798–1800, but it would return, and when it did the principles Jefferson had invoked against the Alien and Sedition Laws would sustain delusions of state sovereignty fully as violent as the Federalist delusions he had combated.

His decision to take a stand in the states was carefully meditated. The action on the Cabell presentment set the course. When Madison came out of retirement in the spring and offered himself for election to the General Assembly, Jefferson remarked on the great good that might be done by "a proper direction of the local force." Still he did not then share the desperation of some of his friends and counseled against extreme measures. In May, John Taylor was saying it was time to consider, as men were considering, Virginia's secession from the Union. Jefferson agreed that Virginia and her neighbors were ridden hard by the eastern states. "But our present situation is not a natural one," he told Taylor. The cunning of Hamilton, played off behind the popularity of Washington, followed by the untoward events and the artifices of the Adams administration, disguised the weakness of the Federalist party. "Be this as it may," he continued philosophically, "in every free and deliberating society, there must, from the nature of man, be opposite parties, and violent dissensions and discords; and one of these, for the most part, must prevail over the other for a longer or shorter time. Perhaps this party division is necessary to induce each to watch and relate to the people the proceedings of the other. But if on a temporary superiority of one party, the other is to resort to a scission of the Union, no federal government can ever exist." And where would the evil stop? One confederacy would become two, then three, then four, until there was nothing left. "Seeing, therefore . . . that we must have somebody to quarrel with, I had rather keep our New England associates for that purpose, than to see our bickerings transferred to others." He concluded on an optimistic note: "A little patience, and we shall see the reign of witches pass over, their spells dissolved, and the people recovering their true sight, restoring their government to its true principles."

To this Taylor soberly replied that if the violence was "indeed owing to witchraft, the spell must be broken by incantations on the part of the Republicans." He suggested several. For example, "The right of the State governments to expound the constitution, might possibly be made the basis of a movement towards its amendment. If this is insufficient, the people in state conventions, are incontrovertibly the contracting parties and possessing the impinging rights, may proceed by orderly steps to the object." Jefferson carefully scored and underscored the planter's proposal for future reference. Taylor, with a hard knot of Virginia Republicans, had never overcome the Anti-Federalist dogma on the Constitution. Wrong in essential principles, the compact necessarily produced vicious effects, as in the centralized privilege and corruption of the Hamiltonian system, and no mere change of men or of party could set the government aright. Jefferson, on the other hand, with the mass of Republicans, believed the disease was in the governors rather than in the government, hence political change could be effective. The object was to restore the Constitution, not to reform it. His conviction weakened in 1798, however, and partly for this reason Virginia Republicans of the Taylor breed expected a good deal more of him in the way of reform than he was prepared to deliver when placed in the presidency.

In June, when he left Congress, Jefferson believed time was on the side of the Republicans; in August he was not at all sure. The delusion of the war party seemed limitless. "There is no event . . . , however atrocious, which may not be expected." Vigorous enforcement of the Sedition Act would crush the Republican press, terrorize public opinion, and block the regular avenues of change through the electoral process. Those laws were merely "an experiment on the American mind," he said, to see to what degradation it would submit. "If this goes down we shall immediately see attempted another act of Congress, declaring that the President shall continue in office during life, reserving to another occasion the transfer of the succession to his heirs, and the establishment of the Senate for life." No reliance could be placed in the federal judiciary, a party stronghold, to check the mad career. Some counterforce was necessary. And where could it be found but in the state legislatures? There was no novelty in the proceeding. As early as 1790 the Virginia assembly had declared its opinion that certain acts of the federal government were unconstitutional. Hamilton had denounced the action, yet it was well founded in the theory of the federal system, even as expounded by Hamilton. "It may safely be received as an axiom in our political system," he had written in *The Federalist*, "that the State governments will, in all possible contingencies, afford complete security against invasions of the public liberty by the national authority . . . . They can discover the danger at a distance; and possessing all the organs of civil power, and the confidence of the people, they can at once adopt a regular plan of opposition, in which they can combine all the resources of the community. They can readily communicate with each other in the different States, and unite their common forces for the protection of their common liberty." Jefferson would have found it difficult to improve on this statement. The right of a state legislature to expound the Constitution and, where necessary, to oppose usurpations by the national government not only safeguarded the liberties of the citizen but also maintained the balance of the federal system upon which the preservation of the Union depended.

On these general principles Jefferson and Madison drafted the Kentucky and Virginia Resolutions of 1798. An air of secrecy surrounded the business. Not for many years were the true authors of the documents known to the public. Perhaps Jefferson discussed ways and means of counteracting the Federalist program when he stopped at Madison's place on his return from Congress, but they did not agree upon a plan of action at this early date. Perhaps they conferred later in the summer, though the record bears no trace. At any rate, early in the fall Jefferson drafted a series of resolutions intended for the North Carolina legislature. He put the document in the hands of Wilson Cary Nicholas for disposition. Acting on his own, Nicholas entrusted it to John Breckinridge, a former resident of Albemarle and friend of Jefferson's, now prominent in Kentucky politics. Visiting his old home, Breckinridge probably convinced Nicholas that Kentucky offered more fertile ground for Jefferson's seed than North Carolina. In Kentucky, as in Virginia, a wave of local protests against war and the "unconstitutional" measures of the federal government rolled across the state. Jefferson approved the choice of Kentucky for the political test. Breckinridge steered clear of Monticello, lest a visit there expose the Vice President's part in the plan afoot. The Kentuckian packed the momentous document in his saddlebag and rode across the mountains the second week of October. A week or so later Madison saw a copy of Jefferson's resolutions at Monticello. Undoubtedly they discussed the question of parallel action in Virginia, as well as Jefferson's new plan, revising that of the previous year, for taking the selection of jurors away from executive and judicial authorities and placing it directly in the hands of the people. (The legislature was not ready for this radical democratic step.) The resolutions Madison then drafted for introduction in the Virginia assembly asserted the same fundamental theory of the Constitution without, however, entering into Jefferson's bolder conclusions. These were too extreme even for

Breckinridge, with the result that the Kentucky Resolutions, adopted at Frankfort on November 10, were milder than Jefferson had planned.

The Resolutions set forth the theory of the union as a compact among the several states. Certain powers only were delegated to the central government; acts beyond its powers were unconstitutional, void, and of no force; and since the contracting parties had created no ultimate arbiter of the Constitution, each state had "an equal right to judge for itself, as well of the infractions as of the mode and measure of redress." Jefferson thus extended the logic of the compact theory and of limited government—a logic almost no one openly disputed—to a conclusion few had faced and fewer still had reached before him. His doctrinaire friend Taylor had preceded him, but Jefferson required neither Taylor's prompting nor his political bias to take this step. It followed naturally from the principles of constitutional law Jefferson and his colleagues had been elaborating for eight or nine years, and its execution only awaited the impetus of legislation as potent as the Alien and Sedition Laws. Five of the nine resolutions were devoted to proving the unconstitutionality of these laws. Except for crimes specified in the Constitution, such as counterfeiting and treason, the federal government had no criminal jurisdiction. Freedom of speech and press had the same standing under the First Amendment, Jefferson maintained, as freedom of religion. Congress could legislate in no matter whatsoever. Yet he did not enter a broadly philosophical plea for freedom of speech, preferring rather to rest his case on state rights ground. It was for the states to determine, he said, "how far the licentiousness of speech and of the press may be abridged without lessening their useful freedom." The Alien Law fell for want of power, for violation of a specific constitutional provision relating to immigration (Article I, Section 9), and for the denial of jury trial and other fair procedures in the deportation of aliens. The sweeping claim made in the name of state rights transcended the immediate issue of civil liberties. The seventh resolution passed a blanket condemnation on federal actions taken under color of the "general welfare" and "necessary and proper" clauses. Matters of less urgency, they were allowed to stand for legislative correction at an early date.

It was in the action resolutions, numbers eight and nine, that the legislature departed from Jefferson's draft. Kentucky declared its opinion that the Alien and Sedition Laws were unconstitutional and communicated the Resolutions to the various state legislatures, and to its senators and representatives in Congress, in order to obtain their repeal. Jefferson's proposal went further. Making a valid distinction between *abuses* of delegated powers, in which the electoral process offered the constitutional remedy, and *assumptions* of powers not delegated, he declared that "a nullification . . . is the rightful remedy" for the latter. There was a certain ambiguity in his statement of the doctrine. Significantly, however, he did not say nullification was the constitutional remedy, holding rather "that every State has a natural right in cases not within the compact . . . to nullify of their own authority all assumptions of power within their limits." The right pertained to each state independently; nevertheless, Jefferson would have Kentucky communicate its actions to the other parties of the compact, inviting each of them to "concur in declaring these acts void and of no force" and to "take measures of its own providing that neither . . . shall be exercised within these respective territories." Had the legislature followed Jefferson's instructions to the letter, Kentucky would have placed itself in defiance of federal laws; and it would have made little practical difference whether the appeal was to natural or to constitutional right. Jefferson's Latinism, "nullification," which three decades later became a political shibboleth, did not appear in the Kentucky Resolutions. Although Breckinridge subscribed to the doctrine in the debate on the resolutions, he trusted with the majority that an early repeal of the obnoxious laws would make unnecessary the resort to nullification. In a second series of resolutions the following year, after the failure of repeal, the legislature declared its opinion in favor of nullification, using that specific term, yet pointedly disclaimed any idea of practicing the doctrine.

As a rule Madison was a man of cooler judgment than Jefferson, and the parts played by these two principals in the Virginia and Kentucky Resolutions illustrate the different traits of character. The younger man once remarked on "a habit in Mr. Jefferson as in others of great genius of expressing in strong and round terms, impressions of the moment." The habit was disclosed in the bolder expressions of Jefferson's draft, which did not come under Madison's judicious eye before its dispatch to Kentucky. The Virginia Resolutions were, by contrast, brief, cautiously worded, and softly spoken. The legislatures of the sister states were asked to join Virginia in adjudging the Alien and Sedition Laws unconstitutional and in taking necessary steps to maintain the rights and liberties reserved to the states or to the people. Nicholas, again the intermediary, took Madison's draft to Monticello. In Jefferson's view it did not take high enough ground. To overcome the impression of a mere declaration of opinion, he proposed adding the phrase, "that the said acts are, and were *ab initio*, null, void and of no force, or effect." Nicholas made the change, and the resolutions were introduced in this form by John Taylor on December 10. But in the course of debate, probably at Madison's instigation, Taylor moved to strike the voiding phrase and restore the declaratory wording of the original. The motion passed. The resolutions were adopted as a solemn expression of opinion, or at least so Madison always held. He plainly did not adhere to the extremity of Jefferson's logic by which the legislature of a single state could nullify federal laws within its borders. If there was an ultimate judge anywhere it was the people of the states, who were the true parties to the compact, not the legislatures. Madison thought the point important enough to bring to his friend's attention in December, for his resolutions seemed to subordinate the true sovereigns to their legislative agents. Confusion was compounded by his description of nullification as a "natural right," which could only mean the right of revolution, necessarily accompanied, in the instance of a compact, by secession.

In the final analysis it is impossible to say precisely what Jefferson's theory was in the Resolutions of '98. They were not conceived in the oracular realm of constitutional law but in a desperate struggle for political survival. Acts unconstitutional had passed, liberty was in jeopardy, war in prospect, and specters of monarchy loomed on the horizon. Jefferson, therefore, pursued "a political resistance for political effect," without much regard for nuances and ambiguities of doctrine. The important point was to declare the Alien and Sedition Acts unconstitutional, leaving the sequel to later decision as events might prudently dictate. "I would not do anything at this moment which would commit us further," he wrote to Taylor in November, "but reserve ourselves to shape our future measures or no measures, by the events which may happen." Politics was an art of maneuver, as Jefferson understood; and although some of the expressions in his draft resolutions were embarrassingly dogmatic, he clearly had no intention of committing himself, his party, or the legislatures to an inflexible position. By resistance on constitutional grounds he hoped to avoid extremes, yet he was prepared for them if pushed by events.

The same practical wisdom that shaped Jefferson's course in this regard was evident in his decision to address the defense of personal and political liberty to the immediate enemy, the federal government. No danger came from the states—it was not a live political question. So it was no part of his purpose to compose a philosophical manifesto of freedom of speech and press; nor could this purpose be encompassed within the strategy of state protest against federal usurpations. The limits of state authority in these vital areas of freedom was another matter altogether. He believed, unquestionably, that the states could regulate "the licentiousness of speech and of press" under statutory or common law. He was not an absolutist. But the republican experiment was insupportable without freedom of speech and press at all levels of government and in the widest latitude compatible with the experiment itself. The emphasis fell, realistically, on state rights in 1798. Jefferson's commitment to the revolutionary principles of freedom and self-government was not, for that reason, any less than it had ever been. The following year he wrote a ringing reaffirmation of the larger faith to a college student: "To preserve the freedom of the human mind . . . and freedom of the press, every spirit should be ready to devote itself to martyrdom; for as long as we may think as we will, and speak as we think the condition of man will proceed in improvement. The generation which is going off the stage has deserved well of mankind for the struggles it has made, and for having arrested the course of despotism which had overwhelmed the world for thousands and thousands of years. If there seems to be danger that the ground they have gained will be lost again, that danger comes from the generation your contemporary. But that the enthusiasm which characterizes youth should lift its parricide hands against freedom and science would be such a monstrous phenomenon as I cannot place among possible things in this age and country."

As the Resolutions went abroad to work on the public mind, Jefferson returned to Philadelphia for the short session of the Fifth Congress. Notwithstanding peace feelers from France, the Federalists voted substantial increases in the army and navy and authorized a loan of $5,000,000 to make good the deficit. Business was sluggish, money scarce; the Treasury floated the loan at 8 per cent interest, and Jefferson doubted the money could be raised even at that price. Spiraling taxes, expenses, and debt caused alarms. The fiscal picture was not as bleak as Jefferson painted it, but considering the poverty of the nation's productive resources, the drain into the federal Treasury was a legitimate concern. The revenue of $10,000,000 amounted to one-third the value of domestic exports, the principal source of national wealth. Interest charges on the debt took a huge bite in taxes, approximately 40 per cent of the total every year. The debt grew with the growth of the military establishment, for more new taxes would not be borne, even at the alternative of borrowing at usurious interest. An annual levy of from two to three dollars on every man, woman, and child was perhaps little enough for the people to bear in defense of the nation; still it was no small burden when the annual income per capita did not much exceed $200, when every resource was needed for productive growth, and when, alas, there was no enemy to fight.

Dr. Logan had returned from his mission in November with tidings of peace. Hundreds of American privateers roamed the seas; the infant navy patroled the harbors and went in hot pursuit of French men-of-war to the West Indies; and Washington came out of retirement to lead the provisional army that really belonged to Major General Hamilton, his second in command over the objection of the President. Yet Logan reported, straight from the horse's mouth, that France earnestly desired peace. The Federalists were enraged. The day Jefferson resumed the chair in the Senate, the leadership in the lower house initiated legislation to punish persons who usurped the executive authority by communicating with the government of a foreign state. In four hours of feverish eloquence Harper unraveled the skein of treason and subversion contrived, he made quite clear, by the Vice President. Whatever the merits of the Logan bill, as it was called, it had less to do with the conduct of diplomacy than with attainting the Republican party and its leader. Through Logan the Federalists sought to get at Jefferson, whose "poor addled cat's paw" the doctor allegedly was. The transparency of their motives was obvious to all, Jefferson noted, yet the bill would pass. When it came before the Senate, only two Republicans dared to vote against it.

The good Quaker's report fell in with mounting evidence of the Directory's desire for reconciliation. The warlike posture of the United States had something to do with the turnabout, though it was a factor Jefferson could never credit. Far more compelling, in his opinion, was Admiral Nelson's defeat of the French fleet at the Nile, surprising reverses on land, the regrouping of the monarchical coalition, and the ruin of Franco-American commerce, all of which must produce a recovery of sanity in the French government. Letters from American friends in France—Joel Barlow, John Brown Cutting, Fulwar Skipwith, and others—pointed out the path of accommodation. Jefferson had already helped to blaze the path, not by conspiratorial transactions but by assurances to Volney, Kosciusko, and Victor Dupont, men of substance who returned to France in 1798, that the American people would trade the sword for the olive branch if given the opportunity. Dupont was especially helpful. This young man, the son of Jefferson's physiocratic friend, had been sent to the United States as consul general in 1798 only to be turned back by Adams. Jefferson had talked to him in the spring. If the Directory would revise its decrees against the neutral trade, recall its corsairs from the West Indies, and declare its willingness to resume negotiations, he told Dupont, the tide would turn, sweeping before it all the feeble artifices of the war party. The recommendation was conveyed to Talleyrand, who followed it exactly. When Gerry departed later in the summer he brought with him an order revoking the most obnoxious of the decrees, and Talleyrand promptly commenced overtures through The Hague for a pacific settlement.

Jefferson found a letter from Gerry on his return to Philadelphia. His reply was a ten-page work of political art, combining a profession of republican faith, a partisan history of the XYZ furor, and a calculated appeal to this Massachusetts moderate to come over to the Republicans. Had not the Federalists abandoned him? He had risked himself by staying in Paris to preserve the peace, while his quondam colleague Marshall, followed by Pinckney, came back with tales branding him a traitor. "They openly wished you might be guillotined, or sent to Cayenne, or anything else." The Republicans, on the other hand, uniformly praised Gerry's conduct, a few only wishing he had done what the Federalists maliciously accused him of attempting and boldly made a treaty beyond his authority. Gerry had the choice, Jefferson frankly told him, either of sinking into "the humble oblivion" to which the Federalists had condemned him or of being borne aloft on the shoulders of a grateful citizenry. For glory would be his if he would communicate fully all the details of his mission. The people had a right to this information. "It is their sweat which is to earn all the expenses of the war, and their blood which is to flow in expiation of the causes of it." Jefferson counted on these disclosures to bring forth the radiant republicanism of the American mind. Needless to say, he also counted the political value of such a recruit as Gerry to the arduous Republican cause in New England.

Within six months Gerry, whose talent for political zigzag became legendary, was the Republican candidate for governor of Massachusetts. He had visited Adams at Quincy in October and found him a willing listener. Adams worried about the army. It was a dangerous engine, especially with Hamilton second in command; and he began to sense the public backlash to measures predicated on war. "If this nation sees a great army to maintain, without an enemy to fight," he warned the Secretary of War, "there may arise an enthusiasm that seems to be little foreseen. At present there is no more prospect of seeing a French army here, than there is in Heaven." About this time he received dispatches from William Vans Murray, American Minister at The Hague, reporting Talleyrand's devious overtures for peace. What he had learned at Quincy contributed to the moderation of his opening address to Congress. He gave a reluctant ear to Dr. Logan, a reluctant eye to what the scoundrel Barlow —"Tom Paine is not a more worthless fellow"—had written to Washington, only then to discover that his own son John Quincy, chargé d'affaires in Berlin, held the same opinion of French intentions. Finally, he received the required assurances from Talleyrand himself. On February 18, without forewarning or consultation, the President nominated Murray as minister plenipotentiary to the French republic.

Jefferson, reading the special message to the Senate, was no less amazed than the High Federalists by this "event of events." "Never did a party show a stronger mortification, and consequently, that war had been their object." Jefferson should have been delighted. Grasping the olive branch, Adams acted on the policy of his opponents. But this was incredible. Supposing the President as anxious for war as the Hamiltonians around him, Jefferson was unable to accept the nomination of Murray at face value. He conjectured that Adams, knowing he could not conceal the French assurances, took a step "which should parry the overture while it wears the face of acceding to it." He nominated Murray on the expectation the Federalists in the Senate would "take on their own shoulders the odium of rejecting it." But they would not; instead, they forced the President to adopt tactics of obstruction and delay which, if they did not negate the mission, "must at least keep off the day so hateful and so fatal to them, of reconciliation, and leave more time for new projects of provocation." This was the object, Jefferson thought, of the decision within a week of Murray's nomination to add two envoys to the mission under conditions that made it problematical whether they would ever leave home.

Jefferson was less than charitable in thus seeking to account for the President's conduct. Yet nothing had taken place to suggest that Adams was any less infatuated with the war policy than the ultras in Congress and the cabinet. He had gone on inflaming the public mind and treating the French republic in the most arrogant manner. He signed the Logan Act even as he profited from Logan's counsel; he enforced the Sedition Act and signed blank warrants for the arrest of aliens; and he gave no check to war preparations. On the very day of Murray's nomination, the new army bill for an eventual force of 30,000 regulars and 75,000 volunteers cleared the Senate for his signature. Several days earlier the Senate approved his appointment of envoys to negotiate treaties of commerce with Russia and Turkey, both new accessions to the second coalition against France. "All this helps," Jefferson said of this transaction, "to fill up the measure of provocation towards France, and to get from them a declaration of war, which we are afraid to be the first in making." And why, he wondered, if the President sincerely wished for reconciliation, did he wait until the end of the session, when all the war measures had passed, to spring his surprise? If Jefferson was mistaken in his view of Adams's intentions, it was not without reason.

What staggered belief among Republicans infuriated High Federalists. Secretary of State Pickering called the projected mission "the most unfortunate and the most humiliating event to the United States . . . since the commencement of the French Revolution." To appease his critics, Adams agreed to a three-man commission. Chief Justice Oliver Ellsworth and William R. Davie, of North Carolina, were joined with Murray. The result was delay, as Jefferson had predicted, and more than that, sabotage by Pickering and his colleagues. There was no appeasing them. They cried betrayal. Adams had been tricked by the combined sophistries of Jefferson and Talleyrand, they charged. The prospects of the Federalist party, soaring since the XYZ Affair, rested on opposition to France. The success of the war system hung on the public conviction of its necessity to force honor and justice from France. To act on the contrary proposition was like declaring "the emperor has no clothes." How was it possible to stamp out sedition, consolidate the national government, recruit an army, and go filibustering in the Spanish dominions when the rationale for these enterprises was taken away? Hamilton, still flirting with the Miranda project, had drawn up a far-reaching program for the Federalist warriors. A force should be collected to put Virginia, headquarters of the opposition, to "the test of resistance," Hamilton said. The great states should be subdivided to reduce their influence, the army should be established on its present footing, the planned naval force completed, a military academy instituted, the judicial arm of the federal government extended into every town and county, a more sweeping sedition law enacted, and all the "renegade aliens" still in the country sent away. Hamilton advocated these measures regardless of a settlement with France, though their prospects would be improved by war. The risk of civil war seems not to have disturbed him; indeed, to make the national authority "a question of force" was a necessary part of the plan. Similar sentiments were espoused by John Fenno, Jr., who took over the *Gazette of the United States* on his father's death in the fall epidemic that also claimed Bache of the *Aurora*. With Cobbett and several others of the press tribe, young Fenno bitterly assailed Adams's peace policy. But unlike Hamilton, who saw that the policy, once started, could not be undone, Fenno called for an immediate declaration of war on France, Spain, and Holland, and the conquest of their West Indies' possessions in collaboration with Britain. He would also do away with the state governments, "those egregrious baubles of sovereignty, those pestiferous incitements of demagogy," and revise the franchise so as to place the government securely in the hands of "the proprietors of the country." Declaring for peace, Adams unwittingly exposed naked reaction in the Federalist ranks.

It was a pity Jefferson could not appreciate the irony of the situation. Adams plunged a sword into the Federalist party, one which many of its leaders thought a betrayal to Jeffersonianism, but which to Jefferson was only a "parry" of French advances. Whether or not anything came of the new mission, its very existence rendered the war party desperate and must, Jefferson supposed, speed the progress of reform. "The spirit of 1776 is not dead. It has only been slumbering." As Congress neared adjournment a rebellion against the direct tax broke out in the eastern counties of Pennsylvania. (It was led, not by a Jacobin, but by a Federalist, John Fries.) The people were opening their eyes. "Pennsylvania, Jersey, and New York are coming majestically around to true principles." Petitions for repeal of the Alien and Sedition Laws poured into Congress. The first victim of the latter, Matthew Lyon, the Vermont congressman and editor, who had served his term in prison and whose fine had been paid by Jefferson and his friends, again sat in the House. Just before the session ended a special committee submitted a report in defense of the Alien and Sedition Laws. When the Republicans attacked it on the floor a strange scene ensued: the Federalists fell into laughing and coughing until, Jefferson reported, one would have needed "the lungs of a vendue-master to have been heard." As it was impossible to proceed, the report quickly passed. Several Federalist-dominated state legislatures, either at this time or soon after, also defended these laws in action on the Virginia and Kentucky Resolutions.

What, if anything, should be done about these Resolutions was one of the problems Jefferson took home with him in March. On the one hand, it was apparent that their doctrine, regardless of the public clamor against the federal laws, raised Unionist alarms in the states, even among Republican moderates in Virginia. To press the issue might very well arrest the "revolution of opinion" in midcourse. "Anything rash or threatening," he told Madison, "might check the favorable dispositions of the middle states, and rally them again around the measures which are ruining us." On the other hand, to let the doctrine lie idle in the face of rebuke, directly by several legislatures, indirectly by Congress, might be interpreted as a sign of weakness. Sometime during the long summer Jefferson decided that Virginia and Kentucky should renew their protests of the previous year. He was motivated, in part, by the clearer recognition of a danger only vaguely discerned in 1798. This was the threat of common law criminal jurisdiction in the federal courts. Edmund Randolph had taken up the subject and the two men exchanged opinions. Of all the claims ever made by the federal government it was, said Jefferson, the most dangerous. "All their other assumptions of un-given powers have been in detail. The bank law, the treaty doctrine, the sedition act, the alien act . . . , etc., etc., have been solitary, unconsequential, timid things, in comparison with the audacious, barefaced and sweeping pretension to a system of law for the U.S., without adoption of their legislature, and so infinitely beyond their power to adopt." The state courts might as well shut up. Perhaps the state legislatures too, for Congress might legislate on any matter within the boundless field of jurisdiction thus opened to the federal courts. It portended a complete consolidation. The claim, absurd as it was, should not go unchallenged. At least two Supreme Court justices openly championed it; many Federalists espoused the doctrine. "But, great heavens!" Jefferson exclaimed, "Who could have conceived in 1789 that within ten years we should have to combat such windmills."

On a Sunday in August, Madison came to Monticello to map plans for a second set of resolutions. Nicholas, though invited, was unable to attend. He was about to go over the mountains to look after the affairs of his late brother, long a leader in Kentucky politics, and so could arrange concerted action between that state and Virginia. Several days before the meeting Jefferson sketched his ideas in a letter to Madison. Not only should the principle of nullification be asserted but the protesting states should announce their intention, should the usurpations persist, to sever themselves from the Union. Such a statement would eliminate some of the ambiguity of the original doctrine by justifying secession as its sequel. If the

Hamiltonians were prepared to put the Union to the test of force, Jefferson seemed prepared to put it to the test of secession "rather than give up the rights of self-government which we have reserved, and in which alone we see liberty, safety and happiness." Six months earlier he had warned against extreme measures of this kind, believing they would check the progress of opinion. He now seemed to think the time had come to wield the threat of secession for political ends. In his opinion, as in the opinion of most men, the Union was an "experiment in liberty," and whether or not it would succeed was still an open question. The Union was neither imperishable nor indestructible. If it failed to serve liberty, becoming despotic instead, it repudiated the end of its being. Jefferson reached the nadir of his hopes for the Union in these notes, hastily sketched, as he admitted to Madison, in August 1799.

But Madison came to dinner—a cool breeze in a hot summer—and at once soothed his friend's feelings. Jefferson receded from the threat of secession, "not only in deference to his judgment, but because we should never think of separation but for repeated and enormous violations, so these, when they occur, will be cause enough of themselves." And so he modified his instructions to Nicholas. At the same time he proposed an addition to the resolutions: a protest against "the new pretensions to a *common law* of the U.S." The subject had doubtless been discussed at Monticello. When Madison came to write his Virginia Report on the Resolutions of 1798, he incorporated a lengthy rebuttal of these pretensions. The point was passed over by the Kentucky legislature. Its Resolutions of 1799 were hastily drawn, as Breckinridge informed Jefferson, and would not have been drawn at all but for Nicholas's appearance at the capital. Going back to Jefferson's draft of 1798, Breckinridge picked up the word and language of nullification, securing the first official usage of the doctrine in a series of resolutions that simply repeated the protest against the constitutionality of the Alien and Sedition Laws. The Virginia Report, adopted by the legislature in January, ran to the same effect. But this document was a masterful exposition of the theory of the federal union and a powerful defense of human rights. An appeal to reason, it affirmed republican liberty without incurring the heresy of disunion. Jefferson was delighted with the

Report, had it reprinted in Philadelphia, and believed it boosted Republican hopes at the opening of the fateful election year.

The Election of 1800

The country mourned the death of George Washington when Jefferson returned to Philadelphia for the meeting of the Sixth Congress in December 1799. He arrived late, too late to participate in the formal ceremonies honoring the first President and to hear Henry Lee proclaim him "first in war, first in peace, and first in the hearts of his countrymen." Black crepe hung from the walls and draped the Vice President's chair when he made his appearance in the Senate several days later. Inevitably, the solemnities of Congress carried partisan overtones. Washington died a Federalist, whether more Hamiltonian or Adamsite it would be difficult to say. He had been partly responsible, not long before his death, for the phenomenal upsurge of the party in Virginia, resulting in the election of Lee, Marshall, and six other Federalists to Congress. To whatever heights the ambitions of party might exalt Washington in death, he could not be more mercilessly exploited than in life. Jefferson must have shared the emotions common to his countrymen at this momentous passage in the nation's history; but he had learned to hide his feelings, especially where Washington was concerned, and so far as the record shows uttered not one word on his death.

Jefferson had small hope for the new Congress, elected months earlier at the peak of the war frenzy. For the first time in years the Federalists held commanding majorities in both houses. All the Republicans could do was to stand their ground, avoid anything rash, let the Federalist warriors consume each other, and prepare for the coming contest. Although worried by Republican backsliding in the southern states, Jefferson was cheered by the recent victory of Thomas McKean at the head of the state Republican ticket in Pennsylvania—evidence that public indignation was beginning to be translated into votes. If Pennsylvania, and perhaps New York, would unite with the Republicans of the southern and western states, there could be no doubt of the outcome in 1800. The balance of political forces was close. Every debate in Philadelphia was an electioneering skirmish. Congress, one observer wrote, was like "a conclave of cardinals, intriguing in the election of a Pope."

The Republican candidate weighed his moves with a view to the election. It was important for him to lead, yet he dared not lead openly. He was especially guarded in his correspondence, wrote few political letters, and declined to trust the post with those he ventured, "knowing that a campaign of slander is now open upon me, and believing that the postmasters will lend their inquisitorial aid to fish out any new matter of slander they can [to] gratify the powers that be." The press was the engine of reform. "Every man must lay his purse and his pen under contribution." He left the pen to others, to old friends like Edmund Pendleton and to unspeakable hirelings like James T. Callender; but he gave freely of his purse. He subscribed to dozens of newspapers (some of them fell victims of the Sedition Law), laid himself and his friends under assessment for new gazettes, and personally saw to the circulation of partisan tracts. In April he sent eight dozen of a single pamphlet, *Political Arithmetic,* by Thomas Cooper, the friend of Priestley, to the chairman of the Republican General Committee in Virginia for distribution to the county committees. Cooper was a seditious character. "I trust yourself only with the secret that these pamphlets go from me," Jefferson admonished the chairman. "You will readily see what a handle would be made by my advocating their contents." The contents, really not so radical, offered a dollars and cents argument on the economic superiority of agriculture and inland commerce to foreign trade supported by an expensive navy and financed by British capital. Jefferson supposed it would appeal to Virginia farmers. With party organization, as represented in the Virginia central committee and similar bodies in other states, he did not directly concern himself. He approved of it, of course, if not in principle, then because such organization seemed necessary to Republican success at the polls, which was the salvation of all principle. Although he was in touch with state leaders, like Burr in New York and McKean in Pennsylvania and John Langdon in New Hampshire, more often his influence at the state level was felt through Republican congressmen, with whom he conversed almost daily over the dinner table at Francis' Hotel. Federalists, seeing the improved Republican machine

—agents dispersed everywhere, committees within committees, every part working in unison—gave Jefferson more credit, or discredit, for the accomplishment than he deserved. He did not build the organization, yet it could not have been built without him. He did not direct it, yet he was the shaft on which the machine turned.

A heterogeneous coalition of the aggrieved, the discontented, and the ambitious, the party had no clearly defined principles and objectives. Jefferson's mind was well furnished with both, however; and although they were not broadcast to the electorate as in a "platform," they gave the Republican party whatever unity of creed it possessed. The creed was stated in private letters, especially those addressed to prospective converts, like Gerry, or to state leaders, like Gideon Granger of Connecticut, who were strangers to Jefferson. The fundamental doctrines were three. First, the preservation of the federal Constitution and the rights of the states. In this connection Jefferson expressed his long-standing opposition to a system of administration and finance that "monarchized" the Constitution, multiplied offices and taxes and debt, and sank the states under a consolidated government. "Our country is too large to have all its affairs directed by a single government. Public servants at such distance . . . , by rendering detection impossible to their constituents, will invite the public agents to corruption, plunder and waste. . . . The true theory of our Constitution is surely the wisest and best, that the states are independent as to everything within themselves, and united as to everyhing respecting foreign nations." Second, freedom of religion, freedom of the press, and the right of the people, inseparable from their sovereignty, to oppose and criticize the governing authorities. "And," he added with a characteristic flourish, "I am for encouraging the progress of science in all its branches; and not for raising a hue and cry against the sacred name of philosophy; for awing the human mind with stories of raw-head and bloody bones to a distrust of its own vision . . . , to go backwards instead of forward to improvement; to believe that government, religion, morality, and every other science were in perfection in the ages of darkest ignorance, and that nothing can ever be devised more perfect than what was established by our forefathers." And third, "free commerce with all nations, political connection with none." Jefferson reaffirmed his belief that the nation should "disentangle" itself from the affairs of Europe. Only in this way could the United States establish its national character and independence, untroubled by the sufferings and rivalries and passions of the Old World. These were his principles, Jefferson said repeatedly. They rested on the mother principle of democracy, since all were unquestionably, he believed, the principles of "the great body of our fellow citizens."

The shiftings and shadings of Jefferson's thought in response to changing circumstances illuminated rather than blurred its basic consistency. Thus the war hysteria, while it caused no change of principle, hardened his broad state rights commitment. The most significant adjustment occurred in the realm of foreign policy. His faith in France had been jolted over the years. He began to speak of disengagement in 1797, but as late as 1798 he justified his faith in the French republic and its cause in Europe. Finally, the 18th Brumaire of Napolean Bonaparte, which overthrew the republic and established the rule of a dictatorial consulate, crushed the last hopes Jefferson had for the Revolution. Once again, as at its birth, the American republic stood alone in the world. He had looked upon France as a commercial ally, but French atrocities on American commerce well-nigh destroyed the country's liberties. He had looked upon France as a spearhead of republicanism in the Old World, but the poor, ignorant peoples' longings for freedom were harnessed to Napoleon's imperial ambitions. He had looked upon the success of the French republic as indispensable to secure the American—nothing was left of this theory in 1800. Darkness had fallen in Europe, and Jefferson was resigned, at last, to an American destiny in a world of its own. "It is very material," he wrote to Breckinridge, "for the [people] to be made sensible that their own character and situation are materially different from the French; and that whatever may be the fate of republicanism there, we are able to preserve it inviolate here. . . . Our vessel is moored at such a distance that should theirs blow up, ours is still safe, if we will but think so." Partiality to France was no longer justified; neutrality, under whatever guise, was no longer enough. Isolation was the true policy. Commerce must go on, of course, but independently of treaties such as he had earlier advocated to upbuild American freedom and power. The French treaties were dead by congressional decree. The Adams administration, while continuing to seek treaties of commerce, had abandoned the liberal principles of the original plan, as had the Jay Treaty. Whatever justification the policy once had was gone. And Jefferson, with most Republicans, believed the system needlessly involved the United States in the quarrels of Europe.

The coming election was omnipresent in Congress. "Our campaign will be as hot as that of Europe," Jefferson philosophized. "But happily indeed in ink only; they in blood." In January, Senator James Ross, the defeated Federalist candidate for governor of Pennsylvania, moved the appointment of a committee to report a bill setting forth the procedures to be followed in the scrutiny of electoral votes cast for President and Vice President. The upshot was the Ross bill. The electoral certificates of the various states, after being opened in Congress, would be referred to a grand committee of six elected members from each house and the Chief Justice. The committee would meet in secret session and throw out any votes cast in an irregular manner or by unqualified electors or under bribery or intimidation of any kind. Its report would be final. Everyone recognized the true purpose of this party measure. The grand committee would be dominated by Federalists, who could be expected to scrutinize the votes for Republican candidates with particular care. William Duane, now editor of the *Aurora*, learned of these secret proceedings, accused the Federalists of a cabalistic plot, and published the bill in full before it passed the Senate. In the arts of exposure and vilification Duane had rapidly proved himself the equal of Bache; and when death cheated the Federalists of enemy number one, they turned to his successor. Duane was no easy mark, however. Pickering had wanted to deport him as a "wild Irishman," but the editor, though he had grown up in Ireland, boasted American birth. Twice arraigned under the Sedition Law, he squirmed free the first time, and by threat of embarrassing disclosures forced the authorities to drop the second case. Now the Federalist senators, enraged by Duane's exposure of the Ross bill, summoned him before the bar of the house to answer for the publication of a false, scandalous, and malicious libel of the Senate.

It made an awkward situation for the Vice President. How could he preside at the trial of the first Republican editor in the land for high breach of the privileges of the Senate? On the other hand, how could he refuse to do his sworn duty? The dilemma might be avoided by stalling the trial. Such was the strategy adopted by Duane's counsel, Alexander Dallas and Thomas Cooper, no doubt in consultation with Jefferson. Duane appeared, denied the jurisdiction of the Senate, and asked to be represented by counsel. The request was granted; counsel, however, would not be permitted to inquire into the question of jurisdiction. In accordance with the strategy, Duane then addressed letters to Dallas and Cooper asking their services, but these gentlemen declined to submit themselves to Star Chamber proceedings. Thus denied the benefit of counsel, Duane informed the Vice President he could not appear for trial. The Senate declared Duane in contempt and instructed the Vice President to issue a warrant for his arrest. Jefferson did his duty. Part of the Federalists' game, he realized, was to put him on the spot. The editor went into hiding at Stenton, out of reach of the process server. Friends and sympathizers, meanwhile, got up a petition and remonstrance in his behalf. On the question of receiving it, the yeas and nays were equal, and Jefferson made the majority with his casting vote. After hearing the petition, the Senate refused to amend its action. But it could not stay in session forever, and so, in a final face-saving gesture, requested the President to prosecute the wily editor for sedition. (He was again indicted in the fall, and again without success.) It was a humiliating defeat for the Federalists. The Ross bill, too, finally met defeat. This piece of Federalist arrogance revolted decency and common sense; fortunately, these virtues had not altogether disappeared in the lower house, which rejected the Senate measure.

Panic descended on the Federalist chieftains as the election approached. The danger of war had passed, but the Sedition Act was enforced even more vigorously, not only against such prominent propagandists as Duane and Cooper and Callender, the monstrous Jacobin trio some High Federalists imagined took their orders from Jefferson himself, but against poor, obscure Republican editors as well. "The onset on the presses is to cripple and suppress the Republican efforts during the campaign which is coming on," Jefferson observed. "In the meantime their own batteries are teeming with every falsehood they can invent for defamation." All signs pointed to returning peace with France. Ellsworth and Davie had finally sailed in November and, with Murray, were received by Napoleon in March. The war machine could no longer be kept up. Washington's death was a blow to the provisional army—Congress began to dismantle it in February. The Federalist engineers, frantic to restore the machine's operation for domestic purposes, only betrayed themselves. "The rapid progress of public sentiment warns them of their danger, and they are passing laws to keep themselves in power," Jefferson said. Having failed with the first line of defense, the Ross bill, they retreated to a second in March. The leadership brought forward a bill to reform the judiciary. The bill would create new courts, many new judges, and greatly extend federal jurisdiction. While not without merits, it was a blatantly partisan measure designed, in part, to make the judiciary a fortress against the rising Republicanism of the nation. By multiplying courts and jurisdiction, the means would be at hand, argued the Massachusetts Federalist Theodore Sedgwick, "to render the justice of the nation acceptable to the people, to aid the national economy, to overawe the licentious, and to punish the guilty." And Wolcott observed, "It is impossible, in this country, to render an army an engine of government, and there is no way to combat the state opposition but by an efficient and extended organization of judges, magistrates, and other civil officers." By the narrowest of margins, Republicans and moderates blocked passage of the bill. The morale of the opposition, at low ebb two years before, had fully revived when Congress broke up in May.

The election of the New York legislature in April provided the first crucial test of party strength. In that state, as in several others, the legislature appointed the presidential electors; as the legislature went, so too would go New York's electoral vote. And the result in the legislature would be controlled by the contest in New York City. There Burr concentrated his efforts. They were rewarded. The Republican ticket, which Burr had framed for the maximum popular appeal, including names of Revolutionary fame—George Clinton, Horatio Gates, Brockholst Livingston—was swept into the Assembly. The Federalists were deposed. Jefferson seemed virtually assured of New York's electoral vote. By his own calculations, victory in New York would mean victory in the nation. Others agreed. When he stopped to see Adams on some official business after the upset in New York, he was accosted with, "Well, I understand that you are to beat me in this contest. . . ." (Jefferson replied that it was not a contest between them but between two systems of political principles: "Were we both to die today, tomorrow two other names would be put in the place of ours, without any change in the motion of the machinery.") So alarmed was Hamilton by Burr's coup that he urged his old friend John Jay, the Governor, to convene the lame-duck legislature in order to nullify the Republican victory by a change of the electoral law. Otherwise, said Hamilton, "the OVERTHROW of the GOVERNMENT . . . a REVOLUTION, after the manner of BONAPARTE," was the prospect. Revolted by the proposition, Jay quietly buried it.

Thus the opening battle spread gloom in one party and irrepressible optimism in the other. The Republicans owed so much to Burr that his candidacy for the vice presidential nomination could not be denied. It should go to a New Yorker anyway. Clinton was approached but declined. Burr, though still bristling at the southerners for their treatment of him in 1796, agreed to stand if he would be fairly supported. When Republican congressmen caucused in Philadelphia in May, Burr was the unanimous choice for Jefferson's running-mate.

The Federalists also went into caucus to choose nominees and map strategy. Their decision to support Adams and Charles Cotesworth Pinckney equally was, in effect, a vote of "no confidence" in the President. As Hamilton saw it, Adams was a necessary sacrifice if the Federalists were to be saved from "the fangs of Jefferson." He assumed the two candidates would, in fact, be equally supported in every state except South Carolina, where the vote would be split between Jefferson and the native son Pinckney, who would, therefore outdistance Adams and, it was to be hoped, the Virginian. The party was still badly torn by Adams's second mission to France; and the principal cabinet officers, Pickering, Wolcott, and McHenry, still took their orders from Hamilton. This intramural conflict, while less public, was more fatal than the conflict with the Republicans. Adams at last woke up to the treachery of his ministers, or at least two of them, Pickering and McHenry, and while the party reeled from the shock of the New York election, dismissed them from office in May. This was the crowning insult to the Hamiltonians. "If Mr. Adams should be reelected," a Marylander wrote, "I fear our constitution would be more injured by his unruly passions, antipathies, and jealousies, than by the whimsies of Jefferson." The President's enemies accused him of striking a bargain with Jefferson: the two men would join forces in the election and swap offices. The cabinet dismissals were part of the bargain, as was Jefferson's casting vote confirming the President's nomination of his father-in-law as a commissioner of the stamp tax. "Mr. *Adams* and his dear friend Mr. *Jefferson* have been *twice closeted* together," wagged one Federalist tongue, "and it is generally understood to be agreed on between them that General Pinckney is not to be President—Adams declares for Mr. Jefferson—the only man in America qualified to fill the appointment, except himself." Malice alone inspired these rumors. Jefferson had no need for Adams's support, nor did he wish it. As for Adams, no doubt he considered the Virginian a small evil compared to the Federalist madmen of the "British faction," but the idea of a secret Adams-Jefferson coalition in 1800 was absurd. As Jefferson had said to Adams of the contest, "Its motion is from principle, not from you or myself."

When Jefferson climbed into the stage at Philadelphia on May 15, he took final leave of the city that had been the principal scene of his public life. Before his return to Congress, the government would be seated on the Potomac. Except for the loss of his associates in the scientific circle, he infinitely preferred the new capital to the old. He continued to view great cities "as pestilential to the morals, the health, and the liberties of man." Philadelphia, for all its charms, had given abundant evidence of that. Realizing he might never be so far east again, he abandoned his usual itinerary and took the long route down the eastern shore to Norfolk, thence along the southside of the James, some of it through country he had never seen. He intended to bypass Richmond but stopped briefly, without becoming "a mannikin of ceremony," to talk with Governor Monroe. From there he went to Mont Blanco, Maria's new home, where horses and servant waited. Maria had lost her first-born child. Anxious for her health, he took her to Monticello with him. He was soon busy with house and farm. He had taken a heavy loss on last year's tobacco because of the suspension of commerce with France. Fortunately, the wheat harvest was the finest ever in Albemarle, and the market was good.

While occupied with domestic cares, he found time to complete a manual of parliamentary procedure begun in February. *Jefferson's Manual* laid down rules for the conduct of the Senate. This was a matter of concern to him from the moment he became Vice President. Fair and orderly procedure in legislative bodies was, he recognized, an essential ingredient of representative government. Neither house of Congress was above criticism in this regard. Jefferson, faced with the task of presiding over the Senate, began to collect his thoughts on "parliamentary science" and later determined to make a permanent digest of precedent and practice before his term of office ended. Although he took account of the experience of American legislative bodies, he went back to the fountainhead, the English Parliament, for his standard. The *Manual*, first published in 1801, is still in use in the Senate of the United States.

He was a passive and, on the whole, silent observer of the presidential campaign. Around his own person the Republican party had achieved a unity of action and of feeling beyond anything previously known. His mind was at ease as the fall elections came on. He would have felt better about the outcome, however, had the Pennsylvania legislature broken the stalemate that threatened to deprive the state of its electoral vote. (The two houses, one Federalist, the other Republican, could not agree on an electoral law.) The persistence of Federalist strength in certain states, such as the Carolinas, also troubled him. Correspondents in the different states kept him abreast of developments. From New England, especially from Connecticut, came pitiful accounts of Republican helots pitted against an entrenched Federalist aristocracy. "There are at least four hundred Men of public education and possessed of public confidence for four or five of us to contend with," wrote Gideon Granger. It was a "System of Terror" managed by clerics and lawyers. "They are now bold enough to tell us that we must be destroyed *root* and branch." Jefferson had no hope of cracking this Federalist stronghold, or Massachusetts either; indeed New England's isolation from the prevailing Republicanism of the country made him anxious for his administration of the government. "It can never be harmonious and solid," he told Granger, "while so respectable a portion of its citizens support principles which go directly to a change of the federal constitution, to sink the state governments, consolidate them into one, and to monarchize that."

Even in Virginia sedition had its day. About the time Jefferson passed through Richmond, James T. Callender was indicted for the publication of *The Prospect Before Us,* his principal contribution to the Republican campaign. Two days later Jefferson advised Monroe, "I think it essentially just and necessary that Callender should be substantially defended." By this he meant the commonwealth should take a hand in the defense, thereby making the trial a test not only of freedom of the press but of state authority as well. Callender was a hard test. It was not simply that he thrived on scandal; he was himself a scandal. "The wretch has a most thief-like look, he is ragged, dirty, has a downcast with his eyes, leans his head towards one side, as if his neck had a stretch, and goes along working his shoulders up and down with evident signs of anger against the fleas and lice." Justice Samuel Chase, the most fanatical Federalist on the bench, had chosen his victim after Luther Martin, in Maryland, gave him a copy of the free-swinging tract in which Adams was called "a hoary headed incendiary." The ablest counsel in Virginia, including the state's attorney general, defended Callender, so far as Chase would permit. The trial, a travesty of justice, ended in conviction by an all-Federalist jury and sentence of a $200 fine and nine months in jail. Of comparatively little importance in the election of 1800, the trial was the central event in what would become the most damaging personal relationship of Jefferson's career.

The relationship began in 1797. Encouraged by the distinguished patronage he then received, Callender put his fangs into Jefferson and would not let go. With the passage of the Sedition Act, he was a marked man in Philadelphia, and so, leaving four motherless children behind him, fled to the asylum of Senator Mason's home in northern Virginia. He was sick of politics. He complained of being ill-used by the Republicans and hunted by the Federalists. Describing himself as "alone in the land of strangers," he implored Jefferson to give him a job at Monticello. The last place Jefferson wanted to see this miserable refugee from Grub Street was at Monticello; still he sympathized with Callender's plight and through a carefully disguised transaction sent him $50. The next year Callender went to Richmond where his talents were employed by the *Richmond Examiner*, the state's leading Republican newspaper. At the same time he began writing *The Prospect*, primarily, it seems, as a money-making venture. Jefferson saw some of this in page proof, predicted the "best effect" from it, and instructed his agent in Richmond to pay Callender $50 on account of the book. All these payments Jefferson later justified as "mere charities . . . , no more meant as encouragements to his scurrilities, than those I give to the beggar at my door are meant as rewards for the vices of his life." Interestingly, the confession acknowledged that Callender wrote "scurrilities" and omitted the premise on which the "charities" were given and, for that reason, concealed. It was a scurrilous time, of course. Political partisans sucked venom as if it were mother's milk. But Callender was no ordinary scandalmonger. His letters to Jefferson reveal a paranoic, embittered against the world, contemptuous of "the rascally society of mankind"—an unscrupulous hireling less interested in the Republican cause than in the money he could make by scandalizing the opposition. No one seemed to like Callender, and some of the most ardent Republicans feared him. John Taylor, for instance, sought to warn Jefferson that the Scotsman was quite capable, at the slightest provocation, of turning on his benefactor. And Jefferson became more guarded. Callender sent him ranting letters from the Richmond jail and advance sheets of the second volume of *The Prospect*. Jefferson made no acknowledgment, except to send another $50 to the wretch, again under the fiction of covering purchases of the book. Motives of charity and of politics had become thoroughly confused, yet it seems unlikely at this point that Jefferson regarded Callender as a worthy object of either one. Probably he considered more the harm than the good Callender could now do to him. At any rate, he had placed himself in the hands of a man not at all loath to blackmail a President or, failing in that, smear him with scandal.

The vilification Jefferson received in the campaign of 1800 was hardly calculated to excite his disgust of Republican hatchet-men like Callender. For nearly a decade the Federalists had been fashioning an ugly image of Jefferson. Little was added in 1800, but everything was raised to the *nth* dimension. The fear and distrust dedi-

cated Federalists felt for Jefferson presumably had psychological validity in the Federalist political mind. And the more they voiced
their apprehensions the more they were possessed by them. In 1800
they became the victims of a self-induced hysteria; yet it did not
seize them blindly. Angry, humiliated, desperate, they set out quite
deliberately to terrorize the American public with the monster of
their imagination. So many things operated to divide and embarrass
the Federalists, the thing to do, Fisher Ames advised, was to "sound
the tocsin about Jefferson." And sound it they did. Infidelity, Jacobinism, Disunionism—these were the most dreadful evils the people
had to fear from the lean and crafty Virginian.

The conception had a certain coherence. The source of Jefferson's malignity was French philosophy. He was a visionary theorist,
"a *philosophe* in the modern French sense of the word," not only a
dangerous profession but one that incapacitated him for the chief
magistracy of a great nation. This was more, much more, than jest
and satire; the threat was real, and the Federalists treated it with an
earnestness that betrayed deep-seated suspicion of philosophical intelligence in affairs of state. Jefferson's democratic ideas, being imported from France, were bizarre. The propagandists could not decide whether democracy would prostrate the government by the
dissipation of its energies or bring the people under the tyranny of a
demagogue; but either result, impotence or despotism, would destroy constitutional government in the United States. Playing up the
worst of these dangers, the Federalists stigmatized Jefferson as a Jacobin and predicted his reign would follow the same course as revolutionary democracy in France. "Murder, robbery, rape, adultery,
and incest will be openly taught and practiced, the air will be rent
with the cries of distress, the soil will be soaked with blood, and the
nation black with crimes." And yet, while portraying Jefferson as
this prodigious Robespierre-Danton-Bonaparte, the Federalists did
not neglect the other side of his character, the side of weakness, vac-
ilation, and cowardice, as first exhibited in the Virginia governorship. Here, too, the fatal French influence was at work: a head full
of dreamy Rousseauist ideas could not govern a state. The Jeffersonian dogmas of state rights represented the extension of these ideas
to the federal system. National breakdown must be the consequence.
Jefferson's views favorable to emancipation of the slaves evinced ei-

ther cruel hypocrisy or speculative delusion. Southerners, at least, might be frightened by the specter of Santo Domingo, another violent offspring of the French Revolution. The Gabriel Conspiracy in Virginia, uncovered in September 1800, dramatized the danger. In the Federalist press it was reported that Gabriel was not, in fact, a Negro slave but the notorious Callender acting on Jefferson's orders. Whether a misguided child of light or a demonic child of darkness, Jefferson was more Frenchman than American, and between the treachery of the one and the treachery of the other there was not much to choose.

Both press and pulpit rang with anathemas on Jefferson the Infidel. The *Gazette of the United States* emblazoned the issue:

THE GRAND QUESTION STATED

At the present solemn moment the only question to be asked by every American, laying his hand on his heart, is "Shall I continue in allegiance to

GOD—AND A RELIGIOUS PRESIDENT;

or impiously declare for

JEFFERSON—AND NO GOD!!!"

Of course, Jefferson's infidelity stemmed from French philosophy. In 1798 New England religionists set up a hue and cry on the world-wide conspiracy against Christianity masterminded by a secret order, the Illuminati, which had overspread Europe under the aegis of the French Revolution and infiltrated seditious societies in the United States. This absurdity was exploded by 1800; but the notion of atheistical democracy seemed peculiarly congenial to many Federalists, and Jefferson offered an inviting target. Some of the shots were wild rumors, for example, that he had done away with the Sabbath and introduced the French calendar in his family. Some were twisted anecdotes. The two most prominent clerical pamphleteers, the Reverends John M. Mason and William Linn, published the story told by still another man of the cloth, John B. Smith, deceased, who had supposedly heard it from Philip Mazzei. While riding with Jefferson through the country, so the story went, Mazzei remarked on the rundown appearance of a church, and his companion declared "it is good enough for him who was born in a manger." Linn drew the moral: "Such a contemptuous fling at the

638

blessed Jesus, could issue from the lips of no other than a deadly foe of his name and cause." (A Republican newspaper, the *Vermont Gazette*, printed what it attested to be the true story. Mazzei, commenting on the church, said that Italian priests would refuse to enter such a shabby place, to which Jefferson replied, "And yet meaner places were deemed grand enough to dispense truth in, by HIM who was born in a manger.") Principally, however, the accusers relied on the *Notes on Virginia*, elated that the culprit convicted himself out of his own mouth. His disbelief in the deluge, his opposition to Bible reading in the schools, his impious declarations—"What *is* he, what *can he be*, but a decided, a hardened infidel?"

Jefferson attributed the vehement attack to his role in overthrowing the establishment in Virginia. Emboldened by the success of political delusion, the Federalist clergy had revived the hope of "obtaining an establishment of a particular form of Christianity thro' the U.S." Whatever the clerical intent—and the record does not support Jefferson's worst fears—the premises of the argument ran directly counter to the principles underlying the disestablishment. These principles were so widely accepted by 1800 that Republicans did not hesitate to acclaim Jefferson for them. As they pointed out, the Federalist censure implied there should be a religious test for high office. Was orthodoxy to be prescribed in religion as well as in politics, all in the face of the First Amendment? Although they marshaled evidence to prove the purity of Jefferson's Christian belief, the Republicans preferred to take the ground—the only one Jefferson could have approved—that the entire question was irrelevant. Between this position and the Federalist religionists no compromise was possible. To the latter, the voice of the nation in calling a deist or infidel to the first magistracy would be "no less than rebellion against God." It would assuredly end in the destruction of the churches and the reign of infamy. Christian belief was the test of moral character. Jefferson, lacking belief, was a bad man. His relations with Washington illustrated his besetting vice, duplicity. Federalists kept the Mazzei letter in the public eye. Moreover, he had obtained his property by fraud, fraud upon his British creditors and—a pure invention—upon a poor widow in his capacity as executor of an estate. But it would take a renegade Republican, Callender, to fill up the catalogue of slander at a later date.

Although personally hurt by the smear campaign, Jefferson

639

nursed his wounds in quiet. What his friend Cooper said in reference to Adams, he probably considered good philosophy for himself: "Calumny is a tax which every man high in office must sometimes pay, but truth like gold will come out unsullied and un-
dimmed from the fire of discussion." He patiently bore the tax, confident he would enjoy the ultimate reward. "I know that I might
have filled the courts of the United States with actions for these
slanders," he wrote to a sympathetic stranger, "and have ruined perhaps many persons who are innocent. But this would be no equivalent for the loss of character. I leave them, therefore, to the reproof
of their own consciences. If these do not condemn them, there will
yet come a day when the false witness will meet a judge who has
not slept over his slanders." He could rely on his Republican friends
to defend his character and principles. John Beckley was one. His
Address to the People of the United States raked through most of the
charges and appended a brief biography of the Republican candidate, the first to be written of him and the first of all campaign lives.
Five thousand copies were printed and it was liberally excerpted in
the Republican press. Out of the enthusiasm was born the first of
America's election songs, "Jefferson and Liberty." Republican hearts
exulted in this hymn of victory—

> Rejoice, Columbia's sons, rejoice
> To tyrants never bend the knee
> But join with heart with soul and voice
> For Jefferson and Liberty.

Federalists were astounded by the industry and organization of the
Republicans, even in New England where they were "trouped,
officered, regimented . . . in a manner that our militia have never
yet equalled," according to Ames. "Every threshing floor, every
husking, every party work on a house-frame or raising a building,
the very funerals are infected with bawlers or whisperers against
government." The report of Jefferson's "funeral" afforded momentary relief. A Massachusetts divine noted in his diary: "In the morning we had news of the death of Mr. Jefferson. It is to be hoped that
it is true." First printed in the *Baltimore American*, a Republican gazette, on June 30, the rumor or hoax was credited even by

some of Jefferson's closest associates; but on July 4, a day Republicans claimed as their own, the *American* rejoiced "Jefferson Lives."

In the enveloping gloom Federalist leaders wrung their hands, bickered and swore, conspired and commiserated with each other. "Have our party shown that they possess the necessary skill and courage to deserve . . . to govern?" wrote the deposed Secretary of War to Wolcott. "What have they done? . . . They write private letters. To whom? To each other, but they do nothing to give a proper direction to the public mind. . . . They meditate in private. Can any good come out of such a system?" Obviously not. A quarreling elite, distrustful of democracy, the Federalists were poorly equipped to conduct a campaign in the electorate. Adams inveighed against the British faction and the Essex Junto, its supposed north of Boston headquarters, "like one possessed," as Ames said. "His language is bitter even to outrage and swearing and calling names." He was reported to speak in friendly terms of his Republican rival; extremists like Ames believed he would see Jefferson President before he would yield to a true Federalist. For many Hamiltonians the choice between Adams and Jefferson was, at best, a choice between evils. The plot to abandon Adams for Pinckney was more easily conceived than executed, however. Hamilton's warmest admirers despaired of its success and feared it would expose the whole party to defeat. The New Yorker persevered. He wrote a vindictive brief against Adams intended for private circulation among the Federalist leaders. When part of the polemic fell into Republican hands, Hamilton threw caution to the winds and published it in full. Coming late in the campaign, in October, the sensational pamphlet had no effect on the outcome of the election, already determined in most states, but it exposed the sickness of the Federalist party more effectively than anything that appeared under Republican auspices.

At Monticello Jefferson kept tabs on the expected electoral vote. By December he counted 58 sure votes for the Republicans, 53 for the Federalists. The remaining 27 belonged to Rhode Island (4) and South Carolina (8), where he rated the chances as even, and to Pennsylvania (15), which stood little chance of voting at all. Adams had shown surprising strength in Maryland and North Carolina. Federalist hopes revived. The race was closer than men on either side had expected. Rhode Island soon joined her New England sisters in the Federalist column. The Republicans had proved their superiority at the polls in Pennsylvania, but a bare Federalist majority in the Senate still blocked the adoption of an electoral law. At the last moment the two houses reached a compromise which split the electoral vote 8 and 7, a disappointing net gain of one for the Republicans. So the two candidates were nearly even as the country awaited word from South Carolina. There the Republican cause was in the able hands of Charles Pinckney, United States senator and kinsman of General Pinckney, the Federalist candidate who was expected to draw votes away from Adams and given an outside chance of winning the presidency. The Republican manager sent Jefferson blow by blow reports on the contest. Since the choice of electors fell to the legislature, the state election was decisive. While disheartened by his party's poor showing in Charleston, always a Federalist stronghold, Pinckney confidently expected the inland counties to furnish a Republican majority. Taking nothing for granted, he went to Columbia, set up his command post, and caucused, coaxed, and bargained to ensure the success of the electoral slate pledged to Jefferson and Burr. On December 2 he dispatched a breathless note to Jefferson: "The election is just finished and we have (thanks to Heaven's goodness) carried it." Jefferson, then in Washington, received the news on December 12. At the same time he was reliably informed from Columbia that one vote would be withheld from Burr, thereby eliminating the possibility of a tie. In the electoral count, though the margin poorly reflected the popular standing of the two parties, Jefferson was the choice over Adams 73 to 65.

Republicanism had triumphed! The bright day dawned—no more "gags, inquisitions and spies," no more "herds of harpies" or "lordlings with gorging jaws" or "bigots with their holy laws." "The Jig's Up!" shouted the *Baltimore American*. "Be glad America!" rejoiced the *Readinger Adler*. Dismayed Federalists wore such long faces, it was said, that barbers doubled their prices. Direst consequences were predicted from seating a visionary, a demagogue, and a "howling atheist" at the head of the nation. But in the victory celebrations even church bells rang for Jefferson. The people had consummated a peaceful revolution in government. "Here ends the 18th Century," one enthusiast marked the year's end. "The 19th begins with a fine clear morning wind at S.W.; and the political horizon affords as fine a prospect under Jefferson's administration, with returning harmony with France—with the irresistible propagation of the Rights of Man, the eradication of hierarchy, oppression, superstition and tyranny over the world. . . ."

In fact, however, the horizon had clouded. Entry into the promised land of "Jefferson and Liberty" was blocked by the terrible abyss of the electoral system. For several days after December 12, Jefferson assumed with most men that his election to the presidency was secure. To be sure, certain states—Kentucky, Tennessee, Georgia, and Vermont—had not been heard from, but no one doubted how they would vote; and the possibility of a tie between the first and second Republican candidates, tossing the choice to the House of Representatives, was too great an absurdity to be credited. Jefferson began putting together his cabinet. On the 14th, in a long letter touching on steam engines and mammoth bones, he offered the Navy post to Robert R. Livingston. The next day he sent congratulations to Burr and expressed regret over the loss of his services to the new administration. "It leaves a chasm in my arrangements, which cannot be adequately filled up." He simply assumed that Burr had been elected Vice President. He mentioned the report from South Carolina and also the expectations as to Tennessee and Georgia: enough votes would be withdrawn from Burr to prevent a deadlock but he would surely top Adams in the final tally. "However," he went on, "it was badly managed not to have arranged with certainty what seems to have been left to hazard." Decency required that he take no part in these arrangements, but Jefferson supposed they had been made. Otherwise a Republican victory would be at least partially nullified, either by loss of one-half the ticket or, in the event of a tie, by political wheeling and dealing that risked everything. The desired result might have been secured in the Virginia "college of electors," allowing the Republicans elsewhere to display their unanimity. But the sting of Burr's accusation of bad faith in 1796 caused Madison, possibly with Jefferson's consent, to demand a unanimous vote for Burr in Virginia. He got it only because he was able to offer anxious Virginia Jeffersonians the assurances of Burr's personal agent that votes would be thrown away from the New Yorker in other states. If there was honor among politicians, Burr was bound to take steps that would place Jefferson's majority beyond hazard. He did not, and so Republican electors, North and South, played Alphonse and Gaston to each other.

The trace of apprehension Jefferson expressed in his letter to Burr increased from day to day. The earlier report from South Carolina was finally discredited; the state's electors were unanimous for Jefferson and Burr. On the 19th "an absolute parity" between the Republican candidates seemed certain, he told Madison. "This has produced great dismay and gloom on the Republican gentlemen here, and equal exultation on the Federalists." The last faint hope of breaking the stalemate vanished on the 23rd when the votes from Georgia and Tennessee were reported in Washington. "Seventy-three for Mr. Jefferson and seventy-three for Mr. Burr," Adams brooded. "May the peace and welfare of the country be promoted by this result!" The fate of the election, perhaps of the nation, would be decided in the lame-duck House of Representatives elected in the year of terror.

What would the Federalists do? The virgin capital buzzed with speculation and rumor. Huddled together in a few boarding houses, with nothing else to amuse them, politics was the congressmen's sole element. "A few, indeed, drink, and some gamble," Gallatin informed his wife, "but the majority drink nought but politics, and by not mixing with men of different or more moderate activities, they inflame one another." Excitement first centered on a Federalist plan to prevent an election altogether and in the interregnum to commit the first magistracy to the president *pro tem* of the Senate or some other officer. "This opens upon us an abyss, at which every sincere patriot must shudder," Jefferson said. Usurpation was the only name for such an act. The Republicans would resist by force if necessary; and groups were soon said to be organizing in neighboring states to march on Washington and put to death any man bold enough to offer himself as the usurper. It was "a wild measure," as Gouverneur Morris, now the junior senator from New York, acknowledged. Only the most desperate Federalists would actually carry it through, though others supposed the threat of the project would frighten the Republicans into imbecility. Jefferson was sufficiently alarmed to call on the President. The plan to make a President by law was fraught with "incalculable consequences," he told Adams, which it was in his power to prevent by executive veto. But the defeated President, with more than a trace of irritation, thought such an act might be justified, and observed that Jefferson could end the crisis in an instant by making certain pledges to the Federalists—pledges he consistently refused to make. For the first time in their long acquaintance, Jefferson recalled the interview, he and Adams parted with displeasure—and it was probably their last parting. The Vice President was not powerless in this situation. As the Senate's presiding officer, he could rule out of order any motion to legislate a President, and he had, in fact, promised to do just that before he talked to Adams. But the danger of usurpation and interregnum gradually receded as the Federalist leadership in Congress decided to make a President of Aaron Burr.

For a time Jefferson seemed little disturbed by this alternate project to upset the will of the people. Under the Constitution a majority of the representatives of each of nine states was needed to elect in the House; and the Federalists simply could not produce the necessary votes for Burr. Republican defections were possible, of course, but the party was firmly united on Jefferson. More likely, if he could not win nine states, stalemate would revive the danger of usurpation. To cover this eventuality Madison proposed in January that Jefferson and Burr jointly convene the new Congress to choose the President. The Republicans in Washington passed over the plan because they did not think it necessary. Burr himself declined all competition with Jefferson. "Be assured," he wrote to Samuel Smith, the Maryland Republican leader, "that the Federal party can entertain no wish for such an exchange. As to my friends, they would dishonor my views and insult my feelings by a suspicion that I would be instrumental in counteracting the wishes and expectations of the people of the United States." Smith published the letter, immensely reassuring to the Republicans.

The fact that Burr's letter was dated December 16, from Albany, when northern Republicans were celebrating Jefferson's election on the basis of the erroneous report from South Carolina, should have prompted second thoughts. At that time Burr had little reason to think the election would go to the House. Nor could he be certain on the point a week later when he pledged his loyalty in a letter to Jefferson. Nonetheless, most Republicans, including the chief, took Burr's disclaimer in good faith. "His conduct has been honorable and decisive, and greatly embarrasses" the Federalists, Jefferson stated. If embarrassed, the Federalists were not dismayed. As if to prove the theory it takes a rascal to know one, they claimed to understand Burr better than the Jeffersonians did. "Burr is a cunning man," one of them wrote. "If he cannot outwit all the Jeffersonians I do not know the man." James A. Bayard, the Delaware congressman, told Hamilton that the Federalists interpreted the letter to Smith either as proceeding from "a false calculation" of the electoral vote or as "a cover to blind his own party." "By persons friendly to Mr. Burr," Bayard said, "it is distinctly stated, that he is willing to consider the Federalists as his friends, and to accept the office of President as their gift." This was all they needed to know, and having let it be known, all that Burr could do to promote his candidacy. Active intervention on his part would give the game away.

As the congressional Federalists closed ranks around Burr, Gouverneur Morris felt like the man who stays sober while the rest of the company drinks itself to death. Adams's feelings were not very different. Burr's good fortune exceeded that of Bonaparte, he reflected. "All the old patriots, all the splendid talents, the long experience, both of Federalists and Antifederalists, must be subjected to the humiliation of seeing this dexterous gentleman rise, like a balloon, filled with inflamable air, over their heads. . . . What a discouragement to all virtuous exertion, and what an encouragement to party intrigue and corruption! What course is it we steer, and to what harbor are we bound?" In this moment of truth men like Morris and Adams, who had worked with Jefferson and who knew him as a dedicated public official, could look with a degree of equanimity on his election to the presidency.

But his leading apologist in the ultimate contest was another former cohort, Alexander Hamilton. "I admit," said Hamilton, "that his politics are tinctured with fanaticism, that he is too much in earnest with his democracy . . . , that he is crafty and persevering in his objects; that he is not scrupulous about the means of success, nor very mindful of the truth, and that he is a contemptible hypocrite." But it was not true, Hamilton insisted, that he was an enemy of the executive authority or a slave to his principles. On the contrary, he was likely to temporize and to acquiesce in established systems; and added to these merits, he was incapable, unlike Burr, of being corrupted. "He is by far not so dangerous a man; and he has pretensions of character." Burr was an unprincipled adventurer, bold enough to institute "the Jacobin system," and if the Federalist party foolishly raised this Catiline to the presidency, it would die. It was rather late in the day for Hamilton, of all people, to be fretting over the suicide of the Federalist party. The congressional leaders, many of them angry at Hamilton for his clumsy attack on Adams, spurned his advice. Casting the balance between the candidates, they argued that Jefferson was weak, Burr strong; Jefferson theoretical, Burr practical; Jefferson imbued with Jacobinical principles, Burr imbued with passion for power. "In public affairs," Griswold observed, "it is much better to trust a knave than a fool." Burr's vices were those of more than ordinary ambition; and to gratify it he would bargain and conciliate with the Federalists. Jefferson's vices, being founded in democratic principles, were incurable and deadly. Secretary of State Marshall, soon named Chief Justice by the departing President, had "insuperable objections" to his Virginia cousin. He would weaken the presidency, sap the foundations of government, and at the head of the majority party "embody himself in the House of Representatives," thereby increasing his personal power at the expense of constitutional authority. The estimate stood in marked contrast to Hamilton's. Neither would be proven right, but neither would be proven entirely wrong. Right or wrong, Hamilton's plea fell on deaf ears in Washington.

Republicans were bewildered by the enemy's resolution to support Burr despite his disavowal of candidacy. Early in January, Smith, to whom the disavowal had been made, went to Philadelphia as the party's emissary to obtain positive assurances from Burr. From Benjamin Hichborn of Massachusetts, who joined Smith, Jefferson at once learned the disappointing results of the meeting. Several years later, in 1804, Hichborn filled in the details of his conversation with Burr.

"We must have a President, and a constitutional one, in some way," Burr said.

"How is it to be done?" Hichborn asked. "Mr. Jefferson's friends will not quit him, and his enemies are not strong enough to carry another."

"Why," said Burr, "our friends must join the Federalists, and give the President."

Jefferson was prepared to believe the worst of Burr in 1804. Whatever his measure of trust in him in 1801, it was shaken by Burr's refusal, at Philadelphia, flatly to withdraw from the contest. As the time of decision neared, the capital was alive with rumors of Burr's agents trading and bribing for votes. "What is it you want, Colonel Lyon?" the Vermonter later claimed to have been asked. "Is it office, is it money? Only say what you want, and you shall have it." These "agents" may have acted without Burr's knowledge; but if he did not actively enter the Federalist plot, he declined to aid his party in foiling it.

Congress, meanwhile, went on with its business. In the Senate a French treaty signed by the American envoys at Morfontaine in October 1800 was at first rejected and then ratified. Republicans applauded the treaty, known as the Convention of 1800. While it superseded the old treaties, it preserved their commercial principles and, of course, restored normal relations between France and the United States. The Federalist bill to strengthen and enlarge the judiciary, scaled down somewhat, moved toward certain passage. "I dread this above all the measures meditated," Jefferson said, "because appointments in the nature of freehold render it difficult to undo what is done." Such measures kept partisan feelings at a high pitch. One January evening a group of Connecticut Federalists called on the Vice President at Conrad's boarding house, where he lodged in congenial Republican company, to lay before him the firearms manufactured on the principle of interchangeable parts by the ingenious Connecticut Yankee Eli Whitney, already known for the invention of the cotton gin. While in France Jefferson had had an enthusiastic first glimpse of this revolutionary development in the industrial arts, and he pronounced Whitney's achievement even more remarkable. Regardless of partisan animosities and jibes of "philosophism," Jefferson qualified as an expert in the arts and sciences.

On Wednesday, February 11, the members of the House retired to the Senate chamber to hear the results of the electoral vote everyone knew. Jefferson, as presiding officer, broke the seals on the state certificates, handed them one by one to the tellers, and at the conclusion announced the totals. The representatives then returned to their hall, closed the doors, and in accordance with procedures already agreed upon began a marathon of balloting, without formal adjournment or interruption by other business. The first ballot showed eight states for Jefferson, six for Burr, and two divided. The shift of a single vote to Jefferson in one of the divided states, Maryland and Vermont, or in Delaware, whose lone representative, Bayard, voted for Burr, would settle the matter. Republicans were hopeful. A Maryland Federalist said he would switch to Jefferson if need be; some looked to Lyon's Vermont colleague, others to Bayard, to break the deadlock. Both sides were impenetrable, however, and the war of attrition commenced. Six additional ballots followed in rapid succession. An hour's respite for a bit to eat, then eight more, another breather, resumption at nine p.m., and continued balloting throughout the snowy night. "The scene was now ludicrous. Many had sent home for night-caps and pillows, and wrapped in shawls and great-coats, lay about the floor of the committee-rooms, or sat sleeping in their seats. At one, and two, and at half past two, the tellers roused the members from their slumbers and took the same ballot as before." And so it went through the 27th ballot at sunrise. The pace slackened now: one more ballot on Thursday, two on Friday, three on Saturday.

"Four days of balloting have produced not a single change of a vote," Jefferson reported to Monroe on Sunday. "Yet it is confidently believed by most that tomorrow there is to be a coalition." (Actually, several congressmen had switched from Burr to Jefferson, all in delegations already decided.) In his quarters at Conrad's, Jefferson knew of no foundation for this belief. Yet the arrangements were going on under his nose. The key man was Bayard. He could end this war of nerves in an instant. Tiny Delaware tipped the scales of the Union. The sudden taste of power went to Bayard's head. He had fallen in with the Federalist scheme to support Burr. But after 33 ballots he was ready to give up the New Yorker. The election was in Burr's power, Bayard said, yet he declined to bid for

Jefferson's votes. Military measures, precautionary to a usurpation in Washington, were reported from the capitals of Virginia and Pennsylvania. Feeling that continuation of the stalemate risked the Constitution and civil war for no purpose, Bayard resigned himself to Jefferson's election.

But the Delaware congressman, still beguiled by the king-maker role, supposed he could exact terms of capitulation from Jefferson. He had, in fact, opened communication with Jefferson's friends while still soliciting votes for Burr. He first approached John Nicholas of Virginia, asking him to obtain assurances from Jefferson on three points of cardinal interest to the Federalists: support of the public credit, maintenance of the navy, and guarantees against the removal of certain federal officers. Nicholas, while foreseeing no difficulty on these points, refused to take the proposition to Jefferson. Bayard then, on Friday, turned to Samuel Smith. The Marylander lodged at Conrad's and had already conversed with Jefferson on the first two of the three points mentioned by Bayard, for other Federalists had made similar inquiries. Smith now agreed to sound out the Virginian on the subject of political removals. He did so that evening, and the next day gave Bayard the assurances he had requested. On the basis of this transaction, it was later charged, most prominently by Bayard, that Jefferson bargained his way into the presidency. This was another libel. Smith talked with Jefferson, but as he later testified, "without his having the remotest idea of my object." Jefferson talked freely on many subjects with his friends, including Federalists like Gouverneur Morris. Even if he had known the object of Smith's conversation, he had not authorized the communication; nor could the honest expression of his opinions be fairly construed as terms of capitulation. He rebuffed all overtures of this kind. "Many attempts have been made to obtain terms and promises from me," he wrote to Monroe on the 15th. "I have declared to them unequivocally, that I would not receive the government on capitulation, that I would not go into it with my hands tied." He deserved no medals for political valor, for he did not need to bargain his way into the presidency. Perhaps Smith thought he did, and in his self-appointed role as intermediary took unwanted liberties with Jefferson's conversation. As for the Delaware Federalist, his delusion would have collapsed without the idea of extortion and bargain.

Bayard expected to break the deadlock when the balloting resumed on Monday. The Federalists in angry caucus persuaded him to wait another day in the hope that Burr, now in Baltimore, might be heard from. On Tuesday, February 17, the 36th ballot, Jefferson was elected. South Carolina and Delaware, previously for Burr, cast blank ballots, and the Federalist members from Vermont and Maryland abstained, presumably on the plan devised by Bayard, thereby giving Jefferson a majority of ten states to four. "Thus has ended the most wicked absurd attempt ever tried by the Federalists," Gallatin sighed. No leader of that party ever undertook to defend its conduct in this crisis. Henceforth, the American people might wonder at the party's professions of fidelity to the Constitution, the Union, and republican government, all recklessly jeopardized in this contest. Even in defeat they acted a miserable part, most Federalists withholding their votes from Jefferson to the bitter end—"a declaration of perpetual war," Jefferson supposed.

But the picture had its brighter side too, and Jefferson was sure to find it. The bitter-enders had little support outside of Congress. The mass of Federalists might be brought back to genuine republicanism. "I am persuaded," he wrote an old friend, "that weeks of ill-judged conduct here, has strengthened us more than years of prudent and conciliatory administration could have done. If we can once more get social intercourse restored to its pristine harmony, I shall believe we have not lived in vain; and that it may, by rallying them [the mass of Federalists] to true republican principles, which few of them had thrown off, I sanguinely hope." With this spirit he turned from the long night of Federalism to the dawn of a new day.

CHAPTER NINE

President:

First Administration

*The people, under such a government [representative democracy], would
seem to be naturally more engaged in preserving and enjoying what they
already possess, than solicitous of acquiring what was not necessary to
their security or happiness; or, at least, that they should resort to no
other means of acquiring it than the exercise of their individual faculties;
nor think of obtaining authority, or power, by the invasion of the rights
of other individuals, or an improper appropriation of the public wealth;
that from the principle of attachment to the rights which vest in them
all, each citizen should feel and be affected by the injustice done to his
neighbor by the public force, as a danger which menaced and concerned
them all, and for which no personal favor could compensate.*

* * *

*This form of government does not call for nor need the constraint of
the human mind, the modification of our natural sentiments, the forcing
of our desires, nor the excitement of imaginary passions, rival interests, or
seductive illusions; it should, on the contrary, allow a free course to all
inclinations which are not depraved, and to every kind of industry which
is not incompatible with good order and morals: being conformable to
nature, it requires only to be left to act.*

Destutt de Tracy, A Commentary and Review of Montesquieu's
Spirit of Laws. *Philadelphia, 1811*

Washington was a city of promises in the first year of the nineteenth century. Nowhere else on the American landscape was the contrast between resplendent ideals and insistent realities so poignantly stated. Without wealth or industry or society, the embryo capital lived on the grandiose image of itself, in which Roman elegance and ambition mingled with American small-town boosterism. Strangers to the scene thought themselves "in the company of crazy people" suffering delusions of grandeur. In the sprawling vastness between Georgetown and Anacostia, three thousand people dwelled in scattered settlements redeemed from nature but little softened by the amenities of civilization. The village pretending to be a capital, "a place with a few bad houses, extensive swamps, hanging on the skirts of a too thinly peopled, weak and barren country," was a grotesque symbol of the aspiring nation itself.

The public sector of the city was fixed by two points, the President's House, elegant and gleaming under its coat of whitewash, and the Capitol, a great torso of a building, the north wing alone awkwardly dominating the summit. These "shining objects [stood] in dismal contrast to the scene around them." Along the mile and a half axis between them, a straight, broad clearing, Pennsylvania Avenue, had been cut through the forest and marsh. Carriages ventured at peril upon the roadway, still beset with stumps and mud holes, though pedestrians traveled more or less at ease on a newly laid stone footway. The avenue, unrelieved by a single house, passed through a deep morass fed by a creek the natives called Tiber long before they were dazzled by Roman dreams. Duck and snipe and partridge infested the marsh, and in the spring the Tiber was so thick with perch "that by shooting in among them one may get a good dish full, for as many will leap on shore with fright . . . as can be killed with the shot".

From Capitol Hill the panorama was breathtaking—wide Potomac, virgin forest, picturesque clearings, and distant heights. Men who came to Washington on the nation's business scoffed at the city's pretensions and groaned at its discomforts, but even the worst groaners and scoffers conceded that no city was ever more beautifully situated. The area just north of the President's House appeared

653

thickly settled. A new community clustered around the Capitol. Tailor, shoemaker, and printer plied their trades; there was a grocery, a stationer's shop, a dry goods store, and an oyster house, as well as seven or eight boarding houses erected for the accommodation of congressmen. The finest of these, the hostelry of Conrad & McMun, perched on the hillside just south of the Capitol, where the House Office Building now stands. Here the Vice President continued to lodge with his Republican friends while he waited to move into the house on Pennsylvania Avenue. Rooms were in short supply —most congressmen doubled up—but Jefferson had a bedroom and a parlor to himself. Everyone was equal at mess, however, "and he occupied during the whole winter the lowest and coldest seat at a long table at which a company of more than thirty sat down." Nor did he command a better seat on the 4th of March.

At twelve noon on that day the 57-year-old statesman, surrounded by friends and well-wishers, walked up New Jersey Avenue, through the square, and into the Capitol to be inaugurated President of the United States. Except for the parade of riflemen and the roar of artillery, the procession was without pomp or ceremony, as befitted the man, the place, and the occasion. The upstart capital was full of visitors and most of them had crowded into the Senate chamber, a cavernous, circular room with a spacious gallery, ranged with arches and massive Doric columns, richly entablatured in appropriate classical style, and withal trying very hard to be elegant. On the platform Aaron Burr, already sworn as Vice President, sat at Jefferson's right, and at his left John Marshall, the new Chief Justice, who would administer the oath of office. John Adams, at his inauguration, had been honored by the presence of his predecessor; but now Adams, embittered by defeat, was on the road to Quincy. The story of his early morning flight buzzed through the gallery. It seemed—more than the petulant act of a proud old warrior—a blunt gesture of Federalist defiance to the new President. What had occurred in 1797 was a succession; what was occurring on this blustery March day four years later was a transfer of power, indeed in Republican eyes and in Jefferson's a revolution in American government as momentous as the Revolution of 1776. The test of this idea lay in the future; it was enough for the present—a truly revolutionary achievement in itself—that power was changing hands by the peaceful and orderly processes of democratic government. The spectacle, for all its simplicity, was the most moving a free people could ever witness. "The changes of administration," a Washington lady noted in her diary, "which in every government and in every age have most generally been epochs of confusion, villainy and bloodshed, in this our happy country take place without any species of distraction, or disorder."

Without further ado, the tall, lanky Virginian, indistinguishable by garb or manner from the multitude, rose to deliver his Inaugural Address. He was no orator, as everyone knew, and few heard anything above the low mumble of his words. But this was an address to be studied and pondered in the cool reflection of the written word. One of the most elaborate of Jefferson's compositions, it had gone through three drafts before he was satisfied with it. Every word, phrase, and nuance had to be right. In style, as in content, it bore the personal insignia of its author. Never had he soared to higher or lovelier peaks of republican ideality. Never was his happy faculty of condensing whole chapters into aphorisms more brilliantly displayed.

The genius of the address lay in its seemingly artless elevation of the Republican creed to a creed of Americanism. Summing up "the essential principles of our government," Jefferson gave a national cast to the principles that had guided his party in the stormy years just past. The list was a long one. Of particular note were the following: "peace, commerce, and honest friendship with all nations—entangling alliances with none"; "the support of the State governments in all their rights, as the most competent administrations for our domestic concerns and the surest bulwarks against anti-republican tendencies; the preservation of the general government in its whole constitutional vigor, as the sheet anchor of our peace at home and safety abroad"; "economy in the public expense, that labor may be lightly burdened"; "the diffusion of information and arraignment of all abuses at the bar of public reason; freedom of religion; freedom of press; freedom of person. . . ." These principles, said Jefferson, were the gifts of American sages and heroes. "They should be the creed of our political faith—the text of civil instruction—the touchstone by which to try the services of those we trust; and should we wander from them in moments of error or alarm, let us hasten to retrace our steps and to regain the road which alone leads to peace, liberty, and safety." In the manner of stating these principles, the cutting edge of partisanship was softened or removed, doctrinaire rigidities were abandoned. Nine-tenths of the American people professed this creed, in Jefferson's opinion. As he once said, "the Republicans are the nation." No more than his predecessors was he reconciled to the permanence of party divisions and party warfare. He looked, rather, to the rapid disappearance of this pestilence and "a perfect consolidation" of political sentiments under Republican auspices.

Spelling out the principles on which the nation should unite, the address made a lofty appeal for the restoration of harmony and affection. Why should Americans emulate the fanaticism and the violence of European politics? "We have called by different names brethren of the same principle. We are all republicans: we are all federalists." The statement was as baffling as it was startling. Jefferson was always stingy with capital letters, otherwise he might have written, "We are all Republicans: we are all Federalists," which was the way many heard it and nearly everyone read it, usually with capitals, in the newspapers. In this sense it was a bold appeal for reconciliation of parties or, more accurately, a converting ordinance for erring Federalists. By erasing imaginary fears of Republicanism, the new President hoped to draw over the mass of Federalists to his cause. But the declaration had a deeper meaning at the foundation of Jefferson's conception of the American polity. Every true republican was a friend of federalism, that is, of the harmony and union of the states under the Constitution, not of the party that had corrupted this concept. The old polarities of liberty and power, rights and duties, individual enterprise and national purpose, the state and the central governments—these were swept away as the new President identified the principles of the federal union with the principles of republican freedom. "If there be any among us," he said, alluding to the delusions of '98, "who would wish to dissolve this Union or to change its republican form, let them stand undisturbed as monuments of the safety with which error of opinion may be tolerated where reason is left free to combat it."* And following this ringing

* In the first draft of the address Jefferson wrote, "I do not believe there is one native citizen of the United States who wishes to dissolve this Union.

affirmation of political freedom, he continued, "I know, indeed, that some honest men fear that a republican government cannot be strong; that this government is not strong enough. But would the honest patriot, in the full tide of successful experiment, abandon a government which has so far kept us free and firm, on the theoretic and visionary fear that this government, the world's best hope, may by possibility want energy to preserve itself? I trust not. I believe this, on the contrary, the strongest government on earth. I believe it is the only one where every man, at the call of the laws, would fly to the standard of the law, and would meet invasions of the public order as his own personal concern. Sometimes it is said that man cannot be trusted with the government of himself. Can he, then, be trusted with the government of others? Or have we found angels in the form of kings to govern him? Let history answer this question." Here was a radical conception of American power and purpose never gleaned by Alexander Hamilton and the Federalist leaders. Under the tyranny of Old World ideas, they supposed the strength of nations and governments consisted in armies and navies, aristocratic patronage, the support of "the rich, the well born, and the able," great treasury, central command, ministerial mastery, the panoply of office and the splendor of state. Jefferson, whom the Federalists had labeled "visionary" for supposing that the United States could dismiss the usual arms and armor of power, now turned around to rebuke them for *their* "theoretic and visionary fear," while declaring his own conviction that this government, in all its weakness by Old World standards, was "the strongest government on earth." The American republic found its unity in an idea. It drew its strength from the energies of a free, enlightened, and virtuous society; and, unlike great monarchies, it would remain strong only as it grew in the affections of the people.

This transmutation of freedom into power, if Jefferson won the stake placed in it, would solve the riddle of the ages. It was an audacious venture in the world of Pitt and Bonaparte. It would require "courage and confidence," Jefferson told his countrymen. Bright promises scarcely glimpsed before the American Revolution were

I am confident there are few native citizens who wish to change its republican features." Dissatisfied with this flat one-dimensional statement, he worked it over with the result quoted above, one of his most famous sentences.

within their grasp. "Kindly separated by nature and a wide ocean from the exterminating havoc of one quarter of the globe; too high-minded to endure the degradations of others; possessing a chosen country, with room enough for our citizens to the hundredth and thousandth generation; entertaining a due sense of our equal right to the use of our faculties . . . ; enlightened by a benign religion . . . ; with all these blessings, what more is necessary to make us a happy and prosperous people? Still one thing more, fellow citizens—" Jefferson answered, "a wise and frugal government, which shall restrain men from injuring one another, which shall leave them otherwise free to regulate their own pursuits of industry and improvement, and shall not take from the mouth of labor the bread it has earned. This is the sum of good government, and this is necessary to close the circle of our felicities." A just government, while necessary, was only a small arc of the circle formed by the blessings of American nature, the freedom of American society, and the virtues of American character. With the government restored to first principles, the republican experiment could now be put to the test. It was a solemn and elevated moment. "We can no longer say there is nothing new under the sun," Jefferson reflected to Joseph Priestley. "For this whole chapter in the history of man is new."

After taking the oath of office the new President left the hall and returned to his lodgings, where congressmen, officers, foreign dignitaries, and prominent citizens greeted him. It was a festive time not only in Washington but in towns across the land. "Drunken frolicks is the order of the day," a New York Federalist pouted, "and more bullocks and rams are sacrificed to this newfangled deity than were formerly by the Israelitish priests." In Richmond a public pageant dramatized the theme, "Union can only be maintained by preserving Liberty." In Philadelphia a great procession wound its way from the State House to the German Reformed Church, where the assemblage heard the Declaration of Independence, "Jefferson's March," an oration, and a hymn of praise, "The People's Friend," to the new President.

> Rejoice, ye States, rejoice,
> And spread the patriot flame;
> Call'd by a Nation's voice,

To make his country's fame,
And dissipate increasing fears,
Our favorite JEFFERSON appears.

Henceforth for Republicans the 4th of March was a red-letter day, like the 4th of July.

The inaugural address rapidly made its way in the public mind. A citizens' committee in Lexington, Kentucky, reported to Jefferson: "Printers have vied with each other in printing it upon Satin, and the whole of the large sized window glass to be found in the state [has been] used to set it in frames for parlours—Teachers of schools are causing the youths under their care to commit it to memory—and your political creed is considered as a masterpiece." Republicans called it "a Magna Charta in politics." "In fact," said William B. Giles, "it contains the only American language I ever heard from the Presidential chair." Federalists—many of them—were not backward in praise. The Chief Justice, while he thought the address gave the lie to the violent party declamation that had elected Jefferson, nevertheless considered it "well judged and conciliatory." Henry Knox, Jefferson's old cabinet colleague, sent warm congratulations. If the rhetoric of concilation was followed by deeds, the enemy would quietly fold their tends. This was Jefferson's wish, and in the euphoria of the inaugural many Federalists embraced it gladly. "His public assurances . . . ," one editor confessed, "Have inspired us with a hope that *he is not the man we thought him.*—We thought him a philosophist, and have found him a virtuous and enlightened philanthropist—We thought him a Virginian, and have found him an American—We thought him a partisan and have found him a president." Benjamin Rush was astonished by the effects in Philadelphia. Old friends too long separated by party names were reunited. Some of the Doctor's Federalist acquaintances read the address again and again. "It never occurred to them 'till last week, that a Republic was a government of *more* energy than a monarchy." The inaugural address opened a new era and every eye fixed on its author.

He did not remain long in Washington after the inauguration. It had been a long siege, since the end of November; he was tired, mentally and physically, and needed a rest. Congress had adjourned.

659

No crisis threatened. The country was calm, calmer than it had been for years. The work of organizing his administration, though far from finished, went steadily forward. Nothing he did in this period jarred the "lullaby effect" of the inaugural address. Let it settle in the public mind, Jefferson reasoned, before the shock waves of reformation commenced. Meanwhile, his own domestic arrangements called for attention in Virginia as in Washington. Near the end of March he moved into the cavernous mansion on Pennsylvania Avenue and began to assemble his household. On April 1 he set out for Monticello. It was only a four-day trip now, but he had eight rivers to cross, without bridges or ferries, and the roads were so punishing he preferred the saddle or a one-horse chair to the gig or carriage. While at home he collected a parcel of books—there were few in Washington. Everything attended to, he was back at his post four weeks after he left it.

Reconciliation and Reform

"If I had a universe to choose from," Jefferson said not long after assembling his cabinet, "I could not change one of my associates to my better satisfaction." He never found occasion to revise this opinion and in retrospect considered the harmony of his official family during eight years a thing without parallel in political annals. It was, in truth, a remarkable feat, one which his own personality made possible as well as necessary.

Two of the four secretaries were indispensable to him. James Madison, the Secretary of State, was well qualified for his office, of course, but it was less in his public than in his private capacity that he made himself necessary to the President. In most important matters Jefferson would be his own Secretary of State, and no one could hold the portfolio who was not tuned in to his mind. The two Virginians acted in perfect friendship, intimacy, and trust. With Albert Gallatin, the Secretary of the Treasury, the case was somewhat different. The Pennsylvanian shared Jefferson's Republican principles and his scientific interests. He was thoroughly conversant with the perplexing politics of his own state and, through marital connection, was rapidly becoming an expert on New York.

660

He was completely loyal to his chief. These were not the qualifications that made him indispensable to the President, however. Gallatin was a financier, the only one the Republicans had; and in so far as the political reformation hung on fiscal management, as it did to no small extent, his importance to the new administration rivaled Hamilton's to the first. Were politics alone consulted, there were grave risks in the appointment of the 41-year-old congressman, whose Swiss birth, forensic prowess, and wizardry with Treasury figures had combined to make him a Federalist whipping boy. But Jefferson never considered a lesser man for the Treasury post. Rather than risk his loss to the administration by the lame-duck Senate's rejection of his nomination, he deferred formal action and in May gave Gallatin a recess appointment, afterwards confirmed by a Republican Senate.

The remaining cabinet posts, War and Navy, together with the attorney generalship, went to men of more ordinary talents. Henry Dearborn, the Secretary of War, was a physician by profession who had learned the arts of soldiering in the Revolution. Jefferson hardly knew him before the appointment, but Dearborn was reputed to be an excellent "man of business" and also the leading Republican in Maine, the appendage of Massachusetts that had the power to swing the commonwealth into the Republican column. This was a great object with Jefferson. It undoubtedly influenced the choice of Levi Lincoln for Attorney General. Lincoln, a Harvard graduate, a leader of the Massachusetts bar, a man long experienced in state politics, was new to the national scene. At 52 years of age he stood, next to the President himself, the oldest member of the official family. The attorney generalship remained a part-time office of something less than full cabinet status. Normally, Lincoln lived at home, in Worcester, where he acted as Jefferson's eyes and ears in the Bay State.

The designation of Robert Smith as Secretary of Navy, unlike the other appointments, was an act of desperation. Jefferson had first offered the post to his philosophical friend Robert R. Livingston, who occupied a pivotal position in New York politics. When he declined, becoming Minister to France instead, Jefferson turned successively to three prominent Republicans and was refused, not once but twice, by each of them. No man of stature wished to preside over the liquidation of the infant navy, which seemed decreed by the return of peace with France, the rage for economy, and Jefferson's supposed hostility. "I believe I shall have to advertise for a Secretary of the Navy," the President sighed in May. Two months later the fifth choice, Smith, accepted. A Baltimore lawyer with almost no experience in public office, Smith's principal claim to recognition was his brother, General Samuel Smith, the prominent Maryland congressman and merchant who had been Jefferson's second choice for the post and who, in fact, ran the affairs of the department until his brother came on in July. The Smiths were connected by marriage with important Virginians, Wilson Cary Nicholas, one of Jefferson's closest political friends, and Peter Carr, his beloved nephew. The circumstances of his appointment were not very flattering, but Robert Smith proved to be an able minister, popular with the navy, amiable in the cabinet, though he and Gallatin were often at loggerheads, and, like the others, loyal to his chief.

These men revolved around the President like satellites around a planet. The model of presidential unity had been set by Washington, but Jefferson dominated his administration more completely than Washington had done. There was rarely any doubt, in cabinet, in Congress, in the public mind, who was master. The importance of unity in the executive to unity in the party was generally understood, and for most Republicans the destiny, even the survival, of the American republic depended on the fortunes of the party. Jefferson, of course, had a deep aversion to dissension and controversy. By some magic of personality he inspired the same amiable temper and restraint in his colleagues. He led without having to command; he dominated without ruling. The cabinet was run like a Quaker meeting; on the rare occasions when a vote was taken, the President counted as one. Differences of opinion among his colleagues invariably yielded to unanimity in matters of policy. But this would not have happened, he once reflected, whatever the temper of his colleagues, had each acted independently. "Ill-defined limits of their respective departments, jealousies, trifling at first, but nourished and strengthened by repetition of occasions, intrigue without doors of designing persons to build an importance to themselves on the division of others, might from small beginnings, have produced persevering oppositions. But the power of decision in the President left no object for internal dissension, and external intrigue was stifled in embryo by the knowledge which incendiaries possessed, that no division they could foment would change the course of executive power." No doubt he remembered, in these observations, his quarrel with Hamilton as well as the breakdown of the Adams administration. It was the latter chapter that most impressed him. Thus he reversed the tendency toward ministerial independence that, he thought, had undermined his predecessor, and returned to Washington's practice of routing everything through the President and centering powers of decision in him. Business was dispatched, not primarily in the cabinet, which met infrequently, but in day-to-day consultation and communication with department heads. The procedures were quite informal, yet they secured the object of executive unity and responsibility because of the confidence that existed in his official family.

Although he was a very able administrator, Jefferson's leadership was not administrative in character. He did not believe, as Hamilton most assuredly did, in administration as a political engine. He was more concerned with the control than the organization of power, with responsibility than with energy, with administration as a simple tool rather than an awesome machine. Recalling the observation of Tocqueville, who epitomized his own view, "the grandeur is not in what the public administration does, but in what is done outside it or without it." He was perfectly capable of using the administrative arts, and did so with a fine hand when crisis forced him to it, but his theory of government gave little scope to them. After the initial reformation, returning the government to the original tack, "let alone" would be his watchword. "A noiseless course, not meddling in the affairs of others, unattractive to notice, is a mark that society is going on in happiness. If we can prevent the government from wasting the labors of the people, under the pretext of taking care of them, they must be happy." This was a faith in what free men could do for themselves, not in what government could do for them. It made more sense in his age than in ours.

Gallatin and Madison arrived on the scene in May, and the administration, makeshift until then, began to function as a unit. The cabinet took a fateful step on May 15. The conduct of the Barbary states had not improved since Jefferson last dealt with them. Several years past the United States had entered into treaties with all four of the pirate states. The peace purchased by tributes and presents to the tune of two million dollars only whet the appetites of the Mediterranean potentates. American commerce in the Mediterranean steadily increased—158 vessels cleared for those ports in 1801—but it was subjected to continued insult, humiliation, and blackmail. Tripoli was the main offender when Jefferson took office. The Pasha, weighing the paltry settlement Tripoli had made against the annual tribute and splendid presents given to Algiers, demanded a new and munificent treaty under the threat of war. For fifteen years Jefferson had opposed submission to the powers. It seemed obvious now, if not before, that there was no reliance on their agreements or any end to their demands. Perhaps the time had come for the United States to reply with cannon instead of gold. The navy was unemployed. Under the terms of the act fixing the peacetime establishment, signed by Adams on March 3, many of the vessels were to be sold, others laid up, and of course most of the officers discharged. Two squadrons consisting of six frigates and two schooners were to remain in service. Where could they be better employed than in the Mediterranean? It was hardly more costly to keep them there than in American waters, where they were unwanted. Jefferson had always advocated a navy to cruise against the Barbary states; and, in fact, Congress had founded the United States Navy in 1794 with this distinct purpose in mind. The Tripolitan ultimatum furnished the occasion to put an old theory to the test. Whether any European states would join in the enterprise, as he had hoped, remained to be seen; and there were limits beyond which he could not commit Congress. In the cabinet discussion, Gallatin alone seemed reluctant to proceed, holding that war would be more costly than tribute, but he supported the decision to send the first squadron under Commodore Richard Dale to protect American commerce in the Mediterranean from Tripolitan or other attacks. Dale was not authorized to start a war; on the contrary, he was instructed to soothe wounded feelings in Tripoli, as well as in Algiers and Tunis. Should war be declared, as seemed likely, he was to defend the American flag and punish the aggressor. The squadron sailed on June 1. When it arrived in the Mediterranean, Tripoli was already at war with the United States.

The rumbles from the Mediterranean barely ruffled the calm of America's foreign relations. The Atlantic storm that had engulfed the Adams administration had blown over, and the promise of peace in Europe held out the most flattering prospects. While the war continued the administration would adhere to the principles of neutral rights without, however, going to war or entering into any arrangements to secure them. "Peace is my passion," Jefferson repeatedly affirmed. Some Federalists feared, some Republicans hoped, the new administration would join the "armed neutrality" of the Northern powers. France backed the League of Armed Neutrals as a maritime weapon against Britain; indeed, Napoleon regarded the Convention of 1800, embodying the rule of free ships–free goods, in the same light. But Jefferson emphatically rejected this policy. "Determined as we are to avoid, if possible, wasting the energies of our people in war and destruction," he wrote to Thomas Paine, an advocate of the League, "we shall avoid implicating ourselves with the powers of Europe, even in support of principles which we mean to pursue." European interests were so different from the American, and so disruptive of American councils, it was better to have nothing to do with them.

One of the first acts of the administration was to suppress the embassies in Lisbon, Berlin, and The Hague—a preliminary declaration of withdrawal from Europe. Ministries were kept up with Spain, France, and Britain. Charles Pinckney went to Madrid, a reward for clinching the Republican victory of 1800. Unfortunately, his skills did not extend to diplomacy. Rufus King, the New York Federalist, was allowed to remain in London over vocal Republican opposition. Jefferson was the beneficiary of an Anglo-American rapprochement carefully nurtured by King for several years. A change of ministry at Westminster, coinciding with the Republican accession in Washington, brightened the picture even more. King was putting the finishing touches on a settlement of the old issue of Revolutionary debts. Other matters were in negotiation. The ministry opened the ports of Gibraltar, Minorca, and Malta to the American squadron in the Mediterranean. "The change of administration here," Jefferson boasted on receiving this news, "has impressed them with a necessity of treating this country with more justice and conciliation." And lest the ministry be misled by propaganda representing him as a creature of France and an enemy of Britain, he made it a point to assure Edward Thornton, the British chargé, of his friendliness and impartiality. Although Britain continued to violate America's neutral commerce, for the present this was not a fighting issue. More serious was the practice of impressment. If Britain would remove this "stumbling-block," nothing more would be wanting. As to France, the partiality Jefferson had once felt was gone. He viewed the Convention of 1800, writing terminus to the alliance of 1778, as another signpost on the road of withdrawal from European politics. The Convention had not yet been ratified in Paris, and certain matters remained to be disposed of under it. Livingston would handle these details; in fact, when he was appointed it did not appear he would have much else to do. But in May, about the time of the first cabinet meeting, rumors reached Washington of the secret Spanish cession of Louisiana to France. The prospect of Napoleonic rebirth of French empire in North America chilled the atmosphere in Washington. It was involved in so many contingencies, however, that Jefferson refused to take alarm, and instead slowly, quietly, set in motion a course of diplomacy that would end two years later in the greatest triumph of his presidency.

Nothing gave the President more trouble in these early months than the disposition of the federal offices. It took more time, caused more pain, personal and political, and made more enemies than all the other business of government. The agony was worse at the beginning but Jefferson never found any relief from it. "The transaction of the great interests of our country costs us little trouble or difficulty," he remarked in 1804. "But the task of appointment is a heavy one indeed. He on whom it falls may envy the lot of a Sisyphus or Ixion. . . . Yet, like the office of hangman it must be executed by someone." What made the office so irksome was Jefferson's effort to strike a balance between the twin principles of reconciliation and reformation enunciated in his inaugural address. Had he clung to one or the other, had he either acquiesced in the Federalist monopoly of the offices or thrown them out in favor of the Republican faithful, his problem would have been much simpler; but his politics made either solution quite impossible. So he rode the horns of the dilemma, now leaning to one side, now to the other, and though the dexterity of his performance was admirable, it failed to satisfy either his friends or his enemies.

Jefferson had been struggling with the problem since December, when the applications of office-seekers began to litter his desk. By the time of the inauguration he had set the guidelines. His object, clearly, was to make as few removals as possible in order to consolidate the mass of Federalists to his administration. "If we can hit on the true line of conduct which may conciliate the honest part of those who were called Federalists," he said, "I shall hope to be able to obliterate, or rather to unite the names Federalists and Republicans." He was repelled by the principle, already reduced to practice in Pennsylvania and New York, of making party affiliation the sole, or even the primary, test of service. The politics of spoils and proscription degraded republican government. Nothing more should be asked of civil servants than that they be honest, able, and loyal to the Constitution. As important as the principle might be considered abstractly, it was far more important practically from its obvious fitness to Jefferson's political strategy. Partisan removals would revolt converts from Federalism, ensure a following to the leaders of that exploded faction, invite foreign intrigue together with the dissensions of European politics, and thus defeat the great goal of "a perfect consolidation" on the "ancient Whig principles" of 1776.

Hearing this line, many Republicans were apprehensive. The Federalists were incorrigible, they said; any temporizing with them would only disgust the Republicans and subvert the administration. It was incumbent on the President "to clear the Augean stables." "A pretty general purgation of offices has been one of the benefits expected by the friends of the new order of things . . . ," William B. Giles candidly advised. "It can never be unpopular to turn out a vicious one and put a virtuous one in his room; and I am persuaded from the prevalence of the vicious principles of the late administration, and the universal loyalty of its adherents in office, it would be hardly possible to err in exclusions." A New York editor put the matter bluntly: "If this," a clean sweep of the offices, "should not be the case, for what, in the name of God, have we been contending." The idea of uniting the parties was a delusion, others warned. Principles of light and darkness, of democracy and royalty, could not be united or compromised; and the Republicans could not be satisfied unless the revolution of principle made itself manifest in a revolution of men throughout the federal establishment. Still others elevated partisan interest to a democratic theory of office. *"Rotation in office,"* a press columnist wrote, "is the essence of Republicanism by keeping the people on a level, disposing them to pursuits of industry, instead of making a trade of the public service, diffusing a knowledge of office more generally among the citizens . . . ; keeping awake and in action the power and energy of so many minds leads to improvement in system, fidelity in practice, general habits of vigilance among the people, with so many political advantages to society." Jefferson could not ignore these partisan pleadings. They had realism, perhaps even democracy, in their favor. But he held his ground.

The policy worked out in March limited removals to two classes of officeholders. First, Adams's "midnight appointments" and, on second thought, all executive appointments (except judges in good behavior) made after December 12, the day Adams knew he had been defeated. On March 3 the Senate was in session late into the night confirming a last batch of nominations, and Adams spent his final hours in the executive chair hurriedly signing nocturnal commissions. The indecency of the proceeding capped two crowded months of Federalist office-packing. What was this for unless to stack the cards against the new regime? Jefferson considered appointments in this category "nullities," therefore not chargeable as removals. The second class, officers guilty of negligence or misconduct, were the only proper subjects of removal. Here Jefferson especially had in mind federal marshals and district attorneys who had forfeited the public trust by their enforcement of the Sedition Act, the former packing juries, the latter prosecuting their fellow citizens with the bitterness of party. "The courts being so decidedly federal and irremovable," Jefferson said, "it is believed that Republican attorneys and marshals being the doors of entrance into the courts, are indispensably necessary as a shield to the Republican part of our fellow citizens." Other grounds for misconduct removal were electioneering, official favoritism, and delinquency or defalcation in accounts. A list drawn up by Jefferson in January 1802 counted twenty-one "midnight appointments," considered null and void, and fifteen removals for misconduct of any kind.

Jefferson bound himself by these rules only so long and so far as they furthered the political consensus he had in view. By making few removals, on the fairest grounds, he hoped to disarm the opposition, prove his political tolerance, and show that principle, not spoils, was the Republican cause. This required unusual patience from his followers while the stake was won. Death and resignation would open some places, careful spotting of delinquent officers would open others; inevitably, however, under a self-denying ordinance against partisan removals, the Republicans would be slow to realize their just claims to participation in the patronage of the federal government. If the policy failed to impress the administration's enemies and only succeeded in alienating its friends, Jefferson was quite prepared to make the necessary adjustments. When the subject came up for review in May, he decided that the case of New York, in particular, called for special treatment.

Every state was a case unto itself. It was the peculiarity of the Republican organization in New York to be split into three factions, each the bailiwick of a notable family or personage: the Clintons, the Livingstons, and Aaron Burr. At the outset Jefferson deferred to the Vice President in patronage matters. Burr submitted a slate of candidates endorsed by the New York congressional delegation. John Swartwout, a Burrite, was promptly named federal marshal and Edward Livingston, not on the slate but half a Burrite himself, became district attorney. The Livingstons held an enviable position, courted by both Clintonians and Burrites, and no one could be certain which way the clan's loyalties would gravitate. Jefferson did not understand the struggle for power then going on in New York, and he wanted as little to do with it as possible; but it soon became apparent to him that the Clintonians, who controlled the state's party machinery, would not tolerate Burr's rivalry. Fresh reports of Burr's intrigues in the electoral contest just passed reached Jefferson's ear. For reasons of policy he had deferred action on the three main recommendations made by Burr and the New York delegation, and now, in May, heeding the remonstrances of men in the Clinton interest, he wrote to the old patriarch, Governor George Clinton, asking his advice. A second channel, hostile to the Burr connection, was thus opened up between Washington and Albany, where De-Witt Clinton, the Governor's brilliant nephew, rapidly became the leading voice. Clinton controlled the Council of Appointment, and with that marvelous patronage machine was not only purging the Federalists from state offices but also securing his own domination. With the spoils of a great state in his hands, Clinton need not be greedy for federal patronage; Burr, on the other hand, had no other place to go. Jefferson shied away from the disgraceful "spirit of persecution" in New York, but he was reconciled to further appointments and removals in the state in order to mollify the warring factions, neither of which he thought very respectable. "We shall yield a little to their pressure," he said, "but no more than appears absolutely necessary to keep them together. And if that would be as much as to disgust other parts of the union, we must prefer the greater to the lesser part."

As it turned out, Jefferson's efforts to close the breach only helped to widen it. In July he appointed one of Burr's candidates, David Gelston, collector of the New York customhouse, but passed over the other two. Instead, a Clintonian was named supervisor and the incumbent naval officer, a reputed Tory named Rogers, was allowed to remain in his post. It had been slated by Burr for Matthew L. Davis, his young friend and political lieutenant who had helped engineer the Republican victory of 1800 in New York City. Burr repeatedly urged Davis's appointment. As the months passed and nothing materialized it came to be seen as the decisive test of Jefferson's political allegiance in New York. It was all very embarrassing to Davis, as well as to Burr, for they had counted on this lucrative office and every politician in New York knew it. In September, armed with letters, Davis pursued the President all the way to Monticello to plead his case. One of the letters was from Gallatin, whom Davis had stopped to see in Washington. If Rogers should be removed Gallatin knew no better man for the office than Davis, but he was revolted by the administration dirtying its hands in the spoils of New York. Dissatisfied with this, Gallatin hastily penned a second letter in which he carefully pointed out the implications of the Davis affair for Jefferson and his administration. After all that had been said on the subject, the rejection of Davis would be a deliberate affront to Burr and he, surely, would take it as "a declaration of war." Davis met with a cool reception at Monticello. Jefferson's doubts about his qualifications had centered on the question of "respectability," doubts not in the least overcome by the unheralded visit of this brash and importunate young man. He told him nothing had been decided, and Davis returned to New York empty-handed. In fact the decision was as plain as day. Jefferson made it quite aware of the political dynamite Matt Davis packed on his shoulders. He was not the cause of the explosion in New York Republicanism, as William Duane held, but he was, in a manner of speaking, the fuse. The explosion was still several months away. Jefferson had hoped by the discriminate use of patronage to avert it. Instead, he was forced to choose between Burrites and Clintonians. His increasing suspicions of the Vice President, carefully cultivated by the Clinton interest, together with a realistic appraisal of the political forces in New York, made that choice inevitable.

The problem of too many Republicans, rivals among themselves, such as Jefferson found in New York, had its counterpart in the problem of Republican poverty and weakness, which was the case in Connecticut. There the Republicans were few, outcasts of society, and systematically excluded from the state government. In this "land of steady habits," politics and religion worked hand in hand— "preachers were politicians, and politicians preachers." Republicans hovered in the shadows of Jacobinism and infidelity, while the Federalist elite stood secure behind massive barricades of law and opinion. Jefferson's election brought no change in the system of persecution and proscription; if anything, it only aroused the Federalist oligarchs to greater exertions. Not only was conciliation producing no converts in Connecticut, it was dimming the faint hopes of the beleaguered band of Republicans. "They are all mortified," the leadership protested, "to see their enemies triumphing in a day when they expected triumph and to be daily insulted and abused as not having merited the confidence of the administration, whose advocates they have been." In most of the states the Republican organization was secure, buttressed by opinion, lavishly furnished with offices. In Connecticut the cause would be lost without the aid of federal patronage. And yet it was a dangerous experiment to force Republicans into offices against the decided will of the community. The issue came to a head on the President's nomination of a Republican for the collectorship at New Haven, currently filled by a "nullity" of Adams's appointment.

Wishing not to ruffle the sensibilities of the state any more than necessary, Jefferson emphasized the importance of finding a Republican of some standing in society for this important post. The unanimous recommendation of the party leadership was Samuel Bishop, mayor of New Haven, chief judge of the county court, a deacon of the Congregational Church, and a firm Republican. In May, Bishop was appointed. At once a "hideous brawling" went up from the Federalists. On June 18 a large group of merchants, who claimed to own seven-eighths of the shipping in New Haven, drew up a remonstrance against the appointment. Elizur Goodrich, the Federalist congressman Adams had named to the post, suited the merchants exactly; Samuel Bishop, on the other hand, was a man of 77 years, so infirm he could hardly write his own name, ignorant of accounting and all things commercial, and entirely unsuitable. To be sure, he held certain offices from the legislature, but on commissions granted long ago and continued out of charity. Moreover, the merchants said, he had been recommended to the President in order to gratify the son, Abraham Bishop, to whom the work of the office would fall, unhappily with no better results. Young Bishop was a strutting democrat. He had earned the hatred of Connecticut Federalists by two orations, one on political delusion delivered at Yale College, of all places, and widely circulated in the election of 1800, the other, which contained an extended parallel between Thomas Jefferson and Jesus Christ, spouted at a Republican victory celebration. The burden of the remonstrance was clear: the President had been "taken in" by the Republican rabble of Connecticut.

Jefferson grew warm on this matter even before the remonstrance reached his desk. He read the reports from the state, the pitiful appeals of the Republicans, the unyielding hostility of the Federalists. On his return to Worcester, Levi Lincoln, the President's chief liaison with the New England Republicans, had endeavored to interpret the administration's conciliatory policy. Everywhere removals were the topic of conversation, he informed Jefferson; "vague reports and individual clamors had clothed the subject with many false circumstances," but on the whole the picture was bright. Connecticut offered the main exception. There the opinion was decidedly and unanimously for removals at full blast. It would be necessary for the administration to go along, though gradually, one blast at a time, so as not to revive the sinking Federalists. While still optimistic about his policy, Jefferson saw the need for flexibility to meet the circumstances of particular states. "In Connecticut alone a general sweep seems to be called for on the principles of justice and policy," he wrote in June. Ecclesiastical dominance made Connecticut a desperate case—she would "follow the bark of liberty only by the help of a tow-rope." When the New Haven remonstrance arrived, he seized the occasion for a public statement of the policy that, until now, had floated on the airy rhetoric of the inaugural address.

Jefferson's reply to the New Haven merchants began with a careful defense of the controversial appointment, then inquired whether his call for the restoration of harmony and affection could be fairly construed, as the Federalists had done, into assurances against removals from office. When all the facts were considered— the monopoly under the late administration and its defeat at the polls—was it to be imagined that the old establishment was to be left undisturbed? "Is it *political intolerance* to claim a proportionate share in the direction of the public affairs? Can they [the Federalists] not *harmonize* in society unless they have everything in their own hands? If the will of the nation . . . calls for an administration of government according with the opinions of those elected; if, for the fulfillment of that will, displacements are necessary, with whom can they so justly begin as with persons appointed in the last moments of an administration, not for its own time, but to begin a career at the same time with their successors. . . . If a due participation of office is a matter or right, how are vacancies to be obtained? Those by death are few; by resignation, none. Can any other mode than that of removal be proposed?" Heretofore the answer to the last question had been yes, the mode of patience and conversion, of making friends by extinguishing enmities. Heretofore the argument that tenure in subordinate offices should rotate with the popular will had been rejected. Heretofore political opinion and party allegiance in themselves had been inadmissible grounds of removal. By suggesting that the Republicans should receive a "proportionate share" of the offices, Jefferson, without quite realizing it, altered the terms of the original policy. "I lament sincerely that unessential differences of opinion should ever have been deemed sufficient to interdict half the society from the rights and blessings of self-government, to proscribe them as unworthy of every trust." Had the case been different he would have resigned himself to time and accident to right the injustice to the Republicans. "But their total exclusion calls for prompter corrections. I shall correct the procedure; but that done," he concluded, "return with joy to that state of things when the only questions concerning a candidate shall be, Is he honest? Is he capable? Is he faithful to the Constitution?"

The answer to New Haven, whatever its intention, dispelled the warm afterglow of the inaugural. Federalist irreconcilers dipped their pens in vinegar and gall to accuse the President of the vilest hypocrisy. "Is this the language of the mild, the philosophic, the wise, the patriotic and conciliatory Jefferson?" they asked. No, it was the language of Jacobinical bigotry and extermination. Republicans hailed the letter for its liberality, candor, and timely correction of sophistical reasonings drawn from the magnanimous clauses of the inaugural address. On the whole the reception pleased Jefferson. The answer to the New Haven merchants was really meant for the Republicans, he said, especially those who were beginning to think that conciliation had wiped out the hopes of reformation. "Appearances of schismatizing from us have been entirely done away." Unfortunately, however, escaping Scylla there was danger from Charybdis. The letter gave more expectation to the "Sweeping Republicans" than he thought the terms justified. This was especially true in Philadelphia where, in contrast to New York, the political nerve center of the federal establishment, the customhouse, remained a Federalist monopoly. His fears that the reply would check the current of "republican federalists" toward the administration were not borne out. Do not be alarmed by the newspaper barrage, Lincoln wrote. "Be assured it is contemptible, and kept alive by a few lying scribblers." The spirit of accommodation was still abroad in New England, he continued with more optimism than the case warranted, and nothing like a general retreat was in order. Jefferson seemed to agree. To heal the wounds of partisanship, restore harmony, rally all shades of Federalists except the monarchical, and thereby make the nation one: this was the real business of the administration. "I am satisfied it can be done," he told Governor McKean, "and I own that the day which should convince me of the contrary would be the bitterest in my life." Expressions of this kind suggest that Jefferson had not accurately calculated the impact of his own words, which plainly set patronage policy on a new course. If the inaugural address was in some sense a converting ordinance for the Federalists, the answer to New Haven was a covenant to secure the Jeffersonian church with the elect of Republicanism.

The conflict between the ideal of reconciliation and the realities of partisanship was never resolved, but as a political matter Jefferson increasingly faced up to the unpleasant responsibilities party government forced upon him. Just after the answer to New Haven, Gallatin forwarded for the President's approval a circular he proposed to issue to the collectors of customs. They would be instructed to award the subordinate offices in their gift wholly on the basis of merit and to abstain from electioneering or political activity of any kind. Jefferson approved the principle but thought the circular should be deferred until the Republicans achieved an equality in the federal offices. (Actually, at that time the restraints would have worked primarily on Federalists, not Republicans. Three years later, after the customhouses had been renovated, Jefferson told Gallatin the Republican officers were "meddling too much with the public elections" and asked that it be stopped. Recalling his proposal in 1801, Gallatin said the circumstances were now so different it would be "very delicate" to decree a political interdict, and he did not.) In the early months Jefferson had not been averse to appointing Federalists to office and did so in New England, much to the consternation of eager Republicans. In August, however, he urged his colleagues to be "inflexible against appointing Federalists." It was more important to satisfy the Republican faithful than to make Federalist converts.

Jefferson's public conscience led him to assign removals to almost any cause other than the political one of opening places for Republicans. He repeatedly drew up lists of removals catalogued under as many as nine headings according to the grounds of decision. While the lists testify to his uneasiness, and are accurate in the main, they are not an adequate record of his motivations in the disposition of patronage. What number of officeholders were removed for political reasons alone, it is impossible to say, but they were probably not many at any time. In 1803, after two years, Jefferson listed only fourteen in this category. Double the figure and it is still a small percentage of the roughly 330 significant civil offices, of which about one-half changed hands during Jefferson's first term. The Federalists, of course, had their own system of bookkeeping which charged every transaction to political persecution. Instead of acknowledging the moderation of his policy, as Jefferson remarked a year after the New Haven remonstrance, these zealots made it the ground for more strenuous opposition; and so he went on, rewarding his friends, punishing his enemies, when he had every wish to stop.

While Jefferson often yielded to Republican patronage demands, he was also capable of monumental efforts to protect his design for political unity. Many cases might be cited. In New York, for example, he withstood for eight years the combined pressure of Republican politicians and merchants to keep in office the Federalist collector of the port of Hudson. But the case of Allan McLane, collector at Wilmington, Delaware, best illustrates the point. In Jefferson's report of the first cabinet discussion of removals, McLane enjoyed the distinction of being the only Federalist officeholder explicitly confirmed in his post. Perhaps this was because his name had figured in the February negotiations between Samuel Smith and James A. Bayard, for the latter has sought assurances of McLane's tenure in office and Smith had mentioned it to Jefferson. If so—and Bayard later testified it was so—the explanation fails to account for the removal of the other officeholder for whom Bayard had sought the same assurances, nor can it fairly account for Jefferson's extraordinary adherence to McLane. McLane had served his country long and ably during the Revolution, always a plus in Jefferson's book; he was well regarded by the Treasury Department and by the merchants along the Brandywine; even more important, Jefferson apparently decided to make him an example of principle, and he clung to it like the rock of salvation when the surrounding political terrain shook beneath him. The Delaware Republicans, still a minority party, panted for McLane's prestigious office. Young Caesar A. Rodney, their leader and a brilliant lawyer, whom the President liked at once, presented the case against McLane: he was unpopular; he had worked for Adams in 1800; he had used his office for personal advantage. The latter charge traced back to 1799, when Secretary of Treasury Wolcott investigated and acquitted the collector. The administration now conducted its own inquiry, with the same result.

The matter slept for a time, but the following spring Washington was again bombarded with demands for McLane's removal. Addresses came from Wilmington, in New Castle County, where the Republicans were strong, as well as from the heavily Federalist county of Kent. (The third and smallest county, Sussex, was also Federalist.) No man was more obnoxoius to the party than McLane, wrote Governor David Hall, the first Republican victor in the state. Rodney voiced the same opinion, though with obvious distaste. Conceding that the authors of the attack on the collector fixed their hungry gaze on the spoils of office rather than the good of the country, admitting the justice of McLane's acquittal, Rodney nevertheless felt that the current for removal could not be resisted without imperiling the Republican cause. "The county of Kent, and particularly the leading men will be paralyzed, unless their remonstrances succeed," he warned. Rodney was then preparing for the state-wide congressional contest in which he had agreed, at Jefferson's urgent solicitation, to take on the Federalist champion, Bayard. Without a respectable showing in Kent, Rodney could not hope to win. He painted a bleak picture of Federalist hegemony. The people needed a clear sign that power had changed hands nationally and Delaware was out of step. The sacrifice of McLane would be such a sign. "The consequences will be wonderful," Rodney said. To these pleadings Jefferson answered he could do nothing unless furnished with substantial evidence pointing to McLane's misconduct. He had at this time, July 1802, just learned of the life appointment of Napoleon as First Consul of France. This melancholy event, the latest of a series blasting republican hopes in Europe, may help to explain the elevated tone of his reply to Hall. "Nor are we," he said, "acting for ourselves alone, but for the whole human race. . . . The leaders of Federalism say that man cannot be trusted with his own government. We must do no act which shall replace them in the direction of the experiment. We must not by any departure from principle, disgust the mass of our fellow citizens who have confided in us this interesting cause." After Hall and Rodney conferred with Jefferson in Washington, he seemed satisfied they would acquiesce so long as McLane abstained from politics.

McLane, meanwhile, was active in his own defense. He had a good friend in John Steele, the moderate Federalist Gallatin had retained as Auditor. Through Steele, principally, the Collector's version of the plot to remove him reached the President. McLane blamed his persecution on personal enmity, political jobbery, and commercial ambition. The last was represented by the city of New Castle, which had been outstripped by Wilmington in the trade of Delaware Bay and had sought, unsuccessfully, to be made a port of entry of the United States. McLane had opposed New Castle's pretensions, a service to Wilmington that earned him the gratitude of its merchants whether Federalist or Republican. But jobbery was the main consideration, McLane thought. If the struggling Republicans in the lower counties succeeded there would be "an Inspector for every Creek." "Here lays the whole matter," he told Gallatin, "the Collector . . . provides for a Deputy, a temporary Surveyor at New Castle, a temporary Surveyor at Lewis Town, an Inspector at Wilmington, a weigh master, a quaser measurer, etc."

Calls for McLane's scalp again went up after the October election. Rodney barely won his contest, but the loss of Kent ensured a continued Federalist majority in the legislature with the probability that Bayard, whom the President had ticketed for oblivion, would be named to the Senate. Rodney charged the defeat to the non-removal of McLane. Fortunately, the problem might soon solve itself, for McLane was quietly talking of retirement. He had concluded his enemies would not rest until the President was forced to remove him, and rather than suffer this disgrace, he asked Steele to seek the administration's indulgence until the coming spring when he would be able to close his books. Jefferson grabbed at the proposal, interpreted McLane's letter as a letter of resignation, and conferred with Rodney on a successor. This was more than McLane had bargained for; at least, so he contended in December when he went to Washington and had a long talk with the President. All he had meant to say, he now told Jefferson, was that *if* his removal was decreed he would like the privilege of resigning. So Jefferson, as unyielding as

678

ever on the principle of the case, was still on the hook with the Delaware Republicans. Out of his loyalty to the President, Rodney tried to pacify them. It was a hopeless task. In 1804, by suffering McLane, Jefferson sacrificed the expectations of the Delaware Republicans together with his own hopes for a clean sweep of the electoral vote. Still he stood firm. And the Federalist collector, who never recanted his political opinions, was still in office when Jefferson left the presidency. Several factors accounted for the prolonged resistance: McLane's Revolutionary services, his powerful connections, especially among Brandywine merchants and manufacturers, the inability of the Delaware Republicans to unite on a candidate whose claims were too impressive to be ignored, and, most of all, the mantle of principle Jefferson had draped over Allan McLane.

As the case suggests, the problem of turning out Federalists was often complicated by the problem of finding suitable successors among the Republicans. Candidates were plentiful enough. Jefferson likened his predicament to that of a man with "one loaf and ten wanting bread." American society was still simple, not poor but far from rich, and the careers open to modest talent were few. The offices in the President's gift held the promise of status and influence, if not of great wealth, and hordes of men sought them. Finding the right candidate was never easy, however. The Republicans, east of the Hudson especially, lacked the high proportion of educated talent of their opponents. Jefferson's standards were high, and every appointment had political ramifications at some level, local, state, or national. Sometimes it seemed better to tolerate a Federalist holdover than by the choice of a successor to alienate a portion of Republicans. Jefferson spent countless hours sifting and weighing the qualifications of candidates. He sought the advice of state and congressional leaders, of course; and since the bulk of federal patronage lay in Gallatin's jurisdiction, he became the principal channel of influence to the President. Gallatin's counsel generally worked for moderation, but he had learned the political trade in Pennsylvania, a tough school, and was less squeamish than his chief in plying it.

For posts in the upper branches of the civil service, Jefferson actively sought men who measured up to his standards of education and respectability. He believed in a "natural aristocracy," which he considered perfectly compatible with republican government and indeed essential to its virtuous leadership. It was part of the conceit of Federalism that these materials did not exist in the Jeffersonian following. The Federalist base had been narrow, overweighed with eastern men of wealth and station who, in too many instances, were blood or affinal relations. Jefferson broadened the base, taking into the official elite more westerners, more men of talents without privileges of birth, and more of respectability without high social status. In marked contrast to his predecessor, he avoided appointments that smacked of nepotism and, leaving out the Livingstons, clannish preferments. As a result, Jefferson made the higher civil service significantly more representative of American society; and despite his elitist idea of the public service, which became an anachronism in the age of democracy, he nevertheless commenced the line of development usually supposed to have begun with Andrew Jackson a generation later.

It is equally true that Jefferson, not Jackson, introduced the partisan standard of removals in the federal government. This came about, however, only because the Federalist had adhered to a partisan standard of appointments, and they, as Jefferson saw it, violently rejected the hand of conciliation held out to them in 1801. When conciliation failed, Jefferson moved toward partisanship, yet never quite reached it. He was always too partisan for infatuated Federalists, never partisan enough for his more zealous followers. Taking the whole country and all the offices into view, his course was both gradual and moderate, slower and softer in the South, faster and harder in the northern states, though exceedingly flexible at all times. In New Jersey only five of 256 party "activists" received appointment to federal posts under Jefferson; the state posts, on the other hand, were manned by these people. In New York the impact of federal patronage was also slight. During his first term alone Jefferson gave appointment to forty New Yorkers, twelve of them to posts abroad; during both terms he removed only eight Federalists, for varying reasons, and in 1809 one-third of the appointees of Washington and Adams remained in office. In Massachusetts no collector was removed in the first year of the administration; five were ousted the next year, all in Essex County, where a strong cadre of Republicans successfully challenged the notorious Essex Junto. In

Boston, where conciliation made steady progress, the old collector, Benjamin Lincoln, enjoyed the rewards of his office almost to the end of Jefferson's presidency. In Massachusetts and New England generally, resistance to the embargo in 1808 probably produced more removals than in all the preceding years. Moderation, gradualism, flexibility: these points of Jefferson's policy cannot be too much emphasized. Because of them he found no rest from problems of removal and appointment, nor from any of the related problems of federal patronage, during eight long years.

President, Congress, and Court

Jefferson was still optimistic about the future of the political *détente* when he went to Monticello at the end of July 1801. While there the newspaper assault triggered by his answer to New Haven gave him something to think about. The attack on the removals policy rapidly slid into an attack on his personal character. Winthrop Sargent, for example, published a vindictive pamphlet in Boston, *Political Intolerance*, which accused the President of lying duplicity in the manner of forcing him out of the governorship of the Mississippi Territory. A Philadelphia gazette accused the President of "killing" John Wilkes Kittera, federal attorney for the eastern district of Pennsylvania, whose sudden death, it was said, had been brought on by insupportable grief over his removal. The Federalists raised a terrible commotion when they learned by way of Paris that Jefferson had invited Thomas Paine to return to the shores of liberty in an American warship. "What! Invite to the United States that lying, drunken, brutal infidel, who rejoiced in the opportunity of basking and wallowing in the confusion, devastation, bloodshed, rapine, and murder in which his soul delights?" Jefferson still honored Paine—the Paine of *Common Sense* and *The Rights of Man*— and wished the adopted country he had nurtured in liberty also to honor him; but many Americans detested the old revolutionary whose scoffing attack on Christianity, *The Age of Reason*, had made him in their eyes the arch apostle of infidelity. Jefferson must have realized that his patronage of Paine might inflame the embers of religious and political bigotry. Yet he risked the venture, relying on sentiments of national gratitude and the country's return to the sanity of former times to sustain him. But this virtuous act proved to be a political blunder. The darts Federalists flung at Paine were really meant for Jefferson who, they said, threw "the weight of presidential influence . . . into the scale of infidelity and vice." More than a year passed before Paine returned to the United States; the issue subsided in the interim, but Federalist editors manufactured others to feed the engines of alarm. They blamed a student riot at the College of William and Mary on "the Jeffersonian system of religion," and held him responsible for the vogue of William Godwin's rationalistic works, which he had allegedly imported to corrupt the nation's youth. They accused him of slavishly submitting to French demands for a million-dollar loan—a pure invention. They spread the rumor that he had ordered the removal of federal arms from the Springfield arsenal, in Massachusetts, to the southward. Thus the irrational fears Jefferson had hoped to allay were kept alive. And despite his efforts to create a national image, he still appeared in the Federalist prints "a caricature, a creature of imagination, a mere image of party, dressed up and exhibited for an electioneering fright."

There were cannon to the left of him as well. Among Republican ideologues who formed a cult around the "doctrines of '98," the patronage issue, which rank politicians viewed simply as a matter of spoils, involved the much greater question of whether the administration moved in the direction of consensus or reform. They were alarmed by the temporizing tone of the inaugural address. A magnanimous gesture was one thing, conciliation on the level of policy quite another. And they feared that Jefferson, in a mistaken quest for unity and calm, would let pass the glorious opportunity of returning the government to true Republican principles. The task called for aggressive assault on the Treasury establishment, reform of the judiciary, reduction of the powers of the "monarchical" executive and the "aristocratic" Senate, restriction of the treaty power, firmer lines of demarcation between the national and the state governments, and so on. Virginia was the center of this Republican unrest. Governor James Monroe was perhaps its principal spokesman to the President, though he heard these rumblings of discontent from other quarters as well. His old friend Edmund Pendleton wrote the platform of the Virginia militants in a tract, *The Danger Not Over*, published in October. Republicanism had triumphed but it would be folly to rely on the purity of its leaders for security. The true principles of the government ought to be fixed beyond reversal or contradiction, and Pendleton proposed a series of eight amendments to the Constitution to complete the work. Jefferson, while sympathetic to these pleas, hoped to contain reform within the limits of a growing national consensus. He was more attentive to the voices of prudence, especially to Madison and Gallatin, who had a different conception of the "revolution of 1800." This incipient division of opinion within the Republican ranks caused no immediate difficulty for the administration; but the seeds of a dangerous schism were already planted.

Jefferson found a useful diversion from politics at Monticello that summer. He had learned of the work of Dr. Benjamin Waterhouse, of Boston, in employing the cowpox virus as an inoculation against smallpox. Waterhouse had introduced the epic-making discovery of Edward Jenner into American medical practice. In December he had sent to Jefferson an account of his experiment. Impressed, deeply interested, the new President actively enlisted in this public health cause, and by his own patronage greatly contributed to its progress in the United States. Waterhouse badly needed such an ally to combat professional inertia and public fears. Early trials of the vaccine, in other hands than his, often failed, hence increasing the prejudice against it. Such was the result of the first two supplies sent to Jefferson in June and administered by an able physician in Washington. The vaccine had lost its potency in transit, probably because of exposure to heat, Jefferson thought; and so he made the ingenious suggestion of shipping the vial in a water filled container. In August Waterhouse sent two fresh supplies to Monticello, one that had come from Jenner in England, the other taken from his own patients. Jefferson now proceeded, with the assistance of a local physician, to vaccinate his plantation family. By the time he returned to Washington about 200 persons, including some of the neighbors, had been vaccinated with excellent results. Waterhouse was delighted.

Methodical in his conduct of the experiment, Jefferson paid particular attention to the rule laid down by Waterhouse to withdraw the live virus from the pustule exactly eight days after vaccination, thereby keeping up a constant supply of vaccine. So successful was Jefferson in this part of the undertaking that he was able to supply pioneer vaccinators in Washington, Richmond, Philadelphia, and elsewhere, and to introduce this gift of the Great Spirit among the Indians. The results were encouraging, but always a skeptic in medical matters, he preferred to await the evidence, and partly for this reason declined to permit his name to be used as an endorsement of vaccination. Waterhouse, however, sent one of Jefferson's letters to a medical friend in London, whence it appeared in an English treatise and immediately in another published in Philadelphia. He thus became publicly identified with the movement that promised to wipe out one of the ancient scourges of mankind. By 1806, when he penned a noble tribute to Jenner, he was convinced the vaccine would, in fact, fulfill its promise. "Medicine has never before produced any single improvement of such utility," he said with characteristic emphasis. "Harvey's discovery of the circulation of the blood was a beautiful addition to the knowledge of the animal economy. But on a review of the practice of medicine before and since that epoch, I do not see any great amelioration which has been derived from that discovery. You," he lauded Jenner, "have erased from the calendar of human afflictions one of its greatest. Yours is the comfortable reflection that mankind can never forget you have lived. Future nations will know by history only that the loathsome smallpox has existed and by you has been extinguished."

In 1806, or even in 1801, Jefferson would gladly have traded for such a fame any of the accolades reserved to statesmen. At Monticello, the "Summer White House," his principal business was to prepare an agenda for the Seventh Congress. Madison came over from Orange, and Jefferson regularly communicated with the other secretaries. Actually, the preparations had been going on since March. The secretaries had canvassed their departments, written reports, and made recommendations, all keyed to a reformation of government along moderate lines. Gradually the pieces fell into place and Jefferson drew up the critical statement of policy that became, on December 8, his first annual message to Congress.

Unlike the "state of the union" messages of his predecessors, Jefferson's was communicated in writing and read by a clerk. The customary practice smacked of the monarch's speech from the throne, in his opinion, and the tedious formalities of an answer embarrassed both Congress and President. Doing away with it was a simple republican gesture Jefferson all the more willingly made because of his aversion to public address; but the innovation endured through a score of presidents who did not feel this aversion and long after monarchical forms and ceremonies ceased to be an issue.

The message itself seemed as self-effacing as the method of its presentation. Those who expected bold utterance and bold reforms pitched to the strains of partisan warfare were disappointed. The message was tame. Jefferson began by felicitating the Congress on the long-awaited return of peace in Europe, alluded to the spirit of friendship among the Indians, then discussed the Tripolitan war as the one exception to this "state of general peace," and finally, announced the happy result of the census of 1800. A population in excess of five million, doubling itself every 22 years, suggested the almost unlimited possibilities of the species in the free American environment. Government could make but a small addition to the spontaneous energies of a free society. "Agriculture, manufactures, commerce, and navigation, the four pillars of our prosperity, are the most thriving when left most free to individual enterprise." Protection from "casual embarrassments" might sometimes justify departures from this rule, as in the instance of the carrying trade, the only one of the four pillars recommended to the care of Congress. The thrust of the message ran toward *laissez faire* and simple government, in accordance with the doctrines of the inaugural address. "When we consider," he said, "that this government is charged with the external and mutual relations only of these states; that the states themselves have principal care of our persons, our property, and our reputation, constituting the great field of human concerns, we may well doubt whether our organization is not too complicated, too expensive; whether offices and officers have not been multiplied unnecessarily, and sometime injuriously to the service they were meant to promote."

The President made no specific recommendations in this matter, nor indeed, with the exception of the judiciary, did he propose to dismantle any of the machinery of government the Federalists had built. "Some things," he remarked privately, "may perhaps be left undone from motives of compromise for a time, and not to alarm by too sudden a reformation, but with a view to be resumed at another time." The judiciary was another matter, especially the new circuit courts created by act of Congress in February. He had at once slated this act for repeal and now, in December, hinted the object to Congress. He also requested repeal of the law of 1798 fixing a residence of fourteen years for naturalization. "Shall oppressed humanity find no asylum on this globe?" he asked. As for the Sedition Law, the first draft of the message had included a paragraph developing the theory of the equal right of each of the three branches of government to decide questions of constitutionality for itself. The hated law expired upon Jefferson's entry into office, so he could not negate it by his own decision; but he promptly pardoned the unfortunate Republicans still suffering its penalties and dropped the prosecution of William Duane still pending under a resolution of the Senate. The latter action, particularly, was branded unconstitutional in the Federalist prints. In his own defense, and in defense of the principle enunciated in the Virginia and Kentucky Resolutions, Jefferson had thought to make a straightforward declaration of his opinion holding the Sedition Act "in palpable and unqualified contradiction to the Constitution, considering it then as a nullity." However, prodded by Gallatin, Smith, and probably Madison, Jefferson eliminated the entire paragraph "as capable of being chicaned, and furnishing something to the opposition to make a handle of." His silence implied a reluctance, in his official station, to broach doctrines sure to be controverted and to defend executive actions of doubtful constitutionality, as he knew the *nolle* entry in the Duane case to be. The message throughout was elaborately deferential to Congress. Jefferson and his party rose to power preaching the Whiggish doctrine of legislative supremacy against the allegedly monarchical tendencies of the Federalist administrations. To reduce executive influence and return the direction of the government to the legislative branch was a logical first step in the Republican reformation. Jefferson honored the theory, renouncing powers and begging legislative restraints; at the same time, however, he devised a subtle language of indirection with Congress, in which recommendations were suggestions and demands were veiled in obscurity. His actions with respect to the Sedition Law ill comported with the Whig theory, so silence seemed best.

So far as the message aimed at a reformation of the federal establishment, it was bottomed on fiscal policy. In the Jeffersonian scripture, debt and taxes were public evils of the first magnitude. They drained capital from the mass of citizens, diverted it from productive enterprise, and supported a system of coercion, corruption, and privilege that was the bane of every government and necessarily fatal to a free one. "Economy and liberty, profusion and servitude." A decade of opposition to Hamiltonian practice had polarized the issue, with the result that the Republicans could see no escape from these simple alternatives. If Jefferson was doctrinaire on the point, Gallatin was more so. The paramount concern of the administration must be the extinguishment of the debt and the reduction of taxes. If it was not done under Jefferson, it would never be done, Gallatin argued, and all the evils of oppressive taxes, moneyed influence, temptations to foreign wars, encroaching government, and so on would be entailed on future generations. In November, Gallatin worked out a plan to cut the revenue and yet extinguish the debt—an unprecedented piece of financial wizardry.

Reversing the usual order of things, the Secretary began with the needs of the debt rather than the operational needs of the government. The government could be rid of debt in four administrations (his first calculations had been for two) by the annual appropriation of $7,300,000 to service and retirement. When it is considered that the debt had increased ten million dollars during the Federalist years, the project for its extinguishment in 16 or 17 Republican years was amazing. Gallatin conservatively estimated the annual revenue at $10,500,000, more than 90 per cent of it from the impost, the remainder from internal taxes, public lands, and the post. This income, after the huge slice for the debt, would leave $3,200,000 for the operation of the government, an amount well below expenditures in any year since 1793. But Gallatin was also determined to reduce taxes, hence the income. The internal taxes produced $600,000 yearly, most of it from the whiskey excise so much detested in the interior parts of the country. Gallatin was reluctant to give up these taxes, not because he approved of them but because of his paramount interest in paying the debt. As they were the only federal taxes that touched the people directly, the political argument for doing away with them was unanswerable, and the great expense, patronage, and inconvenience involved in their collection made them difficult to defend on economic grounds. (As for the patronage, Jefferson rejoiced in the loss, though it would make his task of finding places for Republicans much harder.) Pressed by his chief, the Secretary relented; "let them all go," he said, "and not one remain on which internal taxes may hereafter be engrafted." With only $2,-600,000 to run the government, savings on the order of a million dollars would be necessary. Modest economies had already been effected, as in the diplomatic establishment, and others were anticipated by the suppression of revenue officers, the new judgeships, and the mint. But these were paltry items. The big budgetary items were the army and the navy. Defense expenditures could be expected to fall to a normal peacetime level of about $3,000,000. Gallatin proposed to cut the figure almost in half, taking the biggest bite from the army, which would be reduced to approximately 3000 men scattered between Michilimackinac and the Tombigbee. The cabinet ratified the plan, and Jefferson's message opened it to view, leaving the details to the Secretary's report to Congress.

The system was liable to the objection that it risked national development and national defense to prove a doubtful theory of political economy. If the theory was sound, government would be saved from manifold dangers and private capital would be "set afloat," as Jefferson expressed it, "to be employed in rescuing our commerce from the hands of foreigners, or in agriculture, canals, bridges, or other useful enterprises." The federal government might aid in this work of economic development. In due time it should, and Jefferson and Gallatin were anxious for that time to arrive. But it was first essential for the government to put the people in full possession of their own energies and resources. The idea that the nation could grow out of its debt by federal investment in economic development—by growing deeper into debt—assailed common sense and lay under the Hamiltonian incubus. But even assuming the success of the Jeffersonian experiment in the light of political economy, would the system of "wise and frugal government" secure the nation's respect abroad and its frontiers at home? Jefferson thought it would.

688

The Peace of Amiens in Europe buoyed his confidence. "It removes the only danger we have to fear. We can now proceed without risk, in demolishing useless structures of expense, lightening the burdens of our constituents, and fortifying the principles of free government." The prospect of war could never be dismissed, he conceded, "but sound principles will not justify our taxing the industry of our fellow citizens to accumulate treasure for wars to happen we know not when, and which might not perhaps happen but from temptations offered by that treasury." Furthermore, the vast circumference of the United States could be secured from invasion or attack only at astronomical cost. Later estimates placed the cost of fortifying the principal harbors at $50,000,000 and 2000 soldiers; even then the defenses would be vulnerable. Jefferson referred the matter to Congress, together with naval preparedness, but offered his own opinion that the most effectual defense would be found in a well-ordered militia.

The fiscal model was calculated on peace. Indeed, in a larger sense peace was its object. It expressed the Jeffersonian animus against systems of energy, force, and command, whether fiscal or military, which were simply different faces of a statecraft at war with the liberties and happiness of the people. Jefferson's plan to reverse the natural tendency of every government toward power and aggrandizement placed him on unassailable ground with Republicans, while in Europe, where the message did not pass unnoticed, men rubbed their eyes in disbelief at the spectacle of a chief magistrate renouncing patronage and power. It promised, said an English journal, "a sort of Millennium in government."

It required power to vanquish power, however, and the more the President exercised power with righteous purpose the less scrupulous he became toward the abjurations of Republican theory. This was to be the story of his administration, first disclosed in the solution he and his colleagues found for the control of Congress. In the Republican theory, of course, Congress should control the executive. The deferential clauses of official discourse honored the theory, as Jefferson was bound to do; but he was also bound to recognize that the political system demanded executive leadership if any majority, Federalist or Republican, was to carry out its program. Congress could not lead. During the Federalist ascendancy it had performed most effectively under Hamilton's ministerial guidance. The problem had been easier for the Federalists. They had had no dogmas to overcome and compared with the Republicans had formed a fairly cohesive body. The Republican majority was a coalition of widely assorted interests, experienced in opposition and obstruction, dogmatic on the point of legislative ascendancy, but thus far untried in the constructive work of government. Even when they had earlier controlled the House of Representatives, the Republicans had shown little talent for policy formation and legislation. Jefferson had frequently criticized their lack of discipline and would do so again and again. How then could he, consistent with the Republican theory, make Congress an effective instrument of the reformation in view?

The solution was found in the network of party leadership outside constitutional channels. As the unchallenged head of the Republican party, Jefferson acted with an authority he did not possess, indeed utterly disavowed, in his capacity as President. This was not the first time he had played a double role—the official and the unofficial, the public and the private, the open and the devious—but for the first time he filled both roles in amplitude. Toward the end of diminishing the powers of government, he did not hesitate to employ means that increased his personal power. The long arm of the President reached out, often through the cabinet, to Capitol Hill. Leaders of both houses of Congress were the President's lieutenants. Speaker of the House Nathanial Macon, a ten-year veteran liked by everyone, appointed the standing committees for the transaction of legislative business. He named his young friend John Randolph chairman of the important Ways and Means Committee. Between this erratic and haughty Virginian and the President there was always a barrier and an impasse would develop in time, but Randolph began as a faithful servant of the administration. He and Macon were especially friendly with Gallatin, who turned his home on Capitol Hill into a kind of Republican club and through this nest of associations exercised an influence on the course of legislation nothing short of Hamilton's in his time. William B. Giles, cooler and wiser now, was Jefferson's principal agent in the House and also the majority leader, the "premier or prime minister," as some called him. Through Giles, presidential leadership was locked into congressional leadership. Unfortunately, illness overtook Giles after the first session and Randolph tried to manage the majority. Effective for a brief time, Randolph was not cut out for the role. The success of Jefferson's system of command depended on trust and loyalty, a willingness to work behind doors, to hear hints as orders, to subordinate personal caprice to the business in hand, none of which suited a man of Randolph's vanity, morbid suspicions, and erratic temperament. Jefferson did not openly move against him but quietly cast about for a "man of business" who would work with the administration and "undertake to keep a file of the business before Congress and press it as he would his own docket in court." He hoped that Caesar Rodney would come into the Eighth Congress in 1803 and take charge; but Rodney was no match for Randolph on the floor of the House, and Jefferson watched his system turn into a "rope of sand." Things went a little more smoothly in the Senate. Until his death in 1803, Stevens Thompson Mason, a Virginian, was the recognized leader, ably assisted by Wilson Cary Nicholas and John Breckinridge. Their devotion to Jefferson was complete. Giles succeeded Mason, and his power was such, so it was said, that if he should move to expel a senator on account of his looks, it would probably be done.

Although his method with Congress never worked with unerring precision, and would not have worked at all without his personal magnetism, Jefferson effectively converted party leadership into executive leadership, thereby creating a strong presidency responsive to the majority will of the community. This was no small accomplishment in a party that contained many jarring elements, and with a volatile Congress. He utilized the press, especially the *National Intelligencer* established in Washington as a more or less official administration organ; he kept up a steady stream of communication to Congress and the public on the nation's business; he drafted bills and with his colleagues originated nearly all the important legislation during eight years; he spent countless weary hours and a large part of his salary entertaining congressmen; and at all times exerted great influence through his friends at the Capitol. Hamilton had been right in his prediction that Jefferson would be no enemy to the powers of the executive; yet Marshall too had been right, or partly so, for Jefferson embodied himself in Congress. Federalists bitterly complained of influences felt but unseen. "The President has only to act and the majority will approve"; *"behind the curtain,* [he] directs the measures . . . while in each house a majority of puppets move as he touches the wires"; "the whole system of administration seems founded upon this principle of carrying through the legislature measures by his personal or official influence." The face behind the mask, so gentle and reserved, was a face of power and intrigue. So thought the Federalists.

The system achieved remarkable results in the Seventh Congress. The internal taxes were repealed and 400 federal officers vanished with them. Congress approved Gallatin's plan for the redemption of the debt. The army was reduced to 3000 men. Naval expenditures were cut back despite the Tripolitan war, which Congress authorized the President to prosecute with such force as he saw fit. The Republicans restored the naturalization act of 1795, making new citizens in five years. The Indian Trade and Intercourse Act carried forward the humane policy begun by Washington, with certain additions recommended by Jefferson, among them a prohibition of the liquor traffic. An act authorizing statehood for Ohio and a compact with Georgia for the cession of the vast acreage—the last of the old western claims—between the Chatahoochee and the Mississippi manifested the President's interest in the West. All these measures passed easily, usually on straight party votes.

The Jeffersonian program for the judiciary brought on a long and arduous contest finally won by the Republicans, though at later times it would seem a sham victory. The Federalist-sponsored Judiciary Act of 1801 created a new system of circuit courts with sixteen new judgeships vested with trial jurisdiction in all cases of law and equity arising under the Constitution and laws of the United States. The arrangement would unquestionably facilitate the removal of litigation from the state to the federal bench, thereby strengthening the central government at the expense of the states. Moreover, it relieved the Supreme Court justices of the irksome duty of riding circuit in the far reaches of the Union—a persistent complaint with the justices. The entire matter came to a head in the Adams administration. The Federalists wished to expand the jurisdiction of the federal courts both as an aid to commercial and financial interests, handicapped by a multitude of state jurisdictions, and as a check on the Republican opposition mounted on a cavalry of political heresy. Their object was to make the judiciary an "engine of government" more acceptable than standing armies, more subtle than sedition laws, more enduring than fiscal systems. It had been anything but this during the first decade. The limping third wheel of government, without prestige or popular favor, the judiciary was an equal partner of the executive and the legislature in name only. While these two branches were elegantly—too elegantly in the opinion of some—provided for in the new capital, the Supreme Court was shunted into a parlor-sized office that had been designated for the Clerk of the Senate. The federal courts attained public notoriety in the suppressive atmosphere of 1798. Their ambitions were disclosed in the prostitution of justice to partisan purposes. It was then, and only then, that Jefferson and his followers felt the menace of a judicial establishment more formidable perhaps than the Hamiltonian system. Jefferson had always favored an independent judiciary as the guardian of individual rights against legislative and executive tyranny. His quarrel with the courts was, in fact, that they failed to check these overreaching powers and became the destroyers rather than the protectors of the Constitution and the liberties of the citizen. Under the circumstances, when the courts checked the people rather than the government, when they were the monopoly of a party from the marshals who packed the juries to the judges who harangued them, when they had not enough business to justify expansion unless by manufacturing litigation through sedition and bankruptcy laws, common law jurisdiction, and encroachment on state judicatures—under the circumstances Jefferson could not acquiesce in any enlargement of the offices and powers of the federal judiciary.

As finally passed in the last breathless weeks of Federalist supremacy, the Judiciary Act reached neither the hopes of one party nor the fears of the other. Yet it did create many new judgeships, with the marshals, attorneys, and clerks to go with them, and it expanded federal jurisdiction in several significant areas. The case of disputed land titles between claimants of different states was especially sensitive. Litigation of this type, already of massive proportions in Kentucky, Virginia, and Georgia, grew out of land speculation. So long as the states maintained control, resident claimants tended to be favored over absentees. The act of 1801 threatened to undermine the local authorities, throw land laws into confusion, and enrich the speculators, including a number of Federalist congressmen. Jefferson's sentiments were naturally on the side of the states and the mass of small holders. But this was a secondary consideration in his opposition to the law. He was outraged, as were his followers, by a discredited majority enacting legislation of such momentous consequences in plain defiance of public opinion. The crowning insult, which he could not help but feel personally, came with the appointment of the "midnight judges." Adams hurriedly put together a full list of nominations for the new judgeships (nineteen in all, counting a three-judge court for the District of Columbia) and the Senate just as hurriedly ratified them. All were prominent Federalists; one had captained a Loyalist regiment during the Revolution; some were political casualties of the recent election; one was John Adams's nephew and three were brothers or brothers-in-law of John Marshall. He was the reputed author of the new system he would also head as Chief Justice of the Supreme Court.

Determined upon the repeal of this last act of a dying administration, Jefferson occupied the firmest Republican ground. His enemies had retired to the judiciary as a stronghold, he said. "There the remains of Federalism are to be preserved and fed from the treasury and from that battery all the works or Republicanism are to be beaten down and erased." Repeal touched the sensitive point of tenure. It was easy enough to remove marshals and attorneys, but judges appointed to terms in good behavior could not be legislated out of their seats, even if they had yet to warm them, without seeming to jeopardize the independence of the judiciary. The objection gave Jefferson pause. The Constitution made judges irremovable except by impeachment. But could this protection be fairly used to support a fraud? Could it be used to sanction and maintain a Federalist phalanx in the judicial branch? Who but the Federalists had struck the first blow against the independence of the judiciary? In an era when party affiliation split society in two, not a single Republican sat on the federal bench! And after the election of 1800 not a single judge could claim to possess the full confidence of the people. So Jefferson finally saw the issue as the restoration, not the destruction, of judicial integrity. To bring the courts into line, to chastise them, what could be more appropriate than the elimination of this "parasitical plant" engrafted on the judicial body in 1801?

Jefferson's initial doubts on this question were erased by fresh instances of judicial arrogance in the months following his inauguration. One of these was a prosecution for libel against his young friend Samuel Harrison Smith, editor of the administration newspaper in Washington. In June, Smith published an article defending the President's removals of attorneys and marshals and assailing the irresponsibility of the judges to public opinion. The courts, it was charged, "have been prompt to seize every occasion of aggrandizing executive power, of destroying all freedom of opinion, of executing unconstitutional laws, and of inculcating by the wanton and unsolicited diffusion of heterodox politics, the doctrines of passive obedience and non-resistance." This was a comparatively mild piece of denunciation in a newspaper that was almost a model of political restraint. Nevertheless, the newly established circuit court for the District of Columbia promptly ordered prosecution. The grand jury returned a presentment, but then refused to indict. The matter was dropped. If the article in question had been found libelous, many editors and writers, including Jefferson's old mentor Edmund Pendleton, might have been indicted, for Republican resentment against the judiciary was widespread and, as in Pendleton's case, it often involved the demand to ensure responsibility by making judges removable on the concurrent vote of both houses of Congress.

In December, just after his message to Congress, the Supreme Court issued a direct challenge to the President. The action led to the case of the "midnight judges," known to history as *Marbury v. Madison*. William Marbury with three others alleged that, on March 3, 1801, they had been appointed justices of the peace for the District of Columbia but that their commissions, though complete in every respect, had been withheld by the incoming administration. By some oversight these four commissions in a batch of forty made out for justices of the peace had not been delivered before the midnight hour. On coming into office Jefferson intended to treat the whole lot as nullities (justices of the peace did not enjoy life tenure) and so at once suppressed the tardy commissions. He subsequently named thirty, not forty, District justices of the peace, of whom twenty-three were the original Adams appointees; but Marbury and associates, not being recipients of this generosity, challenged the legality of the administration's action. Accordingly, they petitioned the Supreme Court for a writ of mandamus ordering the Secretary of State to deliver their commissions. The issue was delicate. Not prepared to decide it at once, the Court granted a preliminary motion for a rule to the Secretary to show cause why the writ should not issue. This was enough to raise the hair on Republican heads. Whatever the legal propriety of the "show cause" order—and there was precedent for it—the circumstances made it a political act. Republicans saw it as a bold challenge to the administration, an invasion of the executive power, an incrimination of the President through his agent, Madison. The President's feelings can only be guessed. He and Madison ignored Marshall's order, and it seemed for a time nothing more would be heard of the case. For the present, the Chief Justice had overcome any hesitancy the President may still have felt toward repeal of the Judiciary Act.

Such was the background of the repeal. John Breckinridge, a man known to be close to the President, introduced and shepherded the bill through the Senate. He did not attack the judiciary but took the line that the new courts were unnecessary. The line had been laid down by Jefferson, who had appended to his annual message a statement of the cases instituted and pending in the circuit courts from their inception. There were embarrassing errors in this statement, which Jefferson subsequently corrected, yet the figures showed clearly that the dockets were not so crowded as to warrant an expensive addition to the system. The corrected statement counted 8358 cases during ten years, 1629 of them pending. The largest volume of business had been in the southern states, Virginia at the head, which helps to explain the special sensitivity of the southern Republicans to the federal judiciary. Breckinridge could fairly argue, however, that the amount of litigation was in decline. For instance, hundreds of suits of British creditors had been referred to an Anglo-American commission and would, in fact, soon be settled by a lump payment to Britain. Moreover, it could not be argued that the Supreme Court justices were too busy to travel the circuits. In twelve years the Court had heard but sixty cases and its annual business could be transacted in five or six weeks. Of course the past history of the federal judiciary offered no measure of Federalist aspiration for it. Much new business was contemplated; this, in turn, would call into existence national legislation of equal scope. If these pretensions reached the realm of common law jurisdiction, consolidation would be complete. Jefferson knew this, as did Breckinridge, but for tactical reasons he favored an oblique approach to the question of judicial power. Carefully avoiding the real, the substantial, issue of the scope of federal authority, he turned the spotlight on the side issue of money and efficiency.

The Federalists were no more forthright in their defense of the Judiciary Act. Gouverneur Morris, their leading spokesman in the Senate, lavished his eloquence on the inviolability of contract. Abolition of the offices, he said, struck down the independence of the judiciary. Morris painted a ghastly picture of democratic despotism. "Why are we here?" he asked. "To save the people from their greatest enemy; to save them from themselves." Unfortunately for his argument, the Constitution, of which he had been a framer and on which he professed to stand, left the establishment of the federal judiciary below the Supreme Court to the discretion of Congress, and it was absurd to hold that the shadow of an office remained after Congress abolished the substance. Having blazed their path on this ground, the Federalists then dragged across it the red herring of judicial review, specifically, that is, the power of the federal courts to declare acts of Congress unconstitutional. The question was irrelevant to the debate, said the Republicans, but since a fuss had been raised about it, a reply was in order. Breckinridge, Mason, and others denied the power if it was assumed to be ultimate, for that would make the courts rather than the people the true sovereigns of the country. Their theory conformed exactly to the one Jefferson had stated in the stricken passage of his annual message: each of the co-ordinate branches of the government is supreme in its sphere and may judge for itself the constitutionality of actions of the other branches. Judicial review was thus conceded, though not as a supreme power binding on the executive and the legislature or, indeed, on the people and the states. If Jefferson ever subscribed to another theory he never stated it. The "tripartite" balance belonged to the general theory of the functional separation of powers. It was part of Republican orthodoxy, while the theory of judicial supremacy as asserted by the Federalists had little to support it in 1802.

The prolonged debate did not much clarify the issue, so momentous for the American polity, since the conflict was political through and through.

The Repeal Act cleared the Senate early in February and the House, after a marathon of oratory, a month later. Federalists bewailed the death of the Constitution. "It is dead, it is dead," Morris was heard to moan. Republicans congratulated themselves, the President and the Congress, for thus annihilating Federalist jobbery, extravagance, and influence. "It demonstrates the inflexible determination of those who now hold the reins of authority, to adhere in power to the same principles, avowed by them out of power." Not one American in a thousand, said the *National Intelligencer,* would disapprove the Repeal Act. The act returned the judiciary to its original foundation, somewhat modified in April, however, by a law which, among other things, eliminated one of the semi-annual terms of the Supreme Court. The practical effect was to prevent the meeting of the Court for nearly a year, an expedient dictated, Federalists charged, by the administration's fear of judicial reprisal against the Repeal Act. On the contrary, answered the Republicans, the new arrangement would afford the justices more leisure to attend their circuits, where the bulk of the business lay, without any neglect of the high Court's work; and besides, if the justices meant to declare the Repeal Act unconstitutional they could do so as well in 1803 as in 1802. When the Supreme Court met in February 1803, it prudently upheld the constitutionality of the repeal. Not until after the Civil War was the federal judiciary placed upon the broader foundations projected by the Judiciary Act of 1801.

Only six days before the Court's decision in this matter, Chief Justice Marshall delivered the opinion in the case of *Marbury v. Madison.* In the absence of co-operation from Madison and the Senate, the Court could not prove that Marbury had, in fact, been confirmed and commissioned a justice of the peace. Nevertheless, Marshall, who had been Secretary of State on March 3, 1801, assumed he had been, went on to hold that non-delivery of the commission did not affect the plaintiff's legal right to the office, and that the proper remedy was a writ of mandamus to the Secretary of State. But, alas, the Supreme Court could not grant the remedy. With tortuous reasoning Marshall held that the power of the Court to issue writs of mandamus in the exercise of its original jurisdiction, although given by Congress in the Judiciary Act of 1789, violated the explicit provision of the Constitution and was, therefore, null and void. There is no need to enter into the fallacies of Marshall's reasoning. Jefferson thought it a piece of sophistry, and constitutional historians, while lost in admiration of Marshall's dexterity, have been inclined to agree. What is important is that the Chief Justice, after reading a lecture to the executive on the duty of performing valid contracts with federal appointees, backed away from an open confrontation in which the Court would certainly be the loser. The fact that the retreat was masked under an apparent show of strength by the assertion of judicial authority over acts of Congress made no impression on Republicans at the time, and, in truth, set up a highly ambiguous precedent for the later development of the doctrine of judicial review.

So far as the case excited notice, it was in its character as a duel between the executive and the judiciary. A Federalist gazette exulted, "it has been solemnly decided in the Supreme Court that Mr. Jefferson, the idol of democracy, the friend of the people, has trampled upon the charter of their liberties." The Republicans left to the Court its face-saving gesture. The *National Intelligencer* and Duane's *Aurora* were silent. So was the President. Yet he could not be dispassionate toward anything John Marshall did, and his reflections on the case years later disclose deep resentment, not because the Court claimed the ultimate power to interpret the Constitution, for in fact it did not go that far in the mandamus case, but because Marshall traveled out of the case, pretending a jurisdiction he then disclaimed, in order to make a gratuitous stab at the President. Politics alone, not law, could account for the Chief Justice's behavior. Jefferson passed over the Court's declaration against the constitutionality of an act of Congress, presumably because he regarded this as a proper exercise of power in a matter directly affecting a co-ordinate branch of the government. It should have stopped there—nothing more was needed to dispose of the case—but Marshall ran on into the political field and accused the executive of a trespass on constitutional rights.

Jefferson was not finished with the judiciary. The Repeal Act and the mandamus case were but two skirmishes in a long campaign.

In retrospect, he must have wondered if in his anxiety to achieve reform within the limits of conciliation he had not been too gentle with the judiciary. The Virginia dogmatists later came to this conclusion. In things that counted the courts were remarkably acquiescent to the Jeffersonian regime, and partly for that reason the foundations of judicial power, even if somewhat narrowed, remained intact, ready for Marshall to build upon when the political climate was right. A more radical assault might have secured important Jeffersonian objectives; but the President was not prepared for it in 1802–03. Firmness in the executive and in the Congress, vigilance in the states, would hold the judiciary within constitutional limits. If this trust proved unjustified, he was quite ready to revive the subject in one shape or another. And so the problem of the Federalism of the bench was not solved but surrendered to political contingencies which, as it turned out, made impossible any constructive Republican solution.

Pitched on the horns of his dilemma, reformation and reconciliation, Jefferson agonized a good deal more about the fiscal system than about the judiciary. "When the government was first established," he said, "it was possible to have kept it going on true principles, but the contracted, English, half-lettered ideas of Hamilton destroyed that hope in the bud. We can pay off his debt in 15 years; but we can never get rid of his financial system. It mortifies me to be strengthening principles which I deem radically vicious, but the vice is entailed on us by the first error. In other parts of the government we shall be able by degrees to introduce sound principles and make them habitual. What is practicable must often control pure theory." His intellectual bent was toward the organization of government around principles that embodied political truth, but he was too much the statesman to deny the claims of practice. The conflict ran throughout his life, one accent succeeding the other as the mood or the occasion or the circumstances dictated. Hamilton's legacy was especially annoying. The machine he had erected could be made to work with more efficiency, the nuts and bolts could be tightened, its accountability to the public secured; but it could not be dismantled without ruining the economy together with the hopes of conciliation.

Banking was a case in point. Jefferson believed the government should separate itself from the banks of the country. At the head of the system stood the Bank of the United States, which he thought an institution of "the most deadly hostility . . . against the principles and form of our Constitution." A creature of privilege, it was also too large, too independent, and too centralized. "I deem no government safe which is under the vassalge of self-constituted authorities, or any other authority than that of the nation, or its regular functionaries," he lectured Gallatin in 1803. Looking to the day eight years hence when Bank's charter would expire, he urged the secretary to "make a beginning towards an independent use of our own money," wherein the government would be its own banker. But Gallatin thought the BUS a highly servicable institution both to the government and to the economy. He actually expanded its operations by the addition of new branches and kept the bulk of federal funds in its vaults, where they supported the loans and note issues of capitalistic enterprise. Jefferson was equally distrustful of state banks. Between 1801 and 1811 their number grew threefold, from thirty to ninety, and most of the new ones were Republican. The demand for bank credit in an expanding economy was insatiable. Republican administrations in the state capitals would have courted disaster had they made no provision for it, and, of course, they were eager for a share of the fiscal spoils that, like the patronage spoils, had been a Federalist monopoly. A banking interest rose up in the Republican party. Jefferson felt its pressures and on occasion gave in to them. He instructed the Treasury to distribute the banking business as widely as possible in order to keep it competitive and to attach the banks to "the reformed order of things." Speaking of a politically well-disposed bank in Providence, he told Gallatin, "I am decidedly in favor of making all the banks Republican, by sharing deposits among them in proportion to the dispositions they show." Yet he did not press the point—it ran against the grain. On the whole, the administration conducted its business through the BUS and made no positive effort to create a competing system centered in the Republican state banks. Either system played havoc with Jefferson's faintly archaic ideal of a plain and dignified republican order. But unable to discover a workable alternative, he acquiesced in Gallatin's essentially Hamiltonian practice as well as in the relentless expansion of bank credit. "What is practicable must often control pure theory."

These problems of judicial and fiscal power went beyond the

first Jeffersonian Congress when the reforms were, if incomplete, nevertheless exceedingly gratifying to the Republicans. The Federalists muttered prophesies of doom. Everything was crumbling in ruins, they said. "Many of the members of Congress think there will not be another session under the present government." (Presumably the President would drop the hocus pocus of Congress and come forth openly as a dictator.) Jefferson rejoiced in the record of Congress. "They will pretty completely fulfil all the desires of the people," he wrote as the session drew to a close in April. "They have reduced the army and navy to what is barely necessary. They are disarming executive preponderance, by putting down one-half the offices of the United States, which are no longer necessary. These economies have enabled them to suppress all the internal taxes, and still to make provision for the payment of the public debt as to discharge that in eighteen years. They have lopped off a parasitic limb, planted by their predecessors on their judiciary body for party purposes; they are opening the doors of hospitality to fugitives from the oppressions of other countries; and we have suppressed all those public forms and ceremonies which tended to familiarize the public eye to the harbingers of another form of government." Indeed, so satisfactory was the reformation worked by Congress that later in the year, when he turned his thoughts to the coming session, the President scarcely knew what remained to be done. "We have almost nothing to propose to them but 'to let things alone'. . . . My chief object is to let the good sense of the nation have fair play, believing it will best take care of itself." Gallatin congratulated the President on the difficulty of collecting stuff for a message, since it suggested that the administration would afford "but few materials to historians." Fortunately or unfortunately, the historian of Jefferson's administration has not suffered from the want of materials.

Man in the White House

The phenomenon of Jefferson's popularity, mounting rapidly in the second year of his administration, made a puzzling problem for his political enemies. The country was going to ruin, but the man who, Nero-like, presided over the disaster was the hero of the populace.

Were the people corrupt or corrupted? Probably both. In 1800 the nation had sold its soul to a demagogue; the republic of 1787 had been overturned, the vile temple of democracy reared in its place; and all history testified that worship at this altar led straight to the graves of despotism. "The hopes and fears of the people are two windlasses, which the political machine obeys, as implicitly as any machine can. Those who turn the windlass, are as blind as the French revolutionists to the ruin that is sure to reach them." Old Fisher Ames, who wrote thus, was among the gloomiest of the Cassandras, but the Burkian theme of democratic despotism ran through the Federalist discourse. The true hero of democracy is the demagogue. The demagogue feeds on popularity; all his measures are calculated to obtain it. The younger Adams ascribed to Jefferson an irrepressible "itch for popularity," while the father spoke of "a mean thirst for popularity." Whether itch or thirst, it obliterated all truth, all morality, all nobler ambition, all interests of state beyond the apprehension of the multitude. The multitude is flattered by these attentions but cannot rule; it surrenders itself to the demagogue, and so by a new route the nation is conducted back into tyranny. The Federalists had sought to save the people from themselves; the Republicans, by exalting the popular will, consolidated their own power. Jefferson's "trust the people" was either a cunning façade or an insane delusion.

It hardly needs saying that these classical notions of democracy run through the mill of the French Revolution had little or no relevance to the new style of popular leadership Jefferson embodied. A free government grew strong not by opposing the popular will but by sympathizing with it. "He who would do his country the most good he can," Jefferson observed, "must go quietly with the prejudices of the majority until he can lead them into reason." What was "reason" for him, in the final analysis, was perhaps not very different from that of most Federalists, but he preferred to find it in the majority opinion of the community rather than in the conceits of self-styled guardians of the public interest. Hence popularity was a positive value; had he not possessed it, Jefferson would have deemed his presidency a failure. It held no terrors for him. "If I know myself I have no passion adverse to the interests of man. I have no pleasure in the exercise of power . . . ," he wrote, touching an old theme at the height of his power. "The love of popularity may induce some of those who come after me to practice what their natural dispositions might not otherwise lead them to." But this need not happen if, as in his own case, popularity was a means to virtuous ends. And he added, "If a sense of correct principles can be established among our citizens . . . they will be enabled to keep their governors in the right way."

The more popular Jefferson became, the deeper became the gloom of the shrinking Federalist remnant. "Our country is too big for union, too sordid for patriotism, too democratic for liberty," Ames lamented. The best that could be hoped for was that the cycle would quickly run its course—democracy to despotism to anarchy—after which the saving remnant of the wise and the good would restore the ravished republic. Hamilton, now a practicing lawyer in New York, often slipped into this mood; at other times, his morbidity reached the outer limits of despair. "Mine is an odd destiny," he wrote in 1802. "Perhaps no man in the United States has sacrificed or done more for the present Constitution than myself; and contrary to all my anticipations of its fate . . . I am still laboring to prop the frail and worthless fabric. . . . Every day proves to me more and more, that this American world was not made for me." If it was, indeed, a Jeffersonian world, Hamilton by his own pertinacity had helped to make it so. Young Adams, no admirer of the New Yorker, agreed with his pessimistic diagnosis of the national condition but, puncturing false hopes, pronounced the Federalist system dead and best forgotten. "The experiment . . . has failed, and to attempt its restoration would be as absurd, as to undertake the resurrection of a carcass seven years in the grave." After the election of 1802 the Republicans controlled all but two or three state governments and their majority in the next Congress would be unbeatable. Adams could not understand why "the pilots at the helm" remained so sensitive to opposition. "What they take for breakers are mere clouds of unsubstantial vapour."

Jefferson was disposed to agree and act accordingly. Yet the vapors were peculiarly obnoxious, and despite impressive electoral gains, the results fell below Republican expectations. This was true in Massachusetts, for instance, where Elbridge Gerry, the hope of Republican conciliation, lost the party stronghold, Boston, and met defeat in his third successive contest for the governorship. Young recruits to the Federalist ranks were renewing the vigor of the party as older leaders seemed to give up in dismay. The *Palladium*, a newly renovated Federalist newspaper, spewed venom upon the President and Republicans generally. Jefferson's Massachusetts friends concluded that a daring opposition would be pursued with all possible rancor. "There can be no reconciliation," Lincoln reported sadly in October. The demand for removals rose. Jefferson had made but a handful in Massachusetts. In Boston the weight of the collector's office could tip the scale against the Republicans in any election. Yet Jefferson ran the risk. Without hiding his disappointment over the election, he refused to admit failure in the Bay State and struck the line he would maintain, with but momentary lapses, against the violent Federalists. "This bitterness increases with their desperation," he told Lincoln. "They are trying slanders now which nothing could prompt but a gall which blinds their judgment as well as their consciences. I shall take no other revenge, than, by a steady pursuit of economy and peace, and by the establishment of republican principles in substance and in form, to sink Federalism into an abyss from which there shall be no resurrection for it."

Although Jefferson did not say what particular slanders he had in mind, he probably meant those fathered by James T. Callender, the most notorious of which had been published in Virginia several weeks before and had since made the rounds of the enemy press. The Sedition Act victim got out of jail just as Jefferson became President. Expecting to be rewarded for his past services—crowned for his martyrdom—he at once cast covetous eyes on the Richmond post office. It was beyond his grasp. Jefferson made a point to Monroe of finding "a gentleman of respectable standing in society" for this post. Callender proceeded to make himself obnoxious to the administration by raising a storm over the remission of the $200 fine imposed upon him by Judge Chase. Jefferson, holding the Sedition Act a nullity, at once issued a pardon and ordered remission of the fine. The money was still in the hands of the marshal at Richmond, a Federalist, and he was slow to co-operate. Callender blamed the President who, he said, was sacrificing him as "a scapegoat to political decorum." After five years' labor in the Republican cause he had no money, no job, no reputation, no prospects. "In a word," he raved, "I have been equally calumniated, pillaged, and destroyed by all parties." In hopes of placating this angry man, Jefferson asked Monroe to see if the refund could not be paid by private charities. He would give fifty dollars. Two or three days later Callender appeared in Washington. He pressed his claims, job and fine, upon Madison, who was amazed to discover that to his less endearing passions Callender had added the passion of love—a Richmond damsel in a station above him but hopefully his if he could be named postmaster. To relieve his distress, Jefferson sent fifty dollars. His private secretary returned from this mission with an alarming account of Callender's behavior. "He intimated that he was in possession of things which he could make use of in a certain case; that he received the $50 not as a charity but as a due, in fact as hush money; that I [the President] knew what he expected, viz. a certain office, and more to this effect." The threat of blackmail, intimated before, was now real. This put an end to his charities, Jefferson told Monroe, adding assurances on the idleness of Callender's boasts. "He knows nothing of me which I am not willing to declare to the world myself."

Callender returned to Virginia empty-handed (though he soon collected the $200) and apparently determined to make the President squirm. The Richmond Federalists now sheltered the man they had earlier chased out of town. Augustine Davis, the Federalist editor and postmaster, whose job Callender had sought, and David M. Randolph, the marshal, who had jailed him and repaid his fine, became his partners in libel. A new Federalist weekly, the *Richmond Recorder; or Lady's and Gentleman's Miscellany*, which catered to the taste for scandal, employed Callender. For several months he stored his depraved mind with scraps of gossip about Jefferson that circulated in Virginia, then in the spring of 1802 opened his infamous campaign by charging the President with aid and encouragement in the publication of the pamphlets that had led to the writer's conviction for seditious libel. Mortified by this "base ingratitude," which perverted "charities" into patronage of a lying renegade, Jefferson authorized Monroe to make a full disclosure of his connections with Callender should the Governor think it wise. Callender kept the initiative by printing Jefferson's letters which mingled money with politics in such a way that it required an act of naïveté to separate them. Now that he had dragged his victim down to his own level, Callender smeared him with the dirty gossip of his private life. On September 1 there appeared in the *Recorder* a slanderous little piece, "The President Again," signed by Callender in the conviction that Jefferson would realize at last the heavy cost of his betrayal. "It is well known," the article began, "that the man *whom it delighteth the people to honor*, keeps, and for many years past has kept, as his concubine, one of his own slaves. . . . By this wench, Sally, our President has had several children. . . . The African Venus is said to officiate as housekeeper at Monticello."

Thus was launched the prolific public career of a tale that had titilated Jefferson's enemies in the neighborhood of Monticello for years. The African Venus, Sally Hemings, was apparently the mulatto offspring of John Wayles and Elizabeth Hemings, his concubine, and hence the half-sister of Jefferson's departed wife. Sally it was who had accompanied Polly to Paris in 1787. After her return she had a number of children, all light skinned, whose paternity some wanton men ascribed to Jefferson. Like most legends, this one was not created out of the whole cloth. The evidence, highly circumstantial, is far from conclusive, however, and unless Jefferson was capable of slipping badly out of character in hidden moments at Monticello, it is difficult to imagine him caught up in a miscegenous relationship. Such a mixture of the races, such a ruthless exploitation of the master-slave relationship, revolted his whole being. It is of no historical importance, but the best guess is that Sally's children were fathered by Peter Carr, the same wayward nephew who was responsible for the Langhorne letter and who was now married to Hetty Smith of Baltimore, sister of the Maryland congressman and of the Secretary of the Navy. This circumstance, if true, taken together with a desire to shield his own family from the truth of the Hemings genealogy—a point of delicacy with him—may account for the tight-lipped silence Jefferson maintained on this matter not only when Callender brought it into the open but to the end of his days. His friends issued indignant denials, but succeeded only in feeding the scandal. It was too enticing, too good a snare for the lofty Jefferson, too neat an offset to the tale of Hamilton's amours told by Callender, and coming from him too smashing an example of retributive justice. Political poetasters had a gay time with Jefferson and his African harem. * And so a popular legend was born. Callender had his revenge. It was not sweet, however. He had proved himself a more dangerous friend than enemy. Federalists spread his libels but did not trust him. Damned in infamy for his dirty work, in July 1803, still at it, he drowned, drunk, in the James River.

To one of the malicious charges aired by Callender, Jefferson pleaded guilty. He had, he confessed, "when young and single . . . offered love to a handsome lady," Mrs. John Walker, the

---

* The most widely repeated verses were the following, published originally in the *Boston Gazette:*

A Song
supposed to have been written by the
Sage of Monticello
(to the tune of Yankee Doodle)

Of all the damsels on the green
   On mountain, or in valley,
A lass so luscious ne'er was seen
   As Monticellian Sally.

Yankee doodle, who's the noodle?
   What wife were half so handy?
To breed a flock, of slaves for stock,
   A blackamoor's the dandy.

Search every town and city through,
   Search market street and alley;
No dance at dusk shall meet your view,
   So yielding as my Sally.

Verse

When pressed by loads of state affairs,
   I seek to sport and dally,
The sweetest solace of my cares
   Is in the lap of Sally.

Verse

Let Yankee parsons preach the worst—
   Let Tory Wittling's rally!
You men of morals! and be curst,
   You would snap like sharks for Sally.

Verse

wife of his good friend. The story had been bandied about for some time before Callender got hold of it. Walker had demanded satisfaction fifteen years or so after the event. After the election of 1800, Henry Lee, a political turncoat still seeking to recover solvency and reputation as a Federalist, took up Walker's cause out of malice toward Jefferson. Knowledge of the affair passed from Lee and other Virginia Federalists to the press. During the fall elections of 1802 it was hinted at in Washington, rumored in New York, and freely circulated in Connecticut, allegedly by the agency of the Federalist attorney David Daggett, who, in turn, was said to have got it from Hamilton. (Jefferson later said that Hamilton had threatened disclosure at the time he was put on the carpet for the Reynolds affair.) Walker was still seeking satisfaction when the old scandal cropped up in debate in the Massachusetts legislature in January 1805. This was quickly followed by the "celebrated letter" of Thomas Turner, a Virginian connected with the Walker family, first published in a Boston journal. The letter traversed the whole field of Jefferson libels and became a kind of text for the Federalists. Here and elsewhere the seduction yarn was bawdily elaborated until it read like a chapter in a Richardsonian novel. The rake lewdly assailed the lady's virtue but, alas, was repulsed by a pair of scissors! Not finally, however, for he pursued her for ten years. "We have heard of a ten year siege of Troy," Paine remarked incredulously, "but who ever heard of a ten year siege to seduce?" Meanwhile, negotiations were going on through Lee for honorable amends. Walker demanded that the President make an apology before the whole world. He would not go that far, but in 1806 he formally acknowledged his youthful transgression in a document presented to Walker, who seemed satisfied with this private apology. But nothing could quiet the public slander.

The intricate relationship between these assaults on Jefferson's private character and ordinary political skirmishes is well illustrated by the case of the Geffroy letters. Early in the administration an informant who signed himself Nicholas Geffroy reported official favoritism and waste in the construction of fortifications at Newport, Rhode Island. It seemed just the kind of malfeasance Jefferson expected to uncover when he came into office—and to his distress never did—so he ordered Dearborn to launch an investigation and politely thanked his informant. Only then did he learn from Christopher Ellery, Republican senator from Rhode Island, that the Geffroy letters (there was a second one) were forgeries. Ellery pointed an accusing finger at John Rutledge, Jr., the South Carolina Federalist, who summered at Newport. Just why Rutledge, or any Federalist, should have written these letters was never made clear. It certainly was not clear to Jefferson who, accepting the idea of forgery, promptly dropped the matter. The next year the Republican legislature in South Carolina juggled the congressional districts so as to deprive Rutledge of his seat. He recklessly blamed the President for this maneuver and at the same time joined the little band of Federalists who secretly brooded over the eggs Callender dropped in their midst months before they were ready to hatch. When they hatched, Ellery attacked Rutledge as the trouble-making author of the Geffroy letters, a charge later detailed at length by William Duane. Vehemently denying the charge, Rutledge claimed he had been framed by Jefferson, Ellery, and Duane in order to divert attention from the Callender scandals. In October he asked Jefferson's permission to see the incriminating letters. Apparently he never received a reply. Jefferson knew of his connection with Callender—with what right did he ask any favor of the President? He had once held high hopes for this scion of a distinguished Revolutionary family, but like many of the Carolina aristocrats, Rutledge had gone over to Federalism in the 'nineties and rendered himself useless to his country.

The Callender libels, as Jefferson believed, opened the floodgates of personal vilification. One thing led to another. Thus "Clerk John" Nicholas, the Charlottesville gossip, came to Rutledge's aid by offering to publish a Jefferson forgery, the "Langhorne letter" of 1797, and in fact did publish it in 1803. Thus the Walker scandal triggered the revival of accusations of misconduct and cowardice— "a dastardly traitor to the trust reposed in him"—in his governorship of Virginia. This was part of Turner's catalogue. Charles Symmes, still in 1805 collector of the port at Alexandria, by Adams's appointment and Jefferson's grace, had first aired the subject in 1796. Jefferson's young friend and Virginia congressman, William A. Burwell, now gathered a vast array of evidence for a public vindication in the *Richmond Enquirer*. A Virginian who had loaned fifty pounds to Jefferson in 1773 charged that his offer six years later to discharge the debt in depreciated Revolutionary currency had been a dishonest, nay a criminal act. Similar accusations, all groundless, had been made before. In this instance Jefferson made an exception to his rule against noticing Federalist calumnies and wrote out a statement subsequently printed, quite anonymously, in the *Enquirer*. By these attacks on his private character the Federalist enemies hoped to deflate his immense popularity with the public. "There is not a feature of that character allowed to be fair," the *National Intelligencer* pointedly observed. "Candor is stigmatized as hypocrisy, decision rashness, and learning pedantry." It is doubtful if they accomplished anything aside from stiffening their own last-ditch resistance to the Jeffersonian regime and Republican ardor to maintain it at all cost.

If Jefferson was, in some sense, responsible for Callender, he also had some responsibility for Thomas Paine, another problem visited upon him in 1802. The prophet of reason and revolution arrived in Baltimore on October 30 and hastened to Washington. He had returned to America aboard a private vessel, not the public one earlier offered, but this did not in any way deter the bigoted Federalist sect. "My arrival has struck it as with an hydrophobia," Paine wrote; "it is like the sight of water to canine madness." The President gave him a warm embrace: the prophet was not without honor in his own country. Jefferson's fireside was brightened that winter by a visit from his daughters; they had known Paine in Paris, and though never a favorite with the ladies, he was a frequent guest at the President's House. Paine was a great talker (especially with the assistance of brandy), a supreme egotist, earthy, anecdotal, and full of ideas on all manner of things. He was sixty-five now, bloodied but unbowed by his revolutionary experience. Like the Abbé Sieyes he could say, "I survived," and add mockingly for his detractors, "by the protecting favor of heaven." He was sad about France. "You see they have conquered all Europe, only to make it more miserable than it was before." America, having recovered its sanity, was again the light of the world. He talked to Jefferson of these things, showed him the latest model of the ingenious iron bridge he was still promoting, and exchanged ideas about dry docks, gunboats, Louisiana, the Barbary pirates, and other subjects of current interest to both men. Various stories were afloat: that Paine would receive a post in the administration, that Jefferson had brought him back as a hack writer, that he was preparing a sequel to the *Age of Reason*. In the Federalist press he was "that creeping thing," lower than vermin; at the hotel where he dined curious people came and stared, it was said, as at an orang-outang; in Boston a young poet of the same name petitioned the General Court to permit him to take "a Christian name." A series of public letters, "To the Citizens of the United States," which Paine commenced soon after his arrival, fanned the flames of controversy. Even warm Republicans, like Duane, grew uneasy when Paine, in his third letter, started up the subject of religion. No one could talk him out of it, though if he continued to ride this hobby he would lose the last friends he had. Old Samuel Adams pleaded with him in the name of the people of New England: "Will you excite among them the spirit of angry controversy at a time when they are hastening to unity and peace?" But Paine called "all this war-whoop of the pulpit" a Federalist "stalking horse" and went his own way.

Jefferson, too, felt concern over the unruliness of Paine's opinions, particularly on religion. The two men, whose tempers were as different as fire and water, agreed in the essentials of their theistic faith, but Paine was a zealot, a propagator of the gospel, a prophet of a new religion as well as a new society, while Jefferson was tolerant of religious differences, only wishing that they might not foul the republican nest. In answer to a Connecticut Baptist address some months earlier, he had declared his conviction that the First Amendment erected "a wall of separation between church and state"; however, wishing not to offend the church order in New England, he struck from his reply an explicit refusal to follow his predecessors in proclaiming fast days and thanksgivings, and instead let it ride as an inference from the stated principle. Not long after Paine's visit he composed a "Syllabus . . . of the Doctrines of Jesus," which he described as a statement of his religious creed. It was done for his personal satisfaction, for his children and a handful of intimate friends. The public had no right to know his religious profession, nor did he have any desire to proselytize in its behalf. In these matters of separation of church and state and freedom of religious conscience, he differed from Paine not in principle but in the manner of pursuing it. After Congress convened in December it was said that Jefferson grew very sensitive to criticism of his friendliness with Paine, saw less of him, and made it a point regularly to attend Sunday worship in the Capitol. Paine himself detected a coolness in the President's attitude and, nothing abashed, reprimanded him for it before leaving the city in January. Jefferson had, "by a sort of shyness, as if . . . in fear of federal observation," precluded conversation, Paine said, adding that he was "not the only one who makes observations of this kind." Jefferson denied anything of the sort; on the contrary, he had been perfectly open with Paine, not only out of respect but in defiance to Federalist censure. "As to fearing it, if I ever could have been weak enough for that, they have taken to cure me of it thoroughly!" Yet he may, in fact, have shown the reserve he denied. Paine had imposed on their friendship for years and proven himself imprudent and overbearing. Jefferson could not risk, and did not want, a personal intimacy with him. Whatever the cause, the reunion of the old comrades failed of consummation, and Paine went north, lonely, unloved, literally a man without a country, to live out the remainder of his days in the obscurity of a New York village.

Jefferson had been reading an old favorite, Seneca, when he remarked to a European correspondent: "Nero wished all the necks of Rome united in one, that he might sever them at one blow. So our Federalists, wishing to have a single representative of all the objects of their hatred, honor me with that post, and exhibit against me such atrocities as no nation has ever before heard or endured." He had no intention of playing Nero. From a political standpoint the newspaper opposition was beneath contempt. It made a great noise, being concentrated in the commercial cities, but produced few reverberations in the vast agricultural spaces of America. Jefferson had the good sense not to confuse newspaper opinion with public opinion. He read dozens of newspapers, Republican and Federalist (his account books show that he personally subscribed to about a hundred dollars' worth annually), and thought the bulk of it trash. "When I read the newspapers and see what a mass of falsehood and what an atom of truth they contain, I am mortified with the consideration that 99/100ths of mankind pass through life imagining they have known what was going forward when they would have been nearer the truth had they heard nothing." Still, bad as the journalism of the time was, the press had a right to exist and even at its worst performed a useful service to society.

He was capable of being quite philosophical on the point. "They [the Federalists] fill their newspapers with falsehoods, calumnies and audacities far beyond anything you witnessed while here," he informed his friend Volney, "and happily these vehicles, like the flues of our chimneys, give an innocent conveyance and discharge to smoke and vapours which might be dangerous if pent up in their bowels." He then went on in the language of a true liberal to describe the "experiment" he was making "whether freedom of discussion, unaided by coercion, is not sufficient for the propagation and protection of truth, and for the maintenance of an administration pure and upright in its actions and views." Conducted under the auspices of one who was the object of so much malignity, what a noble experiment this would be! Jefferson stated his commitment in unequivocal terms. "I shall protect them," his libeling critics, he said, "in the right of lying and calumniating, and still go to merit the continuance of it, by pursuing steadily my object of proving that a people, easy in their circumstances as ours are, are capable of conducting themselves under a government founded not on the fears and follies of man, but on his reason. . . . This is the object now nearest my heart." It was still close to heart two years later, in 1804, when the German scientist Alexander von Humboldt visited him in Washington. Glancing at a violent newspaper in the President's office, the Baron asked, "Why are these libels allowed?" And he was answered, "Put that paper in your pocket, Baron, and should you hear the reality of our liberty, the freedom of our press questioned, show this paper, and tell where you found it."

But Jefferson was not always so philosophical. The Callender libels, especially, jarred his faith in the experiment; a press that was capable of inhaling these noxious vapors could not be considered either innocent or useful. Republican leaders in several states took alarm. In Pennsylvania, for instance, Governor McKean told the legislature it was time "that the good sense of the people, aiding the authority of the magistrate, should interpose to rescue us from a tyranny, by which the weak, the wicked and the obscure, are enabled to prey upon the fame, the feelings and the fortunes of every conspicuous member of the community." The following February,

McKean protested to the President that the "infamous and seditious libels" published almost daily had become intolerable. "If they cannot be altogether prevented, yet they may be greatly checked by a few prosecutions." He was quite ready to make the attempt under Pennsylvania law, but as the problem was a national one he wished to clear it with the President. Jefferson took over a week to answer, and when he did yielded to the Governor's pleas. "Not a general prosecution," he said, "for that would look like a persecution: but a selected one." And he enclosed a newspaper that might serve as a starter. In thus departing from his own far nobler experiment, Jefferson succumbed to partisan political pressures. His own preference, as he told another Republican leader, was to acquiesce in the atrocities of the press, but he could not demand this from numberless Republicans who frothed with indignation. He did not doubt, no more than when he wrote the Kentucky Resolutions, the lawfulness of state prosecutions for defamatory publications. Truth should be admitted as a defense, which amended the common law, but he continued to hold that government could be criminally assaulted by the publication of malicious falsehoods, by bad words, as well as by deeds of violence.

In his letter to McKean he offered still another justification for proceedings against journalistic scandalmongers. "The Federalists having failed in destroying the freedom of the press by their gag-law," he said, "seem to have attempted it in an opposite form, that is by pushing its licentiousness and its lying to such a degree of prostitution as to deprive it of credit. And the fact is that so abandoned are the tory presses in this particular that even the least informed of the people have learned that nothing in a newspaper is to be believed. This is a dangerous state of things and the press ought to be restored to its credibility if possible." In short, the aim was not to suppress freedom but to save it, not to muzzle political debate but to make it meaningful, not to destroy the press—it was destroying itself—but to lead it into a career of "useful freedom." Jefferson's statement may be interpreted as a mask for tyranny or, conversely, as a responsible answer to a sickness that demanded some rather strenuous purgatives. The Federalist press seemed to exist for no higher purpose than calumny, and Jefferson's opinion of its Republican counterpart was not much better. Until the condition was corrected the press must fail to fulfill its essential role in a free government. He once told Paine that the licentiousness of the press produced the same effect as the restraint of the press was intended to do. "The restraint was to prevent things being told, and the licentiousness prevents things being believed when they are told." He was not, then, by his own reckoning, engaging in masquerade when he spoke of restoring the integrity of newspapers. It is equally clear, however, that the means he approved in this instance were badly suited to the end in view. Either he did not recognize the danger a few "wholesome" prosecutions posed to all freedom of opinion or he had allowed the vomit of defamation to poison his vision of the truth.

There were very few principles he held as absolutes, and freedom of the press was not one of them. A press unrestrained to truth had not earned the right to unrestrained freedom. To be useful in the larger strategy of freedom the press must be truthful. It was not that; nevertheless, with rare exceptions, Jefferson stuck to high principle. His waverings were momentary, followed by more and more emphatic declarations of faith. Trust the people! And so he could say to John Taylor in 1804 just the opposite of what he had said to Governor McKean in 1803. "The firmness with which the people have withstood the late abuses of the press, the discernment they have manifested between truth and falsehood," he wrote, "show that they may safely be trusted to hear everything true and false, and to form a correct judgment between them." Republicans in New York tried a Federalist editor for seditious libel in 1804, and Pennsylvania did the same in 1805. Jefferson did not intervene in either of these suits under state jurisdiction. When he came to his second inaugural address, he dwelled at length on the experiment, not uninteresting to the world, "whether freedom of discussion, unaided by power, is not sufficient for the propagation and protection of truth—whether a government, conducting itself in the true spirit of its constitution, with zeal and purity, and doing no act which it would be unwilling the whole world should witness, can be written down by falsehood and defamation." The experiment, he went on with justifiable pride, had been fairly made and the suffrages of the people had pronounced the verdict. A free press could not be dangerous to republican government; it remained to be seen whether it could be useful.

The major test of Jefferson's commitment occurred in his second term. In 1806 the federal circuit court in Connecticut indicted several editors and ministers on charges of libeling the President. The Federalist terror persisted in that state. In the two-year period 1804–06, several Republican editors or printers were tried and convicted of seditious libel; a county judge who had turned Republican was dismissed for marching in a procession celebrating the Louisiana Purchase; Josiah Meigs, professor of mathematics at Yale College, was cashiered for his party affiliation; and a group of local justices, all Republicans, were hauled before the General Asssembly and summarily removed from office because they had dared to question the legitimacy of the state government still without a *bona fide* constitution. These circumstances help to explain Jefferson's initial acquiescence in the Connecticut prosecutions. "That a spirit of indignation and retaliation should arise, when an opportunity should present itself," he wrote to one of the Republican martyrs, "was too much within the human constitution to excite either surprise or censure, and confined to an appeal to truth only, it cannot lessen the useful freedom of the press." Yet this endeavor to recall the press within the pale of truth not only ran in the face of the great experiment but also contradicted the Republican principle against common law jurisdiction in the federal courts. Moreover, as Gideon Granger, the Postmaster General from Connecticut, warned the President, the prosecutions would supply the Federalists with martyrs to the injury of the arduous Republican cause. "Let the Federalists tyranize but let us maintain the correct principles of civil liberty," Granger pleaded. As a matter of principle, also of policy, Jefferson agreed; but, as always, he was reluctant to interfere in state contests. Only when he learned that one of the libels touched the Walker affair did he decide to act on the principle. The affair had, at last, been settled to everyone's satisfaction. None of the principals, neither Walker nor Jefferson nor Lee nor others who might be called to testify, wished to see it revived in a court of law. The prospect, Jefferson said, was "harrowing all our feelings." At his request Granger arranged for the dismissal of the prosecution for want of jurisdiction. (Five years later, in 1813, the moot case was taken up by the Supreme Court as the *United States v. Hudson and Goodwin* in order to determine the question of common law jurisdiction, with a result entirely favorable to the Republican opinion.)

The career of Federalist defamation continued throughout Jefferson's presidency, and well beyond, though nothing further occurred in the way of prosecution. It was a great thing to have made the experiment in freedom of the press; it would have been greater still had Jefferson never relaxed his faith in the ultimate result.

People who formed their mental images of the President from what they read in the gazettes usually discovered upon acquaintance that the supposed Satan had no horns. "He appears to be a gentleman of polite manners," a new Massachusetts congressman wrote, "and had I been entirely free from prepossession I should have viewed him in a favorable point of light." Some Federalists overcame their prepossessions. William Plumer, the New Hampshire senator, after four years in Washington was prepared to concede, at least to himself, that he had done the President injustice. A more striking case was Margaret Bayard Smith, the charming bride of the young man Jefferson brought to Washington in 1800 to publish the Republican newspaper. From an elegant Federalist family in Philadelphia, she possessed the prejudices of her class; but they were at once dissolved in Jefferson's presence. "And is this," she asked herself after their first meeting, "the violent democrat, the vulgar demagogue, the bold atheist and profligate man I have so often heard denounced by the Federalists? Can this man so meek and mild, yet dignified in his manners, with a voice so soft and low, with a countenance so benignant and intelligent, can this be that daring leader of a faction, that disturber of the peace, that enemy of all rank and order?" The Smiths became part of the small circle Jefferson drew from the new Washington society and in which he found more pleasure than in the hordes of congressmen.

The qualities of openness, modesty, gentleness, benevolence, and intelligence so much admired by Mrs. Smith struck other friendly observers as well, and they are the qualities young Rembrandt Peale captured in his portrait of 1800, which quickly became the best known likeness of the President. If not a handsome man, he was equally far from being the "tall, large-boned farmer" of Federalist caricature. The lean and lanky frame, spare of flesh—his most striking physical characteristic—easily lent itself to caricature, whence the unflattering appellative "Long Tom." The frame's attire came in for special remark. Men generally agreed it was casual and plain, whatever the color of the breeches, but some thought it coarse and slovenly as well. After calling at the President's House in 1804, Plumer described him as better dressed than usual. "Though his coat was old and threadbare, his scarlet vest, his corduroy small clothes, and his white linen hose, were new and clean—but his linen was much soiled, and his slippers old.—His hair was cropt and powdered." Even his worst enemies thought him among the most agreeable of men in society, "naturally communicative" on small and large subjects alike, "goodnatured, frank and rather friendly." One who was his friend thought him a bit grave, "but without any tincture of pomp, ostentation, or pride, and occasionally [he] can smile, and both hear and relate humourous stories as well as any other man." He relished anecdote and only humorless men supposed he lacked a sense of humor. He tended to be reticent with strangers, yet this was not always the case. Joseph Story, on first encounter, found himself immediately at ease. "Open to all, he seems willing to stand the test of inquiry. . . . You may measure if you please, and cannot easily misjudge." An English Quaker traveling in America dropped by the President's office and was received as if he were an old friend. "From his disregard of all useless forms and ceremonies, not excepting those in religion," the Englishman said, "his enemies accuse him of being deficient both in religion and politeness. But there are men, that have seen a good deal of the world, who believe, on good grounds, that where true religion and true politeness most abound, there we see least of forms and ceremonies, and that true religion and true politeness positively go hand in hand." In truth, Jefferson was no Quaker; but in his august station he endeavored to substitute natural good humor and common civility for the artificial forms of foreign courts. If manners were judged on the standard not of refinement but of consideration, the President had few peers. "He has more ease than grace—" Mrs. Smith keenly observed, "all the winning softness of politeness, without the artificial polish of courts."

The presidency was not all business. Outside the strict line of official function, Jefferson hit upon a course of conduct that dramatized the democratic character of the office. One of the first accomplishments of the new administration, he felt, was the suppression of "all those public forms and ceremonies which tended to familiarize the public eye to the harbingers of another form of government." The annual speech to Congress fell into this category, as did the appointment of fast days, the elegant birthday balls of his predecessors (he even refused to make his birth date public), the splendors of livery and equipage, and, above all, the weekly levees. "What a contrast!" exclaimed a visitor who knew the old regime. "Coteries and drawing rooms are no more; the promenade of superciliousness and dissipation, no longer excites disgust. . . . No vanities obstruct duties. No pomp or show is now seen to puzzle the unthinking, no etiquette is established to impede business or forbid the access of simply clad honesty." Instead, the simple grace of a young republic, whose rugged hills and rude winds and plain manners rebuked all regal ostentation! Conceiving of himself as one of the people, their chosen servant for the time being, Jefferson wished to relieve the presidency of any suggestion of age-old notions of kingship, arrogance, and lofty superiority. He gave an openness, an accessibility, even a familiarity to the office. As John Adams said, though he did not mean it as a compliment, "Jefferson's whole eight years was a levee." While this democratic approach was a deliberate expression of his own mind, it was so much aided and abetted by the conditions of life in the village capital that it might well have been impossible in Philadelphia.

Sociability was built into the President's daily routine. He rose at sunrise, breakfasted at a fixed hour, worked at his desk until one p.m., rode on horseback for an hour or two, in mid-afternoon entertained at dinner, in the evening withdrew to the privacy of his domestic circle, and generally retired at ten. In the morning hours he kept his door ajar for callers both official and unofficial. While he did not seek out common citizens, many accounts testify to the cordiality with which they were met when, perhaps responding to the image of "the man of the people," they sought him out. For instance, a Pennsylvania farmer and his daughter traveling on horseback to Virginia stopped in Washington and begged their congressman to be taken to the President. It was the dinner hour, but the congressman consented, and the three of them soon found themselves seated at the President's table, conversing of clover, stock, and fertilizer. The moral was readily drawn: Jefferson was one "who in his inter-

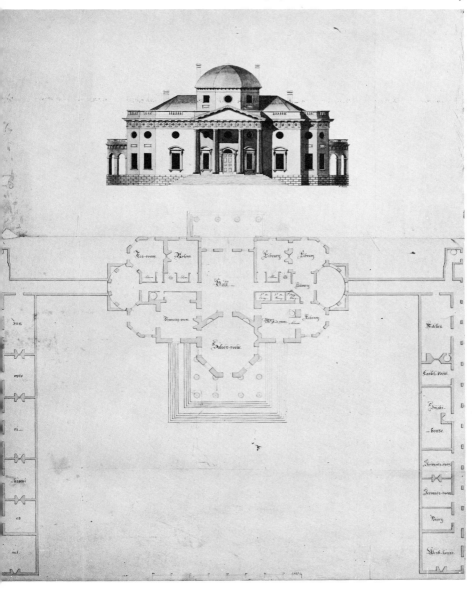

Monticello renewed. Elevation, west front, and plan of first floor and
dependencies. Drawn by Robert Mills, about 1803.

The President. Portrait
by Gilbert Stuart, 1805.

The President.
Medallion portrait
by Gilbert Stuart, 1805.

The President. Portrait by Rembrandt Peale, 1805.

Sage of Monticello. Portrait by Thomas Sully, 1822.

course with his fellow man was as plain, as simple and as free from artificiality or sham as the humblest man in the nation."

The daily ritual of riding horseback acquainted the President with every foot of ground in and around the capital and brought him into contact with all manner of men—the workmen at the navy yard, the mechanics in their shops, gardeners, builders, and so on. He rode alone, usually on his handsome bay Wildair, as obscure as any rider one was apt to meet. Once, it was said, he fell into conversation with a stranger who upbraided the President mercilessly, and Jefferson, without giving the game away, won the gentleman's consent to be introduced to this horrible personage on the morrow. When he called and at last realized his plight, the stranger was full of apology, but Jefferson quickly put him at ease by disclaiming any relationship with the imaginary being to whom apology was owing, and after a long talk the stranger went away as good a friend as he had been an enemy. The enemies labeled his equestrian saunterings a species of democratic ostentation. He sank the dignity of his station, which he well knew how to maintain, in an artful appeal to popular feelings. Thus Joseph Dennie, the same Federalist editor who would be tried for libel in Pennsylvania, made this entry in his "Imaginary Diary of the President:" "Ordered my horse—never ride with a servant—looks proud—mob doesn't like it—must gull the boobies—Adams wouldn't bend so—would rather lose his place—knew nothing of the world."

Actually, although Jefferson wished to be a people's President, there is no need to search the political recesses of his mind for an explanation of his solitary rides. Immediately upon becoming President he had ordered a suitable carriage, "as neat as it can possibly be without any tawdriness," made for him in Philadelphia. Counting the plated harness and the two postillion saddles, the outfit cost him over $1200, to which must be added the cost of four full-blooded bays, $1600, acquired in Virginia. But Washington, its roads rutted and muddy, was no place for a coach and four. If anyone on his domestic staff had a sinecure, it was the coachman, who saw service only at the rare intervals when Jefferson played host to his children. Furthermore, riding horseback was a kind of therapy both mental and physical. For several years Jefferson's health had been so good that he sometimes dreaded the prospect of living too long. But a flaw appeared, a persistent diarrhea, occasionally violent, just at the time he became President. He mentioned the complaint to Benjamin Rush, who prescribed the usual regimen of diet, exercise, bathing, and medication, together with cessation of Jefferson's practice—his prescript against colds—of bathing his feet every morning during the winter. Said Rush, "The bowels sympathize with the feet above any other external part of the body, and suffer in a peculiar manner from the effects of cold water upon them." Well, Jefferson never had much confidence in physicians, even the learned Dr. Rush. Yet he was put on the right track, or so he came to believe, by another physician, Dr. William Eustis of Boston, who evidently believed the bowels sympathized with that part of the body most exercised by a horse. For more information on the "trotting cure," Eustis referred him to the great Dr. Sydenham, "the English Hippocrates." Jefferson got Sydenham's book and at once began to ride a couple of hours daily; by 1804, the bowels strengthened, he was completely cured of his "visceral complaint." One thing is sure: in this instance the bowels sympathized with democracy.

Emblematic of the popular image Jefferson projected, of "Jeffersonian simplicity," was the presentation of the "mammoth cheese" on New Year's Day, 1802. This free-will offering by the farmers of the town of Cheshire in the Berkshire hills of Massachusetts measured four feet four and one half inches in diameter, 15 inches thick, and weighed 1235 pounds. If Federalists could deride, Republicans could exalt Jefferson's fame as the champion of American mammoths. The cheese had been made in the summer, strictly from "Republican cows"—900 of them—then transported by land and by sea in the charge of Parson John Leland, an indefatigable Jeffersonian, Baptist, and crusader for religious liberty. It arrived in Washington on the first morning of the new year in a wagon drawn by four horses richly caparisoned. "It is an ebullition of the passion of Republicanism in a state where it had been under heavy persecution," Jefferson wrote with obvious delight. The present was accompanied by an address inscribed "The Greatest Cheese in America, for the Greatest Man in America." It was a trifle, "a peppercorn," not the enforced offering of a lord to his monarch nor a bribe for lofty titles or offices, but, said the address, "a mite [cast] into the scale of democracy" and a token of the esteem free men felt for their President. (Actually, Jefferson paid a sum of $200 for the cheese in keeping with a strict personal rule against the acceptance of gifts.) Federalist wits made easy jest of the cheese, "this monument of human weakness and folly," to which Republicans returned, "Do what they can —and say what they please, Rats love to nibble at good Cheshire Cheese." Federalist congressmen were insulted by the introduction of Parson Leland in the Capitol pulpit the following Sunday, especially as he chose as his text, the President in attendance, "And behold a greater than Solomon is here." For a year and a half the great cheese reposed in the "mammoth room," as Jefferson dubbed the unfinished east room of the mansion, where it was an object of curiosity. Finally, on July 4, 1803, in celebration of the Louisiana Purchase, Jefferson broke into this "far fam'd and far fetch'd" cheese and served it to his guests. Republicans raved, while Federalists pronounced it wretched.

Twice a year, on New Year's Day and the 4th of July, the President threw open his doors to the public. The latter, he said, was the only birthday he ever celebrated. The festivities in Washington followed the same pattern from year to year. A dawn salute, a military parade, the President in mufti standing in review on his steps, then an oration. At noon the citizens, a hundred or two hundred, flowed into the Executive mansion, greeted by the President himself. Four large sideboards in the dining room offered cake, wine, punch, and other refreshments. From an adjacent room the Marine Band played partiotic airs. (Less than satisfied with the band, which also played at the Sunday services in the Capitol and summer concerts on the grounds of the Executive mansion, the President, in 1805, imported a band of Italian musicians such as he had dreamed of at Monticello.) There were always picturesque additions to the company: the turbaned Tunisian minister and his entourage, all richly garbed, or a delegation of Osage Indians in full regalia from the great Missouri. At two p.m. the citizens departed to wind up the festivities at a public dinner.

The President took only a modest part in the social life of the city. Public dinners, the dancing assembly, theatrical performances (by a touring company from Philadelphia) could boast his patronage but rarely his presence. He was a widower, of course, and that made a difference. Dolley Madison graciously filled the role of first lady as occasion required, and so did his daughter Martha during her visits. Martha possessed none of Dolley's buxom beauty and bubbling charm. She was described as "rather homely, a delicate likeness of her father." But she won the admiration of everyone. Jefferson had put the amusements of the *bon ton* behind him with one exception, horse racing. The turf season in the fall, on the heights beyond Georgetown, was the social event of the year. The races featured the finest blooded-stock of Virginia and Maryland, the human with the equinine. Congress, if it happened to be in session, found excuses to adjourn; hundreds of fashionable carriages surrounded the turf; four or five hundred people of both sexes, all ages and conditions, from the President to the meanest beggar, attended the races. In his love of the turf, Jefferson showed his Virginia colors. Some New Englanders were offended, regarding it as the sport of nabobs, extravagant, immoral, and vulgar; yet they too could be seen at the races. Senator Plumer talked with the President after a day at the turf: "His conversation was vapid—mere commonplace observations on the weather—crops and sickness of particular districts. From these he went into an elaborate defense of horse racing—he said it was an effectual means to improve the breed of horses . . . that all people will have their amusements—that horse racing is less injurious to the people than playing at cards or dice as the Bostonians do."

For eight long years the President played host to congressmen and, in fact, to all official Washington. One of his successors, John F. Kennedy, on the occasion of a dinner for Nobel laureates of the Americas, called his guests "the most extraordinary collection of talents . . . that has ever been gathered together at the White House, with the possible exception of when Thomas Jefferson dined alone." But the President seldom dined alone. Nothing in the presidency, he once remarked, equaled the trials of the table. The burden of entertaining 176 congressmen, as well as foreign diplomats, cabinet officers, and local or visiting dignitaries, was thrust upon him by the meager conveniences of social life in the capital. The President's House, unfinished, scantily furnished though it was, offered to congressmen trapped in this wasteland the only certain refuge from social misery.

By nature and training a hospitable man, Jefferson would have opened his doors to these poor creatures without any ulterior motive. Given the situation, however, he could not help but recognize the political value of what he was doing. In the opinion of unfriendly observers, it was all part of the game of subverting Congress to the executive will. Jefferson ignored the criticism when it came from Federalists who, after all, were pleased to accept his hospitality; but when it came from a Republican who wished to place his independence beyond the shadow of suspicion, he explained the practice in terms which, though political, disclaimed any motive of improper influence. "I cultivate personal intercourse with the members of the legislature," he said, "that we may know one another and have opportunity of little explanations of circumstances, which, not understood might produce jealousies and suspicions injurious to the public interest, which is best promoted by harmony and mutual confidence among its functionaries. I depend much on the members for the local information necessary on local matters, as well as for the means of getting at public sentiment." The President did not turn his house into a kind of congressional club for nothing. He expected, and apparently got, a more sympathetic Congress because of it.

His procedure was well described by a Federalist representative three weeks after the opening of the Seventh Congress: "Under the new order of things, there are no Levees, but the members are invited to dine with the President in rotation, and what is strange . . . only Federalists or only Democrats are invited at the same time. The number in a day is generally eight, and there is one of the heads of Departments, which makes nine." The entertainment of Federalists and Republicans, occasionally called Democrats in derision, was thus separate but equal. Also, Jefferson tried to break down the political cohesiveness of certain boardinghouse groups by mixing the congressmen together. Eight or ten was the usual number; but with other guests, as many as eighteen dined at Jefferson's table. Every other day or so he sent a batch of billets to the Capitol. Guests were invited for 3:30 p.m., the hour Congress usually rose. Down Pennsylvania Avenue they came, to the great white house barren of landscape and (until late in Jefferson's presidency) surrounded by a crude post and rail fence. Servant or private secretary met them at the door and ushered them into a reception room, where the President joined the party and conversed for perhaps half an hour before dinner. Pell-mell was the rule of the house; the guests, accordingly, found what place they could at the table. The dining room, needless to say, was not the resplendent state dining room of the present-day White House. Jefferson had furnished the smaller dining room with an oval table, which he considered more democratic than the rectangular table used by his predecessors. There was neither head nor foot. Green canvas, instead of a bothersome Brussels carpet, covered the floor. Clergymen remarked that no blessing was ever offered. To facilitate the service Jefferson introduced some of his own contrivances, for example, a set of circular shelves on a revolving door that quickly dispatched dishes between kitchen and dining room with the minimum traffic, and dumb waiters sometimes set beside the guests at the table. The food was abundant and good, a combination of French and Virginia cookery, and if hardly of gourmet quality a great treat in this "land of hog, hominey and hoecake." Manesseh Cutler of Massachusetts described the menu of a dinner he rated below par for the President's table: "Rice soup, round of beef, turkey, mutton, ham, loin of veal, cutlets of mutton or veal, fried eggs, fried beef, a pie called macaroni. . . . Ice cream very good, crust wholly dried, crumbled into thin flakes; a dish somewhat like pudding—inside white as milk or curd, very porous and light, covered with cream sauce—very fine. Many other jim-cracks, a great variety of fruit, plenty of wines, and good." Cutler had never tasted macaroni before, thought it some kind of onion, and did not like it. Ice cream was a delicacy, though Jefferson served it in all seasons by virtue of his ice house, filled every winter with two-inch thick cakes of ice cut from a pond below the house. As for the wines, they gave a truly Epicurean finish to the dinners. There were many kinds, all sent to Jefferson by consuls and friends in a dozen ports. No healths or toasts were ever drunk. "You drink as you please, and converse at your ease." The ladies, when ladies were present, retired to another room; tea and coffee were served; games of cards, the usual evening diversion in other houses, were never played, general conversation taking its place. The guests were gone by eight o'clock. "We enjoyed ourselves very well," Cutler wrote, "were social, and handsomely received and entertained."

Part of the enjoyment was the President's talk. Everyone expected him to take the lead, and he usually did, tactfully drawing out even the most retiring guests in conversation that encompassed the table. He made it a rule to avoid political talk lest it cause any uneasiness to his guests. Politeness, he once lectured his grandson and namesake, is "artificial good humor," the sacrifice of one's own little preferences and conveniences to the gratification of others. "Good humor and politeness never introduce into mixed society a question on which they foresee there will be a difference of opinion." At any other table than Jefferson's conversation on such a rule was almost sure to be insipid. But he could discourse on so many subjects, from travels in France to the natural history of parrots, there was never a void. Benjamin Latrobe rated a dinner at the President's House "an elegant mental treat." "Literature, wit, a little business, with a great deal of miscellaneous remarks on agriculture and building, filled every minute." John Quincy Adams, who came into Congress from Massachusetts in 1803, had long ago severed his youthful attachment to the Virginian, yet could still be enchanted by his talk. "You never can be an hour in this man's company without something of the marvellous." Once when the conversation turned to the French Revolution, Jefferson reflected how contrary to all expectations "this great bouleversement" had ended, as if the last dozen years had been a dream, and then said with casual aplomb that the French should return where they had started in 1789 and call back the old family. With an eye to good table talk, Jefferson played certain favorites among the congressmen. Dr. Samuel L. Mitchill, of New York, was his special delight. A physician educated at Edinburgh, learned in many scientific fields, actively associated with Robert Livingston and DeWitt Clinton in both scientific and political enterprise, Mitchill exemplified enlightened republicanism. Jefferson called him his "Congressional Dictionary."

Concern over the President's backstairs influence dampened the pleasure of the Federalist guests. The concern seemed justified. "No one can know Mr. Jefferson and be his personal enemy," one Federalist observed. And political enmity was no certain proof against the charms of his personality. Federalist anxiety on this point went back several years to the time when, as Secretary of State and Vice President, Jefferson had supposedly made many good men dupes by his "philosophizing dinners." Moreover, it soon became apparent that he was not averse to using his hospitality, or rather withholding it, as a political whip. In 1803 he declined to send invitations to the most forward Federalists, Bayard, Rutledge, and Griswold, who had offended him personally in one fashion or another. Word of this "marked neglect" passed through congressional corridors. In February four Connecticut members indignantly refused presidential invitations, and at the last minute Jefferson had to scurry to Georgetown for gentlemen to fill their places at the table. When Congress assembled in November 1804, Senator Plumer noted that the President had altered the form of his invitations. No longer "The President of the United States" but "Thomas Jefferson" requested the congressmen's pleasure at dinner. Asking Giles about this change, Plumer was told it was introduced to give Jefferson greater freedom, since as a private gentleman he was under no obligation to invite any member who abused him. "It discovers a littleness of mind unworthy of the President of the United States," Plumer noted. "As President—he ought never to act toward an individual as if he knew what was said for or against him or his measures." An excellent rule, one which Jefferson took into the presidency and always approved in the abstract. But, as he saw it, certain Federalists had traveled outside the bounds of political opposition and muddied the waters of social intercourse by participating in slanderous attacks on his personal character. Why should he honor men who thus trafficked in dishonor? And how could the easy sociability of his dinners be maintained in the presence of such men? Unfortunately, what began as a selective exclusion traced the typical route of a vicious circle—insult from one side produced insult from the other, until in his second term many Federalists were refusing to call on him even at New Year's, and he, at the same time, was refusing to invite them to dinner.

By then, too, dissension in the Republican ranks caused Jefferson to strike the names of schismatics from his guest lists. The chief of these was John Randolph. There is in Jefferson's papers a detailed record in his most minikin hand of the persons entertained at every dinner from December 1, 1804, to the end of his presidency. The record for the previous years has not survived, though the general picture that emerges for the later period probably holds good for the former. During the second session of the Eighth Congress, a total of 110 days, the President entertained upwards to 600 guests on fifty occasions. The great number were congressmen, and three of them, Randolph, Giles, and Mitchill, were his guests as many as five times. Randolph was eliminated in 1806. Clearly, Republicans as well as Federalists could fall from executive grace. It does not follow that those who remained in his grace, supping at his table, voted any differently in Congress because of it, though this was sometimes said. Asked to explain the Senate's consent to an unpopular executive appointment, Vermont Republican Stephen Bradley snapped, "The President's dinners have silenced them." In these matters the lines of cause and effect cannot be traced.

Entertainment on so large a scale required a well-managed household and considerable expense. The President's annual salary of $25,000 adequately covered his expenses, or so it would seem, but made no contribution toward the solvency of his still precarious estate. The principal items in his Washington accounts were food, wine, and servants. The first ran in the neighborhood of $6500 a year. Wine was an extravagance he could not do without. During his first term he spent about $2400 annually on wines; in his second, the cellar being stocked, considerably less. He personally attended to the wines, no small job in itself, and after a time computed his orders on the basis of actual consumption. Over a given period champagne, for instance, was consumed at the rate of one bottle to three and one-seventh persons, so he fixed the annual requisition at 500 bottles. There were usually eight to ten servants, whose combined wages came to something over $200 annually.

The day-to-day management of the household belonged to the *maître d'hotel* Etienne Le Maire, who Jefferson retained in August 1801, instructing him "that while I wish to have everything good in its kind, and handsome in style, I am a great enemy of waste and useless extravagance, and see them with real pain." One observer described Le Maire as "a very smart man, well educated, and as much a gentleman in his appearance as any man." He evidently met the President's exacting standards, for he remained in his service to the end. Almost any morning of the week he could be seen in the market at Georgetown purchasing supplies of meat and eggs, fruit and vegetables, often to the tune of $50 a day. The French chef, M. Julien, ran the kitchen under Le Maire's supervision, but no detail of domestic management, least of all this one, escaped Jefferson's personal attention. He still imported from abroad certain more or less standard items in his menu, macaroni, for example, and acquired others from Richmond or elsewhere. His unfailing interest in all things botanical and culinary is exhibited in an elaborate table arranged under the heading "A Statement of the Vegetable market at Washington, during a period of 8 years, wherein the earliest and latest appearance of each article within the whole 8 years is noted." Here it becomes apparent that he and his guests generally enjoyed broccoli for only two weeks in April, artichokes from early June to mid-July, tomatoes from mid-July until November, raspberries for but one week in the spring, lima beans for but three short weeks in late summer, and so on. On his daily excursions Jefferson often talked to gardeners with a view to improving the market of the federal city. In the winter months, salads were a special problem. "Would it be within the scope of Mr. Bailey's plan of gardening for the common market," he inquired in 1802, "to make a provision of endive for the ensuing winter, so as to be able to furnish Th. J. with a salad of endive every day through the winter till the spring salading shall commence . . . ?" Evidently it was not, for in December two and one-half years later Jefferson was sending to Baltimore for lettuce and endive.

The President's hospitality, easy and informal in the Virginia manner, presented no problem to his American guests—it was the custom of the country—but to foreign diplomats trained in another school, taught to insist on points of honor, it could be a jolt. The introduction into official society of "the principle of equality, or *pêle-mêle*," was the sequel to his revolt against the "courtly" forms of his predecessors; and although he might have excepted foreign envoys from the rule, he determined not to do so. For a time things went swimmingly. The only foreign minister of rank, Don Carlos Martinez de Yrujo, spent most of his time in Philadelphia, some of it in search of a French chef for the President. He had recently married the daughter of Governor McKean, and being indebted to Jefferson for interceding with the Spanish court to prolong his tour of duty in the United States, he made no protest against the new democratic canons. Nor did the new Dutch minister. This was reserved for Anthony Merry, the first British minister credited to the Jeffersonian court, who arrived in November 1803. He had been portrayed by Rufus King as "a plain, unassuming, and amiable man," as perhaps he was; but his imperious lady, certainly, had pretensions of another order.

The Merrys arrived in a dreary season. They could not find a decent house, and when they acquired an indecent one (actually two small houses side by side) could not find the servants to staff it. They despised Washington from the first moment. "Why it is a thousand times worse than the worse parts of Spain!" Merry exploded. The manner of his reception by the President contributed to these jaundiced feelings. He went with Madison and, finding the reception room empty, they proceeded down the hall to the President's study when he suddenly appeared, as casual as may be, and there in the awkwardness of the hallway Madison made the introductions. "Mr. Jefferson's appearance soon explained to me that the general circumstances of my reception had not been accidental, but studied," Merry reported. "I, in my official costume, found myself at the hour of reception he had himself appointed, introduced to a man as president of the United States, not merely in undress, but *actually standing in slippers down at the heels,* and both pantaloons, coat, and under-clothes indicative of utter slovenliness and indifference to appearances, and in a state of negligence actually studied." It was a deliberate insult to his government, Merry concluded. Perhaps it was. Perhaps Jefferson recalled that morning the insults Americans had received from British ministers and chose this occasion to return the injury. More likely, however, his appearance and conduct were quite unaffected. He was in his usual working attire, the same casual morning dress he wore to receive all and sundry, and presumably saw no reason to affect another appearance for the British Minister. He may have hoped to dispel false expectations and bring the Englishman promptly to American ground. If Merry failed to take the hint and, instead, chose to interpret the reception as a humiliating affront to his sovereign, it could not be helped.

A day or two later Jefferson entertained the Merrys at dinner. The Madisons were there, as were the Yrujos and the Pichons (Louis Pichon, the French chargé d'affaires) and several others. Supposing that the dinner was in his honor, Merry silently fumed at

Pichon's presence, a mere chargé and an enemy Frenchman to boot. He did not realize that the President gave no official dinners, eschewed rank, and, as Madison later explained, at his table threw a mantle of oblivion over hostile relations. When dinner was announced Jefferson offered his arm to Dolley Madison and over her demurring whispers, "Take Mrs. Merry," escorted her to the place at his right. Mrs. Merry was two seats further down the table, while her poor husband scurried to find any seat at all. "This will be cause of war," the Marchiones Yrujo was heard to remark. Four days later the Merrys received the same treatment at a dinner given by the Secretary of State. So it went. Merry poured his heart out to his government, thereby threatening to turn a social spat into an international incident. He refused further social intercourse with the President. Yrujo, who had had a falling-out with the administration, took sides with Merry. The two diplomats' wives turned heel on the cabinet wives. It was, said Madison, a "display of diplomatic superstition, truly extraordinary in this age and in this country."

The arrival on the embattled social scene of Jerome Bonaparte and his American bride introduced a new element which tended to confirm Merry in his belief that he was the victim of a rapprochement between the United States and France following upon the Louisiana Purchase and the resumption of hostilities in Europe. Several months earlier, while on a visit to the United States, Napoleon's youngest brother had dazzled, courted, and wed Elizabeth Patterson of Baltimore. She was not only a raving beauty but also a niece of the Maryland Smiths, who prated on this remarkable family alliance. Jefferson felt uncomfortable about the marriage. It was sure to invite Napoleon's wrath, and he might think the President of the United States should have prevented it. Yet Jefferson did not wish to displease the Smiths or allow reasons of state to come between the course of true love. He entertained the glittering young couple, with the Smiths and others, at a gala dinner. Merry exploded when he learned that the President, who had snubbed his wife, had escorted Mme Bonaparte to dinner. Etiquette did not justify this discrimination, but the ladies themselves did. Mrs. Merry was a large puffed-up woman, as gaudy as a peacock. Everybody in Washington tittered over her grotesque attire—a mélange of satin and crepe and spangles with shawl fantastically draped from head to heels—and her garish display of diamonds at the Robert Smiths' ball for the Bonapartes. Mme Bonaparte, on the other hand, was a bewitching young lady clothed in the highest, and scantiest, of Parisian fashions. Her appearance at the ball "threw all the company into confusion . . . , no one dared to look at her but by stealth," and men who did said "they could put all the clothes she had on in their vest pocket."

If the President was amused by this comic opera, he was not unaware of possibly serious repercusions. It was his turn to be snubbed. When he invited Merry and Yrujo alone to dine with him, they excused themselves, saying they would have to write to their governments for instructions. "It is unheard of," Jefferson fumed, "that a foreign minister has need of the permission of his court to sit down at the table of the head of state: I shall be highly honored when the King of England is good enough to let Mr. Merry come and eat my soup." He wrote an explanation of the whole affair to Monroe, at that time the American envoy in London. Merry himself should not be blamed; he appeared to be an amiable enough man, but his wife, a perfect virago, "has established a degree of dislike among all classes which one would have thought impossible in so short a time." As to the sticking point of precedence, "We have told him [Merry] that the principle of society as well as of government with us is the equality of the individuals composing it; that no man here would come to a dinner where he was to be marked with inferiority to any other; that we might as well attempt to force our principle of equality at St. James's as he his principle of precedence here." Of course, nothing in the application of the principle to social and public occasions was meant to degrade a foreign government or its minister, only, rather, that where the latter happened to sit at dinner, who escorted his wife to the table, and so on had no bearing whatever on the respect accorded him and his government. Jefferson had been in the habit, he explained, of asking one of the cabinet wives "to come and take care of the company, and as she was to do the honors of the table I handed her to dinner myself." Merry had objected, seconded by Yrujo, and so he had discontinued the practice in favor of strict adherence to pell mell, that is, giving his hand to the lady who happened to be nearest him. Alas, the practice was no more acceptable to the dissident ministers. The pretension, he said, "that agents of

733

foreign nations should assume to dictate to us what shall be the laws of our society" had excited emotions of indignation and contempt in the United States, and he feared that the Merrys would "put themselves in coventry" because of it. This proved to be the case. Officially, Merry went about his business in the usual fashion. But unable to enlist the support of the foreign office for his claims, unwilling to yield to the rule of pell mell, he and his wife remained virtual exiles from Washington society to the detriment of Anglo-American relations.

As ludicrous as this little drama was, it was acted on a stage and with players that gave it sober meaning and purpose. Jefferson, in his role, endeavored to fashion a national style in the forms, the ceremonies, the manners of the state. It was an old but as yet unfulfilled passion. He had winced at Washington's levees, at Adams's pomposity, at an American diplomacy alternately futile and servile —the spirit of the nation rebelled at these expressions of the government. To adapt the outward demeanor of the government to the inner spirit of the people was a work of enduring importance beyond the trifles that occasioned it. The work took tangible form in a series of "Rules of Etiquette" approved by the cabinet and published in the press. The rules codified the experience of the administration in the Merry affair: foreign ministers were to pay the first visit to executive heads (Merry had expected the first visit), differences of rank or grade among diplomats and their wives gave no precedence, and when brought together in society they were perfectly equal to everyone else. The experience that led to these rules helped to put the nation in possession of itself. Viewed in this light the President's duel with Anthony Merry was a gesture, modest but dramatic, on behalf of American nationality.

The constant round of entertainment together with weighty affairs of state left Jefferson little time for intellectual pursuits. "It is rare I ever indulge myself in the luxury of philosophy," he apologized to a kindred spirit in 1802, and he would have to repeat himself many times during the next seven years. Year after year he was reelected president of the American Philosophical Society, although he never actually presided and his main service was as a transmission belt of other men's ideas. His presence at the head of the nation lent prestige to scientific endeavor. The National Institute of France elected him, alone among Americans, one of eight foreign associates. He continued to act as a kind of Johnny Appleseed for European flora. Being a farmer on leave, as it were, he tried to keep abreast of things agricultural. On the hint of a Pennsylvania agriculturist, he adapted the pointed toe to his moldboard of the plow, had new models made, and a circular printed to describe the method. According to Mrs. Smith, his favorite room in the elephantine house on Pennsylvania Avenue was the one he called his "cabinet." Books, maps, and charts lined the walls; scientific instruments, garden and carpenter tools lay on the table; in the window recesses were the flowers and plants he tended; and suspended over the roses and geraniums was a mocking bird in a cage. When alone he often opened the cage and the bird perched on his shoulder and sang as he worked at his desk.

Believing that he and his party embodied the sentiments of the great majority of farmers of the country, Jefferson wished his administration to make a positive contribution to agricultural science. He at once took steps to implement an idea drawn from the example of the English Board of Agriculture and first recommended to Congress by Washington in 1796. The project was to unite all the state agricultural societies through a central organization in the capital. Madison, Dr. Mitchill, and the versatile Isaac Briggs, of Maryland, helped to bring this incipient national board of agriculture into being in 1803. Each local society designated delegates, usually congressmen, to the national society. Madison was elected president at the first meeting. The society laid plans to establish an experimental agricultural garden in Washington and resolved to publish nationally the best contributions sifted from the proceedings of the local associations, thereby ensuring, in Jefferson's words, "that not a useful thought of any individual of the nation at large may be lost." Unfortunately, however, an entirely voluntary society, without an active executive secretary, without government subvention, lacked the most important attributes of the English Board, as Arthur Sinclair, its secretary, pointed out to Jefferson. For all his expressed opposition to government intervention in the economy, Jefferson was usually quite prepared to suspend the principle where a scientific purpose could be shown. In this instance, apparently, he did not think the national interest would be served by the creation of a quasi-public agency for the encouragement of agriculture. Of the more esoteric sciences paleontology remained his principal interest. In 1801 Charles Willson Peale, that wonderful impresario of American science, was excavating the bones of a mammoth discovered on a New York farm. The place was deep in water, and Peale asked Jefferson for the loan of a pump from a naval vessel. The loan was promptly authorized, but Peale, with money borrowed from the American Philosophical Society, devised his own scheme for draining the pit. Jefferson must have marveled at Peale's ingenuity: a great wheel 20 feet in diameter, wide enough for men to walk within "as squirrels in a cage," which turned a revolving chain of buckets that conveyed the water out of the pit, and thus enabled the workmen to dig the bones from the mud. (The scene is wonderfully portrayed in Peale's painting, "Exhuming the Mastadon.") It was a precious cache. Within a few months Peale mounted the first skeleton of the mammoth (or mastadon), indeed the first fossil skeleton ever mounted in America and probably the second in the world—the megatherium in Madrid, about which Jefferson had learned in 1797, being the first. It would have made an interesting addition to the *Notes on Virginia* had the author ever found time to revise that prophetic work. Peale exhibited the skeleton in his famous museum in Philadelphia, where it attracted unusual attention. His artist sons Raphael and Rembrandt took a second skeleton, also mounted from the New York remains, for exhibition in Europe, whose savants had never seen this curiosity of the New World. (To celebrate their departure Peale staged a "feast within the breast of the mammoth" for a dozen men!) Jefferson was a distant spectator to these proceedings, but he kept in close touch with Peale, Caspar Wistar, and others, and served as an unofficial clearing house for all discoveries in paleontology. Later, in his second term, he sponsored a private venture of his own at the Big Bone Lick on the Ohio, the legendary source of ancient remains which George Rogers Clark had first tapped for him in 1781. Now, a quarter-century later, he sent William Clark (of Lewis and Clark fame) to the Lick to unearth everything he could. From the great collection of fossil bones Clark shipped to Washington, Jefferson presented some to the Society in Philadelphia, kept a few for his cabinet at Monticello, and gave the rest to the National Institute in Paris. The last were promptly displayed in the Museum of National History, where they enabled George Cuvier to reconstruct not one but two extinct species of the mammoth.

Jefferson's connections with Peale went beyond paleontology. Philosophical Hall could no longer contain his museum. In 1802 he revived his old dream of a national institution and wrote to Jefferson proposing such an establishment in Washington. The vision was grand—Jefferson would have loved to forward it. But he pointed to the constitutional obstacle, and without stating his own opinion of congressional power to encourage science and learning, declined to take up this hazardous cause, at least for the present. Two years later he was meditating a plan for the support of the museum in Washington by contributions from the several states. On his own scale of values, the advancement of science had more importance than political concepts like state rights; but, with the natural history museum as with the agricultural institution, he was unwilling to run the gamut of opposition sure to be formidable, especially among his own followers who possessed his constitutional scruples without his commitment to enlightenment. In the field of invention Peale introduced Jefferson to two new marvels sprung from the mechanical genius of John Isaac Hawkins, who had built him a piano some years before. The physiognatrace was a device for making silhouettes. Raphael Peale visited Washington to take Jefferson's profile, which was reproduced in quantity and distributed as a souvenir to viewers of the mammoth at Peale's Museum. This was a bagatelle. More useful was the polygraph, a new type of copying machine, which Jefferson pronounced "a most precious invention." It was a desk mounting two pens in such a way that what was written by one was perfectly duplicated by the mechanical arm of the other. At Peale's instigation Jefferson introduced the polygraph in his office in February 1804, and as any researcher in the President's letters (duplicates for the most part) can testify it was a vast improvement on the copying press. Jefferson suggested many refinements, and Peale, who took over the machine from Hawkins, incorporated them in later models that often got their first test in the President's office. He was the machine's best salesman, actually wrote a testimonial for Peale's use, and sent polygraphs to friends and heads of state on three continents.

During the first two weeks of June 1804, Jefferson was honored with a visit from the brilliant young scientist-explorer Baron Alexander von Humboldt. He had just completed a five-year expedition in Spanish America, from the Caribbean to the remote provinces of the southern continent, a thousand miles on the Orinoco by canoe, to Quito and Lima in the Andes, thence to Acapulco by sail, and a year's exploration of Mexico. Announcing himself from Philadelphia, Humboldt said he had been inspired by Jefferson's liberalism from his earliest youth. Peale, who afterwards painted his portrait, escorted Humboldt and his companions to Washington. The Baron came to see not the President of the United States but Thomas Jefferson, author of the *Notes on Virginia*, votary of New World enlightenment, and luminary of science and freedom. Although the visitor stayed at Stelle's Hotel on Capitol Hill, he was given the freedom of Jefferson's house and spent many hours in easy conversation with him. On one occasion the Baron came upon his host romping on all fours with his grandchildren in the drawing room. "You have found me playing the fool, Baron," Jefferson remarked, "but I am sure to you I need make no apology." In truth, the Baron was as modest and friendly as he was enlightened. He admired the village capital, did not condescend, unlike so many foreigners, and from the vastness of his knowledge of Mexico and the southern hemisphere was able to capture the immensity of the American future in the year after the Louisiana Purchase. Just at the time New Spain came within the orbit of Jefferson's plans and transactions, Humboldt generously provided maps, statistical reports, information on mines, roads, crops, Indian tribes, settlements, and so on, information that until then had been locked up in Spanish archives. "We all consider him a very extraordinary man . . . ," Gallatin said. "I am not apt to be easily pleased, and he was not prepossessing to my taste, for he speaks . . . twice as fast as anybody I know, German, French, Spanish, and English all together." He poured forth his knowledge—geographical, geological, meterological, ethnological—in volcanic eruptions at Jefferson's table. There were at least three dinners at the President's House. According to Peale, "Not a single toast was given or called for, or politics touched on, but the subjects of Natural History, and improvements of the conveniences of life, manners of different nations described, or other agreeable conversation animated the whole company." The eighteenth century had passed but its spirit still glowed in the conversation of scientists and philosophers of the Old World and the New gathered around the President's table. When Humboldt departed, Jefferson did not hesitate to name him "the most scientific man of his age he had ever seen." The Baron, for his part, went away more convinced than before that the future of civilization lay with America, and that Jefferson, "the most virtuous of men," was its prophet.

The boundaries between science and government overlapped vaguely in a number of areas, some already noted, others still to be observed, while in quite another area, architecture, as related to the planning of the federal city, the President's responsibility was not only definite but cheerfully accepted. Since his association with the early planning of the city, it had fallen on hard times. Very few government lots had been sold at auction, and great private speculators in real estate had failed and landed in debtors' prison. Public morale had been shattered. The original scheme of financing public buildings and improvements by the sale of lots had of necessity been abandoned to a considerable degree, and loans from Maryland and Virginia became the last resort, amounting to $250,000 when Jefferson took office. Revenue from sales proved insufficient to service the loans, to say nothing of repaying them. It was difficult to see how the city, so deficient in active capital, could ever become a going concern. "The situation of Washington is certainly very fine," a visiting Philadelphian observed, "but it has long been ascertained that people cannot live much less grow rich upon prospects. . . . No houses are building; those already built are not finished and many are falling rapidly to decay." In the ghoulish vision of some men Washington was already beginning to resemble the ruins of Palmyra or some other ancient city. Because of the chronic complaints of the city, the capital suffered. Shortages of money, workmen, and materials delayed progress on the public buildings, and congressmen grew impatient at the inconveniences they endured. Bills were introduced to move the capital to Baltimore or Philadelphia. They found little support, but a dissident minority, appealing to the local sentiment for self-government in the District of Columbia, launched a movement to retrocede large portions of the "ten mile square" to Maryland and Virginia, and this could only be seen as a first step in the liquidation of the Potomac capital. Jefferson had to contend with this opposition and at the same time contribute what he could to fulfilling the grand design of the federal city.

In 1801 the President's authority continued to be exercised through the Board of Commissioners; the following year, however, Congress abolished the board, devolving its functions on a superintendent. The same legislation incorporated Washington as an independent municipality, thereby placing it on an equal footing with the sister cities of Georgetown and Alexandria, except that the mayor, like the superintendent, was a presidential appointee. The mayor, Robert Brent, who presided over an elected council, was a personal friend, as were most of the men at the center of the city's affairs. Jefferson's influence was constant. He found some difficulty determining where his authority started and stopped in the perfect maze of jurisdiction—state, congressional, presidential, municipal—that had grown up around the city and the district. Clearly he had responsibility for the execution of the original plan of the city, which included streets, squares, parks, buildings, and so on for the use of the United States. These concerns could not be separated into air-tight boxes, however, so Jefferson's hand reached into almost every phase of the city's development, from the granting of liquor licenses to the building of the navy yard, from markets and canals to schools and militia.

In the condition of the city as he found it, the L'Enfant plan was still largely a blueprint dependent upon the appropriation of money by Congress. Jefferson at once directed the commissioners to give top priority to two projects. First, the completion of a good roadway from Georgetown down Pennsylvania and New Jersey Avenues, a distance of four miles, to the Eastern Branch. By 1804 Pennsylvania Avenue assumed the form Jefferson had designed for it: a broad thoroughfare bordered by rows of trees, behind these on either side narrow roadways, a second row of trees, gutters, and footpaths. The trees were Lombardy poplars, a special favorite, though he loved all trees, planted them at every opportunity, and could not bear to see precious specimens destroyed. (Once in conversation with Mrs. Smith, he exclaimed, "How I wish that I possessed the power of a despot!" Met with disbelief, he went on, "Yes, I wish I was a despot that I might save the noble and beautiful trees that are daily falling sacrifice to the cupidity of their owners, or the necessity of the poor," who cut them for firewood.) The grandeur of a mall, such as he had conceived and L'Enfant had embellished, was a luxury far out of reach in his time; but Pennsylvania Avenue brought to the city a touch of splendor and it endured in the form Jefferson gave to it for over thirty years. The second priority item was the construction of the south wing of the Capitol for the accommodation of the House of Representatives. The Capitol had been a colossal headache form the beginning. A succession of superintendents had struggled with William Thornton's grand design; no sooner had the Senate taken possession of the north wing than it was in need of major repairs and alterations; and another ten years passed before the House moved into its own quarters. The expense, inconveniences, and delays nettled Congress and spurred on opponents of the Washington venture.

Acutely aware of these problems, Jefferson made up his mind to place the Capitol, together with the other buildings, under the superintendence of the best man he could find. In March 1803, three days after he signed into law a far-reaching act of Congress appropriating $50,000 to the public buildings, Jefferson appointed Benjamin H. Latrobe to the post. Nothing in the letter of the statute authorized this appointment, but seeing in the law an opportunity to banish forever all doubts as to the future of the capital, he determined to make the most of it. Latrobe, born and trained in England, had come to Virginia in 1796. There he had planned the penitentiary in Richmond and completed the façade of Jefferson's capitol. Jefferson had known him personally for five years, first in Philadelphia when at work on his Greek Revival building for the Bank of Pennsylvania. Only the year before Jefferson had called him to Washington to plan a dry dock for the navy yard. Latrobe's combination of architectural and engineering genius (he was currently the engineer for the Delaware and Chesapeake Canal) could not be matched by anyone in the United States. He admired Jefferson both as a statesman and as the father of the arts in his adopted country. The respect each man had for the other became the foundation of a fruitful partnership, one that actually benefitted from their contrasting tastes in architecture. Both were classicists, but Latrobe confessed to being "a bigoted Greek," while Jefferson, if not so ready to confess it, was an equally bigoted Roman. The enthusiasm of one checked the enthusiasm of the other.

Latrobe formed his plan for the Capitol after consultation with the President. He was to adhere to the Thornton design so far as practicable, not because it was beyond improvement in Jefferson's eyes but because it had been emphatically endorsed by Washington and accepted without question for a decade. Latrobe obeyed reluctantly, for he was "shocked" by Thornton's conception. Of course, the exterior style was already set: the south wing must repeat the façade of the north wing. The interior was another matter. Jefferson himself put forth the idea of raising the Senate chamber from the basement level to the main floor. And this was done, releasing the lower floor to the Supreme Court after extensive repair and remodeling of the entire wing. As to the House wing, its inner walls in the elliptical shape Thornton had prescribed were already partially built, covered over with a temporary roof under which the House had met since December 1801 when work on the Capitol stopped. But the walls were faulty and had to come down. Starting from the foundations, Latrobe was free to propose his own ideas for the House chamber. Jefferson met him halfway, insisting that the principal feature of the hall, a semicircular colonnade supporting a gallery, be retained, but allowing Latrobe to straighten the sides of Thornton's oval chamber. Thornton objected, the architects quarreled, and Jefferson tried to sooth feelings on both sides. To carve the frieze, the capitals for the columns (Corinthian on his orders) and other decorative stone work, he sent to Italy for craftsmen more richly endowed than native sculptors of ships' heads and mantelpieces. In 1806 his faithful friend Mazzei sent Giuseppe Franzoni and Giovanni Andrei, the vanguard of an Italian invasion in the decorative arts. The former executed an American eagle (specifications provided by Peale) to adorn the frieze and a statue of liberty placed above the Speaker's chair. These did not withstand the British torch in 1814, but the "corn cob capitals"—ears of corn rising upon columns fluted as cornstalks—carved in the basement of the north wing from Latrobe's highly original design, survived the wreckage. While Jefferson applauded this touch of Americanism, he was revolted by Latrobe's plan to raise a lantern (a cupola-like ornament to admit light) above the roof of the House wing. No classical

742

model showed lantern, belfry, or cupola, and Jefferson considered them among the "degeneracies of modern architecture." Conceding the historical point, Latrobe nevertheless thought they might be beautiful in the proper place, as atop the Capitol. He lost this little skirmish yet finally prevailed. In his reconstruction of the Capitol after the War of 1812, Latrobe placed a lantern above each wing.

Jefferson's only serious problem with Latrobe was holding him to the appropriation sparingly doled out by Congress year by year. In his eagerness to finish the House chamber in 1807, Latrobe ran a deficit of $52,000, about 70 per cent over his total budget. Jefferson apologized to Congress and read the architect a stiff lecture on public economy and the principles of American government. Piled on top of the criticism he was receiving for acoustical and other defects in the new chamber, together with partisan rumors of executive displeasure, this was the last straw. The harassed architect threatened to resign. Jefferson hastened to reassure him; no one else, he was convinced, could do the job. Latrobe stayed on, finishing the two wings not long after Jefferson left the presidency. "I think," he then wrote to the architect, "that the work when finished will be a durable and honorable monument to our infant republic, and will bear favorable comparison with the remains of the same kind of the ancient republics of Greece and Rome." It is a pity that Jefferson never saw Latrobe's post-war reconstruction of the Capitol, complete with the modestly domed middle building, for it was, as he always believed it would be, "the first temple dedicated to the sovereignty of the people, embellishing with Athenian taste the course of a nation looking far beyond the range of Athenian destinies."

His own residence, the White House as it would later be called, remained in a half-finished state throughout his presidency. For the first several years the roof leaked, no elegant staircase was in place, the bedrooms were without paint, the east room (where Jefferson kept mammoth cheese and mammoth bones, hence called the mammoth room) had yet to receive plaster, furnishings were sparse, and the grounds barren of landscape. Gradually, under Latrobe's supervision, most of these deficiencies were removed: a new roof went on (sheet iron, by direction of the President, who had used it at Monticello and would direct Latrobe to use it on the Capitol as well), the staircase went up, the apartments were painted, new furniture, though never enough, went in; finally, stone wall and stone steps rose outside, and the grounds—the President's sheep pasture—were gracefully sloped and seeded with grass. Jefferson developed a plan for landscaping the mansion but never found the money to carry it out. He did succeed in building colonnaded terraces on either side, like those he had designed for Monticello, and committed to the same services—meat house, wine cellar, storage, privies, stable, and so on.

Jefferson was a planner by instinct, of governments, buildings, farms, gardens, and towns. The last, town planning, is usually overlooked except in connection with Washington. Actually, his vision ranged much farther, and had the times been different and he free to practice his ideas, the face of America might have been changed for the better. The year before he became President, in the course of conversation with William Henry Harrison of the Northwest Territory, Jefferson spoke of the epidemics that so often besieged American cities and suggested that a remedy might be found in a modification of the common gridiron, or checkerboard, pattern of urban design. Leave every alternate square open, he said, and the infection would not spread. He had noted in Philadelphia that the yellow fever raged at its worst in the most crowded parts of the city, that it did not reach into the country and, in fact, that the contagion could not even be carried into this pure atmosphere. His theory as to the disease was wrong, of course, though he was not the only one to hold it at the time. Noah Webster set forth a similar theory, ascribing epidemics to the morbid state of the atmosphere in congested places, in his *Treatise on Pestilential Diseases* in 1801. It convinced Benjamin Rush and confirmed Jefferson's opinion, which, it might be observed, went along with his general prejudice against cities. Harrison, at any rate, liked Jefferson's idea. In 1802, after becoming Governor of Indiana Territory, he directed that a new town planned near the falls of the Ohio and called Jeffersonville be laid out on the Jeffersonian principle. The President was delighted by this innovation. "In Europe," he wrote, "where the sun does not shine more than half the number of days . . . it does in America, they can build their towns in a solid block with impunity. But here a constant sun produces too great an accumulation of heat to admit that. Ventilation is indispensably necessary." Unfortunately, when

Jeffersonville, Indiana, was finally laid out, diagonal streets in imitation of the L'Enfant plan were superimposed on the grid, cutting every open square into four small triangles; and within two decades the irrepressible commercial spirit had invaded what was left of Jefferson's "ventilating system." He recommended the plan to Governor Claiborne in New Orleans with no visible results; and apparently the only town in the United States built on the Jeffersonian grid was Jackson, Mississippi. The country being a Jeffersonian paradise of opportunity, above all in real estate, had little patience with the beauties and the pleasantries of the Jeffersonian style of life.

Louisiana!

The two administrations of Thomas Jefferson turned on two gigantic facts of geography, the Mississippi River and the Atlantic Ocean. In the first administration, the Mississippi occupied the foreground, and the President's efforts to secure the freedom of its navigation culminated in the Louisiana Purchase. The great effort of the second administration, directed to the freedom of America's seafaring frontier with Europe, met with crushing defeat. The two frontiers, of land and of ocean, westward and eastward, had divided American energies from the beginning; but now, with the acquisition of the vast spaces beyond the Mississippi, the nation's destiny seemed fixed in its direction, and so fabulous was the triumph of Jefferson's western vision that it greatly mitigated the costs of defeat in the Atlantic.

The vision took form in Jefferson's mind about the time of the American Revolution. In confronting the problems of Virginia's far-flung frontiers, he caught the idea of an "empire of liberty," an empire not of the ocean's deep where Albion roamed but a contiguous landward empire formed by the accretion of free and equal states as the Americans took possession of a nearly vacant continent. There were, in fact, almost no limits to his dreams of expansion. "Our confederacy must be viewed as the nest from which all America, North and South is to be peopled," he wrote in 1786. "We should take care not to think it for the interest of that great continent [South America and its appendages] to press too soon on the Spaniards.

745

Those countries cannot be in better hands. My fear is that they are too feeble to hold them till our population can be sufficiently advanced to gain it from them piece by piece. The navigation of the Mississippi we must have. This is all we are as yet ready to receive." In his inaugural address he spoke of the United States as "a chosen country, with room enough for our descendants to the hundredth and thousandth generation." What country? Surely not the one bounded by the 31st parallel, the Great Lakes, and the Mississippi, when nearly a million Americans already lived beyond the Appalachians; the country, rather, of Jefferson's imagination, certain to materialize in easy stages as Americans multiplied and pressed westward. Several months after the inaugural, he was meditating a resolution of the Virginia legislature, forwarded by Monroe, for the colonization of insurgent slaves and free Negroes in the empty spaces of North America or elsewhere. While in sympathy with the object, he opposed the settlement of the blacks any where on the continent. "However our present interests may restrain us within our limits," he explained, "it is impossible not to look forward to distant times, when our rapid multiplication will expand itself beyond those limits, and cover the whole northern, if not the southern, continent, with a people speaking the same language, governed in similar forms, and by similar laws; nor can we contemplate with satisfaction either blot or mixture on that surface." He did not think it necessary that this "empire" be united under one government, but it must be of one people united in the enterprise of freedom, his own country serving as common parent, midwife, and nurse of the entire "American system."

In 1801, as before, the Spanish colonies of Louisiana and the Floridas presented obstacles to American expansion. The danger lay, as Jefferson said, not in Spain's possession of these lands, but in Spanish dispossession by a strong and vigorous power, either Britain or France. So long as Spain remained lord of this domain it was America's for the asking. The Americans might, paraphrasing Montesquieu, thank God for putting Spain in the world, since of all nations she knew best how to possess a great empire with insignificance. There were but 50,000 people in Louisiana and the Floridas, the whole garrisoned with 1500 troops; the American trade at New Orleans outstripped the Spanish two to one; and the colonies showed a deficit of several hundred thousand dollars a year in the imperial accounts. The Spanish governors tried various schemes to check the onrushing Americans, but nothing seemed to work. "Their method of spreading themselves, and their policy [of forming new states] are so much to be feared by Spain as are their arms," one of the governors had said. For these reasons His Catholic Májesty had not been averse to using the North American colonies as pawns in the power plays of European diplomacy. In 1796 he had offered to give Louisiana to France if France could deliver Gibraltar to Spain. French interest in the recovery of the great colony she had lost in 1763 went back a number of years. Moustier, the second French Minister to the United States, had written an enthusiastic memoir on the subject in 1789. After the collapse of the Family Compact during the Revolution, the Girondists espoused liberation of the Spanish colonies, and Edmond Genêt sought to enlist American aid to foment rebellion in Louisiana. Then, in the aftermath of the Jay Treaty, the threat of an Anglo-American alliance, presaging an attack on Louisiana and the Floridas, isolating the French Antilles, closing all North America to French vessels, and wiping out, perhaps forever, the only basis for the re-establishment of French empire in the New World—these considerations impressed the Directory and its successors, including Napoleon Bonaparte.

In 1800 France was supreme in Europe, peace was in the offing, and Napoleon turned his fantastic energies to rebuilding the overseas empire. Louisiana and the Floridas were essential elements of a grand design centered on Santo Domingo, the richest of the colonies, then in the hands of the rebel blacks led by Toussaint L'Ouverture. The mainland colonies would provide the necessary economic and strategic support for a reconquered Santo Domingo and ensure French hegemony not only in the wide littoral from Florida to the Rio Grande but, ultimately, in the West Indies as well. By the Treaty of San Ildefonso, in October 1800, Spain secretly ceded Louisiana to France conditioned on an Italian throne for the Duke of Parma, Charles IV's brother-in-law. The King was content. France could far better defend Louisiana, and its principal value to Spain was as a buffer between the Americans and Mexico. He refused to part with the Floridas, however, despite the importunities of Napoleon's emissaries in Madrid. These negotiations continued. Meanwhile, Napoleon mounted an expedition to take possession of Louisiana at the great port of New Orleans.

Jefferson got wind of the retrocession in May 1801. At once an ominous shadow fell over his administration, so promising in every other aspect. Ominous, but nothing more at this time or for some months to come. Napoleon's plans of New World empire were involved in so many contingencies that they might never materialize. A bargain had presumably been made, but Napoleon had yet to fulfill his part of it. (He would, though not to Spain's satisfaction.) Whether or not the Floridas were included was unknown to the Americans, but without the Floridas Louisiana would be of doubtful value to France. And how could France take possession of Louisiana, much less garrison and colonize it, without first subduing the blacks in Santo Domingo? Moreover, Britain would surely not be indifferent to the revival of French power in the New World. The Peace of Amiens lay only a few months ahead (the preliminary articles were announced in November) but any Napoleonic peace was likely to prove unstable, and without peace in Europe the First Consul could not raise an empire in America. In view of these contingencies, Jefferson wisely resisted the temptation to sound alarms. While prudently moving to strengthen the American force at Fort Adams, just above the Spanish line on the Mississippi, he seemed anxious to make as little noise as possible. It was important to keep the country calm if diplomacy was to work. And given the ambiguity of the situation itself, a strategy of delay and maneuver improvised to meet events as they unfolded seemed to be called for.

Santo Domingo, as Jefferson appreciated, was the nub of Napoleon's problem. American policy toward that tormented island underwent a change with the coming of the new administration. During the Franco-American conflict of 1798–1800, Toussaint, the military commander of the colony, assumed the character of an independent ruler, and in order to maintain the island's commercial lifeline, he entered into a secret agreement with Britain and the United States which secured to those countries a trading monopoly. The arrangement lapsed, of necessity, with the Convention of 1800. The United States quit the rebels as part of the price of peace. But while acknowledging French sovereignty in Santo Domingo, Jefferson was also anxious to preserve America's flourishing trade with the island,

and this was impossible without dealing with the *de facto* sovereign, Toussaint. Inevitably, then, American policy was pitched to ambiguity, an ambiguity France must dispel as she fought to regain control of Santo Domingo. Assigned this task, Pichon, the newly arrived chargé d'affaires in 1801, sought positive assurances from Madison that the United States would uphold French sovereignty in Santo Domingo even in the face of a declaration of independence, which Toussaint had threatened to issue from time to time. Dissatisfied with the Secretary's yes-and-no response, Pichon took the problem to the President in July. France did not wish the cessation of American commerce with the island, since that would only drive Toussaint into British arms, Pichon said, but he was anxious for American cooperation in the restoration of French rule. To this Jefferson replied, first make peace with Britain, "then nothing will be easier than to furnish your army and fleet with everything and to reduce Toussaint to starvation." He reminded the chargé that the country had no love for the Negro leader: his example menaced every slaveholding state. Britain too, he believed, with good reason, would join in the concert, both to secure her own colonies and to put down "another Algiers in the seas of America." Pichon reported the conversation to Talleyrand, the Foreign Minister, and it apparently played some part in Napoleon's decision to go ahead with his plans for Santo Domingo. In the light of events still to come, Jefferson had aroused false expectations of American collaboration in the destruction of this incipient black republic in the Caribbean. Perhaps he had, in fact, promised too much to Pichon. But whatever he promised as to Santo Domingo carried an implicit warning as to Louisiana, which in his mind called for the same consideration of American interests on the Mississippi as France requested for her interests in the Caribbean.

In 1802 Jefferson not only failed to deliver the support allegedly promised for the subjugation of the rebel government but showed every disposition to let the French army rot in Santo Domingo. General Victor Leclerc, Napoleon's esteemed brother-in-law who was given command of the reconquest, landed his first army of 10,-000 men in January. He had been instructed to obtain money and supplies and other assistance from the United States. Pichon, pressing these claims, found the President "reserved and cold," hearing from him as from Madison the familiar story that while the government wished France success it dared not make an enemy of Toussaint. When Leclerc proclaimed a blockade of the ports in rebel control, Jefferson refused to co-operate. Most of the supplies of both armies, rebel and French, were American, and Leclerc's high-handed treatment of merchants and expulsion of the consul were added irritants. For a time the war went well for the French. Toussaint, betrayed by his own generals and acting on Napoleon's assurances of his liberty and the liberty of the blacks, gave himself up to Leclerc. On first hearing of this event, Jefferson was incredulous. "What has been called a surrender of Toussaint to Leclerc, I suspect was in reality a surrender of Leclerc to Toussaint." Wish was father to the thought, and he erred in this detail. Yet his intuition proved sound. Toussaint's surrender was followed by arrest and deportation and imprisonment high in the Jura Mountains, ending in cold and solitary death a few months later. When the authentic report reached Jefferson he predicted that Leclerc's perfidy would be his undoing: "some other black leader will arise, and a war of extermination will ensue: for no second capitulation will ever be trusted by the blacks." And so it happened. "Rid us of these gilded Africans," Bonaparte lectured his general, "and we shall have nothing more to wish." Slavery would be restored, the island's sugar, coffee, indigo, and other tropical produce would again enrich French commerce, and the troops in Santo Domingo would be sent to possess Louisiana. But black arms and yellow fever annihilated one French army after another. In October, Leclerc estimated the nine months' loss at 24,000 men, and still he was not master of the island. A month later he too was dead. The implications of this catastrophe for Louisiana were, throughout, as clear to Jefferson as they were to Bonaparte. A great expedition destined for the Mississippi was mounting at Dunkirk in the summer of 1802, but no sooner were troops and supplies assembled than they were diverted to Santo Domingo. The Louisiana expedition never sailed.

Meanwhile, Robert R. Livingston, the American Minister in Paris, tried to conduct negotiations on Louisiana. Livingston was deaf, spoke no French, and quarreled with every public agent—the consul, the secretary of legation—with whom he had anything to do. As if these handicaps were not enough, neither his own government nor the French ministry paid much attention to him. Talleyrand, recalled to service by Napoleon to direct the imperial policy he had himself largely conceived, despised the Americans. Jefferson traced his enmity to the XYZ incident, but it probably went back to his unhappy experience in the United States as a refugee from revolution. He had, at any rate, been badly burned by the Americans in 1798 and did not intend to make the same mistake again when so much depended on American good will. On matters of claims and other business left over from the Convention of 1800, Talleyrand was eminently approachable, but he turned into a Sphinx at the mention of Louisiana. Only in June 1802 did Livingston learn that the Floridas were not included in the bargain with Spain, though the matter was still in negotiation.

Livingston's original instructions on Louisiana were as mild as the situation would permit. He was to press reasons against the cession, but should he meet with resistance, he was to do nothing that would "unnecessarily irritate our future neighbors, or check the liberality which they may be disposed to exercise in relation to the trade and navigation through the mouth of the Mississippi." This was the first and only imperative of American policy. It seemed little enough—the continuation of existing Spanish policy on the river. But France had other plans for control of the trade and refused to budge. "There never was a government in which less could be done by negotiation than here—," Livingston reported. "There is no people, no legislature, no councillors—One man is everything. He seldom asks advice and never hears it unasked—his ministers are mere clerks and his legislators and councillors parade officials." Communication between Washington and Paris was painfully slow. Partly for these reasons, Jefferson and Madison conducted their own negotiation quite apart from Livingston's. Their official channel was Pichon. In dispatches to Talleyrand he presented the American case against the French policy more effectively than an interested native could possibly do. He cited the pertinent figures on trade and population in Louisiana, pointed to the dangers of again making enemies of the Americans, argued that a strong and independent United States was France's best hope, and begged his country to accede to "that which the force of events will give them in spite of us." The same words in Livingston's mouth seemed not to be heard. Frustrated, Livingston turned to Rufus King, hoping to arouse a sympathetic response in Whitehall. But Britain would not risk the Peace of Amiens on the chance of strengthening ties with the United States. Britain acquiesced in the reconquest of Santo Domingo. As to Louisiana, King reported, Lord Hawkesbury only grunted "highly interesting." If the United States could no longer play off one European power against another, it was difficult to see what leverage the country had left in the tasks of diplomacy.

Undismayed, Jefferson nevertheless struck a new course in April predicated on an old theory, in this case that he could summon the winds of Albion to carry him safely into port. His good friend Dupont de Nemours, who had come to the United States with his family in 1799 and plunged into various enterprises destined to make his name a household word, was returning to France, and out of his deep friendship for the President ("the American Turgot," Dupont called him, after his own master) offered his services in the matter of Louisiana. Unlike Pichon, unlike an influential group of Americanists in Paris, sometimes called the Ideologues, Dupont was not inalterably opposed to the Napoleonic policy. He was going home partly to raise capital for his American enterprises, partly with a view of making peace with the First Consul and securing a high post in the government. Napoleon might listen to him. As a sincere friend of both countries, anxious for a mutually advantageous settlement between them, he seemed peculiarly fitted for the role of an honest broker in the Louisiana negotiation. Jefferson seized the opportunity to use him. He had written an important letter to Livingston which he now entrusted to Dupont and left open for his inspection.

The letter began gravely. The retrocession of Louisiana formed a new epoch in America's foreign relations. Heretofore the country had looked upon France, of all the great powers, as its natural friend, but France astride the lower Mississippi assumed the attitude of defiance. "There is on the globe one single spot, the possessor of which is our natural and habitual enemy. It is New Orleans, through which the produce of three-eights of our territory must pass to market, and from its fertility it will ere long yield more than half of our whole produce and contain more than half our inhabitants. . . . The day that France takes possession of New Orleans fixes the sentence which is to restrain her forever within her low water mark. It seals the union of two nations who in conjunction can maintain exclusive possession of the ocean. From that moment we must marry ourselves to the British fleet and nation." After flourishing this thunderbolt, after warning that the first cannon fired in the next European war would be the signal for tearing up any settlement France may have made on the Mississippi, Jefferson returned to his usual posture of peace and friendship. If in the face of an enlightened view of her own interests France persisted in the present policy, she ought, at least, to cede the island of New Orleans and the Floridas, since this would put off the threatened alliance with Britain and compensate the United States for the risk of a quarrel with France on the Mississippi. "Every eye in the United States is now fixed on the affair of Louisiana. Perhaps nothing since the revolutionary war has produced more uneasy sensations through the body of the nation." Yet Jefferson refused to be an alarmist, and lest the American Minister be inclined in that direction, he pointed out that time was on the American side and Livingston would be able "to return again and again to the charge, for the conquest of St. Domingo will not be short work." In covering this letter, Jefferson underscored several of its points for Dupont's benefit. The cession of New Orleans and the Floridas would be a "palliative" only. Repossession of Louisiana must eventually annihilate France on the ocean and appropriate all America to Britain and the United States as a consequence. The New World, he warned, could no longer be considered a plaything of Europe, "a mere make-weight in the general settlement of accounts,—this speck," Louisiana, "which now appears as an almost invisible point in the horizon, is the embryo of a tornado which will burst on the countries on both sides of the Atlantic, and involve in its effects their highest destinies."

The President's letters stunned Dupont. Gestures of bravado were not apt to impress the conqueror of Europe, the man who, in the words of the Abbé Sieyes, "knows everything, wants everything, and can do everything." And if Jefferson seriously contemplated an alliance with Britain he was sadly deceived. Nothing had changed as to that power: Britain still saw in the United States a formidable rival to her commercial dominion. Dupont did not mention, though both he and Jefferson understood the point, that the proposed marriage to the British fleet would be difficult to manage under the European peace just now, in April, being signed at Amiens. He probably suspected the President was bluffing. Perhaps he was. But the gravity of his analysis of the American position, taken together with the fragility of the Peace of Amiens, raised great risks for the nation that would call his bluff. Dupont thought France would listen if the American demands were limited to the left bank of the Mississippi, and he advised Jefferson to offer gold for New Orleans and the Floridas, assuming the latter were France's to sell.

The proposition of a purchase did not originate with Dupont. It had been earlier mentioned in Washington. On May 1, just before the Frenchman's letter arrived, Madison asked Livingston to ascertain the price, though without any commitment to buy. A startling idea, it could only have arisen in a nation and with an administration determined to settle international disputes without resort to force. In Paris, Livingston redoubled his diplomatic efforts and wrote a powerful memoir against the French course in North America. But the timing was off. Leclerc was taming the "gilded Africans," or so it seemed, and the Louisiana expedition was going forward. Talleyrand refused to bargain. Nor did Dupont succeed in mediating the dispute. Still he was highly useful. He had an audience with Napoleon and talked with Talleyrand and other high officials. Louisiana figured in these discussions. In contrast to Livingston, whose patience was nearly exhausted, Dupont kept up the hopes of the administration in a negotiated settlement.

As the months passed, and Jefferson summered at Monticello and returned to Washington at the first touch of fall, the Louisiana imbroglio seemed no closer to resolution. Simply to bide his time, waiting for something to turn up, may have been a poor excuse for a policy, yet his only alternative was a rupture with France, and this was premature. The situation remained fluid—he did not wish to freeze it beyond the possibilities of chance. Napoleon had yet to make good his policy; a British accord must await a *démarche* in Europe; and war with all its calamities was the last resort. In October he cautioned Livingston against any impetuous move that might commit the United States to one side or the other of the European power balance. We stand, he said, "completely corrected of the error, that . . . France has any remains of friendship for us," moreover "that no consequence, however ruinous to them, can secure us with certainty against the extravagance of her present rulers." Nevertheless, the country would wage unremitting peace with France. "No matter at present existing between them and us is important enough to risk a breach of peace—peace being indeed the most important of all things for us, except the preserving an erect and independent attitude." France was about to possess herself of the Mississippi, yet, without denying anything said from the other side of his mouth, Jefferson insisted that nothing in the present situation warranted a breach with France.

He was still playing for time. In October, within a week of his letter to Livingston, an event at New Orleans turned the clock ahead dramatically. The Spanish intendant revoked the right of deposit in violation of the Pinckney Treaty. Some Americans believed this virtual stoppage of the river traffic had been secretly ordered by Napoleon as a step preparatory to French occupation. Suspicions were also directed at the government in Madrid, which might have ordered the closure with a view to embarrassing their successors in New Orleans. In Washington, fortunately, neither government was blamed. Yrujo assured Jefferson and Madison that the intendant, acting on some mistaken idea of his authority, was alone responsible for the provocative measure. Informed Americans at New Orleans made the same report. Prudence lay on the side of accepting this explanation, especially as Yrujo moved rapidly to heal the breach. A letter from Dupont arrived at this anxious moment to check suspicions of French intrigue. Dupont named a price: six million dollars for New Orleans and the Floridas on condition that France receive the same commercial rights as the Americans. "If you are willing to go that far, I do not despair of success." Dupont wrote with some semblance of authority. As long as diplomatic channels remained open, there was no cause for panic.

In fact, the closure of the Mississippi had been authorized from Madrid, primarily in retaliation for American abuses of the privileges of the entrepôt; but even had the truth been known in Washington, it would not have served Jefferson's purposes nearly so well as the fiction that blamed the crisis on an erratic colonial official. The President sought to calm the soaring war fever among his friends in the West as well as his enemies in the East, who together, whatever the contrary nature of their motives, might topple his administration and throw away the opportunity to gain the Mississippi via the surer pacific route. The crisis came at a busy time. Jefferson was secretly preparing an expedition to explore the Trans-Mississippi country. Congress convened in an agitated frame of mind. He made no mention of the closure of the Mississippi in his message at the opening of the session. When information was demanded, he adroitly persuaded the House to let the administration handle the problem. The West assumed a higher tone, called for troops, and talked of marching on New Orleans. The West did not disturb him. He could control the West, though up to a point its ardor now served his diplomatic objectives. The Federalists were less tractable. Almost to a man they demanded war, not from any sudden conversion to Western interests (they had, many of them, looked upon the retrocession of Louisiana as a political blessing) but from a desire to embarrass the administration. Jefferson viewed the agitation under its varied aspects in January: "In the western country it is natural and grounded on honest motives. In the seaports it proceeds from a desire for war which increases the mercantile lottery; in the Federalists generally and especially those of Congress the object is to force us into war if possible, in order to derange our finances, or if this cannot be done, to attach the western country to them as their best friends, and thus get again into power." The measures thus far taken, being invisible, had not quieted these clamors. Something "sensible," yet in the diplomatic line, had become necessary.

Thus it was that on January 11 Jefferson nominated James Monroe minister extraordinary to join Livingston in negotiations for the purchase of New Orleans and the Floridas. Monroe was an ideal choice. He possessed the confidence of the West; he knew France and, after Jefferson himself, had been the only American minister to win the confidence of that nation. He was ending his term as Governor of Virginia, and although he toyed with the idea of retiring to the practice of law, he was, as Jefferson once remarked, one of those men "born for the public" and bound to serve. As Jefferson's neighbor in Albemarle, Monroe had seen the President often during the summer; doubtless they had conversed at length on the Mississippi question. The appointment was a *fait accompli* before Monroe even knew about it. "The measure has already silenced the Federalists here," Jefferson told him on the 13th. "Congress will no longer be agitated by them: and the country will become calm as fast as information extends over it. All eyes, all hopes, are now fixed on you; and were you to decline, the chagrin would be universal, and would shake under your feet the high ground on which you stand with the public. Indeed I know nothing which would produce such a shock, for on the event of this mission depends the future destiny of this republic." Closure only offered the excuse for Monroe's appointment—a gesture to calm the war hawks—for that problem was silently on its way to solution. The trade of New Orleans, in fact never effectively closed, regained its old footing in April. The larger problem remained. Upon the mission depended, as Jefferson saw it, whether by purchase of New Orleans and the Floridas the United States would "insure to ourselves a course of perpetual peace and friendship with all nations" or go to war with France at no distant time, "get entangled in European politics, and . . . be much less happy and prosperous" than now.

The purchase project, as strongly recommended by Dupont, was taking form. Jefferson felt vaguely distrustful of Livingston in a negotiation of this kind. It was apt to assume so many shapes that he preferred to send a minister who could speak "straight from the horse's mouth," as it were, and upon whom he could rely implicitly. Livingston had lost caste in Washington by including in his memorial to the French government a blatant appeal to Franco-American solidarity against British "tyranny," just when the administration waved a British alliance as its trump card. London protested and Washington hastened to cover its embarrassment. The errant Minister's response to the news of closure and of near disaster in Santo Domingo was to open a new channel of negotiation, Joseph Bonaparte, the elder brother, through whom he hoped to reach the First Consul. Livingston offered a whole series of propositions, some of them wild (the cession of the Florida littoral as a future refuge for the Bonapartes), all of them hinting at bribery, and one of them involving for the first time the acquisition of territory beyond the Mississippi. This proposal called for the sale of New Orleans and the small province to the east, West Florida, as well as that part of Louisiana above the Arkansas River. It raised no enthusiasm in

Washington since it appeared to install France on the Gulf and to make the United States a buffer between British Canada and the French in lower Louisiana. Not surprisingly, Livingston was nettled by Monroe's appointment. When he learned of it in March he was still angling with Joseph Bonaparte—New Orleans in exchange for certain "personal advantages"—but promptly gave it up. "With respect to Louisiana," he wrote despondently, "I fear nothing will be done here."

Yet at this very time the affair rapidly approached a climax. In Washington the Federalists resumed the drumbeats of war, and the administration, while muffling these alarms at home, amplified them for foreign ears. Things threatened to get out of hand in February when James Ross, the Pennsylvania Federalist, introduced in the Senate an inflamatory resolution authorizing the President to take New Orleans by force. "Plant yourselves on the river, fortify the banks, invite those who have an interest to defend it . . . ," said Ross, "and leave the event to him who controls the fate of nations." The resolution failed. Keeping the crisis in the track of diplomacy, Jefferson and Madison played upon Pichon's nerves, and he, in turn, transmitted every perturbation to Paris. "I noticed at his table," Pichon reported after one of the President's dinners, "that he redoubled his civilities and attentions to the British chargé." To the British chargé, Jefferson declared that should the United States be forced to it, "they would throw away the scabbard." No overture was actually made to Britain, though it was well understood, at least by Pichon, that one would be made if Monroe failed in his mission.

Jefferson gave Monroe a letter to Dupont in which he reiterated his view in an urgent manner. "For our circumstances are so imperious as to admit of no delay to our course; and the use of the Mississippi so indispensable, that we cannot hesitate one moment to hazard our existence for its maintenance. If we fail in this effort to put it beyond the reach of accident, we see the destinies we have to run, and prepare at once for them." The preparations went forward in silence: army recruitment was stepped up, arms, troops, and supplies concentrated at Fort Adams, Indian tribes on the left bank pressed to cede their lands, and the passage of western mail expedited. Of course, Jefferson told Dupont, the country would go on in peace if the rights of navigation and deposit were respected by France. Realistically, however, French control of the Mississippi must produce such a state of irritation that the two countries could not long remain at peace. "And how long would it be hers, with such an enemy, situated at its door, added to Great Britain?" Jefferson asked. "I confess, it appears to me as essential to France to keep at peace with us, as it is to us to keep at peace with her." Monroe's instructions authorized the purchase of New Orleans and the Floridas for upwards to ten million dollars—a tremendous stretch on the part of the economy-minded President and Congress. Should the offer be rejected, the ministers were to make the best bargain they could to ensure the rights of navigation and deposit. An addendum after Monroe's departure covered the last resort: alliance with Britain.

But the Louisiana Purchase was made in France, not in America, and it owed more to the vagaries of Bonaparte's ambition than to Jefferson's cautious diplomacy. The dream of New World empire faded fast in the early months of 1803. After Leclerc's death, Napoleon despaired of Santo Domingo. Because of it precious time, to say nothing of blood and treasure, had been lost in the planting of the French flag on the Mississippi; and without Santo Domingo, without the Gulf ports of the Floridas, which Spain would not yield, Louisiana was useless to France. Napoleon still had empire in his eyes. Turning from failure in the Western seas, he revived the dream of empire in the East—Egypt, the Levant, India. Malta stood in his way. He had surrendered the island fortress to Britain in 1800 and now demanded it back. War was again imminent in Europe. Jefferson, hearing this news early in May, convened the cabinet, which decided that on the outbreak of hostilities American neutrality would be withheld and used as a weapon of bargain for New Orleans and the Floridas. "In this conflict," he wrote, "our neutrality will be cheaply purchased by a cession . . . , because taking part in the war, we could certainly seize and securely hold them and more." A British alliance, so much deprecated, would probably not even be necessary. The United States would win its objectives with the armory Jefferson had always advocated. He had calculated at long-range on war coming to his rescue, and now, *mirabile dictu*, the gamble was paying off.

In Paris, meanwhile, everything was settled. Napoleon could not defend Louisiana while marching to the East. He could not march without gold, gold Louisiana would buy. He could not destroy the remains of British power without American friendship, and he could not have that without removing the causes of dissension on the Mississippi. "Irresolution and deliberation are no longer in season," he declared at St.-Cloud on April 11. "I renounce Lousiana." Monroe arrived in Paris the next day. Livingston, to whom Talleyrand had already made the extraordinary proposition of selling the whole of Louisiana, had been so taken aback that he could only repeat the litany of New Orleans and the Floridas. When it dawned on him and Monroe, who joined in the final negotiations, what a noble acquisition this would be, they did not hesitate to conclude a treaty beyond their instructions. After some haggle, the price was set at $15,000,000, one-fourth of which represented the assumption of French debts owed to American citizens. For this the United States received the immense uncharted country between the Mississippi and the Rocky Mountains or beyond. No one knew its size, its limits were obscure, but it virtually doubled the land area of the United States at a cost, omitting the interest, of approximately 13-1/2 cents an acre. "We have lived long," Livingston said at the signing of the treaty, "but this is the noblest work of our whole lives. . . . From this day the United States take their place among the powers of first rank."

News of the treaty reached Washington on the eve of the 4th of July, befitting an event many hailed as the greatest since the Declaration of Independence. All but the most choleric Federalists were overjoyed. Fifteen million dollars for a howling wilderness! Why, said the Federalists, stack the dollars one upon another and the pile would be three miles high. Twenty dollars from every taxpayer in the United States. And for whose benefit? Southern planters and western frontiersmen. The country was already too big—if the distant domain ever grew to statehood, its congressmen would have to go to Washington by way of Cape Horn! The transaction made no sense unless as tribute Thomas Jefferson paid to Napoleon Bonaparte for the conquest of Britain. Well, if the triumph was not enough to turn every fair-minded Federalist into a Republican, then the petulant utterances of the lunatic fringe were certain, in Jefferson's opinion, to bury the Federalist party under a heap of scorn.

Jefferson never boasted that *he* bought Louisiana. Yet he resented the grumblers and doubters who would deny to him and his administration any credit for the accomplishment. To those who had demanded war as the only solution, the President had looked too much "like Sterne's ass, which when . . . kicked, cuffed, and spat upon, turns up his piteous, imploring eyes and says 'pray don't beat us.' " From such a posture, obviously, no good could come. But Jefferson's posture, while pacific, was far more subtle than any political caricature and much better attuned to realities than the warmongering of his critics. In the two-year-long campaign, he never overextended himself, never cut off his lines of retreat, never risked the consequences of an armed encounter, yet kept the objective steadily in view. Inaction was as much a part of his strategy as action, and he knew when to wave the sword and when to sheath it. While not neglecting defensive preparations, he made them without bluster or fanfare. While holding control of the warlike propensities of the West, he was able to use them for diplomatic effect. From easy beginnings he steadily tightened the springs of diplomacy. The entire proceeding was an impressive vindication of the ways of peace in the conduct of American affairs. In the final analysis, of course, he was saved by European war. But this was not simply a piece of dumb luck. The prospect of war, like the prospect of French defeat in Santo Domingo, entered into his calculations. He correctly weighed the imponderables of the European power balance, shrewdly threatened to throw his weight into the British scale, gauged the effect of renewed war on Napoleon's imperial design, and prepared to take advantage of the *démarche* when it came. He wrote in retrospect: "I did not expect he [Napoleon] would yield till a war took place between France and England, and my hope was to palliate and endure, if Messrs. Ross, Morris, etc. did not force a premature rupture, until that event," when the country could be obtained as the price of neutrality or in reprisal for wrongs sure to be received. "The war happened somewhat sooner than was expected," he said, "but our measures were previously taken, and the thing took the best turn for both parties."

Great affairs of state are always surrounded in chance, and victory hangs as much upon making the right wagers in the matters depending on the will of others as it does upon the efficient marshaling of one's own forces. In the Louisiana crisis Jefferson played the game to perfection. Indeed he won much more than he played for, the whole of Louisiana instead of New Orleans and the Floridas. The negotiations centered on the latter because, realistically, the United States was not threatened in Louisiana, and making it an object would only have weakened the force of a claim involving the nation's vital interests. This does not mean that Jefferson had no eyes for Louisiana, itself of small importance to France, only that it was not an immediate object. From the first and primary acquisition, the rest would certainly follow. Instead it came all at once, which altered the timetable of American expansion but not its destination.

For several months Jefferson had been planning to chart the path of destiny to the farthest shore. By happy coincidence the man he had chosen for this task, Meriwether Lewis, set out from Washington on July 4th with the acclaim of the Louisiana Purchase ringing in his ears. From the sixteenth-century conquistador Cabeza de Vaca to Alexander Mackenzie, who traversed the continent on the Canadian side in the 1790's, the work of exploration had gone forward, impelled by the centuries old dream of a Northwest Passage; yet the country of the Missouri River and beyond was still virtually unknown, either a blank on the map, often the only honest cartography, or filled up with imaginary seas, mountains, rivers, and deserts. Jefferson had long been fascinated by the challenge of this great country, first in his relationship with George Rogers Clark during the American Revolution, then with the eccentric Yankee traveler John Ledyard while in France, and in 1793 with the politically aborted expedition of André Michaux. The first requisite was to possess the country for the mind. Geographical knowledge would prepare the way for economic penetration, to be followed eventually by political mastery. The fact that a country held neither title nor jurisdiction in unknown lands and seas was not considered by enlightened rulers and philosophers a bar to "voyages of discovery." "The field of knowledge," Jefferson later said in defense of an expedition into the Spanish borderlands, "is the common property of all mankind, and any discoveries we can make in it will be for the benefit . . . of every other nation, as well as our own."

Both ruler and philosopher, he felt a keen desire to distinguish his administration in works of science as well as of government. His political creed was not well adapted to this purpose, however, and he had been in the presidency nearly two years without taking a single significant step toward the union of the hopes of science with the hopes of republicanism. Some of his philosophical friends candidly confessed their disappointment. "No naturalist travels at the public expense to explore our immense Country and make us acquainted with the infinite resources it contains upon its surface, in its waters and within its bowels, from whence great national advantages would result . . . ," William Dunbar complained, "but it would seem that the speculations of the generality of our politicians are confined within the narrow circle of the customs and the excise, while literature is left to weep in the background." The Mississippi savant still had hopes that under the illustrious Jefferson "Arts, Sciences, and Literature may take a flight, which will at length carry them as far beyond those of our European brethren, as we soar above them in the enjoyment of national liberty." In the end Dunbar would not be disappointed; in fact, he would have a part in the on-going enterprise of exploration launched by the Lewis and Clark Expedition.

The expedition had been in preparation since November 1802. Lieutenant Meriwether Lewis, the President's private secretary, had served in the 1st Infantry; he knew the posts above the Ohio, and had ranged far into the interior. This knowledge of the western country, combined with Jefferson's long acquaintance with his family and upbringing in Albemarle, had prompted the President to call him to Washington in 1801. He came to know the young man intimately. So impressed was he with Lewis's qualities of leadership, talent for observation, knowledge of the Indians, honesty, understanding, and so on—all the qualifications providentially united in one person for the mission Jefferson had in mind—that he did not hesitate to place him in command. Of Lewis's ardor for exploration there could be no doubt: a decade earlier, when only eighteen years of age, he had applied to Jefferson to head the expedition confided to Michaux. "To fill up the measure desired," Jefferson later wrote, "he wanted nothing but a greater familiarity with the technical language of the natural sciences, and readiness in the astronomical observations necessary for the geography of his route." To acquire these he was sent to Philadelphia and placed under the tutelage of its eminent scientists: Benjamin Smith Barton and Caspar Wistar in natural history, Robert Patterson and Andrew Ellicott (in Lancaster) in astronomy, Benjamin Rush in medicine. And, of course, he pored over the maps and travels of Mackenzie and others. After this brief exposure, Lewis hardly qualified as a learned man in any branch of science; nor was his second in command, William Clark of Kentucky, or any member of his party, a scientific specialist. But Jefferson's judgment of Lewis proved correct. He was a remarkably astute observer, and possessing this untrained intelligence under the gloss of science, together with the ability to lead men and the "know how" to survive in the wilderness, he possessed all that was necessary, unencumbered by the superfluous, for blazing the trail to the Pacific in which others might follow.

Jefferson announced the plan of the expedition to Congress in a secret message on January 18. The explorers would trace the Missouri to its source, cross the highlands—how high and how far no one knew—and follow the best water course to the Pacific. This was straightforward, but the purpose of the mission was quite ambiguous, deliberately so. To the ministers of foreign countries, like Yrujo, whose king remained the sovereign of the territory pending its actual transfer to France, Jefferson indicated that the mission was of a "literary" nature. To Congress, which would never approve anything so speculative, he emphasized its commercial aspect. The peltry trade of the Indians along the whole course of the Missouri and beyond might be diverted from Canada to a continuous line of navigation in the lower latitudes all the way to the Atlantic coast. The opening of water communication across the continent was a proper object of congressional legislation under the power to regulate commerce.

Commerce and Indian relations were certainly among the purposes Jefferson had in mind; of first importance, however, was geographical and, more generally, scientific knowledge. In his message he alluded to these objects as merely "incidental." "While other civilized nations have encountered great expense to enlarge the boundaries of knowledge, by undertaking voyages of discovery, and for other literary purposes, in various parts and directions," he said, "our nation seems to owe to the same object, as well as to its own interests, to explore this, the only line of easy communication across the continent, and so directly traversing our own part of it." Here spoke the philosopher-statesman, and it is impossible to read the detailed instructions he penned for Lewis in April without realizing the importance the acquisition of knowledge had in his conception of the expedition. Observations of latitude and longitude were to be taken with "great precision and accuracy" at all points along the route, carefully recorded, and kept in multiple copies. An acquaintance with the various Indian tribes—their languages, customs, occupations, moral and physical circumstances—had obvious bearing on commerce. Among other things meriting attention: "the soil and face of the country . . . the animals . . . the remains . . . the mineral productions of every kind . . . volcanic appearances . . . climate . . . the dates at which particular plants put forth or lose their flowers, or leaf, times of appearance of particular birds, reptiles or insects." Of course, Lewis could not unveil the whole arcanum of western nature. His mission was exploratory. What Jefferson later said to Dunbar in connection with the Red River expedition, he might have said to Lewis: "The work we are now doing is, I trust, done for posterity, in such a way that they need not repeat it. . . . We shall delineate with correctness the great arteries of this great country: those who come after us will extend the ramifications as they become acquainted with them, and fill up the canvas we begin."

Public interest in the expedition rose after the news of the Louisiana Purchase. "The Federalists alone treat it as philosophism, and would rejoice in its failure," Jefferson wrote to Lewis at his winter quarters near the mouth of the Missouri. The vein of raillery, "philosophism," began to flow in the fall when Jefferson sent to Congress a most remarkable document, An Account of Louisiana, in which Indian lore, western apocrypha, and similar scraps of knowledge were mixed with much hard data on the strange new world. The President told of Indian tribes of gigantic stature, of soil too rich for the growth of trees, and of astounding geological phenomena. A paper received from an army officer in the West, sent to Congress and published, reported a great salt mountain—180 miles of glittering white rock salt.* Fabled land indeed! Why, the New York *Evening*

* Jefferson later said he had not read the paper when it was posted through him to Congress and first learned of the salt mountain from lampooning Federalist writers who ascribed the prodigious tale to him. Yet he soberly

Post wondered, had not the President gone on to tell of "the immense lake of molasses" and the "extensive vale of hasty pudding, stretching as far as the eye could see." Perhaps Louisiana overexcited Jefferson's "itch for telling prodigies," which was John Quincy Adams's way of describing his capacity for enchantment; still, even if Lewis and Clark did not meet with fantastic mammoth or Indians descended from Welchmen or mountain "sous'd in pickle"—items mentioned in a satire from Adams's pen—the land proved to be as fabulous as Jefferson's imagination. From Fort Mandan 1600 miles up the Missouri, Lewis described the country he and his party had traversed on the first leg of the journey as "one of the fairest portions of the globe"; and from this point he sent back a barge full of specimens, of soil, plants, animals, Indian artifacts, and so on, which excited great curiosity when they finally arrived in Washington in August 1805. Some of these specimens, like the prairie dog (American badger) were unknown to science, others, like the magpie, heretofore unknown in America. Jefferson experimented with the maize sent by the explorers, filed the Indian vocabularies for future reference, and mounted the great horns of a wapiti in the entrance hall at Monticello. Nearly everything else was sent on to the scientists in Philadelphia. Meanwhile, the explorers descended the Columbia River, wintered near its mouth, then commenced the 3500-mile return trek, reaching St. Louis in September 1806.

Many years would be required to sort out and organize the wealth of information gained by the explorers. As a scientific enterprise, the expedition was a spectacular success. In terms of its practical purpose, the discovery of a feasible commercial route to the Pacific, it was not. The gap between the Missouri and the Columbia proved much greater than anyone had imagined in 1803: 340 miles, much of it, as Lewis said, "over tremendous mountains . . . covered with eternal snows." But such formidable obstacles did not discourage Jefferson nor the many Americans touched by his vision of a continental destiny. As Henry Nash Smith has said, "The importance of the Lewis and Clark expedition lay on the level of imagina-

entertained the possibility of its truth. Nothing in nature was against it. Salt mountains had been mentioned by Pliny and described by modern explorers in various places. In 1804 Osage Indians told him of a great salt plain on the Arkansas. Many laughed at this too.

tion: it was drama, it was the enactment of a myth that embodied the future."

The Louisiana Purchase did not solve the problem of the American West but changed its terms radically. In the summer of 1803, while Lewis descended the Ohio on his way to the continent's end, Jefferson and his colleagues turned their attention to urgent questions of law, government, and diplomacy arising under the treaty of cession. What were the boundaries of Louisiana? The treaty did not declare. The acquisition amounted to a revolution in the American Union. Was it warranted? Could the Union withstand the shock? Could the new lands be governed under the Constitution? How? As colonies subject to the will of Congress or as free and independent states? The people of Louisiana were predominantly French. Could they, or should they, be assimilated to American institutions? What were the bearings of Louisiana on Indian relations, on slavery, on land policy, on foreign policy? A great new frontier—a whole series of frontiers—had been created. How should it be secured and settled?

To these questions Jefferson had no certain answers, and they would be decided finally, like the event that produced them, more by forces of circumstance than by his own agency. On July 16, ten days after the treaty came into his hands, he convened the cabinet to take the first measured steps toward implementation. Congress was called into session October 17. Ratification was a foregone conclusion, but Jefferson made a point of urging prompt attendance on the Kentucky congressmen in particular. The American Consul in New Orleans, Daniel Clark, and the Governor of the Mississippi Territory, William C. C. Claiborne, were put on the alert should any problems arise in the transfer of Louisiana. Since Spain was still in possession, the territory must be handed to the French before it could be handed to the Americans; and in this process everything might be lost unless Washington was prepared to back its claim with force. Congress must provide a government for the province. For this work reliable information was essential. With the help of the secretaries, Jefferson drew up a long list of "Queries as to Louisiana," which he dispatched to the men most likely to supply the answers, such as Claiborne, Clark, and Dunbar. Gallatin, meanwhile, attended to the financial arrangements according to a separate convention coupled with the treaty of cession. The terms were not entirely to his liking, but blessed with an abundant treasury and hopeful of further economies, especially in the Navy Department, Gallatin managed to pay for Louisiana by ready money and the sale of new government stock, without resort to taxes or borrowing.

The treaty gave no precise limits to Louisiana, thereby opening one of the most tortuous and least edifying chapters in the history of American empire. France sold to the United States what she had acquired from Spain. And what was that? "Louisiana with the same extent as it now has in the hands of Spain, and that it had when France possessed it." But these were different things. When France possessed Louisiana it included the whole of the Mississippi Valley between the Great Lakes and the Gulf of Mexico. The portion east of the Mississippi, including the Floridas, passed to Great Britain at the conclusion of the Seven Years War, while the western part, with the Isle of New Orleans, went to Spain. When Spain obtained the Floridas by the treaty of peace in 1783, she did not reincorporate them into Louisiana but governed them as separate colonies. The retrocession of 1800 must have referred to the province France had ceded to Spain in 1762, and its eastern boundary was fixed at the Mississippi and the Iberville encompassing New Orleans. Such was the simple logic of the matter, the logic Livingston had consistently advocated in Paris when Spain's title to the Floridas, unmutilated, comported with American interest. But now that the United States had acquired Louisiana, Livingston found it convenient to read the vague clauses of the treaty as covering West Florida at least to the Perdido River east of the Bay of Mobile. (When he broached the claim to Talleyrand, the old fox snapped, "You have made a noble bargain for yourselves, and I suppose you will make the most of it"; and Napoleon, who could play the fox as well as the lion, commented on the boundary enigma, "If an obscurity did not exist, perhaps it would be good policy to put it there.") Jefferson read Livingston's preliminary argument of the point several days before the cabinet met on July 16. If it was discussed, it was not adopted. Instead, the cabinet decided Monroe should endeavor to purchase the Floridas, the West if not the East, and failing that fall back on the "natural right" Jefferson had always claimed against Spain, to wit, the navigation of rivers rising within American limits through Spanish territory to the Gulf. "We are more indifferent about pressing the purchase of the Floridas, because of the money we have to provide for Louisiana," Jefferson noted this decision, "and because we think they cannot fail to fall into our hands." The conviction that the Floridas would remain Spanish only so long as it suited American convenience was the point on which Jefferson's policy turned.

Still he could not be complacent about the Floridas. The American settlements on the Tombigbee and Alabama demanded access to Mobile, and Mobile was in some ways a superior harbor to New Orleans. The revenue of the Gulf trade, which Gallatin eyed with Midas delight, would waste away if American collectors were confined to New Orleans. Security was also a consideration, for Spanish presence on the east bank of the Mississippi would prove troublesome and the transfer of the Floridas to Britain could never be dropped out of the reckoning. When he retreated to Monticello near the end of July, Jefferson plunged into the books, maps, and documents in his collection of western Americana in order to see to what limits the United States might legitimately press its claims, not only on the east but on the west as well. The western limits were, in fact, more confused than the eastern. Whether they lay on the far or the near side of the Rocky Mountains in the north, whether the Sabine or the Rio Bravo or some river between formed the southwestern boundary, were questions veiled in obscurity. In time Jefferson would consider the distant Oregon country part of the acquisition, but he was not prepared for this leap in 1803. He summed up the results of his investigation in a somewhat hesitant fashion in August: "The unquestioned bounds of Louisiana are the Iberville and Mississippi, on the east, the Mexicana (Sabine) or the highlands east of it, on the west. . . . We have some pretensions to extend the western territory of Louisiana to the Rio Norte, or Bravo; and still stronger the eastern boundary to the Rio Perdido between the rivers Mobile and Pensacola." He marshaled the evidence for these pretensions in a brief memoir, An Examination of the Boundaries of Louisiana. Apparently he was not yet convinced of their legitimacy. While escalating the treaty as far as possible in order to strengthen his bargaining position with Spain, he was unwilling to commit the government to points he regarded as negotiable. But by the following February, the pretended limits had become the true limits in Jefferson's mind, though he would sacrifice Texas for all the Floridas and throw a million dollars into the bargain.

The brilliance of the Louisiana Purchase was somewhat dimmed for Jefferson from the first moment by the gagging conviction it exceeded the limits of the Constitution. For a President, an administration, a party that made a boast of constitutional morality, the problem seemed inescapable. Jefferson had seen it in January when shaping up the purchase offer. The Attorney General had then advised that since the Constitution predicated the Union as it was in 1787, an amendment would be necessary to sanction the acquisition of territory and the addition of new states carved from it. Lincoln's logic had been promptly demolished by Gallatin, who argued that despite the absence of explicit provision, the United States, as a sovereign nation, might acquire territory by treaty, govern it or, Congress approving, incorporate it into the Union. Jefferson appeared to be satisfied, at least to the point of authorizing a bargain in the national interest. "You are right . . . ," he told Gallatin, "there is no constitutional difficulty as to the acquisition of territory, and whether, when acquired, it may be taken into the Union by the Constitution as it now stands, will become a question of expediency." Yet he wished to hold expediency within the limits of principle, adding, "I think it will be safer not to permit the enlargement of the Union but by amendment of the Constitution."

When news of the cession reached him in July, he promptly drafted an amendment intended, in part, to sanction the treaty retroactively. "The Constitution has made no provision for our holding foreign territory, still less of incorporating foreign nations into our Union," he explained to Senator Breckinridge. "The executive in seizing the fugitive occurrence which so much advances the good of this country, have done an act beyond the Constitution. The legislature in casting behind them metaphysical subtleties, and risking themselves like faithful servants, must . . . throw themselves on their country for doing for them unauthorized, what we know they would have done for themselves had they been in a situation to do it." In his opinion this "act of indemnity" would "confirm and not weaken the Constitution, by more strongly marking out its lines." And indeed, on the premises of the Virginia and Kentucky Resolutions and the first inaugural address, no other opinion was respectable. To suppose that the whole shape and substance of the nation could be revolutionized on "fugitive occurrences" by the exercise of the treaty power was so outlandish that Federalist apostles of "implied powers" and "inherent sovereignty" might weep at their timidity.

But Jefferson's contemplated amendment had a prospective as well as a retrospective purpose. In the latter character it authorized the incorporation of Louisiana into the Union; this, however, was the lesser part, actually about one-fifth of the 375 words of Jefferson's draft. The greater part established a policy for all but the most southerly portion of the ceded territory. It would be "locked up," the lands reserved to the Indians, American settlement prohibited for an indefinite period, and no territorial government or state could be erected above the 33rd parallel except by further amendment of the Constitution. This was a startling bid to control the future of the Trans-Mississippi West. Unheralded in Jefferson's thinking, its sources may be discovered in considerations of national unity, defense, political economy, disposition of lands, and, above all, Indian policy.

In the President's eyes the acquisition opened a grand new chapter in the "empire of liberty." "The world will here see such an extent of country under a free and moderate government as it has never yet seen." But, while raising these hallelujahs, he was not blind to certain sobering realities. The country must for some time be virtually as defenseless under the Americans as it was under the Spanish. Would it not be wise, then, to create an Indian buffer between the Mississippi and the nation's borders with the British and Spanish dominions, and allow it to recede as the Americans themselves actually occupied the land? The title deeds still belonged to the savage tribes. To extinguish them peacefully and fairly would require years of patient negotiation; to open the wild lands to indiscriminate settlement would cost incalculable blood and treasure in Indian wars and let loose a whirlwind of speculation not unlike the Yazoo land frauds in the Georgia claim from which the country, and the administration, was only beginning to grope its way toward an honorable solution.

Louisiana promised to fulfil the prophesies of economic abundance, natural increase, and freehold farming, all contained within Jefferson's design of republican empire. While wrestling with the problems of policy, he again read Thomas Malthus's *Essay on Population,* now in revised edition. He thought it "masterly," no doubt true for the mass of mankind in its dismal forecast of population remorselessly outrunning food supply, yet fortunately "inapplicable" to the United States. Indeed the United States, after the Louisiana accession if not before, when the country already had 120 acres of land per capita, reversed the Malthusian rule. "Our food then," Jefferson wrote, "may increase geometrically with our laborers, and our births, however multiplied, become effective." But land wrested from cultivators by the avarice of speculators, land—an unprecedented immensity of virgin land—spread too thin with settlers and too hastily draining labor and capital from the still impoverished East could become more a curse than a blessing. The economic argument against the dispersal of American resources would be made repeatedly, especially by New England Federalists attached to oceanic commerce and fearful of waning political power in the Union. Their motives were suspect. Jefferson paid little attention to them, though he recognized the force of the argument in other hands, including his own.

He discounted too, as politically inspired, the curious revival under Federalist auspices of old Anti-Federalist fears of a union too big to survive in liberty. "We rush like a comet into infinite space," Ames declared. The western country would separate from the eastern and form a confederation of its own, some said. This was all speculation on remote contingencies. Yet, Jefferson asked, what if it should finally come to that? "The future inhabitants of [both] the Atlantic and Mississippi states will be our sons. . . . We think we see their happiness in their union, and we wish it. Events may prove it otherwise; and if they see their interest in separating why should we take side with our Atlantic rather than our Mississippi descendants? It is the elder and the younger son differing. God bless them both, and keep them in union if it be for their good, but separate them if it be better." Liberty was the ultimate value, Union the means, to be cherished only so long as it furthered the end of its being. Such was Jefferson's philosophical view of the matter, drawn out, it should be noted, in answer to captious Federalists.

Nothing could be more mistaken than to suppose that he resigned himself to separation and disunion. On the contrary, he believed the acquisition would strengthen the Union even as it strengthened liberty. The American experiment that upset Malthus also upset Montesquieu. "By enlarging the empire of liberty," Jefferson observed, "we multiply its auxiliaries, and provide new sources of renovation, should its principles at any time degenerate, in those portions of our country which gave them birth." The federal system bottomed on the equality of individuals and of states overcame the objection to republican government in a large empire. The acquisition shut the avenues of foreign intrigue, so dangerous to freedom and union. It extended the agricultural base of a virtuous republic and enabled the nation to cultivate its own garden at peace with the world. It opened the way to orderly possession of the continent, first of the vacant lands east of the Mississippi, then in progressive stages westward. "When we shall be full on this side, we may lay off a range of states on the Western bank from the head to the mouth, and so, range after range, advancing compactly as we multiply."

Advancing compactly as we multiply: the key to the program lay in Indian policy. The tribes east of the Mississippi would be resettled in Louisiana, thereby eliminating the Indian problem where it existed, filling up the eastern country, and garrisoning the western until the Americans were ready to possess it. "If our legislature dispose of it with the wisdom we have a right to expect," Jefferson explained, "they may make it the means of tempting all our Indians on the east side of the Mississippi to remove to the west, and of condensing instead of scattering our population." Searching for a policy to govern the new problem, Louisiana, Jefferson was led to the point of abandoning the policy he had consistently pursued toward the old problem, the Indians. That policy aimed at the rapid acquisition of Indian lands by treaty, the control of the tribes by commercial intercourse under federal supervision, accompanied by a variety of expedients to draw the savages into agriculture, thus by degrees civilizing them until ultimately they were incorporated with the whites. "In truth," Jefferson had recently written to his old friend Benjamin Hawkins, agent to the Creeks, "the ultimate point of rest and happiness for them is to let our settlements and theirs meet and blend together and to intermix, and become one people." Hawkins was the chief exemplar of this assimilationist policy, and Jefferson stood by him against the wrath of Georgians who believed his first loyalty was to the Indians. The Jeffersonian policy had the appearance of deviousness, even hypocrisy: the great white father runs his red children into debt, kills off the game, acquires one tract of land after another, crowding the savages into smaller and smaller reserves, until they are compelled to take the white father's view of their own interests and turn to agriculture and the domestic arts. Whatever the appearances, Jefferson insisted the policy breathed "pure morality" toward the Indians; for, realistically, the only alternative to assimilation was destruction, and if they had to be drawn into the paths of civilization by devious routes, the end justified the means.

The policy seemed to be working in 1803. Millions upon millions of acres were being acquired from the Indians, mostly above the Ohio. Hawkins, at least, was experiencing some success in his civilizing agency to the Creeks. Protestant missionaries, like Samuel Kirkland among the Iroquois, were helping tribes to discover avenues of accommodation. Still, where the problem was critical, where frontiersmen swarmed and the government pressed for land, roads, trading houses, and other concessions, among the confederacies of Creek, Cherokee, Choctaw, and Chickasaw in the booming cotton lands south of the Tennessee, frustrations bore hard upon the President. The tribes in the Mississippi Territory resisted every advance, yet the compact with Georgia in 1802 obligated the government to extinguish Indian titles in return for the state's cession of western claims extending to the Mississippi. The process was proving slow, tedious, and costly. The removal of the southern tribes west of the Mississippi would not only solve this problem but several others as well. So attractive a prospect warranted, in Jefferson's mind, suspension of the enlightened goals of civilization and amalgamation in favor of the entirely different set of directives contained in the policy of Indian removal. "Instead of inviting Indians to come within our limits," Jefferson now said, "our object is to tempt them to evacuate them."

Such was the prospective intent of Jefferson's planned amendment of the Constitution. His more pressing concern was with the constitutional difficulty, however. Dispatches from Livingston reached him in August urging prompt ratification without fuss or bother. "Be persuaded that France is sick of the bargain; that Spain is much dissatisfied; and that the slightest pretense will lose you the treaty." The Minister's fears might be groundless, but Jefferson could not afford to ignore them. In September, Yrujo submitted the caviling protest of his government, which was quite futile, and Senator Nicholas pointedly warned the President not to raise the issue of the competency of the treaty power lest he furnish the Federalists the lever to upset the treaty. Nicholas himself, like most Republicans, denied the want of constitutional power. Jefferson stuck to his opinion. He still wanted the amendment. But given the hazards, he concluded that the less said about it the better and asked his friends in the Senate to do what was necessary *sub silento*. "I had rather ask an enlargement of power from the nation, where it is found necessary, than to assume it by construction which would make our powers boundless," he told Nicholas. "Our peculiar security is in the possession of a written Constitution. Let us not make it a blank paper by construction." Yet what is practical, as he was want to say, must sometimes control what is true in theory, and if ever an instance proved the rule it was the Louisiana Purchase. So without yielding the principle he yielded the position. "If . . . our friends shall think differently," he advised Nicholas, "certainly I shall acquiesce with satisfaction; confiding, that the good sense of the country will correct the evil of construction when it shall produce ill effects."

The matter was dropped. Jefferson made no mention of the constitutional difficulty in his message to Congress on October 17. Federalists raised the issue but to no avail. A revolution in the American Union became, perforce, a revolution in the Constitution. A momentous act of Jeffersonian statesmanship unhinged the Jeffersonian dogmas and opened, so far as precedent might control, the boundless field of power so much feared. Critics then and since found the President inconsistent. In the narrow view he was, but a statesman riding the current of events cannot indulge narrow points of consistency. In the larger view of the national interest, Jefferson's dominant purpose remained what it had always been, indeed leaped far ahead of him, and he would deal with any untoward side-effects when they occurred.

Yielding the constitutional point, he also yielded his far-sighted plan for the disposition of the country between the Red River and the far reaches of the Missouri. The plan was an altogether separate matter; it might have been the subject of a constitutional amendment or put on the more hazardous footing of statutory law. Neither was done. Jefferson talked about it with certain congressmen, with Breckinridge, for instance, who approved the "lock up" in principle but doubted that a constitutional barricade floated on the waters of the Mississippi would check the westerners. Congress did, in 1804, empower the President to offer Trans-Mississippi lands to eastern tribes in exchange for their homelands. In his numerous addresses to visiting tribal delegations in Washington, Jefferson often recommended this course. (These addresses have a rhetoric all their own—child-like, metaphorical, bucolic, and affectedly naïve—which he did not originate but developed into a literary art.) The chiefs showed little interest, however, and Americans on the Mississippi filed indignant protests. By 1805 Jefferson had returned to the old theme of amalgamation. In truth, he had never actually given it up. The policy ran against the grain of both red men and white, and its chances of success dimmed with each passing year, yet Jefferson clung to it as the only humane solution. A quarter-century later the federal government adopted the alternate policy of Indian removal. Jefferson's early gestures in the same direction, and in quite another context, had been forgotten.

The machinery of government worked smoothly to effect the transition of authority in Louisiana. Jefferson reconvened the cabinet in Washington the first week of October. Gallatin had completed the financial arrangements. Information on the conditions and prospects of Louisiana was flowing in and being digested in Madison's department, which held administrative responsibility for territorial government. Dearborn dispatched orders to General James Wilkinson at Fort Adams, near Natchez, to prepare a force competent to take New Orleans should the Spanish refuse to deliver the province to the French. The Senate, meanwhile, quickly approved the treaty and with the House proceeded to frame legislation to implement it.

Jefferson signed the Enabling Act on October 21. The act empowered the President to take possession of Louisiana and, until Congress made provision for its government, vested him or his agents with full powers civil and military. Federalists said this provisional government made the President "as despotic as the Grand Turk" and marveled that the Republican cry of "monarchy" had so soon lost its sting. Directed by the statute to protect the inhabitants of Louisiana in their "liberty, property and religion" during the transition, Jefferson simply continued the local Spanish law in force, in accordance with historical precedent drawn from the example of conquered provinces. He appointed W. C. C. Claiborne temporary governor. He and Wilkinson were charged with seeing that the territory was delivered, first into French, then into American custody. Wilkinson's small force of regulars and militia paraded the colors. On November 30 France came into possession; twenty days later, at the Cabildo in New Orleans, in a ceremony so meager it seemed an impertinence, the Tricolor came down and the Star Spangled Banner waved over Louisiana. When the news reached Washington a thousand miles away near the end of January, cannon dragged up from the navy yard boomed on Capitol Hill and a great festival, in which the President joined, hailed the conclusion of a transaction that still staggered the imagination.

For many weeks Congress labored to bring forth a regular government for the territory. "There appear to be about as many opinions as to the mode of governing Louisiana as there are members of the National Legislature," Gideon Granger informed Claiborne. Like everything else about the Louisiana Purchase, the problem of the form of government answered to no precedent and challenged every theory. Never before had a republic set out to incorporate an alien province almost as big as itself. The rules of conquest did not apply, not only because the relation of conqueror and conquered violated the American scheme of things but also because the purchase treaty bound the United States to admit, "as soon as possible," the ceded territory and its inhabitants into the Union. The legal obligation only reinforced the nation's moral commitment, one that Jefferson himself had laid deep in the polity twenty years before, and he had no thought of backing away from it. But how it should be managed, through what preliminary stages the territory should pass, and on what timetable—on these questions he was flexible, governed by facts not theories, and responsible to the test of practice.

His plans for upper Louisiana have been noted. As to the lower settled portion, soon to become the Orleans Territory, with the same limits as the present state of Louisiana, Jefferson's first thought was to annex it to Mississippi. Of the approximately 50,000 inhabitants nearly half were slaves, and a majority of the whites were natives of French descent, Creoles, who knew nothing of American government. "We shall certainly endeavor to introduce American laws there," Jefferson had written in July, "and that cannot be done but by amalgamating the people with such a body of Americans as may take the lead in legislation and government." Actually, Mississippi was the last place to look for leadership. The eastern territory had similar problems to the western. Claiborne encountered the same difficulties as his Federalist predecessor, Sargent, in governing this refractory populace. "In no part of the Union are the citizens less informed of the principles of our government, and (generally speaking) involved in as much mental ignorance," he had written. On reflection, Jefferson decided against annexation. Mississippi was governed by the provisions of the Northwest Ordinance of 1787, except for the no-slavery proviso, and had just passed from the first to the second grade of territorial government. Jefferson had supposed the government of lower Louisiana might be founded on the same basis. Early in November, he changed his mind. The old ordinance would not do for Louisiana—"it would turn all their laws topsy turvy." As indeed it would. An instrument framed for state-making in vacant domain would not do for a settled province formerly the colony of France and Spain. So Jefferson turned his thoughts to a plan of government adapted to the specific case.

What led him on, down paths of government never ventured in his political philosophy, was the detailed information funneled into Washington. The picture was discouraging. By American standards the old Spanish government was a complete despotism. Supreme authority, civil and military, rested in a governor who reported to the captain-general in Havanna. There was a kind of executive council, the Cabildo, which also acted as a court, and which represented the interests of the great Creole planters. The offices of the Cabildo were purchased; in fact, venality, bribery, and corruption ruled in all things. Except for 6 per cent duties on imports and exports, commonly evaded by smuggling and bribery, there were no taxes, and the Crown met the whole cost of the civil and military establishment. The law, like the church, was Roman, being based on Spanish codes and compilations as ancient as the thirteenth century, though in actuality the law was largely executive or dispensative. The common law was unknown, so too the palladium of Anglo-American liberty, trial by jury. French was the language of the courts, and lawyers had no place in the judicial system. Land titles were in a state of confusion. Not one-fourth of the lands granted by the colonial government were held on complete titles; most of the remainder depended on the written provision of some commandant. Moreover, according to one estimate, 30,000,000 acres of Louisiana had been bargained away by Spanish officials in fraudulent grants, some to Americans who descended on the territory like a flock of buzzards, subsequent to the Treaty of San Ildefonso or even the French cession. So troublesome was the inherited land system that the matter of titles would not finally be disposed of until 1879. Slavery existed, of course, the brutal slavery of the sugar plantations that consumed Negroes as fast as they could be imported. The large, concentrated slave population, together with several thousand free Negroes in and around New Orleans, aroused fears that Louisiana might become another Santo Domingo. Nor was this the only worry for the territory's security. Many of the Creoles, Washington was warned, wished for the return of the province to France, possibly Spain, and they could count the deposed colonial officials as allies.

Ignorance, the unfailing legacy of despotism, was perhaps the worst curse of all. Religious bigotry abounded. Schools were all but non-existent; over half the people were illiterate; at Point Coupee, the second largest place, renowned for wealth and polish, not one-third of the free inhabitants could write their own names. The Quaker Isaac Briggs, Surveyor General south of the Tennessee, spoke of the "vicious, luxurious, and oppressive habits" of the Louisianans, which in his opinion barred their entrance into the "blessings of Republican liberty." Claiborne thought the natives mild and submissive, a good people, but peculiarly vulnerable to the intrigues of ambitious men, Creole or American. "Sudden and total reformation is best calculated for enlightened minds; the experiment may prove

779

hazardous with Creole ignorance." Claiborne agreed with other informants on the need for a firm and strong hand, though he did not go as far as some, Wilkinson and Clark, for example, who advocated virtually a military government. Daniel Clark, the Irish-born consul, rich and ambitious, was by all odds the most knowledgeable American on the civil state of lower Louisiana. His memoranda reached Washington about the first of November and made a deep impression on the President and his colleagues. The imprint could be seen in the Account of Louisiana sent to Congress on November 14. More than any other report, Clark's seems to have crystalized the President's thoughts on the plan of government for lower Louisiana.

Clearly, in his opinion, the Louisianans must serve an apprenticeship before entering the estate of American liberty. They were ignorant of its principles, laws, and forms. The introduction of representative government on the American model would almost certainly put the territory at the hazard of the dominant Creole class, retard improvement, foment discord, and check the influx of Americans who alone could lay the foundations of a free state. Jefferson envisioned a gradual transition to republicanism paced to the advance of American settlement. "In proportion as we find the people there ripe for receiving these first principles of freedom," he told Gallatin, "Congress may from session to session confirm their employment of them." Sometime after the middle of November he discussed his ideas with Breckinridge, who apparently agreed to draw up a plan of government, but sensing the Senator's reluctance, Jefferson began the task himself.

The plan he sketched gave the people of Louisiana no voice in their government. The President would appoint the governor and the secretary for a term of years. Judges, too, would be appointed by the President, not to terms in good behavior but for four years. This was a necessary safeguard, Jefferson said, for "shall the judges take a kink in their heads in favor of leaving the present laws of Louisiana unaltered, that evil will continue for their lives unamended by us, and become so inveterate that we may never be able to introduce the uniformity of law so desirable." Otherwise, except for the elimination of the requirement of large freehold estates for territorial officers, the provisions for the executive and judiciary conformed to the first grade of government under the Northwest Ordinance.

With respect to the legislative power, Jefferson's plan went beyond the first grade, wherein governor and judges made the laws, and yet did not attain the second, wherein the power was shared with a representative assembly. Lower Louisiana easily satisfied the population requirement for the latter, but Jefferson declined to trust the largely alien populace with legislative power. Instead, he proposed an "assembly of notables": twenty-four distinguished characters annually appointed by the governor and sharing with him the lawmaking power. The concept was French, of course. Jefferson supposed it would be more acceptable to the Louisianans than "a legislature of judges." Still, as he confessed to Breckinridge, it was "a sudden conceit" to which he was not attached.

Jefferson also proposed in the government bill a ban on the importation of slaves from abroad—the same as had been imposed on the Mississippi Territory five years before. Moreover, to cover the peculiar case of South Carolina, which had reopened its doors to the African trade, slaves could be brought in only from those American states that prohibited foreign importation. Since the treaty obligated the United States to protect the property of the inhabitants, including slave property, the only place the institution could be legally attacked was at the gates to the territory. Jefferson proposed to close the foreign entrance but leave open the domestic. Realistically, he could do no more. To lock up this rich country to slaves, to prohibit southern planters from migrating there, to force the territory into an economic pattern alien to itself and to its neighbors—Jefferson never even considered these propositions. He did, at one point, consider tacking on a clause pledging emancipation to the grandchildren of slaves henceforth carried to Louisiana. But he quickly dropped the idea. Lower Louisiana was not very promising ground on which to test the federal power to restrict slavery in the territories.

Jefferson sent his plan to Breckinridge in the strictest confidence. No one should know he had even "put pen to paper" on the subject. "I am this particular," he said, "because you know with what bloody teeth and fangs the Federalists will attack any sentiment or principles known to come from me, and what blackguardisms and personalities they make it the occasion of vomiting forth." Eleven days later the Kentuckian moved the appointment of a committee to prepare a plan of government for Louisiana. The bill reported to the Senate on December 30 was in all essentials Jefferson's, though known then and to history by the name of the reporting chairman, Breckinridge. It was vigorously attacked in both houses, and not only by Federalists. "It really establishes a complete despotism," said a Tennessee congressmen. Other Republicans spoke of "the wear and tear of conscience" they suffered from the measure, as well as from the revenue bill (taxation without representation!) that accompanied it. The issue of principle traced back to the fountainhead, the Declaration of Independence. If the United States could tax and govern the people of Louisiana without their consent, the American Revolution had been a sham. Adams, more a purist than most, returned to the charge again and again. The United States had no right to make laws for Louisiana. He conceded that theory could not always control practice. The bandying of the people from one sovereign to another by scratches of a pen violated natural right, yet the treaty of cession was justified. But between "a momentary departure from the inflexible rigor of theory" and "the total sacrifice of all principle" there was a wide difference. Nothing in the situation prevented the United States from obtaining the consent of the Louisianans to a government formed for them.

Adams, who also stoutly advocated a constitutional amendment to take the new country into the Union, would insist for the rest of his life that the management of the Louisiana Purchase subverted every sound principle of the Jeffersonian party. "It made the Union totally different from that for which the Constitution had been formed," he wrote in 1821. "It gives despotic power over territories purchased. It naturalizes foreign territories in a mass. It makes French and Spanish laws a large part of the laws of the Union. It introduced whole systems of legislation abhorrent to the spirit and character of our institutions, and all this done by an administration which came in blowing a trumpet against implied power. After this," he concluded, "to nibble at a bank, a road, a canal, the mere mint and cummin of the law was but glorious inconsistency." And so it was, if Republicanism demanded consistency of this kind. Jefferson, for his part, justified the departure from principle in the permanent interest of liberty and Union. He had little patience with purists who let theory tyrannize over facts. He had seen the consequences of this passion in France. Louisiana was unique, yet perhaps not unlike France under the Old Regime. The only responsible statesmanship was to deal with it on its own terms. "Although it is acknowledged that our fellow citizens are as yet as incapable of self-government as children," Jefferson observed, "yet some cannot bring themselves to suspend its principles for a single moment." It was a suspension, not a subversion, of principle that he called for.

As finally passed in March (51 to 45 in the House) the Breckinridge Act was limited to one year, all power being vested in the President and his appointees during that time. The act prohibited the foreign slave trade. It annulled Spanish land grants after October 1800. Many federal laws were extended to lower Louisiana, or the Orleans Territory as it was named. The country above the 33rd parallel, called the District of Louisiana, was temporarily annexed to the Indiana Territory, interdicted to slavery.

New Orleans already seethed with discontent. Planters and merchants complained of the loss of ancient privileges. The trade with Spain and her colonies had previously been free; now, of course, it paid the same duties as all other trade. The sugar growers had been privileged under the laws of the Indies to pay their debts with the product of their harvest; but the court of justice introduced by Claiborne knew nothing of these laws, it was said, and executions for debt, in lands, slaves, and equipment, were ruining the planters. This court, like the city council, conducted its business in the English language, a grievance voiced repeatedly, usually coupled with complaint against the Governor, whose ignorance of the language and the customs of the country affronted the native populace. Trivial events rising out of the conflict of cultures threatened to explode into international incidents. For example, at a public ball in January, French officers and civilians boisterously interrupted an American country dance, *contre danse, anglais* in their lingo, hence partial to the English, and demanded a waltz instead. Swords were drawn, a riot ensued, a French officer was arrested. No blood flowed but tempers flared for weeks to come. The French commissioner took an interest in the matter. His continued presence, along with the former Spanish officials, proved a constant irritant and an invitation to intrigue by the disaffected of every nationality.

Thrown into this cauldron of troubles, the government act

brought things to a boil. Etiénne Boré, mayor of New Orleans by Claiborne's appointment, resigned his office charging that the new government scheduled to begin October 1 annihilated the rights of the people. Boré joined the growing party of malcontents. While mainly French, it counted among its leaders several ambitious Americans. Clark was one of these. Hating Claiborne, wishing the governorship himself, he was especially dangerous because of his close association with the old Spanish officialdom and the Creole merchants and planters. Another troublemaker, Edward Livingston, had just arrived in the territory, seeking a fresh start for a blighted career. As Jefferson's attorney general for New York, he had defaulted to the government in a huge amount. Forced to resign, he had then joined a battery of lawyers to argue Madrid's contention that France, not Spain, as Washington insisted, was responsible for the spoliations of American commerce in Spanish waters before the Peace of Amiens. A Jeffersonian outcast, Livingston had nothing to lose in taking up the cause of the opposition in Louisiana.

At a public meeting called by this party on June 1, it was decided to prepare a memorial to Congress. Livingston wrote the memorial—a petition of rights and grievances mimicking the style of American petitions to George III a generation before. Adopted at a second public meeting a month later, it then circulated far and wide for signatures. The memorial complained of many things: the tyranny of the English language, the unsettlement of land titles, the substitution of licensing for monopoly in the Indian trade, the high import duties, and so on. But the principal thrusts were against a system of government in which the people had no voice and the prohibition of the slave trade. Taxation without representation, the domination of the executive, the dependence of the judiciary—these forms of tyranny had been repudiated in 1776 and American government had been raised on opposite principles "fundamental, indefeasible, self-evident, and eternal." "Are truths, then, so well founded, so universally acknowledged, inapplicable only to us?" the petitioners asked. "Do political axioms on the Atlantic become problems when transferred to the shores of the Mississippi?" The memorialists, having thus shoved Jefferson's own words down his throat, went on to construe the third article of the treaty of cession as a guarantee of immediate statehood, since only by statehood could the inhabitants be "incorporated in the Union." Jefferson would find little merit in the argument. Whatever that ambiguous phrase meant, it clearly did not impose an obligation of immediate statehood. The strident demand became more understandable when linked with the demand for reopening the slave trade. As a state Louisiana would be free to import slaves, at least until 1808 when the federal constitutional prohibition would take effect. The demand for slaves was urgent and emphatic. The Louisianans, observed the former French commissioner, "could not have been attacked in a more vulnerable spot." On this point alone, Claiborne told Washington, the memorial accurately reflected the opinion of the inhabitants both French and American. Jefferson became convinced that the bar to the slave traffic lay at the bottom of the dissension in Louisiana. And he must have reflected sadly on the irony of a people petitioning for their rights that they might import and enslave Africans.

During the summer Jefferson tended the tedious business of filling offices in the territory. The principal difficulty was with the legislative council which Breckinridge had substituted for his "assembly of notables" and then made appointive of the President instead of the Governor. He tried to appoint bilinguists only and to strike a balance between the French and the American, giving the edge to the latter on the 13 member council. Unfortunately, he had to proceed with the commissions before receiving Claiborne's recommendations reflecting the shift of political loyalties since June. As a result, most of those nominated for the council, Clark and Boré at the head of the list, declined to serve. Not until December was Claiborne able to fill out enough blank commissions to make a quorum in the council and thus put the government in motion.

The decision to retain Claiborne as Governor was no more popular in Congress than in the territory. Claiborne had come into Congress from Tennessee in 1797, having barely attained his majority, and grown men continued to think of him as a mere boy. Jefferson recognized his limitations for the office he now considered the second most important in the United States. Inability to speak French was only his most obvious handicap. Observers described him as "awkward," "slovenly," and "below his place." He had neither the wealth nor the fame nor the dignity Louisianans seemed to expect in a governor. Jefferson had hoped to allay discontents with a master stroke: the appointment of the Marquis de Lafayette. The Revolutionary hero had been stripped of fame and fortune in France. In 1802, at Jefferson's bidding, Congress had voted Lafayette a huge grant of land north of the Ohio in the hope that he would return to live and die in the country of his dreams. With the acquisition of Louisiana, reason and interest came to the aid of sentiment. Jefferson asked Congress to amend the terms of the grant so as to permit Lafayette to take up his lands in Louisiana. This was done, but Lafayette became an absentee lord and declined the governorship. Monroe had been the President's next choice, but he could not be spared from diplomatic assignment in Europe and, when that was finished, spurned the offer. After canvassing other prospects Jefferson reluctantly concluded to stick with Claiborne. He had a year's experience (and two years in Mississippi); he was loyal, trustworthy, and well intentioned; and his rejection while under fire would only embolden the opposition. Claiborne proved a sound choice after all. Nonetheless, it was perhaps the most unpopular appointment Jefferson ever made.

As the plot thickened in New Orleans, Jefferson decided that even if the Louisianans were not ready for representative government, Congress should go ahead and introduce it in order to avoid a calamity infinitely worse. The grievances alleged by the malcontents did not impress him, yet it would be foolhardy to ignore them. Mounting dissension, disunionism, appeals to the First Consul, foreign intervention—vague reports of these dangers came to Jefferson from New Orleans, from Paris, even from London. Whatever the evils to be anticipated from the extension of representative government to the Louisianans, he told Madison in August, they "will not be so serious as leaving them the pretext of calling in a foreign empire between them and us." He returned to the point a week later: "I am so much impressed with the expediency of putting a termination to the right of France to patronize the rights of Louisiana, which will cease with their complete adoption as citizens of the United States, that I hope to see that take place on the meeting of Congress." No hasty retreat to the safety of republican dogma, no sudden conversion to the immutable rights of untutored Creoles, produced this decision. It was a political response to a political situation, one that still wore a dangerous foreign complexion in the President's eyes. The same "expediency" that caused him to oppose representative government for Louisiana in 1803 caused him to advocate it in 1804. Without changing his direction, he changed his timetable, advancing the stage of representative government ahead of the gradual process of Americanization that he still believed the only permanent solution.

Jefferson came to this decision before he read the Louisiana Memorial. Three deputies of the opposition group, Derbigny, Destréhan, and Sauvé, presented the memorial to Congress in the fall. Their principal object, Claiborne advised Madison, was the opening of the African trade, the demand for statehood being only a convenient façade. Republican rhymsters got the point, as evidenced by the concluding lines of "The Louisiana Memorial Abridged":

> O spread lov'd Freedom far and wide.
>
> Receive us to your arms as Brothers
>
> And grant us *to make slaves of others.*

Federalists welcomed and Republicans shunned the Creole deputies. The President's reception was especially frigid; by their own account "he studiously avoided conversing . . . upon every subject that had relation to their mission." They found a better listener in the Vice President, to whom they were introduced by General Wilkinson. These two gentlemen had already concocted plans for a conspiracy in the Southwest that depended on the agitation at New Orleans for its success.

Although Congress rejected the petition for immediate statehood, the act of March 2, 1805, introduced the second stage of territorial government, including a representative assembly, on the plan of the Northwest Ordinance, omitting its freehold qualification for the franchise. A companion bill called local land titles into question and demanded that they be proved to the satisfaction of the United States. The three deputies found little consolation in these measures. They returned to New Orleans mortified and discouraged. Creole opposition grew bold. To no one's surprise the first legislature, convened in November, was dominated by the old inhabitants. A virtual stalemate ensued in the government. Backed by the President, Claiborne endeavored to speed the progress of Americanization. The assembly worked just as hard to turn it back. Plans for an educational system in which Claiborne, like Jefferson, placed great stock came to nothing. He vetoed bills to introduce a black code and to restrict membership in the assembly to native Louisianans. The showdown came when he vetoed legislation to retain the old Spanish civil law. The assembly quit in protest. Claiborne and Clark thought to settle their differences with dueling pistols, alas, without success. (It was not the Governor's only duel. He had been wounded once, his secretary had been killed in defense of the Governor's honor, and disease had robbed him of a wife and daughter.) The presence of the Spanish in West Florida contributed to this persistent hostility to Americanization. Jefferson would make almost any sacrifice to get West Florida, not just for itself but for its bearing on the future of Louisiana. This chronicle of misadventure began with the government's claim under the treaty and continued its troubled course in Jefferson's second administration. Claiborne, meanwhile, discovered the path of political conciliation. Smuggling, tolerated if not approved by the government, together with relaxation of controls over domestic imports, overcame the shortage of slave labor. In 1808 the Governor acquiesced in the adoption of Livingston's civil code derived from the Roman law, thus terminating happily what had seemed an irresoluble conflict. The road to statehood in the Orleans Territory would never be smooth, yet after nearly a decade of strife and confusion born of the clash of cultures, laws, and nationalities, the end would be reached in 1812.

It was, all considered, an unprecedented achievement. The nation incorporated a foreign dominion and committed it to the status of equality in a union of free men. Freedom followed the flag in Louisiana. First one, then many new states fastened on the land; and the nation grew by accretion rather than by conquest and domination. None of this was fated to happen. Under a different leadership it might not have happened. To be sure, the principles of the American polity set the direction and the Northwest Ordinance provided a working formula, but neither the principles nor the formula had been made with a view to foreign territory, foreign laws and institutions, or a foreign populace. The acquisition of Louisiana presented the government with a situation quite new. To have imposed, arbitrarily, rules addressed to another condition would have been the height of folly in Jefferson's opinion, not because they were wrong —on the contrary they were eternally right—but because they would be permanently jeopardized by dogmatism and precipitancy in their application. Jefferson's approach was eminently pragmatic. Never losing sight of the end, he improvised the means, constantly making adjustments to the changing balance of risks in Louisiana, so far as he was able to assess them in Washington. He could not always be right in such a situation. He overreacted to fears of subversive foreign influence, for instance. But he did not make any big mistakes, and whatever the faults of his improvisation, it was vindicated in its workings over the longer run of history.

An event of the magnitude of the Louisiana Purchase profoundly affected everything to come after. Because of it the prospects of the Union were at once far grander and far more terrifying than before, and government must assume new responsibilities addressed to this condition. Because of it the United States acquired greater independence and self-assurance in the affairs of nations, which would be reflected in the diplomacy Jefferson practiced toward Spain and in the developing crisis over neutral rights. Because of it the Republicans tightened their political grip on the nation, growing bold in power and making freaks and fanatics of their opposition. These tendencies would show themselves in Jefferson's second administration, but they were already in evidence at the close of the first.

Triumph on the Mississippi made the President ten feet tall in the public eye, his re-election a foregone conclusion many months before the long, drawn-out contest began. The election did not pass without the usual Job-like utterance from Jefferson. Oh what he would give to exchange "the deadly feuds of party" for "the affections of domestic society"! The protest had become almost a ritual, transparently false, some thought, for no man could go on living in what he hated and despised. But so it had been for many years, and the death of his younger daughter Maria in April gave a peculiar poignancy to the old sadness. Maria, always the delicate one, never recovered from the birth of a second child earlier in the year. Jefferson reached her near the end of a lingering illness, immediately transported her four miles on a litter from Martha's home at Edgehill to Monticello, nursed her, and watched her die in the bright flush of spring. He poured out his grief to the oldest of his friends,

John Page. "Others may lose of their abundance, but I, of my want, have lost even the half of all I had. My evening prospects now hang on the thread of a single life. . . . The hope with which I had looked forward to the moment when, resigning public cares to younger hands, I was to retire to that domestic comfort from which the last great step is to be taken, is fearfully blighted." There had been so much affliction and slaughter since he and Page had come on the scene in the first moments of the Revolutionary torrent that he felt like a lonely straggler marking the footsteps of the fallen. He put on no mourning this sad spring and quickly resumed his usual rounds. People said, "What a Stoic Mr. Jefferson is." But it was not that. "I have had experience enough in the school of affliction," he said, "to know that time and silence are its best medicines and occupation as soon as the state of mind can bear it." One of the letters of condolence came from Abigail Adams, who had taken Polly to her heart many years ago in London. Jefferson was pleased by the letter, not just for the sentiments it contained but for the opportunity to renew a friendship that ought to have been safe from the slings and arrows of party warfare. Whatever their differences of opinion, he had never closed his heart to John Adams nor to his wife, Jefferson wrote. He went on to say in a spirit of candor that only one act of Adams's political life, the midnight appointments, ever gave him a moment's personal displeasure. Instead of grasping this overture, Abigail replied in a tone of political recrimination. Another exchange of letters closed the correspondence on a discordant note. The time had not yet come for the revival of the old friendship.

While Jefferson had no desire to prolong his confinement in office, he was far less willing to gratify his enemies by going into retirement. Apparently he did not commit himself to a second term until early in the election year. The "unfounded calumnies of the Federal party," he said at that time, had obliged him to throw himself on the verdict of the country despite his "decided purpose" to retire. He realized too that his continued leadership was necessary to secure the permanent ascendancy of the party that carried all his hopes for the American experiment. Whatever his misgivings about a second term, he was quite ready to undertake it.

Virtually unanimous in support of the President, Republicans centered their attention on the vice presidential nomination. A constitutional amendment, the 12th, then in the process of ratification by the states, would prevent any recurrence of the near abortion of the popular will in 1801 by requiring separate ballots for President and Vice President. The amendment would close the only loophole through which the Federalists might evict the President, and they fought it vigorously for two years. Some of them were still flirting with Aaron Burr. Burr had lost caste in his own party. Suspicions aroused by his conduct in the contest of 1801 were never quieted and, in fact, tended to be confirmed by his less than ardent support of the administration and his cautious pandering to Federalists in Washington. Jefferson's coolness toward the wily New Yorker first showed itself in patronage decisions. His political death warrant was signed, however, not in Washington, not by the President, but by DeWitt Clinton in New York. The ensuing factional struggle went on for three years, in the press, in the courts, at the polls, and on the dueling grounds. For sheer political violence the spectacle was unsurpassed. Jefferson watched from afar with mingled horror and fascination. Through James Cheetham, a Clintonian editor, whom the administration employed to publish the laws in New York and who regularly supplied the President with pamphlets and newspapers, he received a blow by blow account of the proceedings. It was a biased account, of course, constantly insinuating that the would-be usurper of 1801 still plotted to snatch the presidency from Jefferson by an unprincipled coalition with the Federalists. Burrites, on the other hand, accused the Clintons, uncle and nephew, of using the President as a front for their schemes while waiting in ambush for the administration. Caught between this crossfire, Jefferson must have been puzzled to distinguish his friends from his enemies. The choice was difficult morally, politically much easier, for the Clintonians controlled the state organization.

In January 1804 Burr came to Jefferson and offered to give up the battle, thus ending a dangerous schism in the party, if he could avail himself of an honorable retreat, some mark of favor, perhaps appointment as Livingston's successor in Paris, which would declare to the world that he retired in the President's confidence. Jefferson coolly parried this overture. In 1800 he had needed Burr; now Burr, this "modern Machiavel," as Republicans called him, was a political liability. Reflecting on the interview, he said he had never trusted Burr, who seemed a man "always at market," and their association being entirely political, had never been intimate with him. Burr returned to New York and at once plunged into a race for the governorship against the Clintonians, or regular Republicans. Both factions laid claim to Jefferson's support. He honestly deplored the schism, saying, in effect, "a plague on both your houses." Officially he was neutral, but his "secret wishes" were all on the side of the Clintonians and their candidate, Morgan Lewis.

Near the end of February, as the New York campaign gathered momentum, the congressional Republicans caucused in Washington to nominate candidates for President and Vice President. Jefferson maintained his hands-off policy. The caucus was just as unanimous in its rejection of the Vice President as it was in its endorsement of the President. Burr received not a single vote, and as if to underscore the humiliation, the caucus nominated George Clinton. Burr was virtually read out of the party. The frightful din set up in New York embarrassed the party nationally, and the reverberations of the state conflict convinced Republicans nation-wide that Burr had indeed intrigued against Jefferson in the election of 1800. Jefferson and his friends had been reluctant to draw this conclusion, even less to admit it publicly. It disgraced the party. But what would have been disgrace if admitted in 1801 had the appearance of political valor in 1804. Repudiated in Washington, Burr nevertheless clung to Jefferson's coattails in the gubernatorial contest. The New York Federalists supported him almost to a man. It was 1801 all over again. Voting for Burr, Federalists hoped to sow seeds of discord in the Republican ranks, rally northern Republicans against Virginia domination, perhaps even create in New York the nucleus of the Northern Confederacy some of the Federalist witch-doctors had been prescribing since the affliction of the Louisiana Purchase. Again, as in 1801, Alexander Hamilton opposed their scheme. Through the New York *Evening Post*, established largely under his auspices, Hamilton had kept up a constant barrage against the administration. He had no love for Jefferson or his works; but he hated Aaron Burr and again tried to turn the Federalists from him. His pleas were no more heeded than before, but Burr, crushed in the election, chose to take his revenge on Hamilton, killing him on a bright July morning on the dueling grounds at Weehawken. Checked at every turn, hunted as a murderer, Burr became a political desperado. Jefferson himself, thus far a silent partner in his destruction, would have to bring the culprit to justice at last.

Although Burr was defeated, the New York contest underscored the importance of vigilance and unity in the Republican ranks. The problem was not confined to New York; intramural quarrels split the party in Pennsylvania, for instance, and each faction accused the other of flirting with the Federalists. Jefferson dissected the motives of the opposition in a letter to the Postmaster General. "The Federalists know, that, *eo nominie,* they are gone forever. Their object, therefore, is how to return into power under some other form. Undoubtedly, they have but one means, which is to divide the Republicans, join the minority, and barter with them for the cloak of their name. . . . Thus a bastard system of federo-republicanism will rise on the ruins of the true principles of our revolution." He did not think this "crooked scheme" would work—the mass of Republicans were sound—but the danger was ever-present and, henceforth, never far from his mind. Partly for this reason he became more and more insistent that recipients of the federal patronage have Republican credentials. Any adulteration of the official corps, any schism in the party, any insurgency in Congress, any agitation of a crisis atmosphere played into Federalist hands and must, accordingly, be suppressed.

Disunionism and foreign intrigue, Jefferson generally assumed, entered into the schemes of ultra Federalists. In the early months of 1804 the political air wafted rumors of a disunionist conspiracy in New England. They undoubtedly reached Jefferson's ear, and he could hardly fail to suspect some connection between Burr's candidacy in New York and the alleged plot of Senators Pickering, Tracy, Griswold, Plumer, and their followers in New England. For these men, New England, omitting Rhode Island, was the last refuge of sanity in an America gone mad with democracy. Time was running out. The Virginians ruled the nation with "a rod of iron," New England's power waned as the Union expanded westward, while at home Republicans beat at the doors of the state houses. The only solution lay in secession and the formation of a Northern Confederacy. Leading New York Federalists were let in on the plot, as was Burr, who smiled agreeably without committing himself, and Anthony Merry, who gleefully reported it to his government. The conspiracy collapsed after Burr's defeat and Hamilton's death. Very likely it would have met the same fate in any event, for most ultraists, while they sympathized with the disunion scheme, thought it foolhardy in 1804 and preferred to wait for the redeeming crisis democracy was sure to produce at no very distant time. The inner secrets of this misadventure were quite beyond Jefferson's ken in 1804. But he knew enough to realize that New England, at least, was still vulnerable to Federalist intrigue, for which the only certain remedy was the Republicanization of these states.

The secession plot, engineered by men who had helped raise the structure of federal union and power, was the most extreme partisan reaction to a Jeffersonian nationalism that increasingly used this structure for its own ends. The Louisiana Purchase threatened the power of the eastern states. The interests of dominant groups in these states had been well served by Federalist nationalism. Jeffersonian nationalism, on the other hand, seemed designed for the aggrandizement of the South and the West with interests of another kind. The sectional politics of the dispirited Federalists was thus a logical sequel to nationalism on the constricted Hamiltonian model. And the author of the Kentucky Resolutions of 1798 occupied six years later broader national ground than any president before him. The ultra Federalist fear of Jeffersonian nationalism combined also the fear of democracy. Democracy was the country's real disease, Hamilton lectured the disunionists the day before his death; separation might briefly retard but could not cure it. By relaxing restraints on the popular will and investing its agents with paramount authority, by perfecting the party machinery in every state, the Jeffersonian system worked relentlessly toward a democratic consolidation of power much more awesome than the Federalist version based on elitist politics, fiscal manipulation, and ministerial leadership.

The issue was most clearly drawn in the partisan encounter over the impeachment of two federal judges, John Pickering of the New Hampshire District and Samuel Chase of the Supreme Court. The Repeal Act of 1802 had not touched the foundations of judicial power. As the branch of the government still in Federalist control, the judiciary possessed the means to humble and humiliate the Republican administration and make a farce of democratic principle. Were the people or the judges sovereign? "We shall see who is master of the ship," Caesar Rodney boldly stated the issue. "Whether men appointed for life or the immediate representatives of the people agreeably to the Constitution are to give laws to the community." Since the federal judiciary was largely the creation of Congress, the issue might have been settled in more or less permanent fashion by legislation curtailing the jurisdiction of the courts, by packing them with Republicans, or by devices to secure their responsibility. None of these avenues was taken, as Jefferson and his friends stumbled upon the least effective and most offensive of all expedients, impeachment.

In February 1803, three weeks before Marshall's opinion in the case of *Marbury v. Madison,* Jefferson referred the complaint against Judge Pickering to the House of Representatives, the body charged with the power of impeachment for "high crimes and misdemeanors." The judge was a Federalist, but his bizarre conduct proceeded from intoxication and insanity, and it was this condition, not political malice or criminal behavior, that called for his removal from the bench. Unfortunately, while the Constitution provided for the appointment of judges in "good behavior," it made no provision for removal in cases of "bad behavior" unless by way of impeachment, limited, however, to offences indictable at law. In England and in a number of the states, judges were subject to removal by the executive on the address of the legislature. Jefferson and most Republicans favored a federal procedure of this kind. Had it existed, it would have reached the peculiar case of the New Hampshire judge as well as the general problem of partisanship on the federal bench. But amending the Constitution seemed a risky and tedious business. Although advocated by doctrinaire Virginians, it was not seriously considered in Washington. Nor were other reforms, such as an appellate jurisdiction in the legislature over controverted judicial opinions, which the Chief Justice himself seemed willing to concede. Jefferson resorted to the constitutional process, impeachment, without realizing its pitfalls. To impeach and then convict Pickering, the Republicans were forced to argue that the constitutional provision extended to cases of misbehavior, hence could be used to remove a judge who had committed no crime. The process was transformed from a criminal proceeding into a method of removal. Federalists accused the administration of launching a reign of terror in the judiciary. "The Judges . . . are, if possible, to be removed. Their judicial opinions, if at all questionable through mere errors of judgment, are interpreted into crimes and to be ground of impeachment." And so what began as an honest attempt to remove an unfit judge developed into a heated political controversy in which the two parties became more and more committed to opposed doctrines of judicial responsibility and judicial supremacy.

The Chase impeachment seemed to justify the worst Federalist fears. On May 2, 1803, Justice Chase, one of the most irascible Federalists, delivered a slashing attack on democratic tendencies to the federal grand jury in Baltimore. In the course of his harangue he assailed equal rights, universal suffrage, the Repeal Act, and outrages against property. "Our republican Constitution," he predicted, "will sink into a mobocracy—the worst of all possible governments." Tory language from a signer of the Declaration of Independence! A few days later Jefferson wrote to Joseph Nicholson, a Republican stalwart who was managing the Pickering impeachment in the House. "Ought this seditious and official attack on the principles of our Constitution . . . go unpunished," he asked, "and to whom so pointedly as yourself will the public look for the necessary measures?" In this roundabout fashion Jefferson invited the impeachment of Chase, declining at the same time any further interference in the matter. Republicans remembered Chase as the violently partisan judge in several sedition trials, especially Callender's, and in the treason trial and conviction of John Fries for opposing the direct tax of 1798. His charge to the grand jury again brought politics into the administration of justice and, in addition, announced principles that to Republican ears were incompatible with the Constitution he was sworn to uphold. Inevitably, the impeachment of Chase was a political act. Jefferson had no illusions on the point. Of course, the Federalists held him responsible. In their opinion the Chase impeachment was only one of a series intended to drive every Federalist from the bench. The fact that the House voted the indictment on the same day, March 12, 1804, that the Senate passed the verdict of guilty on Pickering seemed to substantiate their fears. But if Jefferson pursued a grand strategy against the judiciary, he left no record of it. The

Chase impeachment was a piece of improvisation, like every other encounter in the so-called "war on the judiciary," and when the smoke of battle finally cleared no one should have been surprised by how little had been accomplished.

Despite party schism, judicial arrogance, Federalist malice, and the treacherous shoals navigated in Louisiana, the President rode the crest of the wave as the election of 1804 came on. In foreign affairs, where he had been especially fortunate, three problems claimed his attention, and toward each of them he acted with the greater freedom and assurance born of the Louisiana Purchase. The defense of neutral rights, primarily against British infractions, increasingly troubled the administration. The Anglo-American rapprochement commenced by the Federalists had been carried forward by the Republicans under the incentive of French danger on the Mississippi. Considerable progress had been made. The long vexatious issue of Revolutionary debts had been settled. And prospects held out for settlement of the boundary with Canada, liberalization of commerce, and perhaps even curtailment of the British practice of impressment. The Louisiana Purchase relieved the pressure for conciliation on the American side. Edward Thornton, the former British chargé, now back in the foreign office, comparing Merry's reports with his before the Louisiana Purchase, could scarcely credit the evidence of deterioration in "the manifest ill-will discovered toward us." On the British side, the exigencies of war with France led to renewed naval activity in American waters, impressments, and captures on a rising scale. France, too, offended against neutral rights. But her rivalry on the paths of commerce had never threatened the Americans. Moreover, in 1804, Jefferson pandered to France in order to secure her support for American demands against Spain. In this turn of affairs, he took a higher tone with Britain.

West Florida was an especially sticky problem. Having set up a claim to the colony under the Louisiana treaty, Jefferson hastened to use the European war to force the concession of the claim. The theory was that Spain could not defend West Florida, and that France, preferring to see it in American than in British hands, would press the cession on the Spanish court. In order to cover this eventuality and, at the same time, to impress Spain with the earnestness of American intentions, the President asked Congress for authority to establish a customs district in the area of Mobile. Congress obliged with the so-called Mobile Act in February 1804. Since Mobile Bay belonged to Spain and the act gave no clue of a hypothetical character, as something contingent on Spanish cession, it had the appearance of an arrogant invasion of foreign sovereignty. Yrujo, already short-tempered with the administration, went into a rage, unappeased by Madison's reassuring words or the President's careful exclusion of lands outside American jurisdiction from the revenue district on the Mobile. Jefferson later stated publicly that the act had been misunderstood by Spain, that it was wholly prospective; but even Gallatin thought the explanation less than candid. Yrujo finally carried his campaign to the newspapers, writing in the disguise of an American. When he was found out, as he soon was, Jefferson and Madison wanted nothing more to do with him. A similar fate overtook Pinckney in Madrid. This man, a political appointee Jefferson had come to regard as "a standing reproach" to himself, boiled over because Spain made the Mobile Act an excuse for refusing to ratify the claims convention he had negotiated two years earlier. Spanish-American relations were in a torrid state in the fall. Spanish officials rallied the Indians in the Floridas; Jefferson ordered more troops to the borderlands; and both ministers were discredited.

The Mediterranean was the third theater where Jefferson stiffened his posture. The Tripolitan campaign dragged on from year to year with feeble results. "We are . . . now exactly where we were 18 months ago," he wrote dejectedly in September 1803. The "two years' sleep," as he was soon calling it, had been induced by Commodore Morris, Dale's successor in command, who cruised the Mediterranean instead of blockading Tripoli. Jefferson also blamed meddling American consuls more interested in trade with the Barbary states than in their chastisement. Back home Gallatin took an appeasing tone, while Secretary of the Navy Smith consistently advocated a hard line in the modest debate between "hawks" and "doves" in the administration. The President repeatedly demanded a peace forced on Tripoli without a cent of tribute, yet seemed unwilling to supply the fighting ships necessary to the task. He angrily recalled Morris and then, after a court-martial finding of negligence, cashiered him from the service.

When Louisiana was secure, the President gave more attention to this "little speck of Tripoli" that alone marred the horizon. He entrusted the command to a resourceful young officer, Commodore Edward Preble. Indignities continued to pile up. The frigate *Philadelphia* ran aground and gave up its crew to the pirate-enemy. Soon, however, the tide turned. Preble blockaded and bombarded Tripoli, winning a hero's fame. Stephen Decatur's gallant exploit, destroying the captive frigate under the Pasha's nose, earned him the same renown and struck a decisive blow for American honor and courage. Jefferson now determined to push matters to a victorious conclusion. The Mediterranean squadron was powerfully reinforced— scarcely a sea-worthy vessel remained in American waters. Confident that peace could be won by diplomacy backed with naval force, he refused to endorse more extreme measures, such as the audacious plan put forth by William Eaton, formerly consul at Tunis, to lead a motley insurrectionary army overland against Tripoli. The intrepid adventurer was nevertheless permitted to return to the Mediterranean and await the progress of events. Instead he proceeded at once with his fantastic scheme. And he might have won his stake but for the fact that the stepped-up naval bombardment and blockade, assisted by the real threat of his desert army, brought the Pasha to his senses before Eaton could reach Tripoli. In 1805, after four years of war, the Pasha signed a peace that freed commerce of tribute, though the United States paid $60,000 to ransom prisoners. It was not all the President had hoped for, and Smith was downright disappointed by the treaty. But Jefferson had waited twenty years for this victory—when it came he rejoiced in it.

This leaps ahead of the story, beyond Jefferson's electoral victory at home, into the thickening morass of foreign affairs. He stood on the highest public ground in 1804. Federalists seemed resigned to their fate, a shrinking minority, though they fielded a national ticket. The candidates, C. C. Pinckney and Rufus King, were virtually invisible, as the Republicans ran against John Adams, conveniently revived as the monster symbol of the evils from which the Republican Moses had delivered the people. The contrast between four years of Adams and four of Jefferson was striking: new taxes —no taxes; profusion—economy; mounting public debt—rapid extinguishment of the debt; multiplication of offices—elimination of judges, tax-gatherers, and other useless functionaries; Indian wars—

peaceful acquisition of Indian lands; alien and sedition laws—freedom and equality; judicial arrogance—judicial chastisement; oppressive armies and wasteful navies—defensive arms only; trade burdened with restrictions—flourishing commerce; war and subservience to foreign powers—peace, independence, and national expansion.

Republicans stood on the President's record and the people responded. The seventeen states (Ohio had been added) cast 162 electoral votes for Jefferson and Clinton against 14 for Pinckney and King. Only Delaware and Connecticut, with two Maryland electors, landed in the Federalist column. Even Massachusetts went Republican. Nothing gave the President greater satisfaction. "This is truly the case wherein we may say, 'this our brother was dead, and is alive again: and was lost, and is found.'" As long as Massachusetts strayed "out of the fold," the Union could not be sound. Everything would now turn to rights; Connecticut and the remaining grumblers and disorganizers would succumb, and the "perfect consolidation" Jefferson had prophesized four years before would come to pass. "The new century opened itself by committing us on a boisterous ocean," the President mused. "But all this is now subsiding, peace is smoothing our paths at home and abroad, and if we are not wanting in the practice of justice and moderation, our tranquility and property may be preserved, until increasing numbers shall leave us nothing to fear from without." And at the close of another four years he might embrace "the nunc dimittis Domine with a satisfaction leaving nothing to desire but the last great audit."

CHAPTER TEN

President:

Second Administration

And many have imagined republics and principalities which have never been known to exist in reality; for how we live is so far removed from how we ought to live, that he who abandons what is done for what ought to be done, will rather learn to bring about his own ruin than his preservation. A man who wishes to make a profession of goodness in everything must come to grief among so many who are not good. Therefore it is necessary for a prince, who wishes to maintain himself, to learn how not to be good, and to use this knowledge and not use it, according to the necessity of the case.

Machiavelli, The Prince, *1532*

IN MARCH 4, 1805, three months after Napoleon Bonaparte crowned himself Emperor of France midst the splendor of Notre Dame in Paris, Thomas Jefferson rode up Pennsylvania Avenue to the half-finished Capitol, strolled into the half-empty Senate chamber, and in a ceremony more austere than the last again swore the Presidential oath, delivered, inaudibly, an inaugural address, and quietly departed. He conceived of this address as a *compte rendu*, showing the conformity of his administration to the principles of the first inaugural. "The former was *promise:* this is *performance.*" Jefferson's empire was one of principles, and if principles could have worn a crown, he would have crowned them. A self-congratulatory tone pervaded the address, though he was careful to remove any impression of self-applause, ascribing the merits of his administration, rather, "to the reflecting character of our citizens at large." Of foreign affairs he said little other than to reiterate his belief "that with nations, as with individuals, our interests, soundly calculated, will ever be found inseparable from our moral duties." But he was effusive about domestic affairs. Because of the elimination of internal taxes, he observed, "it may be the pleasure and pride of an American to ask, what farmer, what mechanic, what laborer, ever sees a tax-gatherer of the United States." The rapid retirement of the debt and the continuing promise of peace and prosperity pointed to the day, not far distant, when the federal revenue would be liberated, after constitutional amendment, for internal improvements—"rivers, canals, roads, arts, manufacturing, education, and other great objects." The expansion of the Union had given an urgency to this task unfelt before. He took the occasion to rebuke those who feared for the survival of the Union from the great enlargement of territory. "But who can limit the extent to which the federative principle may operate effectively?" he asked. The larger the association, the more remote its extremities, the more varied its interests, the less would the center be shaken in any crisis of affairs; and expansion within continental limits secured the nation from foreign enemies.

The longest passage of the address was a kind of allegory in which Indian savages stood in the place of bigoted Federalists, the "anti-social doctrines" of the latter being condemned by inference from the pitiful state of the former. Jefferson explained his civilizing policy toward the Indians overwhelmed by progress, his efforts to enlighten and bring them to reason against the obstacles of ignorance, prejudice, pride, and the influence of crafty chieftains who inculcated "a sanctimonious reverence for the customs of their ancestors." In short, he said, "they, too, have their anti-philosophers, who find an interest in keeping things in their present state, who dread reformation, and exert all their faculties to maintain the ascendancy of habit over the duty of improving our reason, and obeying its mandates." The force or even the recognition of the allegory was lost by cautious pruning of the address at the behest of his colleagues, Gallatin especially, who thought the terms too broad and unnecessarily offensive to "old school" New Englanders. Thus, for instance, Jefferson eliminated an allusion to the charge of "philosophism" against him: "that science disqualifies men for the direction of the public affairs of the nation is one of the artful dogmas of ignorance and bigotry." In his discussion of press and pulpit, too, he cut out the thornier passages. The draft throughout was more direct, more pungent, and more personal than the final product.

Jefferson had planned to declare in this second inaugural address that he would not again seek re-election to the presidency. He had stated his intentions privately to personal friends. As he wrote to one of them, he had come to believe that a single constitutional term of seven years, his earlier preference, was not as good as the term of four years with re-eligibility, and although the danger persisted "that reelection through life shall become habitual, and election for life follow that"—the way of France to Napoleonic despotism—the example of Washington offered a safeguard which Jefferson hoped to force into an unwritten tradition of the Constitution. In the draft he approached this question indirectly through the discussion of freedom of the press. The experiment he had made proved that truth could not be put down by the calumnies of a licentious press; the people had pronounced their verdict at the polls. But instead of going on to say, as he had intended, that it would not now be necessary for him to appeal to the public again, he held his tongue and substituted a new paragraph in defense of state laws against false and defamatory publications. It was best, Jefferson had been persuaded, "not to put a continuance [in office] out of my power in defiance of all circumstances."

This was sound judgment; unfortunately, by privately confessing his true sentiments, Jefferson signaled the race for the next presidential election three years in advance, dangerously widening factional rifts among Republicans and undercutting his own position politically. Looking confidently now, in the second inaugural, to the completion of that "harmony of sentiment" envisioned in the first—to that "entire union of opinion, which gives to a nation the blessings of harmony, and the benefit of all its strength"—he was also uncomfortably aware that the problem of recalcitrant Federalists was being succeeded by the problem of dissident Republicans. Writing to Nicholas he said he had thought his situation four years ago, facing a humiliated opposition, the most unenviable to be imagined. "But I consider that as less painful than to be placed between conflicting friends. There my way was clear and my mind made up. I never for a moment had to balance between two opinions." Division and discord among friends, all Republicans, contributed to the ordeal of his second administration.

Within a week of the inauguration Jefferson went to Monticello for his usual spring holiday. The Eighth Congress, climaxed by the trial and acquittal of Justice Chase, had adjourned on March 3—many congressmen fled the capital before the inauguration. The President returned to his desk in April, then in mid-July, at the onset of the "sickly season" in the tidewater, again made the bruising four-day trek to Monticello, this time for a long stay, until early October. Such was the regular pattern. During this season the department heads scattered to their homes as well, and government was carried on by underlings in Washington through a network of postal communication. Jefferson said he passed more hours in public business at Monticello than he did in Washington, and it was more laborious because everything had to be written. In August or September Madison usually came over from Montpelier, some twenty miles distant, to take stock with his friend; on occasion one of the other secretaries visited the mountain with his family. Except for an annual excursion to his plantation in Bedford County, Jefferson did not stir from home.

The Republicans in Massachusetts, after scoring impressive gains in the spring canvass, begged him to make a tour through the Northeast; but he declined popular exposure of this kind, offering the press of business as an excuse for what he found personally distasteful. Had politics or popularity been paramount considerations with him he would have undertaken the northern tour, perhaps a southern as well, as President Washington had done before him; but "the man of the people" would not stoop to the little arts of leadership that his own political convictions, and his own legend, far more than Washington's, recommended. He was still anxious to complete the rout of the Federalists in Massachusetts. Lincoln's resignation opened the way for a cabinet reshuffle that would strengthen the Bay State's influence in the administration. Jacob Crowninshield, the

Salem merchant and congressman, was slated to become Secretary of the Navy, replacing Smith who would take the more congenial office of Attorney General. But Crowninshield backed out in March, and Jefferson, after prevailing on Smith to stay in his post, spent the next several months shopping for an Attorney General. He finally had to rob the Senate of one of his most reliable lieutenants, John Breckinridge; but no sooner was the Kentuckian appointed in December than he died. Jefferson now robbed the House of a primary leader, Caesar A. Rodney. With his appointment the cabinet was again complete and would not be disturbed until Jefferson's last days in office.

Trials of Foreign Policy

During these months between the old Congress and the new the administration engaged in a major reassessment of foreign policy. With the formation of the Third Coalition against Napoleon all Europe was engulfed in war. Jefferson could again, as he had written to an English friend, "bless the almighty being who in gathering together the waters under the heavens . . . divided the dry lands of your hemisphere from the dry lands of ours, and said 'here, at least, be there peace.'" But war ravaged the blessed ocean too, hence there could be no easy peace for America; and such were the stakes in the European conflict that Jefferson's system of manipulating American neutrality to force concessions from the great adversaries faced its severest trial. The nature of the problem would become clearer in the fall, after Trafalgar ensured British supremacy on the seas, and clearer yet in December, after Austerlitz heralded the collapse of the Third Coalition. "What an awful spectacle does the world exhibit at this instance," Jefferson would then observe. "One nation bestriding the continent of Europe like a Colossus, and another roaming unbridled on the ocean." If there was comfort in the division of the continent and the ocean between the belligerents, it was also this division that made America's position increasingly difficult. For Britain could play fast and loose with the United States in the Atlantic with little danger to herself, and France, master of a continent, had small need of any assistance the United States might supply. Jefferson continued to perceive the European power balance in the conventional image of scales—a balancing machine—which if depressed on one side caused reciprocal action on the other. But with the polarization of European power this conception grew obsolete. The damage the United States could inflict on British sea power was scarcely enough to engage Napoleon's interest; and the United States could do virtually nothing for Britain on the Continent. Between these extremities of power, neutral America could discover little leverage for action, though Jefferson would grasp at every elusive opportunity. The lesson he had been painfully learning was now driven home: The enemy was not Britain or France or Spain but Europe itself.

All the signs in the early months of 1805 pointed to the end of the decade-long Anglo-American rapprochement. The commercial articles of the Jay Treaty had expired. William Pitt had returned to power and in a few month's time moved the country from complacent to aggressive belligerency. The Third Coalition had been formed, embracing the Northern powers, Russia and Sweden, heretofore the fitful champions of neutral rights in Europe, now leaving the United States alone in their defense. The Royal Navy stepped up its harassment of American commerce; the impressment of American seamen soared to new heights; privateers infested American waters and plundered American trade. Before he left Washington in July, Jefferson sent out a small naval force to cruise against the privateers and, without a stitch of authority, ordered the arrest of any found within the limits of the Gulf Stream.

On July 23 the British vice-admiralty judge Sir William Scott abruptly reversed the country's policy on the neutral carrying trade from enemy colonies. This decision in the case of the ship *Essex* marked a return to strict interpretation of the Rule of 1756, which Britain had tried to interpolate into international law during the Seven Years War. According to the rule, a trade closed in time of peace could not be legitimately opened in time of war; hence a neutral, like the United States, could not carry the produce of the French and Spanish West Indian colonies to the Continent. Strictly British, the rule had no standing in international law, and Great Albion herself observed it only at convenience. She had revived it with devastating effect on American carriers late in 1793. The United

States then evaded the restriction by doing indirectly what it allegedly could not do directly. Enemy cargoes were landed in American ports, passed through customs, and re-exported to belligerent ports on the Continent. For a time the British admiralty courts contended this was fraudulent: the insertion of a neutral port did not neutralize cargoes in "continuous voyage" from one enemy port to another. But by 1801 the judges, without retracting the Rule of 1756, had accepted the principle of the "broken voyage": the landing of the cargo and the payment of duties, even if withdrawn on re-export, broke the continuity of the voyage and neutralized the trade. Now, in 1805, the esteemed Scott ruled that unless the neutral shipper could prove original intent to terminate the voyage in an American port, ship and cargo were subject to seizure and condemnation. Intent being subjective, the ruling could not be fairly applied, and it transferred the burden of proof from the captor to the shipper. The re-export trade floated American prosperity. By 1805 over one-half the country's exports were re-exports, from the colonies of all belligerents including the British. The United States had become the great entrepôt for Europe. Quite aside from the rights of the case, the trade was too valuable to be put to hazard.

What had motivated this shift of policy in Britain? A quasi-official explanation soon appeared in the form of a pamphlet, *War in Disguise; or the Frauds of the Neutral Flags*, whose anonymous author was James Stephen. After a long sleep Britain had awakened to the true character of the American re-export trade, the argument began. It was not a *bona fide* trade, pursued on its own account, but a fraudulent trade, a war in disguise, in tacit alliance with the enemy. Its effect was to negate British maritime and naval superiority in a struggle for survival against the land monster, Napoleon. The military costs of surrendering this superiority were quite evident; what was particularly notable in Stephen's defense of the new policy was the emphasis placed on the commercial costs of the old. The United States, as the last neutral of consequence, took possession of a great trade from which Britain had previously reaped huge profits, from freights, insurance, duties, and mercantile charges. By repossessing this trade Britain would put down a dangerous commercial rival and force it back into channels profitable to herself, even at the risk of supplying her own enemies on the Continent. At the same time, British West Indian commodities, currently under-sold on the Continent because of the American competition, would regain the market; British seamen fled to American vessels would return; and a license to plunder neutral traders would be extended to the whole British marine. Such was the spirit of the new policy. Meanwhile, in the United States, Madison assembled the legal ammunition to demolish it. His learned report, published in January, tore away the fictitious defenses of the *Essex* policy and revealed the real motive as British jealousy of American commerce. He and Jefferson had been fighting on this front for a quarter century. Reason revolted, as Jefferson observed, at the idea that "a belligerent takes to himself a commerce with its own enemy which it denies to a neutral, on the ground of its aiding that enemy in the war." The pretension, inconsistent in itself, was yet entirely consistent with British strategy since the Revolution to subvert American wealth and power.

On the very day of the *Essex* decision Monroe returned to England, where he had succeeded Rufus King. He at once sensed the stiffening of British posture toward the United States. The new policy, with the wave of seizures in the West Indies, was an experiment, he said, to see how much the Americans would bear. It must be resisted. But could the country take on both Britain and Spain at the same time? Having just come from a special mission to Spain, Monroe was impressed by the interconnections between these two American quarrels and inclined to think success with one, as proof of strength, would promote success with the other. France, moreover, was the crucial link to both. A satellite of France, weak and depressed, Spain was at Napoleon's command. He had no interest now in the Floridas or in an altercation between Spain and the United States; and he must see that the sooner this dispute was settled the sooner the United States could give its full attention to Britain. The fact that money would change hands or, better yet, that American stock would be thrown to European speculators in any transaction for the Floridas, seemed to offer further inducement to Napoleon, Talleyrand, and company. Monroe had passed through Paris to obtain the good offices of the French government on his way to Spain to negotiate a settlement. Amazingly, France shunned these overtures and, instead, by taking sides with her ally ensured the defeat of Monroe's mission.

For five months Monroe and the discredited minister, Pinckney, had pressed the American demands at Aranjuez. These demands were harsh. First of all, Spain must ratify unconditionally the spoliations convention of 1802. The convention provided for the settlement of claims, estimated at between five and eight million dollars, arising from depredations in Spanish waters since 1796. Much of the damage had been inflicted by French cruisers, for which Spain said she could not be held responsible, and Yrujo assembled a battery of Philadelphia lawyers to support this position. Washington insisted that since the spoliations had occurred in Spanish jurisdiction, Madrid was responsible; and contrary to a later argument invented in Madrid, neither the Convention of 1800 nor the Louisiana Treaty with France covered the indemnification claim. In January 1804 the Senate had reluctantly ratified Pinckney's compromise reserving the disputed claims for subsequent negotiation. Don Pedro de Cevallos, the Spanish Foreign Minister, now required the suppression of this article and revocation of the offensive Mobile Act as well. The claims issue was less important in itself than as an irritant, both in Madrid and in Washington, where Jefferson saw it as further evidence, along with vexatious border incidents, of Spanish hostility. The issue might be circumvented, Monroe was instructed, by a general settlement that camouflaged the indemnification claim. Such a settlement would reach the greater issues of the Floridas and the western boundary of Louisiana. First, West Florida, to the Perdido, must be acknowledged as American under the Louisiana Treaty. Not only was this right, in the administration's view, but a title dated 1803 would annul the lavish Spanish land grants in the interim, while the United States would be stuck with them under a title dated 1805. Second, Spain must cede East Florida, for which the envoys were authorized to offer two million dollars. The negotiation of this demand might easily take account of the indemnification claim. Third, the western limit: the United States claimed, as had France, to the Rio Bravo; however, this was negotiable in the light of the arrangement on the Floridas. Humboldt, during his visit in June, had impressed the President with the value of the lands lying beyond the Sabine and the Colorado. Madison at once informed Monroe of the President's new felt aversion to the perpetual relinquishment of any of this domain, though he was agreeable to a neutral barrier state between the Rio Bravo and the Colorado or the Sabine for a term of twenty to thirty years. By still later instructions the envoys were authorized to fix the Colorado as the boundary if Spain demanded it in return for the Floridas. This was part of the final offer tendered to Cevallos in May. It was firmly rejected. And Monroe returned to more bad news in England. "It is evident that we have no sincere friends anywhere," he wrote from London, "that all the powers, with whom we have the most immediate relations are jealous of us, by some motives which are common to all." The Americans would have to stop playing games with European rivalries, take the country's interest into their own hands, and repel insult and injury with force.

The news from Cadiz reached Monticello near the end of July. Jefferson's immediate reaction was to conjure again, as in the Louisiana crisis, with a British alliance. "I infer a confident reliance on the part of Spain on the omnipotence of Bonaparte," he wrote to Madison, "but a desire of procrastination till peace in Europe shall leave us without an ally." A pacific settlement with Spain turned on the continuation of the European war; moreover, after a victorious peace the Emperor of France might turn his guns on the United States. "I am strongly impressed with a belief in the hostile and treacherous intentions against us on the part of France, and that we should lose no time in securing something more than a mutual friendship from England." To this startling proposition, Madison demurred. Any bargain struck with Britain, involving as it must a commitment to British arms, would prove more costly than the gains sought from Spain. Jefferson appreciated the point; nevertheless, fresh dispatches in the early weeks of August strengthened his attachment to the idea of a British alliance. He explained himself further to Madison. "The treaty should be provisional only, to come into force on the event of our being engaged in war with either France or Spain during the present war in Europe. In that event we should make common cause, and England should stipulate not to make peace without our obtaining the objects for which we go to war, to wit, the acknowledgment by Spain of the rightful boundaries of Louisiana . . . and 2, indemnification for spoliations, for which purpose we should be allowed to make reprisal on the Floridas and *retain them* as an indemnification." Britain would find sufficient inducement in the American pledge of co-operation, Jefferson thought, and the event of American belligerency would probably never materialize, since the mere fact of the treaty would force France and Spain to seek a settlement. He had not abandoned his old strategy of conquest through peace and diplomacy but simply proposed a change of tactics that, if Britain was willing, still kept the game in American hands.

The Spanish dispatches circulated among the secretaries in four cities and Jefferson collected their opinions at Monticello. Dearborn's cannot be documented; presumably he gave it directly to the chief during a September visit. Smith, as usual, took an aggressive stance: build the naval force for an offensive war, but if there was no time for this, ally with Britain and take Cuba and both the Floridas. Gallatin, surprisingly, agreed with Smith on the need for naval expansion to combat the European idea of the "passive endurance" of the United States; however, he opposed anything war-like including, it seems, a provisional alliance with Britain. American claims on Spain were excessive, in his opinion; surely they offered no just cause for war, a war that would destroy prosperity, plunge the country into debt, and, all together, cost far more than the adventure was worth. Gallatin called for a resumption of negotiation on more modest American demands backed up by defensive preparations. Madison's advice was similar, though he came halfway around —just far enough to appear sympathetic—to the chief's idea of a British alliance. By the middle of September, Jefferson also had the latest counsel of the American minister, John Armstrong, who had succeeded Livingston in Paris. The former Revolutionary general, with a mind that ran more to military than to diplomatic arts, advised the administration to seize Texas as hostage, suspend intercourse with the Spanish colonies, and then negotiate. France, having herself claimed to the Rio Bravo, while declining to claim the Floridas, would take the American side to settle this quarrel. Monroe seemed to concur in Armstrong's opinion, certainly in spirit if not in detail. Jefferson blended these various opinions with his own notion of an alliance and communicated the whole package to Madison. "Supposing a previous alliance with England to guard us in the worst event," he wrote, "I should propose that Congress should pass acts (1) authorizing the Executive to suspend intercourse with Spain at discretion; (2) to dislodge the new establishments of Spain between the Mississippi and Bravo; (3) to appoint commissioners to examine and ascertain all claims for spoliation." With this formulation he was ready to meet the cabinet on October 4 in Washington.

The cabinet met but reached no definite conclusion. Madison had been detained in Philadelphia by his wife's illness, and Jefferson was reluctant to proceed in his absence, especially on the question of a British alliance. Madison inclined to think it best at present to do nothing, and before he returned to Washington at the end of the month, Jefferson had come to the same conclusion. Not knowing which way to move, surrounded by dangers, it was perhaps best to stand still. The latest intelligence from Europe pointed to a long war, while a month or so earlier Jefferson had feared a short one. "This gives us our great desideratum, time," he said. "In truth it places us quite at our ease." The sense of crisis disappeared. All thought of a British alliance vanished, never to materialize again. "This new state of things [in Europe]," he observed, "is the more fortunate in proportion as it would have been disagreeable to have proposed closer connections with England at a moment when so much clamor exists against her for her new encroachments on neutral rights." Relieved of this embarrassment, which ought to have been equally obvious in August when driven to it by a kind of desperation, he fell back on the more congenial tactics skewed to French interest in Spanish affairs. "Our question now is what way to give Spain another opportunity," he wrote Gallatin, and by his rhetorical questions supplied the answer: "Is not Paris the place? France the agent? The purchase of the Floridas the means?"

On November 12, only three weeks before the President's message would go to Congress, the cabinet met and adopted the new plan of proceeding with Spain. First, purchase of both the Floridas: "the exciting motive with France, to whom Spain is in arrears for subsidies, and who will be glad also to secure us from going into the scale with England." Second, American cession of the land between the Rio Bravo and the Guadalupe, the Texas stream south of the Colorado: "the soothing motive with Spain which France would press bona fide because she claimed to the Rio Bravo." Third, Spanish payment of spoliations under her own flag only, before and since the abortive convention of 1802, in an amount not to exceed $5,-

ooo,ooo, for which she would hypothecate to the United States the strip between the Guadalupe and the Bravo. After two years of failure Jefferson was still speculating on France's good offices. Marvelously, on the next day a dispatch from Armstrong gave renewed substance to the speculation. Talleyrand had sent a confidential agent to Armstrong inviting the United States to resume negotiations with Spain and outlining the plan France would support. The old fox struck a hard bargain but, in general, his proposition fell within the range of accommodation, and Jefferson at once reconvened the cabinet. The United States, it was now decided, would pay $5,000,000 (Talleyrand had said ten and the agent had come down to seven) for the Floridas, fix the western boundary on the Colorado, and agree to settlement of spoliations under the Spanish flag by a joint commission, reserving the land south of the Colorado as security for payment of these indemnities.

So agonizing weeks and months of vacillation and indecision terminated in a Spanish policy. Jefferson proceeded with cautious optimism. Congress would have to co-operate, instantly, before a change in the winds at the Tuileries, and secretly, as diplomacy required in a transaction of this kind. He had thought to send immediate orders to Armstrong to arrange for the purchase of the Floridas or, at the very least, to pledge the government for the down-payment. But Gallatin had objected: the assent of Congress, while probable, was not certain and might take time. The cabinet agreed to suspend instructions until Congress could act. To throw the matter into Congress in any shape called for the utmost finesse. Money was wanted —$2,000,000 at the start—for a specific object in secret diplomacy at Paris. If Congress inquired too closely into the object, if it scrupled with the proposition of paying France for Spanish possessions or, indeed, for one possession, West Florida, the United States already claimed to own, the game might be lost. Jefferson had buried his scruples on these points. The claim that the nation had already paid for West Florida was a detail, one Monroe had willingly sacrificed in his efforts at Aranjuez. As to the money, "We need not care who gets that," Jefferson said; even if it were paid in Madrid it would find its way into Napoleon's coffers. Congress, in addition, must be willing to adopt secretly one policy looking to peace and bargain, and another policy, in public, pitched to war in defense of American demands on Spain. This seemed a necessary precaution against diplomatic failure and a useful means of exerting influence on France and Spain. Every part of the President's plan made excellent sense viewed as a whole, while each part was vulnerable to attack if left to itself. The difficulty came in blending the parts together to the satisfaction of Congress.

The hazards on the other side, in France, were largely beyond Jefferson's control. Again, as with Louisiana, the whim of Napoleon was likely to prove decisive. Whether or not he would dictate terms to Spain depended on any number of variables: the circumstances of the war, the adroitness of the American negotiator, the profitability of the transaction, his estimate of American determination and, above all perhaps, of the administration's willingness to subordinate neutrality to French objectives. On the last point Jefferson was ready to offer assurances within the generous limits of neutrality. The matter of profit went beyond the Emperor; it concerned Talleyrand, whose talent for turning public business into private lucre was well known, and a nest of bankers and speculators in Paris, including some Americans, who eyed the Floridas purchase as a handsome job for themselves. Their avarice had been excited by the administration's success in floating the Louisiana Purchase, which pushed American stocks to new heights; but this job had brought no money into their shop. Beginning with Livingston a year and a half before, every informed American in Paris warned the administration that a deal for the Floridas could not be arranged unless the money-lenders and stockjobbers got into the act and, in fact, could not fail if they did. This meant payment in securities, which afforded opportunity for speculation and had all the effect of a *douceur*. The final November cabinet decision provided that the $5,000,000 to be offered for the Floridas would be in the form of stock redeemable in three years. If that turned the proposition into a "French job," it could not be helped.

While wrapping up the Spanish policy, Jefferson drafted his fifth annual message, delivered on December 3. The Republicans dominated the Ninth Congress without hindrance except from themselves. In the Senate were only seven Federalists, though they moved as a phalanx against weak Republican leadership. The huge majority in the House—even the Massachusetts delegation was now predominantly Republican—continued to be led by the triumvirate of Speaker Macon, John Randolph, and Joseph Nicholson. As everyone expected, the message focused on foreign affairs. Jefferson denounced the British system of "hovering" on American coasts and harbors to the annoyance of commerce, and he pledged "effectual and determined opposition" to new principles "interloped into the law of nations." His tone towards Spain was perhaps a little higher. Alluding to the various grievances—spoliations, boundaries, obstructions at Mobile, and aggressions across the Sabine—he seemed to despair of a peaceful settlement. But he quickly broke off, deferred Spanish affairs to a subsequent message, and went on to recommend defensive preparations against belligerent powers generally. "We ought still to hope that time and a more correct estimate of interest, as well as of character, will produce the justice we are bound to expect. But should any nation," he warned, "deceive itself by false calculations, and disappoint that expectation, we must join in the unprofitable contest of trying which party can do the other the most harm. Some of these injuries may perhaps admit a peaceful remedy. Where that is competent it is always the most desirable. But some of them are of a nature to be met by force only, and all of them may lead to it." So the seaport towns should be fortified and furnished with gunboats, the militia system reformed, the export of arms and ammunition prohibited; and consideration should be given to building ships-of-the-line and strengthening the army. Jefferson had planned to call for a reduction of taxes. The Mediterranean Fund, serviced by a small added duty on imports, was scheduled to expire with the termination of the Tripolitan war; instead, Jefferson preferred to keep this revenue derived mainly from the rich and to eliminate the salt tax, which fell on the poor and brought about equal value to the Treasury. Some might think it improvident, he had written in the draft, to abolish taxes in the present circumstances, but he answered, "if we never discontinue taxes while there is a cloud of war visible on our horizon, all taxes will become perpetual." This was carrying economy too far for Gallatin. If the great war should end, the revenue would fall, as it would also if the United States undertook commercial retaliation against Britain. Aside from fiscal considerations, Gallatin pointed out that the tenor of the passage on taxes contradicted the tenor of the passages

815

on foreign affairs. The belligerents, he said, "never can think us serious in any intention to resist if we recommend at the same time a diminution of our resources." Besides, the Treasury would need all the money it could get to pay for the Floridas without impairing the planned retirement of the debt. Jefferson struck all mention of reduced taxes. Nor did he return to the idea thrown out in the inaugural address of applying the surplus revenue, running at a million dollars a year, to internal improvements. Arms and defense would swallow up the surplus. Such was the sad reality again forced on the young nation that pursued wealth and power in an Atlantic world constantly torn by war.

Some quarters heard the message as "war-like." So far as it addressed foreign ears, this was Jefferson's intention. He meant to produce an effect in the Tuileries; and lest that effect, with respect to Spain, be lessened by too mild a notice of "the greater enormity" arising from the British system, Jefferson tried to balance his strictures. He did not mean to arouse belligerent dispositions at home, but in a message addressed to the American public as well as to foreign chancelleries he could not avoid giving the same impression to both; moreover, he fully realized now, if not before, that success abroad demanded challenge to the Quakerish reputation of the administration in Europe and manifest readiness to back up appeals to justice and interest with force. But the military preparations were still calculated on peace. They were meant to overcome the "false calculations" of belligerents who imagined they could kick and cuff the United States with impunity and hence had lost the incentive to pursue peace with the last great neutral.

On December 6, Jefferson communicated his confidential message on Spain, together with a bundle of diplomatic documents. After briefly reviewing the history of the controversy, he alluded to France's interest in preventing a rupture and indications of support for a comprehensive settlement on a plan acceptable to the United States. "The present crisis in Europe is favorable for pressing such a settlement: and not a moment should be lost in availing ourselves of it. Should it pass unimproved, our situation would become much more difficult. Formal war is not necessary. It is not probable it will follow. But the protection of our citizens, the spirit and honor of our country, require that force should be interposed to a certain degree. It will probably contribute to advance the cause of peace. But the course to be pursued will require the command of means which it belongs to Congress exclusively to yield or to deny." The language was obscure: Jefferson neither named the object nor the means wanted. Such were the counsels of prudence. The diplomacy on the French side was secretive and unofficial; he wished to keep it in the same course on the American, so far as the forms of government would permit. He recognized the political risks of the proceeding. Every Federalist editor would raise the cry of French influence and blackmail, and eastern jealousy of southerly expansion of the Union would again rear its head. It was part of his style of personal leadership to employ hints instead of commands, to move circuitously, to rule by a show of submissiveness to Congress. The system had worked in the past. In fact, the congressional procedure with respect to the Spanish business followed precisely the course pursued with respect to Louisiana. It was, Gallatin argued, "the smoothest mode of doing business in Congress." Read by itself the confidential message seemed to call for an act of clairvoyance; but it was meant to be read as part of a system, in relationship to the public message and the real views of the administration. Only the details were wanting, and they could be privately obtained from the executive by those charged with the business in Congress.

Randolph was the man in charge. He had effectively handled the Louisiana appropriation under similar circumstances. The House at once referred the Spanish message to a special committee under his chairmanship. He promptly called on the President and learned, what he already knew vaguely, that $2,000,000 was wanted to purchase the Floridas. He said he could never agree to the measure. The President had not publicly asked for the money but thrown the whole responsibility upon the House; even if he were to make an explicit request, however, Randolph would oppose the grant because, after the failure of the Spanish negotiation, the payment of money would be a kind of extortion and would disgrace the country forever. Nicholson joined Randolph in opposition, leaving only one of the seven members of the House committee to whom the President could confidently turn. This was Barnabas Bidwell, a prestigious lawyer from Massachusetts who had just come into the House and already caught the President's eye as the leader he was seeking. Without any prompting from the President, Bidwell unhesitatingly interpreted the message as a request for money and moved the grant. Randolph adopted the fiction that no such grant was meant, rather the message looked to war-like measures on the southern frontier. The committee rejected Bidwell's motion, he alone voting for it, and did not meet again for two weeeks. Meanwhile, Randolph's hauteur rose. He talked to Madison, who frankly told him that a peaceful settlement with Spain depended on the payment of money to France. "I considered it a base prostration of the national character," Randolph later wrote of the interview, "to excite one nation by money to bully another nation out of its property." The administration pleaded the costs of delay. Snubbing the plea, Randolph galloped off to Baltimore for a week. On his return Gallatin pressed him for action. The Virginian said he would not vote a shilling for the purchase of the Floridas and blurted, "I do not understand this double set of opinions and principles—the one ostensible, the other real; I hold true wisdom and cunning to be utterly incompatible." The administration now confided its cause to Bidwell. The committee continued to support Randolph; finally, on January 3, it reported a resolution calling upon the President to raise troops for the southern frontier and chastise the aggressor. After a week's stormy debate behind closed doors, the House rejected Randolph's motion and adopted Bidwell's substitute, 76 to 54, appropriating $2,000,000 for extraordinary expenses of foreign intercourse. The Senate concurred in the Two Million Act on February 7. Formal instructions finally went to Armstrong in March, six months after the secret overture from Talleyrand.

Randolph's revolt spread confusion and dismay in Washington. For four years, in the service of the administration, he had terrorized the House with his bludgeoning talents, his javelin-like wit, and his loss to the administration could not be easily repaired. As the session wore on his revolt became permanent and systematic, causing the only notable party schism of Jefferson's presidency. At first, during the odious Spanish business, it appeared that Randolph would draw off a large troop of Republicans. But he soon astounded everyone by his mad ravings and conceits, and at the end was left with but a handful of ardent followers, mostly Virginians, who took the name Quids. The Federalists, of course, rallied to him simply to embarrass the administration. With a huge majority, Jefferson could still control Congress, though he would never find a satisfactory replacement for Randolph in the House leadership. The real damage of the schism was this: it rattled the confidence of Republicans in an administration that had seemed invincible, sent waves of suspicion and distrust through the ranks, and shook the pedestal under the President himself. Jefferson's loss was less of followers than of prestige—the aura of invincibility that surrounded him—and as prestige declined so did the zeal and trust and unity of his followers. The crisis of morale appeared not only in Congress but in crucial Republican states such as Virginia, Pennsylvania, and New York. In March, before the troubles in Congress became public knowledge, William Duane informed Jefferson of pernicious reports circulating in Pennsylvania. It was said the President had abandoned the firm Republicans of the South and thrown himself into the arms of a New England party, that he was building a third party composed of moderates, both Federalist and Republican, that he had lost control of his cabinet, and so on. Contributing to this infectious discontent was the question of the Presidential succession, not yet in the open but gnawing at the Republican vitals.

Whether or not any of this might have been avoided had the President taken a different course in Spanish affairs is questionable. As to Randolph, at least, he was spoiling for a fight and would doubtless have found excuse for one on some issue. His principal accusation against the administration, that it followed a double set of opinions, one ostensible and honorable, to go before the public, the other real, devious, and dishonorable, was true in a naïvely moralistic view of politics and diplomacy. Jefferson, preparing materials for an answer to Randolph's exposé of the affair under the mask of "Decius" in the Richmond *Enquirer* in August, denied any duplicity or contradiction of opinions. Both were parts of a single system, both equally official, both the responsibility of the Executive. The two messages perfectly harmonized; the latter, he said, without directly requesting an appropriation, "asked the means of negotiation in such terms as covered the purchase of Florida as evidently as it was proper to speak it out." Perhaps he had carried caution too far in this instance. But if he had chosen to "speak it out," trusting Congress to protect the policy, Randolph would still have found fault on grounds of "double dealing," "bribery," and "backstairs influence." As to the first of these, Jefferson thought it necessary if he was to cover both possibilities, negotiation and force, with Spain. The second was pious nonsense. Even Randolph had declared "there is no Spain," no Pyrenees, no sovereignty except at the sufferance of Napoleon. So the Floridas could be obtained only through France; and for such an accession to the peace and well-being of the nation, Jefferson could neither close his eyes to European realities nor wash his hands of European methods. The charge of "backstairs influence" came with ill grace from a man who had been its principal beneficiary for four years. "But," said Jefferson indignantly, "when he differed from the executive in a leading measure, and the executive, not submitting to him, expressed its sentiments to others, the very sentiments (to wit, the purchase of Florida) which he acknowledges they expressed to him, then he roars out on backstairs' influence." This cant got under the President's skin. Defending his methods to Bidwell, he observed, "if the members [of Congress] are to know nothing but what is important enough to be put into a public message, and indifferent enough to be made known to all the world, and if the executive is to keep all other information to himself, and the House to plunge on in the dark, it becomes a government of chance and not design."

The Florida business was the occasion of Randolph's revolt, not the cause. It was foreclosed in the previous session. His strident opposition to the administration-backed compromise in the case of the Yazoo lands revealed traits of political purism, exhibitionism, and hauteur that were scarcely tolerable in a deliberative body, let alone in a majority leader. In 1795 some 35,000,000 acres in the wild Yazoo country of Mississippi and Alabama had been fraudulently deeded away to speculative companies by the Georgia legislature, which then rescinded the sale after the companies had begun to unload on innocent buyers. The federal government fell heir to the problem of conflicting claims when Georgia ceded its western lands in 1802, and a commission, which included Madison and Gallatin, recommended a settlement that would award 5,000,000 acres to Yazoo purchasers. It was a fair and just compromise; moreover, because of the large New England interest in the Yazoo claims, it was important for the developing national consensus in the Republican party. But Randolph, who despised this consensus, thundered against the settlement as a national disgrace—a legislative reward of fraud and corruption —and his opposition kept "Yazooism" alive for ten years. Successful in this bitter encounter, his self-esteem suffered a crushing blow in the next, the impeachment trial of Justice Samuel Chase. Randolph was the manager, or chief prosecutor, of the case. Indeed he boasted "that this was *his* impeachment—that every article was drawn by *his* hand, and that *he* was to have the whole merit of it." This was true in the main. Jefferson, although he had suggested the move against Chase twenty months before, no longer believed in the efficacy of impeachment and took little interest in the Chase trial. In the end, while the judge was acquitted, Randolph practically hanged himself. His long closing summation, Adams noted, "was without order, conviction, or argument; consisting altogether of the most hackneyed commonplaces of popular declamation, mingled up with panegyrics and invectives upon persons, with a few well-expressed ideas, a few striking figures, much distortion of face and contortion of body, tears, groans, and sobs, with occasional passes of recollection, and continual complaints of having lost his notes." Randolph's management, some observers thought, had determined the verdict. Jefferson never expressed himself on the point, but Madison, it was said, rejoiced in his fellow Virginian's disgrace.

In view of his temperament and politics it is remarkable that Randolph submitted to the role of a backstairs councillor for four years. His corrosive talents demanded opposition. He was notoriously sensitive to any personal affront. As a young friend observed, "He was a man without a skin," though in appearance, gaunt face on a slight frame, he seemed to be all skin. Sullen and angry after the humiliation of the Chase trial, he returned to Washington in December half convinced by rumors that the administration had lost confidence in him. These rumors were not without foundation, especially as they touched Bidwell, actively courted by the administration and the personal representative, for Randolph, of the New England interest. He was despondent, as were many of his friends in Virginia, over the course of the administration. A doctrinaire Virginia Republican, his creed had been firmly fixed in 1798, when he came on the national scene, and with others of this school he felt the administration had strayed from the true path, put conciliation ahead of reform, sacrificed principles to prudence, and continued under different forms the dangerously "monarchical" practices of its predecessors. The evil genius of this betrayal, as Randolph saw it, was the Secretary of State. The symbol of political appeasement, Madison was tainted with Federalism, with Yazooism, and in foreign affairs, Bonapartism. His succession to the presidency would be a disaster. Randolph, therefore, sought to discredit him and at the same time to induce Monroe to contest the succession. The Quids courted Monroe for two years, finally to no avail because the mass of Republicans, including many who preferred Monroe or some other candidate, closed ranks behind the President to avert disaster. All of these factors—personal temperament, ideological disagreement, and animosity to Madison, as well as the collision on foreign policy—entered into Randolph's insurgency. (Randolph himself, ruminating many years later, blamed everything on a game of chess in which he had dared to beat the President!) It was later said of this classic Virginian, who flaunted Virginia manners and prejudices in Congress for years of madness to come, "He has so long spoken parables, that he now thinks in them." And so he was thinking even in 1806. In the final analysis the clash of these two Virginians, Jefferson and Randolph, so antithetical as types it affronts reason to embrace them in the same category, was a paradigm of the conflict between the pragmatic statesman and the political ideologue, the one yielding to circumstances, the other ceremoniously clinging to dogma, the one actively seeking realizable goals within the limits of principle, the other careless of prudence, wary of power, and exalting principle to a fetish.*

* Several stanzas of John Greenleaf Whittier's "Randolph of Roanoke," although written after the Virginian had become a symbol of the "slave power," accurately capture the perverse brilliance of the earlier Randolph.

> Mirth, sparkling like a diamond shower,
> From lips of life-long sadness;
> Clear picturings of majestic thought
> Upon a ground of madness
>
> While others hailed in distant skies
> Our eagle's dusky pinion,
> He only saw the mountain bird
> Stoop o'er his Old Dominion!

Several items of congressional business related to the negotiation for the Floridas. Jefferson nominated Armstrong and James Bowdoin as the special commissioners, an unfortunate pairing as it turned out. Bowdoin, also from Massachusetts, had been earlier appointed to Madrid as Pinckney's successor. The Senate made no objection to him, but so odious had Armstrong become that he was only finally confirmed, with the casting vote of the Vice President, in March. The result was further delay. A bill prohibiting intercourse with rebel-held Santo Domingo genuflected toward Napoleon. The blacks on the western part of the island (Haiti) had declared their independence in 1804. France did not recognize the claim, nor did any other nation; in international law, if not in fact, the island remained a French possession. The Americans carried on a lucrative trade with the rebels, which Jefferson wished to continue and Napoleon could not prevent. Strictly speaking, the trade was illicit; but when Pichon complained Madison told him it was up to France to stop it. The government's responsibility could not be so lightly dismissed, however. Because the trade was unprotected, American ships armed (the law prohibiting the arming of private vessels had expired in 1802) and also carried on a large traffic in arms with the rebels. French and Spanish privateers set upon the American traders. And Merry complained that the trade violated the law of neutrality because both armed vessels and arms, by capture or purchase, became the property of the King's enemies. (He did not mention Britain's interest in eliminating the Americans and monopolizing the trade for herself.) Responding to those pressures the President had laid the problem before the second session of the Eighth Congress. A bill passed to regulate the clearance of armed vessels and to require them to post bond against the use of their armament except in self-defense. The act, limited to one year, had no effect on the illicit trade. Through General Turreau, the scrappy new minister, France filed bitter complaint. But Jefferson made no mention of the matter in his annual message.

It was left to his old friend George Logan, senator from Penn-

> All parties feared him; each in turn
> Beheld its schemes disjointed,
> At right or left his fatal glance
> And spectral finger pointed.

823

sylvania, to take up the subject on his own initiative. When the Clearance bill was before the Senate, Logan had tried unsuccessfully to set it aside in favor of his own bill calling for total non-inter-course; and now, a year later, he sought enactment of this stiffer measure. Merchant Republicans, like Senator Smith of Maryland, vehemently objected, pointing to the loss of profits and revenue from a trade interdict that could be of no benefit to France and only enrich Britain. Undecided, the Senate called on the President for information. He sent notes from Talleyrand and Turreau demanding the trade be stopped. With little ado the Senate gave leave to Logan to bring in his bill, and it rapidly passed through both houses, the Federalists alone objecting. Randolph, it might be noted, steered clear of this matter altogether. Southern Republicans generally thought the black republic a menace to themselves and would gladly see it abandoned. These fears had no bearing on Jefferson's shifting policy toward Santo Domingo. Black rule of the island was a *fait accompli* in his opinion; nothing the United States or France could do would reverse the course. Commerce and diplomacy were his springs of action. That he was willing to sacrifice the former to the latter, to stop the American trade in order to advance his territorial ambitions in the Floridas, seemed the obvious explanation for the Logan bill, and the Federalists at once pounced on it. When the bill was before the House, Timothy Pickering dispatched an eleventh hour warning to the President. All the world knew—Logan had declared it in the Senate and the President's own son-in-law, John W. Eppes, had echoed it in the House—that the bill was before Congress on French demand. "Sir, the moment you sign this act (and you will sign it, if it passes the House of Representatives) you seal the disgradation of your country. . . . One act begets further unwarrantable demands. . . . While we thus yield obedience to France, we shall become the object of her contempt, and the pawn of Europe. Save then your country, while you may, from such ignominy and thralldom."

Pickering would make good his warning. The Santo Domingo bill was a sop to Napoleon, the Federalists said, and from the moment of its passage to the end of Jefferson's administration they accused him of subservience to the French Emperor. The old canard, now fully revived, would merit no attention were it not for the grain of truth it contained with respect to the Santo Domingo legislation. Although the bill originated with the Quaker senator from Philadelphia who, at this very time, strongly opposed the whole Florida venture, it became, in effect, an administration measure. A fortnight before he signed the act, Jefferson pointedly brought it to Armstrong's attention as a means of scoring a hit at the Tuileries. Yet he knew very well that the statute was unenforceable. It simply required bond and clearance for American vessels sailing *under orders* for rebel-held ports; but vessels seldom sailed for the West Indies under orders to specific ports—they surely would not now—and the act contained no effective penalties for violation or fraud. Every congressman considered it "a dead letter," according to Adams. Jefferson found the legislation chiefly valuable as another piece of "double dealing": a gesture of good will toward Napoleon, earning, it was hoped, his gratitude, and a signal to the merchants to continue the lucrative trade with the rebel island at their own peril. The little truth in the Federalist accusation was thus more subtle than they perceived or were willing to admit.

But in Spanish affairs nothing seemed to go right for the President. Randolph "assassinated" the negotiation. From New York, in February, Francisco de Miranda, the inveterate Latin American adventurer, embarked his vessel, the *Leander*, on an expedition against Caracas that the Spanish minister angrily charged, and many Americans believed, had the clandestine backing of the administration. Meanwhile, in Europe, the Third Coalition collapsed and Napoleon marched to hegemony. No sooner did the two envoys, Bowdoin and Armstrong, take up their business in Paris than they quarreled. Armstrong seemed to resent the newcomer; and Bowdoin unfairly suspected the New Yorker of jobbery. Because of the cloud Armstrong was under, tending to jeopardize any treaty he might make, Jefferson wished to add a third member to the commission and asked Nicholas to take the assignment. He declined, and no suitable alternate appeared; sometime later, when the situation became desperate, he wanted to send William Short but believed the Senate would reject the nomination. Hope remained despite difficulties. Napoleon did not want the annoyance of a Spanish-American war and he valued American neutrality, especially if it put the United States on a collision course with Britain. He consented to aid the purchase settlement with Spain, and the Prince of Peace, Manuel Godoy, agreed to name a negotiator in Paris. But as Godoy played for time, Napoleon talked as if the business belonged wholly to Spain and declined to mandate terms. Nothing had been accomplished when the Emperor went off to Prussia in September. The Battle of Jena, eliminating Prussia, occurred in October. With that the game was probably lost. Napoleon's domination over Europe, and the Berlin Decree inaugurating the Continental System, forced the United States into a line of neutrality that virtually removed the risk of war; and both he and Jefferson became preoccupied with British affairs. Tensions on the Mobile and the Sabine mounted. But Jefferson patiently avoided every occasion for war, even as he continued to threaten it. "We ask but one month to be in possession of the City of Mexico"; yet, as he reminded Bowdoin after waving this thunderbolt, he had just suppressed Burr's conspiracy in that direction as evidence of pacific dispositions. Bowdoin felt that Jefferson had over-impressed Spain and France on this point. Fearing nothing, they would grant nothing. But the stockjobbers were the principal obstacle, in his opinion. Not satisfied that they could make money on the American plan, they refused to throw their weight into the scale. France kept up the pretense of seeking a settlement for many months. Finally, in 1808, the Spanish revolt against Napoleon upset all the old calculations. Jefferson returned to consideration of a military solution; but when he left office the Spanish problem was still unsettled—the greatest single defeat of his statesmanship.

If the President dictated Spanish policy to the Congress, he seemed remarkably quiescent about British policy. In January he forwarded several memorials from the seaport cities protesting British invasions of neutral rights and acknowledged that the government's representations in this matter, as also in the matter of impressment, had not been met; but he declined to point out a course of action. Monroe, to whom the case had been committed two years before, had no hopes for an agreement and only awaited word from Washington to return home. The Pitt ministry adhered to the *Essex* decision, which put at hazard every American ship and cargo in the re-export trade to the Continent. Embarked on a war of survival, Britain showed little patience with American claims, though she wished to maintain her ascendancy in the American market and the flow of supplies to her ports.

Until the wave of captures following the *Essex* decision caused an uproar among the coastal merchants, the administration viewed impressment as the more vital issue. To merchants and shipmasters seamen were an expendable commodity, but to a sovereign state the forcible seizure and impressment of its citizens into foreign service was an attack on the nation itself. Every forcible seizure of American citizens was a stinging reminder of the revolutionary nation's continued subservience to the imperious mother country. The problem was peculiar to Anglo-American relations. No other civilized nation practiced impressment on the British plan; no other nation suffered its penalties like the United States. And, of course, it had no sanction in international law. The problem went back to 1790, first became serious in 1796, and then alarming during the last two or three years. Since the beginning of the present European war in 1803, Madison reported to Congress in March, 2273 American seamen had been impressed, on the record, that is—additional hundreds and thousands had been lost without a trace. Every ship in His Majesty's navy was manned in part by American seamen. The navy and marine consumed seamen and justified impressment not only to obtain them but also to check desertion from the barbarous British to the safer, better paid, and generally more humane American service. The American marine, growing by leaps and bounds, actively encouraged desertion; many of the impressed seamen, though a fraction of the total, were undoubtedly His Majesty's subjects. Washington did not claim that the American flag protected absconding British subjects, nor did London claim the right to impress citizens of the United States. But who was British and who was American? Both spoke the same language. Physical identification was difficult, if not impossible, and efforts to get seamen to carry citizenship papers failed. The root of the problem was the conflict of law. In English law a natural-born subject could never throw off his allegiance; so Britain denied the efficacy of American naturalization of British emigrants. Only natives and resident Englishmen in the United States in 1783 were considered *bona fide* American citizens. Under this rule thousands of naturalized American seamen were claimed as British subjects.

Thus impressment assaulted the very existence of American nationality. It forced Jefferson back to one of his fundamental principles, the right of expatriation, embracing the equivalent right of free

827

citizenship. "Every man has a right to live somewhere on the earth, and if somewhere, no one society has a greater right than another to exclude him." The only proper line, he said, was between transient persons and *bona fide* residents of a country. But he did not expect to impose this sweeping principle on Great Britain or even to secure the protection of the American flag for everyone sailing under it. Monroe was authorized to offer two concessions. First, Britain might impress her own subjects aboard American ships in her own ports. Rufus King had gained this point—the abandonment of the practice on the high seas—with the Foreign Office in 1802, only to lose it at the last minute when the Admiralty insisted on the reservation of the "narrow seas" around the British Isles. Second, as a *quid pro quo,* the United States would agree to a plan for the return of deserters. Britain considered any alien seaman in the national service for two years a British subject; Madison proposed to apply the same rule to American seamen, in effect naturalizing every seaman in American sanctuary for two years. London refused to negotiate a convention on these terms. American nationality could concede no more.

Congress was moved more by the losses of trade than by the scourge of seamen. General Smith, himself a great merchant, seized the initiative in the Senate. He had already pressed the administration to adopt a selective non-importation act in retaliation against British discriminatory tonnage duties and extraordinary duties levied on exports to the United States. (Smith estimated the cost of the latter to American consumers at over half a million dollars annually.) The Baltimore senator now united this project with a comprehensive protest against British captures, impressments, and other aggressions on neutral rights. The plan that finally materialized in the Senate embraced two related courses of action. Resolutions strongly advised the President to seek redress and indemnification through the agency of an extraordinary mission. As an aid to the mission, a selective non-importation act was passed to take effect November 15, 1806, barring satisfactory adjustment. The House proceeded along similar lines. After several weeks, during which Randolph bottled up the British business in the Committee on Ways and Means, the House took the matter into its own hands. Andrew Gregg, the veteran Pennsylvania congressman, now startled everyone by proposing a total non-importation on British goods. This was at once attacked by Republicans of varying hues as a war-like measure. Randolph now upbraided the President for failing to show the way to Congress. A whirling tornado, he exhausted himself against the Gregg resolution as if the administration were for it. "After shrinking from the Spanish jackal,'" he fumed, "do you presume to bully the British lion!" Nicholson offered a substitute calling for selective non-importation, similar to, though milder than, the ban proposed by Smith. Madison summarized the confused situation for Monroe's benefit in early March. "The merchants are zealous for an extraordinary commission for the negotiating experiment. In this they are seconded by those who are averse to any legislative remedies [e.g. Randolph], and by some, perhaps generally, by those who wish a negotiation to be armed with legislative provision. The President has decided nothing on this point as yet." And he did not. He was nevertheless grateful to Nicholson for burying the Gregg resolution. The Marylander's weaker motion passed, followed by a bill to implement it, in which the Senate concurred. "What is it?" Randolph asked scornfully. "A milk and water bill, a dose of chicken broth to be taken nine months hence. Good God!" For once his scorn was merited.

Offering no plan of his own, Jefferson acquiesced in this congressional determination of policy toward Britain. Smith said it was forced on him by the Senate, and Jefferson admitted as much at least as to the extraordinary mission. The Senate demanded it under the cover of resolutions, he later told Monroe. "The members of the other House took up the subject, and set upon me individually . . . , and represented the responsibility which failure to obtain redress would throw on us both, pursuing a conduct in opposition to the opinion of nearly every member of the Legislature. I found it necessary, at length, to yield my own opinion to the general sense of the national council, and it really produced a jubilee among them." Non-importation, like a sword suspended over the British, seemed to arouse no more conviction in him than it would at Downing Street. Commercial coercion, on a meaningful scale, was his trump card with Britain and he was not ready to play it in the spring of 1806. Monroe had written eloquently of the stubbornness, almost the futility, of negotiation. A comprehensive settlement such

as Congress proposed must take the form of a treaty, with concessions on both sides; and Jefferson wanted no successor to the Jay
Treaty, preferring, rather, to deal with British problems *ad hoc* as
they arose. An extraordinary mission must also involve an associate
with Monroe. The joint commission was the usual practice, to
which Jay had been the main exception, as if to prove the rule. Jefferson may have guessed Monroe's sensitiveness on this point; and he
could hardly fail to see that some of the sponsors of the treaty project were interested in furthering their own political ambitions at
Monroe's expense. At any rate, Jefferson was stuck with an unwanted policy. In its legislative aspect it marked the revival of old
Republican doctrine of commercial retaliation. While Congress debated, Republican editors dug into the archives and reprinted Madison's commercial resolutions of 1794 and other more distant land-
marks of the doctrine. It still had an important place in Jefferson's
strategy. Significantly, however, it was not Jefferson, or even Madison, though he was more sympathetic, but the Republicans in Congress who resurrected this doctrine in 1806 before, in his judgment,
the country was ready to prove its usefulness.

The President nominated William Pinkney to join Monroe in
the special mission and then succeed him as minister. A Maryland
lawyer with diplomatic credentials and a Federalist background,
Pinkney was not a popular choice, certainly not among Republicans
vexed by Jefferson's temporizing politics. (Had they known of his
first choice for the post, Rufus King, they would have been outraged.) The fact that Smith, and perhaps Randolph, wanted the
commission for himself contributed to the discontent. Monroe was
deeply offended. The appointment of an associate envoy, his successor as well, reduced him to a cypher, he later said. "From that day I
considered myself as nothing." Monroe suffered the anxieties of a
politician too long absent from home. He felt neglected, unappre-
ciated, and now stabbed in the back by his fellow triumvers; and
friends to encourage him in this delusion were not wanting. Jefferson and Madison believed they were acting in accordance with his
stated desire to return home, and they were the more inclined to indulge him in order to protect themselves from the political charge
of keeping a rival for the presidency disarmed in Europe. Monroe
may have felt, too, as Randolph insinuated, that he was being made

to hold the candle for high-toned demands in Britain while the administration pussyfooted with France and Spain. Jefferson sensed his friend's displeasure and went out of his way to reassure him, but three years passed before their friendship regained its old footing.

Suddenly, before diplomacy could be put on the new track, the entire situation changed to the advantage of the United States. News of Napoleon's victories at Austerlitz and Pressburg reached Washington the latter part of March, accompanied by the announcement of Pitt's death and the formation of a new government which brought Charles James Fox, a long-time friend of the United States, into the foreign ministry. A bright prospect opened. From his first interview with Fox, Monroe confidently predicted a fair settlement of differences. Jefferson felt the same optimism. He now hoped the swords rattled by Congress would not perplex negotiations. Explaining the awkward predicament to Monroe, he wrote, "We had committed ourselves in a line of proceedings adapted to meet Mr. Pitt's policy and hostility, before we heard of his death, which self-respect did not permit us to abandon afterwards. . . . It ought not to be viewed by the ministry as looking towards them at all, but merely as a consequence of the measures of their predecessors, which this nation has called on them to correct." In the formal instructions of May 17 Madison also explained away the threatening legislation. The non-intercourse act looked to the encouragement of domestic manufactures, he said. The abandonment of impressment remained the ultimatum of any settlement. Pursuant of the example of the Anglo-Russian treaty of 1801, the United States would relinquish, during the present war, the principle of "free ships make free goods," conditional on full protection of neutral rights in the colonial re-export trade. The guiding principle was that neutrals may trade with all ports of the enemy not in effective blackade and in all articles except military contraband. There must be provision to curb the hovering of British cruisers in coastal waters; American commerce and navigation, generally, must be fairly treated; and indemnities for captures and injuries demanded, though this might be sacrificed in the interest of future safeguards. The problem of "hovering" had been recently aggravated by the *Leander* affair. The captain of this British cruiser, while searching for seamen and contraband at the entrance to New York harbor, fired a "warning" cannon shot that struck a vessel and killed an American sailor. Amidst great public outrage, Jefferson received a solemn apology from Merry and assurances that the *Leander*, her captain, and the two sister vessels would be recalled. The forbearance of the American government and Britain's prompt response boded well for the upcoming negotiations in London.

Unfortunately, the negotiations were in suspension for over two vital months while Monroe awaited Pinkney's arrival and the formal instructions. Jefferson grew anxious in July. Reports continued to be favorable. But, he observed, "the best founded hopes of an advantageous accommodation with England may possibly be blasted by our own indiscretions." Publications had appeared in the Federalist press, and copied in London papers, charging the administration with pursuing opposite lines of conduct toward Britain and Spain and offering a bribe of two million dollars to Napoleon. Randolph's exposé followed in August. These irresponsible political attacks would arm Fox's opponents, perhaps fatally. "Our affairs there, therefore, are in danger of being all in the wind." Jefferson's fears on this score may have been exaggerated. More fatal, certainly, to the American project was Fox's death in September. Illness had overtaken the Foreign Secretary about the time of Pinkney's arrival; further delay resulted, and in August, as Fox slowly slipped away, the negotiation he had begun on the British side was transferred to Lords Holland and Auckland, neither of whom inspired Jefferson with confidence. The bargaining went forward in the fall, but from the moment he learned of Fox's death Jefferson sealed his hopes for a favorable treaty with Britain.

In his annual message Jefferson had called for the rapid acceleration of the nation's defenses. Not all injuries admitted peaceable remedies, and European warlords must understand the defensive capabilities of the United States. Military force was accessory to a foreign policy premised on the efficacy in nearly all cases of American commerce and neutrality to secure the respect of European powers, but the credibility of this policy required disposable military force in the United States. So Jefferson had recommended improved fortifications of seaport cities, gunboats in considerable number, reorganization of the militia, and consideration of building six ships-of-the-line (74 guns) for which materials were already at hand. Congress responded by appropriating $150,000 for fortifications, insufficient for the defense of a single harbor, and $250,000 for 50 gunboats, well below the number wanted. The legislators voted no money for 74's and returned the navy—a victim of Randolph's blunderbuss—to a peacetime establishment of 900 men and three frigates plus a few smaller vessels. Congress rejected the administration's bill to put the militia on a firm basis, though it gave the President authority he did not ask, and did not use at this juncture, to require the governors of the several states to maintain 100,000 militia in readiness. The army remained at the old level of 3000 men, primarily on western stations. Having earlier put Congress on the track of peace and economy, the President seemed unable to switch it to another.

His proposals, which he would repeat in subsequent years, formed part of a comprehensive system of national defense. He never articulated the system in entirety and only isolated parts of it were enacted into law. On land the system placed primary reliance on the militia. Republican ideology from the Revolution forward had enforced the axiom against standing armies. In a country where peace was a moral commitment and the normal state of things, a regular army was as wasteful and unnecessary as it was dangerous. "Were armies to be raised whenever a speck of war is visible on our horizon, we never should have been without them," Jefferson told Congress in 1806. "Our resources would have been exhausted on dangers which have never happened, instead of being reserved for what is really to take place." And should war actually take place, a well-trained militia, promptly called into the field, could hold the ground until sufficient regulars were raised. But the present "promiscuous militia" would never do. That system, loosely governed by the act of Congress of 1792, slightly improved in 1803, lumped all able-bodied men together, abdicated responsibility to the states, and was generally inefficient. Jefferson's report to Congress on the state of the militia in 1804—the first of its kind—showed over half the state militias unarmed and other shocking deficiencies.

In the fall of 1805, before Congress met, Jefferson developed with Dearborn and Smith a new "classification" system, which provided, essentially, for a national military reserve, incorporating a naval militia as well. It seems to have been suggested to him by Napoleon's success with a similar, if more rigorous, system. His secret, Jefferson said, lay in conscripting the service of the young, the healthy, and the enthusiastic; and he would conquer the New World after he finished with the Old unless Congress formed the militia on the same principle. The bill provided for the enrollment of all able-bodied white males betwen the ages of 18 and 45, except those enrolled in the naval militia, and their division into four classes: minor (18–20), junior (21–25), middle (26–34), and senior (35–45). The burden of training and service would rest on the junior class, enrolling approximately 40,000 new recruits annually. They would be furnished with arms at the expense of the United States, trained one day each month, and be liable for active service for one year within the United States or adjacent countries. The minor class would receive the same training but, with the seniors, be liable to service only within their own states. The middle class, mustered twice a year, could be called to duty in adjacent states for three months. Under this plan the entire nation would be in arms within a few years. The country would be able to meet sudden emergencies wherever they arose.

Jefferson "earnestly" recommended the classification system to Congress. In the House a select committee under Joseph B. Varnum of Massachusetts reported against the bill. The plan was too systematic, too rigorous, too expensive, too centralizing for the committee's taste. Whatever the faults of the present loose and heterogeneous system, the committee thought it the only realistic one for a people spread over a vast terrain, governed under different local laws, and little inclined to compulsory service of any kind. Another favorite scheme, viewed by Jefferson as a companion measure, also met defeat. Addressed to the twofold problem of the defense and the Americanization of the Orleans Territory, the bill offered land bounties in return for two years' liability for military service to able-bodied men who settled in the territory. "If by giving 100 miles square of that country we can secure the rest," he observed, "and at the same time create an American majority before Orleans becomes a state, it will be the best bargain we ever made." If it worked in Orleans, the plan would be extended to other frontier areas. Devised to meet an urgent need of his own time, Jefferson's plan looked back to colonial practice and forward to the Homestead Act of 1862. He again pressed it on Congress in 1807, again without success. The classification system, especially, he considered "the most essential thing the United States have to do," and he would rather have it than new regiments of regulars. "No efforts should be spared to bring the public mind to this great point," he said in referring some material for publication in the *National Intelligencer*. But the verdict in Congress again went against him.

Jefferson's naval system took shape gradually in the debate on two issues. Should American naval power be for the protection of commerce or for territorial defense only? This was the first and larger question, and it proved too difficult for Jefferson. He never decided it definitely. His Mediterranean policy, the policy that gave birth to the United States Navy, returned one answer, and his invitation to Congress to built a fleet of 74's seemed consistent with it. But a naval skirmish against pirate nations did not decide the question, nor would the building of a few ships-of-the-line where mighty Albion was the adversary. The question was as old as the republic. Northern commercial interests had generally favored a navy as an arm of trade, while the staple producers of the South, relying mainly on British bottoms, had objected both on grounds of costly discrimination and the inability, practically, of a national fleet to defend the long exposed coastline from the Chesapeake southward. Considerations of cost and practicality influenced Jefferson's thinking. While a friend of foreign commerce in the still undeveloped state of the national economy, he did not believe its defense warranted the expense of a large navy and the attendant risk of war. European experience proved that large navies bred wars, sank a nation's finances, cruelly oppressed thousands upon thousands of seamen, all for the enrichment of a few merchants. Gallatin constantly preached the wastefulness of navies, including Smith's tiny fleet, and the President heard the same line from Thomas Cooper and Tench Coxe, who spoke as political economists, as well as from southern Republicans steeped in prejudice. Jefferson's fundamental objection was economical: not the original costs of a navy but the costs of upkeep, the costs of decay, during long intervals of peace. Reflecting on the problem years later, he wrote, "It has been estimated in England that, if they could be sure of peace a dozen years it would be cheaper for them to burn their fleet, and build a new one when wanting, than to keep the old one in repair during that term."

Jefferson hit on a novel solution to this problem during his second year in the presidency. He proposed to build a "lock-dock" at the navy yard in Washington for laying up ships of war on stocks, out of the water, and protected from the weather. The plan incorporated the principle of the drydock with a canal and lock and a storage facility or "naval arsenal." Benjamin Latrobe was called in to work out the engineering, draw the plans, and produce a model. Vessels would be floated up from the tidal basin, via lock, canal, and the Tiber, to Stoddert's Spring, there dried out, masts lowered, and settled on stays under a great domed roof constructed in the manner of the Halle aux Bleds, free of supports interfering with the movement of vessels in and out. As many as twelve frigates could be kept this way, ready to launch at a moment's notice, for a capital investment estimated by Latrobe at $417,000. The scheme was unprecedented, though Jefferson had heard of something similar in Venice and Benjamin Vaughan brought to his attention Peter the Great's experiment along the same line. The principal defect, as another old Philadelphia friend pointed out, was the impossibility of launching one ship without floating all the rest, and this ingenious man, Robert Leslie, suggested the remedy. Jefferson exhibited Latrobe's model to members of Congress. Aside from its other merits he thought it offered the basis of compromise between commercial and agricultural interests: the former would have their ships and the latter would be spared the ruinous costs of maintaining them. "But," as he recalled the episode, "the advocates for a navy did not fancy it, and those opposed to building of ships altogether were equally indisposed to provide protection for them. Ridicule was also resorted to, the ordinary substitute for reason, when that fails, and the proposition was passed over." He did not again press the plan with Congress; but it remained a part of his naval system, and he would have been much readier to build ships had there been some means of preserving them in times of peace.

Once the choice was made for a mainly defensive navy, the issue became "gunboats versus fortifications." The Federalists had gone into the latter system, that is conventional harbor forts and batteries. Jefferson estimated it could not be completed for less than $50,000,000 and an army to man it of 2000 in peacetime and 5000 in war. Even then fortifications promised no secure defense of certain seaports, such as New York. In 1805 DeWitt Clinton proposed that the administration erect four forts in New York harbor. The cost was astronomical; and ships could easily slip by the batteries through the mile-wide channel. A fort rested on geometrical principles; where a place, like New York, did not lend itself to enclosure or protection by a polygon, the defense was ineffectual. Other expedients were considered. Dearborn later investigated the idea of running a chain with heavy blocks across the harbor entrance, but this figured out to a million dollars and looked impractical besides. In 1805 Jefferson turned from fortifications to the gunboat system of defense for the fifteen principal seaports from Portsmouth to New Orleans. Fortifications were not abandoned altogether, but mobile land batteries, such as he recommended in his message to Congress, were viewed as adjuncts to the gunboat system.

The use of a guerrilla-like "mosquito fleet" in harbor defense had been first suggested in the crisis of the closure of New Orleans in 1802. The crisis passed before the law of Congress authorizing the construction of fifteen gunboats could be implemented, and the administration deferred the project until various models of these small vessels could be studied. Meanwhile, American naval officers in the Mediterranean were discovering the utility of gunboats. In 1804 Commodore Preble obtained six 25-ton craft on loan from Sicily; and on his return to a hero's acclaim the following year he prevailed upon the President to send gunboats to the Mediterranean. Nine of ten already built or building were at once equipped and manned; they sailed from different ports and, amazingly, all reached their destination in July, then played a prominent role in the final stage of operations. Jefferson was delighted. The test helped to convince him of the expediency of gunboats for American coastal defense. Even before he talked to Preble, prompted perhaps by Clinton's outrageous proposal, he had sketched the outlines of the gunboat system: 240 vessels, costing perhaps a million dollars, built as circumstances required over a period of years, hauled up under sheds or partly or fully manned, again as circumstances dictated. The cost of the system was a pittance compared with land fortifications, and Jefferson believed it superior. History had proven the effectiveness of gun-boats many times. Mediterranean and North European nations concerned, like the United States, with territorial defense against great naval powers, had used them extensively. Russia offered the most famous example: in 1788, in the Liman Sea at the mouth of the Dniester, a Russian flotilla of 22 gunboats and 27 galleys destroyed the greater part of a Turkish fleet consisting of 16 ships-of-the-line and several frigates. Gunboats had many advocates in the United States, but their most indefatigable champion was Thomas Paine. In 1798 Paine had submitted to Napoleon the plan of a gunboat armada for the invasion of England. He furnished Jefferson a copy of this plan, and on his return to the United States adapted his ideas to American coastal defense, repeatedly advocating the gunboat solution in letters to Jefferson and in the press. Specifications varied, but the gunboats built in the United States were generally 50 feet long, rigged with oars and sails, mounted with medium cannon in bow and stern, and fully manned with a crew of twenty or more. A hundred gunboats could be bought, at about $5000 each, for the cost of a single ship-of-the-line. One of their principal advantages was the shallow draft that gave the boats superior maneuverability in American bays, inlets, and rivers. They presented a difficult target and the low trajectory of their cannon improved the gunners' accuracy against an enemy. Gunboats were flexible: they could be moved from one place to another with ease or be laid up when not wanted. They multiplied the opportunities for young officers to command, which helps to explain the navy's early tolerance of the system.

With all these advantages, attested by experience, seemingly so well adapted to the extended coastline and pacific dispositions of the United States, Jefferson fully subscribed to the gunboat system in 1805. Unfortunately, even more than his "lock-dock," it lent itself to ridicule. Things got off to a bad start in the fall of 1804 when the first of the diminutive fleet, Gunboat Number 1, was blown by a hurricane off the Georgia coast into a cornfield on Whitemarsh Island. "Every federal *type sticker*, from 'Marshall Coleman' down, down, down, took up the subject, and *hammered* their noodles for weeks together to *make* a paragraph about it." * Gunboats were

* Coleman was the editor of the New York *Evening Post*. A specimen of his lampooning voyage in command of Gunboat Number 1 follows: "Marshall

humbug, visionary, Jeffersonian "philosophism" run amuck. The President absorbed this punishment and went right on pressing his system with Congress. Congress followed, but without enthusiasm, and after 1806 lagged behind. When he left office approximately 180 gunboats were stationed in American ports; if he had had his way there would have been at least three hundred.

Much of the criticism of the system, so far as it was serious, turned on the invidious comparison of gunboats with frigates or other seagoing fighting ships. The boats were not intended to go to sea; their mission was inner-coastal defense; they were mainly a substitute for land fortifications, indeed sometimes described as "movable fortifications." But the system was subject to criticism on other grounds. As James Fenimore Cooper, himself a midshipman in 1808, later observed, one of the arguments Jefferson advanced for the system, the extended coastline, was equally an argument against it, for that defense required outer as well as inner-coastal maneuverability. Gunboats offered no effective defense against blockade, for instance. In the long run these unheroic objects of jest and ridicule probably lowered rather than raised naval morale. In the long run too, the costs gun for gun were perhaps not less than for frigates or 74's, which proved their superiority in every situation other than shoal waters. The gunboat system did not exclude other means of defense, but because of his faith in this particular weapon Jefferson tended to downgrade the importance of supporting weapons at sea and on shore. The gunboats tended to become a substitute for frigates and land fortifications rather than a valuable adjunct to them; as a result the system lacked the balance necessary for its success. The navy turned against the system, and when war came in 1812 it was abandoned.

Congress adjourned on April 21, 1806. Jefferson must have breathed a sigh of relief—it had been an ordeal. His leadership had

C. left 'Carter's Mountain' on the 6th ult. and met with a variety of 'highly interesting' incidents on his passage—among them are the following. In the lat. of Carolina, discovered a 'field of corn,' bore down upon her and fired a gun—she hove to, and after examining how many bushels she produced to an acre, left her. Capes of Virginia in sight, spoke 'Black Sal' and her two tenders, steering for 'Monticello.'—Saw 'Gabriel Jones' . . . and heard a ship, supposed to be the 'Prairie *Dog*,' firing signal guns. Same day, hailed 'Mrs. Walker' bound, bound to Boston. . . ."

been seriously challenged for the first time. Randolph had sent shivers through the party and embarrassed the administration at home and abroad. In the closing hours of the session the Virginian's unbridled fury threatened the President's personal peace as well, as an exchange of insults produced an affair of honor between the Randolph cousins in Congress, the other member of the pair being Thomas Mann Randolph, the President's son-in-law; but a duel was happily averted. Congress gave the President most of the legislation he wanted, some he did not really want, and defeated or passed over other items he considered important. He pretended to be satisfied. The Randolph schism, except for its side-effects on diplomacy, did not disturb him. Randolph had made a scene, indeed a whole drama in which he cast himself as the tragic hero; but his performance was pathetic, and he destroyed himself politically by his own recklessness and violence. To contain it all but a handful of Republicans rallied to the administration. It was a case of rebellion strengthening the government, Jefferson thought. Summing up for Monroe's benefit at the end of the session, he wrote, "Timid men consider it as a proof of the weakness of our government, and that it is to be rent into pieces by demagogues, and to end in anarchy. I survey the scene with a different eye and draw a different augury from it. In the House of Representatives of a great mass of good sense, Mr. Randolph's popular eloquence gave him such advantages as to place him unrivaled as the leader of the House. . . . The sudden defection of such a man could not but produce a momentary astonishment, and even dismay; but for a moment only. The good sense of the House rallied around its principles; and without any leader pursued steadily the business of the session, did it well, and by a strength of vote which has never before been seen." This calmly philosophical view, while not unwarranted as to the danger of Randolph himself, passed too easily over the real damage he had done by discomfiting the Republican majority. Henceforth it would support the administration on great points but prove uncontrollable on lesser ones; and the loyalty of many would be given less in trust than in fear of injuring the party that revolved on the prestige of the President. He might have rid Congress of Randolph by kicking him into a foreign mission, which he craved, but that would be exchanging one risk for another. He did get rid of the principal confederate, Nicholson, by appointing him to a district judgeship; and he tried to smooth over relations with Speaker Macon and to retain or recruit men of trust and talent for leadership roles in Congress.

The summer was quiet. Jefferson made his usual excursion, surveying the worst drought in Virginia since 1755. Nothing of consequence came from American ministers abroad. But mysterious rumblings of disunion and conspiracy in the West, vaguely audible before, grew in volume and became a matter of national concern when he returned to Washington in October. "Having been so long in the midst of a family," he wrote sadly to Martha, "the loneliness of this place is more intolerable than I ever found it. My daily rides too are sickening for want of some interest in the scenes I pass over, and indeed I look over the two ensuing years as the most tedious of my life." And so they proved to be.

The Burr Conspiracy

Rumors of a great conspiracy in the West with Aaron Burr at its head had been afloat for over a year when the President convened the cabinet on October 22, 1806, to ponder an official course of action. Burr's designs were still involved in mystery, but fragmentary evidence pointed to criminal and possibly treasonable acts, and implicated General James Wilkinson, the commanding officer of the United States Army and Governor of Louisiana. To move fast might be tilting at windmills or perhaps arresting the evidence of the crime before it was ripe, the ringleaders going free; to move cautiously, on the other hand, might prove disastrous. In this dilemma the cabinet finally decided, at its third meeting on October 25, on a policy of watchful waiting. A confidential agent, John Graham, was sent down the Ohio to investigate, uncover the designs of the conspirators, and put civil and military authorities on guard. More vigorous steps approved only the day before, such as ordering a naval force under Preble's command to New Orleans, were rescinded. Legal technicalities entered into this decision, much to Smith's irritation. The navy was starved for funds and the statutes gave no authority for the use of the public forces of the United States to suppress conspiracies or insurrections. As to Wilkinson, it was decided to leave him alone pending further information.

Burr's conspiracy had been germinating for over two years. His political career ruined, indictments for the murder of Alexander Hamilton hanging over him in two states, New York and New Jersey, neither fame nor fortune in prospect, this indomitable adventurer turned his gaze to the convulsive Southwest frontier. In the summer of 1804, while still Vice President, he communicated to the British minister a scheme for separating the western states and creating an independent confederacy south of the Ohio. Money and a small fleet, to secure the Mississippi and possibly take the Floridas, were wanted from Britain. Merry at once forwarded this interesting proposition to his government. The ensuing winter in Washington, Burr courted the Creole delegates from New Orleans and in conversations with Merry centered his designs on Louisiana. The Minister again pressed the project with the Foreign Office in London. Just when Burr linked his vague scheme for revolutionizing the West to General Wilkinson's old ambition for the conquest of Mexico is uncertain; but from 1805 the two projects were so deceptively blended that it would be impossible to separate them.

The General was also active in Washington in the early months of the year. His talent for intrigue, his intimacy with Burr, his popularity with the old inhabitants of Louisiana were well known. For years he had been suspected of being in Spanish pay, as indeed he had been intermittently, but Jefferson's predecessors in the chief magistracy had passed over these suspicions, and so did he. A scoundrel to the core, Wilkinson had nevertheless rendered useful service to the government, especially in Jefferson's administration, as in the negotiation of treaties with the southern tribes and the transfer of Louisiana to the United States. The latter event, unknown to the administration, provided him the occasion for renewing his old connections with the Spanish authorities. After Congress created the Louisiana Territory, Jefferson named Wilkinson governor. The appointment provoked a good deal of criticism, less from suspicions of the middle-aged general than from the principle of separation of civil and military authority. Jefferson subscribed to the principle; in fact, on this ground he had earlier withstood the pressure of Wilkinson's ardent friends in Congress to appoint him governor of the Mississippi Territory. "But in the appointment to Louisiana," Jefferson said in answer to congressional strictures, "I did not think myself departing from my own principle, because I consider it not as a civil government, but merely as a military station." He was still working on the theory that closed Louisiana to American settlement. Wilkinson agreed with this policy and went to St. Louis in 1805 with orders to plan the removal of all settlers to the east bank of the Mississippi. Viewing Louisiana as a great Indian reserve, Jefferson associated it with military government and Indian affairs, both within the jurisdiction of the War Department. Moreover, the danger of war with Spain, involving action on the frontier, suggested the wisdom of blending civil and military authority in the office of a commandant. Wilkinson seemed admirably qualified for the post. What Jefferson overlooked was the danger the vainglorious general himself presented to the peace and harmony of the Union. At St. Louis he was in an enviable position to carry on conspiratorial enterprises either with Burr or the dons as he chose.

Burr set out to reconnoiter the West in April 1805. He had already recruited several prominent associates, and as he moved down the Ohio, across Kentucky to Nashville, thence down the Cumberland and the Mississippi to New Orleans, he picked up others. Without disguising his bitterness toward the administration, he artfully conveyed the idea of an expedition against New Spain with the covert support of the government. At New Orleans he fell in with Clark, Livingston, and the Creole opposition to the Claiborne regime. The city was ripe for revolt, Burr concluded. Here the revolution of the western states might begin, or alternately, or perhaps in conjunction with that revolution, an expedition launched against Mexico. Burr conferred with Wilkinson both on the downward leg of his journey, at Fort Massac on the Ohio, and on his return at St. Louis, the base of Wilkinson's overland maneuvers. Western newspapers followed Burr's movements with suspicion. That he was engaged in conspiratorial intrigue seemed likely, but he had so effectively decoyed his object that no one could be sure of it.

Back in Washington in November, Burr reported enthusiastically to Merry. With British assistance the western revolt might commence in the spring. If Britain abstained, he warned, France would regain control of the dissevered country. Nothing official came from London. The ministry, while interested in Burr's project, was preoccupied with France on the Continent. Disappointed, Burr now sought to sell the scheme to Spain. In Philadelphia he sent his trusted aide Jonathan Dayton, the former New Jersey senator, to the disgraced Spanish minister, Yrujo, who was still feuding with the administration. Yrujo at first backed off, but after Dayton fabricated for his benefit the story of Madison's clandestine support of Miranda's expedition against Caracas, Yrujo took him seriously. The plot changed. It still aimed at revolution in the West but not at Mexico or the Floridas, as Yrujo had earlier believed when Britain was to be the protector. A *coup d'état* in Washington would commence the revolution. The President and other officers of the government would be seized, the banks plundered, the navy yard taken, and a naval expedition sent to New Orleans, where it would operate jointly with Wilkinson's army. Such a project only appeared insane, the Marquis wrote to the government in Madrid. Actually, given a host of adventurous men, who were not wanting, and the soft-headedness of the professors of goodness in Washington, it was perfectly easy of execution; and it would be well worth a million Spanish dollars to destroy the American colossus. But Spain declined to speculate in this venture. In fact, it may not have been the venture Burr had in mind. Perhaps he was simply engaging in a swindle of Spain on his own account, as Wilkinson and other Americans had done in the past. Or perhaps he was only trying to quiet apprehensions of a filibustering expedition against Mexico.

But neither of these contingencies was present in Burr's invitation to General William Eaton to join the conspiracy. Yet the plot he unfolded to Eaton was much the same as the one Dayton had described to Yrujo, with the added touch of assassination of the President. " 'Hang him!'—'throw him into the Potomac!'—'send him to Carter's mountain!' " Such was Eaton's recollection under oath of Burr's language. It is easy enough to understand Burr's approach to him. The hero of Derne was also something of a desperado. He had been, he felt, shabbily treated by the administration for his services in the Tripolitan campaign; and he had impressive military and political connections in Washington. But Eaton possessed the saving virtue of patriotism. In March, after hearing Burr's proposition, he went to the President and in a roundabout way warned him of the impending insurrection. Could not Burr be sent on a mission abroad? "The President . . . seemed to think the trust too important, and expressed something like a doubt about the integrity of

Mr. Burr," Eaton later testified. But if Burr was not put out of the way, Eaton warned, there would be a revolution on the western waters within eighteen months. "The President said he had too much confidence in the information, the integrity and attachment of the people of that country to the Union, to admit any apprehensions of that kind." Jefferson's response might have been different had Eaton disclosed all the facts and their source, but he feared Burr would "turn the tables" on him. As a result, his guarded warning carried no more weight with Jefferson than the general run of rumor and gossip. Eaton was scarcely to be trusted anyway. Known to be friendly with Burr, his errand to the President may have been at Burr's instigation. Only a few weeks before Burr himself had begged Jefferson for high employment of some kind and warned him of the great harm he could do from outside the government. Jefferson politely informed him that he no longer possessed the public confidence; as to the threat of injury, he had never conducted business on motives of this kind and had no fear of injury from Burr.

What injury could the serpentine New Yorker have in mind? Jefferson believed with most men that he was capable of almost any treachery. "I never . . . thought him an honest, frank-dealing man," he later said, "but considered him a crooked gun, or rather perverted machine, whose aim or shot you could never be sure of." But Burr was no fool: he could not undertake anything so chimerical as a western revolution. Averse on principle to considering any man his personal enemy, Jefferson continued to treat Burr politely for several weeks and entertained him at dinner—for the last time—on April 8. A week later he learned from Senator Smith that Burr had been actively soliciting depositions in Washington in proof of the Federalist canard that Jefferson had bargained his way into the presidency in 1801. Smith and Bayard were the principal deponents. Their testimony being contradictory proved of little value to Burr, who had hoped to transfer the onus of his own downfall to the President's head. Jefferson was indignant. He may have seen Burr's threat embodied in this fabrication. At any rate, it probably did more to discredit the New Yorker in Jefferson's eyes than anything he had seen or heard of the rumored western conspiracy in the spring of 1806.

An early warning had come from a responsible source, Joseph

H. Daveiss, the federal district attorney for Kentucky. His first confidential letter in January pointed the finger of suspicion at Wilkinson; subsequent letters implicated him with Burr in a conspiracy with Spain, and Daveiss named Dayton and John Brown, the Ohio senator, together with several prominent Kentucky Republicans. Daveiss later accused the President of heedless indifference to this intelligence. In fact, when the first report reached him in February, Jefferson at once showed it to the secretaries and within a week instructed Daveiss to communicate any new information he could turn up. The attorney diligently pursued his investigation, but the evidence he forwarded was of little use. Much of it belonged to ancient history: the old Spanish conspiracy of the 1780's and '90's, including the old suspicions of Wilkinson. Daveiss piled up hearsay and conjecture, gossip and rumor; nothing in his reports firmly linked Burr to Wilkinson or offered evidence respectable in a court of law. There was also the question of the attorney's credibility. He was a Federalist carried over from the Adams administration. The possibility that he was engaged in a political game, actuated as well perhaps by personal or family resentments, could not be discounted. His list of suspects read like a roster of Kentucky Republicanism. Even John Breckinridge, the President's deceased attorney general, appeared on the list. That some of these men, old friends like Brown and Judge Harry Innes, had once dallied with Spain, Jefferson did not doubt, but that was all in the dim past before the opening of the Mississippi and the acquisition of Louisiana. Suspicions of Daveiss on this head increased in July when John Wood, an unprincipled Federalist editor, formerly associated with Burr and more recently with Augustine Davis and his libeling crew in Richmond, established a newspaper, *The Western World*, in Frankfort, devoted to sinking the Republicans under the weight of the old Spanish conspiracy. Brown alerted Jefferson to this development and mentioned Daveiss, an inveterate personal enemy, together with John Marshall's brothers-in-law, as partners in Wood's press. Daveiss, angered by the President's neglect, filed his last report in August. He shuffled the list of suspects and said that the nature of the conspiracy had changed. It was no longer with Spain but directed against the Spanish colonies, though still premised on the severance of the western states and territories. After all this Daveiss concluded, "I must further observe, that I have often doubted whether the whole of this matter might not be a mere swindling trick played off on the Spaniards by our countrymen." This possibility had occured to the men in Washington. In Wilkinson's history, particularly, a vague line separated swindle from treason; and the former was no crime in public law.

Beginning in September, however, the administration received weighty items of information on the unfolding conspiracy that fit into the picture Daveiss had sketched. By then Burr, having done all he could in the East, had already gone to the Ohio to make final preparations for the expedition down the river. In this connection he visited the home of Colonel George Morgan just below Pittsburgh. Without revealing his plans he talked freely to Morgan and his sons of the imbecility of the federal government ("with two hundred men he could drive the president and congress into the Potomac") and western separatism ("the separation of the Union must take place"). To this the Colonel exclaimed, "God forbid!" and wrote to the President. About the same time a former New York congressman reported that one Comfort Tyler had recently returned from the West much richer than he had ever been and begun recruiting men for an expedition on the Ohio. Other reports identified Harman Blennerhassett, a well-to-do Irish émigré who lived on an island opposite Marietta, Ohio, as the author of newspaper articles advocating western separation; moreover, Burr had visited Blennerhassett's Island, the staging area of the expedition, in the fall. In October, Gideon Granger brought to Jefferson the unabridged version of Burr's overture to General Eaton. The pieces of the puzzle fell into place; the picture, while still mysterious, the object still obscure, clearly revealed Burr at the head of a western conspiracy. Such was the state of Jefferson's knowledge near the end of October when he took the first hesitant steps to cope with the conspiracy, a conspiracy so strangely public by then that men wondered at the timidity of the government. Jefferson's hesitancy stemmed from two main considerations. First, the dilemma already mentioned: to spring the trap before crimes had been committed would be to let the traitors, if traitors they were, go free. Second, he had too much confidence in the loyalty of the West, and just enough in General Wilkinson, to believe that Burr could cause any real damage to the Union. So, for the present, he sent Graham on Burr's trail and put governors and commanders in the West on guard.

Wilkinson, meanwhile, had gone to the Sabine to deal with Spanish encroachments on the Texas frontier. Ordered on this mission in May, the General had only finally descended the river in September. Jefferson was shocked by the commander's disobedience to orders and supposed it related in some way to Burr's plans. Cautiously suspending judgment on Wilkinson's complicity with Burr, he grasped the opportunity to ease him out of the governorship of Louisiana. The House had censured the appointment on principle; the territorial government had been in turmoil since Wilkinson's arrival in St. Louis; and judges, junior officers, and prominent civilians clamored for his removal. He had powerful pleaders for his cause in Washington, none more powerful than Senator Smith of Maryland. Smith staunchly defended his comrade of Revolutionary days against the "cabal" in St. Louis and the vicious rumors of disloyalty. Only two days before ordering the General to the Sabine, Jefferson assured Smith that he had no intention of dumping Wilkinson the Governor. But Smith interpreted the orders as just that, a convenient way of dumping the Governor; and so did Wilkinson, and so, in fact, did Jefferson. He at once pressed the office on Monroe, and when Monroe was detained in England held it open for Meriwether Lewis, who came to his long journey's end in the fall. Mortified by the military order, his enemies jubilant, Wilkinson was sorely tried, and he tarried in St. Louis as long as he dared to take stock of his future. If he chose he could ignite war with Spain on the Sabine. This fit the prescription of the twofold plan of conquest and revolution he had concocted with Burr. If, on the other hand, he wished to recover power and prestige with the government, he could make peace on the Sabine, turn on Burr, and present himself as the savior of both his own country and New Spain.

He had probably not committed himself to either of these interesting options before he reached the post at Natchitoches, east of the Sabine. But his actions led to the prevention, not to the instigation, of war. The Spanish commander at once responded to his threat by withdrawing across the river into Texas. Several weeks later Wilkinson marched to the Sabine and signed the neutral ground treaty which secured peace on the frontier pending the final determination of boundaries. At the same time he grandly dispatched an aide to the Viceroy in Mexico City with his bill of $120,000 for services rendered His Catholic Majesty! Between these two events, the Spanish retreat and the treaty, an emissary bearing a ciphered dispatch from Burr reached Wilkinson's camp. All was in readiness. British protection was secured. Commodore Thomas Truxton, the hero of the quasi-war with France who had resigned from the navy under unpleasant circumstances after Jefferson came to power, was going to Jamaica to pick up a British squadron, sail to New Orleans, and join parts of the American fleet at the mouth of the Mississippi. Detachments from various quarters would rendezvous on the Ohio in November; Burr would lead the first of 500 or a thousand men and coalesce with Wilkinson at Natchez in early December. They would then decide the exact course of the campaign. "The gods invite to glory and fortune; it remains to be seen whether we deserve the boon." Wilkinson questioned the emissary on military objectives. Presumably Louisiana would be revolutionized, New Orleans seized, an expedition sent to Vera Cruz, thence to Mexico. If Wilkinson had not by this date, October 8, decided to abandon Burr, the contents of the dispatch turned him toward that treachery rather than the harder one. To conquer Mexico without a war was absurd; to revolutionize the West, if that was still an object, almost as difficult when the plot had become a scandal from Pittsburgh to New Orleans. And Wilkinson must have known that Burr lied in boasting British support. Still the General hesitated for nearly a fortnight; then, on October 21, he sent a fast riding courier with a dispatch to the President. He described the "daring enterprise" and professed to be uninformed of its "prime mover and ultimate objects," but expecting a revolt in the territory, he had decided to make peace with the Spaniards and throw his army into the defense of New Orleans. Two days later Wilkinson marched to the Sabine; a month later he reached New Orleans.

On the receipt of Wilkinson's dispatch, November 25, the President convened the cabinet. There was no longer room to doubt a conspiracy, its general design, or its prime mover. Jefferson at once issued a proclamation denouncing the "criminal enterprise," enjoining all participants to withdraw, and calling all authorities to take appropriate action. Orders went out to officers from Pittsburgh to New Orleans. Graham had already spurred Ohio's governor to action; and Wilkinson had nicely anticipated the President's orders to him to arrange an accommodation on the Sabine and hurry to New Orleans. The proclamation, while vigorous, was also guarded: it neither named Burr nor so much as implied treason, positing rather an unlawful enterprise against the Spanish dominions. But Jefferson was probably now convinced of Burr's complicity in treason. Clearly, he had two main objects in view and, depending on the circumstances, would pursue either or both. One was an attack on Mexico, the other Western disunion and independence. Given the military requirements of the first, it could not be accomplished without the aid of the second, at the very least the possession of New Orleans. A possible third object entered the picture in November. On leaving Blennerhassett's Island, Burr passed through Kentucky and along the way purchased part of an old disputed Spanish land claim, the Bastrop grant, on the Washita River. The grant, which was quite worthless, figured in Burr's plans as a cover or refuge. As Jefferson later said, "This was to serve as the pretext for all his preparations, an allurement for such followers as really wished to acquire settlements in that country, and a cover under which to retreat in the event of final discomfiture of both branches of his real design." The desperate and disaffected had joined Burr for obvious reasons; some of his confederates were obsessed with dreams of western empire; many well-meaning citizens had been seduced by assurances of the government's secret patronage; and still others had been lured by the promise of land.

Congress convened in a state of alarm. The spectacle of conspirators stalking the land in broad daylight struck astonishment. Few, if any, congressmen doubted the reality of the conspiracy. Some questioned the energy of the administration in quelling it. Others secretly hoped for its success and Jefferson's disgrace. Yet as to Burr, the reports strained credulity. Senator Plumer, who remembered Burr's sympathy with the New England disunionists two years earlier, observed, "Burr is capable of much wickedness—but not so much folly." Jefferson, too, was puzzled whether to treat Burr as a Catiline or a Don Quixote. In his December message to Congress he stuck to the premise of the proclamation: the expedition was against the Spanish provinces—the criminal attempt of private individuals "to decide for their country the question of peace or war." If this was not the whole truth it was still a necessary fiction, for the government did not have the authority, which he now requested, to employ the nation's public forces to suppress enterprises "preparing against the United States."

Jefferson waited anxiously through the month of December to learn the fate of the conspiracy. It became in his mind a test of the loyalty of the West, and even more, a test of the power of a free government to maintain itself. He expected his faith to be vindicated. The proclamation, which he later described as "an instantaneous levee en masse," would mobilize the citizens to crush the conspiracy. Burr's true strength was unknown in Washington. Yet only Smith, in the cabinet, pushed for more vigorous measures. Jefferson agreed they would be needed if the expedition now on the Ohio was not broken up before the end of the year. In the West, meanwhile, where the President's proclamation had yet to be heard, the conspirators celebrated the only kind of triumph they would ever know, in the courts in law. In the district court at Frankfort, Daveiss secured a grand jury to inquire into Burr's enterprise. When the attorney's principal witness failed to appear he moved dismissal. Two weeks later he applied for a new grand jury, only this time to be foiled by the rulings of the judge as well as the absence of a key witness under subpoena. The jury returned no indictment. Daveiss thus proved the honorableness of his intentions throughout, even if his precipitancy embarrassed the government. (When he sometime later issued a diatribe against the President for the opposite of precipitancy he was at once removed from office.) For the hardy Federalist attorney to win an indictment in Kentucky against the former Vice President who professed to be acting in concert with the government in a popular cause against Spain—this was impossible in early December. The conspirators were upset on the river, however. The first blow fell on Blennerhassett's flotilla on the Ohio. Many of the recruits drew off when the President's proclamation became known. Few boats ever reached the Mississippi.

By the beginning of the new year Jefferson believed the conspiracy had been crushed. Burr remained at large with a few stragglers on the Mississippi, where he learned of the proclamation, the Ohio seizures, and Wilkinson's betrayal. The General turned New Orleans into an armed camp, subverted the civil authority, arrested several of Burr's associates, and when they were released on writs of habeas corpus bound two of them under military escort to Washington for trial. His zeal could not have been greater, but he wantonly induced panic and trampled on the law. Jefferson excused these actions without approving them. "We are obliged to estimate them," he wrote the General reassuringly, "not according to our own view of the danger, but to place ourselves in your situation and only with your information." Wilkinson expected a British fleet from below, Jefferson thought, and an expedition of several thousand men descending on the city from above. In that situation the law of self-preservation became the higher law, and Wilkinson had earned the nation's gratitude for risking himself to save the country. This, of course, is precisely what the turncoat commander wanted his chief to believe. Jefferson had remained anxious about the General even after the fall dispatches. He had gone this far with him on the hunch he was a safer friend than enemy, less dangerous inside the government than outside of it, and in the final reckoning a more prudent patriot than frontier adventurer. That he had been embarked in some way with Burr seemed likely, especially if the design was Mexico in a national war on Spain; but that he would abandon rank, reputation, and power to become a dubious second in Burr's fantastic scheme seemed incredible. All doubts were dispelled by Isaac Briggs, the Quaker surveyor, who broke into the New Year's festivities at the President's House with dispatches from New Orleans. "Is Wilkinson sound in this business?" he asked the trusted Briggs. "There is not the slightest doubt about it." From this moment Jefferson never wavered in his support of Wilkinson's conduct.

The principal malefactor remained at large but Jefferson felt justified in announcing the suppression of the conspiracy in a special message to Congress on January 22. Sent in response to resolutions of the House, the message gave a clear and straightforward account of what had taken place so far as it was known to the executive. Unfortunately, Jefferson allowed himself to declare that Burr's guilt had been "placed beyond question." This was very likely the case. The President voiced the prevailing opinion. Even Senator Plumer, for a long time "an infidel" on the subject, asserted, "There cannot now remain any doubt of Burr's seditious and treasonable designs—unless multitudes . . . have conspired to establish falsehood." Old John Adams, in Quincy, doubtless agreed. "But if his guilt is as clear as the noonday sun," he remarked, "the first magistrate of the nation ought not to have pronounced it so before a jury had tried him." The message disclosed that three of Burr's associates had been liberated by habeas corpus in New Orleans and, further, that two of them had been sent hither in the belief they could not receive an impartial trial in that turbulent city. The next day William B. Giles, who had returned to the post of leadership in the Senate, moved the suspension of habeas corpus for a limited time. A bill was at once reported, restricted to arrests for treason or other high crimes under the authority of the President, and passed over one dissenting voice on the same day. This was not the President's bill. It originated with Giles and Smith, in fact with both Smiths, for the secretary had been advocating suspension of the writ for a month; and as friends of Wilkinson, these gentlemen were enraged by judicial trifling with his stern measures in New Orleans. William Burwell, the Virginia congressman, formerly the President's private secretary, asked Jefferson about the suspension bill on the day it passed the Senate. He said it could not be justified and if approved in the House would give him great pain. Burwell and Eppes, Jefferson's son-in-law, fought the bill in the House, where it met defeat in some measure because of the covert hostility of the administration.

Burr's western odyssey came to a close on February 19. Three weeks earlier he had prudently surrendered to civil authority in Mississippi. Again a grand jury refused to indict. Burr had not committed any offence in the jurisdiction of the territorial court of Mississippi, and for this reason the attorney general had moved to send the prisoner to Washington, but the court overruled him. Still under recognizance in the sum of $10,000 to the court, Burr fled to the sanctuary of West Florida. In the Tombigbee country, just above the boundary, the fugitive was captured, placed under military arrest, then conducted under armed guard more than a thousand miles to Richmond.

Just where Burr should be tried was a problem. The trail of conspiracy ran its devious course from the Atlantic coast to the mouth of the Mississippi, but if he was to be convicted of treason in a court of law it was necessary to hold him to overt acts, with witnesses to these acts, at some particular place. On the whole, Blennerhassett's Island seemed the most eligible spot, and that being in Virginia jurisdiction the case would go to the federal circuit court in Richmond, where John Marshall, the President's old enemy, would preside. The judge tipped his hand at the end of February when he released the two prisoners, Eric Bollman and Samuel Swartwout, Wilkinson had sent from New Orleans, on grounds of insufficient evidence. This decision, Nicholson's release of two other accomplices in Baltimore on the same grounds, the rising outrage against Wilkinson, the instinctive public sympathy for the hunted, the persecuted, the heroes of misfortune, artfully sounded for political effect—already in March the trial of Burr and company threatened to become a trial of the President and his commanding general.

Jefferson had never underestimated the difficulty of securing legal evidence of Burr's guilt. This had been the problem from the beginning, and it continued to plague him as he turned to the task of gathering the evidence. The culprit was guilty beyond a shadow of doubt in Jefferson's mind. Burr had earned his hatred, but this was not a vindictive personal judgment, though that played a part inevitably. It was, rather, the judgment of the President who viewed the conspiracy in its totality and in the light of his responsibility for the peace and safety of the nation. Whether Burr could be convicted in a court of law conducted on other views was a different matter, but he was guardedly optimistic. It was more important that the conspiracy had been crushed. "On the whole," he wrote, "this squall, by showing with what ease our government suppresses movements which in other countries require armies, has greatly increased its strength by increasing the public confidence in it." The event had vindicated republican government against the old canard of weakness and imbecility, vindicated the experiment of republican liberty over a vast territory, vindicated the federal system and the virtue of the people, and above all, the power of the law where every citizen has a stake in its preservation.

In the tumult and confusion of the Burr Conspiracy, Congress mercifully finished its business in three months and went home. When the session opened no change had occurred in the nation's foreign relations. In January, after the revelations of Eaton and

854

Truxton started public speculation of foreign assistance in Burr's schemes, Jefferson spiked these rumors which, he said, were "to be imputed to the vauntings of the author of the enterprise, to multiply his partisans by magnifying the belief of his prospects and support." Except for quickening the pace of defense preparations nothing was wanted but patience in foreign affairs. Much of the President's annual message dealt with western affairs, not only the conspiracy and the neutralization of the Sabine, but with such subjects as Indian relations, defense, settlement, and exploration. The return of Lewis and Clark gave great satisfaction. Jefferson also reported the exploration of the Red River by Thomas Freeman and Zebulon Pike to the sources of the Mississippi. Not all the contours of the immense country had been traced but enough was now known to commence an accurate map of the Mississippi and its waters. Jefferson especially recommended to Congress enactment of the bounty bill for settling Americans on the river above New Orleans. Burr's enterprise pointed up the vulnerability of the territory, and Jefferson saw no real security apart from planting young and hardy men on the spot to defend it. Congress again passed over the recommendation. A more fundamental one, associated with western development but national in scope and aim, met the same fate.

Jefferson called for amendment of the Constitution to authorize the federal government to apply its resources to "the great objects of public education, roads, rivers, canals, and such other objects of public improvement as may be thought proper." He had tossed out the idea in the second inaugural address, when the plan was to distribute the funds among the states. Since then Gallatin had persuaded him to retain federal control. "By these operations," Jefferson said to Congress, "new channels of communication will be opened between the states; the lines of separation will disappear, their interests will be identified, and their union cemented by new and indissoluble ties." Roads and canals would knit the Union together, facilitate defense, furnish avenues of trade, break down local prejudices, and consolidate that "union of sentiment," so essential to the national polity, that had been his polestar since entering the presidency. This was a new departure, but it did not mark any shift of principles. He had never flatly opposed public improvements under federal auspices. In the past, however, his hostility to privilege in any shape and his concern for the sanction of the Constitution had led him to oppose various plans and projects in this line, including some his judgment otherwise approved. He had not moved earlier to secure the constitutional authority mainly for fiscal reasons. The debt had first claim on the revenue. Now, thanks to the profits of the neutral trade, the debt was well on the way to extinction and still the surplus piled up, exceeding the new outlays for defense and such hypothetical demands as the Florida purchase. The source of these profits produced a strong motive for investment in the country's internal development. A national prosperity founded on an extraordinary war in Europe was highly precarious. Whether in a state of war or of peace, the carrying trade was no more than a temporary mainstay of the economy, essential until the country got on its feet but to be gradually replaced by the home market. The object of political economy, Adam Smith had taught, was to increase the productive resources of a nation, and to that end a capital employed at home was generally many times more productive than a capital employed in the roundabout and uncertain traffic of foreign commerce. At least for the United States, Smith's example of China, with its extensive interior and virtual isolation, was a better model than the example of Britain with which the nation had set up a perilous rivalry on the oceans. Jefferson had always recognized this. The primacy he had given to agricultural industry reflected his view, in perfect accord with Smith's, of the natural order of economic development. But powerful circumstances had impinged on theory. The inducements offered by foreign commerce and the primitive state of the home economy had given ascendancy to the carrying trade. This would change in time, and it would change sooner if the federal government lent a hand to the development of arteries of internal commerce, the primary infrastructure of the home market. Investment of the national capital in works of peace instead of war strongly appealed to the President. Nor did he confine his views to such mundane things as roads and canals. His proposal gave equal rank to "a national establishment for education," despite Gallatin's plea to subordinate this unpopular innovation to the business-minded interest in routes of trade. But whether Congress would be sufficiently enlightened to adopt any part of the plan, or whether the warring powers would permit the country to invest its resources in works of peace, remained to be seen.

Certain Republican precedents were available. In 1806 Congress authorized the President to lay out a road, by commissioners of his appointment, from Cumberland, Maryland, on the Potomac, to Ohio. Gallatin had conceived this measure. When Ohio became a state in 1802 he had arranged for 5 per cent of the proceeds from the sale of public lands in Ohio to be paid into a fund for the making of roads to link the state to the East. By subsequent legislation the take had been lowered to 2 per cent, but enough money had been accumulated by 1806 to warrant the beginning of what would become the National Road, running all the way to Illinois. When the commissioners reported two years later Jefferson learned at firsthand the political hazards of federal responsibility for fixing routes of trade. Every town considered the road for its benefit. The commission's route bypassed the aspiring metropolis of Washington, in southwestern Pennsylvania, which at once roared its disapproval. The county, Gallatin reminded the President, had always given a 2000-vote majority to the Republican party, and if its allegiance shifted the Federalists might win Pennsylvania in the next election. From these political pressures Jefferson recoiled in disgust; still he submitted, directing the commissioners to survey a route through Washington. Because of the uniqueness of the Ohio fund, the National Road offered a doubtful precedent. So, too, did western roads through the Indian country principally for postal communication. In 1804 Jefferson had directed Briggs, going out to New Orleans as surveyor-general, to map a better and shorter route to that distant quarter than the existing 1200-mile passage over Indian traces and treacherous mountains and rivers. Briggs accomplished his mission, and Congress voted money for the new post road. (Since Congress had not authorized Briggs's expenses, Jefferson reimbursed him out of his own pocket.) Money had previously been voted for lighthouses and harbor improvements. In 1806, by an appropriation for the survey of the coast between Cape Hatteras and Cape Fear, the government began under Jeffersonian auspices the United States Coastal Survey. But neither this nor the Lewis and Clark Expedition nor anything thus far undertaken could be considered on the same plane with the systematic planning and construction of roads and canals through the states. A constitutional amendment seemed expedient for the innovation, and had it been obtained the political morass that trapped and muddled federal enterprise in this area over the next thirty to forty years might have been avoided.

Congress did not respond to Jefferson's proposal. Except for a Senate resolution calling on Gallatin to submit a comprehensive report on roads and canals, which eventuated in an admirable plan of development, no further action was recorded before the gusts of war shriveled this enlightened venture of Jeffersonian nationalism. The chances for the educational part of the plan had never been good. The idea of a national university had originated with George Washington. Its champions were not politicians but statesmen of science, art, and literature who regarded Jefferson as their leader. They were men like Dr. William Thornton, designer of the Capitol and superintendent of patents; Benjamin Latrobe, the architect and engineer; Dupont de Nemours, who had prepared a national plan of education at Jefferson's request; George Logan, senator and agriculturist; and, above all, Joel Barlow, that wayfaring poet and propagandist of revolution, who returned to his native land in 1805 seventeen years after Jefferson met him in Paris at the beginning of his European odyssey. All these men felt a deep interest in national pursuits of peace, in commercial freedom, and in the hardware of internal improvements, as well as in higher education under the patronage of the federal government. For years Barlow had been associated with Robert Fulton, the inventor-promoter of the submarine and torpedo, which would supposedly render naval power ineffectual against seagoing commerce, and the steamboat, already tested on the Seine and by others in American waters, which seemed providentially designed for the inland waterways of the United States. Jefferson failed to grasp the full significance of the steamboat. Few men did; Robert Livingston, Fulton's partner and patron of the *Clermont* voyage in 1807, was the exception. Barlow introduced his ingenious friend to the President, and he showed much more interest in the torpedo, as a weapon against British naval power, than in the steamboat. But Barlow and Fulton, together with Latrobe and perhaps others, all enthusiasts for canal navigation, undoubtedly influenced Jefferson's thinking on this phase of internal improvements; and Barlow, in particular, sparked the idea of a national university.

Barlow settled in Washington in the fall of 1805. For several years Jefferson had been urging him to come home and write a history of the United States. Marshall's *Life of Washington,* now beginning to appear, horrified the President. During the ensuing winter he set Barlow to work, with boxes upon boxes of material supplied from Monticello and easy access to all the offices of government, to write a Republican history of the new nation. The past did not seriously interest Barlow, however, and he turned his restless mind to the university project. He discussed it at length with the President, wrote a prospectus for him, and at his direction drafted a bill which Logan introduced in the Senate. Influenced in part by Napoleon's National Institute, the bill contemplated both a scientific academy and an educational institution, combining teaching and research in a fashion unknown to American universities of that time. Jefferson hoped that Peale's Museum might find shelter in this national institution. The result, had it materialized, would have had the characteristics of the American Philosophical Society, the University of Virginia, and the Smithsonian Institution all rolled into one. But Congress showed little interest. The mass of Republicans were indifferent or hostile from niggardly views of public economy or state rights, while the Federalists feared political influence, despite the safeguards contained in the bill. Jefferson's recommendation in his sixth annual message gave the project higher standing than before, but the sequel confirmed Gallatin's judgment that it was too unpopular to be considered. Jefferson did not press the measure again. A year later, at the commencement of the Tenth Congress, he wrote disappointingly to Barlow, "I had fondly hoped to set those enterprises [internal improvements generally] into motion with the last legislature I shall meet. But the chance of war is an unfortunate check." Roads and canals were more popular than science and education, of course, but "the narrow and niggardly views of ignorance working the suffrage of ignorance" doomed both halves of the system. "There is a snail-paced gait for the advance of new ideas on the general mind, under which we must acquiesce," he philosophized. "A forty years' experience of popular assemblies has taught me that you must give them time for every step you take. If too hard pressed, they balk, and the machine retrogrades." An ultimate faith in the machine—this was the final solace.

Toward the close of the session Jefferson was able to communicate two items of good news from abroad. The American ministers in London had concluded a treaty, and Armstrong had been reliably informed in Paris that Napoleon's Berlin Decree, making lawful prize of all traffic with Britain, would not extend to American carriers. Without this exemption or the protection of Britain, American neutrality was obliterated. If Monroe and Pinkney had, in fact, secured a treaty "satisfactory on all points," then Britain had presumably yielded to the American ultimatum on impressment under the alarm of the Berlin Decree. For in November the envoys had informed the administration that the British commissioners would not recede from impressment in the treaty, though they would deliver informal assurances of caution and forbearance in the practice. The American team considered the Auckland-Holland note on the subject satisfactory and were proceeding on their own responsibility to conclude the treaty. This startled Jefferson. "I believe the *sine qua non* we made is that of the nation," he told Madison, who entirely agreed, "and that they would rather go on without a treaty than one which does not settle this article." He convened the cabinet on February 2. The question was put: Should the United States yield the principle of the non-importation act in return for a treaty, even if satisfactory on other points, that did not secure its citizens against impressment? "Unanimously not. Because it would be yielding the only peaceable instrument for coercing all our rights." In other words, it was not simply the failure of the *sine qua non* that caused dissent but this failure in conjunction with treaty stipulations that would undoubtedly annihilate commercial legislation against Britain. As to neutral rights generally, Jefferson again expressed his belief that the two emperors, Napoleon and Alexander, would enforce them in the eventual peace treaty, surely with more latitude than Britain would now allow. The cabinet agreed to maintain a friendly attitude, to renew the executive suspension of the non-importation act, and to adhere to the original ultimatum. Writing to the envoys the next day, Madison said flatly that no treaty omitting firm guarantees against impressment would be acceptable. He recognized, of course, a treaty might already have been signed. Such was the case, on December 31, but by then Britain would have had time for sober second thoughts under the duress of the Berlin Decree and might have yielded to the American demand. This was Jefferson's hope when he announced the accord to Congress on February 19. In fact, the British ministry's reaction to the decree had been just the opposite; in the end it was Monroe and Pinkney, not Auckland and Holland, who had been frightened by Napoleon.

A copy of the treaty reached David Erskine, the new, young, and likeable British Minister, on March 3, the day before the expiration of the Ninth Congress. Erskine rushed the document to Madison who, in turn, took it to the President. Not only was the treaty silent on impressment but a British note had been annexed reserving to His Majesty's government the right to reciprocate the Berlin Decree and, in this connection, to violate engagements with the United States unless France revoked the decree or the American government openly combated it. That evening a joint committee of Congress rode in a carriage to the President's House to inquire of any last-minute business. When the treaty was mentioned, Dr. Mitchill asked if the Senate might expect an early call to consider it. "Certainly not!" Jefferson snapped. His irritability was compounded by a migraine attack. He could not imagine why his envoys had signed such a humiliating treaty, unless they had panicked at the first news of the Berlin Decree, supposing war with France inevitable. Talking to Erskine the next day, he said the informal note on impressment was worthless and waxed indignant at the pre-condition binding the United States to resist the injuries of another nation while Britain, an equal party to the contract, left herself free to wreak whatever injuries she pleased. Congress wound up its affairs agog at the President's peremptory rejection of the treaty. He took a heavy responsibility on himself, Senator Smith observed. Coerced into making the treaty by the Senate, he nevertheless refused its advice on acceptance. And why? Because he did not get everything asked. If British depredations increased would not he be responsible? Would not Monroe and Pinkney be insulted? Would not he and Madison be accused of seeking to discredit Monroe and curry favor with Napoleon? All these embarrassing questions had no effect whatever on the President's determination to refuse "a hard treaty" with Britain.

Indeed the more he pondered the treaty the worse it became in his eyes. When the official text arrived he subjected it to close scrutiny, arranging his "observations" in three columns: the specific article and the *pros* and *cons*. Most of the ink was in the third column. He had at first, somewhat impulsively perhaps, brushed the accord aside for two or three reasons; now he eagerly searched out and found many additional objections. The prior objections focused on the notes rather than the treaty itself. In the absence of an article on impressment the question became whether the United States could accept the note of the British commissioners as an "implied abandonment" of the practice. Monroe insisted this was the case: the note conceded the substance without the shadow of the right. It ought to be viewed, Monroe said, as if it were a stipulation of the treaty itself. He should have known better. On the British side the assurances were cautionary only, made no part of the treaty, and had no application to "British seamen," however they might be defined. Jefferson, for his part, viewed the omission of security against impressment as constructive recognition of the right, hence prejudicial to the American claim in the future. Without again entering into the argument over impressment, he thought Britain better able than the United States to make the necessary concession. More American than British seamen were seized on the high seas and the practice assailed the sovereignty of the United States, itself a greater consideration than any on the other side. Two additional things should be said of Jefferson's reaction to the note on the Berlin Decree. First, the British ministry waited only seven days after its commissioners signed the treaty before retaliating against the decree. The American government was given no time to comply with the demand, and the order in council of January 7, throwing a "paper blockade" along most of the European coast, attacked an American-dominated trade between Continental ports. After this blow, what reliance could be placed in British engagements? Second, the note in particular, but certain articles of the treaty as well, would force the United States into an unneutral attitude toward France. Jefferson said it "clearly squinted at the expectation that we would join in resistance to France, or they [Britain] would not regard the treaty." The country could not permit itself to be bullied into war. While Napoleon straddled the Continent, while the Florida purchase still depended on his good offices with Spain, Jefferson wished to avoid a fiasco with France, such as the Jay Treaty had invited a decade before.

But what of the treaty articles themselves? On a superficial view Article XI was the most valuable. It secured the re-export trade on the landing of the cargo and the payment of token duties in the American port. But as Jefferson read the article it restricted the re-export of colonial produce to European markets and the supply of the colonial markets to European articles. Moreover, this British retreat from the *Essex* decision was confined to the period of "the present hostilities." So if peace were made tomorrow the concession would be worthless. Article III covered the East India trade, highly prized by American merchants. Monroe thought it was returned to the footing of the Jay Treaty. Actually, the new provision put an end to indirect voyages to East India ports. The cargoes and the capital for this labyrinthian trade were obtained by coastal voyages in Europe and at other intermediate points; limited to direct voyages, it would be severely handicapped to the advantage of the British East India Company, even more so now than at the time of Jay's Treaty because fewer native princes were independent of British control. The treaty provided for equal tonnage duties, but this remained a fiction because of the added town port charges levied in Britain though not in the United States. The treaty acquiesced in the discriminatory duties on exports to the United States. Since the Constitution denied to Congress the power to lay export duties, reciprocity in this area was impossible, at great cost to American consumers and also to traders placed at a competitive disadvantage in the trans-shipment of British wares. The articles on contraband and blockade marked some advance for the American position, but recognition of the British doctrine on neutral flags, the status of the cargo determining the status of the ship, was a retrograde step. Other articles secured to British cruisers favorable treatment in American ports and to British privateers privileges that the United States was bound to deny the enemies of France. This was inadmissible. Finally, the "most favored nation" article barred the United States from retaliatory legislation against Great Britain. While so many wrongs remained to be righted by that power, "we will never," Jefferson emphatically declared, "tie our hands by treaty, from the right of passing a non-importation or non-intercourse act, to make it in her interest to become just."

Expert testimony confirmed Jefferson's judgment on the commercial articles of the treaty. In April, Madison laid these articles before Tench Coxe, Jacob Crowninshield, William Jones, and Senator Smith, perhaps others, all men who qualified as experts on the intricacies of foreign trade. The result was wholesale condemnation. Coxe, for instance, said that Britain surrendered nothing of importance and secured every present advantage in the Anglo-American trade. Better the United States should withdraw from the ocean and concentrate on internal trade and manufactures, he thought. Smith, who had earlier upbraided the President for cavalierly dismissing the treaty, now said it would "completely prostrate our commerce at the foot of Great Britain." The Senate would never ratify it. There was no informed public opinion of the accord since only its general outlines were known. The fact that it was silent on impressment justified its rejection to most Republicans. The President's popularity was unbounded, Nicholson wrote sourly to Monroe, and his will that of the nation. The only criterion of judgment on events was his approval or disapproval. If he were in favor of Jay's Treaty, the people would enthusiastically applaud it. "Such is our present infatuation," said Nicholson.

The treaty, meanwhile, was in the course of re-negotiation in London. That, at least, was the fiction adopted by the administration. Monroe and Pinkney had been instructed to renew the negotiation before the treaty reached Washington, so nothing had been concluded for the advice and consent of the Senate. In April, before Jefferson went to Monticello, the cabinet approved a long list of revisions to be sought. It considered Madison's proposal to surrender the employment of British seamen in exchange for the abolition of impressment. Pending Gallatin's report on the impact of this measure on the American marine, the new bill of particulars for the envoys was held up. When Gallatin estimated that nearly one-half the able seamen in the foreign trade were British—an estimate Jefferson thought high—the cabinet shelved Madison's plan and returned to the earlier proposition to reciprocate the British practice of nationalizing alien seamen after two years' service. The formal instructions were dispatched on May 20, just after Jefferson's return to Washington. An understanding on impressment thus remained the primary object; it was not in itself the decisive one, however. The United States might have shuffled along without an impressment article had it not been for the annex on the French decree, the unsatisfactory commercial articles, and the utterly intolerable sacrifice of commercial coercion.

By this time a new Tory, or "Pittite," ministry had come to power in Britain. The cabinet change doomed what slender hope Jefferson still had for an accommodation. Indeed, from the receipt of the treaty he viewed the continued negotiations in London as a kind of shadow play to save Monroe's face, to keep up expectations at home, and to gain precious time. He wrote to Gallatin in April, "Time strengthens my belief that no equal treaty will be obtained. . . . Perhaps we may engage them to act on certain articles, including their note on impressment, by a mutual understanding, under the pretext of further time to arrange a general treaty. Perhaps too the general peace will in the meantime establish for us better principles than we can obtain ourselves." Procrastination was his policy. While the negotiation took "a friendly nap," time, always "the most precious thing to us," would again be granted the opportunity to rescue the country from difficulties. He had not really wanted a treaty in the first place, preferring, rather, separate accords on critical issues. And when the envoys returned a treaty that dealt badly with the minor issues, made no provision on the major one in direct violation of their instructions, put the United States in hostile relation to France, and disarmed the country of its most potent weapon of defense, Jefferson felt justified in trotting this abomination out the back door. Having rejected accommodation with Britain, he now had to see if he had other means to vindicate American claims.

The opportunity would arise sooner than he expected. Meanwhile, the Burr trial got under way at Richmond. The executive officer responsible for the government's case was the Attorney General, Caesar A. Rodney, who was handicapped by illness in his family at Wilmington. Partly for this reason, but also because he knew that he as well as Burr was on trial, Jefferson took a more active role in the collection of evidence and the conduct of the prosecution than constitutional duty alone seemed to require. When Burr arrived in Richmond and appeared before Judge Marshall, the court decided to hold him on no higher charge than misdemeanor and admit him to bail in the amount of $10,000. Jefferson exploded. Demanding proof of overt acts of treason in order to commit the prisoner on that charge, Marshall placed an impossible burden on the government and twisted the law itself in the interest of the criminal. "We had always before understood that when there was reasonable ground to believe guilt, the offender must be put on his trial," Jefferson observed. "That guilty intentions [of treason] were probable, the judge believed. And as to overt acts, were not the bundles of letters of information in Mr. Rodney's hands, the letters and facts published in local newspapers, Burr's flight, and the universal belief or rumor of his guilt, probable ground for presuming the facts of enlistment, military guard, rendezvous, threats of civil war, or capitulation, so as to put him on trial? Is there a candid man in the U.S. who does not believe some one, if not all, of these overt acts to have taken place?" But the evidence could not be collected and the witnesses brought to Richmond under several months. Burr's crimes were sown from the Atlantic through all the western waters to New Orleans. Why are the crimes not proved? the judge asked. "As if an express could go to Natchez, or the mouth of the Cumberland, and return in five weeks, to do what has never taken place in twelve," Jefferson acidly retorted. Why, if troops were assembled on the Ohio in November or December, had not affidavits been obtained by the end of March? "But I ask the judge where they should have been lodged? At Frankfort? at Cincinnati? at Nashville? St. Louis? Natchez? New Orleans? These were the probable places of apprehension and examination. It was not known at *Washington* till the 26th of March that Burr would escape from the Western tribunals, be retaken and brought to an Eastern one: and in 5 days after (neither 5 months nor 5 weeks as the judge calculates) he says, it is 'impossible to suppose the affidavits could not have been obtained.'" The decision was bad enough in its immediate effect; far worse were its implications for the trial still to come. For under a rigid interpretation of the Constitution's treason clause—two witnesses to the same overt act—Burr and his accomplices might go free. "The first ground of complaint was the supine inattention of the administration to a treason stalking through the land in open day. The present one, that they have crushed it before it was ripe for execution, so that no overt acts can be produced." Still impaled on the horns of this dilemma, Jefferson nevertheless felt that the government, if given a little time, could produce the evidence to convict the malefactors of treason even in a partisan court.

In April, and throughout the ordeal at Richmond, the President channeled his feelings not against Burr or his poor deluded followers but against the court and the circle of Federalists who made Burr's cause their own. Of course, he wished the culprit hanged for his crime. It was no ordinary crime. The integrity of the nation had been assaulted. This was the root of his passion, not the person of Aaron Burr, who had already destroyed himself regardless of the verdict at the bar of justice. In any fair and impartial trial that verdict must be guilty. The President himself had pronounced it and the public had thundered its approval. So when the course of justice opened in seeming defiance of the nation, Jefferson fell back on his old conviction in the Federalism of the bench. The mass of Republicans shared his opinion on the politicization of the trial. When Burr came out on bail in April, Marshall attended a dinner party hosted by John Wickham, a leading Richmond Federalist and chief counsel of the accused, who was also a guest. Thomas Ritchie, editor of the Richmond *Enquirer,* denounced the Chief Justice for this "wilful prostration of the dignity of his own character" and "wanton insult" to his country. To the Governor of Virginia, a mild and usually soft-spoken Republican, William H. Cabell, this notorious incident gave the plot away. "The Federalists have completely made this [trial] a party question," he wrote to a brother. "They unblushingly say that the prosecution originated with Mr. Jefferson in revenge and is kept up by the Republicans from the same motives. God damn their souls, they do not see that it is their enmity to Mr. Jefferson that makes them in love with misdemeanors and treasons, provided they can bring his administration into contempt." A year before the Federalists had used the Miranda case in the same way. The defendants then, charged with aiding and abetting an unlawful enterprise against Spain, were hailed as the martyred victims of a deceitful and persecuting administration. The government's chief prosecutor at Richmond, federal attorney George Hay, commented philosophically, "There is amongst mankind a sympathy for villainy, which sometimes shows itself in defiance of every principle of patriotism and truth." But with the Federalists it was more than that. They patronized and lionized Burr—the murderer of Hamilton—in order to assassinate the President politically. As the trial developed, Jefferson and Burr changed places and it rapidly became, on their side, a prosecution of the President, also of his general-in-chief, for driving an innocent lamb to slaughter.

"There never was such a trial from the beginning of the world," Hay remarked. Never, certainly, in the United States had a trial aroused so much interest or been accompanied by so much fanfare nation-wide. Late in May Burr and several accomplices were arraigned before a grand jury. Hay sought indictment for treason as well as misdemeanor, but things began inauspiciously. Several prospective jurors, including the distinguished Republicans Giles and Nicholas, though not John Randolph, were successfully challenged by the defense. The final complement of two Federalists, four Quids, and ten Republicans struck the President as unrepresentative. He traced it to the error of a wholly independent judiciary, "which from the citadel of the law can turn its guns on those they [the judges] were most meant to defend." Setting up a dispatch rider between Richmond and Washington, he was in constant touch with counsel. Hay complained of the court's rejection of affidavits on technical grounds of form, though it seemed to admit others similarly at fault from the defense side. The government had counted on the damaging testimony of Eric Bollman, one of the confederates earlier brought in custody to Washington, where he had given his story to the President orally and in writing on the pledge it would never be used against him or go out of executive hands. Jefferson had honored this man, the famed rescuer of Lafayette from prison, when he came to the United States; but he had fallen in with Burr. He was expected to give the same testimony in court, under the protection of executive pardon, he had given in Washington. Now Bollman refused the pardon and stood on the right against self-incrimination. At the same time he accused the President of betrayal of trust by delivering the Washington statement to Hay—a delicate point of ethics perhaps but one Jefferson resolved easily enough in his own mind on the ground that the offer of pardon fulfilled the promise and that Hay was a hand of the executive. At any rate,

Bollman's testimony was lost to the government. The man on whom the prosecution's case principally turned was General Wilkinson. Days and weeks passed and Wilkinson did not appear. Burr's partisans gloated: the Janus dared not show himself. He finally arrived, however, with ten witnesses wrested from the arms of the courts in New Orleans, and promptly opened a noose large enough for his own neck together with Burr's.

The defense counsel realized that the acquittal of their client depended on the conviction of Wilkinson. Partly for this reason, partly to harass the President, Burr himself moved that Jefferson be subpoened to appear in court with certain letters bearing on Wilkinson's actions. Marshall issued the subpoena on an opinion that could only be interpreted, like *Marbury v. Madison,* as a slap at the President. Jefferson's temperature had been mounting steadily. The judge tolerated the grossest invective against him from the defense counsel's most vocal member, Luther Martin, the "unprincipled and impudent Federal bull-dog," as Jefferson called him. And on one occasion Marshall openly avowed his opinion that the prosecution seemed more interested in a conviction than a fair trial—a statement he blushingly retracted when called to account by one of Hay's associates, William Wirt. The subpoena further strained Jefferson's feelings, yet he never lost control. The same maneuver had been attempted in the Miranda case; within two months it would be attempted, on Madison, in the Connecticut libel case. Were the President and his executive officers to be hailed into courts all across the country? "The Constitution enjoins his constant agency in the concerns of six millions of people. Is the law paramount to this, which calls on him on behalf of a single one?" Jefferson asked. He went on to reiterate his tripartite theory of the federal balance. "But would the executive be independent of the judiciary, if he were subject to the *commands* of the latter, and to imprisonment for disobedience; if the several courts could bandy him from pillar to post, keep him constantly trudging from north and south and east and west, and withdraw him entirely from his constitutional duties?" With this parade of horribles the question answered itself, so convincingly, in fact, that Marshall might have squirmed had he seen the opinion. But it was written for Hay's benefit; Jefferson would not dignify the subpoena with a formal answer and he would resist any effort to enforce it. Actually, as Hay pointed out, the President's appearance on the scene was the last thing wanted by the defense. No demand to enforce the subpoena embarrassed the judge. Nor did justice require it. Jefferson co-operated promptly and fully with the request for papers and offered to give testimony by way of deposition should the court desire. It was never requested.

On June 24–25 the grand jury returned indictments for treason and misdemeanor against Burr, Blennerhassett, Dayton, Smith, Tyler, and two others. The chief accuser, Wilkinson, barely escaped indictment himself. For Jefferson the General's part in suppressing the conspiracy covered the multitude of his sins, and he could readily sympathize with the man whose plight—the scapegoat of criminals—was similar to his own. Burr was thrown into the Richmond jail; two days afterwards, on the plea of counsel, the court permitted him to lodge under guard in the comfort of the house occupied by Luther Martin. The other defendants received no such generosity. On August 3, Burr's treason trial began. Impaneling a jury was tedious work. After several days, forty-eight had been called and only four chosen. Nearly everyone, Hay reported, was convinced of Burr's guilt and said so. "Have you not said that Col. Burr ought to be hung?" went one interrogatory. "No, I said hanging was too good for him." A jury was finally secured and Hay opened the case for the government. The indictment charged Burr with assembling troops and "levying war" against the United States at Blennerhassett's Island on December 10, 1806, and further with descending the western rivers in order to take possession of New Orleans. Hay dwelt at length on the fine line between conspiracy and treason, between the design and the act of treason, between the procurement of a treasonable force and the actual levying of war. It was incumbent on the prosecution to show, he concluded, that Burr had a treasonable design and assembled a force to effect that design. In this Hay believed he was supported by Marshall's opinion in the habeas corpus case of Bollman and Swartwout only a few weeks before. If there is "an actual assemblage of men for the purpose of executing a treasonable design," Marshall declared, "all those who perform any part, however minute, or however remote from the scene of action, and who are actually leagued in the general conspiracy are traitors." This seemed to adhere to the common law rule, "in treason all are principals." It followed, then, that the testimony of two witnesses to Burr's *procuring* a treasonable assemblage on the island, regardless of his whereabouts or war-like acts, would constitute proof of treason.

The testimony of Eaton, the Morgans, and others went to establish Burr's treasonable designs. Several witnesses to the goings-on at the island proved that armed men, boats, military stores, and provisions had been assembled, and that Blennerhassett, Tyler, and company had named the division of the Union as one of their objects. But it soon became apparent, before most of the witnesses had been called, that the prosecution could not fix Burr's presence on the island at the time of the overt act laid in the indictment or prove by the positive testimony of two witnesses that he procured such an assemblage in force as constituted "levying war." At this point the defense moved to arrest the evidence. After ten days of argument Marshall, on August 31, delivered his opinion accepting the motion and sent the case to the jury. The opinion, if it did not contradict that in the former case, unraveled its obscurities in favor of the defendant. In *Bollman* the judge had emphasized "the assemblage of men"; he now required "the employment and exhibition of force" in proof of "levying war." The question of Burr's procurement of treasonable acts became irrelevant unless the acts procured were, in fact, treasonable. "The legal guilt of the person who planned that assemblage on Blennerhassett's island depends . . . on the criminality of that assemblage. If those who perpetrated the fact be not traitors, he who advised the fact cannot be a traitor. His guilt, then . . . depends on theirs; and their guilt can only be established in a prosecution against themselves." The opinion amounted to a directive of acquittal to the jury. The jury returned an unusual verdict. The defendant, it said, "is not proved to be guilty by any evidence submitted to us."

Jefferson, quiet throughout this trial, had prepared himself for the decision. "The event has been what was evidently intended from the beginning . . . ," he wrote to Hay, "that is to say, not only to clear Burr but to prevent the evidence from ever going before the world." The whole conduct of the trial—the assault on him personally, the flattering attentions to Burr, the Jesuitical reading of the law—had been political, in his opinion. At first he seemed disinclined to go to trial on the lesser charge of misdemeanor for mounting an expedition against the Spanish dominions. Hay advised against it, at least in Richmond and before Marshall, where everything must again turn on the events at Blennerhassett's Island. But Jefferson ordered Hay to proceed, perhaps less with a view to the conviction of Burr than the embarrassment of Marshall. "If defeated," he said, "it will heap coals of fire on the head of the Judge; if successful, it will give time to see whether a prosecution of treason against him [Burr] can be instituted in any, and what other court." The trial commenced immediately. Another subpoena issued to the President, which he ignored as before; and the final result was much the same as before. The court arrested the evidence at the threshold by excluding any testimony not directly connected with the spot laid in the indictment. Hearings were then begun on the commitment of Burr and Blennerhassett for treason and misdemeanor in Ohio and Kentucky. The court, on October 20, remanded the prisoners for trial in the former state on the lesser charge only. Burr posted a small bail, at once forfeited, and fled to England.

Jefferson supposed the rulings at Richmond "equivalent to a proclamation of impunity to every traitorous combination which may be formed to destroy the Union." Fortunately, however, the public revulsion against the court would produce a more than adequate compensation in the form of a constitutional amendment making the federal judiciary, "this colossal power, which bestrides the legislative and executive authorities," responsible to the will of the nation. In November he laid the trial proceedings before Congress so that it might judge whether the defect lay in the testimony, or in the law, or in the administration of justice, and furnish whatever remedy needful to secure the nation from treason. The legislatures of Massachusetts and Pennsylvania instructed their respective delegations to work for a constitutional amendment rendering judges removable by the President on the address of both houses of Congress. Giles and Randolph introduced legislation to widen the scope of the treason clause beyond the construction Marshall had given to it. Jefferson was a silent observer of these proceedings; and Congress, preoccupied with foreign affairs, as he was, came to no final resolution of the problem. The Senate, at least, left no doubt of its opinion of the Burr Conspiracy. A committee under Adams's chairmanship moved the expulsion of John Smith, the Ohio senator, for his participation in the criminal combination "against the *peace, Union,* and *liberty* of the people of the United States." Adams's report warmly commended the administration for suppressing the conspiracy that would, "in a very short lapse of time, have terminated not only in war, but in a war of the most horrible description, in a war at once foreign and domestic." It went on to declare, without entering into technical legal questions of criminality, "that if the daylight of evidence, combining one vast and complicated intention, with overt acts innumerable, be not excluded from the mind by the curtain of artificial rules, the simplest understanding cannot but see what the subtlest understanding cannot disguise, crimes before which ordinary treason whitens into virtue—crimes of which war is the mildest feature." Several Republicans stood by Smith in the belief he had been duped by Burr. The vote on the expulsion resolution, 19 to 10, fell one short of the two-thirds needed. But the Senator resigned under the force of censure.

"Some circumstantial evidence is very strong, as when you find a trout in the milk." Thoreau's aphorism fits the case nicely. The verdict of common sense, of morality, and of history on Burr was, and must remain, guilty; the verdict of law was, and must remain, innocent. He might have been convicted on a less stringent interpretation of the treason clause, and but for Marshall's political bias this would surely have been the result. In the long run, however, the nation was better served by his bias than by Jefferson's. For conviction would have introduced into American law the ancient English principle of "constructive treason," founded in this case on Burr's "constructive presence" at Blennerhassett's Island, where the evidence failed to pin overt acts of treason on him. It was better that the scoundrel go free than be convicted on evidence outside the indictment or on a constructive definition of the act of "levying war." Jefferson could hardly be expected to take this view of the matter. Although he knew all along the defect of the evidence, the unfortunate constraints of the indictment, and so on, he also believed these difficulties could be surmounted by a court that placed the protection of the government above the protection of criminal assailants. In cases where the nation itself was attacked, as he believed it was in this case, the judiciary ought not to conjure with the law to cover traitors. At another time, in another place, he might have condemned reasoning of this kind as dangerous to liberty; but with the responsibilities of the chief magistrate at a time when the experiment in liberty and union was still perilous, he could not afford the luxury of abstract opinion. Democracy, too, placed him at odds with the Chief Justice. Jefferson had exchanged the independence of the judiciary, once thought an essential safeguard of civil liberties, for a vaguely plebicitarian conception—a judiciary responsible to the will of the nation. There could be no doubt of that will in the case of Aaron Burr. Over and over Jefferson emphasized the judgment of the people, so alarmingly at issue with the judgment of the court.

In the last analysis it was the popular judgment that counted, and partly for this reason Jefferson could tame his anger at the court. The Catiline went into exile. First in London, then in Paris, he tried to market a disunionist conspiracy with much the same western plot as before. He failed, of course. The foreign offices distrusted him. At times he lived on the edge of starvation. Finally, in 1812, he returned home in disguise and disgrace. How the mighty had fallen! If Jefferson took any comfort from the perdition that pursued Burr to his grave, he never mentioned it. Wilkinson fell too, but with the agility of a cat landed on his feet. Jefferson astutely anticipated the uproar in Congress against Wilkinson, and referred the charges of collaboration with Spain to a military court of inquiry. The artful dodger passed through this ordeal, another and longer and inconclusive one in Congress, and finally, in 1811, won acquittal from a court-martial. Through all this Jefferson stood by him, not from any fondness for the blustering commander but because his actions, crooked or straight, defeated the Burr Conspiracy. "As to the rest of his life," Jefferson wrote in 1812, "I have left it to his friends and his enemies, to whom it furnished matter enough for disputation. I classed myself with neither." In the end it seemed to him that the evils of Burr or Wilkinson or Marshall were small and transient compared with the permanent good wrought by the Burr Conspiracy in fixing the Union in the affections of the American people.

The Embargo

On June 25, when Jefferson was supposedly under subpoena to appear in Richmond, Captain Charles Gordon of the USS *Chesapeake* burst into the President's House to report the outrage committed on his ship off Norfolk three days before. The *Chesapeake*, under way for the Mediterranean, had been hailed by the HMS *Leopard*, one of a squadron patrolling off Hampton Roads, and ordered to submit to search for British deserters. Refused by Commodore James Barron, in command, the *Leopard* poured repeated broadsides into the defenseless frigate, killing three and wounding eighteen before its flag could be struck. Four alleged deserters were then removed and the *Chesapeake* limped back to port. The British government, in all the extremity of its pretensions, had never claimed the right to search national vessels. The assertion of the claim was an insult; accompanied by force, in the attack on the *Chesapeake*, it was an act of war.

Jefferson learned from Gordon that the captain of the *Leopard* acted under orders from Vice Admiral George C. Berkeley, commander of the fleet in American water. Berkeley, a typical specimen of admiralty arrogance and influence that intimidated government itself, was responsible for intercepting enemy vessels and contraband from the St. Lawrence to the Caribbean. His ships—roughly a score of different sizes and descriptions, with others building in Bermuda —depended on the services of American ports, and the same ports constantly depleted their crews. In May he learned that several British deserters had enlisted aboard the *Chesapeake* at Norfolk and, in addition, that three vessels of his fleet, earlier proscribed on the President's order for the *Leander* affair in New York, had been forced to leave Charleston. Boiling angry, he issued the order to search the *Chesapeake*. Of the four seamen taken, one was a genuine deserter, and he would later hang at Halifax; the other three were American citizens who had "deserted" from impressment aboard the HMS *Melampus*. They, too, would be condemned at Halifax, and then pardoned on condition of returning to the British service.

As the news of the *Chesapeake* affair spread across the country, the populace rose with thunderous voice against Britain. "I have never seen so large an assemblage—" Senator Smith wrote of the public meeting in Baltimore, "every man almost of respectability of whatever party was present—There appeared but one opinion— War." The same sentiment echoed and re-echoed in mass meetings up and down the land during the next several weeks. In Virginia, Governor Cabell ordered the militia into the Norfolk area. In Philadelphia the public assaulted a British armed brig, believed to be loading provisions for the Norfolk squadron, and left her crippled and dismantled. "This country has never been in such a state of excitement since the battle of Lexington," Jefferson remarked. And even Lexington had not produced the same unanimity. With such ardor did the Federalists rally to the administration that the President was tempted to exclaim with the Psalmist, "Lord, what have I done that the wicked should praise me!"

What he did, essentially, was to tap the war fever for vigorous measures in pursuit of peace, if possible, in preparation for war, if necessary. The cabinet officers reassembled in Washington and met on July 2. By proclamation the President proscribed all British warships from American waters. The Mediterranean squadron was recalled. The frigate *Revenge* was dispatched to Britain with instructions for the American ministers. They were to demand disavowal of the attack and the principles on which it rested, reparations for injuries, return of the four seamen, Berkeley's recall, and security against future outrages. Since the last could not be obtained while impressment existed, the demand was linked to the old ultimatum. The policy was redress, not war. But placing this price tag on his suit for redress, the President realized he ran the risk of war. We operate on three principles, he said in explaining the policy to his son-in-law Randolph: first, that the usage of nations calls for seeking satisfaction before going to war and, besides, peace is still a great object; second, that 40,000 seamen and property worth many millions scattered through all the seas and oceans ought to be brought home before a declaration of war; third, that Congress is the arbiter of war and should not be committed by any act of the President. Interestingly, he did not convene Congress at once, though some war-minded advisers urged him to do so. The call went out for more than three months hence, on October 26, by which time tempers would have cooled and the *Revenge* should have returned with the verdict of the British ministry on the suit for redress. Even if the verdict proved negative, it was by no means certain in his mind that war should follow. Non-intercourse, or commercial coercion in some form, had not yet been tried, only threatened; and this, not war, was the next logical step. In July, such was "the torrent of passion," Jefferson had only to snap his fingers to plunge the country into war with the old enemy. Instead he used the power in his hands for peace. As so often before in foreign crises, he played for time: Napoleon's time, time for military preparations at home, time for Britain to show her hand.

In the immediate crisis it could not be known whether Berkeley, the admiralty, or the ministry had been the author of the attack on the *Chesapeake*. If the orders were ministerial, as Jefferson first suspected, Britain had already thrown down the gauntlet and no American vessel was safe on the seas. But perhaps the Admiral's orders were equivocal, leaving him free to employ force in given circumstances; perhaps they had been timed to exploit the expected turmoil of the Burr Conspiracy or to coincide with renewed Indian incitements on the Great Lakes frontier. The main fear in July was an attack on Norfolk. "Blows may be hourly possible," Jefferson warned on the 7th. Governor Cabell, while keeping up his guard, was under strict orders not to strike the first blow. An anomalous situation existed at Hampton Roads. The men and ships of the British squadron, by virtue of defying the President's proclamation, were considered "enemies *de facto*." Communication with them was by flag only. When a small party foraging on shore for supplies was captured, Jefferson agreed with Cabell on the right to treat them as prisoners-of-war but prudently directed their release lest an enemy *de jure* be recognized. He was satisfied by the end of July that the squadron's intentions were pacific, though it did not withdraw beyond the capes until October. All the while the administration made extensive military preparations. These were defensive in part, addressed immediately to the enforcement of the proclamation in American harbors; but they also contemplated offensive war. The governors of the several states were ordered to ready their respective quotas of 100,000 militia for a winter campaign against Canada. Artillery, ammunition, and camp equipage were ordered to rendezvous points near the frontier. The discretionary act of the last Congress for the acceptance of volunteer companies, organized and placed on stand-by, was put into effect. The Army and Marine Corps were brought up to authorized limits, and the naval complement raised above the maximum fixed by law. Materials for additional gunboats were procured in anticipation of congressional appropriation. Fortifications were pushed, especially at New York, Charleston, and New Orleans.

And Gallatin quietly sounded out the banks on annual loans to support a war. The public knew nothing of these preparations. Rather than manufacturing a war hysteria around national defense, as his predecessor had done in another crisis, Jefferson worked silently, made no answer to the numerous addresses he received, and said "our greatest praise shall be, that we *appear* to be doing nothing."

Cooling the crisis in the hope of peace, Jefferson nevertheless remained skeptical of its chances. Where British pride and jealousy were concerned, the nation had learned not to expect justice, least of all from a Tory ministry. "I suppose our fate will depend on the successes or reverses of Bonaparte," he mused. This was a hard fate indeed. "It is really mortifying that we should be forced to wish success to Bonaparte and to look to his victims as our salvation." But, as he said repeatedly, "the English being equally tyrannical at sea as he is on land, and that tyranny bearing on us in every point of either honor or interest, I say 'down with England,' and as for what Bonaparte is then to do to us, let us trust to the chapter of accidents. I cannot, with the Anglomen, prefer a certain present evil to a future hypothetical one." Near the end of August news of the Battle of Friedland and the Treaty of Tilsit, conscripting Russia in Napoleon's Continental System, reached him at Monticello. Once again the fortunes of European war seemed to come to America's rescue. British reflexes to this blow ought to prove conciliatory, yet he reminded himself that Tory behavior upset all the laws of reason and nature. If war should come he intended to make the most of it, not only in Canada but in the Floridas as well. "I had rather have war against Spain than not, if we should go to war against England," he told Madison. "Our southern defensive force can take the Floridas, volunteers for a Mexican army will flock to our standard, and rich pabulum will be offered to our privateers in the plunder of their commerce and coasts. Probably Cuba would add itself to our confederation." This was boldly stated, as if in relief from the pent-up tensions of peace. War was an easy temptress; still he remained faithful to the demanding mistress of peace.

In London the brilliant young foreign secretary, George Canning, who gloated in the Tory name, learned of the *Chesapeake-Leopard* encounter only a week after the Emperor Alexander's betrayal at Tilsit. Canning's response when cornered was to attack, specifically in this instance the Danish and Russian fleets; and as for the United States, he would rather invite hostilities with contempt than surrender to an "insidious neutrality." He had powerful support. Monroe dispatched his estimate of the situation in early August. "There has been at all times . . . a strong party here for extending [the war's] ravages to the [United States]," he wrote. "This party is combined of the ship-holders, the navy, the East and West India merchants, and certain political characters of great consideration in the State. So powerful is this combination that it is most certain that nothing can be obtained by this government on any point, but what may be extended of necessity. The disasters of the North ought to inspire moderation, but it seems to have produced directly the opposite effect." A month later Monroe presented his formal note on the *Chesapeake* affair. The government had already disavowed the act and recalled Berkeley; the only question remaining, in Canning's view, was the amount of the reparations to families of the victims. With colossal arrogance Canning turned everything around: the real act of aggression was the President's proclamation. (In Washington his minister, Erskine, had demanded indemnification for some British water casks destroyed by the people of Hampton after the *Chesapeake* murders, a demand which reminded Jefferson of the man who broke his cane over the head of another and then sued for the cost of the cane.) By the proclamation the President took reprisal into his own hands and could not, accordingly, demand anything of Britain, said Canning, though she generously volunteered reparations. And since the attack was unauthorized there was no basis for joining the general issue of impressment in the settlement. Jefferson, on the other hand, considered an abuse of impressment in one branch of practice as involving every other and flowing from what was authorized. "Certain it is," he added, "there can never be friendship, nor even the continuance of peace with England so long as no American citizen can leave his own shore without danger of being seized by the first British officer he meets." Canning, on his side, discovered "extraordinary circumstances" for Berkeley's attack in the employment of deserters on American ships of war. These cavils, combined with the imperatives of British naval supremacy in the fall of 1807, doomed the prospect of settlement. The Monroe-Pinkney treaty met the same fate. It was buried by mutual consent in October. Near the end of that month Canning transferred this annoying little *Chesapeake* business to a special envoy, George Rose, to the United States. Rose's instructions barred any proposition on impressment, and placing the United States in the wrong, demanded the recall of the President's proclamation prior to negotiations. The mission had no chance of success.

Meanwhile, the Tenth Congress convened. The *Revenge* had not yet returned, but the President was pleased to discover—what he had hardly dared to hope—that the war spirit had cooled and the members of Congress, almost to a man, seemed disposed to peace or, at most, to coercive measures short of war. He found encouragement in the withdrawal of the British squadron from Hampton Roads and mercantile reports of fewer captures at sea since the *Chesapeake* encounter. Peace was still his passion, peace was still pending, and if it failed let the onus be on Britain. So he had no idea of provoking Congress to war. He worked through three drafts of his annual message in order to strike just the right balance between patriotic indignation and pacific intentions. In the opinion of Gallatin and Smith, who, strangely, found themselves doves together, the first draft had the appearance of a war-like manifesto. Jefferson softened a few expressions without altering the substance or the tone of the message, which was firm but calm and not at all war-like. While warning the nation that it might not long be permitted to remain in the quiet pursuits of peace, he called for patience pending the outcome of negotiations and accelerated military preparations while the outcome was uncertain. In due time Congress would appropriate several million dollars for national defense.

It was an open secret in Washington that Jefferson would not meet another Congress. He had made his decision to retire long ago. The pleas of Republican leaders had alone restrained him from public announcement. "The pivot we have been spinning upon is yourself," one of them had written. Without his leadership, it was feared, the party would fly apart, each faction or sect spinning into a little orbit of its own. And the fate of the republic itself was bound up with the fate of the Republican party. Some thought the Randolph schism and the party turmoils in Pennsylvania and elsewhere had been produced by the reports two years past of the President's decision to retire in 1809. Officially, Jefferson had given no credence to these rumors; privately, however, all his words and actions pointed to retirement. Congressmen noted as early as February 1807 that he was beginning to send his things to Monticello; and when he went there the ensuing spring he carried a great quantity of trees and shrubs for the gardens of repose that increasingly occupied his idle moments. Newspaper subscriptions were allowed to expire, beginning—no better place, he said—with the *Evening Post* in November. Since the first reports of his intentions, Republican committees, legislative assemblies, religious associations, and citizens in number had showered him with addresses and resolutions urging him to stay on the job. Occasionally he answered private citizens. The infirmities of age and the principle of rotation in office were his pleas. The former were not only physical—rheumatism, an infected jaw, and so on—but psychological. "The principal effect of age . . . ," he observed, "is an indisposition to be goaded by business from morning to night, from laboring in an Augean stable, which cleared out at night presents an equal task the next morning." Duty to principle supported desire. "If some period be not fixed, either by the Constitution or by practice, to the services of the First Magistrate," he wrote to one petitioner, "his office, though nominally elective, will in fact, be for life; and that will soon degenerate into an inheritance." Yet Randolph accused him of creating a "masked monarchy."

Finally, in December, because he could wait no longer, despite the critical juncture of national affairs, the President announced his impending retirement by way of answer to the addresses of the state legislatures. "The die is cast," a Pennsylvanian wrote. And while the President's decision was a matter of profound regret, the principle at the bottom of it entitled him to immortal renown. "If anything were wanting to stamp Jefferson great and good; to place him highest on the list of the benefactors of mankind, the voluntary surrender of the first office in the gift of a free people, entitles him to precedence." The succeeding January the Republican caucus met in Washington, and with surprising ease, though not without opposition from Clintonians in New York and Quids, mainly Virginians, whose reluctant candidate was James Monroe, the party nominated Madison for President and renominated George Clinton for the second office. Thus, in the face of increaisng factionalism, Jefferson managed to control the choice of a successor and to hold the party together.

Administration and Congress marked time for several weeks awaiting dispatches from abroad. From Erskine, late in November, Madison learned of Canning's uncompromising position in the *Chesapeake* affair. London newspapers teemed with speculation on more drastic measures of impressment and new orders in council that would place the entire European continent under blockade. Some American merchants voluntarily kept their ships in port. Napoleon, partly in anticipation of the British move, announced that the Berlin Decree would be extended to the United States. The regulations had yet to be promulgated and, of course, Napoleon could no more blockade the British Isles than he could the United States; but between the tightening Continental System and the expected British orders, American commerce was caught in the jaws of a vise, a maniacal war of blockades, from which there seemed to be no appeal to reason or justice or right. The ruthless had combined to slaughter the innocent.

In this rapidly deteriorating situation, Jefferson's cabinet met on three successive days at the end of November. Nothing final was decided, but between war, a total embargo on American commerce, and acquiescence in the European decrees, Jefferson reported to his son-in-law, "the middle proposition is most likely." Madison clearly favored this course. Gallatin favored something less drastic, perhaps a sweeping non-importation act against Britain to take effect two months hence. The long-suspended selective non-importation law was allowed to go into operation in December. On the 18th, after further consultation, Jefferson sent a brief confidential message to Congress calling attention to "the great and increasing dangers with which our vessels, our seamen, and merchandise, are threatened on the high seas and elsewhere," and to the efficacy of a general embargo for the protection of "these essential resources." The message communicated the papers on the new construction of the Berlin Decree and the proclamation of George III recalling all his natural-born subjects from foreign service and ordering the vigorous enforcement of impressment to this end. Both houses closed their doors. The Senate, suspending its rules, passed the Embargo Act on the same day (22 yea, 6 nay), the House three days later (82 yea, 44 nay), and it became law on December 22. A self-blockade of the nation's commerce, the embargo prohibited American vessels from sailing to foreign ports and foreign vessels from taking on cargo in the United States.

With barely a ripple of protest the government launched an experiment of incredible magnitude, one that dwarfed all previous undertakings and held momentous consequences for the peace of the United States and the world. There was nothing novel in the idea of an embargo; it was part of the Jeffersonian canon, and as an expedient of defense or diplomacy had been in the course of speculation for two years. But no one, not even Jefferson himself, fully grasped the significance or in December 1807 foresaw the consequences of the Embargo Act. A certain obscurity surrounded the measure, which would be the source of abuse and recrimination in the months to come. In part this resulted from the President's failure to present to Congress one of the principal grounds of action, the British orders in council of November 11. Briefly, these orders made fair prize of neutral carriers trading with Continental ports controlled by the enemy, unless under license from Britain. The Continent was placed under quarantine to neutrals with the object of forcing their trade into British channels. At the commencement of the Rose mission, Canning designedly held back the communication of these decrees. They had not been officially received in Washington when Jefferson sent his embargo message to Congress, so he omitted any notice of this new outrage. But the orders had been anticipated for several weeks. They were widely rumored in the English press and confirmed by foreign correspondents. Years later Jefferson said he distinctly recalled having seen the King's proclamation of the state of siege against the Continent in the London newspapers; and Madison went further, saying a copy of the unsigned orders lay on the President's desk when he wrote his message. The first draft of the message referred to the fact as something known, yet not officially communicated, and pointedly declared "the whole world is thus laid under interdict by these two nations." But Jefferson struck both reference and declaration, apparently at Madison's cautious suggestion, with the result that the administration opened itself to the charge of embarking on unprovoked commercial warfare against Britain, presumably at the dictate of Napoleon. Among Federalists and Randolphians the dogma was implanted that the embargo originated in hostility to Britain and friendship for France. The dogma would have taken root, indeed it already had, regardless of anything Jefferson might have said. His critics were undaunted by the receipt and publication of the British orders in January. Yet the embargo would have been better understood and protected from malice had it been grounded unequivocally in the renewed British aggression against neutral rights.

A greater error in this regard was the President's failure to inform the public of the objectives of the embargo. He called the nation to surrender its foreign commerce, the basis of prosperity, furl the sails of hundreds of ships, discharge tens of thousands of seamen from employment, renounce markets for grain, cotton, tobacco, lumber, fish, and other products, hitting the producers as well as the merchants, and shrivel the profits and revenue of foreign imports. Why were these sacrifices required? Jefferson did not explain. He issued no proclamation. To Congress he stated, at most, half his thought, and that without elucidation. The embargo was wanted, he said, to protect the "essential resources" of the country employed in foreign commerce. According to one reliable estimate, 1500 vessels, 20,000 seamen, and $60,000,000 worth of cargo were on the high seas when the embargo became law. (This was about one-third less than in the summer just past, for in the interim many shipholders had voluntarily embargoed their vessels.) The intention of the embargo, then, seemed to be protective and precautionary: to secure from marauding belligerents as much of the nation's seaborne wealth as possible, meanwhile closing the ports to departures and meditating measures to be taken when the ships were safely home. The usual period allowed for this maneuver was ninety days, though the Indiamen required up to twice as long. In that interval, too, the outcome of the Rose mission would become known and the nation's defenses strengthened. Depending on events, war with either, conceivably both, of the belligerents seemed likely. From the President on down, everyone agreed that war was preferable to *permanent* embargo. Of his advisers, however, only Gallatin argued for a statutory time limit scaled to the immediate objective, and Congress hurriedly passed the legislation without fixing a terminal date. To have done so, in Jefferson's opinion, while consistent with the theory of the embargo as a protective measure, would have been to weaken its effect as a coercive measure, and he also had this undisclosed theory in view.

In Jefferson's conception the embargo was not simply a short-run measure preliminary to war but an experiment at longer run—how long he did not know—to discover a peaceable substitute for war. The antecedents of the policy went back over four decades, and its varied career included the non-importation associations before the American Revolution, Madison's retaliatory measures in the First Congress, Jefferson's Report on Foreign Commerce, followed by the resolutions of January 1794, and the non-importation act of 1806. That the United States could enforce justice on European nations by withholding or restraining its commerce in some fashion was a first principle of Jeffersonian diplomacy and of Jeffersonian Republicanism. The dependence of the European colonies in the West Indies on American provisions, especially in wartime, the importance of American neutral carriers and their cargoes of grain, naval stores, tropical produce, and raw materials for European belligerents, the enormous value of the American market, above all to British merchants and manufacturers—these factors in the transatlantic economy placed an ultimate weapon of peace in American hands which, if put to a fair test, Jefferson believed, might not only secure his own country from the ravages of European war but also demonstrate the efficacy of commercial coercion to peace-loving peoples everywhere. "I place immense value in the experiment being fully made," he said, "how far an embargo may be an effectual weapon in [the] future as well as on this occasion." But this aim, which must appear visionary to many at home and unfriendly as well to governments abroad, was held in reserve until the rescue of American property from the seas forced the acknowledgment of a rationale for the continuation of the embargo other than the one first advanced.

Yet the history of Republican ideology and statecraft, especially as exhibited in the public careers of the President and the Secretary of State, pointed to this rationale from the beginning. While they maintained official silence, the *National Intelligencer* at once expounded the general theory of the embargo in several articles which discerning readers ascribed to the Secretary. "It is singularly fortunate that an embargo, whilst it guards our essential resources," the first article stated, "will have the collateral effect of making it the interest of all nations to change the system which has driven our commerce from the ocean." Universal and impartial in its terms, the embargo offered no cause for war to any nation, though on the author's own reckoning it would prove more injurious to Britain than to her enemies. What counted, at any rate, were the injuries and the privations certain to be inflicted by this great weapon on nations abroad, not the injuries and privations at home. The latter were of small moment, the second article endeavored to show, while the third pointed to positive economic benefits, as in the liberation of the country from debilitating foreign fashions and luxuries, the growth of domestic manufactures, and the expansion of the home market. Finally, the experiment promised to secure the American people, through the virtuous practice of peace rather than the dubious glories of war, the "national character" that had so long eluded them. "Let the example teach the world that our firmness equals our moderation; that having resorted to a measure just in itself, and adequate to its object, we will flinch from no sacrifices which the honor and good of the nation demand from virtuous and faithful citizens." These articles in the administration gazette explained the embargo better than anything else published at the time. Yet they were not a substitute for a declaration by the President himself. If political and diplomatic considerations made such a declaration unwise in December, this was not the case in April or May. But even then he failed to take the nation into his confidence and to establish in public opinion the credibility of a policy no longer defensible on protective grounds. He betrayed his own principles of leadership, which underscored official openness and public trust, and contributed to the bewilderment and confusion surrounding the embargo. The field of exegesis was left to his enemies while his friends were reduced to pleading implicit faith in him.

Confidence ran high during the early months of the experiment. Jefferson put himself personally in charge of enforcing the embargo. He did not expect the task would be easy, but it proved far more difficult than he imagined at the outset. Administratively the law fell within Gallatin's jurisdiction. Although he had approved the policy with reservations, Gallatin labored like a Hercules to ensure it the fair trial he, no less than his chief, wanted. He at once discovered several deficiencies in the basic law. If the embargo was to be effective it must control the coastal trade and hold navigation within its confines; but the law levied no extraordinary penalties on ships sailing without clearance and omitted coasting vessels from the bonds—double the value of craft and cargo—exacted of ocean-going vessels. To close these loopholes Congress promptly passed the first supplementary act. A second suppplementary act, in March, laid additional penalties and, further, extended the embargo to exports by land as well as by sea. The latter provision slammed the gates on the flourishing traffic across the Canadian frontier. Six weeks later, in the waning hours of the session, Congress passed still another act, the fourth in the series of embargo laws. Again the coastal trade was the object. Collectors were empowered to search and detain vessels ostensibly bound coastwise but suspected of fraudulent trading, and the President was fully authorized to employ the navy in enforcement. This piling up of legislation, each law more severe than the last, also injured the experiment. Had the basic law been more carefully drawn, habits of evasion—hard to stop once started—might never have started, and the sense of mounting federal tyranny might have been avoided. As the mere recital of these laws suggests, the administration had the bear by the tail and could neither tame him nor let go.

Considering the dimensions of the task and the paucity of administrative means, the embargo was diligently and, on the whole, effectively enforced. It was manifestly impossible to plug all the leaks by sea and by land. Congress opened a huge leak by inserting in the second supplementary act "an insidious clause," as Jefferson labeled it, permitting anyone, with the President's approval, to send a ship for valuable property held abroad. Administering this provision Jefferson tried to maintain the integrity of the embargo while also meeting the intention of Congress. If, as was said, Jamaica owed two million dollars to New York merchants, 30 or 40 vessels would be required to settle the account in sugar and rum, whereas three or four could settle it in specie. Obviously, then, the latter course was preferred. The complexity of cases was such that Jefferson declined to formulate general rules and, instead, judged each application on its merits. Some New York merchants owned $100,000 worth of sandalwood in the Friendly Islands. The Orient was its only market.

Should they be permitted to send a ship, sell the sandalwood in the Orient, and bring home the proceeds in a return cargo, despite the legal provision barring traffic and trade in retrieved property? Yes, said Jefferson. "The bringing home of property being the main object, if it be in an impracticable form, it affects the intention of the law to let it be commuted into a practicable form." Before he called a halt to applications under the provision in August, 594 vessels had sailed to foreign ports, and many of them did not return, gladly forfeiting bond for the freedom and profits of the neutral trade.

On the coast infractions were serious from New York eastward. The most zealous of Gallatin's collectors could not always detect vessels loading secretly and sailing without clearance for foreign parts. The penalties of the supplementary acts, followed by increasing naval surveillance, reduced this leak to a trickle, however. The consul in Havana reported that in the period January 17–February 25, forty-five American flags arrived there compared with only four in a second period March 1–April 11. To be sure, American traders continued to ply the seas. Yankees reportedly landed thirty cargoes of cotton at Liverpool in the spring; and General Armstrong warned the President of Americans who came in under French colors, saying they were from the French islands when they were really from Baltimore. But this was expected and within tolerable limits. Many of the strays never returned. Some carriers jumped the embargo, of course. But the ships trading abroad at their own risk were a tiny fraction of the American marine, probably less than 5 per cent. Ingenious merchants and shipmasters quickly discovered new and, for a time, safer ways of evading the embargo. For example, ships went off without clearances or supposedly bound coastwise, and put their cargoes aboard British vessels hovering offshore, then sneaked back to the mainland or sailed to Nova Scotia or the West Indies. From these ports captains were likely to plead distress. The excuse, "blown off course," became the mariners' tiresome refrain. Jefferson's patience finally gave way under petitions of this kind. "We know that the fabrication of proofs of leaking ships, stress of weather, cargoes sold under duress, are a regular part of the system of infractions of the embargo, with the manufacture of which every foreign port is provided, and that their oaths and forgeries are a regular merchandise in every port. We must therefore consider them as nothing," he said, "and that the act of entering a foreign port and selling the cargo is decisive evidence of an intentional breach of the embargo." Most coastal merchants were loyal and law-abiding; some of them zealously supported the embargo. But Jefferson's encounters with mercantile avarice and knavery lowered still further his estimate of the class generally, especially the New Englanders.

Transactions of the market place that had been of no consequence to government suddenly assumed major importance under the embargo. As the commissar of the nation's economy, Jefferson made decisions on such trifling matter as the flour bakers used, the bread people ate. This particular question arose because of the amazing increase of flour shipments from the Middle Atlantic ports, ostensibly in the coastal trade. The President thought every seaboard city, Charleston excepted, ought to be able normally to supply itself with flour from the hinterland, even if of inferior quality to flour from the Delaware. Hence all flour cargoes were suspect. A Treasury circular to the collectors on May 6 called attention to the powers of detention they now possessed and urged their exercise on shipments of grain, flour, provisions, and so on to places where they could not be required for actual consumption. At the same time Jefferson instructed the governors of Georgia, South Carolina, Massachusetts, New Hampshire, and the Orleans territory, where local flour stocks might prove insufficient, to issue import licenses to reliable merchants directed, in turn, to the collector at the place of export. Gallatin was unhappy with this system. He did not trust all the governors; licensing risked mercantile favoritism or monopoly; and the unexpected flood of applications caused a massive administrative problem. The country, it appeared, was more specialized in its productions, more interdependent economically, than had been realized. With the extension of cotton cultivation in South Carolina and Georgia those states were substantial importers of provisions; and northern seaport towns, like Boston, imported more flour coastwise than they brought from the interior. The licensing system was relaxed within a month. Coastal shipments of flour and provisions not exceeding one-eighth of the cargo were permitted to move freely. The limitation, it was thought, would remove temptations to evasion and speculation and at the same time meet the needs of the people. "I do not wish a single citizen to be deprived of a meal of bread,"

Jefferson said, "but I set down the exercise of commerce, merely for profit, as nothing when it carries with it the danger of defeating the objects of the embargo." The licensing system remained, however, to cover emergency situations.

Massachusetts, alone of the states, seemed to be in a perpetual emergency. When Governor James Sullivan continued to issue licenses in large number, Jefferson ordered him to stop. Sullivan, the Bay State's first Republican executive, said he would, if demanded, but within three weeks the scarcity of bread would produce "mob riots and convulsions" and the enemies of the embargo would triumph. The people would then believe, as they did not now, the Federalist accusations "that the President has no confidence in the northern part of the nation, but relies on Virginia, etc., etc., etc." Jefferson reconsidered. Still suspecting the honesty of this traffic, he asked Levi Lincoln to investigate. Sullivan was a political alarmist, always in a bustle; Lincoln, cool and composed, could correctly estimate the situation in Massachusetts. The former Attorney General acknowledged that some of the imported flour had been carried out of the country but, on the whole, vindicated the Governor. The superfluity of flour for Massachusetts continued to vex the President on into the fall. It was small comfort perhaps, but of all the crimes charged against him in that quarter, he could not be accused of taking bread from the mouths of its citizens.

Another critical area for the enforcement of the embargo was the northern frontier of New York and New England. On and about Lake Champlain, in particular, a brisk smuggling trade was carried on with Canada by boat, wagon, and sled. Rising prices of potash, lumber, pork, and other articles returned exorbitant profits. By the summer, it was said in Plattsburg, "there was not a poor man in debt in the country." The Canadians encouraged the traffic and paid the Americans, in part, in proscribed English wares. The collectors, harassed and intimidated, were unable to suppress the traffic; and the second line of defense, manned by federal marshals, district attorneys, and judges, was ineffectual in the hostile environment. Here, as on the Passamaquoddy, actual shooting broke out, revenue boats were fired on, and smuggling gangs forcibly recaptured property legally seized by collectors. (There was a frontier traffic in the South as well, on the St. Mary's, but it was small by comparison.) In April, on Gallatin's advice and with cabinet approval, Jefferson issued a proclamation placing the Champlain region in a state of insurrection. The insurgents were ordered to disperse and the Governor authorized, if necessary, to call out the militia. Jefferson did not contemplate the use of the army, though he possessed the authority under the act of Congress provoked by the Burr Conspiracy. Very soon, as the situation deteriorated, Gallatin asked for and got a small force of regulars to aid in quelling the disturbance. The citizenry of the area treated the President's proclamation with contempt. Resolutions from one town called it an act of "military despotism." There was no insurrection, it was said, only violations of the law by a few desperate characters, but the law being arbitrary and wrong, the people refused to aid in its enforcement.

In the summer, the area of Oswego, on Lake Ontario, became a trouble spot. By this time, Gallatin confessed, commercial avarice and Federalist politics had combined to "baffle all our endeavors" along the northern frontier. Collectors and district attorneys wanted energy and even Republican juries declined to convict malefactors. The President himself, after the first humiliation, hesitated to risk a second proclamation of insurrection. Gallatin went to the Governor of New York, Daniel D. Tompkins, and prevailed upon him to call out the militia on his own authority, which did not require a public declaration. Tompkins doubted an insurrection actually existed at Oswego. Perhaps not in the popular sense, Jefferson conceded, but men arrayed in war-like manner against the laws, firing on public guards, and seizing confiscated property fell within the legal definition of insurrection. "I think it is so important in example to crush these audacious proceedings, and to make the offenders feel the consequences of individuals daring to oppose a law by force, that no effort should be spared to compass this object." Tompkins yielded to the President's appeal. To the two companies of New York militia, the administration added, in September, a small contingent of regulars. The situation improved, but half the army of the United States could not have put a stop to illicit trade on the wide northern frontier.

Dwelling on infractions, one is apt to lose perspective on the embargo. The mass of people everywhere obeyed the law. Indeed, Jefferson's zeal against violators stemmed as much from his concern for equitable enforcement throughout the Union as from concern for the embargo's impact abroad. A harsh law could not be maintained with justice anywhere if hundreds or thousands exploited it for personal gain in one section of the Union. Most collectors were reliable. Those who were not, commonly Federalist holdovers, resigned or were removed. With rare exceptions the federal machinery of law enforcement stood up under the ordeal. In general, public suppport of the embargo was excellent in the South, reasonably good in the Middle Atlantic states, and fair to poor east and west of the Hudson. Beginning in the spring, public morale declined in all sections and fell precipitously in the eastern states in the fall. Many factors, varying from place to place, caused this deterioration over the months but most of them may be grouped under three general headings: economic hardship and denial, partisan political opposition, and the growing sense of the failure of the experiment in its effects abroad. Running through all this was the belief that the embargo, however noble or ignoble its purposes, exacted too high a price from a free people.

The embargo struck a hard blow to the economy, but a comfortable cushion of prosperity saved the country from disaster. Most merchants and farmers had large reserves from the profits of previous years. So, too, did the federal Treasury, a whopping $17,000,000 surplus, part of which Jefferson still hoped to divert to internal improvements. Except for a few imported materials (antimony, wire, dyestuffs) the country suffered no acute shortages. Inventories were high when the embargo took effect, and omitting the banned "luxury" items from Britain, foreign goods continued to come into the country, at about half the normal rate. The prices of most articles were surprisingly stable. Many merchants covered their losses by raising prices on import goods in stock. Their maritime capital, if partially immobilized, was not seriously impaired, and may have been improved by diversion to manufactures. Domestic prices declined, of course. The southern staples, cotton and tobacco, were hardest hit, falling 40 to 50 per cent. Wholesale commodity prices, on the average, fell about 15 per cent in 1808.

The seaport cities showed the most immediate and dramatic effects of the embargo. An estimated 30,000 seamen were idled, together with longshoremen, ships' craftsmen, and other workers in maritime industry. Many seamen, British and American, signed on foreign vessels as if in mockery of Jefferson's effort to secure this national resource; but the seamen probably suffered more than any other economic group. And Massachusetts, with one-third of the nation's tonnage in foreign commerce, as well as a great fishing fleet, perhaps had more reason to complain of the embargo than any other state. Yet the loudest complainants, merchants generally, suffered little shrinkage of capital, and the stories of ships' rotting at the wharves and grass growing in the streets were embellished for political effect. Chancellor Livingston, after touring coastal New England in the winter of 1808–09, reported to Madison, "Never have I at any time witnessed more ease and comfort, more building and improvement." Livingston hardly qualified as an unbiased observer. He was pro-embargo, pro-French, and, like the host of Republican merchants, outside the British trading orbit. But he was not alone in his estimate, and if he erred on the brighter side, observers with a different bias erred on the darker side. Things were worse in New York than in Boston. In May an English observer, actually a spy sent down from Halifax, reported eighty bankruptcies, hundreds of debtors in jail, and thousands out of work. Philadelphia approved the embargo and, in fact, turned it to good account, as did some of the cities in New England, by the diversion of mercantile capital to manufactures and the exploitation of markets in the interior. Jefferson rejoiced in Philadelphia: the city exemplified that "spring" to manufactures which in the end became his solace, almost his vindication. Household manufactures sprang up everywhere in 1808; textile mills and other factories increased at a rapid rate, above all in Pennsylvania.

The economic incidence of the embargo in the vast agricultural spaces of the country, while less visible, was at least as severe and, in the South, more damaging in the long run. Farmers had no control over their prices; they could, however, withhold crops from market for a time, indeed almost indefinitely in the case of non-perishables, if sufficiently affluent. But few were affluent. An astute Vermonter described the chain of pressures in that state, the same as in most rural areas: "The staple commodities . . . are reduced to low prices, consequently money is scarce. They [the farmers] cannot remit.

The merchant delivers his account to an attorney. He sues A, B, C, etc. A, B, C, etc., curse the embargo, because they cannot sell their produce and pay their debts. And sue D, E, F, etc., indebted to them, who in turn curse the embargo and sue G, H, I, etc., who in turn curse the embargo and proceed to persecute those indebted to them in a course of eternal litiguity." Lawyers as a class, it need hardly be said, blessed the embargo. In Virginia, where debt was a chronic disease, creditors showed more leniency than elsewhere. Courts closed in some counties. The legislature, in February, revived an old relief law permitting the extension of debts for twelve months under certain conditions. Executions in federal courts continued, of course, and reports from some quarters indicate that British and urban merchants out-of-state pushed the country debtors hard. In the southern states generally, where the embargo found its best support, it also caused the most enduring economic damage. The South was the nation's leading exporter. Its destiny remained agricultural, while the North's lay in the direction of manufacturing, which the embargo promoted. Southern planters, unlike northern merchants, had enjoyed only modest profits from the neutral trade; and unlike their farming counterparts above the Potomac, they manufactured almost nothing for themselves, had a permanent labor force to keep up, and discovered no collateral sources of income, legitimate or otherwise, from the embargo. Ultra-Federalists invented the myth of a Virginia experiment to destroy eastern commerce and navigation; in fact, no other section suffered as much as the South, which seemed to be martyring itself to save the eastern carrying trade. The President himself, with many planters more opulent than he, would never recover from the blow.

While not insensitive to the distresses of the citizens, the President's cold and lofty response to petitioners for relief failed to meet the reality of their sufferings. They blasted the embargo—"O grab me" in reverse—and cursed the President. Better their petitions be addressed to London and Paris, to the enemies of mankind who had brought this grievous stringency on the nation, he replied. Every complaint, every obstruction, every unrest gave aid and comfort to the enemies and prolonged the real cause of distress. The government, at any rate, could do nothing to relieve personal hardships incident to a measure for the nation's good. Playing for higher stakes,

Jefferson hardened himself to censures often grounded, he felt, in petty profit-seeking motives. His philosophy taught him that the embargo was an easy scapegoat for virtually all the ills men suffered. Among the numerous scraps of song and verse inspired by the embargo was one that expressed his view exactly:

> There's knaves and fools and dupes and tools
>   Debas'd enough to argue
> That every ill the people feel
>   Is owing to *The Embargo*
>
>   . . .
>
> Do party men incline to pen
>   A false and foolish farr'go,
> No other theme so fruitful seem
>   As *"Jefferson's d—d Embargo"*
>
>   . . .
>
> Should Hessian Fly our wheat destroy,
>   Or granaries crowd with weevil,
> *The Embargo's* curst in language worst
>   As source of all the evil.

The second of these verses points to what Jefferson considered a still more powerful motive of complaint and opposition. His political enemies exploited the embargo for all it was worth, and it was worth a good deal, especially in New England, where Federalism had still to be reckoned with. The bulk, perhaps nine out of ten, of the ever increasing addresses and resolutions against the embargo came from that quarter of the Union. That distress should be translated into political opposition was natural; but that the assault on the law should be directed by extreme Federalists suggested a power play aimed at political revolution or something worse. Opposition on the score of hardship caused the President little pain. The problem became serious when a dangerous faction hitched a ride on these disturbances and converted them into a political engine against the Republican administration.

The embargo was a screaming partisan issue from the first—only the volume changed during its fourteen-month history. Arguments that would become hackneyed in press and assembly were heard in acrimonious debate on the supplementary legislation in Congress.

Barent Gardenier, a New York Federalist, shocked the House by the violence of his speech on the second supplementary bill in February. The proposed interdiction of land commerce bore no relationship to the alleged purposes of the original act. That "sly, cunning measure" must now be seen for what it was: an act not to protect the nation's resources but to destroy its trade. And for whose benefit? "Do not go on forging chains to fasten us to the car of the Imperial Conqueror," he declared. Cries of "order" did not deter him. "Yes, sir, I do fear that there is an unseen hand which is guiding us to the most dreadful destinies—unseen, because it cannot endure the light. Darkness and mystery overshadow this House and the whole nation. We know nothing—we are permitted to know nothing. We sit here as mere automata. . . ." Replying to Gardenier, the majority leader, George W. Campbell of Tennessee, patiently examined the causes of the embargo. One of its objects, he said, though not the principal one at the beginning, was coercion of the belligerents by a denial of American commerce, and he went on to denounce the charges of acting under French influence as "infamous, groundless falsehoods." Gardenier promptly challenged him. The two gentlemen met on the dueling ground, and the challenger barely escaped with his life. Leading Federalists also questioned the motives of military measures. The administration asked for, and got, authorization for the President to raise 6000 regulars. The request wrenched the President's principles, but he was getting used to that. This, with other measures, was all part of a two-stage policy, first to back up the persuasions of the embargo abroad, and second to prepare the nation for war should it fail. Wrong, said the Federalists: the bill secretly aimed at an army to enforce the embargo at home with bullets and bayonets. It was marvelous how their imaginings of the starry-eyed visionary faded into delusions of the dark Machiavel.

As the spring elections came on in New York and Massachusetts, the Federalists mounted the dragons of discontent in a bold bid to return to power, immediately to the state houses and just beyond to the national capital. In March the President's inveterate foe, Senator Pickering, published a blast in the form of a letter to Governor Sullivan. Had not the embargo been mandated by Napoleon? (Why else, Pickering mused privately, would the President destroy his popularity?) Why had the President secretly withheld intelligence from Paris? Had Britain done the United States any "essential injury"? Was not the embargo enacted in hostility to northern commerce? Pickering defended the British ministry against the administration, predicted national ruin from the embargo, and warned the northern states to look to their defenses. Twenty thousand copies of the pamphlet were said to have circulated in Massachusetts alone. Jefferson wrote to Lincoln with some alarm. The petty scribblings of the newspaper herd were beneath contempt, but lies were freighted with influence when they came from the pen of an honorable senator. Lincoln calmly reassured the President. The letter was regrettable but it would have little effect. "It is the comparative few that make all the noise, the desperate in politics, the desperate in property. . . . The great body of the people, all the Republicans and many Federalists, believe in the necessity of the [embargo]." Yet the Federalists, stirred by Pickering's blast, regained control of the legislature, narrowly, though Sullivan won re-election as governor. In New York, where Pickering's letter also fired up the Federalists, the Republicans scored a hard victory. Nearly all the newspapers were Federalist or Clintonian, and the latter would not defend the embargo. "At present the arguments appear to be all on the other side," a worried Republican wrote to Madison. Like many others, he wished the administration would make a public case for the embargo. So far as diplomatic documents could speak the administration had done that. Near the end of March the President sent a veritable flood of papers to Congress covering the Monroe-Pinkney negotiations, the *Chesapeake* imbroglio, and the Rose mission, just terminated in stalemate, as well as Armstrong's correspondence. Jefferson believed this mass of papers, which were published, contained the best and ablest answers to the brawlers against the embargo. Perhaps they did. Lincoln thought the publication helped to discredit Pickering and save the Republicans from disaster in Massachusetts. But diplomatic correspondence was not a substitute for executive appeal to the public understanding.

Assessing the damage from the attack, Jefferson feared, above all, its ill effects abroad. The madcap Federalists, he said in June, were playing a dangerous game without perhaps being aware of it. "They are endeavoring to convince England that we suffer more by the embargo than they do, and if they will hold out awhile, we must abandon it." Of course we must, to be followed by war if the embargo failed in its mission. "But the fact is, that if we have war with England, it will be solely produced by their maneuvers." Increasingly, Jefferson transferred the blame of failure from himself and his policy to the party that opposed both. If most Federalists knew not what they were doing, Timothy Pickering surely did. He was trying to revive the disunionist plot of 1804, drawing the eastern states into a separate confederacy under British protection. Adams, his Massachusetts colleague in the Senate, warned the President in March of British collusion in these designs. (Since the *Chesapeake* affair Adams had gravitated toward the administration, causing the Massachusetts Federalists to deprive him of his seat in 1808.) Sullivan backed this warning with hysterical predictions of a British expedition to Halifax to receive the returning eastern states. Rose carried Pickering's inflamatory pamphlet to London in the spring, where it was at once reprinted, widely read, and applauded by the ministry as evidence of the administration's collusion with France and groaning public opposition to the embargo.

By this time the experiment appeared for what it was, peaceable coercion, and the administration pretended nothing else. Everything, Jefferson said, must be subordinated to the test of this great weapon until it became more burdensome than war. Time was required for it to work on the belligerents; unfortunately, as Jefferson began to realize, every hour gained abroad was an hour lost at home. In this race he steadily tightened the screws of the enforcing machine and, against the efforts to subvert the embargo, endeavored to make it a convincing measure in foreign courts. He outlined the diplomatic strategy to Madison in March. Armstrong and Pinkney should demand revocation of the obnoxious decrees. If both belligerents complied, the United States would remain neutral. If not, they should be told, without any bullying gestures, that when the time came to drop the embargo, if either one withdrew its decrees we would war on the other, and if neither relented we would choose the enemy. The policy seemed to hinge success of the experiment with one power to war on the other—a sorry half-victory for peaceable coercion. Actually, of course, Jefferson reasoned that success with one must produce success with the other, since neither would risk American belligerency. Prompted by the administration, Congress passed resolutions in April authorizing the President to suspend the embargo against any or all belligerents. For the present then, and until Congress resumed in the fall, the duration of the embargo hung on the decrees. The ministers were at once instructed on the offer to suspend, holding out the idea of American hostilities against the power that persisted in its edicts.

In Britain, meanwhile, the embargo was just beginning to be felt. Leading Whigs and spokesmen of manufacturing and mercantile interests in the American trade—Lord Grenville, Alexander Baring, Lord Erskine, Henry Brougham, the editors of the *Edinburgh Review*, and others—launched a campaign against the orders in council. The orders formed a system, adopted under the fiction of military reprisal, to establish Britain as the grand emporium of trade with the Continent. In 1793 Britain had tried to starve the enemy into submission; now she intended to feed it by forcing the produce of the empire upon the market and making the Americans either carry it and pay the price in British ports or retire from the oceans. The government frankly conceded the monopolitic purpose. Canning's instructions to Erskine stated it, and Spencer Perceval, Chancellor of the Exchequer, summed it up when the November orders were signed: "Our orders . . . say to the enemy, 'If you will not have *our* trade, as far as we can help it you shall have *none*." The policy was ruinous, said the adversaries. Britain could not expect to command the American market, worth 12,000,000 pounds a year to her manufacturers alone, and rob the Americans of ability to pay by forcing them from the neutral trade. No respectable nation, no neutral, could submit to the monopolistic license system. American neutrality was advantageous to Britain. The produce of the West Indies found vent through it and the planters were fed by it, though in their rage against the competition of the enemy islands they had blindly turned on the Americans. Stores for the navy, cotton for the spindles, food for the people came from the United States; the trade gave employment to factory workers, artisans, and seamen; and the growing country was Britain's best customer. Even if the embargo were removed, the orders would still be ruinous, Brougham declared in Commons. For the orders, not the embargo, which were cause and effect respectively, produced the stoppage of the American trade.

Jefferson was delighted by these strictures. They were his own, and they proved him right, at least in the light of reason. He was being condemned for destroying American commerce, Canning the British, one by embargo, the other by monopoly, one sacrificing gain for peace, the other prosecuting war for profit. It was only a question of who would yield first. Unfortunately for Jefferson the forces ranged behind Canning were much more powerful than his opposition, which centered in a manufacturing interest still weak and isolated politically. The embargo threw seamen out of work, merchants out of business, farmers out of markets instantly in the United States; its impact on the British economy took time, though when it occurred it would be felt in men's stomachs as well as in their pocketbooks. Manchester manufacturers were laying off workers in March—the distress began. But in the spring and on through the summer, morale was high in Britain, the press spoke of the embargo with contempt, and the Tory ministry had nothing to fear from King or Parliament. When Congress adjourned without lifting the embargo, no change of policy or opinion occurred.

Jefferson attributed this obstinance to two factors. First, the misrepresentation of the law's effectiveness and support, together with the belief it would produce a political revolution in the United States, threw dust in the eyes of the nation. Second, the unforeseen Spanish revolt against Napoleonic domination revived British fortunes in the war and opened a vast new market, the peninsula and the Spanish colonies, to her commerce. This turn of affairs, Jefferson remarked in August, put the British "on their stilts again." The new trade more or less compensated for the loss of the old. Jefferson felt the jolt at home too. Merchants, eager to enter the race for the riches of the crumbling Spanish empire, pressed for the removal of the embargo as to that sector. He thought the request preposterous, given the objectives of the embargo and the utter confusion of Spanish affairs, knowing full well, however, the advantage conceded to the British rival. "Considering the narrow and selfish policy of the present cabinet," Madison observed, "it is possible that it may be tempted to continue its orders lest a removal of our embargo should interfere with her in the new commercial prospect. But I suspect she is still more swayed by the hopes of producing a revolution in the public counsels here, which might be followed by a coalition with her in the war."

The embargo was never intended to have the same effect in France as in Britain. An impartial measure in law, its potential for economic damage was much greater on the island empire than on the continental one. Moreover the sister measure, non-importation, applied to Britain alone. The administration's diplomacy with France turned on this differential effect of peaceable coercion. "The embargo which appears to hit France and Britain equally," Jefferson told Turreau, "is for a fact more prejudicial to the latter than the other by reason of a greater number of colonies which England possess and the infirmity in local resources." These were only two items in the comparative balance. What the Federalists interpreted as a partiality of motive and cause was, in fact, a partiality in effect produced by the very different circumstances of the belligerents. By impressing Napoleon with the strength of the American commitment to neutral rights against British pretensions, Jefferson expected two favors in return: first, the revocation of his decrees as to American trade, and second, his aid in securing the Floridas from Spain. The decrees were largely futile against the United States for the same reason that the embargo was largely futile against France: neither effectively reached the object. But the former were the pretext for the British orders; hence by their revocation Napoleon would place the United States in position to demand British repeal at the penalty of war.

Instead of snatching at this bait, Napoleon toyed with Jefferson and played games with the embargo. The Milan Decree, in retaliation against the November orders, declared every vessel going to or coming from a British port, trading under her regulations, as in effect British and lawful prize. Many American vessels fell captives of this extension of the laws of the Continental System to the sea. Armstrong learned they would be sequestered, not confiscated, pending Washington's declaration of war on Britain. This tilt at blackmail was followed in April by the Bayonne Decree. American flags entering Continental ports were seized on the pretext that, in view of the embargo, they must be British in disguise. The American loss ran to $10,000,000. Napoleon said he was simply helping Jefferson enforce the embargo! Mocking Jefferson's system, believing American commerce hopelessly entangled with the British, and American pacificism incorrigible, the Emperor would not abate any part of his own system. "This is no doubt madness," Armstrong wrote, "and what is worse it is . . . incurable." Once again he advised the United States to take its interests into its own hands, beginning with the seizure of the Floridas. No one could be sure from one moment to the next who was the protector of the Floridas in 1808. Jefferson's first concern, as always, was to prevent the Floridas from falling to either major power, and near the end of the year he let it be known to officials in Cuba and Mexico that the United States was "extremely unwilling" that either of these colonies should pass into the hands of Britain or France. This was the germ of the "no transfer" principle of the Monroe Doctrine fifteen years later.

The spectacle of both belligerents cynically trampling on American rights, neither consenting to be "played off" against the other in Jefferson's neutral game, led him to embark on diplomatic relations with Russia. Alexander's reputation for liberalism impressed the President. His hostility to British maritime pretensions, his commitment to neutral rights and freedom of the seas, and the superficial resemblances between his empire and the American, convinced Jefferson that Russia was "the most cordially friendly to us of any power on earth." He was pleased in 1804 when the Emperor, who reciprocated these feelings, invited a correspondence. An exchange ensued. In 1806 Alexander presented Jefferson with a bust of himself, and he, in return, endeavored to satisfy the Emperor's curiosity about the government of the United States. Pacific nations, he said, looked to Alexander's influence to secure their rights when peace finally came to Europe. In addition to neutral rights, Jefferson suggested that the treaty of peace make provision for collective economic sanctions against aggressor nations. In 1808, when there were persistent rumors of an Austrian mediated peace, he grew more anxious for Alexander's patronage of principles abandoned by every other sovereign, including the French Emperor. So he decided to send William Short on a secret mission as minister plenipotentiary to St. Petersburg. The chief object, he told Short, was "to avail ourselves of the Emperor's marked dispositions of friendly regard for us, whenever a treaty of peace shall be on the tapis, and to engage him to patronize our interests there, so as the benefit of the maritime rights which shall then be settled, may be extended to us, and nothing plotted to sacrifice us by France or England, neither of which wish us success." Short sailed in September. Not until the following February, in his last official communication to Congress, did Jefferson present his name to the Senate. Secrecy had been called for, in large part, because of apprehensions that neither Short nor the mission would be approved. The apprehensions proved correct. The Senate rejected the nomination of Short and then, on Madison's authority, that of J. Q. Adams, though Adams was later approved; and in 1810 the Emperor sent a minister to the United States. Diplomatic relations between the two countries thus began as a sidewind of embargo diplomacy. Jefferson's purpose was perfectly clear but his confidence in the Emperor of Russia proved delusory.

During the early summer the President was guardedly optimistic about his "last appeal to the reason and reputation of nations." The mass of Americans regardless of section, interest, or party supported the embargo, and but for the criminal rage of Tory Federalists, "subjects for a mad-house," all would be well. The irksome business of enforcing the law claimed nearly all the President's energies. The embargo was the government—government was the embargo. Defense preparations suffered except as they related to current operations. Always on the lookout for new and unconventional weapons of coastal defense, the President took an interest in Robert Fulton's torpedo. The French and British had passed up this invention, and Smith was skeptical, but Jefferson ordered the Navy Department to co-operate with Fulton in a demonstration finally performed at Kalorama, Barlow's Washington residence, the succeeding February. The threat of Indian warfare in the Illinois country, very alarming a year ago, had receded. Jefferson concluded that the agitation of the Shawnee chief Tecumseh and his brother the Prophet turned not on hostile alliance with the British, as earlier feared, but on the rejection of advancing civilization and reversion to "the ancient habits, customs and superstitions of their fathers." It was only a transient delusion, Jefferson said, and he continued to press his policy of land cessions followed by "intercourse, civilization, and incorporation." The Indians above the Ohio ceded their lands by the millions of acres but got precious little "civilization" in return. The negative half of Jefferson's policy succeeded brilliantly; the positive half failed from administrative and, more fundamentally, moral inadequacy. Demoralization and the reviving primitivism of Tecumseh and the Prophet were the upshot in the Northwest. Jefferson was right: their system could not prevail. But neither could his. The program red men spurned white men would not support. West of the Mississippi, control, not civilization, was the policy. The President was delighted by John Jacob Astor's formation of the American Fur Company to trap and trade on the far Missouri. Jefferson promised "every reasonable patronage" of the government. American merchants, taking possession of this trade, would exclude foreigners who poisoned the minds of the Indians against us, Jefferson said, and their factories would have the same effect as so many armies.

On the 4th of July the President set the style for the nation by appearing at his noon reception in a suit of homespun. His guests on that occasion could view the great collection of bones recently brought from Big Bone Lick on the Ohio and displayed in the "mammoth room." Several days later Caspar Wistar came down to study the collection and take back to the American Philosophical Society the parts necessary to complete the specimen he was mounting. Jefferson shipped the remainder to the National Institute in Paris, then set out for home. Monticello, during August and September, offered no refuge from the toils of the embargo. Petitioners cried out for suspension and relief, so many that Jefferson had a standard printed reply prepared; and every mail brought venomous productions directed at him personally, some ribald:

> Thomas Jefferson
> You are the damdest
>   fool that God put
>   life into
>   God damn you.

and some threatening:

> I have agreed to pay four of my friends $400 to shoot you if you don't take off the embargo by the 10th of October. . . .

Libelous verse filled the columns of the Federalist press. Among the most elaborate of these productions was "The Embargo" by a youthful prodigy of thirteen, William Cullen Bryant.

> Go, wretch, resign the president's chair,
> Disclose secret measures foul or fair,
> Go, search with curious eye, for horned frogs,
> 'Mongst the wild wastes of Louisiana bogs;
> Or where Ohio rolls his turbid stream,
> Dig for huge bones, thy glory and thy theme.
> Go sean, philosophist, thy . . . charms,
> And sink supinely in her sable arms;
> But quit to abler hands the helm of state,
> Nor image ruin on the country's fate.

Jefferson continued to trace the vehemently personal attack to the desperation of an opposition bereft of principles. "Lamentations and invective were all that remained to them. . . . I became of course the butt of everything which reason, ridicule, malice and falsehood could supply. They have concentrated all their hatred on me, till they have really persuaded themselves that I am the sole source of all their imaginary evils."

The libels and lampoons, while painful, had no weight with him politically; the waywardness of respectable Republicans, on the other hand, gave cause for concern. One of the first danger signals came from the judiciary. On the circuit bench in South Carolina, Justice William Johnson, a political associate who had been Jefferson's first appointment to the Supreme Court in 1804, issued a writ of mandamus to the collector at Charleston obliging him to clear a vessel detained under regulations of the executive for the enforcement of the Fourth Embargo Act. That the President and the Secretary of Treasury could prescribe uniform rules for the collectors in the execution of an act of Congress seemed reasonable, but Johnson ruled that the whole discretion to detain a suspicious vessel lay with the collector. The decision amazed Jefferson, especially in view of its source, and on the opinion of the Attorney General sustaining the executive authority, he directed the collectors to conduct themselves as before. Federalists screamed "executive usurpation" and "subservience of the judiciary." On Jefferson's theory, of course, the President was not bound to obey every judicial mandate, and certainly not one where a court's own authority was doubtful (Rodney denied the circuit court's right to issue writs of mandamus) and where a single opinion, if allowed to prevail, would bring down a whole system of legislation. Collectors continued to be harassed with suits, mostly private, in state courts. Surprisingly, in the only test of constitutionality in a federal court, the Massachusetts district bench emphatically upheld the embargo as a proper exercise of the congressional power to regulate commerce. Ironically, the judge, John Davis, was a firm Federalist. The Federalist doctrine of loose construction thus came to the aid of a measure Jefferson would have found difficulty defending on the constitutional doctrine he took into office.

Rising opposition to the embargo frightened the party cadre in New York and New England. Their first commitment was to office, not to policy, and they would sacrifice the President before they would sacrifice their standing at the polls. Sullivan warned of the turn things were taking. "These men consider the embargo as operating very forcibly to the subversion of the Republican interest," he said. And should the measure continue much longer without decisive effect abroad, it would surely sink all the Republicans east of the Delaware. Gallatin was of the same opinion. New England would be Federalized—the Essex Junto mounted for disunion—probably New York and New Jersey, possibly even Pennsylvania. Casting the odds in August, he feared the presidential contest was lost.

The Secretary was tired and sore. Despite all his efforts the frauds of the embargo persisted. "The consciousness of having done what was right in itself is doubtless sufficient," he wrote gloomily, "but for the inefficacy of the measure on the Lakes and to the northward there is no consolation, and that circumstance alone is the strongest argument that can be brought against the measure itself." Yet he did not despair. Barring redress abroad, the embargo must be continued with means of enforcement equal to the ends of the measure itself. Two things were essential, he told his chief: first, not a single vessel should be permitted to move without the permission of the executive; and second, collectors should be empowered to seize property anywhere, not just along the frontiers, without liability to personal suit and with the assistance of military force. "I am sensible that such arbitrary powers are equally dangerous and odious," he said. But they had been made necessary by Federalist incitement to evasion and the natural selfishness incited by a system so far above the common understanding as to render ordinary patriotism of little account.

Jefferson himself, so deeply committed to the policy he could not entertain the thought of abandoning it, entered fully into Gallatin's resolution to put the embargo to the test of force. He must have sometimes recalled his experience in the Virginia governorship, when he had been called to account for jeopardizing the safety of the commonwealth by feeble and temporizing measures. In this crisis he would not run the same risks. "The embargo law is certainly the most embarrassing one we have ever had to execute," he replied cheerlessly to Gallatin. "I did not expect a crop of so sudden and rank growth of fraud and opposition by force could have grown up in the United States. I am satisfied with you that if the orders and decrees are not repealed, and a continuance of the embargo is preferred to war (which sentiment is universal here), Congress should legalize all *means* which may be necessary to obtain its *end*." No one could dissent from the general proposition that the means, if legitimate, should be equal to the end. As Jefferson said on another occasion, it is the responsibility of the executive to do whatever he can to save the public the benefit of the law. "Its intention is the important thing: the means of attaining it quite subordinate." Yet a measure like the embargo, which would strain the capacities of an authoritarian government, could not long co-exist with the ends of a free one. The main question was not whether it was being enforced. Obviously it was, otherwise there would not have been such a hue and cry against it; and doubtlessly enforcement powers could be strengthened. But was the end of coercion abroad any longer supportable in the face of increasing deprivation, loss of liberties, alienation of opinion, division of the Union, and Republican collapse at home? How much was it worth to the American people to discover another arbiter than war among nations? How far could the experiment in peaceable coercion be carried against the dynamics of American freedom? How long could the nation endure an experiment submitted to the sufferance of foreign powers? These questions transcended the relationship of means to ends and weighed different ends themselves in the balance.

Jefferson was not oblivious to these considerations. He took it as axiomatic that at some point the embargo would become more costly than war. No other alternative was available. He had committed the nation to a system from which there could be no honorable escape but war. Yet, on the premises of the system itself, war was the great behemoth of evil; and to concede now, after so much sacrifice for peace, that the American people could no more avoid war than the common run of humanity was to concede his best hopes not only for his own country but for the rule of reason and enlightenment among nations. Other more immediately practical questions had to be asked. War with whom? With what honor could the United States align itself with either of the tyrant nations of Europe? With what risks of danger from the other? And at what costs to unity and sanity at home? Weighing the alternatives, Jefferson unhesitatingly stuck with the embargo. The experiment was not yet desperate. All reports spoke of squirming and suffering in Britain. Bonaparte had his hands full in Spain. Peace might suddenly return to Europe. A little more patience, more strength of means, more loyalty to government, more tolerance of trifling sacrifices in the interest of great ends, he reasoned, would lead to success.

Nothing happened to change Jefferson's opinion between his return to Washington in October and the meeting of Congress on November 7. First the *St. Michael* and then the *Hope* brought dispatches from Britain. Pinkney urged the government to persevere in its course. Repeal of the embargo would be fatal. Britain would never tolerate the rivalry of our neutral trade, and war would only open "a new career in vassalage and meanness." "The embargo, and the loss of our trade, are deeply felt here, and will be felt with more severity every day," the minister advised. "The wheat harvest is likely to be alarmingly short, and the state of the continent will augment the evil. The discontents among their manufacturers are only quieted for the moment from temporary causes. Cotton is rising, and will soon be scarce. Unfavorable events on the continent will subdue the temper, unfriendly to wisdom and justice, which now prevails." But this temper, as expressed in Canning's communications of September 23 to Pinkney, showed no disposition to reform. Responding to the proposition to suspend the embargo, Canning evaded the issue in an idle parade of insult and recrimination. Since the November orders had not been known in Washington when the President moved the embargo, their repeal could not be linked to the suspension of that measure. It was "manifestly unjust" to Britain and came to the aid of the Continental System at a critical hour. Alluding to conversations between the two, Canning treated Pinkney's offer to suspend as "unauthorized," as something advanced privately but not on the instructions of government, and therefore requiring nothing official from him. With this ruse he dismissed embargo repeal, persisted in the policy of commercial warfare, and left Jefferson to get out of the scrape as best he could. The tone as well as the substance of Canning's letters distressed the President. They were "written in the high ropes," he told Erskine, and when known "would be stinging to every American breast." He included one of them in the foreign correspondence sent to Congress at the time of the annual message; the other, on the offer to suspend, was held back pending Pinkney's vindication.

The message reported the unhappy outcome of the overture to Britain and the silence of France on the similar overture to her. Considering that each government had pledged to withdraw retaliatory decrees on the action of the other, it was "reasonably expected that the occasion would have been seized by both for evincing the sincerity of their profession, and for restoring to the commerce of the United States its legitimate freedom." But the appeal to justice had fared no better under peaceable coercion than before. What was to be done? In cabinet discussions prior to the meeting of Congress, none of the secretaries had a new policy to suggest, except Smith who would call home the ministers and prepare for war against both powers, and he stood alone in this opinion. All agreed the embargo should not be continued much longer; but when it should be taken off, under what formula, and with what replacement—minds boggled at these questions. Federalists trooped into Congress, backed by new electoral victories in the eastern states, demanding immediate repeal and careless of the consequences. Some of Jefferson's Republican friends sought to prepare his mind for acceptance of the inevitable. Nicholas, for example, tried to switch the train of Jefferson's thought from the rightness of the measure to the reality of failure. The experiment had been fairly tried. Its defeat because of unforeseen events abroad and misconduct in one section of the Union was no reproach to the President. He should get clear of the tottering system as fast as possible in order to control the alternative, which otherwise would be forced on the government by a desperate opposition. Jefferson's popularity was identified with the national welfare, Nicholas said; hence the burden of leadership rested squarely on his shoulders. The implication, apparently, was that Madison's shoulders were not big enough. Jefferson did not like the implication or respond to the plea. On the contrary, he virtually surrendered his leadership when the electoral result became known in November. Madison won handily over the Federalist candidate C. C. Pinckney—122 to 47 in the final tally of electoral votes. The result marked a decline in Republican strength, but it was far from the disaster many had predicted, and viewed as a referendum on the embargo genuinely encouraging to the President.

The President's message spoke of failure but offered no suggestion for recovery. It belonged to Congress to "weigh and compare the painful alternatives out of which a choice is to be made." In his own mind, though he did not disclose it to Congress, the alternatives were submission, war, and embargo for another six months if necessary. The first was out of the question, the second painful in the extreme and the last thing wanted, unless against France, by the vociferous enemies of the embargo. After surveying the state of the national defenses, he called Congress to fix its attention "unremittingly" on "the safety of our country." The message was grim. But Jefferson introduced several cheerful notes. Retirement of the debt continued. During seven and one-half years over $33,000,000 of funded debt had been extinguished, liberating the treasury of $2,000,000 annual interest. Jefferson was understandably proud of this achievement, though it had not come about by way of economy in operating expenses, which had risen, and owed less to Gallatin's fiscal management than to the bonanza of European war. Defense now laid first claim on the surplus, yet Jefferson again asked Congress to inaugurate "a system of improvement." He congratulated the country on the conversion of industry and capital from foreign commerce and navigation to domestic manufactures, and expressed confidence that these establishments formed behind the protective wall of the embargo would become permanent. The passage was bolder as originally written. But Gallatin had objected to the suggestion of positive benefit to the nation from the annihilation of foreign commerce. Even as amended, Jefferson's encomium on manufactures fed the jealousies and fears of commercial interests already convinced the embargo aimed at their destruction; and the same anxieties were now felt by spokesmen of the agricultural interest. From Virginia, where Federalists and Quids had never accepted the embargo, John Taylor, one of the latter, read Jefferson a lecture on the rise of a "tyrannical manufacturing interest" that threatened to plunder the farmers as Hamilton's paper and stock interest had done in the past. Taylor was prophetic. In time Jefferson would understand the merits, if not the validity, of his fears.

But Jefferson's conspectus of the state of the Union in 1808 foreshadowed a significant revision of the principles of his political economy. Instead of the old reliance on agriculture with commerce as its handmaid, looking to an expansive foreign trade, he now spoke of "a due balance between agriculture, manufactures and commerce," focusing on the home market. The opposition of the commercial interest was, indeed, wonderful. The carrying trade had kept the nation in "hot water" from the beginning until the embargo, the very measure complained of, was undertaken to protect it. "Their doctrine goes to the sacrificing agriculture and manufactures to commerce," Jefferson wrote privately, "to the calling all our people from the interior country into a city of Amsterdam." The embargo had rescued the United States from this delusion, negatively by disclosing its costs, positively by disclosing the undeveloped potential of the national economy. Neither navigation nor agriculture had anything to fear from the rise of manufactures. All would benefit by the shift from the primacy of external to the primacy of internal trade. "My idea is that we should encourage home manufactures to the extent of our own consumptions of everything of which we raise the raw materials. . . . Our agriculture will still afford surplus produce enough to employ a due proportion of navigation."

Throwing the embargo into the hornets' nest on Capitol Hill was an act of supreme folly. Gallatin and Madison, whose own indecision contributed to the act, soon realized the error and begged the President to point out a "precise and distinct course" to Congress. You must, Gallatin said, "decide the question absolutely." But Jefferson declined. "On this occasion," he had already stated, "I think it is fair to leave to those who are to act on them, the decisions they prefer, being . . . myself but a spectator." Madison and Gallatin, the latter slated for Secretary of State, were the principal executors. And they did, on the President's retreat from responsibility, endeavor to lay out a path for Congress; but lacking Jefferson's prestige, uncertain what the path should be, and timid to pursue it when known, the executors lost control of the options to a leaderless herd of the demoralized, the faint-hearted, and the disgusted. Jefferson's policy was what it had always been: embargo or war, the latter to be determined, and the enemy chosen, when the former could no longer be borne, allowing perhaps another six months to the trial. The election, the testimony of support from three-quarters of the Union, strengthened enforcement of the embargo, the manifest fairness of the government's dealings with France and Britain as disclosed in diplomatic correspondence read by the entire nation, Bonaparte's reascendancy in Spain which, if it did not put him on better terms, would compel Britain to be more accommodating—these events sustained his fantastic expectations of public endurance which would allow him to go out of office without a humiliating reversal of policy.

"A great confusion and perplexity reign in Congress," Gallatin observed. Despite the avalanche of petitions against the embargo, the House refused to debate a motion for its repeal, and the Senate defeated such a motion by the same margin, 25 to 6, as was recorded on the passage of the measure a year before. While senators pummeled their colleagues with tiresome arguments, a committee under Giles's chairmanship drafted the fifth and last of the embargo laws, the Enforcing Act. Tailored to Gallatin's specific request, in accordance with the determination to legalize "all means to the end," Giles's bill drastically raised the bonds on coastal traders, gave collectors a free hand to seize suspicious property anywhere, and authorized the President to employ the army, navy, and militia to enforce the embargo laws. Republicans discovered legal precedents for these provisions. Yet some of them clearly violated guarantees of

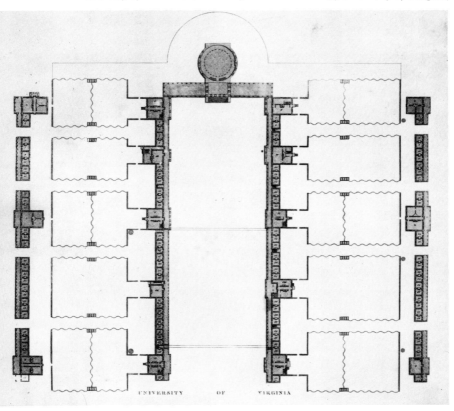

Plan of the University of Virginia. Engraving by Peter Maverick from a drawing by Jefferson in 1822.

The University of Virginia. Engraving by B. Tanner, 1827.

Jefferson at eighty-two. Plaster life mask by John H. I. Browere, 1825.

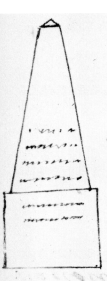

could the dead feel any interest in Monu-ments or other remembrances of them, when, as Anacreon says: Ολιγη δε κεισομεσθα
Κονις, οςεων λυθεντων
the following would be to my Manes the most gratifying.

On the grave a plain die or cube of 3.f without any mouldings, surmounted by an Obelisk of 6.f. height, each of a single stone: on the faces of the Obelisk the following inscription, & not a word more

Here was buried
Thomas Jefferson
Author of the Declaration of American Independance
of the Statute of Virginia for religious freedom
& Father of the University of Virginia.'

because by these, as testimonials that I have lived, I wish most to be remembered. ~~to be~~ to be of the coarse stone of which my columns are made, that no one might be tempted hereafter to destroy it for the value of the materials.

my bust by Ciracchi, with the pedestal and truncated column on which it stands, might be given to the University if they would place it in the Dome room of the Rotunda.

on the Die, of the Obelisk, might be engraved
Born apr. 2. 1743. O.S.
Died ——   ,

Jefferson's design and inscription for his tombstone.

Monticello, west front, after Jefferson's death. Engraving after a
painting by George Cooke.

personal liberty (the searches and seizures clause of the Fourth Amendment, for instance) and, over-all, so vast was the concentration of power in the President and in minor functionaries, the measure mocked every principle Jefferson held except the one principle, that of the embargo itself, which he believed the crisis of affairs had made a national imperative. The bill passed the Senate on the usual party division; the House stiffened the measure and approved it, 71 to 32. If Congress represented the will of the people, no more decisive test of public support for the embargo was ever recorded.

It was a hollow victory, however. Public support nationally had never been in question; the politically manipulated opposition in the Northeast, especially in Massachusetts, was the critical problem. Now, in January, the Enforcing Act hurried Massachusetts to the brink of resistance and, possibly, disunion. Pickering and associates grew bold. Warned ten months earlier by Adams of this brewing conspiracy, repeatedly alarmed by Sullivan, Jefferson said it was now believed the Bay State legislature just coming into session would call a convention and propose the separation of the New England states. The *New England Palladium*, in Boston, spiced the discontents with the publication of the Canning to Pinkney letter Jefferson had withheld from Congress. The insinuation of government duplicity and the sarcastic tone of the British minister delighted the ultraists, while the publication itself suggested the complicity of the Essex Junto in the policy of a foreign power against their own government. No Federalist congressman undertook to defend the publication and one of them, the Marylander Francis Scott Key, roundly denounced this "direct and insidious attempt of a foreign government to take advantage of and influence the parties of this country." But the spirit of revolt in Massachusetts rose higher. Collectors resigned before the wrath of an angry public. Newspapers and handbills portrayed the President as a tyrant—worse than George III in 1776—and called for open resistance. "Nerve your arms with vengeance against the despot who would wrest the inestimable germ of independence from you, and you shall be conquerors. Give ear no longer to the siren voice of democracy and Jeffersonian liberty. It is a cursed delusion, adopted by traitors, and recommended by sycophants." All along the coast town meetings passed defiant resolutions in an awesome display of grassroots democracy that impressed Jefferson even as he reeled under its blows. Early in February the Bay State legislature, while not calling a convention, adopted a report directing Congress to repeal the embargo forthwith, resume trade with Britain, and "unfurl the republican banner against the imperial standard" of Bonaparte. It further declared the Enforcing Act "unconstitutional, and not legally binding." The Connecticut legislature followed this action by declaring the state's non-compliance with the "unconstitutional and despotic acts" of the federal government.

In Congress, meanwhile, the administration forces tried to ride out the storm. On January 20 the House passed a resolution calling for a special session of the new Congress on the fourth Monday of May. In the course of debate a caustic young Massachusetts representative, Josiah Quincy, arraigned the President for imposture and deceit and declared the administration so patently spineless it could not be kicked into war. Yet Quincy opposed war; *laissez faire*, including submission to Britain, was his policy, as it was Randolph's. The Republican majority held firm and the resolution passed 80 to 26. The implicit assumption, as Jefferson explained to his son-in-law in Virginia, was that Congress would lift the embargo in June, if it had not done its work by then, and letters of marque and reprisal would at once issue against either or both belligerents as the preliminary to hostilities. This was satisfactory to him, and he hoped it would quiet discontents to the eastward. Nicholas made the next move: a resolution declaring that beyond a certain date, to be supplied, the embargo would be repealed, navigation resumed, and also defended by marque and reprisal against nations persisting in their decrees. Nicholas moved to fill the blank with June 1.

But now the New England Republicans bolted. Joined by Clintonians, Randolphians, and assorted Republicans frightened by war, disunion, and loss of office, they defeated the administration repeal date, 73 to 40, then approved with three additional votes the substitution of March 4. This revolution would not have occurred but for the fumbling and tardiness of the administration. The plan embodied in the Nicholas resolution would surely have passed earlier in the session; brought forward after nearly three months of tearing dissension in Congress and explosion in Massachusetts, it was too late. The troubles in the East, Jefferson said, communicated "a kind of panic" to several representatives from that quarter and produced "this sudden and unaccountable revolution of opinion." In the retrospect of eighteen months he was more specific: "I ascribe all this to one pseudo-Republican, Story. He came on . . . and stayed only a few days; long enough, however, to get complete hold of Bacon, who giving in to his representations became panic struck, and communicated his panic to his colleagues, and they to a majority of the sound members of Congress. They believed in the alternative of repeal or civil war, and produced the fatal measure of repeal." Whether the shame or the glory of embargo repeal belonged primarily to Joseph Story or to his Massachusetts colleague Ezekiel Bacon —Story gave the credit to Bacon—is of no importance, but they were the exciting force. Until January no sounder Republicans sat in the House. Young Story, who came on just before Christmas in replacement of Crowninshield for the Salem district, at first stood out against repeal, defended the Enforcing Act, and deplored the seditious tactics of the Essex Junto, which he held responsible for British obstinacy. He voted for the June session but then became convinced that the embargo would have to be sacrificed to allay the dangerous spirit of rebellion and disunionism in New England. Nicholas, Campbell, and other administration leaders pressed him to stick with them. "In the course of these consultations," Story later recalled, "I learned the whole policy of Mr. Jefferson; and was surprised as well as grieved to find, that in the face of the clearest proofs of the failure of his plan, he continued to hope against facts. . . . The very eagerness with which the repeal was supported by a majority of the Republican party ought to have taught Mr. Jefferson that it was already considered by them as a miserable and mischievous failure."

The only honorable alternative to repeal, the administration held, was war. But the·anti-war party outnumbered the anti-embargo party. And instant war was out of the question. Desperate to salvage a policy of some kind, the administration fell back on the plan of non-intercourse first broached in November. As finally passed near the end of February, the Non-Intercourse Act reopened trade with all countries except Britain and France, and authorized the President to resume trade with either of them upon the repeal of the offensive edicts. A provision directing marque and reprisal against the refractory nation was stricken by the House—a final crushing defeat for the administration. The new policy exposed the country to all the risks of war without any of the coercive benefits of the old. Its saving grace, its only excuse, was profit. No one doubted that the belligerents would get everything wanted from the United States via indirect or covert channels and that British goods would be smuggled wholesale into the country. The United States would indeed become "a city of Amsterdam, a mere headquarters for carrying on the commerce of all nations," and a city of smugglers besides. "Thus were we driven," Jefferson sadly concluded, "from the high and wise ground we had taken, and which, had it been held, would have either restored us our free trade or have established manufactures among us."

To the end of his days Jefferson believed that the embargo, if endured a little longer, would have forced justice from Britain and thus put a stop to the long train of degradation that finally terminated, ingloriously, in the War of 1812. The case was a hard one, he conceded. At any other time, with any other nations, the fairness and liberality of the American effort would have won respect, but the hurricane then blasting the world—the twin furies of the "tyrant of the ocean" and "the scourge of the land"—prostrated all principles of reason and right. "All those calculations which, at any other period, would have been deemed honorable, of the existence of a moral sense in man, individually or associated, of the connection which the laws of nature have established between his duties and his interests, of a regard for honest fame and the esteem of our fellow men, have been a matter of reproach to us, as evidences of imbecility. As if it could be folly for an honest man to suppose that others could be honest also, when it is in their interest to be so. And when is this state of things to end?" For Jefferson, the hopes of the Enlightenment, of a new nation, even a world, conceived in its spirit, were wrapped up in the experiment of peaceable coercion. Hence its defeat, his defeat, was more than personal or political or diplomatic; it was a moral defeat as well, and the whole revolutionary edifice of peace and benevolence, reason and law, and freedom of intercourse among nations was involved in the destruction. The New Englanders were only the agents of this disaster. The experiment was undertaken because of the mania of Europe, above all because of Britain's inveterate hostility to the nation wrenched from her loins in revolution; and Britain crushed the experiment, not because her survival demanded it but for commercial monopoly and profit, and not from her intrinsic power but from the persistent colonial subserviency of the new nation. All his life, it seemed, he had been combating the "mother country," and now he and the embargo were going out together—poignant testimony to the nation's untransacted destiny. "The proof she exhibited on that occasion," Jefferson confessed some months later, "that she can exercise such an influence in this country as to control the will of its government and three-fourths of its people, and oblige the three-fourths to submit to one-fourth, is to me the most mortifying circumstance that has occurred since the establishment of our government."

Justifying the embargo to himself, Jefferson closed his eyes to the faults of the policy. Perseverance for six months might very well have brought Britain to her knees. The American minister, Pinkney, fervently shared this conviction. Riots in Manchester, disorders in the countryside, the sufferings of workers, artisans, and West Indian slaves, rising food prices, shortages of raw materials, shrinkage of mercantile income, the damaging loss of the Amercian market—a nation at war could bear great hardships for a time and government could risk the consequences; but the limits of endurance were breached in the early months of 1809, and the ministry did, in fact, relax its orders in April partly because of the embargo's impact, though not until after its repeal became known. This consideration lost its force, however, when weighed in the balance with the mounting discords, casualties, and sufferings of the embargo at home. The nation plunged from unparalleled prosperity into an economic decline from which it would not fully recover for a quarter of a century. And despite Jefferson's plea in the name of manufactures, there were no solidly redeeming economic rewards of the policy. The political damage reckoned in Republican losses and Federalist revival, in torn morale and shrinkage of principle as well as of votes, in subversive plots and disunionism, and the shock to Jefferson's hopes of harmony and reconciliation—these injuries were also incalculable. It was a tribute to the President's power and the trust he inspired that the people endured the embargo for so long and would, in fact, have endured it longer but for the revolt in one quarter of the Union.

But to have contained the rising discontents in 1809 would have required more force and energy than the American government could command and more obedience than a free and enterprising people could give. They had gone a long way with Jefferson's project to prove a principle they never fully understood, in part because he never fully explained it. Patriotism beyond the ordinary degree was required, but the motives of loyalty and sacrifice available to a nation at war were not so readily enlisted or maintained for a hard experiment in the ways of peace. When it appeared to exact more from them than from the intended victims many lost heart while others turned on the government in savage rage. It was the "failure of nerve" among the Republicans, more than the opposition of the Federalists, that defeated the embargo. Jefferson, for all the freight of idealism, had always steered a close-reefed political craft. The voyage of the embargo was under full sail, and the helmsman's single-minded commitment to the principle, with the rational hope it embodied, obscured his view of the navigational hazards. They were false, mere phantasms, in his vision of the truth; but they were, in fact, very real, and as such demanded recognition from a government he had himself made responsive to the popular will and from a federal union that, on his own principle, exacted compromise as the price of existence. Not only politically but diplomatically as well he had allowed himself to become the captive of a policy. When it failed, when the European powers refused to play his neutral game, when foreign events turned up nothing favorable to American aims, when commercial coercion was treated as a "paper tiger," Jefferson had no retreat but to war—the last of all evils—a war he might have had but did not want in 1807 and which neither he nor his executors nor the Congress had the courage to undertake in 1809. The result was drift. His popularity, though shaken, remained high during his last months in office. He might have controlled the sequel, but considering himself a "lame-duck," choosing not to meddle, policy was surrendered to the turbulence in Congress; and not until Andrew Jackson would a President regain control of the reins of government.

A deluge of addresses, all congratulatory, many championing the doomed embargo, poured in upon the President as the hour of retirement neared. They came from Republican meetings, from state legislatures, municipal bodies, colleges, military units, churches and religious associations, and associations of all kinds. The words of the prophet, "Every man has sat under his own vine and under his fig tree, and none to make him afraid," ran like a theme through the encomium. And whatever the errors or failures of his presidency, the public seemed to say, they arose from nothing vicious but from the virtuous heart of a statesman who repelled the Machiavellian teachings of "how not to be good." The "affectionate farewell" of the Virginia General Assembly, penned by William Wirt, was especially eloquent:

> We have to thank you for the model of an administration conducted on the purest principles of republicanism; for pomp and state laid aside; patronage discarded; internal taxes abolished; a host of superfluous offices disbanded; the monarchic maxim "that a national debt is a national blessing" renounced, and more than thirty-three millions of our debt discharged; the native right to nearly one hundred millions of acres of our national domain extinguished; and without the guilts or calamities of conquest, a vast and fertile region added to our Country, far more extensive than the original possessions, bringing along with it the Mississippi and the port of Orleans, the trade of the West to the Pacific Ocean, and in the intrinsic value of the land itself, a source of permanent and almost inexhaustible revenue. These are points in your administration, which the historian will not fail to seize, to expound and teach posterity to dwell upon with delight. Nor will he forget our peace with the civilized world, preserved through a season of uncommon difficulty and trial, the good will cultivated with the unfortunate aborigines of our Country, and the civilization humanely extended among them; the lesson taught the inhabitants of the coast of Barbary, that we have the means of chastising their piratical encroachments and awing them into justice; and that theme on which, above all others, the historic genius will hang with rapture, the liberty of speech and of press preserved inviolate, without which genius and science are given to man in vain.

Jefferson answered these numerous addresses with flourishes to freedom, union, and peace—and a pang of regret that the dragons still breathed. To the citizens of Washington he offered a somewhat anxious reaffirmation of the revolutionary faith declared in 1776 and embellished in 1789:

> Trusted with the destinies of this solitary republic of the world, the only monument of human rights, and the sole depository of the sacred fire of freedom and self-government from hence it is to be lighted up in other regions of the earth, if other regions of the earth shall ever become susceptible to its benign influence, all mankind ought then, with us, to rejoice in its prosperous, and sympathize in its adverse fortunes, as involving everything dear to man. And to what sacrifices of interest or convenience ought not these considerations to animate us, and to what compromises of opinion and inclination, to maintain harmony and union among ourselves, and to preserve from all danger this hallowed ark of human hope and happiness.

Madison asked Jefferson to ride with him in his carriage to the inauguration, but he declined, saying all the honors of the day belonged to him. The retiring President rode up Pennsylvania Avenue on horseback, unattended, hitched his steed to the paling, and went into the Capitol with the rest of the procession. "This day I return to the people and my proper seat is among them." He dined with but a solitary guest, his young grandson Jeff, and that night attended the Inaugural Ball. "Am I too early?" he asked a friend when he found himself among the first arrivals. "You must tell me how to behave, for it is more than forty years since I have been to a ball." With what deliverance he had looked forward to this day is suggested by a letter he wrote to Dupont. "Never did a prisoner, released from his chains, feel such relief as I shall on shaking off the shackles of power," he said. "Nature intended me for the tranquil pursuits of science, by rendering them my supreme delight. But the enormities of the time in which I have lived, have forced me to take a part in resisting them, and to commit myself to the boisterous ocean of political passions. I thank God for the opportunity of retiring from them without censure, and carrying with me the most consoling proofs of public approbation."

He took a week to wind up his personal affairs in Washington and then, following a caravan of wagons, set out for Monticello. The roads were especially treacherous at this season; he rode the last

three days in the saddle, part of the time through a blinding snowstorm, and came safely into port at the last on the 15th. His friends
and neighbors, the citizens of Albemarle, presented him a cordial address. No testimony, Jefferson said in reply, could be more grateful
than that of "the triers of the vicinage." "Of you, then, my neighbors, I may ask, in the face of the world, 'whose ox have I taken, or
whom have I defrauded? Whom have I oppressed, or of whose hand
have I received a bribe to blind mine eyes therewith?' On your verdict I rest with conscious security."

Sage of Monticello

Oh, the blessings of privacy and leisure! The wish of the powerful and eminent, but the privilege only of inferiors, who are the only people that live to themselves; nay, the very thought of it is a consolation, even in the tumults and hazards that attend greatness. . . . But it is one thing to retire for pleasure, and another thing for virtue, which must be active even in that retreat, and give proof of what it has learned: for a good and wise man does in privacy consult the well-being of posterity. Zeno and Chrysippus did greater things in their studies than if they had led armies, borne offices, or given laws, which in truth they did, not to one city alone, but to all mankind: their quiet contributed more to the common benefit than the sweat and labor of other people.

Seneca, Moral Essays.

A LL MY WISHES END where I hope my days will end, at Monti-cello." Many more days than Jefferson calculated, seventeen years and four months of days, lay before him, during which the dream of felicity became a delusion, yet with his confidence in a universe framed on benevolence and his affirmative response to life, he remained a cheerful worker in the vineyard until the end.

The mansion was finished now, all but the final touches, just in time for the decay to commence. Jefferson had turned his thoughts to the gardens, nothing elaborate on the style of English landscape such as he had once envisioned and so much admired in William Hamilton's "Woodlands," in Philadelphia, which would have been awkward in the thick woods and hanging hollows and ridges of Monticello, but flower and vegetable gardens on an ample plan. Trees had always been his passion, he wrote to Madame de Tessé, whom he continued to keep in American seed and whose courage in planting trees he admired; as for himself, he thought it was time to begin planting flowers. "The labors of the year, in that line, are repaid within the year, and death, which will be at my door, shall find me unembarrassed by long-lived undertakings." He said he had scarcely ever planted a flower, and though he had laid out whole orchards of fruits and gardens of vegetables, he had never been free to indulge his calling in this direction. "No occupation is so delightful to me as the culture of the earth, and no culture comparable to that of the garden," he said in the third year of retirement. "Such a variety of subjects, some are always coming to perfection, the failures of one being repaired by the successes of another, and instead of one harvest a continued one through the year." How much more rewarding than the political calling! The flower gardens on the west lawn, planned in 1807 but not completed for five years, featured a winding walk, bordered on either side, with oval beds set in the hollows. "I remember well," one of his granddaughters recalled, "when he first returned to Monticello, how immediately he began to prepare new beds for his flowers." A great variety was planted, and he felt renewed by the annual cycle. A new vegetable garden was laid out, too, in three long tiers on the sunny slope of the mountain; and for the second and last time Jefferson renewed the orchard that had gone to decay while he was attending to public business.

Jefferson's estate was in sad repair when he left the presidency. His farms had suffered grievously, he felt, from the absence of close personal supervision, and he expected to remedy this by becoming a farmer again. Yet by his own admission he was an indifferent farmer. The causes of deterioration lay deeper: in the cursed labor system, in soil exhaustion and erosion, and the depression of the market. Hazards of pests and weather the farmer always had with him, but they were especially unkind to Jefferson during several successive seasons. And under the restraints of embargo, non-intercourse, and war, the market was seldom favorable. On paper he suffered no loss of assets. He continued to own approximately 10,000 acres of land and 200 slaves. The total value of his estate has been

estimated at $200,000. But Virginia lands declined more or less stead-
ily in value and produced a paltry return. At the time of his retirement Jefferson estimated an annual income from his farms of $4000,
to which might be added perhaps $1500 to $2000 from other
sources, such as the flour mill, the naillery (this too had to be restored, with poor results), a cooper's shop, and slave hire on occasion. He intended to tighten his belt at Monticello and live as a plain
farmer; but he would be denied this fate. Living expenses at home
increased without improvement of capital or income. Worst of all
he was still plagued with debts. The blight ate into his happiness and
finally consumed a great part of his estate.

Winding up his affairs during the winter in Washington, Jefferson suddenly found himself overwhelmed with a multitude of forgotten accounts, $10,000 to $12,000 above his resources. It dawned
on him for the first time how far he had lived beyond his income.
Recalling the shock in later years, he said the deficit arose from
turning the President's House into "a general tavern" for the Washington community. Whatever the cause, he had to borrow to pay
these debts. Eight thousand dollars came from a private lender in
Virginia, the remainder from the Bank of the United States on a
note endorsed by James Madison. Uneasy about the liability thus assumed by the President, Jefferson soon transferred this debt to
Thaddeus Kosciusko, whose American investments he had managed
for many years. (He was a much better manager of other men's
money than of his own.) These were only the debts run up in
Washington. He had not altogether rid himself of the old debts dat-
ing back to the Revolution. Altogether, he owed something like
$25,000 at the time of his retirement; and no sooner would he begin
to see the end of this bondage than new liabilities would befall him.
As before, his Bedford plantation, Poplar Forest, much the more
productive of the two, was mortgaged to his creditors. He tried to
sell several small detached parcels of land, but this was slow work
and had no appreciable effect on his estate until the last years of life.
To round-out his holdings in Albemarle and Bedford, he also
bought some additional acreage. He considered his property and
Randolph's "common stock," and since his son-in-law was also heavily in debt, Edgehill, too, operated under mortgage.

The Randolphs and their children, reaching the number of

eleven in 1818, lived with the patriarch at Monticello. With Francis Eppes, Maria's offspring, a part-time resident, the grandchildren came to an even dozen. To say that they worshiped their grandfather is an understatement. "Cheerfulness, love, benevolence, wisdom, seemed to animate his whole form," one of them recalled. "I cannot describe the feelings of veneration, admiration, and love that existed in my heart towards him. I looked upon him as a being too great and good for my comprehension; and yet I felt no fear to approach him, and be taught by him some of the childish sports I delighted in. When he walked in the garden, and would call the children to go with him, we raced after and before him. . . . He would gather fruit for us, seek out the ripest figs, or bring down the cherries from on high above our heads with a long stick, at the end of which there was a hook and a little net bag. . . . One of our earliest amusements was in running races on the terrace or around the lawn. He placed us according to our ages, giving the youngest and smallest the start of all the others by some yards, and so on; and then he raised his arm high with his white handkerchief and we started off to finish the race by returning to the starting-place and receiving our reward of dried fruit—three figs or prunes or dates to the victor, two to the second, and one to the lagger who came in last." Their mother managed the busy household at Monticello, tutored the children, and received the same adoration as her father. Everyone observed the resemblance of father and daughter. One of the neighboring Gilmers, who formed part of the Albemarle circle centered at Monticello, thought Martha Randolph the most accomplished woman he ever knew: "her person tall, largely, loosely made, and awkward, but her actions and manners are graceful, easy, and engaging; her face not what would be esteemed beautiful, but her features are flexible and playful and agreeable. An expression of intelligence always animates her countenance; a turn for the ludicrous, a sweet and variable voice, the contraction of muscles about the eyes when she speaks, vast and various information, frankness and eloquence far above what I have ever met with in any person of her sex. . . ." Between these two paragons, Martha and her father, Randolph cut a poor figure. For all his talents, such as raised him to the governorship of the commonwealth in 1819, he was volatile, eccentric, and little loved by his children. Even Jefferson slowly cooled in his affection for him. The Monticello family had its trials and tribulations like any other. What distinguished it finally was the virtuous character of the patriarch, honored and loved in his domestic circle "above all earthly beings."

Monticello was not only a home; it was a monument. People came from all over: "People of wealth, fashion, men in office, professional men, military and civil, lawyers, doctors, Protestant clergymen, Catholic priests, members of Congress, foreign ministers, missionaries, Indian agents, tourists, travellers, artists, strangers, friends." Some came as idle curiosity seekers, some as seekers of Delphi, others as pilgrims to Mecca. They came to see the renowned Sage of Monticello, statesman, scientist, philanthropist, whose life was identified with the prodigy of the New World, and whose home was among the most interesting of his creations. The monument was even a kind of museum. Visitors noticed "the strange furniture on its walls." In the entrance hall hung heads of elk, deer, buffalo, and mammoth, Indian curiosities from the Lewis and Clark journey, and a variety of paintings, which overflowed into the parlor—portraits of New World discoverers, of Franklin, Adams, Paine, and other Americans, some native landscapes, several of Trumbull's historical canvases, and many Biblical scenes from European galleries—together with busts of various luminaries, including Ceracchi's of Jefferson and Hamilton, who, it was said, stood opposed on marble pedestals in the great hall.

Among the numerous visitors were many Jefferson enjoyed; as for the rest, he had not the heart to turn them away. They came, most of them, to do him honor; hospitality was the custom of the country, and there was no nearby inn to which they could go. So Monticello became a tavern, as the President's House had been. During the summers, when travel commenced from the lowcountry, they came in gangs, Edmund Bacon, the farm manager recalled, "the whole family, with carriage and riding horses and servants; sometimes three or four such gangs at a time." Often the stable, which would take twenty-six horses in addition to the family's stock, was full. Martha put up as many as fifty guests a night on the mountain. Of course, they had to be fed. "I have killed a fine beef, and it would all be eaten in a day or two," Bacon said. More than anything else, he felt that the expense of so much company sank Jefferson's fortune. However that may be, he never complained of the company or the expense, though it was a far cry from the simple, quiet retirement he had imagined. Always on display at Monticello, he escaped two or three times a year to Poplar Forest, ninety miles and two days to the south. Before he left the presidency, as building drew to a close at Monticello, he began to build a house at this plantation, and it became more necessary to him when he retired. This second home and refuge, a lovely brick octagon, occupied him for a dozen years.

In 1810, after a year's retirement, Jefferson described his daily routine to Kosciusko. "My mornings are devoted to correspondence. From breakfast to dinner, I am in my shops, my garden, or on horseback among my farms; from dinner to dark, I give to society and recreation with my neighbors and friends; and from candle light to early bed-time, I read." His health was excellent for a man of sixty-seven years. He used spectacles only to read at night, and another decade passed before he lost a tooth. He said he read but a single newspaper, Thomas Ritchie's *Richmond Enquirer*, though he continued to subscribe to Duane's *Aurora* and the *National Intelligencer*. "But I wish at length to indulge myself in more favorite reading, in Tacitus and Horace and the writers of that philosophy which is the old man's consolation and preparation for what is to come." He occasionally read new books and grew fond of the *Edinburgh Review*. But the ancient writers were his favorites. "I saw him more frequently with a volume of the classics in his hand than with any other book," a granddaughter recalled. He once told an old political associate that he knew more of what passed two or three thousand years ago, "of the heroes of Troy, of the wars of Lacedaemon and Athens, of Pompey and Caesar, and of Augustus too," than of what passed from day to day. Still he was not dead to the world around him. "I talk of ploughs and harrows, of seeding and harvesting with my neighbors," he said, "and of politics too, if they choose, with as little reserve as the rest of my fellow citizens, and feel, at length, the blessings of being free to say and do what I please, without being responsible to any mortal." Among his most pleasing occupations was the direction of the studies of youths who came to him for books and learning and inspiration, often settling nearby. Some, like William Cabell Rives, had distinguished careers before them. "I endeavor," Jefferson said, "to keep their attention fixed on the main object of all science, the freedom and happiness of man."

Less pleasing, in time a drudgery against which he revolted, was a mammoth correspondence. In a single year he received over 1200 letters. "They are letters of inquiry, for the most part, always of good will, sometimes from friends whom I esteem, but much oftener from persons whose names are unknown to me, but written kindly and civilly, and to which therefore, civility requires answers." Many went unanswered of necessity, but he wrote literally thousands of letters, on every conceivable subject, some of them masterpieces of the epistolary art, and all with his own hand until the last years of his life. The early morning hours from sun-up until breakfast were set aside for this task; often, however, Jefferson sat at his writing table, "under the whip and spur, from morning to night." "Is this life?" he once asked John Adams, his most famous correspondent, who was not afflicted in the same way. "At best it is but the life of a mill-horse, who sees no end to his circle but death. To such a life, that of a cabbage is paradise." The stiffness of his right wrist, the legacy of misadventure in Paris now compounded by the miseries of age, led him to declare a "state of insurgency" in 1817. But he never found any relief from this burden of his life.

The Sage of Monticello was many times blessed. Good health, good conscience, benign temperament, indefatigable industry, loving family, pleasant country society, honors of a life well spent—all these and more were his. But for his debts and the perilous state of Virginia agriculture, he said in 1810, his private happiness would be unalloyed. For a decade he remained cheerful about the prospects, only then to discover that his hopes were blasted. It was not a tranquil retirement, a life of study and ease and affection untroubled by the cares of the world, such as had always been his dream for Monticello. Once again he realized how much his private happiness belonged to his public happiness. Every renunciation of interest in affairs of state was followed by ejaculations of deep concern. During forty years in the public service he had accumulated quite an agenda of unfinished business. He could not attend to all of it but certain items, above all education, made an irresistible claim upon him. In his private station, aged and remote from the seats of power, he was still a public man, and in the eyes of many the chief personage in the United States. No one, certainly, embodied so well the history and the hopes of the new nation; and although this dream, too, dimmed for him in the last years of life, he remained its most authentic voice until his death on the fiftieth anniversary of its birth.

Kaleidoscope in Twilight

Many people found it difficult to believe that Jefferson had really surrendered the helm of state. The idea that he secretly directed the administration of his successor from Monticello was wholly mistaken, but Madison had stood for so long in Jefferson's shadow it seemed unlikely he could stand in the sunshine of his own. Jefferson naturally had a stake in the new administration, nor only for reasons of friendship and patriotism but because Madison was, in a very positive sense, the heir of measures he had started. The ultimate fate of his own presidency was involved with the fate of his successor. Conscious of this, conscious of Madison's unfortunate reputation as "a mere appendage" of himself, Jefferson leaned over backwards not to interfere. Each man knew the other's mind almost as well as his own, and they had implicit confidence in each other, so advice was rarely asked or volunteered. As in the past, Madison and his wife usually visited at Monticello in September. What passed in these conversations it is impossible to say, but their correspondence in these years was neither voluminous nor especially informative on matters of state.

Jefferson's influence with the President was most often requested in the business of patronage. Considering himself *hors de combat*, he at once had a circular printed to answer all the pleading office-seekers. Only in the cases of two or three Virginia friends of many years did he actively intercede. In 1810 the death of Justice William Cushing at last opened the way to a Republican majority on the Supreme Court. Jefferson could not be indifferent to this event. For ten years the Court had "braved the spirit and the will of the nation," and at this very time he found himself the defendant in a huge damage suit likely to be heard at Chief Justice Marshall's bench. The vacancy fairly belonged to Massachusetts, Cushing's state. Jefferson recommended Levi Lincoln, a Republican tried and true. Madison offered the seat to Lincoln, who declined, and then, again on his friend's recommendation, to Gideon Granger, whom the Senate rejected. Only after all other possibilities failed did Madison name Joseph Story, the man he may have wanted in the first place but whom Jefferson had ruled out for his insurgency against the embargo.

The former President rendered an important political service by helping to restore the friendship of Madison and Monroe. Monroe had found no new public employment since his return from England. Alienated from Madison, associated with the Randolph junto, there seemed to be no place for him in the administration. He soon returned to Albemarle, and Jefferson made it his business to draw him away from his quondam friends and to revive the old cordiality between the second and third of the Virginia triumvirs. When Meriwether Lewis took his own life in October 1809, Madison offered the Louisiana governorship to Monroe. Jefferson had pressed the same office on him in the past and now did so again, again without success. The next year the General Assembly brought Monroe back to the governorship; but no sooner did he take up the reins than a cabinet shake-up in Washington led him to resign to accept the post of Secretary of State under Madison. From that moment, barring misadventure, Monroe's eventual succession to the presidency was assured, to Jefferson's enormous satisfaction.

The cabinet shake-up, which might better be described as an explosion, had its origins in the rivalry between Albert Gallatin and Robert Smith. These gentlemen had suppressed their differences and worked more or less in unison while Jefferson was at the helm; but the harmony he had managed during eight years Madison could not manage during one. Gallatin had wanted and been promised the State Department. Madison, at the last minute, fearing the opposition of Gallatin's enemies and Smith's friends in the Senate, not only Samuel Smith but William B. Giles and others as well, named Smith to this first post in the cabinet and kept Gallatin in the Treasury. Visiting at Monticello in the fall, Gallatin poured his heart out to his former chief and threatened to resign. Jefferson urged him to stay on, emphasizing the importance of finally sinking the debt and moving ahead with works of improvement and peace. Gallatin stayed on but dissension increased. William Duane, who blamed Gallatin for the ascendancy of the more moderate faction of Pennsylvania Republicans, launched a torrid campaign of invective in the *Aurora*. The spreading feud split the administration and threatened to split the party in 1810. Several Republicans begged Jefferson's intervention to restore harmony. He declined but exhorted Duane, with the other dissidents, to curb their zeal in the interest of unity. The Republicans were not just a party—the name was degrading— "the Republicans are the *nation*," he thundered. "The last hope of human liberty in the world rests on us. We ought, for so dear a stake, to sacrifice every attachment and every enmity." Poor Duane, hopelessly in debt, harassed by creditors, slapped with one libel suit after another, all in the cause of Republicanism, seemed doomed to spend his life in courts of law. Just before leaving office, Jefferson had commissioned him a lieutenant colonel in the provisional army (the editor was a student of the art of war), and despite his vexation at him for "schismatizing" the administration, he now undertook to raise $8000 among Virginia Republicans to keep the *Aurora* in operation. It was a hard cause, and it became desperate the succeeding April when the peppery editor turned on the President himself. Forced at length to choose between Gallatin and Smith, Madison chose Gallatin without hesitation. Smith was dismissed and Monroe brought in. Jefferson, with nine-tenths of the Republican party, would have chosen the same way. He put no credence in reports of Gallatin's enmity to him on the score of Anglophobism—they emanated from David Erskine, the former British minister—and his merits placed him in a class by himself. To Madison he explained his efforts on Duane's behalf, for his "incalculable services to Republicanism," lest the President suppose he endorsed the editor's attack on the administration. He made one last effort to reform Duane and save the *Aurora* but feared the editor had become so much the victim of his passions that he would go the way of Randolph. And so he went, yet Jefferson never abandoned him.

For three years the country drifted toward war. Within a few weeks of his retirement, Jefferson watched the hope of peace dawn brightly and then sink as suddenly as it rose. On the assurances of Erskine that the orders in council would be revoked in June, Madison issued a proclamation restoring trade with Britain. Jefferson hailed this "triumph of our forbearing and yet persevering system." But George Canning at once disavowed the Erskine Agreement and recalled the errant minister. The embarrassed President restored non-intercourse. It was a "dirty trick," Jefferson commiserated with his friend. "Should Bonaparte have the wisdom to correct his injustice towards us, I consider war with England inevitable." Bonaparte ran true to form; even so, after other awkward passages in the pursuit of peace, war with Britain became inevitable in 1812.

Jefferson expressed mingled feelings of disappointment and relief. War, on the one hand, would cut out the lingering cancer of British influence: "the second weaning from British principles, British attachments, British manners and manufactures will be salutary, and will form an epoch of the spirit of nationalism and of consequent prosperity, which would never have resulted from a continued subordination to the interests and influence of England." The American strategy, obviously, was to attack Canada and drive Britain from the continent. "The acquisition of Canada this year, as far as the neighborhood of Quebec, will be a mere matter of marching," Jefferson boasted. Halifax would fall in the next campaign. The Floridas, too, would become an object. The world would then see such an "empire of liberty" as had never been surveyed since the creation. This conception of the war as an epoch of liberty and nationality had firm roots in Jefferson's thought. It was a war against Britain, of course, but in the larger sense it was against Europe, the Old World, and in this sense it promised the consummation of that hemispheric "American system" toward which New World ideology had aimed from the beginning. "What in short is the whole system of Europe towards America but an atrocious and insulting tyranny," Jefferson wrote to one of his unknown correspondents. "One hemisphere of the earth, separated from the other by wide seas on both sides, having a different system of interests flowing from different climates, different soils, different productions, different modes of existence, and its own local relations and duties, is made subservient to all the petty interests of the other, to *their* laws, *their* regulations, their passions and wars, and interdicted from social intercourse, from the interchange of mutual duties and comforts with their neighbors, enjoined on all men by the laws of nature." A war commenced under such favorable auspices as he believed this one to be, holding the promise of so much gain in liberty and dignity and independence, he had almost come to think a blessing to the nation.

On the other hand, what was war itself but the curse of the Old World blighting the hopes of the New? Jefferson contemplated this chapter as a mournful necessity. "Farewell all hope of extinguishing the public debt! Farewell all visions of applying the surplus revenue to the improvements of peace, rather than the ravages of war. Our enemy has indeed the consolation of Satan on removing our first parents from Paradise; from a peaceful and agricultural nation he makes us a military and manufacturing one." The country was meant to be, and might have become, "a garden for the delight and multiplication of mankind," he said. "But the lions and tigers of Europe must be gorged in blood, and some of ours must go, it seems, to their maws, their ravenous and insatiable maws." The United States would win the contest, of course, and get back on the track of destiny, but it would never shine quite so brightly for Jefferson again.

The conduct of the war was itself disillusioning. The crushing military defeats of 1812, beginning with General William Hull's "treacherous" surrender of Detroit in August, shattered Jefferson's easy optimism. It was farewell to Canada too. "So wretched a succession of generals never before destroyed the fairest expectations of a nation," he wrote in disgust. Some Republicans cherished the hope that he might be called back into service, perhaps as President or, more likely, as Secretary of State in Madison's cabinet, relieving Monroe to energize the feeble War Department. Jefferson refused to consider it and counseled the despondent to rally to the administration. The military failures, he felt, proved the case for the reinvigorated militia system he had first recommended to Congress in 1805. Monroe, when he became Secretary of War in 1814, took up the plan, but Congress again registered its opposition. On no problem did Jefferson express himself as strongly as that of war finances. The Bank of the United States died with the expiration and non-renewal of its charter in 1811, which was gratifying; but Congress, instead of adopting his system of Treasury notes redeemed by taxes, abandoned its control over the currency to a multiplying horde of state banks, which flooded the country with worthless paper, drove out specie, drove up prices, and upset property values everywhere.

"Instead of funding issues of paper on the hypothecation of specific redeeming taxes (the only method of anticipating in time of war, the resources of times of peace, tested by the experience of nations)," he wrote, "we are trusting to tricks of jugglers of the cards, to the illusions of banking schemes for the resources of the war, and for the cure of colic to inflations of more wind." His views were well known to the administration, yet when it finally came to grips with financial disaster after two years of war, the remedy chosen was a second national bank, the Hamiltonian solution, rather than his own. He felt the effect of inflation in his own purse, for although it should have raised his income with his expenses, and helped him pay his debts, it did not even by half, largely because the British blockade of the Chesapeake barred access to foreign markets. He pleaded with Madison to send a naval force to break the blockade, but frigates could not be spared and gunboats, though Jefferson seemed to think them servicable in this situation, could not do the job. As a result, at any rate, he and his neighbors were feeding their wheat to the horses in 1814 and tobacco was not worth the pipe that smoked it. Whiskey was one recourse, "but all mankind must become drunkards to consume it," Jefferson quipped. "To me this state of things brings a sacrifice of all tranquillity and comfort through the residue of life. . . . [By] the total annihilation in value of the produce that was to give me subsistence and independence, I shall be like Tantalus, up to the shoulders in water, yet dying of thirst." Thus the war was a great personal as well as national misfortune.

Jefferson took what pleasure he could in the Peace of Ghent at the end of 1814. Andrew Jackson's victory at New Orleans, even if it came after the signing of the peace, had not been wasted, he said. It proved once again that the West was sound and "that our militia are heroes when they have heroes to lead them." The peace was, he thought, only an armistice. The treaty returned the belligerents to the status quo ante bellum, omitting provisions on impressment and neutral rights that had caused the war in the first place. So the country must prepare for the resumption of hostilities at the first crack of the cannon in Europe. The Hartford Convention, called at the invitation of the Massachusetts legislature in December, bespoke the strength of British attachments and disunionist sentiments in that quarter of the Union. "Oh Massachusetts! How have I lamented the degradation of your apostacy!" Fortunately, the peace made a laughing-stock of the New England Federalists and the Hartford Convention a synonym of political degradation. "The cement of the Union is in the heart-blood of every American," Jefferson wrote. "I do not believe there is on earth a government established on so unmovable a basis. Let them, in any state, even in Massachusetts itself, raise the standard of separation, and its citizens will rise in mass, and do justice themselves on their own incendiaries." Still, in other letters, Jefferson did not dismiss this threat to peace and union. British jealousy and hostility, now unchecked by Bonaparte, had yet to run its course. "We were safe from the British fleets because they had Bonaparte at their back," he warned nine months after the war ended, "but the British fleets and the conquerors of Bonaparte being now combined, and the Hartford nation drawn off to them, we have uncommon reason to look to our own affairs." The only limits on the overwhelming power of Britain were bankruptcy and the "ascendancy which nature destines for us by immutable laws."

Distrusting Britain as before, even as he ardently wished peace and friendship with her, Jefferson could not take unalloyed pleasure in the downfall of Napoleon. If the allies succeeded in carving up Europe to suit themselves, he said, "we can expect no other favor than that of being the last devoured." He had penned many scorching indictments of "the beast," the "moral monster" who had "inflicted more misery on mankind than any other who . . . ever lived," and some of them had found their way into the press against his will and to the chagrin of Republicans, like Duane, who in their hatred of Britain persisted in seeing Napoleon as the champion of liberty. On balance, despite the unlucky loss of France in the scales of European power, Jefferson thought the downfall of Napoleon a blessing to humanity. The return of the Bourbons offered the only solution for France. This melancholy event, writing *finis* to the epoch of European liberty commenced with such glorious hopes in 1789, led Jefferson to reflect with Lafayette, Dupont, and other old comrades on the causes of the catastrophe. "Possibly you may remember," he wrote to the Marquis, "at the date of the *jeu de paume* (June 20, 1789), how earnestly I urged yourself, and the patriots of my acquaintance, to enter into a compact with the King, securing freedom of religion, freedom of the press, trial by jury, habeas corpus, and a national legislature, all of which it was known he would yield, to go home, and let them work on the amelioration of the condition of the people. . . . This was as much as I then thought them able to bear, soberly and usefully for themselves. You thought otherwise, and that the dose might be larger. And I found you were right, for subsequent events proved they were equal to the constitution of 1791. Unfortunately, some of the most honest and enlightened of our patriotic friends . . . thought more still could be obtained and borne. They did not weigh the hazards of a transition from one form of government to another, the value of what they had already rescued from those hazards, and might hold in security if they pleased, nor the imprudence of giving up the certainty of such a degree of liberty, under a limited monarch, for the uncertainty of a little more under the form of a republic . . . , and from this fatal error of the republicans . . . flowed all the subsequent sufferings of the French nation." For it to be a matter of congratulation that France, and Europe, had reverted to the ante-revoltuionary condition was mournful in the extreme. "I fear from the experience of the last 25 years that morals do not, of necessity, advance hand in hand with the sciences," Jefferson confessed. Still he could not rest in darkness and doubt. Conceding to John Adams that he had been the better prophet on the French Revolution, Jefferson nevertheless felt that in the longer race of history Adams and his faithless tribe would be left at the starting gate. "But altho' your prophesy has proved true so far," he wrote in 1816, "I hope it does not preclude a better final result. The same light from our West seems to have spread and illuminated the very engines employed to extinguish it. It has given them [the Europeans] a glimmering of their rights and their power. The idea of representative government has taken root and growth among them . . . ." And so he continued to steer "with Hope in the head, leaving Fear astern."

The light of the American Revolution had spread to the southern precincts of the New World too. Jefferson rejoiced in the colonial revolts and the new independent states of Latin America. Although he trembled for their survival against the maraudings of Old World imperialism and feared their governments would end in priestly ignorance and military despotism, Jefferson placed this development in the ongoing epoch of American liberty. "But in whatever governments they end," he wrote to Humboldt in 1813, "they will be *American* governments, no longer to be involved in the never ceasing broils of Europe. The European nations constitute a separate division of the globe; their localities make them part of a distinct system, they have a set of interests of their own in which it is our interest never to engage ourselves. America has a hemisphere to itself." This conception of a hemispheric "American system," rooted in the Jeffersonian "empire of liberty," would not be realized in a year or a decade but its day would surely come. For a time Jefferson hoped that the European powers, excluding Britain because of her naval supremacy, might mutually guarantee the peace and independence of the Latin American states until they could stand on their own legs. But the Holy Alliance was little inclined in this direction; and in 1823 Jefferson counseled and supported the declaration of President Monroe that sought to close the hemisphere to Old World powers and make the United States the guardian of the "American system."

All during the war Jefferson made improvements in his Rivanna mill, in agricultural economy, and, above all, in household manufactures. The flour mill had cost him a great deal and continued to involve him in expense and litigation that consumed most of the meager profits. As finished in 1806 the mill incorporated certain improvements, including elevators, conveyor buckets, and hopperboys, on which the ingenious Oliver Evans claimed patents. Evans's agent later presented Jefferson with a bill for $89.60 for the use of these improvements. He paid willingly, as a tribute to a man whose talents were so useful to mankind, but at the same time denied he was under legal obligation to pay. In 1813, when Evans sued for his patent claim in Baltimore, Isaac McPherson, of that city, wrote to ask Jefferson's opinion of the case. His reply was a remarkable essay not just on patent law but on the rights of mankind to ideas. The Rivanna manufacturing mill, he said, had been erected after the expiration of Evans's first patent and before his second. But this was a technicality. By consulting a number of books on the mechanical arts, he showed that the principles of Evans's patent were very old and had been applied to many uses the world around. A man cannot, he went on to argue, patent a new application of a known principle

937

or an old machine. "If nature has made any one thing less susceptible than all others of exclusive property, it is the action of the
thinking power called an idea, which an individual may exclusively
possess as long as he keeps it to himself; but the moment it is di-
vulged, it forces itself into the possession of every one, and the re-
ceiver cannot dispossess himself of it. Its peculiar character, too, is
that no one can possess the less, because every other possesses the
whole of it. He who receives an idea from me, receives instruction
himself without lessening mine; as he who lights his taper at mine,
receives light without darkening me. That ideas should freely spread
from one to another over the globe, for the moral and mutual instruction of man, and improvement of his condition, seems to have
been peculiarly and benevolently designed by nature, when she
made them, like fire, expandable over all space, and like the air in
which we breathe, move, and have our physical being, incapable of
confinement or exclusive appropriation." This was fundamental—a
law of nature. Yet Jefferson had written the patent law under which
Evans claimed monopoly. Explaining the history of this misadventure, he said that under the original law Evans's patent would have
been refused on the principle stated, but the inability of the patent
commissioners to examine each request for title had led to the registration system, which installed the English principle of monopoly
and left the only challenge to litigants in the courts. Evans won his
suit in Baltimore. McPherson then published a pamphlet attacking
the claim and offering Jefferson's letter in evidence. The pamphlet
went to every member of Congress in the form of a memorial for
revision of the patent law. Evans replied publicly, and privately to
Jefferson. To adapt and combine known mechanisms for a new purpose, he claimed, vested in him an exclusive right to the use. Jefferson, who had always admired and encouraged Evans, repeated the
argument of his letter to McPherson. If the patent law conferred
monopoly on the application of ideas that had become the property
of mankind, it took much more from the nation than it gave in return.

The rage for household manufactures, begun under the embargo,
continued thoughout the war. The spinners and weavers were more
daring adversaries of Britain than all the generals, Jefferson remarked. In 1812 he hired a married couple to manage his works at

Monticello. Two years later he and Randolph together had four jennies in operation, a total of 112 spindles, and the carders and looms to go with them. Chiefly, he aimed to clothe his plantation family with 2000 yards of coarse linens, cottons, and woolens yearly, looking to finer things once this was accomplished. Apparently he never got much beyond the first object. He experimented with new and larger spinning machines, but patent fees again became a problem, and their complexity was such that no one could keep them in repair; so he favored the ancient jenny. To make woolens he must have sheep. Jefferson had been raising sheep, mainly for mutton, for twenty years. Now he went into woolgrowing and shared the fantastic hopes of his countrymen for the silken wool of the Spanish merinos. The country became "sheep mad"—above all merino mad. The first merinos had been smuggled out of Spain by David Humphreys, Robert Livingston, the Duponts, and others about 1800. Jefferson supposed some of his flock, the offspring of European imports in the 1790's, were genuine merinos, but learned in 1809 that their wool fell far below the grade. Not until the next year, when prices of merinos soared out of sight, did he obtain a ram and ewe, of the variety called Acquines, as a gift from William Jarvis in Lisbon. "What shall we do with them?" he asked Madison, similarly blessed. "I have been so disgusted with the scandalous extortions lately practiced in the sale of these animals, and with the description of patriotism and praise to the sellers, as if the thousands of dollars apiece they have not been ashamed to receive were not reward enough, that I am disposed to consider as right, whatever is the reverse of what they have done." He proposed that they make gifts of the offspring to Virginia farmers less fortunate than themselves; in seven years the whole state would be covered with this valuable breed. Some farmers bred their stock at Monticello, and apparently Jefferson gave away some of his merino lambs, for two years later he had only a ram and two ewes. But the ravages of dogs and disease took others. And by 1812 the merino craze had so far subsided in Virginia, he said, that farmers would not even take them as gifts. The merinos produced less wool than hardier breeds and of a finer quality than was wanted for Virginia household manufactures. Few farmers understood the husbandry of merinos. All over the United States, when the breed failed to live up to expectations, whole flocks were slaughtered for mutton. Within a few years the merino enthusiasm turned into a fiasco.

Jefferson's experience in his own household strengthened his commitment to manufacturing enterprise as a branch of national economy. An English traveler, John Melish, who had interviewed him in Washington, and whose *Travels* appeared in 1812, was perhaps the first to call the public's attention to Jefferson's revision of the well-known opinion of domestic manufactures advanced in the *Notes on Virginia*. Melish's two volumes, in turn, with their wealth of detail on the progress of American manufactures, astonished Jefferson. In a number of private letters he explained that while he had earlier believed the workshops should remain in Europe and the United States should concentrate on what it could most advantageously produce "as a member of the great family of mankind," exchanging its agriculutral surpluses for European manufactures, he had been forced to conclude the world was not ready for this system—it was two worlds rather than one—and, therefore, "we must endeavor to make everything we want within ourselves, and have as little intercourse as possible with Europe in its present demoralized state." "We must now place the manufacturer by the side of the agriculturist," he declared in the most widely publicized of these letters, addressed to the Massachusetts Republican Benjamin Austin, in 1816. The independence and welfare of the nation required it. And to this end protectionism on a moderate scale won Jefferson's endorsement. He had come by degrees to the conception of a balanced economy of agriculture, commerce, and manufactures, fulfilling the Revolutionary prophesy of the new nation as "a world within itself." Yet he had not embraced the spirit and substance of the industrial revolution. As he did not wish his country to become "a city of Amsterdam," so he did not wish it to become "a city of Manchester." The usual insignia of industrialism—cities of spindles and smoke and steam, great stock companies, masses of propertyless operatives huddled in the poet's "dark satanic mills"—had no place in his thought. The clatter of spindles and the smoke of shops at Monticello was one thing; massed in a different environment, unredeemed by the virtues of nature, quite another. "I concur with you," he wrote to his old friend Peale, "in doubting whether the great establishments, by associated companies, are advantageous in this country. It is the household manufacture which is really precious." It was moral, healthy, and paternal within the beneficent circle of nature. What he embraced, then, was the household-handicraft-mill complex of an advanced agricultural society. He realized, of course, that manufacturing on a larger and more sophisticated scale, by "associated companies," would accompany this growth, at least in the populous eastern centers; but he hoped, quite literally, to place the manufacturer *by the side* of the husbandman and in this way to preserve the values of an agricultural society within an emerging manufacturing one.

Manufacturing was his hobby, agriculture his business, during these years. He continued to experiment with crops and rotations, fertilizers, plows, and threshing machines. For a time he was an enthusiast for benne (sesame), supposedly planted with great success in South Carolina and Georgia, and expected its oil would replace olive oil, butter, and lard in the American diet. But after a trial of three successive seasons in Albemarle, the net product extracted by the cast-iron press he had built was one gallon of oil. The good earth of Albemarle had deteriorated under his feet. To restore it he experimented with plaster, as a fertilizer, on the "Loudoun system" popularized by John A. Binns. In addition to deeper plowing, Jefferson championed the horizontal, or contour, plowing introduced in the Albemarle region by his son-in-law. The innovation materially reduced erosion and leaching. "The improvement of our soil from this course . . . ," Jefferson reported, "strikes everyone with wonder." And in point of beauty nothing could equal "the waving lines and rows winding along the face of the hills and vales." In 1817 he joined with other prominent planters of the region in founding the Albemarle Agricultural Society, a lively center of improving science for many years. Yet the condition of Virginia agriculture went from bad to worse. The sequel to peace was drought. Seeing that his own situation was becoming desperate, Jefferson placed his grandson Jeff in charge of the Albemarle farms in 1815 and several years later gave him the management of Poplar Forest as well. In effect, Jefferson ceased to be a practicing farmer.

Pressures of debt mixed with motives of patriotism in his decision to sell his great library to the nation in 1815. The consummate act of British barbarity, the burning of the Capitol near the close of

941

the war, made ashes of the little congressional library. Three weeks after learning of this event, Jefferson wrote to Samuel Harrison Smith, asking him to act as his agent in the tender of his library to Congress. "You know my collection, its condition and extent," he said. "I have been fifty years making it, and have spared no pains, opportunity or expense, to make it what it is." Into the making had gone books purchased from Virginia estates, from Parisian booksellers, from friends and agents all over Europe, from American publishers and dealers, scoured from attics and the dustbins of courthouses, and many acquired *gratis* or by way of legacy, as from George Wythe. Jefferson supposed the library now numbered 9000 to 10,000 volumes (an overestimate), and while it embraced all branches of knowledge, it was peculiarly a library for American statesmen. "It is long since I have been sensible it ought not to continue private property, and had provided that, at my death, Congress should have the refusal of it, at their own price. But the loss they have incurred makes the present the proper moment for this accommodation without regard to the small remnant of time and the barren use of my enjoyment." Perhaps he might be permitted to retain during his life a few books chiefly classical and mathematical, which were the favorite amusements of his declining years. He enclosed the catalogue commenced in 1783 and kept up ever since. Included in its three main divisions, History, Philosophy, and Fine Arts, and the numerous sub-divisions, were 6500 volumes, not only books but rare colonial newspaper files and precious manuscripts in Virginia history, some of incalculable value, such as the records of the Virginia Company of London. They were arranged in his study in plain pine cases, stacked in tiers nine feet high, and so sturdy and compact that the cases needed only to be boarded and nailed up in front for shipment.

When Congress met in October the joint library committee at once reported a resolution authorizing a contract for purchase of the library. Some opposition arose in the House, chiefly from Massachusetts Federalists. The library was much too large, they said, and it contained many philosophical and infidel productions of no use to congressmen and insulting to the nation. The resolution passed with an amendment requiring the sanction of Congress before the purchase was completed. A Washington bookseller, Joseph Milligan, who knew the collection and was acceptable to both parties, returned an appraisal of $24,000. This was arbitrary to say the least. Milligan simply took the catalogue and allowing $10 for a folio, $6 for a quarto, $3 for an octavo, and $1 for a duodecimo added up the total. Had the library been appraised volume by volume, whether on original cost or replacement value, the figure would have been much higher. William Thornton, for one, thought Congress paid less than half the true value. But Jefferson seemed satisfied, and in December, over renewed opposition, Congress appropriated $23,950 for the acquisition. In March Jefferson described himself as "to the elbows in the dust of my book-shelves." Many books on loan had to be called in, each volume labeled and placed in accordance with the catalogue, and the cases nailed up. Eleven wagons carried the library to Washington in May. There it reposed in temporary quarters for four years before a commodious room in the north wing of the Capitol, now restored, was ready to receive it. Jefferson's books thus became the nucleus of one of the great libraries of the world. Unfortunately, the pyromania that took his first library also eventually consumed his second—two-thirds of the volumes were lost in the Library of Congress fire of 1851.

Jefferson applied three-quarters of the money received from Congress to the payment of pressing debts and at once laid out several hundred dollars of the remainder in the purchase of books. (He had, finally, reserved nothing from the sale.) Thus began his third library, a highly personal collection, especially notable for new editions of classical authors, running eventually to about a thousand volumes. While still in the dust of his old books, he was visited by a brilliant young Bostonian, George Ticknor, and his companion Francis C. Gray, who bore flattering letters of introduction from John Adams. Gray's journal of the visit is a poignant reminder that Monticello, in the waning years of Jefferson's life, was not the resplendent mansion it is today. Unkempt grounds, cluttered house, furnishings falling into decay: the picture, for Gray, was one of genteel shabbiness. Jefferson took to Ticknor at once, called him "the best bibliograph" he had ever encountered, and commissioned him to purchase a whole catalogue of books in Europe, whither he was bound to study modern languages and literature. He finally settled at the University of Gottingen together with another Massa-

943

chusetts son, Edward Everett, later joined by a third, George Bancroft. This "Gottingen trio," drawn to new fountainheads of learning while Virginia's sons basked in twilight at home, later returned to their native land and opened exciting vistas of German romantic philosophy and literature to the mind. Ticknor saw that Jefferson's catalogue was attended to, though most of the books came from other hands in Paris and London. Common sense told Jefferson that he ought to leave off buying books. Consulting the morality tables some years earlier, in his sixty-ninth year, he discovered that he had but seven years to live. Of all the books he then owned there were not many he cared to read and he would probably decamp before he could read fifty by choice. Solicited to subscribe to a compendius European atlas, he said, "I have, at different periods, bought several 'present states of Europe, geographical and political,' and while I have been reading them, Bonaparte has shuffled all together and dealt out new hands." Riding had become more important than reading: "This is more likely to baffle the tables of morality than reading a $30 book." Still he could not live without books—certain books—and never ceased to acquire them.

In the varied intellectual life of retirement, Jefferson was midwife and nurse to several books, helped to translate two, and, while he wrote none himself, published a lengthy pamphlet in 1812 that was a dazzling piece of erudition. This purported to be a history of the facts and the law arising on them in the angry controversy between Edward Livingston and the government of the United States over the ownership of the Batture St. Marie adjacent to New Orleans. The batture was a long shoal or beach formed by the silt of the Mississippi. Covered with water during half the year, it was used as a free anchorage by the thousands of boats and rafts that descended the river; and during the other months, when above water-level, it served as a quay and source of sand and dirt for the city inhabitants. From time beyond memory the batture had been considered public property. Livingston, having defaulted to the Treasury and accepted a judgment in the amount of $100,000, had gone to New Orleans in 1803 to recoup his fortune. He at once became active against the Claiborne regime, of course; and realizing the great potential value of the batture, by some estimates in the neighborhood of half a million dollars, he acquired a financial stake in the property by taking up the legal case of the landholder fronting the beach. In 1807 the supreme court of the territory ruled, in behalf of Livingston and his client, that the batture, as alluvium, rightfully belonged to the owner of the land bordering the river. The public was outraged. Riot and bloodshed threatened when Livingston, now the principal claimant, commenced improvements that would, some feared, alter the channel of the river, embarrass navigation, and possibly even drown New Orleans during the annual spring inundation. Governor Claiborne, supposing title to the batture passed to the United States with the acquisition of Louisiana, appealed to Washington for aid. In November 1807, after full cabinet discussion and approval, Jefferson ordered Livingston's eviction, by force if necessary, as an intruder on the public lands. The decision of the territorial court was considered a nullity. The United States had not been a party to it and, besides, answered to no court on account of the national domain. The eviction notice was served, in part, under provision of the Squatters' Act of 1807. Jefferson viewed the action as a restoration of the batture to its former condition pending any adjudication of the title by Congress or land commissioners. Driven off in January, Livingston then went to Washington to argue his case. He was unsuccessful. Jefferson had laid the matter before Congress but it acquiesced in the executive's defense of the public title. Livingston did not acquiesce, however; and in May 1810, with amazing effrontery, he filed suit for trespass against Jefferson in the circuit court at Richmond and asked personal damages of $100,000, the same amount, as it happens, for which he was still in hock to the Treasury.

The suit broke like a summer's storm over Monticello. On the face of it, the idea that a former President could be hauled into court and possibly sent into bankruptcy for official actions taken on his judgment of the public interest seemed absurd. Jefferson trusted the government would come to his rescue if that became necessary; for the present, however, he had to defend himself, and indeed preferred the government to keep hands off lest the Federalists make a partisan scandal of the case. He would have felt little anxiety for the outcome but for the court, which was Marshall's circuit, and depending on the result there the case might go to the Supreme Court. Livingston, who had been a thorn in Jefferson's side for seven years, had obviously calculated the Chief Justice's "twistifications" of the law and enmity to the defendant in lodging the suit at Richmond. Jefferson retained three prestigious Virginia lawyers, George Hay, William Wirt, and Littleton W. Tazewell, and began to prepare a statement of the case for their guidance. It was hard work. Quite a volume of literature had already accumulated. The batture had a long and involved history. The law of the case ramified into French, Spanish, and Roman sources and called up the whole history of sovereign and riparian rights to navigable waters from Herodotus forward. Thirty years had passed since Jefferson had been at the bar, but he had not lost his touch with the law. Aided by his friends in Washington, especially Gallatin, his coadjutors in New Orleans, and the Richmond counsel, he developed his statement over eighteen months. How to plea presented a dilemma. He had three main options: the merits of the case, embracing defense of the public title; the discretion of the executive acting, even if in error, in the people's interest; the want of jurisdiction in the court at Richmond for a trespass committed in New Orleans. He preferred the first course, which would place the case before the public and, it was to be hoped, confirm the government's title to the batture. Still, in the torpor of years, he shrank from the immense labor and prolonged anxiety this must entail. Counsel finally presented all three pleas, plus three others, to the court in December 1811. The first, dismissal for want of jurisdiction, prevailed—reluctantly on the part of one of the two judges, Marshall.

Now Jefferson felt it was his duty to lay the facts before the public. He arranged to have 250 copies of his statement printed under the title, *The Proceedings of the Government of the United States in Maintaining the Public Right to the Beach of the Mississippi.* . . . The details are intricate. Basically, he argued that the batture, even if alluvium, belonged to the sovereign in French law governing navigable waters, and therefore passed to the United States in 1803; however, the batture was, in fact, part of the bed of the river and as such could never be alienated. A single individual, Livingston, had no right "to drown the city of New Orleans, or to injure, or change, of his own authority, the course or current of a river which is to give outlet to the productions of two-thirds of the whole area of the United States." Jefferson could scarcely restrain his indignation. And suppose his executive action had been in error, he asked, did he therefore become liable for his whole fortune? Certainly he could not be accused of malice or corruption when his conduct accorded with the custom of the city, the will of the people, the opinion of the governor, the attorney general, and the legislature of the territory, as well as of his own cabinet and, apparently, of Congress. "If a functionary of the highest trust, acting under every sanction which the Constitution has provided for his aid and guide, and with the approbation, expressed or implied, of its highest councils, still acts on his own peril, the honors of his country would be but snares to ruin him." Wirt described Jefferson's production very well when he called it "a piece of Greecian architecture" uniting airiness and solidity, beauty and power. Livingston published his answer; and by sheer persistence he eventually obtained title to the batture, enabling him, at last, to close his account with the government in 1830. It is pleasing to record that he enjoyed a friendly correspondence with the Sage of Monticello before his death.

Frequent requests came to Jefferson to revise the *Notes on Virginia*. He had collected materials for this purpose and recognized, of course, that certain opinions expressed in this pivotal work, while still spoken as gospel in some quarters, had undergone change or required elucidation; but he never found time to revise the *Notes*. Requests came for permission to publish his familiar letters to deceased friends, such as George Wythe, Thomas Paine, and Benjamin Rush. He declined. "To fasten a man to all his unreflected expressions, and to publish him to the world in that as his serious and settled form is a surprise on his own judgment and character." If the world would show a little patience, it would have time enough to judge his acts and character from the ample record of his life. He declined autobiography as well, except for the benefit of his family, and while he assembled personal notes and memoranda on the political history of the 1790's, he left this time-bomb to explode after his death. He was not indifferent to posthumous fame, otherwise he would not have so systematically preserved his papers, but he was remarkably patient about it.

His labors as a translator were in connection with two manuscripts of the French political economist, Destutt de Tracy. One of the group of *Idéologues*, which included several of Jefferson's friends in France, Tracy had written a critical commentary on Montesquieu which he feared to publish at home. He asked Jefferson to attend to its translation and publication, anonymously, in the United States, whence its influence would reverberate back to France. Jefferson admired the work, thought it soundly republican and liberal, a useful corrective of Montesquieu's heresies, and, on the whole, "the most valuable political work of the present age." He induced Duane to undertake the translation and publication, though he contributed to the former, and the work appeared in 1811 under the title *A Commentary and Review of Montesquieu's Spirit of Laws*, with Jefferson's "author's preface" in the disguise of an unnamed Frenchman. So true, in fact, were its doctrines to those of the Sage of Monticello that the book was adopted as a text at William and Mary and some Frenchmen ascribed the authorship to him. Even Dupont was fooled and began to translate the book back into French. Jefferson persuaded him to desist. After Napoleon's exile, Tracy appeared publicly as the author of the original French version. So successful was this venture that he asked the same favor of Jefferson for his treatise on political economy. Duane botched the translation. Jefferson had to revise the whole—a daily drudgery of many weeks in the winter of 1815–16—and Milligan finally published it, with Tracy's name, in Washington.

As the years passed and death took its toll of the Founding Fathers, Jefferson and Adams became the great patriarchs of the nation's heritage. For the Virginian, at least, remembrance did not come easily. He derived little enjoyment from looking back over the ground he had traveled, the field strewn with the bodies of dead friends, himself standing "like a solitary tree . . . , its trunk indeed erect but its branches fallen off and its neighboring plants eradicated from around it." With the decay of memory, and its damnable tricks, he sometimes felt like a stranger to his own life. Public events—a remorseless crowding of events—had passed with such rapidity and confusion, he said, that they seemed like scenes in a magic lantern, vanishing quickly, leaving only a blur in the mind. He was little inclined to stare into the shadows of his own reflection and generally preferred to broach the future rather than recall the past. Still the history of his country was of immense importance to posterity. He could not and would not write it; but he opened himself freely to those who would, and there were many calls upon him for assistance.

His principal venture thus far in this enterprise was with Joel Barlow. It came to nought, as Barlow in 1811 returned seven boxes of Jefferson's papers and set off on a futile mission to bring Napoleon to his senses, dying instead with his retreating army in the snows of Poland in 1812. Another project, William Waller Hening's collection of the laws of Virginia, which Jefferson may be fairly said to have inspired, came to fruition after he left the presidency. He had gone to much trouble and expense to collect texts of the missing or forgotten laws of the province from the legislative beginnings in 1619. In 1796, when he loaned some of "these precious monuments of our history" to Wythe for an edition of the laws relative to lands, Jefferson wrote a letter, subsequently published by the General Assembly, imploring an edition of all the laws ever passed in Virginia. Hening, then a young Albemarle lawyer, undertook this work a decade later. Jefferson placed his indispensable collection at Hening's disposal and gave him every encouragement. The monumental *Statutes at Large*, the first work of its kind in the United States, began to appear in 1809 and concluded with the 13th volume in 1823. Jefferson had earlier loaned historical materials to John Daly Burk, whose *History of Virginia*, in three volumes to the Revolution, was dedicated to him "by a sort of national right." Louis Hue Girardin and Skelton Jones continued the work in a fourth volume, published in 1816, over which Jefferson's muse presided pencil in hand. Especially notable was the book's defense of his wartime governorship; indeed in these chapters it could be read as his personal vindication. His lawyer-friend Wirt, who had married an Albemarle lady and resided in the neighborhood in earlier years, repeatedly pumped him for recollections of Revolutionary times and, more especially, of Patrick Henry, whose biography he had undertaken to write. "Mr. Henry," said Wirt confidently in 1810, "seems to me a good text for a discourse on rhetoric, patriotism and morals." Jefferson could not unreservedly accept the premise; still, Wirt had literary as well as legal talents, as demonstrated by many Addisonian essays, so Jefferson encouraged him. Recalling Henry in all candor, lauding him as the greatest orator who ever lived, yet portraying him neither as saint nor as hero but as a lazy and ignorant backwoodsman, Jefferson sent the admiring author into a tailspin. "I despair of the subject," he declared. Torn between his splendid conception and unheroic, even impious, image Jefferson set before him, Wirt was sorry he had ever taken it up. He kept returning to the biography, however, and in 1816 pleaded with Jefferson to read the nearly complete manuscript. He agreed and offered some rather withering criticisms in the form of polite suggestions: "that Mr. Henry read Livy thro' once a year is a known impossibility," many passages were "too flowery for the sober taste of history," and some should be stricken altogether. Still he pronounced the work excellent. The judgment seemed more courteous than candid. Wirt shot back, should he publish it? Yes, by all means, said Jefferson, suppressing his fears. Published it was—a landmark in American hagiography.

While Jefferson steadfastly refused to dredge up his own past for the benefit of would-be biographers, he wrote a number of felicitous sketches of famous contemporaries, some of which became famous themselves. In the aftermath of the second war with England the nation decided to celebrate itself. A virtual industry grew up around the publication of elegant "repositories" of the lives and portraits of Revolutionary heroes and signers of the Declaration of Independence. The fame of that document soared, and the fame of its author, who was often consulted on its history, soared with it. Several of his biographical sketches, of Wythe and Franklin and Peyton Randolph, were written at the solicitation of compilers and publishers of Revolutionary lives. Others, such as the brilliant characterization of General Washington, occurred in the normal course of correspondence. In all this patriotic ferment little controversies arose. Was the Revolution set in motion by Massachusetts or Virginia? Marshall credited the former province with the origination of committees of correspondence. Wirt's *Henry* cited Jefferson's authority for the prior claim of Virginia and, also, of Henry over the Bay State hero, James Otis, in the Revolutionary vanguard. Jefferson did not become a polemicist in these matters, however. Undoubtedly his most important contribution to the annals of biography was the fifteen-page sketch of the life of Meriwether Lewis published in the two-volume *History* of the Lewis and Clark Expedition in 1814.

Jefferson had waited impatiently for this work for several years. Lewis had arranged for the publication of a definitive record before his death, and on that event General Clark assumed the responsibility. But neither knew anything of writing or publishing. What finally materialized, unfortunately, was not the journals themselves but a hurried narrative derived from the journals by two young authors in Philadelphia. A great deal remained to be done before this momentous chapter of history and science could be closed. The most precious parts—geographical, botanical, zoological, linguistic, and so on—had yet to go before the world. But despite Jefferson's continuing interest, the skill that presided over the performance of the expedition was not available for its liquidation.

Nature meant him to be a scientist, Jefferson had told himself many times, and he fancied he might take up this calling at last in studious retirement at Monticello. But it was too late: "Forty-two years of entire absorption by political duties scarcely permitting me as much attention to the more beloved studies of the natural sciences as would keep me where I once was, disqualify me from instructing those daily versed in their exercise and practice." Whole new worlds of natural science and philosophy and literature were coming into existence beyond his ken. Ticknor gave him glimpses of the astounding new intellectual world of Germany; but knowing neither the language nor the climate of romanticism he was barred from entrance. The principal diversions of his old age, as of his youth, were the ancient classics and mathematics. "My business," he wrote in his seventy-sixth year, "is to beguile the weariness of declining life, as I endeavor to do by the delights of classical reading and of mathematical truths and by the consolations of a sound philosophy, equally indifferent to hope and fear." In the realms of science, he advanced nothing new. One important contribution he had hoped to make, on the Indian languages, had been washed away in the waters of the James River as the trunk containing his collection of vocabularies fell to pirates on its passage from Washington in 1809. He remained president of the American Philosophical Society, very much in his climate, for six more years, finally insisting that he withdraw from this "sinecure" at the end of 1814. His learned letters ranged over a wide, and generally familiar, terrain: the "poison" of Hume and Blackstone, the moral sense, Epicurean philosophy, the history of the Greek ablative, Lord Napier's theorem for the solution of right-angled spherical triangles, the superiority of Linnaean classification to the systems of Cuvier and Blumenbach, the comparison of the American and Siberian mammoth, the new Spanish constitution, the history of hopperboys, weights and measures on a universal standard, and the value of neology in the enrichment and growth of language. Of the latter it might be observed that he had often been criticized, from the *Notes on Virginia* forward, for using words not to be found in standard dictionaries. As late as 1820 the citadel of New England letters, *The North American Review,* called him to account for *location, centrality, sparse,* and *grade.* To these purists who made grammar rather than strength or usage their guide, he replied that necessity obliged the Americans to invent new words for new things, to write and speak anew as they must think anew, "and should the language of England continue stationary, we shall probably enlarge our employment of it, until its new character may separate it in name as well as in power, from the mother tongue."

Jefferson was the magnet of the country intellectual circle in Albemarle. Over the years some of its brightest stars, like William Short and Robert Mills, had fled to Philadelphia, others to Richmond or elsewhere, and Jefferson's hope of attracting enlightened Europeans, like the French political economist Jean-Baptiste Say and the Portuguese savant Correa de Serra, never materialized, though his university became a magnet of another sort. But the prominent families, Randolphs, Carrs, Coleses, Cabells, Gilmers, and others, contained a wealth of talent, to which newcomers like Louis Girardin, William C. Rives, Nicholas P. Trist, and so on made impressive additions. Monticello was a country philosophical hall. In the late afternoons, when Jefferson gave himself up to society, friends and neighbors gathered around and were enthralled by his conversation, "light and attic," one observed, "having sometimes the agreeable levity of the French, at others the graver instruction of a philosopher, but always the simplicity and pleasantry which are among the characteristics of greatness." A stranger who had spent only a few days in this Socratic company said he could have spent an age without ennui: "so much freshness of character; nothing worn out or exhausted; such a magnanimous carelessness in the promulgation of his opinions; such various knowledge, so easy and cheerful a hospitality." Within the Albemarle circle, young Francis Walker Gilmer, earlier a pupil, was now his greatest pride. "In the vast dearth of scientific education in our state he presents almost the solitary object," Jefferson said of Gilmer. It was a melancholy confession of Virginia backwardness. Even Gilmer, with his fine talents for science of literature, became a slave to the law, like nearly every member of the Albemarle circle. The Abbé Correa, a regular summer guest from Philadelphia during eight years, shone in the opinion of everyone. He came on in 1813 with flattering introductions from Caspar Wistar, Dupont and others. Jefferson at once pronounced him "the greatest collection and best digest of science in books, men, and things" he had ever met with, "and with these the most amiable and engaging character." Correa was an *encyclopédist* of the old school, though especially well versed in geology and botany. During the fall of 1815 he and Gilmer accompanied Jefferson on a tour of the Peaks of Otter, the highest in Virginia's Blue Ridge, which he measured, and of the Natural Bridge, that "most sublime of nature's works," his own property, which he had not viewed for several decades. Jefferson had hoped that Correa might become a permanent member of the country circle, but he returned to Portugal in 1820.

The finest literary legacy of these autumn years was his correspondence with John Adams. The first essay toward renewal of the old friendship occurred in 1804 when Mrs. Adams wrote a letter of condolence to Jefferson on the death of his younger daughter. Jefferson had then invited a reunion, but political wounds had not healed and the exchange terminated on a sour note. In 1810 Benjamin Rush, a great friend of both men, took up the task of reconciliation. In response Jefferson sent his correspondence with Mrs. Adams to explain the difficulty. Some months later Edward Coles, Madison's private secretary at the time, called on Adams at Quincy. He talked freely of Jefferson and their political differences, and complained of his treatment by him; but after Coles assured him of Jefferson's continued affection, Adams burst out, "I always loved Jefferson, and still love him." When Coles's report reached Monticello, Jefferson at once wrote to Rush. "This is enough for me," he declared. Rush passed the word to Quincy, and Adams seized the olive branch. On January 1, 1812, he opened the correspondence with greetings on the new year and the promise of "two pieces of homespun" produced in his quarter of the Union. Jefferson, caught off-guard by Adams's humor, responded with a lecture on domestic manufactures, only the next day to discover that the "homespun" consisted of two volumes of *Lectures on Rhetoric and Oratory* by John Quincy Adams.

In a sense the contrast between humor and gravity in these opening letters characterized the entire correspondence of over fourteen years. Adams tended to be rollicking, Jefferson serious; Adams garrulous, Jefferson spare of diction; Adams bold, even reckless, in expression of opinion, Jefferson studied and reserved; Adams egocentric, Jefferson detached and, on the whole, much more interested in things observed and reflected upon than in himself. Adams's letters, which are the more sprightly, ran off in half-a-dozen directions at once. Jefferson's, more felicitous, tended to be rounded essays on some topic of learning—Indian ethnology, Greek pronunciation, the uses and abuses of grief, Christianity and the common law. Adams liked to speculate on history and politics and theology; Jefferson, while he ventured in these realms, was more drawn to scientific ones. Adams inclined to look back and reflect over the ground they had traversed, even to settle an old score or two; Jefferson seldom looked back and never engaged in recriminations. Adams wrote much more, about four times as much. The correspondence was a godsend to him. Jefferson, burdened with correspondents, could not keep up with him. The Quincy sage read more too. "Forty-three volumes read in one year, and twelve of them quartos!" Jefferson exclaimed. "Dear Sir, how I envy you! Half a dozen 8 vos. in that space of time are as much as I am allowed." Both men were keenly aware of their place in history, and as their Revolutionary comrades passed away one by one (Rush went in 1813), the bond between them strengthened.

"You and I ought not to die, before we have explained ourselves to each other," Adams declared. This seemed much more important to him than it did to Jefferson, who resisted all the way; and in the end, at least in the branch of Adams's chief concern, political philosophy, it cannot be said that they succeeded. About most things they agreed, or at any rate did not choose to differ, from the metaphysical nonsense of Plato to the despotism of Napoleon. But between them there remained fundamental differences of opinion. One that was aired, quite pleasantly, concerned aristocracy. Adams broached the subject. Aristocracy had always been his *bête noire*, but considering it inevitable and in some ways valuable in any society, he had supposed even republican constitutions must arrange for it. Jefferson, in reply, distinguished between *natural* and *artificial* aristocracy, the former founded on virtue and talents, the latter on wealth and birth. "The natural aristocracy I consider as the most precious gift of nature, for the instruction, the trusts, and government of society. . . . May we not even say," he opined, "that that form of government is the best, which provides most effectually for a pure selection of these natural aristoi into the offices of government? The artificial aristocracy is a mischievous ingredient in government, and provision should be made to prevent its ascendancy." How? Adams would lock "the pseudo-aristoi" into a separate chamber of the legislature. But that would institutionalize the evil. It was an unjust intrusion on the popular will; nor was it necessary to protect wealth from numbers. "I think the best remedy," Jefferson said, "is that provided in all our constitutions, to leave to the citizens the free election and separation of the aristoi from the pseudo-aristoi, of the wheat from the chaff. In general they will elect the really good and wise." And he went on to speak of the one thing, the general diffusion of knowledge, still wanted in his own state to secure the happy result. Adams, answering with his usual candor, rejected Jefferson's basic distinction. The natural and the pseudo-aristoi were one and the same, he said, and every aristocracy tends to become hereditary. While he could match Jefferson's expletives against Calvinism, there was still a gloomy predestinarianism in Adams's view of society, which suggested his Puritan lineage, and which the sunny Virginian repelled. Again and again Adams gloatingly recalled his friend to the exploded hopes—Jefferson's, not his—of the French Revolution. "Let me ask you, very seriously my friend, Where are now in 1813, *the perfection and perfectibility* of human nature? Where is now, the progress of the human mind? Where is the amelioration of society?" *Touché!* Nevertheless, despite the shock to his best hopes, Jefferson serenely pointed to progress in the face of catastrophe and voiced his faith in the ultimate triumph.

The reconciliation was but a year and a half old when Adams called Jefferson to account for portraying him as a kind of vandal against science and progress in a letter written to Joseph Priestley in 1801. The letter had turned up in the *Memoirs of the Late Reverend Theophilus Lindsay*, published in London. Jefferson offered a tactful explanation and expressed indignation at the publication of his private letters. He was less anxious about this particular letter, offensive to Adams, than another to Priestley in April 1803 on the subject of religion. In this epistle, now published, he had sketched the plan of a comparative view of the moral doctrines of the ancients, the Jews, and Jesus. He had hoped Priestley might undertake this work. The great philosopher-theologian died a few months later, though not before he had written *The Doctrines of Heathen Philosophy Compared with Revelation* in response to Jefferson's request. Adams now, in 1813, encouraged his friend to take up the work on his own account. Jefferson explained that he had, just after his letter to Priestley, written a brief syllabus, or outline, of the proposed inquiry. Only Priestley and Rush, to whom he had sent copies, were let in on the secret. Actually, the privileged circle had been somewhat larger, and Jefferson now admitted Adams to it.

This important chapter in the history of Jefferson's religious opinions had its beginnings in a promise made to Rush, a devout Christian, in the course of evening conversations in 1798–99 which, as Jefferson remembered, "served as an anodyne to the afflictions of the crisis through which our country was then laboring." Rush believed Christianity laid the groundwork of republicanism. Jefferson could not follow him to the acceptance of revelation or sectarian dogma of any sort but promised to give him a view of the subject, the result of a life of inquiry and reflection, very different from the "anti-Christian system" ascribed to him by clerical and political enemies. Rush reminded him of the promise during the election of 1800. Jefferson had not forgotten it. His views, he said, while they should be acceptable to rational Christians, would probably not reconcile the *genus irratabile vatum* who had seized upon the recent delusion to aid their pretensions of establishing a particular form of Christianity in the United States. "The returning good sense of our country threatens abortion to their hopes, and they believe that any portion of power confided to me will be executed in opposition to their schemes, and they believe truly, for I have sworn upon the altar of God eternal hostility against every form of tyranny over the mind of man." As the tone of this passage suggests, Jefferson's religious libertarianism became more deeply involved in anti-clericalism under the attack of pulpit politicians in 1800.

Not until April 1803 did he fulfill, in some part, his commitment to Rush. At the moment of leaving Monticello he received Priestley's little book, *Socrates and Jesus Compared*. This touched his own view, and he ruminated the subject on the road back to Washington. There he at once set down his Syllabus of an Estimate of the Merit of the Doctrines of Jesus, Compared with Those of Others. In this outline of less than a thousand words he reached the conclusion that the system of morals broached by Jesus, "if filled up in the true style and spirit of the rich fragments he left us, would be the most perfect and sublime that has ever been taught by man." The ancient heathen moralists, their teachings uncluttered by the corruptions and superstitions of Christianity, had won his allegiance when young, but he now thought them deficient on two serious counts. So far as they aimed at "tranquillity of mind" they were "really great." This was always an important consideration with Jefferson, and he continued to seek instruction from Seneca, Cicero, Epicurus, and other ancient moralists to the day of his death. But they had not developed man's duties to his fellows "within the circle of benevolence" or pushed their scrutinies into the recesses of the human heart. Neither had the Jews, whose ideas of the deity were degrading and whose ethics were "repulsive and anti-social." This was left to Jesus. Many disadvantages attended his teachings: he wrote nothing himself; the rich patrons of learning opposed him, and so the commitment of his teachings to writing fell to unlettered men who, moreover, wrote from memory after the transactions of his life had passed; a victim of the "combination of the altar and the throne" at an early age, he was not spared the time or the maturity to perfect his system; only fragments survived, which descended to posterity "mutilated, misstated, and often unintelligible," and still more disfigured by "the corruptions of schismatizing followers." Even so, the universal philanthropy Jesus inculcated, gathering all mankind into one family, together with his juster notions of God, his appeal to the tribunal of the heart, and his teaching of a future state of rewards and punishments as an incentive to moral conduct—in this his system was sublime.

Such is "my religious creed," Jefferson said. Whether or not it made him a Christian in the theological sense, he did not care. The moral branch of religion alone concerned him; the dogmatic branch of the priests and metaphysicians corrupted the pure and simple principles of Jesus. "I am a Christian," he declared, "in the only sense he wished any one to be; sincerely attached to his doctrines, in preference to all others; ascribing to himself every *human* excellence; and believing he never claimed any other." The question of Christ's humanity or divinity, being theological, was purposely omitted from the Syllabus. He sent copies to Rush, Priestley, several members of the cabinet, John Page, and his two daughters. All were under strict instructions not to expose it to anyone. It was a matter between God and himself; nor did he wish to countenance by any act of his the presumption of those who would erect a public tribunal over the rights of conscience. He had placed the document in these few friendly hands, he said, that they might judge the libels published against him and, presumably, secure the sanctity of his grave after death. He did not proselytize; he had no public object in view. Still he believed that his opinions, if fully developed, might form the basis of a broad common faith, a *consenus gentium*, uniting all men of reason and liberality around a hard core of morality, discovered in the moral sense, and a benevolent god discovered by inquiry into nature. Christianity might thus be saved from both the priests and the infidels. He was fond of saying, with Bolingbroke, "there would never have been an infidel, if there had never been a priest." Jesus was the greatest reformer of morals and scourger of priestcraft who ever lived, Jefferson declared, and on these points natural religionists like himself had underestimated his character. For this reason he encouraged Priestley to take up the work of inquiry and reconciliation along the lines sketched in the Syllabus and, indeed, already carried some way by the great Unitarian. Jefferson had been deeply influenced by Priestley's *Corruptions of Christianity* (1782) and other works which, with Conyers Middleton's writings, he said, formed the groundwork of his religious faith. Priestley was a Socinian, who denied the Trinity, virgin birth, original sin, vicarious atonement, the divine inspiration of Scripture, and so on. Yet he subscribed to revelation and the miracles, preached such curious doctrines as the resurrection of the body, though not of the soul, and prophesied a second coming—a millennium of the Enlightenment. If much of Priestley's theology was unacceptable to the secular-minded Jefferson, he fully entered into the spirit of his return to primitive Christianity. And Priestley, who championed Jefferson's political cause, recognized in him a religious friend as well, and even had the temerity to dedicate his last major book, the huge *General History of the Christian Church* (1802–03), to Jefferson.

There was still a second part of the work Jefferson had in mind. On the premises of the Syllabus the teachings of Jesus had been disfigured and corrupted; so it was necessary to strip away the impurities and lay bare the plain and unsophisticated moral texts. Sometime after Priestley's death, during several desultory evenings in Washington, Jefferson took a New Testament, cut from the books of the Evangelists those verses that had the authentic stamp of Jesus' mind and imagination, "as easily distinguished as diamonds in a dunghill," and arranged the text in an octavo of forty-six pages which he called the "Philosophy of Jesus." He mentioned this to no one until several years after his retirement. The publication in 1813 of his letters to Priestley alerted him to the danger of his Syllabus bursting upon the public. When Rush died in that year, Jefferson implored his son to return this document. The Syllabus remained a secret. In 1816 Francis Adrian Van der Kemp, a versatile scholar and Unitarian preacher who had come to the United States in 1788, a refugee of the abortive Dutch revolution, asked Jefferson for a copy of the Syllabus he had seen while visiting Adams at Quincy. Jefferson complied, adding the usual injunction. Van der Kemp liked it so much he begged Jefferson to permit its publication, quite anonymously, in an English theological journal. Surprisingly, he consented; and it appeared in the *Monthly Repository of Theological and General Literature* in 1816 with ascription to "an eminent American statesman." This was more ascription than Jefferson had bargained for. Fortunately, so obscure was the journal in the United States, it was never picked up.

Yet at this very time the word circulated that Jefferson had changed his religious opinions and planned to publish a book on the subject. He received letters welcoming his conversion to Christ. Part of the the mysterious infection stemmed from the republication of the letters to Priestley in a Boston volume, *American Unitarianism*.

The principal source, however, was a letter to Charles Thomson, his old comrade, who had let it go into the press. In the letter Jefferson spoke of his Philosophy of Jesus. "It is a document in proof that *I am a real Christian*, that is to say, a disciple of the doctrines of Jesus, very different from the Platonists, who call *me* infidel. . . ." He went on to say that if he had the time he would improve this first essay by the addition of Greek, Latin, and French texts ranged in columns side by side with the English, perhaps subjoining a translation of Gassendi's Syntagma of the doctrines of Epicurus, which he still thought the most virtuous and rational system of the ancients. To those who inquired, mainly on the basis of this letter, of his conversion to Christianity, Jefferson denied it, at least in so far as any change of opinion was implied, and as for writing a book he "should as soon think of writing for the reformation of Bedlam." All he had in mind, solely for his personal satisfaction, was the project mentioned to Thomson: a bible of primitive Christianity. For this he needed New Testaments in the four languages, all of roughly the same typography. (The Hebrew text should have been included but Jefferson did not know the language.) He began to assemble these in 1816. Either because the bibles or the time failed him, the work was not completed until 1819. He called this scissors-and-paste book of 164 pages, two columns to the page, "The Life and Morals of Jesus of Nazareth," and had it bound in red morocco. Apparently no one, not even in his immediate family, knew of its existence until after his death. The Syllabus with this work constitute what is sometimes called The Jefferson Bible.

Jefferson said he was a sect to himself so far as he knew. He continued, as in younger days, to aid churches of different denominations in his neighborhood and often attended their services; but he belonged to no church. He followed with interest the Unitarian controversy in New England and once predicted "there is not a young man living in the United States who will no: die a Unitarian." In Unitarianism he saw the possibilities of a unifying religion of humanity, and this new accent counterpointed the earlier individualism of Jefferson's religious creed. But he was not a Unitarian. Rather than seeking "the country of spirits," he preferred to rest his head on "that pillow of ignorance which the benevolent Creator has made so soft for us, knowing how much we should be forced to use it." Deep or moving religious experience seems never to have touched him. He had discovered in his youth that reason was the only oracle given to man by God. And as he wrote confidently in 1814: "I have followed it faithfully in all important cases, to such a degree at least as leaves me without uneasiness, and if on minor occasions I have erred from its dictates, I have trust in him who made us what we are, and knows it was not his plan to make us always unerring. He has formed us moral agents, not that, in the perfection of his state, he can feel pain or pleasure from anything we may do: he is far above our power: but that we may promote the happiness of those with whom he has placed us in society, by acting honestly towards all, benevolently to those who fall within our way, respecting sacredly their rights bodily and mental, and cherishing especially their freedom of conscience, as we value our own. I must ever believe that religion substantially good which produces an honest life, and we have been authorized . . . to judge the tree by its fruits. Our particular principles of religion are a subject of accountability to our god alone. I inquire after no man's and trouble none with mine: nor is it given to us in this life to know whether yours or mine, our friend's or our foe's, is exactly right." Given this summation, what had he changed? Not much. He still rejected revelation, the divinity of Christ, the miracles, the atonement, and so on, without which Christianity was nothing in the eyes of believers. He did not even accept Jesus on his own terms, for Jesus was a spiritualist by the grace of God and he a materialist by the grace of science. But he had brought the morals of Jesus, above all the love of man, within the perimeters of the older faith of the Enlightenment. The simple precepts of Jesus infused a universal ethic founded on the natural rights of man. In this sense Jesus *was* the savior, not of priests and metaphysicians only, but of all men; and Jefferson was the *real* Christian he professed to be.

Founding the University

On his agenda of unfinished business the septuagenarian Jefferson gave first place to education. "I have two great measures at heart, without which no republic can maintain itself in strength," he wrote soon after his retirement. "1. That of general education, to enable every man to judge for himself what will secure or endanger his freedom. 2. To divide every county into hundreds, of such size that all the children of each will be within reach of a central school in it." On these "two hooks," he often said, the future of republican government depended. The wards, or hundreds, while associated with primary education, would be miniature republics, drawing every citizen immediately into the administration of local affairs and voicing the will of the people through all the expanding circles— county, state, and federal—of Jefferson's concentric commonwealth. The wards would be the Virginia equivalent of New England townships, which had proven their strength and vitality in the embargo repeal. Both proposals, wards and general education, traced back to Jefferson's Bill for the More General Diffusion of Knowledge in 1778. The crucial defeat of his young years, he hoped it might ripen into the triumph of his old age.

Virginia had never been very hospitable to his reforms, and was perhaps less so now than at the crest of the Revolutionary wave. The prophet was honored but unarmed in his native country. The constitution of 1776 still stood as an obstacle to democratic government. A new movement for its reform arose west of the Blue Ridge. Jefferson furnished it with an ideology and a platform, marking the farthest advance of his democratic thought, but he declined to become a gladiator in this embattled cause. Reform, such as it was, came only after his death and could not have come sooner because of conservative fears of his influence. Slavery emancipation, on the gradual plan he had formed during the Revolution and publicized, like the constitutional reforms, in the *Notes on Virginia*, was another crucial item on the agenda. But Jefferson despaired of its success; and he would not waste the waning energies of the years that remained to him in a cause certain to deprive him of all power for good in other and more promising directions. So he made education, arduous yet not impossible of fulfillment, his "holy cause." "I have only this singular anxiety in the world," he wrote in 1817. "It is a bantling of 40 years birth and nursing, and if I can once see it on its legs, I will sing with sincerity and pleasure my nunc dimittis." In the end he could sing indeed, though not for the plan of general education. Again it went down to defeat. In the process, however, he brought to fruition his dream of a university. This had been part of the original plan—the apex of a comprehensive system of public education arising like a pyramid from the primary schools. To erect the apex without the base was doubtless an act of folly; yet this is what the Virginians attempted, and Jefferson, knowing it was folly, took what pleasure he could in the result.

The University of Virginia, chartered in 1819, was as much his personal creation as Monticello, the Declaration of Independence, or the Lewis and Clark expedition. And perhaps nothing contained so well the dominant forces of his life and mind, of democracy and enlightenment and nationality, as his vision of a great university. The vision passed through several phases before it came to realization. Initially, in 1779, Jefferson sought to transform William and Mary into a secular institution of university caliber. He failed in this and gradually lost all hope of reforming his alma mater. In 1794 he felt keen interest in the proposal of a Swiss exile from revolution, François d'Ivernois, to remove the whole College of Geneva to the United States. When the General Assembly passed up the opportunity, Jefferson recommended it to President Washington in the belief that this seminary, one of the finest in Europe in his opinion, might become the foundation of a national university. But Washington thought the hazards of transplanting a foreign college, and a foreign-speaking faculty, too great. Jefferson himself had earlier warned against one experiment in this line, the establishment of a French academy of arts and sciences in Richmond under the direction of Quesnay de Beaurepaire, which had already failed.

In 1800 he first seriously turned his thoughts to the creation of a wholly new institution in his native state. From his friends Priestley and Dupont he requested the plan of a university "so broad and liberal and modern as to be worth patronizing with public support, and be a temptation to the youth of other states to come and drink of the cup of knowledge and fraternize with us." Priestley offered a series of useful suggestions, while Dupont furnished an elaborate plan of national education. Neither altogether suited Jefferson's purposes. At this stage he aimed at a state university, modestly begun but large in conception, and national in spirit and service and outline. In January 1805 he wrote a four-page prospectus for such a university in reply to the request of Littleton Waller Tazewell, who seemed to believe the General Assembly had been brought to the point of action. Already Georgia, North Carolina, South Carolina, and Tennessee had established state universities, and though they existed mostly on paper, Virginia could not be indifferent to this movement. The letter to Tazewell was the genesis of Jefferson's plan for the University of Virginia. Emphasizing the modernity of his conception, he called not only for a redefinition of higher education but for a university geared to the constantly advancing knowledge of the times. "Science is progressive," he wrote. "What was useful two centuries ago is now become useless; e.g., one half of the professorships of William and Mary. What is now deemed useful will in some of its parts become useless in another century. . . . Everyone knows that Oxford, Cambridge, the Sorbonne, etc. are now a century or two behind the sciences of the age." Perhaps as an inducement to the legislature, Jefferson offered the legacy of his library to the meditated university. But it was not to be. When Virginia remained mute after the passage of two years, Jefferson set aside his hopes in this direction, and in December 1806 recommended a national university to Congress. The project concerted with Joel Barlow and others was still another engagement in the forty-year campaign.

Jefferson had been in retirement for five years before he became associated with the enterprise that led to the establishment of the University of Virginia. Several of his neighbors, including Peter Carr as president of the board, were endeavoring in 1814 to set up a private secondary school, Albemarle Academy, in Charlottesville. Petty academies of this kind, Jefferson told Adams, dotted the state. "They commit their pupils to the theatre of the world with just taste enough of learning to be alienated from industrious pursuits, and not enough to do service in the ranks of science." Placed on the board of the fledgling academy, he at once set out to escalate it into a college and then into a university. In September he drafted a bill to accomplish the first step, the conversion of Albemarle Academy into Central College. The bill failed in the ensuing session of the legislature but passed in February 1816. By the act of incorporation Central College was a private non-sectarian seminary with no other resources than it could raise from the sale of the two glebes in Albemarle (the parish lands of the old Established Church), from voluntary subscriptions, and from lottery. However, the charter provided for a liberal enlargement of the educational plan to reach the objects of a state university and divested the college of its local character by placing the appointment of the Board of Visitors in the governor and making him an ex officio member. The Governor, Wilson Cary Nicholas, named Jefferson's friends, including Madison and Monroe, to the board. In the space of two years a lifeless academy had been transformed into the design of a state university.

But Jefferson aimed at more than a university. That remained, as in 1778, the capstone of a general plan of public education. He revived this plan in his letter to Carr transmitting the college bill in 1814. Three grades of instruction, elementary, general, and professional, corresponded more or less to the three classes of society, the laboring, the gentry, and the learned. The primary schools, again as in 1778, contemplated the division of counties into wards and three years of rudimentary education at the public expense to ensure that everyone was equipped for the business of life and the duties of citizenship. In 1796 the General Assembly had given the county courts the option of laying out aldermanic districts, like Jefferson's wards, and assessing the populace for public schools. But the local magistrates had not exercised this option, which aroused Jefferson against these "oligarchs," and Virginia slid into deeper ignorance than she had known at her birth. The "General Schools" of Jefferson's second grade combined the features of a secondary or grammar school and a college. They would be terminal for youth whose position or calling required modest polish, while they would be preparatory for those destined to the pursuits of science and the learned professions. Essentially classical schools, they would also embrace philosophy, mathematics, and natural science. These "colleges," as Jefferson began to call them, would be established by the commonwealth in districts within a day's ride of every citizen. Although aided by the state, they would not be free except for the few "public foundationers," the natural aristoi of the poor, as proposed in the original plan. In the third grade, the professional, "each science is to be taught in the highest degree it has yet attained." His conception was still vague, but he envisioned a university with specialized instruction in the useful sciences and learned professions of the time. The most novel feature of this plan was the provision for a school of technical philosophy serving artisans and workmen—machinists, brewers, shipwrights, glassmakers—through evening courses and maintained, like the ward schools, at public expense. While one might wish Jefferson had persevered with this idea of an evening trades school, he probably realized its impracticality in Virginia and, accordingly, dropped it from later plans. The letter to Carr throughout was quite abstract, a philosophical view, and addressed to no specific institution.

Over a year later the scheme Jefferson had sketched for his nephew, who had died in the interim, came prominently into the deliberations at Richmond. It was published, and Charles Fenton Mercer drafted a general education bill based on the plan. The bill passed the House but came to grief in the Senate. Both houses concurred in February 1816 in a resolution requesting the Directors of the Literary Fund to report a comprehensive plan of education from the primary schools through the university. The Literary Fund had been set up in 1810 to receive state income from miscellaneous sources and to aid, principally, the education of the poor. Jefferson eyed this resource for the state university postulated by the February resolution. If the Literary Fund went to the support of primary schools nothing would be left for the university or the district colleges. The decision of the legislature on the destiny of the Literary Fund would largely determine the future of public education in Virginia. While he proceeded to build Central College as the shell of the state university, Jefferson worked to shape the whole system of education. The Governor, Nicholas, gave him a sympathetic ear, of course, as did certain members of the assembly; but his principal liaison with that body, and his leading coadjutor in the establishment of the university, was Joseph C. Cabell.

A friend and neighbor, deeply interested in the cause of public education, one of the trustees of Central College, and the representative of the Albemarle district in the Senate, Cabell headed the cadre of "Monticello men" at Richmond. He conferred at length with Jefferson in the summer of 1817. At his request Jefferson drafted bills for the three grades of education. The Bill for Establishing Elementary Schools was on the usual plan. Requiring the support of these schools by tax levies on the residents of each ward, proportioned to property, Jefferson's system reserved the Literary Fund for the colleges and the university. Cabell presented this bill, with the companion Bill for the Establishment of District Colleges and University, to the chairman of the Committee on Schools and Colleges, after striking certain interesting provisions. Jefferson had wished to exclude clergymen as visitors (trustees) of the elementary schools, to bar religious instruction inconsistent with the tenets of any sect or denomination, and, borrowing from the example of the new Spanish constitution, to impose a test of literacy for citizenship on the rising generation. On the advice of Nicholas, Thomas Ritchie, and others, Cabell omitted these invitations to political cavil. Objections to the plan arose on the score of practicality; the mass of people, it was said, would not submit to taxation for education, and the rich would not contribute to the education of the poor. Jefferson answered in a letter to Cabell published in Ritchie's *Enquirer*. Among other things, he pointed out that the cost of the lower schools amounted to only three and three-quarter cents per capita for the entire state and that the rich had an important stake in raising up honest and useful citizens from the mass of poor. Indeed, in the equalitarian society of the United States, their children or grandchildren might well be poor. But Jefferson's bill did not emerge from the committee. Offered as a substitute in the House, it received few votes. What passed was an act providing for appropriations of the Literary Fund to the education of the poor only in "charity schools," so far as they might be conducted in the counties. This was a grave disappointment, and it proved decisive for elementary education in Virginia until after the Civil War. Nor was any provision made for district colleges. Yet the defeat breathed life into the university. When the school bill came to the Senate, Cabell engrafted upon it a $15,000 annuity from the Literary Fund for the support of a state university. A commission was to be appointed by the Governor to fix the site of the institution and develop its educational plan.

Jefferson rejoiced in this half-victory. He felt confident that the commission would choose the site of Central College for the university. During the past year the board under Jefferson's direction as Rector had bought 200 acres of high ground just west of Charlottesville, commenced the building, and even begun to assemble a faculty. Precious little money had been raised. Determined to call attention to this struggling infant, Jefferson assumed the disguise of an itinerant correspondent to write a flattering prospectus of the university-to-be for publication in the *Richmond Enquirer*. The cornerstone of the first building was laid with appropriate ceremony in the presence of Jefferson, Madison, and Monroe on October 6, 1817.

By then the architectural plan had been settled. The conception of an "academical village" had taken form in Jefferson's mind at least a dozen years before. He had broached it in his letter to Tazewell. Consulted in 1810 on a new college in Tennessee, he advised against the common practice of erecting a large central building, unfriendly to health, study, morals, and manners. "It is infinitely better," he said, "to erect a small and separate building for each separate professorship, with only a hall below for his class, and two chambers above for himself; joining the lodges by barracks for a certain portion of students, opening into a covered way to give a dry communication between all the schools. The whole of these arranged around an open square of grass and trees, would make it, what it should be in fact, an academical village, instead of a large and common den of noise, of filth and of fetid air." What evolved from this conception in 1817 was a rectangle open at one of the longer sides, alternating modest two-story pavilions with a series of flat-roofed barracks, or dormitories, of one story, the whole united in front by a covered colonnade. Jefferson wished the pavilions to be "chaste models of the orders of architecture taken from the finest remains of antiquity," not alone for their inherent beauty but in order to instruct and elevate the taste of the students. He asked William Thornton and Benjamin Latrobe to sketch their ideas. Both responded generously. They influenced the design of some of the pavilions, no two alike, though in the final analysis the architectural work, like everything else, was Jefferson's. Latrobe suggested the idea of a dominant central building, which Jefferson matured into the Rotunda, a scale model of the Roman Pantheon adapted to the service of a library.

The plan underwent some change when Jefferson became better acquainted with the terrain. The site offered a narrow ridge declining from north to south and allowing but 200 feet of level ground between the buildings on either side. So Jefferson rearranged the three-sided rectangle into two long porticoed rows, descending in three levels with the slope of the ground, and open at both ends, though to be filled at the north by the Rotunda. Latrobe objected to the east-west exposure thereby given to the conjoined residences of professors and students. The west winds would freeze them in winter and the sun bake them in summer. Jefferson conceded the objection but the terrain was a law of nature. Other parts of the plan were settled as the building went forward. The gardens of the professors would be placed at the rear of their pavilions and separated by serpentine walls. The "hotels" for feeding the students, conducted by French families speaking their native tongue, would be thrown on rear streets, and joined by additional dormitories in arcaded ranges paralleling the rows on the lawn. How far Jefferson would be able to go with his plan remained to be seen. In 1817, in the *Enquirer* article, he hoped for four professors, hence four pavilions and the dormitories to go with them, by 1820. But he was then writing under the restraint of a college plan. The university bill drafted for Cabell called for ten professors, each a separate school, each with its own pavilion.

Jefferson lavished his love of classical architecture on the pavilions. "We are sadly at a loss here for a Palladio," he wrote to Madison in November 1817. All of his three editions had gone to Washington and nobody in the neighborhood had one. Obviously Madison or someone came to his rescue, for the façades of the pavilions were derived from Palladio and, in some instances, from the antique models themselves, such as the Theater of Marcellus and the Bath of Diocletian. Some of the first occupants of the buildings complained of Jefferson's "logarithmic" adherence to Palladian rule for the sake of external appearance to the sacrifice of interior livability. The criticism may have been just. He believed a degree of splendor would contribute to the success of the institution, most immediately in the attraction of a superior faculty. And certainly his great achievement was not in the individual buildings themselves, whether viewed from the outside or the inside—only the Rotunda qualified in this respect as a monument of architectural genius—but in the unified articulation of the whole, not alone for its dramatic beauty but for its exquisite adaptation to the educational purposes to be served. Ticknor, when he first gazed on this serried mass of red brick and white columns in 1824, called it "more beautiful than anything architectural in New England, and more appropriate to a university than is to be found, perhaps, in the world." And Lewis

Mumford, a century later, placed Jefferson's creation in a rank by itself in the nation's architecture for the succeeding fifty years. Imitative in classical details, the over-all design was one of unparalleled originality. No prototype has ever been discovered for it. Reference has sometimes been made to the Reverend Samuel Knox's *Essay on the Best System of Liberal Education*, winner of an Amercian Philosophical Society prize in 1799. Jefferson had surely read this essay and learned from it; indeed, Knox was the first man offered an appointment to the faculty of Central College. In his discussion of the physical design of a university, Knox proposed the grouping of buildings around a square in a manner similar to Jefferson's "academical village"; but he imposed smaller squares, like graduated blocks, one inside the other until all freedom and openness was lost. Classical sources have sometimes been cited. And undoubtedly the layout of Roman country villas entered into Jefferson's conception, as it did into Monticello, which itself bears visual resemblances to the University; but this is the most that can be said. During these years Jefferson designed a number of buildings in the Albemarle region—courthouses, jails, country houses, even a church—but before the University they pale into insignificance. This was a masterpiece, and a heroic one at that, for the raising of columns, capitals, and entablatures in the Virginia upcountry was not easy work, and Jefferson made himself personally responsible for every last detail.

In the spring of 1818 he was appointed to the commission charged with choosing the site and developing the plan of the state university. The principal competition to Charlottesville came from Williamsburg, in the tidewater, and Lexington and Staunton in the Valley. William and Mary, at the former place, feared the rivalry of a state university. The old college had declined steadily. Jefferson never gave a thought to its rehabilitation, nor did he consider it a serious threat to his ambitions for Central College. The claims of the Valley were more troublesome from the standpoint both of geography and population. The Valley was the fastest growing section of Virginia. Jefferson supported its claims, and the claims of the Transmontane beyond, for political equality through the reform of the Virginia constitution. Staunton aspired to become the new capital of the commonwealth, and feared the location of the university in Charlottesville would impair its chances. Lexington, farther to the south, boasted a going seminary, Washington College (later Washington and Lee), for elevation to higher status. Sectarian religionists gathered around both William and Mary and Washington College, the former Episcopal, the latter Presbyterian; and neither could look with equanimity on a secular institution fathered by the Sage of Monticello. The commission, being formed on senatorial districts, gave the balance of influence to the country east of the Blue Ridge. During the summer Jefferson confidently developed his strategy and wrote a report that might serve as a draft for the commission's educational plan.

The commission met at Rockfish Gap, high in the Blue Ridge nearly thirty miles west of Monticello, on August 1-4. Jefferson made the strenuous journey on horseback. From the moment the commission gathered around tables in the room of a local tavern and chose him to preside, everything went his way. He had prepared a large map showing Charlottesville's location exactly at the geographical and population center of the state. If this argument was not conclusive in itself, there were the added persuasions of his fame and reputation, his leadership in the cause of education, and the prospects of a new institution neither wearied by age nor fettered by parochial or sectarian ties. The commission chose Charlottesville and Central College with little difficulty. And as chairman of a committee to draw up the proposed plan of education, Jefferson offered the report he had already written.

The Rockfish Gap Report, one of the great documents from his pen, was not addressed to "an assembly of philosophers," he said, but to the Virginia General Assembly, which must act on the recommendations of the commission. Written with a view to influencing the legislative decision, it was, in this sense, a political production, and should not be taken as a complete or definitive guide to Jefferson's mind on the subject of higher education. In his educational labors, as in others, he never articulated his whole thought. His ideas were in constant motion and seldom abstracted from immediately practical objectives. Still the Report of 1818 has exceptional theoretical interest. He began with definitions of the aims and character of primary and secondary education. It was impossible to plan a university in an educational vacuum or to expect it to succeed in its mission without strong foundations in the lower schools. So he entered an impassioned plea for public education in general. "Education . . . engrafts a new man on the native stock, and improves what in his nature was vicious and perverse into qualities of virtue and social worth. And it cannot be but that each generation succeeding to the knowledge acquired by all those who preceded it, adding to it their own acquisitions and discoveries, and handing the mass down for successive and constant accumulation, must advance the knowledge and well-being of mankind, not *infinitely*, as some have said, but *indefinitely*, and to a term which no one can fix or foresee." Voicing once again this hope of the Enlightenment, Jefferson showed little patience with owl-like creatures only fitted for the habitations of the night. The values of education, moral, political, and economical, were above all estimate, not alone for the individual but for the state and the nation. Education was the only road to "the prosperity, the power, and happiness of a nation."

Jefferson collected the useful sciences to be taught in the university into ten branches: Ancient Languages (Latin, Greek, Hebrew), Modern Languages (including Anglo-Saxon), Pure Mathematics (adding military and naval architecture), Physico-Mathematics (mechanics, optics, pneumatics and so on, plus astronomy and geography), Natural Philosophy (physics, chemistry, mineralogy), Natural History, Anatomy and Medicine, Government (including civil history), Law, and Ideology (the science of thought, embracing moral philosophy, belles lettres, and fine arts). The actual grouping of the subjects in the schools would be finally determined by the ten professors in the light of their qualifications. The conception, over-all, broke completely with the traditional classical curriculum in higher education. In England certainly, to a lesser extent in the United States, the colleges and universities had been at the service of wealth and religion, dispensing a mixture of humanistic refinement and Christian piety. Some American educators were beginning to recognize the need to reform the curriculum in directions both secular and modern, giving scope to new sciences like chemistry and political economy, to modern languages, and to professional and applied subjects. Innovations along this line had been attempted at some places, but without much success. The University of Pennsylvania, as Jefferson knew, had made a promising start in modern studies a quarter-century ago. Recent reports from Wistar and others had been discouraging, however, and by 1818 Jefferson thought better of Harvard than of Pennsylvania. Abroad only the Scottish universities, Edinburgh most notably, had reached out to the larger community and introduced the practical element into the higher learning. The educational plan, like the architectural plan, of the University of Virginia had no model; still the University of Edinburgh, with which Jefferson and many Virginians had affinities, scientific or theological, exerted a pervasive influence.

Jefferson hoped to dispense altogether with conventional study of the ancient languages, not because he, with so many modernists, thought them dead and useless, but because these languages were "the foundations common to all the sciences," and so should form the core of instruction in the collegiate or secondary schools. He worried lest the University be dragged down to the level of a classical school full of "the noisy turbulence of a multitude of small boys." He again entered a plea for the district colleges, which would take boys to the fifteenth year of age or beyond. "These institutions . . . ," he wrote, "might then be the passage of entrance for youths into the University, where their classical learning might be critically completed, by a study of the authors of highest degree; and it is at this stage only that they should be received at the University." While he would have liked to embrace such applied studies as agriculture, commerce, diplomacy, and manufacturing in his scheme, he was unwilling to do so at the expense of the basic sciences and, practically, knew the legislature would never support more than ten schools. (He finally had to settle for eight.) Medicine, occupying the shady ground between science and charlatanism, would be taught only in its theoretical aspects and as a part of general culture. It could not be taught clinically, or professionally, without a hospital, which did not exist in Charlottesville. Young men preparing to become physicians and surgeons would have to complete their education elsewhere.

The Report called attention to the unprecedented omission of religious instruction and a chair of divinity. The constitutional principles of religious freedom and equality presented an insuperable bar, Jefferson said. He sometimes spoke of theology as "the charlatanism of the mind," as medicine was "the charlatanism of the body," and so far as this view prevailed he could not consider it a branch of

973

useful knowledge to be taught in any university, public or private. He did not express this view in the Report. On the contrary, anticipating pious objections to a godless university, he emphasized that religion in its moral, literary, and historical aspects had a place in the curriculum. These would be taught as a branch of ethics, through the languages, and so on. Since the study of languages involved for Jefferson the whole history of civilization, the student of Hebrew, Greek, and Latin, for instance, would learn a great deal of primitive Christianity. In a larger sense all education was moral. It exercised man's moral sense, overcame any of its "innate obliquities," and developed one's duties to others and to God. By purely secular studies, cultivating those moral obligations in which all sects agree, Jefferson prophesied, "a basis will be formed common to all sects." A common faith uniting the multitude of Americans in a secular religion of peace and reason and humanity would surely advance hand in hand with the progress of enlightenment.

Jefferson addressed himself briefly to certain "accessories" of formal education—manual exercise, manual arts, and "the arts which embellish life, dancing, music, and drawing"—which, while not incorporated in the schools, would be available to the students; and also to the parietal functions of a resident university. Here he expressed an unusually liberal attitude. Most American colleges and universities were nurseries for growing boys. Discipline was a serious problem everywhere; and such was the reputed indulgence of southern parents toward their children that the president of Yale had once declared there could never be a university below the Potomac. Nevertheless, Jefferson repudiated the common appeal to motives of fear in the government of youth. "Hardening them by disgrace, to corporal punishments, and servile humiliations cannot be the best process for producing erect character." He recommended instead "the affectionate deportment" of the home environment. And noting the experience of some universities abroad in allowing the students to police and govern themselves, he thought the example worthy of emulation in America for the initiation of youth into the duties of civil life. The government of a university, unlike that of a school, ought to be a portico to manhood. If founded in reason and comity, he said, "it will be more likely to nourish in the minds of our youth the combined spirit of order and self-respect, so congenial with our political institutions, and so important to be woven into the American character."

One of Jefferson's most liberal ideas was not contained in the Rockfish Gap Report, presumably because it had not yet occurred to him. This was the principle of free election. Jefferson came to it in 1820. He had sent his grandson Francis Eppes to Columbia College, in South Carolina, where Thomas Cooper was teaching while waiting to take up his appointment in Charlottesville. Young Eppes soon found himself in a regimented curriculum, forced into courses he did not want or need, and to proceed, not as he was capable, but in the lockstep of the four-class system. In this respect Columbia College (later the University of South Carolina) was like every other. The regimen was wasteful and arbitrary, Jefferson wrote sympathetically to young Eppes. It will be "the fundamental law of our university to leave everyone free to attend whatever branches of instruction he wants, and to decline what he does not want." And so it became. Furthermore, the marshaled classes (freshman, sophomore, and so on) would be abolished. Students became simply students, all on an equal footing, and free to proceed according to ability. Very likely Jefferson would have arrived at this position without the shock of his grandson's experience. It was a logical outcome of the revolt against the standard curriculum, of the introduction of specialized courses of study, and the spirit of individualism. George Ticknor, just beginning his tenure as Professor of Modern Languages at Harvard, soon hit on the same idea in his efforts to reform that institution. The reform did not take hold, not at Harvard or anywhere outside the University of Virginia, for half a century. The "elective system," like most of the liberal reforms proposed in the Report of 1818, was admired in theory but had little practical influence in the educational world of the time.

The published Report made a strong impression in Richmond. Sectarian and local interests in the General Assembly opposed the commission's site recommendation, but many legislators, east and west, Episcopal and Presbyterian, set aside their prejudices and voted, in January 1819, to charter the University of Virginia in Charlottesville. The pride and the interest of the commonwealth demanded a university; it was too late in the day to quarrel about location or other details. A new Board of Visitors was constituted in the shell of the old, Jefferson still the Rector, and the University arose on the foundations of Central College. Nothing but the name had changed. The University existed on paper only. With but one pavilion completed and a meager $15,000 a year committed by the state, its future was still at hazard. Jefferson at once pressed Nicholas and Cabell for additional funds. Most of the counties had not claimed the money in the Literary Fund for the support of local charity schools. Jefferson proposed the diversion of these derelict funds, amounting to $45,000, to the University. The assembly would not now hear of it or vote another cent for the University, Cabell informed him. One victory at a time was all the "Monticello men" could expect. Some legislators feared the University would drain the Literary Fund. Very few shared Jefferson's splendid conception of the institution. Motives of mean economy were reinforced by economic disaster. Unfortunately, the University came into existence in the year of the Panic of 1819, the nation's first great depression. Retrenchment was the order of the day, and for the next several years Jefferson's pleas for help fell on reluctant ears in Richmond.

He was determined not to open the institution until it could be opened in style, buildings completed, faculty assembled, and all the insignia of a university in evidence. He had a horror of its becoming a petty college filled with mediocre professors and student cast-offs of Harvard or Princeton or Pennsylvania. Tentatively, the opening was scheduled for 1822. Meanwhile, Jefferson and the board arranged for a classical school to be set up in Charlottesville to prepare youth for the University. On the grounds Arthur S. Brokenborough, named Proctor, assumed oversight of the building; but Jefferson and John Hartwell Cocke, the board's committee of superintendence, were constantly active. The buildings had first priority and Jefferson gave them steady attention. To carve the Ionic and Corinthian capitals of several façades, he imported two Italian artisans, only then to discover that the native stone, even some hauled from a quarry 70 miles distant, was not susceptible to this delicate art. So he arranged for the capitals to be executed in Carrara and shipped to Charlottesville. Later the capitals and marble blocks of the Rotunda came in this way.

He also began to recruit a faculty. Indeed one professor, Thomas Cooper, had already been appointed and invitations had gone out to others before the University was chartered. In October 1818, on his return to Monticello from Warm Springs, which he had visited after the meeting at Rockfish Gap, seeking relief of rheumatism and becoming desperately ill instead, Jefferson invited Ticknor and Nathaniel Bowditch to join the faculty of the embryo university. Bowditch, also of Massachusetts, he considered the nation's premier mathematician. And had he obtained their services, together with Cooper's, he would have had the nucleus of a faculty without peer in the United States. But Ticknor and Bowditch declined. Discouraged, Jefferson felt he had no choice but to go abroad for a faculty. From the beginning, as far back as 1800, he had insisted that the professors be of the first order of science, "supereminent professors," American if possible, European if necessary. They should be scholars as well as teachers, consistent with his idea of a university dedicated both to the discovery and the dissemination of knowledge. Edinburgh best exemplified this idea. Aided by Dugald Stewart, the luminary of Scottish "common sense" philosophy, whose friendship Jefferson had made in Paris, he hoped to recruit several of the professors from Edinburgh and her sister institutions. Oxford, the citadel of classical studies, Cambridge, of mathematics—these too, and possibly the new German universities, should be explored. Brushing aside difficulties, Jefferson exuded optimism. "With scientists and men of letters," he said, "the globe itself is one great commonwealth, in which no geographical divisions are acknowledged; but all compose one fraternity of fellow citizens." The school of law and government alone must go to an American. Although several talented Americans applied for one chair or another, none measured up to Jefferson's standards. By 1819 he was not only resigned to a mainly European faculty but exultant over the celebrity it would confer on the University at the outset.

The one American already named, Cooper, "the greatest man in America in the powers of mind and acquired information," in Jefferson's opinion, was lost to the institution in 1820. The storm that blew up around this man of all science, Priestley's companion and disciple, victim of the Sedition Law, Republican ideologue and Unitarian publicist, threatened irreparable harm to the University. At the last meeting of the old board in February 1819, which Jefferson, sick and weary, braved a snowstorm to attend at Madison's place, he proposed to bring Cooper on at once to teach the upper classes in the classical school. Several of the Visitors, including Cabell, expressed surprise that the College, or University, was still obligated to Cooper, who had taken a position in South Carolina. They also raised the question of his moral character. Jefferson assured them of the obligation—the post at Columbia was temporary—and of Cooper's good character, as evidenced during his visit at Monticello the previous fall. The first meeting of the new board in March confirmed Cooper in his appointment, on leave, as it were, in South Carolina. He would teach chemistry, mineralogy, and natural philosophy, perhaps law for a time. Jefferson considered him "the cornerstone of the edifice."

Now the evangelical clergy, spearheaded by the Presbyterians, attacked Cooper's appointment. John Holt Rice, the pope of Virginia Presbyterianism, climaxed the campaign in January 1820 with a long article in his *Evangelical Magazine*. Cooper's theological writings, Rice argued, showed little philosophy and much prejudice, and his Socinianism would alienate a substantial portion of the people of Virginia from the state university. Rice feared an invasion of Unitarianism. He did not call for a Calvinistic university but for one where religion had a respectable place in the curriculum, in the faculty, in divine worship. In his eyes a university without religion was a monstrosity. He was equally concerned for the success of the institution, however. As Cabell informed Jefferson, Rice and the Presbyterians had rallied to the charter bill in the assembly. And the University, Rice felt, could not succeed in hostility to the prevailing opinion of the community. A university conducted without preference as to religious sect was one thing, a university without religion, or indeed motivated by rationalistic zeal against orthodoxy, quite another. Well, Jefferson had been on this hook before—forty years before. The priests driven out of their monopoly, sought reentrance under cover of equality; and when he attempted to exclude them, in affairs of education as in affairs of state, they accused him of proselytizing infidelity.

Jefferson reacted to the furor on several levels. Privately he was outraged at this assault on the integrity of the University, and he flailed the Presbyterians in characteristic fashion. All the priests, he wrote to Correa, "dread the advance of science as witches do the approach of daylight; and scowl on the fatal harbinger announcing the subversion of the duperies in which they live." The Presbyterians were the loudest, he declaimed to Short: "The most intolerant of all sects, the most tyrannical, and ambitious; ready at the word of the lawgiver, if such a word could be obtained, to put the torch to the pile, and to rekindle in this virgin hemisphere the flames in which their oracle Calvin consumed the poor Servetus." This reflex action, wired into Jefferson's brain and nerves and tissue over fifty years, was neither quite fair to the Presbyterians nor responsive to the real issue he faced. How could a democratic state university, supported by the people of the state and in their service, maintain its integrity without alienation of its constituency? Jefferson never really saw the issue. It was inconceivable to him that freedom of mind—academic freedom in this case—could be opposed to the will of a free people in "this virgin hemisphere." Democracy could not defeat enlightenment. In fact, of course, the history of the higher learning in America proved that it could, not generally but sometimes. However that may be, Jefferson realized, practically, something had to be done to appease the sectarians. Cooper himself offered no problem. He was being well paid in Columbia, better than he would be in Charlottesville; and he doubted Jefferson's prodigy would ever spring to life. The clergy would not permit it. At Columbia, as earlier at Carlisle, in Pennsylvania, he was assailed by bigotry. He had not the courage to face the *odium theologicum* still another time and offered to resign. Jefferson at first refused to accept his resignation; but he relented gracefully, reluctantly, at the April meeting of the board, convinced by Cabell and others that the cornerstone had become the millstone of the University. Cooper's contract of three years' standing was annulled by mutual consent in October.

The crusade continued despite Cooper's sacrifice. Fighting for money in the assembly, Cabell repeatedly warned the Rector of the widespread opinion in evangelical circles, Presbyterian especially, "that the Socinians are to be installed at the University for the purpose of overthrowing the religious opinions of the country." (Had the clergy known of the overtures to Ticknor and Bowditch, both Unitarians, though of the mild New England variety, the alarm would surely have been greater.) "The clergy have succeeded in spreading the belief of their intended exclusion," Cabell said, "and in my opinion it is the source of much of our trouble." At the meeting of the Visitors in October 1822, someone, probably Jefferson himself, brought forward a resolution to conciliate the sectarians. The various denominations would be invited to establish theological schools "on the confines" of the University and entirely independent of it. The Visitors adopted the proposal and it formed part of their annual report to the legislature. The purpose was not, as has sometimes been said, to enable the University students to obtain formal religious instruction, though they might avail themselves of the religious services of these schools outside regular University hours; the purpose, rather, was to extend the secular instruction of the University to the theological students. Without in any way compromising the University, the arrangement might open the minds of a new generation of clergy. "And by bringing the sects together," Jefferson explained to Cooper, "and mixing them with the mass of other students, we shall soften their asperities, liberalize and neutralize their prejudices, and make the general religion a religion of peace, reason and morality." The schools "on the confines" resolution was an astute move to placate the sectarians. Cabell credited it with great influence in Richmond. "It is the Franklin that has drawn the lightning from the cloud of opposition." Jefferson confidently expected some of the churches to take up the invitation. They did not, and the evangelicals eyed the University with suspicion and jealousy for years to come.

From beginning to end a grudging legislature offered the main obstacle to Jefferson's plans for the University. "All the states but our own are sensible that knowledge is power," he wrote. Kentucky, the daughter of Virginia, already boasted a going university. Must Virginia send her sons to Kentucky, or to Harvard or Princeton or Columbia, for their education? Jefferson estimated Virginia's annual debt to the other states on account of education at $300,000. Constantly, he appealed to the pride and reputation of the state, not only in behalf of the University but of education generally. Massachusetts, one-tenth the size of Virginia and the fourth smallest state, had more influence than any other. "Whence this ascendancy?" he asked. "From her attention to education, unquestionably. There can be no stronger proof knowledge is power, and . . . ignorance is weakness." Virginia, by contrast, seemed destined to become "the Barbary of the Union." The degeneration over half a century was indeed appalling. "The mass of education in Virginia before the Revolution placed her with the foremost of her sister colonies. What is her education now? Where is it?" he demanded. "The little we have we import, like beggars, from other states; or import their beggars to bestow on us their miserable crumbs."

These appeals to pride and interest were joined in 1820 by appeals to political sentiment. Jefferson had envisioned the University as a national institution; increasingly, under the reaction produced by the Panic of 1819 and the Missouri Compromise south of the Potomac, he came to think of it as a state or sectional bulwark of Old Republicanism against the advance of "consolidation" and kindred political heresies in the North. The line of division between free and slave states marked out by the Missouri Compromise pointed up the gravity of "trusting to those who are against us in position and principle to fashion to their own form the mind and affections of our youth." Send them to Harvard, Jefferson warned, and they will be returned "fanatics and tories." Yet there were probably, in 1821, some 500 of Virginia's future leaders enrolled in northern seminaries, learning the lessons of "anti-Missourism" and imbibing heretical opinions. "This canker is eating at the vitals of our existence," he lectured, "and if not arrested at once will be beyond remedy." The appeal accurately expressed Jefferson's deep distress over the course of national affairs, yet it must also be seen as part of his strategy of argument with a legislature that shared his political anxieties and might discover more enthusiasm for an institution devoted to Virginia's, and the South's, sovereign interests that for one devoted to liberality and enlightenment in the abstract. At any rate, whether conviction or strategy, Jefferson tended to give a political cast to his conception of the University; and while he did not abandon the ideal of a fountainhead of learning for the entire nation, it slowly receded from view.

Jefferson and his friends waged a relentless five year campaign to obtain the money to build the University. The General Assembly had committed the state to $15,000 a year. The legislature would not divert the surplus of the Literary Fund, as Jefferson wanted, but it would permit the Visitors to borrow the capital for the buildings.

Three loans of $60,000 each were authorized over a four-year period. The trick then became, first to liberate the loans of interest, which must otherwise be paid from the annuity, or possibly the meager private subscriptions, and finally to sponge the principal. The state had a claim on the government of the United States for expenses incurred in the prosecution of the War of 1812. Jefferson angled for legislative extermination of the whole of the University's debt by means of this hypothetical claim. While he failed in this, he succeeded in liberating the annuity of interest and, in 1824, obtained an outright grant of $50,000 for the purchase of books and scientific apparatus, contingent on Washington's payment of the Virginia claim. Pressure from Jefferson, Cabell, and others, with the personal intervention of President Monroe, led to prompt settlement of the claim. As for the $180,000 debt, Jefferson never gave it another thought; it was already remitted in the eyes of everyone, including the enemies of the institution.

During these years Jefferson's hopes for the University sometimes faltered. "I perceive that I am not to live to see it opened," he wrote gloomily to Cabell in 1821. Cabell was struggling to obtain approval of the second loan; and convinced that the legislature would never again vote one cent for the institution, he announced his intention to retire. Jefferson begged him to reconsider. He did, and continued his leadership of the cause at Richmond. Senators and delegates complained that the University was on too grand a scale, that too much money went into finery, that it was costing twice as much as originally estimated, and so on. Jefferson answered these critics and also those, including some of the Visitors, who wanted to open the University before the library was completed and all the essentials of academic excellence secured. "It would be an impatience defeating its own object, by putting on a subordinate character in the outset, which never would be shaken off," he said. Jealous local interests continued to snipe at the University. Staunton and Richmond feared that behind its elegant façade the state capital would be seated in Charlottesville. William and Mary had not altogether given up the fight. In 1823, after the assembly voted the third loan to build the Rotunda, Cabell thought the resistance of the College had been broken, in fact that all the enemy battalions had struck their colors. But the friends of William and Mary made one last challenge the next year, proposing to transfer the College, lock, stock, and barrell, to Richmond, where it would have all the advantages of location at the seat of government. Jefferson countered this move by threatening legislation to consolidate the endowment of the College with the University. The former would lose its identity and the latter would become the beneficiary of $6000 a year, easily making up the deficit of two professors in Jefferson's plan, for the annuity alone, he realized, would support only eight professors of distinction. Although he did not expect the old college to submit to this death decree, he did expect the threat to quiet the removal petition in the legislature. Apparently it did, for the petition was withdrawn.

While fighting for the University, Jefferson kept the whole system of education steadily in view. It was mortifying to be charged, as he was, with sacrificing primary to higher education. He denied this and blamed the curious reversal of priorities on the legislature. If the state chose to place the cart before the horse, he could only make the best of it. "If we cannot do everything at once, let us do one thing at a time," he philosophized. The system of charity schools, after several years experience, was a complete bust. The money might better have been spent on the University, he felt, pending the institution of common schools on the ward plan, which required no preliminary outlay by the legislature. When the third loan was on the carpet, in 1823, he wrote to Cabell: "Were it necessary to give up either the Primaries or the University, I would rather abandon the last, because it is safer to have a whole people respectably enlightened than a few in a high state of science and the many in ignorance. This last is the most dangerous state in which a nation can be. The nations and governments of Europe are so many proofs of it." Young Rives had gone to Richmond with his mentor's encouragement to push a new plan of primary schools. Cabell now told Jefferson this was a mistake. The odious reputation of the charity schools had produced a reaction in favor of the University and nothing should be done to divert the current. Persuaded by Cabell's reasoning, Jefferson asked Rives to let the primaries sink, meanwhile "availing ourselves of the present state of discredit under which that plan is, and profiting of the current it produces toward the University." The regional colleges must also wait. Expediency dictated his course, but in championing the University he did not sacrifice anything attainable at the lower levels of the educational pyramid.

In May 1824 the Visitors announced the opening of the University nine months hence. Ten pavilions, 109 dormitories (for 218 students), and 6 hotels had been completed. The Rotunda was up, though the columns stood gaping for their capitals en route from Italy and the vast cavernous interior awaited books and ornamentation. In the summer Jefferson drew up a catalogue of the library— 6860 volumes—and arranged for the purchase of the books. A faculty remained the principal problem. None of the professors, reluctantly only eight at the start, had been appointed. (Law and Government, separate schools in the Rockfish Gap Report, were combined, and the chair in Physico-Mathematics dropped.) Cabell, who was familiar with the British and Continental universities from a grand tour twenty years ago, had been scheduled to undertake the recruiting mission abroad. He was not well, however, and declined. Jefferson entrusted this delicate responsibility to Francis Walker Gilmer, throwing the law professorship into the bargain. Gilmer hesitated on the professorship but agreed to the mission. The 34-year-old attorney, almost a son to Jefferson, set forth in the spring with flattering letters of introduction to Richard Rush, the American Minister in London, to Dugald Stewart and others. He was to go to Oxford for a classicist, to Cambridge for a mathematician, to Edinburgh for an anatomist; either Edinburgh or Cambridge might provide professors of natural history or natural philosophy, while a scholar in modern languages should be obtained from the Continent. This last was the first secured. George Blaetterman, a German earlier recommended by Ticknor, talked to Gilmer in London and agreed to terms. On the other posts Gilmer met with great difficulty. No one knew anything of this embryo university in the wilds of Virginia; and while Gilmer spoke eloquently of the buildings, the Rector, and the prospects, he had mountains of ignorance and prejudice and conceit to overcome. Moreover, the income of British university professors turned out to be much greater than Jefferson had been led to believe. (Virginia offered $1500 in salary, plus student tuitions of perhaps $500 a year and a house and garden.) Expansion at places like Cambridge had suddenly brightened the opportunities for younger scholars; and the Britishers did not look with favor on the long term, practically the year around, or the assortment of subjects they would be expected to cover in Virginia.

Hearing all this from Gilmer in October, Jefferson said he had never received a greater blow to his hopes. "I think therefore," he wrote to Madison in the depths of dismay, "he had better bring the best professors he can get, although of secondary standing." The whole idea of going abroad was to obtain professors of the first rank, which struck some patriots as un-American to begin with; and if Jefferson had to settle for foreigners of "secondary standing," he might better have recruited his faculty at home. But within a week another letter from Gilmer revived his spirits. Before he left England in the fall Gilmer had engaged five of the six professors sought abroad: Blaetterman (modern languages), Thomas Key (a Cambridge M.A., for mathematics), George Long (a fellow of Trinity College, Cambridge, for classics), Charles Bonneycastle (son of a noted mathematician, for natural philosophy), and Robley Dunglison (a London physician, for anatomy and medicine). Gilmer arranged for the sixth, in natural history, in New York. Thomas Addis Emmet, nephew of the Irish refugee-patriot, took this post. On the whole, they were men of broad general culture and able scholars. But they were not the "supereminent professors" Jefferson had hoped for, nor is it certain that the chairs could not have been filled by Americans of equal or higher rank.

The chairs of law and, subsequently, of moral philosophy had been reserved for Americans. The latter, including *belles lettres,* went to George Tucker on Madison's suggestion. Fifty years of age in 1825—much the eldest of the eight professors—Tucker belonged to a prominent Virginia clan, had served three terms in Congress, published two volumes of essays, at least one of them known to Jefferson, and recently completed a long novel, *The Valley of the Shenandoah.* All considered, he was one of the most literate Virginians of his day. Jefferson summoned him to Monticello and finally argued him into the professorship just as the University opened. The law chair remained empty for another year. Jefferson insisted the occupant be politically sound—none of "the honied Mansfieldism of Blackstone" or the "toryism" of Marshall and his ilk was admissible—and this requirement, together with the loss of income any prominent lawyer must suffer in the post, made the prospects desperate. Gilmer finally accepted but died before he could occupy the chair; and it was offered to six other Virginia Republicans before a Fredericksburg lawyer, John Tayloe Lomax, consented in April 1826.

Jefferson's anxiety for the political purity of the law school led him to propose the prescription of certain texts in government. There was nothing unusual about this; as he said, it was the common practice for the trustees of colleges and universities to determine the *norma docendi* in the various schools. The founders of the University of Virginia, by leaving this matter to the professors, registered another advance for educational liberalism. But in the case of the law school, so far as it was a school of government, Jefferson thought the Visitors had a duty to lay down the first principles to be taught. He sent the proposal to Madison and Cabell in Feburary 1825, when the occupant of the law chair remained very uncertain. "He may be a Richmond lawyer, or one of that school of quondam Federalism, now consolidation," Jefferson observed. "It is our duty to guard against such principles being disseminated among our youth, and the diffusion of that poison, by a previous prescription of the texts to be followed in their discourses." He suggested Locke on civil government, Sidney's *Discourses*, and with particular reference to the United States, the Declaration of Independence, *The Federalist*, and Madison's Virginia Report of 1799 on the Alien and Sedition Laws. Madison and Cabell concurred in the proposal. The former suggested the addition of Washington's Farewell Address, to which Jefferson readily agreed. At its next meeting, in March, the Board adopted the Rector's resolution. Its intent was somewhat ambiguous, as if the author knew he transgressed the legitimate boundaries of academic freedom. It began with a mere expression of *opinion* that the *best guides* to the true principles of government were to be found in the given texts; but it ended with the statement that they *shall be used as the texts and documents of the school.* Clearly, if the resolution meant to prescribe certain texts, it did not mean to proscribe others. The purpose was to ensure that the students received the correct principles of government, "in the common opinion" of their elders, before they trusted the researches and convictions of their own minds. Whatever the intent, the resolution assailed the libertarian spirit of the University. "This institution,"

Jefferson had written, "will be based on the illimitable freedom of the human mind. For here we are not afraid to follow truth wherever it may lead, nor to tolerate any error so long as reason is left free to combat it." But the personal and political distresses of the final years of the founder's life eroded this conception. The resolution on political texts expressed his deepening anxieties for the survival of the Union and Republicanism. In a sense it was not partisan, for the canon was acceptable to men of all parties—"all federalists, all republicans"—yet it would not have been ventured at all but for the partisan fears of consolidation in the surrounding political environment of Jefferson's last unquiet years.

The faculty arrived, the library filled up, and the students dribbled in, only fifty or so at the start but over a hundred a year later. Jefferson was pleased with the professors, all but Tucker utter strangers to him. The young Europeans faced a season of acclimatization both educational and environmental. Trifling problems arose but, in the main, they adjusted satisfactorily; and at Monticello all the professors learned of the founder's prejudices in the different schools of instruction—his rage against Hume and Blackstone, his skepticism of medicine, his enthusiasm for Anglo-Saxon. The students were less pleasing. They had been very poorly prepared by Jefferson's lights. At once the University had to relax its admission standards and recede from the lofty conception of a post-collegiate institution. There were no "classes," but had there been most the entrants would have qualified as freshmen or sophomores rather than as the juniors and seniors contemplated by Jefferson's plan. And there were no degrees, only diplomas offered by the several schools, but had there been the only realistic degree would have been the B.A., though in 1831 when the faculty bowed to the univeral practice of awarding degrees, it chose to award the M.A. Moreover, the students were inclined to rowdy and riotous behavior quite beyond Jefferson's expectations. The idea had got into circulation of a lax "democratic" code of government in the University. Hearing this from Philadelphia in August, Jefferson blandly answered that two-thirds of the students, the older ones, required no government and their example controlled the younger third. "The University may be said to be as quiet as a Convent." Within a month rampage and riot rolled over the tranquil lawn. Three students were expelled and

987

eleven severely reprimanded. Jefferson, 82 years of age, rode down from Monticello to help restore order; and the Visitors, meeting just after the disturbance, stiffened the regulations governing students. The refusal of the students to bear witness against their fellows undermined Jefferson's plan for the denizens to police themselves.

Other hopes and plans would also fail, but a dream had become a reality and the founder would not live to trace its tortuous history. Jefferson's labors for the University absorbed him almost to the hour of his death. At the end of April 1826, he laid out the plan of a botanical garden. On his last visit to the grounds, as he watched the raising of the great marble capitals atop the columns of the Rotunda, he must have reflected on the agony and the ecstasy of this triumph. "I have long been sensible," he had written three months before, "that while I was endeavoring to render my country the greatest of all services, that of regenerating the public education, and placing the rising generation on the level of our sister states . . . , I was discharging the odious function of a physician pouring medicine down the throat of a patient insensible of needing it." Yet with courage, faith, and skill rarely equalled, he had succeeded—at least with the University. It was *his* monument. If Emerson's aphorism, "An institution is the lengthened shadow of one man," has any truth, it belongs to Jefferson and the University of Virginia. It contained himself. Jefferson knew this. So when he came to write his epitaph, reflecting on his varied services, he chose for inscription on his tombstone, " 'Author of the Declaration of Independence, of the Statute of Virginia for Religious Freedom, and Father of the University of Virginia,' because by these, as testimonials that I have lived, I wish most to be remembered."

Unquiet Sage

Jefferson's last years were etched with sadness and even a little bitterness. A siege of illness came upon him in the fall of 1818, and he was never really free of bodily misery again. The waters of insolvency rose steadily until he despaired of his estate. Deterioration was all around him, not only at Monticello but in his beloved Virginia, shriveling into drab decay only half a century after the sun rose and without ever reaping the promises of the green springtime. Perhaps the University would charm back the sun; but the affliction ran too deep, as Jefferson knew in his heart, and so far as the University was committed to peculiar Virginia principles and tired Virginia defenses it became an ally of the mournful sickness it was intended to cure. The years 1819–20 were years of crisis for the entire nation. Economic depression and sectional discord were succeeded by rancorous political discontent. The crisis involved several vital areas of national policy but settled most grievously on the issue of slavery restriction, eventuating in the Missouri Compromise. This "firebell in the night," as Jefferson called it, shook his hopes for the Union and, in association with other tendencies in the national government, drove him back to old political fears, back to the "principles of '98," overlaid now with a sectional consciousness he had not known before. For a decade in retirement he had quietly drifted with the currents of nationalism. His political feelings revived in 1819, not with the zest of new wine, but with the musty acridity of a wine soured by age. The anguish of his personal affairs entered into the reaction. To an extent he transferred the burden of his own problems to the public, particularly to the national government, whose disastrous course had brought on himself, on his family, and on his state great vexations of life and spirit.

The Panic of 1819 struck when Jefferson's fortunes were at low ebb yet still showed promise of improvement. In 1815, after years of Napoleonic wars, the starved European markets soaked up American agricultural surpluses and prices soared. Unfortunately, Jefferson, like many Virginia farmers, derived little benefit from this boom. Two years of drought were followed by invasion of fly, which left him, in 1817, only enough wheat to seed the next year's crop. His Bedford tobacco was so miserably bad during successive seasons that he discharged the two overseers there. Prospects improved in 1818. Plaster and clover were restoring his farms in Albemarle. Fields that formerly produced five or six bushels to the acre, he said, were yielding two or three times as much under his grandson's management. But for his debts he might have trusted in God, husbandry, and the weather. Not until Jeff took a hand in the plantation business did Jefferson realize how far his estate was mortgaged to his creditors. His total indebtedness at this time is not easily calculated, but it was probably not less than when he returned to Monticello. Borrowing from Richmond banks to pay interest on his old debts and to make up deficiencies in accounts with his Richmond factor, he steadily increased his obligations without substantially improving his income.

The chain of pressures released by the panic began with these banks, specifically in Jefferson's case with the Richmond branch of the Second Bank of the United States. The BUS, after feeding the post-war inflation by allowing the state banks recklessly to expand their note issues, suddenly put on the brakes in the summer of 1818. Just as he was setting out for Rockfish Gap, Jefferson learned that the Richmond branch had curtailed his credit 12-1/2 per cent. So on his $3000 loan he had to come up with $375 at once. This, he said, "is really like a clap of thunder to me, for god knows I have no means in the world of raising money on so sudden a call, my whole and sole dependence being only in the annual income of my farm." It was only the beginning. Contraction by the BUS forced contraction by the state banks, among them the Bank of Virginia, to which Jefferson was indebted; and one curtailment was followed by a second, then a third, until the early months of the next year he had to borrow an additional $4000, most of it from still another Richmond bank, in order to meet the demands and keep up his credit. His bank debt alone rose to over $10,000. Meanwhile, as money vanished, agricultural prices dropped precipitously. "Never were such times seen as we have now here," Jefferson wrote despondently. "Not a dollar is passing from one to another. Everyone had been so pressing and so pressed that finding it useless they from necessity give it up and bear and forbear with one another." The price deflation and the money stringency, he estimated with pardonable extravagance, had tripled his debts. He tried to sell land but there were few buyers, though he did manage to dispose of one tract. Bankruptcy knocked at his door, as at so many others, in 1819, just when improved management and husbandry and markets had once again brightened his hopes of a better tomorrow.

Jefferson blamed the panic on the banks, above all the national bank at the head of a vicious system. Banks, by their easy paper issues, seduced ambitious farmers from the labors of the plow into careers of gambling and speculation, then to save their own skins bankrupted the farmers. Jefferson had sworn many Jeremiads against the system; now, for the first time, he was himself a victim of it. "We have been truly sowing the wind, and are now reaping the whirlwind." The distresses, he said, were no greater than he had always expected and freely predicted from the moment of the creation of the Bank of the United States in 1791. "Hamilton . . . let in this torrent of swindling institutions which have spread ruin and wretchedness over the face of our country." But he could take small comfort in this political vindication, if vindication it was, amidst personal catastrophe in 1819.

What he called the *coup de grâce* to his fortunes was administered by one of his dearest friends, Governor Nicholas, who sank under the weight of the panic and took part of Jefferson's estate with him. On May 1, 1818, he had endorsed two BUS loans, each of $10,000, for Nicholas. This was more than a routine service in view of Jefferson's circumstances and the precarious state of the Virginia economy. But Nicholas, a director of one of the Richmond banks, had endorsed for him and been helpful in other ways. As Governor he had been a good friend of the University. Through the marriage of a daughter to Jeff he had become almost a member of the family. The two promissory notes were for twelve months only, and Nicholas was thought to be worth upwards to $300,000. But the panic "revolutionized" his fortune. Nicholas defaulted, the bank protested the notes, and the liability fell on the first endorser. Jefferson was at Poplar Forest, wracked by rheumatism, in August 1819 when he learned of this new affliction. "A call on me to the amount of my endorsements for you," he wrote Nicholas, "would indeed close my course by a catastrophe I had never contemplated." The bankrupt's property would be committed to trustees with the hope, of course, it might prove sufficient to protect his endorsers and cover his debts. Jefferson took encouragement from a recent ruling of the state Court of Appeals freeing usurious debts from liability—this would wipe-off nine-tenths of Nicholas's, he casually remarked. Meanwhile, to cover the $20,000 obligation at the bank, Jefferson executed a bond which, in effect, mortgaged part of Poplar Forest. The interest itself now drained off $1200 yearly from his income and ate into his capital. He pressed some of Nicholas's debtors, but without success, and tried to sell more land, with the same result. He never got free of the debt. Amazingly, in all this he showed not a trace of enmity toward Nicholas, tried to persuade Monroe to give him a federal office, and remained an affectionate friend until the penniless man went to his death three years later.

Prices turned upward in 1821 but Jefferson dropped farther and farther behind every year. Unable to sell land he sold slaves, realizing $3500 in one transaction to furnish a labor force for his grandson Francis Eppes. Jefferson consoled himself that the Negroes at least remained in the family. His bank loans increased, although on one occasion, in 1822, all three Richmond banks turned him down for additional credit. A statement of the next year listed debts in excess of $40,000, as well as the $20,000 obligation on Nicholas's account. Randolph's position was similar. He fell into despondency, withdrew from his family, and finally became quite alienated from Jefferson. In order to protect his property from liability for the Colonel's debts, and thus to secure it for Martha and the children, Jefferson named his dutiful grandson, Jeff, executor of his estate— another blow to Randolph's pride. In the end, all else failing, Jefferson was reduced to the humiliation of begging permission of the legislature to dispose of most of his property by way of lottery in the expectation of saving the splendid remnant, Monticello, for Martha.

These anxieties drove Jefferson back on his political heels. While he did not inspire, he gave aid and comfort to the Virginia revival of state rights politics led by a phalanx of Old Republicans, which included his former nemesis John Randolph of Roanoke, the planter-philosopher John Taylor, Judge Spencer Roane of the state's supreme bench, Thomas Ritchie, editor of the *Richmond Enquirer*, William B. Giles, and other lesser lights. With these men he made a *bête noire* of "consolidation" and from this protean enemy sought to save Virginia, indeed the entire South, by drawing the national government back into the narrow channels of the "principles of '98." Awakened from his political slumbers by the Panic of 1819, the Sage of Monticello was haunted for the rest of his life by ghosts of departed Federalism. Banking, as already noted, was the root of the evil; but it was associated in his mind with a whole system of measures, sometimes called "the American System," for the development of national wealth and power. The protective tariff for the

support of manufactures and internal improvements for the creation
of a home market were integral parts of the system. These measures,
while they may have been Hamiltonian in origin, had been assimilated into Jeffersonian nationalism. The American System, generally,
was the legitimate offspring of Jefferson's mature politics. Yet in
1819 he disowned these latter-day children: the national bank,
which Madison and Gallatin had approved if he had not, because of
the rage of speculation; the tariff because it taxed agriculture,
chiefly southern and western, for the support of manufactures,
chiefly northern; and internal improvements because, without the
safeguard of a constitutional amendment, they hastened the federal
government down the disastrous road of consolidation. Even more
alarming was the aggressive underpining of consolidation by the
federal judiciary, highlighted by several broad nationalistic opinions
of Chief Justice Marshall in and around 1819. The Federalism of the
bench seemed incurable, unless by drastic surgery; and Jefferson
feared that the old political hydra, Federalism, nothing changed but
its name, had sneaked back into power under the camouflaged
"good feelings" of the Monroe era and renewed its grip on the entire federal establishment. Most alarming of all was the Missouri
Compromise of 1820. This new species of Federalist trickery, as he
saw it, "fanaticized" the North against the South, and it drove him
toward sectionalism in spite of himself.

In all this Jefferson's political feelings consorted with the ascendant Old Republican ideology in Virginia. He did not take an active
role but neither did he disguise his approval of this movement. To
Judge Roane, who led the state judiciary's fight against encroachments of the federal courts, Jefferson said he subscribed to "every
tittle" of his essays in the *Enquirer*. "They contain the true principles of the revolution of 1800, for that was as real a revolution in
the principles of our government as that of '76 was in its form."
The principles denied the supremacy of the Supreme Court to decide constitutional questions for the other branches of the government, for the states, and for the people. "The judiciary of the
United States," he wrote in 1820, "is the subtle corps of sappers and
miners constantly working under ground to undermine the foundations of our confederated fabric. They are construing our Constitution from a coordination of a general [national] and special [state]

government to a general and supreme one alone. This will lay all things at their feet . . . ." Jefferson read John Taylor's turgid polemics, beginning in 1820 with *Construction Construed and Constitutions Vindicated*, a slashing attack on the Supreme Court, especially its opinion in *McCulloch v. Maryland* upholding the constitutionality of the Second Bank on the Hamiltonian logic of implied powers. To Ritchie, Roane, and the Caroline planter himself, Jefferson did not hesitate to pronounce this work orthodox. Taylor's writings against the Court, the tariff, internal improvements, and every other avenue of consolidation ought to be "standing instruction" to Congress, he said. For six months he stoutly resisted the pressures of Old Republicans to bring him forth publicly, "like a Priam in armor," in support of Taylor's doctrines. He finally yielded, however. The endorsement, drawn from Jefferson's previous letters, declared that on all important public questions Taylor espoused "the true political faith, to which every Republican should stedfastly hold."

But many Republicans of the nationalist persuasion, friends of the American System and the coalescence of parties in the "era of good feelings," expressed surprise and regret at this evidence of Jefferson's patronage of a new state rights party. "I am pelted for it in print," he observed unhappily. Further efforts to draw him into the leadership of this cause were unavailing. Yet when Ritchie, pressed to defend the partisan conscription of Jefferson's name and reputation, disclosed his authorship of the Kentucky Resolutions of 1798, the Sage of Monticello confessed "the naked truth." The truth should be known at last, he said in 1821, for after the passage of twenty-three years the country faced another crisis such as that of '98, only now the federal judiciary spearheaded the assault on the Constitution. This spiritual return to the partisan climate of the 1790's, this revival of the Republican feelings and symbols and slogans of '98, had a profound influence on the course of American politics in the ensuing decade; and in the South especially, the cause of state rights, strict construction, and limited government paraded under the Jeffersonian banner of "nullification" nailed to the Kentucky Resolutions.

The judiciary was the great unresolved problem of Jeffersonian Republicanism, as the Hamiltonian outburst of 1819 made abundantly clear. Jefferson's prescription for reform contained two main elements. First, in order to secure the responsibility of the federal courts to the Constitution and the people, judges should be appointed to six-year terms renewable by the President with the consent of both houses of Congress. Judicial independence, running to judicial absolutism, could not coexist with democracy. "Independence can be trusted nowhere but in the people in mass," Jefferson declared. Nor could the Union survive if the Supreme Court arrogated to itself the authority to decide fundamental issues arising in the federal system. The Court seemed not to realize that the Constitution "is a compact of many independent powers, every single one of which claims an equal right to understand it, and to require its observance. However strong the cord of compact may be," he warned, "there is a point of tension at which it will break." But, it was usually said in reply, there must be an ultimate arbiter somewhere. To be sure, Jefferson answered: the people of two-thirds of the states. They had adopted the Constitution and were competent to amend it. "Let them decide to which they meant to give an authority claimed by two of their organs. And it has been the peculiar wisdom and felicity of our Constitution to have provided this peaceable appeal, where that of other nations is at once to force." Jefferson also called for the courts, above all the Supreme Court, to adopt the practice of seriatim opinions, each judge pronouncing for himself rather than through the mouth of a single one. He pressed the point with Justice William Johnson, who acknowledged its merits but was not entirely convinced. Marshall dominated his fellows and huddled up unanimous opinions in secret conclave, Jefferson believed. By forcing each judge on his mettle, he hoped to neutralize the engine of consolidation under the Chief Justice's command. Neither reform made headway. The Court, while never impervious to political influence, remained impervious to reform; and Jefferson went to his death badly worsted in the recurrent battle of a quarter-century with John Marshall.

It was slavery, raising a mighty storm in national affairs for the first time, that gave a peculiar pungency to Jefferson's fears of judicial nationalism, bank mania, and the consolidating American System. The Missouri Question, brought on by the application of the territory for admission to statehood, embraced the larger issue of congressional authority to prohibit slavery in the Louisiana Purchase lands and, ultimately, to control the destiny of the institution itself. "In the gloomiest moments of the Revolutionary War," Jefferson wrote at the height of the debate in February 1820, "I never had any apprehensions equal to what I feel from this source." A compromise resolved the immediate crisis. Missouri was admitted as a slave state, Maine (a simultaneous applicant) as a free state, thereby maintaining the sectional balance in Congress, and slavery was henceforth prohibited above the latitudinal line 36° 30'. Jefferson vehemently disapproved of the Missouri Compromise. The fact that former Federalists like Rufus King, now United States Senator from New York, headed the anti-slavery forces in Congress bore out his fears of resurgent Toryism within the Republican amalgam. "The Missouri question is a mere party trick," he declared. "The leaders of Federalism, defeated in their schemes of obtaining power by rallying partisans to the principles of monarchism . . . have changed their track, and thrown out another burr to the whale. They are taking advantage of the virtuous feelings of the people [against slavery] to effect a division of parties by a geographical line. They expect that this will insure them, on local principles, the majority they could never obtain on the principles of Federalism." Having labored to build a national party to cement the Union together, Jefferson perceived not merely a revival of the old party conflict but of a conflict fanaticized by sectionalism. "The old schism of Federal and Republican," he explained to Short, "threatened nothing because it existed in every state, and united them together by the fraternism of party. But the coincidence of a marked principle, moral and political, with a geographcial line, once conceived, I feared would never more be oblitered from the mind; that it would be recurring on every occasion and renewing irritations until it would kindle such mutual and mortal hatred as to render separation preferable to eternal discord. I have been among the most sanguine in believing that our Union should be of long duration," he continued gravely. "I now doubt it much, and see the event [of disunion] at no great distance, and the direct consequence of this question." It was, he prophesied, "the knell of the Union."

While he did not deny the moral aspect of the question, Jefferson believed the northern restrictionists were politically motivated or, in some instances, honestly deluded by their righteousness against slavery. "They are wasting Jeremiads on the miseries of slaves as if we were advocates for it." For himself, at least, the cession of slave property was "a bagatelle" unworthy of a second thought *if* a scheme of emancipation and expatriation could be effected. "But as it is," he sighed, "we have the wolf by the ears, and we can neither hold him, nor safely let go. Justice is in one scale, self-preservation in the other." The dangers of slave revolt and racial warfare, embedded in every southerner's mind, surfaced in Jefferson's in 1820. "Are our slaves to be presented with freedom and a dagger?" he asked Adams. For if Congress could regulate the condition of the inhabitants of new states it could presumably declare all the slaves free in the existing states. "In which case," he told Gallatin, "all the whites south of the Potomac and Ohio must evacuate their states; and most fortunate those who can do it first." Virtue would become vice if pushed to the lengths of destruction and disunion. Who then would be the sinners, the slaveholders or the abolitionists? Moreover, the restriction of slavery would not, in fact, free a single human being. Restriction had only the semblance of morality; morality itself, Jefferson said, indulging a delusion of his own, lay on the side of the diffusion of slaves into the territories, "because by spreading them over a larger surface their happiness would be increased, and the burden of their future liberation lightened by bringing a greater number of shoulders under it." In truth, between a question of power and a question of existence, North and South, morality was hard to find anywhere. In 1784 Jefferson had proposed the exclusion of slavery from the territories. Indeed he was the father of the principle he now opposed in circumstances so entirely different he could not recognize the claim of the principle upon him.

Amidst the deluge of woe, the Missouri Compromise threw Jefferson into the deepest political malaise of his entire life. "I regret," he wrote seven weeks after the measure became law, "that I am now to die in the belief, that the . . . sacrifice of themselves by the generation of 1776, to acquire self-government and happiness to their country, is to be thrown away by the unwise and unworthy passions of their sons, and that my only consolation is to be that I live not to weep over it. If they would but dispassionately weigh the blessings they will throw away, against an abstract principle more

997

likely to be effected by union than by scission, they would pause before they would perpetrate this act of suicide on themselves, and of treason against the hopes of the world." The melancholy testament of an old man in a dark season, it was not, fortunately, his final one.

If this chapter had any power for good it should spur the country to adopt a plan of gradual emancipation and colonization such as he had advocated in the Revolutionary era. Black slavery, this first and last curse visited on the country by European despotism, still mocked the nation's pretensions and blighted the promises of the American Revolution. All of Jefferson's values and goals dictated the extermination of slavery. This was as self-evident as the principles of 1776 themselves. But the Revolutionary generation could not be brought up to the mark. The Virginians of that day, Jefferson reflected, daily nursed and educated in the habits of slavery, had no more doubted the legitimacy of this species of property than of horses and cattle. "The quiet and monotonous course of colonial life had been disturbed by no alarm, and little reflection on the value of liberty." And drawn into the tasks of nation-building, choosing not to waste his influence in the advocacy of an untimely cause, he had patiently awaited the "revolution of opinion" sure to come. "I had always hoped that the younger generation," he wrote in 1814, "receiving their early impressions after the flame of liberty had been kindled in every breast, and had become, as it were, the vital spirit of every American, that the generous temperament of youth, analogous to the motion of their blood and above the suggestions of avarice, would have sympathized with oppression wherever found, and proved the love of liberty beyond their own share of it." He had been disappointed in this hope; and contrary to all reasonable expectations, domestic slavery had taken deeper root despite the bar to the African trade, and interest, instead of going over to the side of morality, had found new sustenance of exploitation in the burgeoning cotton lands of the South. While President, in response to resolutions of the Virginia legislature seeking an asylum for free Negroes and criminal slaves, he had endeavored to make arrangements with a British company colonizing Negroes in Sierra Leone. A similar overture had been made to the government of Portugal. These efforts failed; but the principle of colonization, which Jefferson and nearly all liberal southerners considered the *sine qua non* of emancipation, had been set in motion. Virginians were prominent in the American Colonization Society founded in 1817. Under its auspices Liberia was soon established as an independent republic for the colonization of freed blacks from the United States. Although Jefferson encouraged, and in a larger sense inspired, this movement, he neither took an active role in the Society nor supposed that a tiny colony on the distant coast of Africa (he favored Santo Domingo as an asylum) offered a realistic solution to the mammoth problem of slavery in the United States.

In 1814 Jefferson's young friend and neighbor, Edward Coles, beseeched him to become a Hercules against slavery. "This difficult task [of emancipation] could be . . . more successfully performed by the revered father of our political and social blessings than by any succeeding statesman," Coles argued, "and would seem to come with peculiar propriety and force from those whose valor, wisdom and virtue have done so much in meliorating the condition of mankind. And it is a duty, as I conceive, that devolves particularly on you, from your known philosophical and enlarged view of subjects, and from the principles you have professed and practiced through a long and useful life." Coles had already embarked on an experiment to free and educate his own slaves, an experiment that necessitated his removal to free soil and took him, finally, to Illinois in 1819. Jefferson welcomed his "solitary voice" but thought his proposed course mistaken. He tried to persuade Coles to remain in Virginia, becoming, even as a slaveholder, the public missionary of emancipation and persevering until it was accomplished. As for himself, it was out of the question. "No, I have outlived the generation with which mutual labors and perils begat mutual confidence and influence. This enterprise is for the young—for those who can follow it up, and bear it through to its consummation." Instead he took up another and more agreeable cause, education.

Whether he might have effectively wielded the club against slavery, as Coles thought, is very doubtful. And it was not now, nor had it ever been, a labor consonant with his personal or political style. He could preach emancipation, plan it, encourage it, all from high principles and humanitarian feelings; but he could not lead so unpopular or so desperate a cause. That required moral enthusiasm

999

and political audacity he neither possessed nor trusted. At bottom he did not care enough to sacrifice himself, or even put himself to great inconvenience, for the freedom of slaves, certainly not in the declining years of life. His dear friend Kosciusko, dying in Swizerland in 1817, had named Jefferson executor of his estate and provided for the disposition of his property in the United States, about $17,000 in securities, to the purchase, manumission, and education of young blacks. Jefferson declined this testamentary trust. He tried to get his younger neighbor John Hartwell Cocke, whose sentiments were in perfect accord, to take it on, but he too declined, citing the obstacle of Virginia laws. The object of the will was lost. Had Jefferson felt stronger about the object he would have ventured the experiment, despite statutory obstacles and the shortness of years, for the experiment was one he often commended to others and, indeed, one he may have himself suggested to Kosciusko, whose will was executed in Philadelphia prior to his departure under the shadow of the Alien Law in May 1798.

Jefferson adhered to the plan of gradual emancipation sketched in the *Notes on Virginia* in 1785. All the slaves born after a certain day would be emancipated, left in the care of their families until able to work, placed under state guardianship, and then deported at a proper age to Santo Domingo or elsewhere. "This would give time for a gradual extinction of that species of labor, and substitution of another, and lessen the severity of the shock, which an operation so fundamental cannot fail to produce." The expenses of the plan might be met by revenue from the public lands, a large part of which had been ceded by the southern states. Until 1820 Jefferson had thought the entire burden must fall on the slaveholding states. With the Missouri Compromise he concluded that the survival of the Union itself depended on the solution of this problem; accordingly, that the responsibility belonged jointly to the federal and state governmets. Such was the fillip of hope in that egregious measure. The magnitude of the object overcame Jefferson's constitutional scruples. The plan was difficult but feasible. "And who could estimate its blessed effects?" he asked. "I leave this to those who will live to see their accomplishment, and to enjoy a beatitude forbidden to my age. But I leave it with the admonition, to rise and be doing." For in another generation the problem would escape control and the country would go the way of Santo Domingo multiplied to the hundredth power. He did not despair utterly. What was right and good must prevail in the end, he philosophized. But would right prevail before disaster? Or would righteousness itself, exalted to hysteria in one section, hysterically resisted in the other, produce disaster? There was a solemn note of resignation in Jefferson's last letter on the subject only two weeks before his death. "A good cause is often injured more by ill-timed efforts of its friends than by the arguments of its enemies," he wrote partly as warning, partly as justification. "Persuasion, perseverance, and patience are the best advocates on questions depending on the will of others. The revolution in public opinion which this cause requires, is not to be expected in a day, or perhaps in an age; but time, which outlives all things, will outlive this evil also. My sentiments have been forty years before the public. Had I repeated them forty times, they would only have become the more stale and threadbare. Although I shall not live to see them consummated," he concluded, "they will not die with me; but living or dying, they will ever be in my most fervent prayer."

Jefferson's anti-slavery opinions, while generally known, only scratched the surface of the public mind during these last unquiet years. His political reaction, on the other hand, moving with the current of Virginia opinion, exposed him to the buffetings of parties and gave him an unwanted prominence in the presidential election of 1824. He had been disappointed in Monroe. Consolidation had reared its ugly head during his administration. Monroe had nursed the illusion of an amalgamation of parties, "that the lion and the lamb are lying down together," and while this might seem the culmination of Jefferson's own strategy of conciliation—"all federalists, all republicans"—it had, in fact, permitted the lions to return in the disguise of the lambs. Monroe approved of the Missouri Compromise, gave up Texas to Spain, acquiesced in rising protectionism, and even yielded on internal improvements without benefit of constitutional amendment. Of course, with some of the President's measures Jefferson concurred, above all the Monroe Doctrine, on which he was fully consulted. The famous pronouncement, declaring the Western Hemisphere off-limits to European powers, expressed the true spirit of Jeffersonian foreign policy, summed up in one of the former President's letters to Monroe while the doctrine was being formulated in Washington: "Our first and fundamental maxim should be, never to entangle ourselves in the broils of Europe. Our second—never to suffer Europe to intermeddle with cis-Altantic affairs. America, North and South, have a set of interests distinct from those of Europe, and perculiarly her own. She should therefore have a system of her own, separate and apart from that of Europe. While the last is laboring to become the domicile of despotism, our endeavor should surely be, to make our hemisphere that of freedom." So long as Jefferson's differences with Monroe were political, they did not intrude on an old friendship. In 1824, however, he asked the favor of a federal office, the Richmond postmastership, for his long-suffering commercial agent, Bradford Peyton, and was turned down. "I asked it as for myself . . . ," he.explained bitterly to Peyton. "It was the first opportunity, too, I had ever given him of obliging me. I have miscalculated, and shall better understand my place hereafter." The friendship survived but never recovered its old footing of intimacy.

With the passing of the Virginia Dynasty, the incipient revival of parties, and rising political passions, the succession to the presidency aroused unusual interst. As early as December 1821 attempts were made to enlist Jefferson's name and reputation on the side of one candidate or another. "Numerous have been the attempts to entangle me in the imbroglio," he said a year and some months later. Scrupulously withholding public endorsement of any one of the four or five leading candidates, he nevertheless made it abundantly clear in private letters that William H. Crawford, of Georgia, a Republican of "the old school" was his favorite. And some of these letters were dressed-up for partisan purposes and published in the press, causing the usual perturbations at Monticello. Death eliminated Crawford. No candidate receiving a majority of the electoral vote, the choice fell to the House of Representatives, where John Quincy Adams emerged victorious over Andrew Jackson. Adams represented the consolidationist wing of the amalgamated party, the National Republicans; and while Jefferson had reservations about Jackson, he at once became the rallying point for the Democratic Republicans committed to Jeffersonian restoration on the principles of 1800.

Adams's first message to Congress, in December 1825, produced consternation and dismay at Monticello. Boldly nationalistic, laying out a vast program of internal improvements, embracing not only roads and canals but moral and intellectual objects as well, the message again transported Jefferson back to the Federalist decade. Virginia Republicans turned to him for counsel. He drafted for the legislature a solemn protest against federal usurpations, but then suppressed it on the appearance of firm resolutions from South Carolina and resistance in Congress to the Adams regime. "We had better at present rest awaile on our oars and see which way the tide will set," he prudently advised. Patience and longer endurance was also his directive to Giles, now Governor, who tried, unsuccessfully, to enlist him in the campaign to discredit the motives of Adams's "political conversion" of 1808 and to reveal him as a pseudo-Republican. But in a second and confidential letter to Giles, Jefferson lashed out at the new breed of Republicans, "who having nothing in them of the principles of '76 now look back to a single and splendid government of an aristocracy, founded on banking institutions and monied incorporations under the guise and cloak of their favored branches of manufactures, commerce, and navigation, riding and ruling over the plundered ploughman and beggared yeomanry." With this Taylor-like utterance, he also fixed the limits to patience and endurance. The states must be ever vigilant, he said, and when the sole alternatives become "dissolution of our Union . . . or submission to a government without limitation of powers," there should be no hesitation in the choice of liberty. Giles sat on this bombshell while the Sage of Monticello lived; releasing it soon after his death, it created havoc in the National Republican camp and inspired the motley assemblage of democrats and state rightists, northerners, southerners, weterners, aristocratic planters and petty bourgeois, nostalgic Old Republicans and freewheeling entrepreneurs following Andrew Jackson back, figuratively, to the "revolution of 1800."

So, nursing his wounds at Monticello, Jefferson helped to transact the political future. Ironically, the rebel against the past, the prophet of progress and enlightenment, the champion of the living generation ended his days haunted by demons he had vanquished a quarter-century before and left a legacy of fetish and dogma, jealousy and fear, to American politics. This was not the whole of it, of course—only the sadder part. The political shadows that darkened

Jefferson's last years had a reality of their own—they were not imaginary—yet they loomed larger than they were and grew darker still from the gloom around him. The decay of his own fortune was simply an incident to the decay of Virginia. From the richest and most populous state at the beginning of the new nation, Virginia had become one of the poorest, giving up her unfortunates to people the West, and falling farther and farther behind in the race for improvement and power. Too many of her talented sons in the sciences and the arts went north to Philadelphia or elsewhere; those who stayed behind faced blighted careers with a dilettantish sideboard of learning and wit or condemned to the galleys of law and politics. Virginia was not barren culturally or intellectually, as the little circle in Albemarle attested, but she was living on old capital and an ineradicable amateurism lay over everything. Nothing is more likely to evoke the sense of degeneracy than the sense of a "golden age"; and in Virginia the fame of the Revolutionary generation hung like a pall over the sons. In culture as in politics Virginia cherished this grandiose image of herself. Its various parts, truncated and distorted now, held the mind enthralled. In the North things were starting into life—a new age—not only industrially but intellectually. Jefferson's granddaughter Ellen, who married Joseph Coolidge of a prominent Boston family in 1825, felt she was entering a whole new world on her journey northward. The prosperous look of the people, the lands, and the villages, the great improvements of art and industry—why, she exclaimed, "they are at least a century in advance of us." The future lay with Ellen, not with Jeff in Albemarle or the other grandchildren. Jefferson sensed this. Had he not given the last dozen years of his life to rescuing Virginia from that awful destiny,"the Barbary of the Union," by building the University? But he had better reason to know than William Short that it had been "got up against the grain" and that redemption was beyond his powers. (Short predicted the University would collapse within two or three years of the founder's death.) Perhaps there was no redemption, from slavery or ignorance or debt; but the crisis of 1819–20 sent him charging back to 1800 for a political cure of the Virginia malaise. It was indeed the sadder part of a chapter otherwise glorious and full of faith.

Men who visited the Sage of Monticello near the end of his life said he appeared a man twenty years younger than he was. The ravages of age were more evident to him than to the casual observer, but his mind remained lively, his senses sharp, his countenance warm, his manners as bright and urbane as ever. He attributed his good health, generally, to temperate habits of living. He ate moderately, an essentially vegetable diet, and drank light wines only. He kept regular hours, exercised daily on horseback, and bathed his feet every morning in cold water, as he had done for sixty years, to which he ascribed his remarkable freedom from colds. With little trust in physic and less in physicians—three of them together were enough to bring buzzards to the neighborhood, he jested—he was fortunate in rarely needing either.

Nevertheless, the toll of physical affliction mounted from his seventy-fifth year. After the conference at Rockfish Gap, it may be recalled, he rode to Warm Springs to seek relief from the aches and pains of rheumatism. But the waters, finding no disease to heal, made one instead. He returned home prostrated by a severe intestinal disturbance, which grew worse under treatment, and actually brought him to death's door for a time. The illness lasted many months and he never got entirely free of it. In 1822 he broke his left arm in a fall; the crippled state of his right hand and wrist, badly swollen from the old dislocation, made writing increasingly painful. On occasion he employed one of the grandchildren as a secretary. Except at brief intervals, until the final illness came on in 1825, he was able to continue his accustomed rounds. He could often be seen trudging to and from the University. Horseback riding had long ago replaced walking as the "sovereign invigorator" of mind and body; indeed, said Jefferson, "so delightful and so necessary is this daily revival to me, that I would wish to lose that and life together."

Monticello continued to receive its stream of visitors. The rising University offered an additional attraction to some. Early in November 1824, General Lafayette, then on a triumphal tour of the United States—an unparalleled patriotic extravaganza—wound up the mountain in a wave of Revolutionary banners, stepped from his carriage at the east lawn, and met Jefferson halfway to the door, where the old comrades fell tearfully into each other's arms. They traversed a vast field of history during the General's visit of several days. Jefferson, ill and feeble, attended a great banquet for the "nation's guest" in the Rotunda, still under scaffolding, at the University. Three Presidents of the United States sat at the head-table. It was Jefferson's last public appearance. He made a little address, through the voice of another, extolling Lafayette's services in war and peace and closing with a prayer for the eternal duration of the nation's freedom.

Perhaps the best description of Jefferson at this time comes from Daniel Webster, then a rising political star, though in another firmament than Jefferson's. Tall and thin, head set forward on the shoulders, neck wiry and limber, hair long and graying—Thomas Sully captured the main features in his full-length portrait of 1821 which, adding the life-mask by J.H.I. Browere in 1825, offers the best likeness of the aged Sage. "His eyes are small," said Webster, "very light, and now neither brilliant nor striking. His chin is rather long, but not pointed. His nose small, regular in its outline, and the nostrils a little elevated. His mouth is well-formed and still filled with teeth; it is strongly compressed, bearing an expression of contentment and benevolence. His complexion, formerly light and freckled, now bears the marks of age and cutaneous affection. His limbs are uncommonly long; his hands and feet very large, and his wrists [both swollen from fractures] of an extraordinary size. His walk is . . . easy and swinging. He stoops a little . . . . When sitting, he appears short, partly from a rather lounging habit of sitting and partly from the disproportionate length of his limbs." Webster thought his dress neglected but not slovenly. Even in the house—it was December 1824—he wore a long gray overcoat (surtout) and two waistcoats underneath. "His pantaloons are very long and loose, and of the same color as his coat." He wore glasses only to read at night and his hearing was good. His conversation, easy and natural, touched everything with lightness and grace. On the whole, Webster thought, he showed "an extraordinary degree of health, vivacity, and spirit."

The last illness, urinary in nature, descended the following May. For long intervals Jefferson lay on a couch of pain. But he was often up and about, if not in the saddle then in the carriage. "The little of the powers of life which remains to me I consecrate to our university," he wrote in October. But for the specter of bankruptcy he could go peacefully in the confidence of Seneca that "he who had dedicated his mind to virtue, and to the good of human society, whereof he is a member, had consummated all that is either profitable or necessary for him to know or to do toward the establishment of his peace." But on his death the creditors would flock like buzzards over the mountain, and his family, even his beloved daughter, would be driven penniless and propertyless from the land of their birth. From this gloomy prospect he sought relief in January 1826 by appealing to the legislature for permission to dispose of most of his property by lottery. This last mortifying solution had become "almost a question of life and death." Lotteries were not uncommon in Virginia for eleemosynary purposes, but the privilege had very rarely, in recent decades, been extended to individuals and in no instances analogous to Jefferson's. For the first time in his life he begged a personal favor from the state he had served. Mainly he urged the prostration in the value of lands, which if sold on the market must be sacrificed at one-third or one-fourth of their true worth. Raffled in a lottery on a fair valuation, his property should realize enough money to pay his debts and leave to him and Martha Monticello with an adjoining farm. The General Assembly, after some hesitation, bowed to his request in February. As the lottery was set in motion, the American public learned of Jefferson's plight. Gratitude, it had often been said, is a virtue unknown to republics. As if to refute the slur, Jefferson's friends and admirers in New York, Philadelphia, Baltimore, and elsewhere organized subscription funds in his behalf. The lottery was suspended. Jefferson died in the belief, quite delusory as it turned out, that this outpouring of public sympathy and affection would save his estate.

He slowly sank from the middle of February. The urinary disease, compounded by a renewed attack of diarrhea, drained the life from his body. In March, knowing he must die, he drew his last will. It provided for the emancipation, subject to legislative confirmation, of five of his ablest and most faithful slaves. Neither the state of his property nor the state of the laws, he felt, permitted him to do more. The fatal crisis arrived in June. (The last entry in his account book was on June 20: "Isaacs for cheese 4.84.") Dr. Dunglison, the University Professor of Medicine who was at his bedside, remarked on the clarity and vigor of his mind to the end. "Until the 2nd and 3rd of July," the Doctor recalled, "he spoke freely of his approaching death; made all his arrangements with his grandson, Mr. Randolph, in regard to his private affairs; and expressed his anxiety for the prosperity of the University and his confidence in the exertion in its behalf of Mr. Madison and the other Visitors . . . . In the course of the day and night of the 2nd of July, he was affected with stupor, with intervals of wakefulness and consciousness; but on the 3rd, the stupor became permanent. About seven o'clock of the evening of that day, he awoke, and seeing my staying at his bedside exclaimed, 'Oh Doctor, are you still there?' in a voice, however, that was husky and indistinct. He then asked, 'Is it the Fourth?' to which I replied, 'It soon will be.' These were the last words I heard him utter."

The patriarch died at Monticello, surrounded by his family, at approximately one o'clock in the afternoon on the fiftieth anniversary of the Declaration of Independence. (On his reading table were two French political pamphlets, Aristotle's *Politics*, and a volume of Seneca.) John Adams also died on that memorable day at Quincy. His last words, "Thomas Jefferson still survives," prophesied a long history still to come, for Jefferson could not escape the future. More than any of his great contemporaries he had given form to the ideas, the values, even the dilemmas of the new nation, and thus involved himself with its destiny. He had inspired its democracy, which was egalitarian and progressive and inherently centralizing, yet within a coherent frame of law committed to the protection of individual and provincial rights and to the guardianship of enlightened intelligence. He had inspired the nationality of the Americans, not only the elements of independence and empire but those of character and ethos as well, yet under an overarching vision of the revolutionary nation's responsibilities to the freedom and peace and happiness of mankind. He had inspired the new nation with the hopes of the Enlightenment, embracing the paired directives toward nature and progress, science and humanism, power and civility, self-discovery and universality.

It was a mighty legacy. Posterity could comprehend it only in fragments. Lying on his deathbed, Jefferson's mind wandered backwards to the American Revolution, when the dream of the new nation was born. He had been invited to attend the anniversary ceremonies in Washington. Ten days before he died he penned his last letter, declining the invitation but affirming the faith of his life in a noble last testament to the nation on its jubilee. "May it be to the world, what I believe it will be (to some parts sooner, to others later, but finally to all), the signal of arousing men to burst the chains under which monkish ignorance and superstition had persuaded them to bind themselves, and to assume the blessings and security of self-government. That form which we have substituted, restores the free right to the unbounded exercise of reason and freedom of opinion. All eyes are opened, or opening, to the rights of man. The general spread of the light of science has already laid open to every view the palpable truth, that the mass of mankind has not been born with saddles on their backs, nor a favored few booted and spurred, ready to ride them legitimately, by the grace of God. These are grounds of hope for others. For ourselves, let the annual return of this day, forever refresh our recollections of these rights, and an undiminished devotion to them." And so he went to his death in the knowledge that the end of a man is nothing weighed in the scales with the history he has made.

Select

Bibliography

THE BIBLIOGRAPHY lists the sources of principal interest for this study. The bibliographical essay in *The Jefferson Image in the American Mind* offers a view of the literature from the time of Jefferson's death. Many items cited there are not repeated here. Also omitted are the books that Jefferson read—the books that shaped and informed his mind—to which the best guide is Sowerby's *Catalogue* of Jefferson's library, cited below.

PRIMARY SOURCES

a) *Jefferson Papers*

Three major manuscript collections:

Library of Congress. (Principally letters to and from Jefferson, it is of first importance for his public career.) Microfilm Edition.

Massachusetts Historical Society. (Sometimes called the Coolidge Collection, it is of special interest for Jefferson's private affairs.) Microfilm Edition.

University of Virginia. (A varied collection most useful for family and local concerns. A calendar is available: *The Jefferson Papers of the University of Virginia*, Constance E. Thurlow and Francis L. Berkeley, Jr., comp.)

The Account Books (1767–1826). Typescript photocopy, University of Virginia.

Published Editions:

The Writings of Thomas Jefferson. 10 v. Paul L. Ford, ed. (New York, 1892–99)

The Writings of Thomas Jefferson. 20 v. A. A. Lipscomb and A. E. Bergh, eds. (Washington, 1903)

The Papers of Thomas Jefferson. 17 v. to date. Julian P. Boyd and others, eds. (Princeton, 1950–65)

Other Published Works:

The Commonplace Book of Thomas Jefferson. Gilbert Chinard, ed. (Baltimore, 1926)

The Literary Bible of Thomas Jefferson. Gilbert Chinard, ed. (Baltimore, 1928)

Thomas Jefferson's Garden Book, 1766–1824. Edwin M. Betts, ed. (Philadelphia, 1944)

Thomas Jefferson's Farm Book. Edwin M. Betts, ed. (New York, 1953)

Notes on the State of Virginia. William Peden, ed. (Chapel Hill, 1955)

"A Memoir on the Discovery of Certain Bones of a Quadruped of the Clawed Kind in the Western Parts of Virginia," American Philosophical Society *Transactions*, v. 4 (1799)

The Complete Anas of Thomas Jefferson. F. B. Sawvel, ed. (New York, 1903)

Catalogue of the Library of Thomas Jefferson. 5 v. E. Millicent Sowerby, ed. (Washington, 1952)

The Complete Jefferson. Saul K. Padover, ed. (New York, 1943)

b) *State Papers and Related Documents*

American Archives. 9 v. Peter Force, ed. (Washington, 1837–53)

American State Papers. 38 v. Walter Lowrie and Matthew S. Clarke, eds. (Washington, 1836–61)

Calendar of Virginia State Papers and Other Manuscripts. 11 v. W. P. Palmer and others, eds. (Richmond, 1875–93)

Collection of Interesting and Important Reports and Papers on Navigation and Trade. (London, 1807)

A Compilation of the Messages and Papers of the Presidents. 10 v.
J. D. Richardson, ed. (Washington, 1907)

Correspondence of the French Ministers to the United States, 1791–97. F. J. Turner, ed. American Historical Association *Annual Report, 1903.* (Washington, 1904)

Debates and Proceedings in the Congress of the United States, v. 1–19 (Washington, 1834–53)

Instructions to the British Ministers to the United States, 1791–1812. Bernard Mayo, ed. American Historical Association *Annual Report, 1936.* (Washington, 1941)

Journal of the House of Delegates of Virginia, 1776–1790. (Richmond, 1827–28)

Journals of the Council of State of Virginia, 1776–1781. 2 v. H. R. McIlwaine, ed. (Richmond, 1931–32)

Journals of the Continental Congress. 34 v. Worthington C. Ford, ed. (Washington, 1904–36)

Louisiana Under the Rule of Spain, France, and the United States, 1785–1807. 2 v. James A. Robertson, ed. (Cleveland, 1911)

Papers Relating to America. (London, 1810)

Reports of the Trials of Aaron Burr. 2 v. D. Robertson, ed. (Philadelphia, 1808)

The Statutes at Large . . . Virginia. 13 v. W. W. Hening, ed. (Richmond, 1809–23)

The Territorial Papers of the United States, 24 v. Clarence E. Carter, ed. (Washington, 1934–52)

c) *Contemporary Letters, Journals and Writings*

(Letters are incorporated in some of the biographical works listed under Secondary Sources—Other Books.)

Adams, Abigail: *Letters of Mrs. Adams.* 4th ed. Charles F. Adams, ed. (Boston, 1848)
New Letters of Abigail Adams, 1788–1801. Stewart Mitchell, ed. (Boston, 1947)

Adams, John: *Works.* 10 v. Charles F. Adams, ed. (Boston, 1850–56)
Diary and Autobiography. 4 v. L. H. Butterfield, ed. (Cambridge, 1961)
Papers of John Adams. (Letters 1797–1801) Microfilm Edition.
The Adams-Jefferson Letters. 2 v. Lester Cappon, ed. (Chapel Hill, 1959)

The Spur of Fame: Dialogues of John Adams and Benjamin Rush, 1805–1813. John A. Schutz and Douglass Adair, eds. (San Marino, Calif., 1966)

Adams, John Quincy: *Memoirs.* 12 v. Charles Adams, ed. (Philadelphia, 1874–77)

Writings. 7 v. Worthington C. Ford, ed. (New York, 1913–17)

Adams, Samuel: *Writings.* 4 v. H. A. Cushing, ed. (New York, 1904–08)

Ames, Fisher: *Works.* 2 v. Seth Ames, ed. (Boston, 1854)

Bayard, James A.: *Papers.* Elizabeth Donnan, ed. American Historical Association *Annual Report,* 1913 (Washington, 1915)

Bland, Theodorick, Jr.: *Papers.* 2 v. Charles Campbell, ed. (Petersburg, Va., 1840–43)

Bond, Phineas: *Letters.* J. F. Jameson, ed. American Historical Association *Annual Report,* 1896–97 (Washington, 1897–98)

Bowdoin, James: *The Bowdoin and Temple Papers,* Part II. Massachusetts Historical Society *Collections,* 7th ser., v. 6 (Boston, 1907)

Burwell, William A.: "Private Memoir . . . ." MS, Library of Congress

Cabell, Joseph C.: *Early History of the University of Virginia as Contained in the Letters of Thomas Jefferson and Joseph C. Cabell.* Nathaniel F. Cabell, ed. (Richmond, 1856)

Carter, Landon: *Diary . . . , 1752–1758.* 2 v. Jack P. Greene, ed. (Charlottesville, 1965)

Clark, George Rogers: *Papers, 1771–1781.* James A. James, ed. Illinois Historical Society *Collections.* (Springfield, 1912)

Cutler, Manasseh: *Life, Journals and Correspondence.* 2 v. (Cincinnati, 1888)

Daggett, David: "Selections from the Letters Received . . . , 1786–1802." Franklin B. Dexter, ed. American Antiquarian Society *Proceedings,* new ser., v. 4 (1855–87)

Duane, William: "Letters." Worthington C. Ford, ed. Massachusetts Historical Society *Proceedings,* 3rd ser., v. 20 (1906–07)

Dunbar, William: *Life, Letters and Papers.* Mrs. Dunbar Rowland, ed. (Jackson, Miss., 1930)

Dunlap, William: *Diary.* 3 v. (New York, 1930)

Dupont de Nemours, Pierre Samuel: *Correspondence . . . Jefferson.* Dumas Malone, ed. (Boston, 1930)

Erskine, David M.: "Letters from America, 1798–1799." Patricia H. Menk, ed. *William and Mary Quarterly,* 3rd ser., v. 6 (1949)

Fenwick, Joseph: "Letters . . . , 1787–1795." Richard K. MacMaster, ed. *Maryland Historical Magazine*, v. 60 (1965)

Few, Frances: "Diary . . . , 1808–1809." Noble E. Cunningham, Jr., ed. *Journal of Southern History*, v. 29 (1963)

Fithian, Phillip V.: *Journal and Letters* . . . , *1773–1774*. H. D. Farish, ed. (Williamsburg, 1943)

Foster, Sir Augustus: *Jeffersonian America*. Richard Beale Davis, ed. (San Marino, Calif., 1954)

Gallatin, Albert: *Writings*. 3 v. Henry Adams, ed. (Philadelphia, 1879)

Grenville, William W.: *The Manuscripts of J. B. Fortesque*. . . . v. 9. Royal Historical Manuscripts Commission (London, 1915)

Griswold, Roger: Papers (1797–1801). Library of Congress. Microfilm Edition.

Hamilton, Alexander: *Works*. 7 v. John C. Hamilton, ed. (New York, 1850–51)

Works. 12 v. Henry Cabot Lodge, ed. (New York, 1904)
Papers. v. 1–14. Harold Syrett and others, eds. (New York, 1961–69)

Higginson, Stephen: "Letters . . . , 1783–1804." J. F. Jameson, ed. American Historical Association *Annual Report*, 1896. (Washington, 1897)

Honyman, Robert: "Diary and Journal . . . , 1776–1782." MS, Library of Congress

Howe, John: "Secret Reports . . . , 1808." David W. Parker, ed. *American Historical Review*, v. 17 (1911–12)

Iredell, James: *Life and Correspondence*. 2 v. G. J. McRee, ed. (New York, 1857–58)

Jay, John: *Correspondence and Public Papers*. 4 v. Henry P. Johnston, ed. (New York, 1890–93)

Jones, Joseph: *Letters* . . . , *1777–1787*. Worthington C. Ford, ed. (New York, 1889)

King, Rufus: *Life and Correspondence*. 6 v. Charles R. King, ed. (New York, 1894–1900)

Latrobe, Benjamin H.: *Journal* (New York, 1905)

Lee, Richard Henry: *Letters*. 2 v. James C. Ballagh, ed. (New York, 1911–14)

Letters of Members of the Continental Congress. 8 v. Edmund C. Burnett, ed. (Washington, 1921–36)

Lewis, Meriwether, and William Clark: *Letters of the Lewis and Clark Expedition*. Donald Jackson, ed. (Urbana, Ill., 1962)

Original Journals of the Lewis and Clark Expedition, 1804–06. 8 v. Reuben G. Thwaites, ed. (New York, 1904–05)

Liston, Henrietta: "Letters . . . , 1796–1801." Bradford Perkins, ed. *William and Mary Quarterly,* 3rd ser., v. 11 (1954)

Maclay, William: *Journal.* E. S. Maclay, ed. (New York, 1890)

Madison, James: *Letters and Other Writings.* 4 v. (Washington, 1894)

> *Writings.* 9 v. Gaillard Hunt, ed. (New York, 1900–10)

> *Papers.* v. 1–5. William T. Hutcheson and Willam M. E. Rachel, eds. (Chicago, 1962–69)

> Presidential Papers. Library of Congress. Microfilm Edition.

Marshall, Christopher: *Passages from the Diary.* William Duane, ed. (Philadelphia, 1849)

Miscellaneous State Department Papers, 1801–09. Microfilm Edition.

Mitchill, Samuel L.: "Letters from Washington, 1801–1813." *Harper's Magazine,* v. 58 (1879)

Monroe, James: *Writings.* 7 v. S. M. Hamilton, ed. (New York, 1898–1903)

> Presidential Papers. Library of Congress. Microfilm Edition.

Morris, Gouverneur: *A Diary of the French Revolution.* 2 v. Beatrix C. Davenport, ed. (Boston, 1939)

Murray, William Vans: "Letters . . . to John Quincy Adams, 1797–1803." Worthington C. Ford, ed. American Historical Association *Annual Report,* 1912 (Washington, 1914)

Nicholas, Wilson Cary: Papers. Library of Congress. Microfilm Edition.

Otto, Louis W.: "A French Diplomat's View of the First Congress, 1790." Margaret M. O'Dwyer, ed. *William and Mary Quarterly,* 3rd ser., v. 21 (1964)

Paine, Thomas: *Writings.* 2 v. Philip Foner, ed. (New York, 1945)

Pendleton, Edmund: *Letters and Papers.* 2 v. David J. Mays, ed. (Charlottesville, 1967)

Pickering, Timothy: *Calendar of Pickering Papers.* Massachusetts Historical Society *Collections,* v. 58 (Boston, 1896)

Plumer, William: *Memorandum of Proceedings in the Senate, 1803–07.* E. S. Brown, ed. (New York, 1923)

Riedesel, Friederich von: *Memoirs, Letters and Journals.* 2 v. W. L. Stone, tr. (Albany, 1868)

Riedesel, Madame: *Letters and Journals.* W. L. Stone, tr. (Albany, 1867)

Rush, Benjamin: *Letters.* 2 v. Lyman H. Butterfield, ed. (Princeton, 1951)
Old Family Letters (Philadelphia, 1892)

Simcoe, John Graves: *Military Journal.* (New York, 1844)

Smith, Abigail Adams: *Journal and Correspondence of Miss Adams.* Ed. by her daughter. (New York, 1841)

Smith, John Cotton: *Correspondence and Miscellanies.* (New York, 1847)

Smith, Robert: "Some Papers . . . ." Bernard C. Steiner, ed. *Maryland Historical Magazine,* v. 15 (1925)

Smith, Samuel: Papers. Library of Congress. Microfilm Edition.

"South Carolina Federalist Correspondence, 1789–1797." Ulrich B. Phillips, ed. *American Historical Review,* v. 14 (1909)

Steele, John: *Papers.* 2 v. H. M. Wagstaff, ed. (Raleigh, N.C., 1924)

Taggart, Samuel: "Letters . . . , 1803–1814." George H. Haynes, ed. American Antiquarian Society *Proceedings,* new ser., v. 33 (1923)

Taylor, John: "Letters, 1793–1823." *John P. Branch Historical Papers of Randolph-Macon College,* v. 2 (1908)

Thornton, Edward: "A Young Englishman Reports on the New Nation . . . , 1791–1793." S. W. Jackman, ed. *William and Mary Quarterly,* 3rd ser., v. 18 (1961)

Von Humboldt, Alexander: "Correspondence with Jefferson, Madison and Gallatin." Helmut de Terra, ed. American Philosophical Society *Proceedings,* v. 103 (1959)

Washington, George: *Correspondence of the American Revolution, Being Letters of Eminent Men to George Washington,* 4 v. Jared Sparks, ed. (Boston, 1853)
Diaries, 1748–1799. 4 v. J. C. Fitzpatrick, ed. (Boston, 1925)
Washington's Farewell Address. Victor H. Paltsits, ed. (New York, 1935)
Writings. 39 v. J. C. Fitzpatrick, ed. (Washington, 1931–41)

Webster, Noah: *Letters.* Harry R. Warfel, ed. (New York, 1953)

Wilson, James: *Works.* 2 v. James D. Andrews, ed. (Chicago, 1896)

d) *Contemporary Newspapers, Magazines, Pamphlets, and Political Miscellany*

Newspapers:

Aurora (Philadelphia), 1797–1809
Gazette of the United States (New York, Philadelphia), 1790–93, 1798–1800

General Advertiser (Philadelphia), 1790–93
National Gazette (Philadelphia), 1791–93
National Intelligencer (Washington), 1800–09
Niles' Weekly Register (Baltimore), 1811–26
Virginia Gazette(s) (Williamsburg), 1769–76

Magazines:

American Museum (Philadelphia), 1787–92
North American Review (Boston), 1815–26

Pamphlets and Miscellany:

Austin, Benjamin, *Constitutional Republicanism* (Boston, 1803)

Baring, Alexander, *An Inquiry Into the Causes and Consequences of the Order in Council . . . .* (London, 1808)

Barlow, Joel, *Advice to the Privileged Orders* (New York, 1794)

[Beckley, John], *An Address to the People of the United States with an Epitome and Vindication of the Public Life and Character of Thomas Jefferson* (Philadelphia, 1800)

Brougham, Henry, *The Speech . . . Before the House of Commons . . . April 1, 1808* (London, 1808)

Callender, James T., *The Political Progress of Britain.* 2 v., 3rd ed. (Philadelphia, 1795)
   The Prospect Before Us. 3 v. (Richmond, 1800–01)

Cobbett, William, *Porcupine's Works.* 12 v. (London, 1801)

Cooper, Thomas, *Political Essays* (Northumberland, Pa., 1799)

Coxe, Tench, *Reflections on the State of the Union* (Philadelphia, 1792)
   A View of the United States of America (Philadelphia, 1794)

Daveiss, Joseph Hamilton, *A View of the President's Conduct Concerning the Conspiracy of 1806* (Frankfort, Ky., 1807)

Fenno, John, Jr., *New Political Aspects* (Philadelphia, 1799)

[Fessenden, William G.], *Democracy Unveiled.* 2 v., 3rd ed. (New York, 1806)

Hay, George, *An Essay on the Liberty of the Press . . . .* (Richmond, 1803)

Knox, Samuel, *A Vindication of the Religion of Mr. Jefferson* (Baltimore. 1801)

An Essay on the Best System of Liberal Education (Baltimore, 1799)

Magruder, Allan B., *Political, Commercial, and Moral Reflections on the Late Cession of Louisiana to the United States* (Lexington, Ky., 1803)

Mason, John M., *The Voice of Warning to Christians* . . . . (New York, 1800)

Moore, Frank, comp., *Diary of the American Revolution, from Newspapers and Original Documents*. 2 v. (New York, 1859–60)

Pickering, Timothy, *A Letter to the Honorable William Sullivan* . . . . (Hartford, 1808)

Pownall, Thomas, *A Memorial . . . to the Sovereigns of Europe*. . . . 2nd ed. (London, 1780)

Price, Richard, *Observations on the Nature of Civil Liberty* (London, 1776)
Observations on the Importance of the American Revolution (London, 1784)

Roscoe, William, *Consideration on the Causes, Objects, and Consequences of the Present War* (London, 1808)

Schlegel, J. F. W., *Neutral Rights* . . . . (Philadelphia, 1801)

Sheffield, Lord [John Baker Holroyd], *Observations on the Commerce of the United States* (London, 1783)

[Smith, William Loughton], *The Politicks and Views of a Certain Party Displayed* (n.p., 1792)
The Pretensions of Thomas Jefferson to the Presidency Examined . . . . (Philadelphia, 1796)

[Stephen, James], *War in Disguise; or The Frauds of the Neutral Flags* (London, 1805)

Taylor, John, *Arator*. 2nd ed. (Georgetown, 1814)
An Examination of the Late Proceedings of Congress Respecting the Official Conduct of the Secretary of the Treasury (Philadelphia, 1793)
An Inquiry Into the Principles and Policy of the Government of the United States (New Haven, 1950)
Construction Construed and Constitutions Vindicated (Richmond, 1820)

Tucker, St. George, ed., Notes and Appendices, *Blackstone's Commentaries*. 5 v. (Philadelphia, 1803)
A Dissertation on Slavery (Philadelphia, 1796)

Reflections on the Cession of Louisiana to the United States (Washington, 1803)

e) *Travels*

Anburey, Thomas, *Travels Through the Interior Parts of America.* 2 v. (London, 1789)

Bayard, Ferdinand-Marie, *Travels of a Frenchman in Maryland and Virginia . . . , in 1791.* Ben C. McCary, ed. (Williamsburg, 1950)

Bernard, John, *Retrospections of America, 1797–1811* (New York, 1887)

Boudinot, Elias, *Journey to Boston in 1809.* M. H. Thomas, ed. (Princeton, 1955)

Bradbury, John, *Travels in the Interior of America* (Liverpool, 1817)

Brissot de Warville, J. P., *New Travels in the United States of America.* 2nd ed. (London, 1794)

Burnaby, Andrew, *Travels through North America.* [1759–60] Rufus R. Wilson, ed. (New York, 1904)

Caldwell, John Edwards, *A Tour Through Part of Virginia in . . . 1808.* (New York, 1809)

Chastellux, Marquis de, *Travels in North America, 1780, 1781.* Howard C. Rice, tr. and ed. (Chapel Hill, 1963)

Crevecoeur, M. G. St. Jean de, *Letters from An American Farmer* (London, 1782)

Davis, John, *Travels in the United States* (New York, 1803)

Du Roi, August Wilhelm, *Journal.* Charlotte S. J. Epping, tr. (New York, 1911)

Hunter, Robert, Jr., *Quebec to Carolina in 1785–1786.* Louis B. Wright and Marion Tinling, eds. (San Marino, 1943)

Kendall, Edward A., *Travels Through the Northern Parts of the United States, in 1807–1808.* 3 v. (New York, 1809)

La Rochefoucauld Liancourt, Francois A. F., Duc de, *Travels Through the United States of North America.* 2 v. (London, 1799)

Melish, John, *Travels in the United States of America, in the Years 1806 and 1807.* 2 v. (Philadelphia, 1812)

Moreau de Saint-Méry, *American Journey, 1793–1798.* Kenneth Roberts and Anna M. Roberts, tr. and ed. (Garden City, 1947)

Schoepf, Johann David, *Travels in the Confederation.* 2 v. Alfred J. Morrison, tr. and ed. (Philadelphia, 1911)

Smyth, John F. D., *A Tour of the United States of America, 1784.* 2 v. (Dublin, 1784)

Strickland, William, *Observations on the Agriculture of the United States of America* (London, 1801)

Sutcliffe, Robert, *Travels in Some Parts of North America in the Years 1804, 1805, and 1806.* (Philadelphia, 1812)

Weld, Isaac, Jr., *Travels Through the States of North America . . . During the Years 1795, 1796, and 1797* (London, 1799)

Young, Arthur, *Travels in France During the Years 1787, 1788, 1789.* M. Betham-Edwards, ed. (London, 1913)

SECONDARY SOURCES

a) *Books on Jefferson*

Berman, Eleanor D., *Thomas Jefferson Among the Arts* (New York, 1947)

Boorstin, Daniel, *The Lost World of Thomas Jefferson* (New York, 1948)

Bullock, Helen D., *My Head and My Heart* (New York, 1945)

Caldwell, Lynton K., *The Administrative Theories of Hamilton and Jefferson* (Chicago, 1944)

Chinard, Gilbert, *Thomas Jefferson, The Apostle of Americanism.* Rev. ed. (New York, 1939)

Dumbauld, Edward, *Thomas Jefferson, American Tourist* (Norman, Okla., 1946)

Frary, I. T., *Thomas Jefferson, Architect and Builder* (Richmond, 1931)

Healey, Robert M., *Jefferson on Religion in Public Education* (New Haven, 1962)

Honeywell, Roy J., *The Educational Work of Thomas Jefferson,* (Cambridge, 1931)

Kimball, Fiske, *The Life Portraits of Jefferson and Their Replicas* (Philadelphia, 1944)
Thomas Jefferson, Architect (Boston, 1916)

Kimball, Marie, *Jefferson: The Road to Glory* (New York, 1943)

Jefferson: War and Peace (New York, 1947)

Jefferson: The Scene of Europe (New York, 1950)

Koch, Adrienne, *Jefferson and Madison: The Great Collaboration* (New York, 1951)

The Philosophy of Thomas Jefferson (New York, 1943)

Lehman, Karl, *Thomas Jefferson, American Humanist* (Chicago, 1947)

Levy, Leonard, *Jefferson and Civil Liberties* (Cambridge, 1963)

Malone, Dumas, *Jefferson the Virginian* (Boston, 1948)

Jefferson and the Rights of Man (Boston, 1951)

Jefferson and the Ordeal of Liberty (Boston, 1962)

Martin, Edwin T., *Thomas Jefferson, Scientist* (New York, 1952)

Nichols, Frederick D., *Thomas Jefferson's Architectural Drawings* (Boston, 1960)

Nock, Albert J., *Jefferson* (New York, 1926)

Parton, James, *Life of Thomas Jefferson* (Boston, 1874)

Peterson, Merrill D., *The Jefferson Image in the American Mind* (New York, 1960)

Randall, Henry S., *Life of Thomas Jefferson*. 3 v. (Philadelphia, 1857)

Randolph, Sarah N., *The Domestic Life of Thomas Jefferson*. American Classics Edition (New York, 1958)

Tucker, George, *Life of Thomas Jefferson*, 2 v. (Philadelphia, 1837)

Wiltse, Charles M., *The Jeffersonian Tradition in American Democracy* (Chapel Hill, 1935)

b) *Other Books*

Abel, Anna H., *The History of Events Resulting in Indian Consolidation West of the Mississippi*. American Historical Association *Annual Report*, 1906 (Washington, 1908)

Abernethy, Thomas P., *The Burr Conspiracy* (New York, 1954)

The South in the New Nation, 1789–1819 (Baton Rouge, 1961)

Western Lands and the American Revolution (New York, 1937)

Acomb, Frances, *Anglophobia in France, 1763–1789* (Durham, N.C., 1950)

Adams, Henry, *History of the United States During the Administrations of Jefferson and Madison*. 9 v. (New York, 1891–93)

The Life of Albert Gallatin (Philadelphia, 1879)

ed., *Documents Relating to New England Federalism, 1800–1815* (Boston, 1877)

Adams, Herbert B., *The College of William and Mary* (Washington, 1887)

Thomas Jefferson and the University of Virginia (Washington, 1888)

Adams, Randolph G., *Political Ideas of the American Revolution* (Durham, N.C., 1922)

Agar, Herbert, *The Price of Union* (Boston, 1950)

Alden, John R., *John Stuart and the Southern Colonial Frontier* (Ann Arbor, 1944)

The South in the Revolution, 1763–1789 (Baton Rouge, 1957)

Allen, Harry C., *Great Britain and the United States: A History of Anglo-American Relations* (London, 1954)

Alvord, Clarence W., *The Mississippi Valley in British Politics.* 2 v. (Cleveland, 1917)

Anderson, Dice R., *William Branch Giles* (Menasha, Wisc., 1914)

Arendt, Hannah, *On Revolution* (New York, 1963)

Arieli, Yehoshua, *Individualism and Tradition in American Ideology* (Cambridge, 1964)

Aronson, Sidney H., *Status and Kinship in the Higher Civil Service* (Cambridge, 1964)

Bacon-Foster, Corra, *The Potomac Route to the West* (Washington, 1912)

Bailyn, Bernard, "General Introduction," *Pamphlets of the American Revolution.* v. 1 (Cambridge, 1965)

Baldwin, Simeon E., *Life and Letters of Simeon Baldwin* (New Haven, 1918)

Balinky, Alexander, *Albert Gallatin: Fiscal Theories and Policies* (New Brunswick, 1958)

Barnes, Harry Elmer, *The Evolution of Penology in Pennsylvania* (Indianapolis, 1927)

Barnhart, John D., *Henry Hamilton and George Rogers Clark . . . .* (Crawfordsville, Ind., 1951)

Beard, Charles A., *Economic Origins of Jeffersonian Democracy* (New York, 1915)

and Mary R. Beard, *The American Spirit* (New York, 1942)

Becker, Carl, *The Declaration of Independence* (New York, 1922)

Bemis, Samuel F., *Jay's Treaty* (New York, 1923)

John Quincy Adams and the Foundations of American Foreign Policy (New York, 1949)

ed., *The American Secretaries of State and Their Diplomacy.* v. 1 and 2 (New York, 1927)

Bernhard, Winfred E. A., *Fisher Ames, Federalist Statesman, 1758–1808.* (Chapel Hill, 1965)

Beveridge, Albert J., *Life of John Marshall.* 4 v. (Boston, 1916–19)

Blake, John B., *Benjamin Waterhouse and the Introduction of Vaccination* . . . . (Philadelphia, 1957)

Boorstin, Daniel, *The Americans: The Colonial Experience* (New York, 1958)

Borden, Morton, *The Federalism of James A. Bayard* (New York, 1955)

Boudinot, Jane J., ed., *The Life of Elias Boudinot.* 2 v. (Boston, 1896)

Boulton, James T., *The Language of Politics in the Age of Wilkes and Burke* (Toronto, 1963)

Boyd, Julian P., *The Declaration of Independence: The Evolution of the Text.* . . . (Washington, 1943)

Number 7, Alexander Hamilton's Secret Attempts to Control American Foreign Policy (Princeton, 1964)

Brant, Irving, *James Madison: The Virginia Revolutionist* (Indianapolis, 1941)

James Madison: Father of the Constitution (Indianapolis, 1950)

James Madison: Secretary of State (Indianapolis, 1953)

James Madison: The President (Indianapolis, 1959)

James Madison: Commander-in-Chief (Indianapolis, 1961)

Bridenbaugh, Carl, *Myths and Realities: Societies of the Colonial South* (Baton Rouge, 1952)

Seat of Empire: The Political Role of Eighteenth Century Williamsburg (Charlottesville, 1963)

Briggs, Herbert W., *The Doctrine of Continuous Voyage* (Baltimore, 1926)

Brown, Everett S., *Constitutional History of the Louisiana Purchase, 1803–1812* (Berkeley, 1920)

Brown, Glenn, *History of the United States Capitol.* v. 1 (Washington, 1900)

Brown, Robert E., and B. Katherine Brown, *Virginia, 1705–1786: Democracy or Aristocracy?* (East Lansing, Mich., 1964)

Brown, Roger H., *The Republic in Peril: 1812* (New York, 1964)

Bruce, Philip Alexander, *History of the University of Virginia.* v. 1 and 2 (New York, 1920)

Bruce, William C., *John Randolph of Roanoke* (New York, 1939)

Bruchey, Stuart, *The Roots of American Economic Growth* (New York, 1965)

Bryan, Wilhemus B., *A History of the National Capital*. v. 1 (New York, 1914)

Brydon, George M., *Virginia's Mother Church*. 2 v. (Philadelphia, 1952)

Bryson, Gladys, *Man and Society: The Scottish Inquiry of the Eighteenth Century* (Princeton, 1945)

Bulfinch, Ellen S., ed., *The Life and Letters of Charles Bulfinch* (Boston, 1896)

Burk, John Daly, and others, *History of Virginia*. 4 v. (Richmond, 1804–16)

Burnett, Edmund C., *The Continental Congress* (New York, 1941)

Burt, A. L., *The United States, Great Britain, and British North America* . . . . (New Haven, 1940)

Butts, R. Freeman, *The American Tradition in Religion and Education* (Boston, 1950)
The College Charts Its Course (New York, 1939)

Callender, Guy S., ed., *Selections from the Economic History of the United States* (Boston, 1909)

Carroll, John A., and Mary W. Ashworth, *George Washington*. v. 7 (New York, 1957). *Cf.* Freeman, Douglas S.

Cassirer, Ernst, *The Philosophy of the Enlightenment*. Fritz C. A. Koelln and James P. Pettegrove, trs. (Boston, 1951)

Chambers, William N., *Political Parties in a New Nation* (New York, 1963)

Channing, Edward, *A History of the United States*. 6 v. (New York, 1905–25)

Charles, Joseph, *The Origins of the American Party System* (Williamsburg, Va., 1951)

Chitwood, Oliver P., *Justice in Colonial Virginia* (Baltimore, 1905)

Clark, Allen C., ed., *Life and Letters of Dolly Madison* (Washington, 1914)

Clauder, Anna C., *American Commerce as Affected by the Wars of the French Revolution* . . . . (Philadelphia, 1932)

Colbourn, H. Trevor, *The Lamp of Experience* (Chapel Hill, 1965)

Commager, Henry S., and Elmo Giardonetti, eds., *Was America a Mistake? An Eighteenth Century Controversy* (Columbia, S.C., 1967)

Conant, James B., *Thomas Jefferson and the Development of American Public Education* (Berkeley, 1962)

Conway, Moncure D., *Omitted Chapters of History Disclosed in the Life and Public Papers of Edmund Randolph* (New York, 1888)

The Life of Thomas Paine. 2 v. (New York, 1892)

Cooper, James Fenimore, *The History of the Navy of the United States*. 2 v. (Philadelphia, 1839)

Corwin, Edward S., *The Doctrine of Judicial Review* (Princeton, 1914)

John Marshall and the Constitution (New Haven, 1919)

The President: Office and Powers (New York, 1940)

Cox, Isaac J., *The West Florida Controversy, 1789–1813* (Baltimore, 1918)

Craven, Avery, *Soil Exhaustion as a Factor in the Agricultural History of Virginia and Maryland, 1606–1860* (Urbana, Ill., 1926)

Cresson, William P., *James Monroe* (Chapel Hill, 1946)

Crosskey, William W., *Politics and the Constitution in the History of the United States*. 2 v. (Chicago, 1953)

Cunningham, Noble E., Jr., *The Jeffersonian Republicans: The Formation of Party Organization, 1789–1801* (Chapel Hill, 1957)

The Jeffersonian Republicans in Power (Chapel Hill, 1963)

Curtler, W. H. R., *A Short History of English Agriculture* (Oxford, 1909)

Dangerfield, George, *Chancellor Robert R. Livingston of New York* (New York, 1960)

The Era of Good Feelings (New York, 1952)

Darling, Arthur B., *Our Rising Empire, 1763–1803* (New Haven, 1940)

Dauer, Manning J., *The Adams Federalists* (Baltimore, 1953)

Davis, David Brion, *The Problem of Slavery in Western Culture* (Ithaca, N.Y., 1966)

Davis, Joseph S., *Essays in the Earlier History of American Corporations*. 2 v. (Cambridge, 1917)

Davis, Matthew L., *Memoirs of Aaron Burr*. 2 v. (New York, 1936–37)

Davis, Richard Beale, *Francis Walker Gilmer: Life and Learning in Jefferson's Virginia* (Richmond, 1939)

Intellectual Life in Jefferson's Virginia (Chapel Hill, 1964)

De Conde, Alexander, *Entangling Alliance: Politics and Diplomacy Under George Washington* (Durham, N.C., 1958)

The Quasi-War: The Politics and Diplomacy of the Undeclared War with France, 1797–1801 (New York, 1966)

Dewey, Davis R., *Financial History of the United States.* 12th ed. (New York, 1936)

Dewey, John, *Freedom and Culture* (New York, 1939)

Dickerson, Oliver M., *The Navigation Acts and the American Revolution* (Philadelphia, 1951)

Dictionary of American Biography. 22 v. Allen Johnson, Dumas Malone, Harris E. Starr, eds. (New York, 1928–58)

Dorfman, Joseph, *The Economic Mind in American Civilization.* v. 1 and 2. (New York, 1946)

Douglass, Elisha P., *Rebels and Democrats* (Chapel Hill, 1955)

Echeverria, Durand, *Mirage in the West: A History of the French Image of American Society to 1815* (Princeton, 1957)

Eckenrode, Hamilton J., *The Revolution in Virginia* (Boston, 1916)
Separation of Church and State in Virginia (Richmond, 1910)

Ellery, Eloise, *Brissot de Warville* (Boston, 1915)

Ernst, Robert, *Rufus King, American Federalist* (Chapel Hill, 1968)

Ferguson, E. James, *The Power of the Purse* (Chapel Hill, 1961)

Fischer, David H., *The Revolution of American Conservatism* (New York, 1965)

Foster, Roger, *Commentaries on the Constitution of the United States.* v. 1 (Boston, 1895)

Freeman, Douglas S., *George Washington: A Biography.* v. 5 and 6. (New York, 1952–54) Cf. Carroll and Ashworth.

Gaines, William H., *Thomas Mann Randolph* (Baton Rouge, 1966)

Garlick, Richard C., Jr., *Philip Mazzei, Friend of Jefferson* (Baltimore, 1933)

Gay, Peter, *The Enlightenment: An Interpretation. The Rise of Modern Paganism* (New York, 1966)

Gibbs, George, *Memoirs of the Administrations of Washington and Adams.* 2 v. (New York, 1846)

Gilbert, Felix, *To the Farewell Address* (New York, 1961)

Godechot, Jacques, *France and the Atlantic Revolution of the Eighteenth Century, 1770–1799.* Herbert Rowen, tr. (New York, 1965)

Goldsborough, Charles W., *The United States Naval Chronicle.* v. 1 (Washington, 1824)

Goodman, Paul, *The Democratic-Republicans of Massachusetts* (Cambridge, 1964)

Gottschalk, Louis, *Lafayette, 1783–1789* (Chicago, 1950)

Gough, J. W., *John Locke's Political Philosophy* (Oxford, 1950)

Graham, Gerald S., *Sea Power and British North America, 1783–1802* (Cambridge, 1941)

Gras, N. S. B., *A History of Agriculture in Europe and America* (New York, 1925)

Gray, Francis C., *Thomas Jefferson in 1814. Being an Account of a Visit to Monticello* (Boston, 1924)

Gray, Lewis C., *History of Agriculture in the Southern United States to 1860.* 2 v. (Washington, 1933)

Graydon, Alexander, *Memoirs of His Own Time.* J. S. Littell, ed. (Philadelphia, 1846)

Green, Constance M., *Washington, Village and Capital, 1800–1878* (Princeton, 1962)

Greene, Jack P., *The Quest for Power . . . , 1689–1776* (Chapel Hill, 1963)

Grigsby, Hugh Blair, *The Virginia Convention of 1776* (Richmond, 1855)

Griswold, Rufus W., *The Republican Court; or American Society in the Days of Washnigton* (London, 1854)

Gummere, Richard M., *The American Colonial Mind and the Classical Tradition* (Cambridge, 1963)

Guttridge, G. H., *English Whiggism and the American Revolution* (Berkeley, 1942)

Haines, Charles G., *The Role of the Supreme Court in American Government and Politics, 1789–1835* (Berkeley, 1944)

Hammond, Bray, *Banks and Politics in America from the Revolution to the Civil War* (Princeton, 1957)

Handler, Edward G., *America and Europe in the Political Thought of John Adams* (Cambridge, 1964)

Haraszti, Zoltan, *John Adams and the Prophets of Progress* (Cambridge, 1952)

Harlow, Vincent T., *The Founding of the Second British Empire, 1763–1793* (London, 1952)

Harrell, Isaac S., *Loyalism in Virginia* (Durham, N.C., 1926)

Harris, Neil, *The Artist in American Society: The Formative Years, 1790–1860* (New York, 1966)

Hart, Freeman H., *The Valley of Virginia in the American Revolution* (Chapel Hill, 1942)

Hartz, Louis, *The Founding of New Societies* (New York, 1964)

Hastings, G. E., *Life and Works of Francis Hopkinson* (Chicago, 1926)

Hatcher, William B., *Edward Livingston* (Baton Rouge, 1940)

Hawke, David, *A Transaction of Free Men: The Birth and Career of the Declaration of Independence* (New York, 1964)

Hazelton, John H., *The Declaration of Independence: Its History* (New York, 1960)

Hazen, Charles D., *Contemporary American Opinion of the French Revolution* (Baltimore, 1897)

Hechscher, Eli, *The Continental System: An Economic Interpretation* (Oxford, 1922)

Heimann, Edward, *History of Economic Doctrines* (New York, 1945)

Henderson, Archibald, *Dr. Thomas Walker of the Loyal Company of Virginia* (Worcester, 1951)

Herr, Richard, and Harold T. Parker, eds., *Ideas in History: Essays Presented to Louis Gottschalk* . . . . (Durham, N.C., 1965)

Higginbotham, Sanford W., *The Keystone in the Democratic Arch: Pennsylvania Politics, 1800–1816* (Harrisburg, 1952)

Higgins, Earl Leroy, ed., *The French Revolution as Told by Contemporaries* (Cambridge, 1938)

Hildreth, Richard, *The History of the United States*. 6 v. (New York, 1849–56)

Hindle, Brooke, *The Pursuit of Science in Revolutionary America* (Chapel Hill, 1956)

Holmes, Jack D. L., *Gayoso. The Life of a Spanish Governor in the Mississippi Valley, 1789–1799* (Baton Rouge, 1965)

Hook, Sidney, *The Paradoxes of Freedom* (Berkeley, 1962)

Horsman, Reginald, *The Causes of the War of 1812* (Philadelphia, 1962)

Expansion and American Indian Policy, 1783–1812 (East Lansing, Mich., 1967)

Howe, John R., Jr., *The Changing Political Thought of John Adams* (Princeton, 1966)

Humphrey, Edward F., *Nationalism and Religion in America, 1774–1789* (Boston, 1924)

Humphreys, Francis L., *Life and Times of David Humphreys*. 2 v. (New York, 1917)

Hunt, Gaillard, *The Department of State of the United States* (New Haven, 1894)

Hutcheson, Harold, *Tench Coxe* (Baltimore, 1938)

Hynemann, Charles S., *The First American Neutrality* (Urbana, Ill., 1934)

Irwin, Ray W., *Diplomatic Relations of the United States with the Barbary Powers, 1776–1816* (Chapel Hill, 1931)

Jackson, Henry F., *Scholar in the Wilderness, Francis Adrian Van der Kemp* (Syracuse, 1963)

Jacob, John I., *A Biographical Sketch of the Life of the Late Michael Cresap* (Cincinnati, 1866)

Jacobs, James R., *The Beginnings of the United States Army, 1783–1812* (Princeton, 1947)
    Tarnished Warrior, Major General James Wilkinson (New York, 1938)

James, Charles F., *Documentary History of the Struggle for Religious Liberty in Virginia* (Danville, Va., 1900)

[Jefferson, Isaac], *Memoirs of a Monticello Slave*. Rayford W. Logan, ed. (Charlottesville, 1951)

Jennings, Walter W., *The American Embargo, 1807–1809* (Iowa City, 1921)

Jensen, Merrill, *The Founding of a Nation* (New York, 1968)
    The New Nation . . . (New York, 1950)

Jones, Howard Mumford, *O Strange New World* (New York, 1965)

Jordon, Winthrop D., *White over Black: American Attitudes toward the Negro, 1550–1812* (Chapel Hill, 1968)

Kaplan, Lawrence S., *Jefferson and France: An Essay* . . . . (New Haven, 1967)

Kapp, Friedrich, *The Life of Frederick William von Steuben*. 2nd ed. (New York, 1859)

Kehoe, Vincent, *Virginia 1774* (Málaga, Spain, 1958)

Keller, Charles R., *The Second Great Awakening in Connecticut* (New Haven, 1942)

Kennedy, John P., *Memoirs of the Life of William Wirt*. 2 v. (New York, 1872)

Koch, Adrienne, *Power, Morals, and the Founding Fathers* (Ithaca, N.Y., 1961)

Koebner, Richard, *Empire* (Cambridge, England, 1961)

Kurtz, Stephen G., *The Presidency of John Adams* (Philadelphia, 1957)

Landers, H. L., *The Virginia Campaign and the Blockade and Siege of Yorktown* . . . . (Washington, 1931)

Leary, Lewis G., *That Rascal Freneau* (New Brunswick, 1941)

Leder, Lawrence H., *Liberty and Authority: Early American Political Ideology, 1689–1763* (Chicago, 1968)

Lee, Henry, *Memoirs of the War in the Southern Department of the United States* (Philadelphia, 1812)

Lefebvre, George, *The Coming of the French Revolution.* R. R. Palmer, tr. (New York, 1960)

Levy, Leonard W., *The Legacy of Suppression: Freedom of Speech and Press in Early American History* (Cambridge, 1960)

Lewis, O. F., *The Development of American Prisons and Prison Customs, 1775–1845* (New York, 1922)

Lingley, Charles R., *The Transition in Virginia from Colony to Commonwealth* (New York, 1910)

Lipset, Seymour Martin, *The First New Nation* (New York, 1963)

Little, Lewis P., *Imprisoned Preachers and Religious Liberty in Virginia* (Lynchburg, Va., 1938)

Lodge, Henry Cabot, *The Life and Letters of George Cabot* (Boston, 1877)

Logan, Deborah, *Memoir of Dr. George Logan of Stenton* (Philadelphia, 1899)

Logan, John A., Jr., *No Transfer: An American Security Principle* (New Haven, 1961)

Logan, Rayford W., *The Diplomatic Relations of the United States with Haiti, 1776–1891* (Chapel Hill, 1941)

Lokke, Carl L., *France and the Colonial Question . . . , 1763–1801* (New York, 1932)

Lough, John, *An Introduction to Eighteenth Century France* (New York, 1960)

Lyon, E. Wilson, *Louisiana in French Diplomacy, 1759–1804* (Norman, Okla., 1934)

Macmillan, Margaret B., *The War Governors in the American Revolution* (New York, 1943)

Magrath, C. Peter, *Yazoo: Law and Politics in the New Republic . . . .* (Providence, 1966)

Mahan, Alfred Thayer, *Sea Power in Its Relation to the War of 1812.* 2 v. (Boston, 1905)

Mahon, John K., *The American Militia: Decade of Decision, 1789–1799* (Gainesville, Fla., 1960)

Main, Jackson T., *The Antifederalists: Critics of the Constitution* (Chapel Hill, 1961)

Malone, Dumas, *The Public Life of Thomas Cooper* (New York, 1926)

Martin, Francis-Xavier, *The History of Louisiana* (New Orleans, 1882)

Marx, Leo, *The Machine in the Garden: Technology and the Pastoral Ideal in America* (New York, 1964)

Mayo, Bernard, *Myths and Men: Patrick Henry, George Washington, Thomas Jefferson* (Athens, 1959)

Mays, David John, *Edmund Pendleton, A Biography.* 2 v. (Cambridge, 1952)

Maxwell, Lloyd W., *Discriminatory Duties and the American Merchant Marine* (New York, 1926)

Maxwell, William, *Memoir of the Reverend John H. Rice* (Philadelphia, 1835)

Mazzei, Philip, *Memoirs. . . .* Howard R. Marraro, tr. (New York, 1942)

McBain, Howard L., *De Witt Clinton and the Origin of the Spoils System in New York* (New York, 1907)

McCaleb, Walter F., *The Aaron Burr Conspiracy.* Rev. ed. (New York, 1936)

McColley, Robert, *Slavery in Jeffersonian Virginia* (Urbana, Ill., 1964)

McDonald, Forrest, *We the People: The Economic Origins of the Constitution* (Chicago, 1958)

McIlwain, Charles H., *The American Revolution: A Constitutional Interpretation* (New York, 1924)

McLean, Robert C., *George Tucker, Moral Philosopher and Man of Letters* (Chapel Hill, 1961)

McLaughlin, Andrew C., *A Constitutional History of the United States* (New York, 1935)
    The Foundations of American Constitutionalism (New York, 1932)

McMaster, John B., *A History of the People of the United States.* v. 1 and 2 (New York, 1883)

Meade, Robert, *Patrick Henry: Patriot in the Making* (Philadelphia, 1957)

Meade, William, *Old Churches, Ministers and Families of Virginia* 2 v. (Philadelphia, 1861)

Miller, John C., *Alexander Hamilton: Portrait in Paradox* (New York, 1959)
    Triumph of Freedom, 1775–1783 (Boston, 1948)

Miller, Samuel, *A Brief Retrospect of the Eighteenth Century.* 2 v. (New York, 1803)

Minnigerode, Meade, *Jefferson, Friend of France, 1793* (New York, 1928)

Mitchell, Broadus, *Alexander Hamilton.* 2 v. (New York, 1957–62)

Mitchell, Julia Post, *St. Jean de Crevecoeur* (New York, 1916)

Mordecai, Samuel, *Richmond in By-Gone Days* (Richmond, 1946)

Morgan, Edmund S., *Virginians at Home* (Charlottesville, 1963) and Helen M. Morgan, *The Stamp Act Crisis* (Chapel Hill, 1953)

Morison, Samuel E., *The Life and Letters of Harrison Gray Otis.* 2 v. (Boston, 1913)

Morris, Richard B., ed., *The Era of the American Revolution* (New York, 1939)

Morton, Louis, *Robert Carter of Momini Hall* (Williamsburg, Va., 1941)

Mudge, E. T., *The Social Philosophy of John Taylor of Caroline* (New York, 1939)

Mumford, Lewis, *The South in Architecture* (New York, 1941)

Munroe, John A., *Federalist Delaware, 1775–1815* (New Brunswick, 1954)

Nagel, Paul C., *One Nation Indivisible: The Union in American Thought, 1776–1861* (New York, 1964)

Nelson, William H., *The American Tory* (New York, 1962)

Nettels, Curtis P., *The Emergence of a National Economy, 1775–1815* (New York, 1962)

North, Douglass C., *The Economic Growth of the United States, 1790–1860* (Englewood Cliffs, N.J., 1961)

Nye, Russel B., *The Cultural Life of the New Nation, 1776–1830* (New York, 1960)

Palmer, Robert R., *The Age of the Democratic Revolution.* 2 v. (Princeton, 1959–64)

Pattison, William D., *Beginnings of the American Rectangular Land Survey System, 1784–1806* (Chicago, 1957)

Paullin, Charles O., *The Navy and the American Revolution* (Cleveland, 1906)

Pearce, Roy Harvey, *The Savages of America: A Study of the Indian and the Idea of Civilization* (Baltimore, 1953)

Perkins, Bradford, *The First Rapprochement: England and the United States, 1795–1805* (Philadelphia, 1955)
Prologue to War: England and the United States, 1805–1812 (Berkeley, 1961)

Perry, Ralph Barton, *Puritanism and Democracy* (New York, 1944)

Philbrick, Francis S., "Introduction," *The Laws of Illinois Territory, 1809–1818*, Illinois State Historical Library *Collections*, v. 25 (Springfield, 1950)

The Rise of the West, 1754–1830 (New York, 1965)

Pickering, Octavius, and C. W. Upham, *The Life of Timothy Pickering*. 4 v. (Boston, 1867–73)

Pierson, Hamilton, W., *Jefferson at Monticello* (New York, 1962)

Pitkin, Timothy, *A Statistical View of the Commerce of the United States of America* (New Haven, 1835)

Pocock, J. G. A., *The Ancient Constitution and the Feudal Law* (Cambridge, England, 1957)

Pole, J. R., *Political Representation in England and the Origin of the American Revolution* (New York, 1966)

Porter, Albert O., *County Government in Virginia* (New York, 1947)

Pound, Merritt C., *Benjamin Hawkins, Indian Agent* (Athens, Ga., 1951)

Powell, J. H. *Bring Out Your Dead: The Great Plague of Yellow Fever in Philadelphia in 1793* (Philadelphia, 1949)

Prince, Carl E., *New Jersey's Jeffersonian Republicans* (Chapel Hill, 1967)

Prucha, Francis P., *American Indian Policy in the Formative Years* (Cambridge, 1962)

Purcell, Richard J., *Connecticut in Transition, 1775–1818* (Washington, 1918)

Quaife, Milo M., ed., *The Capture of Old Vincennes* (Indianapolis, 1927)

Quincy, Edmund, *Life of Josiah Quincy of Massachusetts* (Boston, 1867)

Ragatz, Lowell J., *The Fall of the Planter Class in the British Caribbean, 1763–1833* (New York, 1928)

Reps, John W., *The Making of Urban America: A History of City Planning in the United States* (Princeton, 1965)

Risjord, Norman K., *The Old Republicans: Southern Conservatives in the Age of Jefferson* (New York, 1965)

Ritcheson, Charles R., *British Politics and the American Revolution* (Norman, Okla., 1954)

Robbins, Caroline, *The Eighteenth-Century Commonwealthman* (Cambridge, 1959)

Rogers, George C., *Evolution of a Federalist: William Loughton Smith of South Carolina* (Columbia, 1962)

Rose, Lisle A., *Prologue to Democracy: The Federalists in the South, 1789–1800* (Lexington, Ky., 1968)

Rossiter, Clinton, *Alexander Hamilton and the Constitution* (New York, 1964)

Seedtime of the Republic (New York, 1953)

Rowland, Kate Mason, *Life of Charles Carroll of Carrollton, 1737–1832* . . . . 2 v. (New York, 1898)

Life of George Mason, 1725–1792. 2 v. (New York, 1892)

Rudolph, Frederick, *The American College and University* (New York, 1962)

Rush, Benjamin, *Autobiography*. George W. Corner, ed. (Princeton, 1948)

Rutman, Darrett B., ed., *The Old Dominion: Essays for Thomas Perkins Abernethy* (Charlottesville, 1964)

Saricks, Ambrose, *Pierre Samuel Du Pont de Nemours* (Lawrence, Kans., 1965)

Schachner, Nathan, *Aaron Burr* (New York, 1937)

Schaff, Philip, *Church and State in the United States* (New York, 1888)

Scharf, J. T., and Thompson Westcott, *History of Philadelphia, 1609–1884.* 3 v. (Philadelphia, 1884)

Scott, Arthur P., *Criminal Law in Colonial Virginia* (Chicago, 1930)

Sears, Louis, *George Washington and the French Revolution* (Detroit, 1960)

Jefferson and the Embargo (Durham, N.C., 1927)

Sellers, Charles Coleman, *Charles Willson Peale.* 2 v. (Philadelphia, 1947)

Semmes, John E., *John H. B. Latrobe and His Times, 1803–1891* (Baltimore, 1917)

Semple, R. B., *History of the Rise and Progress of the Baptists in Virginia* (Richmond, 1810)

Setser, Vernon G., *The Commercial Reciprocity Policy of the United States, 1774–1829* (Philadelphia, 1937)

Shulim, Joseph I., *The Old Dominion and Napoleon Bonaparte* (New York, 1952)

Singleton, Esther, *Story of the White House.* v. 1 (New York, 1907)

Smallwood, William M., *Natural History and the American Mind* (New York, 1941)

Smelser, Marshall, *The Congress Founds the Navy, 1787–1789* (South Bend, Ind., 1959)

Smith, Henry Nash, *Virgin Land: The American West as Symbol and Myth* (Cambridge, 1950)

Smith, James Morton, *Freedom's Fetters: The Alien and Sedition Laws and American Civil Liberties* (New York, 1956)

[Smith, Margaret Bayard], *The First Forty Years of Washington Society*. Gaillard Hunt, ed. (New York, 1906)

Smith, Page, *John Adams*. 2 v. (New York, 1962)

Spalding, E. Wilder, *His Excellency George Clinton* (New York, 1938)

Sparks, Jared, *The Life of Gouverneur Morris*. 2 v. (Boston, 1832)

Sprout, Harold, and Margaret Sprout, *The Rise of American Naval Power, 1776–1918* (Princeton, 1939)

Spurlin, Paul M., *Montesquieu in America, 1760–1801* (Baton Rouge, 1940)

Staples, William R., *Rhode Island in the Continental Congress* (Providence, 1870)

Steiner, B. C., *The Life and Correspondence of James McHenry* (Cleveland, 1907)

Stephen, Sir Leslie, *History of English Thought in the Eighteenth Century*. 2 v. Harbinger Ed. (New York, 1962)

Stewart, Robert A., *History of Virginia's Navy of the Revolution* (Richmond, 1933)

Stillé, Charles J., *The Life and Times of John Dickinson* (Philadelphia, 1891)

Stokes, Anson P., *Church and State in the United States*. v. 1 and 2. (New York, 1950)

Story, William W., ed., *Life and Letters of Joseph Story*. 2 v. Boston, 1851)

Stourzh, Gerald, *Benjamin Franklin and American Foreign Policy* (Chicago, 1954)

Sullivan, William, *Familiar Letters on Public Characters and Public Events* (Boston, 1834)

Sydnor, Charles, *The Development of Southern Sectionalism, 1819–1843* (Baton Rouge, 1953)

    Gentlemen Freeholders: Political Parties in Washington's Virginia (Chapel Hill, 1952)

Tarleton, Banastre, *History of the Campaign of 1780 and 1781* (London, 1787)

Thayer, Theodore, *Nathanael Greene: Strategist of the American Revolution* (New York, 1960)

Thom, William T., *The Struggle for Religious Freedom in Virginia: The Baptists* (Baltimore, 1900)

Thomas, Charles M., *American Neutrality in 1793* . . . . (New York, 1931)

Thompson, J. M., *The French Revolution* (Oxford, 1945)

Tinkcom, Harry M., *Republicans and Federalists in Pennsylvania, 1790–1801* (Harrisburg, 1950)

Tocqueville, Alexis de, *The Old Regime and the French Revolution.* Stuart Gilbert, tr. (Garden City, 1955)

Tolles, Frederich B., *George Logan of Philadelphia* (New York, 1953)

Trumbull, John, *Autobiography.* Theodore Sizer, ed., (New Haven, 1953)

Turner, Lynn W., *William Plumer of New Hampshire* (Chapel Hill, 1962)

Van Doren, Carl, *Benjamin Franklin* (New York, 1938)

Van Tyne, Charles, *Loyalists in the American Revolution* (New York, 1929)

Varg, Paul A., *Foreign Policies of the Founding Fathers* (East Lansing, Mich., 1963)

Vile, M. J. C., *Constitutionalism and the Separation of Powers* (Oxford, 1967)

Von Eckhardt, Ursula M., *The Pursuit of Happiness in the Democratic Creed* (New York, 1959)

Walters, Raymond, Jr., *Albert Gallatin: Jeffersonian Financier and Diplomat* (New York, 1957)

Alexander James Dallas (Philadelphia, 1943)

Warren, Charles, *A History of the American Bar* (Boston, 1911)

The Supreme Court in United States History. 2 v., Rev. ed. (Boston, 1937)

Jacobin and Junto (Cambridge, 1931)

Odd Byways in American History (Cambridge, 1942)

Watkins, Frederick, *The Political Tradition of the West* (Cambridge, 1948)

Watson, John S., *The Reign of George III, 1760–1815* (New York, 1960)

Weinberg, Albert K., *Manifest Destiny. A Study of Nationalist Expansion in American History* (Baltimore, 1935)

Welch, Richard E., Jr., *Theodore Sedgwick, Federalist* (Middletown, Conn., 1965)

Whitaker, Arthur P., *The Spanish-American Frontier, 1783–1795* (Boston, 1927)

The Mississippi Question, 1795–1803 (New York, 1934)

White, Leonard D., *The Federalists: A Study in Administrative History* (New York, 1948)

The Jeffersonians . . . . (New York, 1951)

Whitney, Lois, *Primitivism and the Idea of Progress in the English Popular Literature of the Eighteenth Century* (Baltimore, 1934)

Willey, Basil, *The Eighteenth Century Background* (London, 1949)

Wilkinson, James, *Memoirs of My Own Times.* 3 v. (Philadelphia, 1816)

Willcox, William B., *Portrait of a General. Sir Henry Clinton in the War of Independence* (New York, 1964)

Wirt, William, *The Letters of the British Spy.* 10th ed. (New York, 1832)

Sketches of the Life and Character of Patrick Henry (Philadelphia, 1817)

Wolf, A., *A History of Science, Technology, and Philosophy in the 18th Century.* Torchbook Edition. 2 v. (New York, 1961)

Woodress, James, *A Yankee's Odyssey: The Life of Joel Barlow* (Philadelphia, 1958)

Woods, Edgar, *Albemarle County in Virginia* (Charlottesville, 1901)

Woodward, C. Vann, ed., *The Comparative Approach to American History* (New York, 1968)

Woolery, William K., *The Relation of Thomas Jefferson to American Foreign Policy* (Baltimore, 1927)

Wright, Benjamin F., *American Interpretations of Natural Law* (Cambridge, 1931)

Wright, Louis B., *The Atlantic Frontier* (New York, 1947)

The Cultural Life of the American Colonies (New York, 1957)

Young, Alfred, *The Jeffersonian Republicans of New York. The Origins, 1763–1797* (Chapel Hill, 1967)

Young, James Sterling, *The Washington Community, 1800–1828* (New York, 1966)

Zahniser, Marvin L., *Charles Cotesworth Pinckney* (Chapel Hill, 1967)

Zimmerman, James F., *Impressment of American Seamen* (New York, 1925)

c) *Articles and Essays*

Two anthologies may be consulted: *The Jefferson Reader*, Francis Coleman Rosenberger, ed. (New York, 1953) and *Thomas Jefferson: A Profile*, Merrill D. Peterson, ed. (New York, 1967). The latter contains articles or essays by Dixon Wecter, Carl Becker, John Dos Passos, Robert R. Palmer, Merrill D. Peterson, William D. Grampp, Dumas Malone, Julian P. Boyd, Louis B. Wright, Horace M. Kallen, and George Harmon Knoles, none of which is cited below.

Adams, Mary P., "Jefferson's Reaction to the Treaty of San Ildefonso," *Journal of Southern History*, v. 21 (1955)

Adams, Randolph G., "Thomas Jefferson, Librarian," in *Three Americanists* (Philadelphia, 1939)

Ammon, Harry, "The Formation of the Republican Party in Virginia," *Journal of Southern History*, v. 19 (1953)

"The Genêt Mission and the Development of American Political Parties," *Journal of American History*, v. 52 (1966)

"James Monroe and the Election of 1808 in Virginia," *William and Mary Quarterly*, 3rd ser., v. 20 (1963)

"The Jeffersonian Republicans in Virginia: An Interpretation," *Virginia Magazine of History and Biography*, v. 71 (1963)

Anderson, Dice R., "Jefferson and the Virginia Constitution," *American Historical Review*, v. 21 (1916)

Appleby, Joyce, "The Jefferson-Adams Rupture and the First French Translation of John Adams' *Defence*," *American Historical Review*, v. 73 (1968)

Arena, C. Richard, "Landholding and Political Power in Spanish Louisiana," *Louisiana Historical Quarterly*, v. 38 (1955)

Bailyn, Bernard, "Boyd's Jefferson: Notes for a Sketch," *New England Quarterly*, v. 33 (1960)

"Butterfield's Adams: Notes for a Sketch," *William and Mary Quarterly*, 3rd ser., v. 19 (1962)

"Political Experience and Enlightenment Ideas in Eighteeth Century America," *American Historical Review*, v. 67 (1962)

Bestor, Arthur, "Thomas Jefferson and the Freedom of Books," in Bestor and others, *Three Presidents and Their Books* (Urbana, Ill., 1955)

Bigelow, John, "Jefferson's Financial Diary," *Harper's Magazine*, v. 70 (1885)

Bowman, Albert H., "Jefferson, Hamilton, and American Foreign Policy," *Political Science Quarterly*, v. 81 (1956)

Boyd, Julian P., "The Megalonyx, the Megatherium, and Thomas Jefferson's Lapse of Memory," *American Philosophical Society Proceedings*, v. 102 (1958)

"Two Diplomats Between Revolutions: John Jay and Thomas Jefferson," *Virginia Magazine of History and Biography*, v. 66 (1958)

Brant, Irving, "Edmund Randolph, 'Not Guilty'," *William and Mary Quarterly*, 3rd ser., v. 7 (1950)

Brown, Ira V., "The Religion of Joseph Priestley," *Pennsylvania History*, v. 24 (1957)

Buron, Edmund, "Statistics on Franco-American Trade, 1778–1806," *Journal of Economic and Business History*, v. 4 (1931–32)

Busey, Samuel C., "The Centennial of the First Inauguration of a President at the Permanent Seat of the Government," Columbia Historical Society *Records*, v. 5 (1902)

Butterfield, Lyman H., "Elder John Leland, Jeffersonian Itinerant," American Antiquarian Society *Proceedings*, v. 62 (1952)

Chinard, Gilbert, "Eighteenth Century Theories on America as a Human Habitat," American Philosophical Society *Proceedings*, v. 91 (1947)
"Jefferson Among the Philosophers," *Ethics*, v. 53 (1943)
"Jefferson's Influence Abroad," *Mississippi Valley Historical Review*, v. 30 (1943)

Coatsworth, John H., "American Trade with European Colonies in the Caribbean and South America, 1790–1812," *William and Mary Quarterly*, 3rd ser., v. 24 (1967)

Coles, Harry L., Jr., "The Confiscation of Foreign Land Titles in Louisiana," *Louisiana Historical Quarterly*, v. 38(1955)

Cometti, Elizabeth, "John Rutledge, Jr., Federalist," *Journal of Southern History*, v. 13 (1947)

Corwin, Edward S., "The 'Higher Law' Background of American Constitutional Law," *Harvard Law Review*," v. 42 (1928–29)

Cox, Isaac J., "Hispanic-American Phases of the Burr Conspiracy," *Hispanic-American Historical Review*, v. 12 (1932)
"The Pan-American Policy of Jefferson and Wilkinson," *Mississippi Valley Historical Review*, v. 1 (1914–15)

Dauer, Manning J., "The Two John Nicholases: Their Relationship to Washington and Jefferson," *American Historical Review*, v. 45 (1940)

De Conde, Alexander, "Washington's Farewell Address, the French Alliance, and the Election of 1796," *Mississippi Valley Historical Review*, v. 38 (1957)

Detwiler, Philip F., "The Changing Reputation of the Declaration of Independence: The First Fifty Years," *William and Mary Quarterly*, 3rd ser., v. 19 (1962)

Downes, Randolph, "Thomas Jefferson and the Removal of Governor St. Clair in 1802," *Ohio Archeological and Historical Quarterly*, v. 36 (1927)

Duff, Stella F., "The Case Against the King: The *Virginia Gazettes* Indict George III," *William and Mary Quarterly*, 3rd ser., v. 6 (1949)

Dungan, James R., "Sir William Dunbar of Natchez, Planter, Explorer, and Scientist, 1792–1810," *Journal of Mississippi History*, v. 23 (1961)

Evans, Edith R., "Thomas Jefferson in Annapolis," *Maryland Historical Magazine*," v. 41 (1946)

Evans, Emory G., "Planter Indebtedness and the Coming of the Revolution in Virginia," *William and Mary Quarterly*, v. 19 (1962)

Ewers, John C., "Chiefs from the Missouri and Mississippi," *Smithsonian Journal of History*, v. 1 (1966)

Fabian, Bernhard, "Jefferson's *Notes on Virginia:* The Genesis of Query XVII . . . ," *William and Mary Quarterly*, 3rd ser., v. 12 (1955)

Farnham, Thomas J., "The Federal-State Issue and the Louisiana Purchase," *Louisiana History*, v. 6 (1965)

Faulkner, Robert K., "John Marshall and the Burr Trial," *Journal of American History*, v. 53 (1966)

Fischer, David H., "The Myth of the Essex Junto," *William and Mary Quarterly*, 3rd ser., v. 21 (1964)

Fisher, John E., "Slavery and the Slave Trade in the Louisiana Purchase, 1803–1812," *Essays in History*, v. 13 (1968)

Fowler, Samuel, "The Political Opinions of Jefferson," *North American Review*, v. 101 (1865)

Franklin, Mitchell, "The Place of Thomas Jefferson in the Expulsion of Spanish Medieval Law from Louisiana," *Tulane Law Review*, v. 16(1942)

Friis, Herman, R., "Baron Alexander von Humboldt's Visit to Washington . . . ," Columbia Historical Society *Records* (1960–62)

Gaines, Edwin M., "Governor Cabell and the Republican Schism in Virginia, 1805–08," *Essays in History*, v. 2 (1955)

Ganter, Herbert L., "William Small, Jefferson's Beloved Teacher," *William and Mary Quarterly*, 3rd ser., v. 4 (1947)

Graham, Gerald S., "The Migration of the Nantucket Whale Fishery . . . ," *New England Quarterly*, v. 8 (1935)

Greene, Jack P., "The Currency Act of 1764 in Imperial-Colonial Relations, 1764–1776," *William and Mary Quarterly*, 3rd ser., v. 18 (1961)

Greene, John C., "Some Early Speculations on the Origin of Human Races," *American Anthropologist*, v. 56 (1954)

Hatfield, Joseph T., "William C. C. Claiborne, Congress and Republicanism, 1797–1804," *Tennessee Historical Quarterly*, v. 24 (1964)

Haynes, Robert V., "The Revolution of 1800 in Mississippi," *Journal of Mississippi History*," v. 19 (1957)

"Historical Philadelphia," American Philosophical Society *Transactions*, new ser., v. 43 (1953)

Howell, Wilbur Samuel, "The Declaration of Independence and Eighteenth Century Logic," *William and Mary Quarterly*, 3rd ser., v. 18 (1961)

Hunt, Gaillard, "Office Seeking During Jefferson's Administration," *American Historical Review*, v. 3 (1898)

Hyslop, Beatrice F., "The American Press and the French Revolution of 1789," American Philosophical Society *Proceedings*, v. 104 (1960)

"American Press Reports of the French Revolution, 1789–1794," *New York Historical Society Quarterly*, v. 42 (1958)

Jellison, Charles A., "That Scoundrel Callender," *Virginia Magazine of History and Biography*, v. 67 (1959)

Jensen, Merrill, "Democracy and the American Revolution," *Huntington Library Quarterly*, v. 20 (1957)

"The Idea of a National Government During the American Revolution," *Political Science Quarterly*, v. 58 (1943)

Keim, C. Ray, "Primogeniture and Entail in Colonial Virginia," *William and Mary Quarterly*, 3rd ser., v. 25 (1968)

Kenyon, Cecilia M., "Republicanism and Radicalism in the American Revolution: An Old-Fashioned Interpretation," *William and Mary Quarterly*, 3rd ser., v. 19 (1962)

Koch, Adrienne, and Harry Ammon, "The Virginia and Kentucky Resolutions: An Episode in Jefferson's and Madison's Defense of Civil Liberties," *William and Mary Quarterly*, 3rd ser., v. 5 (1948)

Krislov, Samuel, "Jefferson and Judicial Review: Refereeing Cahn, Commager and Mendelson," *Journal of Public Law*, v. 9 (1960)

Laub, C. H., "Revolutionary Virginia and the Crown Lands, 1775–1783," *William and Mary Quarterly*, 2nd ser., v. 11 (1931)

Lerche, Charles O., Jr., "Jefferson and the Election of 1800: A Case Study of the Political Smear," *William and Mary Quarterly*, 3rd ser., v. 5 (1948)

Leubke, Fred C., "The Origins of Thomas Jefferson's Anti-Clericalism," *Church History*, v. 33 (1963)

Lewis, Anthony M., "Jefferson and Virginia's Pioneers, 1774–1781," *Mississippi Valley Historical Review*, v. 34 (1948)

"Jefferson's *Summary View* as a Chart of Political Union," *William and Mary Quarterly*, 3rd ser., v. 5 (1948)

Loehr, Rodney C., "The Influence of English Agriculture on American Agriculture," *Agricultural History*, v. 11 (1937)

Lokke, Carl L., "Jefferson and the Leclerc Expedition," *American Historical Review*, v. 33 (1928)

Lovejoy, Arthur O., "The Parallel of Deism and Classicism," *Modern Philology*, v. 19 (1932)

Low, W. A., "Merchant and Planter Relations in Post-Revolutionary Virginia, 1783–1789," *Virginia Magazine of History and Biography*, v. 61 (1953)

Lyon, E. Wilson, "The Directory and the United States," *American Historical Review*, v. 43 (1938)

Macloed, Julia H., "Jefferson and the Navy: A Defense," *Huntington Library Quarterly*, v. 8 (1945)

Main, Jackson T., "The Distribution of Property in Post-Revolutionary Virginia," *Mississippi Valley Historical Review*, v. 41 (1954)

"Government By the People: The American Revolution and the Democratization of the Legislature," *William and Mary Quarterly*, 3rd ser., v. 23 (1966)

Marraro, Howard R., "The Four Versions of Jefferson's Letter to Mazzei," *William and Mary Quarterly*, 2nd ser., v. 22 (1942)

Mayo, Bernard, "A Peppercorn for Mr. Jefferson," *Virginia Quarterly Review*, v. 19 (1943)

McDonald, Forrest, "The Anti-Federalists, 1781–1789," *Wisconsin Magazine of History*, v. 46 (1963)

Merriam, J. M., "Jefferson's Use of the Executive Patronage," *American Historical Association Papers* (1888)

Miller, Ralph N., "American Nationalism as a Theory of Nature," *William and Mary Quarterly*, 3rd ser., v. 12 (1955)

Mott, Royden J., "Sources of Jefferson's Ecclesiastical Views," *Church History*, v. 3 (1934)

Nash, Gary B., "American Clergy and the French Revolution," *William and Mary Quarterly*, 3rd ser., v. 22 (1965)

Nussbaum, F. L., "American Tobacco and French Politics," *Political Science Quarterly*, v. 40 (1926)

"The French Colonial Arrêt of August 30, 1784," *South Atlantic Quarterly*, v 27 (1928)

"The Revolutionary Vergennes and Lafayette versus the Farmers General," *Journal of Modern History*, v. 3 (1931)

Palmer, Robert R., ed., "A Neglected Work: Otto Vossler on Jefferson and the Revolutionary Era," *William and Mary Quarterly*, 3rd ser., v. 12 (1955)

Pancake, John S., "Aaron Burr: Would Be Usurper," *William and Mary Quarterly*, 3rd ser., v. 8 (1951)

Peden, William, "Some Notes Concerning Thomas Jefferson's Libraries," *William and Mary Quarterly*, 3rd ser., v. 1 (1944)

——— ed., "A Book Peddler Invades Monticello," *William and Mary Quarterly*, 3rd ser., v. 6 (1949)

Pocock, J. G. R., "Machiavelli, Harrington, and English Political Ideologies in the Eighteenth Century," *William and Mary Quarterly*, 3rd ser., v. 22 (1965)

Praeger, Frank D., "Trends and Developments in American Patent Law from Jefferson to Clifford, Part Two," *American Journal of Legal History*, v. 6 (1962)

Pritchard, Walter, "Selecting a Governor for the Territory of Orleans," *Louisiana Historical Quarterly*, v. 31 (1948)

Pulley, Judith P., "An Agent of Nature's Republic Abroad: Thomas Jefferson in Pre-Revolutionary France," *Essays in History*, v. 11 (1966)

Randolph, Edmund, "Essay on the Revolutionary History of Virginia,"*Virginia Magazine of History and Biography*, v. 43–45 (1935–37)

Reid, David S., "An Analysis of British Parliamentary Opinion on American Affairs at the Close of the War of Independence," *Journal of Modern History*, v. 18 (1946)

Reynolds, Donald E., "Ammunition Supply in Revolutionary Virginia," *Virginia Magazine of History and Biography*, v. 73 (1965)

Rhinesmith, W. Donald, "Joseph Dennie, Critic of Jeffersonian Democracy," *Essays in History*, v. 7 (1962)

Rice, Howard C., Jr., "Jefferson's Gift of Fossils to the Museum of Natural History in Paris," American Philosophical Society *Proceedings*, v. 95 (1951)

Risjord, Norman K., "The Virginia Federalists," *Journal of Southern History*, v. 33 (1967)

Ritcheson, Charles R., "The London Press and the First Decade of American Independence, 1783–1793," *Journal of British Studies*, v. 2 (1963)

Robbins, Caroline, "Honest Heretic: Joseph Priestley in America," *American Philosophical Society Proceedings*, v. 106 (1962)

Scanlon, James E., "A Sudden Conceit: Jefferson and the Louisiana Government Bill of 1804," *Louisiana History*, v. 9 (1968)

Schneider, Herbert W., "The Enlightenment in Thomas Jefferson," *Ethics*, v. 53 (1943)

Sée, Henri, "Commerce Between France and the United States," *American Historical Review*, v. 31 (1926)

Seeber, Edward D., "Critical Views on Logan's Speech," *Journal of American Folklore*, v. 60 (1947)

Sifton, Paul G., ed., "Otto's Memoir to Vergennes, 1785," *William and Mary Quarterly*, 3rd ser., v. 22 (1965)

Simpson, George Gaylord, "The Beginnings of Vertebrate Paleontology in the United States," *American Philosophical Society Proceedings*, v. 86 (1942)

Smelser, Marshall, "The Jacobin Phrenzy: The Menace of Monarchy, Plutocracy, and Anglophilia, 1789–1798," *Review of Politics*, v. 21 (1959)

Smith, T. V., "Thomas Jefferson and the Perfectibility of Mankind," *Ethics*, v. 53 (1943)

Sowerby, E. Millicent, "Thomas Jefferson and His Library," *Bibliographical Society of America Publications*, v. 50 (1956)

Steel, Anthoney, "Impressment in the Monroe-Pinkney Negotiations, 1806–1807," *American Historical Review*, v. 57 (1952)

Stover, John F., "French-American Trade During the Confederation, 1781–1789," *North Carolina Historical Review*, v. 35 (1958)

Tanner, Douglas W., "Thomas Jefferson, Impressment, and the Rejection of the Monroe-Pinkney Treaty," *Essays in History*, v. 13 (1968)

Tate, Thad W., "The Coming of the Revolution in Virginia: Britain's Challenge to Virginia's Ruling Class, 1763–1776," *William and Mary Quarterly*, 3rd ser., v. 19 (1962)

Terra, Helmut de, "Motives and Consequences of Alexander von Humboldt's Visit to the United States," *American Philosophical Society Proceedings*, v. 104 (1960)

Thomas, Robert, "The Virginia Convention of 1788," *Journal of Southern History*, v. 19 (1953)

Trent, William P., "The Case of Josiah Philips," *American Historical Review*, v. 1 (1895–96)

Turner, Kathryn, "Federalist Policy and the Judiciary Act of 1801," *William and Mary Quarterly*, 3rd ser., v. 22 (1965)

"The Midnight Judges," *University of Pennsylvania Law Review*, v. 109 (1960–61)

Verner, Coolie, "The Maps and Plates Appearing with the Several Editions of Mr. Jefferson's 'Notes on the State of Virginia'," *Virginia Magazine of History and Biography*, v. 59 (1951)

Viner, Jacob, "Power versus Plenty as Objectives of Foreign Policy in the Seventeenth and Eighteenth Centuries," *World Politics*, 1 (1948)

Wall, A. J., "The Story of the Convention Army," New York Historical Society *Quarterly Bulletin*, v. 11 (1927–28)

Waterman, Julius S., "Thomas Jefferson and Blackstone's *Commentaries*," *Illinois Law Review*, v. 27 (1933)

Wheat, Carl I., "Mapping the American West, 1540–1857," American Antiquarian Society *Proceedings*, v. 64 (1954)

Wolford, Thorp L., "Democratic-Republican Reaction in Massachusetts to the Embargo of 1807," *New England Quarterly*, v. 15 (1942)

Wood, Gordon S., "Rhetoric and Reality in the American Revolution," *William and Mary Quarterly*, 3rd ser., v. 23 (1966)

Woodfin, Maude H., "Contemporary Opinion in Virginia of Thomas Jefferson," in *Essays in Honor of William E. Dodd*, Avery Craven, ed. (Chicago, 1935)

Zook, George F., "Proposals for a New Commercial Treaty Between France and the United States, 1778–1793," *South Atlantic Quarterly*, v. 8 (1909)

d) *Unpublished Theses and Dissertations*

Adams, Mary P., "Jefferson's Military Policy with Special Reference to the Frontier, 1805–1809," Ph.D. Dist., Univ. of Va., 1958

Brewer, Paul, "Jefferson's Administration of the Patronage: New York, 1801–1804," M.A. Thesis, Univ. of Va., 1968

Coyner, M. Boyd, "John Hartwell Cocke of Bremo: Agriculture and Slavery in the Ante-Bellum South," Ph.D. Dist., Univ. of Va., 1961

Cross, Jack L., "Thomas Pinckney's London Mission," Ph.D. Dist., Univ. of Chicago, 1957

Dabney, William M., "Jefferson's Albemarle: History of Albemarle County, Virginia, 1727–1819," Ph.D. Dist., Univ. of Va., 1951

Elsmere, Mary Jane Shaffer, "The Impeachment Trial of Justice Samuel Chase," Ph.D. Dist., Indiana Univ., 1962

Gaines, Edwin M., "Outrageous Encounter: The Chesapeake-Leopard Affair of 1807," Ph.D. Dist., Univ. of Va., 1960

Harrison, Joseph Hopson, Jr., "The Internal Improvements Issue in the Politics of the Union, 1783–1825," Ph.D. Dist., Univ. of Va., 1954

Harrison, Lowell H., "John Breckinridge, Western Statesman," Ph.D. Dist., New York Univ., 1951

Knudson, Jerry W., "The Jefferson Years: Response by the Press, 1801–1809," Ph.D. Dist., Univ. of Va., 1962

Lacy, Alex B., "Jefferson and Congress: Congressional Methods and Politics, 1801–1809," Ph.D. Dist., Univ. of Va., 1963

McGrath, Rosemarie, "The Issue of the Foreign Slave Trade in the Louisiana Territory," M.A. Thesis, Univ. of Va., 1967

Mumper, Jamse M., "The Jefferson Image in the Federalist Mind, 1801–1809," Ph.D. Dist., Univ. of Va., 1966

Pancake, John S., "The General from Baltimore: The Public Life of General Samuel Smith, 1752–1812," Ph.D. Dist., Univ. of Va., 1947

Pulley, Judith P., "Thomas Jefferson at the Court of Versailles: An American *Philosophe* and the Coming of the French Revolution," Ph.D. Dist., Univ. of Va., 1966

Rasmusson, Ethel Elise, "Capital on the Delaware: The Philadelphia Upper Class in Transition, 1789–1801," Ph.D. Dist., Brown Univ., 1962

Shackelford, George Green, "William Short, Jefferson's Adopted Son, 1758–1849," Ph.D. Dist., Univ. of Va., 1955

Sheehan, Bernard W., "Civilization and the American Indian in the Thought of the Jeffersonian Era," Ph.D. Dist., Univ. of Va., 1965

Smith, Robert H., "Albert Gallatin's Fiscal Policy," Ph.D. Dist., Syracuse Univ., 1954

Stampp, Norman, "Political Parties in Connecticut," Ph.D. Dist., Yale Univ., 1952

Stewart, Donald H., "Jeffersonian Journalism: Newspaper Propaganda and the Development of the Democratic-Republican Party, 1791–1801," Ph.D. Dist., Columbia Univ., 1951

Wheeler, William Bruce, "Urban Politics in Nature's Republic: The Development of Political Parties in the Seaport Cities in the Federalist Era," Ph.D. Dist., Univ. of Va., 1967

Index

(Thomas Jefferson is abbreviated TJ. All entries refer to him directly or indirectly.)

Abbaye Royale de Pentemont, 295, 356, 385
Account of Louisiana, An (TJ), 765, 780
Act of Toleration, 136
Adams, Abigail, 294, 405; friendship with TJ, 298, 302, 345, 355, 356; alienation from TJ, 790, 953; quoted, 359, 420, 596, 597
Adams, John, 22, 31, 98, 288, 294, 309, 310, 312, 345, 471, 936, 943, 948, 964, 1008; political theory, 64, 65, 381-82, 438-39, 995; in Revolutionary movement, 73, 80, 81, 86, 87, 88; opinion of TJ, 80, 298, 516, 544, 508-69, 703, 953; TJ begins correspondence with, 161; in France, 286, 298, 332; TJ's opinion of, 298, 438, 559, 560, 953; Minister to England, 302, 308, 363, 398; and Barbary powers, 313, 314; tour with TJ, 342-44; and Dutch bankers, 363, 364, 366; Vice President, 405-6, 417-18; controversy with TJ, 438-39, 440-43; presidential candidate, 545, 557; administration of, 560-75, 590-651 passim; inauguration of, 562-63; alienation from TJ, 568-69, 654; in election of 1800, 632-33, 641, 644, 645, 646; "midnight appointments" of, 668, 694; renewal of correspondence with TJ, 928, 953-56; quoted, 65, 80, 86, 87-88, 97, 99, 305, 479, 594, 853
Adams, John Quincy: young friend of TJ, 298; as Publicola, 440; in Congress, 703, 704, 766, 821, 872-73;

and Louisiana government bill, 782; and embargo, 898; Minister to Russia, 903; President, 1002-3
Adams, Samuel, 80, 712
Adet, Pierre: in election of 1796, 555-56; quoted, 507, 556-57
agricultural economy, in TJ's thought, 290, 459, 773, 856, 940-41. See also commercial policy, political economy
agricultural science: experiments in Mediterranean culture, 159-60, 353, 327, 537; importance of, 350, 352; the plow, 365-66, 589-90; at Monticello, 493, 526-33; activities as President, 735-36; in retirement, 941
Agricultural Society of Paris, 590
air balloons, 287, 299
Albemarle Academy, 964
Albemarle Agricultural Society, 941
Albemarle County: in TJ's youth, 5-10; elects TJ to Burgesses, 22; in Revolution, 77; instructions of 1776, 103; welcomes TJ in 1790, 393; TJ's affection for, 518; farms in, 524, 528, 924, 941; welcomes TJ in 1809, 921; intellectual circle, 952-53
Alexander I, and TJ's diplomacy, 860, 878, 902-3
Algiers, 310, 664; negotiations with, 312, 367, 368, 422, 510
Alien Enemies Act, 603-4
Alien (Friends) Act, 604-5, 606, 613, 620, 622
Alliance of 1778, see France
Ambler, Jacquelin, 20

American Colonization Society, 999
American Committee, 319, 320-21, 346
American Fur Company, 904
American Philosophical Society, TJ and, 248, 265, 419, 497, 517, 563, 579, 589; president of, 576, 580, 586, 734, 859, 904, 951
American Revolution: coming of in Virginia, 33-45, 69-79 *passim*; as intellectual movement, 45-68; proceedings in Congress (1775-76), 81-92; and France, 87, 370, 380; and internal reform, 98-100 (*see also* Virginia); and Europe, 142, 255-56, 387, 389; commercial principles of, 289-90, 292-93, 303-4; Republican appeal to, 593, 657; history of, 949-50; and TJ's death, 1008-9
"American System," in domestic policy, 992-93, 994
"American system," hemispheric, 746, 932, 937
Ames, Fisher, quoted, 409, 570, 608, 637, 641, 703, 704, 772
Andrei, Giovanni, 742
Angeville, Comte d', 347
Anglo-French (Eden) treaty, 324
Anglo-Russian Treaty of 1801, 831
Anglo-Saxonism: TJ and, 17-18, 57-61, 64, 74, 98, 114, 987; language, 60, 608, 972
animal husbandry, 531, 939-40
Annapolis, Maryland, 269
Anti-Federalists: in ratification, 360-61; in Virginia, 392, 412, 436, 610
Anville, Duchesse d', 347
archaeology, 259
architecture: TJ's early ideas of, 24, 30; Monticello, 25-26, 521, 538-43; Virginia Capitol, 340-42, 352-53, 539; importance of, 352-543; in national capital, 448, 449, 539, 739, 741-43; in other buildings, 927, 970; and University of Virginia, 968-70, 976
Aristotle, 61, 1008
armed neutrality, 545, 665
Armstrong, John, Minister to France, 811, 813, 818, 823, 825, 860, 888, 898, 901, 902
Army, U.S.: in Quasi War, 599, 617, 619, 620, 631; in TJ's administration, 688, 692, 833; and the embargo, 891, 896, 912
Arnold, Benedict, invades Virginia, 203, 206-8, 209; plan to capture, 220-22

Arnoux, Abbé, 351
Articles of Confederation, 97, 119, 218; executive in, 275; and national domain, 278, 280; treaty power in, 291, 305; and Constitution, 359-60
Assembly of Notables, 349, 356, 370
Association, The: of 1769; 35-36; of 1774, 70, 77
Assumption bargain, 411-14
Astor, John Jacob, 904
astronomy, 160, 265, 336
attainder, 131-32
Attorney General, U.S., 395, 397, 661
Auckland, Lord, 822, 860, 861
Aurora, The, 556, 558, 563, 621, 629, 699, 927, 931
Austerlitz, battle of, 805, 831
Austin, Benjamin, 940
autobiography, TJ and, 3, 948-49, 950

Bache, Benjamin F., 446, 556, 560, 602, 607, 621
Bacon, Edmund, 926
Bacon, Ezekiel, 915
Bacon, Francis, 386; quoted, 48
Bacon, Matthew, 18
Bailyn, Bernard, cited, 67, 93
balanced government: idea of in TJ's thought, 57, 61-65; and "separation of powers," 65; and Virginia constitution, 104-5; and French Revolution, 373, 378, 381-82, 438; and federal judiciary, 697
Bancroft, George, 944
Bank of the United States (First): as proposed by Hamilton, 432; TJ's opposition to, 433-34, 435-36, 701; constitutional issue of, 433-35; expiration of, 933
Bank of the United States (Second), 934, 990
banking, TJ's opinions of, 435-36, 700, 933-34, 990-91
Baptists, in Virginia, 135-36, 143
Barbary powers: TJ's actions as President, 292, 367; negotiations with, 310-12, 510; plan of confederacy against, 312-14; TJ's report on, 422. *See also* Tripoli, Algiers
Barclay, Thomas, 311, 510
Baring, Alexander, 899
Barlow, Joel, 296, 618, 619, 903; and TJ, 658, 949; plan of national university, 859-60, 964
Barré, Colonel Isaac, 74; quoted, 32
Barron, Commodore James, 875
Barton, Benjamin Smith, 419, 587, 763

Bartram, John, 5
Bartram, William, 420
Bastrop grant, 850
Batture St. Marie, and TJ, 944-47
Bayard, James A., 676, 677, 678, 728; in Burr-TJ contest, 646, 649-51, 845
Bayonne Decree, 901
Beaurepaire, Quesnay de, 963
Beccaria, Marchese di, 47, 124, 126, 128
Beckley, John, 437, 468, 554, 555, 575, 640
Beckwith, Major General George, 416, 417, 428, 439
Bérard, Simon, 319, 328
Berkeley, Admiral George C., 875, 876, 877, 879
Berlin Decree, 826, 860, 861, 862, 882, 901
Bermuda, 188, 216, 617
Berni agreement, 320, 321, 356
Beverley, Robert, quoted, 166
Bible, The, TJ and, 959-60
Bidwell, Barnabas, 817-18, 820, 821
Big Bone Lick, 736, 904
Bill of Rights, U.S., TJ and, 106, 360-61. *See also* Constitution, First Amendment, Kentucky Resolutions
Bingham, Mrs. William, 420
Binns, John A., 941
Bishop, Abraham, 672
Bishop, Samuel, 672
Blackstone, William: TJ's view of, 16, 17, 951, 985, 987; on allegiance, 73, 154; on escheat, 123
Blaetterman, George, 984, 985
Blanchard, Jean Pierre, 479
Bland, Richard, 44; imperial theory of, 72, 77; TJ on, 72
Bland, Theodorick, 414
Blennerhassett, Harman, 847, 870, 871
Blennerhassett's Island, 847, 850, 854, 871, 872
blockade, 546, 831, 863
Board of Agriculture (English), 527, 589, 735
Bolingbroke, Lord, 50, 51, 53, 63, 64, 958
Bollman, Eric, 854, 868, 870, 871
Bonaparte, Jerome, 732
Bonaparte, Mme (Elizabeth Patterson), 732-33
Bonaparte, Joseph, 757-758
Bonaparte, Napoleon, 565, 732, 833-34, 954; TJ's opinion of, 628, 677, 878, 935; and Convention of 1800, 631, 665; First Consul, 677; and

Louisiana, 747-62; and Florida negotiations, 768, 808, 814, 825-26; Emperor, 801; and Berlin Decree, 882; and TJ's embargo diplomacy, 901-2; and War of 1812, 932
Bonneycastle, Charles, 985
Boone, Daniel, 119
Boré, Etienne, 784, 785
Boston Port Act, 71, 75
Boston Tea Party, 70
"botanizing excursion," 439-40
botany, 250; American-European exchanges, 335-36, 337-38, 735
Botetourt, Norborne Berkeley, Baron de, 33, 35, 36
Boulton, Matthew, 343, 402
Bowditch, Nathaniel, 977, 979
Bowdoin, James, 823, 825, 826
Boyd, Julian P., quoted, 112, 415
Bracton, Henry, 18, 60
Bradley, Stephen, 729
Brand-Hollis, Thomas, 342
Brant, Irving, cited, 586
Braxton, Carter, 101, 104, 120
Breckinridge, John: and Kentucky Resolutions, 612, 613, 614, 624; Senate leader, 691, 696-97; and Louisiana, 770, 776, 780-82; Attorney General, 805, 846
Breckinridge Act, TJ and, 780-83
Brehan, Marquise de, 369
Brent, Robert, 740
Brienne, Comte de, 372
Briggs, Isaac, 735, 779, 852, 857
Brodhead, General William, 218
"broken voyage," doctrine of, 807
Brokenborough, Arthur S., 976
Brougham, Henry, 899
Browere, J. H. I., 1006
Brown, James, 583
Brown, John, 846
Brown, Mather, 345
Brunswick, Duke of, 479
Bryant, William Cullen, quoted, 905
Buffon, Comte de, 47, 262, 287, 577; and degeneracy theory, 253, 254, 255, 256, 258, 578, 581; TJ meets in France, 338-39
Burgh, James, 59, 63
Burk, John Daly, 949
Burke, Edmund: on the sublime, 23-24; on American character, 67; on imperial relationship, 72-73; and French Revolution, 384, 437, 439
Burr, Aaron: elected to Senate, 439; TJ's relations with, 553, 557, 570, 671, 791-92, 845; vice presidential

Burr, Aaron (*continued*)
candidate in 1796, 555, 557; in election of 1800, 626, 631, 632, 642, 643, 644, 645-51; Vice President, 654, 669, 670-71, 787; political demise, 792-94; western conspiracy, 841-55; trial, 854, 865-72; flight and return, 872, 873
Burr Conspiracy, 826, 877; cabinet discussions of, 841, 847-48; germination of, 841-42, 843-45; Wilkinson's role in, 842-43, 846-47, 848-49; knowledge of, 846-47; staging on the Ohio, 847, 850; objectives of, 849, 850; TJ's proclamation against, 849-50, 850-51; defeat of, 851-53; message to Congress, 852-53
Burr trial: law of treason in, 853-54, 866-67, 870-72; problems of jurisdiction and evidence, 854, 865-66; politicization of, 867-68; grand jury proceedings, 868-70; treason trial, 870-72; TJ's response to verdict, 871-72
Burwell, Rebecca, 19-20, 84
Burwell, William A., 710, 853
Byrd, William, 6
Byrd, William, III, 39

Cabell, Joseph C., and founding of University of Virginia, 966-88 *passim*
Cabell, Samuel J., 605
Cabell, William H., 875, 877; quoted 867
Cabell presentment, 605-6
Callender, James T., 569-70, 575, 626, 635-36, 705-8, 710
Calonne, Charles-Alexandre de, 317, 318-20, 322, 323, 356, 371, 372
Calvin, John, 979
Cambridge University, 964, 977, 984
Camden, Battle of, 197, 203
Campbell, George W., 869, 915
Campbell, William, 193, 194
Canada, 83, 418, 797, 878, 887, 890, 932, 933
Canning, George, 932; and *Chesapeake* affair, 878-80, 882, 883; and embargo, 899, 908-9, 913
capital punishment, limitation of, 125
Care, Henry, 58
Carmichael, William, 311, 312, 362, 398, 400, 417, 430, 456
Carondelet, Baron de, 431
Carr, Dabney, 8, 9, 69, 70, 244

Carr, Peter, 244, 336, 573, 662, 707, 964
Carrington, Edward, 464
carrying trade, U.S., 288, 320, 322-25, 422-29, 508-10, 513-15, 546-47; versus internal trade, 290-91, 856, 911; and re-export trade, 807-8, 863; and East India market, 863. *See also* commercial policy, embargo, political economy
Carter, Landon, 39, 163
Carter, "Wild Bob," 39
Carter's Mountain, 236
Cary, Archibald, 254, 265
Cassirer, Ernst, quoted, 47
Catherine, Empress, 339, 587
Central College, 964-65, 966, 967, 971, 976
Cevallos, Don Pedro de, 809, 810
Chalut, Abbé, 351
Charles IV, of Spain, 747
Charleston, fall of, 167, 194, 195
Charlottesville, Virginia, 162, 233, 235, 236, 534, 536; and University of Virginia, 967, 970, 971
Chase, Justice Samuel: in trial of Callender, 635, 705; impeachment and trial of, 796-97, 804; and Randolph's humiliation, 821
Chastellux, Chevalier de, 293, 295, 334, 338; visits at Monticello, 245-46, 538
Chateaubriand, René François, quoted, 420
Cheetham, James, 791
Cherokee, 193, 714
Chesapeake affair, 874-80, 882, 897
Chickasaw, 774
Choctaw, 774
Christianity: and the Enlightenment, 49, 50-52, 54, 56; and common law, 60-61, 136; plan to establish in Virginia, 139-41; reflections on, 353-54; pure doctrines of, 956-57, 959-60. *See also* religion
Chubb, Thomas, 50
Church, Angelica Schuyler, 356
Church, Kitty, 356
Church of England: and William and Mary College, 11; TJ's views of, 44, 66; TJ and disestablishment of, 133-45
church and state, TJ's views of, 139-45, 712, 973-74. *See also* religion
Cicero, 49, 53, 73, 154, 957; quoted, 519
citizenship: in Virginia, 153; among

nations, 309-10; and impressment of seamen, 827

Claiborne, Richard, 222-23, 232

Claiborne, William C. C., 767, 945; Governor at New Orleans, 745, 777, 778, 779, 784, 785-86, 787-88

Clark, Daniel, 767, 780, 784, 785, 788, 843

Clark, George Rogers, 6, 156, 177, 208, 254, 736, 762; Kentucky delegate, 120; conquest of Vincennes, 176, 178-79, 180, 181; military operations in West, 182-83, 193, 198; expedition against Detroit, 216, 217-19; and Genêt, 498; and Chief Logan, 585-86

Clark, William, 6; and paleontology, 255, 736; western expedition, 764, 951

Clarke, Samuel, 50

Classical civilization: influence of, 7, 14, 29, 527, 927; in architecture, 24-25, 341, 539, 741-43; in the Enlightenment, 49-50; and Christian morals, 957; and University of Virginia, 968, 969, 973

Clay, Reverend Charles, 143, 469

Claypole, John, 230

Clérisseau, Charles, 341

Clermont, 858

Clinton, DeWitt, 670, 727, 791, 837, 838

Clinton, George: wartime governor, 174, 214; New York Republican leader, 440, 469, 506, 631, 632, 669; vice presidential candidate, 792, 882

Clinton, General Sir Henry, 167-68, 185, 195, 198, 200, 228

Coastal Survey, U.S., 857

Cobbett, William, 580, 603, 604, 621

Cocke, John Hartwell, 976, 1000

Coercive Acts, 70, 77

coinage, 275-78, 336-37, 402, 444

Coit, Joshua, 592

Coke, Sir Edward: TJ's study of, 16, 17-18, 19, 22; and Whig history, 58, 59

Coles, Edward, 953, 999

Colle, 159, 163

College of New Jersey, 10

Collier, Admiral Sir George, 168

Collinson, Peter, 5

colonization, of freed Negroes, 260, 746, 997, 988-99

Columbia College, 974, 978, 979

commerce, American foreign: conditions in 1784, 288; plan of treaties,

289, 291-93, 304-6; in Mediterranean, 310, 313, 422, 510, 664; with France, 315-30, 388, 483-85, 488, 564; and Jay Treaty, 546-47; Pinckney Treaty, 551-52; and re-export trade, 807-8, 863; in 1807, 882

commercial policy: in imperial controversy, 36, 70, 74-75; in Revolutionary War, 171-72; in Confederation, 286-87, 290-93, 303; reciprocity treaties, 291-93, 305-10, 422; toward France, 315-30, 388; and Constitution, 359; as Secretary of State, 398, 421-29, 429-30, 455-56, 459-60, 473, 509-10, 512-15; as Vice President, 566-67, 591, 627-29; as President, 808, 829-30, 856-57, 883, 885, 911 (see also peaceable coercion)

committees of correspondence, 69-70, 950

common law: in England, 59; and Christianity, 60-61, 136; in America, 74; adapted in Virginia, 112, 116, 125; and federal courts, 607, 623, 624, 697, 717; and seditious libel, 607, 616, 715, 716; and treason, 870-71

"Commonwealthmen," 58-59, 63

Condorcet, Marquis de, 262, 315, 331, 334, 425; and French Revolution, 373, 376, 382; quoted, 297

Confederation, and Western claims, 119, 183, 218; "new plan of finance" in 1780, 190-91; in 1783, 270-71, 275, 288; commerce and, 291, 309, 359; diplomatic establishment of, 301-2

Connecticut: Republican party in, 634, 671; and TJ's patronage policy, 671-75; political persecution and TJ libel case, 716-17; and embargo, 914

consolato del mare, 485, 509, 546

Constitution, U.S.: TJ and ratification of, 357-61; TJ's opinions of, 359-60, 412, 433-34, 460-61, 471, 484, 494, 613-14, 623-24, 627, 655-58, 685, 869, 993-94, 995; presidential re-eligibility, 360, 803; Hamilton and, 409, 434, 472; and Louisiana Purchase, 770-71, 775-76; impeachment under, 795; treason clause, 853-54, 866-67, 870-72; and internal improvements, 855, 858, 1001; and embargo, 906, 912-13; and American System measures, 992-96, 1002-3

constitutional convention, idea of, 102-4

Consular Convention, 495

Continental Army, Virginia Line, 170, 184, 195, 229
Continental Congress: First, 66-67, 69, 71, 76, 77; Second, 79-92
Continental System, 826, 878, 882, 901, 909
contraband, 546, 831, 863
Convention Army, 162-65, 188, 200, 217
Convention of 1800, 648, 665, 666, 748
Cook, Captain James, 339
Coolidge, Joseph, 1004
Cooper, James Fenimore, 839
Cooper, Thomas, 835; in election of 1800, 626, 630, 640; and University of Virginia, 975, 976, 977-79
Cornwallis, General Lord Charles: in southern campaign, 195, 197, 200, 219, 226-27, 232; in Virginia, 203, 234, 236, 239
Cosway, Maria, 347-49, 352, 354, 380, 386
Cosway, Richard, 347, 348
county courts, Virginia, 21, 155, 965
Coxe, Tench, 429, 444, 835, 864
Crawford, William H., 1002
Creeks, 431, 587, 773, 774
Cresap, Michael, 581-82, 584-86
Crèvecœur, Hector St. Jean de; Letters, 257, 293; and TJ, 293, 334; and American dream, 331, 334, 369; quoted, 340
crimes and punishments, TJ's bill on, 125-33
Crowninshield, Jacob, 804-5, 864, 915
Cuba, 878, 902
Currie, Dr. James, 555
Cushing, Justice William, 929
Cutler, Manesseh, on TJ, 726
Cutting, John Brown, 618
Cutting, Nathaniel, 386
Cuvier, George, 577, 579, 737, 952

Daggett, David, 709
Dale, Commodore Richard, 664, 798
Dallas, Alexander J., 498, 499, 504, 630
Dalrymple, Sir John, 58
Dane, Nathan, 284
Daveiss, Joseph H., 846-47, 851
David, Jacques Louis, 352
Davie, William R., 621, 630
Davies, William, 210, 230, 233
Davis, Augustine, 706, 846

Davis, Matthew L., 670-71
Dayton, Jonathan, 844, 846, 870
Deane, Silas, 107
Dearborn, Henry, Secretary of War, 661, 709, 776, 811, 837
Decatur, Captain Stephen, 799
decimal system, 277-78, 285, 402-5
Declaration of the Causes and Necessity of Taking Up Arms, 81-82
Declaration of Independence, 14, 45, 75, 99, 141, 154, 157, 316, 387, 537, 963; resolution on, 86; Congress appoints committee, 87; TJ drafts Declaration, 87-91; debated in Congress, 91-92; philosophy of, 93-96; fame and reputation of, 96, 294-95, 342, 950; and recognition doctrine, 482; and Louisiana government, 782, 784; fiftieth anniversary of, 1008-9
Declaration of the Rights of Man and Citizen, 380
Declaratory Act, 34, 69, 73
Dejean, Phillip, 176, 179, 181
Delaware, 649, 800; and TJ's patronage policy, 676-79
Démeunier, Jean Nicholas, 346
democracy, 1008; in English heritage, 46, 57-65; in Declaration of Independence, 93-96; in constitution-making, 102-7; in government of West, 282, 284-85; and U.S. Constitution, 358-59; and French Revolution, 372-73, 376, 380; and TJ's administration, 703-4, 720, 794, 874; and university education, 979
Democratic Societies, 492, 548, 605
Dennie, Joseph, 721
De Pauw, Cornelius, 253
Derbigny, Pierre, 787
descents, law of, 115
Destouches, Chevalier, 225
Destréhan, Jean, 787
Detroit: in Revolutionary War, 177, 182, 183, 198, 217, 218; fall of in 1812, 933
Dickinson, John, 71, 72, 77, 80, 81-82, 86
Dickson, Adam, 525
Diderot, Denis: Encyclopédie, 202, 336; quoted, 47
diplomatic establishment, U.S.: during Confederation, 301-2; in Washington's administration, 398-400, 430; in Adams's administration, 593; in TJ's administration, 665
D'Ivernois, François, 963

"doctrines of '98," in Republican ideology, 682-83, 686, 989, 994
Dodge, John, 179, 181
Dorchester, Lord, 417
Douglas, Reverend William, 7-8
Droz, Jean Pierre, 336-37, 402
Duane, William, 671, 710, 712, 927; prosecution of, 629-30, 686, 819; TJ's loyalty to, 931, 948
Duer, William A., 366-67, 462, 463, 471
Duer Panic, 462-63
Dunbar, William, 587, 588, 765, 767; quoted, 763
Dungeness, 4-5
Dunglison, Robley, 985, 1007-8
Dunmore, Lord, Governor of Virginia, 69, 78; flight and military operations of, 79, 83, 98
Dunmore's War, 78, 581, 584
Dupont, Victor, 618
Dupont de Nemours, Pierre Samuel, 920, 935, 939, 948, 953; and Franco-American commerce, 315, 319, 425; and French Revolution, 373, 382; and Louisiana Purchase, 752, 753-54, 755, 758-59; and national education, 858, 963

Eaton, General William: and Tripolitan war, 799; and Burr Conspiracy, 844-45, 847, 854, 871
Eden, William, 124
Edgehill, 522, 789
Edinburgh Review, 899, 927
education: in Virginia, 145-46, 928, 961-63, 983-84; TJ's plan of 1778, 146-48, 150-52, 965; and Europe, 332, 387; national, 856, 858, 859-60, 964. See also University of Virginia
Eighth Annual Message (TJ), 909, 910
election of 1796, 543-45, 554-58
election of 1800, 625-42, 643-51, 845
election of 1804, 789, 799-800
election of 1808, 881, 910
election of 1824, 1001, 1002-3
Elk Hill, 28, 236, 242, 350, 524
Ellery, Christopher, 710
Ellicott, Andrew, 588, 764
Ellsworth, Oliver, 621, 630
Embargo, The: message on, 882, 883; first law, 882-83; motives and objectives of, 883-86, 901; second law, 887; third law, 887, 896; fourth law, 887, 905; infractions and enforcement of, 887-92, 906-8; New England opposition to, 889, 895, 906, 913-14, 914-15; economic incidence of, 892-94, 910-11; political attack on, 895-98, 905; diplomacy of, 897-903, 908-9; alternatives to, 908, 910, 915; repeal of, 909-15; fifth law, 912-13, 914; reflections on, 916-18
Emerson, Ralph Waldo, quoted, 988
Emmet, Thomas Addis, 985
"empire of liberty," in TJ's thought, 68, 177-78, 282-83, 745-46, 771, 932, 937
empire theory, in pre-Revolutionary controversy, 71-77, 84-85, 89
Encyclopédie méthodique, 335-36, 346, 382
English law and government: in TJ's thought, 29, 57-65, 72-77; and American Revolution, 93; and French Revolution, 373, 378, 381-82
Enlightenment, The, 739, 1008; TJ as man of, 29, 47-56; and American Revolution, 93; and criminal law, 124; and nature, 255; and Negroes, 262; and diplomacy, 305; and decimal system, 402-3; and Christianity, 961; and education, 972
entail, law of, 113-15
Epictetus, 53
Epicureanism, 49, 53-54, 951
Epicurus, 957, 960
Episcopal Church, Virginia, 143, 144
epitaph, TJ's, 134, 988
Eppes, Elizabeth Wayles, 265, 355, 356, 394
Eppes, Francis, 303, 355
Eppes, Francis (grandson), 925, 975, 992
Eppes, John Wayles: marries Mary Jefferson, 542; in Congress, 824, 853
equality: TJ's doctrine of, 93-94; in Virginia constitution, 105-6; and Negroes, 261-64; and Union, 282; of generations, 382-84. See also education, freedom, religion
equity, 155
Erskine, David, British Minister, 861, 879, 882, 899, 909, 931
Erskine, Lord, 899
Erskine agreement, 931-32
Essex decision, 806-7, 826, 827, 863
ethnology, 259, 339. See also Indians
Europe: opinion of U.S. in, 300; TJ's ambivalence toward, 300-332, 387; influence on TJ, 314, 331, 365, 387-

Europe (*continued*)
89, 521, 539, 541; TJ's travels in, 327, 334, 342-44, 350-55, 363-65; and America, 331-32, 352; withdrawal from, 566, 628, 665, 666, 806, 932-33
Eustis, Dr. William, 722
Evans, Oliver, 937, 938
Everett, Edward, 944
Examination of the Boundaries of Louisiana, An (TJ), 769-70
expatriation, TJ's doctrine of, 73-74, 77, 154, 827-28

Fabbroni, Giovanni, 160, 164
Farewell Address, 556, 566, 572, 986
Farm Book (TJ), 532
Farmers-General, 316-17, 318-19, 321, 322, 425
farming: TJ and, 27-28, 493; idealization of, 256-57; in France, 350-51; in Albemarle, 523-34, 923, 940, 989
Fauquier, Francis, 14-15, 33, 41
Federalist, The, 396, 611, 986
Federalists: in ratification, 360; image of TJ, 464-66, 554-55, 571-72, 637-40, 682, 703, 721; and Genêt episode, 505, 508; and Jay Treaty, 515-16, 545-49; in election of 1796, 554-58, 563; and Washington's fame, 572, 573; and TJ's scientific reputation, 580-82; and war hysteria, 596-99, 600-603, 607; and Alien and Sedition Laws, 603-7; split on Adams's second commission to France, 621-22, 631, 632-33; in election of 1800, 629-30, 626-41; First Inaugural appeal to, 656, 659; attack TJ's patronage policy, 667, 674, 681; allege subservience of Congress, 692-93, 725, 727-28; and judiciary, 692-93; oppose Louisiana policies, 756, 760, 765-66, 772; collusion with Burr, 791, 792, 867-68; and Northern Confederacy scheme, 793-94; portrayed by TJ in Second Inaugural, 802-3; allege his subservience to Napoleon, 817, 824-25; oppose his naval system, 838-39; and embargo, 883-84, 894, 895-98, 903, 905; and War of 1812, 935; and consolidation, 992-93, 996, 1003
Fenno, John, 406, 446, 469, 470, 474
Fenno, John, Jr., 621-22
Ferguson, Adam, quoted, 390
Fifth Annual Message (TJ), 814-16
Fine Creek, 4, 7

First Amendment, and Sedition Act, 606-7, 613; in TJ's political creed, 627, 639, 655, 656-57, 712
First Inaugural Address (TJ), 655-59, 746
Fisheries, 426. See also Whale Fishery
Fitzhugh, Peregrine, 568
Flahut, Mme de, 376
Floridas, 397-98; TJ's policy toward, 416, 417, 429, 456, 497, 566, 746, 878; in Louisiana diplomacy, 747-48, 751; whether included in Louisiana Purchase, 768-70; negotiation to purchase, 808-10, 816-17, 825-26; and embargo diplomacy, 901, 902; and War of 1812, 932. See also West Florida
Forest, The, 27, 175
foreign debts, U.S.: in Holland, 362-64, 366, 367-68; in France, 362, 366-67, 471; and Hamilton's program, 409, 410
Forrest, Uriah, 568-69
fortifications, in TJ's defense policy, 832, 833, 837, 877
Fox, Charles James, 831, 832
Fox's Libel Act, 607
France: and American Revolution, 87, 370; TJ declines mission to, 107; Alliance of 1778, 158, 172, 357, 368, 387-88, 398, 415, 422-25, 483-85, 488, 494-95, 500, 506, 512, 628, 666; naval support in Virginia, 221, 225, 228, 234, 240; and American commerce, 292, 308-9, 314-30, 388, 422-24, 425, 488; TJ, Minister to, 301-70 *passim*; TJ's travels in, 350-55; U.S. debts in, 362, 366-67, 482, 495; Consular Convention, 368-69; TJ's policy as Secretary of State, 398, 455-56, 473, 479-86, 509, 512; and Jay Treaty, 555-56, 561, 564, 566; Adams's first commission to, 560-62, 564, 565, 591, 594-95; second commission, 618, 630; TJ's changing policy toward, 566, 628, 666, 754-55; and Louisiana, 601, 647, 747-62; and Florida negotiations, 808, 812, 813, 814, 816, 825-26, 862-63, 901; Continental System, 826, 860, 882; and embargo, 901-2; and Napoleon's downfall, 935. See also French Revolution
Franklin, Benjamin: 98, 253, 273, 288, 292, 315, 340, 343, 401, 419, 950; and American ideal, 66; population theory, 68; in Continental Congress,

79, 80, 84, 87, 88; in France, 107, 286, 297, 332, 340, 368; TJ's opinion of, 257, 388; TJ succeeds, 302-3; death of, 394, 425
Franzoni, Giuseppe, 742
Frederick the Great, 204, 306
"free ships make free goods," 305, 485, 509, 546, 665, 831, 863
freedom: and American character, 67; of trade, 74-75, 289, 304, 329-30, 388; in Declaration of Independence, 93-96; in Virginia constitution, 106-7; of religious conscience, 134, 141-45, 655; of mind, 134, 141, 144, 616, 986-87; and slavery, 260; in U.S. Constitution, 360; and Europe, 370; and science, 579, 581; of speech and press, 606-7, 613, 616, 655, 714-18, 803; in political creed of 1800, 627-28; of ideas, 937-38
freehold tenure, 113-17
Freeman, Thomas, 855
French Revolution: TJ and, 332, 370-85, 389, 398, 425, 438-39, 443, 480, 500, 504, 519, 548, 628; Assembly of Notables, 356, 370; aristocratic revolt, 371-72; Estates General, 373-77; National Assembly, 377-80; storming of Bastille, 379-80; "Great Fear," 380; formation of constitution, 380-82; mercantilist reaction, 425; in American opinion, 437, 439, 443, 479-81; "conspiracy of kings," 479; republic, 479, 506, 747; Directory, 548, 555, 601, 618, 747; 18th Brumaire of Bonaparte, 628; First Consul, 677; later reflections on, 727, 935-36, 955; Emperor, 801
Freneau, Philip, and National Gazette, 444-45, 446, 468, 469, 470, 474, 502, 508
Friedland, Battle of, 878
Fries, John, 622, 796
frontier, influence of, 5-6. See also West, western lands
Fry, Joshua, 6
Fulton, Robert, 858-59, 903
Funding system, 409-11, 432; TJ's view of commercial and diplomatic effects, 424, 428-29, 515; of speculative mania, 436, 462-63; of political corruption, 468, 472; in TJ's administration, 700, 702

Gabriel Conspiracy, 638
Gallatin, Albert, 663, 686, 690, 798, 803, 820, 864, 878, 880, 946; in Con-

gress, 569, 592-93, 644, 651; Secretary of Treasury, 660-61; and patronage policy, 670, 675, 678, 679; and fiscal policy, 687-89, 701, 815-16, 910; and Louisiana, 767-68, 770; and Floridas, 798, 811, 813, 817, 818; and internal improvements, 855, 856, 857, 858; and embargo, 882, 884, 886, 888, 891, 906-7, 911-12; and Madison's administration, 930-31; quoted, 738, 835
Gardenier, Barent, 896
gardening: TJ's style in, 26, 343-44; importance of, 352; President's House, 744; in old age, 923
Gardoqui, Diego de, 358
Gaspee, 69
Gassendi, Pierre, 54, 960
Gates, General Horatio, 216, 631; commands Southern Army, 197, 198, 203
Gay, Peter, cited, 49
Gazette de Leide, 408, 446
Gazette of the United States, 408, 438, 464, 469, 621, 638
Geffroy letters, 709-10
Geismar, Baron de, 365
Gelston, David, 670
Gem, Dr. Richard, 383
Genêt, Edmond Charles, 402, 556; French Minister, 481-507 passim, 509, 512-13, 747
geographical exploration, TJ and, 738; Ledyard, 339-40; Lewis and Clark, 340, 756, 762-67; Michaux, 496-97
geology, 251-52
George III, 342, 882, 883; and imperial controversy, 33, 49, 62-63, 64, 75, 76, 78, 83-84, 84-85; arraigned in Declaration of Independence, 89, 90, 91, 92, 99, 153
Georgia, 326, 431; compact of 1802, 692, 774; and Yazoo land frauds, 771, 820
Gerry, Elbridge: in Congress, 79-80, 294; Minister to France, 561, 565, 596, 601, 618; in Republican politics, 567-68, 570, 618-19, 627, 704
Gibbs, James, 24
Gibson, General John, 584, 585
Giles, William Branch, 492, 553, 868, 930; leads attack on Treasury, 477-78; in TJ's administration, 667, 690-91, 728, 729, 853, 872, 912; in Virginia state rights' revival, 992, 1003; quoted, 559, 659

Gilmer, Francis Walker, 953, 984-85, 986

Girardin, Louis Hue, 949, 952

Girondins, 481, 488, 496, 498, 506, 747

Godoy, Manuel, 826

Godwin, William, 682

Goodrich, Elizur, 672

Gordon, Captain Charles, 874-75

Gordon, Thomas, 58, 59

Graham, John, 841, 850

Grand, Ferdinand, 362

Grand Ohio Company, 43

Granger, Gideon, 627, 635, 930; Postmaster General, 717, 777, 847; quoted, 634

Gray, Francis C., 943

Great Britain: and coming of Revolution, 34-38, 62-65, 67, 73, 76; policy in Northwest, 176-77, 345, 427, 431, 453, 454, 497, 546; and American commerce, 289-90, 292, 304, 307-8, 311, 317-18, 322, 324-25, 329, 398, 422-23, 426-27, 546-47; TJ's hostility toward, 300, 342, 453, 455, 567; danger of war with, 300, 357, 567; Nootka Sound affair, 415-18; TJ's policy as Secretary of State, 425-28, 429-30, 473; negotiations with Hammond, 451-55; and neutrality of 1793, 500, 508-10; and Jay Treaty, 545-47; in TJ's opinion as Vice President, 567-68, 591; and Miranda project, 600-601; U.S. *rapprochement* with, 665-66, 797; in Louisiana diplomacy, 752, 753-54, 758, 759; in War of Third Coalition, 806-8; alliance meditated by TJ, 811, 812; congressional policy toward, 826-30; Monroe-Pinkney treaty project, 860-65; in *Chesapeake* affair, 875-80, 882; November 1807 orders in council, 882, 883, 884; and embargo, 899-901, 908-9, 913, 917; and War of 1812, 931-32, 934-35

Great George, 536

Great Seal, U.S., 98

Greathouse, Daniel, 584-85

Greene, General Nathanael, commander of Southern Army, 203, 204, 206, 210, 216, 219, 220, 223, 226, 227, 234, 239

Gregg, Andrew, 828-29

Grenville, Lord, 452, 545, 899

Grimm, Baron de, 333-34, 339

Griswold, Roger, 592, 728, 793; quoted, 647

Grotius, Hugo, 73, 484, 527

gunboat system, 836-39

Hale, Edward Everett, 589

Hale, Sir Matthew, 60

Hall, David, 677, 678

Hallet, Stephen, 449

Hamilton, Alexander, 278, 554, 661, 663, 709; nationalist, 270, 367; Secretary of Treasury, 396-517 *passim;* funding system, 396, 409-11, 428-29, 462-63, 468, 472, 794; character of, 397, 478-79, 575-76n, 594, 700, 704; constitutional doctrine of, 409, 434-35, 442-43, 460, 472, 611-12, 657; on TJ, 464-65, 646-47, 691; and neutrality of 1793, 482-86, 489-90, 499-502, 503-4, 505, 509, 511; and Jay Treaty, 515-16, 546; and Whiskey Rebellion, 548; and Adams's administration, 558, 564, 600, 617, 621-22; in election of 1800, 632, 641, 646-47; death of, 792-93

Hamilton, Sir Henry, 176-82

Hamilton, William, 922

Hammond, George, British Minister, 427-28; TJ's negotiations with, 431, 451-55, 509, 511, 549

Hannibal, 353

Hardy, Samuel, 274

Harmer, General Josiah, 431

Harper, Robert Goodloe, 593, 617; quoted, 580, 604

Harpers Ferry, 251, 268

Harrison, Benjamin, 81, 109, 110, 156, 172, 206, 216-17, 274

Harrison, William Henry, 744

Hartford Convention, 934-35

Harvard University, 972, 975, 981

Harvey, William, 684

Harvie, John, 158

Harvie, John, guardian of TJ, 10

Hawkesbury, Lord, 752

Hawkins, Benjamin, 587, 773

Hawkins, John Isaac, 737

Hay, George, 946; in Burr trial, 867-68, 870

Heckwelder, John, 583-84

Helvetius, Claude Adrien, 124

Helvetius, Mme, 335

Hemings, Bob, 535

Hemings, Elizabeth, 707

Hemings, James, 535

Hemings, Sally, 355, 707

Henderson, Richard, 119, 121

Hening, William Waller, 949

Henry, John, 583

Henry, Patrick, 185, 319, 345; as lawyer, 13, 16, 20-21, 22; in colonial politics, 41-42; TJ's opinions of, 42-43, 949-50; in Revolutionary movement, 42, 69, 71, 78, 80, 83; in Virginia reform, 102, 108, 110, 140; Governor of Virginia, 108, 131, 156, 165, 177; retires, 166-67; returns to assembly, 191, 237; and U.S. Constitution, 361, 408, 433

Hichborn, Benjamin, 647-48

history, TJ's views: general, 29, 57, 65, 157; of ancient 49-50; of English, 57-61, 62-65, 73-76; in education, 147, 974; as archivist, 150, 949; natural and civil, 249; of U.S., 858, 948-51

Hoban, James, 449

Hobbes, Thomas, 55

Hogarth, William, 26, 343-44

Hogendorp, Gijsbert Karel van, quoted on TJ, 269-70, 275

Holbach, Baron d', 335; quoted, 48

Holbach, Mme d', 335

Holland, Lord, 832, 860, 861

Holland, 228; democratic republic defeated in, 357, 372-73, 374; U.S. loans in, 362-64, 367-68; travels in, 363, 364

Holy Alliance, 937

Homer, 343

Hood's on James, 206, 208, 210-12, 231, 232

Hopkinson, Francis, 343, 417, 419

Horace, 927

Houdetot, Comtess de, quoted, 334

Howard, John, 124

Howell, David, 278

Hull, General William, 933

Hulme, Obadiah, 58, 59

Humboldt, Alexander von, 714, 809, 937; visits Washington, 738-39

Hume, David, 262; and religion, 51; *History of England*, 58; TJ on, 59, 951, 987

Humphreys, David, 295, 296, 298, 510, 939

husbandman, ideal of, 116-17, 256-57

Hutcheson, Francis, 55

Hutchinson, Dr. James, 419, 450, 508

Ideologues, 752, 948

Illuminati, 638

impeachment, of federal judges, 794-97, 804

impressment of seamen, 428, 546, 666, 797, 826, 827-28, 831, 860, 861, 862, 864-65, 875, 879-80

Indian Trade and Intercourse Act, 962

Indiana Company, 121

Indians: in TJ's youth, 5, 6; at William and Mary, 11, 149; and western lands, 118, 280; in Revolutionary War, 169, 176, 193; TJ's policy toward, 193, 258, 450-51, 802, 904; opinions of in *Notes on Virginia*, 253, 258-59, 263; origins and languages of, 258, 339, 586-88, 766, 951; and Spanish colonies, 397-98; in Northwest, 431, 450-51, 877, 903-4; plan of Indian removal, 771, 773-74, 776; in Far West, 904

Ingenhousz, Jan, 336

Innes, Harry, 437, 583, 846

Innes, James, 230; quoted, 214

Intercourse Bill, 1790, 300-400

Internal improvements, 816, 855-58, 910, 993

Iredell, Justice James, 605

Iroquois, 774

Isaacks, Jacob, 450

Italy, TJ and, 159-60, 163, 353-54

Izard, Ralph, quoted, 488

Jackson, Andrew, 918, 934, 1002, 1003

Jacobins, 506

Jarvis, William, 939

Jay, John, 80, 287, 326, 358, 469, 632; Secretary of Foreign Affairs, 288, 309, 311, 312, 314, 366, 367, 368, 369; Chief Justice, 395, 417-18, 504; treaty with Britain, 515-16, 545-48

Jay Treaty, 515-16, 545-52; TJ's views of, 547, 548, 566, 571, 596, 629, 830, 863; French reaction to, 555-56, 561, 566, 747; expiration, 806

Jefferson, Isaac, 536, 538

Jefferson, Jane, sister, 9

Jefferson, Lucy, daughter, 265, 301

Jefferson, Martha, sister, 8, 244

Jefferson, Martha, wife, 27, 100, 113, 159, 207, 242, 243, 246

Jefferson, Martha (Patsy), daughter, 27, 244, 246, 265, 267, 287, 724, 789; TJ's instructions to, 268-69; in Paris, 295, 356, 385; marries Thomas Mann Randolph, 392, 394; family of, 447, 522, 540, 924-25, 1007

Jefferson, Mary (Maria, Polly), daughter, 159, 265, 303; in Paris, 355, 356, 376, 385; at Monticello, 394, 447, 521; in Philadelphia, 447,

Jefferson, Mary (*continued*)
449-50, 493, 506; marries John Wayles Eppes, 542; family of, 633, 925; death, 789-90
Jefferson, Peter, father, 3-5, 6, 7, 9, 25, 30, 41
Jefferson, Randolph, brother, 9
Jefferson, Thomas: personal estate and finances, 9, 27-28, 123, 302, 345, 394, 474, 523-24, 533-34, 729, 923-24, 934, 989-92, 1007-8; personal features, 10, 399-400, 519, 718-19, 731, 735, 1006; traits of mind and character, 28-31, 266, 268, 269-70, 330-32, 343-44, 348, 351-52, 387-89, 397, 520-21, 528, 531-32, 590, 718-19, 727, 927; health of, 84, 242-46, 300-301, 349, 382, 405, 721-22, 1005, 1006-8; life portraits of, 340, 345, 347, 420, 718, 1006
Jefferson, Thomas, Jr., grandfather, 4
"Jefferson and Liberty," 640
Jefferson's Manual, 634
Jeffersonville, Indiana, 744
Jenner, Edward, 683-84
Jesus, TJ on, 52, 53, 957-60
Johnson, Justice William, 904-5, 995
Jones, Gabriel, 120
Jones, John Paul, 302, 332, 340, 510
Jones, Joseph, 279
Jones, Skelton, 949
Jones, William, 864
Jouett, Jack, 235
judicial review, doctrine of, 697, 699, 905-6, 995
Judiciary, U.S.: in Federalist strategy, 631, 648, 686, 692-94; TJ's view of, 668, 693, 694-95, 699-700, 869; impeachment proceedings, 794-97; and trial of Burr, 867, 868, 872-73; and embargo, 905-6; and renewed consolidation, 933-95
Judiciary, Virginia, 154, 993
Judiciary Act of 1801, 631, 648, 686, 692-94; repeal of, 696-98, 702, 794
Julien, M., 729-30
jury trial, right of, 155

Kalm, Peter, 253
Kames, Lord, 55, 58, 124, 527
Kennedy, John F., quoted, 724
Kentucky, 846, 980; in Revolutionary War, 119-20, 177, 180, 229; statehood, 279; and Mississippi navigation, 397 497-98
Kentucky Resolutions of 1798, 612, 613-14; of 1799, 614, 622-24, 770-71, 794, 994

Key, Francis Scott, 913
Key, Thomas, 985
King, Rufus, 284, 504, 799, 830; Minister to Britain, 600, 604, 665, 731, 752, 808, 828; and Missouri Compromise, 996
King's Mountain, Battle of, 198, 200, 212
Kirkland, Samuel, 774
Kittera, John Wilkes, 681
Knox, Henry, 659; Secretary of War, 397, 417, 418, 483, 490, 494, 499, 502, 504, 506
Knox, John, 151
Knox, Samuel, 970
Koch, Adrienne, cited, 54
Kosciusko, General Thaddeus, 604, 605, 618, 924, 1000

Lafayette, General Marquis de, 301, 335, 340, 350, 398, 425, 935; Virginia campaigns of, 221-22, 224-26, 231, 234, 235, 239; TJ's friend in France, 299, 302, 311, 312, 314, 315, 319, 320, 322, 323, 326; and American dream, 315-16, 331; opinion of TJ, 316; and French Revolution, 356, 371, 373, 375, 377, 380; land grant and offer of Louisiana governorship, 786; triumphal tour, 1005-6; quoted, 360, 868
Lamb, John, 311, 312
Lambert, M., 321, 322
La Mothe, Guillaume, 176, 179, 181
Land Office, Virginia, establishment of, 121-22, 171
Land Ordinance of 1785, 278, 285
landscape gardening, *see* gardening
Langdon, John, 80, 626
Langhorne letter, 573-74, 707, 710
La Place, Marquis de, 336
La Rochefoucauld, François, Duc de, 334, 346, 373
La Rochefoucauld, Duchesse de, 400
La Rochefoucauld-Liancourt, François Alexandre Frédéric, Duc de: visits at Monticello, 519-23, 528, 529; quoted, 342
Las Casas, Bartolomé, de, 259-60
Latrobe, Benjamin, 538, 590, 723, 858; superintends government buildings, 741-43; and TJ's "lock-dock," 836; and University of Virginia, 968-69
Lavoisier, Antoine, 334
law: TJ and study of, 12-13, 16-19; practice of, 20-22, 244; English, 57-65; attitude toward, 111; courts of, 155

law of nations, 457, 483-85, 546, 806-7
Leander affair, 831-32, 875
Leclerc, General Victor, 749, 750, 754, 759
Ledyard, John, 339-40, 762
Lee, Arthur, 274, 401
Lee, Francis L., 69
Lee, Henry, 444-45, 573, 625, 709, 717
Lee, Richard Henry, 160, 202; in colonial politics, 41-42; in Revolutionary movement, 69, 80-81, 83, 86, 87; in Virginia politics, 110, 156; quoted, 189, 237
Lee, Thomas Ludwell, 111
Leland, John, 722, 723
Le Maire, Etienne, 729
Le Maire, Jacques, 188
L'Enfant, Major Pierre Charles, 448-49, 450, 588, 740, 741
Leopard, HMS, 875
Leslie, Major General Alexander, 199, 200, 203
Leslie, Robert, 403, 836
Lewis, Meriwether, 6; and western expedition, 762-64, 848, 930; TJ's sketch of his life, 950-51
Lewis, Morgan, 792
Lewis, Nicholas, 394
Lewis and Clark Expedition, 340, 756, 762-67, 855, 857, 950-51, 963
lex talionis, 127-28, 131
libels, of TJ, 555, 705-8, 710, 714
Liberia, 999
libraries, TJ's first, 27; second, 50, 72, 333; catalogue of, 50, 53, 249, 265; TJ proposes state library, 149-50; sold to Congress, 941-43; third, 943-44
Library of Congress, 266, 943
Life and Morals of Jesus of Nazareth (TJ), 959
Lincoln, Benjamin, 681
Lincoln, Levi, 890, 897, 930; Attorney General, 661, 672-73, 674, 705, 770, 804
linguistics, 259, 586-87, 951. *See also,* Indians
Linn, William, 587
Linnaeus, Karl, 47, 250
Liston, Robert, 600
Livingston, Brockholst, 631
Livingston, Edward, 550-51, 669; and Louisiana opposition, 784, 788, 843; and Batture case, 944-47
Livingston, Robert R., 86, 87, 274, 437, 439, 643, 727, 858, 939; Minister to France, 661, 666, 750-54, 757-58, 760, 768, 775, 811, 814; quoted, 893

Livingston, William, 174
Livy, 49, 52, 336
"lock-dock," plan of, 741
Locke, John, 18, 47, 55, 64, 73, 147, 154, 386; political theory, 94-95, 986; theory of property, 117, 383; toleration, 136, 138, 139; quoted, 3, 62
Logan, Chief, legend of, 259, 581-86
Logan, Dr. George, 419, 493; as agriculturist, 527, 530; his mission to France, 602-3, 617-18, 619; and Santo Domingo trade, 824, 825; and national university, 858
Logan, Mrs. George, 602-3
Logan Act, 617, 620
Lomax, John Tayloe, 986
Long, George, 985
lottery, of TJ's estate, 992, 1007
Louis XVI, 302, 315, 356, 357, 371, 373, 374, 376, 377, 378, 379, 401, 480
Louisiana, 397-98; TJ's policy as Secretary of State, 416, 429, 497, 566; and Miranda project, 600-601; ceded to France, 666, 747; conditions under Spain, 778-80, 783
Louisiana Memorial, 784-85, 787
Louisiana Purchase, 745-62; geographical boundaries of, 768-70, 809, 812-13, 848-49, 855; and land policy, 771; and Indian policy, 771, 773-74, 776; and political economy, 771-72; and the Union, 772-73, 794; and territorial government, 777-89; Federalist hostility to, 717, 777; and slavery, 781, 995-96
Louisiana Territory (District), 783
Louisiana Treaty, 760, 767, 784-85
L'Ouverture, Toussaint, 747, 748-50
Loyal Company, 6, 44, 121
Loyalists, in Virginia, 122, 135; sequestration of property, 123; confiscation, 123-24, 171; test oath, 132; in war, 169, 194, 198, 220; in peace, 271, 405, 451, 453
Lucretius, 49
Luzerne, Chevalier de la, 227, 302, 401
Lynch, Charles, 194
Lyon, Matthew, 592, 622, 648, 649

McCleod, Captain, 235, 236
McCulloch v. Maryland, 994
McHenry, James, 563, 632, 641
Machiavelli, Niccolò, 55, 61; quoted, 801
McKean, Thomas, 625, 626, 675, 714-15, 716

Mackenzie, Alexander, 762, 764
McLane, Allan, and TJ's patronage policy, 676-79
Maclay, William: on TJ, 399-400; on Washington, 406; quoted, 411
Macon, Nathaniel, 690, 815, 841
McPherson, Isaac, 937-38
Madison, Dolley, 553, 724, 732
Madison, James, 217, 249, 254, 266, 279, 298, 301, 308, 309, 340, 358, 366, 372, 382, 384, 418, 447, 485, 488, 489, 527, 575, 645, 869, 924; in Virginia assembly, 109; and TJ's Revision of the Laws, 112, 130-31, 141, 142, 150; on religious persecution, 135; on TJ, 243; relationship with TJ, 266, 390-93, 614-15; as nationalist, 270, 360, 396; and Bill of Rights, 360, 361; and Treasury measures, 410, 413, 422-23, 431, 432, 433, 434; opposition leader, 437, 444-45, 461-62, 468, 470, 471, 477; excursion with TJ, 439-40; Hamilton's opinion of, 464; and neutrality of 1793, 494, 501, 505; resolutions of 1794, 515-16, 885; and Jay Treaty, 546, 547, 550-51; marries and plans retirement, 553; and *rapprochement* with Adams, 557-62; enters Virginia assembly, 609-10; drafts Virginia Resolutions of 1798, 612, 614-15, of 1799-1800, 623-24; Secretary of State, 660, 663, 683, 684, 686, 696, 706, 731, 732, 749, 750, 798, 804, 809, 827; and British diplomacy, 808, 828, 830, 831-32, 861; and Florida diplomacy, 810, 811, 812, 818; and John Randolph, 820, 821, 822; nominated and elected President, 881, 910; and embargo, 882, 883, 898, 911-12; President, 903, 920, 929-31, 933-34; and University of Virginia, 965, 968, 986, 1008; quoted, 190, 280, 369, 406
Madison, Bishop James, 8, 336
Magill, Charles, 219
Maison Carrée, 341, 352-53, 539
Malthus, Thomas, 772, 773
mammoth (mastadon), 254-55, 577, 578, 722, 736-37, 952
"mammoth cheese," 722-23
Mandeville, Bernard de, 55, 435
manufactures: in Revolutionary Virginia, 172, 188; importance of, 352, 514-15, 940-41; Hamilton's report on, 458-60; at Monticello, 534-37, 937, 938-39; embargo's encourage-

ment of, 892, 893, 910-11, 917. *See also,* commercial policy, political economy
Marbois, François, 202, 247, 250, 287
Marbury v. Madison, 695-96, 698-99
Marie Antoinette, 299, 356, 376, 377, 378, 379
Marine Corps, U.S., 723, 877
Marmontel, Jean François, 334
Marshall, John, 550, 555, 625, 929, 945, 946; Minister to France, 565, 601, 618; TJ's opinion of, 601, 985, 995; on TJ, 647, 659, 691; Chief Justice, 654, 694, 696, 698-99, 700, 795, 993; in Burr trial, 854, 866-73; *Life of Washington,* 859
Martin, Luther: attacks TJ, 581-82, 583, 586, 635; in Burr trial, 869, 870
Maryland, 557, 739
Mason, George: and western lands, 43, 121; and Virginia constitution, 89, 101, 102; and Virginia reforms, 109, 111; and federal government, 437, 474
Mason, Stevens Thompson, 635, 691, 697
Massachusetts: circular letter of 1768, 34; and Coercive Acts, 70, 77; and Lexington and Concord, 78; commerce of, 322; rebellion in, 358; Republican party in, 634-35, 704-5, 804-5, 814; and TJ's patronage policy, 680-81; in election of 1804, 800, of 1805, 804; and embargo, 890, 893, 896, 897, 913-14; and War of 1812, 935; education in, 980-81
mathematics, 951, 952
Mathurins, 367, 368
Maury, James, 8, 9
Maury, Reverend James, 8
Maxwell, Captain James, 231
Mazzei, Philip: in Albemarle, 159-60, 163; in Europe, 172, 334, 382, 570-71 742; quoted, 225
Mazzei letter, 570-74, 575, 592-93, 639
Meade, Bishop William, quoted, 144
mechanical arts, 300, 336-37, 343, 352, 354, 365-66, 459, 531, 589-90, 648, 737, 937-38
medicine, TJ's views of, 684, 973, 987
Mediterranean fund, 815
megalonyx, 577, 578, 579
megatherium, 577, 579, 736
Meigs, Josiah, 717
Melampus, HMS, 875
Melish, John, 940
"Memoir on the Discovery of Cer-

tain Bones of a Quadruped . . ."
(TJ), 577-79
Mercer, Charles Fenton, 966
Mercer, John F., 274
merino sheep, 939-40
Merry, Anthony, British Minister,
794, 797, 823, 832, 842, 843; recep-
tion of, 731-34
Merry, Mrs. Anthony, 731, 732-33
Mesmer, Friedrich Anton, 299-300
meteorology, 30, 39, 160
Mexico, 738, 902
Michaux, André, 496, 762, 763
Middleton, Conyers, 50, 51
"midnight appointments," 668-69, 694,
695
Mifflin, Thomas, 498, 499, 504
Milan Decree, 901
Militia, U.S.: in TJ's defense policy,
689, 833; classification system, 833-
34; and enforcement of embargo,
891, 912
Militia, Virginia, in Revolutionary
War, 169, 186-87, 197, 198, 212-16,
229
Milligan, Joseph, 942-43, 948
Mills, Robert, 538, 952
Milton, Virginia, 534, 536
Mirabeau, Comte de, 335, 375, 376
Miranda, Francisco de, 496; project
in 1798, 600-601, 621; Leander ex-
pedition, 825, 844, 867, 869
Missouri Compromise, 981, 989, 995-
98, 1000
Missouri River, trade and navigation,
764, 904
Mississippi River, trade and navigation, 182, 279-80, 358, 397, 416,
417; TJ claims right to, 456-57; and
Genêt, 496-98; under Pinckney
Treaty, 551-52; and Louisiana diplomacy, 746, 752-53, 755-56
Mississippi Territory, 588, 774, 778,
781
Mitchill, Dr. Samuel L., 727, 729, 735,
861
Mobile Act, 799, 809
Molesworth, Sir Robert, 58, 59
"monarchical tendencies," TJ and,
405-6, 438-39, 440-43, 571, 593-94
money unit, U.S., 97, 275-78, 444
Monroe, James, 301, 312, 313, 413,
428, 470, 381, 485, 496, 605, 635, 786,
848; wartime relationship with TJ,
196; friendship, 243, 269, 831, 930,
1002; in Congress, 269, 274, 283-84;
Minister to France, 547, 548, 556; recalled, 561, 574-75; in Virginia Republicanism, 575, 633; Governor, 649,
650, 706, 746; Minister to Britain,
733, 808, 826; envoy to France,
756-57, 758, 760; mission to Spain,
768, 808-10, 811, 813; as Quid candidate against Madison, 822, 881;
Pinkney associated with, 830; and
Monroe-Pinkney treaty, 830-31, 860-
61; and Chesapeake affair, 879; in
Madison's administration, 930-31,
933; and University of Virginia,
965, 968, 982; President, 1001-2
Monroe Doctrine, 902, 937, 1001-2
Monroe-Pinkney treaty, 860-65, 879-
80, 897
Montesquieu, Baron de, 47, 124, 746,
773; theories of, 61, 66, 260, 294;
TJ's opinion of, 62, 948
Monticello, 9, 31, 201, 267, 301, 447,
466, 469, 506, 517, 553, 607, 612, 624,
633, 660, 671, 683, 736, 754, 881, 904,
963; building of, 23-26; TJ on, 24;
moves to, 26; rebuilding of, 26, 521,
538-43; improvements, 159; TJ
chased from, 235-36, 242; Chastellux
on, 245-46; TJ returns to in 1789,
391-93; plans improvements at, 474,
493, 537; retires to in 1794, 518-23;
farm at, 528; naillery at, 536-37, as
cultural ideal, 543; as "summer
White House," 684, 804; in TJ's
retirement, 920-21, 922-23, 924-29,
943; household manufactures at,
938-39
Montmorin, Comte de, 325, 326, 368,
369, 382, 401, 425
moral sense, philosophy of, 55-56, 94
More, Sir Thomas, quoted, 130
Morellet, Abbé, 315, 334, 381
Morgan, Colonel George, 847, 871
Morocco, 310; treaty with U.S., 311-
12
Morris, Gouverneur: and French
Revolution, 376, 380; London mission in 1790, 399, 417, 425-26; Min-
ister to France, 430, 480, 482, 503,
506; in Congress, 644, 646, 650, 697,
698, 761; quoted, 329
Morris, Commodore Richard, 798
Morris, Robert, architect, 24, 25
Morris, Robert, 376; and monetary
system, 275-77; and tobacco trade,
319, 320
Morris, Mrs. Robert, 420
Morse, Jedediah, 264
Moustier, Comte de, 369, 401, 747

Muhlenberg, General J. P. G., 209, 231

Mumford, Lewis, cited, 969-70

Murray, William Vans, 619, 620, 621, 631

music, TJ and, 15, 27, 164, 333, 343, 723

Muter, George, 210

National Capital: New York, 405-7; Philadelphia, 419-20, 420-21, 492-93, 505-6, 507-8; Washington, 644, 653-54, 721, 723-24, 731, 739; permanent site determined, 412-14; TJ in planning of, 418, 447-49, 739-44

National Capitol, 449, 653, 741, 742-43

national domain: creation of, 278, 280; land system, 285

National Gazette, 445-46, 461, 464, 470-71, 473-74, 490, 508

National Institute, of France, 734-35, 736-37, 859, 904

National Intelligencer, 691, 698, 699, 711, 927

National Road, 857

national university, 858-60, 964

nationality, American, 1008; before Revolution, 65-68; in *Notes on Virginia*, 247-48, 254-59, 265; and TJ's European experience, 314, 331-32, 338, 380, 387-89; and foreign policy, 566-68, 627-29; and TJ's presidency, 734, 794, 854, 858; War of 1812, 932-33

"natural aristocracy," 152, 679, 955

Natural Bridge, Virginia, 246, 251, 953

natural history, in *Notes on Virginia*, 249-65. *See also* ethnology, paleontology, etc.

Natural History Museum (Peale's), 419, 737, 859

natural law, 25, 29, 31, 47, 49, 64, 66, 255, 404

natural rights: in general, 57, 64; in Declaration of Independence, 93-96; in landholding, 113-15, 118-19; in criminal justice, 129; in religion, 134; and expatriation, 154; and slavery, 260; in trade, 304, 329-30, 388; on navigable waters, 457; of speech and press, 606; and state rights, 615

naturalization, TJ on: bill in Virginia, 153; as President, 686, 692, 827

Naturalization Act, 603; repeal of, 686, 692

Nature, American: and nationality, 251, 253-57, 265, 337-38, 338-39; and civilization, 255, 257, 369, 1008

Navy, U.S.: TJ's proposed creation of, 312-14; in Quasi War, 599, 600, 617; founded, 664; peacetime establishment in 1801, 664; and fiscal policy, 688, 692; establishment in 1806, 833; character of the naval system, 835-37; TJ's "lock-dock," 836; gunboats, 836-39; after *Chesapeake* encounter, 877; embargo and, 887, 912

Navy, Virginia, in Revolutionary War, 168-69, 222, 231

Navy Department, 599, 661-62

Navy Yard, Washington, 740, 741

Necker, Jacques, 335, 375, 377, 379

Necker, Mme, 335

Negroes, TJ's thoughts on, 259-64

Nelson, Admiral Horatio, 618

Nelson, Thomas, 108

Nelson, General Thomas, 199, 206, 207, 212; succeeds TJ as Governor, 236, 239

Nelson, William, 43

neology, 952

neutrality, U.S., 292, 329, 357, 389; in TJ's policy, 416; in 1793, 481-513; and Jay Treaty, 546, 566; in War of Third Coalition, 805-8, 826, 831, 860, 862, 863, 882, 899-901

New Haven Remonstrance, 672; answer to, 673-75

New Jersey, 680

New Orleans: TJ on its importance, 752-53; closure of, 755-56, 757; U.S. authority in, 776-77, 783, 786; and Burr Conspiracy, 849, 850, 852, 853, 854; and Batture St. Marie, 944-46

New World: images of, 66-68, 255-56, 331, 369; degeneracy theory of, 252-53; TJ's attack on, 254-59, 265, 338-39, 578; in TJ's conception, 745-46, 932

New York: and Revolution, 34-35; party contests in, 439, 469; in election of 1800, 625, 631-32; in TJ's patronage decisions, 669-71, 680; Burr-Lewis contest, 791-93; and embargo, 896, 897

New York *Evening Post*, 792, 881

newspapers: English, 300, 408; European, 408; U.S., 408, 444-46; partisan warfare in Philadelphia, 464, 466, 469, 470-71, 473-74; in election of 1800, 626; TJ's views of, 713-14, 715-16, 927

Newton, Sir Isaac, 47, 54, 386, 403

Nicholas, George, 237; and censure of TJ, 237-39, 241-42
Nicholas, John, 650
Nicholas, "Clerk John," 573, 710
Nicholas, Robert Carter, 70, 109, 120, 140
Nicholas, Wilson Cary: TJ's political associate, 575, 612, 615, 623, 624; and TJ's administration, 662, 691, 775, 825, 909-10, 915; and University of Virginia, 965, 967; bankruptcy of, and TJ, 991-92
Nicholson, Joseph, 796, 815, 817, 829, 840, 854, 864
Nock, Albert J.: quoted, 29; cited, 531
Nolan, Philip, 588-89
Non-Importation Act, of 1806, 828-30, 882, 885, 901
Non-Intercourse Act, of 1809, 915-16
Nootka Sound affair, 415-18
North, Lord Frederick, 36, 69, 76; his "conciliatory proposition," 78; TJ's replies to, 78-79, 82
North American Review, 952
Northern Confederacy, in 1804, 793-94, 898
Northwest Ordinance, 278, 284, 778, 780, 787, 788
Notes on Coinage (TJ), 276-78
Notes on Virginia (TJ), 153, 237, 245, 267, 302, 587; writing of, 247-48; publication of, 248-49, 334, 381; as work of natural history, 249-65, 586; influence and reputation of, 264-65, 295, 334, 581, 584, 639, 738, 940, 947, 952, 962; appendix to, 584; quoted, 137, 289-90
nullification, doctrine of, 614, 624, 994

Observations on the Whale-Fishery (TJ), 325-26
Ohio, 692, 857. *See also* Indians, Northwest
Ordinance of 1784, 278, 281-84
Orleans Territory, 783; TJ's policy for defense of, 834-35, 855
Osborne's, 231
Ossian, 245, 302
Otis, James, 72, 950
Otto, Louis Guillaume: protests Tonnage Act, 423; on TJ, 424; quoted, 409, 556
Oxford University, 964, 977, 984

Page, John, 17, 166, 958; quoted, 19, 98, 144, 202

Page, Mann, 583
Paine, Thomas, 63, 241, 440, 560, 665, 709, 947; *Common Sense*, 85-86, quoted 67-68, 68, 85, 95, 96, 289; and TJ, 337, 360, 444; and French Revolution, 384, 437, 438, 439; return to U.S., 681-82, 711-13; champion of gunboats, 838
painting, TJ and, 351-52
paleontology, 255, 576-79, 736-37
Palladio, Andrea, and TJ's architecture, 24-26, 341, 354, 539, 969
Panic of 1819: and University of Virginia, 976, 981; and TJ's personal fortune, 989-92; and political reaction, 992-94
Parson's Cause, 8, 22
Parton, James, quoted, 31
patents, TJ and, 450, 589-90, 937-38
Patterson, Robert, 589
Peace of Amiens, 754
Peace of Ghent, 934
peaceable coercion, 829-30, 863-64, 865, 883-86, 898, 916-18. *See also* commercial policy
Peale, Charles Willson, 738, 742; museum, 419-20, 737; and the mammoth, 736; and polygraph, 737
Peale, Raphael, 736
Peale, Rembrandt, 718, 766
Pendleton, Edmund, 126, 288; as lawyer, 13, 20; in colonial politics, 41, 71, 81, 83, 101; and Virginian reforms, 102, 104, 108, 109, 110, 111, 114, 115, 140; in election of 1800, 626; and after, 682-83, 695
Penet, Windel & Company, 172, 188
penitentiary system, 130
Pennsylvania: in Revolution, 81, 91; in election of 1796, 554, 555-56, 557; of 1800, 625, 634, 641, 642; in TJ's administration, 667, 714-15, 793, 857
Perceval, Spencer, 899
Pestalozzi, Johann, 148
Peter the Great, 836
Petersburg, Virginia, 230, 231, 234
Peterson, Jeffrey and Kent, dedication page
Petit, Adrien, 355, 400, 421
Petite Démocrate, 498-501
Petrarch, 354
Petty, Sir William, quoted, 152
Peyton, Bradford, 1002
Philadelphia, USS, 199
Philips, Josiah, 131, 156
Phillips, Major General William, 163, 164, 165, 180-81; campaign in Virginia, 226, 230-31

Pichon, Louis, French chargé d'affaires, 731, 749, 749-50, 751, 752, 758, 823
Pickering, Judge John, impeachment of, 794-96
Pickering, Timothy, 444, 549; Secretary of State, 563, 600, 621, 629, 632; and Northern Confederacy, 793-94; and opposition to embargo, 824, 896-98
Pike, Zebulon, 855
Pinckney, Charles: in election of 1800, 642; Minister to Spain, 665, 798, 809, 823
Pinckney, Charles Cotesworth: Minister to France, 561, 565, 618, 632; presidential candidate, 641, 799
Pinckney, Thomas: Minister to Britain, 430, 475, 485, 509; Spanish treaty, 551-52; vice presidential candidate, 557, 558
Pinckney Treaty, 551-52, 588, 755
Pinkney, William, Minister to Britain, 830, 860-61, 898, 908, 913, 917
Pitt, William, 308, 508, 806, 831
Pitt, William (Lord Chatham), 72, 79
Plato, 51, 954
plow, TJ's moldboard, 365-66, 531, 589-90, 735
Plumer, William: on TJ, 718, 719, 724, 728, 793; on Burr, 850, 852-53
poetry, TJ and, 30, 245
Point of Fork, on James, 230, 233, 234, 235
political economy, TJ's views of: early, 286-93; as President, 685, 688, 702, 772, 856, 911; in retirement, 940-41, 993. See also carrying trade, commercial policy, manufactures
political parties: beginnings of, 437, 443, 444-46, 463-64, 469, 478-79; TJ's opinions of, 565, 593-94, 656, 996. See also Federalists, Republican party
polygraph, 737
Poplar Forest, 28, 242, 245, 523-24, 924, 927, 991
Porcupine's Gazette, 580, 581
Portsmouth, Virginia, 168, 208, 209, 220, 225, 232
Portugal, 510; treaty negotiations with, 306, 309, 320, 343, 345
Post Office, U.S., 444
postal system: TJ on, 161; in war, 196; in federal government, 444, 423
Pownall, Thomas, quoted, 297

Preble, Commodore Edward, 799, 837, 841
Presbyterians: and disestablishment, 136, 141, 143, 150; and University of Virginia, 978-79
Presidency, TJ's: First Inaugural Address, 655-59; cabinet, 660-63, 804-5; foreign affairs of, 663-64, 745-62, 768-70, 797-99, 805-32, 860-65, 874, 883, 897-903, 908-9; federal offices, appointments and removals, 666-81, 688, 793; First Annual Message, 684-87; fiscal policy, 687-89, 700-701, 815-16, 910; defense policy, 688-89, 815-16, 832-39, 877-78, 896; control of Congress, 689-92, 725, 817, 820, 840-41; attack on judiciary, 692-700, 794-97; "experiment" in free press, 714-18, 803; personal style of, 718-34, 817; government of Louisiana, 770-89; Second Inaugural Address, 801-4; presidential succession, 803, 822, 880-82, 910; Burr Conspiracy and trial, 841-55, 865-74; internal improvements, 855-60; 910; embargo, 882-918; retirement, 918-20
Presidency, U.S.: re-eligibility of chief magistrate, 360, 803; powers in foreign affairs, 399, 484, 494, 551, 552; ceremonies and forms of, 405, 406, 407, 571, 685, 702, 719-20, 733-34; development of cabinet, 451, 489, 501
President's House: TJ's plan of, 449, 539; during his occupancy, 653-54, 722, 724, 725-26, 735, 743-44, 924
Pressburg, Battle of, 831
Preston, William, 194
Price, Richard, 342; quoted, 291
Priestley, Joseph, 576, 580, 626, 658, 963; TJ and his theological works, 956, 958
primogeniture, law of, 113-14
Prince of Orange, 357, 363, 373
Princess of Orange, 357
prisoners-of-war, in Revolutionary War, 162-65, 179-80, 220
Proceedings of the Government of the United States in Maintaining the Public Right to the Beach of the Mississippi . . . (TJ), 946-47
Proclamation of Neutrality, 484-86, 490, 494
Proclamation of 1763, 43
Prophet, The, 903, 904
Provision Order, of 1793, 508-10

Prussia, 508; treaty of 1785, 305-6; travels in, 365
public credit: Virginia's in Revolution, 122-24, 170-71, 189-91, 215, 228; nation's, TJ on, 364, Hamilton on, 409
public debts, U.S.: TJ opposes transfer to Europe, 363, 364, 366; Hamilton's plan for, 409-11; domestic speculation in, 414-15; in 1798-99, 617; TJ's policy as President, 687, 700, 856, 910. *See also* Funding system
Pufendorf, Baron von, 484

Quartering Act, 34
Quasi War: causes of, 555, 561, 564; defense preparations, 564, 595, 599-600, 617; domestic aspects of, 607-8, 617, 622; TJ's peace efforts, 618; Adams's peace mission, 619, 630; Convention of 1800, 648
Quids, 818, 822
Quincy, Josiah, 914

race, TJ's theory of, 256-64, 339, 773-74
Ramsay, David, 326-27
Randolph, Anne, granddaughter, 447, 474
Randolph, David M., 706
Randolph, Edmund, 106, 298, 623; Attorney General, 397, 433, 454, 455, 470, 490, 491-92, 502, 504, 511; TJ's opinion of, 491-92, 549; Secretary of State, 549; quoted, 20-21, 71, 102, 237, 243, 444
Randolph, Ellen Wayles, granddaughter, 542, 1004
Randolph, Isham, grandfather, 5
Randolph, Jane, mother, 4, 5, 9, 84
Randolph, John, attorney general, 84
Randolph, John, of Roanoke, 868, 872, 881, 914, 992; as congressional leader, 690, 691, 728, 729, 815; opposes Two Million Act, 817-20; and policy toward Britain, 828-29, 830; effects of his revolt, 818, 832, 840, 880
Randolph, Peter, 10
Randolph, Peyton, 13, 15, 33, 42, 71, 79, 83, 950
Randolph, Thomas Jefferson, grandson, 474, 920, 941, 989, 991, 1004, 1008
Randolph, Thomas Mann, 7, 392, 522

Randolph, Thomas Mann, son-in-law, 392, 447, 474, 476, 522, 523, 840, 876, 925-26, 941
Randolph, William, 5, 7
Rapin-Thoyras, Paul de, 58, 59
Raynal, Abbé: *Histoire,* 66, 346; and degeneracy theory, 253, 256, 257
recognition, diplomatic, 482
Red River Expedition, 765, 855
religion: TJ's early views of, 15, 29, 50-53, 54-56; disestablishment of, 133-45; as enemy of, 580, 587, 608, 638-39; TJ's views and Paine's, 712-13; TJ's ultimate creed, 956-61; and education, 967, 973-74, 978-80. *See also* Christianity, Church of England, church and state
Report on the Cod and Whale Fisheries (TJ), 426
Report on Commerce (TJ), 426-27, 452, 510, 512-15, 885
Report on Manufactures (Hamilton), 458-59, 463
Report on the Mediterranean Trade (TJ), 422
Report on Public Credit (Hamilton), 409-11
Report on the Tonnage Law (TJ), 422-24
Report on Weights and Measures (TJ), 400-405
Republican party: and Giles resolutions, 475-78; and French Revolution, 479-81; and Genêt, 505, 508; and Jay Treaty, 515-16, 544-52; in election of 1796, 545, 554-58; and *rapprochement* with Adams, 557-60, 563; TJ assumes leadership, 569-70, 574-75; and "terror of '98," 590-625; in election of 1800, 625-42, 643-51; credo in TJ's Inaugural Address, 655-58; and federal patronage, 667-81; and Virginia ideologues, 682-83; TJ's leadership as President, 689-92; and federal judiciary, 692-97, 794-97; factional divisions, 728, 729, 791-92, 793, 803-4; and election of 1804, 790-94; New England interest in, 804-5, 814, 817-18, 819, 821-22; Randolph schism, 817-22, 840, 931; and election of 1808, 880-82; and embargo, 885, 905, 914-15; and Madison's administration, 929-31; deterioration of, 992, 1001, 1003. *See also* political parties
Residence Act, 412-14, 447

Revision of the Laws, Virginia, 111-112 ff, 146, 152-53
revolution, right of, 96
Revolutionary debts, 344-45, 451, 453, 665, 696, 797
Revolutionary War, 81, 158; Southern campaign, 167-68; in Virginia, 167-240 *passim;* conclusion of, 267, 271-72
Reynolds affair, and Hamilton, 575, 575-76n, 709
Rice, Reverend John Holt, 978
rice: in TJ's French negotiations, 326-28; smuggles Piedmont, 327, 353; introduces upland variety, 327, 537
Richmond, Virginia, capital, 156; TJ's plan for, 175; abandoned to Arnold, 207, 208-9; in Phillips's invasion, 230, 231, 233; Burr trial in, 867
Richmond *Enquirer,* 710, 711, 819, 927, 967, 968
Riedesel, Major General Friederich von, 163
Riedesel, Baroness von, 163
Ritchie, Thomas, 867, 927, 967, 992, 994
Rittenhouse, David, 160, 252, 257, 265, 403, 419, 450, 576, 577
Rivanna River, navigation of, 23, 537
Rives, William Cabell, 927, 952, 983
Roane, Judge Spencer, 992, 993, 994
Robertson, William, 253
Robinson, John, 41, 42, 43
Rochambeau, General Comte de, 233
Rockfish Gap Report (TJ), 971-75
Rodney, Caesar A.: Delaware Republican leader, 676-79, 795; Attorney General, 805, 865, 866, 905-6, 691
Rogers, Richard, 670
Rose, George, British Minister, 880, 883, 884, 897, 898
Ross, David, 228
Ross, James, 629, 758, 761
Ross Bill, 629, 630, 631
Rousseau, Jean Jacques, 148, 255
Rule of 1756, 806-7, 863
Rumsey, James, 337
Rush, Benjamin, 419, 436, 599, 659, 722, 744, 764, 947; intermediary between Adams and TJ, 953; and TJ's religious opinions, 956-57, 958
Rushworth, John, 70
Russia, 508, 620, 806, 838, 878, 902-3
Rutledge, Edward, 80, 86, 91, 327, 570
Rutledge, John, 80, 91

Rutledge, John, Jr., 574-75, 710, 728

St. Clair, General Arthur, 431, 450-51, 454
St. Etienne, Rabout, 377
St. Eustatius, 228
St. Lambert, M., 334
Santo Domingo: insurrection, 430, 495, 505, 509, 535, 638; in Louisiana diplomacy, 747, 748-50, 752, 753; TJ and U.S. trade with, 748-49, 759, 761, 823; Clearance Act, 823; Logan Act, 824; as asylum for freed slaves, 999, 1000
Sappington, John, 584
Saratoga, Battle of, 158, 162
Sargent, Winthrop, 681, 778
Sauvé, Pierre, 787
Say, Jean-Baptiste, 952
Schuyler, Philip, 439
science: in early education, 11, 29; and architecture, 25, 30-31; in Enlightenment, 47-48; attitude in TJ, 252, 255, 264, 532-33, 579-80, 803, 951; TJ's reputation in, 264-65, 576-90 *passim;* and republicanism, 335, 338, 579, 581, 627; and West, 496, 578, 588; internationalism of, 579, 590; and progress, 627, 964; and federal government, 735, 737, 739, 762-63; and university education, 972-73
Scott, Sir William, case of *Essex,* 806-7
sculpture, 340, 351, 352
Second Inaugural Address (TJ), 801-4, 855
Sedgwick, Theodore, 631
Sedition Act, 605, 606-7, 620, 622, 635, 668, 686, 705
Seneca, 49, 53, 713, 957, 1008; quoted, 30, 923, 1007
Senf, Colonel John Christian, 199, 211
Serra, Correa de, 952, 953
Servetus, 979
Seven Years War, 38, 43, 65, 768, 806
Seventh Annual Message (TJ), 880
Shadwell, 5, 7, 27, 537, 937
Shaftesbury, Lord, 55
Shakespeare, William, 18, 344
Shawnee, 176, 183, 229, 903
Shays' Rebellion, TJ's response to, 358-59
Sheffield, Earl of, 290
Shelburne, Earl of, 289, 290, 342
Shenstone, William, 26
Sherman, Roger, 87

Shippen, Thomas Lee, 333, 419
Shippen, William, 419
Short, William, 825, 952, 1004; secretary to TJ, 287, 295, 301, 345, 349, 353, 365, 377, 385, 401, 403, 425; chargé d'affaires in France, 400, 417, 424; envoy to Spain, 430, 456; Minister at The Hague, 430, 480; aborted mission to Russia, 902-3
Sidney, Algernon, 18, 58, 986
Sierra Leone, 453-54, 998
Sieyes, Abbé, 376; quoted, 711, 753
Simcoe, Colonel John Graves, 234, 235
Simitière, Pierre Eugene de, 98
Sinclair, Arthur, 735
Sinclair, Sir John, 590
sinking fund, 462-63
Sixth Annual Message (TJ), 855, 859
Skelton, Martha Wayles, marries TJ, 27
Skipwith, Fulwar, 618
slavery: TJ's early effort to ameliorate, 44; African trade denounced in Declaration of Independence, 91-92, and closed in Virginia, 152; in revision of laws, 152-53; TJ's denunciation of, 260, 998; colonization policy, 260, 746, 997, 998-99; plan of emancipation, 260, 535, 902, 998, 1000; restricted in territories, 283, 284, 995-97; congressional debate in 1790, 408-9; in British negotiations, 451, 453-54, 998; and Santo Domingo revolt, 535, 638, 749, 824; and Louisiana Purchase, 779, 781, 783, 784, 785; diffusion of, 997
slaves, TJ's, 27, 236, 391, 474, 521, 534-35, 992, 1007
Small, Dr. William, 12, 14, 15, 19, 55
smallpox, 265, 683-84
Smith, Abigail Adams, 298, 345, 346
Smith, Adam, 513, 856; quoted, 68, 289, 383, 435
Smith, Henry Nash, quoted, 766-77
Smith, John, 870, 872, 873
Smith, Jonathan B., 437
Smith, Margaret Bayard, on TJ, 718, 719, 740
Smith, Robert: Secretary of Navy, 660-61, 686, 798, 799, 805, 810, 841, 851, 853, 880, 903, 909; and Madison's administration, 930-31
Smith, Samuel: in Burr-TJ contest, 645-46, 647-48, 650, 676, 845; in TJ's administration, 662, 824, 848, 853, 875; and Non-Importation Act, 828,

829, 830; and Monroe-Pinkney treaty, 861, 864
Smith, Samuel Harrison, 695, 942
Smith, William, 346, 388
Smith, William Loughton, 465-66, 554-55
Smithsonian Institution, 859
Society of the Cincinnati, 286, 346, 572
Society for the Encouragement of Useful Manufactures, 463
Society of United Irishmen, 604
South America, 600, 738, 745-46, 936-37
South Carolina: 411, 557, 710, 781; in Revolutionary War, 167, 194; and TJ's commercial diplomacy, 326, 327-29; in election of 1800, 641-42, 644
South Carolina Agricultural Society, 328
South Sea Bubble, 462
Southern Army, Virginia's support of, 195-98, 200-201, 204-5, 227. See also Revolutionary War
"sovereignty of the living generation," in TJ's thought, 382-84
Spain: Jay-Gardoqui affair, 358, 398; Nootka Sound affair, 415-18; TJ's policy toward, 397-98, 429, 456-57, 497-98, 510-11, 511-12; Indian policy in Southwest, 431, 458; negotiations with, 457-58, 510-11; TJ declines mission to, 522; Pinckney Treaty, 551-52; in Louisiana diplomacy, 746-47; and Florida controversy, 768, 808-10; and western limits of Louisiana, 769-70, 809-10, 848-49; and spoliations convention, 798; in TJ's reappraisal of 1805, 810-14, 815, 816-17; revolt against Napoleon, 826, 900, 908
Stael, Mme de, 335
Stamp Act, 34, 36, 42
Stamp Act Resolves, Virginia, 43
state debts: assumption of, 410-11, 468; Virginia protest, 433
State Department, office of, 391, 392, 395
"state of nature," in Locke, 66, 102; TJ on, 157
state rights: in response to Cabell presentment, 605-6; in Virginia and Kentucky Resolutions, 609-16, 623-24; in election of 1800, 627; in First Inaugural, 655; revival of, 992-97, 1003

Statute for Religious Freedom (TJ), 134, 141-43, 334, 537, 988
Staunton, Virginia, 236, 536, 970, 982
Steele, John, 678
Stephens, James, 807-8
Steuben, General Frederick William von, 215, 286; commands in Virginia, 203-4; in Arnold's invasion, 206, 207, 209; champions fort at Hood's, 210-12; ineptness and arbitrary attitude of, 212, 220, 223, 225, 239; plan to capture Arnold, 221, 224, 225; and Greene, 223, 224, 226, 234; humiliation of, 235
Stevens, General Edward, 197
Stevens, John, 382
Stewart, Dugald, 977, 984
Stiles, Ezra, 293
Stoicism, 49, 53-54
Story, Joseph: on TJ, 719; in embargo repeal, 915; named Justice, 930
Strickland, William, visits Monticello, 524, 527, 530, 589
Stuart, John, 577, 579
Sullivan, James, 890, 897, 898
Sullivan, John, 338-39
Sully, Thomas, 1006
A Summary View of the Rights of British America (TJ), 69, 70-77, 84, 89, 114, 117
Supreme Court, U.S.: and rules of neutrality, 501; and common law jurisdiction, 623, 717; and TJ's administration, 692, 695-96; opposed by TJ in 1819-20, 929-30, 993
Swartwout, John, 669, 854, 870
Swift, Jonathan, quoted, 533
Sydenham, Dr. Thomas, 712
Syllabus of an Estimate of the Merit of the Doctrines of Jesus . . (TJ), 712, 956-58
Symmes, Charles, 710

Tacitus, 49, 52, 57, 58, 927
Talleyrand-Périgord, Charles Maurice de, 403, 824; and XYZ affair, 596, 601, 618, 619, 621; and Louisiana diplomacy, 749, 751, 754, 760; and Florida negotiation, 768, 808, 813, 814
Tarleton, Colonel Banastre, 234, 235
Taylor, John, 555, 716, 911; and agriculture, 529-30; and crisis of 1798, 610-11, 615, 636; and Virginia state rights' revival, 992, 994

Tazewell, Littleton W., 946, 963-64, 968
Tea Act, 70
Tecumseh, 903, 904
Ternant, Jean Baptiste, 425, 430, 455, 481-82, 490
Tessé, Mme de, 335, 352, 923
Test oath, in Revolutionary Virginia, 132
Thomson, Charles, 80, 248, 250, 343, 419, 960
Thoreau, Henry David, quoted, 873
Thornton, Edward, 666, 797
Thornton, William, 449, 741, 742, 858, 943, 968
Ticknor, George, 943, 951, 969, 975, 977, 979, 984
Tilly, Commodore Arnaud de, 221
Tindal, Matthew, 50, 51
tobacco trade, 288, 425; in TJ's French negotiations, 317, 318-21, 346
Tocqueville, Alexis de, quoted, 373, 479, 663
Todd, Reverend John, 145
Tompkins, Daniel D., 891
Tonnage Act, 422-24, 863
Tories, see Loyalists
torpedo, 858
town planning, TJ and, 744-45
Townshend, Charles, 32, 34
Townshend Acts, 34, 35
Tracy, Destutt de: TJ and his writings, 947-48; quoted, 653
Tracy, Nathaniel, 295
Tracy, Uriah, 793
Trafalger, Battle of, 805
Transylvania Company, 119-20
treason: TJ and Virginia statute, 132-33; in Burr trial, 853-54, 866, 870-72, 873
Treasury Department, 395, 397, 477, 660-61
treaties of commerce, TJ appointed to negotiate, 286-87; plan of, 289-90, 291-93, 304-5; with Prussia, 305-6, with France, 289, 315-30, 423, 425, 455-56, 494-95; TJ opposes in 1800, 628-29
Treaty of Peace, 1783, 219, 267, 271-72, 344-45, 453-54, 456, 546, 768
treaty power, 291, 304-5, 550, 551
Treaty of San Ildefonso, 747, 768, 779
Treaty of Tilsit, 878
Trenchard, John, 58, 59
Tripoli, war with, 664, 685, 798-99; peace with, 799, 815; 310, 320, 343

Trist, Nicholas P., 952
Trumbull, John, TJ and, 345, 347, 386, 492
Truxton, Commodore Thomas, 849, 855
Tuckahoe, 5, 7, 207
Tucker, George, 985, 987
Tucker, St. George, 116, 535
Tull, Jethro, 526
Tunis, 310
Turgot, A. R. J., 381, 752
Turkey, 620
Turner, Thomas, 709, 710
Turreau, General Louis M., French Minister, 823, 824, 901
Twelfth Amendment, 791
Two Million Act, 818
Tyler, Comfort, 847, 870, 871
Tyson, Edward, 262

Union, The: in Confederation, 305, 309, 313; under Constitution, 413, 434-35, 461-62, 609, 623-24, 656-57; and Louisiana Purchase, 772-73, 775; and internal improvements, 802, 855; and Burr Conspiracy, 851, 854, 874; anxieties for, 987, 994, 995, 996, 1003
Unitarianism, 137, 959-61, 978, 979
U.S. v. Hudson and Goodwin, 717
University of Edinburgh, 392, 973, 977, 984
University of Pennsylvania, 420, 972
University of Virginia, TJ and founding of, 961-88; genesis of, 961-68; architectural plan, 968-70; site and educational plan, 970-75; religion and, 973-74, 978-80; founding and building, 975, 980-84; recruitment of faculty, 976-77, 984-85; school of law and government, 985-87; opening, 987-88

Vaca, Cabeza de, 762
Valley Forge, 158
Van der Kemp, Francis Adrian, 959
Varina, 394, 522
Varnum, Joseph B., 834
Vattel, Emerich de, 484, 495, 527
Vaughan, Benjamin, 342, 836
Vergennes, Comte de, 425; negotiations with, 315, 316-20, 325
Vice Presidency, office of, 545; TJ elected to, 557, 560; inaugurated, 562; conciliation with Adams, 557-60, 560-63; in opposition to administration, 565-69, 574, 594-96,

598-99, 607-8, 611-16, 618-19, 620-21
Vincennes, conquest of, 176, 177-78
Virginia: and the frontier, 5-6, and coming of Revolution, 33-45, 69-79 passim, 83, 84, 86; planter debts in, 40-41, 123; constitution of 1776, 99-101; revision of the laws, 111-12; religion, 133-45; education, 145-46; slavery, 152-53; courts, 154-55; wartime government in, 168-74; capital of, 156; TJ on deterioration of, 1004. See also University of Virginia, western lands, etc.
Virginia Constitution of 1776: TJ and, 99-107, 118, 133; draft of 1783, 132, 267, 381; executive in, 173; efforts to reform, 267, 962
Virginia Declaration of Rights, 89, 101, 133
Virginia Resolutions: of 1798, 612; of 1799-1800, 623-25, 986
Volney, Comte de, 520, 576, 580, 604, 618, 714
Voltaire, François Marie Arouet de, 47, 252, 255, 330

Walker, John, 8, 709, 717
Walker, Mrs. John, 708-9, 717
Walker, Dr. Thomas, 6, 43, 44
War Department, 395, 397, 661
War of 1812: coming of, 916, 931-32; TJ's reaction to, 932-33; conduct of, 933-34; and peace, 934-37
wards, TJ's conception of, 147, 150, 962
Washington, George, 185, 204, 232, 235, 237, 280, 316, 357, 360, 527, 561; and the West, 43; in Revolutionary movement, 71; Commander in Chief, 81, 158, resignation as, 272-73; and the southern theater, 168, 195-96, 199, 227; and Governor Hamilton, 181-82; warns TJ of invasion, 206; orders Lafayette to Virginia, 221; meditates southern campaign, 233-34, 240; TJ's opinion of, 257, 273, 406-7, 478, 516, 548-49, 570-74, 950; and Society of the Cincinnati, 286; Houdon statue of, 340; President, 390-517 passim, 548-52, 858, 963, conduct as, 395-96, 406-7, 516, 662; in partisan conflict, 466-68, 470-75, 478; re-election of, 478; and neutrality, 484, 490-91, 500-501, 502, 504, 511; retirement of, 545, 562-63; as Federalist aegis, 545, 549-50, 571, 572-73, 639; aliena-

Washington, George (*continued*) tion from TJ, 573-74; death of, 625, 631
Washington College, 971
Waterhouse, Dr. Benjamin, 683-84
Watt, James, 343
Wayles, John, 27-28, 39, 41, 707
Wayne, General Anthony, 233, 234, 239
Webster, Daniel, visits TJ, 1006
Webster, Noah, 744
Weedon, General George, 209, 226
Weld, Isaac, 520
West, Benjamin, 340
West, American: in TJ's thought, 6, 68, 117, 176-77, 180, 183, 219, 496, 588, 745-46; commerce of, 182, 250, 279-80, 291, 354, 358, 397; TJ's plans for, 278-85; redemption and pacification of, 397-98, 416; and Louisiana Purchase, 745; and Lewis and Clark, 762; and Burr Conspiracy, 851; and Sixth Annual Message, 855
West Florida, U.S. claim to, 768, 788, 797, 813
western lands, Virginia: in coming of Revolution, 43-44, 78; in TJ's reforms, 117-22; ceded to Union, 169, 217-18, 278-79; in Revolutionary War, 176-78, 182-83, 219
western states: creation of, 118, 282; and continental expansion, 745, 747, 788
Westham, 172, 206, 207
Westover, 24, 206, 208, 231
Whale Fishery: U.S., 288, 322; British, 322; French, 322; and TJ's French negotiations, 322-26
Whately, Thomas, 26, 343
Whig principles, TJ and, 17, 58-59, 63-65, 158, 174; in England, 73, 76; in Virginia, 101, 104-5, 173; in French Revolution, 372-73, 377-78, 381-82; in federal government, 468, 472, 494, 593-94, 686-87, 689-90, 697
whiskey excise, 463, 468
Whiskey Rebellion, 523, 448
Whitney, Eli, 336, 648
Whittier, John Greenleaf, quoted, 822-23n
Wickham, John, 867
Wilkes, John, 45, 63
Wilkinson, Brigadier General James,

589, 776, 777, 780, 787; and Burr Conspiracy, 841-55 *passim;* Governor of Louisiana, 842-43; neutral ground treaty, 848-49; quits Burr, 849; actions in New Orleans, 852, 853, 854; at Burr trial, 869, 870; and thereafter, 874
William and Mary, College of, 6, 336, 682, 964; TJ enters, 10; described, 11-12; TJ's education at, 12; efforts to reform, 146, 148-49, 161, 963; and founding of university, 970, 971, 982-83
Williamsburg, Virginia, 11, 33, 70-71, 108, 156, 209, 230
Williamson, Hugh, 283, 285
Willink and Van Staphorst, 362, 363, 368
Wilson, James, 73, 76, 86
wines, TJ and, 351, 355, 365, 385, 421, 726, 729
Wirt, William, 869, 919, 946; life of Henry, 949-50
Wistar, Caspar, 419, 450, 736, 904, 953, 972
Wolcott, Oliver, 444, 463-64, 549, 562, 631, 641; Secretary of Treasury, 563, 602, 632, 677
women, TJ and, 20, 27, 268-69, 348, 351, 385
Wood, John, 846
Woodford, General William, 185
Wythe, George, 99, 100, 108, 109, 125, 151, 249, 505, 942, 947, 950; in TJ's youth, 13, 14, 15, 17, 20; in Revolutionary movement, 71, 101; reviser, 111

XYZ affair, 594-96, 601-2; TJ's view of, 596-97, 618-19

Yale College, 293
Yazoo land frauds, 771, 820-21
yellow fever, 505-6, 507-8, 744
Yorktown, Battle of, 216, 240
Young, Arthur, 351, 355, 526, 527, 530, 531
Yrujo, Don Carlos Martinez de, Spanish Minister, 730, 731, 732, 733, 755, 764, 775, 798, 809, 844

Zane, Isaac, 160
zoology, 252-55, 338-39